S0-BQX-040

SOUTH AMERICA

8th Edition

Where to Stay and Eat
for All Budgets

Must-See Sights
and Local Secrets

Ratings You Can Trust

Fodor's Travel Publications   New York, Toronto, London, Sydney, Auckland
www.fodors.com

718
Fod

FODOR'S SOUTH AMERICA

Editors: Laura Kidder and Kelly Kealy (lead project editors); Erica Duecy, Alexis Kelly, Margaret Kelly, Josh McIlvain, Adam Taplin

Writers: Eddy Ancinas, Tom Azzopardi, Aviva Baff, Ruth Bradley, Lucy Bryson, Brian Byrnes, Daniel Corry, Ana Cristina, Andy Footner, Nicholas Gill, Doug Gray, Katya Hodge, Michell Hopey, Katy Hutter, Anna Katsnelson, Paul Kaye, Brian Kleupfel, Jimmy Langman, Richard McColl, David Miller, Katy Morrison, Victoria Patience, Tim Patterson, Stephen Silva, Mark Sullivan, Simon Tarmo, Alistair Thompson, Jeffrey Van Fleet, Oliver Wigmore, Jonathan Yevin

Production Editor: Tom Holton

Maps & Illustrations: Ed Jacobus, Craig Cartographic Services, David Lindroth, Mark Stroud, *cartographers*; Bob Blake, Rebecca Baer, *map editors*; William Wu, *information graphics*

Design: Fabrizio La Rocca, *creative director*; Guido Caroti, Siobhan O'Hare, *art directors*; Tina Malaney, Chie Ushio, Ann McBride, Jessica Walsh, *designers*; Melanie Marin, *senior picture editor*

Cover Photo (Victoria water lily, Amazon River, Peru): Andoni Canela/age fotostock

Production Manager: Angela McLean

COPYRIGHT

8th Edition

ISBN 978–1–4000–0686–1

ISSN 0362–0220

SPECIAL SALES

This book is available at special discounts for bulk purchases for sales promotions or premiums. Special editions, including personalized covers, excerpts of existing books, and corporate imprints, can be created in large quantities for special needs. For more information, write to Special Markets/Premium Sales, 1745 Broadway, MD 6-2, New York, New York 10019, or e-mail specialmarkets@randomhouse.com.

AN IMPORTANT TIP & AN INVITATION

Although all prices, opening times, and other details in this book are based on information supplied to us at press time, changes occur all the time in the travel world, and Fodor's cannot accept responsibility for facts that become outdated or for inadvertent errors or omissions. So **always confirm information when it matters,** especially if you're making a detour to visit a specific place. Your experiences—positive and negative—matter to us. If we have missed or misstated something, **please write to us.** We follow up on all suggestions. Contact the South America editor at editors@fodors.com or c/o Fodor's at 1745 Broadway, New York, NY 10019.

PRINTED IN THE UNITED STATES OF AMERICA

10 9 8 7 6 5 4 3 2 1

Be a Fodor's Correspondent

Your opinion matters. It matters to us. It matters to your fellow Fodor's travelers, too. And we'd like to hear it. In fact, we need to hear it.

When you share your experiences and opinions, you become an active member of the Fodor's community. That means we'll not only use your feedback to make our books better, but we'll publish your names and comments whenever possible. Throughout our guides, look for "Word of Mouth," excerpts of your unvarnished feedback.

Here's how you can help improve Fodor's for all of us.

Tell us when we're right. We rely on local writers to give you an insider's perspective. But our writers and staff editors—who are the best in the business—depend on you. Your positive feedback is a vote to renew our recommendations for the next edition.

Tell us when we're wrong. We're proud that we update most of our guides every year. But we're not perfect. Things change. Hotels cut services. Museums change hours. Charming cafés lose charm. If our writer didn't quite capture the essence of a place, tell us how you'd do it differently. If any of our descriptions are inaccurate or inadequate, we'll incorporate your changes in the next edition and will correct factual errors at fodors.com immediately.

Tell us what to include. You probably have had fantastic travel experiences that aren't yet in Fodor's. Why not share them with a community of like-minded travelers? Maybe you chanced upon a beach or bistro or B&B that you don't want to keep to yourself. Tell us why we should include it. And share your discoveries and experiences with everyone directly at fodors.com. Your input may lead us to add a new listing or highlight a place we cover with a "Highly Recommended" star or with our highest rating, "Fodor's Choice."

Give us your opinion instantly at our feedback center at www.fodors.com/feedback. You may also e-mail editors@fodors.com with the subject line "South America Editor." Or send your nominations, comments, and complaints by mail to South America Editor, Fodor's, 1745 Broadway, New York, NY 10019.

You and travelers like you are the heart of the Fodor's community. Make our community richer by sharing your experiences. Be a Fodor's correspondent.

Happy traveling!

Tim Jarrell, Publisher

CONTENTS

CONTENTS

ABOUT THIS BOOK

OUR RATINGS

Sometimes you find terrific travel experiences and sometimes they just find you. But usually the burden is on you to select the right combination of experiences. That's where our ratings come in.

As travelers we've all discovered a place so wonderful that its worthiness is obvious. And sometimes that place is so experiential that superlatives don't do it justice: you just have to be there to know. These sights, properties, and experiences get our highest rating, **Fodor's Choice**, indicated by orange stars throughout this book.

Black stars highlight sights and properties we deem **Highly Recommended**, places that our writers, editors, and readers praise again and again for consistency and excellence.

By default, there's another category: any place we include in this book is by definition worth your time unless we say otherwise. And we will.

Disagree with any of our choices? Care to nominate a place or suggest that we rate one more highly? Visit our feedback center at www.fodors.com/feedback.

BUDGET WELL

Hotel and restaurant price categories from ¢ to $$$$ are defined in the opening pages of each chapter. For attractions, we always give standard adult admission fees; reductions are usually available for children, students, and senior citizens. Want to pay with plastic? **AE, D, DC, MC, V** following restaurant and hotel listings indicate if American Express, Discover, Diners Club, MasterCard, and Visa are accepted.

RESTAURANTS

Unless we state otherwise, restaurants are open for lunch and dinner daily. We mention dress only when there's a specific requirement and reservations only when they're essential or not accepted—it's always best to book ahead.

HOTELS

Hotels have private bath, phone, TV, and air-conditioning and operate on the European Plan (aka EP, meaning without meals), unless we specify that they use the Continental Plan (CP, with a continental breakfast), Breakfast Plan (BP, with a full breakfast), or Modified American Plan (MAP, with breakfast and dinner) or are all-inclusive (including all meals and most activi-

ties). We always list facilities but not whether you'll be charged an extra fee to use them, so when pricing accommodations, find out what's included.

Many Listings	
★	Fodor's Choice
★	Highly recommended
✉	Physical address
✛	Directions
🕮	Mailing address
☎	Telephone
🖷	Fax
⊕	On the Web
✍	E-mail
🎫	Admission fee
☉	Open/closed times
Ⓜ	Metro stations
🖃	Credit cards

Hotels & Restaurants	
🖼	Hotel
↵	Number of rooms
⚅	Facilities
🍽	Meal plans
✕	Restaurant
⚄	Reservations
↘	Smoking
ᚨᚱ	BYOB
✕🖼	Hotel with restaurant that warrants a visit

Outdoors	
⛳	Golf
⛺	Camping

Other	
☾	Family-friendly
⇨	See also
✉	Branch address
☞	Take note

WHAT'S
WHERE

1 Venezuela. Just a few hours from the eastern United States, Caracas, Venezuela's crowded capital, is a futuristic blend of glass office towers and concrete apartment buildings built with oil money. Along the Caribbean coast are stretches of pristine white sand, including those on Isla Margarita. In the Andean city of Mérida, the world's longest and highest cable car carries you to the foot of glacier-topped Pico Bolívar. In the southeast, huge table-top mountains tower over grasslands in Parque Nacional Canaima. Here Angel Falls plummet more than 2,647 feet.

2 Colombia. Colombia is the continent's only country to touch both the Pacific and the Atlantic. Thanks to the Andes, the major cities sit at different altitudes, and with each comes a different attitude. Bogotá, the sprawling capital, sits at 8,700 feet and has a formal air that recalls its colonial past. The atmosphere grows more relaxed, however, if you descend 2,000 feet to Medellín, a small but vibrant city whose mild climate has earned it the name "city of eternal spring." At sea level, the historic port of Cartagena is an exuberant town with strong Afro-Caribbean influence.

3 Ecuador. A living quilt of terraced green plots covers this nation's lower slopes of cloud-capped volcanoes, where corn grows twice as tall as the sturdy farmers. Quito, the capital, lies at the foot of Volcán Pichincha, which sometimes sputters to life. Cuenca, Colonial, offers both architectural charm and an outstanding market. The coast is home to the port of Guayaquil, a departure point for the Galápagos Islands, home of the remarkable wildlife that sparked Darwin's theories of evolution.

4 Peru. Peru contains a wealth of history within its borders. Cusco, once the capital of the Inca empire, is one of the hemisphere's most beautiful cities. On a hilltop outside of Cusco is the massive fortress of Sacsayhuaman. It's a great introduction to Inca culture before you head to that unforgettable maze of structures, and stairways that make up Machu Picchu. Lima, the capital is the safekeeper of colonial treasures. Few cities enjoyed such power during the colonial era. For an entirely different side of Peru, visit the Amazon rain forest near Puerto Maldonado.

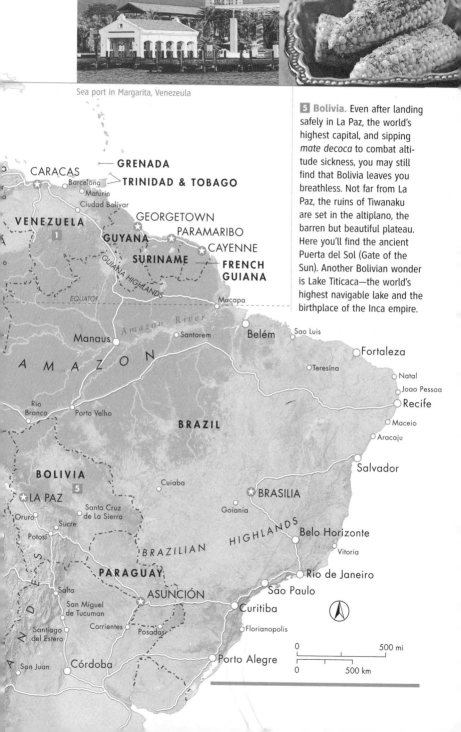

Sea port in Margarita, Venezuela

5 Bolivia. Even after landing safely in La Paz, the world's highest capital, and sipping *mate decoca* to combat altitude sickness, you may still find that Bolivia leaves you breathless. Not far from La Paz, the ruins of Tiwanaku are set in the altiplano, the barren but beautiful plateau. Here you'll find the ancient Puerta del Sol (Gate of the Sun). Another Bolivian wonder is Lake Titicaca—the world's highest navigable lake and the birthplace of the Inca empire.

CARACAS

GRENADA

Barcelona

TRINIDAD & TOBAGO

Maturin

Ciudad Bolivar

VENEZUELA **1**

GEORGETOWN

GUYANA

PARAMARIBO

SURINAME

CAYENNE

FRENCH GUIANA

GUIANA HIGHLANDS

EQUATOR

Macapa

Amazon River

Manaus

Santarem

Belém

Sao Luis

Fortaleza

Teresina

Natal

Joao Pessoa

Recife

A M A Z O N

Maceio

Rio Branco

Aracaju

Porto Velho

BRAZIL

Salvador

BOLIVIA **5**

Cuiaba

BRASILIA

LA PAZ

Goiania

Oruro

Santa Cruz de La Sierra

Sucre

Potosí

BRAZILIAN HIGHLANDS

Belo Horizonte

Vitoria

Rio de Janeiro

PARAGUAY

Salta

ASUNCIÓN

São Paulo

San Miguel de Tucuman

Curitiba

Corrientes

Posadas

Santiago del Estero

Florianopolis

0   500 mi

San Juan

Córdoba

Porto Alegre

0   500 km

WHAT'S WHERE

Piura

Chiclayo

Trujillo

Chimbote

PERU

LIMA

Ica

6 Brazil. Portuguese-speaking Brazil is the world's fifth-largest country and has an oversized vitality to match. To most visitors, Brazil is Rio de Janeiro, famous for its spectacular bay-side setting, fabulous beaches, skimpy string bikinis, and riotous Carnaval. But Brazil goes far beyond Rio's beaches and hedonistic pleasures. Skyscrapers, stock markets, and agribusiness set the pace in the megalopolis of São Paulo. Far to the southwest is the mighty Foz de Iguaçu (Iguaçu Falls). A unique Afro-Brazilian culture thrives in tropical Salvador, capital of Bahia State. And then there's the Amazon, a gargantuan waterway flowing for more than 4,000 mi, so wide in places you can't see the shore from a riverboat's deck, and banked by a rain forest that houses the greatest variety of life on earth.

7 Chile. You're never far from the ocean in this 4,267-km-long (2,650-mi-long) country, as it averages only 177 km (110 mi) in width. Chile is justly famous for its twin resorts of Valparaíso and Viña del Mar, with their wide swaths of sand and nonstop nightlife. In the north, the Atacama Desert is so dry that in some areas no rain has ever been recorded. Next come the copper mines that

brought great wealth to the country, followed by the fertile Central Valley region that's home to the sprawling capital of Santiago and the wine regions around it. The green and aquamarine waters of the Lake District are to the south. Finally, in the extreme south lies the forbidding landscape of windswept Tierra del Fuego.

8 Paraguay. Paraguay may be short on trendy eateries and luxurious accommodations, but it's long on charm. Asunción is a provincial capital whose pleasures are simple: a stroll through the botanical gardens or a leisurely alfresco lunch. In the countryside, motorcycles and pop music compete with oxcarts and traditional *polca* music. The country's original inhabitants were the Guaraní, and the ruins of missions near Encarnación are an impressive reminder of their fascinating legacy. Here Jesuits converted the native population and organized a unique communal society. Several colonial-era buildings, abandoned when the Jesuits were expelled from the region in 1767, are being restored.

9 Argentina. Gauchos and tango dancers have given Argentina a mystique, but these images tell only half the story. Duck into the boutiques of Buenos Aires's Palermo district or drop by for tea at an elegant *confitería,* and you'll realize that *porteños* (the residents of this port city) are educated, and urbane. Away from the capital the pace is slower, the people more open, and the landscape striking. North of Buenos Aires are Iguazú Falls—in all, some 300 separate waterfalls that thunder over a 4-km-wide (2½-mi-wide) precipice on the border of Brazil, Argentina, and Paraguay. West of Buenos Aires, Mendoza and its environs are famous for wineries that are often set in the foothills of the Andes. In Patagonia to the south, you'll find the ski resort of Bariloche; the icy monoliths of Parque Nacional los Glaciares; and the famous Parque Nacional Tierra del Fuego at the very tip of the country.

Islas de Juan Fernandez (Chile)

Penguin off coast of Chile

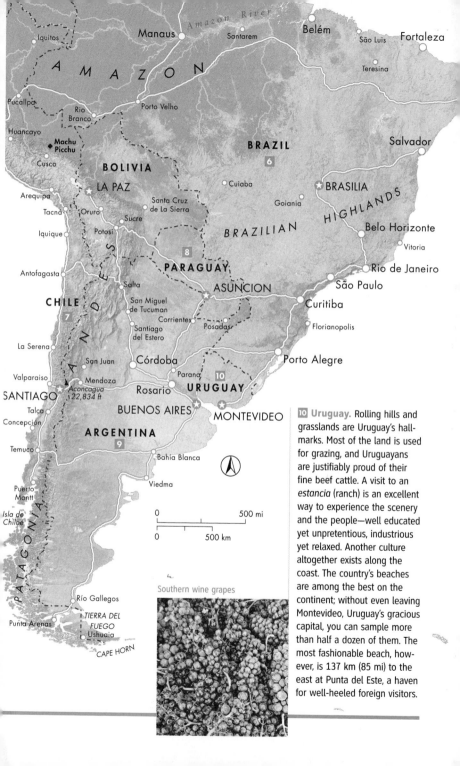

Southern wine grapes

10 Uruguay. Rolling hills and grasslands are Uruguay's hallmarks. Most of the land is used for grazing, and Uruguayans are justifiably proud of their fine beef cattle. A visit to an *estancia* (ranch) is an excellent way to experience the scenery and the people—well educated yet unpretentious, industrious yet relaxed. Another culture altogether exists along the coast. The country's beaches are among the best on the continent; without even leaving Montevideo, Uruguay's gracious capital, you can sample more than half a dozen of them. The most fashionable beach, however, is 137 km (85 mi) to the east at Punta del Este, a haven for well-heeled foreign visitors.

IF YOU LIKE

The Wild, Wild World

Volcanoes, some still smoldering, run the length of the Andes; at their feet lie everything from desolate sand dunes to bubbling hot springs. The 30,000-year-old Perito Moreno Glacier broods in Argentina's Parque Nacional los Glaciares. A mighty roar fills the air as the raging waters of Iguazú Falls plunge over basalt cliffs at the point where Argentina, Paraguay, and Brazil meet. Angel Falls crash nearly two-thirds of a mile down a cliff in a remote corner of Venezuela. And simply nothing is more amazing than the Amazon, the world's largest rain forest area, which extends from Brazil into eight other South American nations.

Amazon Rain Forest. A visit to the world-famous Amazon is one of those "life-list" experiences. Its scope and natural wealth are truly awe-inspiring.

Angel Falls, Canaima National Park, Venezuela. The world's highest waterfall is the centerpiece of this beautiful national park the size of Belgium.

Atacama Desert, Chile. The most arid spot on Earth is in El Norte Grande's Atacama Desert; no measurable precipitation has ever been recorded there.

Brazil's Beaches. Copacabana and Ipanema have Rio's best "scenes," but Barra da Tijuca, Prainha, and Grumari are its most beautiful sandy stretches. Búzios has some gorgeous shoreline, too. Ilhabela, in São Paulo State, is a paradise of more than 25 beaches. Bahia's Praia do Forte has plenty of leisure activities, 12 km (7 mi) of sand, and sea turtles.

Galápagos Islands, Ecuador. The islands not only provide close contact with marine and island-bound wildlife, they also provide a unique perspective on Charles Darwin's theory of evolution.

Glaciar Perito Moreno, Patagonia. Tons of ice regularly peel off this advancing glacier and crash into Lago Argentino.

Iguazú Falls/Foz do Iguaçu. Iguazú Falls National Park protects 275 waterfalls and countless species of bird, mammal, insect, and amphibia. Trails disappear into a greenhouse of lianas, creepers, epiphytes, bamboo, orchids, and bromeliads.

Mitad del Mundo, Quito, Ecuador. The exact latitudinal center of the earth, determined in 1736, is 26 km (16 mi) north of Quito. You can take an elevator up the Middle of the World monument, an obelisk crowned with a 2.5-ton metal globe.

Parque Nacional da Chapada Diamantina, west of Salvador. One of Brazil's most spectacular parks, Chapada Diamantina was a former diamond mining center. Today it's a center for hard and soft adventure.

Parque Nacional Torres del Paine, Chile. Glaciers that swept through Patagonia millions of years ago created the ash-gray spires that dominate this national park.

Península Valdés, Argentina. This is the best place to view Patagonia's southern right whales as they feed, mate, give birth, and nurse their offspring. Seals and penguins keep you company, too.

Río Tebicuary, Paraguay. Fish for dorado from a launch on the river, whose banks are home to monkeys, capybaras, and the occasional alligator.

Salar de Uyuni, Bolivia. Visit the world's biggest and highest desert of salt near Potosí, where you'll find red and green mineral-tinted lagoons and an island with towering cacti.

Archaeological Sites

The mysteries of ancient ruins such as the windswept streets at Tiwanaku in Bolivia and the stately temple at Ingapirca in Ecuador never fail to tantalize. Peru alone has a wealth of pre-Columbian sites that would take weeks to fully explore. Almost every major archaeological site in the country is worth seeing, but the must-see sights include Machu Picchu and the fortress of Ollantaytambo. If you have more time, visit the Nazca lines, gigantic, mysterious drawings in the desert.

Cerros Pintados, Reserva Nacional Pampa del Tamarugal, Chile. Here you'll find the world's largest group of geoglyphs (more than 400). Scientists believe these figures of birds, animals, and geometric patterns—which ancient peoples may have used to help them navigate the desert—date from AD 500 to 1400.

Isla del Sol, Bolivia. According to legend, the Inca Empire was founded on Sun Island, in shimmering Lake Titicaca. Here you'll see beautiful coves sheltering white sandy beaches, steep Inca steps, and a sacred fountain at the port of Yumani as well as the ruins of the Inca palace of Pilkokaina.

Machu Picchu, Peru. The most important archaeological site in South America, the "lost city of the Incas" is rediscovered every day by adventurous travelers. Crowded or not crowded, misty rains or clear skies, Machu Picchu never ceases to enthrall, and the Inca Trail is still the great hiking pilgrimage. Stay in Aguas Caliente for the best access.

Museo Chileno de Arte Precolombino, Santiago, Chile. Personal items from Central and South America's indigenous peoples are on display in the city's beautifully restored Royal Customs House.

Museo Histórico Regional, Ica, Peru. A visit to this museum provides an excellent overview of the area's ancient cultures, with fine displays of Paracas weavings and Nazca ceramic sculptures.

Museo Rafael Larco Herrera, Lima, Peru. This museum was constructed on the site of pre-Columbian pyramid houses. It's mostly known for its impressive pre-Columbian erotic pot collection. If you're not into titillating art, check out the more than 40,000 other ceramics, textiles, and gold pieces on display.

Nazca Lines. Twelve miles north of the town of Nazca is one of the world's greatest mysteries, 11 giant engravings of animals and shapes known as the Nazca Lines.

Ollantaytambo. Sixty kilometers northwest of Cusco, the enormous Inca terraces of Ollantaytambo was one of the few locations where the Incas managed to defeat Spanish conquistadors. The fortress also served as a temple, with a ceremonial center greeting those who manage to get to the top.

Sacsayhuaman, Cusco, Peru. The massive fortress of Sacsayhuaman, perhaps the most important Inca monument after Machu Picchu, is built of blocks of stones weighing up to 361 tons.

Temples at Ingapirca, Cuenca, Ecuador. At this ancient city is an elliptical stone structure acknowledged to be a temple to the sun that was built by the Incas. A small museum houses artifacts found at the ruins.

IF YOU LIKE

Art, Culture & History

The colonizers brought a legacy of greed, corruption, and slavery to South America. But they also left the continent with some wonderful architecture. To see it, you need only stroll the ramparts of Cartagena or the cobblestone streets of Quito's Old City. In southern Paraguay and northeastern Argentina Jesuit ruins reflect the blending of missionary and indigenous cultures. The continent's great museums house pieces that range from ancient textiles to contemporary Latin American masterworks.

Casa Real de Moneda, Potosí, Bolivia. The Royal Mint was once used to forge coins from the silver mined in the nearby hills.

Cerro Rico, Potosí, Bolivia. If you don't mind tight spaces, descend into one of the 5,000 tunnels that crisscross Cerro Rico, the "Rich Hill" that filled Spain's coffers with silver until the reserves were exhausted in the early 19th century.

Colonia del Sacramento, Uruguay. One of South America's most beautiful colonial cities has preserved architecture, cobblestone streets, and a tranquillity evident in its people and pace.

Compañía de Jesús, Quito, Ecuador. Almost 1½ tons of gold were poured into the ceilings, walls, pulpits, and altars during construction of South America's wealthiest Jesuit church.

Donación Botero collection, Bogotá, Colombia. Fernando Botero's artwork interprets his subjects from a distinctly Latin-American standpoint—Colombians affectionately refer to him as "the man who paints fat people."

Museu Afro-Brasileiro, Salvador, Brazil. Africa's strong influence on this region of the country is displayed in a collection of musical instruments, masks, costumes, and artifacts.

Museo de Arte Contemporáneo de Caracas Sofía Imber. With works by Picasso, Miró, and Bacon, this museum has an outstanding collection of modern art.

Museo de Arte Latinoamericana de Buenos Aires (MALBA). One of the world's few museums specializing in Latin American art is in a stunningly simple building.

Museu de Arte Naif do Brasil, Rio, Brazil. The canvases that grace the walls bring to art what Brazilians bring to life: verve, color, and joy.

Museo Jesuítico, San Ignacio, Paraguay. Paraguay's first Jesuit mission is now a museum of wood carvings by the indigenous Guaraní people.

Museo de Oro, Bogotá, Colombia. In weight, more than $200 million in gold, gathered from indigenous cultures, and the largest uncut emerald in the world are housed here.

Museo Textil Etnográfico, Sucre, Bolivia. This museum showcases Andean weavings and tapestry art.

Palacio de la Inquisición, Cartagena, Colombia. This former headquarters of the South American branch of the Spanish Inquisition displays racks, thumbscrews, and other torture devices.

Teatro Amazonas, Manaus, Brazil. No other structure better represents the opulence of the rubber boom.

Trinidad, Southern Paraguay. Red sandstone structures make up Paraguay's most impressive Jesuit ruins.

WHEN TO GO

Seasons below the Equator are the reverse of those in the north—summer in Argentina, Bolivia, Chile, Paraguay, Peru, and Uruguay, and portions of Brazil and Ecuador, runs from December to March and winter from June to September. Prices in beach resorts invariably are higher during the summer months. If you're looking for a bargain, stick to the off-season.

Climate

Because of the great variety of latitudes, altitudes, and climatic zones on the continent, you'll encounter many different kinds of weather in any given month. The highland areas of the Andes—which run north to south down the west coast of South America from Colombia through Ecuador, Peru, Bolivia, Chile, and Argentina—are at their most accessible and most comfortable in the dry season, May–October. July–September is ski season in Chile and Argentina.

An entirely different climate reigns in the Amazon basin, whose tropical and subtropical rain forests spread from Ecuador and Peru across the northern third of Brazil. The dry season runs from May to September—which means it's simply less rainy than at any other time. Contrary to what you may have heard, the rainy season is a great time for an Amazon River trip; the waters are higher then and boats can venture farther upriver into the tributaries.

Certain ocean regions—the Atlantic coast from Brazil all the way down to the famous resort of Punta del Este in Uruguay, as well as the Caribbean shore of Venezuela—are at their hottest and most crowded when it's North America's winter. The sea moderates temperatures in most South American cities year-round, even as far south as Buenos Aires. The Pacific coast is bordered mainly by a strip of desert, where the climate is always hospitable. Argentine and Chilean Patagonia hold countless fjords, perfect for cruising from November to March.

Weather wise, May and June are probably the best months to visit South America, as you can expect both good weather and off-season prices. These months, as well as September and October, are also relatively uncrowded.

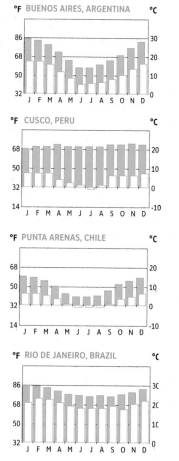

Argentina

WORD OF MOUTH

Back to work now—my 12-day Argentina trip is over. We started out in BA for 4 days, where we met up with our son . . . shopped, ate, saw the city's highlights, [and took day trips]. . . . From BA we flew down to Tierra del Fuego and [visited Ushuaia, Tierra del Fuego National Park, El Calafate, and Glacier National Park]. We left El Calafate . . . and flew to BA and then on to Iguazú. Straight from deep winter to the subtropical rain forest—it was great! This was our whirlwind tour. We had 9 flights and 7 different airports in 12 days. We were tired but so extremely happy that all the flying didn't matter. I'd love to go back and spend more time at these places and explore new ones. Next time.

—Chery

MOST TRAVELERS THINK THEY'VE STUMBLED upon a long-lost European country when they get to Argentina. Most Argentines, too, are convinced they're more European than South American. A quick look at the people walking down the avenues of any Argentine city confirms the impression. There are more Italian surnames than Spanish, and the largest colony of Yugoslavs outside of their fractured homeland. There are tens of thousands of descendants of Jewish immigrants from Eastern Europe, and communities of British, French, and German families enjoy cultural and financial clout far beyond their insignificant numbers.

But in spite of the symbiosis with Europe, the country has had a chaotic past, politically and economically. The pitfalls of Argentine politics weren't inappropriately characterized in the musical *Evita*: "Truth is stranger than fiction" is a maxim confirmed by the musical-chairs–like process that has placed both soldiers and civilians in the country's presidency. Further, Argentina is a me-first society that considers government a thorn in its side, and whose citizens avoid paying taxes with the finesse of bullfighters. As a community, it's totally chaotic, but as individuals, Argentines are generous and delightful, full of life, and eager to explain the intricacies of their complex society. They're also philosophers, anxious to justify their often enviable existence. Friendship is a time-consuming priority, and family connections are strong. Argentines work longer hours than New Yorkers—just not so efficiently—and rival Madrileños at dining until dawn.

Argentina stretches more than 5,000 km (3,000 mi) from north to south and encompasses everything from snow-covered mountains to subtropical jungle. In the north, nature is ravenous and rampant in the sultry province of Misiones; here the spectacular Iguazú Falls flow amid foliage that is rain-forest thick. In the pampas, or plains, of central Argentina, the countryside recalls the American West: In the west, the Andean backbone Argentina shares with Chile attracts wine-lovers to Mendoza, climbers to Mt. Aconcagua, and skiers to Bariloche and other resorts. Patagonia, in the south, is like no other place on earth. Monumental glaciers deposit icebergs into lakes. Penguins troop along beaches. Whales hang out with their tails emerging from the sea.

ORIENTATION & PLANNING

GETTING ORIENTED

Updated by Victoria Patience

Buenos Aires is the nation's political, economic, and cultural capital and the gateway to the rest of the country. The pampas—vast plains of cattle ranches and home of the gauchos—extend south from the cityl. Iguazú Falls are roughly 1,300 km (800 mi) to the city's northeast on the border with Paraguay and Brazil. Nestled in the shadow of the Andes, Mendoza was a desert before irrigation transformed it into the world's fourth-largest wine-producing region. Patagonia's rough and largely uninhabited territory extends south to Tierra del Fuego and consumes a third of Argentina. It's divided into two regions: the Atlan-

TOP REASONS TO GO

Dance the Night Away. From its beginnings in portside brothels at the turn of the 19th century, tango has marked the character of Buenos Aires and its inhabitants. Although you probably associate tango with dance, for locals it's more about the music and lyrics. Regardless, this the place to experience the best of this impassioned, art form.

Indulge Your Inner Carnivore. The beef here is so good, most Argentines see little reason to eat anything else, though pork, lamb, and chicken are tasty alternatives, and civito (kid), when in season, is outstanding. Carne asado (roasted meat) usually means grilled a la parrilla (on a grill over hot coals), but it can also be baked in an oven or roasted at a barbecue (asado).

Worship the Vine. Argentines drink a lot of vino tinto (red wine); Malbec and Cabernet are the most popular. If you prefer vino blanco (white wine), try a sauvignon blanc or chardonnay from Mendoza, or lesser-known wineries from farther north, such as La Rioja and Salta, where the Torrontés grape thrives. This varietal produces a dry white with a lovely floral bouquet.

Get Outdoors. Fishing in Patagonia's northern Lake District is legendary (especially in Bariloche). Hiking and mountain biking in national and provincial parks provide unique memories of a vast wilderness. Since Argentina's seasons are the opposite of North America's, you can ski or snowboard from June to September.

tic, with an incomparable variety of marine life, and the Andes, with frozen lakes, glaciers, and thousand-year-old forests.

Buenos Aires. Elegant boulevards and quirky cobbled streets give the capital a European air, but the chaotic traffic and protest marches are distinctly Latin American. The home of the tango is *the* place to learn the dance or take in a show. It's also a place filled with world-class boutiques, restaurants, and museums.

Iguazú Falls. On the Argentine-Brazilian border, some 1.7 million gallons of the Iguazú River plummet over a precipice each second, forming a 275-meter-wide (900-foot-wide) wall of water. Trails, metal catwalks, and Zodiacs all allow for spray-soaked close-ups.

Mendoza. Mendoza is the heart of the winelands, and its wineries enjoy the greatest reputation. Vintners here use desert sun, mountain snow, and extreme altitudes to craft distinctive wines—especially Malbec, the area's signature red. The region's other thrills include river rafting, horseback riding in the Andes, and skiing.

Patagonia. Alpine scenery on a gigantic scale is one way to describe the pine forests and snowcapped peaks of northern Patagonia's Lake District. The region's hub, Bariloche, is near some of Argentina's best ski spots. Farther south and east, penguins, whales, and sea lions are the entertaining natural attractions on the windswept, wave-battered Atlantic coast. Southern Patagonia really is the end of the world: Tierra del Fuego is closer to Antarctica than to Buenos Aires, and Ushuaia is the Earth's southernmost city. The monumental beauty of the Perito Moreno glacier is alone worth the trip south. For many, though, Patagonia's romance lies in its sheer desolation.

ARGENTINA PLANNER

WHEN TO GO

Buenos Aires is least-crowded in January and February, when locals beat the heat at resorts outside the city. City sightseeing is most pleasant during the temperate spring and fall. Try to visit Iguazú Falls in August through October, when temperatures are lower, the falls are fuller, and the spring coloring is at its brightest.

Mendoza's wine harvest season is celebrated in late February and early March with the vendima (wine festival). Winter is the time for pruning and tying vines. Ski season begins in July.

If you're heading to the Lake District or Patagonia, visit during the shoulder seasons of December and March. Southern seas batter the Patagonia coast year-round and winds there often reach gale-force. In Tierra del Fuego, fragments of glaciers cave into lakes with a rumble throughout the thaw from October to the end of April.

CLIMATE

Because of Argentina's great variety of latitudes, altitudes, and zones, you can encounter many different climates in any given month. The following are average daily maximum and minimum temperatures for Buenos Aires and Bariloche.

BUENOS AIRES

Jan.	85F	29C	May	64F	18C	Sept.	64F	18C
	63	17		47	8		46	8
Feb.	83F	28C	June	57F	14C	Oct.	69F	21C
	63	17		41	5		50	10
Mar.	79F	26C	July	57F	14C	Nov.	76F	24C
	60	16		42	6		56	13
Apr.	72F	22C	Aug.	60F	16C	Dec.	82F	28C
	53	12		43	6		61	16

BARILOCHE

Jan.	70F	21C	May	50F	10C	Sept.	50F	10C
	46	8		36	2		34	1
Feb.	70F	21C	June	45F	7C	Oct.	52F	11C
	46	8		34	1		37	3
Mar.	64F	18C	July	43F	6C	Nov.	61F	16C
	43	6		32	0		41	5
Apr.	57F	14C	Aug.	46F	8C	Dec.	64F	18C
	39	4		32	0		45	7

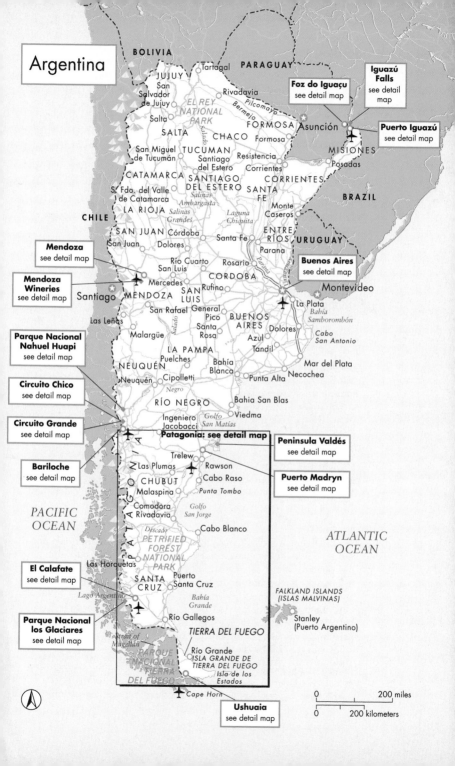

HOLIDAYS

New Year's Day; Day of the Epiphany (January 6); Veteran's Day (April 2); Labor Day (May 1); Anniversary of the 1810 Revolution (May 25); Semana Santa (Holy Week; 4 days in April leading up to Easter Sunday); National Sovereignty Day (June 10); Flag Day (June 20); Independence Day (July 9); Anniversary of San Martín's Death (August 17); Día de la Raza (Race Recognition Day) (October 12); Day of the Immaculate Conception (December 8); and Christmas.

Scores of performances and classes mark the Festival Buenos Aires Tango, the world's biggest tango festival, which culminates in a massive outdoor milonga along Avenida Corrientes. Carnaval comes in many guises throughout February. Mendoza celebrates the Festival de La Vendimia, the grape-harvest festival, during the first week of March. The Fiesta Nacional de la Nieve aka National Snow Festival is a monthlong winter carnival that takes place in August in and around Bariloche. The last two weeks of July sees La Rural, Argentina's biggest agricultural show, which includes displays of gaucho riding skills.

GETTING HERE & AROUND

BY AIR

There are direct daily flights, including those by flagship carrier Aerolíneas Argentinas, between Buenos Aires and several North American cities, with New York and Miami as primary departure points.

Buenos Aires' Aeropuerto Internacional de Ezeiza Ministro Pistarini (EZE)—known as Ezeiza—is 35 km (22 mi) southwest of and a 45-minute drive from city center. Most domestic flights operate out of Aeroparque Jorge Newbery (AEP). It's next to the Río de la Plata in northeast Palermo, about 8 km (5 mi) north of the city center. Both it and Ezeiza are run by the private company Aeropuertos Argentinos 2000.

Elsewhere in Argentina are mostly small, well maintained, and easy to get around. Flying times to Buenos Aires are 11–12 hours from New York, 9 hours from Miami, 10½ hours from Dallas or Houston, and 13 hours from Los Angeles, via Santiago de Chile.

BY BOAT

There's frequent ferry services across the Río de la Plata between Buenos Aires and the Uruguayan cities of Colonia and Montevideo. Buquebus operates direct services to both cities on large car-and-passenger ferries, which take three hours (return tickets cost 169 pesos to Colonia and 451 pesos to Montevideo). Both Buquebus and Colonia Express also run faster catamarans to Colonia, which take an hour or less, and cost 219 pesos and 234 pesos return, respectively. The more modest Ferrylíneas also serves the Buenos Aires–Colonia route on a smaller scale with fewer boats per day.

Buquebus and Ferrylínas both leave from terminals at the northern end of Puerto Madero. The Colonia Express terminal is in the port area near Retiro, a five-block walk from the long-distance bus station.

BY BUS

Frequent, dependable, and comfortable—with toilets, a/c, videos, and snacks—long-distance buses connect Buenos Aires with cities all over Argentina and with neighboring countries. Bus travel is substantially cheaper than flying, and far less prone to delays. Travelers often choose overnight sleeper services for trips up to 12 hours long.

Most bus companies have online timetables; some allow you to buy tickets online or by phone. Web sites also list *puntos de venta* (sales offices)—in many cases you don't need to go to the terminal to buy tickets, though you can usually buy them there right up until departure time. Be prepared to pay cash.

In general, long-distance buses depart from Buenos Aires' Terminal de Omnibus de Retiro, which is often referred to as the Terminal de Retiro or simply Retiro. You can buy tickets from the *boleterías* (ticket offices) on the upper level; there are also two ATMs here. The terminal's excellent Web site lists bus companies by destination, including their phone number and ticket booth location.

BY CAR

Argentina's long highways and fabulous scenery make it a great place for road trips. However, if you're only going to be staying in Buenos Aires and other big cities, a car isn't useful.

Ultramodern highways usually connect major cities. Gradually these become narrower routes, and then county roads—which often aren't divided or in great condition. City streets throughout Argentina are notorious for potholes, and lanes are poorly marked. Elsewhere street signs are often hard to see and sometimes nonexistent. Local driving styles range from erratic to downright psychotic, and the road mortality rate is shockingly high, especially in summer.

If you don't fancy dealing with traffic yourself, you can arrange a *remis con chofer* (car and driver) throughout hotels or taxi companies in most cities. For trips to and from a specific destination, you pay a pre-agreed-upon flat fare. Otherwise most companies charge an hourly rate of 35–50 pesos (sometimes with a two- or three-hour minimum). Rental companies also offer this service, but are more expensive.

GAS STATIONS Along highways, most *estaciones de servicio* are open 24 hours and are full service, with convenience stores and sometimes ATMs. In rural areas, stations have small shops and toilets but are few and far between and have reduced hours. Attendants don't expect a tip, though most locals add a few pesos for a full tank. Credit cards aren't always accepted—look for signs saying *tarjetas de crédito suspendidas* (no credit cards).

The major service stations are YPF, Shell, Petrobras, and Esso. Locals say that YPF gas is the highest quality. It also tends to be the cheapest. Prices are often more expensive in the north of Argentina. There are three grades of unleaded fuels, as well as diesel and biodiesel. GNC is compressed natural gas, an alternative fuel. Stations with GNC signs may sell only this, or both this and regular gas.

ESSENTIALS

ELECTRICITY

The electrical current in Argentina is 220 volts, 50 cycles alternating current (AC); wall outlets usually take Continental-type plugs, with two round prongs, though newer hotels are moving to plugs with three flat, angled prongs.

ENTRY REQUIREMENTS

As a U.S. citizen, you need only a passport valid for at least six months to enter Argentina for visits of up to 90 days—you'll receive a tourist visa stamp on your passport when you arrive. You should carry your passport or other photo ID with you at all times.

Officially, children visiting Argentina with only one parent do not need a signed and notarized permission-to-travel letter from the other parent to visit Argentina. However, as Argentine citizens *are* required to have such documentation, it's worth carrying a letter just in case.

For information on passport and visa requirements to visit the Brazilian side of Iguazú Falls, see the Iguazú section below.

HEALTH & SAFETY

No vaccinations are required, but the Centers for Disease Control (CDC) recommend vaccinations against hepatitis A and B, and typhoid for all travelers. A yellow fever vaccine is also advisable if you're traveling to Iguazú. Each year there are cases of cholera in northern Argentina, mostly in the indigenous communities near the Bolivian border; your best protection is to avoid eating raw seafood. Malaria exists only in low-lying rural areas near the borders of Bolivia and Paraguay; cases of dengue fever, another mosquito-borne disease, are also reported occasionally.

In the Andes, to remedy *apunamiento,* or altitude sickness—which results in shortness of breath and headaches—walk slowly, eat lightly, and drink plenty of fluids (avoid alcohol).

Argentina is safer than many Latin American countries. However, recent political and economic instability has caused an increase in street crime—mainly pickpocketing, bag-snatching, and occasionally mugging—especially in Buenos Aires.

Emergency Contacts **General Numbers** (📷 *107 for ambulance, 101 for police, 100 for fire).* **U.S. Embassy** (✉ *Av. Colombia 4300, Palermo, Buenos Aires* 📷 *11/5777–4554, 11/5777–4873 after hours* ⊕ *http://argentina.usembassy.gov).*

LANGUAGE

Argentina's official language is Spanish, known locally as *castellano* (rather than *español*). It differs from other varieties of Spanish in its use of *vos* (instead of *tú*) for the informal "you" form, and there are lots of small vocabulary differences, especially for everyday things like food. Porteño (as natives of Buenos Aires are known) intonation is rather singsong, and sounds more like Italian than Mexican or peninsular Spanish. And, like Italians, porteños supplement their words with lots and lots of gesturing. Another peculiarity is pronouncing the letters "y" and "ll" as a "sh" sound.

Services geared toward tourism generally employ an English-speaking staff. It's also common to find English-speaking staff at commercial and entertainment centers.

MONEY MATTERS

CURRENCY & EXCHANGE
Argentina's currency is the peso, which equal 100 centavos. Bills come in denominations of 100 (violet), 50 (navy blue), 20 (red), 10 (ocher), 5 (green), and 2 (blue). Coins are in denominations of 1 peso (a heavy bimetallic coin); and 50, 25, 10, and 5 centavos.

At this writing the exchange rate is 3.20 pesos to the U.S. dollar. You can change dollars at most banks (between 10 AM and 3 PM), at a *casa de cambio* (money changer), or at your hotel. All currency exchange involves fees, but as a rule, banks charge the least, and hotels the most. You need to show your passport to complete the transaction.

PRICING
Although prices in Argentina have been steadily rising, Buenos Aires is still surprisingly cheap if you're traveling from a country with a strong currency. Eating out is very good value, as are mid-range hotels. Room rates at first-class hotels approach those in the United States, however.

Sample prices: cup of coffee and two *medialunas* (croissants), 5–6 pesos; litre bottle of beer, 8–14 pesos; glass of wine, 11–16 pesos; steak and fries in a cheap restaurant, 12–15 pesos; 1-mi taxi ride in Buenos Aires, 3.10 pesos; bus ride in Buenos Aires, 90 cents.

TAXES
Argentina has 21% V.A.T. (known as IVA) on most consumer goods and services. The tax is usually included in the price of goods and noted on your receipt. You can get nearly all the IVA back on locally manufactured goods if you spend more than 70 pesos at stores displaying a duty-free sign. You're given a Global Refund check to the value of the IVA, which you get stamped by customs at the airport, and can then cash in at the clearly signed tax refund booths. Allow an extra hour to get this done.

Argentina has an international departure tax of $18, payable by credit card or in cash in pesos, dollars, or euros. There's an $8 domestic departure tax, but this is often included in the price of tickets. Hotel rooms carry a 21% tax. Cheaper hotels and hostels tend to include this in their quoted rates; more expensive hotels add it to your bill.

TIPPING
Propinas (tips) are a question of rewarding good service rather than an obligation. Restaurant bills—even those that have a *cubierto* (bread and service charge)—don't include gratuities; locals usually add 10%. Bellhops and maids expect tips only in the very expensive hotels, where a tip in dollars is appreciated. You can also give a small tip (10% or less) to tour guides. Porteños round off taxi fares, though some cabbies who frequent hotels popular with tourists seem to expect more. Tipping is a nice gesture with beauty and barbershop personnel—5%–10% is fine.

PHONES

The country code for Argentina is 54. To call landlines from the United States, dial the international access code (011) followed by the country code (54), the two-to-four-digit area code without the initial 0, then the five-to-nine-digit phone number. Any number that is prefixed by a 15 is a cell. To call these from the United States, dial the international access code (011) followed by the country code (54), Argentina's cellphone code (9), the area code without the initial 0, then the seven- or eight-digit cell phone number without the initial 15.

All of Argentina's area codes are prefixed with a 0 (e.g., the code for Buenos Aires is 011), which you need to include when dialing within the country. You don't need to dial the area code to call a local number. Confusingly, area codes and phone numbers don't all have the same number of digits. For local directory assistance (in Spanish), dial 110.

Argentina's two phone companies—Telecom and Telefónica—operate public phones and phone centers, called *locutorios* or *telecentros*. Although service is efficient, and direct dialing—both long-distance and international—is universal, public phones aren't abundant and are often broken. All accept coins; some have slots for phone cards.

RESTAURANTS & HOTELS

RESTAURANTS Whether eaten at home or in a restaurant, meals in Argentina are events. Sobremesa (chatting at the table after the meal) is just as important as the meal, and people linger over wine or coffee long after the dishes have been cleared away. Breakfast is usually served until 11 [am]; lunch runs from 12:30 to 3:30; dinner is from 8 to around midnight.

ACCOMMO-DATIONS Buenos Aires has an array of hotels, inns, apart-hotels (short-term rental apartments), and hostels. Mendoza has many good, small to medium-size hotels. Idyllic lake-view lodges, cozy cabañas (cabins), vast estancias (ranches), and inexpensive hospedajes or residenciales (bed-and-breakfasts) are found in towns and in the countryside throughout Patagonia.

WHAT IT COSTS (IN ARGENTINE PESOS)				
¢	$	$$	$$$	$$$$
RESTAURANTS under 8	8–15	15–25	25–35	over 35
HOTELS under 80	150–280	140–220	220–300	over 300

Restaurant prices are based on the median main course price at dinner. Hotel prices are for two people in a standard double room in high season.

VISITOR INFORMATION

Contact **Argentine Secretariat of Tourism** ☎ *800/555-0016 in Argentina* ⊕ *www.turismo.gov.ar.*

BUENOS AIRES

Updated by Brian Byrnes, Andy Footner & Victoria Patience

Incredible food, fresh young designers, and a thriving cultural scene—all these Buenos Aires has. Yet less-tangible things are at the heart of the city's sizzle. Here, a flirtatious glance can be as passionate as a tango; a heated sports discussion as important as a world-class soccer match. It's this zest for life that's making Buenos Aires one of Latin America's hottest destinations. And, whether they're screaming for a soccer team or enjoying an endless barbecue with friends, porteños (as the city's citizens are called) are always demonstrating that enjoying the here and the now is what life is all about.

GETTING HERE & AROUND

BY AIR Flagship Aerolíneas Argentinas operates direct flights between Buenos Aires and New York JFK and Miami. The airline and its partner Austral operate flights, generally from Buenos Aires's Aeroparque Jorge Newbery, to many Argentine cities, including Puerto Iguazú, Salta, Mendoza, Córdoba, Bariloche, Ushuaia, and El Calafate.

Transfers Between Airports: A taxi ride between the international Ezeiza and the Aeroparque costs 80–90 pesos and takes an hour in normal traffic. Manuel Tienda León shuttles make the same trip for 38 pesos.

Transfers from Ezeiza: A cab costs about 70 pesos (you pay the metered price and tolls) and takes 45–60 minutes. Manuel Tienda León shuttles run to and from the airport and their terminal in the Retiro district leave roughly every half hour; some include free drop-off at downtown hotels. A one-way ticket costs 35 pesos. Bus 86 leaves from a shelter in the parking area opposite the Aeropuertos Argentinos 2000 building (turn left out of Terminal B). You need change for the 1.50 peso ticket and patience for the 2–3 hours it takes to reach San Telmo and Plaza de Mayo (it runs along Avenida Paseo Colón).

Transfers from Aeroparque: A taxi to Microcentro or San Telmo costs 10–15 pesos and takes anything from 15 to 45 minutes depending on downtown traffic. Manuel Tienda León also operates shuttle buses to and from their terminal and to downtown hotels, but as a ticket costs 14 pesos, it makes more sense to take a taxi. Several city buses run along Avenida Rafael Obligado, outside the airport: the 160 and 37 go to Plaza Italia, and the 33 and 45 go to Retiro and the Microcentro. All cost 90¢.

BY BUS Most long-distance buses depart from the Terminal de Omnibus de Retiro, which is often referred to as the Terminal de Retiro or simply Retiro. Ramps and stairs from the street lead you a huge concourse where buses leave from more than 60 numbered platforms. There are restrooms, restaurants, public phones, lockers, news kiosks, and a tourist office on this floor.

Colectivos (city buses) connect the city's barrios and the greater Buenos Aires area. Ticket machines on board only accept coins (fares within the city are a flat 90¢). Bus stops are roughly every other block, but you may have to hunt for the small metal route-number signs: they could be stuck on a shelter, lamppost, or even a tree. Stop at a news kiosk and buy the *Guía T,* a handy route guide.

BY CAR　Avenida General Paz is Buenos Aires' ring road. If you're driving into the city, you'll know you're in Buenos Aires proper once you cross it. That said, having a car here is more hassle than it's worth; there are ample taxis and public transportation options. A more convenient option than driving yourself is to have your travel agent or hotel arrange for a *remis* (car and driver), especially for a day's tour of the suburbs. Black-and-yellow taxis fill the streets and take you anywhere in town and short distances into greater Buenos Aires. Fares start at 3.10 pesos with 31¢ per 650 feet. You can hail taxis on the street or ask hotel and restaurant staffers to call for them.

BY SUBTE　Service on the *subte* (subway) is quick, but trains are often packed and strikes are common. Four of the six underground lines (A, B, D, and E) fan out west from downtown; lines C and H (only partly open) connect them. Single-ride tickets cost a flat 90¢. The subte shuts down around 11 PM and reopens at 5 AM.

SAFETY & PRECAUTIONS

Although Buenos Aires is safer than most Latin American capitals, the country's unstable economy means crime is a concern. Pickpocketing and mugging are common, so avoid wearing flashy jewelry, be discreet with money and cameras, and be mindful of bags. Take taxis as much as possible after dark. Police patrol most areas where you're likely to go, but they have a reputation for corruption, so locals try to avoid contact with them.

Protest marches are a part of life in Buenos Aires: most are peaceful, but some end in confrontations with the police. They often take place in the Plaza de Mayo, in the square outside the Congreso, or along the Avenida de Mayo connecting the two.

ESSENTIALS

Airport Info **Aeropuertos Argentinos 2000** ⊕ *www.aa2000.com.ar).*

Airport Shuttle **Manuel Tienda León** (☎ *11/4383–4454 or 810/888–5366* ⊕ *www.tiendaleon.com.ar).*

City Bus Info **Los Colectivos** (⊕ *www.loscolectivos.com.ar).*

Remises **Remises Full-Time** (☎ *11/4775–1011).* **Remises Traslada** (☎ *11/5128–8888).*

Subte Info **Metrovías** (☎ *800/555–1616* ⊕ *www.metrovias.com.ar).*

Taxis **Pídalo** (☎ *11/4956–1200* ⊕ *www.radiotaxipidalo.com.ar).* **Radio Taxi Ciudad** (☎ *11/4923–7007* ⊕ *www.radiotaxiciudad.com.ar).*

Visitor Info **Turismo Buenos Aires** (⊕ *www.bue.gov.ar).*

BUENOS AIRES TOURS

The Web site of the city tourist board, Turismo Buenos Aires has lively, downloadable MP3 walking tours in English. Bright orange info booths at the airports and seven other locations provide maps and have English-speaking personnel. The super-personalized service—for tours in town and out—you get from Isabel at **Buenos Aires Tours** (⊕ *www.buenosaires-tours.com.ar*) is almost heroic. For a local's perspective, contact the **Cicerones de Buenos Aires** (☎ *11/4431-9892* ⊕ *www.cicerones.org.ar*), a free service that pairs you with a porteño to show you parts of town you might not see otherwise. Highly informed young historians from the University of Buenos Aires lead the cultural and historical tours at **Eternautas** (☎ *11/5031-9916* ⊕ *www.eternautas.com*). It offers orientation tours, neighborhood walks, themed outings (e.g., Evita, the literary city, Jewish Buenos Aires), and excursions outside town.

Through **La Bicicleta Naranja** (☎ *11/4362-1104* ⊕ *www.labicicletanaranja.com.ar*) you can rent a bicycle and gear to follow one of the routes on their excellent maps or go with a guide on general or theme trips. See Buenos Aires from the river on a 2½-hour sailboat tour with **Smile on Sea** (☎ *11/15-5018-8662* ⊕ *www.smileonsea.com*). Large onboard screens make the posh minibuses used by **Opción Sur** (☎ *11/4777-9029* ⊕ *www.opcionsur.com.ar*) part transport and part cinema. Each stop on their city tour is introduced by relevant historical footage (e.g., Evita rallying the masses at Plaza de Mayo).

EXPLORING BUENOS AIRES

Little remains of Buenos Aires's colonial days. This is due in part to the short lifespan of the adobe (mud and straw) used to build the city's first houses, and also to the fact that Buenos Aires's elite have always followed Europe's architectural trends. The result is an arresting hotchpotch of styles that hints at many far-off cities—Rome, Madrid, Paris, Budapest. With boulevards lined with palatial mansions and spacious parks, Palermo, La Recoleta, and some parts of the downtown area are testament to days of urban planning on a grandiose scale (and budget); San Telmo and La Boca have a distinctly working-class Italian feel.

CENTRO & ENVIRONS

Office workers, shoppers, sightseers, and traffic fill the streets around Centro each day. Locals profess to hate the chaos; unrushed visitors get a buzz out of the bustle.

❸ **La Manzana de Las Luces** *(The Block of Illumination)*. More history is packed into this single block of buildings southwest of Plaza de Mayo than in scores of other city blocks put together. Among other things, it was the enclave for higher learning: the metaphorical *luces* (lights) of its name refer to the "illuminated" scholars who worked within. The block's earliest occupant was the controversial Jesuit order, which began construction here in 1661. The Jesuits honored their patron saint at the **Iglesia de San Ignacio de Loyola** *(Saint Ignatius of Loyola*

Church) (⊠*Corner of Alsina and Bolívar*). The first church on the site was built of adobe in 1675; within a few decades it was rebuilt in stone. The Iglesia de San Ignacio is open to the public, but you can only visit the rest of Manzana de las Luces on guided tours led by excellent professional historians. Call ahead to arrange English-language visits. ⊠*Entrance and inquiries at Perú 272, Plaza de Mayo* 🕾*11/4342–6973* 💷*5 pesos* ⊗*Visits by guided tour only; Spanish-language tours leave daily at 3, 4:30, and 6* PM; *call to arrange tours in English* Ⓜ*A to Plaza de Mayo, D to Catedral, E to Bolívar.*

❹ **Plaza de Mayo.** Since its construction in 1580, this has been the focal
★ point of Argentina's most politically turbulent moments, including the uprising against Spanish colonial rule on May 25, 1810—hence its name. Thousands cheered for Perón and Evita here; anti-Peronist planes bombed the gathered crowds a few years later; and there were bloody clashes in December 2001 (hence the heavy police presence and crowd-control barriers). Here, too, you can witness the changing of the Grenadier Regiment guards; it takes place weekdays every two hours from 9 until 7, Saturday at 9 and 11, and Sunday at 9, 11, and 1.

The eclectic Casa de Gobierno, better known as the **Casa Rosada** (⊠*Hipólito Yrigoyen 219 Plaza de Mayo* 🕾*11/4344–3802* ⊕*www. museo.gov.ar* 💷*Free* ⊗*Weekdays 10–6, Sun. 2–6*), or Pink House, is at the plaza's eastern end, with its back to the river. It houses the government's executive branch (the president works here but lives elsewhere) and was built in the late 19th century over the foundations of an earlier customhouse and fortress. The balcony facing Plaza de Mayo is a presidential podium. Evita rallied the *descamisados* (the shirtless—meaning the working class) here, and Madonna sang her filmed rendition of "Don't Cry for Me Argentina." Check for a small banner hoisted alongside the nation's flag, indicating "the president is in." Ⓜ*Line A, Plaza de Mayo; Line D, Catedral; Line E, Bolívar.*

❺ **Teatro Colón.** Its magnitude, magnificent acoustics, and opulence (grander than Milan's La Scala) position the Teatro Colón (Colón Theater) among the world's top five operas. It has hosted the likes of Maria Callas, Richard Strauss, Arturo Toscanini, Igor Stravinsky, Enrico Caruso, and Luciano Pavarotti, who said that the Colón has only one flaw: the acoustics are so good, every mistake can be heard. The theater is currently dark owing to restoration work that's slated to end in 2010. Until then, tours of the theater—once very popular—are suspended, and performances are being held in other theaters. ⊠*Main entrance: Libertad between Tucumán and Viamonte; box office: Pasaje Toscanini 1180, Centro* 🕾*11/4378–7100 tickets, 11/4378–7132 tours* ⊕*www.teatrocolon.org.ar* Ⓜ*D to Tribunales.*

SAN TELMO & LA BOCA

No longer do southern neighborhoods like San Telmo and La Boca play second fiddle to posher northern barrios. The hottest designers have boutiques here, new restaurants are booked out, and the south is also the linchpin of the city's tango revival, appropriate given that the dance was born in these quarters.

1 **Calle Museo Caminito.** Cobblestones, tango dancers, and haphazardly
★ constructed, vividly painted conventillos have made Calle Museo
Caminito the darling of Buenos Aires' postcard manufacturers since
this pedestrian street and open-air museum–art market opened in 1959.
Artists fill the block-long street with works depicting port life and
tango, which is said to have been born in La Boca. It's all more commercial than cultural, but its embrace of all things tacky make it a fun
outing. Many of La Boca's tenements have been recycled into souvenir
shops. The plastic Che Guevaras and dancing couples make the shops
in the **Centro Cultural de los Artistas** (⊠*Magallanes 861* ☺*Mon.–Sat.
10:30–6*) as forgettable as all the others on the street, but the uneven
stairs and wrought-iron balcony hint at what a conventillo interior was
like. ⊠ *Caminito between Av. Pedro de Mendoza (La Vuelta de Rocha
promenade) and Olivarría, La Boca* 🖼*Free* ☺*Daily 10–6.*

2 **Estadio Boca Juniors.** The stadium that's also known as La Bombonera
★ (meaning candy box, supposedly because the fans' singing reverberates
as it would inside a candy tin) is the home of Argentina's most popular club. Inside the stadium is **El Museo de la Pasión Boquense** (The
Museum of Boca Passion), a modern, two-floor space that chronicles
Boca's rise from neighborhood club in 1905 to its current position as one
of the world's best teams. On the tour, lighthearted guides take you all
over: to press boxes, locker rooms, underground tunnels, and the field
itself. ⊠*Brandsen 805, at del Valle Iberlucea, La Boca* 🕾*11/4309–
4700 stadium, 11/4362–1100 museum* ⊕*www.museoboquense.com.
ar* 🖼*Museum: 14 pesos. Stadium: 14 pesos. Museum and stadium: 22
pesos* ☺*Museum daily 10–6 except when Boca plays at home; stadium
tours hourly 11–5; English usually available, call ahead.*

RECOLETA & ALMAGRO

For the most-illustrious families, Recoleta's boundaries are the boundaries of the civilized world. The local equivalents of the Vanderbilts
throw parties in the Alvear Palace Hotel, live in spacious 19th-century
apartments, and wouldn't dream of shopping elsewhere. By contrast
Almagro to the southwest is a gritty, working-class neighborhood that
spawned many tango greats.

6 **Cementerio de la Recoleta.** The ominous gates, Doric-columned portico,
Fodor'sChoice and labyrinthine paths of the city's oldest cemetery (1822) lead to final
★ resting place for the nation's most-illustrious figures. These 13½acres
are rumored to be the most expensive real estate in town. The cemetery has more than 6,400 elaborate vaulted tombs and majestic mausoleums, 70 of which have been declared historic monuments. The
mausoleums resemble chapels, Greek temples, pyramids, and miniature
mansions. Among the cemetery's highlights are the embalmed remains
of Eva Perón, who made it (almost intact) here after 17 years of post-
humous wandering, are in the Duarte family vault. The city government runs free guided visits to the cemetery in English on Tuesday and
Thursday at 11. If you prefer an independent tour, the administrative
offices at the entrance can provide a free map, and caretakers throughout the grounds can help you locate the more-intriguing tombs. These

are also labeled on a large map at the entrance. ✉*Junín 1760, Recoleta* ☎*11/4803–1594* ✉*Free.* ⊙*Daily 8–6.*

❼ Museo Nacional de Bellas Artes. The world's largest collection of Argentine art is displayed in this huge golden-color stone building. The 24 ground-floor galleries contain European art. Upstairs, the Argentine circuit starts in Room 102 with works from colonial times through the 19th century. Follow the galleries around to the right and through 20th-century art. Head straight for the first-floor Argentine galleries while you're feeling fresh, and keep the European collection for later. For English information, check out one of the MP3 audio guides (15 pesos) in the scant gift shop at the bottom of the stairs. ✉*Av. del Libertador 1473, Recoleta* ☎*11/4803–0802 tours (in Spanish)* ⊕*www. mnba.org.ar* ✉*Free* ⊙*Tues.–Fri. 12:30–7:30, weekends 9:30–7:30.*

FodorsChoice
★

PALERMO

Whether your idea of sightseeing is ticking off museums, flicking through clothing rails, licking your fingers after yet another long lunch, or kicking up a storm on the dance floor, Palermo can oblige.

❿ Museo Evita. Eva Duarte de Perón, known universally as Evita, was the wife of populist president Juan Domingo Perón. She was both revered by her working-class followers and despised by the Anglophile oligarchy of the time. The Museo Evita shies from pop culture clichés and concentrates on Evita's life and works, particularly the social aid programs she instituted and her role in getting women the vote. Evita's reputation as fashion plate is also reflected in the many designer outfits on display, including her trademark working suits and some gorgeous ball gowns. The museum's excellent guided visits are available in English but must be arranged by phone in advance. That said, laminated cards with just-understandable English translations of the exhibits are available in each room and at the ticket booth. ✉*Lafinur 2988, 1 block north of Av. Las Heras, Palermo* ☎*11/4807–9433* ⊕*www. museoevita.org* ✉*10 pesos* ⊙*Tues.–Sun. 1–7* Ⓜ*D to Plaza Italia.*

★

❽ Museo de Arte de Latinoamericano de Buenos Aires (MALBA, Museum of Latin American Art of Buenos Aires). The fabulous MALBA is one of the cornerstones of the city's cultural life. Its centerpiece is businessman and founder Eduardo Constantini's collection of more than 220 works of 19th- and 20th-century Latin American art in the main first-floor gallery. Young enthusiastic guides give great tours in Spanish; you can call ahead to arrange group English-language tours. ✉*Av. Presidente Figueroa Alcorta 3415, Palermo* ☎*11/4808–6500* ⊕*www.malba.org. ar* ✉*12 pesos, free Wed.* ⊙*Thurs.–Mon. noon–8, Wed. noon–9.*

FodorsChoice
★

❾ Parque Tres de Febrero. Known locally as Los Bosques de Palermo (Palermo Woods), this 200-acre green space is really a crazy quilt of smaller parks. Rich grass and shady trees make this an urban oasis, although the busy roads and horn-honking drivers that crisscross the park never quite let you forget what city you're in. South of Avenida Figueroa Alcorta you can take part in organized tai chi and exercise classes or impromptu soccer matches. You can also jog, bike, or in-line skate here, or take a boat out on the small lake. ✉*Bounded by Avs. del Lib-*

Ⓒ
FodorsChoice
★

ertador, Sarmiento, Leopoldo Lugones, and Dorrego, Palermo Ⓜ*D to Plaza Italia.*

WHERE TO EAT

Buenos Aires is the most cutting-edge food town in the Southern Hemisphere. Here, three things have come together to create a truly modern cuisine: diverse cultural influences, high culinary aspirations, and a relentless devotion to aesthetics, from plate garnishes to room decor. And yet, at their core, even the most modern international restaurants in Buenos Aires are informed by this city's appreciation of a good bottle of wine shared with friends and family over a long meal.

CENTRO & ENVIRONS

CENTRO

¢ **Confitería La Ideal.** Part of the charm of this spacious 1918 coffee shop–

CAFÉ milonga is its sense of nostalgia: think fleur-de-lis motifs, timeworn European furnishings, and stained glass. No wonder they chose to film the 1998 movie *The Tango Lesson* here. La Ideal is famous for its *palmeritas* (glazed cookies), tea service, and the scores of locals and foreigners who attend milongas here. Tango lessons are offered Monday through Saturday at varying times throughout the day and night; concerts take place every evening except Tuesday and Thursday. ⊠*Suipacha 384, at Av. Corrientes, Centro 11/5265–8069* ⊕*www.confiteriaideal.com* 🚍*No credit cards* Ⓜ*C to C. Pellegrini, D to 9 de Julio.*

¢ **El Cuartito.** This porteño classic has been making pizza and empanadas

PIZZA since 1934, and the surroundings have changed little in the last 70 years. The brusque waitstaff is part of the charm. Drop in for a slice at the *mostrador* (counter) or make yourself comfortable under the portraits of Argentine sporting greats for fantastic, no-nonsense food and cold Quilmes beer. Try a slice of *fainá* (like a chickpea-flour flat bread), one of the traditional Argentine variations on pizza. ⊠*Talcahuano 937, Centro 11/4816–4331* 🚍*No credit cards* Ⓜ*D to Tribunales.*

$ **Gran Café Tortoni.** In the city's first confitería, established in 1858, art

CAFÉ nouveau decor and high ceilings transport you back in time. Tango star Carlos; writer Jorge Luis Borges; local and visiting dignitaries; and intellectuals have all eaten and sipped coffee here. Don't miss the *chocolate con churros* (thick hot chocolate with baton-shape doughnuts for dipping). Reserve ahead of time for the nightly tango shows; there's a 50-peso cover. ⊠*Av. de Mayo 825, Centro 11/4342–4328* ⊕*www.cafetortoni.com.ar* 🚍*AE, MC, V* Ⓜ*A to Perú.*

$$$$ **Tomo I.** The famed Concaro sisters have made this restaurant, on the

ARGENTINE mezzanine of the Hotel Panamericano, a household name. The French-inspired menu has excellent fried, breaded calf brains. The chocolate tart oozes warm, dark ganache. White linen–covered tables set far apart in the romantic red room allow for quiet conversation. Service is tops. Reservations are recommended. ⊠*Carlos Pellegrini 521, Centro 11/4326–6698* ⊕*www.tomo1.com.ar* 🚍*AE, DC, MC, V* ☾*Closed Sun. No lunch Sat.* Ⓜ*B to Carlos Pellegrini, D to 9 de Julio.*

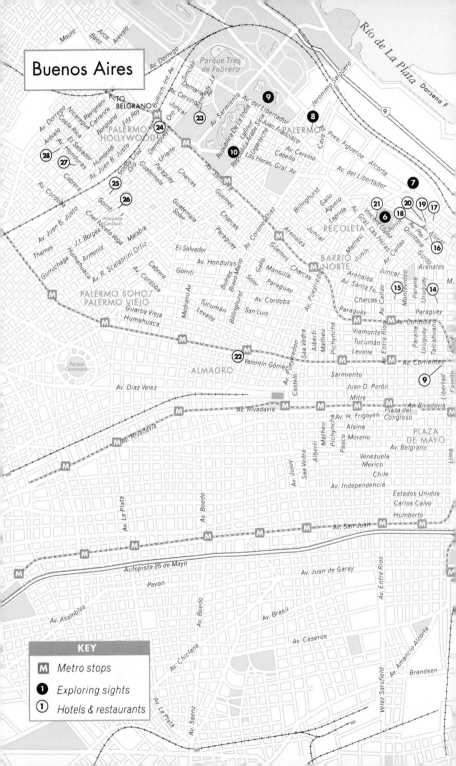

0

0

1 km

Darsena E

Darsena D

Darsena C

Darsena B

Darsena A

1

PUERTO MADERO

$$ **La Caballeriza.** Locals in the know come to this big, lively, informal steak
STEAK   house, where the prices are very reasonable for good, quality meat. Sip
champagne at the friendly bar while you wait for a table. The parrilla is
wood-fired, Uruguayan style, and the *asado de tira* (rack of beef short
ribs) is a highlight, but you also can't go wrong with the classic *bife de
chorizo* (bone-in sirloin or rump steak). There's another branch by the
Recoleta mall next to the cemetery, but this one is superior. ⊠*A.M. de
Justo 580, Puerto Madero 11/4514–4444* ⊕*www.lacaballerizapuerto
madero.com* ▭*AE, DC, MC, V* Ⓜ*B to L.N. Alem.*

SAN TELMO & LA BOCA

SAN TELMO

¢   **Bar Dorrego.** Bar Dorrego probably hasn't changed much in the last
CAFÉ   100 years or so. Dark wood and politely aloof waiters set the stage;
good coffee, *tragos* (alcoholic drinks), sangria, and snacks complete the
scene. When the weather is warm, sit at a table outside, order a cold
Quilmes beer and some salty peanuts, and soak in the scene. ⊠*Defensa
1098, at Humberto I, on Plaza Dorrego, San Telmo 11/4361–0141*
▭*No credit cards* Ⓜ*C or E to Independencia.*

$$ **La Farmacia.** Mismatched tables and chairs, comfy leather sofas, and
ARGENTINE   bright colors fill this cute, century-old corner house that used to be
☾   a traditional pharmacy. Generous breakfasts and afternoon teas are
served on the cozy ground floor, lunch and dinner are served in the dining room, and you can have late-night drinks on the bright-yellow roof
terrace. Arts and dance workshops are run upstairs, and the building
has two boutiques selling local designers' work. The modern Argentine
dishes are simple but well done, and the fixed-price lunch and dinner menus are deals. ⊠*Bolívar 898, San Telmo 11/4300–6151* ▭*No
credit cards* ☾*Closed Mon.* Ⓜ*C or E to Independencia.*

LA BOCA

$ **El Obrero.** For 50 years El Obrero has served juicy grilled steaks,
STEAK   sweetbreads, sausages, and chicken. The blackboard menu includes
rabas (fried calamari) and puchero. Try the *budín de pan* (Argentine
bread pudding). This spot is popular with tourists and local workmen
alike, so expect a short wait. La Boca is sketchy at night, so lunch is
preferable; in any case, take a taxi. ⊠*Augustín R. Caffarena 64, La
Boca 11/4363–9912* ▭*No credit cards* ☾*Closed Sun.*

RECOLETA

$$$$ **La Bourgogne.** White tablecloths, fresh roses, and slick red leather chairs
FRENCH   emphasize the restaurant's elegance. A sophisticated waitstaff brings
Fodor'sChoice   you complimentary hors d'oeuvres as you choose from chef Jean-Paul
★   Bondoux's creations, which include foie gras, rabbit, escargots, cha-
teaubriand, *côte de veau* (veal steak), and wild boar cooked in cassis.
The fixed-price tasting menu is more affordable than à la carte selec-
tions and features a different wine with each plate. ⊠*Alvear Palace
Hotel, Ayacucho 2027, Recoleta* ☎*11/4805–3857 or 11/4808–2100*
⚐*Reservations essential. Jacket and tie* ▭*AE, DC, MC, V* ☾*Closed
Sun. No lunch Sat.*

$$$$ **Duhau Restaurante & Vinoteca.** Just as the Palacio Duhau Hotel changed
MODERN the game of luxury in Buenos Aires, so has its eponymous restaurant.
ARGENTINE This wonderful spot serves some of the best food in the city, com-
Fodor'sChoice plimented with impeccable and friendly service. The menu is French-
★ inspired, but with proud touches of Argentine cuisine: sweetbreads
with Patagonian berries, king prawns from Tierra del Fuego, and trout
from Bariloche. The beef is all certified Black Angus from the province
of Santa Fe. The wine list reads like a book: more than 500 varieties are
available. After dinner, visit the Cheese Room, which offers 45 different
cheeses. ⊠*Av. Alvear 1661, Recoleta* 11/5171–1340 ⊕*www.buenos
aires.park.hyatt.com* ▤*AE, D, MC, V* ⊙*No lunch weekends.*

$ **El Sanjuanino.** Northern Argentine fare is served at this long-estab-
ARGENTINE lished, if touristy, spot. El Sanjuanino is known for its tamales,
☺ *humitas* (steamed corn cakes wrapped in husks), and especially its
empanadas, which crowds line up to take out for a picnic in the park
(they're 20% cheaper to go). But they also make good *locro, pollo
a la piedra* (chicken pressed flat by stones), venison, and antelope
stew. Skip the boring, hamlike *lomito de cerdo* (pork steak). The decor
includes hanging hams and a stuffed deer head, but the vibe is still fun.
⊠*Posadas 1515, at Callao, Recoleta* 11/4804–2909 ▤*AE, MC, V*
⊙*Closed Mon.*

PALERMO

PALERMO

$$ **Rio Alba.** In terms of quality, price, and charm, this is the best parrilla in
STEAK Buenos Aires. Period. It consistently serves the tastiest and most tender
Fodor'sChoice cuts of beef. The asado de tira is particularly good, as is the flavorful
★ entrana. Ask for a minigrill at your table to keep your meat warm;
you're going to need time to finish the enormous servings. It's packed
every night of the week. ⊠*Cervino 4499, Palermo* 11/4773–5748
▤*AE, D, MC, V.*

PALERMO HOLLYWOOD

$ **El Encanto.** It's a sports, cinema, and theater museum *and* a fantastic
STEAK parrilla. Walls are covered with sports and film memorabilia, and glass
cases are packed with trophies from soccer championships. The food
is fantastic, too. The bife de chorizo and ojo de bife are top-notch, as
are the salads and desserts. Service is touch-and-go, but the chaos and
eclectic crowd make for an unforgettable evening. ⊠*Bonpland 1690,
Palermo Hollywood* 11/15–5809–2240 ▤*No credit cards.*

PALERMO SOHO

$$$ **La Baita.** In a city filled with first- and second-generation Italians, it's
ITALIAN surprisingly hard to find a good Italian meal. Look no further than La
Baita, a cozy corner spot in the heart of Palermo Soho that attracts
highbrow porteños and Europeans. They do fantastic fresh pastas,
and nice meat dishes. The main dining room is quaint, and some of
the tables are too close together, but the romantic atmosphere, live
music, and friendly service make up for it. ⊠*Thames 1603, Palermo
Soho* 11/4832–7234 ▤*MC, V* ⊙*No lunch Mon.*

¢   **Club Eros.** A basic dining room attached to an old soccer club, Club Eros
ARGENTINE   has developed a cult following for its downscale charm. The excellent
fare at rock-bottom prices has begun to draw young Palermo trend-
ies as well as older customers who have been loyal to the club for
decades. There's no menu, but you can confidently order a crispy milanesa (breaded meat cutlet), or, if available, a bife de chorizo and fries.
Pasta sauces fall flat, but the flan is terrific. ⊠ *Uriarte 1609, Palermo
Soho 11/4832–1313* ▭ *No credit cards.*

WHERE TO STAY

Centro and Puerto Madero are teeming with international hotel chains,
and most of them are well located. But once you close your door, it's
easy to forget where you are. In San Telmo, hotels are primarily grand
old mansions with soaring ceilings and impressive wooden doors.
Across town in Palermo, it's a hipper, more urbane feel, but hotels are
so new they haven't had time to develop their own character yet.

CENTRO & ENVIRONS

CENTRO

$$ **Buenos Aires cE Design Hotel.** This hotel drips coolness. The lobby's
glass floor looks down to a small pool, just one example of the trans-
parency theme here. Floor-to-ceiling windows afford amazing views,
and mirrors are placed for maximum effect. Rooms have rotating flat-
screen TVs that let you watch from bed or from one of the leather
recliners. Mattresses are high and mighty and covered in shades of
brown and orange. **Pros:** Supermodern and spacious suites; great loca-
tion. **Con:** The basement lounge feels like, well, a basement. ⊠ *Marcelo
T. Alvear 1695, Centro* ☎ *11/5237–3100* ⊕ *www.designce.com* ⤵ *21
rooms, 7 suites* ⚼ *In-room: safe, kitchen, Ethernet, Wi-Fi. In-hotel:
bar, pool, gym, laundry service, public Wi-Fi* ▭ *AE, DC, MC, V* Ⓜ *D
to Callao.*

$$ **Marriott Plaza Hotel.** This Buenos Aires landmark brims with old-
Fodor'sChoice   school style. Built in 1909 and renovated in 2003, the hotel sits at the
★   top of pedestrian-only Florida Street and overlooks the leafy Plaza San
Martín. The elegant lobby, crystal chandeliers, and swanky cigar bar
evoke Argentina's opulent, if distant, past. Rooms are comfortable and
clean, if not particularly spacious. **Pros:** Great prices; every area of the
building offers a fascinating city view. **Cons:** The main lobby is small;
check-in can be lengthy. ⊠ *Florida 1005, Centro* ☎ *11/4318–3000,
800/228–9290 in U.S.* ⊕ *www.marriott.com* ⤵ *313 rooms, 12 suites*
⚼ *In-room: safe, Ethernet. In-hotel: 2 restaurants, room service, bar,
pool, gym, concierge, laundry service, public Wi-Fi* ▭ *AE, DC, MC, V*
⦿| *BP* Ⓜ *C to San Martín.*

¢   **Milhouse Hostel.** This hostel goes the extra mile with pool tables, televisions, and concierge services. The house, which dates from the late
1800s, has been tricked out with funky artwork and accessories. Its
three floors overlook a tiled patio and all lead out to a sunny terrace.
Morning yoga classes may well be followed by rowdy beer-swilling
asados (barbecues). At night, the surrounding streets can be dodgy, so
take precautions. **Pros:** It's lovely and lively. **Cons:** It's a hostel; hygiene

standards are sometimes below par. ⊠*Hipólito Irigoyen 959, Centro* ☎*11/4345–9604 or 11/4343–5038* ⊕*www.milhousehostel.com* ⟿*13 private rooms, 150 beds total* ♿*In-room: no a/c, no phone, no TV, Ethernet, Wi-Fi. In-hotel: restaurant, bar, laundry facilities, parking (fee)* ⊟*No credit cards* ⊠*CP* Ⓜ*A to Piedras, C to Av. de Mayo.*

PUERTO MADERO

$$$$

FodorśChoice

★

▧ **Faena Hotel + Universe.** Argentine fashion impresario Alan Faena and famed French architect Philippe Starck set out to create a "universe" unto itself. Rooms are feng shui perfect with rich reds and crisp whites. Velvet curtains and Venetian blinds open electronically to river and city views; velvet couches, leather armchairs, flat-screen TVs, and surround-sound stereos lend more luxury. Other highlights are two excellent restaurants and an elaborate spa with a Turkish bath. **Pros:** Quite simply, one of the most exhilarating hotels on the planet. **Cons:** An ever-present "are you cool enough?" vibe. ⊠*Martha Salotti 445, Puerto Madero* ☎*11/4010–9000* ⊕*www.faenahotelanduniverse.com* ⟿*110 rooms, 16 suites* ♿*In-room: safe, DVD, Ethernet, dial-up, Wi-Fi. In-hotel: 2 restaurants, room service, bars, pool, gym, concierge, laundry service, parking (fee), no-smoking rooms* ⊟*AE, DC, MC, V.*

SAN TELMO

$

FodorśChoice

★

▧ **Gurda Hotel.** The Gurda will give you glimpse into what life was like at the turn of the 19th century. Seven rooms line the long, open-air hallway with exposed brick, green plants, and bamboo sticks. Each room is named after something or someone decidedly Argentine—Jorge Luis Borges, Malbec, Patagonia—with decorations to match. (In the Borges room you can find volumes of his work and a colorful portrait of the literary legend.) Rooms are basic, but charming. **Pros:** The young friendly staff can organize wine tastings with local sommeliers, and tango lessons. **Cons:** The entrance is on a busy street; the restaurant and bar are noisy. ⊠*Defensa 1521* ☎*11/4307–0646* ⊕*www.gurda hotel.com* ⟿*7 rooms* ♿*In-room: safe, Wi-Fi. In-hotel: restaurant, room service, bar, concierge, laundry service, parking (fee), no-smoking rooms* ⊟*AE, DC, MC, V* Ⓜ*C to Constitucion.*

$$

FodorśChoice

★

▧ **Moreno Hotel.** A gorgeous art deco building dating back to 1929, the Moreno's architects were posed with the challenge of restoring the 80-year-old site without disturbing its original elements, like mosaic tiling and stained-glassed windows. The seven-floor hotel has spacious and sexy rooms, each decorated in a color motif complete with chaise lounges, Argentine cowhide rugs, and big fluffy beds. The top-floor terrace has an outdoor fireplace, big wooden recliners, and amazing city views. **Pros:** There's a top-notch restaurant and 130-seat theater on-site. **Con:** Some rooms are just steps from the main lobby and elevator. ⊠*Moreno 376* ☎*11/6091–2000* ⊕*www.morenobuenosaires.com* ⟿*39 rooms* ♿*In-room: safe, refrigerator, Ethernet, dial-up, Wi-Fi. In-hotel: restaurant, room service, bar, gym, concierge, parking (fee), no-smoking rooms* ⊟*AE, MC, V* Ⓜ*A to Plaza de Mayo.*

RECOLETA & ALMAGRO

RECOLETA

$$$$ **Alvear Palace Hotel.** If James Bond were in town, this is where he'd

Fodor'sChoice   hang his hat. In fact, Sean Connery *has* stayed here, because when

★   it comes to sophistication, the Alvear Palace is the best bet in Buenos Aires. It has hosted scores of dignitaries since opening its doors in 1932, and although new and more-affordable hotels are making it something of a gray ghost, the Alvear is still swanky. It's all about world-class service and thoughtful touches. **Pros:** The lunch buffet is out of this world, and the French restaurant, La Bourgogne, is one of the city's best. **Cons:** You'll pay dearly to stay here. ⊠ *Av. Alvear 1891, Recoleta* ☎ *11/4808–2100, 11/4804-7777, 800/448-8355 in U.S.* ⊕ *www.alvearpalace.com* ☞ *100 rooms, 100 suites* ♿ *In-room: safe, Ethernet, dial-up, Wi-Fi. In-hotel: 2 restaurants, room service, bar, pool, gym, concierge, laundry service, no-smoking rooms* ⊟ *AE, DC, MC, V* ⦿| *BP.*

$ **Art Hotel.** It has an impressive ground-floor gallery where exhibits of works by acclaimed Argentine artists change monthly. Rooms are classified as "small and cozy," "queen," or "king" and many have wrought-iron bed frames with white canopies. The building's 100-year-old elevator will take you to the rooftop patio, where there's also a hot tub. **Pro:** Its bohemian vibe will make you feel like you've joined an artists' colony. **Con:** Rooms are dark and somewhat antiquated. ⊠ *Azcuenaga 1268, Recoleta* ☎ *11/4821–4744* ⊕ *www.arthotel.com. ar* ☞ *36 rooms* ♿ *In-room: safe, Ethernet. In-hotel: bar, laundry service, public Wi-Fi* ⊟ *AE, MC, V* Ⓜ *D to Pueyrredón.*

$ **Hotel Bel Air.** Given the fancy French-style facade, you could mistake the Bel Air for a neighborhood hotel somewhere in Paris. Inside, a more-modern feel takes over, with a round wood-panel lobby bar and a snazzy café that looks onto exclusive Arenales Street, dotted with art galleries, fashion boutiques, and furniture stores. Rooms have handsome wooden floors and simple but stylish furnishings in an array of earth-tone colors. **Pros:** Great price and location on a posh street. **Cons:** Staff is easily distracted; hallways and common areas are cramped. ⊠ *Arenales 1462, Recoleta* ☎ *11/4021–4000* ⊕ *www.hotelbelair.com. ar* ☞ *77 rooms* ♿ *In-room: safe, dial-up, Wi-Fi. In-hotel: restaurant, room service, bar, gym, laundry service, airport shuttle, no-smoking rooms* ⊟ *AE, DC, MC, V* Ⓜ *D to Tribunales.* ⦿| *BP.*

$$$$ **Park Hyatt Palacio Duhau.** Its two buildings, a restored 1930s-era

Fodor'sChoice   mansion and a 17-story tower, are connected by an underground art

★   gallery and a leafy garden. The rooms are decorated in rich hues of wood, marble, and Argentine leather. Mansion rooms are larger and more charming. Sip a whiskey at the Oak Bar and visit the Ahin Spa, next to the city's largest indoor pool. **Pros:** Understated elegance; great restaurant; the 3,500-bottle Wine Library and "Cheese Room" are unique attractions. **Cons:** A long walk from one side of the hotel to the other; although elegantly decorated, common areas lack warmth. ⊠ *Av. Alvear 1661, Recoleta* ☎ *11/5171–1234* ⊕ *www.buenosaires. park.hyatt.com* ☞ *126 rooms, 39 suites* ♿ *In-room: safe, Ethernet,* *dial-up, Wi-Fi, DVD. In-hotel: 2 restaurants, room service, bar, pool, gym, spa, concierge, laundry service* ⊟*AE, MC, V.*

ALMAGRO

$$ ⛨**Abasto Plaza Hotel.** This place is *all* about the tango. Photos and paintings of famous musicians line the walls that surround the checked-marble dance floor, which is next to a boutique selling sequined skirts, stilettos, and fishnets. Suites each have their own dance floor for private lessons, or you can join other guests for nightly tango lessons and a live show. Rooms are large and elegant with—surprise—a tango theme. The enormous Abasto Shopping Center is across the street. **Pros:** If you're here to tango, this is your place. **Cons:** Tango overload is a real possibility; furnishings and bedding are tired. ⊠*Av. Corrientes 3190, Almagro* ☎*11/6311–4466* ⊕*www.abastoplaza.com* ⇔*120 rooms, 6 suites* ♿*In-room: Ethernet, dial-up, Wi-Fi. In-hotel: restaurant, room service, bar, pool, gym* ⊟*AE, DC, MC, V* ⏻*BP* Ⓜ*B to Carlos Gardel.*

PALERMO

HOLLYWOOD

$$ ⛨**Home Buenos Aires.** It oozes coolness and class. Each room is decorated with vintage French wallpaper and has a stereo, a laptop-friendly safe, and either a bathtub or a wet room. On-site there's a vast garden; a barbecue area; an infinity pool; a holistic spa; and a funky lounge bar where you can sip a cocktail and listen to mood music. **Pros:** Hip and fun; always has interesting guests. **Con:** Lots of nonguests come here to hang out, reducing the intimacy factor. ⊠*Honduras 5860, Palermo Hollywood* ☎*11/4778–1008* ⊕*www.homebuenosaires.com* ⇔*14 rooms, 4 suites* ♿*In-room: safe, Ethernet, Wi-Fi. In-hotel: restaurant, room service, bar, pool, spa* ⊟*AE, MC, V* Ⓜ*D to Ministro Carranza.*

SOHO

¢ ⛨**Giramondo Hostel.** The funky Giramondo has all a hostel needs: plenty of beds and bathrooms, a kitchen, a TV and computer lounge, and a patio, where backpackers from around the world grill up slabs of Argentine beef. The dark, dank underground bar serves up cheap drinks; it also has a small wine cellar. Giramondo is two blocks from buses and the subte on Avenida Santa Fe, so there's access to Palermo's pulsing nightlife and to downtown. **Pros:** They have the budget traveler in mind, and cater to short-term and long-term travelers. **Con:** The surrounding streets are chaotic and loud. ⊠*Guemes 4802, Palermo Soho* ☎*11/4772–6740* ⊕*www.hostelgiramondo.com.ar* ♿*In-room: no a/c, no phone, kitchen, no TV, Ethernet. In-hotel: bar, no elevator, laundry facilities* ⊟*No credit cards* Ⓜ*D to Palermo.*

AFTER DARK

BARS & CLUBS

FodorśChoice **Bahrein.** Sheik—er, chic and super-stylish, this party palace is in a
★ 100-year-old former bank. Eat upstairs at Crizia, or head straight to the main floor's Funky Room, where beautiful, tightly clothed youth groove to pop, rock, and funk. The downstairs Excess Room has elec-

tronic beats and dizzying wall visuals. For 500 pesos, get locked in the vault and guzzle champagne all night with strangers. ⊠*Lavalle 345, Centro* ☎*11/4315–2403* Ⓜ*B to Alem.*

★ **Le Bar.** Le Bar is a stylish addition to the Centro drinking scene. Up the stairs from the cocktail lounge is a clever sunken seating arrangement; farther still is a smokers' terrace. Office workers get the evening started; DJs start a bit later and play till 2 AM. ⊠*Tucuman 422, Centro* ☎*11/5219–8580.*

Bar 6. Somewhat of a Palermo Soho institution, Bar 6 suffers from the indifferent waitstaff that such a reputation demands. If you can get past that, it's a convenient Palermo meeting point (it opens at 8 AM), a stylish bar, and a decent restaurant. A DJ often plays good music in the evenings. ⊠*Armenia 1676, Palermo Soho* ☎*11/4833–6807.*

Cava Jufre. There aren't any wild nights at this wine bar, but gather around for plenty of earnest and good-natured appreciation of the output of lesser-known Argentinean bodegas. The decoration is simple and woody, and there's an impressive cellar downstairs. This is a good place to discover some new varietals—and do call ahead to see if there are any wine-tasting events planned. It's closed Sunday. ⊠*Jufre 201, Palermo* ☎*11/4775–7501* ⊕*www.lacavajufre.com.ar.*

Gran Bar Danzon. At this hot spot local business sharks and chic internationals sip wine and eat sushi by candlelight. It's extremely popular for happy hour, but people stick around for dinner and the occasional live jazz shows, too. The wine list and the appetizers are superb, as is the flirting. ⊠*Libertad 1161, Recoleta* ☎*11/4811–1108* Ⓜ*C to Retiro.*

The Kilkenny. A popular pub that spawned a whole street of imitators, the Kilkenny serves surprisingly good Irish food and has Guinness on draft. Celtic or rock bands play every night, entertaining the after-work crowd from nearby government and commercial buildings who come for the 8 PM to 11 PM happy hour. ⊠*Marcelo T. De Alvear 399, Centro* ☎*11/4312–7291* Ⓜ*C to San Martín.*

Fodor'sChoice ★ **Niceto.** The former home of the outrageous Club 69 boasts one of the city's most interesting lineups with everything from indie rock to minimal techno; it turns into one of the city's biggest cumbia venues every Wednesday at midnight with Club night Zizek. The larger main room with a balcony holds live shows and lots of dancing and there's usually something contrasting and chilled taking place in the back room, too. ⊠*Cnel. Niceto Vega 5510, Palermo Hollywood* ☎*11/4779–9396.*

TANGO

DINNER SHOWS

Fodor'sChoice ★ **Rojo Tango.** Five-star food, choreography, and glamour: you wouldn't expect anything less from the Faena Hotel + Universe. Crimson velvet lines everything from the walls to the menu at the Cabaret, and tables often hold celebs both local and global. As well as classic tangos, the implausibly good-looking troupe does jazz-tango, semi-naked numbers, and even the tango version of Roxanne from *Moulin Rouge*. It's worth breaking the piggy bank for. ⊠*Martha Salotti 445, Puerto Madero* ☎*11/5787–1536* ⊕*www.rojotango.com.*

★ **El Viejo Almacén.** This place was founded by legendary tango singer Edmundo Rivero, but he wouldn't recognize the slick outfit his rootsy

1

bar has become. Inside the colonial building lurks a tireless troupe of dancers and musicians who perform showy tango and folk numbers. ⊠*Balcarce 786, at Independencia, San Telmo* ☎*11/4307–6689* ⊕*www.viejo-almacen.com.ar.*

MILONGAS

La Catedral. Behind its unmarked doors is a hip club where the tango is somehow very rock. Casual milongas take place on Tuesday, Friday, and Saturday, and it's a cool night out even if you're not planning to dance. ⊠*Sarmiento 4006, doorbell 5, Almagro* ☎*11/15–5325–1630.*

Fodor's Choice ★ **La Ideal.** Soaring columns and tarnished mirrors are part of La Ideal's crumbling old-world glamour. The classic tearoom hosts milongas organized by different groups in its first-floor dance hall every day of the week. Many include live orchestras. ⊠*Suipacha 384, Plaza de Mayo* ☎*11/4601–8234* ⊕*www.confiteriaideal.com.*

Fodor's Choice ★ **Salón Canning.** Several milongas call this large dance hall home. The coolest is Parakultural, which takes place Monday, Wednesday, and Friday. Originally an alternative, "underground" milonga, it now attracts large numbers of locals (including longtime expats). ⊠*Av. Scalabrini Ortíz 1331, Palermo* ☎*11/4832–6753* ⊕*www.parakultural.com.ar.*

12 de Octubre *(El Bar de Roberto).* Cobweb- and dust-covered bottles line the walls of this tiny venue, with maybe the most authentic tango performances in town. From behind a heavy wooden bar, owner Roberto dispatches *ginebra* (a local gin) to old-timers and icy beer and cheap wine to students. When the singing gets going at 2 or 3 AM, it's so packed there's no room to breathe, but the guitar-and-voice duos manage gritty, emotional tango classics all the same. ⊠*Bulnes 331, Almagro* ☎*11/6327–4594* ☾*Thurs.–Sat. after midnight.*

SHOPPING

CLOTHING: MEN'S & WOMEN'S

CASUAL & COOL

Antique Denim. Burberry meets Diesel at Antique Denim, where smart, dark jeans are worn with colorful tweed jackets with leather elbow patches. The denim cuts are sharp and tailored, made for cruising the town. ⊠*Gurruchaga 1692, Palermo Viejo* ☎*11/4834–6829.*

A.Y. Not Dead. Rainbow vinyl, fake snakeskin, truckloads of nylon: it's all very synthetic at A.Y. Not Dead. Seen anywhere other than under a strobe, the clothes may be hard to take, but to carve a space for yourself on a heaving club floor, shopping here's the way forward. ⊠*Soler 4193, Palermo Viejo* ☎*11/4866–4855* ⊕*www.aynotdead.com.ar.*

Fábrica de Bananas. The entrance is small, but inside there's a vast warehouse filled with clothes by scores of young designers. Street wear predominates, but there's space for accessories, hats, underwear, art books, and even sex toys. On weekend nights, the sofas in the middle of the store become Espacio Björk, a laid-back bar. Note that late nights mean the store doesn't open until 1 PM. ⊠*Arévalo 1445, Palermo Hollywood* ☎*11/4777–6541* ⊕*www.fabricadebananas.com.ar.*

Kosiuko. Branches of Kosiuko, the ultimate local teen brand, are always packed with trendy adolescents served by hip-wiggling staff not much older than they are. The girls come for the improbably small, low-cut pants, the guys for budding metrosexual-wear. Kosiuko's fragrances and deodorant are a favorite with the population's most perspiring age group. ⊠*Av. Santa Fe 1779, Barrio Norte* ⊠*Abasto Mall, Av., Corrientes 3247, Almagro* ☎*11/4707–4091* ⊕*www.kosiuko.com.ar.*

Un Lugar En El Mundo. San Telmo's hippest shop showcases young designers, whose men's and women's clothing is both wearable and affordable. Bolsas de Viaje's vinyl and canvas creations evoke the golden age of air travel, Mir's satchels and totes in heavily stitched chestnut leather make you want to go back to school, and Paz Portnoi's cowhide heels are perfect for dressing up. ⊠*Defensa 891, San Telmo* ☎*11/4362–3836* Ⓜ*C or E to Independencia.*

María Aversa. There's a touch of gypsy in María Aversa's colorful knitwear, and the two-story town house store gives you plenty of room to roam. In addition to large-gauge knits, look for more unusual offerings, such as a velvet jacket with crocheted sleeves. ⊠*El Salvador 4580, Palermo Viejo* ☎*11/4833–0073* ⊕*www.mariaaversa.com.ar.*

Ona Saez. The ultrafitted jeans at Ona Saez are designed to be worn with sky-high heels and slinky tops for a sexy night out. The menswear is equally slick, mixing dressed-down denim with cool cotton shirts and tees. ⊠*Florida 789, Centro* ☎*11/5555–5203 Abasto Mall, Av. Corrientes 3247, Almagro* ☎*11/4959–3602 11/4775–1151* ⊕*www.onasaez.com.*

Refans A+. Futballers, soap-opera stars, clubbers: everyone seems to be wearing one of Refans's trademark T-shirts. They come in ultrabright colors, emblazoned with quirky Italian phrases like *siamo fuori* ("We are out," a reference to the World Cup). Lucas Castromán, a local futball star himself, is behind the brand. Anoraks, hoodies, jeans, and messenger bags round up the offerings. ⊠*El Salvador 4577, Palermo Viejo* ☎*11/4777–7251* ⊠*Arévalo 2843, Las Cañitas* ⊕*www.refans.net.*

Tienda Porteña. Browsing the building is almost as fun as browsing the clothes here. This multibrand boutique takes up the whole of a traditional San Telmo casa chorizo. Each room opens onto another, all containing simple railings hung with different small designers. Belocca's tango-inspired shoes are one reason to come; the cheerful baubles that dangle above the original bathroom sink are another. At night, the back turns into a bar serving microbrewery beers. ⊠*Carlos Calvo 618, San Telmo* ☎*11/1362–3340* Ⓜ*C to San Juan; C or E to Independencia.*

HIGH DESIGN

Giesso. A classic gents' tailor for nearly a century, Giesso is now pulling a Thomas Pink by adding jewel-color ties and shirts to its range of timeless suits. A new women's-wear line includes gorgeous linen suits and cashmere overcoats. ⊠*Av. Alvear 1882, Recoleta* ☎*11/4804–8828* ⊠*Florida 997, Centro* ☎*11/4312–7606* ⊕*www.giesso.com.ar.*

Kostüme. It's all very space odyssey at Kostüme. Extra-brief dresses might be made of netting or bunched-up nylon, worn over drainpipe trousers. Many tops are asymmetrical, and pants come with saddlebag-like protrusions. Menswear includes unusual Jedi-esque hooded robe-jackets.

✉*República de la India 3139, Palermo Botánico* ☎*11/4802–3136* ⊕*www.kostume.net* Ⓜ*D to Plaza Italia.*

Nadine Zlotogora. Bring your sense of humor to Nadine Zlotogora: her way-out designs are playful yet exquisitely put together. Sheer fabrics are embroidered with organic-looking designs, then worn alone or over thin cotton. Even the menswear gets the tulle treatment: military-look shirts come with a transparent top layer. ✉*El Salvador 4638, Palermo Viejo* ☎*11/4831–4203* ⊕*www.nadinez.com.*

FodorsChoice **Pablo Ramírez.** His tiny shop front is unadorned except for "Ramírez" ★ printed on the glass over the door—when you're this big, why say more? Pablo's couture doesn't come cheap, but given the peso prices, his perfectly tailored numbers are a (relative) bargain. He favors black for both waspishly waisted women's wear and slick gent's suits, though a few other shades are beginning to creep in. ✉*Perú 587, San Telmo* ☎*114342–7154* ⊕*www.pabloramirez.com.ar* Ⓜ*E to Belgrano.*

★ **Varanasi.** The structural perfection of Varanasi's clothes is a clue that the brains behind them trained as architects. Equally telling is the minimal, cavernous shop, fronted by plate glass. Inside, A-line dresses built from silk patchwork and unadorned bias cuts are some of the night-out joys that local celebs shop for—indeed, few others can afford to. ✉*Costa Rica 4672, Palermo Viejo* ☎*11/4833–5147* ✉*Libertad 1696, Recoleta* ☎*11/4815–4326* ⊕*www.varanasi-online.com.*

SPORTSWEAR

Stock Center. The official pale-blue-and-white shirts worn by the Argentine soccer team, the Pumas (the national rugby team), and the Leonas (women's hockey team) are some of the best sellers at this sporting megastore. The Nike, Adidas, and Puma clothing is all made in Brazil, and so is relatively cheap. Über-trendy Gola sneakers are another reason to come. ✉*Corrientes 590, Microcentro* ☎*11/4326–2131.*

Topper. Impossible as it may seem, the coolest footwear on Buenos Aires' dance floors in the '80s were yellow Wellington boots from this local sportswear brand. They're still selling them, together with the football shirts and bargain gym wear that's kept Topper popular despite competition from big international names. ✉*Gurruchaga 1573, Palermo Viejo* ☎*11/4832–6667* ⊕*www.topper.com.ar.*

HANDICRAFTS, SILVER & SOUVENIRS

★ **Aire del Sur.** Alpaca, carved deer bone, onyx, and leather are some of the materials that might be combined into perfectly crafted trays, candelabras, or photo frames at Aire del Sur. The winning mix of these traditional materials with contemporary designs has won the hearts of stores like Barneys in New York and Paul Smith in London. Call ahead to arrange a visit to the Recoleta showroom. ✉*Arenales 1618, 9th fl., Recoleta* ☎*11/5811–3640* ⊕*www.airedelsur.com.*

★ **Fundacín Silataj.** This small handicraft shop is run by a nonprofit organization, which trades fairly with around 30 indigenous communities in Argentina. The shop smells like the aromatic palo santo wood used to make the trays, platters, cutting boards, and hair combs they carry. Other offerings include carnival masks, handwoven textiles, beaten tin ornaments, and alpaca jewelry. Prices, though higher than in markets, are reasonable, quality is excellent, and you know your money is going to the artisans. Note that the store closes for lunch. ✉ *Vuelta de Obligado 1933, Belgrano* ☎*11/4785–8371* ⊕*www.fundacionsilataj. org.ar* Ⓜ*D to José Hernández.*

★ **Juan Carlos Pallarols Orfebre.** Argentina's legendary silversmith has made pieces for a mile-long list of celebrities that includes Frank Sinatra, Sharon Stone, Jacqueline Bisset, Bill Clinton, Nelson Mandela, the king and queen of Spain, and Princess Máxima Zorrequieta—Argentina's export to the Dutch royal family. A set of his ornate silver-handled steak knives is the perfect way to celebrate cow country, though you'll part with a few grand. ✉ *Defensa 1039, San Telmo* ☎*11/4362–0641* ⊕*www.pallarols.com.ar* Ⓜ*C or E to Independencia.*

Khori Wasi. Indigenous crafts from all over Latin America are chaotically arrayed in this vast, rust-color store. They're particularly strong on animal carnival masks and ceramics from Peru and Bolivia. There are also replicas of archaeological finds; cards next to each display explain the origins of the original. ✉*Peru 863, San Telmo* ☎*11/4300–3784* ⊕*www.khori-wasi.com.ar* Ⓜ*C or E to Independencia.*

Lappas. The classic silver trays, cutlery sets, tea sets, and ice buckets are favorites on porteño high-society wedding lists. Department stores worldwide stock Lappas silverware, but why pay export prices? ✉*Florida 740, Microcentro* ☎*11/4325–9568* Ⓜ*B to Florida* ✉*Santa Fe 1381, Barrio Norte* ☎*11/4811–6866* ⊕*www.lappas.com.*

★ **Materia Urbana.** The quirky, postmodern souvenirs this store specializes in are a welcome variation from all those mates and gaucho knives. The ubiquitous cow comes as a bright leather desk organizer here, while the national human icons Evita and Che adorn rolls of packing tape. Fridge-magnet poetry will help you remember your Spanish, and if you still can't manage more than "Hola," there's a hilarious illustrated dictionary of Argentine gestures to keep you going. Beautiful designer bags, jewelry, home ware, tango CDs, and prints by local artists are less ironic options. ✉*Defensa 707, San Telmo* ☎*11/4361–5265* ✉*Gorriti 4791, Palermo Viejo* ☎*11/4831–6317* ⊕*www.materiaurbana.com.*

Platería Parodi. This über-traditional store is chockablock with everything a gaucho about town needs to accessorize right, all in top-quality silver. There are belt buckles and knives for the boys, and the no-nonsense Pampa-style women's jewelry would go great with Gap and Ralph Lauren alike. ✉*Av. de Mayo 720, Plaza de Mayo* ☎*11/4342–2207* Ⓜ*A to Piedras.*

★ **Tierra Adentro.** Beautiful indigenous crafts come with a clean conscience at Tierra Adentro, which insists on trading fairly with the native Argentine craftsmen whose work they stock. Fine weavings are the shop's hallmark, but wide silver bracelets and gobstopper-size turquoise beads are other tempting offers. ✉*Arroyo 882, Retiro* ☎*11/4393–8552* ⊕*www.tierraadentro.info* Ⓜ*C to San Martín.*

MALLS

Abasto. The soaring art deco architecture of what was once the city's central market is as much a reason to come as the three levels of shops. Although Abasto has many top local chains, it's not as exclusive as other malls, so you can find bargains at shops like Ver, Yagmour, and

Markova. You can also dress up at Ayres, Paula Cahen d'Anvers, Akiabara, or the Spanish chain Zara, famous for its cut-price versions of catwalk looks. Levi's, Quiksilver, Puma, and Adidas are among the casual international offerings; for something smarter, there's Dior. Men can hit such trendy shops as Bensimon and Mancini or go for the *estanciero* (estate owner) look with Legacy chinos and polos. Take a break in the fourth-floor food court beneath the glass panes and steel supports of the building's original roof. The mall also has a cinema; if you prefer live entertainment, near the food court is a Ticketek booth. ⊠ *Av. Corrientes 3247, Almagro* ☎ *11/4959–3400* ⊕ *www.abasto-shopping. com.ar* Ⓜ *B to Carlos Gardel.*

★ **Alto Palermo.** A prime Palermo location, choice shops, and a pushy marketing campaign have made Alto Palermo popular. Giggly teenage hordes are seduced by its long, winding layout. Ladies who lunch sip espresso in the cafés of its top-level food hall. The 154 shops are strong on local street-wear brands like Bensimon and Bowen for the boys and Akiabara, Ona Sáez, Las Pepas, and Rapsodia for the girls. Check out trendy local designers María Vázquez and Allo Martínez for way-out party frocks, and Claudia Larreta for more staid numbers. Paruolo, Sibyl Vane, and Lázaro are the best of many good shoe and handbag shops. Surf-and-skate store Cristobal Colón does board shorts and All-Stars; local versions of Puma and Adidas footwear disappear fast despite high price tags. Other international names include Levi's and Miss Sixty. ⊠ *Av. Santa Fe 3251, at Av. Colonel Díaz, Palermo* ☎ *11/5777–8000* ⊕ *www.altopalermo.com.ar* Ⓜ *D to Bulnes.*

Galerías Pacífico. Upscale shops line the three levels of this building, which was designed during the city's turn-of-the-20th-century golden age. Stores are organized along four glass-roofed passages, which branch out in a cross from the central stairwell; the cupola above it is decorated by Argentine greats like Antonio Berni. Top local menswear brands Etiqueta Negra and La Dolfina Polo Lifestyle have large stores here. Paula Cahen d'Anvers and Uma are some of the options for younger women, while Janet Wise and Claudia Larreta do more sophisticated looks. There are a basement food court, a cinema, and the Centro Cultural Borges, whose small international art exhibitions have featured Andy Warhol, Salvador Dalí, and Henri Cartier-Bresson. ⊠ *Calle Florida 753, at Av. Córdoba, Microcentro* ☎ *11/4319–5100* Ⓜ *B to Florida.*

★ **Paseo Alcorta.** If you're a serious shopper and have time to visit only one mall, make it this one. Local fashionistas favor it for its mix of high-end local chains and boutiques from some of the city's best designers, all under one roof. Trendsetters like Trosman, Jazmín Chebar, and María Vázquez do cool clothes for girls, while for more classic chic there's Claudia Larreta and Portsaid. The men can hold their own up at Hermanos Estebecorena and Etiqueta Negra. Ultrahip accessories come as handbags at Jet, or as glasses at EXE, and Mishka and Paruolo sell cute but dressy shoes. The international presence is strong, too, with stores from Armani Exchange, Hilfiger, Lacroix, and Cacharel, as well as the usual sports brands. A classy food hall and Wi-Fi round off the reasons to come. ✉*Jerónimo Salguero 3172, at Av. Figueroa Alcorta, Palermo* ☎*11/5777–6500* ⊕*www.paseoalcorta.com.ar.*

Patio Bullrich. The city's most upscale mall was once the headquarters for the Bullrich family's meat-auction house. Inside stone cow heads mounted on pillars still watch over the clientele. A colonnaded front, a domed-glass ceiling, and curlicued steel supports are other reminders of another age. Top local stores are relegated to the lowest level, making way for the likes of Lacroix, Cacharel, and Maxmara. Urban leather-ware brand Uma has a shop here, as does Palermo fashion princess Jessica Trosman, whose spare women's clothes are decorated with unusual heavy beadwork. The enfant terrible of Argentine footwear, Ricky Sarkany, sells dangerously pointed stilettos in colors that walk the line between exciting and kitsch. Edgy but elegant menswear line Etiqueta Negra has its first store outside the snooty northern suburbs here. When the gloriously huge bags these shops pack your purchases into begin to weigh you down, stop for a calorie-oozing cake at Nucha, on the Avenida del Libertador side of the building. ✉*Enter at Posadas 1245, or Av. del Libertador 750, Recoleta* ☎*11/4815–3501* ⊕*www. shoppingbullrich.com.ar* Ⓜ*C to Retiro.*

MARKETS

Feria de San Pedro Telmo. This market packs a small San Telmo square every Sunday. Elbow your way through the crowds to pick through antiques and curios of varying vintages as well as tango memorabilia, or watch dolled-up professional tango dancers perform on the surrounding cobbled streets. The unofficial "stalls" (often just a cloth on the ground) of young craftspeople stretch several blocks up Defensa, away from the market proper. As it gets dark, the square turns into a milonga, where quick-stepping locals show you how it's done. ✉*Plaza Dorrego, Humberto I y Defensa, San Telmo* ☎*11/4331–9855* ⊕*www. feriadesantelmo.com* ⊘*Sun. 10–dusk* Ⓜ*E to Independencia, then walk 9 blocks east along Independencia to Defensa. Alternatively, A to Plaza de Mayo, D to Catedral, E to Bolívar, then walk 8 blocks south on Bolívar.*

Feria de Artesanías de la Plaza Vuelta de Rocha (Caminito). In the heart of colorful La Boca, Caminito showcases local artists all week long. You can find attractive port scenes in watercolors as well as stylish photographs of the neighborhood's old houses, though don't expect any budding Picassos. The market expands on weekends with stalls selling handicrafts and tacky souvenirs. As shoppers here are almost exclusively tourists, prices tend to be overambitious—sometimes irritatingly so. ✉*Av. Pedro de Mendoza and Caminito, La Boca* ⊘*Art market daily 10–6; crafts market weekends 10–6.*

Feria Artesanal de la Recoleta. It winds through several linked squares outside the Recoleta Cemetery. Artisans sell handmade clothes, jewelry, and housewares as well as traditional crafts. ✉*Avs. Libertador and Pueyrredón, La Recoleta* ☎*11/4343–0309* ⊘*Weekends 10–dusk.*

Feria de Plaza Serrano. The business conducted in this hip Palermo Viejo market rivals that done in the neighborhood's trendy boutiques. In a small square—which is actually round—artisans sell wooden toys, ceramics, and funky jewelry made of stained glass or vintage buttons.

1

TANGO TO GO

Need we remind you that Buenos Aires is the best place in the world to stock up on tango music, memorabilia, and serious dance wear? Some of the best tango shoes in town, including classic spats, 1920s T-bar designs, and glitzier numbers for men and women are all made to measure at **Flabella** (⊠*Suipacha 263, Microcentro* ☎*11/4322–6036* ⊕*www.flabella.com*). For foxier-than-thou footwear that's kicking up storms on milonga floors worldwide, head to **Comme Il Faut** (⊠*Arenales 1239, Apt. M, Barrio Norte* ☎*11/4815–5690* ⊕*www.commeil faut.com.ar*); dedicated dancers love its combination of top-notch quality and gorgeous, show-stopping colors

like teal or plum, usually with metallic trims. Animal-print suede, fake snakeskin, and glittering ruby take-me-home-to-Kansas numbers are some of the wilder options. **Tango Brujo** (⊠*Esmeralda 754, Microcentro* ☎*11/4326–8264* ⊕*www.tango brujo.com*) is a one-stop tango shop selling shoes, clothes, and how-to videos. Recordings by every tango musician under the sun can be found at **Zivals** (⊠*Av. Callao 395, Congreso* ☎*11/5128–7500* Ⓜ*B to Callao* ⊠*Serrano 1445, Palermo Viejo* ☎*11/4833–7948* ⊕*www. tangostore.com*). They stock CDs of classics, modern performers, and electro-tango as well as DVDs, sheet music, books, and even T-shirts.

This is also a great place to buy art: the railings around a playground here act as an open-air gallery for Palermo artists, and organizers control the quality of art on display. The feria continues unofficially at many nearby bars, which push their tables and chairs aside to make room for clothing and accessory designers: expect to find anything from cute cotton underwear and one-off T-shirts to clubbing dresses. Quality is often low, but so are prices. ⊠*Plazoleta Cortázar (Plaza Serrano) at Honduras and Serrano, Palermo Viejo* ⊗ *Weekends 11–dusk.*

WINE

FodorśChoice ★ **Grand Cru.** Don't let the small shop front put you off: as with all the best wine shops, the action is underground. Grand Cru's peerless selection includes wines from Patagonian vineyard Noemia, one of the country's best and exclusive to the shop. Incredibly savvy staffers will guide you, and they can FedEx up to 12 bottles anywhere in the world. ⊠*Av. Alvear 1718, Recoleta* ☎*11/4816–3975* ⊕*www.grandcru.com.ar.*

★ **La Finca.** Unusual wines from boutique vineyards are among the great finds here. Like their stock, the staff hails from Mendoza, capital of Argentine oenology, and they're a friendly, knowledgeable crew. Past the rustic shelving piled high with bottles are a few tables where you can sample wines like Carmelo Patti or Bramare, accompanied by a light *picada* (snack) of goat cheese and black olives, also from Mendoza. ⊠*Honduras 5147, Palermo Viejo* ☎*11/4832–3004.*

Ligier. Ligier has a string of shops across town and lots of experience guiding bewildered shoppers through their impressive selection. Although they stock some boutique-vineyard wines, they truly specialize in the big names like Rutini and Luigi Bosca. Their leather wine carrying cases make a great picnic accessory. ⊠*Av. Santa Fe 800, Retiro* ☎*11/4515–0126* Ⓜ*C to San Martín.*

Terroir. A wine-lovers' heaven is tucked away in this white stone Palermo town house. Expert staffers are on hand to help you make sense of the massive selection of Argentine wine, which includes collector's gems like the 1999 Angélica Zapata Cabernet Sauvignon. Terroir ships all over the world. ⊠*Buschiazzo 3040, Palermo* ☎*11/4778–3443* ⊕*www.terroir.com.ar.*

IGUAZÚ FALLS

Updated by Victoria Patience

1358 km (843 mi) north of Buenos Aires; 637 km (396 mi) west of Curitiba, Brazil.

Iguazú consists of some 275 separate waterfalls—in the rainy season there are as many as 350—that plunge more than 200 feet onto the rocks below. They cascade in a deafening roar at a bend in the Iguazú River (Río Iguazú/Río Iguaçu) where the borders of Argentina, Brazil, and Paraguay meet. Dense, lush jungle surrounds the falls: here the tropical sun and the omnipresent moisture make the jungle grow at a pace that produces a towering pine tree in two decades instead of the seven it takes in, say, Scandinavia. By the falls and along the roadside, rainbows and butterflies are set off against vast walls of red earth, which is so ubiquitous that eventually even paper currency in the area turns red from exposure to the stuff.

The falls and the lands around them are protected by Argentina's Parque Nacional Iguazú (where the falls are referred to by their Spanish name, the Cataratas de Iguazú) and by Brazil's Parque Nacional do Iguaçu (where the falls go by the Portuguese name of Foz do Iguaçu). The Argentine town of Puerto Iguazú and the Brazilian town of Foz do Iguaçu are the hubs for exploring the falls (the Paraguayan town of Ciudad del Este is also nearby).

ARGENTINA INFO

GETTING HERE & AROUND

Aerolíneas Argentinas flies four to six times daily between Aeroparque Jorge Newbery in Buenos Aires and the Aeropuerto Internacional de Puerto Iguazú (20 km/12 mi southeast of Puerto Iguazú); the trip takes 1¾ hours. LAN does the same trip three to four times daily. Normal rates are about 350–400 pesos each way. Four Tourist Travel runs shuttle buses from the airport to hotels in Puerto Iguazú. Services leave after every flight lands and cost 12 pesos. Taxis to Puerto Iguazú cost 40 pesos.

> **DOOR-TO-DOOR**
>
> Argentinean travel agencies **Sol Iguazú Turismo** (☎*3757/421–008* ⊕*www.soliguazu.com.ar*) and **Caracol Turismo** (☎*3757/424–242* ⊕*www.caracolturismo.com.ar*) organize door-to-door transport to both sides of the falls, and can reserve places on the Iguazú Jungle Explorer trips. Both also run day trips to the Jesuit ruins in San Ignacio, the Itaipú Dam, and to other areas of Misiones Province.

Vía Bariloche operates several daily bus services between Retiro bus station in Buenos Aires and the Puerto Iguazú Terminal de Omnibus in the center of town. The trip takes 16–18 hours, so it's worth paying the little extra for *coche cama* (sleeper) or *cama ejecutivo* (deluxe sleeper) services, which cost 200–240 pesos one-way (regular semi-cama services cost around 180 pesos). You can travel direct to Rio de Janeiro (22 hours) and São Paolo (15 hours) with Crucero del Norte; the trips cost 250 and 200 pesos, respectively.

From Puerto Iguazú to the falls or the hotels along RN 12, take El Práctico from the terminal or along Avenida Victoria Aguirre. Buses leave every 15 minutes 7–7 and cost 8 pesos round-trip.

There's little point in renting a car around Puerto Iguazú: daily rentals start at 150–200 pesos, more than twice what you pay for a taxi between the town and the falls. A hire car is useful for visiting the Jesuit ruins at San Ignacio, 256 km (165 mi) south of Puerto Iguazú on RN 12, a two-lane highway in excellent condition.

ARGENTINA ESSENTIALS

Airline Contacts **Aerolíneas Argentinas** (☎ *800/2228–6527* ⊕ *www.aerolineas. com.ar*). **LAN** (☎ *810/999–9526* ⊕ *www.lan.com*).

Banks & Currency Exchange **Argencam** (✉ *Av. Victoria Aguirre 1162*). **Banco de la Nación** (✉ *Av. Victoria Aguirre 179* ⊕ *www.bna.com.ar*).

Bus Contacts **Crucero del Norte** (☎ *11/5258–5000 in Buenos Aires, 3757/421–916 in Puerto Iguazú* ⊕ *www.crucerodelnorte.com.ar*). **Four Tourist Travel** (☎ *3757/422–962 at airport, 3757/420–681 in Puerto Iguazú*). **Vía Bariloche** (☎ *11/4315–7700 in Buenos Aires, 3757/420–854 in Puerto Iguazú* ⊕ *www. viabariloche.com.ar*).

Medical Assistance **Farmacia Bravo** (✉ *Av. Victoria Aguirre 423* ☎ *3757/420–479*). **Hospital Samic** (✉ *Av. Victoria Aguirre 131, Puerto Iguazú* ☎ *3757/420–288*).

Taxis **Remises Iguazú** (✉ *Puerto Iguazú* ☎ *3757/422–008*).

Visitor Info **Cataratas del Iguazú Visitors Center** (✉ *Park entrance* ☎ *3757/420–180* ⊕ *www.iguazuargentina.com* ⊙ *Apr.–Sept. 8 AM–6 PM; Oct.–Mar. 7:30 AM–6:30 PM*). **Puerto Iguazú Tourist Office** (✉ *Av. Victoria Aguirre 311, Puerto Iguazú* ☎ *3757/420–800* ⊙ *Daily 7–1 and 2–9*).

BRAZIL INFO

GETTING HERE & AROUND

There are direct flights between Foz do Iguaçu and São Paulo (1½ hours; R$380), Rio de Janeiro (2 hours; R$440), and Curitiba (1 hour; R$250) on TAM, which also has connecting flights to Salvador, Recife, Brasilia, other Brazilian cities, and Buenos Aires. Low-cost airline Gol operates slightly cheaper direct flights on the same three routes.

The Aeroporto Internacional Foz do Iguaçu is 13 km (8 mi) southeast of downtown Foz. The 20-minute taxi ride should cost R$35–R$40; the 45-minute regular bus ride about R$3. Note that several major hotels are on the highway to downtown, so a cab ride from the airport to these may be less than R$30. A cab ride from downtown hotels directly to the Parque Nacional in Brazil costs about R$90.

Via bus, the trip between Curitiba and Foz do Iguaçu takes 9–10 hours with Catarinense (R$90; R$180 for sleeper service). The same company operates the 17-hour route to Florianópolis (R$120). Pluma travels to Rio de Janeiro, which takes 11½ hours (R$130), and São Paolo, which takes 14 hours (R$130; R$205 for sleeper). The Terminal Rodoviário in Foz do Iguaçu is 5 km (3 mi) northeast of downtown. There are regular buses into town, which stop at the Terminal de Transportes Urbano (local bus station, often shortened to TTU) at Avenida Juscelino Kubitschek and Rua Mem de Sá. From here, buses labeled Parque Nacional also depart every 15 minutes (7–7) to the visitor center at the park entrance; the fare is R$4. The buses run along Avenida Juscelino Kubitschek and Avenida Jorge Schimmelpfeng, where you can also flag them down.

> ### CROSS-BORDER BUS
>
> **Tres Fronteras** (☎3757/420–377 in Puerto Iguazú ⊕www.tresfron teras.com.ar) runs an hourly cross-border public bus service between the centers of Puerto Iguazú and Foz do Iguaçu. Locals don't have to get on and off for immigration but be sure you do so. To reach the Argentine falls, change to a local bus at the intersection with RN 12 on the Argentine side. For the Brazilian park, change to a local bus at the Avenida Cataratas roundabout.

There's no real reason to rent a car in Foz do Iguaçu: it's cheaper and easier to use taxis or local tour companies to visit the falls, especially as you can't cross the border in a rental car. There are taxi stands (*pontos de taxi*) at intersections all over town, each with its own phone number. Hotels and restaurants can call you a cab, but you can also hail them on the street.

BRAZIL ESSENTIALS

Airline Contacts GOL (☎300/115–2121 toll-free, 45/3521–4230 in Foz do Iguaçu ⊕www.voegol.com.br). **TAM** (☎800/570–5700 toll-free, 45/3528–8500 in Foz do Iguaçu ⊕www.tam.com.br).

Bus Contacts Catarinense (☎300/147–0470 toll-free, 45/3522–2050 in Foz do Iguaçu ⊕www.catarinense.net). **Pluma** (☎800/646–0300 toll-free, 045/3522–2515 in Foz do Iguaçu ⊕www.pluma.com.br).

Banks & Currency Exchange Banco do Brasil (⊠Av. Brasil 1377 ⊕www.bb.com.br).

Medical Assistance FarmaRede (pharmacy) (⊠Av. Brasil 46 ☎45/3572–1363). **Hospital e Maternidade Cataratas** (⊠Rua Santos Dumont 714 ☎45/3523–5200).

Taxis Ponto de Taxi 20 (☎45/3523–4625).

Visitor Info Foz do Iguaçu Tourist Office (⊠Praça Getúlio Vargas 69, Brazil ☎45/3521–1455 ⊕www.iguassu.tur.br ⊘7 AM–11 PM).

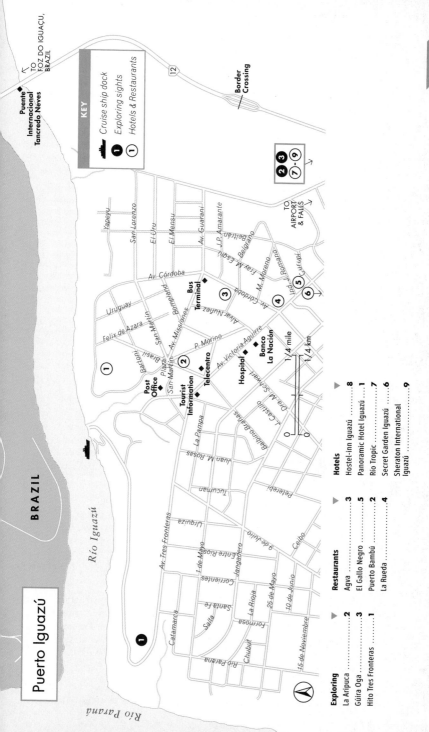

Puerto Iguazú

BRAZIL

Río Paraná

Río Iguazú

↖ TO FOZ DO IGUAÇU, BRAZIL

Puente Internacional Tancredo Neves

KEY
- ⛴ Cruise ship dock
- **1** Exploring sights
- ① Hotels & Restaurants

Border Crossing

TO AIRPORT & FALLS →

Exploring ▶
La Aripuca **2**
Güira Oga **3**
Hito Tres Fronteras **1**

Restaurants ▶
Agva **3**
El Gallo Negro **5**
Puerto Bambú **2**
La Rueda **4**

Hotels ▶
Hostel-inn Iguazú **8**
Panoramic Hotel Iguazú .. **1**
Río Tropic **7**
Secret Garden Iguazú **6**
Sheraton International
Iguazú **9**

0   1/4 mile
0   1/4 km

1

BORDER CROSSINGS

U.S., Canadian, and British citizens need only a valid passport for stays of up to 90 days in Argentina. Crossing into Brazil at Iguazú is a thorny issue. In theory, *all* U.S. citizens need a visa to enter Brazil. Visas are issued in about three hours from the Brazilian consulate in Puerto Iguazú (as opposed to the three days they take in Buenos Aires), and cost approximately 430 pesos. The Buenos Aires consulate also has a reputation for refusing visas to travelers who don't have onward tickets from Brazil.

If you stay in Foz do Iguaçu, travel on to other Brazilian cities, or do a day trip to Brazil by public bus or through an Argentinean company, you'll need a visa. There have been reports of getting around this by using a Brazilian travel agent or by using local taxis (both Argentine and Brazilian) that have "arrangements" with border control. Though the practice is well established (most hotels and travel agents in Puerto Iguazú have deals with Brazilian companies and can arrange a visa-less visit), it *is* illegal. Reinforcement of the law is generally lax but sudden crackdowns and on-the-spot fines of hundreds of dollars have been reported.

BRAZILIAN CONSULATES

In Buenos Aires ⊠ *Carlos Pellegrini 1363, 5th fl., Buenos Aires* ☏ *11/4515–6500* ⊕ *www.conbrasil.org.ar.*

In Puerto Iguazú ⊠ *Av. Córdoba 264, Puerto Iguazú* ☏ *3757/421–348.*

EXPLORING IGUAZÚ FALLS

To visit the falls, you can base yourself in the small Argentine city of Puerto Iguazú, or its sprawling Brazilian counterpart, the city of Foz do Iguaçu. The two cities are 18 km (11 mi) and 25 km (15 mi) northwest of the falls, respectively, and are connected by an international bridge, the Puente Presidente Tancredo Neves. Another bridge links Foz do Iguaçu with Ciudad del Este in Paraguay. Together, the three cities form the *Triple Frontera* (Tri Border).

Originally a port for shipping wood from the region, Puerto Iguazú now revolves around tourism. This was made possible in the early 20th century when Victoria Aguirre, a high-society porteña, funded the building of a road to the falls to make it easier for people to visit them. Despite the constant stream of visitors from Argentina and abroad, Puerto Iguazú is small and sleepy: there are only 32,000 inhabitants, and many of its roads still aren't paved.

The same was once true of Foz de Iguaçu, but the construction of the Itaipú dam (now the second largest in the world) in 1975 transformed it into a bustling city with 10 times more people than Puerto Iguazú. Many have jobs connected with the hydroelectric power station at the dam, while others are involved with trade (both legal and illegal) with the duty-free zone of Ciudad del Este, in Paraguay.

In general it makes more sense to stay in tourism-oriented Puerto Iguazú: hotels and restaurants are better, peso prices are lower, and it's

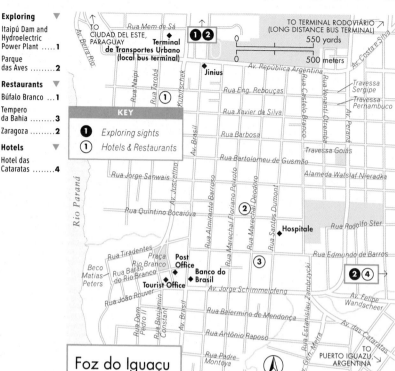

much safer than Foz do Iguaçu, which has a bad reputation for violent street crime. There's also more to do and see on the Argentine side of the falls, which take up to two days to visit. The Brazilian side, though impressive, only warrants half a day.

Many travel agencies offer packages from Buenos Aires, São Paulo, or Curitiba that include flights or bus tickets, transfers, accommodation, and transport to the falls. These packages are usually more expensive than booking everything yourself but you do get round-the-clock support, which can be useful for rescheduling transfers around Argentina's delay-prone flights. WOW! Argentina's Iguazú packages include flights, two nights' accommodation at the Sheraton Iguazú, airport transfers, and a boat ride (but not transport to the Brazilian side), and costs around $700 per person. Buenos Aires Tours does a similar package but with accommodation in Puerto Iguazú; it includes transport to the Argentine side of the park (but not the Brazilian) and costs around $400 per person.

If you're staying in town, rather than at the hotels in the parks, you can easily reach the falls on your side of the border by public bus, private shuttle (most hotels work with shuttle company), or taxi. Travel agencies and tour operators in Puerto Iguazú and Foz de Iguaçu also offer day trips to the opposite sides of the border. Most are glorified shuttle

Iguazú Falls

Sheraton Internacional Iguazú

Visitor Center

Salto Lanusse

Salto Dos Hermanas

Circuito Inferior

Salto Alvar Nuñez

Tropical das Cataratas

Salto Ramirez

BRAZIL

Salto Bossetti

Isla San Martín

Circuito Superior

Salto Méndez

Salto San Martín

Ferrocarril Proyectado

Salto Santa Maria

Salto Floriano

Rio Iguazú

Salto Deodoro

Salto Peñon de Bella Vista

Garganta del Diablo

0 — 1/8 mile

0 — 1/8 kilometer

TO ESTACIÓN GARGANTA DEL DIABLO ↓

services that save you the hassle of changing buses and get you through immigration formalities quickly. Use them to facilitate getting to the park, but avoid those that include in-park tours: most drag you around with a huge group of people and a megaphone, which rather ruins the fabulous natural surroundings.

Both parks are incredibly well organized and clearly signposted, so most visitors have no trouble exploring independently. Once in the park, be sure to go on a boat trip, an unmissable—though drenching—experience that gets you almost under the falls. You can reserve these through tour operators or hotels, or at booths inside the parks.

THE ARGENTINE SIDE

Argentina's side of the falls is in the **Parque Nacional Iguazú,** which was founded in 1934 and declared a World Heritage Site in 1984. The park is divided into two areas, each of which is organized around a train station: Estación Cataratas or the Estación Garganta del Diablo. (A third, Estación Central, is near the park entrance.) Paved walkways lead from the main entrance past the Visitor Center, called Yvyrá Retá—"country of the trees" in Guaraní. Colorful visual displays provide a good explanation of the region's ecology and human history. To reach the park proper, you cross through a small plaza containing a food court, gift shops, and ATM. From the nearby Estación Central, the gas-propelled

Tren de la Selva (Jungle Train) departs every 20 minutes. ☎3757/49–1469 ⊕www.iguazuargentina.com ✉40 pesos; 20 pesos on 2nd day ⏲Apr.–Sept. 8–6; Oct.–Mar. 7:30–6:30.

TOUR OPERATORS

Iguazú Jungle Explorer ☎3757/42–1696 ⊕www.iguazujungleexplorer. com runs trips within the Argentine park. Their standard trip, the Gran Aventura, costs 100 pesos and includes a truck ride through the forest and a Zodiac ride to San Martín, Bossetti, and the Salto Tres Mosqueteros (be ready to get soaked). The truck carries so many people that most animals are scared away: you're better off buying the 50-peso boat trip—Aventura Nautica—separately.

It's all about adrenaline with **Iguazú Forest** ☎3757/42–1140 ⊕www. iguazuforest.com. Their full day expedition involves kayaking, abseiling, waterfall-climbing, mountain-biking, and canopying all within the Argentine park.

Argentine park ranger Daniel Somay organizes two-hour Jeep tours with an ecological focus through his Puerto Iguazú–based **Explorador Expediciones** ☎3757/42–1632 ⊕www. hotelguia.com/turismo/explorador-expediciones. The tours cost 50 pesos and include detailed explanations of the Iguazú ecosystem and lots of photo ops. A specialist leads the birdwatching trips, which cost 215 pesos and include the use of binoculars.

THE BRAZILIAN SIDE

In Brazil you can see the falls in the **Parque Nacional Foz do Iguaçu**. Much of the park is protected rain forest—off-limits to visitors and home to the last viable populations of panthers as well as rare flora. Buses and taxis drop you off at a vast, plaza alongside the park entrance building. As well as ticket booths, there's an ATM, a snack bar, gift shop, and information and currency exchange. Next to the entrance turnstiles is the small Visitor Center, where helpful geological models explain how the falls were formed. Doubledecker buses run every 15 minutes between the entrance and the trailhead to the falls, 11 km (7 mi) away; the buses stop at the entrances to excursions run by private operators Macuco Safari and Macuco Ecoaventura (these aren't included in your ticket). The trail ends in the Porto Canoas service area. There's a posh linen-service restaurant with river views, and two fast-food counters the with tables overlooking the rapids leading to the falls. ☎045/3521–4400 ⊕www.cataratasdoiguacu.com.br ✉R$20.50 ⏲Apr.–Sept. 9–5; Oct.–Mar. 9–6.

TOUR OPERATORS

You can take to the water on the Brazilian side with **Macuco Safari** ☎045/3574–4244 ⊕www.macucosafari.com.br. Their signature trip is a Zodiac ride around (and under) the Salto Tres Mosqueteros. You get a more sedate ride on the Iguaçu Explorer, a 3½ hour trip up the river. In Brazil, Cânion Iguaçu ☎045/3529–6040 ⊕www.campodede safios.com.br offers rafting and canopying, as well as abseiling over the

IGUAZÚ ITINERARIES

LIGHTNING VISIT

If you only have one day, limit your visit to the Argentine park. Arrive when it opens, and get your first look at the falls aboard one of Iguazú Jungle Explorer's Zodiacs. The rides finish at the Circuito Inferior: take a couple of hours to explore this. (Longer summer opening hours give you time to squeeze in the Isla San Martín.) Grab a quick lunch at the Dos Hermanas snack bar, then blitz the shorter Circuito Superior. You've kept the best for last: catch the train from Estación Cataratas to Estación Garganta del Diablo, where the trail to the viewing platform starts (allow at least two hours for this).

BEST OF BOTH SIDES

Two days gives you enough time to see both sides of the falls. Visit the Brazilian park on your second day to get the panoramic take on what you've experienced up-close in Argentina. If you arrive at 9 am, you've got time to walk the entire trail, take photos, have lunch in the Porto Canoas service area, and be back at the park entrance by 1 pm. You could spend the afternoon doing excursions and activities from Macuco Safari and Macuco EcoAventura, or visiting the Itaipú dam. Alternatively, you could keep the visit to Brazil for the afternoon of the second day, and start off with a lightning return visit to the Argentine park (halfprice entrance on second visit) and see the Garganta del Diablo with the sun rising behind it.

SEE IT ALL

With three days you can explore both parks at a leisurely pace. Follow the oneday itinerary, then return to the Argentine park on your second day. Make a beeline for the Garganta del Diablo, which looks different in the mornings, then spend the afternoon exploring the Sendero Macuco (and Isla San Martín, if you didn't have time on the first day). You'll also have time to visit Güira Oga bird sanctuary or La Aripuca (both on RN 12) afterwards. You could spend all of your third day in the Brazilian park, or just the morning, giving you time to catch an afternoon flight or bus.

river from the Salto San Martín. They also offer wheelchair-compatible equipment.

Macuco Ecoaventura ☎*045/3529–6927* ⊕*www.macucoecoaventura. com.br* is one of the official tour operators within the Brazilian park. Their Trilha do Pozo Negro combines a 9-km guided hike or bike ride with a scary boat trip along the upper river (the bit before the falls). The aptly-named Floating trip is more leisurely; shorter jungle hikes are also offered.

EXPLORING OTHER SIGHTS

Surprisingly, Iguazú is not the only site to see in these parts, though few people actually have time (or make time) to go see them.

IN ARGENTINA

Numbers in the margin correspond to numbers on the Puerto Iguazú map.

2 **La Aripuca.** It looks like a cross between a log cabin and the Pentagon, but this massive wooden structure—which weighs 551 tons—is a large-scale replica of a Guaraní bird trap. La Aripuca officially showcases different local woods, supposedly for conservation purposes—ironic, given the huge trunks used to build it, and the overpriced wooden furniture that fills the gift shop. ⊠*RN 12, Km 5, Puerto Iguazú* ☎*3757/423–488* ⊕*www.aripuca.com.ar* ✑*10 pesos* ⊙*Daily 9–7.*

3 **Gúira Oga.** Although Iguazú is home to around 450 bird species, the parks are so busy these days that you'd be lucky to see so much as a feather. It's another story at Gúira Oga, which means "house of the birds" in Guaraní, although "bird rehab" might be more appropriate. Injured birds, birds displaced by deforestation, and birds confiscated from traffickers are brought here for treatment. The large cages also contain many species on the verge of extinction, including the harpy eagle and the red macaw, a gorgeous parrot. The sanctuary is in a forested plot just off RN 12, halfway between Puerto Iguazú and the falls. ⊠*RN 12, Km 5, Puerto Iguazú* ☎*3757/423–890* ✑*Free* ⊙*Daily 8:30–6:30.*

1 **Hito Tres Fronteras.** This viewpoint west of the town center stands high above the turbulent reddish-brown confluence of the Iguacú and Paraná rivers, which also form the *Triple Frontera,* or Tri Border. A mini pale-blue-and-white obelisk reminds you you're in Argentina; across the Iguazú River is Brazil's green-and-yellow equivalent; farther away, across the Paraná, is Paraguay's, painted red, white, and blue. A row of overpriced souvenir stalls stands alongside it. ⊠*Av. Tres Fronteras, Puerto Iguazú.*

IN BRAZIL

Numbers in the margin correspond to numbers on the Foz do Iguaçu map.

1 **Itaipú Dam and Hydroelectric Power Plant.** It took more than 30,000 workers eight years to build this 8-km (5-mi) dam, voted one of the Seven Wonders of the Modern World by the American Society of Civil Engineers. The monumental structure produces 25% of Brazil's electricity and 78% of Paraguay's, and will be the largest hydroelectric power plant on Earth until China's Three Gorges (Yangtze) Dam is completed. You get plenty of insight into how proud this makes the Brazilian government—and some idea of how the dam was built—during the 30-minute video that precedes hour-long guided panoramic bus tours of the complex. Although commentaries are humdrum, the sheer size of the dam is an impressive sight. To see more than a view over the spillways, consider the special tours, which take you inside the cavernous structure and includes a visit to the control room. Night tours—which include a light-and-sound show—begin at 8:30 Friday and Saturday.

At the **Ecomuseu de Itaipú** (Itaipú Eco-Museum) (⊠*Km 10, Av. Tancredo Neves* ✑*R$8* ⊙*Daily 8–5:30*) you can learn about the geology, archaeology, and efforts to preserve the flora and fauna of the area since the dam was built. Note that it's funded by the dam's operator Itaipú Binacional, so information isn't necessarily objective. ⊠*Km 11, Av.*

Tancredo Neves ☎800/645–4645 ⊕*www.itaipu.gov.br* ✉*Panoramic tour R$13, special tour R$30* ⊙*Panoramic tours Mon.–Sat. 8, 9, 10* AM, *2, 3, 3:30* PM. *Special tours Mon.–Sat. 8, 8:30, 9:30, 10* AM, *2, 2:30, 3:30* PM.

❷ Flamingos, parrots, and toucans are some of the more-colorful inhabitants of the privately run **Parque das Aves** (Bird Park). Right outside the Parque Nacional Foz do Iguaçu, it's an interesting complement to a visit to the falls. A winding path leads you through untouched tropical forest and walk-through aviaries containing hundreds of species of birds. Iguanas, alligators, and other nonfeathered friends have their own pens. ⊠*Km 17, Rodovia das Cataratas* ☎*045/3529–8282* ⊕*www.parquedasaves.com.br* ✉*$10* ⊙*Apr.–Sept., 8:30–5:30; Oct.–Mar., 8:30–6.*

WHERE TO EAT

Booming tourism is kindling the restaurant scenes of Puerto Iguazú and Foz do Iguaçu, and each has enough reasonably priced, reliable choices to get most visitors through the two or three days they spend there. Neither border town has much of a culinary tradition to speak of, though most restaurants at least advertise some form of the local specialty *surubí* (a kind of catfish), although it's frequently out of stock. Instead, parrillas or churrascarias abound, as do pizza and pasta joints.

PUERTO IGUAZÚ, ARGENTINA

$$
SEAFOOD
✕**Aqva.** Locals are thrilled: finally, a date-night restaurant in Puerto Iguazú. Although the high-ceilinged split-level cabin seats too many to be truly intimate, they make up for it with well-spaced tables, discreet service, and low lighting. Softly gleaming timber from different local trees lines the walls, roof, and floor. Local river fish like *surubí* and *dorado* are the specialty: have them panfried, or, more unusually, as empanada fillings. Forget being romantic at dessert time: the chef's signature dessert, fresh mango and pineapple with a torrontés sabayon, is definitely worth keeping to yourself. ⊠*Av. Córdoba at Carlos Thays* ☎*3757/422–064* ⊟*AE, MC, V.*

$$
ARGENTINE
★
✕**El Gallo Negro.** A gaucho in full regalia mans the barbecue, which has pride of place outside the hefty wooden cabin that houses this classy parrilla. The rustic-looking trestle tables on the wide veranda afford a great view of your sizzling steak; at night, they get the white tablecloth and candle treatment. It's not all barbecued beef: caramelized suckling pig in an apple-and-honey sauce or lamb slow-cooked in red

wine are some of the standouts from the kitchen. Their tempting take on Iguazú's only regional specialty, *surubi*, which they sauté in coconut milk, is sadly rarely available. ⊠*Av. Victoria Aguirre 773, at Curupí* ☎*3757/422–465* ▤*AE, MC, V.*

$ ✕**Puerto Bambú.** Iguazú's warm evenings make this popular pizzería's
PIZZA outdoor tables perfect for a casual meal. Their thin-crust pizzas are cooked *a la parrilla* (on a barbecue), so there's a pleasantly smoky edge to them. Reggae plays quietly in the background until around midnight, when they crank up the volume and bring out the cocktails as Puerto Bambú turns into a bar. ⊠*Av. Brasil 96* ☎*3757/421–900* ⌲*Reservations not accepted* ▤*No credit cards.*

$$–$$$ ✕**La Rueda.** This parrilla is so popular with visitors that they start serv-
ARGENTINE ing dinner as early as 7:30 PM—teatime by Argentine standards. The local beef isn't quite up to Buenos Aires standards, but La Rueda's bife de chorizo is one of the best in town. Surubi is another house specialty, but skip the traditional Roquefort sauce, which rather eclipses the fish's flavor. They've stayed true to their rustic roots, however: hefty tree trunks hold up the bamboo-lined roof, and the walls are adorned by a curious wooden frieze carved by a local artist. ⊠*Av. Córdoba 28, 3370* ☎*3757/422–531* ⌲*Reservations essential* ▤*AE, DC, MC, V.*

FOZ DO IGUAÇU, BRAZIL

$$ ✕**Búfalo Branco.** The city's finest and largest churrascaria does a killer
BRAZILIAN *rodizio* (all-you-can-eat meat buffet). The picanha stands out from the 25 meat choices, but pork, lamb, chicken, and even—yum—bull testicles find their way onto the metal skewers they use to grill the meat. The salad bar is well stocked, a boon for vegetarians. ⊠*Av. Rebouças 530* ☎*45/3523–9744* ▤*AE, MC, V.*

$$–$$$$ ✕**Tempero da Bahia.** If you're not going as far as Bahia on your trip, you
SEAFOOD can at least check out its flavors at this busy tangerine-painted restaurant. It specializes in northeastern fare like *moquecas* (a rich seafood stew made with coconut milk and palm oil); their delicious versions are unusual for mixing prawns with local river fish. Spicy panfried sole and salmon are lighter options. The flavors aren't quite so subtle at the all-out seafood (and river food) buffets they hold several times a week, but they're tasty and cheap enough to pull in crowds. ⊠*Rua Marechal Deodoro 1228* ☎*45/3025–1144* ▤*AE, MC, V* ☽*No dinner Sun.*

$$–$$$$ ✕**Zaragoza.** On a tree-lined street in a quiet neighborhood, this tra-
SPANISH ditional restaurant's Spanish owner is an expert at matching Iguaçu's fresh river fish to authentic Spanish seafood recipes. Brazilian ingredients sneak into some dishes—the *surubi à Goya*, catfish in a tomato-and-coconut-milk sauce—definitely merits a try. ⊠*Rua Quintino Bocaiúva 882* ☎*45/3028–8084* ▤*AE, DC, MC, V.*

WHERE TO STAY

Once you've decided which country to base yourself in, the next big decision is whether to stay in town or at the five-star hotel inside each park. If you're on a lightning one-night visit and you only want to see one side of the falls, the convenience of staying inside the park might offset the otherwise unreasonably high prices for mediocre levels of luxury. Otherwise, you get much better value for money at the establishments in town or on highways BR 489 (Rodavia das Cataratas) in Brazil, or RN 12 in Argentina. During the day you're a 20-minute bus ride from the falls and the border, and at night you're closer to restaurants and nightlife (buses stop running to the park after 7 or 8; after that, it's a 70-peso taxi ride into town from the park). Hotels in Argentina are generally cheaper than in Brazil. During low season (late September–early-November and February–May, excluding Easter), rooms are often heavily discounted.

⚠ Staying on the Brazilian side (apart from at the Hotel das Cataratas in the park) isn't recommended. It's dangerous, especially after dark, and more expensive. What's more the hotels generally aren't as good as those on the Argentine side.

PUERTO IGUAZÚ, ARGENTINA

¢   ▢ **Hostel-Inn Iguazú.** An enormous turquoise pool surrounded by classy wooden loungers and well-kept gardens lets you know this hostel is far from typical. Spacious double rooms with private bathrooms, huge windows, and lots of light attract couples and families. Partying backpackers love the great-value dorm accommodations (but be sure to book one with air-conditioning) and organized weekend bar expeditions. The Hostel-Inn is on the road halfway between Puerto Iguazú and the falls so you can get to the park early, but you're only a short bus or taxi ride from the restaurants and bars in town. You can sort out excursions, including visa-less visits to the Brazilian side, through the in-house travel agency. The kitchen churns out simple sandwiches, salads, and burgers, and there's an all-out asado several times a week. **Pros:** Beautiful pool area; rooms are simple but clean and well designed; location between town and the falls gives you the best of both worlds. **Cons:** Impersonal service from indifferent staff; lounge and kitchen are run-down; very basic breakfast. ⊠*Ruta 12, Km 5,* ☎*3757/421–823* ⊕*www.hostel-inn.com* ⇋*52 rooms* ⌂*In-room: no a/c, no phone, no TV (some), Wi-Fi. In-hotel: restaurant, pool, bar, no elevator, laundry service, public Internet* ⊟*No credit cards* ⫯⊙⫯*CP.*

$$$ ▢ **Panoramic Hotel Iguazú.** The falls aren't the only good views in Iguazú: ★   half the rooms of this chic hotel look onto the churning, jungle-framed waters of the Iguazú and Paraná rivers. The view inside the rooms is lovely, too. Taupe throws and ocher pillow shams offset the clean lines of the contemporary dark-wood furniture. You don't miss out on luxury by booking a standard, as all have king-size beds, flat-screen TVs, and hot tubs. Even the pool, set on a large terrace, looks over the river. The view gets seriously panoramic from the top-floor bar, one of the best sundowner spots in town. **Pros:** River views; great attention to detail in the beautifully designed rooms; the gorgeous pool. **Cons:** The in-house casino can make the lobby noisy; indifferent staff aren't up to the price tag; it's a short taxi ride to the town center and in-house transport is overpriced. ⊠*Paraguay 372, 3370* ☎*3757/498–133* ⊕*www. panoramic-hoteliguazu.com* ⇋*91 rooms* ⌂*In-room: safe, refrigerator, Wi-Fi. In-hotel: 3 restaurants, bar, pool, public Internet, no-smoking rooms* ⊟*AE, MC, V* ⫯⊙⫯*CP.*

¢ ★ **Río Tropic.** Friendly owners Rémy and Romina give you a warm welcome at this rootsy B&B, which is surrounded by a lush garden. Rooms open onto a shady veranda that runs all the way along the wooden building; from there it's a couple of more steps to the pool. Pine paneling gives the rooms a country vibe, and though simple, they're spotlessly clean and have firm beds. **Pros:** The wonderfully helpful and attentive owners; peaceful surroundings; abundant homemade breakfasts served on a terrace in the garden. **Cons:** Too far from the town center to walk to; the rooms with no air-conditioning are stuffy in summer; low on luxury. ⊠*Montecarlo s/n, at Km 5, RN 12* ☎*3757/1541–6764* ⊕*www.riotropic.com.ar* ⇖*10 rooms* &*In-room: no a/c (some), no phone, no TV. In-hotel: bar, pool, bicycles* ⊟*No credit cards* ⍓*CP.*

$ **Secret Garden Iguazú.** Dense tropical vegetation overhangs the wooden walkway that leads to this tiny guesthouse's three rooms, tucked away in a pale-blue clapboard house. There's nothing fancy about them, but the wood and wicker furniture and brightly painted paneling are cheerful and welcoming. So is the owner, John Fernandes. He's full of information and advice about Iguazú, which he shares with you over high-octane caipirinhas at the nightly cocktail sessions. **Pros:** Wooden deck overlooking the back-to-nature garden; knowledgeable owner John's charm and expert mixology; home-away-from-home vibe. **Cons:** The three rooms book up fast; no pool; comfortable but not luxurious. ⊠*Los Lapachos 623, 3370* ☎*3757/423–099* ⊕*www. secretgardeniguazu.com* ⇖*3 rooms* &*In-room: no phone, no TV, Wi-Fi. In-hotel: Public Wi-Fi.* ⊟*No credit cards* ⍓*CP.*

$$$$ **Sheraton International Iguazú.** That thundering you can hear in the distance lets you know how close this hotel is to the falls. The lobby opens right onto the park trails and half the rooms have big balconies with fabulous falls views—be sure to reserve one of these well in advance (note that they're about 30% more expensive). The proximity is what you pay for: the rooms are perfectly serviceable, but the dated furniture, worn bathrooms, and drab linens aren't up to the price. And although the spa is a step in the right direction, with a gorgeous hot tub and treatment tents on an outdoor deck, you have to pay extra to use it. You can see the rising mist over the falls from the beautiful swimming pool, which is surrounded by palm trees and jungle. **Pros:** The falls are on your doorstep; great buffet breakfasts; well-designed spa. **Cons:** Drab rooms are in need of a complete makeover; mediocre food and service at dinner; other restaurants are an expensive taxiride away. ⊠*Parque Nacional Iguazú, Argentina* ☎*3757/491–800* ⊕*www.sheraton.com* ⇖*176 rooms, 4 suites* &*In-room: safe, refrigerator. In-hotel: 2 restaurants, room service, pools, gym, spa, tennis courts, laundry service, public Internet, airport shuttle, no-smoking rooms* ⊟*AE, DC, MC, V* ⍓*CP.*

FOZ DO IGUAÇU, BRAZIL

$$$$ ★ **Hotel das Cataratas.** Not only is this stately hotel *in* the national park, with views of the smaller falls from the front-side suites, but it also provides the traditional comforts of a colonial-style establishment: large rooms, terraces, vintage furniture, and hammocks. The main building, surrounded by verandas and gardens, is almost 100 years old and is a

National Heritage Site. Although the rooms are comfortable, it's the setting and atmosphere that you pay for, rather than luxury fittings. Still, for many, the chance to wander the paths to the falls before and after the hordes of day visitors arrive is priceless. The Itaipú restaurant serves traditional Brazilian dinners, including feijoada and a variety of side dishes. There's also an all-you-can-eat barbecue and salad buffet each night in the Ipê grill near the pool. The hotel is undergoing extensive renovations through 2009: it will remain open, but with fewer rooms. **Pros:** Right inside the park, a short walk from the falls; serious colonial-style charm; friendly, helpful staff. **Cons:** Rooms aren't as luxurious as the price promises; far from Foz do Iguaçu so you're limited to the on-site restaurants; only the most-expensive suites have views of the falls. ⊠*Km 28, Rodovia das Cataratas* ☎*045/2102–7000 or 0800/726–4545* ⊕*www.hoteldascataratas.com.br* ⇌*198 rooms, 5 suites* ⏚*In-room: safe, refrigerator. In-hotel: 2 restaurants, tennis courts, pool, gym, laundry service, public Internet, airport shuttle* ⊟*AE, MC, V* ⎶*CP.*

MENDOZA

1,060 km (659 mi) southwest of Buenos Aires; 250 km (155 mi) east of Santiago, Chile.

Updated by
Eddy Ancinas

Mendoza Province, its eponymous capital, and the capital's environs (departments) are home to about 1,600,000 people, with roughly 110,000 of them living in Mendoza City. Most of the major vineyards and bodegas are in departments south of the city (Maipú, Godoy Cruz, Luján de Cuyo) and farther south across the Río Mendoza, in the regions of Agrelo and Perdriel. Still more vineyards are farther south in the Uco Valley. Each department has its own commercial areas, with shopping centers, hotels, and restaurants.

Mendoza City is shaded from the summer sun by a canopy of poplars, elms, and sycamores. Water runs along its sidewalks in acéquias, disappears at intersections, then bursts from fountains in the city's 74 parks and squares. Many acéquias were built by the Huarpe Indians and improved upon by the Incas long before the city was founded in 1561 by Pedro del Castillo.

Thanks to the booming wine and tourism industry, Mendoza bustles with innovative restaurants and lodgings that range from slick high-rises with conference rooms for serious wine tasting, to low-key inns and B&Bs for serious relaxing. Low-rise colonial buildings with their high ceilings, narrow doorways, and tile floors house restaurants and shops. In the afternoon, shops close, streets empty, and siesta-time rules—until around 5, when the city comes back to life and and goes back to work.

GETTING HERE & AROUND

Mendoza's Aeropuerto Internacional Francisco Gabrielli is 6 km (4 mi) north of town on Ruta Nacional 40. Aerolíneas Argentinas has flights (about two hours) from Buenos Aires. LAN Chile has 55-minute flights from Santiago, Chile.

Busy Terminal del Sol is in Guaymallén, an eastern suburb about a 10-minute cab ride to or from town. From here, buses travel to every major Argentine city and to Santiago, Chile. Transport companies include Andesmar and La Cumbre, with service to San Juan (3 hours); Chevallier with daily service to Buenos Aires (14 hours); El Rápido, with daily buses to Buenos Aires and Santiago, Chile (8 hours).

Driving from Buenos Aires (along lonely but paved Ruta Nacional 7, aka Ruta Pan Americano or the Panamerican Highway) or Santiago (again, on Ruta Nacional 7, which is sometimes closed along this stretch in winter) is an option, provided you have plenty of time and speak some Spanish. There's little need of a car in town, and it's hard to find wineries in outlying areas on your own—even when you *do* speak Spanish. Further, Mendocinos are known for their cavalier attitude toward traffic rules. Pay attention to weather and road information. If you fear getting lost or breaking down in remote areas, hire a remis (a car with a driver) or arrange a tour. ⚠ **Downtown streets have ankle-breaking holes, steps, and unexpected obstacles, so watch where you're going.**

ESSENTIALS

Air Contacts **Aerolíneas Argentinas** (☎ *261/420–4101*). **LAN Chile** (☎ *261/425–7900 in Mendoza, 0800/222–2424 elsewhere*).

Banks **Banelco** (⊠ *Av. San Martín at San Lorenzo* ⊠ *San Marín at Sarmiento*). **Banco de la Nación** (⊠ *Av. San Martín at Gutiérrez*) **Citibank** (⊠ *Av. San Martín 1098*).

Bus Contacts **Andesmar** (☎ *261/438–0654* ⊕ *www.andesmar.com*). **Chevallier** (☎ *261/431–0235*). **El Rápido** (☎ *261/431–4094*). **Terminal de Ómnibus** (⊠ *Av. Gobernador Videla at Av. Acceso Oeste* ☎ *261/448–0057*).

Car Rentals **Avis** (⊠ *Primitivo de la Reta 914* ☎ *261/447–0150* ⊕ *www.avis.com*). **Hertz** (⊠ *Espejo 415* ☎ *2627/423–0225*). **Localiza** (⊠ *Primitivo de la Reta 0800* ☎ *261/429–6800* ⊕ *www.localiza.com*).

Medical Assistance **Farmacia del Puente** (⊠ *Av. Las Heras 201* ☎ *261/423–8800*). **Hospital Central** (⊠ *José F. Moreno and Alem, near bus station* ☎ *261/420–0600*).

Taxis **La Veloz del Este** (☎ *261/423–9090*).

Visitor Info **Mendoza Tourist Board** (⊠ *Av. San Martín 1143, at Garibaldi* ☎ *261/420–1333* ⊕ *www.turismo.mendoza.gov.ar*).

EXPLORING THE SIGHTS

In 1861, an earthquake destroyed the city, killing 11,000 people. Mendoza was reconstructed on a grid, making it easy to explore on foot. Four small squares (Chile, San Martín, Italia, and España) radiate from the four corners of Plaza Independencia, the main square. Their Spanish tiles, exuberant fountains, shaded walkways, and myriad trees and flowers lend peace and beauty. Avenida San Martín, the town's major thoroughfare, runs north–south out into the southern departments and wine districts. Calle Sarmiento intersects San Martín at the tourist office and becomes a *peatonal* (pedestrian mall) with cafés, shops, offices, and bars. It crosses the Plaza Independencia, stops in front of the Hyatt Plaza, then continues on the other side of the hotel.

NEED A BREAK?

For a fresh cup of coffee, stop at Bonafide Espresso (⊠ *Peatonal Sarmiento 102* ☎ *261/423-7915*) on the corner of Sarmiento and 9 de Julio. *Medialunas* (croissants) and *alfajores* (cookies with dulce de leche, sweet carmelized milk) add to the enjoyment of this lively café.

MAIN ATTRACTIONS

Parque General San Martín. This grand public space has more than 50,000 trees from all over the world. Fifteen kilometers (9 mi) of paths and walkways meander through the park, and the rose garden has about 500 varieties. You can observe nautical competitions from the rowing club's balcony restaurant, visit the zoo, or play tennis or golf. Scenes of the 1817 Andes crossing by José de San Martín and his army during the campaign to liberate Argentina are depicted on a monument atop Cerro de la Gloria (Glory Hill) in the park's center. The soccer stadium and Greek theater (capacity 22,500) attract thousands during vendimia, the annual wine-harvest festival.

Plaza Independencia. In Mendoza's main square, you can sit on a bench in the shade of a sycamore tree and watch children playing in the fountains, browse the stands at a weekend fair, or take a stroll after lunch to the historic Plaza Hotel (now a Hyatt) on your way to the shops and outdoor cafés on the pedestrian-only Calle Sarmiento, which bisects the square. The **Museo Arte Moderno** (☎ *261/425-7279* ⊠ *45 pesos* ☉ *Mon.–Sat. 9–1 and 4–9, Sun. 4–9*), right in the plaza, exhibits paintings, ceramics, sculptures, and drawings by Mendocino artists from 1930 to the present.

IF YOU HAVE TIME

Museo del Area Fundacional. On the site of the original *cabildo* (town hall), the Foundation Museum explains the region's social and historical development. Of note is the display of a mummified child found on Aconcagua, with photos of his burial treasures. Excavations, made visible by a glass-covered viewing area, reveal layers of pre-Hispanic and Spanish remains. ⊠ *Beltrán and Videla Castillo* ☎ *261/425-6927* ⊠ *5 pesos* ☉ *Tues.–Sat. 8 AM–10 PM, Sun. 3–8.*

Museo del Pasado Cuyano. This 26-bedroom, 1873 mansion, the home of former governor and senator Emilio Civit, was the gathering place of the belle époque elite.

TOURING TIPS
In winter, a *bus turístico* (tourist bus) departs at 9:30 AM and 2:30 PM from the tourist office (where you can buy tickets for 15 pesos) and travels along a tour route, letting you on and off at designated stops. Also, you can pick up a free walking-tour map (the Circuitos Peatonales) at hotels or the tourist office.

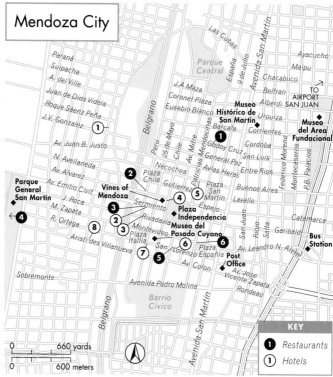

Mendoza City

Today it's the Museum of the Cuyo's Past, a gallery and archive with paintings, antiques, manuscripts, and newspapers. ⊠*Montevideo 544* ☎*261/423–6031* 🖾*Donation suggested* ⊙*Weekdays 9–12:30.*

Museo Histórico de San Martín. The San Martín Historical Museum has a decent library and a token collection of artifacts from campaigns of the Great Liberator. ⊠*Av. San Martín 1843* ☎*261/425–7947* 🖾*3 pesos* ⊙*Weekdays 8:30–1:30.*

NEED A BREAK?

More than 40 ice-cream flavors, including *dulce de leche* (sweet caramelized milk) with *granizado* (chocolate chip) and many fresh berry and chocolate concoctions, will make you want to visit Soppelsa (⊠*Emilio Civit and Belgrano, Mendoza*).

EXPLORING THE WINERIES

The department of Maipú, south and slightly east of Mendoza City, has some 12 wineries in the districts of General Gutierrez, Coquimbito, and Cruz de Piedra. To the south, the department of Luján de Cuyo borders both sides of the Mendoza River and has 27 wineries in the districts of Agrelo, Carodilla, Chacras de Coria, Drummond, Perdriel, Ugarteche,

INSIDER INFO

Before heading out to the wineries, stop by the **Vines of Mendoza** (✉ *567 Espejo, between Chile and 25 de Mayo, Mendoza* ☎ *0261/438–1031* ⊕ *www.vinesofmendoza.com*) tasting room and information center. (Their Web site is a great place to get info before you even leave home.) It's owned by two American entrepreneurs who visited the area and fell enough in love with it to quit their jobs, move down, and establish a central place where English-speaking visitors can get insider wine and winery information.

In addition to offering 50 boutique wines by the glass and by the flight, they have weekly wine events and classes. Their knowledgeable staff can offer guidance on area tour guides, wineries, and wine stores.

Vines of Mendoza also makes it possible to continue your wine experience at home. By joining the Acéquia Wine Club you receive shipments of four to six bottles of locally produced wine four times a year (each shipment costs US$145–US$245).

Feel like investing in a really big way? Through the Vines' private vineyard program you can buy 4- to 12-acre parcels of a Valle de Uco vineyard. As an owner, you—in consultation with a team of vineyard managers and winemakers—would participate in everything from choosing what to plant to designing your own label. It's the ultimate way to be an insider.

and Vistalba. ■**TIP→** **Aceso Sur (Ruta Nacional 40), the main highway south, is the fastest way to get to the area.**

GODOY CRUZ

❶ **Bodega Escorihuela.** Founded in 1884 by Spaniard Miguel Escorihuela Gascón, this large winery features a 63,000-liter French barrel—the largest in the province. In 1993, a group of investors led by pioneer vintner Nicolás Catena bought the interests in the Bodega Escorihuela. Experimentation and innovation continue here with art exhibits and Francis Mallmanns' renowned restaurant, 1884. ✉*Belgrano 1188, Godoy Cruz* ☎*261/499–7044* ⊕*www.escorihuela.com.ar* ☉*Weekdays 9:30–12:30 and 2:30–3:30; guided tours on the hr.*

MAIPÚ

❸ **Bodega la Rural.** In 1855, Felipe Rutini left the hills of Italy to found a winery in the raw land of Coquimbito, Argentina. His descendants planted the first grapes (Chardonnay and Merlot) in the now-popular Tupungato District of the Valle de Uco. Today, Bodega la Rural is still family-owned and -operated. The winery's well-known San Felipe label was created by Alejandro Sirio, a famous Spanish artist. Inside the original adobe barns, the Museo del Vino (Wine Museum) has machinery; vintage carriages; 100-year-old leather, wood, and copper tools; and even an amazing mousetrap. ✉*Montecaseros 2625, Coquimbito, Maipú* ☎*261/497–2013* ⊕*www.bodegalarural.com.ar* ☉*Tours every 30 mins Mon.–Sat. 9–1 and 2–5, Sun. 10–1 with reservations.*

4 **Bodegas y Viñedos López.** Wines up to 60 years old are stored in the main cellar of this traditional family winery, established in 1898. After a tour of the winery, tastings take place in the cave, where lunches can be arranged with a two-day notice. ⊠ *Ozamis 375, Maipú* ☎*261/497–2406* ⊕*www.bodegaslopez.com.ar* ☉ *Weekdays tours hourly 9–5, Sat. tours at 9:30, 10:30, 12:30, Sun. open only by appt.*

2 **Familia Zuccardi.** In 1950, Don Alberto Zuccardi, a civil engineer, developed a more modern system of irrigation for his vineyards in Maipú and later in Santa Rosa. He and his team of 450 workers continue to discover new approaches to viniculture and wine tourism; their newest innovation, the Cava de Turísmo, is an air-conditioned cave where you can join tours of the bodega led by family members or an oenologist. A soft, soothing light glows on cobblestone floors, concrete walls, and warm woodwork in the tasting room and gift shop. Outside, you can walk shoulder to shoulder with the neatly labeled vines to the garden restaurant for a wine-tasting lunch or tea. During harvest time (February and March), Vení a Cosechar (Come and Harvest) is a program for wannabe grape-pickers that includes an early-morning pickup at your hotel, breakfast, and a morning of hard work in the vineyards (guided by agronomists and oenologists). This is followed by a wine tasting and lunch. From June to August, a similar program teaches the art of pruning. Cooking classes, music, and art exhibits also take place here. ⊠ *RP33 Km 7.5, Maipú* ☎*261/441–0000* ⊕*www.familiazuccardi.com* ☉ *Mon.–Sat. 9–5:30; Sun. 10–5.*

Fodor'sChoice ★

8 **Finca Flichman.** In 1873, Don Sami Flichman, a Jewish immigrant, planted the first vines in the stony soil of a former riverbed in the *barrancas* (ravines) next to the Mendoza River. His son Isaac acquired the property during the 1930s depression and had the foresight to produce only high-quality grapes. In 1983 the Wertheim family bought the winery, introduced new technology, and added another winery. Underground cellars—some ancient, some new—stainless-steel tanks, and computerized temperature controls make this one of Argentina's most modern wineries. ⊠ *Munives 800, Maipú* ☎*261/497–2039* ⊕*www.flichman.com.ar* ☉ *Wed.–Sun. 10–5.*

LUJÁN DE CUYO

17 **Bodega Catena Zapata.** A faux Mayan pyramid rising from the vineyards fronts the towering snow-clad Andes at this landmark winery, where the architecture rivals the wine. You descend from a crystal cupola through concentric spaces to the tasting room, which is surrounded by 400 oak barrels. Columbia University economics professor Nicolás Catena planted his vineyards at varying altitudes, then blended varietals from these different microclimates to create complex, distinctive wines. Special tastings with meals can be arranged for groups by prior notice. ⊠ *Calle J. Cobos s/n, Agrelo, Luján de Cuyo* ☎*261/490–0214* ⊕*www.catenawines.com.*

7 **Bodega Lagarde.** Founded in 1897, Lagarde is one of the oldest and most traditional wineries in Mendoza. The third generation of the Pescarmona family now cultivates the grapes, producing limited quantities of

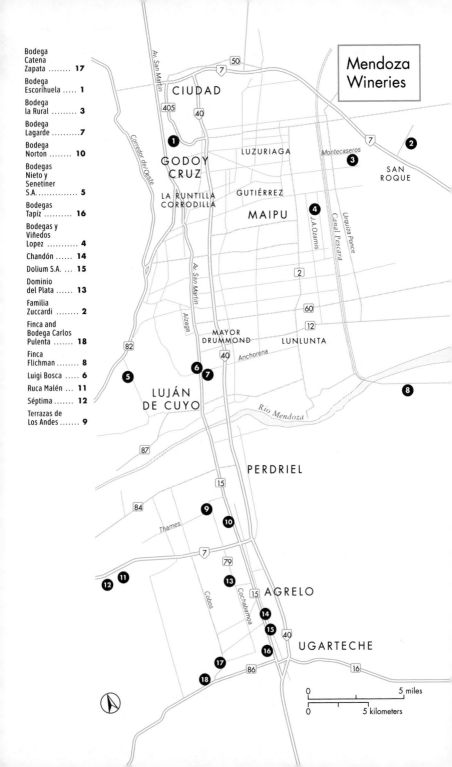

Mendoza Wineries

CIUDAD

LUZURIAGA

Montecaseros

SAN ROQUE

GODOY CRUZ

LA RUNTILLA CORRODILLA

GUTIÉRREZ

MAIPU

J.A.Ozamis

Canal Pescara

Urquiza Ponce

MAYOR DRUMMOND

Anchorena

LUNLUNTA

LUJÁN DE CUYO

Río Mendoza

PERDRIEL

Thames

AGRELO

Cobos

Cochabamoa

UGARTECHE

0   5 miles

0   5 kilometers

quality wine and searching for ways to improve while avoiding fleeting trends. ⊠*San Martín 1745, Mayor Drummond, Luján de Cuyo* ☎*261/498–0011* ⊕*www.lagarde.com.ar* ⊗*Weekdays 10–5.*

⓾ Bodega Norton. In 1895, English engineer Sir Edmund Norton built the first winery in the valley south of the Mendoza River. Part of the old adobe house and a wing of the winery demonstrate the traditional construction of beamed ceilings with bamboo reeds under a zinc roof. In 1989 an Austrian businessman purchased the company, and his son continues to modernize and expand the 100-year-old vineyards. ⊠*RP15 Km 23.5, Perdriel, Luján de Cuyo* ☎*261/490–9700* ⊕*www. norton.com.ar* ⊗*Hourly tours daily 9–noon and 2–5.*

❺ Bodegas Nieto y Senetiner S.A. White adobe walls, tile roofs, flower-bed-lined walkways, and huge shade trees welcome you to this bodega. From March 10 to mid-April, volunteer pickers arrive for breakfast, a brief explanation of harvest technique, and an introduction to their foreman. Then, with tools in hand, it's off to the vineyards with the agronomist until baskets are inspected to see who wins the prize for the best pick. From mid-August until the end of September, pruning (*podar*) takes place, and you can join the experts in cutting, tying, and modifying vines. Perhaps the most unusual tour is a three-hour, 2-km (1-mi) horseback ride to a hilltop for a view of the mountains and vineyards. During a maté (a tealike beverage) and muffin break, an oenologist explains the varietals growing around you. All of these activities include lunch at the bodega, tasting, and a tour, and all require reservations. ⊠*Guaradia Viaje, between RN7 and Rosque Sáenz Peña s/n, Vistalba, Luján de Cuyo* ☎*261/498–0315* ⊕*www.nietosenetiner.com. ar* ⊗*Summer: tours weekdays at 10, 11, 12:30, and 4; Other seasons: tours weekdays at 10, 11, 12:30, and 3.*

⓰ Bodegas Tapíz. When the Ortiz family bought this modern bodega from Kendall Jackson in 2003, CEO Patricia Ortiz, a medical doctor and mother of five, decided to take a different approach to winemaking. She and oenologist Fabián Valenzuela want to make "happier wines" that are easier to drink and more food-friendly. Inside the bodega, walls of loose river rocks held in place by wire mesh contrast the slick granite walls and long corridors. In summer a two-horse carriage driven by a local gaucho takes you on a learning tour of the vineyard. Club Tapiz, a seven-room inn with a spa, restaurant, and bicycles, is only 20 minutes away. ⊠*RP15 Km 32, Agrelo, Luján de Cuyo* ☎*261/490–0202* ⊕*www.tapiz.com* ⊗*Weekdays 9–5.*

⓮ Chandón. The president of Moët & Chandon was so impressed by the *terroir* (soil, climate, and topography that contribute to making each wine unique) in Agrelo that he decided to build the first foreign branch of his family's company here. Today, the winery is producing wine and *vino spumante* (sparkling wine) in great quantities. In a one-hour class for groups of 2 to 15, an oenologist will guide you through the process of blending wine, and you can take your new private label home with you. During harvest (February, March, and April), an agronomist takes groups to work in the vineyard with modern equipment; lunch is included. Special workshops can be arranged for business groups, wine clubs, and wannabe winemakers. ✉ *RN40 Km 29, Agrelo, Luján de Cuyo* ☎ *261/490–9968* ⊕ *www.chandon.com.ar* ⊗ *Hourly tours weekdays 10–1 and 2–5; winter weekday tours at 11:30, 2, 3:30, and 5. Sat. tours require reservation.*

⑮ Dolium S.A. "Dolium" is the Latin word for the amphoras used by the Romans to store wine underground. Here modern, simple, and innovative winemaking occurs in what appears to be a small gray box set in the middle of a vineyard. The winery works are actually underground; you simply taste the wines upstairs in a glass-and-steel reception area that looks down into the action. ✉ *RP15 Km 30, Agrelo, Luján de Cuyo* ☎ *261/490–0200* ⊕ *www.dolium.com* ⊗ *Weekdays 9–5, weekends by appointment.*

⑬ Dominio del Plata. Since 2001 Susana Balbo and her husband, viticulturalist Pedro Marchevsky, have combined their formidable skills with the newest technology and a passion for the care and cultivation of their land. Balbo, Argentina's first licensed female oenologist and an internationally known winemaking consultant, can look out her living room window across a sea of vineyards to the sparkling Cordón de Plata mountain range. From her dining room window, she can see the stainless-steel tanks and pipes of the bodega she designed. ✉ *Cochebamba 7801, Agrelo, Luján de Cuyo* ☎ *261/498–6572* ⊗ *Weekdays 9–1 and 3–5* ⌂ *Reservations essential.*

⑱ Finca and Bodega Carlos Pulenta. Carlos Pulenta has been referred to as the "Robert Mondavi of Argentina." During his seven years as president of Salentein, a Dutch company with three bodegas, he increased the number of European varietals, installed the latest technology, and put Salentein wine on the tables of the world. He left in 2004 and returned to his family's land in Vistalba, where he built his own bodega in the middle of the vineyard. The courtyard entrance frames a perfect view of the 4,900-meter (16,000-foot) Cordón de Plata mountain range. More than a bodega, the light stone and polished concrete complex houses an ultramodern 12-room inn, perhaps the best restaurant in the region (La Bourgogne), elegant meeting rooms, an underground salon for private parties, and a conference center. Inside the bodega, glass walls expose the tumbled rocks and dirt that Malbec thrives in. You'll find architectural surprises around every corner as you explore the cellars. Pulenta and his team of family advisers and oenologists have created three blends using Malbec, Cabernet, Merlot, and Bonarda, plus a delicate Sauvignon Blanc. ✉ *Roque Saenz Peña 3531, Vistalba, Luján de Cuyo* ☎ *261/498–9400* ⊕ *www.carlospulentawines.com.*

Fodor'sChoice ★

⑥ Luigi Bosca. Albereto, Raul, and Roberto Arizú—descendants of Leoncio Arizú, who brought the original vines from Spain in 1890—believe that a winemaker's job is to preserve what nature has delivered. Here, nature is on their side. The terroir has much to do with the unique character of Luigi Bosca's wine. This bodega is an architectural gem, with carved reliefs depicting the history of wine in Argentina, tile floors, inlaid wood ceilings, and painted arches. ✉ *San Martín 2044, Drum-*

mond, Luján de Cuyo ☎261/498–0437 ⊕*www.luigibosca.com.ar* ⊙*Daily tours at 10, 11, 12:30, and 4 (3 in winter).*

⓫ Ruca Malén. Jon Pierre Thibaud brings 10 years of experience as president of neighboring Chandon vineyards to this modern, compact boutique winery situated just back from Ruta Nacional 7. Thibaud and his French partner, Jacques Louis de Montalembert, have dedicated their collective skill and passion to selecting the finest grapes for quality wines. Wine tours are led by an oenologist. With one day's notice, a gourmet lunch and wine tasting is available for 55 pesos per person. For reservations, contact Ruca Malén by phone or e-mail. ⊠*RN7 Km 1059, Agrelo, Luján de Cuyo* ☎261/410–6214 ⊕*http://bodegaruca malen.com* ⊙ *Weekdays 10–5, Sat. 10–1.*

⓬ Séptima. When the Spanish wine group Codorniú decided that Argen-
★ tina would be their seventh great wine investment, they constructed their winery in the *pirca* style, in which natural stones are piled one atop the other. The Huarpe natives used this technique to build walls, dwellings, and sacred places. Inside the massive walls is a state-of-the-art winery with sleek wood and glass corridors. Visitors climb over hoses and machinery while they follow the grapes from vineyard to bottle in a natural working atmosphere. A rooftop terrace is available for private lunches, weddings, or sunset wine tastings. A rosé blend of Malbec and Pinot Noir is an interesting invention. ⊠*RN7 Km 6.5, Agrelo, Luján de Cuyo* ☎261/498–5164 ⊕*www.bodegaseptima.com. ar* ⊙ *Weekdays 10–5* ⚠*Reservations essential.*

❾ Terrazas de Los Andes. Four vineyards situated at different heights (terraces)—Syrah at 800 meters (2,600 feet), Cabernet Sauvignon at 980 meters (3,200 feet), Malbec slightly higher, and Chardonnay at 1,200 meters (3,900 feet)—take advantage of different microclimates, allowing each varietal to develop to its maximum potential. Bare brick walls, high ceilings, and a labyrinth of soaring arches store premium wines in stainless-steel tanks and oak barrels. Built in 1898 and restored in the mid-1990s, everything in the tasting room—from the bar to the tables to the leather chairs—is made with recycled barrels. A six-room guesthouse and a dining room are available for family or business gatherings. Reservations are required one day in advance by phone or e-mail. ⊠*Thames and Cochebamba, Perdriel, Luján de Cuyo* ☎261/448–0058 ⊕*www.terrazasdelosandes.com* ⊙ *Weekdays 10–noon.*

WHERE TO EAT

MENDOZA CITY

$ ✕**Azafrán.** It's as much a gourmet grocery and wine shop as it is a res-
WINE BAR taurant—one that offers a break from parrilla fare, at that. In the wine
★ bar, an old wine press has been converted into a tasting table. Outside on the sidewalk or inside this 19th-century brick building you can enjoy cheeses, pâtés, and hot and cold tapas served on wooden platters. Shelves are stocked with olive oils, smoked meats, dried herbs, mushrooms, olives, jams, and breads. ⊠*Sarmiento 765, Mendoza* ☎261/429–4200 ⊠ *Villanueva 287* ▤*MC, V* ⊙*Closed Sun.*

$ ✕ **La Florencia.** Sidewalk tables invite you to stop and peruse the menu:
ARGENTINE grilled, baked, and broiled meats and fish; pastas; pizzas; game; and
a variety of salads, along with a lengthy wine list. Inside are eclectic
displays of antique weapons, telephones, and gaucho artifacts. The
upstairs dining room has a breezy street view. ⊠*Sarmiento and Perú,
Mendoza* ☎*261/429–1564* ⊟*AE, DC, MC, V.*

$$$ ✕ **La Marchigiana.** They've served homemade pasta since 1950. The
ITALIAN woman behind it all often dines here with her family, and her cook-
books are for sale. The old restaurant burned down in 2006, but a
modern version with underground parking is just as popular with Men-
docinos looking for a reasonably priced meal. ⊠*Patricias Mendocinas
1550, Mendoza* ☎*261/423–071* ⊠*Palmares Shopping Mall, Godoy
Cruz* ☎*261/439–1961* ⊟*AE, DC, MC, V.*

$$$ ✕ **Mi Tierra.** It's in an old house with tall narrow doors, high ceilings,
ARGENTINE and five dining rooms. Chicken or rabbit *al disco* (in a wok) comes with
grilled vegetables. Leave room for the *volcan de frutas* (fruit in a merengue). ⊠*Mitre 794, at corner of San Lorenzo, Mendoza* ☎*261/425–
0035* ⊟*AE, DC, MC, V* ☉*No lunch.*

$$ ✕ **La Tasca de Plaza España.** If the bright red walls, the strange faces
MEDITERRANEAN painted above the entrance, and the eclectic art inside don't grab you,
the tapas and Mediterranean dishes probably will. Seafood tapas, veal-
and-artichoke stew, and a casserole of zucchini, onions, and peppers
in a cheese sauce are a few of the tempting dishes served in this ven-
erable—though irreverent—old house. ⊠*Montevideo 117, Mendoza*
☎*261/423-3466* ⊟*AE, MC, V.*

$$ ✕ **Terrazas del Lago.** It's a 15-minute taxi ride from downtown to this
ARGENTINE restaurant in Parque General San Martín. The long wood-and-glass
building overlooks a lake and two pools that are part of an aquatic club
(open for day use by nonmembers). A buffet fills one room. The master
of the pasta bar waits to help you—first with choosing from four kinds
of ravioli and eight types of noodles, then with selecting a sauce from a
simmering pot, and finally with piling your plate with all kinds of other
items. Seating is outdoors on a deck or indoors with air-conditioning
(essential for summer lunches). Reservations are a good idea. ⊠*Av. Las
Palmeras s/n, on Parque Gral San Martín, Mendoza* ☎*261/428–3438*
⊟*AE, MC, V* ☉*No dinner Sun.; no lunch Mon.*

GODOY CRUZ

$$$ ✕ **1884 Restaurante Francis Mallman.** The soft glow of candles on the
ARGENTINE patio under the prune trees at the 100-year-old Bodega Escorihuela
★ sets the tone for Francis Mallman, who put Argentina on the map of
international *alta cocina* (haute cuisine), to present his version of Pata-
gonian cuisine. Empanadas and baby goat are baked in mud ovens, a
custom derived from the Incas, and the 36-page wine list has detailed
information on grapes and bodegas. ⊠*Belgrano 1188, Godoy Cruz*
☎*261/424–2698* ⊟*AE, DC, MC, V.*

MAIPÚ

$$$ ✕ **Terruño.** Light from a whimsical chandelier high in the timbered ceil-
ARGENTINE ing highlights the Malbec-color walls and worn floors of this 1890
★ vintner's residence. Appetizers, such as Andean trout with mushrooms

or a corn, tomato, and onion tart, are as good as the entrées. An experienced staff knows how to pair local wine with each course, including dessert. ⊠*Club Tapiz, Pedro Molina (RP60) s/n, Maipú* ☎*261/496– 4815* ⚑*Reservations essential* ⊕*www.tapiz.com.*

LUJÁN DE CUYO

$$$$ ✕**La Bourgogne.** "Cooking comes from regional traditions. My cuisine is tied to the land," says Jean-Paul Bondoux, Argentina's only
FRENCH   Relais Gourmand chef. He applies his French culinary skills to the best
Fodor'sChoice   local produce, and every bite is a fork-stopper in this casually elegant
★   restaurant at Carlos Pulenta's winery. Lunch and cocktails are served on a porch overlooking the vineyards. ⊠*Roque Sáenz Peña 3531, Vistalba, Luján de Cuyo* ☎*261/498–9400* ⊕*www.carlospulenta wines.com* ⚑*Reservations essential* ▤*AE, MC, V* ☉*No dinner Sun. Closed Mon..*

WHERE TO STAY

MENDOZA CITY

¢   ⊞**Damajuana.** It's easy to feel at home inside or out: a bar, restaurant, fireplace, and TV are in the living room, and the spacious backyard has a grill and hammocks. It's a popular hostel with rooms for two, four, or six people that are half the price per person of the one double. All rooms have lockers and shared baths. The neighborhood—steps from bars, boutiques, and cafés—is popular with young Mendocinos. **Pros:** Great neighborhood, especially for young people; steps from bars, boutiques, and cafés. **Cons:** Little peace or privacy. ⊠*Aristedes Villanueva 282, Mendoza* ☎*261/425–5858* ⊕*www.damajuanahostel.com.ar* ⚑*8 rooms* ⚐*In-hotel: restaurant, bar, pool, public Wi-Fi* ▤*MC, V.*

$$$$ ⊞**Executive Hotel.** The tall, elegant tower of this downtown hotel looks
★   out on the Plaza Italia in a quiet residential area just blocks from shops and restaurants. The lobby and dining area are all slick marble, glass, and mirrors. The staff is welcoming—from the front-desk staff to the waiters to the concierge. If you're here for a longer stay, opt for a suite; each has a sitting room with a couch, a desk, and a counter for snacks or drinks. **Pros:** Sauna, tasting rooms with free wine from local vinters. **Con:** Windowless bar-restaurant. ⊠*San Lorenzo 660, Mendoza 5500* ☎*261/524–5000* ⊕*www.parksuites.com.ar* ⚑*49 rooms, 32 suites* ⚐*In-room: safe, Wi-Fi. In-hotel: restaurant, pool, gym, parking (fee)* ▤*AE, DC, MC, V* ⓐ*CP.*

$$$$ ⊞**Hotel Aconcagua.** The service is efficient at this modern hotel on a quiet street near shops and restaurants. Classic gray granite creates a businesslike atmosphere throughout the lobby and in meeting and guest rooms. Los Parrales, the restaurant, uses a mud oven and wood-fired grill to create typical Mendocino meals. **Pros:** Central location; business suites with attendant on top floor. **Con:** Public areas often crowded with wine-business and tour groups. ⊠*San Lorenzo 545, Mendoza* ☎*261/520–0500* ⊕*www.hotelaconcagua.com* ⚑*159 rooms, 9 suites* ⚐*In-hotel: restaurant, pool, executive floor, public Wi-Fi, parking (no fee)* ▤*AE, DC, MC, V* ⓐ*CP.*

$$$ ⛁**Hotel Crillón.** The loyal clientele of this small hotel returns for the neighborhood: it's tranquil yet it's within walking distance of plazas, restaurants, museums, and shops. Small suites have separate workstations, and the helpful staff can plan excursions. **Pros:** Good value and location; quiet street. **Cons:** Older building; basic décor. ⊠*Perú 1065, Mendoza* ☎*261/429–8494* ⊕*www.hcrillon.com.ar* ⇱*67 rooms, 6 suites* ♻*In-room: Wi-Fi. In-hotel: bar, pool, public Wi-Fi* ▤*AE, DC, MC, V* ⏣*CP.*

$$$$ ⛁**Hotel NH Cordillera.** Sometimes a simple, straightforward hotel is all you need. Here plenty of the amenities and a welcoming staff make up for the rather impersonal surroundings. Suites have a wooden deck overlooking the Plaza San Martín. **Pros:** Convenient location; babysitting services; sauna; Jacuzzi; business center. **Cons:** Lack of personality; pool is small. ⊠*España 1324, Mendoza M5500DWN* ☎*261/441–6464* ⊕*www.nh-hotels.com* ⇱*100 rooms, 5 suites* ♻*In-room: Wi-Fi. In-hotel: restaurant, bar, pool, gym, parking (no fee), public Internet, public Wi-Fi* ▤*AE, DC, MC, V* ⏣*CP, EP.*

$$$$ ⛁**Park Hyatt Mendoza.** Hyatt has preserved the landmark Plaza Hotel's
Fodor'sChoice   19th-century Spanish colonial facade: a grand pillared entrance and
★   a wide veranda that extends to either side of the street. Lunch, afternoon tea, and dinner are served on this gracious terrace overlooking Mendoza's main square. A two-story wine wall separates the restaurant from the lobby. Minimalist bedrooms are softened by plump white pillows and duvets covering the simple ebony beds. Bathrooms have plenty of mirrors to complement chrome and marble accents. **Pros:** Good snacks and atmosphere in wine bar; dining on front porch. **Con:** Glass walls in bathroom don't allow for privacy. ⊠*Calle Chile 1124, Mendoza 5500* ☎*261/441–1234* ⊕*http://mendoza.park.hyatt.com* ⇱*171 rooms, 15 suites* ♻*In-room: safe, Ethernet. In-hotel: restaurant, bar, pool, gym, spa, parking (no fee)* ▤*AE, DC, MC, V* ⏣*CP.*

$$$ – $$$$ ⛁**Posada de Rosas.** Don't be fooled by this ordinary house on an ordinary street—inside, bright rooms are decorated with modern art and ancient Andean weavings and have just the places to enjoy breakfast (inside or out on the patio) or tea or to curl up with a *New Yorker* or one of the English-language wine magazines that are set out. American expat owners Ellen and Riccardo share their knowledge and passion for Mendoza through their tour company, Amazing Mendoza (⊕*www. amazingmendoza.com*). Three rooms with kitchenettes in an outside building face the garden. **Pros:** Peaceful location; helpful English-speaking owners. **Con:** Long walk to town. ⊠*Martínez de Rozas 1641, Mendoza 5500* ☎*261/423–3629* ⊕*www.posadaderosas.com* ⇱*8 rooms* ♻*In-room: refrigerator. In-hotel: pool, no elevator, public Wi-Fi* ▤*AE, DC, MC, V* ⏣*CP.*

$$$$ ⛁**Villagio Boutique Hotel.** There's a high-tech Italian feel to this modern boutique hotel a block from the main plaza and shopping street. Expect such details as polished wood or stainless-steel trim; beige, black, and tan furnishings; and modern artwork throughout. **Pros:** Spacious rooms; artful architecture and design; sauna; Jacuzzi with a mountain view. **Cons:** Small rooms; some guests complain of thin walls and noise from neighbors; some rooms have views of air shaft. ⊠*25 de Mayo*

1010, Mendoza5500 ☎*261/524–5200* ⊕*http://hotelvillaggio.com.ar*
🖙*26 rooms* ♿*In-room: Wi-Fi. In-hotel: restaurant, bar, pool, gym, public Wi-Fi* ⊟*AE, DC, MC, V* ⫶◯⫶*CP.*

MAIPÚ

$$$ 🖿**Club Tapiz.** This 1890 governor's mansion feels like a private villa.
★   Stroll through the old winery, lounge on the enclosed patio, or gaze at the Andes from the outdoor pool or indoor Jacuzzi. Evening wine tastings will whet your appetite for dinner in Terruña (Terroir). **Pros:** Great restaurant; close to vineyards. **Con:** Far from shops or town. ⊠*Pedro Molina (RP60) s/n, Maipú* ☎*261/496–4815* ⊕*www.tapiz.com* 🖙*7 rooms* ♿*In-hotel: restaurant, bar, spa, bicycles* ⊟*AE, MC, V.*

LUJÁN DE CUYO

$$$$ 🖿**Cavas Wine Lodge.** Inside a gracious colonial villa surrounded by
★   mountains and vineyards, a reception hall is washed in sunlight from high windows, and common areas are appointed in white, gold, wood, and leather. Imagine yourself in one of the white adobe guesthouses, with your own patio and plunge pool, and your own roof deck with a fireplace. Bedrooms are painted a soothing cream that contrasts with the bold red throws and pillows. Bathrooms have natural stone walls and what seems like all the amenities ever invented. Enjoy the Jacuzzi or an aromatherapy or vinotherapy treatment in the on-site spa. Ask the concierge to arrange visits to nearby bodegas; make reservations at restaurants; or organize horseback-riding, rafting, or biking excursions. **Pros:** Luxurious; private; spacious; good service. **Cons:** Expensive; far from shops, restaurants, and other urban activities. ⊹*RN40 south, west on RN7, turn onto Cosa Flores just before Ruca Malen Winery. Follow signs for 2.2 km (1.4 mi)* ⊠*Lujan de Cuyo* ☎*261/410–6927* ⊕*www.cavaswinelodge.com* 🖙*14 rooms* ♿*In-room: safe, DVD, Ethernet (some). In-hotel: restaurant, bar, pool, gym, spa, bicycles* ⊟*AE, DC, MC, V* ⊘*Closed June* ⫶◯⫶*CP.*

$$$ 🖿**Chacras de Coria Lodge.** A stay at this lodge puts you in an upscale residential area 15 minutes from Mendoza and close to wineries in Maipú and Luján de Cuyo. The staff here can arrange custom tours with oenologists as well as catered meals, golf, tennis, horseback riding, mountain biking—even tango lessons. On-site, the atmosphere is intimate at the evening wine tastings, outdoor cooking classes, *asados* (barbecues), and candlelit dinners on the veranda. **Pros:** Personalized tours; close to vineyards; good restaurant. **Con:** In a residential suburb. ⊠*Viamonte 4762, Chacras de Coria, Luján de Cuyo* ☎*261/496–1888* ⊕*www.postalesdelplata.com* 🖙*6 rooms, 1 apartment* ♿*In-hotel: restaurant, bar, pool* ⊟*AE, MC, V* ⫶◯⫶*CP.*

$$$$ 🖿**La Posada Carlos Pulenta.** The enormous rooms on the second floor
Fodor's Choice of this Tuscan terra-cotta building face east, where the sun rises over
★   vineyards, or west, where it sets over the Andes. Cream-color tile floors, dark wicker furniture, and taupe-and-café-au-lait-covered furnishings are luxurious. Sumptuous chairs await you on the veranda for lunch, wine tasting, or daydreaming. The restaurant, La Borgogne, has an open kitchen where you can join a cooking class. The staff can arrange wine tours. **Pros:** Good views; modern business center;

all meals included in rate and can be served in your room. **Cons:** Few rooms; no pool. ⊠*Roque Sáenz Peña 3531, Vistalba, Luján de Cuyo* ☎*261/498–9400* ⊕*www.carlospulentawines.com* ⇄*4 rooms* ⟨&⟩*In-room: Wi-Fi. In-hotel: restaurant, bar* ⊟*AE, MC, V* ⟨◎⟩*MAP.*

AFTER DARK

Avenida Arístedes Villanueva wakes up at around 11 PM, when the bars, boutiques, wine shops, and cafés open their doors. As the evening progresses, crowds get bigger, and the music—rock, tango, salsa—gets louder. The action peaks after midnight. Inexpensive, casual **El Bar del José** (⊠*Arístedes Villanueva 740 Mendoza* ☎*No phone*) was the first gathering place in the trendy Villanueva neighborhood.

Por Acá (⊠*Arístedes Villanueva 557Mendoza*) attracts a cosmopolitan crowd of locals and Europeans. Live rock music begins after 10 PM. The **Regency Casino** (⊠*25 de Mayo and Sarmiento Mendoza* ☎*261/441– 2844*) at the Park Hyatt Mendoza has blackjack, stud poker, roulette tables, slot machines, and an exclusive bar.

SHOPPING

Pick up leather goods, shoes, and clothing along the pedestrian part of Sarmiento and its cross streets, or on Avenida La Heras, where you'll find regional products to eat, drink, wear, or decorate your house with. On weekends, Plaza Independencia becomes a market with stands selling jewelry, handmade sweaters, ponchos, maté gourds, olive oil, and other regional wares.

CLOTHES & ACCESSORIES

Talabarterías sell fine leather goods and everything equestrian, from saddles and handmade tack to hats, vests, and other gaucho-inspired items. Mendocinos shop at **La Matera** (⊠*Villanueva 314, Mendoza* ☎*261/425–3332*) for boots, vests, belts, scarves, and riding gear. On the peatonal, **Cardón** (⊠*Sarmiento 224Mendoza*) carries gaucho clothing and accessories: *bombachas* (baggy, pleated pants), leather jackets and vests, boots, belts, scarves, ponchos, and knives.

FOOD & WINE

There's a huge selection of wine at **La Casa del Vino** (⊠*Villanueva 160, Mendoza* ☎*261/425–0659*). **Pura Cepa** (⊠*Peatonal Sarmiento 664, Mendoza*) conducts in-store wine tastings. Before your picnic, grab a bottle of Malbec at **Juan Cedrón** (⊠*Peatonal Sarmiento 278, Mendoza*). **Azafrán** (⊠*Sarmiento 765, Mendoza* ☎*261/429–4200*) is a wine bar, café, wine shop, and delicatessen with regional olive oil, jams, meats, and cheeses.

In a beautiful old country house, **Historias & Sabores** (*Histories and Flavors* ⊠*Carril Gómez 3064, Coquimbito-Maipú* ☎*261/155–744–614 reservations* ⊙*Mon.–Sat. 11–6*), conducts guided tours and tastings of fruits, olives, chocolates, and liquors. Learn how chocolate-covered cordials are made.

MARKET

The 1884 **Mercado Central** (⊠*Av. Heras and Patricias Mendocinas, Mendoza*) is the oldest market in Mendoza. Ponchos, Indian weavings, olive oil, fruit, and handicrafts are sold in open stalls daily from 9 to 1:30 and 4:30 to 9.

SPORTS & THE OUTDOORS

The high peaks of the Andes provide a natural playground of ski slopes in winter, mountains to climb in summer, and miles of trails to hike, bike, or ride on horseback. Rivers roar out of the mountains in spring, inviting rafters and kayakers to test the water. Country roads in and around the vineyards make great bike paths.

Some of the most wild and remote mountain areas are made accessible by the Ruta Nacional 7, which crosses the Andes right by Parque Provincial Aconcagua (⇨*below*). Such mountain towns near the park as Potrerillos and Uspallata offer lodging and a base close to the action.

Tour operators in Mendoza City offer a variety of adventures. **AymaraTurismo** (⊠*9 de Julio 1023, M5500, Mendoza* ☎*261/420–2064* ⊕*www.aymara.com.ar*) handles guided horseback rides, trekking, mountain climbing, and river rafting on the Mendoza River.

Tras Andino Turismo (⊠*Chile 1443 Loc. 04, Mendoza* ☎*261/425–425–6726* ⊠*R82 Km 38, Cacheuta* ☎*262/449–0159* ⊕*www.trasandino turismo.com.ar*) has operations in Mendoza City and in the mountains. They offer trekking to base camp at Aconcagua as well as 15-day ascents. They also offer mountain-biking, rock-climbing, rafting, and horseback trips.

HORSEBACK RIDING

Cabalgata (horseback riding) is an enjoyable and natural way to explore the mountains west of Mendoza. You can ride to the foot of Aconcagua or Tupungato, or follow the hoof prints of San Martín on a seven-day trip over the Andes. **Cordon del Plata** (⊠*Av. Las Heras 341, Mendoza* ☎*261/423–7423* ⊕*www.cordondelplata.com*) offers horseback rides from a day to a week, combination horseback riding/trekking/rafting trips, and mountain-biking trips.

MOUNTAIN BIKING

Many of Mendoza's back roads lead through the suburbs and vineyards into the Andean foothills and upward to mountain villages—or all the way to Chile.

Motor-Bikes (⊠*Urquiza 1606, Maipú* ☎*261/410–6686* ⊕*www.bikes andwines.com*) rents three kinds of mountain bikes for full- or half-day self-guided tours in the wine district of Maipú. Trips include a map, water bottle, lunch, and medical and mechanical assistance. You begin at La Rural winery and museum and along the way visit three wineries, a chocolate and liquor factory, and an olive oil company. The lunch stop is at a deli, where you can eat on a patio.

WHITE-WATER RAFTING

Mendoza-based adventure-tour companies offer half- to two-day Class II to Class IV rafting and kayaking trips on the Río Mendoza near Potrerillos (⇨*Parque Provincial Anconcagua, below*).

With **Argentine Rafting Expeditions** (*Office:* ⊠*Primitivo de la Reta 992 Loc. 4, Mendoza* ☎*262/429–6325* ⊕*www.argentinarafting.com*) you can raft the Río Mendoza, take a kayak class, or combine rafting, horseback riding, and mountain biking in a two-day multisport outing, spending the night in a mountain refugio. **Betancourt Rafting** (⊠*Lavalle 36, Galería Independencia, Loc. 8, Mendoza* ☎*261/429– 9665* ⊠*RN 7, Km 26, Luján de Cuyo* ☎*261/15–559–1329* ⊕*www. betancourt.com.ar*) has three small cabins and a lodge at the Cacheuta Hot Springs.

PATAGONIA

Updated by
Eddy Ancinas,
David Miller,
Tim Patterson
& Jonathan
Yevin

Patagonia, that fabled land of endless, empty, open space at the end of the world, has humbled the most fearless explorers. Many have described it as a cruel and lonely windswept place unfit for humans. Darwin called Patagonia "wretched and useless," yet he was deeply moved by its desolation and forever attracted to it. Today the 800,000 square km (309,000 square mi) that make up Argentine Patagonia continue to challenge and fascinate explorers, mountaineers, nature lovers, sports enthusiasts, and curious visitors from around the world. Because the population in Patagonia is small relative to its land mass, a staggering variety of plants and wildlife exists in pristine habitats.

The addition of an airport in Calafate, with direct flights from Buenos Aires and Bariloche has made the far reaches of Patagonia much more accessible to tourists. Covering the great distances between Bariloche, in the north; Ushuaia, in the south; and El Calafate, Río Gallegos, and Trelew, in the middle, requires careful planning—air travel is essential. Tours to popular sights along the Atlantic coast, to the glaciers, or in and around Bariloche, can be arranged in Buenos Aires or in each destination. If you want to see it all, packaged tours can make the whole trip easier.

BARILOCHE

1,615 km (1,001 mi) southwest of Buenos Aires (2 hrs by plane); 432 km (268 mi) south of Neuquén on R237; 1,639 km (1,016 mi) north of Río Gallegos; 876 km (543 mi) northwest of Trelew; 357 km (221 mi) east of Puerto Montt, Chile, via lake crossing.

Bariloche is the gateway to all the recreational and scenic splendors of the Northern Lake District and headquarters for 2-million-acre Nahuel Huapi National Park. Although planes, boats, and buses arrive daily, you can escape on land or water—or just by looking out a window—into a dazzling wilderness of lakes, waterfalls, mountain glaciers, forests, and meadows.

Patagonia

The town of Bariloche hugs the southeastern shore of Nahuel Huapi Lake, expanding rapidly east toward the airport and west along the lake toward Llao Llao, as Argentines and foreigners buy and build without any apparent zoning plan. Being the most popular vacation destination in Patagonia has not been kind to the town once called the "Switzerland of the Andes." Traffic barely moves on streets and sidewalks during holidays and the busy months of January–March, July, and August.

Nevertheless, the Centro Cívico (Civic Center), with its gray-green stone-and-log buildings, has not lost its architectural integrity. Designed by Alejandro Bustillo, this landmark square, with its view of the lake and mountains, is a good place to begin exploring Bariloche.

GETTING HERE & AROUND

For long excursions, such as the Seven Lakes Route, Circuito Grande, or Tronadór (⇨ *below*), sign up for a tour through your hotel or with a local tour agency. If you prefer the independence of figuring out maps and driving yourself, rent a car. Tour operators for fishing, rafting, and bike trips will pick you up and transport you to your destination. For good maps and a list of tour operators, look for *Guía Busch* at local bookstores, car-rental agencies, and kiosks. A local bus picks up skiers in Bariloche, and many hotels have their own shuttle.

SAFETY & PRECAUTIONS

Driving in Bariloche requires total attention to blind corners, one-way streets, and stop signs where no one stops. Never leave anything in your car. On Bariloche's challenging sidewalks, uneven steps, broken pavement, and unexpected holes are potential ankle-breakers. When students hit Bariloche during holidays, they party until 5 or 6 in the morning, resulting in serious drunk-driving auto accidents.

ESSENTIALS

Bus Contacts **Bariloche Bus Terminal** (✉ *Av. 12 de Octubre* ☎ *2944/432-860*). **Algarrobal** (✉ *9 de Julio 1800* ☎ *2944/427-698*). **Andesmar** (✉ *Mitre 385* ☎ *2944/430-211*). **Don Otto** (✉ *At bus terminal in Bariloche, Mitre 321* ☎ *2944/429-012*). **VIATAC** (✉ *Moreno 138* ☎ *2944/434-727*). **El Valle** (✉ *Av. 12 de Octubre 1884* ☎ *2944/431-444*). **Via Bariloche** (✉ *Mitre 321* ☎ *2944/432-444*).

Currency Exchange **Banco Frances** (✉ *Av. San Martín 332* ☎ *2944/430-325*). **Bansud** (✉ *Mitre 427* ☎ *2944/424-210*).

Medical Assistance **Angel Gallardo** (✉ *Gallardo 701* ☎ *2944/427-023*). **Farmacia Detina** (✉ *Bustillo 12,500* ☎ *2944/525-900*). **Hospital Zonal Ramón Carillo** (✉ *Moreno 601* ☎ *2944/426-119*). **Hospital Sanatorio del Sol** (✉ *20 de Febrero 598* ☎ *2944/525-000*).

Rental Cars **Baricoche** (✉ *Moreno 115* ☎ *2944/427-638* ⊕ *www.baricoche.com. ar*). **Localiza** (✉ *Emilio Frey & V.A. O'Conner* ☎ *2944/435-374, 2944/1562-7708 cell* ⊕ *www.autosurpatagonia.com.ar*).

Visitor & Tour Info **Oficina Municipal de Turismo** (✉ *Centro Cívico, across from clock tower* ☎ *2944/429-850* ⊕ *www.barilochepatagonia.info*) is open daily 8:30 AM–9 PM.

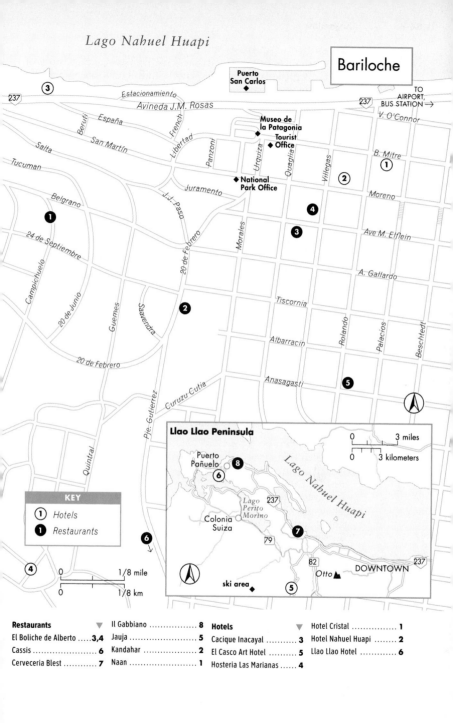

Bariloche

Lago Nahuel Huapi

Restaurants ▼
El Boliche de Alberto **3,4**
Cassis **6**
Cerveceria Blest **7**
Il Gabbiano **8**
Jauja **5**
Kandahar **2**
Naan **1**

Hotels ▼
Cacique Inacayal **3**
El Casco Art Hotel **5**
Hosteria Las Marianas **4**
Hotel Cristal **1**
Hotel Nahuel Huapi **2**
Llao Llao Hotel **6**

EXPLORING: SIGHTS

The **Museo de la Patagonia** tells the social and geological history of northern Patagonia through displays of Indian and gaucho artifacts and exhibits on regional flora and fauna. The history of the Mapuche and the Conquista del Desierto (Conquest of the Desert) are explained in detail. ✉ *Centro Cívico, next to arch over Bartolomé Mitre* ☎ *2944/422–330* 🎫 *2.50 pesos* ☾ *Mon. and Sat. 10–1, Tues.– Fri. 10–12:30 and 2–7.*

For an aerial view of the area around Bariloche, don't miss **Cerro Otto** (Mt. Otto; 4,608 feet). The ride to the top in a little red gondola takes about 12 minutes. Owned by **Teleférico Cerro Otto** (✉ *Av. de los Pioneros* 🎫 *30 pesos* ☾ *Daily 10–5*), all proceeds go to local hospitals. The mountain is 5 km (3 mi) west of town; a free shuttle bus leaves from the corner of Mitre and Villegas, and Perito Moreno and Independencia. You can also hike or mountain bike to the top, or drive 8 km (5 mi) up a gravel road from Bariloche. In winter, cross-country skis and sleds are for rent at the cafeteria. In summer, hiking and mountain biking are the main activities. For a real thrill, try soaring in a paraplane out over the lake with the condors. Call for **information** (☎ *2944/441–035*) on schedules and sled or ski rentals.

EXPLORING: SCENIC JOURNEYS

The **Circuito Chico** (Small Circuit) is a 70-km (43½-mi) half-day scenic trip from Bariloche along the west shore of Lago Nahuel Huapi. As you head west on Avenida Bustillo (R237) toward Península Llao Llao, enjoy the lake views and variety of lodgings on either side of the road until you reach the Península Llao Llao and **Puerto Pañuelo** (Km 25.5) on a little bay on the right—the embarkation point for lake excursions and for the boat crossing to Chile.

Across from the port, the Hotel Llao Llao sits on a knoll surrounded by three different lakes, with a backdrop of sheer rock cliffs and snow-covered mountains. You'll have to admire from afar if you're not a guest (or haven't made a lunch reservation). The Circuito Chico then circumvents the Llao Llao peninsula, following R77 to Bahía Lopez. Following the lake's edge, you glimpse the bay through a forest of ghostly, leafless lenga trees. After crossing the bridge that links Lago Moreno and Lago Nahuel Huapi at Bahía Lopez, the road crosses Arroyo Lopez (Lopez Creek), where you can stop for a hike up to a waterfall, or continue driving above Lago Moreno to Punto Panoramico, a scenic overlook worth a photo stop. Just before you cross the bridge that separates Lago Moreno east and west, an unmarked dirt road off to the right leads to the rustic village of **Colonia Suiza,** a good spot to stop for tea or lunch before exploring further. After crossing the Moreno Bridge, and passing Laguna El Trebol (a small lake on your left), R77 joins R237 back to Bariloche.

NEED A BREAK?

Cheddar Casa de Te. There's a little log house with a corrugated metal roof, a stone terrace and red umbrellas hanging out over the lake, with views through the gnarly branches of a giant coihué tree to blue water and distant

Fishing The Lakes

Fishing season runs November 15–May 1. In some areas, catch-and-release is allowed year-round; catch-and-release is usually compulsory, but in some places catches may be kept. Guides are available by the day or the week. Nahuel Huapi, Gutiérrez, Mascardi, Correntoso, and Traful are the most accessible lakes in the northern Lake District.

If you're seeking the perfect pool or secret stream for fly-fishing, you may have to do some hiking, particularly along the banks of the Chimehuín, Limay, Traful, and Correntoso rivers. Near Junín de los Andes, the Malleo and Currihué rivers, and lakes Huechulafquen, Paimún, and Lácar are good fishing grounds.

Fishing licenses allowing you to catch brown, rainbow, and brook trout as well as perch and *salar sebago* (landlocked salmon) are obtainable in Bariloche at the **Direcciones Provinciales de Pesca** (⊠ *Elfleín 10* ☎ *2944/425–160*). You can also get licenses at the Nahuel Huapi National Park office and at most tackle shops. Boats can be rented at **Charlie Lake Rent-A-Boat** (⊠ *Av. Ezequiel Bustillo, Km 16.6* ☎ *2944/448–562*).

Oscar Baruzzi at **Baruzzi Deportes** (⊠ *Urquiza 250* ☎ *2944/424–922*) is a good local fishing guide. **Martín Pescador** (⊠ *Rolando 257* ☎ *2944/422–275* ✐ *martinpescador@bariloche.com.ar*) has a shop with fishing and hunting equipment. Ricardo Almeijeiras, also a guide, owns the **Patagonia Fly Shop** (⊠ *Quinchahuala 200, Av. Bustillo, Km 6.7* ☎ *2944/441–944* ✐ *flyshop@bariloche.com.ar*).

---

mountains. The trout sorrentinos in pesto sauce are as good as the view. ⊠ *Av. Bustillo (R237), Km 25* ☎ *2944/448–152* ⊙ *Closed Tues.* ☰ *MC, V.*

The **Circuito Grande** (Large Circuit) covers 250 km (155 mi) in an all-day excursion across the lake from Bariloche, and includes two towns where you could spend a night. Leaving Bariloche on R237 heading east, follow the Río Limay into the Valle Encantado (Enchanted Valley), with its magical red-rock formations. Before crossing the bridge at Confluéncia (where the Río Traful joins the Limay), turn left onto R65 to Lago Traful. Five kilometers (3 mi) beyond the turnoff, on a dirt road heading toward Cuyín Manzano, are some astounding sandstone formations. As you follow the shore of Lago Traful, a sign indicates a *mirador* (lookout) on a high rock promontory, which you can climb up to on wooden stairs. The road from Villa Traful dives into a dense forest until it comes to the intersection with the Seven Lakes Circuit (R237). Turn right if you want to add the Seven Lakes Circuit. Otherwise, turn left and follow the shore of Lago Correntoso to the paved road down to the bay at Villa La Angostura.

A less-traveled all-day boat excursion to **Puerto Blest** leaves from Puerto Pañuelo on the Península Llao Llao (accessible by bus, car, or tour). After the boat docks at Puerto Blest, a bus transports you over a short pass to Puerto Alegre on **Laguna Frías** (Cold Lagoon), where a launch waits to ferry you across the frosty green water to **Puerto Fríos** on the other side. Monte Tronadór towers like a great white sentinel. The

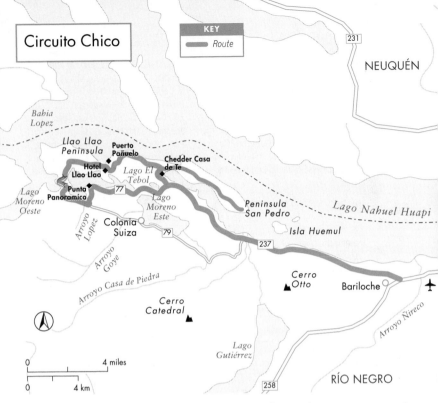

Circuito Chico

KEY
— Route

231

NEUQUÉN

Bahia Lopez

Llao Llao Peninsula

Puerto Pañuelo

Chedder Casa de Te

Hotel Llao Llao

Lago El Tebol

Lago Moreno Oeste

Punta Panoramico

77

Lago Moreno Este

Peninsula San Pedro

Lago Nahuel Huapi

Arroyo Lopez

Colonia Suiza

79

Isla Huemul

237

Arroyo Goye

Cerro Otto

Bariloche

Arroyo Casa de Piedra

Cerro Catedral

Arroyo Ñireco

Lago Gutiérrez

RÍO NEGRO

258

0 ___ 4 miles
0 ___ 4 km

launch returns to the dock at Puerto Alegre, where you can return by foot or by bus to Puerto Blest. From there, the trail to **Cascada Los Cántaros** (Singing Waterfalls) climbs 600 steps to a series of waterfalls cascading from rock to pool to rock. After lunch in **Puerto Blest** at its venerable old hotel, the boat returns to Bariloche. Note: this is the first leg of the Cruce a Chile por Los Lagos.

WHERE TO EAT

$ ✕ **El Boliche de Alberto.** Leather place mats, calfskin menus, and the smell
ARGENTINE   of beef all hint heavily at steak house. Alberto has the best beef in Bariloche. Grilled chicken, lamb, and chorizos all arrive sizzling on a wooden platter, accompanied by empanadas, *provoleta* (fried provolone cheese), salad, fried potatoes, and chimichurri sauce (slather it on the bread). Two locations: ⊠ *Villegas 347* ☎ *2944/431–433* ⊠ *Bustillo 8800* ☎ *2944/462–285* ⊕ *www.elbolichedealberto.com* ▤ *AE, DC, MC, V.*

$$$$ ✕ **Cassis.** Chef Mariana began her culinary career in Argentina's best
ARGENTINE   resorts, until she and her husband found the perfect spot to showcase
Fodor'sChoice   her considerable talent: on lovely Lago Gutiérrez, across the road from
★   the Arelauquen resort (a 30-minute drive from Bariloche). Together they have created dishes like venison baked in rhubarb and blackcurrant sauce; carrot, lime, and lemongrass soup; and fantastic desserts

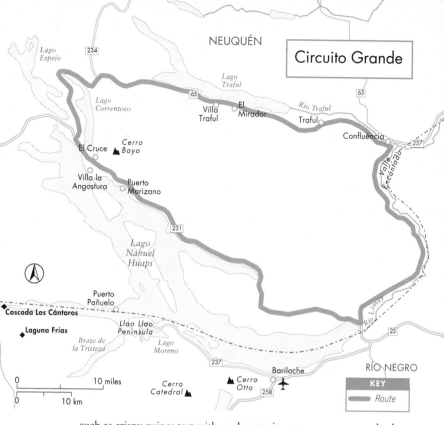

Circuito Grande

such as crispy quince tart with cardamom ice cream or crepes and cakes smothered with fresh berries. ⊠*R82 Arelauquen Point, Lago Gutiérrez* ☎*2944/476–167* ⊕*www.cassis.com.ar* ⚠*Reservations essential* ▤*No credit cards.*

$–$$ ✕**Cerveceria Blest.** This lively spot claims that it was the first brewpub
ARGENTINE in Argentina, and its relaxed bustle hits the spot after a day on the
slopes. Don't miss the excellent bock beer, with a toasty coffee flavor,
or if you prefer hard cider, the Fruto Prohibido. You can come in just
for an après-ski beer sampler, or stay for dinner, which might include
costillitas de cerdo ahumadas con chucrut (smoked pork chops with
sauerkraut—is there a more classic beer food than that?). Pizzas, steak
potpies, and other Anglophilic options round out the menu. ⊠*Av.
Bustillo, Km 11.6* ☎*2944/461–026* ▤*AE, MC, V.*

$$$–$$$$ ✕**Il Gabbiano.** "We don't serve lunch," the folks at this cozy, candlelit
ITALIAN house on the Circuito Chico near Llao Llao boast, "because preparing
dinner takes all day long." It's hard to argue with that philosophy after
you sample the exquisite pastas, which change daily. Look for *tortelli*
stuffed with wild boar, or pumpkin ravioli; they also have a way with
fresh trout. A beautiful wine cellar is open to guests. ⊠*Av. Bustillo,
Km 24.3* ☎*2944/448–346* ⚠*Reservations essential* ▤*No credit cards*
☽*Closed Tues. No lunch.*

$$–$$$ ✕ **Jauja.** Big and friendly, Jauja is a favorite with families for its great
ARGENTINE variety of entrées: meats from Patagonia to the Pampas, fish from both
oceans, local game, and pasta dishes are enhanced by fresh vegetables
and salads. Take-out food is ordered around the corner at the Quaglia
address. ⊠ *Elflein 128* ☎ *2944/429–986* ✉ *Quaglia 366* ☎ *2944/422–
952* ⊟ *AE, DC, MC, V.*

$$$$ ✕ **Kandahar.** A rustic wood building with a woodstove and cozy win-
ARGENTINE dow seats in alcoves is the perfect setting for sipping a pisco sour, and
savoring a plate of smoked trout or salmon and guacamole. Start with
the *tarteleta de hongos* (mushroom tart) and *rosa mosqueta* (rose hip)
soup, followed by wild game and profiteroles with hot chocolate sauce.
⊠ *20 de Febrero 698* ☎ *2944/424–702* ⊟ *AE, MC, V.*

$$$$ ✕ **Naan.** You can go around the world in six courses at this small pri-
ECLECTIC vate home–cum-restaurant in Bariloche's upscale hillside neighborhood,
Barrio Belgrano. Vegetarian Vietnamese rolls, Italian panini, French
mushroom gratin, Thai soup, Lebanese baba ghanoush—even Tex Mex
quesadillas make great shared appetizers. Then come the main courses:
Moroccon pilaf, Chinese beef with shiitake mushrooms and asparagus,
a Brazilian seafood plate, Greek lamb kabob, French grilled trout. Desserts are equally creative concoctions of local berries and chocolate
whipped, moussed, meringued, or creped. ⊠ *Campichuelo 568, Barrio Belgrano* ☎ *2944/421–785* ✍ *Reservations essential* ⊟ *AE, MC,
V* ⊗ *Closed Mon. and 3 wks in Nov.*

WHERE TO STAY

If you don't have a car, it's better to stay in town. If you're looking for
serenity, consider a lake-view hotel or cabins along the route to the Llao
Llao Peninsula. Addresses for out-of-town dining and lodging properties are measured in kilometers from the Bariloche Civic Center.

$$$$ 🏨 **Cacique Inacayal.** Looking out from your bedroom window when the
★ wind whips up the waves on Nahuel Huapi Lake, you'll be glad you're
on land. Perched on a cliff overlooking the lake, Cacique Inacayal has
the reception, bar, and an outdoor patio on the top; fine dining room
for hotel guests down one floor; and lakeview rooms on the three floors
below. In the middle of it all, a glass-covered atrium six stories high
allows light into all floors and interior spaces. Dinner is included in
the price and consists of a cold buffet, soup, and two entrées to choose
from. **Pro:** The maître d' makes every dinner seem like a party. **Con:**
Music in the bar (until 10 PM) could be disturbing to guests on lower
floors, as could be smoke drifting upward. ⊠ *Juan Manuel de Rosas
625, 8400* ☎ *2944/433–888* ⊕ *www.hotelinacayal.com.ar* ⏎ *57
rooms* ⚘ *In-hotel: bar, parking, public Wi-Fi* ⊟ *AE, DC, MC, V.*

$$$$ 🏨 **El Casco Art Hotel.** Intriguing sculptures, perched on marble stands,
FodorśChoice wooden ledges, or freestanding in the garden are part of a collection
★ of more than 200 artworks displayed throughout the hotel. All public
spaces—halls, wine bar, gourmet restaurant—even the downstairs gym,
indoor-out swimming pool, and large Jacuzzi—face the lake, where the
hotel's private launch is docked at the pier. The rooms are huge, done in
the same natural colors, with good art and a great view being the major
attractions. The hotel is only 15 minutes from the ski area, Bariloche,

and two 18-hole golf courses. **Pros:** Art everywhere; activities galore; self-contained luxury. **Con:** Perhaps too much extravagance for some. ⊠ *Av. Bustillo, Km 11.5* ☎ *2944/463–131* ⊕ *www.hotelelcasco.com* 🛏 *57 suites* ⚲ *In-hotel: restaurant, bar, gym, pool, public Wi-Fi* ▭ *AE, DC, MC, V* †⊙†*FAP.*

$$ 🏨**Hostería Las Marianas.** A perfectly proportioned Tyrolean villa, this B&B on a sunny hillside in Barrio Belgrano, the nicest neighborhood in town, is only four blocks from the city center, but it's in a world of its own on a quiet street surrounded by well-tended gardens. The owners are mountaineers and skiers, and their photos decorate the walls of the breakfast room, where homemade breads and jams are served to guests who gather at breakfast or teatime. **Pro:** Away from the crowds. **Con:** Uphill haul from city center. ⊠ *24 de Septiembre 218* ☎ *2944/439–876* ⊕ *www.hosterialasmarianas.com.ar* 🛏 *16 rooms* ⚲ *In-hotel: no elevator, public Internet* ▭ *No credit cards* †⊙†*CP.*

$–$$ 🏨**Hotel Cristal.** A basic businesslike downtown hotel, this recycled old standby in the center of Bariloche has been greatly improved with modern furnishings and better facilities as tour groups and independent travelers discover the flavor of being on the street with all the chocolate shops. The lobby has a nice fireplace and bar. The standard no-frills rooms are tidy and adequate. **Pros:** Central downtown location; good value. **Cons:** Small bathrooms; desultory reception; popular with tour groups. ⊠ *Mitre 355* ☎ *2944/422–442* ⊕ *www.hotelcristal.com.ar* 🛏 *50 rooms* ⚲ *In-hotel: restaurant, bar, public Wi-Fi* ▭ *AE, DC, MC, V* †⊙†*CP.*

$$$–$$$$ 🏨**Hotel Nahuel Huapi.** This slick city hotel on a busy downtown street in Bariloche has a spacious lobby with a wine bar in one corner and a sit-around fireplace in another. Locally made ceramics decorate the interior. Textured beige wallpaper in the large bedrooms show off the deep reds and browns of the woven bedspreads and upholstered chairs. Some rooms have a nice view into the neighbor's garden. **Pros:** Central location; good accessibility for people with disabilities. **Con:** Rooms overlooking street might be noisy. ⊠ *Moreno 252* ☎ *2944/433–635* ⊕ *www.hotelnahuelhuapi.com.ar* 🛏 *86 rooms* ⚲ *In-hotel: restaurant, bar, parking, gym* ▭ *AE, DC, MC, V* †⊙†*CP.*

$$$$ 🏨**Llao Llao Hotel & Resort.** This masterpiece by architect Alejandro Bustillo sits on a grassy knoll surrounded by three lakes with a backdrop of rock cliffs and snow-covered mountains. Local wood—alerce, cypress, and hemlock—has been used for the walls along the 100-yard hallway, where paintings by local artists are displayed. Every room has a view worth keeping the curtains open for. A lunch or dinner reservation will also get you inside to see one of the most beautiful hotels in the world. **Pros:** Beautiful setting; helpful staff; lots of activities. **Con:** The public is allowed to visit this landmark hotel only on a guided tour on Wednesday at 3 PM. ⊠ *Av. Ezequiel Bustillo, Km 25, 25 km (15½ mi) west of Bariloche* ☎ *2944/448–530* ⊕ *www.llaollao.com* 🛏 *153 rooms, 12 suites, 1 cabin* ⚲ *In-room: safe. In-hotel: 2 restaurants, bar, golf course, pool, gym, spa, water sports, bicycles, children's programs (ages 2–12), no-smoking rooms* ▭ *AE, DC, MC, V* †⊙†*CP.*

SHOPPING

Along Bariloche's main streets, calles Mitre and Moreno, and the cross streets from Quaglia to Rolando, you can find shops selling sports equipment, leather goods, hand-knit sweaters, and gourmet food like homemade jams, dried meats, and chocolate. **Ahumadero Familia Weiss** (⊠*Palacios 401* ☎*2944/435–789* ⊠*Av. Bustillo, Km 20* ☎*2944/435–789*) makes pâtés, cheeses, smoked fish, and wild game.

Talabarterís sell items for the discerning equestrian or modern gaucho. **Cardon** (⊠*Av. San Martín 324*) is a fine leather store whose leather jackets, coats, vests, bags, belts, and boots are sold all over Argentina. At **El Establo** (⊠*Mitre 22*), look for shoes, handbags, belts, wallets, and wall coverings with distinctive black-and-white Mapuche designs.

SPORTS & THE OUTDOORS

HORSEBACK RIDING

Argentine horses are sturdy and well trained, much like American quarter horses. *Tábanas* (horseflies) attack humans and animals in summer months, so wear long sleeves on *cabalgatas* (horseback outings). **Carol Jones** is the granddaughter of an early pioneering family, and her ranch north of town does day rides and overnights from the Patagonian steppes into the mountains (☎*2944/426–508* ⊕*www.caroljones.com*). **El Manso** (☎*2944/523–641 or 2944/441–378*) combines riding and rafting over the border to Chile. **Tom Wesley** at the **Club Hípico Bariloche** (⊠*Av. Bustillo, Km 15.5* ☎☎*2944/448–193* ⊕*www.cabalgatastomwesley.com*) does rides lasting from one hour to a week.

SKIING

Cerro Catedral (Mt. Cathedral), named for its Gothic-looking spires, is the largest and oldest ski area in South America, with 39 lifts, 4,500 acres of mostly intermediate terrain, and a comfortable altitude of 6,725 feet. The runs are long, varied, and scenic. One side of the mountain has a vertical drop of 3,000 feet, mostly in the fall line. At the top of the highest chairlift, a Poma Lift transports skiers to a weather station at 7,385 feet, where a small restaurant, **Refugio Lynch,** is tucked into a wind-sculpted snow pocket on the edge of an abyss with a stupendous 360-degree view of Nahuel Huapi Lake. To the southwest, Monte Tronadór, a 12,000-foot extinct volcano, straddles the border with Chile, towering above lesser peaks that surround the lake. August and September are the best months to ski. Avoid the first three weeks of July (school vacation). ⊹*46 km (28½ mi) west of town on Av. Bustillo (R237); turn left at Km 8.5 just past Playa Bonita.*

Villa Catedral (⊕*www.catedralaltapatagonia.com*), at the base of the mountain, has ski retail and rental shops, information and ticket sales, ski-school offices, restaurants, and even a disco. Frequent buses transport skiers from Bariloche to the ski area. For information and trail maps, contact **La Secretaría de Turismo de Río Negro** (⊠*12 de Octubre 605* ☎*2944/423–188*). **Club Andino Bariloche** (⊠*20 de Febrero 30* ☎*2944/422–266*) also has information and trail maps.

PARQUE NACIONAL NAHUEL HUAPI

Created in 1943, the Parque Nacional Nahuel Huapi is Argentina's oldest national park. The park extends over 2 million acres along the eastern side of the Andes in the provinces of Neuquén and Río Negro, on the frontier with Chile. It contains the highest concentration of lakes in Argentina. The biggest is Lago Nahuel Huapi, an 897-square-km (346-square-mi) body of water, whose seven long arms (the longest is 96 km [60 mi] long, 12 km [7 mi] wide) reach deep into forests of *coihué* (a native beech tree), *cyprés* (cypress), and *lenga* (deciduous beech) trees. Intensely blue across its vast expanse and aqua green in its shallow bays, the lake meanders into distant lagoons and misty inlets where the mountains, covered with vegetation at their base, rise straight up out of the water. Every water sport invented and tours to islands and other lakes can be arranged through local travel agencies, tour offices, and through hotels. Information offices throughout the park offer help in exploring the miles of mountain and woodland trails and the lakes.

GETTING AROUND

The easy way to get around is to plan your days with a local tour operator or remis, or hire a rental car, mixing up excursions between land and lake. When planning all-day or overnight trips, remember that distances are long, and unpaved roads slow you down.

ESSENTIALS

Visitor info **Intendencia del Parque Nacional Nahuel Huapi** (⊠ *Av. San Martín 24 [at Civic Center], Bariloche* ☎ *2944/423–111* ⊕ *www.parquesnacionales.gov.ar*).

EXPLORING NAHUEL HUAPI

Having landed in Bariloche, you can explore the park on an organized tour or on your own. Nearby excursions such as the Circuito Chico, Circuito Grande, a trip to Tronadór, or the ski area at Catedral can be done in a day. Since much of the park is covered by Nahuel Huapi Lake (it's 96 km [57 mi] long, covering 346 square mi), some of your exploration will be by boat to islands, down narrow fjords, or to distant shores on organized excursions. Small towns like Villa La Angostura and Villa Trafúl are excellent destinations for further explorations on foot or by horse to smaller lakes with their connecting streams, waterfalls, and surrounding forests and high peaks. Since most of the park is at a low elevation (under 6,000 feet), getting around in winter is not difficult—just cold. Fall foliage, long, warm summer days, and spring flowers are the rewards of other seasons. Park entry is 12 pesos.

The most popular excursion on Lago Nahuel Huapi is the 30-minute boat ride to **Isla Victoria**, the largest island in the lake. A grove of redwoods transplanted from California thrives in the middle of the island. Walk on trails that lead to enchanting views of emerald bays and still lagoons.

The **Parque Nacional los Arrayanes** (⊠ *12 km [7½ mi] along a trail from Península Quetrihué* ☎ *2944/423–111*) is the only forest of arrayanes in the world. These trees absorb so much water through their thin skins that all other vegetation around them dies, leaving a barren for-

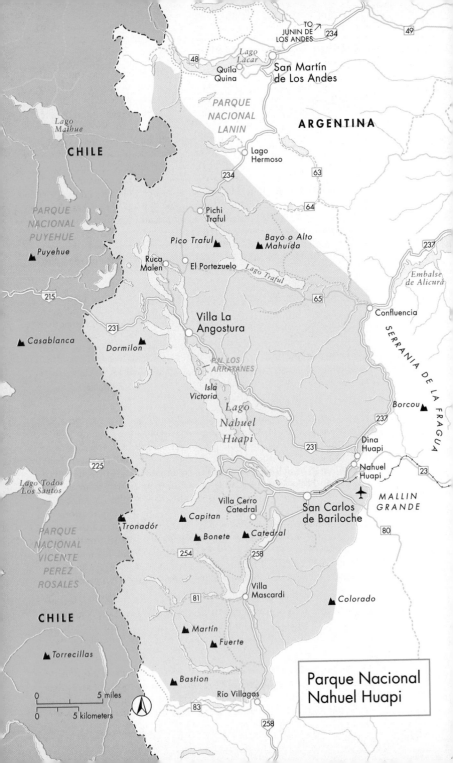

TO JUNÍN DE LOS ANDES

234 **49**

48

Lago Lácar

Quila Quina

San Martín de Los Andes

PARQUE NACIONAL LANIN

ARGENTINA

Lago Hermoso

234 **63**

64

Pichi Traful

▲ Pico Traful

▲ Bayo o Alto Mahuida

Ruca Malen

El Portezuelo

Lago Traful

PARQUE NACIONAL PUYEHUE

▲ *Puyehue*

215

231

▲ *Casablanca*

▲ *Dormilon*

65

Villa La Angostura

P.N. LOS ARRAYANES

Isla Victoria

Lago Nahuel Huapi

Confluencia

Embalse de Alicurá

237

SERRANIA DE LA FRAGUA

▲ *Borcou*

237

Dina Huapi

231

225

Lago Todos Los Santos

▲ *Tronadór*

PARQUE NACIONAL VICENTE PEREZ ROSALES

CHILE

▲ *Torrecillas*

▲ *Capitan*

Villa Cerro Catedral

▲ *Bonete*

▲ *Catedral*

254

258

Nahuel Huapi

✈

San Carlos de Bariloche

MALLIN GRANDE

23

80

Villa Mascardi

▲ *Colorado*

81

▲ *Martín*

▲ *Fuerte*

▲ *Bastion*

Río Villagas

83

258

0 ___ 5 miles

0 ___ 5 kilometers

Parque Nacional Nahuel Huapi

CHILE

CHILE

Lago Malhue

est of peeling cinnamon-color trunks. A one-hour stroll up and down wide wooden steps and walkways is a unique experience, as light filters through the twisted naked trunks, reflecting a weird red glow. You can make this excursion from the pier at Bahía Brava in Villa La Angostura (or by boat from Bariloche via Isla Victoria). In summer months you can walk (three hours) or ride a bike, after registering at the *Guardaparque* office (ranger station) near the pier. Leave in the morning, as entrance to the park closes at 2 PM. A nice combination is to go by boat and return by bicycle (it's all downhill that way). If returning by boat, buy your return ticket at the pier before you leave.

Boats to Isla Victoria and Parque Nacional los Arrayanes leave from Puerto Pañuelo, on the Península Llao Llao. They run twice daily (more in high season), at 10 AM and 2 PM. The earlier departure includes time for lunch on the island in a cafeteria-style restaurant. The later departure is a shorter trip. Boats are run by **Cau Cau** (⊠ *Mitre 139, Bariloche* ☎ *2944/431–372* ⊕ *www.islavictoriayarrayanes.com*) and **Turisur** (⊠ *Mitre 219, Bariloche* ☎ *2944/426–109* ⊕ *www.bariloche. com/turisur*).

A visit to **Monte Tronador** (Thunder Mountain) requires an all-day outing covering 170 km (105 mi) round-trip from Bariloche. The 12,000-foot extinct volcano, the highest mountain in the northern Lake District, straddles the frontier with Chile, with one peak on either side. Take R258 south along the shores of Lago Gutiérrez and Lago Mascardi. Between the two lakes the road crosses from the Atlantic to the Pacific watershed. At Km 35, turn off onto a road marked TRONADOR and PAMPA LINDA and continue along the shore of Lago Mascardi, passing a village of the same name. Just beyond the village, the road forks and you continue on a gravel road, R254. Near the bridge the road branches left to Lago Hess and Cascada Los Alerces—a detour you might want to take on your way out.

As you bear right after crossing Los Rápidos Bridge, the road narrows to one direction only: it's important to remember this when you set out in the morning, as you can only go up the road before 2 PM and down it after 4 PM. The lake ends in a narrow arm (Brazo Tronador) at the Hotel Tronador, which has a dock for tours arriving by boat. The road then follows the Río Manso to **Pampa Linda,** which has a lodge, restaurant, park ranger's office, campsites, and the trailhead for the climb up to the Refugio Otto Meiling at the snow line. Guided horseback rides are organized at the lodge. The road ends 7 km (4½ mi) beyond Pampa Linda in a parking lot that was once at the tip of the now receding **Glaciar Negro** (Black Glacier). As the glacier flows down from the mountain, the dirt and black sediment of its lateral moraines are ground up and cover the ice. At first glance, it's hard to imagine the tons of ice that lie beneath its black cap.

SPORTS & THE OUTDOORS

For information on mountain climbing, trails, refugios (mountain huts), and campgrounds, visit the **Intendencia del Parque Nacional Nahuel Huapi** (⊠*Av. San Martín 24 [at Civic Center], Bariloche* ☎*2944/423–111* ⊕*www.parquesnacionales.gov.ar*).

HIKING

Nahuel Huapi National Park has many forest trails near Bariloche, El Bosón, and Villa La Angostura. For day hikes in the forest along the shore of Nahuel Huapi Lake or to a nearby waterfall, search for trails along the Circuito Chico in the Parque Llao Llao. For altitude and grand panoramas, take the ski lift to the top of Cerro Catedral and follow the ridge trail to Refugio Frey, returning down to the base of the ski area.

West of Bariloche, turn right at Villa Mascardi onto the dirt road to Pampa Linda (⇨ *What to See; Monte Tronadór, above*). From there you can hike a long day or overnight to Otto Meiling hut, or make shorter forays to the glacier or nearby waterfalls. A three-day trek will take you right past Tronadór and its glacier, along the Alerce River and over the Paso de los Nubes (Clouds Pass) to Puerto Bless, returning to Bariloche by boat. Hiking guides can be recommended through local tour offices. For trail maps and information on all of the Lake District, look for the booklet (in Spanish) *Guía Sendas y Bosques* (Guide to Trails and Forests) sold at kiosks and bookstores. For ambitious treks, mountaineering, or use of mountain huts and climbing permits, contact **Club Andino Bariloche** (⊠*20 de Febrero 30* ☎*2944/422–266* ⊕*www. clubandino.org*). Click on the *mapas* link on the Web site.

MOUNTAIN BIKING

The entire Nahuel Huapi National Park is ripe for all levels of mountain biking. Popular rides go from the parking lot at the Cerro Catedral ski area to Lago Gutiérrez and down from Cerro Otto. Local tour agencies can arrange guided tours by the hour or day and even international excursions to Chile. Rental agencies provide maps and suggestions and sometimes recommend guides.

Dirty Bikes (⊠*Vice Almirante O'Connor 681* ☎*2944/425–616* ⊕*www. dirtybikes.com.ar*) offers local day trips all over the Lake District, including long-distance trips to Chile and back, for all ages and abilities. **La Bolsa del Deporte** (⊠*Diagonal Capraro 1081* ☎*944/433–111*) rents and sells bikes.

WHITE-WATER RAFTING

With all the interconnected lakes and rivers in the national park, there's everything from your basic family float down the swift-flowing, scenic Río Limay to a wild and exciting ride down Río Manso (Class II), which takes you 16 km (10 mi) in three hours. If you're really adventurous, you can take the Manso all the way to Chile (Class IV). **Alunco** (⊠*Moreno 187* ☎*2944/422–283* ⊕*www.aluncoturismo.com.ar*) arranges rafting trips throughout the area. **Aguas Blancas** (⊠*Morales 564* ☎*2944/432–799* ⊕*aguasblancas.com*) specializes in the Manso

River and offers an overnight trip to Chile with asado and return by horseback. They also rent inflatable kayacks (*duckies*). **Extremo Sur** (✉ *Morales 765* ☎ *2944/427–301* ⊕ *www.extremosur.com*) arranges trips on the ríos Limay and Manso.

PUERTO MADRYN

67 km (41½ mi) north of Trelew, 450 km (279 mi) north of Comodoro Rivadavia, 1,380 km south of Buenos Aires.

Approaching from the Ruta 3, it's hard to believe that the horizon-line of buildings perched just beyond the windswept dunes and bad-lands is the most successful of all coastal Patagonia settlements. But once you get past the outskirts of town, past the tire-repair places and humble barrios, to the city's downtown, and onto the wide coastal road known as the Rambla, you'll see why. The restaurants, bars, cafés, dive shops, multistory houses and hotels facing the clear and tranquil Golfo Nuevo are full of activity—and tourists from around the world—but not yet overcrowded.

The first economic boom came in 1886, when the Patagonian railroad was introduced, spurring the town's port activities along with salt and fishing industries. Although it isn't likely the original Welsh settlers who arrived here in 1865 could have imagined just how much Puerto Madryn would evolve, a large part of Madryn's success is owed to their hardworking traditions, which continue with their descendants today. The anniversary of their arrival is celebrated every 28th of July here and in other Chubut towns. Only a statue—the Telhueche Indian Monument—serves as a reminder of the indigenous people who once lived here and who helped the Welsh survive.

GETTING AROUND

Madryn is just small enough to walk, and most of the hotels and resi-dences are on or near the 3½-km-long (2-mi-long) Rambla, or pedes-trian walkway along the Golfo Nuevo. A great way to get around is by renting a bicycle. To reach the nature preserves just north and south of town—El Doradillo and Punta Loma—you'll either need to rent a vehicle, travel with a tour, or take a *remis*.

For those flying in and out of Trelew, Transportes Eben-Ezer is the official Airport shuttle to and from Puerto Madryn.

Carlos and Carol de Passera of Causana Viajes have 17 years of experience leading custom and special-interest trips—focusing, for example, on archaeology, birding, botany, natural history, or whale-watching—for American and Canadian adventure-travel companies. Cuyun Co Turismo can arrange all-day tours of the Península Val-dés; reserve ahead, especially if you want an English-speaking guide. They can also organize tours to Punta Tombo, Gaiman, the Dique Ameghino, and Camarones.

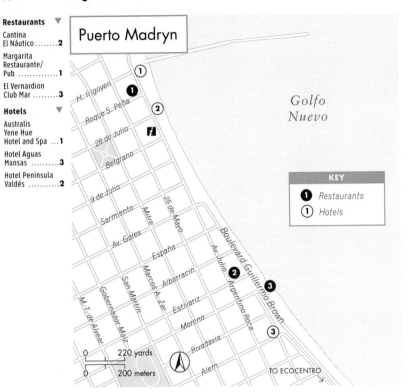

Puerto Madryn

Golfo Nuevo

KEY

❶ *Restaurants*

① *Hotels*

ESSENTIALS

Bus Contacts **Andesmar** (✉ *Terminal de Ómnibus* ☎ *2965/473–764*). **Don Otto** (✉ *Terminal de Ómnibus* ☎ *2965/451–675*).**TAC** (✉ *Hipólito Yrigoyen 331* ☎ *2965/451–537*).

Currency Exchange **Banco de la Nación** (✉ *9 de Julio 127* ☎ *2965/450–465*). **Credicoop** (✉ *Roque Sanez Peña at 25 de Mayo* ☎ *2965/455–139*). **Banco del Chubut** (✉ *25 de Mayo 154* ☎ *2965/471–250* ⊕ *www.bancochubut.com.ar*).

Rental Cars **Patagonia Sur Car** (✉ *Av. Rawson 1190* ☎ *2974/466–768* ⊕ *www. patagoniasurcar.com.ar*).

Visitor & Tour Info **Bottazzi** (✉ *Complejo La Torre, Blvd. Brown at Martín Fierro, Puerto Madryn* ☎ *2965/474–110* ⊕ *www.titobottazzi.com*). **Causana Viajes** (✉ *Moreno 390, Puerto Madryn* ☎ *2965/455–044* ⊕ *www.causana.com.ar*). **Cuyun Co Turismo** (✉ *Julio A. Roca 165, Puerto Madryn* ☎ *2965/454–950 or 2965/451–845* ⊕ *www.cuyunco.com.ar*). **Hydro Sport** (✉ *Av. Julio A. Roca s/n, Puerto Madryn* ☎ *2965/495–065* ⊕ *www.hydrosport.com.ar*). **Puerto Madryn Tourist Board** (✉ *Av. Roca 223* ☎ *2965/453–504 or 2965/456–067* ⊕ *www. madryn.gov.ar/turismo/en/general_information/*).

EXPLORING PUERTO MADRYN

El Doradillo. Following the coastal road 14 km (9 mi) north from Puerto Madryn brings you to El Doradillo Beach. The ocean floor drops steeply, creating a special environment where, between the months of June and mid-December, you can walk up to southern right whales, sometimes with mothers teaching their young to swim. During other times of the year, it's just a regular beach similar to the rest of Puerto Madryn's coastline. *Free*.

EcoCentro. EcoCentro is a modern hands-on museum and research center that promotes the protection of the sea through education. A whale-sounds exhibit and an invertebrates "touch pool" allow visitors to get a personal appreciation for marine life, and a new cave exhibit is especially good for kids. The center is on a cliff at the north end of the city's beach. *Julio Verne 3784* 2965/457–470 *www.ecocentro. ar* 21 pesos Daily 2:30–7:30.

Punta Loma Sea Lion Reserve. Just 14 km (9 mi) southeast of the city (follow signs toward Punta Ninfas), Punta Loma might be your first glimpse of the region's spectacular marine mammals. A colony of some 600 South American sea lions can be seen at the beach below a tall, crescent-shape bluff. 2965/453–504 20 pesos Visit during low tide—check local paper or tourism office for tide schedule.

WHERE TO EAT

$$ ✕ **Cantina El Náutico.** Don't let the corny, yellow-neon sign outside put you off; this local favorite run by three generations of a French Basque family serves fantastic homemade pasta and fresh seafood. Even the "butter" that accompanies the bread is a cut above—a mixture of mayonnaise with garlic, parsley, and pepper. For dessert, try the outstanding *macedonia* (fruit salad with ice cream). *Av. Roca 790* 2965/471–404 *AE, DC, MC, V.*

$$–$$$$ ✕ **Margarita Resto/Pub.** Margarita has long been famous in Puerto
★ Madryn for its cocktails and nightlife. The food here is excellent and it's one of the few places you can find more elaborate vegetarian options. On Wednesday nights at 11 there is live jazz. You can grab a quiet meal at lunchtime, yet the dance-floor lighting, disco ball in the back room, and chill-out beats remind you of the party to come. *Av. Saénz Peña 15, at Roca* 2965/470–885 *www.margaritapub.com AE, MC, V.*

$$–$$$ ✕ **El Vernardino Club Mar.** In the center of the beach, El Vernardino has the best location in Puerto Madryn. Don't let the playground and the stacks of kayaks and windsurfers (El Vernardino also runs a "sea school" and rents equipment) dissuade you from eating here. A diverse menu with twists on classic seafood dishes—like the "wok marino" or seafood stir-fry—makes for some of the best eating in the city. *Blvd. Brown 860* 2965/455–633 *www.vernardinoclubdemar.com.ar/ index.html AE, MC, V.*

WHERE TO STAY

$$$$ **Australis Yene Hue Hotel and Spa.** The Australis Yene Hue is Puerto Madryn's newest luxury hotel. From the cavernous lobby with cascading water garden to the luminous breakfast room, well equipped (by

Argentinian standards) mini-gym, and rooftop pool, the Yene Hue is modern, spacious, and refined. **Pro:** Brand new. **Cons:** Young staff still getting organized; rooms not facing the ocean may not be worth the price. ⊠*Roca 33* ☎*2965/471–214* ⊕*www.australiset.com.ar* ⇱*68 rooms* ⚐*In-hotel: bar, pool, spa, laundry service, public Wi-Fi* ⊟*AE, MC, V* ⦿*CP.*

$$$ 🏨**Estancia San Guillermo.** If you want to experience a Chubut farm filled with snorting pigs, overfriendly guanacos, and strutting roosters, head for Estancia San Guillermo. A few miles outside Puerto Madryn, owners Alfredo and Cristina Casado welcome you to their home with 1,200 sheep that roam their 7,400-acre fossil-filled farm. Watch Alfredo shear a sheep or his helpers prepare the *parrilla* (grill). Stay in roomy, comfortable villas with kitchens and bathrooms; rates include all meals. The estancia has a dining room if you're just coming for the day. **Pro:** You'll have a Patagonian estancia all to yourself. **Con:** You're isolated from the rest of town once you get there. ⊠*Contact info in Puerto Madryn: Av. 28 de Julio 90* ☎*2965/452–150* ⊕*www.san-guillermo.com* ⇱*3 rooms* ⊟*No credit cards* ☉*Closed mid-May–mid-June* ⦿*FAP.*

$ 🏨**Hotel Aguas Mansas.** This hotel is one block from the beach in a pretty residential neighborhood and a few blocks from the center of town. It's nothing fancy—just clean, quiet rooms and good, personable service. It's one of the few lodgings with a pool, especially in this price range. **Pros:** Pool; friendly staff. **Con:** Not as elegant as other hotels. ⊠*José Hernandez 51* ☎*2965/473–103* ⊕*www.aguasmansas.com* ⇱*20 rooms* ⚐*In-hotel: bar, pool, laundry service* ⊟*MC, V* ⦿*CP.*

$$$$ 🏨**Hotel Península Valdés.** After extensive remodeling, the classic Hotel Península Valdés offers a new, elegant cafeteria, new bathrooms throughout the hotel, and modernized elevators. Ask for a *panoramico* (room with a view) on an upper floor for the best experience. **Pros:** Newly remodeled; excellent service. **Con:** Small, nearly unusable gym by American standards. ⊠*Av. Roca 155* ☎*2965/471–292* ⊕*www. hotelPeninsula.com.ar* ⇱*76 rooms* ⚐*In-hotel: restaurant, bar, gym, laundry service, public Wi-Fi* ⊟*AE, DC, MC, V* ⦿*BP.*

SPORTS & THE OUTDOORS

DIVING

One dive shop stands out in particular: **Aquatours** (⊠*Av. Roca 550* ☎*2965/451–954* ⊕*www.aquatours.com.ar*) has dive masters and instructors who have pioneered courses in diving with sea lions, and who offer diving for people with disabilities.Several other dive shops are on Boulevard Brown, including **Scuba Duba** (⊠*Blvd. Brown 893* ☎*2965/452–699*).

FISHING

Costas Patagonicas (☎*2965/451–131*) organizes fishing trips. **Jorge Schmid** (☎*2965/451–511*), a respected guide in the area, offers fishing trips as well as whale-watching and dolphin-viewing trips.

HORSEBACK RIDING

For a completely different view, check out Madryn's beaches from horseback. Rides are available with **Huella y Costas** (✉ *Blvd. Brown 1900* ☎ *2965/1563–7826*).

KAYAKING & WINDSURFING

☾ **Vernardino Club Mar** rents sea kayaks and windsurfers, and runs a "Sea School" (⊕ *www.escueladelmar.com.ar*) for kids, where local instructors work with children aged 6–14 on snorkeling, windsurfing, bait and lure fishing, basic nautical and fishing knots, and identification of local fauna, as well as offering motor and sailboat excursions. There is also a windsurfing school for adults. (✉ *Blvd. Brown 860* ☎ *2965/455–633* ⊕ *www.vernardinoclubdemar.com.ar/index.html*).

PENÍNSULA VALDÉS

Fodor'sChoice
★

Puerto Pirámides is 104 km (64 mi) northeast of Puerto Madryn.

Designated a UNESCO World Heritage site for its important marine mammal populations, and with its unique landscape—the lowest point (132 feet below sea level) on the South American continent—Península Valdés is one of the most spectacular places in Patagonia. Although full-day tours are available from Puerto Madryn, to properly experience Península Valdés you should plan a minimum of two full days of exploring, spending at least a night, but preferably two, at Puerto Pirámides and/or La Elvira near Caleta Valdés. Bring binoculars.

The biggest attraction is the *Ballena Franca* (southern right whale) population, which feeds, mates, and gives birth here. The protected mammals attract some 120,000 visitors every year from June, when they first arrive, through December. Especially during the peak season of September and October, people crowd into boats at Puerto Pirámides to observe at close range as the 30- to 35-ton whales breach and blast giant V-shape spouts of water from their blowholes.

From the visitor center at the entrance to the peninsula—which is worth an hour just for orientation—a series of interconnected 32- to 64-km (20- to 40-mi) dirt roads take you to several major wildlife viewing areas. These extend from the cliff-guarded beaches and elephant-seal colonies at Punta Delgada in the south to Punta Norte at the northern tip, where depending on the season, you can see orcas. There are also three salt lakes of varying sizes, and large inland populations of guanacos, foxes, rheas, and partridges in addition to the ubiquitous Patagonian sheep that are ranched here.

GETTING AROUND

Heading toward the peninsula on Ruta 2, just before entering the isthmus you'll reach the park entrance, where you'll pay a fee of 40 pesos. Some 22 km (14 mi) down the road is the newly remodeled

Information Center and Museum (☎ *2965/1556–5222* ☾ *Daily 8–8*) . An hour spent here studying the various exhibits on marine, coastal, and continental flora and fauna, as well as fossils, climate, and geology, will make for a more informed visit.

From there you'll continue another 24 km (15 mi) to a junction where you can either go an additional 2 km (1.2 mi) south to Puerto Pirámides, or head 5 km (3 mi) east to where the circuit of interconnected roads taking you around the peninsula begins.

EXPLORING PENÍNSULA VALDÉS

Puerto Pirámides has only one main street, Avenida de Ballenas, which rolls down Golfo Nuevo with a scattering of tin-roofed buildings among dunes and flowers. For ecological reasons, only 350 people are allowed to live here, but there is a good selection of campsites, hotels, and restaurants. Bring plenty of money with you, as the ATM may be out of cash. Aside from whale-watching and lounging around with a beer while looking out on the pyramid-shape cliffs of Valdés Bay, activities include scuba diving, sand-boarding, and mountain-biking tours. Whale-watching excursions leave from the little harbor, generally at 8:30 or 9—check with your hotel to reserve with one of the local outfits. Smaller boats, such as the ones operated by Hydro Sport (⇨ *Whale-Watching Tours, below)* are preferable to big ones, as they tend to get closer to the whales.

From Puerto Pirámides it's about 5 km (3 mi) along RP2 to the beginning of a circuit around the peninsula. For starters, you'll see the **Lobería Puerto Pirámides,** a sea-lion colony 4 km (2½ mi) from town (on the way to Punta Delgada), but each vista and wildlife-viewing opportunity here is unique, and you'll want to take your time.

Head southeast (with a full tank of gas) along RP2 for about 70 km (43 mi) to get to the elephant-seal and sea-lion colonies at **Punta Delgada,** on the southeastern tip of the peninsula. The elephant seals' breeding season starts in August when the males compete for beach space, after which females arrive, form harems, and give birth. The seals head out to sea in November. There is an old lighthouse, which you can climb to the top of for open-sea views, and guards' quarters that have been turned into an upmarket hotel and restaurant. You have to walk down stairs and paths to get to the animal observation area, which is open 9:30–4:30.

From there, head up the eastern coast of the island (on RP47, though it's unmarked), about another 35 km (22 mi), to the elephant-seal colony at **Punta Cantor.** You can either take RP52 back across the peninsula, reconnecting with RP3 to return to Puerto Pirámides, or continue up the coast another 22 km (14 mi) or so to **Caleta Valdés.** Here you can stop at Parador La Elvira, a complex with a restaurant, gift shop, and cliff-side walkway to another impressive elephant-seal beach—peak activity is in September.

The northeastern corner of the peninsula, **Punta Norte,** has the most remote and largest sea-lion settlement of all; orcas cruise through town from time to time, and Magellanic penguins roam the land from October through March. From Punta Norte, RP3 is an inland shortcut that

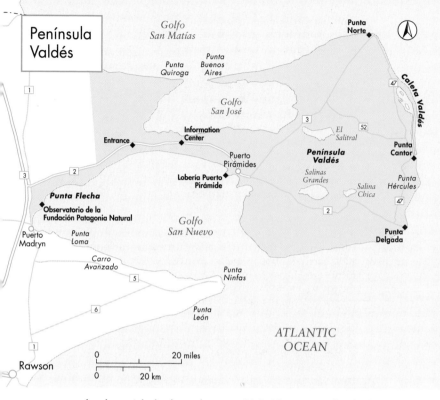

Península Valdés

Golfo San Matías

Punta Norte

Punta Quiroga

Punta Buenos Aires

Caleta Valdés

1

47

Golfo San José

3

El Salitral

52

Information Center

Entrance

Puerto Pirámides

Península Valdés

Punta Cantor

3

2

Lobería Puerto Pirámide

Salinas Grandes

Salina Chica

Punta Hércules

Punta Flecha

Observatorio de la Fundación Patagonia Natural

Golfo San Nuevo

2

47

Puerto Madryn

Punta Loma

Punta Delgada

Carro Avanzado

Punta Ninfas

5

6

Punta León

ATLANTIC OCEAN

0   20 miles

0   20 km

Rawson

1

heads straight back southwest to Pirámides, passing by **El Salitral,** one of the peninsula's three large salt-lake ecosystems.

WHERE TO EAT

$$ ✕**La Estación Pub.** The coolest bar in Pirámides is also the town's best seafood restaurant. Amid the nets and nautical gear is an eclectic collection of music posters leaning heavily toward glam rock—Iggy Pop, David Bowie, Lou Reed, etc. Owner Mario Gadda is also an avid mountain biker and organizes fully equipped biking tours. ⊠*Av. de las Ballenas s/n* ☎*2965/495–047* ✐*mariogadda@gmail.com* ▭*MC, V.*

$$ ✕**La Posta.** A new family restaurant that also serves *minutitias*—hamburgers, sandwiches, and other light fare—La Posta has a great location overlooking the town, and good food. A multitiered patio is on the hillside and next door is an attached mini-mercado where you can buy cold cuts, fruits, vegetables, chips, and drinks. This is a good place to find camping supplies. At night La Posta becomes a resto-bar. ⊠*Av. de las Ballenas s/n* ☎*2965/1564–2051* ✐*lucas_moller84@hotmail. com* ▭*No credit cards.*

WHERE TO STAY

$$$ ▦**Cabañas en el Mar.** These comfortable A-frame cabins have private balconies with views of the ocean, as well as kitchenettes, making them popular with families and biologists here on extended stays. A new ice-cream

shop and café is in the lobby. Each unit accommodates up to six people. **Pro:** Inexpensive, and you can cook in your cabin. **Con:** May be slightly noisy during the day. ⊠ *Av. de las Ballenas s/n* ☎ *2965/495–049* ⊕ *www.piramides.net/cabanas* ⤴ *6 cabañas* ♿ *In-hotel: laundry service* ⊟ *No credit cards.*

$$$ 🏨 **Punta Delgada.** This former light-
★ house (along with a navy station, a post office, and a little school for the guards' families) is a sea-lion colony observation point, and an elegant hotel. Punta Delgada's lux-uries are simple and aristocratically old-fashioned: comfortable beds, a tennis court, a pleasant pub with pool and darts, starry night skies, board games, and utter tranquility. Excursions are organized by the staff. There are no telephones or even cell service, never mind television; there's no electricity 9–noon and 3–7. Nor are there water views from the rooms, unfortunately; the hotel sits too far inland for that. Still, it's one of the most impressively isolated hotels in Patagonia. Dinner is served for hotel guests only, but nonguests can lunch at the restaurant ($$–$$$$), which features chicken curry, king crab, and *cordero al asador* (roasted lamb) at midday. Tour groups tend to stop by for lunch in large numbers. **Pros:** Peaceful; good excursions; completely pleasant. **Cons:** Rooms don't have water views; too isolated for some; tour buses. ⊠ *Punta Delgada, Península Valdés* ☎ *2965/458–444* ⊕ *www.puntadelgada.com* ⤴ *27 rooms* ♿ *In-room: no phone, no TV. In-hotel: restaurant, bar, tennis court* ⊟ *AE, MC, V* ☾ *Closed Apr.–July.*

$$$ 🏨 **Las Restingas.** Built at the very edge of Golfo Nuevo, this is the most
★ luxurious hotel in town, and also the one hotel where it's possible to see whales from your window. Rooms boast crisp linens and huge picture windows. **Pro:** Beautiful rooms, lobby, overall setting and service. **Con:** Rooms facing the village are overpriced. ⊠ *Primera Bajada al Mar at Ribera Marítima* ☎ *2965/495–101* or *2965/495–102* ⊕ *www.lasrestingas.com* ⤴ *12 rooms* ♿ *In-hotel: restaurant, bar, beachfront, laundry service, pool, spa, public Internet* ⊟ *AE, MC, V.*

> **WHALE-WATCHING TOURS**
>
> For whale-watching, **Jorge Schmid** (☎ *2965/295–012* or *2965/295–112*) is a reliable operator. He also rents scuba equipment. **Hydro Sport** (☎ *2965/495–065* ⊕ *www.hydrosport.com.ar*) is another popular whale-watching operation, and is sponsored by the U.S.-based Whale Conservation Institute.

EL CALAFATE & THE PARQUE NACIONAL LOS GLACIARES

320 km (225 mi) north of Río Gallegos via R5, 253 km (157 mi) east of Río Turbio on Chilean border via R40, 213 km (123 mi) south of El Chaltén via R40.

Founded in 1927 as a frontier town, El Calafate is the base for excursions to the Parque Nacional los Glaciares (Glaciers National Park), which was created in 1937 as a showcase for one of South America's most spectacular sights, the Perito Moreno glacier. Because it's on the southern shore of Lago Argentino, the town enjoys a microclimate much milder than the rest of southern Patagonia. During the long summer days between December and February (when the sun sets around 10 PM), and during Easter vacation, tens of thousands of visitors come from all corners of the world and fill the hotels and restaurants. This is the area's high season, so make reservations well in advance. October, November, March, and April are less crowded and less expensive periods to visit. March through May can be rainy and cool, but it's also less windy and often quite pleasant. The only bad time to visit is winter, particularly June, July, and August, when many of the hotels and tour agencies are closed.

To call El Calafate a boomtown would be to put it mildly. Between 2001 and 2008, the town's population exploded from 4,000 to 22,000, and it shows no signs of slowing down; at every turn you'll see new construction. As a result, the downtown has a very new sheen to it, although most buildings are constructed of wood, with a rustic aesthetic that respects the majestic natural environment. One exception is the brand-new casino in the heart of downtown, the facade of which seems to mock the face of the Perito Moreno glacier. As the paving of the road between El Calafate and the glacier nears completion, the visitors continue to flock in—whether luxury package tourists bound for the legendary Hostería Los Notros, backpackers over from Chile's Parque Nacional Torres del Paine, or *porteños* (those from Buenes Aires) in town for a long weekend.

The booming economy means prices are substantially higher than in most parts of Patagonia—they seem to rise every other week—and many longtime locals bemoan the rampant commercialization of their hometown.

GETTING HERE & AROUND

El Calafate is so popular that the flights are selling out weeks in advance, so don't plan on booking at the last minute. Driving from Río Gallegos takes about four hours across desolate plains. Esperanza is the only gas, food, and bathroom stop halfway between the two towns.

Avenida del Libertador San Martín (known simply as Libertador, or San Martín) is El Calafate's main street, with tour offices, restaurants, and shops selling regional specialties, sportswear, camping and fishing equipment, and food.

A staircase in the middle of San Martín ascends to Avenida Julio Roca, where you'll find the bus terminal and a very busy Oficina de Turismo with a board listing available accommodations and campgrounds; there's a multilingual staff to help plan excursions. It's open daily 7 AM–10 PM. The Parques Nacionales Office, open weekdays 7–2, has information on the entire park, the glaciers, area history, hiking trails, and flora and fauna.

Gador Viajes operates glacier tours and can arrange visits to estancias around El Calafate.**Hielo y Aventura** offers mini-trekking and "Big Ice" expeditions on the Perito Moreno glacier.**René Fernández Campbell** is the specialist for boat tours on Lago Argentino and to the Upsala Glacier.

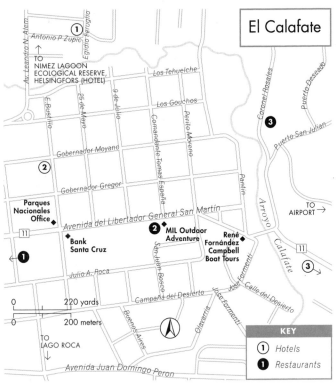

El Calafate

ESSENTIALS

Bus Contacts Bus Sur (☏ *2966/442–765, 2902/491–631 in El Calafate*).**Cal Tur** (✉ *Terminal Ómnibus, El Calafate* ☏ *2962/491–842*). **Interlagos** (✉ *Bus terminal* ☏ *2902/491–179*). **TAQSA** (✉ *Bus terminal* ☏ *2902/491–843* ⊕ *www.taqsa.com. ar*). **Turismo Zaahj** (☏ *5661/412–260*).

Currency Exchange Provincia de Santa Cruz (✉ *Av. Libertador 1285* ☏ *2902/492–320*).

Medical Assistance Hospital Distrital (✉ *Av. Roca 1487* ☏ *2902/491–001*). **Farmacia El Calafate** (✉ *Av. Libertador 1190* ☏ *9405/491–407*)

Remis El Calafate (✉ *Av. Roca* ☏ *2902/492–005*).

Rental Cars Cristina (✉ *Av. Libertador 1711* ☏ *2902/491–674* ✍ *crisrent@arnet. com.ar*). **Dollar Rent a Car** (✉ *Av. Libertador 1341* ☏ *2902/492–634*).

Visitor & Tour Info Hielo y Aventura ✉ *Av. Libertador 935, El Calafate* ☏ *2902/492–205* ⊕ *www.hieloyaventura.com*. **Parques Nacionales Office** (✉ *Av. Libertador 1302* ☏ *2902/491–005*). **Oficina de Turismo** (✉ *Av. Roca 1004* ☏ *2902/491–090* ⊕ *www.elcalafate.gov.ar*). **René Fernández Campbell** ✉ *Av. Libertador 867, El Calafate* ☏ *2902/491–155* ✍ *fernandez_campbell@ infovia.com.ar*.

EXPLORING EL CALAFATE & LOS GLACIARES

The Hielo Continental (Continental ice cap) spreads its icy mantle from the Pacific Ocean across Chile and the Andes into Argentina, covering an area of 21,700 square km (8,400 square mi). Approximately 1.5 million acres of it are contained within the **Parque Nacional los Glaciares,** a UNESCO World Heritage site. The park extends along the Chilean border for 350 km (217 mi), and 40% of it is covered by ice fields that branch off into 47 glaciers feeding two enormous lakes—the 15,000-year-old **Lago Argentino** (Argentine Lake, the largest body of water in Argentina and the third-largest in South America) in the park's southern end, and **Lago Viedma** (Lake Viedma) at the northern end near **Cerro Fitzroy,** which rises 11,138 feet. Plan on a minimum of two to three days to see the glaciers and enjoy the town—more if you plan to visit El Chaltén or any of the other lakes. Entrance to the southern section of the park costs 40 pesos.

The **Glaciar Perito Moreno** lies 80 km (50 mi) away on R11, which is almost entirely paved. From the park entrance, the road winds through hills and forests of *lengas* and *ñires* trees, until suddenly, the startling sight of the glacier comes into full view. Descending like a long white tongue through distant mountains, it ends abruptly in a translucent azure wall 3 km (2 mi) wide and 165 feet high at the edge of frosty green Lago Argentino.

Although it's possible to rent a car and go on your own, virtually everyone visits the park by day-trip tours booked through one of the many travel agents in El Calafate (unless you're staying in Los Notros, the only hotel inside the park—which arranges all excursions). The most basic tours take you to see the glacier from a viewing area composed of a series of platforms wrapped around the point of the Península de Magallanes. The platforms, which offer perhaps the most impressive view of the glacier, allow you to wander back and forth, looking across the Canal de los Tempanos (Iceberg Channel). Here you listen and wait for nature's number-one ice show—first, a cracking sound, followed by tons of ice breaking away and falling with a thunderous crash into the lake. As the glacier creeps across this narrow channel and meets the land on the other side, an ice dam sometimes builds up between the inlet of Brazo Rico on the left and the rest of the lake on the right. As the pressure on the dam increases, everyone waits for the day it will rupture again. The last time was in March 2004, when the whole thing collapsed in a series of explosions that lasted hours and could be heard in El Calafate.

In recent years, the skyrocketing increase in the number of visitors to Glaciar Perito Moreno has created a scene that is not always conducive to reflective encounters with nature's majesty. Although the glacier remains spectacular, savvy travelers would do well to minimize time at the madhouse that the viewing area becomes at midday in high season, and instead encounter the glacier by boat, on a mini-trekking excursion, or by supplementing Perito Moreno with a visit to one of the less crowded glaciers in the region.

Glaciar Upsala, the largest glacier in South America, is 55 km (35 mi) long and 10 km (6 mi) wide, and accessible only by boat. Daily cruises depart from Puerto Banderas (40 km [25 mi] west of El Calafate via R11) for the 2½-hour trip. While dodging floating icebergs (*tempanos*), some as large as a small island, the boats maneuver as close as they dare to the wall of ice rising from the aqua-green water of Lago Argentino. The seven glaciers that feed the lake deposit their debris into the run-off, causing the water to cloud with minerals ground to fine powder by the glacier's moraine (the accumulation of earth and stones left by the glacier). Condors and black-chested buzzard eagles build their nests in the rocky cliffs above the lake. When the boat stops for lunch at Onelli Bay, don't miss the walk behind the restaurant into a wild landscape of small glaciers and milky rivers carrying chunks of ice from four glaciers into Lago Onelli. Glaciar Upsala has diminished in size in recent years, a trend many attribute to climate change.

OFF THE BEATEN PATH

The **Nimez Lagoon Ecological Reserve** is a marshy area on the shore of Lago Argentino just a short walk from downtown El Calafate. It's home to many species of waterfowl, including black-necked swans, buff-necked ibises, southern lapwings, and the occasional flamingo. Strolling the footpaths among grazing horses and flocks of birds may not be as intense an experience as—say—trekking on a glacier, but a trip to the lagoon provides a good sense of the local landscape. For some reason, the gate is sometimes locked until 9 AM, frustrating early morning bird enthusiasts. If you get there early go ahead and hop the fence; no one will mind. ⊠ *1 km (½ mi) north of downtown, just off Av. Alem* 🖃 *2 pesos.*

WHERE TO EAT

$$$
ECLECTIC
✕ **Barricas de Enopio.** The emphasis at this restaurant-bar is on the extensive wine list and great cheeses that accompany each glass. A variety of brochettes and dinner entrées are big enough to share. The menu includes eclectic dishes such as pasta stuffed with venison or wild boar. The space is chic, casual, and cozy, with natural-cotton curtains and tablecloths, handmade lamps, and Tehuelche influences. ⊠ *Av. Libertador 1610* 🕾 *2902/493–414* 🖃 *AE, MC, V.*

$$$
ARGENTINE
✕ **Rick's Parrillá.** It's *tenedor libre* (literally, "free fork," or all you can eat) for 35 pesos at this immensely popular *parrilla* in a big yellow building on El Calafate's main street. The place is packed full of tourists day and night. The room is big and bustling, if not particularly interesting, and the spread includes lamb and *vacío* (flank steak). ⊠ *Av. Libertador 1091* 🕾 *2902/492–148* 🖃 *MC, V.*

$$–$$$
ARGENTINE
Fodor'sChoice
★
✕ **La Tablita.** It's a couple of extra blocks from downtown, across a little white bridge, but this parrilla is where the locals go for a special night out. Patagonian lamb and beef ribs are cooked gaucho-style on an asado, or grill, including steaks, chorizos, and excellent *morcilla* (blood sausage). The enormous *parrillada* for two is a great way to sample it all, and the wine list is well priced and well chosen. ⊠ *Coronel Rosales 28* 🕾 *2902/491–065* ⊕ *www.interpatagonia.com/latablita* 🖃 *AE, DC, MC, V* 🕓 *No lunch Mon.–Thurs. June and July.*

WHERE TO STAY

$$$$
Fodor's Choice
★
☷**Helsingfors.** If we could recommend only one property in southern Patagonia, it would be Estancia Helsingfors, a luxurious, converted ranch house with an absolutely spectacular location in the middle of the National Park on the shore of Lago Viedma. Knowledgeable guides can point out dozens of species of birds; inside, a cozy fire warms the sitting room, friendly staff serve fine food and delicious house wine, and the beds are perhaps the most comfortable in Patagonia. Don't leave without visiting the breathtaking blue lake at the foot of a glacier that's a three-hour hike or horseback ride from the inn. **Pros:** Unique location; wonderful staff. **Con:** Three hours by dirt road from El Calafate. ☒*Reservations in Buenos Aires: Cordoba 827, 11th fl.* ☏*11/4315–1222 in Buenos Aires* ⊕*www.helsingfors.com.ar* ⇝*8 rooms* ☖*In-room: no TV. In-hotel: restaurant* ▤*AE, MC, V* ☽*Closed May–Sept.* ⏁|*FAP.*

$$$$
☼
Fodor's Choice
★
☷**Hotel Kau-Yatun.** From the homemade chocolates and flower bouquets that appear in the rooms each evening to the sweeping backyard complete with swing sets for the kids, every detail of this converted ranch property is tailored to thoughtful hospitality. Guests rave about the attentive staff, the excellent food with a focus on local and organic ingredients, and the building, which feels more well loved than the newer hotels in town. **Pros:** Great food; loving attention to detail. **Con:** Water pressure is only adequate. ☒*25 de Mayo* ☏*2902/491–059* ✑*kauyatun@cotecal.com.ar* ⇝*44 rooms* ☖*In-hotel: restaurant, bar, airport shuttle, bicycles, public Wi-Fi, no elevator* ▤*AE, MC, V* ⏁|*CP.*

$$
☷**Miyazato Inn.** Jorge Miyasato and his wife, Elizabeth, have brought the flawless hospitality of a traditional Japanese country inn to El Calafate. Comfortably removed from the tourist scene downtown, and only a short walk from the Ecological Preserve, each of the five rooms has hardwood floors and comfortable twin beds. The Miyasatos have two young children, and the family atmosphere makes this cozy inn a refuge of intimacy and calm. **Pros:** Clean; homey; good value. **Con:** Neighborhood dogs are noisy. ☒*Egidio Feruglio 150* ☏*2902/491–953* ⊕*www.interpatagonia.com/miyazatoinn* ⇝*5 rooms* ☖*In-hotel: public Wi-Fi, no elevator* ▤*MC, V* ⏁|*CP.*

$$$$
★
☷**Posada los Alamos.** Surrounded by tall, leafy alamo trees and constructed of brick and dark *quebracho* (ironwood), this attractive country manor house uses rich woods, leather, and handwoven fabrics to produce conversation-friendly furniture groupings in the large lobby. Plush comforters and fresh flowers in the rooms, and a deferential staff make this a top-notch hotel. Lovingly tended gardens surround the building and line a walkway through the woods to the restaurant and the shore of Lago Argentino. **Pros:** Nice interiors; beautiful gardens. **Con:** Staff can be overly formal. ☒*Moyano 1355, at Bustillo* ☏*2902/491–144* ⊕*www.posadalosalamos.com* ⇝*140 rooms, 4 suites* ☖*In-hotel: restaurant, bar, golf course* ▤*AE, MC, V* ⏁|*CP.*

Parque Nacional
los Glaciares

SPORTS & THE OUTDOORS

BOAT TOURS

The two most popular scenic boat rides in the Parque Nacional los Glaciares are the hour-long **Safari Náutico,** in which your boat cruises a few meters away from the face of the Glaciar Perito Moreno, and the full-day **Upsala Glacier Tour,** in which you navigate through a more extensive selection of glaciers, including Upsala and Onelli, and sections of Lago Argentino that are inaccessible by land. The Safari Náutico costs 35 pesos, not including transportation from El Calafate. **René Fernández Campbell** (⊠*Av. Libertador 867, El Calafate* ☎*2902/491–155* ✆*fernandez_campbell@infovia.com.ar*) is currently the only local tour operator that runs boat tours to Upsala and Onelli glaciers. Any hotel can arrange reservations.

HIKING

Although it's possible to find trails along the shore of Lago Argentino and in the hills south and west of town, these hikes traverse a rather barren landscape and are not terribly interesting. The mountain peaks and forests are in the park, an hour by car from El Calafate. If you want to lace up your boots in your hotel, walk outside, and hit the trail, go to El Chaltén—it's a much better base than El Calafate for hikes in the National Park. Good hiking trails are accessible from the camping areas and cabins by Lago Roca, 50 km (31 mi) from El Calafate.

HORSEBACK RIDING

Anything from a short day ride along Lago Argentino to a weeklong camping excursion in and around the glaciers can be arranged in El Calafate by **Gustavo Holzmann** (⊠*Av. Libertador 4315* ☎*2902/493–278* ⊕*www.cabalgataenpatagonia.com*) or through the tourist office. *Estancias Turísticas* (tourist ranches) are ideal for a combination of horseback riding, ranch activities, and local excursions. Information on **Estancias de Santa Cruz** is in Buenos Aires at the **Provincial tourist office** (⊠*Suipacha 1120* ☎*11/4325–3098* ⊕*www.estanciasdesantacruz.com*) . **Estancia El Galpón del Glaciar** (⊠*Ruta 11, Km 22* ☎☎*2902/492–509 or 11/4774–1069* ⊕*www.estanciaalice.com.ar*) welcomes guests overnight or for the day—for a horseback ride, bird-watching, or an afternoon program that includes a demonstration of sheepdogs working, a walk to the lake with a naturalist, sheep-shearing, and dinner in the former sheep-shearing barn, served right off the grill and the asador by knife-wielding gauchos. **Estancia Maria Elisa** (☎☎*2902/492–583 or 11/4774–1069* ✆*estanciamariaelisa@cotecal.com.ar*) is an upscale choice among estancias. Other estancias close to El Calafate are **Nibepo Aike** (⊠*50 km [31 mi] from El Calafate near Lago Roca* ☎*2966/492–797* ⊕*www.nibepoaike.com.ar*), **Alta Vista** (⊠*33 km [20 mi] from El Calafate* ☎*2966/491–247* ✆*altavista@cotecal.com.ar*), and **Huyliche** (⊠*3 km [2 mi] from El Calafate* ☎*2902/491–025* ✆*teresanegro@cotecal.com.ar*).

ICE TREKKING

★ A two-hour mini-trek on the Perito Moreno Glacier involves a transfer from El Calafate to Brazo Rico by bus and a short lake crossing to a dock and refugio (mountain hut), where you set off with a guide, put crampons over your shoes, and literally walk across a stable portion of the glacier, scaling ridges of ice, and ducking through bright-blue ice tunnels. It is one of the most unique experiences in Argentina. The entire outing lasts about five hours. Hotels arrange mini-treks through **Hielo y Aventura** (✉*Av. Libertador 935* ☎*2902/492–205* ⊕*www. hieloyaventura.com*), which also organizes much longer, more difficult trips of eight hours to a week to other glaciers; you can arrange the trek directly through their office in downtown El Calafate. Mini-trekking runs about 300 pesos for the day. Hielo y Aventura also runs a longer "Big Ice" trek that traverses a much more extensive area of the glacier and costs 420 pesos. If you're between the ages of 18 and 40 and want a more extreme experience, Big Ice is highly recommended.

MOUNTAIN BIKING

Mountain biking is popular along the dirt roads and mountain paths that lead to the lakes, glaciers, and ranches. Rent bikes and get information at **Alquiler de Bicicletas** (✉*Av. Buenos Aires 173* ☎*2902/493–806*).

USHUAIA

914 km (567 mi) south of El Calafate, 3,580 km (2,212 mi) south of Buenos Aires.

At 55 degrees latitude south, Ushuaia, which began as a penal colony, rightly (if perhaps too loudly) promotes itself as the southernmost city in the world (Puerto Williams, a few miles south on the Chilean side of the Beagle Channel, is a small town).

Above the city, the last mountains of the Andean Cordillera rise, and just south and west of Ushuaia they finally vanish into the often stormy sea. Snow whitens the peaks well into summer. Nature is the principal attraction here, with trekking, fishing, horseback riding, and sailing among the most rewarding activities, especially in the Parque Nacional Tierra del Fuego (Tierra del Fuego National Park). The chaotic and contradictory urban landscape includes a handful of luxury hotels amid the concrete of public housing projects. Scores of "sled houses" (wooden shacks) sit precariously on upright piers, ready for speedy displacement to a different site. But there are also many small, picturesque homes with tiny, carefully tended gardens.

GETTING HERE & AROUND

Arriving by air is the preferred option. Ushuaia's Aeropuerto Internacional Malvinas Argentinas (Peninsula de Ushuaia, 2901/431–232) is 5 km (3 mi) from town, and is served daily by flights to/from Buenos Aires, Río Gallegos, El Calafate, Trelew, and Comodoro Rivadavía. There are also flights to Santiago via Punta Arenas in Chile. A taxi into town costs about 7 pesos.

Arriving by road on the RN3 involves Argentinean and Chilean immigrations/customs, a ferry crossing, and a lot of time. The town is very walkable and taxis are cheap.

There is no regular passenger transport (besides cruises) by sea.

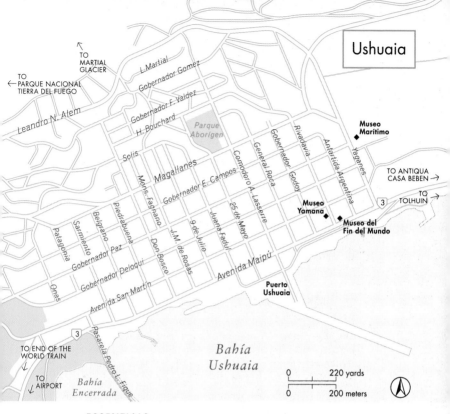

Ushuaia

ESSENTIALS

Bus Services Tecni-Austral (⊠*Roca 157* ☎*2901/431–408*). **Trans los Carlos** (⊠*Av. San Martín 880* ☎*2901/22337*).

Visitor Info Tierra del Fuego Tourism Institute (⊠*Maipú 505* ☎*2901/421–423*). **Ushuaia Tourist Office** (⊠*Av. San Martín 674* ☎*2901/432-000* ⊕*www.e-ush uaia.com*).

EXPLORING USHUAIA

Fodor'sChoice ★ Part of the original penal colony, the Presidio building was built to hold political prisoners, street orphans, and a variety of other social undesirables from the north. In its day it held 600 inmates in 380 cells. Today it holds the **Museo Marítimo** (Maritime Museum), within Ushuaia's naval base, which has exhibits on the town's extinct indigenous population, Tierra del Fuego's navigational past, Antarctic explorations, and life and times in an Argentine penitentiary. You can enter cell blocks and read the stories of the prisoners who lived in them while gazing upon their eerie effigies. Well-presented tours (in Spanish only) are conducted at 3:30 daily. ⊠*Gobernador Paz at Yaganes* ☎*2901/437–481* 🎫*15 pesos* ⊗*Daily 10–8.*

At the **Museo del Fin del Mundo** (End of the World Museum), you can see a large stuffed condor and other native birds, indigenous artifacts, maritime instruments, and such seafaring-related objects as an impressive mermaid figurehead taken from the bowsprit of a galleon. There are also photographs and histories of El Presidio's original inmates, such as Simon Radowitzky, a Russian immigrant anarchist who received a life sentence for killing an Argentine police colonel. The museum is in the 1905 residence of a Fuegonian governor. The home was later converted into a bank, and some of the exhibits are showcased in the former vault. ⊠ *Maipú 173, at Rivadavía* ☎ *2901/421–863* ✉ *10 pesos* ⊘ *Oct.–Mar., daily 9–8; Apr.–Sept., daily noon–7.*

The **Tren del Fin del Mundo** (End of the World Train) takes you inside the Parque Nacional Tierra del Fuego, 12 km (7½ mi) away. The touristy 40-minute train ride's gimmick is a simulation of the trip on which El Presidio prisoners were taken into the forest to chop wood, but unlike them, you'll also get a good presentation of Ushuaia's history (in Spanish and English). The train departs daily at 9:30 AM, noon, and 3 PM in summer, and just once a day, at 10 AM, in winter, from a stop near the national park entrance. If you have a rental car, you'll want to do the round trip, but if not, one common way to do the trip is to hire a *remis* (car service) that will drop you at the station for a one-way train ride, pick you up at the other end, and then drive you around the Parque Nacional for two or three hours of sightseeing (which is more scenic than the train ride itself). ⊠ *Ruta 3, Km 3042* ☎ *2901/431–600* ⊕ *www.trendelfindelmundo.com.ar* ✉ *95 pesos first-class ticket, 50 pesos tourist-class ticket, 20 pesos national park entrance fee (no park fee in winter).*

Tour operators run trips along the **Canal Beagle,** on which you can get a startling close-up view of sea mammals and birds on **Isla de los Lobos, Isla de los Pájaros,** and near **Les Eclaireurs Lighthouse.** There are catamarans that make three-hour trips, generally leaving from the Tourist Pier at 3 PM, and motorboats and sailboats that leave twice a day, once at 9:30 AM and once at 3 PM (trips depend on weather; few trips go in winter). Prices range 60 pesos–140 pesos; some include hikes on the islands. Check with the tourist office for the latest details; you can also book through any of the local travel agencies.

★ If you've never butted heads with a glacier, and especially if you won't be covering El Calafate on your trip, then you should check out **Glaciar Martial,** in the mountain range just above Ushuaia. Take the Camino al Glaciar (Glacier Road) 5 km (3 mi) out of town until it ends (this route is also served by the local tour companies). Even if you don't plan to hike to see the glacier, it's a great pleasure to ride the 15-minute lift (and hiking this stretch is unrewarding), which is open daily 10–5, weather permitting (it's often closed from mid-May until August) and costs 25 pesos. If you're afraid of heights, you can instead enjoy a small nature trail here, and a teahouse. After a steep, strenuous 90-minute hike, you can cool your heels in one of the many gurgling, icy rivulets that cascade down water-worn shale shoots and enjoy the great views.

WHERE TO EAT

$$–$$$$ ✕**Chez Manu.** *Herbes de provence* in the greeting room tip French quasi-
ARGENTINE celebrity chef Manu Herbin's hand: he gives local seafood a French
Fodor'sChoice touch to diversify the Argentine gastronomy and create some of Ush-
★ uaia's most memorable meals. Perched a couple of miles above town,
across the street from the Hotel Glaciar, the restaurant has grand views
of the Beagle Canal. The first-rate wine list includes Patagonian selec-
tions. Don't miss the *trucha fueguina* (local trout) in white wine sauce,
served with buttery rice cooked in fish stock, or the *centolla* (king crab)
au gratin. ✉*Camino Luís Martial 2135* ☎*2901/432–253* ▤*AE, MC,
V* ☉*Closed Mon., May, and June.*

$$–$$$$ ✕**Tía Elvira.** On the street that runs right along the Beagle Channel,
ARGENTINE this is an excellent place to sample the local catch. Garlicky shellfish
appetizers and centolla are delicious, and even more memorable is the
tender *merluza negra* (black sea bass). The room is decked out with
nautical knickknacks that may seem on the tacky side for such a pricey
place. The service is friendly and familial. ✉*Maipú 349* ☎*2901/424–
725* ▤*AE, DC, MC, V* ☉*Closed Sun. and July.*

$$–$$$ ✕**Volver.** A giant king crab sign beckons you into this red tin restaurant,
ARGENTINE which provides some major relief from Avenida San Martín's row of
★ all-you-can-eat parrillas. The name means "return" and it succeeds in
getting repeat visits. Newspapers from the 1930s line the walls in this
century-old home; informal table settings have place mats depicting old
London landmarks; and fishing nets hang from the ceiling, along with
hams, a disco ball, tricycles, and antique lamps. The culinary highlight
is king crab (*centolla*), which comes served with a choice of five different sauces. ✉*Maipú 37* ☎*2901/423–977* ▤*AE, DC, MC, V* ☉*No
lunch May–Aug.*

WHERE TO STAY

Choosing a place to stay depends in part on whether you want to spend
the night in town, out of town several miles west toward the national
park, or above town several miles uphill.

$$$$ ▣**Cumbres de Martial.** This charming wood complex, painted fire-
engine red, is high above Ushuaia at the foot of the ski lift that leads to
the Martial glacier. Each spacious room has an extremely comfortable
bed and a small wooden deck with terrific views down to the Beagle
Channel. The *cabañas* are beautiful self-contained log cabins. There are
also a teahouse and a small nature trail beside the Martial River. There
is, however, no complimentary shuttle service to town, so you'll need
to take a 10- to 15-peso taxi to access Ushuaia. **Pros:** Easy access to the
glacier; views. **Con:** You need to cab it to and from town. ✉*Camino
Luís Martial 3560* ☎☎*2901/424–779* ⊕*www.cumbresdelmartial.
com.ar* ⇆*6 rooms, 4 cabins* ⚒*In-room: safe. In-hotel: restaurant,
bar, laundry service, airport shuttle* ▤*AE, DC, MC, V* ☉*Closed Apr.
and May* ⑩*BP.*

$$ ▣**Hostería Patagonia Jarké.** Jarké means "spark" in a local native lan-
★ guage, and indeed this B&B is a vibrant addition to Ushuaia. This
three-story lodge, cantilevered down a hillside on a dead-end street in
the heart of town, is an amalgam of alpine and Victorian styles on the

outside; inside, a spacious contemporary design incorporates a glass-roofed lobby, several living rooms, and breakfast room. Rooms have polished wood floors, peaked-roof ceilings, artisanal soaps, woven floor mats, bidets, Jacuzzi tubs, and lovely views. **Pro:** Feels like home. **Con:** Steep walk home. ⊠*Sarmiento 310* ☎☎*2901/437–245* ⊕*www. hosteriapatagoniaj.com* ⇆*15 rooms* ⌂*In-room: safe. In-hotel: bar, laundry service, public Wi-Fi* ⊟*AE, DC, MC, V* ⎮⊙⎮*BP.*

$$$$ ⬚ **Hotel y Resort Las Hayas.** Las Hayas is in the wooded foothills of the
Fodor'sChoice   Andes, overlooking the town and channel below. Ask for a *canal* view
★   and, since the rooms are all decorated differently and idiosyncratically, sample a variety before settling in. All feature Portuguese linen, solid oak furnishings, and the Las Hayas trademark: fabric-padded walls. A suspended glass bridge connects the hotel to a spectacular health spa, which includes a heated pool, Jacuzzi, and even a squash court. The wonderful five-star restaurant Le Martial prepares an excellent version of *mollejas de cordero* (lamb sweetbreads) with scallops, and boasts the best wine list in town. **Pros:** Four Internet stations; good restaurant. **Con:** Decor doesn't suit everyone. ⊠*Camino Luís Martial 1650, Km 3* ☎*2901/430–710, 11/4393–4750 in Buenos Aires* ⊕*www.lashayashotel.com* ⇆*85 rooms, 7 suites* ⌂*In-room: safe. In-hotel: restaurant, bar, pool, gym, spa, laundry service, airport shuttle* ⊟*AE, DC, MC, V* ⎮⊙⎮*CP.*

$$$ ⬚ **La Tierra de Leyendas.** The hotel is in the Estancia Río Pipo, on a wind-battered hill 4 km (2½ mi) west of town, in an area once inhabited by canoeist nomads. The five bedrooms—with names such as La Coqueta and La Mision—boast large windows facing the Beagle Channel or the snowcapped Andes; a cozy living room offers a book exchange, board games, video library, and glass display tables with antique arrows, bones, and currency. The restaurant has a top-notch gourmet menu—offering such exotic fare as *conejo a la cazadora* (stuffed Fuegian rabbit)—prepared by the owner. **Pro:** An extraordinarily quaint find for western Ushuaia. **Con:** Insanely windy—hold on to your hat. ⊠*Tierra de Vientos 2448,* ☎*2901/443–565* ⊕*www.tierradeleyendas.com.ar* ⇆*5 rooms* ⌂*In-room: DVD, safe. In-hotel: laundry service, public Wi-Fi* ⊟*AE, MC, V.*

PARQUE NACIONAL TIERRA DEL FUEGO

★   The pristine park, 21 km (13 mi) west of Ushuaia, offers a chance to wander through peat bogs, stumble upon hidden lakes, trek through native *canelo, lenga,* and wild cherry forests, and experience the wonders of wind-whipped Tierra del Fuego's rich flora and fauna. Everywhere, lichens line the trunks of the ubiquitous lenga trees, and "Chinese lantern" parasites hang from the branches.

Visits to the park, which is tucked up against the Chilean border, are commonly arranged through tour companies. Another way to get to the park is to take the Tren del Fin del Mundo (⇨*above*). **Transportes Kaupen** (☎*2901/434–015*), one of several private bus companies, has buses that travel through the park; you can get off the bus, explore the park, and then wait for the next bus (the service operates only in summer).Yet one more option is to drive to the park on R3 (take it until it ends and you see the famous sign indicating the end of the Pan-American Highway, which starts 17,848 km [11,065 mi] away in Alaska, and ends here). If you don't have a car, you can also hire a private *remis*. Trail and camping information is available at the park-entrance ranger station or at the Ushuaia tourist office. At the park entrance is a gleaming new restaurant and teahouse set amidst the hills, **Patagonia Mia** (⊠*Ruta 3, Entrada Parque Nacional* ☎*2901/1560–2757* ⊕*www. patagoniamia.com*); it's a great place to stop for tea or coffee, or a full meal of roast lamb or Fuegian seafood.Highlights of the park include the spectacular mountain-ringed lake, **Lago Roca**, as well as **Laguna Verde**, a lagoon whose green color comes from algae at its bottom. Much of the park is closed from roughly June through September, when the descent to Bahía Ensenada is blocked by up to 6 feet of snow. Even in May and October, chains for your car are a good idea. No hotels are within the park—the only one burned down in the 1980s, and you can see its carcass driving by—but there are three simple camping areas around Lago Roca. Tours to the park are run by **All Patagonia** (⊠*Juana Fadul 26* ☎*2901/433–622 or 2901/430–725*).

SPORTS & THE OUTDOORS

FISHING

The rivers of Tierra del Fuego are home to trophy-size freshwater trout—including browns, rainbows, and brooks. Both fly- and spin-casting are available. The season runs November–March; fees range from 10 pesos a day to 40 pesos for a month. Founded in 1959, the **Asociación de Caza y Pesca** (⊠*Av. Maipú 822* ☎*2901/423–168*) is the principal hunting and fishing organization in the city. **Rumbo Sur** (⊠*Av. San Martín 350* ☎*2901/421–139* ⊕*www.rumbosur.com.ar*) is the city's oldest travel agency and can assist in setting up fishing trips. **Wind Fly** (⊠*Av. 25 de Mayo 143* ☎*2901/431–713 or 2901/1544–9116* ⊕*www.windflyushuaia.com.ar*) is dedicated exclusively to fishing, and offers classes, arranges trips, and rents equipment.

MOUNTAIN BIKING

Good mountain bikes normally cost about 5 pesos an hour or 15 pesos–20 pesos for a full day. Bikes can be rented at the base of the glacier, at the **Refugio de Montaña** (⊠*Base Glaciar Martial* ☎*2901/1556–8587*), or at **D. T. T. Cycles** (⊠*Av. San Martín 903* ☎*2901/434–939*). Guided bicycle tours (including rides through the national park), for about 50 pesos a day, are organized by **All Patagonia** (⊠*Fadul 26* ☎*2901/430–725*). **Rumbo Sur** (⊠*San Martín 350* ☎*2901/421–139* ⊕*www.rumbosur. com.ar*) is the city's biggest travel agency and can arrange trips. **Tolkeyén Patagonia** (⊠*San Martín 1267* ☎*2901/437–073*) rents bikes and arranges trips.

SCENIC FLIGHTS

The gorgeous scenery and island topography of the area is readily appreciated on a Cessna tour. A half-hour flight (US$35, or 102 pesos per passenger; US$50, or 145 pesos for one passenger alone) with a local pilot takes you over Ushuaia and the Beagle Channel with views of area glaciers and snowcapped islands south to Cape Horn. A 60-minute flight (US$70 or 203 pesos per passenger; US$100 or 290 pesos for one passenger alone) crosses the Andes to the Escondida and Fagnano lakes. **Aero Club Ushuaia** (⊠ *Antiguo Aeropuerto* ☎ *2901/421–717* ⊕ *www.aeroclubushuaia.org.ar*) offers half-hour and hour-long trips.

SKIING

Ushuaia is the cross-country skiing (*esqui de fondo* in Spanish) center of South America, thanks to enthusiastic **Club Andino** (☎ *2901/422–335*) members who took to the sport in the 1980s and made the forested hills of a high valley about 20 minutes from town a favorite destination for skiers.

Glaciar Martial Ski Lodge (☎ *2901/243–3712*), open year-round, Tuesday–Sunday 10–7, functions as a cross-country ski center from June to October. Skis can also be rented in town, as can snowmobiles.

Bolivia

WORD OF MOUTH

Drove to Copacabana (really, a pretty beach town), hopped on the boat and went to [Isla del Sol] island. We had nice traditional lunch on the island and took a hike (stopping at ruins along the way) to our eco lodge on top of the island. Just beautiful, more than I had ever imagined.

—quimbymoy

By Paul Kaye

"ROOFTOP OF THE WORLD" IS how people describe Bolivia. The dizzying altitude of parts of this country is almost always mentioned. Bolivia's largest city, La Paz, is the world's highest capital, at 11,942 feet. The city's Aeropuerto Internacional El Alto, at 13,310 feet, is the world's highest commercial airport. Lake Titicaca is the highest navigable lake in the world. They play football on top of mountains.

But these high-flying statistics don't reveal much about the country or the people. Bolivia is larger than Texas and California combined, but most of its 8 million people are concentrated in a handful of urban centers—La Paz, Santa Cruz, Cochabamba, and Sucre—making it a very easy place to get to know. Off the beaten track—and onto the very unbeaten—Bolivia contains every type of terrain, from tropical lowlands to parched desert to rugged mountain peaks. It has the second-largest range of natural environments in the world, after Mexico. Although generally considered an Andean nation, nearly two-thirds of the country sweats it out in the steamy Amazon Basin—remote, overlooked, and as inhospitable as it is soul-stirring. On Bolivia's wildest frontier, indigenous tribes live as they have for centuries, unimpressed, it seems, by the displays of the modern world. In the provinces of Beni and Santa Cruz, near the border of Brazil, tribes still hunt with bows and arrows.

To the west of these tropical lowlands, just beyond Cochabamba and Santa Cruz, the Andes rise sharply to form the backbone of South America's Pacific coast. This two-prong mountain range shelters between its eastern and western peaks a long, rambling plain. Known as the altiplano, this high, cold plateau may seem bleak, but for the adventurous traveler there are treasures to be found, including the mountains themselves, the deep-blue waters of Lake Titicaca, the staggering views of the Salar de Uyuni, and the ancient and bloodstained city of Potosí.

Centuries of Spanish dominion have left their mark, but Bolivia remains a land of indigenous farmers, ranchers, and artisans. On the windswept Andean plateaus you will still see local weavers toting their crafts and red-cheek children to weekly markets. By the time the sun has risen, the brightly dressed Aymara are in place, ready to sell textiles and ponchos, not to mention vegetables, fruits, and medicinal herbs. On city streets you'll see business executives in the latest designer fashions shouting into mobile phones as they buy flowers from bowler-hatted indigenous women. These ladies will also be shouting into mobile phones, but through a mouth-full of coca leaves. And here is the root of Bolivia's magic: the ancient and the modern are conjoined here, and as far as the passing traveler is concerned, seamlessly.

ORIENTATION & PLANNING

GETTING ORIENTED

From the altiplano to the Amazon basin, Bolivia borders five countries and comprises nearly every microclimate and ecosystem imaginable. It's most famous for the Andes, which take up a large chunk of the west. Also well known are the vast jungle regions of Amazonia, which extend all the way east into Brazil. But Bolivia has a surprisingly varied series of ecosystems within those two major regions. Mountain areas vary from cool and dry (as in the high-altitude cities of La Paz and Potosí), to temperate (the cities of Cochabamba and Sucre), to warm and pleasant almost year-round (in the fertile, grape-growing lands near the southern city of Tarija). Jungle areas also vary: from very humid and warm, as in Santa Cruz, to the more temperate climates in the northwest province of Pando. In the northeast province of Beni, encompassing the city of Trinidad, the hot, wet climate is occasionally broken by cold spells called *surazos*.

La Paz. La Paz and its surroundings are what many people expect Bolivia to be: poor, high, desolate, and cold. However, drop down the other side of the city and you are in the sub-tropical Yungas in an hour, and the farther you go the deeper and darker the Amazon becomes.

Lake Titicaca. Lake Titicaca embodies all the mysteries of Bolivia's ancient and not so ancient indigenous societies, and the sacred character of this vast body of water is understandable. Its stunning islands and mountain backdrop give you a real opportunity to step back and reflect.

Central Bolivia. The center of the country is the home of the two "other" cities, Cochabamba and Santa Cruz, and each is distinct and in its own way the capital of its region. Go to the permanent spring of Cochabamba to relax and live well, and Santa Cruz's oil-rich territories to experience a cowboy boomtown grown very big.

Southern Bolivia. The jewel of the south, and some would say Bolivia, is the Salar de Uyuni, the vast otherworldly salt flats, but to appreciate the great tragedies of Bolivia's past and the torments of its present, you need to go to Potosí, the skeleton of a once hugely wealthy city.

BOLIVIA PLANNER

WHEN TO GO

With its extremes of terrain, altitude, and climate, Bolivia has something to appeal to nearly every traveler. During the rainy season from November to March, heavy downpours make overland traveling difficult and dangerous, as many smaller roads are virtually impassable. If you plan to travel this way, it's best to go between April and October, when winter skies mean endless sun and perfect light (and zero burn time).

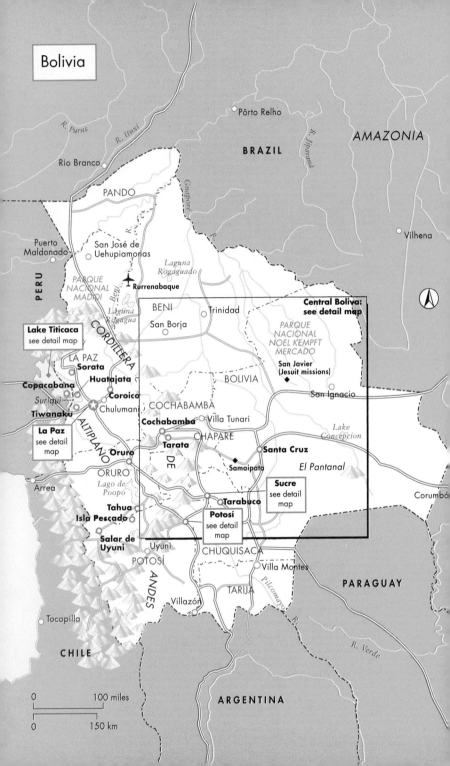

Bolivia

AMAZONIA

BRAZIL

Pôrto Relho

Rio Branco

R. Purus

R. Ituxi

R. Jiparaná

R. Guaporé

Vilhena

PANDO

Puerto Maldonado

San José de Uehupiamonas

Laguna Rogaguado

PERU

CORDILLERA

PARQUE NACIONAL MADIDI

Rurrenabaque

Laguna Rogagua

Beni R.

BENI

Trinidad

San Borja

PARQUE NACIONAL NOEL KEMPFT MERCADO

Central Bolivia:
see detail map

Lake Titicaca
see detail map

LA PAZ
Sorata

Huatajata

Copacabana

Suriqui

Tiwanaku

La Paz
see detail map

Coroica

Chulumani

COCHABAMBA

Cochabamba

Villa Tunari

CHAPARE

BOLIVIA

San Javier
(Jesuit missions)

San Ignacio

Lake Concepción

ALTIPLANO

Oruro

Tarata

DE

Samaipata

Santa Cruz

El Pantanal

ORURO

Lago de Poopó

Tahua

Isla Pescado

Salar de Uyuni

Uyuni

POTOSÍ

Arrea

Tarabuco

Potosí
see detail map

Sucre
see detail map

Corumbá

ANDES

CHUQUISACA

Villa Montes

PARAGUAY

Villazón

TARIJA

Pilcomayo R.

Tocopilla

CHILE

R. Verde

0   100 miles

0   150 km

ARGENTINA

2

CLIMATE

In high-altitude cities like La Paz and Potosí the weather can get very chilly, particularly at night. Lowland cities like Santa Cruz, sitting in the Amazon basin, are hot and humid most of the year. Cochabamba, dubbed the "City of Eternal Spring," enjoys a mild Mediterranean climate year-round.

The following are the average monthly maximum and minimum temperatures for La Paz. Remember this is not indicative of the country as a whole, and that almost all other regions are more temperate.

Jan.	64F	18C	May	66F	19C	Sept.	72F	17C
	43	6		35	2		38	3
Feb.	64F	18C	June	60F	16C	Oct.	65F	18C
	43	6		36	2		40	4
Mar.	64F	18C	July	61F	16C	Nov.	67F	20C
	43	6		34	1		42	6
Apr.	66F	19C	Aug.	62F	17C	Dec.	64F	18C
	40	4		35	2		43	6

HOLIDAYS

During Carnaval and many of Bolivia's other holidays the country virtually shuts down, sometimes for a couple of days before and after. Don't plan to travel on the holiday itself, as transit is practically nonexistent. Major holidays are New Year's Day; Carnaval (weekend prior to start of Lent), Good Friday (April); Labor Day (May 1); Independence Day (August 6); All Saints' Day (November 2); Christmas.

GETTING HERE & AROUND

Traveling around Bolivia is an enjoyable experience if you savor unpredictability, display huge amounts of patience, and have lots of time to hang around in airports, bus stations, and on the wrong side of landslides. Flying is often the best way to go, as it is relatively cheap in-country and very fast. Bus services between cities and to the border can be excellent, but dangerous if they are overnight, or during national holidays. Car rental is expensive, and you need to be a confident and assertive driver to manage Bolivian highways and the off-road experience of minor roads. Renting a taxi for a day is a viable option, but settle on a price first and only pay 50% up front.

BY AIR

All international and domestic flights to La Paz arrive at El Alto airport, which is on the altiplano in the city of El Alto, 12 km (7 mi) from downtown. Many stop first at Santa Cruz's airport, Viru Viru, which also serves as an international hub. American Airlines has daily flights between Miami, Santa Cruz, and La Paz. AeroSur, Bolivia's domestic airline, flies to most major cities in Bolivia, and TAM, the military airline, can offer very good value. Amazonas airline (☎02/222–0848) connects La Paz to Cobija, Santa Cruz, Trinidad, and other eastern points.

TOP REASONS TO GO

Water water everywhere. Carnival in Oruro may seem like the biggest frat-house waterfight in the world, but it's also a stunning realization of Bolivian folklore and dance. The endless procession of groups is wearying after a couple of hours (there are more than 30,000 dancers), and the sun can be brutal—Oruro is 3,700 metres (12,140 feet) above sea level. Keep your trip short, arrive as early as possible, and take waterproofs. You can buy your water pistol there.

Flipper of the Forest. Yes, friends, that *was* a pink dolphin you just saw in the Beni River—and no, you didn't have too much chicha to drink. The Amazonian basin is home to an astonishing array of wildlife, including caimans, Amazonian catfish the size of Volkswagens, sloths, jaguars, and the famed pink dolphins, which the first Spaniards mistook, perhaps understandably, for mermaids.

No salt added. The Salar de Uyuni, the giant salt desert that borders Chile, is an impressive, barren, and unique landscape. The gaping fissures, endless expanse of white, and eerie light give it an otherworldly vibe, and the neighboring lagoons of red, green, and other colors (depending on nearby mineral content) add to the mystique. In the rainy season a thin layer of water turns it into the world's largest mirror.

Mines, all mines. Descending into the muck, humidity, and low-oxygen environment of Potosí's mines isn't everyone's idea of a good time, but if you want to know what kind of work and suffering it took to extract the world's greatest silver fortune from the Cerro Rico, you've got to get a little dirty. While you're in there, make an offering to the spirit of the mountain—the little fellow gladly accepts coins, cigarettes, or a splash of alcohol.

On top of the world. The Isla de Sol, sitting pretty in the middle of Lake Titicaca, not only has the best views of the mountains of the Royal Range and the sacred waters of the lake itself, but it also has sparkling white beaches and more trout than you could eat if you settled down and grew old here. Which wouldn't be a bad idea, the magic energy levels could keep you going for centuries.

Domestic flights can be heavily booked, so always reconfirm your reservation a day or so in advance. If you do not, your reservation may be canceled.

Airlines **AeroSur** (✉ *Av.Irala 616, Santa Cruz* ☎ *03/336–4446* ✉ *Edif. Hotel Radisson, Av. Arce 2177, La Paz* ☎ *02/244–4930* ⊕ *www.aerosur.com* ✉ *Calle Arenales 31, Sucre* ☎ *04/646–2141*). **American Airlines** (✉ *El Prado, Av. 16 de Julio, 1440 Edificio Hermann, La Paz* ☎ *02/235–1360* ✉ *Calle Beni 167, Santa Cruz* ☎ *03/334–1314* ⊕ *www.aa.com*). **Aerolineas Argentinas** (✉ *Edif. Banco de la Nación Argentina, Segundo Piso, Santa Cruz* ☎ *03/333–9776/9777* ⊕ *www. aerolineas.com.ar*).

BY BUS

Private bus companies connect Bolivia's major cities. Because of the often poor roads, bus journeys can be very slow—a trip from La Paz to Santa Cruz, for example, can take more than 24 hours. Securing a

Modern Politics

In 2005, MAS (Movimiento al Socialismo), a political party that emerged from the jungles of the Chapare and the coca leaf industry, won a landslide victory in general elections, and its leader, Evo Morales, became South America's first indigenous president. Seen as the only alternative to the corrupt governments of the past, and by many indigenous as the only true hope for them to achieve recognition, he now faces the almost impossible challenge of making his voters' aspirations reality—hardly an easy task in a country as diverse and poorly integrated as Bolivia. Instead of uniting the country, his prioritizing of indigenous concerns has led to a massive and growing gulf between classes and races. The New Constitution, which was supposed to create a better Bolivia for all, has led to fights, bloodshed, and riots. The antagonism between the lower areas in the east and the predominantly indigenous west has grown; six departments have declared themselves autonomous, which effectively means they seek independence. Bolivia now teeters on the edge of a huge political and social crisis: can it claw its way back, as it has done so many times before?

seat is usually no problem, though you should reserve at least a day in advance for the long and tedious rides between La Paz, Sucre, Potosí, and Santa Cruz. The best way to do this is either through an agency or by going to the bus terminals themselves.

Bus Companies **Expreso Mopar** (☎ 02/237-7443). **Trans Copacabana** (☎ 02/237-7894).

BY CAR

It takes confidence and a thick skin to drive in Bolivian cities, courage to use the big highways between them, and special 4x4 skills to manage the smaller roads; in most cases, it's easier to use public transport or hire a taxi. In the city, drive defensively and assume that vehicles around you are going to do the stupidest thing possible, especially at traffic lights. Before driving outside the city, inquire about the conditions around your proposed destination. Most roads are unpaved and poorly maintained. During the rainy season many are subject to flash floods and landslides, so prepare for long delays. If you can, hire a driver familiar with the area so that you can enjoy the scenery without frazzling your nerves. Avoid driving at night outside built-up areas, especially on the highways—it's terrifying.

Renting a car can be very expensive in Bolivia, particularly because you need a four-wheel-drive vehicle to reach many destinations. The rate for a four-wheel-drive vehicle is $300–$700 per week. Compact cars suitable for short trips cost $150–$250 per week. The minimum age for most car rentals in Bolivia is 25 years. You need a passport, driver's license (some rental companies require an International Driver's License), and a credit card.

The national oil company, YPFB, maintains service stations on most major roads. Many are open 24 hours a day and gas is cheap, approximately $1.70 per gallon. Away from the main roads, GASOLINA signs alert you to private homes where fuel is sold (make sure they filter the gasoline for impurities when they fill your tank). Unleaded gasoline is available at some service stations.

BY TRAIN

Bolivia's great train services all died years ago, and the country is now crisscrossed only by rusty rails. There is still transport between Oruro and towns near the border like Uyuni, Tupiza, and Villazon.

> **TIP**
>
> Unless you are traveling in a risk area, you won't need your yellow fever vaccination, but you will need the certificate if you are traveling on to some of the other countries on the continent, including the international hub airport at São Paulo. Don't get one from the health centers in-country—they are not recognized internationally.

There's also an occasional service from Uyuni to Calama, Chile, though it's a long, rough, high, and cold ride. The classic ride from La Paz to Arica on the coast of Chile stopped running many years ago. Check what's going on at ⊕ *www.fca.com.bo.*

ESSENTIALS

ELECTRICITY

Bolivia's electric current is 110/220 volts AC in La Paz and 220 volts AC in the rest of the country. You'll need adapters for two-pronged outlets, which are used for both types of current. Be very careful to make sure your appliance can take a 220 voltage (usually stated somewhere on the casing) before you plug it in.

ENTRY REQUIREMENTS

American citizens must have a tourist visa, to be organized before arriving or at ports of entry. Requirements are fairly complex, so the latter is not recommended. If you want to stay longer than your free days, you have the option of overstaying your visa and being fined (Bs)10 for each extra day you overstay, purchasing a 30-day extension for (Bs)150, or hopping across the border into Peru and back with a new visa. Citizens of Australia, Canada, the United Kingdom, and New Zealand need only a valid passport, and receive a free 30-day visa upon arrival in Bolivia (however, it doesn't hurt to ask if they will extend it to 90).

ALTITUDE Due to the high altitude in La Paz and Potosí, you may suffer from *soroche,* or altitude sickness when you arrive. Symptoms include dizziness, fatigue, and shortness of breath. Avoid alcohol, drink lots of water, and rest as much as you can in the first few days. Do not take the soroche pills sold in pharmacies within Bolivia—they are a dangerous mix of chemicals banned in the United States and Europe. Symptoms usually disappear within a week. If they do not, consult a doctor, especially if you have a history of high blood pressure. *Mate de coca,* a herbal (and completely legal) tea made from coca leaves, can be very effective. If you suffer from heart or lung diseases, or are pregnant, consult your doctor before traveling.

HEALTH & SAFETY

FOOD & DRINK
Although the higher areas of Bolivia are relatively free of bacteria, lower altitudes harbor some really dangerous strains. To play it safe, do not drink tap water and order beverages without ice. Avoid eating food from street vendors. You can find most of the things you want to try in restaurants and cafés for a slightly higher price. If you buy on the street or from a market, take the U.S. Center for Disease Control and Prevention's advice: "Boil it, cook it, peel it, or forget it."

OTHER PRECAUTIONS
At present, no shots or vaccination certificates are required for entering Bolivia, although you will need a yellow fever vaccine if you are moving on to countries such as Brazil. If you'll be spending time in remote areas, ask your doctor about typhoid, hepatitis A and B, yellow fever, and tetanus vaccinations. If you're headed for the Amazon, consider antimalarial prophylactics.

Bring plenty of sunblock—the high altitudes feel cool, but the sun will burn you within minutes due to the thin atmosphere. Wear sunglasses and a hat as much as possible. In the winter, humidity in La Paz can drop to 0%, and your skin and eyes can get very uncomfortable, so use moisturizing cream and drops if necessary.

Be careful with dogs—in the cities they are friendly, but be very wary in rural areas. Usually picking up a stone is enough to warn them off. Rabies is a real risk in Bolivia, so if you're bitten by anything see a doctor immediately.

SAFETY
Crime is not a major problem in Bolivia compared to other Latin American countries, but it's increasing both in frequency and seriousness. In larger cities such as La Paz, Cochabamba, Sucre, and Santa Cruz, street crime—including pickpocketing, mugging, and purse-snatching—is on the rise. Avoid wearing flashy jewelry and watches, and be aware of your surroundings at all times, especially in busy plazas and on jam-packed buses. Carry only as much cash as necessary when in the city, especially in crowded market areas. Exercise special caution around bus terminals, where there have been several kidnappings and even murders of tourists. Don't trust any "policemen" who ask to see your papers: be assertive, don't let them search you, and walk away fast. Never take an unmarked taxicab, especially in the Cementario area of La Paz. For public transport, use "radio taxis" (they have a telephone number on a sign on the roof), public buses and minibuses, or the fixed-route, shared *trufis*. For further advice, the best sources are the British Embassy's Travel Advice at ⊕*www.fco.gov.uk* and the U.S. Department of State's Country Specific Information at ⊕*www.travel.state.gov*.

LANGUAGE

Spanish is the predominant language in the cities, and Bolivian Spanish is one of the easiest on the continent to understand. Quechua and Aymara are spoken by highlanders who may or may not also speak Spanish, while Guaraní is spoken in some parts of the Amazonian basin. Hotel staffs usually have some knowledge of English, French, or

German. Learning a few words of Spanish will go down well—in many places people will assume you can speak it.

MONEY MATTERS

The unit of currency is the boliviano, which can be divided into 100 centavos. Bolivianos come in bills of 5, 10, 20, 50, 100, and 200. Coins come in denominations of 10, 20, and 50 centavos and 1, 2 and 5 bolivianos. At this writing, the exchange rate was (Bs)7.56 to the U.S. dollar. Bolivians frequently refer to their currency as *pesos*.

You can change U.S. dollars and European currency in banks, casas de cambio, and on the street (not recommended). Most banks in Bolivia's larger cities have ATMs, but muggings at these have become more common, so be careful when using them alone or at night.

Most major credit cards are accepted in most cities and towns in Bolivia, but only in established retail chains, hotels, and restaurants. American Express is generally unpopular. If you are traveling in a rural area, make sure to bring along enough cash and carry it in a variety of small demoninations (coins and notes lower than 10 bolivianos).

PHONES

The international code for Bolivia is 591. Dial the country code, then the departmental area code, then the seven-digit number. If you are calling from abroad, drop the "0" from the area code. Local codes for the departments are as follows: La Paz, Oruro, Potosí, 2; Santa Cruz, Beni, Pando, 3; Cochabamba, Tarija, Chuquisaca (Sucre), 4. To call a Bolivian mobile phone from abroad, use 591 and the mobile number.

Long-distance and international calls can be made from local offices of Entel, Cotel, and AXS. You'll find their offices everywhere. The least-expensive place to make international calls is at an Internet café.

TAXES

Throughout Bolivia, a 13% value-added tax (IVA) is added to hotel and restaurant prices and to items purchased in some stores. If you are charged IVA, you should also be given a receipt or *factura*. It's worth asking for a price *sin factura* (without a receipt) if you are bargaining, as this may mean paying less. Street vendors work strictly in cash.

TIPPING

Bolivia is not a tipping culture, but expect to pay for small favors and "help" everywhere. In restaurants, a tip of 5% to 10% is in order if you are happy with the service. Taxi drivers do not expect tips unless you hire them for the day, in which case 10% is appropriate. Airport porters expect (Bs)5 per baggage cart they handle. Shoeshine boys, who pop up out of the cracks in the pavement on every corner, will try to charge you 10 times the going rate of (Bs)1—their roguish smiles may persuade you to tip more. If someone offers to watch your car, best to accept or they will steal it instead—again, (Bs)1 is standard for this "service."

RESTAURANTS & HOTELS

CUISINE Bolivia is one of the least-expensive countries in South America for travelers. A meal at a basic restaurant should cost no more than (Bs)20, and even at the most elegant restaurants you can eat well for less than (Bs)50.

Bolivian cuisine is healthy, wholesome, and satisfying, if lacking the finer touch. Cheaper eateries go for quantity as much as quality, so avoid over-ordering. Soups make a complete meal in themselves, loaded with meat, potatoes, vegetables, and a ricelike grain called *quinua*, now recognised as a complete, and gluten-free, protein source. Look out for the peanut soup—it'll change your ideas about nuts. Fresh trout from Lake Titicaca is fried, stuffed, steamed, grilled, spiced, or covered in a rich sauce. Another excellent, delicate fish from the lake is *pejerrey,* which is especially good in *ceviche,* a cold marinated fish dish often eaten mid-morning. Set lunch—*almuerzo* or *almuerzo executivo*—is always good value, whether it's in a fancy restaurant or from a market stall. Many meals are served with a spicy sauce called *llajwa,* made from the local hot peppers. It comes in various shades, and you'll soon be addicted.

In the highlands, where carbohydrates are the dietary mainstay, they freeze-dry potatoes, then soak them overnight and boil them. The result, *chuño* and *tunta,* is then used to accompany main dishes, and probably best left on the side of the plate, too. Other traditional fare includes *asado de llama*, roast llama, and *pique macho,* beef grilled with hot peppers, chopped tomatoes, and onions, often served with fried potatoes and gravy. Snacks include *saltenas* and *tucumanas,* pastries filled with meat, chicken, or vegetables. Eating these without having them explode all over your clothes takes skill, so watch how the locals do it. Over your Sunday newspaper you can try *api,* a delicious hot grain drink served with deep-fried pastries.

ACCOMMO- With growing competition for tourist dollars, there has been a push
DATIONS to upgrade older hotels, and, where possible, to build new ones. The style, however, remains very Bolivian, and unless you are paying top dollar you need to be flexible and, to a certain extent, accept what you get. There is now a wider range of accommodations, from cozy guest houses to luxury resorts to themed hotels. Eco-resorts are on the rise, although you may form your own opinion about how green some of them really are. There also growing numbers of backpacker hostels, mostly run by foreigners; the standards may be better, but you may not appreciate the frat-house atmosphere. Many hotels have two pricing systems—one for Bolivians and one for foreigners. Even if you are in the latter category, good accommodation can be found for $15 or less, particularly away from the cities. The most expensive luxury hotels are more pricey, at $120–$150 per night for a double. Do not be afraid to ask to see the room in advance—it's common practice in Bolivia—and take your time when you do.

WHAT IT COSTS IN BOLIVIANOS					
	¢	$	$$	$$$	$$$$
Restaurants	under (Bs)10	(Bs)10–(Bs)20	(Bs)20–(Bs)50	(Bs)50–(Bs)90	over (Bs)90
Hotels	under(Bs)30	(Bs)30–(Bs)100	(Bs)100–(Bs)300	(Bs)300–(Bs)700	over Bs)700

Restaurant prices are based on the median main course price at dinner. Hotel prices are for two people in a standard double room with bathroom in high season.

VISITOR INFORMATION

At the present time there are no official tourist information offices outside Bolivia. In-country, the InfoTur offices—a new state initiative—are well stocked with information, leaflets, and brochures. You can find them at the airports in La Paz, ☎(2)2112008, and Santa Cruz, ☎(3)3369595, also in Uyuni, ☎(2)2622102. You can also check out the growing range of dedicated Web sites, such as ⊕*www.bolivianet. com* or ⊕*www.bolivianweb.com.*

LA PAZ

Perched on the edge of the altiplano, La Paz overlooks a landscape of great—if stark—beauty. If you fly into Aeropuerto Internacional El Alto, the plateau breaks without warning and reveals the deep, jagged valley that cradles the town. At dusk, as the sun sets on the bare flatlands that surround La Paz, a reddish glow envelops the city's greatest landmark: the towering, snow-capped peaks of Illimani.

The city is nestled in a bowl-shape valley and ranges in altitude from 9,951 to 11,930 feet above sea level. The altitude might make things difficult at first, but it also ensures that La Paz is free of heat and humidity, and devoid of mosquitoes and other pesky insects.

Nearly half of La Paz's 2 million residents and most of its indigenous inhabitants live in poorly constructed adobe and brick homes on a barren plateau called El Alto, which has grown so much it is now a separate city—some would say this is an optimistic term. Downtown La Paz is more cosmopolitan, and the south of the city, the Zona Sur, is extremely European in flavor.

GETTING HERE & AROUND

Taxis are the quickest alternative for getting to and from the airport. The current going rate for the 30- to 45-minute journey is around (Bs)45—use a taxi from the rank and you won't be overcharged. Minibuses also service the airport. The cost is approximately (Bs)5, but it's rather a rough introduction to La Paz.

Within the city, taxis and *trufis* (shared taxis), identifiable from the destination sign lodged in the windshield, are cheap and plentiful. Expect to pay less than (Bs)6 for most trips within the city center. Newer radio taxis, identified by the illuminated sign on the roof, are the safest option for tourists. Rates are fixed at (Bs)6 to (Bs)20, depending on the length

TWO WEEKS IN BOLIVIA

It is possible to see many of the most memorable sites in Bolivia in 15 days, but you need to fly at certain stages due to the huge distances, and it's best to start low and work your way up so that you minimize the effects of altitude.

Start in **Santa Cruz**. From here fly northeast to the jungle town of **Trinidad** for a three-day float trip on the Río Mamoré aboard the flotel Reina Enin. The flotel is essentially a large barge with cabins on it; during the day, as you drift, you stop at little villages along the river. Return to Santa Cruz and then fly on to the colonial town of **Sucre**. Spend the fifth day touring its well-ordered colonial streets and museums. Make sure to visit the market in nearby **Tarabuco** if you're there on a Sunday. On your sixth day, take a bus southwest to the colonial mining town of **Potosí**. Remember to take it easy when you get here, as it's very high up. Take a walking tour of the city and visit its churches and museums. On Day 7, take a bus to **Oruro**. Don't hang about here, but take the overnight train to the **Salar de Uyuni**. Drive out onto the Salar and stay the night in the salt hotel, then retrace your steps back to Uyuni, Oruro, and then on to **La Paz**. On your 10th day, visit La Paz's outdoor markets in the morning and then head out to see the **Valley of the Moon** in the afternoon, or just amble along the Prado avenue and people-watch. Visit the fascinating ruins of **Tiwanaku** on the 11th day, then the same day head to Huatajata on **Lake Titicaca** and spend the night at one of the hotels there. On the 12th day, catch the early hydrofoil to **Isla del Sol** to see its sparkling beaches and Inca ruins and spend the night. Wake up for the dawn if you can. On the 13th day, catch the boat back to **Copacabana**. Have a look at the church, grab a final view of the lake from the Cavalry, then get a bus back to La Paz.

of your journey. Cheaper are *micros*, 12-seat minivans that travel roughly the same bus routes. They're quicker and more comfortable, especially if you get the front seat. Listen carefully before you board, as destinations are shouted out the window as the vehicles roll through the city. Better yet, ask a local to help you locate the right one.

Because La Paz is so compact, visiting the city's main sights would seem easy; however, add time if you're walking for climbing the hills and taking frequent breaks to assuage the effects of the altitude. You'll need a couple of days for a thorough exploration, but don't worry about getting lost—if you do, just go down the hill and you'll reach the main avenue eventually.

SAFETY & PRECAUTIONS

Safety never used to be a problem in La Paz, but things are changing, and unfortunately a lot of crime now is directed at tourists. This is unlikely to go any further than opportunistic theft, especially bag-snatching or pickpocketing, but at night and in certain areas it can be worse, particularly around large concentrations of tourists. Be especially careful around Sagárnaga and San Francisco church, and at the Cementario bus terminal, where there have been several cases of kidnappings

Beverages of Bolivia

Even if you're just after a tipple, sipping a glass of wine or having a cool one at high altitude can have a cost. Nonetheless, once you are acclimatized, there are some interesting beverages to sample.

BEER

Each major city still has its own brewery, generally founded by Germans who emigrated here at the same time as they came to the United States, and microbreweries have started to pop up. There's also the CBN, the national beer company. As well as their standard brew, Paceña in La Paz often have special labels, which are always worth trying. Sureña in Sucre is a good bet. Avoid the Carnival beer, Bock—it has more alcohol than Carnival spirit.

LIQUOR

For something a little different, try *singani*, the local liquor. It's best in the potent pisco sour made with lime juice or the slightly smoother *chuflay*, made with lemonade. *Chicha* is a grain alcohol locals concoct by chewing maize, spitting out the resulting mash, adding water, and allowing the mixture to ferment. The sweet, rather cloudy result is drunk mainly in the lowland valleys in and around Cochabamba, and tastes a lot better than it sounds, once you forget how it's made.

WINE

Tarija, in the Andean foothills near the Argentine border, is Bolivia's wine-growing area. Wines have been produced here since the early 17th century. The major producers are La Concepcion and Kohlberg, although you can also buy good unlabeled wines in the *bodegas*. Tarija's Malbec and Cabernet Sauvignon have won international medals.

of tourists. In general, avoid obvious shows of wealth and tourist status such as expensive cameras, keep an eye on your bags at all times, look like you know where you are going, and be aware of what is happening around you. A common scam is for somebody to surreptitiously spray something on you, then help you clean it off, taking everything you have in the process. Be very cautious when using taxis at night—always look for radio taxis or trufis (see the notes earlier in the chapter on safety for more details). This said, La Paz remains in general a safe city and a relief for travelers arriving from other South American countries; a few basic precautions just make this all the more enjoyable.

ESSENTIALS

Buses Expreso Mopar (✉ *Terminal de Buses* ☎ *02/237-7443*). **Trans Copacabana** (✉ *Terminal de Buses* ☎ *02/237-7894*). **Trans El Dorado** (✉ *Terminal de Buses* ☎ *02/235-9153*). **Transporte 20 de Octubre** (✉ *Calle Yanacachi 1434* ☎ *02/231-7391*). **Veloz del Norte** (✉ *Av. de las Américas 283* ☎ *02/231-1753*).

Bus Terminal Terminal de Buses (✉ *Av. Perú* ☎ *02/236-7275*).

Embassies United States (✉ *Av. Arce 2780, Casilla 425, La Paz* ☎ *02/216-8000* 🖶 *02/216-8111* ⊕ *www.usembassy.gov*). **British** (✉ *Av. Arce 2732, La Paz* ☎ *02/243-3424* 🖶 *02/243-1073* ⊕ *www.britishembassy.gov.uk*).

2

Mail Federal Express (✉ *Calle Capitán Ravelo 2401* ☎ *02/244-3437*). **La Paz Post Office** (✉ *Av. Mariscal Santa Cruz at Calle Oruro*).

Rental Cars Hertz (✉ *Av. Heroes del Km 7 #777* ☎ *02/280-0675*). **Kolla Motors Ltda.** (✉ *Calle Rosendo Gutierrez 502* ☎ *02/241-9141* ✍ *kollamotors@zuper.net*). **Imbex** (✉ *Av. Montes 522* ☎ *02/231-6895*).

Taxis Servisur (☎ *02/279—9999*). **Magnifico del Sur** (☎ *02/275—1212*). **Uriarte** (☎ *777—60666*).

Train National Railroad Line (✉ *Fernando Guachilla 494, La Paz* ☎ *02/241-6545* ⊕ *www.fca.com.bo*).

Tour Operators America Tours SRL (✉ *Av. 16 de Julio 1490* ☎ *02/232-8584* ⊕ *www.america-ecotours.com*). **Fremen Tours** (✉ *Calle Pedro Salazar 537* ☎ *02/241-7062* 🖷 *02/241-7327* ⊕ *www.andes-amazonia.com*). **Magri Turismo** (✉ *Calle Capitán Ravelo 2101* ☎ *02/244-2727* 🖷 *02/244-3060* ⊕ *www.bolivianet. com/magri*).

EXPLORING LA PAZ

Heading into La Paz from the airport, the city's main thoroughfare changes names several times: Avenida Ismael Montes, Avenida Mariscal Santa Cruz, El Prado, Avenida 16 de Julio, and Avenida Villazón. The street, a colorful blur of trees, flowers, and monuments, is often clogged with pedestrians and vendors, especially on weekends. On Sunday it's blocked off to traffic completely. At the end of the Prado, the street splits into the Avenida 6 de Agosto and Avenida Arce, which lead to the residential areas of San Jorge and Sopocachi, where many of La Paz's bars and restaurants are located. Continue down the hill on 6 de Agosto and you will eventually reach Obrajes and the Zona Sur.

PLAZA MURILLO

Plaza Murillo and the cobblestone streets that surround it in the downtown area of the city are steeped in history and easy to cover in a morning of wandering. The square dates from 1549, the year after the city was founded, and it's fun just to sit in and watch the world—and the occasional marching band—go by. Nearby you'll find the city's grand governmental buildings and some of its most beautiful churches, as well as the picturesque Calle Jaén.

MAIN ATTRACTIONS

❻
Fodor'sChoice
★
Museo de Instrumentos Musicales de Bolivia. This museum, founded by local musician Ernesto Cavour, is the most complete collection of musical instruments in the nation; if you think it's all *charangos* and *quenas,* you haven't seen half of what Bolivian music has to offer. Seven rooms feature percussion, string, and wind instruments used in the various regions of Bolivia. ✉ *Calle Jaén 711, Casa de la Cruz Verde* ☎ *02/240-8177* 🎟 *(Bs)5* ☽ *Daily 9:30-1:00, 2:30-6:30.*

❸ Museo Nacional de Arte. Commissioned by a Spanish noble in 1775, the National Art Museum holds three stories of paintings and sculpture. The first floor is devoted to contemporary foreign artists; the second to works by Melchor Pérez Holguín, considered to be the master of

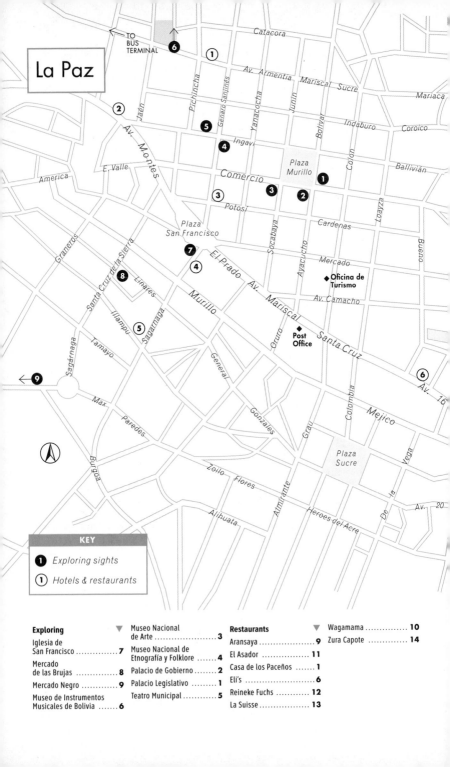

La Paz

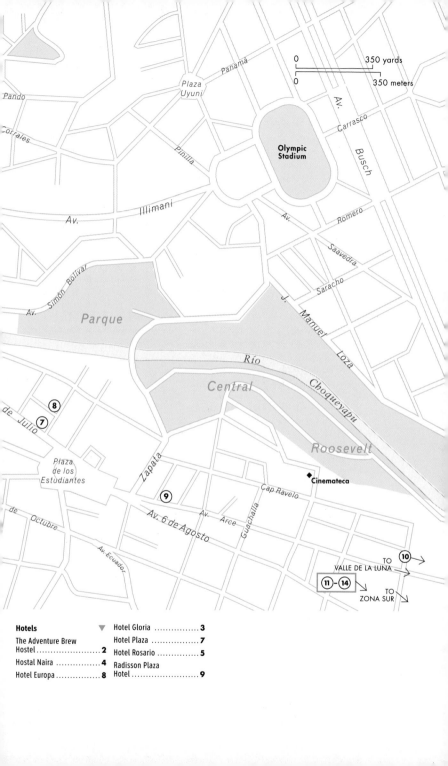

Olympic Stadium

Parque

Central

Río Choqueyapu

Roosevelt

Plaza Uyuni

Plaza de los Estudiantes

Cinemateca

0   350 yards
0   350 meters

Pando

Corrales

Panamá

Av. Carrasco

Av. Busch

Pinilla

Illimani

Av.

Av.

Romero

Saavedra

Saracho

J. Manuel Loza

Av. Simón Bolívar

Av.

de Julio

(8)

(7)

Zapata

(9)

Cap Ravelo

Av. Arce

Guachalla

Av. 6 de Agosto

de Octubre

Av. Ecuador

TO VALLE DE LA LUNA   (10)

(11)-(14)

TO ZONA SUR

Andean colonial art; and the third to a permanent collection of Bolivian artists. You can also relax in the central courtyard beside the lovely alabaster fountain. ⊠ *Plaza Murillo at Calle Comercio, Zona Central (Downtown)* ☎ *02/237–1177* ⊕ *www.mna.org.bo* ⊠ *(Bs)10* ⊙ *Tues.– Sat. 9–12:30 and 3–7, Sun. 9:30–12:30.*

❹ **Museo Nacional de Etnografía y Folklore.** Housed in an ornate 18th-century building, the National Museum of Ethnography and Folklore exhibits feathers, masks, and weavings from indigenous peoples. It has permanent displays on the Ayoreos, who live in the Amazon region, and the Chipayas, who come from the surrounding altiplano. ⊠ *Calle Ingavi 916, Zona Central* ☎ *02/240–8640* ⊕ *www.musef.org.bo* ⊠ *Free* ⊙ *Tues.–Fri. 9–12:30 and 3–7, weekends 9:30–12:30.*

❷ **Palacio de Gobierno.** The imposing Presidential Palace was guarded by tanks and machine gun-toting soldiers until 1982, when the constitutional government was restored following a 1979 coup and three years of military rule. Chocolate-box soldiers now watch the front door instead. In front of the palace is a statue of former president Gualberto Villarroel. In 1946 a mob stormed the building and dragged Villarroel to the square, where he was hanged from a lamppost. The structure, which is closed to the public, is also known as Palacio Quemado (Burned Palace), because it has twice been gutted by fire. ⊠ *Plaza Murillo, Zona Central (Downtown).*

IF YOU HAVE TIME

❶ **Palacio Legislativo.** The meeting place for Bolivia's Congress, the Legislative Palace was built in 1905. This imposing classical structure has a visitor's gallery where you can oberve the legislators in session, which is more entertaining that it sounds. ⊠ *Plaza Murillo, Zona Central (Downtown)* ⊠ *Free* ⊙ *Weekdays 9–noon and 2:30–5.*

❺ **Teatro Municipal.** A handsome building both inside and out as a result of an extensive restoration, the Municipal Theater regularly stages traditional dance and music, as well as classical music performances, theater, and opera. Check the newspaper for upcoming events. ⊠ *Calle Genaro Sanjinés 629, Zona Central (Downtown)* ☎ *No phone.*

PLAZA SAN FRANCISCO

This broad plaza just south of Avenida Mariscal Santa Cruz is the city's cultural heart. Indigenous people come to hawk all sorts of handicrafts, as well as more prosaic goods, such as cassette tapes, watches, and electrical gadgets. If you're lucky, you'll see a wedding at the beautiful Iglesia de San Francisco. Behind this plaza is a network of narrow cobblestone streets full of tourism agencies, craft shops, and travelers' bars and hostels. Try to do your shopping away from Sagárnaga Street, the heart of backpacker land.

❼ Fodor'sChoice ★ **Iglesia de San Francisco.** Considered one of the finest examples of Spanish-colonial architecture in South America, the carved facade of the 1549 Church of San Francisco is adorned with birds of prey, ghoulish masks, pine cones, and parrots—a combination of Spanish and Indian motifs created by local artisans who borrowed heavily from

2

the style then popular in Spain. Crafts stalls line the church wall; most days you'll find colorful weavings and handmade musical instruments. Climb the narrow stairs to the roof for great views of downtown La Paz, or stay grounded in the café inside the church. ⊠ *El Prado at Calle Sagárnaga.*

8 **Mercado de las Brujas.** On Calle Linares, just off bustling Calle Sagárnaga, you'll find the Witches Market, where indigenous women in tall derby hats sell lucky charms, curses, and ingredients for powerful potions. If you are building a new house, you can buy a dried llama fetus to bury in the yard for good luck. Not the best place to find gifts for the folks back home, perhaps.

9 **Mercado Negro.** Near the intersection of Calle Max Paredes and Calle Graneros, the streets are filled with peddlers hawking clothing and household goods, as well as traditional medicines. Tucked into alleys and courtyards are *tambos* (thatch-roof structures) where you can purchase oranges, bananas, and coca leaves. The leaf is chewed by farmers and miners (and tourists) to ward off hunger and the effects of the altitude. It tastes awful.

WHERE TO EAT

La Paz restaurants are becoming increasingly cosmopolitan, and though there is still a lack of sophistication in dining out, the range is improving. Alongside a vast array of establishments serving traditional Bolivian fare, you can now choose between a small but excellent handful of sushi restaurants, get thoroughly carnivorous at one of the many Argentinian grill houses, go upmarket with new Swiss/Bolivian cuisine, or splash out on traditional dishes from the old country, Spain. The area around Plaza de los Estudiantes and the residential neighborhood of Sopocachi have a good selection of cheap eating. For a more international and expensive experience, head down to the southern area of the city, where you will also find the café-terrace set lounging around. Wherever you go, look out for the *almuerzo* if you're after a good-value set lunch.

$$$-$$$$
LATIN
AMERICAN
Fodor'sChoice
★
✕**Aransaya.** From its location on the penthouse floor of the Radisson Plaza Hotel, this upmarket, formal restaurant gives diners spectacular views of the city. The presentation of the Bolivian and international cuisines is excellent, and so is the service, which is good, because you'll have to wait for your dinner. A place to impress your guests. ⊠ *Av. Arce 2177* ☎ *02/244–1111* ⊟ *AE, MC, V.*

$$-$$$
ARGENTINE
★
✕**El Asador.** Eat anything you can cut off a cow at this Argentine-owned grill in the south of the city. There's also chicken and pork, all served on sizzling hot plates. Fast, efficient service, generous portions, and cheap prices, which include side dishes, make this a popular weekend eatery. ⊠ *Av. Montenegro 740* ☎ *02/279–1962* ⊟ *AE, MC, V.*

$$$-$$$$
LATIN
AMERICAN
✕**Casa de los Paceños.** Get the real Bolivian eating experience at this fancier version of all those cheap restaurants you see downtown. Unfortunately the real experience includes the service, which is dismal. Be

CLOSE UP

Bolivian History

Almost everywhere in Bolivia you'll stumble across reminders of the country's long, eventful, and tragic history. A civilization said to be more advanced than the Inca thrived in Bolivia sometime between 600 BC and AD 1200 in an area 90 km (50 mi) west of La Paz called Tiwanaku. It's considered by many to be the "cradle of the American civilizations." When the Inca arrived, the city was already in ruins, possibly destroyed by an earthquake. Spanish conquistadors conquered the Inca civilization in the 1500s—their stay has left its mark, particularly in Sucre and Potosí.

From its earliest days, Bolivia's fortunes have risen and fallen with its mineral wealth. Centuries ago it was the Inca and Aymara who dug deep for precious silver. In the 17th century, Spain's colonization of South America was fueled largely by the vast amounts of silver hidden deep in Cerro Rico, the "Rich Hill" that towers over Potosí in southern Bolivia. Cerro Rico's seemingly inexhaustible lode, first discovered in 1545, quickly brought thousands of prospectors to what was at the time the greatest mining operation in the New World. During the 17th and 18th centuries Potosí was the most populous and wealthiest city in the Americas. For

the Spanish, the phrase *"vale un Potosí"* ("worth a Potosí") became a favorite description for untold wealth. But there's a darker side to the story. Some 8 million indigenous Quechua people died in the mines after being forced to stay inside the airless tunnels for as long as six months. Even today, men who work in the mines have far shorter than average life spans and suffer from the same fates as their ancestors.

Bolivia was named in honor of its liberator, Simón Bolívar, who proclaimed the country's independence from Spain in 1825; until then, it had been simply called Alto Peru. The country was once much, much larger than it is today, but losing wars has been a costly habit. It originally extended to the Pacific, but after rich deposits of nitrates were discovered in the Atacama Desert, Chile began to eye the region. During the War of the Pacific that broke out in 1879, Chile captured Bolivia's short stretch of coastline. Bolivia stubbornly believes that someday it will once again have a seaport. In addition, Bolivia lost 38,000 square mi when Brazil annexed a large part of the Amazon basin in 1903, then twice as much again after a dispute with Paraguay in 1938.

patient, because the food, especially the *chairo* soup, is very good. ⊠ *Av. Sucre 856* ☎ *02/244–1111* ▤ *AE, MC, V.*

$$
AMERICAN ✕ **Eli's.** There are branches of this cheap and cheerful American-style diner all over the city but the oldest and most interesting is inside the Monje Campero cinema. You may not spot James Dean huddled over a coffee in a booth, but he'll certainly be up on the wall with a thousand other stars, none of them as old as the waiters. Huge menu and tiny prices. ⊠ *Av. El Prado 1495* ▤ *No credit cards.*

$$$
GERMAN ✕ **Reineke Fuchs.** Monster sausages, mustard, and brown bread, towering glasses of *weisbier*—you'll get the whole German experience at this popular restaurant, with branches in the center and the south of the city. Imbibe cautiously: the drinks will leave you with a sore head,

2

and wallet. ⊠ *Av. Montenegro/Calle 18 (zona sur) and Pasaje Jauregui 2241 (Downtown)* ☎*02/277–2103* ☰*AE, MC, V.*

$$$–$$$$
LATIN
AMERICAN

✕ **La Suisse.** Don't be fooled by the Swiss-chalet frontage and the name, this is modern Bolivian cuisine at its best. It may feel like you're sitting inside a cuckoo clock, but the dining is excellent. Try sticking with the starters and get a range of things to try, or fork out on a llama steak and a fondue to follow. It's the place to go for birthdays, anniversaries, and funerals, so book your table. ⊠ *Av. Muñoz Reyes 1710* ☎*02/279–3160* ☰*MC, V.*

$$$–$$$$
JAPANESE
Fodor'sChoice
★

✕ **Wagamama.** The specialty is fresh trout from Lake Titicaca cooked Japanese style, but the sushi and noodle dishes are excellent too, and the hot plate is noisy fun. ⊠ *Pasaje Pinilla 2557, off Av. Arce, 1 block downhill from Plaza Isabel la Católica* ☎*02/224–4911* ☰*MC, V* ⊘ *Closed Mon.*

$$$–$$$$
SPANISH

✕ **Zuracapote.** You'd think you were back in the old country at this high-concept Spanish restaurant, and that includes the prices. The wine menu is probably the best in La Paz. Avoid the main dishes—which can be insipid—and choose a selection of tapas and a good Chilean or Argentinian wine. ⊠ *Calle Federico B., 28B* ☎*02/211–9788* ☰*MC, V.*

WHERE TO STAY

Although the number of rooms in La Paz increases every year, hotels are often booked solid during holidays and festivals. Make reservations at least a month in advance when possible. Inexpensive hotels and hostels tend to be located near Calle Sagárnaga and around the bus terminal.

¢

🏨 **The Adventure Brew Hostel.** Probably the most bearable of the recent crop of backpacker hostels staggering drunkenly onto the Bolivian hotel market, this well-run establishment just down from the bus station offers good services—including an on-site microbrewery—and the usual crop of free offers. You do however need to pay in advance by credit card, which may not be entirely convenient. **Pros:** Really well-informed staff, the food, and the endless partying. **Cons:** Located right on a very busy road, the payment policy, and the endless partying. ⊠ *Av. Montes 533* ☎*02/246–1614* 🖷*02/236–0831* ⊕*www.theadventure brewhostel.com* ⌂ *In-hotel: restaurant* ☰*V.*

$$

🏨 **Hostal Naira.** This charming and consistently popular hostel, whose bright, cheerful rooms surround a central courtyard, sits above the famous Peña Naira, where groups perform traditional folk music. There's always hot water—a luxury at this price range—and the service is excellent. **Pros:** Staff really seem to care, pop downstairs for your peña. **Cons:** The tourist-intense neighborhood can be tiring. ⊠ *Sagárnaga 161* ☎*02/235–5645* 🖷*02/231–1214* ⊕*www.hostalnaira.com* ⏎*22 rooms* ⌂ *In-hotel: restaurant, laundry facilities, Internet* ☰*No credit cards.* ⦿*CP*

$$$$
Fodor'sChoice
★

🏨 **Hotel Europa.** The view of snowcapped Mt. Illimani from the rooftop garden sets this downtown hotel apart. There's original artwork on display in the lobby, and the restaurant does great breakfasts. Aside from that, it's a standard five-star range of facilities. The fitness center and pool are popular with expats. **Pros:** The crepes and the bar. **Cons:** Tricky access, endless wedding receptions. ⊠ *Calle Tiahuanacu 64* ☎ *02/231–5656, 0800/10–5656 toll-free in Bolivia* 🖷 *02/231–3930* ⊕ *www.hoteleuropa.com.bo* 🖛 *110 rooms* ⚘ *In-room: dial-up. In-hotel: restaurant, room service, bars, pool, gym, laundry service* 🖃 *AE, MC, V.*

$$$ 🏨 **Hotel Gloria.** This clean, friendly hotel a block from Plaza San Francisco has an inexpensive rooftop restaurant that specializes in international and vegetarian dishes. It also has a tour desk in the lobby. Don't be put off by the clunky English on the Web site. **Pros:** Friendly staff, good location. **Cons:** Rooms can be gloomy, bathrooms even more so. ⊠ *Calle Potosí 909* ☎ *02/240–7070* 🖷 *02/240–6622* ⊕ *www.hotel gloria.com.bo* 🖛 *90 rooms, 2 suites* ⚘ *In-hotel: 2 restaurants, bar* 🖃 *AE, MC, V.*

$$$$ 🏨 **Hotel Plaza.** The rooftop restaurant and bar of this luxurious but now aging business hotel have excellent views of La Paz and the Andes. Ask for a room facing Mt. Illimani; besides good views, you'll have less noise from the street. **Pros:** As central as you can get. **Cons:** Now rather aged, hard to justify its five-star status. ⊠ *Av. 16 de Julio 1789* ☎ *02/237–8311* 🖷 *02/237–8318* 🖛 *175 rooms, 10 suites* ⚘ *In-hotel: 2 restaurants, bars, pool, gym, laundry service* 🖃 *AE, MC, V.*

$$ 🏨 **Hotel Rosario.** This charming, Spanish-style hotel has had a complete makeover and expansion. The sunny courtyard has a fountain surrounded by clay pots overflowing with flowers. Rooms are on the small side, but most have private baths and all are clean and bright; many have spectacular views of Chacaltaya. The restaurant has live music from 8 to 9 Friday and Saturday. The travel agency, Turisbus, has an office in the lobby. **Pros:** The architecture, the no-smoking policy (unusual in La Paz), and the sister hotel at the Lake. **Cons:** Rooms can be very cramped. ⊠ *Calle Illampu 704* ☎ *02/245–1658 or 02/245–6634* 🖷 *02/245–1991* ⊕ *www.hotelrosario.com* 🖛 *41 rooms, 1 suite* ⚘ *In-hotel: restaurant* 🖃 *AE, MC, V.*

Fodor'sChoice

★

$$$$ 🏨 **Radisson Plaza Hotel.** Yet another luxury hotel with great views. The focus at this high-rise business hotel not far from Plaza de los Estudiantes is on luxury and service. Upper-floor rooms have excellent views of the city and the surrounding mountains, as does the rather upscale rooftop restaurant. **Pros:** The genuine focus on clients. **Cons:** Rather antiseptic atmosphere and not very Bolivian. ⊠ *Av. Arce 2177* ☎ *02/244–1111, 800/333–3333 in U.S.* 🖷 *02/244–0402* ⊕ *www.radisson.com/lapazbo* 🖛 *239 rooms, 7 suites* ⚘ *In-room: safe. In-hotel: 2 restaurants, bar, pool, gym, laundry service, airport shuttle* 🖃 *AE, MC, V.*

NIGHTLIFE

Bars and clubs open and close in La Paz in the blink of a llama's eyes, but some have stood the test of more than a couple of months of existence and are worth visiting, especially for live music. To check what's going on and what's still open, pick up a free weekly culture and nightlife guide, such as *Mañana Seguro* or *Afuera*.

Corruption

Like most developing countries, Bolivia has a serious corruption problem. Despite government efforts to take a hard line, the problem continues to run throughout society, from a traffic cop's request for "collaboration" to a government minister's filling up his offshore accounts with federal reserve. You may not notice anything if you are traveling light, but stay any length of time and you will have to deal with it.

You need to decide where you stand. Refuse to cooperate and pay nothing, and you will waste huge amounts of time wrestling with Bolivian bureaucracy—and you can never win against Bolivian bureaucracy. Dig into your pocket whenever you need to, and this will mean digging really deep once people realize you are ready to do this. You can take the middle ground—the average traffic policeman makes less than $40 a month, and your (Bs)1 "fine" for going the wrong way up a one-way street will help him put food on the table. It's your choice, but be aware of the impact either way.

BARS

Even if you are not a party animal, we recommend visiting a bar or two in La Paz. Most have a mixed, friendly crowd, play great music—often live—and are lots of fun. People go to socialize, dance, and celebrate the weekend, even if it's Monday.

Sopocachi, southeast of the Plaza de los Estudiantes, has the largest concentration of bars, many around Plaza Aboroa. Avoid spending too much time in the plaza, especially late at night—it gets a bit rough after midnight. **Mongo's Rock Bottom Cafe** (⊠ *Hermanos Manchego 2444* ☎ *02/244–0714*) has been around for years, but is still one of the most popular bars in town thanks to the music, often live, and the friendly mixed crowd of locals and tourists. It also has one of the most interesting menus in the city. Reserve first to avoid the squeeze. **RamJam** (⊠ *Presbiterio Medina 2421* ☎ *02/242–2295*) is newer, but with a similar vibe for a yuppy crowd: you can mix air with your liquor at the oxygen bar on the second floor of the bar.

Traffic (⊠ *Av. Arce 2549* ☎ *02/211–8033*) is probably the hippest bar in town once the music, techno, trance, and ambient kicks off after 10. It attracts a young, relaxed dance crowd. **Diesel Nacional** (⊠ *Av. 20 de Octubre 2271* ☎ *02/242–3477*) is a high-concept bar up from Aboroa with friendly service and a quirky menu. You can remember your bohemian roots and gawp at La Paz's hippies at lovely old **Boca y Sapo** (⊠ *Indaburo 654*).

Well-to-do thirtysomethings hole up with '60s, '70s and '80s music videos and pricey beer at **Capotraste** (⊠ *Av. Montenegro/Calle 18 San Miguel* ☎ *02/277–2856*). Take a look at their menus—every one is a classic rock album.

DANCE CLUBS

Forum (✉*Calle Víctor Sanjinés 2908* ☎*02/232–5762*) is a cavernous club two blocks from Plaza España. It's frequented mainly by the under-twenty set and American Marines. **Mongo's** (✉*Hermanos Manchego 2444* ☎*02/235–3914*) turns into a lively club in the evening Thursday through Saturday, playing a blend of Latin dance and modern house and disco. Get there early or expect a long wait.

LIVE MUSIC

Almost every bar in La Paz plays live music, but if you want to see what's happening on the modern scene, try **Equinoccio** (✉*Av. Sanchez Lima 2191* ☎*706–12413*). There is live jazz and a real jazz vibe almost every night at **Thelonius** (✉*20 de Octubre 2172* ☎*02/242–4405*).

PEÑAS

Peñas are nightclubs that showcase traditional Bolivian music and dance. The energetic live performances—as popular with Paceños as they are with tourists—cost from $8 to $20 per person. Dinner is usually included. The most famous is **Peña Naira** (✉*Sagárnaga 161* ☎*02/235–0530*), near Plaza San Francisco. Shows are a bargain at $4–$5. **Casa del Corregidor** (✉*Murillo 1040* ☎*02/236–3633*) has performances most evenings.

THE ARTS

For concert, theater, and cinema listings, pick up a copy of the Spanish-language *La Prensa, La Razón,* or *El Diario.* or grab a copy of one of the free weekly culture and nightlife guides, such as *Mañana Seguro* or *Afuera.* You'll find these in most bars and restaurants, and cultural centers such as the *Alliance Française* or the *Goethe-Institut.*

CINEMA

La Paz has a small selection of cinemas showing mainstream releases, but the best place to see both these and art-house stuff is at the **Cinemateca** (✉*Calle Oscar Soria, casi esq. Rosendo Gutierrez* ☎*02/2444090* ⊕*www.cinematecaboliviana.org*). As well as having the most comfortable seats and best equipment, it's also a library of Bolivian film and an exhibition space, the whole thing housed in a stunning new building.

GALLERIES

The **Galería Emusa** (✉*Av. 16 de Julio 1607* ☎*02/375–042*), in El Prado, hosts rotating exhibits of Bolivian sculpture and art. **Arte Unico** (✉*Av. Arce 2895* ☎*02/232–9238*) mounts varied exhibits. For modern work, try the **Arte Espacio Caf** (✉*Av. Arce 2915* ☎*02/243–3333*) or **Galeria Nota** (✉*René Moreno 1335* ☎*02/279–3773*).

THEATER

The **Teatro Municipal** (✉*Calle Genaro Sanjinés 629* ☎*02/237–5275*) stages folk events and traditional music and dance concerts. It's worth going just to see the refurbished building. Check listings for upcoming events.

Bolivian Crafts

Bolivia's rich selection of crafts includes silver jewelry, handwoven rugs, intricate embroidery, and traditional musical instruments such as the *quena* (flute) and *charango* (mandolin). You'll also find sweaters, gloves, scarves, and ponchos made from alpaca or llama wool. Both materials make for excellent fabrics. Crafts shops, like other types of business in Bolivia, are usually grouped together. In La Paz, for instance, most can be found on Calle Sagárnaga. It's always worth looking for cooperatives outside the capital, however. These sell traditional textiles made in rural areas, especially in the provinces of Chuquisaca and Potosí. The shawls, hats, and skirts worn by highland women are sold in most of the local markets and in some stores in La Paz, but shopkeepers sometimes refuse to sell some types of traditional garments to foreigners. However, the felt bowler hats are for sale everywhere, and make an interesting fashion statement back home. Due to the low level of tourism, souvenirs tend to be realistically priced. Although bargaining is expected, many sellers will drop their prices only by small amounts, typically 5% to 10%.

SHOPPING

MARKETS

Calle Sagárnaga, near Plaza San Francisco, is a good place to look for local handicrafts. Along the tiny streets that lead off to the right and left are numerous crafts shops. On Calle Linares, just off Calle Sagárnaga, you'll find the **Mercado de las Brujas.** The Witches Market is where you'll find folk remedies and herbal treatments. For Aymara embroidered shawls, try the **Mercado Negro** on Calle Max Paredes. Prices start at $15 and peak at more than $200 for those made of buttery-soft vicuña wool. Colorful *polleras*, the traditional skirts worn by indigenous women, are priced between $50 and $100; bowler hats start at around $20. For the ultimate flea-market experience, head up to El Alto on Thursday or Sunday to one of the largest markets in the world, where you can buy anything from a forklift truck to a Kalishnikov rifle. There's no address, as it covers almost the whole city. Don't carry anything at all with you: pickpocketing is rife.

SPECIALTY SHOPS

Before you begin bargain hunting for alpaca sweaters, visit one or two stores to get an idea of what to look for. High-quality hand-knit designs that sell for around $100 here fetch three times that amount in the United States. The shops along Calle Sagárnaga, near Plaza San Francisco, are a good place to compare quality and price, but also venture into the streets above for better bargains.

Artesanías Sorata (⊠*Calle Linares 862* ☎*02/231–7701*) carries traditional alpaca knitwear with ethnic designs. **Casa Fisher** (⊠*Av. Mariscal, Handal Center* ☎*02/239–2946*) is known for high-quality knits. One of the best places in town to buy reasonably priced *chompas,* colorful jackets made with traditional textiles, is **Coral** (⊠ *Calle Linares 836* ☎ *02/234–2599*).

If you are interested in Bolivian and South American art, music, and literature, then **Escaparate** (⊠ *Calle 21, 8446* ☎ *02/277–5700* ⊕ *www.boliviacultural.com*) is the best place in La Paz, if not the country. The collection is excellent, and there is usually an art exhibition in the store too. They'll let you sit around for hours, and the owner speaks English.

SPORTS

SOCCER

Bolivians would be lost without their weekly soccer fix. Even the poorest, most remote villages have a playing field. Games are usually played on the only flat piece of land in town, so sheep and cows often graze on the field when there's not a game, and through-traffic may interrupt proceedings. La Paz has two teams: Bolívar and the Strongest. Both compete in the **Estadio Hernando Siles** (⊠ *Plaza de los Monolitos* ☎ *02/235–7342*), in the Miraflores district. The spectacle is always very entertaining, although the soccer can be terrible. You can also watch an entire stadium full of people trying to sit in the shade. Check local press or TV for games.

SIDE TRIPS FROM LA PAZ

TIWANAKU
72 km (44 mi) west of La Paz.

★ An hour's drive west of La Paz, Tiwanaku (also spelled Tiahuanacu) is Bolivia's most important archaeological site. Partial excavations have revealed the remains of five different cities, one built on top of the other. The site's most impressive monument is the 10-ton La Puerta del Sol (Gate of the Sun), an imposing stone fixture believed to be a solar calendar built by a civilization that surfaced around 600 BC and mysteriously disappeared around AD 1200. The gate is part of an elaborate observatory and courtyard that contain monoliths and a subterranean temple. Although the site lacks the sweep and splendor of Peru's Machu Picchu, it does provide a glimpse into the ancestry of the Aymara, who still farm the ingeniously constructed terraces built centuries ago.

Start your visit with the museum next to the ruins. It displays artifacts found at the sight, the most spectacular of which is a 20-ton, 7.3-meter (24-foot) tall monolithic statue sculpted out of red sandstone. The monolith was discovered by an American, Wendell C. Bennett, during excavations in 1934, and since then had been on display in an open-air garden museum in La Paz, where it was being seriously eroded by weather. It was returned to Tiwanaku when the new indoor museum opened in 2002. Admission to the ruins and the museum is around US$10.

CLOSE UP

Festivals

The two-week **Feria de Alasitas** takes place in La Paz beginning January 24. It's an orgy of wishful thinking, as everybody buys miniature versions of the things they long for, including cars, houses, visas to the US, wads of euros, and gigantic penises, and get them blessed by the Pachamama. Even the newspapers are published in tiny editions. The creativity is dazzling, and it's a great souvenir opportunity.

February brings **Carnival,** a weeklong celebration that includes music and dancing all over the country. The biggest bash is held in the mining town of Oruro, 225 km (140 mi) southeast of La Paz. It's a pre-Lenten tradition, started more than 200 years ago, when workers, dressed as devils, danced to honor the Virgin in a festival called La Diablada. Although the Saturday before Ash Wednesday is the biggest day for the huge groups of dancers, festivities last for a week. Away from the religious spectacle, Carnival is an excuse for some serious partying and can get very rowdy.

Pujllay is a colorful festival commemorating the 1816 victory by the Tarabucan people over the Spanish (a rare event in South American history); it takes place the week following Carnival in the village of Tarabuco. The battle is re-created, but without the hand-to-hand fighting, steel claws, and bloodshed. Nonetheless, the spectacle of drunken, sweating warriors marching down the streets to the battle ground is still stirring, as is the sight of all the tourists being overcharged for handicrafts.

Easter and especially **Good Friday** celebrations, characterized by candlelit religious processions by masked supplicants, are held all over the country, but are particularly impressive in Copacabana on Lake Titicaca. They are preceded by the arrival of pilgrims who have walked from La Paz over the preceding three or four days. Book very very early if you want to stay in the town over the Easter period, and get there a couple of days before; the pilgrims move quicker than the traffic jams on Good Friday itself.

June 24, the **Fiesta de San Juan** in La Paz, is traditionally regarded as the coldest day of the year. It's warmed up with bonfires, hot drinks, and hot dogs, and huge firework displays all over the city—many using suborbital size rockets and enough dynamite to bring down the government. Get a view from high up and enjoy the show.

El Día de Todos los Santos (All Saints' Day) and **El Día de los Muertos** (All Souls' Day) take place all over Bolivia on November 1 and 2. On November 1 families prepare a table full of things that those they are commemorating loved in life—beer, soups, and cigarettes are a common feature—and at exactly noon the dead descend on the table. They remain there for 24 hours, then on All Soul's Day they are gone. Many families then go to the cemetery and party around—and on top of—the graves of their ancestors late into the night.

Since it's not always possible to find a guide at Tiwanaku, it's best to book a full-day tour in La Paz. If you decide to come on your own, take a local bus, which takes 90 minutes, and costs US$2. ■TIP→Be sure to ask about the return schedule so you won't get stuck here, and bring a warm sweater or poncho—the area is frequently windy and cold, as there are no trees to break the wind. There's a small café where you can have a light lunch. If you are in La Paz in June, go out to the site for dawn on the day of summer solstice, it's a moving experience.

> ### BIKING WITH DEATH
>
> Well, you might say your chances are just as good biking to Coroico from La Paz as they are taking a bus down what the UN once proclaimed "the world's most dangerous road," and you'd probably be right. But now the public transport goes down the shiny new highway, so it's just you, the subtropics, and some terrifying drops. Choose your agency carefully, make sure your bike has good brakes before you set off, and don't look down.

COROICO
70 km (43 mi) northeast of La Paz.

Your first glimpse of the small resort town of Coroico will be unforgettable as you come around one of the numerous bends in the road on the long descent down from the Andes. People come here to see Los Yungas, an astounding subtropical region as well as an excellent break from the city of La Paz. Work has now finished on the new road down, which makes this peaceful little town an even more attractive proposition. If you really want to earn your sunbed by the pool, hitch onto a bicycle tour down the old road instead. There are lots of companies doing this, but the oldest, safest, and best (and most expensive) is **Gravity Assisted Mountain Biking** (⊕*www.gravitybolivia.com* ☎*02/231–3849*).

WHERE TO STAY & EAT

$$ ⌨**Hotel Esmeralda.** From the sunny patio at this unpretentious hotel up the hill from Coroico's central plaza you'll get astounding views of the valley below and, if you biked, the road you came down. The hotel is also surrounded by gardens. The restaurant, with a charcoal pizza oven, is good, but get there early to beat the scramble for the buffet dinner. From the hotel you can arrange hiking tours of nearby Parque Nacional Madidi. **Pros:** The gardens and ther views. **Cons:** The walk up to the hotel will finish you off if you've been hiking, the shared bathrooms can be grim. ⊠*5 ms uphill from plaza* ☎*02/213–6017* ⊕*www.hotelesmeralda.com* ⌂*In-hotel: restaurant, pool, Internet, no elevator* ⊟*MC, V.*

$$$$ ⌨**Hotel Rio Selva.** Probably the best hotel in the Yungas, and it can get
☺ very busy as a result. Go during the week to unwind and do very little
Fodor's Choice except listen to the river, slide down a tube into a pool or two, and slap
★ bugs. You can choose from a wide range of room types, but ask for something close to the reception area—it's a long walk from the new blocks to the restaurant and bar area. **Pros:** You don't need to leave the hotel for anything, not that there's anywhere to go. **Cons:** The ferocious insects add to the slightly claustrophobic feel of the place, can

get very noisy on holiday weekends. ⊠*Desvio Km 84, Carretera Cota Pata* ☎*02/289–5559* ⚏*In-hotel: restaurant, pool, Internet, gym, spa* ⊟*MC, V.*

$ 👿**El Viejo Molino.** This beautiful Spanish-style resort hotel is perched high above the valley, among clusters of sugarcane and banana trees heavy with fruit. Relax by the pool or play a few games of tennis. At the tour office you can make arrangements for a rafting trip on a nearby river. The grilled steak in the restaurant is one of the excellent entrées. **Pros:** Good service in a stunning location. **Cons:** Overpriced for this jungle location. ⊠*On hwy. into Coroico, Camino Santa Barbara, Km 1* ☎*02/220–1499* 🛏*28 rooms* ⚏*In-room: safe. In-hotel: restaurant, room service, bar, pool, laundry service, Internet* ⊟*MC, V.*

RAIN FOREST

Fodor'sChoice **Parque Nacional Madidi.** The Chalalan Ecolodge in Madidi National
★ Park offers a great chance to experience Bolivia's rain forest. The lodge, owned and operated by the Quechua-Tacana community of San José de Uchupiamonas, immerses you into a culture that has lived in the tropical rain forest for 300 years. While you're here, be on the lookout for hundreds of species of birds, troops of monkeys, herds of wild peccaries, and the elusive jaguar. You reach the park by taking a one-hour flight from La Paz to the jungle town of Rurrenabaque, where you overnight—and on the next day you take a five-hour canoe trip and a 30-minute walk through the rain forest to your thatch-roof cabin facing Lago Chalalan. A 5-day/4-night package, with three nights at Chalalan, is $399 per person (shared bath; $500 with private bath) plus the air fare. For information, contact **America Tours SRL** (⊠*Av. 16 de Julio 1490, La Paz* ☎*02/237–4204* 🖷*02/231–0023* ⊕*www. america-ecotours.com*).

OFF THE BEATEN PATH **Mamore River.** Fremen Tours' four-day riverboat expedition from Trinidad offers you the opportunity to take a shortcut into the heart of the Amazon basin. Fly from La Paz to Trinidad in the Beni region, then it's a short drive (if you're in the dry season) to the river. The program includes opportunities for day and nighttime animal-spotting, and treks
Fodor'sChoice into the jungle itself. The boat is small but has a good kitchen, and
★ the service is excellent. If you risk it in the rainy season, you'll find a smaller group of travelers accompanying you, which is better—it can get claustrophobic and noisy on board. For information, contact **Fremen** in La Paz.(⊕*www.andes-amazonia.com/*).

LAKE TITICACA

At an altitude of 12,506 feet, Titicaca is the world's highest navigable lake and also one of the largest. It covers an area of 7,988 square km (3,474 square mi) in the altiplano, shared between Peru and Bolivia. Some of the highest peaks in the Andes rise along the northeastern shore. The lake is actually two bodies of water joined by the narrow Estrecho de Tiquina (Strait of Tiquina). The smaller section, Lago Huiñaymarca, is the easiest to reach from La Paz. To see the much larger part, Lago Chucuito, travel on to Peru, or to visit the islands which are the highlight of the lake, include Copacabana on your itinerary.

Considered sacred by the Aymara people who live on its shores, Lake Titicaca was also revered by the Tiwanaku and Inca civilizations. Here you'll find the Isla del Sol (Sun Island) and Isla de la Luna (Moon Island), each with ruins in varying states of decay. According to legend, Isla del Sol is where the Inca Empire was founded when Manco Kapac and Mama Ojllo, son and daughter of the Sun God Inti, came down to Earth to improve the life of the altiplano people. This, some might say, is taking some time—tourism has brought few benefits, and life, clawed out of the barren landscape, continues to be hard for the Aymara Indians who inhabit this area.

Major archaeological discoveries continue both around and in the lake, but for the traveler the real attraction is the beauty of the area, and the undeniable power and energy that emanates from it. Few who visit Titicaca fail to be impressed.

GETTING HERE & AROUND

Renting a car and driving yourself is an excellent way to get to Lake Titicaca. Take the El Alto Highway northwest from the city. The road is paved between La Paz, Huatajata, the strait at Tiquina, and Copacabana, and barring heavy traffic, takes less than four hours. If it's your own vehicle, get it blessed at the church while you are there.

Minibuses run regularly from the gates of El Viejo Cementerio in La Paz to destinations along Lake Titicaca, including Batallas, Huatajata, and Tiquina. One-way tickets are about $1. Private bus companies that collect passengers at their hotel charge roughly $10 round-trip to Copacabana (four hours) and $15 to Sorata (six hours). **Diana Tours** (⊠ *Calle Sagárnaga 328* ☎ *02/235–0252*) and **Turibus** ((⊠ *Calle Illampu* ☎ *02/232–5348 or 02/236–9542*) are two well-known companies operating this route. Companies are also at the bus terminal in La Paz, including TransTur (☎ *02/237–3423*) at Caseta 18.

Crillón Tours, one of the oldest tour companies in La Paz, operate the hydrofoils and the Inca Utama Resort on Lake Titicaca, and the Posada del Inca on Isla del Sol. (⊠ *Av. Camacho 1223* ☎ *02/213–6612* ☐ *02/213–6614* ⊕ *www.titicaca.com*).

HUATAJATA

85 km (53 mi) from La Paz.

This popular weekend escape for Paceños is a regular stop on the guided-tour circuit and the easiest way to experience the beauty of the lake. Huatajata is a practical base for exploring the area, and there is a succession of cheap and not so cheap trout restaurants along the road. The fish is fresh in all of them. For picnics, you can try the tree-lined but heavily littered beach at Chúa, the village beyond Huatajata.

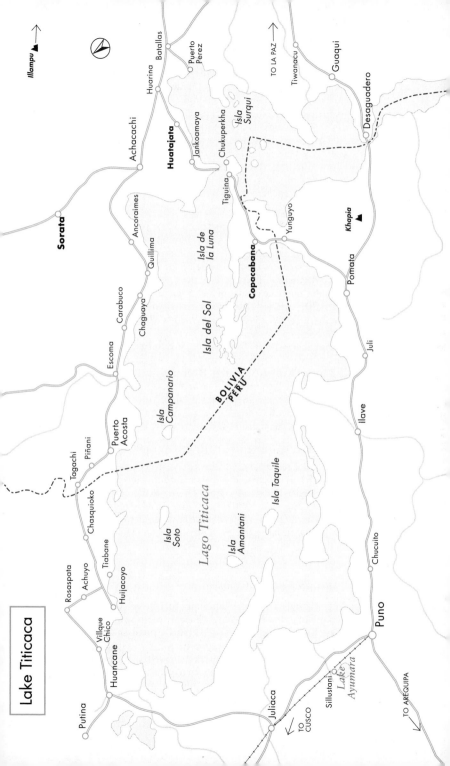

EXPLORING HUATAJATA

Part of the Inca Utama Hotel & Spa is the **Andean Roots Eco Village,** a small but charming museum and exhibition on the culture and history of the region. Replicas of mud houses that many of the Chipaya people of the surrounding altiplano still live in are outside the museum, along with some disgruntled and very shaggy llamas. Probably the most interesting things are the replicas of the tortora boats used by explorer Thor Heyerdahl for his expeditions across the Pacific and Atlantic oceans. The real ones were built just down the coast. The brothers who built these, and who served in the crew for some of these epic journeys, are often here and happy to talk to you for the price of a postcard. The replicas themselves are not only technically impressive but also rather beautiful.

WHERE TO STAY

$$$　🏨 **Hotel Lake Titicaca.** Coming from La Paz, you'll see this well-equipped complex on the lakeshore a few minutes before you reach Huatajata. The furnishings are slightly dated and the pool rather murky, but the sweeping views of the lake make up for it. It's another popular Sunday lunch destination from La Paz. **Pros:** Again, the setting is undeniably special. **Cons:** The hordes of kids from La Paz in the pool on weekends, the indifferent food. ⊠ *Midway between Huarina and Huatajata, look for signs* 🕾 *02/235–6931* 🖷 *02/235–1792* 📞*24 rooms* ♿*In-hotel: restaurant, bar* 🚭*AE, MC, V.*

$$$–$$$$　🏨 **Inca Utama Hotel** This expensive hotel on the Lake includes the Andrean Roots Eco Village, an obervatory, a rather basic spa and gym, and a small children's park. Hydrofoils depart daily from the dock alongside the hotel to the Sun and Moon islands, Copacabana, and Puno (on the Peruvian side of the lake). You can make reservations at the hotel or with Crillón Tours' office in La Paz. The restaurant serves fine international cuisine and is a popular destination for Paceños for Sunday lunch. Your receipt will get you into the **Andean Roots Eco Village.** A boardwalk extends out onto the lake to the Choza Nautica thatch-roof restaurant, which we have never seen open. **Pros:** The setting, the herb garden, and the restaurant. **Cons:** Flavorless decor and service style. ⊠ *Off hwy. from La Paz to Copacabana (Km 45, look for sign), Huatajata* 🕾*02/233–7533, 02/233–9047, 800/488–5353 in U.S.* 🖷*02/213–6614* 🌐*www.titicaca.com* 📞*70 rooms* ♿*In-hotel: 2 restaurants, bar, gym, spa, Internet* 🚭*AE, MC, V.*

COPACABANA

79 km (49 mi) from Huatajata.

After Huatajata the road continues to Tiquina, where you can see the handful of patrol boats that stubbornly persist from what was Bolivia's navy. Your bus or car is loaded onto a small and very unstable raft, which chugs slowly across the strait, while you speed across in a small motorboat. Ask the Navy conscripts manning the crossing for permission if you wish to stay with your vehicle, though you may decide against it once you've seen the rafts. From here it's a 90-minute drive to Copacabana, a pleasant, if touristy, town which provides easy access to the lake and the surrounding countryside. It is also a major pilgrimage destination for devout Bolivians at Easter and lost South American hippies all year.

GETTING HERE & AROUND

You can get a bus to Copacabana from the Cementario in La Paz or much more expensively organize your trip through an agency in town. The most enjoyable option is to rent a car and drive—it takes about three hours and the roads are very good, as are the views. In the center of Copacabana's main plaza, the tourist information booth is the place to find information about the area. The opening hours are erratic, but if they're closed, hotels are more than happy to answer your questions and to help with booking tours.

In Copacabana most hotels will change U.S. dollars, as will many shops along Avenida 6 de Agosto. Some will also change traveler's checks, but don't count on it. Banco Union on Avenida 6 de Agosto in Copacabana exchanges foreign currency and gives cash advances on Visa cards. There are a few casas de cambio at Copacabana's main plaza. At time of writing there are no ATMs.

ESSENTIALS

Post Office **Copacabana Post Office** (⊠ *Av. 6 de Agosto*).

Visitor Info **Information Booth** (⊠ *Av. Abaroa and Av. José Mejía*).

EXPLORING COPACABANA

Copacabana's breathtaking Moorish-style **Cathedral,** built between 1610 and 1619, is where you'll find the striking sculpture of the Virgin of Copacabana. There was no choice but to build the church, because the statue, carved by Francisco Yupanqui in 1592, was already drawing pilgrims in search of miracles. If you see decorated cars lined up in front of the cathedral, the owners are waiting to have them blessed. Walk around to a side door on the left and light a candle for those you wish to remember, then admire the gaudy glitter and wealth of the church interior itself. Throngs of young Paceños do the three-day walk to Copacabana from La Paz to pay homage to the statue with a candlelight procession on Good Friday. You can combine your visit with the semi-scramble up past the stations of the cross on the hill above the town. If the climb doesn't knock you out the view will.

WHERE TO EAT

Copacabana has a wide array of hotels, hostels, international cafés, bars and pizza joints, which reflects its popularity as a weekend destination from La Paz and as the crossing point for travelers from Peru. There's a lot of competition, so most are good value—the best thing to do for lunch or dinner is wander along the two main streets and window-shop first. You can find the famous trout dishes everywhere.

¢–$ ✕ **Snack 6 de Agosto.** Although it serves various entrées, this place is
SEAFOOD   best known for its trout, fresh from Lake Titicaca. There's also a selection of vegetarian dishes. ⊠ *Av. 6 de Agosto* ☎ *02/0862–2040* ⊟ *No credit cards.*

¢–$ ✗**Sujna Wasi.** This Spanish-owned restaurant is tiny, with seating for
VEGETARIAN   fewer than two-dozen people. It's the place to come in Copacabana
for vegetarian food. The restaurant has a small library with books,
maps, and travel information. ⊠*Calle General Gonzalo Jaúregui 127*
☎*02/862–2091* ▭*No credit cards.*

WHERE TO STAY

$$ 🏨**Ambassador Hotel.** This hotel near the lake is aligned with a youth
hostel, which means it offers special rates for students. Although the
rooms are somewhat small, it's hard to beat the view from the rooftop
restaurant. **Pros:** Right on the beach. **Cons:** The rubbish from the lake
close by. ⊠*Calle General Gonzalo Jaúregui, Plaza Sucre* ☎*02/862–
2216* ⤴*42 rooms* ⌂*In-hotel: restaurant* ▭*No credit cards.*

$$ 🏨**Hotel La Cupula.** It's worth staying on in Copacabana just to enjoy this
Fodor'sChoice   alternative-style hotel tucked below the hills at one corner of the bay.
★   Breakfast is exceptional, especially if you're a vegetarian. The recent
addition of five kitchen-equipped bungalows with tranquil lake views,
creative natural designs, and a separate reception area make it all the
more interesting. **Pros:** The alternative vibe, the great vegetarian breakfasts, and the penthouse room—if you can get it. **Cons:** Gets a bit more
than chilly at night, staff can be hard to locate. ⊠*Michel Pérez 1–3*
☎*02/862–2029* ⊕*www.hotelcupula.com* ⤴*39 rooms* ⌂*In-hotel:
restaurant, room service, bar, laundry service* ▭*MC, V.*

$$ 🏨**Hotel Playa Azul.** Many of the comfortable rooms at this hotel over-
look a small courtyard. The most charming thing about this well-located
hotel is its cozy dining room lit with gas lamps. Groups frequently stop
here for the filling and tasty lunches. **Pros:** A good set lunch. **Cons:**
Rather small rooms, can get noisy in that old courtyard. ⊠*Av. 6 de
Agosto* ☎*02/862–2227* ⤴*39 rooms* ⌂*In-hotel: restaurant, room ser-
vice, bar, laundry service* ▭*MC, V.*

$$$ 🏨**Hotel Rosario Del Lago.** One of the nicest accommodations in Copa-
cabana, this colonial-style hotel is a few blocks from the main plaza.
Its clean, homey rooms, including a spacious suite that sleeps six, have
excellent views of the shore. Restaurant Kota Kahuana ("View of the
Lake") specializes (like every eatery in town) in trout caught in Lake
Titicaca, as well as international fare. **Pros:** Friendly staff, good buffet
breakfast, the view of the sunset from any of the rooms. **Cons:** Tiny,
really tiny, showers, and pillows made from local stone. ⊠*Calle Rigoberto Paredes and Av. Costanera* ☎*02/862–2141, 02/245–1341 in La
Paz* ☎*02/862–2140 in La Paz* ⊕*www.hotelrosario.com/lago* ⤴*29
rooms, 1 suite* ⌂*In-hotel: restaurant, Internet* ▭*AE, MC, V.*

ISLA DEL SOL & ISLA DE LA LUNA

12 km (7½ mi) north of Copacabana.

Fodor'sChoice   The largest of Lake Titicaca's islands, **Isla del Sol** is the best place to visit
★   and to stay on the lake. The views of the Cordillera Real mountains
are amazing, especially at dawn and dusk, and the island has beautiful
white sandy beaches and an extraordinary terraced landscape. There
are ruins, including the Inca palace of Pilkokaina and a strange rock

formation said to be the birthplace of the sun and moon, and an excellent Inca trail across the island. Alternatively, you can just laze around and soak up the cosmic energy.

En route to Isla del Sol, boats sometimes stop at **Isla de la Luna,** where the ruins of Iñacuy date back to the Inca conquest. You'll find an ancient convent called Ajlla Wasi (House of the Chosen Women). Stone steps lead up to the unrestored ruins of the convent.

GETTING HERE & AROUND

The most expensive—and comfortable—way to get here is by hydrofoil from the **Inca Utama Hotel** in Huatajata but cheaper boats leave from Copacabana all day. The journey takes about three hours and costs (Bs)30. Once you are on the island, it's walking all the way.

SAFETY & PRECAUTIONS

You may be asked to pay to get onto the Inca trail on the island, and then again at various points along it. The initial payment seems legitimate, and justified, but none of the others, so be firm.

WHERE TO STAY

You will be amply rewarded for your climb up the steps from the port—the higher you go, the cheaper the hostels or *posadas.* They are almost all good, if basic. The north side of the island has more attractive options, including a couple of places on the beach itself.

¢　**Hostal Pacha-Mama.** Located at the north end of the island, this low-budget hostel is a bit unkempt, but it's right on the beach and has hot showers. Ask for a room upstairs; they're cleaner. Breakfast, lunch, and dinner are offered, along with laundry service. **Pros:** Cheap as they come, and the hot water is a novelty. **Cons:** Be prepared to rough it in the rooms, on a very busy road, the payment policy, and the endless partying. *In-hotel: restaurant, laundry* *No credit cards.*

¢　**Hostal Puerta del Sol.** Another budget option at the south end of the island, but this time with private rooms and bathrooms if you pay more. There are excellent views of the Peruvian side of the lake, and the restaurant is good. **Pros:** Right at the southern tip, with quieter and unusual views. **Cons:** Very simple accommodation. *On ridge of island* *73506995/71955181* *www.bolivia-travel.net/puertadelsol* *singles and doubles* *No credit cards.*

$$–$$$　**La Posada del Inca.** Rooms in this beautifully restored colonial-style hacienda on Isla del Sol are small but attractively furnished, and all have private baths. Electric heaters and electric blankets powered with solar energy cut the night chill. The hillside location offers sweeping views of the lake. The restaurant serves meals family-style in the dining room. Rooms must be booked as part of a hydrofoil tour with Crillón Tours in La Paz, making this a very expensive and perhaps unnecessary option. **Pros:** High standard of service and a good restaurant. **Cons:** The pricing, and the fact it's out of place on the island. *02/233–7533* *02/211–6482* *www.titicaca.com* *20 rooms* *In-hotel: restaurant* *AE, MC, V.*

SORATA

45 km (28 mi) north of Huatajata.

Sorata lies nearly 8,200 feet above sea level in a tropical valley at the foot of Mt. Illampu. This is a starting point for serious climbers to climb the snowcapped mountain or for experienced hikers to make the arduous, weeklong trek along the Camino del Oro (Trail of Gold) to the gold-mining cooperatives. Others just come to soak up the stunning scenery and sleep in the shade of the mountains for a while.

GETTING HERE & AROUND

Buses depart half-hourly or when full from the Cementerio in La Paz, cost about (Bs)12. Recommended is **Trans Unificada.** The buses arrive in and depart from Sorata's main plaza. Buses from Sorata to La Paz operate between 4 AM and 6 PM. From Copacabana you can take a Trans Copacabana bus to La Paz, get off in Huarina, and flag a bus to Sorata.

ESSENTIALS

Bus Contact **Trans Unificada** (☎ *02/238–1693*).

WHERE TO STAY & EAT

$$ Hotel Ex-Prefectural Sorata. A sparkling renovation makes the most of this hotel's charming outdoor garden and lovely views across the valley. The restaurant specializes in the traditional dishes of the region. If you are coming from La Paz, the hotel is on the main highway 1 km (½ mi) from Sorata's central square. **Pros:** Lovely setting, and out of town slightly, so quieter. **Cons:** Oh-so-slow service. ⊠ *Carretera Principal Sorata* ☎ *02/272–2846* ☍ *In-hotel: restaurant* ⊟ *AE, MC, V.*

$$ ✕ Pete's Place. Probably the best place to eat in Sorata is actually a res-
ECLECTIC   taurant owned by a Englishman. The menu, however, has something for everyone, meat lover or vegetarian, and the restaurant's owner is a good source of tips and information about Sorata and surroundings. ⊠ *Hostal Don Julio Sorata, Plaza Principal.*

TOURS

You'll get a much clearer idea of the quality of tour operators by looking in Sorata itself than in La Paz. You'll also get a better deal. Below are some recommendations if you want to organize things before you get there:

America Tours normally organize jungle trips, and are very good at it, but they also go to the Laguna Glacier during the April to October climbing season. (⊠ *Office 9, ground floor, 1490 Edificio Av., Av. Prado, La Paz* ☎ *02/237–4204* ⊕ *www.america-ecotours.com*).

Bolivian Mountains offers four-day trekking trips to the Laguna Glacier, as well as most of the peaks in Bolivia. They have very competent guides—a rarity in the mountains of Bolivia—and can organize any routes you'd care to try. (⊠ *Rigoberto Paredes 1401 y Colombia, La Paz* ☎ *02/248–2767* ⊕ *www.bolivianmountains.com*).

CLOSE UP

Trekking Around Sorata

The Camino de Oro and the Illampu Circuit are the two classic treks starting from Sorata, but they are long, arduous, and can be dangerous. Less strenuous undertakings are the two-day trek to the Laguna Chalata or a stunning three-day hike to the Laguna Glacier. Official guides can be found in the office opposite the Residential Sorata. Prices vary depending on what's included, but you should pay around $10 per person per day, with extras bolted on if you need to hire sleeping bags and tents.

The most spectacular trip leaving from Sorata is the six-day bike and boat journey to Ruhrenabaque. Cyclismo Andino (Andean Biking) (☎735–78093) provides a fully provisioned trip with state-of-the-art bikes into the Bolivian rain forest, where you pick up a boat for a river trip to the jungle town. It costs around $250 per person depending on group size.

A good day walk from Sorata is the San Pedro cave, a three-hour walk away around a winding mountain road to the caves, where there is a (Bs)15 entry fee. No guides are needed for this relatively flat hike, which takes in some spectacular views from high above the Sorata River and the valley it has carved in the mountains.

CENTRAL BOLIVIA

The two major cities in central Bolivia, Cochabamba and Santa Cruz, are both southeast of La Paz—but here ends all similarity. Cochabamba, the country's third-largest city, is in a fertile valley in the foothills of the Andes. Often referred to as the "Breadbasket of Bolivia," Cochabamba produces a large share of the country's fruit and vegetables, and much of its meat and dairy products. Nestled in the eastern foothills of the Andes, it is known for its mild, sunny weather. Hot and humid Santa Cruz, Bolivia's second-largest city, is on the edge of the Amazon basin. In addition to agriculture, its economy is fueled by lumber, gas, and oil; the booms of the last few decades have resulted in its being a real economic and political powerhouse state.

GETTING HERE & AROUND

It takes nearly five hours to drive southeast from La Paz to Cochabamba. From La Paz, drive 190 km (118 mi) south to Caracollo, one of the few villages along the way with a gas station, and then head east toward Cochabamba. The drive between Cochabamba and Santa Cruz takes 10 hours on the Nuevo Camino (New Road). It may be new, but don't try this route without a four-wheel-drive vehicle. You can break the trip into almost equal parts by staying overnight at Villa Tunari.

Depending on the state of the road, it takes about seven hours to travel by bus between La Paz and Cochabamba. If you're headed from La Paz to Santa Cruz, figure on a 20-hour trip. One-way tickets for either journey cost between $10 and $15. To avoid standing in the aisle for the entire journey, book tickets at least a day in advance. Many companies have buses that leave several times a day.

SAFETY & PRECAUTIONS

Take the normal health precautions for tropical regions when traveling in this area—drink only bottled water, and don't eat from street stands where food is sitting around. Make sure to bring along plenty of mosquito repellent.

COCHABAMBA

400 km (250 mi) southeast of La Paz.

This bustling metropolis is one of the oldest cities in Bolivia, and many buildings from the 16th century stand along its narrow streets. Built on the traditional grid pattern, the central part of Cochabamba is divided into quadrants beginning at the intersection of Avenida de las Heroínas and Avenida Ayacucho. Streets are labeled *norte* (north), *sur* (south), *este* (east), and *oeste* (west). The quadrant is included as an abbreviation in the address; for example, Hotel Aranjuez is located at Calle Buenos Aires E-0563.

GETTING HERE & AROUND

AeroSur (⊕*www.aerosur.com*) flies daily from La Paz and Sucre to Aeropuerto Jorge Wilsterman in Cochabamba (☎04/422–6548). The airport is 10 km (6 mi) from downtown. A taxi into town is about $5.

ESSENTIALS

Bus Depot **Terminal de Cochabamba** (⊠*Av. Ayacucho at Av. Aroma*).

Currency Exchange **Banco Mercantil** (⊠*Calle Calama E-0201, Cochabamba* ☎*04/425–1865*). **Banco Nacional** (⊠*Calle Nataniel Aguirre S-0198, Cochabamba* ☎*04/425–1860*).

Internet Café **Center Internet** (⊠*Av. de las Heroínas E-0267, Cochabamba* ☎*04/423–3423*).

Post Office **Cochabamba** (⊠*Av. de las Heroínas and Av. Ayacucho*).

Rental Cars **A. Barron's** (⊠*Calle Sucre E-0727, Cochabamba* ☎*04/422–2774*). **Toyota** (⊠*Av. Libertador Bolívar 1567, Cochabamba* ☎*04/428–5703*).

Taxis **Radio Taxi** (⊠*Lanza N-579, Cochabamba* ☎*04/422–8856*).

Visitor Info **Cochabamba** (⊠*Calle General Achá* ☎*04/422–1793* ☉ *Weekdays 9–noon and 2:30–5*).

EXPLORING COCHABAMBA

A gleaming white statue of Christ with his arms outstretched, called **El Cristo de la Concordia,** stands watch on a hilltop overlooking Cochabamba. This is where many people come to get a perspective on this city with a population of more than half a million. There are also astounding views of Cochabamba from La Coronilla, a hill on the outskirts of the city. At the top is a monument called **La Heroínas de la Coronilla,** honoring women who died during Bolivia's protracted War of Independence.

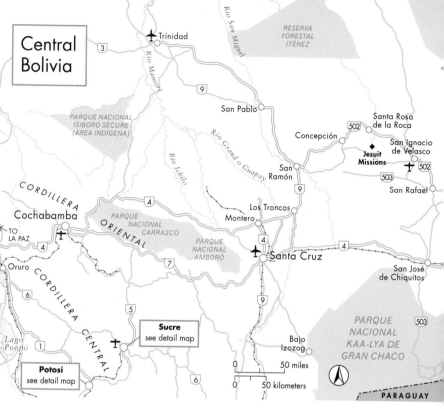

Many of the sights in Cochabamba, a colonial town founded in 1571, are scattered around the palm-lined **Plaza 14 de Septiembre,** where magnolias and jacarandas bloom and pigeons cruise for crumbs. Facing the main square is the **Catedral de Cochabamba,** which was started in 1571 but took more than 150 years to complete. One block southeast from the main square is a church called the **Templo de San Francisco,** a colonial masterpiece built in 1581 but thoroughly renovated in 1782 and again in 1926. Inside the Temple of St. Francis are elaborately carved wooden galleries and a striking gold-leaf altar.

Cochabamba's excellent **Museo Arqueológico** is one of the more comprehensive and interesting collections of artifacts outside of La Paz. On display in the Museum of Archaeology are pre-Columbian pottery, silver and gold work, and strikingly patterned handwoven Indian textiles. ⊠*Jordán and Aguirre* ☎*No phone* 🎟*(Bs)20* ⊙*Weekdays 9–noon and 3–7, Sat. 9–1.*

Across the Río Rocha is the **Palacio Portales,** which was built but never occupied by Simón Patiño, a local tin baron who amassed one of the world's largest fortunes. The mansion and 10-acre gardens reflect his predilection for French Renaissance style. One of the chambers on the upper floor mimics Italy's Sistine Chapel. The mansion, a five-minute taxi ride from the center of town, is now a cultural and educational cen-

ter. ✉ *Av. Potosí 1450* ☎*04/424–3137* 🖶*(Bs)10* ⊙ *Weekdays 5* PM–
6 PM, *Sat. 10* AM–*11*.

WHERE TO EAT

Eating out and eating big is even more important in Cochabamba than
the rest of the country; there may not be international dishes, but for
traditional Bolivian fare the city is unrivalled. Leave yourself lots of
time and don't eat breakfast first. If you are after something lighter—or
resting between lunch and dinner—there are plenty of places for coffee
and cakes, especially in El Prado near Plaza Colon, and in Calle España
and its side streets.

$$$
ARGENTINE
★
✕**Bufalo Rodizio.** At this Argentine-style eatery, all the meat you can eat
is carved at your table by waiters dressed as gauchos. There's also an
excellent salad bar. Reserve a table on Sunday; they are usually packed
with diners enjoying great views of the city. ✉*Edificio Torres Sofer, Av.
Oquendo N-0654* ☎*04/425–1597*.

$$–$$$
LATIN
AMERICAN
✕**Casa de Campo.** This informal and lively restaurant serves traditional
Bolivian dishes—grilled meats and a fiery *picante mixto* (grilled chicken
and beef tongue). You dine outdoors on a shaded patio. ✉*Av. Aniceto
Padilla and Av. Bolívar* ☎*04/424–3937* ▭*MC, V*.

$–$$
CHINESE
✕**Chifa Lai Lai.** This *chifa*, or Chinese restaurant, has the kind of service
usually found only in more expensive places. The food is tasty and
the wines are cheap. Try the Ecuadoran shrimp dishes. ✉*Av. Aniceto
Padilla* ☎*04/424–0469* ▭*MC, V*.

$$–$$$
IRISH
Fodor's Choice
★
✕**Na Cunna.** This Irish pub and restaurant on Avenida Salamanca (near
Lanza) has a wide selection of dishes, a very friendly atmosphere,
and an active role in the city's music scene. A main meal costs about
(Bs)30. Open Tuesday to Saturday from 7.30 PM to about 2.30 AM,
with bands on Friday or Saturday. ✉*Av. Salamanca 577* ☎*04/452–
1982* ▭*MC, V*.

$–$$
LATIN
AMERICAN
✕**Quinta Guadalquivir.** Parrots in cages placed around a small but beautifully landscaped garden lend a tropical vibe to this popular outdoor
eatery. Shady trees make it a pleasant lunch stop. Dishes are a mix of
traditional Bolivian and international food. ✉*Calle J. Bautista 370*
☎*04/424–3491* ▭*AE, MC, V*.

WHERE TO STAY

$$$
🏠**Gran Hotel Cochabamba.** Most of the simple but comfortable rooms
at this two-story hotel overlook the gazebo in the center of the plant-
filled courtyard. The adjoining Restaurante Carillón serves a tasty
pique macho. **Pros:** Reasonable prices and good service. **Cons:** See the
rooms first—away from the courtyard they're rather dark. ✉*Plaza
Ubaldo Anze* ☎*04/411–9986* 🖶*04/448–6911* 📶*43 rooms, 5 suites*
♿*In-hotel: restaurant, bar, tennis court, pool* ▭*AE, MC, V*.

$$$
🏠**Hotel Aranjuez.** This elegant hotel is noted for its lovely gardens
overflowing with bougainvillea. The well-appointed rooms are spacious and comfortable; most have baths attached. A live jazz band
plays in the lobby bar most weekends. **Pros:** Beautiful settings, digital
Internet connection, and welcoming for kids. **Cons:** Rather pricey for
the city. ✉*Av. Buenos Aires E-0563* ☎*04/428–0076 or 04/428–0077*

2

🖨04/424–0158 ⊕www.aranjuezhotel.com ⤵30 rooms, 3 suites ♿In-hotel: restaurant, bar, pool ▤AE, MC, V.

$$$ 🏨**Hotel Portales.** In a quiet residential area in the northern part of the city, this Spanish-colonial-style hotel surrounded by lush gardens is Cochabamba's most luxurious accommodation. It has numerous recreation facilities, from a racquetball court to two heated pools. It's a short taxi ride from the center of town, and local swing bands play in the bar. **Pros:** Nice gardens and a choice of restaurants. **Cons:** The rooms can be rather dilapidated, and no elevator—not good if you are on the top floor. ✉Av. Pando 1271 ☎04/428–5444 🖨04/424–2071 ⤵98 rooms, 8 suites ♿In-hotel: 2 restaurants, bar, pools, gym, laundry service, no elevator ▤AE, MC, V.

$$ 🏨**Hotel Union.** You'll appreciate this hotel's location—a block from the main square. The rooms are simple and clean. Ask for an upper-floor room away from noisy Avenida de las Heroínas. **Pros:** Very central. **Cons:** Service can be indifferent. ✉Calle Baptista S-0111 ☎☎04/423–5065 ⤵43 rooms, 5 suites ♿In-hotel: restaurant, bar ▤AE, MC, V.

SHOPPING

Cochabamba is well known for its alpaca sweaters and leather goods, but don't expect prices much lower than in La Paz. Plaza Colón marks the start of **El Prado** (sometimes called Avenida Ballivián), a shop-lined avenue that stretches north to the Río Rocha. The local market, **La Cancha,** is open daily near Avenida Aroma. It's a good place to browse for less expensive crafts.

Asarti (✉Calle México and Av. Ballivián ☎04425–0455) sells high-quality knits. They also have a showroom at the Radisson Hotel in La Paz. **Casa Fisher** (✉Calle Ramorán Rivero 0204 ☎04/428–4549) sells beautiful alpaca sweaters. **Tipay** (✉Calle Jordán E-0732 ☎04/425–1303) is a clothing cooperative of local women who sell handmade knits in alpaca and cotton.

SANTA CRUZ

900 km (560 mi) southeast of La Paz.

Just 30 years ago, oxen pulled carts through the muddy streets of Santa Cruz and cowboys rode in to wash off the dust and raise some more. Now this is the largest city in Bolivia and the most westernized. Exploitation of massive reserves of natural gas and oil have made the department of Santa Cruz the richest in the country. Add the temperatures to the mix (average 30°C) and you have a very different proposition from the altiplano and La Paz. The people are different, too, more Brazilian in spirit and behavior (especially during Carnival), and the beauty of the women is legendary. Nonetheless, Santa Cruz, with more than 1,300,000 inhabitants, hasn't been completely transformed—you can still find traces of its colonial past in the architecture of the city center. And don't be put off by the discos, country clubs, and burger joints—there are many good reasons to make the trip down, including the Jesuit Missions of Chiquitos, two exceptional national parks (Amboro and Noel Kempf Mercado), and the ancient fortress of Samaipata.

GETTING HERE & AROUND

International flights stop at Aeropuerto Internacional Viru-Viru (☎ *03/334–4411*) in Santa Cruz before continuing to La Paz. Similarly, flights from La Paz stop in Santa Cruz on their way out of the country. The airport is about 15 km (9 mi) north of the city. Buses to the center of town depart every 20 minutes and cost about (Bs)8. Taxis should run about (Bs)50.

Santa Cruz is a driver's town, but taxis are readily available on the streets; exercise caution and always use radio taxis.

SAFETY & PRECAUTIONS

Crime in Santa Cruz is generally not focused on tourists as much as it is in La Paz, for example, but there is more of it, and it's dangerous. Armed robbery, kidnapping, and car theft are more common, and you should take necessary precautions. The best advice is to forget the relative safety of other Bolivian cities and behave as if you are in an average South American capital.

ESSENTIALS

Bus Services **Terminal de Santa Cruz** (✉ *Av. Cañoto at Av. Irala*). **Expreso Mopar** (☎ *02/237–7443*). **Trans Copacabana** (☎ *02/237–7894*).

Currency Exchange **Banco Mercantil Santa Cruz** (✉ *René Moreno at Suárez de Figueroa, Santa Cruz* ☎ *03/334–5000*). **Banco Nacional** (✉ *René Moreno 258, Santa Cruz* ☎ *03/336–4777*).

Internet Café **Café Internet** (✉ *Calle Sucre 673* ☎ *03/335–2161*)

Post Office **Santa Cruz** (✉ *Between Junín and Florida*).

Rental Cars **A. Barron's** (✉ *Av. Alemana 50, Santa Cruz* ☎ *03/342–0160*). **Imbex** (✉ *Calle Monseñor Peña 320, Santa Cruz* ☎ *03/353–3603*).

Taxis **Radio Taxi Equipetrol** (✉ *Av. General Martínez 338, Santa Cruz* ☎ *03/335–2100*).

Visitor Info **Santa Cruz** (✉ *Casa de la Cultura 1st fl., on Plaza* ☎ *03/333–2770* ⊙ *Weekdays 8:30–noon and 2:30–6*).

EXPLORING SANTA CRUZ

The **Basílica Menor de San Lorenzo** was built between 1845 and 1915 on the ruins of a 17th-century cathedral. The imposing church, on Plaza 24 de Septiembre, holds a small museum displaying colonial-era religious icons, paintings, and sculptures. ✉ *Plaza 24 de Septiembre* ☎ *03/332–7381* 🎟 *(Bs)10* ⊙ *Daily 7–noon and 3–8*.

The **Casa de la Cultura** hosts cultural exhibits, recitals, and concerts, in addition to a permanent exhibit of crafts made by indigenous people. ✉ *Plaza 24 de Septiembre* ☎ *03/334–0270* 🎟 *Free* ⊙ *Daily 9–noon and 3–6*.

Fodor's Choice ★ The **Jesuit Missions of Chiquitos**, in the Chiquitania region of Santa Cruz, were built by Jesuit priests in the 17th century for local Christianized Indians. The 10 churches that remain are beautiful examples of a merging of Catholic and local religious influences of that period, as well as the venue of an international festival of Baroque and Renaissance music. It's also a UNESCO World Heritage Site. Ask about tours to the area in agencies in the city.

Lurking in the valleys 200 km (124 mi) from the city of Santa Cruz, the fort of **Samaipata** was once the center of a huge pre-Columbian civilization; there is now doubt that it had any military purpose, but it still impresses. The massive sculptured rock at the heart of the site, best seen from a distance, is a unique monument to Andean culture and development, and one of the largest carved stones in the world. The best way to get to the site is by road from Santa Cruz to the town of Samaipata, (about two hours), then hire a taxi to the fort itself, which is 7 km (4 mi) away. ☎(Bs)20 ☉ Daily 9–5.

WHERE TO EAT

There is a smaller range of hotels in Santa Cruz than in La Paz, and a wider range of restaurants—and both are generally more expensive, reflecting the fact that this is the most business-oriented region of the country.

$$$$
FRENCH ✕**El Candelabro.** International food and a very elegant ambience are provided at this upmarket establishment split into two spaces: a piano bar with live music and a restaurant. Treat yourself before you fly out of the country. ⊠ *Calle 7 Oeste Equipetrol* ☎ *03/333–7248* ▤ *AE, MC, V.*

$$$–$$$$
BOLIVIAN
Fodor'sChoice
★ ✕**La Casa del Camba.** Big and very busy always, but one of the best places to eat regional dishes. The kitchen and service are excellent. The restaurant has a branch out in the countryside too. ⊠ *Av. Cristóbal de Mendoza* ☎ *03/342–7864* ▤ *AE, MC, V.*

$$$–$$$$
BOLIVIAN ✕**Los Hierros.** Barbecue beef is the order of the day, and it's of the finest cuts. Squeeze a little salad on your plate, and if you're brave, an antipasto first. The wine list is huge. ⊠ *Av. Monseñor Rivero 300* ☎ *03/339–2460* ⊕ *www.los-hierros.com* ▤ *AE, MC, V.*

$$$–$$$$
ECLECTIC
★ ✕**Makhassan.** Nice food, nice service, and nice people at this alternative to Yorimichi. The food is European–Asian fusion and it's highly recommended. Only has sushi at night, though. ⊠ *Av. Las Americas 71* ☎ *03/332–2323* ⊕ *www.makhassan.com/* ▤ *MC, V.*

$$$$
JAPANESE ✕**Yorimichi.** One of the most expensive restaurants in the city, and the service is dreadful, but the sushi is excellent, so it's your decision. ⊠ *Av. Busch 548* ☎ *03/334–7717* ▤ *AE, MC, V.*

WHERE TO STAY

$$$ 🏨**Gran Hotel Santa Cruz.** This family-owned hotel dating from the 1930s is a few blocks south of Plaza 24 de Septiembre. Rooms are like a comfortable den; those that overlook the pool have small private balconies. The restaurant serves very good international cuisine. **Pros:** Very comfortable, and well-located. **Cons:** Can get very noisy if your room is next to the pool. ⊠ *Calle Pari 59* ☎ *03/334–8811* ☎ *03/332–4194* ⇆ *40 rooms, 12 suites* ⌂ *In-hotel: 2 restaurants, bars, pool, gym* ▤ *AE, MC, V.*

$$$$ 🏨**Hotel Camino Real.** A free-form pool meanders through the tropical gardens at this low-rise, high-class hotel in a residential neighborhood on the outskirts of Santa Cruz. The Tranquera restaurant serves good international fare. Rooms have air-conditioning. **Pros:** All the amenities you'd expect from an international five-star hotel. **Cons:** Far from the center of town. ⊠ *Calle K 279, Equipetrol Norte* ☎ *03/342–3535* 🖷 *03/343–1515* ⊕ *www.caminoreal.com.bo* ⮐ *104 rooms, 8 suites* ⚂ *In-hotel: 2 restaurants, pool, gym, spa* ⊟ *AE, MC, V.*

$ 🔲 **Hotel Paititi** This comfortable budget option is the sister hotel to the Viru-Viru in Cochabamba. Air-conditioned rooms are available. **Pros:** Good value. **Cons:** The canned music, thunderous a/c, single rooms feel like cells. ⊠ *Av. Cañoto 450* ☎ *03/355–9169 or 03/355–9167* ⊕ *www. hotelviruviru.com/hotelpaititi* ⮐ *40 rooms, 12 suites* ⚂ *In-hotel: Internet* ⊟ *AE, MC, V.*

$$$$ 🔲 **Hotel Los Tajibos.** This sprawling resort hotel on the edge of the city and 15 minutes from the airport is a series of low-slung buildings surrounded by lush gardens. El Papagayo restaurant serves excellent seafood. **Pros:** Huge gardens and lots of water, almost all rooms on the ground floor. **Cons:** It can be a long walk from your room to breakfast, let alone from the hotel to town. ⊠ *Av. San Martín 455* ☎ *03/342–1000* 🖷 *03/342–6994* ⊕ *www.lostajiboshotel.com* ⮐ *185 rooms, 6 suites* ⚂ *In-hotel: 2 restaurants, pool, gym, Internet* ⊟ *AE, MC, V.*

$$ 🔲 **Jodanga.** One of the growing number of backpacker hostels in Bolivia, and a bit more civilized than others. The features are fairly standard for this kind of stay: free beers, Skype address, open kitchen, etc., but they include as much friendly help as they can give you. They even give Spanish classes. **Pros:** Good fun, an airport pick-up (unusual for a hostel), and committed staff. **Cons:** Late-night drinking in the Jacuzzi. ⊠ *El Fuerte No. 1380* ☎ *03/339–6542* ⊕ *www.jodanga.com* ⚂ *In-hotel: Wi-Fi, Internet, laundry, pool, airport shuttle* ⊟ *AE, MC, V.*

$$$$ 🔲 **Yotaú.** The spacious accommodations in this all-suite hotel are more like apartments, complete with kitchens and washing machines. Just outside of Santa Cruz in the suburb of Barrio Equipetrol, this strikingly modern hotel has a landscaped garden. **Pros:** A very wide range of facilities includes a good gym, car rental, and medical care. **Cons:** Very expensive option if you are not with family or friends, and the architecture is not to all tastes. ⊠ *Av. San Martín 7* ☎ *03/336–7799* 🖷 *03/336–3952* ⊕ *www.yotau.com.bo* ⮐ *100 suites* ⚂ *In-hotel: 2 restaurants, bar, pool, gym, laundry* ⊟ *AE, MC, V.*

BARS

Dress to impress and take your credit cards if you're going out in the center of Santa Cruz or in the neighborhood of Equipetrol—most of the bars are very exclusive and very pricey. Nonetheless, it can be very entertaining watching the young and beautiful flaunt it all at one of the high-concept establishments. Have a walk along Avenida San Martín in Equipetrol and take your pick. Fashionable at this writing are **Acqua Blue** (⊠ *162 Beni St.* ☎ *03/339–7435*) in the center and **People's Secret** (⊠ *Av. San Martín entre calles 6 y 7*) in Equipetrol.

SHOPPING

Santa Cruz is not the best place to pick up your handcrafted and hard-bargained-for indigenous piece of art, as most shops are focused on modern creature comforts, but you'll find crafts shops and street vendors scattered around Plaza 24 de Septiembre. **Artecampo** (⊠ *Calle Monseñor Salvatierra 407* ☎ *03/334–1843*) is a cooperative with a colorful selection of handmade hammocks made from locally grown cotton. There are also mobiles and intricate hand-painted woodwork.

2

CENTRAL BOLIVIA TOURS

Recommended day trips in the department of Santa Cruz include the ancient site of Samaipata and Amboro National Park—both are close to the city itself and they can be combined. You can also stay overnight at Amboro and so venture a bit deeper into this excellent park to see its cloud forests and birds. Noel Kempf Mercado Park, on the northeastern border with Brazil, offers a great opportunity to stay in real Amazon jungle, and has a good range of services for tourists. It's best to take five or six days for this and camp in the park. The Jesuit Missions are another highlight of this area, but their distance from the city of Santa Cruz means it's a good idea to have a few days free to visit the churches.

There are numerous tour operators for this area. When looking, make sure the agency you choose is legitimate and worth the money by checking with the municipal tourism authority (☎ *03/378493*) or the tourist office at the airport.

TOUR OPERATORS

Rosario Tours offers trips to all the main attractions of central Bolivia and has an excellent reputation (⊠ *Arenales 193, Santa Cruz* ☎ *03/336-9656* ⊕ *www.rosariotours.com*). **Forest Tours** covers all the main destinations, but with a clear ecotourism focus (⊠ *Cuellar, 22, between 24 de Septiembre and Libertad, Santa Cruz* ☎ *03/337–2042* ⊕ *www.forestbolivia.com*).

Magri Turismo covers all of Bolivia and is a well-established company with offices in many cities. In Santa Cruz you will find them at (⊠ *Guarnes, esq. Potosí, Santa Cruz* ☎ *03/334–5663*).

Viru Viru Travel has a particularly good range of ecotourism tours for the national parks of Santa Cruz, and also covers the baroque music festival at the Jesuit Missions (⊠ *Edificio Oriente, Local 1, Calle Chuquisaca esq. Ballivián, Santa Cruz* ☎ *03/336–4040* ⊕ *www.viruviru travel.com*).

Ruta Verde covers all the main tourist destinations in Bolivia, including the big-three national parks and a trip retracing Che Guevara's last steps. It's Dutch-run, and has a good reputation. (⊠ *Calle 21 de Mayo 318, Santa Cruz* ☎ *03/3396470* ⊕ *www.rutaverdebolivia.com*).

SOUTHERN BOLIVIA

There are some major contrasts in the south of Bolivia, partly because it is so huge. Potosí, steeped in history, most of it bloody, is high, cold, and barren. Tarija, up against the Argentinian border, is warm, friendly, and easygoing. Sucre is somewhere in the middle, an earnest university town and the capital of Bolivia. The Salar de Uyuni is, quite simply, out of this world.

GETTING HERE & AROUND

Although the highways aren't the best, driving can be a nice way to see some areas of southern Bolivia. When visiting Potosí it's best to fly to Sucre and drive from there. You should also consider hiring a car and driver or taking a tour through a travel agency. The highway is good between Sucre and Potosí, but plan to overnight, as it passes through mountains and is not lighted. The best way to get to the wine country of Tarija is by flying direct from La Paz or Santa Cruz.

SUCRE

740 km (460 mi) southeast of La Paz.

Sucre has had many names since it was founded by the Spanish in 1538. The town's first official name was La Plata, but it was just as often called Charcas. In 1776, after splitting the region from Peru, the Spanish changed the name to Chuquisaca. Locals now refer to Sucre as *la ciudad blanca* (the white city)—no wonder, since by government edict all buildings in the center of the city must be whitewashed each year.

It was in Sucre that the region declared its independence from Spain in 1825. The country was named for its liberator, Simón Bolívar. Sucre was the country's original capital, but the main government functions were transferred to La Paz in the late 1800s, leaving the Corte Suprema de Justicia (Supreme Court) as Sucre's main governmental function.

Although its population now tops 200,000, Sucre—with its ornate churches, cobblestone streets, and broad plazas—retains the feel of a colonial town. Its moderate year-round climate and friendly people make it a pleasant if somewhat dull place to stay while taking side trips to Tarabuco or Potosí, or checking out the dinosaur prints outside the town.

GETTING HERE & AROUND

Sucre's Aeropuerto Juana Azurduy de Padilla (☎064/454–445)—about 5 km (3 mi) north of Sucre—has regular flights to La Paz on AeroSur. A taxi ride into town should cost about (Bs)15. Buses bound for Potosí and Sucre leave La Paz daily. The 19-hour trip to Sucre costs less than (Bs)100. Buses between Sucre and Potosí depart approximately every hour. The trip takes about three hours and costs about (Bs)40.

ESSENTIALS

Bus Contacts **Sucre** (✉ *Calle Ostria Gutiérrez* ☎ *04/644–1292*).

CLOSE UP

Sunday Market Foray

If you are in Sucre over a weekend, take a full-day excursion to the village of Tarabuco to experience its famous Sunday market. About 64 km (40 mi) east of Sucre, here you will still see indigenous women wearing tri-cornered hats fringed with coins and men with brightly colored ponchos and leather helmets resembling those worn centuries ago by the Spanish conquistadors. Like many towns in the region, Tarabuco is filled with vendors from end to end selling finely woven belts and *charangos*, a stringed instrument made from armadillo shells. In mid-March Tarabuco is the location of one of South America's liveliest traditional festivals, Pujilay.

Currency Exchange Banco Santa Cruz (⊠ *Calle San Alberto and España* ☎ *04/645–5400*).

Post Office Sucre (⊠ *Av. Argentina 50*).

Rental Cars Imbex (⊠ *Serranoí 165, Sucre* ☎ *04/646–12222*).

Taxis Exclusivo (⊠ *Jaime Mendoza 960, Sucre* ☎ *064/451–414*). Sucre (⊠ *Playa 25 de Mayo, Sucre* ☎ *064/451–333*).

Visitor Info Sucre Oficina de Turismo (⊠ *Nicolás Ortiz 182* ☺ *Weekdays 8–noon and 2–6*).

EXPLORING SUCRE

❶ **Catedral Metropolitana.** Started in 1559, this neoclassical cathedral is famous for its statue of the Virgin of Guadalupe, which is adorned with diamonds, gold, emeralds, and pearls donated during the 17th century by mining barons. ⊠ *Plaza 25 de Mayo* 🖾 *Free* ☺ *Weekdays 10–noon and 3–5, Sat. 10–noon.*

❷ **Museo Charcas.** The most popular exhibits at the Charcas Museum are mummified bodies discovered outside of Sucre in the 1960s. Curators believe the centuries-old mummies were entombed as human sacrifices. Also featured at this university-run museum are galleries of colonial paintings and textiles. ⊠ *Calle Bolívar 698* ☎ *04/645–3285* 🖾 *(Bs)15* ☺ *Mon.–Sat. 2:30–6.*

❸ **Museo de la Recoleta.** Founded in 1601 by Franciscan monks, the Museum of the Retreat displays colonial religious works in a setting of serene courtyards and gardens. Equally noteworthy is the restored chapel with its intricately carved choir seats. ⊠ *Plaza Pedro Anzures* ☎ *04/645–1987* 🖾 *(Bs)10* ☺ *Weekdays 9–11:30 and 3–5:30.*

Fodor'sChoice
★

❹ **Museo Textil Etnográfico.** This museum is housed in the colonial Caserón de la Capellanía. The Textile and Ethnographic Museum preserves the 4,000-year-old weavings and tapestry art of the Andean world, especially communities around Tarabuco. A display of costumes showcases regional fiesta garb; there are also loom demonstrations. ⊠ *Calle San*

Alberto 413 ☎*04/645–3841* ✉*(Bs)16* ⊙*Mon.–Sat. 8:30–12:30 and 2:30–6.*

WHERE TO EAT

Sucre's large student population keeps its many inexpensive restaurants in business. Around Plaza 25 de Mayo, many offer a *menú del día* or *almuerzo* (meal of the day) for $2 or $3. If you're not a fan of spicy food, avoid dishes prefaced with the words *ají* (pepper) or *picante* (spicy).

$-$$
FRENCH
★

✕**Alliance Française la Taverna.** You may not have come to Sucre to eat crepes, but they're very good at this restaurant in the French Cultural Center. The menu also includes coq au vin and ratatouille. Seating is available in the dining room or outside in the courtyard. The location, near Plaza 25 de Mayo and the Universidad San Francisco, makes it a popular spot. ⊠*Calle Aniceto Arce 35* ☎*04/645–3599* ▤*No credit cards* ⊙*Closed Sun.*

$-$$
LATIN AMERICAN

✕**El Huerto.** At this restaurant near the municipal park, adventurous carnivores should try a traditional Bolivian entrée, such as *picante de lengua* (spicy tongue). There's plenty on the menu for vegetarians, too. The outdoor patio has a beautiful garden, and is a pleasant place to linger over a long meal. Bring a sweater at night, as it gets a bit chilly. ⊠*Ladislao Cabrera 86* ☎*04/645–1538* ▤*MC, V.*

$
CAFÉ

✕**Joy Ride Cafe.** As the name suggests, a backpacker café with all that involves, but they also run mountain biking and hiking trips. A great range of Belgian beers, too. ⊠*Nicolás Ortiz 14* ☎*04/642–5544* ⊕*www.joyridebol.com* ▤*No credit cards.*

$
CAFÉ

✕**Penco Penquitos.** For pocket change you can have a sandwich or nibble on an impressive selection of fresh pastries, from eclairs to empanadas, at this café near the university. ⊠*Calle Estudiantes 66* ☎*04/644–3946* ▤*No credit cards.*

WHERE TO STAY

Sucre has many small hotels and hostels, almost all of which are comfortable, clean, and friendly. Most include breakfast.

$$

▨**Hostal de Su Merced.** When you notice the colorful wood ceiling in the reception room—a reproduction of the original painted by a Jesuit priest—you know instantly that this family-owned hotel is a gem. Built as a private home in the late 17th century, the gleaming white colonial structure with a handsome tin roof has large, airy rooms with sunlight streaming in through the tall windows. From the rooftop sundeck you get excellent views of the entire city. **Pros:** A rather beautiful old building. **Cons:** Slightly run-down rooms, and the service is not friendly. ⊠*Calle Azurduy 16* ☎▥*04/644–2706, 04/644-2706, or 04/644–5150* ⊕*www.desumerced.com* ⤢*14 rooms, 2 suites* ♿*In-hotel: restaurant, laundry, Internet* ▤*MC, V.*

¢

▨**Hostal Sucre.** This colonial-style place, just two blocks from Plaza 25 de Mayo, is built around two inner courtyards—which means the rooms are all quiet. A restaurant serves light meals and snacks. **Pros:** A nice old building, lovely courtyards to sit in. **Cons:** Some dark and dingy rooms—stick to the courtyards. ⊠*Calle Bustillos 113* ☎*04/645–1411* ▥*04/646–1928* ⤢*33 rooms* ♿*In-hotel: restaurant* ▤*AE, MC, V.*

Sucre

KEY

- **1** Exploring
- ① Hotels & Restaurants

POTOSÍ

169 km (105 mi) southwest of Sucre.

Potosí has a split and tragic personality. Its soaring churches and opulent mansions call to mind a time when this was the wealthiest city in South America. The sagging roofs and crumbling facades make it difficult to put the town's painful past and difficult present out of your mind.

Silver, tin, and zinc from nearby Cerro Rico made fortunes for the mineral barons who built their grand homes along Potosí's winding cobblestone streets. Tens of thousands of people flocked here hoping to make a little money. In 1650, with a population topping 160,000, Potosí was the largest and most prosperous city, first on the continent and then in the world, and the Spanish even now describe things of great value as "worth a potosí." But that wealth came from the labor of more than 8 million indigenous people forced to work in the mines, most of whom died there.

> **DID YOU KNOW?**
>
> Locals will not only tell you that officially Sucre is still the nation's capital, but they are also prepared to fight for it, and the suggestion to move the seat of government here from La Paz resulted in exactly that, with riots and clashes in the city and mass demonstrations against the move in La Paz. The problem of where the capital should be has become one of the most contentious issues in Bolivia today.

There's another old saying that puts all this wealth into perspective: "Bolivia had the cow, but the other countries got the milk." Potosí is now one of Bolivia's poorest cities. Depleted mines, outdated machinery, and an inhospitable terrain—Potosí sits on a windy plain at 13,452 feet above sea level—are not leading to prosperity. But as more and more buildings are restored (some as an act of contrition by the Spanish), more people are being drawn to one of Bolivia's most interesting cities.

GETTING HERE & AROUND

Potosí has no direct flights, but you can get here directly from La Paz by bus. The journey, via Oruro, takes about 12–14 hours, and can be arduous. A better alternative is to come via Sucre, as the road is better and the journey is short (164 km/3 hours). The only way to get around Potosí itself is to walk. The steep, winding streets and sidewalks are narrow, so pedestrian traffic can often be more of a problem than cars. To visit the museums and historic buildings you'll need a guide. English-speaking guides aren't always available, so consider arranging a tour through a travel agency in La Paz or Santa Cruz.

ESSENTIALS

Buses Potosí Bus Terminal (⊠ *Av. Universitaria* ☎ *02/624-3362*).

Post Office Potosí (⊠ *Av. Lanza 13*).

Taxis I.N.N (⊠ *Calle Frias 58* ☎ *062/222-606*). **Potosí** (⊠ *Zona San Clemente 125* ☎ *062/225-257*).

Visitor Info **Potosí Oficina de Turismo** (⊠ *Cámara de Minería, Calle Quijarro* ☎ *02/225–288* ⊙ *Weekdays 9–noon and 3–6).*

EXPLORING POTOSÍ

1 **Casa Real de Moneda.** The showpiece of Potosí is the Royal Mint, built in 1773 at a cost of $10 million. This massive stone structure, where coins were once minted with silver from nearby Cerro Rico, takes up an entire city block. It now holds Bolivia's largest and most important museum. On display are huge wooden presses that fashioned the strips of silver from which the coins were pressed, as well as an extensive collection of the coins minted here until 1953. There's also an exhibit of paintings, including works by Bolivia's celebrated 20th-century artist, Cecilio Guzmán de Rojas. A guard accompanies all tours to unlock each room as it's visited. The building is cool, so bring along a sweater. To see everything will take about three hours. ⊠ *Ayacucho at Lanza* ☎ *04/622–2777* ⊠ *(Bs)20* ⊙ *Tues.–Sat. 9–noon and 2–6:30, weekends 9–1.*

Fodor's Choice ★ (to left of Casa Real de Moneda)

Fodor's Choice ★ **Cerro Rico.** Five thousand tunnels crisscross Cerro Rico, the "Rich Hill," which filled Spain's coffers until the silver reserves were exhausted in the early 19th century. Today tin is the primary extract, though on the barren mountainside you still see miners sifting through the remnants of ancient excavations. If you don't mind tight spaces, take a tour through one of the mines that are still active. You'll descend into the dark, humid tunnels where hundreds of workers strip down to next to nothing because of the intense heat. ■ TIP➔ **Keep in mind that these mines are muddy, and wear clothes you don't mind getting dirty.** Hard hats, raincoats, boots, and carbide lamps are provided, but take along a flashlight to get a better look at things. The extremely narrow entrance to the mine may scare you off, but go in far enough to give *El Tío* (a statue of a small, grinning devil) a cigarette and add more coca leaves to the pile around his feet. The miners say he brings safety and prosperity.

2 **Convento y Museo de Santa Teresa.** The Convent and Museum of St. Theresa displays a strange mix of religious artifacts. In one room are sharp iron instruments once used to inflict pain on penitent nuns, as well as a blouse embroidered with wire mesh and prongs meant to prick the flesh. Other rooms contain works by renowned colonial painters, including Melchor Pérez Holguín. ⊠ *Calle Chicas* ☎ *02/622–3847* ⊠ *(Bs)25* ⊙ *Weekdays 9–noon and 2–5:30.*

3 **Iglesia de San Lorenzo.** Potosí's most spectacular church, built between 1728 and 1744, has some of the finest examples of baroque carving in South America. Elaborate combinations of mythical figures and indigenous designs are carved in high relief on the stone facade. If the front doors are locked, try to get in through the courtyard. ⊠ *Calle Bustillos* ☎ *No phone.*

4 **Iglesia y Convento de San Francisco.** Built of granite during the colonial period, this was Potosí's first church. It has a brick dome and beautiful arches. On the main altar is the statue of the "Lord of the Veracrúz," the patron of Potosí. It also has many beautiful paintings. A panoramic view of the city can be enjoyed from a viewing platform. ⊠ *Corner of Nagales and Tarija* ☎ *02/622–25399* ⊠ *(Bs)10* ⊙ *Weekdays 2:30–4:30.*

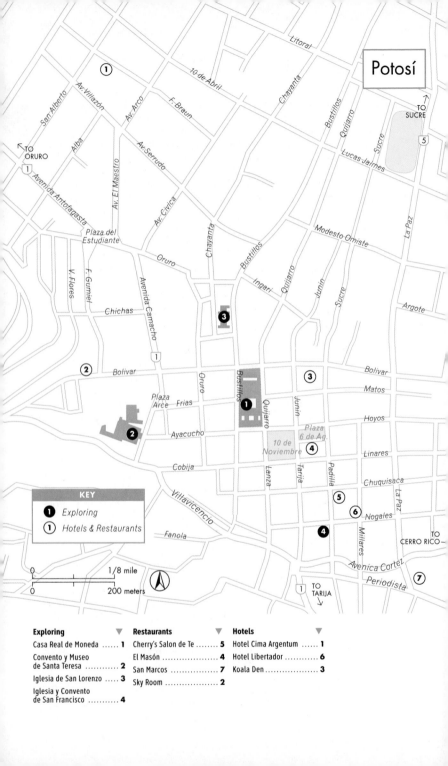

Potosí

TO SUCRE

TO ORURO

TO TARIJA

TO CERRO RICO

KEY
- 1 *Exploring*
- 1 *Hotels & Restaurants*

0 — 1/8 mile
0 — 200 meters

WHERE TO EAT

Potosí is not known for its food, but one thing worth trying is the delicious *kala'purka* soup, made with maize flour and cooked using volcanic stones. You'll be full for days.

$–$$
CAFÉ ✕**Cherry's Salon de Te.** At this delightful coffee shop you can sip mugs of refreshing mate de coca while you ponder the delicious selection of cakes and strudels. ✉*Calle Padilla 8* ☎*02/622–2969* ▱*No credit cards.*

$$
LATIN AMERICAN ✕**El Mesón.** Potosí's most exclusive restaurant has a quiet dining room where you can get both traditional Bolivian and international food. ✉*Calle Tarija at Calle Linares* ☎*04/622–3087* ▱*MC, V.*

$$
LATIN AMERICAN
★ ✕**San Marcos.** Potosí's most unusual restaurant occupies a former silver processing plant. Each piece of ancient machinery has been put to use— the bar, for example, is a platform where stones were once washed. Both local and international dishes are served, including *trucha al gusto* (trout broiled with lemon, garlic, and pesto sauce) and *filete flambé San Marcos* (steak doused with cognac and set aflame). There's live music every Friday night. ✉*La Paz and Betanzos* ☎*02/622–2781* ▱*MC, V.*

$$
LATIN AMERICAN ✕**Sky Room.** You'll be treated to fine sunset views from this aptly named rooftop restaurant. The service can be indifferent, but the restaurant serves good traditional dishes, such as *pichanga* (various types of meats served with salad) and grilled chicken. ✉*Edif. Matilde, Calle Bolívar 701* ☎*02/622–6345* ▱*MC, V.*

WHERE TO STAY

$$ ⌂**Hotel Cima Argentum.** Near the Santa Teresa Convent and six blocks from the Casa de Moneda, this is one of Potosí's more modern hotels. The large rooms and nine suites are spread over three floors, with balconies overlooking a courtyard under a glass dome. The rooms are rather somberly decorated but comfortable. The restaurant is open from 7 AM to 11 PM. **Pros:** Modern design and service standards. **Cons:** Rather gloomy rooms, and they can get chilly. ✉*Av. Villazon 239* ☎*02/622–9538* ▤*02/612–2603* ⊕*www.hca-potosi.com* ⇆*20 rooms, 9 suites* ⌂*In-hotel: restaurant, room service, Internet, laundry* ▱*MC, V.*

$$$ ⌂**Hotel Libertador.** Artwork by local Potosí painters brightens hallways and rooms in this centrally located hotel, probably the best in the city, although you may find this designation relative. There's a small patio on the top floor where you can risk a little sun. The big plus here is central heating. **Pros:** Warm–and you'll need the heating. **Cons:** Indifferent service and facilities for the price. ✉*Millares 58* ☎*02/622–7877* ▤*02/622–4629* ⊕*www.hostal-libertador-potosi.com* ⇆*20 rooms, 3 suites* ⌂*In-hotel: restaurant, bar, Internet* ▱*MC, V.*

¢ ⌂**Koala Den.** This backpacker hostel is a bit pricey for this bracket, but the staff are very helpful, it's heated, and you have your own bathroom. It's also very central. **Pros:** Quieter than average, friendly staff and guests, great breakfast. **Cons:** Run-down on the outside, but then this is a run-down city. ✉*Junin 56* ☎*02/622–6467* ⌂*In-hotel: restaurant* ▤*No credit cards.*

SHOPPING

Despite Potosí's rich mineral wealth, don't expect bargains on handcrafted silver jewelry. Brass and low-grade silver items can be found at the **Mercado Central** at Bustillos and Bolívar. The **Mercado Artesenal,** on the corner of Sucre and Omiste, has locally produced crafts.

SALAR DE UYUNI

Fodor'sChoice

★   *219 km (136 mi) southwest of Potosí.*

One of Bolivia's most spectacular sites, the Salar de Uyuni is the world's highest salt flat, at 3,650 meters (11,975 feet) above sea level, and also the largest, at 10,582 square km (4086 square mi). Once part of a prehistoric salt lake covering most of southwestern Bolivia, it still extends through much of the departments of Potosí and Oruro. As well as the vast expanse of salt, you'll find a series of eerie, translucent lagoons tinted green and red due to high copper and sulfur contents. Living on the salt flat are flamingos (also tinted green and red), rheas, vicuñas, and foxes. Driving across it, whether in the dry or rainy season, is a unique experience.

GETTING HERE & AROUND

It takes four to five hours of travel on very rough roads to reach Uyuni from Potosí and twice that from La Paz, but there is a new road, which makes this more viable, and takes you right to the edge of the Salar at Tahua. Most people choose to make arrangements with a travel agency. Another option is to get a bus to Oruro and the train from there to Uyuni. The site is remote, and can be extremely cold, with night temperatures falling to -25°C (-13°F). While the area is accessible year-round, the most popular time is from March to December, when the Salar should be dry. If you battle through during the rainy season, you will be rewarded with an extraordinarily vivid mirror effect from the shallow water covering the flats. Whenever you go, take plenty of sunblock, sunglasses (with side panels if possible), and lots of warm clothing. In addition, if you are sleeping on the Salar in the salt hotel, take a good sleeping bag.

SAFETY & PRECAUTIONS

If you are driving, avoid the temptation to cross without a good guide: the flats can be treacherous and can hide huge sinkholes. Take a lot of spare fuel for unexpected detours. One of the most common causes of accidents on the flats is drivers making sharp turns and rolling their vehicles.

EXPLORING THE SALAR

The Salar is the obvious draw, and best seen and appreciated by a drive across it. In the middle of the flats you will find the Isla del Pescado (Fish Island) or Incahuasi, which has great views of the vast expanse of white and the distant hills, framed by the gigantic cactus that grow here. You can't stay here, but there is a restaurant run by the owners of Mongos's, in La Paz.

This trip is enough in itself, but many people combine it with (and most tours include) a detour down to the Laguna Colorada (Red Lake) and Laguna Verde (Green Lake) close to the Chilean border. It's well worth it. The two lakes, in the Eduardo Aboroa Reserve, are a haven for birds, as well as providing some of the most striking scenery in Bolivia. Get there in the afternoon for the full, colourful, effect.

WHERE TO STAY

There are almost no places to stay on the Salar itself, except the salt hotel (a hotel made of salt), which is a frequent overnight (and very cold) stop on the numerous tours out of Uyuni. In the town, there are a few possibilities catering to the large numbers of travelers using Uyuni as a base from which to explore. There is an interesting hotel in the village of Tahua, on the northern side of the flats if you are coming directly from La Paz by car.

$ **Hotel Tahua.** This new hotel, and community project, is in the village
Fodor's Choice   of Tahua, a small village right on the edge of the northern side of the
★   flats under the volcano Thunupa. It's more upmarket than other hotels in the region, as reflected in the locally crafted furniture, arty design, and, impressively, Wi-Fi. It also has the great advantage of being at the end of the new road from La Paz and 20 minutes from the Isla del Pescado, meaning you can avoid Uyuni entirely. **Pros:** Modern facilities, staggering location, serious commitment to the community. **Cons:** You need a car to get here. ☎02/2440714, 02/ in La Paz ↝20 rooms ⌂In-hotel: restaurant, Internet, Wi-Fi ▤MC, V.

¢   **Hotel Toñito.** This whitewashed colonial hotel is just two blocks from the colorful Plaza 10 de Noviembre. Many rooms overlook the hotel's two courtyards. Ask to see one of the modern rooms in the back, which are more spacious, and don't miss a pizza in their restaurant. The hotel is part of the Toñito group, which can organize tours onto the Salar from the office just down the road from the hotel. They also have a serious commitment to supporting the local community. **Pros:** The pizza restaurant. **Cons:** Rooms can be claustrophobic, noise from the central courtyard. ⊠60, Av. Ferroviaria ☎02/693-3186, 02/693–3186 in La Paz ⊕www.bolivianexpeditions.com/hotel ↝20 rooms ⌂In-hotel: restaurant ▤MC, V.

TARIJA

570 km (354 mi) south of Sucre.

Tarija is where you go when you've had enough of Bolivia, not just because it's on the way out of the country to Argentina or Paraguay, but also because it's different. The people, the climate, the food, and the culture all have more in common with those of neighboring countries than they do with the surrounding Bolivian territory. It's also different because you may be the only tourist in the entire city. Add to this the excellent weather and the fact it is Bolivia's wine-producing region, and you have an ideal getaway destination.

GETTING HERE & AROUND

You can fly direct to Tarija from La Paz or Santa Cruz, or if you are already in the neighborhood in Sucre then it's a day's bus trip. The overland journey from La Paz is epic, and not recommended. Once you are in the city, walking is a good option. It's not large, and you won't have the inconveniences of La Paz's altitude or Santa Cruz's heat.

ESSENTIALS

Visitor Info **Secretaría del Turismo** (⊠ *Calle 15 de abril entre Sucre y Daniel Campos*).

EXPLORING TARIJA

The best thing to do in Tarija is nothing, but before the easygoing vibes get you take the opportunity to visit one of the many wine cellars, or *bodegas,* dotted around the city. Among the best are Concepcion's **Valle de Concepción,** (⊠ *60, Av. Ferroviaria* ☎ *6651514*) and Kohlberg's **Francisco Lazcano Barrio San Jorge II,** (⊠ *Carretera Panamericana* ☎ *6630002*).

SOUTHERN BOLIVIA TOUR OPERATORS

Candelaria Tours in Sucre organizes trips to Potosí and to nearby Tarabuco for the Sunday market. In Potosí, Sin Fronteras and Hidalgo Tours organize excursions around the city as well as to the Cerro Rico mines. Fremen Tours in La Paz arranges wine tours of the Tarija area.

It is best to organize a trip on the Salar while you are still in La Paz—local agencies in Uyuni are unreliable, to say the least, and this is no place to get stuck. Toñito Tours specializes in tours in southwestern Bolivia. It has a major commitment to the local community in Uyuni, and its hotel does an excellent pizza. Trips to the Salar de Uyuni are usually for four days and cost about $30 a day, including accommodations, a car and driver, and a cook who prepares three meals a day.

Tour Companies **Candelaria Tours** (⊠ *Calle Audiencia 1, Sucre* ☎ *064/461–661*). **Altamira Tours** (⊠ *Av. del Maestro 50, Sucre* ☎ *04/645–3525*). **Fremen Tours** (⊠ *Plaza Abaroa, La Paz* ☎ *02/232–7073*). **Hidalgo Tours** (⊠ *Av. Bolívar at Av. Junín, Potosí* ☎ *062/222–5186*). **Magri Turismo** (⊠ *Calle Capitán Ravelo 2101, La Paz* ☎ *02/244–2727* 🖷 *02/244–3060* ⊕ *www.bolivianet.com/magri*). **Sin Fronteras** (⊠ *Calle Bustillos 1092, Potosí* ☎ *062/224–058*). **Toñito Tours** (⊠ *Sagárnaga 189, La Paz* ☎ *02/233–6250* 🖷 *Av. Ferroviaria 152, Uyuni* ☎🖷 *02/693–3186* ⊕ *www.bolivianexpeditions.com*).

Brazil

WORD OF MOUTH

"Brazil is very child-friendly: children eat out late, stay up late and generally take part in every day life."

—gypsyluce

"On our first day in Rio we restricted ourselves to the beaches at Ipanema and Copacabana. The beach culture of vendors, soccer and volleyball is a tourist sight in itself."

—jrlaw10

"Buzios is the perfect honeymoon destination, great little charming pousadas, beautiful beaches, nice little town with shops, restaurants and bars."

—Dondiega

BRAZIL IS BEST KNOWN FOR its beaches. Its Portuguese colonizers concentrated on the coastal regions, avoiding the inland areas with rare exceptions—a preference that has dictated national life to this day. In the 1960s the government moved the capital from Rio to inland Brasília in an effort to overcome the "beach complex," but three decades later the majority of the population remains concentrated along a narrow coastal strip.

By contrast, the Amazon jungle, which covers 40% of the nation's land mass, has a population of only about 16 million—less than the city of São Paulo alone. Brazil's other hinterland regions are as sparsely populated as they are diverse. The northeast contains the rugged sertão, a region that frequently suffers droughts; the central west is the site of the immense cerrado (savanna) area; still farther west are the Pantanal Wetlands—an enormous swamp.

The country is also a melting pot of races and cultures. Beginning with its Portuguese colonizers, Brazil has drawn waves of immigrants from around the globe, including more than 15 million Africans who were transported here as slaves. The result is the ethnic mix of modern-day Brazil—Italian and German communities in the south, prosperous Japanese and Korean colonies in the state of São Paulo, a thriving Afro-Brazilian culture in Bahia, and remnants of Indian cultures in the north. Brazilians are white, tan, gold, black, brown, red, and seemingly all shades in between. Yet the various groups are united by a common language and a cultural heritage distinct from that of the remainder of South America. Brazilians speak Portuguese, not Spanish, and unlike all their neighbors, they were never a Spanish colony.

The variety of cultures, beliefs, and topographies makes this warm nation a showcase of diversity. An array of nature's bounty—from passion fruit and papaya to giant river fish and coastal crabs—has inspired chefs from all over the world to try their hands in Brazilian restaurants, adding lightness and zest to the country's already exquisite cuisine. Whether you travel to the Amazon rain forest or the urban jungle of São Paulo, you'll plunge into an exotic mix of colors, rhythms, and pastimes.

ORIENTATION & PLANNING

GETTING ORIENTED

Many consider Brazil a continent in its own right. It's larger than the continental United States, four times the size of Mexico, and more than twice as large as India. Occupying most of the eastern half of South America, it borders on all of the other nations of the continent, with the exception of Chile and Ecuador. Its population of 163 million is almost equal to that of the continent's other nations combined, making it South America's true colossus.

TOP REASONS TO GO

LIFE'S A BEACH

Brazil's continuous, 7,700-km (4,800-mi) coast offers a seemingly infinite variety of beaches. Styles range from the urban setting of Rio's Copacabana and Ipanema to isolated, unspoiled treasures along the northeastern coast.

DANCE, DANCE, DANCE!

In the heat of the South American summer (February or March, depending on the date of Easter), the Rio and Salvador explode in gaiety. Hundreds of thousands dance in formal carnival parades and spontaneous street parties.

THE AMAZING AMAZON

Twenty percent of the world's freshwater reserves are found here, and the area is responsible for more than 30% of the earth's oxygen and is home to two-thirds of the world's existing species.

FUTEBOL

South Americans in general are passionate about futebol (soccer), but Brazilians are virtually hysterical about it. Top players are treated like deities and o jogo bonito (the beautiful game) is considered an art form.

Rio. Welcome to the Cidade Maravilhosa, or the Marvelous City, as Rio is known in Brazil. Synonymous with the girl from Ipanema, the dramatic view from Christ the Redeemer atop Corcovado Mountain, and famous Carnival celebrations, Rio is also a city of stunning architecture, abundant museums, and marvelous food. Rio is also home to 23 beaches, an almost continuous 73-km (45-mi) ribbon of sand.

São Paulo. São Paulo is a megalopolis of 19 million people, with endless stands of skyscrapers defining the horizon from every angle. The largest city in South America, São Paulo even makes New York City, with its population of about 8 million, seem small in comparison. And this nearly 500-year-old capital of São Paulo State gets bigger every year: it now sprawls across some 8,000 square km (3,089 square mi), of which 1,525 square km (589 square mi) make up the city proper.

Salvador. In "the land of happiness," as the state of Bahia is known, the sun shines almost every day. Its Atlantic Ocean shoreline runs for 900 km (560 mi), creating beautiful white-sand beaches lined with coconut palms—while inland is Parque Nacional da Chapada Diamantina (Chapada Diamantina National Park), with 152,000 hectares (375,000 acres) of mountains, waterfalls, caves, natural swimming pools, and hiking trails. And in Bahia's capital, Salvador, the beat of bongo drums echoing through the narrow cobblestone streets is a rhythmic reminder of Brazil's African heritage.

Amazon. The world's largest tropical forest seems an endless carpet of green that's sliced only by the curving contours of rivers. Its statistics are as impressive: the region covers more than 10 million square km (4 million square mi) and extends into eight other countries The Amazon forest is home to 500,000 cataloged species of plants and a river that annually transports 15% of the world's available freshwater to the sea, yet it's inhabited by only 16 million people.

PLANNING

WHEN TO GO

Seasons below the equator are the reverse of the north—summer in Brazil runs from December to March and winter from June to September. The rainy season in Brazil occurs during the summer months. Showers can be torrential but usually last no more than an hour or two. The Amazon and the Pantanal have the most pronounced rainy seasons, running roughly from November to May and marked by heavy, twice-daily downpours.

CLIMATE

Rio de Janeiro is on the tropic of Capricorn, and its climate is just that—tropical. Summers are hot and humid. The same pattern holds true for the entire Brazilian coastline north of Rio, although temperatures are slightly higher year-round in Salvador and the northeastern coastal cities. In the Amazon, where the equator crosses the country, temperatures in the high 80s to the 90s (30s C) are common all year. In the south, São Paulo, winter temperatures can fall to the low 40s (5°C–8°C).

RIO DE JANEIRO									
Jan.	84F	29C	May	77F	25C	Sept.	75F	24C
	69	21		66	19		66	19
Feb.	85F	29C	June	76F	24C	Oct.	77F	25C
	73	23		64	18		63	17
Mar.	83F	27C	July	75F	24C	Nov.	79F	26C
	72	22		64	18		68	20
Apr.	80F	27C	Aug.	76F	24C	Dec.	82F	28C
	69	21		64	18		71	22

SALVADOR									
Jan.	87F	31C	May	80F	27C	Sept.	78F	26C
	76	24		70	21		69	21
Feb.	88F	31C	June	80F	27C	Oct.	80F	27C
	79	24		67	19		69	21
Mar.	87F	31C	July	78F	26C	Nov.	83F	28C
	77	25		66	19		72	22
Apr.	84F	29C	Aug.	80F	27C	Dec.	86F	30C
	73	23		67	19		77	25

HOLIDAYS

Major national holidays include: New Year's Day (Jan. 1, but sometimes Dec. 31 is also taken a holiday); Carnaval (the week preceding Ash Wednesday); Good Friday (the Friday before Easter Sunday); Easter Sunday; Tiradentes Day (Apr. 21); Labor Day (May 1); Corpus Christi (60 days after Easter Sunday); Independence Day (Sept. 7); Our

Lady of Aparecida Day (Oct. 12); All Souls' Day (Nov. 1); Declaration of the Republic Day (Nov. 15); and Christmas.

FESTIVALS & EVENTS

Carnival (usually in February) is the best time to soak up the energy of Rio and Salvador. Arrive a few days before the celebrations begin, or stay a few days after they end in order to enjoy the museums and other sights that close for the four days of revelry. You'll have to book your hotel and flight at least one year in advance for Carnival. In São Paulo, cultural events—film and music festivals, and fashion and art exhibits—usually take place between April and December.

GETTING HERE & AROUND

BY AIR

Book as far in advance as possible, particularly for weekend travel. Planes tend to fill up on Friday, especially to or from Brasília or Manaus. For more booking tips and to check prices and make online flight reservations, log on to www.infraero.gov.br

BY BOAT

Cruise itineraries to Brazil change frequently, so contact a travel agent or a cruise company to get the most recent information. Popular Brazilian ports of call include Belém, Fortaleza, Manaus, Recife, Rio, Salvador, and Vitória (in Espínito Santo State).

BY BUS

The nation's *ônibus* (bus) network is affordable, comprehensive, and efficient—compensating for the lack of trains and the high cost of air travel. Every major city can be reached by bus, as can most small to medium-size communities.

BY CAR

Traveling by car is recommended if you meet the following criteria: you're not pressed for time, you enjoy driving even in places you do not know well, you do not want to be limited by airline/bus schedules. It's reasonably safe in most areas, a wonderful way to see the country and to visit lesser-known areas.

GAS STATIONS Stations are plentiful within cities and on major highways, and many are open 24 hours a day, 7 days a week. In smaller towns few stations take credit cards, and their hours are more limited. If you want a receipt, ask for a *recibo*.

ESSENTIALS

ELECTRICITY

The current in Brazil isn't regulated: in São Paulo and Rio it's 110 or 120 volts (the same as in the United States and Canada); in Recife and Brasília it's 220 volts (the same as in Europe); and in Manaus and Salvador it's 127 volts. Electricity is AC (alternating current) at 60 Hz, similar to that in Europe. To use electric-powered equipment purchased in the U.S. or Canada, bring a converter and adapter. Wall outlets take Continental-type plugs, with two round prongs.

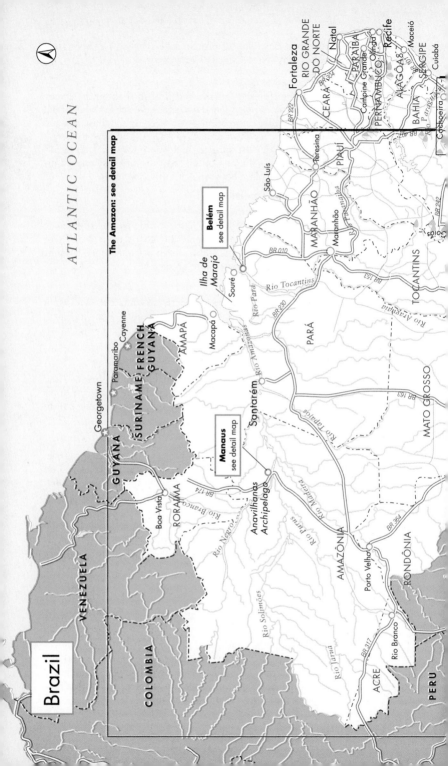

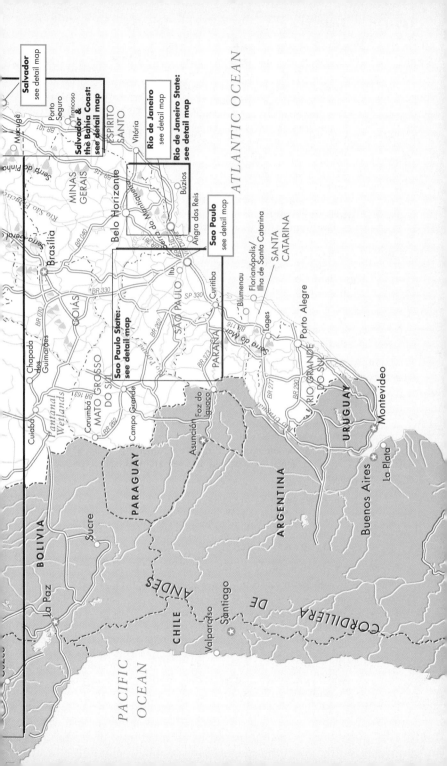

Salvador
see detail map

Mucugê

Porto
Seguro

Trancoso

BR 101

Salvador &
the Bahia Coast:
see detail map

ESPÍRITO
SANTO

Serra do Pinho

MINAS
GERAIS

Vitória

BR 116

Belo Horizonte

Rio de Janeiro
see detail map

Rio de Janeiro State:
see detail map

Rio São Francisco

Serra Geral

Búzios

BR 040

Brasília

São Paulo
see detail map

Angra dos Reis

ATLANTIC OCEAN

BR 330

GOIÁS

BR 070

Ituí

Chapada
dos
Guimarães

BR 364

SÃO PAULO

SP 330

Curitiba

Blumenau

Florianópolis/
Ilha de Santa Catarina

SANTA
CATARINA

Pantanal
Wetlands

MATO GROSSO
DO SUL

BR 262

BR 1631

BR 262

PARANÁ

BR 376

Lages

Serra do Mar

BR 116

Cuiabá

Corumbá

Campo Grande

São Paulo State:
see detail map

Foz do
Iguaçu

BR 277

Porto Alegre

BR 290

RIO GRANDE
DO SUL

Rio Uruguai

BOLIVIA

Sucre

Asunción

PARAGUAY

URUGUAY

Montevideo

La Paz

ANDES

ARGENTINA

Buenos Aires

La Plata

CHILE

Santiago

Valparaíso

CORDILLERA DE

PACIFIC
OCEAN

ENTRY REGULATIONS

A visa is required and must be arranged prior to arrival. At the time of this writing it cost Americans US$100 and Canadians C$72. Requirements change, sometimes at the drop of a hat, and the burden is on you to make sure that you have the appropriate visas.

Yellow fever immunization is compulsory to enter Brazil if you're traveling directly from one of the following countries in South America (or from one of several African countries): Bolivia; Colombia; Ecuador; French Guiana; Peru; or Venezuela. You must have an International Certificate of Immunization proving that you've been vaccinated.

> **WARNING**
>
> It's not safe to drive at night, especially in Rio and São Paulo where drivers commonly run stop signs and traffic lights to avoid robbery. Take special note of motorcyclists at night—they're often used in robberies for a quick getaway. We strongly recommend that women do not drive alone at night.

HEALTH & SAFETY

SAFETY Although there has been a real effort to crack down on tourist-related crime, particularly in Rio, petty street thievery is still prevalent in urban areas, especially in places around tourist hotels, restaurants, and discos. By day the countryside is safe.

SHOTS & Vaccinations agaist hepatitis A and B, menengitis, typhoid, and yellow
MEDICATIONS fever are highly recommended. Consult your doctor about whether to get a rabies vaccination.

Discuss the option of taking antimalarial drugs with your doctor. Note that in parts of northern Brazil a particularly aggressive strain of malaria has become resistant to one antimalarial drug—chloroquine). Some antimalarial drugs have rather unpleasant side effects—from headaches, nausea, and dizziness to psychosis, convulsions, and hallucinations.

For travel anywhere in Brazil, it's recommended that you have updated vaccines for diphtheria, tetanus, and polio. Children must additionally have current inoculations against measles, mumps, and rubella.

RESTAURANTS & HOTELS

Food in Brazil is delicious, inexpensive (especially compared to other countries), and bountiful. A lot of restaurants prepare plates for two people; when you order, ask if one plate will suffice. Many Brazilian dishes are adaptations of Portuguese specialties. Fish stews called caldeiradas and beef stews called cozidos (a wide variety of vegetables boiled with different cuts of beef and pork) are popular, as is bacalhau, salt cod cooked in sauce or grilled. Salgados (literally, "salteds") are appetizers or snacks served in sit-down restaurants as well as at stand-up lanchonetes. One of the most avid national passions is the churrascaria, where meats are roasted on spits over an open fire, usually rodízio style. Rodízio means "going around," and waiters circulate nonstop carrying skewers laden with charbroiled hunks of beef, pork, and chicken, which are sliced onto your plate with ritualistic ardor.

Unlike lodging in European countries, all hotels in Brazil have bathrooms in their rooms. (Budget hotels in the Amazon or northeast don't always have hot water.) Hotels listed with EMBRATUR, Brazil's national tourism board, are rated using stars. Staff training is a big part of the rating, but it's not a perfect system, since stars are awarded based on the number of amenities rather than their quality. **For top hotels in Rio and Salvador during Carnival you must make reservations a year in advance.** Hotel rates rise by 20% on average for Carnival. Not as well known outside Brazil but equally impressive is Rio's New Year's Eve celebration. More than a million people gather along Copacabana Beach for a massive fireworks display and to honor the sea goddess Iemanjá. To ensure a room, book at least six months in advance.

WHAT IT COSTS IN REAIS					
	¢	$	$$	$$$	$$$$
AT DINNER	under R$15	R$15–R$30	R$30–R$45	R$45–R$60	over R$60
FOR 2 PEOPLE	under R$125	R$125–R$250	R$250–R$375	R$375–R$500	over R$500

Restaurant prices are per person for a main course at dinner or for a prix-fixe meal. Hotel prices are for a standard double room in high season, excluding tax.

VISITOR INFORMATION

EMBRATUR, Brazil's national tourism organization, doesn't have offices overseas, though its Web site is helpful. For information in your home country, contact the Brazilian embassy or the closest consulate, some of which have Web sites and staff dedicated to promoting tourism. The official consular Web site in New York, www.brazilny.org, has details about other consulates and the embassy as well as travel information and links to other sites. Cities and towns throughout Brazil have local tourist boards, and some state capitals also have state tourism offices. Viva Brazil provides background and travel info on Brazil's different regions as well as links that will help you arrange your trip.

Contacts **Brazilian Embassy-New York** (⊕ *www.brazilny.org*) **EMBRATUR** (☏ *61/3429-7774 in Brasilia, 646/378-2126 in U.S. East Coast, 310/ 341-8394 in U.S. West Coast* ⊕ *www.embratur.gov.br*) **Viva Brazil** (⊕ *www.vivabrazil.com*).

RIO DE JANEIRO

As you leave the airport and head to Ipanema or Copacabana, you'll drive for about a half hour on a highway from where you'll begin to get a sense of the city's dramatic contrast between beautiful landscape and devastating poverty. In this teeming metropolis the very rich and the very poor live in uneasy proximity. But by the time you reach breezy, sunny Avenida Atlântica—flanked on one side by white beach and azure sea and on the other by condominiums and hotels—your heart will leap with expectation as you begin to recognize the postcard-famous sights. Now you're truly in Rio, where the 10 million *cariocas* (residents of the city of Rio) live life to its fullest.

Prepare to have your senses engaged and your inhibitions untied. Rio seduces with a host of images: the joyous bustle of vendors at Sunday's Feira Hippie (Hippie Fair); the tipsy babble at sidewalk cafés as patrons sip their last glass of icy beer under the stars; the blanket of lights beneath Pão de Açúcar; the bikers, joggers, strollers, and power walkers who parade along the beach each morning. Borrow the carioca spirit for your stay; you may find yourself reluctant to give it back.

Rio's circuit of *praias* (beaches) begins with Flamengo, on Guanabara Bay, but the best strands are farther south. Beaches are the city's pulse points: exercise centers, gathering places, lovers' lanes. Although cariocas wander into the water to cool off, most spend their time sunning and socializing, not swimming.

GETTING AROUND

Cariocas divide their city into four main sections: the suburban Zona Norte (North Zone), the chic Zona Sul (South Zone), the sprawling Zona Oeste (West Zone), and the urban Centro. Most tourist activity is in beach- and hotel-laden Zona Sul, the heartbeat of Rio, where you'll find a mix of residential areas, office buildings, shops, restaurants, bars, and beaches..

The metro extends from the Zona Norte to Copacabana, with shuttles to Ipanema, Leblon, Gávea, São Conrado, and even Barra da Tijuca. Within Ipanema and Copacabana, it's quite easy to get around on foot, but some attractions are far apart, so a taxi might be the way to go. After dark you should always take a taxi, and it's easy to hail taxis on every main street. Few cab drivers speak English; it's a good idea to have your destination written down to show the driver, in case there's a communication gap.

Don't attempt to use the bus unless you know which line to take and you speak enough Portuguese to ask directions (drivers don't speak English). Never take the bus at night. Vans are a form of informal public transportation that are much more frequent, quicker than buses, 100% safe, and only R$2 per ride; if you're staying in Copacabana or Ipanema, vans are a good and inexpensive option because they ride along the beaches.

SAFETY & PRECAUTIONS

IN THE CITY Despite Rio's reputation, many cariocas feel that the city's safety is unfairly portrayed by the media. Most crimes involving visitors occur in crowded public areas: beaches, busy sidewalks, intersections, and city buses. Pickpockets, usually children, work in groups. One will distract you while another grabs a wallet, bag, or camera. Be particularly wary of children who thrust themselves in front of you and ask for money or offer to shine your shoes. Another member of the gang may strike from behind, grabbing your valuables and disappearing into the crowd. Another tactic is for criminals to approach your car at intersections. Always keep doors locked and windows partially closed. Leave valuables in your hotel safe, don't wear expensive jewelry or watches, and keep cameras strapped to your wrist.

ON THE BEACH Don't shun the beaches because of reports of crime, but *do* take precautions. Leave jewelry, passports, and large sums of cash at your hotel; don't wander alone and at night; and be alert when groups of friendly youths engage you in conversation (sometimes they're trying to distract you while one of their cohorts snatches your belongings). A big danger is the sun. From 10 AM to 3 PM the rays are merciless, making heavy-duty sunscreen, hats, cover-ups, and plenty of liquids essential; you can also rent a beach umbrella from vendors on the beach or your hotel. Lifeguard stations, including bathrooms and showers, are found every kilometer.

> ### WHAT'S A CARIOCA?
>
> The term *carioca* was an indigenous word meaning "white man's house" and was used in the city's early history to describe the Portuguese colonizers. Today the word is used more broadly, to identify residents of the city of Rio. But the word defines much more than birthplace, race, or residence: it represents an ethos of pride, a sensuality, and a passion for life. Poor or rich, cariocas share a common identity and a distinct local accent, considered by foreigners and Brazilians alike to be the most beautiful within the Portuguese language.

ESSENTIALS

Airports Aeroporto Internacional Antônio Carlos Jobim (*Galeão, GIG* ☎ *021/3398–4526*). **Aeroporto Santos Dumont** (*SDU* ☎ *021/3814–7070*).

Bus Depots Rodoviária Novo Rio (✉ *Av. Francisco Bicalho 1, São Cristóvão* ☎ *021/2291–5151*). **Menezes Cortes Terminal** (✉ *Rua São José 35, Centro* ☎ *021/2299–1380*).

Currency Exchange American Express (✉ *Av. Atlântica 1702 B, Copacabana*). **Banco do Brasil** (✉ *Rua Bartolomeu Mitre 438 A, Leblon* ✉ *Rua Senador Dantas 105, Centro*). **Banco 24 Horas ATM** (✉ *Av. Nossa Senhora de Copacabana 202* ✉ *Av. Nossa Senhora de Copacabana 599* ✉ *Rua Visconde de Pirajá 174, Ipanema*).

Emergency Services Ambulance and Fire (☎ *193*). **Police** (☎ *190*). **Tourism Police** (✉ *Rua Humberto de Campos 315, Leblon* ☎ *021/3399–7170*).

Medical Services Cardio Plus (✉ *Rua Visconde de Pirajá 330, Ipanema* ☎ *021/2521–4899*). **Copa D'Or** (✉ *Rua Figueiredo Magalhães 875, Copacabana* ☎ *021/2545–3600*). **Galdino Campos Cardio Copa Medical Clinic** (✉ *Av. Nossa Senhora de Copacabana 492, Copacabana* ☎ *021/2548–9966*). **Medtur** (✉ *Av. Nossa Senhora de Copacabana 647, Copacabana* ☎ *021/2235–3339*).

Pharmacies Drogaria Pacheco (✉ *Av. Nossa Senhora de Copacabana 534, Copacabana* ☎ *021/2548–1525*). **Farmácia do Leme** (✉ *Av. Prado Júnior 237, Leme* ☎ *021/2275–3847*).

Rental Cars Avis (✉ *Av. Princesa Isabel 350, Copacabana* ☎ *021/2543–8579*). **Hertz** (✉ *Av. Princesa Isabel 334, Copacabana* ☎ *021/2275–7440 or 0800/701–7300* ✉ *Aeroporto Internacional Antônio Carlos Jobim* ☎ *021/3398–4339* ✉ *Aeroporto*

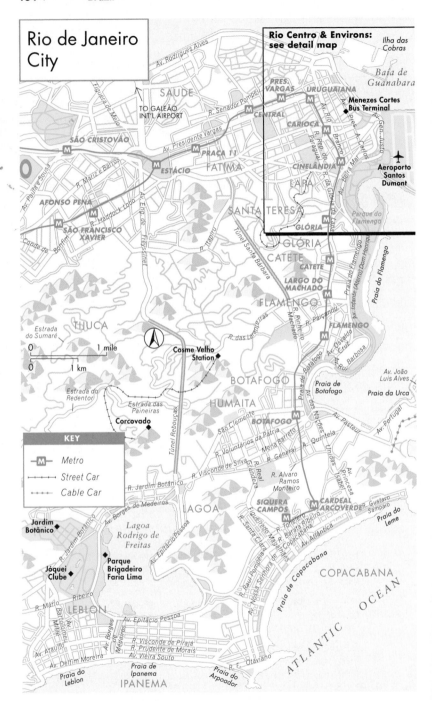

Rio de Janeiro City

Rio Centro & Environs: see detail map

Ilha das Cobras

Baía de Guanabara

Av. Rodrigues Alves

TO GALEÃO INT'L AIRPORT

SAÚDE

PRES. VARGAS

URUGUAIANA

Menezes Cortes Bus Terminal

R. Senador Pompeu

CENTRAL

CARIOCA

SÃO CRISTOVÃO

Av. Presidente Vargas

PRAÇA 11

FÁTIMA

CINELÂNDIA

ESTÁCIO

LAPA

Aeroporto Santos Dumont

AFONSO PENA

SANTA TERESA

SÃO FRANCISCO XAVIER

GLÓRIA

GLÓRIA

CATETE

Parque do Flamengo

Túnel Santa Bárbara

CATETE

LARGO DO MACHADO

Estrada do Sumaré

THIJUCA

FLAMENGO

FLAMENGO

R. das Laranjeiras

Praia do Flamengo

0   1 mile
0   1 km

Cosme Velho Station

R. Pinheiro Machado

Estrada do Redentor

Estrada das Paineiras

BOTAFOGO

Praia de Botafogo

Av. João Luis Alves

Praia da Urca

Corcovado

HUMAITÁ

São Clemente

BOTAFOGO

R. Voluntários da Pátria

Av. Pasteur

Av. Portugal

KEY

Metro
Street Car
Cable Car

R. Jardim Botânico

LAGOA

SIQUEIRA CAMPOS

CARDEAL ARCOVERDE

Jardim Botânico

Lagoa Rodrigo de Freitas

Praia do Leme

Jóquei Clube

Parque Brigadeiro Faria Lima

Av. Atlântica

COPACABANA

LEBLON

Av. Epitácio Pessoa

Praia de Copacabana

Av. Delfim Moreira

R. Visconde de Pirajá
R. Prudente de Morais
Av. Vieira Souto

ATLANTIC OCEAN

Praia do Leblon

Praia de Ipanema

Praia do Arpoador

IPANEMA

Santos Dumont ☎*021/2262–0612*). **Uni-das** (☎*021/4001–2222 for main reservations line* ✉*Aeroporto Santos Dumont, Av. Senador Salgado Filho s/n, Centro* ☎*021/2240–9181* ✉*Av. Princesa Isabel 166, Copacabana* ☎*021/3685–1212* ✉*Aeroporto Internacional do Galeão, Estrada do Galeão s/n, Ilha do Governador* ☎*021/3398–2286*).

Subway Metrô Rio (☎*021/3211–6300 information line* ⊕*www.metrorio.com.br*).

Taxis Centro de Taxis (☎*021/2195–1000*). **Coopacarioca** (☎*021/2518–1818*). **Coopatur** (☎*021/2573–1009*).

Tours Cultural Rio (☎*021/9911–3829* ⊕*www.culturalrio.com.br*). **Favela Tour** (☎*021/3322–2727* ⊕*www.favelatour. com.br*). **Gray Line** (☎*021/2512–9919*). **Private Tours** (☎*021/2232–9710* ⊕*www.privatetours.com.br*). **Rio Hiking** (☎*021/2552–9204 or 021/9721–0594* ⊕*www.riohiking.com.br*).

THE COPS

Once known as the murder capital of the world, Rio is now less dangerous than a decade ago. Simple changes such as installing lights on the beaches have greatly improved safety in certain parts of the city. An increased police presence has also helped. In Rio there are three types of police: the gray-uniformed Military Police, the beige-uniformed Municipal Guard, and the black-uniformed special forces called the BOPE (pronounced "boppy"). For a glimpse at Rio's SWAT team, the BOPE, check out the film *Tropa de Elite* (2007).

Train Estação Dom Pedro II Central do Brasil (✉*Praça Cristiano Otoni on Av. President Vargas, Centro* ☎*021/2588–9494*).

Visitor Info Embratur (✉*Rua Uruguaiana 174, Centro* ☎*021/2509–6292* ⊕*www. embratur.gov.br*). **Riotur** (✉*Rua da Assembléia 10, near Praça 15 de Novembro, Centro* ☎*021/2217–7575 or 0800/707–1808* ⊕*www.rio.rj.gov.br/riotur*). **Riotur information booth** (✉*Av. Princesa Isabel 183, Copacabana* ☎*021/2541–7522*). **Turisrio** (✉*Rua da Ajuda 5, Centro* ☎*021/2215–0011* ⊕*www.turisrio.rj.gov.br*).

Numbers in the text correspond to numbers in the margin and on the Rio Centro & Environs map and the Rio de Janeiro City map.

EXPLORING RIO DE JANEIRO

CENTRO & ENVIRONS

Rio's settlement dates back to 1555, and much of the city's rich history is captured in traditional churches, government buildings, and villas, which are tucked in and around Centro. You can use the metro to get downtown, but wear comfortable shoes and be ready to walk multiple blocks. The metro stations that serve Centro are Cinelândia, Carioca, Uruguaiana, Presidente Vargas, Central, and Praça Onze.

Numbers in the text correspond to numbers in the margin and on the Rio Centro and Environs map.

MAIN ATTRACTIONS

❹ Igreja de São Francisco da Penitência. The church was completed in 1737, nearly four decades after it was started. Today it's famed for its wooden sculptures and rich gold-leaf interior. The nave contains a painting of

CLOSE UP

What's Your Beach Style?

Praia do Flamengo. Power-walkers, volleyballers, and yoga enthusiasts come to Flamengo Beach to work up a sweat. It isn't a tourist destination, and you rarely see people swimming (pollution can be a problem) or sunbathing.

Praia do Botafogo. The view of the bay and the Sugar Loaf from this beach is breathtaking, but it isn't a popular beach with tourists or even locals, due to pollution in the bay waters.

Praia do Vermelha. This tiny beach neighboring the Pão de Açúcar has beautiful scenery but polluted waters. It's generally populated only by cariocas who live nearby.

Praia do Leme. A continuation of Copacabana Beach, Leme has a similar feel. Lined with kiosks and volleyball nets, it's popular with locals and tourists.

Praia do Diabo. Between Ipanema and Copacabana, this small strip attracts surfers. The view is beautiful, and if you're at Ipanema, it's worth the walk to Praia do Diabo.

Praia de Copacabana. The city's grande dame, Copacabana is a 3-km (2-mi) stretch packed to the gills on sunny days with sunbathers, vendors, and athletes. Kiosks along its busy promenade have snacks and drinks. Cafés and high-rise hotels line the waterfront avenue.

Praia de Ipanema. Always-crowded Ipanema is smaller than Copacabana, but equally famous. It's a perfect place to sunbathe and people-watch. At the east end is the dramatic rock formation Pedra do Arpoador; visible to the west, past Leblon, is the Morro Dois Irmaos (Two Brothers Mountain) and the hillside Vidigal favela.

Praia do Leblon. Ipanema Beach extends west to meet Leblon Beach, which has the same feel. It's very popular for exercising on the sand or boardwalk. Water pollution is a problem.

Praia do Vidigal. Sheltered by rock formations, Vidigal doesn't attract many other travelers other than those staying in the nearby hotels, because access is difficult.

Praia de São Conrado. Hang gliders land here after leaping from a nearby peak. The proximity to the Rocinha favela keeps many people away. Tourists are rare.

Praia Barra da Tijuca. Rio's longest beach (18 km/11 mi) has clean and cool waters. Its far end, called Recreio dos Bandeirantes, was a fishing village until the late 1960s. The neighborhood of Barra da Tijuca feels like a suburb, and the beach reflects that. It attracts families with young children and older folks out for a stroll.

Prainha. Just beyond Barra da Tijuca, Prainha has rough seas that make it popular with surfers. It's nearly empty on weekdays.

Praia de Grumari. The copper sands of this lovely beach are packed on weekends. It has little infrastructure but clean sand and water, and is backed by green hills.

St. Francis, the patron of the church—reportedly the first painting in Brazil done in perspective. Part of the Convento do Santo Antônio, this church is partially roped off due to renovations, though its beauty still shines through. ⊠*Largo da Carioca 5, Centro* ☎*021/2262–0197* 🖅*R$2* ⊘ *Wed.–Fri. 11–4* Ⓜ*Carioca.*

❶ **Mosteiro de São Bento.** Just a glimpse of this church's main altar can fill you with awe. Layer upon layer of curvaceous wood carvings coated in gold create a sense of movement. Spiral columns whirl upward to capitals topped by cherubs so chubby and angels so purposeful they seem almost animated. Although the Benedictines arrived in 1586, they didn't begin work on this church and monastery until 1617. It was completed in 1641, but such artisans as Mestre Valentim (who designed the silver chandeliers) continued to add details almost through to the 19th century. Every Sunday at 10, mass is accompanied by Gregorian chants. ⊠*Rua Dom Gerardo 68, Centro* ☎*021/2206–8100* 🖅*Free* ⊘ *Weekdays 7–noon and 2–6.*

❻ **Museu Nacional de Belas Artes.** Works by Brazil's leading 19th- and 20th-
★ century artists fill the space at the National Museum of Fine Arts. The most notable canvases are those by the country's best-known modernist, Cândido Portinari, but be on the lookout for such gems as Leandro Joaquim's heartwarming 18th-century painting of Rio (a window to a time when fishermen still cast nets in the waters below the landmark Igreja de Nossa Senhora da Glória do Outeiro). After wandering the picture galleries, tour the extensive collections of folk and African art. At this writing the museum is in its final stage of a six-phase overhaul of the building. ⊠*Av. Rio Branco 199, Centro* ☎*021/2240–0068* ⊕*www.iphan.gov.br* 🖅*R$4, free Sun. and during construction* ⊘ *Tues.–Fri. 10–6* Ⓜ*Carioca or Cinelândia.*

❺ **Theatro Municipal.** If you visit one place in Centro, make it this theater, modeled after the Paris Opera House and opened in 1909. Carrara marble, stunning mosaics, glittering chandeliers, bronze and onyx statues, gilded mirrors, German stained-glass windows, brazilwood inlay floors, and murals by Brazilian artists Eliseu Visconti and Rodolfo Amoedo make the Municipal Theater opulent indeed. The main entrance and first two galleries are particularly ornate. As you climb to the upper floors, the decor becomes simpler, a reflection of a time when different classes entered through different doors and sat in separate sections—but also due in part to the exhaustion of funds toward the end of the project. The theater seats 2,357—with outstanding sight lines—for its dance performances and classical music concerts. English-speaking guides are available. ⊠*Praça Floriano 210, Centro* ☎*021/2299–1667* ⊕*www. theatromunicipal.rj.gov.br* 🖅*Tours R$4* ⊘ *Guided tours available by request weekdays 1–4* Ⓜ*Cinelândia or Carioca.*

IF YOU HAVE TIME

❷ **Beco do Comércio.** A network of narrow streets and alleys centers on this pedestrian thoroughfare, also called the Travessa do Comércio. The area is flanked by restored 18th-century homes, now converted to offices. The best known is the Edifício Teles de Menezes. Once a

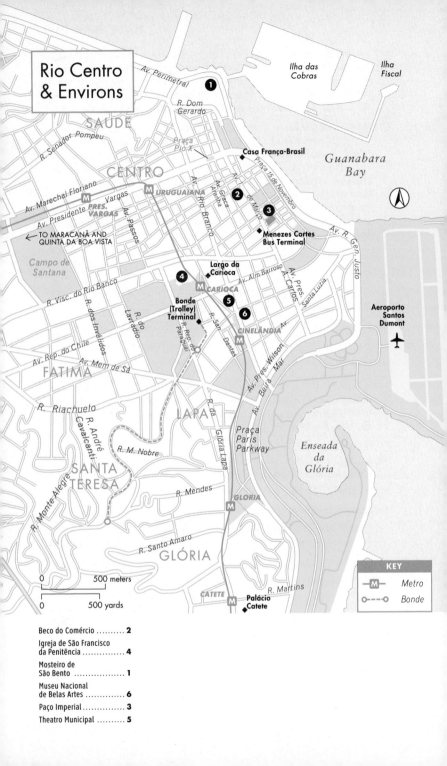

Rio Centro & Environs

Av. Perimetral

SAÚDE

R. Dom Gerardo

R. Senador Pompeu

Praça Pio X

CENTRO

1

Casa França-Brasil

Guanabara Bay

Ilha das Cobras

Ilha Fiscal

Av. Marechal Floriano

URUGUAIANA

Av. Presidente Vargas

PRES. VARGAS

← TO MARACANÃ AND QUINTA DA BOA VISTA

Av. Passos

Av. Graça Aranha

Av. Rio Branco

Praça 15 de Novembro

Av. de Março

2

3

Menezes Cortes Bus Terminal

Av. R. Gen. Justo

Campo de Santana

R. Visc. do Rio Branco

R. dos Invalidos

R. do Lavradio

4

Largo da Carioca

CARIOCA

Av. Alm. Barroso

A. Carlos

Av. Pres. Carlos

Santa Luzia

Aeroporto Santos Dumont

Bonde (Trolley) Terminal

R. Rep. do Paraguai

R. San. Dantes

5

6

CINELÂNDIA Av.

Av. Pres. Wilson

Av. Rep. do Chile

Av. Mem de Sá

FÁTIMA

R. Riachuelo

R. André Cavalcanti

LAPA

R. da Glória Lapa

Av. Beira Mar

Praça Paris Parkway

Enseada da Glória

R. Monte Alegre

SANTA TERESA

R. M. Nobre

R. Mendes

GLÓRIA

R. Santo Amaro

GLÓRIA

CATETE

R. Martins

Palácio Catete

0   500 meters

0   500 yards

KEY

Ⓜ Metro

o---o Bonde

functional aqueduct and the source of water for downtown Rio, the **Arco do Teles,** links this area with Praça 15 de Novembro. A great place to grab a bite to eat, the Beco do Comércio offers dining options from low-end quilo-style restaurants to some higher end restaurants and cafés. ✉*Praça 15 de Novembro 34, Centro* Ⓜ*Uruguaiana.*

❸ **Paço Imperial.** This two-story colonial building with thick stone walls and an ornate entrance was built in 1743, and for the next 60 years was the headquarters for Brazil's captains (viceroys), appointed by the Portuguese court in Lisbon. When King João VI arrived, he made it his royal palace. After Brazil's declaration of independence, emperors Dom Pedro I and II called the palace home. When the monarchy was overthrown, the building became Rio's central post office. Restoration work in the 1980s transformed it into a cultural center and concert hall. The building houses a restaurant, a coffee shop, a stationery-and-CD shop, and a movie theater. The square on which the palace sits, Praça 15 de Novembro, known in colonial days as Largo do Paço, has witnessed some of Brazil's most significant historic moments: it's where two emperors were crowned, slavery was abolished, and Emperor Pedro II was deposed. The square's modern name is a reference to the date of the declaration of the Republic of Brazil: November 15, 1889. ✉*Praça 15 de Novembro 48, Centro* ☎*021/2533–4407* ⊕*www.pacoimperial. com.br* ✉*Free* ☉ *Weekdays 1–5.*

URCA

Tiny sheltered Urca faces Botafogo. The quiet neighborhood with single-family homes and tree-lined streets is separated by the Pão de Açúcar from a small underwhelming patch of yellow sand called Praia Vermelha. This beach is, in turn, blocked by the Urubu and Leme mountains from the 1-km (½-mi) Leme Beach at the start of the Zona Sul. Besides having one of the city's most famous attractions, the Pão de Açúcar, Urca has our favorite branch of the world-famous churrascaria Porcão *(*⇨ *Where to Eat).*

★ **Pão de Açúcar** *(Sugar Loaf).* This soaring 1,300-meter (approximately 4,290-foot) granite block at the mouth of Baía de Guanabara was originally called *pau-nh-acugua* (high, pointed peak) by the indigenous Tupi people. To the Portuguese the phrase seemed similar to *pão de açúcar*; the rock's shape reminded them of the conical loaves in which refined sugar was sold. Italian-made bubble cars holding 75 passengers each move up the mountain in two stages. The first stop is at Morro da Urca, a smaller, 212-meter (705-foot) mountain; the second is at the summit of Pão de Açúcar itself. The trip to each level takes three minutes. In high season long lines form for the cable car; the rest of the year the wait is seldom more than 30 minutes. ✉*Av. Pasteur 520, Praia Vermelha, Urca* ☎*021/2546–8400* ⊕*www.bondinho.com.br* ✉*R$35 adults, R$17.50 children under 13, free for children under 6* ☉*Daily 8* AM*–9* PM.

ZONA SUL

Copacabana is Rio's most famous tourist neighborhood thanks to its fabulous beach and grande-dame hotels like the Copacabana Palace. The main thoroughfare is Avenida Nossa Senhora de Copacabana, two blocks inland from the beach. The commercial street is filled with shops, restaurants, and sidewalks crowded with colorful characters. Despite having some of the best hotels in Rio, Copacabana's heyday is over, and the neighborhood is quite a bit grittier than Ipanema or Leblon. It's no secret to thieves that tourists congregate here, so keep your eyes peeled for shady types when walking around after dark.

Ipanema, Leblon, and the blocks surrounding Lagoa Rodrigo de Freitas are part of Rio's money belt. For an up-close look at the posh apartment buildings, stroll down beachfront Avenida Vieira Souto and its extension, Avenida Delfim Moreira, or drive around the lagoon on Avenida Epitácio Pessoa. Other chic areas near the beach include Praça Nossa Senhora da Paz, which is lined with wonderful restaurants and bars; Rua Vinicius de Moraes; and Rua Farme de Amoedo.

Fodor'sChoice ★ **Praia de Copacabana.** Maddening traffic, noise, packed apartment blocks, and a world-famous beach—this is Copacabana, or Manhattan with bikinis. Walk along the neighborhood's classic crescent to dive headfirst into Rio's beach culture, a cradle-to-grave lifestyle that begins with toddlers accompanying their parents to the water and ends with silver-haired seniors walking hand in hand along the sidewalk. Copacabana hums with activity: you're likely to see athletic men playing volleyball using only their feet and heads, not their hands—a sport Brazilians have dubbed *futevôlei.* As you can tell by all the goal nets, soccer is also popular, and Copacabana frequently hosts the annual world beach soccer championships. You can swim here, although pollution levels and a strong undertow can sometimes be discouraging. Pollution levels change daily and are well publicized; someone at your hotel should be able to get you the information. Copacabana's privileged live on beachfront Avenida Atlântica, famed for its wide mosaic sidewalks designed by Burle Marx, and for its grand hotels—including the Copacabana Palace Hotel—and cafés with sidewalk seating. On Sunday two of the avenue's lanes are closed to traffic and are taken over by joggers, rollerbladers, cyclists, and pedestrians. ⊠ *Av. Princesa Isabel to Rua Francisco Otaviano, Copacabana.*

Praia do Arpoador. This beach, at the east end of Ipanema, has great waves for surfing. Nonsurfers tend to avoid the water for fear of getting hit by boards. But it's popular for sunbathing. ⊠ *Rua Joaquim Nabuco to Rua Francisco Otaviano, Arpoador.*

Fodor'sChoice ★ **Praia de Ipanema.** As you stroll along this beach you catch a cross section of the city's residents, each favoring a particular stretch. One area is dominated by families (near Posto [Post] 10), another is favored by the gay community (near Posto 8). Throughout the day you'll see groups playing beach volleyball and soccer, and if you're lucky you'll even get to see Brazilian Olympic volleyball champions practicing on the beach. There are kiosks all along the boardwalk, where you can get anything from the typical coconut water to fried shrimp and turnovers. ✉ *Rua Joaquim Nabuco to Av. Epitácio Pessoa, Ipanema.*

SÃO CONRADO & BARRA DA TIJUCA

West of the Zona Sul lie the highly residential (and considerably affluent) neighborhoods of São Conrado and Barra da Tijuca. São Conrado's main attractions are the nearby favelas of Rocinha and Vila Canoas and the chic Fashion Mall. Its quiet beach serves as a landing site for hang gliders and paragliders. Barra has more to offer to the shopper, with plenty of malls and high-end restaurants for the middle-upper class that dwells there.

Praia de São Conrado. Undoubtedly the safest beach in Rio, Praia de São Conrado is empty during the week and packed on weekends and holidays. This is the playground of the residents of Rocinha, the world's largest shantytown. It's worth it to stay until sunset; the pumpkin sun makes a beautiful show over Pedra da Gávea. ✉ *São Conrado.*

FodorśChoice **Sítio Roberto Burle Marx** *(Roberto Burle Marx Farm).* Beyond Grumari,
★ the road winds through mangrove swamps and tropical forest. It's an apt setting for the plantation-turned-museum where Brazil's famous landscape designer Roberto Burle Marx is memorialized. Marx, the mind behind Rio's swirling mosaic beachfront walkways and the Atêrro do Flamengo, was said to have "painted with plants," and was the first designer to use Brazilian flora in his projects. More than 3,500 species—including some discovered by and named for Marx as well as many on the endangered list—flourish at this 100-acre estate. He grouped his plants not only according to their soil and light needs but also according to their shape and texture. Marx also liked to mix the modern with the traditional—a recurring theme throughout the property. The results are both whimsical and elegant. In 1985 he bequeathed the farm to the Brazilian government, though he remained here until his death in 1994. His house is now a cultural center full of his belongings, including collections of folk art. The grounds also contain his large ultramodern studio (he was a painter, too) and a small, restored colonial chapel dedicated to St. Anthony. ✉ *Estrada Roberto Burle Marx 2019, Pedra da Guaratiba* ☎ *021/2410–1412* 💲 *R$5* ⊙ *Tues.–Sun. by appointment only; tours at 9:30* AM *and 1:30* PM.

THE LUSH INLAND

In the western portion of the city north of Leblon, trees and hills dominate the landscape in the neighborhoods of Jardim Botânico, Lagoa, Cosme Velho, and Tijuca. In addition to their parks and gardens, these primarily residential neighborhoods have marvelous museums, seductive architecture, and tantalizing restaurants. The architecture is a mix of modern condominiums and colonial houses. Public transportation doesn't conveniently reach the sights here; take a taxi or a tour.

Numbers in the margin correspond to numbers on the Rio de Janeiro City map.

MAIN ATTRACTIONS

Fodor'sChoice **Corcovado.** There's an eternal argument about which view is better,
★ from Pão de Açúcar (Sugar Loaf) or from here. Corcovado has two
advantages: at 690 meters (2,300 feet), it's nearly twice as high and
offers an excellent view of Pão de Açúcar itself. The sheer 300-meter
(1,000-foot) granite face of Corcovado (the name means "hunchback")
has always been a difficult undertaking for climbers.

It wasn't until 1921, the centennial of Brazil's independence from Portugal, that someone had the idea of placing a statue atop Corcovado.
A team of French artisans headed by sculptor Paul Landowski was
assigned the task of erecting a statue of Christ with his arms apart
as if embracing the city. It took 10 years, but on October 12, 1931,
the *Cristo Redentor* (Christ the Redeemer) was inaugurated by then
president Getúlio Vargas, Brazil's FDR. The sleek, modern figure rises
more than 30 meters (100 feet) from a 6-meter (20-foot) pedestal and
weighs 700 tons. In the evening a powerful lighting system transforms
it into a dramatic icon.

There are four ways to reach the top: by cogwheel train (R$36), by taxi
(R$10 per person), car (R$13 per person), or on foot (R$5 per person,
free on Catholic holidays). The fee to enter on foot was instituted in
December 2007 and is a highly controversial matter, with both the
Catholic Church and Rio governor César Maia against the fee. The
train, built in 1885, provides delightful views of Ipanema and Leblon
from an absurd angle of ascent, as well as a close look at thick vegetation and butterflies. (You may wonder what those oblong medicine
balls hanging from the trees are, the ones that look like spiked water-
melons tied to ropes—they're *jaca,* or jackfruit.) Visit Corcovado on
a clear day; clouds often obscure the Christ statue and the view of the
city. Go as early in the morning as possible, before people start pouring
out of the tour buses, and before the haze sets in. ⊠*Estrada da Redentor, Cosme Velho* ⊕*www.corcovado.org.br* ☎*R$36* ☉*Daily 9–6.*

★ **Jardim Botânico.** The 340-acre Botanical Garden contains more than
5,000 species of tropical and subtropical plants and trees, including 900
varieties of palms (some more than a century old) and more than 140
species of birds. The temperature is usually a good 12°C (22°F) cooler
in the shady garden that was created in 1808 by Portuguese king João
VI during his exile in Brazil. In 1842 the garden gained its most impressive adornment, the Avenue of the Royal Palms, a 720-meter (800-
yard) double row of 134 soaring royal palms. Elsewhere in the gardens
the Casa dos Pilões, an old gunpowder factory, has been restored and
displays objects that pertained to both the nobility and their slaves.
Also on the grounds are a library, a small café, and a gift shop that
sells souvenirs with ecological themes. ⊠*Rua Jardim Botânico 1008,
Jardim Botânico* ☎*021/3874–1808 or 021/3874–1214* ⊕*www.jbrj.
gov.br* ☎*R$4* ☉*Daily 8–5. Guided tours in English, Spanish, and
Portuguese available by appointment weekdays 9–4.*

IF YOU HAVE TIME

Museu de Arte Naïf do Brasil. More than 8,000 art naïf works by Brazil's best (as well as works by other self-taught painters from around the world) grace the walls of this colonial mansion that was once the studio of painter Eliseu Visconti. The pieces, in what is reputedly the world's largest and most complete collection of primitive paintings, date from the 15th century through contemporary times. Don't miss the colorful, colossal 7×4–meter (22×13–foot) canvas that depicts the city of Rio; it reportedly took five years to complete. This museum sprang from a collection started decades ago by a jewelry designer who later created a foundation to oversee the art. ⊠ *Rua Cosme Velho 561, Cosme Velho* ☎ *021/2205–8612 or 021/2205–8547* ⊕ *www.museunaif.com. br* ☞ *R$8* ⊙ *Tues.–Fri. 10–6, weekends and holidays noon–6.*

WHERE TO EAT

With more than 900 restaurants, Rio's dining choices are broad, from low-key Middle Eastern cafés to elegant contemporary eateries with award-winning kitchens and first-class service. The succulent offerings in the *churrascarias* (restaurants specializing in grilled meats) can be mesmerizing for meat lovers—especially the places that serve *rodízio* style (grilled meat on skewers is continuously brought to your table— until you can eat no more). Hotel restaurants often serve the national dish, *feijoada* (a hearty stew of black beans and pork), on Saturday— sometimes Friday, too. Wash it down with a *chopp* (the local draft beer; pronounced "shop") or a caipirinha (Brazilian rum, lime, and sugar).

CENTRO

$-$$
SEAFOOD

✗**Alba Mar.** Opened in 1933, Alba Mar is not hard to spot—it's housed in a distinctive circular green building facing Guanabara Bay. While the building's 360-degree views are a draw in themselves, the real reason people come is for the outstanding seafood. The chef works magic with the daily specials, and the haddock soufflé is fluffy, creamy culinary nirvana. If you're just looking to nibble, check out the classic codfish balls, sit back, and take in the spectacular view across the bay. ⊠ *Praça Marechal Âncora 186, Centro* ☎ *021/2240–8428* ⊕ *www.albamar. com.br* ☰ *AE, DC, MC, V* ⊙ *No Dinner* Ⓜ *Carioca.*

¢-$
BRAZILIAN

✗**Amarelinho.** The best spot for city-center people-watching, this vast pavement *boteco* (bar) sits directly in front of the Biblioteco Nacional, and to the side of the imposing Theatro Nacional. A city-center institution since 1921, the bar attracts hordes of lunchtime and afterwork diners, competing for the tables and chairs that sit directly on the flagstones of the busy Praça do Floriano. Waitstaff in bright yellow waistcoats and bow ties flit among the tables delivering simple Brazilian dishes such as the mixed grill (R$20) served with rice and fries. Pizzas are also popular here, as is the ice-cold draft beer. Given the prime location, prices are surprisingly reasonable. Don't confuse Amerelinho with the adjoining bar, Vermelhino. Both have yellow roof canopies and yellow plastic chairs, but Amerelinho serves superior food. ⊠ *Praça Floriano 55 B, Cinelândia, Centro* ☎ *2122408434* ⊕ *www.amarelinhodacinelandia. com.br* ☰ *AE, DC, MC, V* ⊙ *Closed Sun.* Ⓜ *Cinelândia.*

¢   ✕**Confeitaria Colombo.** At the turn of the 20th century this belle epoque
CAFÉ   structure was Rio's preeminent café, the site of elaborate balls, after-
FodorsChoice   noon teas for upper-class *senhoras,* and a center of political intrigue
★   and gossip. Enormous jacaranda-framed mirrors from Belgium, stained
glass from France, and tiles from Portugal add to the art nouveau decor.
Today locals come here to nibble on above-average *salgados* (savory
snacks) and melt-in-the-mouth sweet treats. The waffles here are a local
legend. Savory pastries are stuffed with shrimp and chicken, and vegetarian nosh includes spinach and ricotta quiche and heart-of-palm pie.
You can wash it all down with a creamy coffee, a European lager or, on
a hot day, a fruity cocktail (served virgin or laced with alcohol). Perhaps
the best way to absorb the opulence is to do as Rio's high society did
a century ago: with *chá da tarde,* or afternoon tea (R$50 buys a lavish
spread for two). ⊠*Rua Gonçalves Dias 32, Centro* ☎*021/2232–2300*
⊕*www.confeitariacolombo.com.br* ⊟*AE, DC, MC, V* ☉*Closed Sun.
No dinner* Ⓜ*Carioca.*

COPACABANA & LEME

$–$$ ✕**Azul Marinho.** You'll catch superb sunsets from the beachside tables at
SEAFOOD   this quiet little spot in Arpoador, which serves high-quality seafood and
pasta dishes. The restaurant occupies the ground floor of the Arpoador
Inn hotel, and boasts a giant panoramic window looking out onto a
barely trafficked street across from Arpoador beach. *Moqueca* is the
specialty, made with shrimp, cod, lobster, crab, or octopus—or a mix
of them all. Service is excellent and the seafood is fresh, but our favorite reason to go to Azul Marinho is to sit at its outdoor tables next to
the sands, enjoying early-evening appetizers, drinks, and the sunset.
⊠*Av. Francisco Bhering s/n, Arpoador* ☎*021/3813–4228* ⊕*www.
cozinhatipica.com.br* ⊟*AE, DC, MC, V.*

$$$–$$$$ ✕**Cipriani.** This restaurant is housed in the plush environs of Copaca-
ITALIAN   bana Palace and overlooking the hotel's enormous pool. Start with a
★   Cipriani, champagne with fresh peach juice (really a Bellini), and then
take your pick from an extensive North Italian menu that includes
appetizers like sea-bass salad with fava beans and burrata cheese, and
excellent mains such as wild-rice risotto with asparagus and squid. The
freshly made pasta dishes are prepared with great care, and the meat
and fish entrées are appropriate to their lavish surroundings. Service,
as one would expect, is excellent. The degustation menu is R$191, or
R$342 with wine. ⊠*Copacabana Palace Hotel, Av. Atlântica 1702,
Copacabana* ☎*021/2545–8747* ⊕*www.copacabanapalace.com.br*
⚲*Reservations essential* ⊟*AE, DC, MC, V* Ⓜ*Cardeal Arcoverde.*

$$$–$$$$ ✕**D'Amici.** The diverse menu at D'Amici offers specialties from various
ITALIAN   regions of Italy. Diners can take their pick from Sicilian and Milanese
★   pasta and fish dishes, among others. To keep hunger at bay while the
main course is prepared, the mixed Italian antipasti includes Parma
ham and grana padano cheese (R$34 for four). This place has the larg-
est wine list in Rio, with 300 labels, ranging from R$26 to R$10,000—
for the Romanée Conti—and also serves 30 types of wine by the glass
(R$9–R$26). The restaurant is consistently a hit in Rio for its food
and atmosphere. ⊠*Rua Antônio Vieira 18, Leme* ☎*021/2541–4477*
⊟*AE, DC, MC, V* ⚲*Reservations essential.*

$$$$ ✕ **Le Pré-Catalan.** Considered the best French cuisine in Rio, this is the
FRENCH   *carioca* version of the charming Parisian restaurant of the same name
in the Bois du Boulogne. This highly reputed establishment has several
prix-fixe menus, ranging in price from R$158 for three courses, to
R$215 for R$10. The degustation menu is R$185. À la carte includes
delicious dishes like lamb chops with fondant potato, rosemary, and
ratatouille. ✉ *Sofitel Rio Palace, Av. Atlântica 4240, Level E, Copacabana* ☎ *021/2525–1160* ᴬ *Reservations essential* ☰ *AE, DC, MC, V*
⊘ *No lunch* Ⓜ *No metro.*

$$$–$$$$ ✕ **Siri Mole & Cia.** For seafood served Bahian style (from the northeast),
BRAZILIAN   this is the place. The restaurant takes its name from a soft-shell crab
native to Brazil, and the signature dish here is the moqueca—a Bahian
stew combining dendê oil and coconut milk with seafood. (Beware, this
dish is delicious but very high in saturated fat. It can have disastrous
effects on the digestion if you're not used to it.) You can take your pick
from squid, lobster, fish, or, of course, siri mole crab. There's also a
branch in Centro, or, to sample Siri Mole's northeastern cuisine in a less
formal environment, you can visit the offshoot beach kiosk, right on
the sands at Copacabana. ✉ *Rua Francisco Otaviano 50, Copacabana*
☎ *021/2267–0894* ⊕ *www.sirimole.com.br* Ⓜ *Siqueira Campos, then
shuttle bus to Praça General Osório, get off at last stop in Copacabana*
☰ *AE, DC, MC, V.*

FLAMENGO & BOTAFOGO

$$$$ ✕ **Carême.** This acclaimed bistro offers inventive and high-quality
FRENCH   French cuisine that makes good use of fresh, largely organic, ingredi-
ents. The à la carte menu offers something different each day, or you
can opt for the *menu decouverté*—a selection of entrées, main courses,
and desserts served in miniature portions. The head chef, Flávia Qua-
resma, has become something of a televison celebrity in Brazil. ✉ *Rua
Visconde de Caravelas 113, Botafogo* ☎ *021/2537–2274* ᴬ *Reserva-
tions essential* ⊘ *Closed Sun. and Mon. No lunch* ☰ *AE, DC, MC, V*
Ⓜ *Botafogo.*

$$$$ ✕ **Porcão Rio's.** The ultimate in Brazilian churrascaria experiences, Por-
BRAZILIAN   cão has bow-tied waiters who flit between linen-draped tables, wield-
FodorśChoice   ing giant skewers, and slicing your portions of sizzling barbecued beef,
★   pork, and chicken until you can eat no more. The buffet is huge, with
salads, sushi, and, on Saturday, more than 15 types of feijoada. (Hats
off if you can do churrasco *and* feijoada in one sitting!) Porcão is a
chain, with four restaurants in Rio—including the one in Ipanema
(⇨*below)*—and another in the suburb of Niterói, but the nearly floor-
to-ceiling windows with a view over Guanabara Bay to the Sugar Loaf
make the Flamengo branch our top choice. ✉ *Av. Infante Dom Hen-
rique, Parque do Flamengo* ☎ *021/2554–8535* ☰ *AE, DC, MC, V.*

$$–$$$$ ✕ **Yorubá.** Exotic and delicious dishes are served at this restaurant, one
AFRICAN   of the few places that go beyond traditional African–Brazilian cuisine.
Try the Afro menu, a selection of contemporary West African dishes.
Service can be slow, but you're well rewarded for the wait. The *piripiri*
(a spicy rice with ginger, coconut milk, and shrimp) is worth the price
of R$80 for two. ✉ *Rua Arnaldo Quintela 94, Botafogo* ☎ *021/2541–
9387* ☰ *AE, V* Ⓜ *Botafogo* ⊘ *Closed Mon. and Tues.*

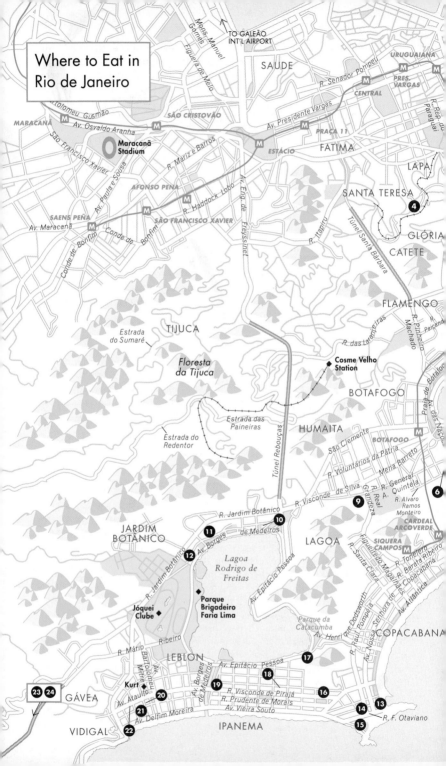

Where to Eat in Rio de Janeiro

Maracanã Stadium

Cosme Velho Station

Jóquei Clube

Parque Brigadeiro Faria Lima

Kurt

4
6
9
10
11
12
13
14
15
16
17
18
19
20
21
22
23
24

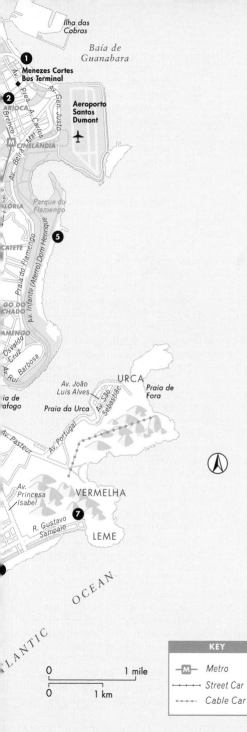

KEY

—Ⓜ— *Metro*

·····› *Street Car*

•◦•◦ *Cable Car*

IPANEMA & LEBLON

$$$-$$$$
PORTUGUESE
Fodor'sChoice
★

✕**Antiquarius.** This much-loved establishment is famous for its flawless rendering of Portuguese classics. A recommended dish is the lobster with rice, lime, and fried greens. The *cataplana*, a seafood stew with rice, is also marvelous, and the *perna de cordeiro* (leg of lamb) is the most-requested dish on the menu. The wine list impresses even Portuguese gourmands. ⊠*Rua Aristides Espínola 19, Leblon* ☏*021/2294–1049* ⊕*www. antiquarius.com.br* ⌨*Reservations essential* ▭*DC, MC.*

$$
BRAZILIAN
★

✕**Casa da Feijoada.** Many restaurants serve Brazil's savory national dish on Saturday, but here the huge pots of the stew simmer every day. You can choose which of the nine types of meat you want in your stew, but if it's your first time, waiters will bring you a "safe" version with sausage, beef, and pork—sans feet and ears. The feijoada comes with the traditional side dishes of rice, collard greens, *farofa* (toasted and seasoned manioc flour), *aipim* (fried yuca), *torresminho* (pork rinds), and orange slices (to lower your cholesterol!). The set meal price includes an appetizer portion of black-bean soup and sausage, a choice of dessert, and a lime or passion-fruit *batida* (creamy cachaça cocktail). Not feeling like the feijoada? The menu also features options such as baked chicken, shrimp in coconut milk, grilled trout, and filet mignon. Desserts include *quindim* (a yolk-and-sugar pudding with coconut crust) and Romeo and Juliet (guava compote with fresh cheese). The caipirinhas are made not only with lime but also with tangerine, passion fruit, pineapple, strawberry, or kiwi. Be careful—they're strong. ⊠*Rua Prudente de Morais 10, Ipanema* ☏*021/2247–2776* ⊕*www.cozinhatipica.com.br* ▭*AE, DC, MC, V* Ⓜ*Sigueira Campos, then shuttle bus to Praça General Osório.*

¢–$
ECLECTIC

✕**Fazendola.** The name means "small farm," and this restaurant is reminiscent of a Brazilian farm with its wooden furniture and dim lighting. Homemade dishes prepared with fresh ingredients are sold by the kilo. The other option is to try their delicious pizza, which you can order either à la carte or rodizio-style (all you can eat). ⊠*Rua Jangadeiros 14B, Ipanema* ☏*021/2247–9600* ▭*AE, DC, MC, V* Ⓜ*Siqueira Campos, then shuttle bus to Praça General Osório.*

¢–$$
CAFÉ
★

✕**Garcia & Rodrigues.** Cariocas breakfast at this cozy combination café, delicatessen, liquor shop, and trendy restaurant. At lunchtime choose from a selection of sandwiches, such as marinated salmon, pastrami, or buffalo-milk cheese. Dinner, based on French cuisine, is served until 12:30 AM Monday–Thursday and until 1 AM Friday and Saturday. Menu choices are broad and it's updated regularly to make the most of seasonal ingredients. On Sunday nights the café is open until midnight, but à la carte meals are not served. ⊠*Av. Ataulfo de Paiva*

1251, Leblon ☎021/2512–8188 ⊕www.garciaerodrigues.com.br ▤AE, DC, MC, V.

¢–$$
BRAZILIAN
✕**Jobi.** Not to be missed, Jobi is a Leblon institution—and since it's open daily from 9 AM to 4 AM, you should be able to squeeze it in. It's the sort of place you can go to in your bikini straight from the beach. Basic sandwiches and salads are on the menu, but the reason to go is the fabulous seafood. Order a full meal or just try various appetizers. The *bolinho de bacalhau* (mini cod cakes) may be the best in town. ⊠*Rua Ataulfo de Paiva 1166, Leblon* ☎021/2274–0547 ▤AE.

$–$$$$
ITALIAN
✕**Margutta.** A block from Ipanema Beach, Margutta has a reputation for outstanding Mediterranean-style seafood, such as broiled fish in tomato sauce and fresh herbs or lobster cooked in aluminum foil with butter and saffron rice. Veggie options include homemade rigatoni with dried wild mushrooms and olive oil flavored with white truffles. ⊠*Av. Henrique Dumont 62, Ipanema* ☎021/2511–0878 ▤AE, DC, MC, V ⊗*No lunch weekdays.*

$$$–$$$$
SEAFOOD
Fodor'sChoice
★
✕**Satyricon.** Some of the best seafood in town is served at this eclectic Italian seafood restaurant, which has impressed the likes of Madonna and Sting. The fish baked in a thick layer of rock salt is a specialty, and the sushi and sashimi are well loved. ⊠*Rua Barão da Torre 192, Ipanema* ☎021/2521–0627 ⊕www.satyricon.com.br ▤DC, MC, V Ⓜ*Siqueira Campos, then shuttle bus to Praça General Osório.*

JARDIM BOTÂNICO

$$$$
FRENCH
Fodor'sChoice
★
✕**Olympe.** This top-notch venue is run by Claude Troisgros, of the celebrated Michelin-starred Troisgros family of France. The menu's all-Brazilian ingredients are a unique trait of this innovative restaurant that blends native flavors with nouvelle techniques. Every dish—from the crab or lobster flan to chicken, fish, and duck prepared with exotic herbs and sauces—is exceptionally light. The passion-fruit crepe soufflé is highly recommended. ⊠*Rua Custódio Serrão 62, Jardim Botânico* ☎021/2537–8582 ⌕*Reservations essential* ▤AE, MC, V.

$$–$$$$
ITALIAN
Fodor'sChoice
★
✕**Quadrifoglio.** Considered by most locals to be the best Italian restaurant in the city, cozy Quadrifoglio is tucked away on a quiet street. The food and the service are impeccable; the restaurant has been around since 1991 and much of the original waitstaff still works there. Some favorite entrée choices are spinach ravioli and the fabulous salads. Leave room for one of the deservedly famous desserts, such as ice cream with baked figs. ⊠*Rua J. J. Seabra 19, Jardim Botânico* ☎021/2294–1433 ▤AE, DC, MC, V ⊗*No dinner Sun., no lunch Sat.*

FOOD ON THE GO

There's a street snack for every taste in Rio—from low-cal treats such as corn on the cob and chilled pineapple slices to less virtuous, but absolutely delicious, barbecued sticks of grilled cheese served with or without herbs. Tasty bags of roasted and salted peanuts and cashews are found everywhere, as are giant hot dogs, served on a stick and covered in manioc flour. Barbecued chicken heart (*coraçao*) is not for the fainthearted, and the grilled shrimp at the beach is best avoided unless you want a side order of food poisoning.

LAGOA

$$$ ✕ **Mr Lam.** Mr Lam, head chef of Mr Chow in New York, leads the
CHINESE kitchen at this glamorous 2006 addition to the Rio dining scene. In
★ a city where Chinese food has long been associated with low-budget
dining, this restaurant has burned the rule book, serving top-quality
Peking cuisine to a discerning clientele. The downstairs dining room
is spacious and well illuminated by enormous windows, but for the
ultimate experience book a table on the top floor—at night the roof
comes right off to allow dining beneath the stars, and you can request
a spot directly beneath the gaze of the Christo Redentor. À la carte is
an option, but most diners choose from one of the set menus (R$75–
R$125 per person). ✉ *Av. Maria Angélica 21, Lagoa* ☎ *21/2286–6661*
⊕ *www.mrlam.com.br* ⌲ *Reservations essential* ▭ *AE, DC, MC, V*
⊘ *No lunch weekdays.*

SANTA TERESA

$$–$$$ ✕ **Aprazível.** A tropical garden filled with exotic plants, monkeys, and
BRAZILIAN birds is the spectacular setting for this family restaurant serving pan-
★ Brazilian dishes. The owner and chef, Ana Castilha, hails from Minas
Gerais but was formally trained at the French Culinary Institute in New
York, and there's a distinctly French twist to the traditional Brazilian
dishes on offer. There are some unusual salads, including one featuring
mixed lettuce with mango, whole green peppercorns, Minas cheese,
and sundried tomatoes (R$24). The all-Brazilian wine list is chosen
with great care, and may surprise those who have previously dismissed
national wines. The outdoor tables enjoy excellent views of downtown
and Guanabara Bay during the day, and at night the garden is illumi-
nated by numerous hanging lanterns. If you're lucky you might spot the
pair of toucans that regularly visit the garden. Grass and bamboo roofs
keep diners dry if the weather takes a turn for the worse, and there are
several indoor tables, too, for those who don't fancy alfresco dining.
✉ *Rua Aprazível 62, Santa Teresa* ☎ *21/2508–9174* ⊕ *www.aprazivel.
com.br* ▭ *AE, DC, MC, V* ⊘ *Closed Mon.*

SÃO CONRADO, BARRA DA TIJUCA & BEYOND

$–$$$ ✕ **476.** At the end of a road with stunning coastal views, 476 is all
SEAFOOD about simplicity, with seven delicious entrées that include *moquecas*
Fodor'sChoice (seafood stews), grilled seafood, and curries. It has only 20 tables, some
★ in a lovely garden at the water's edge. The quiet fishing village 13 km (8
mi) west of Barra da Tijuca is a nice respite from the bustling Zona Sul.
Tell the taxi driver to take you to "Quatro Sete Meia." ✉ *Rua Barros
de Alarção 476, Pedra da Guaratiba* ☎ *021/2417–1716* ⌲ *Reservations essential* ▭ *AE, MC, V.*

$$–$$$ ✕ **Restaurante Point de Grumari.** From Grumari Beach, Estrada de Guara-
SEAFOOD tiba climbs up through dense forest, emerging atop a hill above the
vast Guaratiba flatlands. Here you find this eatery famed for grilling
fish to perfection. With its shady setting, glorious vistas, and live music
performances (samba, bossa nova, jazz), it's the perfect spot for lunch
(it's open daily 11:30–6:30) after a morning on the beach and before an
afternoon at the Sítio Roberto Burle Marx or the Museu Casa do Pon-
tal. Alternatively, come here in the early evening to catch the spectacu-

lar sunset. ⊠*Estrada do Grumari 710, Grumari* ☎*021/2410–1434* ⊕*www.pointdegrumari.com.br* ☰*AE, DC, MC, V* ⊘*No dinner.*

WHERE TO STAY

Most hotels are in Copacabana and Ipanema. Copacabana hotels are close to the action (and the metro), but the neighborhood is noisier than Ipanema (which is itself noisier than São Conrado and Barra da Tijuca). ⚠ **Note that "motels" aren't aimed at tourists. They attract couples looking for privacy and usually rent by the hour.**

3

CENTRO & GLÓRIA

$$$$ 🏨 **Glória.** The grande dame of Rio's hotels, this is the oldest in the city and retains plenty of historic charm. The hotel is in wonderful tropical gardens, and front-facing rooms have a great view over Guanabara Bay and Sugar Loaf. Glória is stuffed full of antique French furniture, and a major renovation in 2005. There are three restaurants and two pools—one of which is absolutely enormous. The fitness center is very well equipped and has good views of the bay. Request a room in the original building as opposed to the new annex, where rooms are uninspired. The hotel's good convention center and location close to Centro makes it popular among business travelers (and a helicopter landing pad on the roof means Lula is a regular guest), but it's a bit of a trek to Zona Sul beaches. **Pros:** Main building is attractive and has plenty of atmosphere. Great gardens and pools. Good restaurant. **Cons:** Annex rooms not good value, bus or cab ride to Zona Sul, Glória not very safe at night. ⊠*Rua do Russel 632, Glória* ☎*021/2205–7272 or 0800/21–3077* 🖨*021/2555–7282* ⊕*www.hotelgloriario.com.br* 🛏*579 rooms, 21 suites* ♿*In-room: safe, refrigerator, Ethernet (some), Wi-Fi (some). In-hotel: 3 restaurants, room service, bars, pools, gym, spa, concierge, laundry service, parking (fee), no-smoking rooms* ☰*AE, DC, MC, V* ⊠◯|*BP* Ⓜ*Glória.*

COPACABANA & LEME

These neighborhoods can be dangerous at night, so it's wise to get around by taxi after dark.

$$$$ 🏨 **Copacabana Palace.** The addition of a seven-room luxury spa in 2007
Fodor's Choice has brought this iconic hotel up to date. Built in 1923 for the visiting
★ king of Belgium and inspired by Nice's Negresco and Cannes's Carlton, the Copacabana was the first luxury hotel in South America, and it's still one of the top hotels on the continent. Marlene Dietrich, Robert De Niro, and Princess Di are among the many famous faces to have stayed here. The hotel's neoclassical facade is beautifully maintained and remains a glimmering white. Inside you can find one of the city's largest and most attractive swimming pools. One of Copacabana Palace's two restaurants, the Cipriani, is rated among the city's best for its northern Italian cuisine, while the Saturday feijoada, served in the less formal Pergula restaurant by the pool, is legendary. The interior of the hotel is as glittering white as its facade, and the look is cool, elegant, and luxurious—from the marble reception desk to the immaculately attired bellboys. Oceanview rooms are more expensive than those at

Where to Stay in Rio de Janeiro

3

KEY

—Ⓜ— *Metro*

┝━━┥ *Street Car*

•••••• *Cable Car*

0 ——————— 1 mile

0 ——————— 1 km

the back, whose view of the Copacabana streets somewhat detracts from the glamorous atmosphere. A genuine Rio landmark, Copacabana Palace remains the stomping ground of the rich and fabulous despite a growing preference for Ipanema and Leblon over Copacabana. However, the nightlife here is less sophisticated, and you're likely to find yourself making nightly cab journeys to Ipanema and Leblon. **Pros:** A historic landmark, front-facing rooms have spectacular views, great on-site restaurant. **Cons:** Dearth of nightlife, dangerous neighborhood at night, "city view" rooms have poor view of backstreets, dated in-room facilities. ⊠*Av. Atlântica 1702, Copacabana* ☎*021/2548–7070, 0800/21–1533, 800/237–1236 in U.S.* ⊕*www.copacabanapalace. com.br* 🛏*122 rooms, 111 suites* ⟡*In-room: safe, DVD (some), VCR (some), Ethernet, Wi-Fi (some). In-hotel: 2 restaurants, room service, pools, gym, spa, beachfront, public Internet, public Wi-Fi, bars, tennis court, pool, gym, spa, concierge, laundry service, no-smoking rooms, some pets allowed* ⊟*AE, DC, MC, V* Ⓜ*Cardeal Arcoverde.*

$–$$ 🏨 **Copacabana Rio Hotel.** Brightly decorated in blues, yellows, and reds, the rooms here are nicer than those you find at many more expensive places. A few rooms have wonderful views of Pedra da Gávea (Gávea Rock). Single, double, and triple rooms and suites are all reasonably priced and are good value for the location—one block back from the beach. From the heated rooftop pool you can see Copacabana Beach and Sugar Loaf, and the on-site restaurant serves buffet-style and à la carte meals. You're practically in Ipanema here, which is handy for nightlife, but it's a 10 block walk to the nearest metro station at Canto Galo. **Pros:** Good price, comfortable rooms, handy for Copacabana and Ipanema beaches. **Cons:** No metro, busy and noisy street. ⊠*Av. Nossa Senhora de Copacabana 1256, Copacabana* ☎*021/2267–9900* ⊕*www.copacabanariohotel.com.br* 🛏*90 rooms, 8 suites* ⟡*In-room: safe. In-hotel: restaurant, pool, gym, concierge, laundry service, parking (fee)* ⊟*AE, DC, MC, V* �*BP* Ⓜ*Siqueira Campos.*

$$–$$$ 🏨 **Luxor Regente Hotel.** The best of the Luxor hotels in Rio, the Regente was renovated in 2004. Rooms are now spic-and-span and reasonably tasteful—some in bright blue-and-yellow hues, and other in more refined off-whites and browns. The downstairs lounge is modern and vibrant, with leather chairs, red sofas, and glass tables. The restaurant Forno e Fogão has a good Saturday feijoada, though it's not as celebrated as that of the Copacabana Palace. The suites have whirlpool baths. The gym area is small, but the hotel is committed to continually updating its equipment. If you choose a standard room, be sure that it's not one that faces south; those rooms have an unfortunate view of a trash-can-filled alley. Other rooms look out over Avenida Atlântica and Copacabana Beach. **Pros:** Good for families, modern, pool. **Cons:** Some rooms have poor views, breakfast has cold dishes only, Copacabana not the safest area. ⊠*Av. Atlântica 3716, Copacabana,* ☎*021/2525–2070 or 0800/16–5322* ⊕*www.luxor-hotels.com* 🛏*228 rooms, 2 suites* ⟡*In-room: safe, Ethernet (some). In-hotel: restaurant, room service, bars, pool, gym, concierge, laundry service, parking (fee), no-smoking rooms* ⊟*AE, DC, MC, V* ⏀*BP.*

$$ ⊞**Miramar Palace.** A mix of old and new, this beachfront hotel has some of the largest rooms in Rio, with some of the best views. Classic accents like the Carrara marble floor of the lobby and the spectacular glass chandeliers that light the restaurant are contrasted with modern amenities like wireless Internet and the contemporary 16th-floor bar with an unobstructed view of the entire sweep of Copacabana. **Pros:** Beachfront location, large rooms, good views. **Cons:** Busy area, must use taxis to Ipanema and Leblon at night. ⊠*Av. Atlântica 3668, Copacabana* ☎*021/956–200 or 0800/23–2211* ⊕*www.windsorhotels.com* ➳*147 rooms, 9 suites* ⌂*In-room: safe, refrigerator, Ethernet, Wi-Fi (some). In-hotel: restaurant, room service, bars, concierge, laundry service, public Internet, public Wi-Fi, parking (no fee), no-smoking rooms* ⊟*AE, DC, MC, V* ⓘ◎|*BP.*

$–$$ ⊞**Ouro Verde Hotel.** Since the 1950s this hotel has been favored for
★ its efficient, personalized service. Quirky touches such as the huge art deco reception desk, enormous gilt-framed mirrors, and reading room with antique furnishings give this hotel an air of old-time decadence, while the modern bar, which features DJs and live music several nights a week, brings things up to date for younger guests. The quiet beachfront location, at the Leme end of Copacabana, is excellent, and the prices are low for Avenida Atlântica, although it should be noted that some of the fixtures and fittings are a little past their prime. All front rooms face the beach; those in the back on the 11th and 12th floors have a view of Corcovado. **Pros:** Good location, good price, quirky hotel with lots of character. **Cons:** Far from Ipanema and Leblon, furnishings are a little worn. ⊠*Av. Atlântica 1456, Copacabana* ☎*021/2543–4123* ⊕*www.dayrell.com.br* ➳*60 rooms, 2 suites* ⌂*In-room: safe, Wi-Fi (some). In-hotel: restaurant, room service, bar, laundry service, public Internet, public Wi-Fi, no-smoking rooms* ⊟*AE, DC, MC, V* Ⓜ*Cardeal Arco Verde.*

$$$$ ⊞**Rio Internacional.** All rooms at this Copacabana landmark hotel have
★ balconies with sea views, a rarity on Avenida Atlântica. The distinctive black- and red-fronted hotel is Swiss-owned, and the tidy and modern Scandinavian design is one of its best assets. Crisp white decor is a trademark of the hotel, and the rooftop pool with its wood-paneled sun deck is first rate, with excellent views across the bay, and of the Corvovado and the Christ statue. The hotel attracts a well-to-do clientele made up of business travelers and holiday-makers alike; all guests are welcomed with a glass of Champagne. **Pros:** Good design and tasteful decor, excellent service, good views, beachfront. **Cons:** Some rooms are smallish, some mattresses lack support ⊠*Av. Atlântica 1500, Copacabana* ☎*021/2543–1555 or 0800/21–1559* ⊕*www.riointernacional. com.br* ➳*117 rooms, 11 suites* ⌂*In-room: safe, Ethernet. In-hotel: restaurant, room service, bars, pool, gym, beachfront, public Internet, public Wi-Fi, concierge, laundry service, parking (fee), no-smoking rooms* ⊟*AE, DC, MC, V* Ⓜ*Cardeal Arco Verde.*

$$$$ ⊞**Sofitel Rio Palace.** Anchoring one end of Copacabana Beach, this huge hotel was given a top-to-bottom face-lift in 2007 and is once again one of the best on the strip. The building's H shape gives breathtaking views of the sea, the mountains, or both from the balconies of all rooms. The hotel has two pools—one catches the morning sun; the other, afternoon rays. All beds are brand new, and wonderfully comfortable. The look is understated yet luxurious, with decor dominated by neutral creams, whites, and light browns. The wooden paneled elevators and corridors have a classic sophistication, and the executive floors combine modern facilities with antique mirrors, clocks, and chests of drawers. Holiday makers enjoy the beachfront location and the picture-perfect views that take in the entire length of Copacabana beach, while business executives appreciate the top-notch business facilities. The restaurant Le Pré-Catalan is as good as its Parisian original. **Pros:** Handy for Ipanema and Arpoador beaches and nightlife, fantastic views. **Cons:** Very large, could feel impersonal, bar and restaurant expensive. ⊠ *Av. Atlântica 4240, Copacabana* ☎ *021/2525–1232 or 0800/703–7003, 800/7763–4835 in U.S.* ⊕ *www.accorhotels.com.br* ⮨ *388 rooms, 53 suites* ♿ *In-room: safe, Ethernet, Wi-Fi. In-hotel: 2 restaurants, bar, pools, gym, laundry service, concierge, executive floor, parking (fee), no-smoking rooms, some pets allowed, public Internet, public Wi-Fi* ☰ *AE, DC, MC, V.*

IPANEMA & LEBLON

$–$$ **Arpoador Inn.** This simple pocket-size hotel occupies the stretch of sand known as Arpoador. Surfers ride the waves, and pedestrians rule the roadway—a virtually traffic-free street allows direct beach access. At sunset the view from the landmark rock that juts out into the ocean at the end of the beach is one of Rio's most beautiful. The spectacle is visible from the hotel's back (deluxe) rooms that face Arpoador Beach. Avoid the front rooms, which can be noisy. Built in the '70s, the hotel has since been renovated and has a good seafood restaurant, Azul Marinho, on the ground floor overlooking the beach. The restaurant has tables right next to the sand, and guests can choose to take their buffet breakfast here. Some rooms are much larger than others, so specify if you have a preference. **Pros:** Great sunset, good restaurant, good price. **Cons:** Some rooms a little noisy, can be busy with groups of surfers. ⊠ *Rua Francisco Otaviano 177, Ipanema* ☎ *021/2523–0060* ⊕ *www.arpoadorinn.com.br* ⮨ *50 rooms* ♿ *In-room: safe. In-hotel: restaurant, room service, bar, laundry service, public Internet* ☰ *AE, DC, MC, V* ⦿ *BP.*

$$$–$$$$ **Best Western Sol Ipanema.** Another of Rio's crop of tall, slender hotels, this one has a great location between Rua Vinicius de Moraes and Farme de Amoedo, where there are several bars, anchoring the eastern end of Ipanema Beach. While it isn't luxurious, the hotel has comfortable accommodations, and the interiors are crisp, clean, and modern. Deluxe front rooms have panoramic beach views, and back rooms from the eighth floor up, which are the same size, have views of the lagoon and Corcovado. **Pros:** Great location, friendly staff, modern. **Cons:** Standard facilities. ⊠ *Av. Vieira Souto 320, Ipanema* ☎ *021/2525–2020* ⊕ *www.solipanema.com.br* ⮨ *90 rooms* ♿ *In-room: refrigerator, Ethernet. In-hotel: restaurant, room service, bars, pool, laundry service, parking (no fee), no-smoking rooms* ☰ *AE, DC, MC, V* ⦿ *BP.*

$$$$ ⊞ **Fasano Rio.** Fasano Rio opened to great fanfare in 2007, and with good reason. The Italian-owned Fasano Group is renowned for its stylish, elegant hotels and restaurants, and Fasano Rio has the added glamour of having been crafted by French designer Philippe Starck. The location, in front of Ipanema Beach, could not be better, and the understated facade of the building masks a wealth of quirky style inside. A key theme is the use of Amazonian wood—the reception desk is carved from a huge tree trunk—and modern glass and chrome. Elsewhere, specially commissioned furnishings re-create the style of the 1950s and '60s. You'll find unique touches everywhere, such as the huge pink-and-white candy-stripe armchairs in the middle of each corridor, but the real star of the show is the white-marble plunge pool on the rooftop terrace. With breathtaking views across Ipanema Beach, it's the ultimate in Rio decadance. A poolside bar and restaurant serves wonderful tropical juices, light meals, and cocktails. Egyptian cotton sheets, goosedown pillows, and plasma-screen televisions are further indulgent touches. The hotel's elegant Italian restaurant, Fasano Al Mare, has already picked up awards, and the intimate lounge bar Londra, which blends English punk-rock attitude with Italian glamour, has a waiting list a mile long. ⊠ *Av. Viera Souto 80, Ipanema* ☎ *21 3202 4000* ⊕ *www. fasano.com.br* ⤳ *82 rooms, 10 suites* ⌂ *In-room: safe, refrigerator, DVD (some), Ethernet, Wi-Fi. In-hotel: 2 restaurants, room service, bar, pool, gym, bicycles, laundry service, public Internet, public Wi-Fi, some pets allowed.*

$$$–$$$$ ⊞ **Ipanema Plaza.** European standards and solid service are the hallmarks of this hotel. The rooms are large, with white-tile floors and modern facilities, and the decor is tastefully tropical. In the center of Ipanema, very close to the beach, the hotel is on a street that's rife with restaurants and bars. From the rooftop pool it's possible to see not only the ocean, but also the lagoon and the statue of Christ the Redeemer. In 2005 the hotel introduced Ipanema Floor—an executive floor with all the bells and whistles, including rooms and suites with spectacular views over Ipanema Beach, elegant Italian fixtures, and fine linens with impossibly high thread counts. **Pros:** Attractive, comfortable accommodation, good views from pool, attention to detail. **Cons:** Pool often used for private parties during high season, pricey neighborhood. ⊠ *Rua Farme de Amoedo 34, Ipanema* ☎ *021/3687–2000* ⊕ *www. ipanemaplazahotel.com* ⤳ *118 rooms, 13 suites* ⌂ *In-room: safe, Ethernet (some), Wi-Fi. In-hotel: restaurant, room service, pool, gym, concierge, laundry service, executive floor, parking (fee), no-smoking rooms* ⊟ *AE, DC, MC, V* ⎜◎⎜*BP.*

$$$$ ⊞ **Marina All Suites.** In front of Leblon Beach and surrounded by designer stores and upmarket restaurants, Marina All Suites is a favorite with chic holidaymakers (Gisele Bundchen and Calvin Klein are regulars). The lofty building is home to 37 spacious suites, and those on the upper floor have each been signed by a different designer. As well as slick design, each of the rooms is equipped with a stereo system, and many have ocean views. The service is superb, and the hotel has some wonderfully eccentric touches such as a home cinema. There's also a shared "living room" with lounge and bar, where you can receive friends.

At the time of writing, the rooftop pool was being completely over-hauled to provide a clearer view of the ocean. The top-floor bar, Bar D'Hotel, is considered one of the best nightlife spots in the area. **Pros:** Good location, well equipped, spacious, excellent service. **Cons:** Leblon Beach is not quite as pretty as Ipanema. ⊠ *Av. Delfim Moreira 696, Praia do Leblon* ⊕ *www.hoteismarina.com.br* ⟳ *37 rooms* ⌂ *In-room: safe, kitchen (some), refrigerator, DVD (some), Wi-Fi. In-hotel: restaurant, room service, bar, pool, gym, bicycles, laundry service, concierge, public Internet, public Wi-Fi, airport shuttle, parking (no fee), no-smoking rooms.*

> **PLAYING IT SAFE**
>
> Safety after dark is of paramount importance in Rio. You should be aware of your surroundings at all times. Always take a taxi after dark, and be sure it has the company name and phone number painted on the outside before you get in. Some drivers are reluctant to go to certain areas of town such as Santa Teresa due to protection rackets; in such situations simply ask to be taken to a taxi rank where they will continue your journey. Pickpockets love Copacabana and Lapa, so keep valuables either at the hotel or at least well hidden.

SANTA TERESA

$$$–$$$$ 🏠 **Relais Solar.** In a leafy courtyard set back from a quiet street, Relais Solar is the perfect boutique hideaway in bohemian Santa Teresa. The expansive colonial building comprises two 2-room suites, plus a separate bungalow. Next to each suite is a smaller room that can only be rented in conjunction with the main suite. Polished wooden floors in the dining room lead to a wide, winding staircase. Each room is flooded with light when the old-fashioned shutters are flung open to reveal a hammock-strewn veranda. A breakfast of tropical fruit, cheeses, breads, meat, and pastries can be had outdoors beneath the trees or indoors at the vast dining table. When night falls a bartender mixes cocktails beneath the stars, and there are occasional live music performances. **Pros:** Quiet and peaceful, gorgeous indoor and outdoor space, lively eating and drinking scene nearby. **Cons:** A long way from the beach, Santa Teresa can feel isolated from the rest of the city. ⊠ *Ladeira do Meirelles 32, Santa Teresa* ☎ *21/2221–2117* ⊕ *www.solardesanta. com* ⟳ *2 suites, 1 bunglow* ⌂ *In-room: refrigerator, Wi-Fi. In-hotel: room service, bar, pool, no elevator.*

NIGHTLIFE

BARS

A much-loved local pastime is drinking a well-chilled *chopp* (draft beer) and enjoying the lively atmosphere of a genuine Rio *botequim* (bar). Every neighborhood has its share of upmarket options (branches of *Belmonte, Devassa,* and *Conversa Fiada* are dotted around town), but no less enjoyable are the huge number of down-to-earth hole-in-the-wall options, offering ice-cold bottles of *cerveja* (beer) and some interesting regulars.

BOTAFOGO & **The Cobal.** More than just a bar, this collection of bars, restaurants, and
FLAMENGO shops in the style of an open-air market is always lively and has great
views of Cristo Redentor. The largely outdoor Espirito Do Chopp is
the best option, weather permitting. ⊠*Rua Voluntarios Da Patria 446,
Botafogo* ☎*21/2266–5599* ⊕*www.espiritodochopp.com.br.*

COPACABANA **Bip Bip.** Here the *roda de samba*—where musicians sit and play instru-
★ ments around a central table (in fact the *only* table in this tiny bar)—is
legendary, as is the help-yourself beer policy. The gnarled old owner
makes drink notations and keeps the crowd in check. ⊠*Rua Almirante
Gonçalves 50, Copacabana* ☎*021/2267–9696.*

Cervantes. This no-frills Copacabana institution marries great beer with
great sandwiches made with fresh beef, pork, and cheese crammed into
French bread (with obligatory pineapple slice). It's closed on Monday,
but merely to give the staff a chance to recover—the rest of the week
they cater to even the most tardy diners. They're known for their lively
late night–early morning crowd. ⊠*Av. Prado Júnior 335, Copacabana*
☎*021/2275–6147.*

IPANEMA **Bar Garota de Ipanema.** This is the original Garota (there are branches
all over the city), where Tom Jobim and Vinicius de Moraes penned
the timeless song "The Girl from Ipanema" back in the '60s. They
serve well-priced food and drink that no doubt originally appealed
to the two great songsmiths. ⊠*Rua Vinicius de Moraes 39, Ipanema*
☎*021/2523–3787.*

★ **Devassa.** Another cross-city chain of bars, Devassa is particularly nota-
ble for its own-brand beers, including delicious Pale Ales and Chopp
Escuro (dark beer). It also has a great menu of meat-related staples.
This branch in particular shines for its plum location a block back from
Ipanema Beach. ⊠*Rua Prudente de Moraes 416, Ipanema* ☎*21/2522–
0627* ⊕*www.devassa.com.br.*

LEBLON **Bracarense.** A trip to Bracarense after a hard day on the beach is what
Rio is all about. Crowds spill onto the streets while parked cars double
as chairs and the sandy masses gather at sunset for ice-cold chopp and
some of the best pork sandwiches, fish balls, and empadas in the neighborhood. ⊠*Rua José Linhares 85B, Leblon* ☎*021/2294–3549.*

★ **Jobi Bar.** Authentically carioca and a smart but down-to-earth must for
taking in the local spirit; on weekends it stays open until the last customer
leaves. ⊠*Av. Ataulfo de Paiva 1166, Leblon* ☎*021/2274–0547.*

NIGHT CLUBS & LIVE MUSIC

BOTAFOGO **Casa Da Matriz.** Undoubtedly one of the more adventurous clubs in Rio
both in terms of appearance and music policy. Young crowds flock to
this shabbily decorated venue that has the appearance of a house party
with its multiroom layout, staircase, and kitchen, and even old school
arcade games and a small junk shop. ⊠*Rua Henrique de Novaes 107,
Botafogo* ☎*021/2226–6342.*

Cinemathèque. Close to Botafogo Metro Station, Cinemathèque is a
new edition to the Matriz empire slowly taking over Botafogo with its

Carnival in Rio

By far the biggest event of the year, planning and preparation start months before the four-day Carnival weekend that's marked on every Brazilian's calendar. What began as a pre-Lent celebration has morphed into the massive affair of street parties, masquerades, and samba parades. Elaborate costumes, enormous floats, and intensive planning all unfurl magically behind the scenes as Brazilians from all walks of life save their money for the all-important *desfile* down the Sambódromo. Even though Carnival has set dates based on the lunar calendar that determines when Lent occurs, the *folia* (Carnival festivities) start at least a week before and end at least a week after the samba schools parade. Five-star hotels like the Sheraton

and Copacabana Palace have balls that are open to the public, as long as you can afford tickets (which run upward of R$3,000). A cheaper option is partying with the Carnival blocks and Carnival bands, which revel along the streets and beaches of the Zona Sul. If you really want to get close to the action, then you'll need to buy tickets (well in advance) for a seat at the Sambódromo. Most samba schools begin their rehearsals around October; if you're in Rio from October to January, visit one of the samba schools *(see Nightlife)* on a rehearsal day. Whether your scene is hanging out at the bars, partying in the street, parading along the beach, masked balls for the elite, or fun in a stadium, Rio's Carnival is an experience of a lifetime.

inventive bars and clubs. Expect a variety of Brazilian music old and new with live shows upstairs from 10:30 PM, or simply relax in the open air garden downstairs. ⊠*Rua Voluntários da Pátria 53, Botafogo* ☎*021/2286–5731.*

COPACABANA **Le Boy.** Right next door to La Girl, this is, unsurprisingly, the gay male mecca, playing pop and house music along with outrageous stage shows at the weekends. ⊠*Rua Paul Pompéia 102, Copacabana* ☎*021/2513-4993* ⊕*www.leboy.com.br.*

Fosfobox. For the more serious dance music enthusiast, Fosfobox, in the heart of Copacabana, plays the best underground dance music as well as rock and pop from Wednesday to Sunday. It's in an industrial-feeling basement and has a newly opened second room, which offers a bit more comfort with its cosy red sofas. ⊠*Rua Siqueira Campos 143, Copacabana* ☎*021/2548–7498* ⊕*www.fosfobox.com.br.*

La Girl. A well-known girls-only gay club that attracts the famous and fabulous females of Rio. ⊠*Rua Raul Pompéia 102, Copacabana* ☎*021/2513–4993* ⊕*www.lagirl.com.br.*

IPANEMA **Lounge 69.** A sleek new option in the heart of Ipanema, Lounge 69 with its attractive wooden facade and dashing interior provides a fresh taste of late night glamour in this happening street. ⊠*Rua Farme de Amoedo, Ipanema.*

LARANJEIRAS **Casa Rosa.** This former brothel is now a stunning bright pink mansion in the Laranjeiras hillside. It's loved by locals for its traditional musical repertoire. Sunday afternoon *feijoada* and samba on the terrace is a must for anyone seeking out a true carioca experience. ⊠*Rua Alice 550, Laranjeiras* ☎*021/8877 8804* ⊕*www.casarosa.com.br.*

LAPA **Carioca da Gema.** The original template for Lapa's samba clubs since
★ opening in 2000, Carioca da Gema remains one of the liveliest spots in the area, with local musical talent six nights a week (closed Sunday). By 11 PM it can be hard to find a place to stand, but regulars still find a way to samba, so call ahead and book a table if you are more keen on spectating. ⊠*Rua Mem de Sá 79, Lapa* ☎*021/2221 0043* ⊕*www. barcariocadagema.com.br.*

★ **Rio Scenarium.** Rio Scenarium has become an absolute staple for those seeking out live samba in Rio, but despite the hordes of tourists it somehow manages to retain its authenticity and magic. This is due in part to its incredible setting in a former junk shop, still rammed to the rafters with old instruments, bikes, furniture, and puppets, but also the great bands and persevering locals who love to show off their moves and entice novices onto the dance floor. Arrive early (before 9 PM) to avoid the queues at the weekends or call ahead and book a table. ⊠*Rua do Lavrádio 20, Lapa* ☎*021/3147–9005* ⊕*www.rioscenarium.com.br.*

SAMBA-SCHOOL SHOWS

Weekly public rehearsals (*ensaio*) attract crowds of samba enthusiasts and visitors alike to the *escolas de samba* (samba schools) from August through to Carnival (February or March). As the schools frantically ready themselves for the high point of the year, the atmosphere in these packed warehouses is often electric, and with Mangueira and Beija Flor, always sweaty. This may prove one of your liveliest and most chaotic nights on the town. Ticket prices range from R$10 to R$25.

Acadêmicos do Salgueiro. Rehearsals are only on Saturday at 10 PM. ⊠*Rua Silva Teles 104, Andaraí* ☎*021/2288–3065* ⊕*www.salgueiro. com.br.*

Beija-Flor. The winning school in 2007, its rehearsals take place on Thursday at 9 PM. ⊠*Pracinha Wallace Paes Leme 1025, Nilópolis* ☎*021/2791–2866* ⊕*www.beija-flor.com.br.*

Estação Primeira de Mangueira. One of the most popular schools and always a challenger for the Carnival title, rehearsals are Saturday at 10 PM. ⊠*Rua Visconde de Niterói 1072, Mangueira* ☎*021/3872–6787* ⊕*www.mangueira.com.br.*

SPORTS & THE OUTDOORS

BOATING & SAILING

Dive Point. Schooner tours around the main beaches of Rio and as far afield as Buzios and Angra are offered here, as well as deep-sea and wreck diving. Be sure to ask if their prices include all the necessary equipment and training (if required). ⊠*Av. Ataulfo da Paiva 1174, basement, Leblon* ☎*021/2239–5105* ⊕*www.divepoint.com.br.*

Saveiro's Tour. Catch one of the daily cruises around Guanabara Bay— views of Sugar Loaf, Botafogo Bay, and the Rio-Niterói Bridge are the highlights. They also hire out speedboats and sailboats by the day. ✉*Rua Conde de Lages 44, Glória* ☎*021/2225–6064* ⊕*www. saveiros.com.br.*

HANG GLIDING

★ **Hilton Fly Rio Hang Gliding Center.** DeHilton and his team have years of experience of flying over Tijuca Forest and landing on São Conrado beach. They can arrange pickup and drop-off from your hotel; price US$125. ✉*Rua Jose Higino 254, Tijuca* ☎*021/2278–3779 or 021/9964–2607* ⊕*www.hiltonfly rio.com.*

> ### RIO SURF BUS
>
> The Oi Surf Bus goes three times a day from Lago Do Machado to Prainha, which is considered to be the best surfing beach close to the city. The two-hour trip takes in the best surf breaks west of Rio, including all 12 km of Barra, Recreio, and Macumba. There's no snobbery if you don't have a board and you're just going along for the ride. Catch the bus from anywhere along Copacabana, Ipanema, or Leblon beachfront for an easy route to some stunning out-of-town beaches. Check outward and return times at ⊕*www. surfbus.com.br*, because you do not want to be left stranded.

Just Fly. For R$200 Just Fly will collect you from your hotel, run you through the basics, and then run you off Pedra Bonita mountain into the sky high above Tijuca Forest. Excellent instructors can also film or photograph the experience for an extra charge. ☎*021/2268–0565 or 021/9985–7540* ⊕*www.justfly.com.br.*

São Conrado Eco-Aventura. This is another reliable and experienced team that can offer you a bird's-eye view of Rio either by hang glider or paraglider. ☎*021/9966–7010* ⊕*www.guia4ventos.com.br.*

HORSE RACING

★ **Jóquei Clube.** This beautiful old stadium manages to conjure a bygone sense of grandeur to even the smallest of race meetings with its impeccably preserved betting hall, 1920s grandstand, and views of the beach in the distance framed by Cristo Redentor and the Dois Irmaos mountain. When the big event of the year, the Grande Premio, comes around every August, expect the crowds to swell as the great and the good seize the opportunity to get dressed to the nines. Entry is free, too, but you need to dress smart–casual, with no shorts or flip-flops allowed in the main stand. ✉*Praça Santos Dumont 31, Gávea* ☎*021/3534–9000* ⊕*www.jcb.com.br.*

SURFING

Escola de Surf do Arpoador. The most consistent break in the city has its own surf school based on the beach; simply call up or stop by to book an early-morning appointment. ✉*In front of posto 7, Arpoador beach, Arpoador* ☎*021/9131–2368* ⊕*www.surfboys.com.br.*

Kitepoint Rio. This is one of several companies based in huts along Avenida do Pepê near Posto 7 that will provide all the equipment and training you need to master the sport of kite surfing. Wind conditions have to be just right though, so patience is a virtue when seeking lessons. ⊠ *Av. do Pepê, Kiosk No. 7, Barra* ☎ *021/9200–0418.*

SIDE TRIPS FROM RIO

The state of Rio de Janeiro is relatively small, yet offers a broad range of distinctly Brazilian attractions, most within three hours of the city. Búzios, with its 23 beaches, temperate climate, and vibrant nightlife, is a popular destination for people from around the world. Northeast of Rio de Janeiro lies Petrópolis, whose opulent imperial palace was once the summer home of the emperor. West of Rio de Janeiro, Angra dos Reis is the jumping-off point for 365 islands that pepper a picturesque bay. The largest, Ilha Grande, is a short ferry ride from Angra dos Reis and is still somewhat unspoiled. Paraty, a UNESCO world heritage site, is a well-preserved imperial town. Its 18th-century Portuguese architecture and secluded beaches make it the highlight of the region.

BÚZIOS

24 km (15 mi) northeast of Cabo Frio, 176 km (126 mi) northeast of Rio.

Fodor'sChoice ★ Little more than two hours from Rio de Janeiro, Búzios is a string of 23 beautiful beaches on an 8-km-long (5-mi-long) peninsula. It was a fishing village until the 1960s, when Brigitte Bardot holidayed here to escape the paparazzi.

Búzios has something for everyone. Some hotels cater specifically to families and offer plenty of activities and around-the-clock childcare. Many offer spa facilities, and some specialize in weeklong retreats. For outdoor enthusiasts, Búzios offers surfing, windsurfing, kite surfing, diving, hiking, and mountain biking.

GETTING HERE & AROUND
From Rio de Janeiro, drive across the Rio-Niterói bridge and bear left, following the BR 101. At Rio Bonito take the exit to the Region dos Lagos. At São Pedro de Aldeia, turn left at the sign for Búzios. The trip takes approximately two hours.

TEAM has weekend charter flights that depart when there are enough passengers. A round-trip ticket is R$575.

SAFETY & PRECAUTIONS
A few simple rules: don't eat fresh oysters sold anywhere but in a restaurant, and make sure the drinks you buy from street vendors are made with commercial ice. (The easiest way to check is to look for a circular hole through the middle.)

Avoid visiting Praia da Foca in the late afternoon and evening. Don't go alone during the day, as there have been muggings on the beach.

A Bit of History

The history of the state of Rio de Janeiro is as colorful as it is bloody. The first Portuguese trading post was established in 1502 in Cabo Frio to facilitate the export of Pau-Brasil (Brazil Wood). This led to confrontations with Tamoios Indians and their French allies.

The discovery of gold in the state of Minas Gerais in 1696 and the construction of the "Caminho de Ouro" (Path of Gold) from the mines to Paraty bought prosperity. In its wake came pirates and corsairs who used the islands and bays of Angra dos Reis as cover while they plundered the ships bound for Rio de Janeiro.

The mines gave out in the late 1700s, but the relatively new crop called

coffee, introduced to the state around 1770, brought another boom. In the mid-19th century the state produced more than 70% of Brazil's coffee. Sadly, vast tracks of Atlantic rain forest were destroyed to make room for the crop across the interior of the state.

In 1808, threatened by Napoléon, King Dom João VI of Portugal moved his court to Rio. He returned to Portugal in 1821 and left his son, Dom Pedro I, behind as prince regent. The following year Dom Pedro I was called back to Portugal, but refused to leave. Instead, he declared Brazil an independent state and himself its emperor. In 1847, his son, Dom Pedro II, inaugurated Petrópolis as the summer capital of Brazil.

ESSENTIALS

Airline TEAM Transportes Aéreos (☎ 021/3328–1616 ⊕ www.voeteam.com. br).

Airport Aeroporto Umberto Modiano (✉ Av. José Bento Ribeiro Dantas s/n ☎ 22/2629–1225).

Banks & Currency Exchange Banco 24 Horas ATMs (✉ Praça Santos Dumont, Centro). **Currency Exchange** Malizia Tour (✉ Av. José Bento R. Dantes 100 ☎ 022/2623–1226).

Bus Contacts Auto Viação 1001 (☎ 021/4004–5001 ⊕ www.autoviacao1001. com.br).

Emergencies & Medical Assistance Clínica Búzios (✉ Estrada J. B. Ribeiro Dantas 3000, Manguinhos ☎ 22/2623–2465).

Taxi Búzios Radio Taxi (☎ 22/2623–2509).

Visitor & Tour Info Búzios Tourism Office (✉ Avenida J.B. Ribeiro Dante s/n, Porceco ☎ 022/2633–6200 ⊕ www.buziosonline.com.br). **Tour Shop** (✉ Orla Bardot 550, Centro ☎ 22/2623–4733 or 022/2623–0292 ⊕ www.tourshop.com.br).

EXPLORING BÚZIOS

☾ **Praia Azeda** and **Praia Azedinha** both have clear, calm waters and are accessible via a trail from Praia dos Ossos, or by boat. It's one of the few places you may find topless bathing. **Praia da Ferradura,** with its calm water and casual bars, captures the spirit of Búzios. It's a great beach for families with young children. **Praia de Geribá** is a half moon

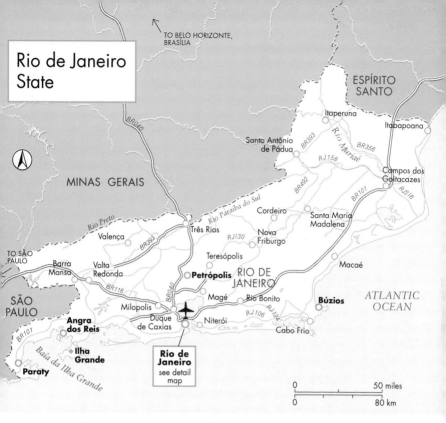

Rio de Janeiro State

of white sand that is fashionable with a young crowd. The waves make it popular choice for surfers and wind surfers. **Praia João Fernandes** and **Praia João Fernandinho** boast calm seas and crystal waters. Bars on the beach serve fresh seafood.

WHERE TO EAT

$$$–$$$$
CONTINENTAL
★

✕**Cigalon.** Widely considered the best restaurant in Búzios, Cigalon is an elegant establishment with a veranda overlooking the beach. Though the waiters are bow-tied and the tables covered with crisp linens and lighted by flickering candles, this place still has a casual feel. The food is French-inspired, and includes lamb steak, braised duck breast, and prawns in a lemongrass sauce with almonds. The R$50 bistro menu—including a starter, a main, and a dessert—is a great deal. ⊠*Rua das Pedras 199 Centro, 28950–000* ☎*022/2623–6284* ▤*AE, DC, MC, V.*

$$$$
SEAFOOD
★

✕**Satyricon.** The Italian fish restaurant famous in Rio has opened up shop here as well. The dishes here are expensive, but always excellent. Go all out and try the grilled mixed seafood plate with cream of Lemon Risotto. Reservations are normally required for parties of four of more on the weekends. ⊠*Av. José Bento Ribeiro Dantas (Orla Bardot) 500* ☎*022/2623–2691* ▤*AE, DC, MC, V* ☉*No lunch.*

WHERE TO STAY

$$$$ ⬚ **Casas Brancas.** If you're looking for complete relaxation, and you've
Fodor'sChoice   got plenty of cash on hand, this is the place to stay in Búzios. The
★   quirky building was constructed on several levels facing the beach,
which makes for interestingly shaped rooms. Each is decorated with
care, but simple cottage style and Zen-like peace and quiet are the hallmarks here. Get an ocean-view room, and one with a private balcony if
you can swing it. The spa is one of the best in town. **Pros:** Great sunset
views, on the beach, close to Rua das Pedras. **Cons:** Often booked up
in high season, limited wheelchair access. ⊠*Alto do Humaitá 10, off
Orla Bardot, Centro* ☎*022/2623–1458* ⊕*www.casasbrancas.com.br*
⬚*32 rooms, 3 suites* ⬚*In-room: safe, refrigerator. In-hotel: restaurant, pool, spa, laundry service, no elevator, public Wi-Fi* ⊟*AE, DC,
MC, V* ⍟*BP.*

$$$ ⬚ **Galápagos Inn.** Overlooking the charming Orla Bardot—the continu-
★   ation of Rua das Pedras, where people congregate at night—this hotel
also has a view of the sea and, best of all, a view of the sunset. Rooms
are comfortable, with decoration inspired by the sea. Verandas have
views to João Fernandinho Beach, and there's bar service at the beach.
The hotel is included in Brazil's esteemed Roteiros de Charme club, a
highly exclusive association of the nation's best places to stay. **Pros:**
All rooms have ocean views, close to center. **Cons:** Beach is crowded
during high season, lots of steps to climb. ⊠*Praia João Fernandinho
3* ☎*022/2620–8800* ⊕*www.galapagos.com.br* ⬚*39 rooms, 5 suites*
⬚*In-room: safe, refrigerator, cable TV. In-hotel: restaurant, room ser-
vice, bar, pool, laundry service, exercise room, no-smoking rooms, pub-
lic Internet, no elevator* ⊟*AE, DC, MC, V* ⍟*BP.*

$$ ⬚ **Pousada dos Gravatás.** Its location right on long Praia de Geribá
☾   makes this pousada the best budget option in Búzios. Both breakfast
and lunch are included in the rates. Suites have verandas and ocean
views. Standard apartments are at the back of the pousada, facing an
inside patio. Rooms aren't big, but they're comfortable, with decor
inspired by the sea. **Pros:** Lunch served on the beach, good value for
money, family-friendly atmosphere. **Cons:** Small rooms, basic restaurant. ⊠*Rua dos Gravatás 67, Praia de Geribá* ☎*022/2623–1218*
⊕*www.pousadagravatas.com.br* ⬚*55 rooms, 8 suites* ⬚*In-room:
refrigerator. In-hotel: room service, bar, pools, gym, beachfront, public Wi-Fi* ⊟*AE, DC, MC, V* ⍟*BP.*

SPORTS & THE OUTDOORS

BIKING   **Nas Trilhas de Búzios** (⊠*Rua canto do Revela 2, Praia de Manguinhos* ☎*22/2623–6365 or 22/9234–6707*) offers everything from half-
day bike tours around the city to seven-day excursions along deserted
beaches and through the mountains.

SURFING   Surf schools set up tents along Geribá Beach, and also rent out boards.
Expect to pay R$45 an hour for a private lesson, including board rental,
and R$15 to rent a board for an hour. In front of the Hotel le Relais
de la Borie, **Ma'rcio's Surf School** (⊠*Praia de Geribá* ☎*22/9215–3880*)
offers personalized classes and a wide range of rental equipment.

PETRÓPOLIS

68 km (42 mi) northeast of Rio.

The highway northeast of Rio de Janeiro rumbles past forests and waterfalls en route to a mountain town so refreshing and picturesque that Dom Pedro II, Brazil's second emperor, moved there with his summer court. From 1889 to 1899 it was also the country's year-round seat of government. Horse-drawn carriages clip-clop between the sights, passing flowering gardens, shady parks, and imposing pink mansions.

GETTING HERE & AROUND

From Rio by car head north along BR 040 to Petrópolis. The picturesque drive—once you leave the city—takes around an hour, depending on the traffic. Única buses leave every 40 minutes—less often on weekends—from Rio's Rodoviária Novo Rio. The easiest and safest way to get to Petrópolis is to arrange a shuttle at your hotel in Rio.

ESSENTIALS

Banks & Currency Exchange Banco 24 Horas ATMs (⊠ *Praça Paulo Carneiro, 25620-140*).

Bus Contacts Rodoviária Petrópolis (⊠ *Rua Doutor Porciúncula 75* ☎ *024/2237-0101*). **Única** (☎ *021/2263-8792*).

Emergencies & Medical Assistance Hospital Municipal Nelson de Sá Earp (⊠ *Rua Paulino Afonso 529, Centro* ☎ *024/2237-4062*).

Taxi Ponto de Taxi Elite (☎ *0800/282-1412 or 24/2242-4090*).

Visitor & Tour Info Petrópolis Tourism Office (⊠ *Praça da Liberdade s/n Petrópolis* ☎ *24/2246-9300* ⊕ *www.petropolis.rj.gov.br*). **Grayline Tours** (⊠ *Av. Niemeyer 121, Rio de Janeiro* ☎ *21/2512-9919* ⊕ *www.grayline.com.br*). **Tourism Radical Rio** (☎ *21/9224-6963* ⊕ *www.rioturismoradical.com.br*).

EXPLORING PETRÓPOLIS

The **Casa de Santos Dumont** *(Santos Dumont House)* was built in 1918 by one of the world's first aviators. Santos Dumont's inventions fill the house, including a heated shower he invented before most homes had running water. The home doesn't have a kitchen because Dumont ordered his food from a nearby hotel—the first documented restaurant delivery service in Brazil. ⊠ *Rua do Encantado 22* ☎ *024/2247-3158* 🖼 *R$5* ☉ *Tues.–Sun. 9:30–5.*

Take a horse-drawn carriage to **Cathedral São Pedro de Alcântara,** the Gothic cathedral containing the tombs of Dom Pedro II; his wife, Dona Teresa Cristina; and their daughter, Princesa Isabel. ⊠ *Rua São Pedro de Alcântara 60, Centro* ☎ *024/2242-4300* 🖼 *Free* ☉ *Tues.–Sun. 8–noon and 2–6.*

The **Museu Imperial** is the magnificent 44-room palace that was the summer home of Dom Pedro II, emperor of Brazil, and his family in the 19th century. The colossal structure is filled with polished wooden floors, artwork, and grand chandeliers. You can also see the diamond-encrusted gold crown and scepter of Brazil's last emperor, as well as other royal jewels. ⊠*Rua da Imperatriz 220, Centro* ☎*024/2237–8000* ⊕*www.museuimperial.gov.br* ⊠*R$8* ☼*Tues.–Sun. 11–6.*

$$$ **Locanda Della Mimosa.** This cozy pousada is in a valley with trails
★ winding through the colorful bougainvillea trees. The handful of suites
are decorated in a classical style with imperial influences. Tea is served
in the afternoon and is included in the price of the room. The Italian
restaurant, run by the talented Danio Braga, who is always cooking up
novelties, is open Thursday through Sunday and includes specialties
from different regions of Italy. **Pros:** Spacious rooms, great restaurant,
afternoon tea service. **Cons:** Need to book in advance. ⊠*Km 71.5,
BR 040, Alameda das Mimosas 30, Vale Florido* ☎*024/2233–5405*
⊕*www.locanda.com.br* ⇆*6 suites* ⤶*In-room: refrigerator, DVD, Wi-
Fi. In-hotel: restaurant, room service, bar, pool* ⊟*MC* ⦿*BP* ☼*Hotel
closed Mon.–Thurs.*

$$ **Pousada de Alcobaça.** Just north of Petrópolis, this is considered by
many to be the region's loveliest inn. The grounds have beautiful gar-
dens and a shimmering swimming pool. The kitchen turns out exceptional breakfasts, lunches, and high teas with an emphasis on fresh
ingredients. Meals ($–$$$), which include savory pastas, are served
in the garden. A pot roast, prepared in a charming farm kitchen, is
a must. The hotel grows its own vegetables and herbs. All rooms in
the early-20th-century house are cozy and decorated in a rustic style.
Pros: Tasty food, great views. **Cons:** Need to book far in advance,
it's a 15-minute drive into the city. ⊠*Agostinho Goulão 298, Cor-
rêas* ☎*024/2221–1240* ⇆*11 rooms* ⊕*www.pousadadaalcobaca.com.
br* ⤶*In-room: DVD. In-hotel: restaurant, room service, tennis court,
pool, laundry service* ⊟*AE, DC, MC, V* ⦿*BP.*

ANGRA DOS REIS

168 km (91 mi) west of Rio.

Angra dos Reis (Bay of Kings) has it all: colonial architecture, beauti-
ful beaches, and clear green waters. Schooners, yachts, sailboats, and
fishing skiffs drift among the bay's 365 islands, one for every day of
the year. Indeed, Angra dos Reis' popularity lies in its strategic location
near the islands. Some are deserted stretches of sand, others patches
of Atlantic rain forest surrounded by emerald waters perfect for swim-
ming or snorkeling.

GETTING HERE & AOURND

Angra dos Reis-bound Costa Verde buses leave Rio every hour. The
2½-hour trip costs R$34. Ferries leave the terminal at Angra dos Reis
for Ilha Grande every day at 3:30 PM. The 90-minute trip costs R$5.

From Rio by car, get onto the Rio-Santos highway (BR 101) and follow
it south for 190 km until you get to Angra dos Reis. Expect the trip to
take between two and three hours, depending on traffic.

TEAM airlines offers an irregular service from Rio to Angra dos Reis.

SAFETY & PRECAUTIONS

Leaving your car unattended on the street is risky. Park your car in one of the many secure lots, expecially if you plan an overnight trip to Ilha Grande.

ESSENTIALS

Airline **TEAM Transportes Aéreos** (☎ 021/3328–1616 ⊕ www.voeteam.com.br).

Airport **Aeroporto Municipal** (✉ Rua Pref. João Galindo s/n, Japuíba ☎ 24/3365–4073).

Banks & Currency Exchange **Banco 24 Horas ATMs** (✉ Rua Júlio Maria 2352, 3900-504).

Bus Contacts **Costa Verde** (☎ 021/2573–1484 ⊕ www.costaverdetransportes. com.br). **Rodoviária Angra dos Reis** (✉ Av. Almirante Jair Toscano de Brito 110 ☎ 024/3365–2041).

Emergencies & Medical Assistance **Santa Casa de Misericórdia** (✉ Rua Doutor Coutinho 8423900-620 ☎ 024/3365–5004).

Taxi **Ponto de Táxi** (☎ 24/3365–1361).

Visitor & Tour Info **Angra dos Reis Tourism Office** (✉ Av. Ayrton Senna 580 ☎ 24/3367–7789 ⊕ www.angra.rj.gov.br). **Mar de Angra** (✉ Av. Júlio Maria 16 ☎ 24/3365–1097 ⊕ www.mardeangra.com.br).

EXPLORING ANGRA DOS REIS

The **Associação dos Barqueiros** (☎ 024/3365–3165) runs boat tours to the islands. Don't miss the tour to Ilha da Gipóia and its beautiful beaches, like the famous Jurubaíba, which is perfect for snorkeling or diving. ⚠ Some boats have a reputation for playing loud music. Check ahead of time if you prefer a more tranquil environment.

WHERE TO STAY

$$$$ ★ ⊞ **Hotel do Frade & Golf Resort.** Guest-room balconies overlook the sea and the private beach at this modern resort hotel. The many sports options include boat rentals (sailboats, motorboats, catamarans), scuba diving and, of course, golf. It's no surprise that seafood is a standout at the buffet restaurant called Scuna ($$$). Other restaurants, which serve a variety of international cuisines, open in summer. Room rates include both breakfast and an additional meal. **Pros:** Top-notch service, spacious rooms, private beach. **Cons:** Impersonal feel, pricey rates, a long way from the city. ✉ Km 123, BR 101, Praia do Frade, 32 km (20 mi) west of Angra do Reis ☎ 024/3369–9500 ⊕ www.hoteldofrade. com.br ⤢ 162 rooms ♿ In-room: safe, refrigerator, Wi-Fi. In-hotel: 5 restaurants, room service, bar, golf course, tennis courts, pool, laundry service, no-smoking rooms ⊟ AE, DC, MC, V ⊙ FAP.

$$ ⊞ **Portogalo Suíte.** Perched on a hill with a wonderful view of the bay, the exposed-brick buildings at this hotel have a rustic appeal. Rooms have balconies with sea view. Although starkly white and cool, with tile floors, the rooms are clean and right above the beach. A cable car takes guests down the hillside to the beach and the marina. **Pros:** Views of the bay and Ilha Grande. All rooms have verandas with ocean views.

Cons: A long way from town, basic rooms. ⊠*Km 71, BR 101, Praia de Itapinhoacanga, 25 km (16 mi) south of town* ☎*024/3361–4343 or 0800/282–4343* ⊕*www.portogalosuite.com.br* ⇆*85 rooms* ⌂*In-room: safe, refrigerator, cable TV. In-hotel: room service, bar, tennis courts, sauna, pool, laundry service, public Wi-Fi* ⊟*AE, DC, MC, V.*

ILHA GRANDE

21 km (13 mi) south of Angra dos Reis or Mangaratiba via 90-minute ferry ride.

Ilha Grande, 90 minutes via ferry from Angra dos Reis, is one of the most popular island destinations in Brazil. It boasts 86 idyllic beaches, some of which are sandy ribbons with backdrops of tropical foliage, while others are densely wooded coves with waterfalls tumbling down from the forest.

Ilha Grande once provided refuge for pirates and corsairs, and was the first point of entry for many slaves brought here from Africa. Later it became a leper colony, but for some its use as a political prison during the military dictatorship from 1964 to 1984 was its most insidious incarnation.

GETTING HERE & AROUND

Ferries to Ilha Grande are run by Barcas S/A. The ferry for Vila do Abraão on Ilha Grande leaves Angra dos Reis daily at 3:30 PM and returns weekdays at 10 AM and weekends at 11 AM.

As there are no cars, it's wise to take only what you can carry. Men waiting at the pier make a living helping tourists carry luggage for about about R$5 per bag.

SAFETY & PRECAUTIONS

Avoid taking unlicensed boats. Verify the condition of any boat you plan to board, and check that it has a life preserver for every person aboard.

ESSENTIALS

Banks & Currency Exchange There are no banks or ATMs on the island, and credit cards are not widely accepted. Be sure to bring some extra cash with you.

Emergencies & Medical Assistance **Posto de Saude** (⊠*Rua Getúlio Vargas).*

Visitor & Tour Info **South America Experience** (☎*021/2513–4091* ⊕*www. southamericaexperience.com).* **Tourist Information Center** (⊠*Rua da Praia s/n* ☎*24/3361–5508).* **Ilha Grande Dive** (⊠*Rua Buganville* ☎*24/3361–5512* ⊕*www.ilhagrandedive.com.br).*

WHAT TO SEE

Blue Lagoon is popular with day-trippers from the mainland. This natural pool that forms at low tide is home to thousands of small fish that will literally eat out of your hands. Be sure to take a mask and snorkel.

Dois Rios has two rivers that flow out of the forest on either side of this beach, providing a bountiful environment for aquatic life. Just inland are the ruins of the old prison.

★ Locals and visitors alike regard **Lopez Mendes**, a 3 km (2 mi) stretch of white with emerald waters, as one of the most beautiful beaches on Ilha Grande. Organize a boat trip from Vila do Abraão if you don't feel up to the two-hour hike through the forest.

WHERE TO EAT

$–$$
SEAFOOD
✕**Lua e Mar.** Expect fresh, well-prepared seafood at this longtime favorite. It's a casual establishment, so you can stroll in from the beach still wearing your Havaianas. Try Dona Cidinha's specialty, fish with half-ripe bananas. ⊠ *Rua da Praia, Vila do Abraão* ☎ *024/3361–5113* ⊟ *AE, DC, MC, V* ☉ *Closed Wed.*

$–$$
SEAFOOD
✕**O Pescador.** Inside the pousada of the same name, this rustic but cozy restaurant mixes local seafood with Italian cooking techniques. The specialties are grilled fish (types of fish vary according to the season), bought from local fishermen. Grilled dourado and grouper are served most of the year. ⊠ *Rua da Praia, Vila do Abraão* ☎ *024/3361–5114* ⊟ *AE, MC, V.*

WHERE TO STAY

$
🏨**Pousada do Canto.** In a colonial-style house, this pousada faces pretty Praia do Canto. The place has tropical atmosphere, with nice touches like the thatched-roofed bar beside the pretty pool. Some rooms face the ocean and have verandas. **Pros:** On the beach, short walk to the village, pretty pool. **Cons:** Rooms can get chilly in winter, small bathrooms. ⊠ *Rua da Praia 121, Vila do Abraão* ☎ *19/3455–0986* ⊕ *www.ilha grande.com.br/pages/pousadas/ilhazul/canto.html* ⤴ *11 rooms* ⟡ *In-room: refrigerator. In-hotel: pool, beachfront, no elevator* ⊟ *AE, DC, MC, V* ⦿ *BP.*

$$
★
🏨**Pousada Sankay.** The colorful rooms at Pousada Sankay have names inspired by sea creatures, like Lagosta (lobster) or Golfinho (dolphin). Kayaks, canoes, and other boats are available for rent, as is diving equipment. A boat from the pousada can pick you up at Angra dos Reis. **Pros:** Plenty of activities, bar extends over the ocean. **Cons:** You need a boat to get to the Vila do Abraão, small rooms. ⊠ *Enseada do Bananal* ☎ *024/3365–4065* ⊕ *www.pousadasankay.com.br* ⤴ *16 rooms* ⟡ *In-room: refrigerator. In-hotel: restaurant, bar, pool, gym* ⊟ *AE, DC, MC, V* ⦿ *MAP* ☉ *Closed June.*

PARATY

99 km (60 mi) southwest of Angra dos Reis, 261 km (140 mi) southwest of Rio.

This stunning colonial city—also spelled Parati—is one of South America's gems. Giant iron chains hang from posts at the beginning of the mazelike grid of cobblestone streets, closing them to all but pedestrians, horses, and bicycles. Until the 18th century this was an important transit point for gold plucked from the Minas Gerais—a safe harbor protected by a fort. In 1720, however, the colonial powers cut a new trail from the gold mines straight to Rio de Janeiro, bypassing the town and leaving it isolated. It remained that way until contemporary times, when artists, writers, and others "discovered" the community and UNESCO placed it on its list of World Heritage Sites.

GETTING HERE & AROUND
From Rio De Janeiro, it's a four-hour drive along the BR 101 to Paraty. Costa Verde buses leave Rio daily every two hours. The journey costs R$42.

SAFETY & PRECAUTIONS
Although downtown is safe, even late at night, be careful about walking alone in other parts of town.

ESSENTIALS
Banks & Currency Exchange **Banco 24 Horas ATMs** (⊠ *Rua Roberto Silveira, Praça Chafariz).*

Banco do Brazil (⊠ *Rua Roberto Silveira 192, Praça Chafariz)* has exchange rates that are better than most in town.

Bus Contacts **Costa Verde** (☎ *21/2573–1484* ⊕ *www.costaverdetransportes.com. br).* **Rodoviária Paraty** (⊠ *Rua Jango Pádua* ☎ *024/3371–1177).*

Emergencies & Medical Assistance **Santa Casa de Misericórdia** (⊠ *Av. São Pedro de Alcântara, Pontal* ☎ *024/3371–1623).*

Taxi **Tuim Taxi Service** (☎ *24/9918–7834* ⊕ *www.eco-paraty.com/taxi).*

Visitor & Tour Info **Paraty Tourism Office** (⊠ *Av. Roberto da Silveira 1* ☎ *024/3371–1897* ⊕ *www.paraty.com.br).* **Paraty Tours** (⊠ *Av. Roberto Silveira 11* ☎ *24/3371–2651* ⊕ *www.paratytours.com.br).* **South America Experience** (☎ *021/2513–4091* ⊕ *www.southamericaexperience.com).*

EXPLORING PARATY
The **Forte Defensor Perpétuo** was built in the early 1700s (and rebuilt in 1822) as a defense against pirates. It's now home to a folk-arts center. ⊠ *Morro da Vila Velha* ☎ *No phone* 🖅 *R$1* ☉ *Wed.–Sun. 9–5.*

The oldest church in Paraty, the simple **Igreja de Santa Rita** was built in 1722 by and for freed slaves. Today it houses a small religious art museum (Museu de Arte Sacra). It's a typical Jesuit church with a tower and three front windows. ⊠ *Rua Santa Rita* ☎ *024/3371–1620* 🖅 *R$1* ☉ *Wed.–Sun. 9–noon and 2–5.*

BEACHES
Sono and **Antigos** are two of the most beautiful beaches in Paraty. They can only be accessed by a trail through the forest. It's an easy hour-long hike, and once here you can catch a ride back by boat.

About 30 km (20 mi) from Paraty, **Trinidade** was once a hippie hangout. Today Trinidade is one of the most happening districts in Paraty, with plenty of activities and even a natural pool that's perfect for children.

WHERE TO EAT

$$–$$$$
ECLECTIC
✗**Merlin o Mago.** The German chef and owner, Hado Steinbrecher, was a former photojournalist and food critic who studied in France and traveled through Asia, mainly in Thailand and India. The cuisine here is an interesting mixture of Brazilian, French, and Thai traditions. Entrées include grilled shrimp flambéed in cognac or snook wrapped in a crepe with yogurt and green pepper, topped with caviar. ⊠*Rua do Comércio 376* ☎*024/3371–2157* ⊕*www.paraty.com.br/merlin* ⊟*DC, MC, V.*

$$$$
SEAFOOD
✗**Refúgio.** Near the water in a quiet part of town, this seafood restaurant is a great place for a romantic dinner. Café tables out front sit under heat lamps. The codfish cakes are excellent. ⊠*Praça do Porto* ☎*024/3371–2447* ⊕*www.eco-paraty.com/refugio* ⊟*MC, V.*

WHERE TO STAY

$$
★
🏨**Pousada Pardieiro.** The houses that make up this property are decorated in a 19th-century colonial style. Rooms have dark-wood carved beds and antique bureaus. There are no TVs in the rooms, but there's a living room with a home theater. A beautiful patio has birds and orchids. **Pros:** Close to the historic center, great pool and garden. **Cons:** No room TVs, cold floors in winter. ⊠*Rua do Comércio 74* ☎*024/3371–1370* ⊕*www.pousadapardieiro.com.br* 🛏*27 rooms, 2 suites* ♿*In-room: no room TV, safe, refrigerator. In-hotel: restaurant, room service, bar, pool, laundry service, public Internet* ⊟*AE, DC, MC V.*

$
Fodor'sChoice
★
🏨**Pousada do Príncipe.** The great-grandson of Emperor Pedro II owns this aptly named inn at the edge of the colonial city. The Pousada of the Prince is painted in the yellow and green of the imperial flag, and its quiet, colorful public areas are decorated with photos of the royal family. Rooms are small, decorated in a colonial style, and face either the interior garden or the swimming pool. The restaurant is impressive, too; its chef turns out an exceptional feijoada. **Pros:** Close to the historic center, beautiful buildings. **Cons:** Unimaginative decoration, so-so service. ⊠*Av. Roberto Silveira 289, Paraty* ☎*024/3371–2266* ⊕*www.pousadadoprincipe.com.br* 🛏*34 rooms, 3 suites* ♿*In-room: refrigerator. In-hotel: restaurant, room service, tennis courts, pool, laundry service* ⊟*AE, DC, MC, V.*

SÃO PAULO

The main financial hub in the country, São Paulo is also Brazil's most cosmopolitan city, with top-rate nightlife and restaurants and impressive cultural and arts scenes. Most of the wealthiest people in Brazil live here—and the rest of them drop by at least once a year to shop for clothes, shoes, accessories, luxury items, and anything else that money can buy. *Paulistanos* (São Paulo inhabitants) work hard and spend a lot, and there's no escaping the many shopping and eating temptations.

Despite—or because of—these qualities, many tourists, Brazilian and foreigners, avoid visiting the city. Too noisy, too polluted, too crowded, they say—and they have a point. São Paulo is hardly a beautiful city;

it's fast-paced and there's lots to do, but it's also a concrete jungle, with nothing as attractive as Rio's hills and beaches. Yet, even as the smog reddens your eyes, you'll see that there's much to explore here. When you get tired of laid-back beaches, São Paulo is just the right place to go.

GETTING AROUND

70 km (43 mi) inland from the Atlantic Ocean with an average elevation of around 800 meters (2,625 feet), São Paulo has a surprisingly flat and featureless metropolitan area, apart from a few elevated areas. A major thoroughfare called the "Marginal"—two one-way expressways on either side of a smelly, Pinheiros river—divides the city from both north to south and east to west, with most business and tourist activity occurring in the southeastern quadrant.

Navigating São Paulo is not easy, and staying either in the central areas or at least near an inner-city subway station is advisable. The subway is quick, easy, inexpensive, and covers much of the city, with stops near the most interesting sites for travelers. Buses can be hard to navigate if you don't speak Portuguese.

Driving in the city isn't recommended because of the heavy traffic, daredevil drivers, and inadequate parking. You'll also need to get a temporary driver's license from *Detran*, the State Transit Department, which can be a very time-consuming endeavor. Cabs rates are reasonable and they're abundant in the popular neighborhoods.

SAFETY & PRECAUTIONS

Stay alert and guard your belongings at all times. Avoid wearing expensive sneakers or watches and flashy jewelry, or carrying cameras or laptops—all of which attract attention. Muggers love to target Centro and Liberdade neighborhoods. Crimes often occur at ATMs throughout the city and at the airports, particularly if you're carrying a laptop.

If you're driving, stay alert during traffic jams and at stop signs, especially at night, and don't deviate from the main streets and beltways. Watch out for motorcycle drivers—there are many who are express couriers, but some are robbers. You should always be wary when there are two people on one bike.

ESSENTIALS

Airports **Aeroporto Internacional de Congonhas** (*CGH* ✉ *Av. Washington Luís s/n, Jabaquara* ☏ *011/5090–9000* ⊕ *www.infraero.gov.br*). **Aeroporto Internacional de São Paulo/Guarulhos** (*GRU* ✉ *Rod. Hélio Smidt s/n, Guarulhos* ☏ *011/6445–2945* ⊕ *www.infraero.gov.br*).

Currency Exchange **Banco do Brasil** (✉ *Av. Paulista 2163, Jardins* ⊕ *www. bancodobrasil.com.br* Ⓜ *Consolação*). **Bank Boston** (✉ *Av. Paulista 800, Jardins* ⊕ *www.bankboston.com.br* Ⓜ *Brigadeiro*). **Citibank** (✉ *Av. Paulista 1111, Jardins* ⊕ *www.citibank.com.br* Ⓜ *Trianon-Masp*).

Emergency **Ambulance** (☏ *192*). **Delegacia de Turismo (Tourism Police)** (✉ *Av. São Luís 91, Centro* ☏ *011/3214–0209* Ⓜ *República*). **Fire** (☏ *193*). **Police** (☏ *190*).

Medical Services **Albert Einstein** (✉ *Av. Albert Einstein 627, Morumbi* ☎ *011/3747–1233* ⊕ *www.einstein.br*). **Beneficência Portuguesa** (✉ *Rua Maestro Cardim 769, Paraíso* ☎ *011/3505–1001* ⊕ *www.beneficencia.org.br* Ⓜ *Vergueiro*). **Sírio Libanês** (✉ *Rua. D. Adma Jafet 91, Bela Vista* ☎ *011/3155–0200* ⊕ *www.hsl.org.br*).

Pharmacies **Droga Raia** (✉ *Rua José Maria Lisboa 645, Jardim Paulistano* ☎ *011/3884–8235, 011/3237–5000 delivery* ⊕ *www.drogaraia.com.br*). **Drogaria São Paulo** (✉ *Av. Angélica 1465, Higienópolis* ☎ *011/3667–6291* ⊕ *www.drogariasaopaulo.com.br*).

Rental Cars **Avis** (✉ *Rua da Consolação 335, Centro* ☎ *011/3259–6868 or 0800/19–8456*). **Hertz** (✉ *Rua da Consolação 439, Centro* ☎ *011/3258–9384 or 011/4336–7300*). **Localiza** (✉ *Rua da Consolação 419, Centro* ☎ *011/3231–3055 or 0800/99–2000*).

Subway **Metrô** (☎ *011/3286–0111* ⊕ *www.metro.sp.gov.br*).

Taxis **Coopertaxi** (☎ *011/6195–6000*). **Ligue-Taxi** (☎ *011/2101–3030*).

Visitor Info **Anhembi Turismo e Eventos da Cidade de São Paulo** (✉ *Anhembi Convention Center, Av. Olavo Fontoura 1209, Santana* ☎ *011/6224–0400* ⊕ *www.cidadedesaopaulo.com* ✉ *Praça da República at Rua 7 de Abril, Centro* Ⓜ *República* **São Paulo Convention and Visitors Bureau** (✉ *Alameda Ribeirão Preto 130, conjunto 121, Jardins* ☎ *011/3289–7588* ⊕ *www.visitesaopaulo.com*). **Secretaria de Esportes e Turismo do Estado de São Paulo** (✉ *Praça Antônio Prado, 9, Centro* ☎ *011/3241–5822* ⊕ *www.selt.sp.gov.br*).

GAROA

One of São Paulo's most famous nicknames is *terra da garoa*, which basically means land of drizzling rain. Although some periods of the year are worse than others, no matter when you visit you'll more than likely get at least a little taste of garoa. An umbrella can be your best friend.

EXPLORING SÃO PAULO

CENTRO

This downtown area has the city's most interesting historic architecture and some of its most famous sights; however, many parts are also quite daunting and dirty, so be prepared. Area highlights include the freshly revamped (2006) Praça da Sé, considered the vortex for the São Paulo municipal district. Parque da Luz is just to the north and next to a number of important buildings, including the Estação da Luz, the former headquarters of São Paulo Railway that now houses the Museum of the Portuguese Language.

Numbers in the text correspond to numbers in the margin and on the São Paulo Centro map.

MAIN ATTRACTIONS

❼ **Catedral da Sé.** The imposing 14-tower neo-Gothic church, renovated in 2002, has tours through the crypt that contains the remains of Tibiriçá, a native Brazilian who helped the Portuguese back in 1554. ✉ *Praça da Sé s/n, Centro* ☎ *011/3106–2709 or 011/3107–6832 for tour informa-*

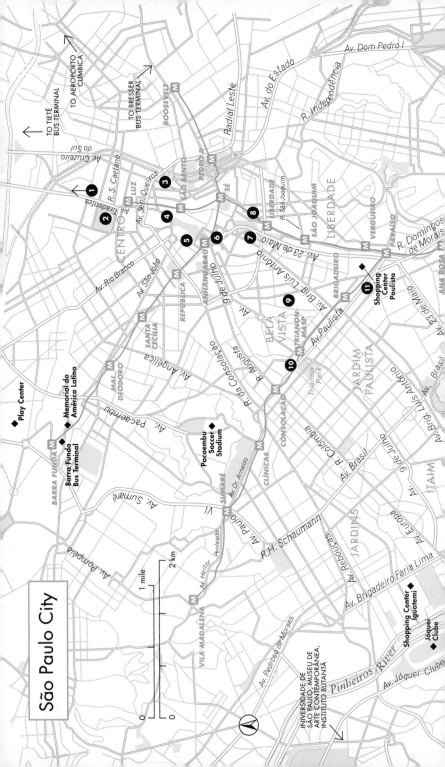

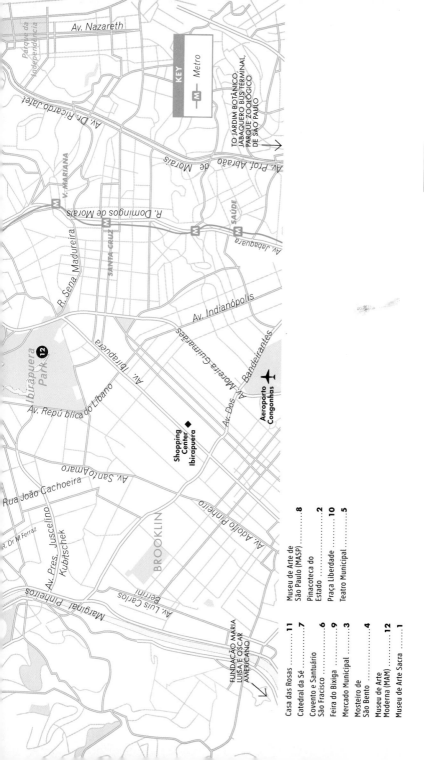

KEY

M — Metro

TO JARDIM BOTÂNICO,
JABAQUERA BUS TERMINAL,
PARQUE ZOOLÓGICO
DE SÃO PAULO →

Aeroporto
Congonhas

Shopping
Center
Ibirapuera

Ibirapuera
Park ⑫

Parque da
Independência

BROOKLIN

FUNDAÇÃO MARIA
LUISA E OSCAR
AMERICANO

Casa das Rosas **11**
Catedral da Sé **7**
Covento e Santuário
São Fracisco **6**
Feira do Bixiga **9**
Mercado Municipal **3**
Mosteiro de
São Bento **4**
Museu de Arte
Moderna (MAM) **12**
Museu de Arte Sacra **1**

Museu de Arte de
São Paulo (MASP) **8**
Pinacoteca do
Estado **2**
Praça Liberdade **10**
Teatro Municipal **5**

3

tion ☎*Tour R$3* ⊙*Mon. and Wed.–Sat. 8–5, Sun. 8:30–6; tour Mon. and Wed.–Sat. 9:30–4:30* Ⓜ*Sé.*

❸ Mercado Municipal. The city's first grocery market, this huge 1928 neo-baroque-style building got a major renovation in 2004 and is now the quintessential hot spot for gourmets and food lovers. The building, nick-named Mercadão (Big Market) by locals, houses 318 stands that sell just about everything edible, including meat, vegetables, cheese, spices, and fish from all over Brazil. It also has restaurants and traditional snack places—don't miss the salt cod *pastel* at Hocca Bar. ⊠*Rua da Cantareira 306, Centro* ☎*011/3228–0673* ⊕*www.mercadomunicipal. com.br* ☎*Free* ⊙*Mon.–Sat. 5* AM*–6* PM*, Sun. 7–4* Ⓜ*São Bento.*

FodorśChoice
★

❹ Mosteiro de São Bento. This unique, Norman–Byzantine church con-
★ structed between 1910 and 1922 was designed by German architect Richard Berndl. Its enormous organ has some 6,000 pipes, and its Russian image of the Kasperovo Virgin is covered with 6,000 pearls from the Black Sea. If you go on Sunday, don't miss the 10 AM mass and the monks' Gregorian chants. ⊠*Largo de São Bento, Centro* ☎*011/3328–8799* ⊕*www.mosteiro.org.br* ☎*Free* ⊙*Weekdays 6* AM*–6:30* PM*, weekends 6–noon and 4–6* Ⓜ*São Bento.*

❶ Museu de Arte Sacra. If you can't get to Bahia or Minas Gerais dur-
★ ing your stay in Brazil, you can get a taste of the fabulous baroque and rococo art found there at the Museum of Sacred Art. On dis-play is a collection of 4,000 wooden and terra-cotta masks, jewelry, and liturgical objects from all over the country (but primarily Minas Gerais and Bahia), dating from the 17th century to the present. The on-site convent was founded in 1774. ⊠*Av. Tiradentes 676, Centro* ☎*011/3326–1373* ☎*R$4* ⊙*Tues.–Fri. 11* AM*–6* PM*, weekends 10* AM*–7* PM Ⓜ*Tiradentes or Luz.*

❷ Pinacoteca do Estado. The building that houses the State Art Gallery was constructed in 1905 and renovated in 1998. The permanent col-lection has more than 5,000 works of art, including more than 10 Rodin sculptures and several pieces by famous Brazilian artists like Tarsila do Amaral (whose work consists of colorful, somewhat abstract portraits) and Cândido Portinari (whose oil paintings have social and historical themes). The building has a restaurant. ⊠*Praça da Luz 2, Centro* ☎*011/3324–1000* ⊕*www.pinacoteca.org.br* ☎*R$4, Sat. free* ⊙*Tues.–Sun. 10–6* Ⓜ*Luz.*

IF YOU HAVE TIME

❻ Convento e Santuário São Francisco. The baroque building is actually two churches, one run by Catholic clergy and the other by lay brothers. One of the city's best-preserved Portuguese colonial buildings, it was built between 1647 and 1790, and restored in 1997. ⊠*Largo São Francisco 133, Centro* ☎*011/3106–0081* ⊕*www.franciscanos.org.br* ☎*Free* ⊙*Daily 7:30* AM*–8* PM Ⓜ*Sé or Anhangabaú.*

❺ Teatro Municipal. Inspired by the Paris Opéra, the Municipal Theater was built between 1903 and 1911 with art nouveau elements. *Hamlet* was the first play presented, and the house went on to host such luminaries as Isadora Duncan in 1916 and Anna Pavlova in 1919. Plays and operas are still staged here; local newspapers have schedules and information on how to get tickets. The fully restored auditorium, resplendent with gold leaf, moss-green velvet, marble, and mirrors, has 1,500 seats and is usually open only to those attending cultural events, although prearranged visits are also available. A dedicated, on-site museum was reopened in 2007. ⊠*Praça Ramos de Azevedo, Centro* ☎*011/3223–3022* ☛*Tickets from R$10* ☉*Tours by appointment Tues. and Thurs. at 1* PM Ⓜ*Anhangabaú.*

LIBERDADE

The red-porticoed entryway to Liberdade (which means "Freedom") is south of Praça da Sé, behind the cathedral. The neighborhood is the center of São Paulo's vibrant Japanese, Korean, and Chinese communities, and features a range of Asian-style streetscapes and shopfronts.

❿ **Praça Liberdade.** Every weekend 10–7, this plaza hosts a sprawling
★ Asian food and crafts fair that exhibits São Paulo's eclectic cultural mix. You may see, for example, Afro-Brazilians dressed in colorful kimonos hawking grilled shrimp on a stick. Several religious celebrations are held here, like April's Hanamatsuri, commemorating the birth of the Buddha. Apart from the fair and special events, another reason to visit this square is to stop by at the nearby Japanese shops and restaurants. The fair will very likely be crowded, so keep your wits about you and do not wander around at night. ⊠*Av. da Liberdade and Rua dos Estudantes, Liberdade* Ⓜ*Liberdade.*

AVENIDA PAULISTA & BIXIGA

The imposing Avenida Paulista is home to some of the city's best hotels, biggest financial companies, and most important businesses. Many of São Paulo's cultural institutions center around this impressive, eight-lane-wide thoroughfare.

Officially called Bela Vista, Bixiga is São Paulo's Little Italy. Here are plenty of restaurants, theaters, and nightlife hot spots. Southwest of Centro and right next to Avenida Paulista, Bixiga is an old, working-class neighborhood—where everybody knows everybody else's business.

MAIN ATTRACTIONS

⓫ **Casa das Rosas.** The House of the Roses, a French-style mansion with gardens inspired by those at Versailles, seems out of place next to the skyscrapers of Paulista. It was built in 1935 by famous *paulistano* architect Ramos de Azevedo for one of his daughters. The building was home to the same family until 1986, when it was made an official municipal landmark. It was later opened as a cultural center, and it's one of the avenue's few remaining early-20th-century buildings. ⊠*Av. Paulista 37, Paraíso* ☎*011/3285–6986* ⊕*www.casadasrosas.sp.gov.br* ☛*Free* ☉*Tues.–Sun. 11–9* Ⓜ*Brigadeiro.*

NEED A BREAK?

A recommended snack is the delicious *bauru*—a sandwich with roast beef, tomato, cucumber, and a mix of melted cheeses—at Ponto Chic (⊠*Praça Osvaldo Cruz 26, Paraíso* ☎*011/3289–1480* ⊕*www.pontochic.com.br*

⊙ *Daily 11 AM–2 AM*), a block east of Instituto Itaú Cultural, across Avenida Paulista.

❽ **Museu de Arte de São Paulo (MASP).** Fodor'sChoice One of the city's premier fine-arts ★ collections, with more than 7,000 pieces, is in this striking low-rise, elevated on two massive concrete pillars 256 feet apart. Highlights of the collection are works by Van Gogh, Renoir, Delacroix, Cézanne, Monet, Rembrandt, Picasso, and Degas. Baroque sculptor Aleijadinho, expressionist painter Lasar Segall, and expressionist/surrealist painter Cândido Portinari are three of the many Brazilian artists represented. The huge open area beneath the museum is often used for cultural events and is the site of a charming Sunday antiques fair. ⊠ *Av. Paulista 1578, Bela Vista* ☎ *011/3251–5644* ⊕ *www.masp.art.br* ☒ *R$10* ⊙ *Tues.–Sun. 11–6* Ⓜ *Trianon*.

IF YOU HAVE TIME

❾ **Feira do Bixiga.** Strolling through this flea market is a favorite Sunday activity for paulistanos. Crafts, antiques, and furniture are among the wares. Walk up the São José staircase to see **Rua dos Ingleses**, a typical and well-preserved fin de siecle Bixiga street. ⊠ *Praça Dom Orione s/n, Bixiga* ☒ *Free* ⊙ *Sun. 8–5*.

PARQUE IBIRAPUERA

Ibirapuera is São Paulo's Central Park, though it's slightly less than half the size and is often more crowded on sunny weekends than its NYC counterpart. The park was inaugurated in 1954, and some pavilions used for the opening festivities still sit amid its 160 hectares (395 acres). It has jogging and biking paths, a lake, and rolling lawns. You can rent bicycles at a number of places near park entrances for about R$5 an hour.

⓬ **Museu de Arte Moderna (MAM).** More than 4,500 paintings, installations, sculptures, and other works from modern and contemporary artists such as Alfredo Volpi and Ligia Clark are part of the Modern Art Museum's permanent collection. Temporary exhibits feature works by new local artists. The giant wall of glass, designed by Brazilian architect Lina Bo Bardi, serves as a window beckoning you to peek inside. ⊠ *Av. Pedro Álvares Cabral s/n, Gate 3, Parque Ibirapuera* ☎ *011/5085–1300* ⊕ *www.mam.org.br* ☒ *R$5.50, free Sun.* ⊙ *Tues.–Sun. 10–6*.

WHERE TO EAT

São Paulo's dynamic social scene centers on dining out, and among the 12,000-plus restaurants, most of the world's cuisines are covered. The most popular options include Portuguese, Japanese, Italian, French, and Lebanese; contemporary fusions are popular and plentiful. Most places don't require jacket and tie, but Paulistanos tend to dress to European standards.

BIXIGA

$–$$
ITALIAN
✕**Montechiaro.** The hardworking folks at this Brazilian-Argentine-owned cantina serve up a massive menu at more than reasonable prices—all of the plates serve two. Lasagna and roasted goat's leg are among the specialties of the house. Tuesday through Friday, they serve a specially priced executive menu, for those on an extra tight budget. Don't leave without picking up one of their cute embroidered bibs. ⊠ *Rua Santo Antonio, 844/846, Bixiga* ☎ *011/3259–2727* ⊕ *www.montechiaro.com.br* ▤ *AE, DC, MC, V* Ⓜ *Brigadeiró.*

$$–$$$$
ITALIAN
★
✕**Roperto.** Wine casks and bottles adorn the walls at this typical Bixiga cantina, located on a street so charmingly human-scaled you'll hardly believe you're still in São Paulo. You won't be alone if you order the ever-popular fusilli—either *ao sugo* (with tomato sauce) or *ao frutos do mar* (with seafood)—or the traditional baby goat's leg with potatoes and tomatoes. ⊠ *Rua 13 de Maio 634, Bixiga* ☎ *011/3288–2573* ⊕ *www.cantinaroperto.com.br* ▤ *DC, MC, V* Ⓜ *Brigadeiro.*

CENTRO

$$–$$$$
FRENCH
✕**La Casserole.** Facing a little Centro flower market, this romantic, Parisian-style bistro has been around for five decades and has witnessed more than its share of wedding proposals during its years. Surrounded by wood-paneled walls decorated with art that nods at famous French artists, you can dine on such delights as *gigot d'agneau aux soissons* (roast leg of lamb in its own juices, served with white beans) and cherry strudel. ⊠ *Largo do Arouche 346, Centro* ☎ *011/3331–6283* ⊕ *www.lacasserole.com.br* ▤ *AE, DC, MC, V* ⊗ *Closed Mon. No lunch Sat.* Ⓜ *República.*

$$$–$$$$
ITALIAN
Fodor'sChoice
★
✕**Famiglia Mancini.** This busy little cantina is well loved for both its cuisine and its location. It's on a singular, unforgettable strip of Rua Avandhandava, where you may find yourself admiring the cobblestones on the street as you wait for a table. An incredible buffet with cheeses, olives, sausages, and much more makes finding a tasty appetizer a cinch. The menu has many terrific pasta options, such as the cannelloni with palm hearts and a four-cheese sauce. All dishes serve two people. ⊠ *Rua Avanhandava 81, Centro* ☎ *011/3256–4320* ⊕ *www.famigliamancini.com.br* ▤ *AE, DC, MC, V* Ⓜ *Anhangabaú.*

CERQUEIRA CÉSAR

$$
BRAZILIAN
✕**Bargaço.** The original Bargaço, in Salvador, has long been considered the best Bahian restaurant in that city. If you can't make it to the northeast, be sure to have a meal in the São Paulo branch. Seafood is the calling card. ⊠ *Rua Oscar Freire 1189, Cerqueira César* ☎ *011/3085–5058* ⊕ *www.restaurantebargaco.com.br* ▤ *DC, MC* Ⓜ *Consolação.*

¢
PIZZA
★
✕**Pedaço da Pizza.** This is one of the few places in the city where pizza is served by the slice. Choose from the traditional favorites like pepperoni, or an innovation, like pizza with shimeji mushrooms and kale. It's a good late-night stop, especially on the bar-filled Centro side of Rua Augusta, since it's open until 6 AM on weekends. The place is crowded with pau-

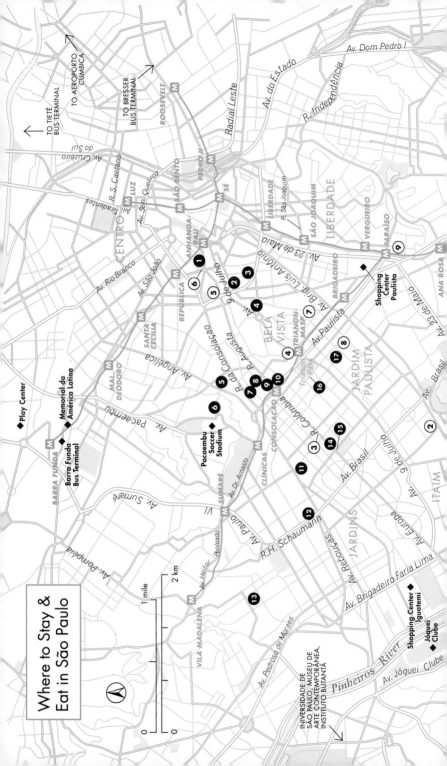

Where to Stay & Eat in São Paulo

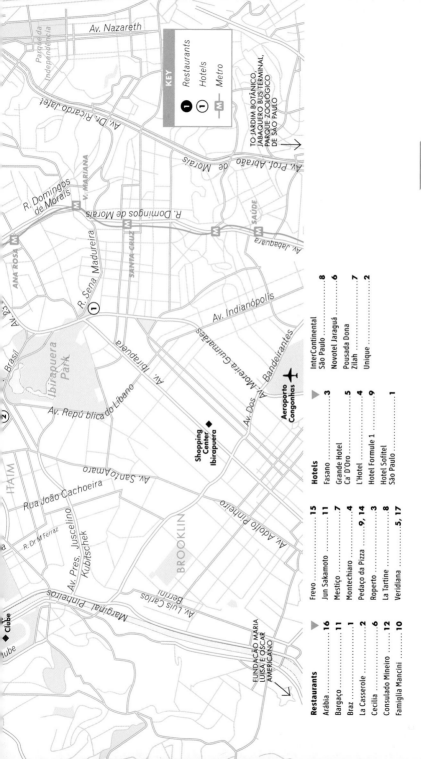

3

KEY

● Restaurants

① Hotels

Ⓜ Metro

TO JARDIM BOTÂNICO,
JABAQUERO BUS TERMINAL,
PARQUE ZOOLÓGICO
DE SÃO PAULO

Restaurants

Hotels

listanos once the nearby movie the-
ater lets out. ⊠*Rua Augusta 2931,
Jardins* ☏*011/3891–2431* ⊠*Rua
Augusta 1463, Cerqueira César*
☏*3285–2117* ▤*No credit cards*
Ⓜ*Consolação.*

CONSOLAÇÃO

$–$$$
ECLECTIC
★
✕ **Mestiço.** Even the fabulous people
have to wait at the bar before get-
ting a table in this large sleek din-
ing room; but for those with a
vegetarian in their party, dishes like
the California, a tofu and veggie
curry, make the wait worth it. The
restaurant also makes a point of using free-range chicken and ecologi-
cally responsible heart-of-palm throughout the eclectic menu, which
also includes Italian, Brazilian, and Bahian dishes. ⊠*Rua Fernando de
Albuquerque 277, Consolação* ☏*011/3256–1539 or 011/3256–3165*
⊕*www.mestico.com.br* ▤*AE, DC, MC, V* Ⓜ*Consolação.*

$–$$$
FRENCH
★
✕ **La Tartine.** An ideal place for an intimate dinner, this small bistro has
a good wine selection and an upstairs bar furnished with mismatched
sofas and armchairs. The menu changes daily; a favorite is the classic
coq au vin, or you can fill up on entrées such as beef tenderloin or soups
and quiches. It's usually crowded with São Paulo's trendy people, and
you might have to wait to get a table on weekends. ⊠*Rua Fernando de
Albuquerque 267, Consolação* ☏*011/3259–2090* ▤*AE, V* ⊘*Closed
Sun.* Ⓜ*Consolação.*

HIGIENÓPOLIS

$
EASTERN
EUROPEAN
✕ **Cecília.** Get your gefilte fish, pickled herring, matzo bread, and potato
latkes at this small restaurant serving traditional (non-kosher) Jewish cuisine. Pastrami sandwiches are popular, and a special "Jewish
feijoada" (with meat, white beans, barley, and potatoes) is served on
weekends. A lunch buffet offering most of the house dishes is open
from Tuesday to Friday for 25 reais. The restaurant is family-run, and
the owner, Cecilia Judkowitch, is always there. ⊠*Rua Tinhorão 122,
Higienópolis* ☏*011/ 3662–5200* ▤*AE, V* ⊘*Closed Mon.*

$$
PIZZA
Fodor'sChoice
★
✕ **Veridiana** Owner Roberto Loscalzo transformed a 1903 mansion into
a remarkable dining space; expansive yet intimate, grandiose yet wel-
coming. At one end of the room a two-story brick oven presides over
diners like a cathedral organ while chefs pull Napoli-style pizzas from
its three different mouths. Different place-names lead to different taste
combinations: Napoli in Beruit blends goat cheese and zaatar spice,
while Napoli in Brasili has sundried meat and Catupiry, the creamy
Brazilian cheese. If you don't feel like globetrotting, go for the Do
Nonno, topped with juicy whole grilled tomatoes. The Jardim's loca-
tion is a luxurious update of the original's aesthetic. ⊠*Rua Dona
Veridiana 661, Higienópolis* ☏*011/3120–5050* ⊕*www.veridiana.
com.br* ▤*AE, DC, MC V.* ⊠*Rua José Maria Lisboa 493, Jardim
Paulista* ☏*011/3559–9151* ▤*AE, DC, MC V.*

> ### CAFEZINHO PLEASE
>
> When you finish the meal, don't
> forget to ask for a *cafezinho*
> ("little coffee"). Served at espresso
> size and strength, it's a great
> homegrown *digestif*. In this land
> of coffee, a cafezinho probably
> won't show up on the bill; a little
> cup at the end of a sumptuous
> meal is a standard way of
> saying thanks.

JARDINS

$–$$$$ ✕**Arábia.** For almost 20 years Arábia has served traditional Lebanese
MIDDLE cuisine at this beautiful high-ceilinged restaurant. Simple dishes such as
EASTERN hummus and stuffed grape leaves are executed with aplomb. The lamb
★ melts in your mouth. The reasonably priced "executive" lunch includes
one cold dish, one meat dish, a drink, and dessert. Don't miss the
crepe-like ataife, filled with pistachio nuts or cream, for dessert. ⊠*Rua
Haddock Lobo 1397, Jardins* ☎*011/3061–2203* ⊕*www.arabia.
com.br* ⊟*AE, DC, MC.*

¢–$ ✕**Frevo.** Paulistanos of all types and ages flock to this Jardins lun-
BRAZILIAN cheonette on the stylish Rua Oscar Freire for its beirute sandwiches,
filled with ham and cheese, tuna, or chicken, and for its draft beer
and fruit juices in flavors such as *acerola* (Antilles cherry), passion
fruit, and papaya. ⊠*Rua Oscar Freire 603, Jardins* ☎*011/3082–3434*
⊕*frevinho.com.br* ⊟*AE, DC, MC, V.*

MOEMA

$–$$ ✕**Braz.** Its name comes from one of the most traditional Italian neigh-
PIZZA borhoods in São Paulo, and no one argues that it doesn't have the
Fodor'sChoice right. Each of the nearly 20 types of crisp-crusted pizzas is delicious,
★ from the traditional margherita to the house specialty, pizza *braz*, with
tomato sauce, zucchini, and mozzarella and Parmesan cheeses. The
chopp (draft beer) is also very good. ⊠*Rua Grauna 125, Moema*
☎*011/5561–0905* ⊕*www.casabraz.com.br* ⊟*DC, MC, V.*

PINHEIROS

$–$$ ✕**Consulado Mineiro.** During and after the Saturday crafts and antiques
BRAZILIAN fair in Praça Benedito Calixto, it may take an hour to get a table at this
★ homey restaurant. Among the traditional *mineiro* (from Minas Gerais
State) dishes are the *mandioca com carne de sol* (cassava with salted
meat) appetizer and the *tutu* (pork loin with beans, pasta, cabbage,
and rice) entrée. The cachaça menu is extensive, with rare, premium,
and homemade brands. Several types of *batidas* (fruit-and-alcohol mix-
tures) and caipirinhas are served. ⊠*Rua Praça Benedito Calixto 74,
Pinheiros* ☎*011/3064–3882* ⊕*www.consuladomineiro.com.br* ⊟*AE,
DC, MC, V* ⊘*Closed Mon.* ⊠*Rua Cônego Eugenio Leite 504, Pinheiros* ☎*011/3898–3241* ⊟*AE, DC, MC, V.*

$$$–$$$$ ✕**Jun Sakamoto.** Arguably the best Japanese restaurant in a town
JAPANESE famous that's for them, Jun Sakamoto is known for using fish of the
highest quality and for employing sushi chefs of the highest caliber and
artistry to cut them. This is haute gastronomy at its haughtiest. You're
best served if you let the waiters wearing futuristic earpieces guide
you through the menu based on what's the freshest fish in the house.
⊠*Rua Lisboa, 55, Pinheiros* ☎*011/3088–6019* ⊕*www.ivitelloni.
com.br* ⊟*AE, DC, MC, V.*

WHERE TO STAY

São Paulo is all about business, and for the most part so are its hotels.
Most of them are near Avenida Paulista, along Marginal Pinheiros, or
in the charming Jardins neighborhood, where international businesses

are located. Breakfast is a sumptuous affair and is oftentimes included in the room rate.

CENTRO & ENVIRONS

$$ 🏨 **Grand Hotel Ca' D'Oro.** A bit like visiting a rich great uncle in Europe, the musty carpet and faded wallpaper of the rooms are more than compensated by the finely worked furniture, gracious staff, and the Continental grandeur of the public spaces. While the cavernous downstairs lobbies are replete with Velázquez replicas, deep leather chairs, and a coffee table made from a giant 1820s English bellows, the panoramic pool is a perfectly preserved window into 1970s splendor: atop the astroturf carpeting sits single-cast plastic pool furniture that would draw crowds at a museum of contemporary design. **Pros:** Classy staff, endless public sitting rooms, unintentional retro charm. **Cons:** Rua Augusta gets a little wild at night. ⊠ *Rua Augusta 129, Cerqueira César* ☎ *011/3236–4300* ⊕ *www.cadoro.com.br* ⇤ *240 rooms, 50 suites* ⚠ *In-room: safe, Ethernet. In-hotel: restaurant, room service, bars, 2 pools, gym, laundry facilities, public Wi-Fi, parking (fee)* ⊟ *AE, DC, MC, V* Ⓜ *Consolação.*

$ 🏨 **Novotel Jaraguá.** Built in 1951 to be the headquarters of one of the
★ main newspapers in the city, the building that now houses this hotel is a landmark in downtown São Paulo. The huge mural created by Di Cavalcanti is one of the 1950s attractions. All 415 rooms were renovated in 2004; their decor hovers somewhere between Scandinavian and airport lounge (albeit a well-maintained airport lounge). The furnishings are all blond wood and brushed steel of an indistinguishable contemporary style, which all-in-all makes for pleasant rooms at good prices. **Pros:** Close to many restaurants and sights, 10-minute taxi to Paulista. **Cons:** Area a little spooky at night, since most nearby businesses are closed. ⊠ *Rua Martins Fontes 71, Centro* ☎ *011/3120–8000* ⊕ *www.novotel. com.br* ⇤ *309 rooms, 106 suites* ⚠ *In-room: Wi-Fi. In-hotel: restaurant, bar, public Wi-Fi, parking (fee)* ⊟ *AE, MC, V* ⏏ *BP.*

JARDINS

$$$$ 🏨 **Fasano.** With a decor that hints at 1940s modern, but is undeniably 21st-century chic, Fasano caters to those for whom money is a mere detail. Rooms have Eames chairs, leather headboards, parquet floors, huge windows, and walk-in closets. The restaurant off the lobby with the same name exudes the same deep sense of luxury. **Pros:** Attentive, knowledgeable staff, beautiful top-floor pool. **Cons:** Paying for it all. ⊠ *Rua Vittorio Fasano 88, Jardins* ☎ *011/3896–4077* 🖷 *011/3896-4156* ⊕ *www.fasano.com.br* ⇤ *56 rooms, 8 suites* ⚠ *In-room: safe, refrigerator, Ethernet. In-hotel: restaurant, room service, bar, pool, gym, spa, concierge, laundry service, airport shuttle, parking (no fee), no-smoking rooms* ⊟ *AE, DC, MC, V* ⏏ *EP.*

$$$$ 🏨 **InterContinental São Paulo.** This exquisite hotel is one of the most
★ attractive of the city's top-tier establishments and consistently gets rave reviews because they pay so much attention to small things—they offer a choice of six different types of pillow. Service is attentive, and both the private and public areas are well appointed. Creams, pastels, and marble come together with seamless sophistication and elegance. **Pros:**

Japanese breakfast, Playstation in rooms. **Cons:** Suites aren't much bigger than normal rooms. ⊠*Al. Santos 1123, Jardins* ☎*011/3179–2600 or 0800/11–8003* 🖶*011/3179–2666* ⊕*www.intercontinental.com* 🛏*189 rooms, 36 suites* 🛎*In-room: DVD, Wi-Fi, Ethernet. In-hotel: restaurant, room service, bar, pool, gym, hair salon, parking (fee)* ▤*AE, DC, MC, V* Ⓜ*Trianon.*

$$–$$$$ 🎦**L'Hotel.** Compared to the top-of-the line chain hotels on Paulista, L'Hotel stands out as truly special experience. Though the famous Parisian hotel of the same name is its declared muse, the luxury here is understated rather than decadent. Rooms are done in soft blue, beige, or rose, the woodwork and cabinets in patina. The French dining room and the English-style piano bar that faces it are twin gems. The top floor pool has a retractable roof, Japanese ofuro baths heated upon request, and every guest gets a complementary brown and gold pair of the famous Havaianas flipflops. **Pros:** Small number of rooms makes for personalized service, L'Occitane bath products. **Cons:** No fitness center. ⊠*Alameda Campinas 266, Jardins* ☎*011/2183–0500* 🖶*011/2183–0505* ⊕*www.lhotel.com.br* 🛏*80 rooms, 7 suites* 🛎*In-hotel: 2 restaurants, room service, bar, pool, gym, laundry facilities, parking (fee)* ▤*AE, DC, MC, V* Ⓜ*Trianon.*

$ 🎦**Pousada Dona Zilah.** Marvelously located in the retail-heavy part of the Jardins district, and easily navigable both to and from, this homey pousada, while not exactly cheap, might be a more affordable alternative if you're seeking to momentarily escape the skyscraper experience. Once you step inside this former private residence, you might easily forget that you're still at the center of a bustling megalopolis. The skylighted café serves breakfast to guests, lunch to those who work at nearby businesses, and a light dinner. Take a peek at the guestbook to see how past guests have raved. ⊠*Alameda Franca 1621, Jardins* ☎*011/3062–1444* 🛏*14 rooms* 🛎*In-hotel: no elevator, restaurant, public Internet* ▤*MC, V* Ⓜ*Consolação.*

$$$$ 🎦**Unique.** It's hard not to see a familiar shape (some say watermelon, some say boat, but neither hits the mark) in the wild but harmonius design of this boutique hotel. Apartments, some with walls that echo the curve of the building's exterior, have plasma TVs with DVD players, mobile phones, king-size beds, and whirlpool baths with remote control, while the pool features a waterslide and submerged hydromassage chairs. The lobby bar and rooftop restaurant are destinations in and of themselves. **Pros:** Steps from Ibirapuera Park and a taxi ride to many top restaurants. **Cons:** Nonstop techno music in public spaces. ⊠*Avenida Brigadeiro Luís Antônio 4700, Jardins* ☎*011/3055–4710 or 0800/770–8771* 🖶*011/3889–8100* ⊕*www.unique.com.br* 🛏*95 rooms* 🛎*In-room: refrigerator, DVD, Ethernet, Wi-Fi. In-hotel: restaurant, pool, gym, spa, public Wi-Fi, parking (fee)* ▤*AE, DC, MC, V* ﺓⓄ|*BP.*

Fodor'sChoice ★

PARAÍSO

¢ 🎦**Hotel Formule 1.** With hotels at both ends of Paulista and in Centro, Formule 1 is a great choice if you value location and price over luxury. Like the cockpit of a racecar, rooms have been stripped down to what's necessary for a comfortable stay; a TV, a double bed with a single bunked over it, and an efficient but small bathroom. Perfect for travelers who plan on spending most of their time out and about. The lobby is always full of groups of young people waiting to embark on an excursion. **Pros:** Close to metro, vending machines and pay phones in lobby. **Cons:** Breakfast

GETTING AROUND
AFTER DARK

For safety reasons, we strongly suggest taking cabs at night—it's convenient and relatively cheap. Ask your concierge about transportation if finding a cab proves difficult.

unspectacular compared to that at other hotels, often fully booked. ⊠ *Rua da Consolação, 2303, Consolação* ☎ *011/3123–7755* ⊕ *www. accorhotels.com.br* ➦ *399 rooms* & *In-hotel: public Internet, parking (fee)* ⊟ *AE* Ⓜ *Consolação.*

VILA MARIANA

$$–$$$$ 🏨 **Hotel Sofitel São Paulo.** Near the Congonhas Airport and Ibirapuera Park, this modern, luxury hotel is noted for its French style. The restaurant serves French cuisine. Dark-wood furniture fills the rooms, many of which have views of the park. It's refreshing to be able to see trees from your window in São Paulo. **Pros:** Many amenities, convenient helipad for millionaires. **Cons:** Afternoon traffic, far from business centers. ⊠ *Rua Sena Madureira 1355, Bloco 1, Vila Mariana* ☎ *011/5087–0800* 🖷 *011/5575–4544* ⊕ *www.accorhotels.com.br* ➦ *219 rooms* & *In-hotel: restaurant, room service, bar, tennis court, pool, gym, laundry facilities, parking (fee)* ⊟ *AE, DC, MC, V.*

NIGHTLIFE

BARS

CENTRO   First opened in 1949, **Bar Brahma** (⊠ *Av. São João 677, Centro* ☎ *011/*
Fodor'sChoice   *3333–3030 reservations* ⊕ *www.barbrahmasp.com* Ⓜ *República*) used
★   to be the meeting place of artists, intellectuals, and politicians. The decor is a time warp to the mid-20th century, with furniture, lamps, and a piano true to the period. This is one of the best places in São Paulo for live music, with traditional samba and Brazilian pop groups.

ITAIM & VILA   Close to the northern border of Itaim is **Na Mata Café** (⊠ *Rua da Mata,*
OLÍMPIA   *70, Itaim* ☎ *011/3079–0300* ⊕ *www.namata.com.br*), considered one of the best live music venues in the city, with shows just about every night of the week.

Featuring a huge wall lined with more than 500 types of rumlike cachaça, **Bar Do Arnesto** (⊠ *Rua Ministro Jesuíno Cardoso, 207, Vila Olímpia* ☎ *011/ 3848–9432* ⊕ *www.bardoarnesto.com.br*) is a great example of the traditional Brazilian *botequim*. These casual bars generally offer something a little different, and specialize in cold bottled beer, snack foods, and caipirinhas.

PINHEIROS & VILA MADALENA

★ The '60s and '70s bohemian-chic decor at **Astor** (⊠*Rua Delfina 163, Vila Madalena* ☎*011/3815–1364* ⊕*www.barastor.com.br*) sends you back in time. The quality draft beer and tasty snacks and meals mean this place is always hopping; the menu is full of specialties from classic bars in Brazil. Don't miss *picadinho à astor* (beef stew with rice and black beans, poached eggs, banana, farofa, and beef *pastel*).

★ The fashionable patrons at **Grazie a Dio** (⊠*Rua Girassol 67, Vila Madalena* ☎*011/3031–6568* ⊕*www.grazieadio.com.br*) may vary in age, but they always appreciate good music. The best time to go is at happy hour for daily live performances. On Saturday it's jazz, and on Friday, bossa nova. The natural decorations, including trees and constellations, complement the Mediterranean food served in the back.

MUSIC CLUBS

ITAIM BIBI

Featuring rock, MPB (música popular brasileira) and samba, **6:01** (⊠*Rua Comandatuba, 26, Itaim* ☎*011/3846–3031 and 3845–7396* ⊕*www.seiseum.com.br*) gets packed at night and is known as a great place for flirting, especially on Wednesday and Friday. As the name suggests, the bar opens just after 6 PM Tuesday to Sunday.

MOEMA

With a name right out of New Orleans, it's no wonder that **Bourbon Street** (⊠*Rua dos Chanés 127, Moema* ☎*011/5561–1643 or 011/5095–6100* ⊕*www.bourbonstreet.com.br*) is where the best jazz and blues bands, Brazilian and international, play. Performances are Tuesday–Sunday, after 9:30 PM. On Sunday you can merengue and mambo at the Caribbean dance party.

PINHEIROS

Canto da Ema (⊠*Av. Brigadeiro Faria Lima 364, Pinheiros* ☎*011/3813–4708* ⊕*www.cantodaema.com.br*) is considered the best place to dance forró in town. *Xiboquinha* is the official forró drink, made with *cachaça* (a Brazilian sugarcane-based alcohol), lemon, honey, cinnamon, and ginger. Doors open at 10:30 PM Wednesday–Saturday and it's open 7–midnight on Sunday; admission is R$14–R$20.

VILA MADALENA

★ The tiny round tables at **Piratininga** (⊠*Rua Wizard 149, Vila Madalena* ☎*011/3032–9775* ⊕*www.piratiningabar.com.br* Ⓜ *Vila Madalena* ⊙*Daily 4* PM), a small bar-restaurant, are perfect for a quiet rendezvous. The live MPB (música popular brasileira), bossa nova, blues, and jazz music, which starts daily between 7 and 9 PM (R$8 per person cover charge), add to the romance.

DANCE CLUBS

Most clubs open at 9 PM, but people tend to arrive late (around midnight), and dance until 5 or 6 AM. Still, you should arrive early to be at the front of the lines. Don't worry if the dance floor appears empty at 11 PM; things will start to sizzle an hour or so later.

PINHEIROS

Housed in an unmissable building, **Avenida Club** (⊠*Av. Pedroso de Morais 1036, Pinheiros* ☎*011/3814–7383* ⊕*www.avenidaclub.com.br*) hosts a range of dance events, such as Caribbean or Brazilian dance parties, while Sunday brings contemporary MPB and rock acts. The large wooden dance floor is one of the finest in town.

Every night except Sunday, **Blen Blen Brasil** (⊠*Rua Inácio Pereira da Rocha 520, Pinheiros* ☎*011/3815–4999*) has live music ranging from reggae to salsa jazz to Brazilian rock and MPB, beginning at 8 PM. Entry from R$25.

VILA OLÍMPIA **Buena Vista Club** (⊠*Rua Atílio Innocenti 780, Vila Olímpia* ☎*011/* **Fodor's**Choice *3045–5245* ⊕*www.buenavistaclub.com.br*) is a good place to take ★ dance classes. On Sunday you can learn to dance *gafieira* and *zouk*. Live music and DJs heat up the dance floor for hours. The club also has good appetizers and drinks and is open Wednesday–Sunday. You might feel like you're on the set of an Austin Powers movie at **Lov.e Club & Lounge** (⊠*Rua Pequetita 189, Vila Olímpia* ☎*011/3044–1613* ⊕*www.loveclub.com.br*). Before 2 AM the music isn't too loud, and you can sit and talk on the '50s-style sofas. After that, the techno and house effects keep people on the small dance floor until sunrise. *Pancadão,* the unique carioca-style funk, can be heard on some nights. The club is open Tuesday to Saturday from midnight.

GAY & LESBIAN BARS & CLUBS

There's a good cluster of watering holes along Avenida Vieira de Carvalho in República, and the Rua Frei Caneca in Consolação (10 minutes from the Consolação metro on Avenida Paulista) is a regular rendezvous point and hangout.

BARRA FUNDA In a huge colonial blue house in an old industrial neighborhood, **Blue** & LAPA **Space** (⊠*Rua Brigadeiro Galvão 723, Barra Funda* ☎*011/3666–1616* ⊕*www.bluespace.com.br* Ⓜ*Marechal Deodoro*) is one of the largest gay nightclubs in São Paulo. Every Saturday and Sunday, two dance floors and four bars, along with lounge and private rooms, fill with a large crowd interested in the house DJs and go-go-boy and drag shows. Popular **The Week** (⊠*Rua Guaicurus 324, Lapa* ☎*011/3872–9966* ⊕*www.theweek.com.br*) has a whopping 6,000-square-meter area. Two dance floors, three lounge rooms, a deck with a swimming pool, six bars, and several DJs who play house, electro, and techno animate an often shirtless-crowd on Friday and Saturday nights.

ITAIM BIBI Popular lesbian spot **Clube Z** (⊠*Rua Tabapuã 1420, Itaim Bibi* ☎*011/3071–0030* ⊕*www.clubz.com.br*), open Friday and Saturday, has Ancient Rome decor, red velvet sofas, and two DJs spinning house and techno.

SIDE TRIPS FROM SÃO PAULO

São Paulo's surroundings are perfect for all types of getaways. The state has the best highways in the country, making it easy to travel by car or bus to its many small, beautiful beaches, and even beyond to neighboring states (Paraná, Rio de Janeiro, and Minas Gerais). Although most sandy stretches require one- or two-hour drives, good side trips from the city can be as close as the 30-minute trip to Embu.

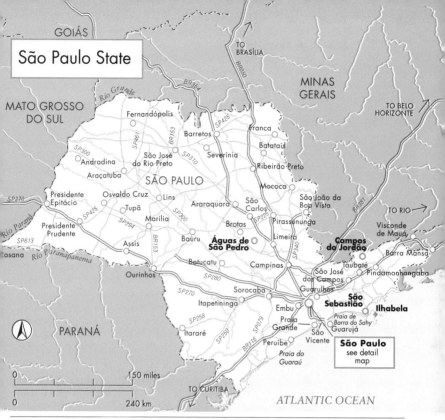

SÃO SEBASTIÃO

204 km (127 mi) southeast of São Paulo.

São Sebastião stretches along 100 km (62 mi) of the Litoral Norte (North Shore). Its bays, islands, and beaches attract everyone from the youngsters who flock to Maresias and Camburi to the families who favor Barra do Sahy. Boating enthusiasts, hikers, and wildlife-seekers also come here, especially on weekends, when hotels are often crowded. Nightlife is good here—the best is in Boiçucanga. The "beautiful island" of Ilhabela *(⇨ below)* is a 15-minute boat ride away from downtown São Sebastião.

GETTING HERE & AROUND

Litorânea buses travel five times daily to São Sebastião (to the ferry dock) from São Paulo and take about 2½ hours.

The drive from São Paulo to São Sebastião is about 2½ hours. Take Rodovia Ayrton Senna–Carvalho Pinto (SP 070), followed by Rodovia Tamoios (SP 099) to Caraguatatuba, and then follow the signs, which lead all the way to the Ilhabela ferry landing.

SAFETY & PRECAUTIONS

Leave jewelry, passports, and your money clip in your hotel safe, or at very least, don't leave your possessions unattended if decide to go for a dip.

ESSENTIALS

Banks & Currency Exchange **Banespa Santander** (⊠ *Avenida Guarda Mor Lobo Viana, Centro*).

Bus Contacts **Litorânea** (☎ *011/6221–0244* ⊕ *www.litoranea.com.br*). **Terminal Rodoviário** (⊠ *Praça Vereador Venino Fernandes Moreira, 10*).

Emergencies & Medical Assistance **Ambulance** (☎ *912*). **Fire** (☎ *193*). **Police** (☎ *190*).

Visitor & Tour Info **Tourist Office Sectur** (⊠ *Av. Altino Arantes, 174, Centro* ☎ *12/3892–2620*).

EXPLORING SÃO SEBASTIÃO

★ Families with young children favor small, quiet **Barra do Sahy** (⊠ *Rio-Santos Hwy., SP 055, 157 km/97 mi southeast of São Paulo*). Its narrow strip of sand (with a bay and a river on one side and rocks on the other) is steep but smooth, and the water is clean and calm. Kayakers paddle about, and divers are drawn to the nearby Ilha das Couves. Area restaurants serve mostly basic fish dishes with rice and salad. Note that Barra do Sahy's entrance is atop a slope and appears suddenly—be on the lookout around marker Km 174.

The young and the restless flock to **Camburi** (⊠ *Rio-Santos Hwy., SP 055, 162 km/100 mi southeast of São Paulo*), to sunbathe, surf, and party. At the center of the beach is a cluster of cafés, ice-cream shops, and bars and the Tiê restaurant. The service may be slow, but Tiê's menu is extensive, and the open-air setup is divine. Camburi is just north of Barra do Sahy. If you're coming from the south, take the second entrance; although it's unpaved, it's usually in better shape than the first entrance, at Km 166.

ILHABELA

7 km (5 mi)/15-min boat ride from São Sebastião.

Fodor's Choice
★ Ilhabela is favored by those who like the beach and water sports; indeed, many championship competitions are held here. This is the biggest sea island in the country, with 22 calm beaches along its western shore, which faces the mainland. The hotels are mostly at the north end, though the best sandy stretches are the 13 to the south, which face the open sea. Eighty percent of the island is in a state park area.

There are two small towns on the island: one is where the locals live; the other is where most visitors stay because of its hotels, restaurants, and stores. During the winter months most businesses that cater to tourists, including restaurants, are open only on weekends.

Scuba divers have several 19th- and early-20th-century wrecks to explore—this region has the most wrecks of any area off Brazil's coast—and hikers can set off on the numerous inland trails, many of which lead to a waterfall (the island has more than 300). ⚠ **Mosquitoes are a problem; bring insect repellent.**

GETTING HERE & AROUND

Balsas (ferries) from São Sebastião to Ilhabela run every 30 minutes from 6 AM to midnight and hourly during the night. The São Sebastião balsa transports vehicles as well as passengers. To get to the ferry dock in São Sebastião, take Avenida São Sebastião from town to the coast. Make advance ferry reservations, particularly December–February.

The best way to get around Ilhabela is by car. There are no rental agencies on the island (or connecting bridges) so be sure to make arrangements beforehand. Public buses also cross the island from north to south daily.

SAFETY & PRECAUTIONS

Ilhabela is a safe little island. Nevertheless, be sure to take common-sense precautions. Don't carry large amounts of money on your person and don't leave your belongings unattended.

ESSENTIALS

Banks & Currency Exchange Banespa (✉ *Rua Dr. Carvalho 98*). **Bradesco** (✉ *Praça Cel. Julião M. Negrão 29*).

Emergencies & Medical Assistance Ambulance (☎ *912*). **Fire** (☎ *193*). Hospital: **Pronto Socorro Municipal Governador Mário Covasú** (✉ *Av. Prof. Malaquias de Oliveira Freitas 154* ☎ *012/3895–8789*). Pharmacy: **Drogaria Nova Esperança** (✉ *Rua da Padroeira 73* ☎ *012/3896–1183*). **Police** (☎ *190*).

Ferry São Sebastião balsa (☎ *0800/704–5510*).

Visitor & Tour Info Ilhabela Secretaria do Turismo (✉ *Rua Bartolomeu de Gusmão 140* ☎ *012/3896–1091* ⊕ *www.ilhabela.sp.gov.br*). **Maremar** (✉ *Avenida Princesa Isabel, 90 Ilhabela* ☎ *012/3896-3679* ⊕ *www.maremar.tur.br* ☞ *Scuba-diving, jeep, horseback-riding, and hiking tours*).

WHAT TO SEE

Praia Grande (✉ *13 km/8 mi south of ferry dock*) has a long sandy strip with food kiosks, a soccer field, and a small church.

At night people gather at **Praia do Curral** (✉ *6 km/4 mi south of Praia Grande*), where there are many restaurants and bars—some with live music—as well as places to camp. The wreck of the ship *Aymoré* (1921) can be found off the coast of this beach, near Ponta do Ribeirão, where you can also look for a waterfall trail.

A small church and many fishing boats add to the charm of **Praia da Armação** (✉ *14 km/9 mi north of ferry dock*). The beach was once the site of a factory for processing blubber and other resources from whales caught in the waters around the island. Today windsurfers stick to capturing the wind and the waves.

To reach **Baía dos Castelhanos** (✉ *22 km/14 mi east of the ferry dock*) you need a four-wheel-drive vehicle, and if it rains even this won't be enough. Consider arriving by sailboat, which demands a 1½- to 3-hour trip that can be arranged through local tour operators. With such an isolated location, you can see why slave ships once used the bay to unload their illicit cargo after slavery was banned in Brazil. If you're lucky, you might spot a dolphin off the shore of this 2-km (1¼-mi) beach—the largest on the island.

WHERE TO STAY & EAT

$$–$$$
SEAFOOD
★

✕ **Viana.** *Camarão* (shrimp) is prepared in various ways at this traditional and petite restaurant with just a few tables. It's popular among locals, who come here to eat and enjoy the gorgeous view and sunsets. Grilled fish is also on the menu. ⊠*Av. Leonardo Reale 1560* ☎*012/3896–1089* ⏁*Reservations essential* ▭*No credit cards* ⊗*Closed weekdays Apr.–June and Aug.–Nov.*

$$$$
Fodor'sChoice
★

▦ **Maison Joly.** Past guests of this exclusive hotel at the top of the Cantagalo Hill range from kings of Sweden to the Rolling Stones. Upon arrival you're given a beach kit complete with mosquito repellent and a hat. Each of the rooms has distinctive furnishings that are part of its theme, such as a piano, a billiard table, or a telescope—and all have balconies facing the sea. The restaurant ($$$$), which now opens to nonguests, is excellent. ⊠*Rua Antônio Lisboa Alves 278, 11630-000* ☎*012/3896–2213* ☒*012/3896–2364* ⊕*www.maisonjoly.com.br* ⏁*9 rooms* ♿*In-room: safe. In-hotel: restaurant, bar, pool, spa, public Internet, no kids under 12, no elevator* ▭*DC, MC, V.*

$
★

▦ **Pousada dos Hibiscos.** North of the ferry dock, this red house has mid-size rooms, all at ground level. The friendly staff serves up a good breakfast and provides poolside bar service. Each room has its own unique decoration, but all have hardwood furnishings, and either tile or stone floors. ⊠*Av. Pedro de Paula Moraes 720* ☎☎*012/3896–1375* ⊕*www.pousadadoshibiscos.com.br* ⏁*13 rooms* ♿*In-room: safe. In-hotel: bar, pool, gym, refrigerator, no elevator* ▭*AE, V.*

SPORTS & THE OUTDOORS

BOATING &
SAILING

You can arrange boating and sailing trips through **Maremar Turismo** (⊠*Av. São João 574* ☎*012/3896–3679* ⊕*www.maremar.tur.br*), one of the biggest tour agencies in Ilhabela. **Ilha Sailing Ocean School** (⊠*Av. Pedro de Paula Moraes 578* ☎*012/9766–6619* ⊕*www.ilhasailing. com.br*) has 12-hour sailing courses that cost about R$500.

SCUBA DIVING

Ilhabela has several good dive sites off its shores. In 1884 the British ship *Darth* sank near **Itaboca** (⊠*17 km/11 mi south of ferry dock*). It still contains bottles of wine and porcelain dishes. **Ilha de Búzios** (⊠*25 km/15 mi offshore; take boat from São Sebastião*), one of the three main Ilhabela islands, is a good place to see a variety of marine life, including dolphins. For beginners, the recommended diving and snorkeling spot is the sanctuary off the shore of islet **Ilha das Cabras** (⊠*2 km/1 mi south of ferry*). It has a statue of Neptune at a 22-foot depth.

SURFING

One of the best places to surf is **Baía de Castelhanos** (⊠*22 km/14 mi east of ferry dock*). **Pacuíba** (⊠*20 km/12 mi north of ferry dock*) has decent wave action.

ÁGUAS DE SÃO PEDRO

180 km (112 mi) northwest of São Paulo.

São Paulo's inland region has beautiful mountains, springs, rivers, and waterfalls perfect for outdoor activities like hiking and rafting. Historic attractions are generally fewer than in other states. Save some time for clothing and crafts shopping, and for the lavish regional cuisine.

Although Águas de São Pedro is the smallest city in Brazil, at a mere 3.9 square km (1.5 square mi), its sulfurous waters made it famous countrywide in the 1940s and '50s. Fonte Juventude is the richest in sulfur in the Americas and is often used to treat rheumatism, asthma, bronchitis, and skin ailments. The waters at Fonte Gioconda have minor radioactive elements (and, yes, they are reportedly good for you), whereas Fonte Almeida Salles's have chlorine bicarbonate and sodium (which are said to alleviate the symptoms of diabetes and upset stomachs).

You can access the springs at the Balneário Publico (public bathhouse) or through some hotels.

GETTING HERE & AROUND

Piracicabana buses run daily from São Paulo to Águas de São Pedro. The trip takes three hours. Águas de São Pedro is about a 2½-hour drive north of São Paulo on Anhangüera-Bandeirantes (SP 330/SP 348) and then SP 304. Águas de São Pedro is compact, so it's easy to get around on foot.

ESSENTIALS

Banks & Currency Exchange **Bradesco** (⌧ *Av. Carlos Mauro 336*).

Bus Contacts **Piracicabana** (☎ *011/6221–0032* ⊕ *www.piracicabana.com.br*).

Emergencies & Medical Assistance **Ambulance** (☎ *912*). **Fire** (☎ *193*). Hospital: **Pronto Socorro Municipal** (⌧ *Rua Antônio Feijó 52* ☎ *019/3482–1721*). Pharmacy: **Drogaria Estância** (⌧ *Av. Carlos Mauro 375* ☎ *019/3482–1347*). **Police** (☎ *190*).

Visitor & Tour Info **Águas de São Pedro Informações Turísticas** (⌧ *Av. Carlos Mauro, in front of Balneário* ☎ *019/3482–2173 or 3482–1096* ⊕ *www.aguasdes aopedro.sp.gov.br*).

EXPLORING ÁGUAS DE SÃO PEDRO

Balneário Municipal Dr. Octávio Moura Andrade has immersion baths in sulfurous springwater. You can swim in the pool or sweat in the sauna while you wait for your private soak, massage, or beauty appointment. A snack bar and a gift shop round out the spa services. ⌧ *Av. Carlos Mauro* ☎ *019/3482–1333* ⌑ *R$8–R$33* ☉ *Mon.–Sun. 7–6.*

☾ A walk through the woods in **Bosque Municipal Dr. Octávio Moura Andrade** is a chance to relax. Horseback riding costs around R$10 for a half hour. It's part of the Balneário complex *(⇨below)*. Saunas, baths, and massages cost R$8–R$33. ⌧ *Av. Carlos Mauro* ☎ *019/3482–1333* ⌑ *Free* ☉ *Weekdays 7–noon, weekends 7–5.*

WHERE TO STAY

¢   **Avenida.** This hotel with an arcaded veranda resembles a large ranch house. Rooms are plain and sparsely decorated, but they're spacious. The restaurant (¢–$$$) serves homestyle Brazilian fare like *filé cubana* (steak with fried bananas) and has live music on Friday and Saturday. ⊠*Av. Carlos Mauro 246* ☎*019/3482–1221* 🖷*019/3482–1223* ⊕*www.hotelavenida.com.br* 🛏*53 rooms* ⚐*In-room: no a/c. In-hotel: restaurant, room service, pool, public Internet, some pets allowed* ▤*No credit cards.*

$$$–$$$$ **Grande Hotel São Pedro.** The beautiful art deco building was a casino during the 1940s. Now it's a teaching hotel and restaurant ($$–$$$) with all the comforts of a full-service spa. Many of the friendly staff members are students—including those who prepare dishes such as salt cod in pistachio sauce. The property is in the middle of a 300,000-square-meter (3.2 million-square-foot) park with more than 1 million trees and local wildlife. ⊠*Parque Dr. Octávio de Moura Andrade* ☎*019/3482–7600* 🖷*019/3482–1665* ⊕*www.grandehotelsenac.com. br* 🛏*96 rooms, 16 suites* ⚐*In-hotel: 2 restaurants, room service, bar, tennis court, pool, gym, spa, refrigerator* ▤*AE, DC, MC, V.*

CAMPOS DO JORDÃO

184 km (114 mi) northeast of São Paulo.

In the Serra da Mantiqueira at an altitude of 5,525 feet, Campos do Jordão and its fresh mountain air are paulistas' favorite winter attractions. In July temperatures drop as low as 32°F (0°C), though it never snows; in warmer months temperatures linger in the 13°C–16°C (55°F–60°F) range.

In the past some people came for their health (the town was once a tuberculosis treatment area), others for inspiration—including such Brazilian artists as writer Monteiro Lobato, dramatist Nelson Rodrigues, and painter Lasar Segall. Nowadays the arts continue to thrive, especially during July's Festival de Inverno (Winter Festival), which draws classical musicians from around the world.

Exploring Campos do Jordão without a car is difficult. The attractions are far-flung, except for those at Vila Capivari.

GETTING HERE & AROUND

Expresso Mantiqueira buses leave São Paulo for Campos do Jordão every two hours daily. The journey takes three hours and costs R$29. To reach Campos do Jordão from São Paulo (a 2½-hour drive), take Rodovia Carvalho Pinto (SP 070) and SP 123.

ESSENTIALS

Banks & Currency Exchange **Bradesco** (⊠*Av. Frei Orestes Girardi 1037*). **Itaú** (⊠*Av. Frei Orestes Girardi 859*).

Bus Contacts **Expresso Mantiqueira** (☎*011/6221–0244* ⊕*www.expressom antiqueira.com.br*). **Terminal Rodoviário** (⊠*Av. Januário Miraglia,12460-000*).

3

Emergencies & Medical Assistance **Ambulance** (☏ *912*). **Fire** (☏ *193*). **Hospital São Paulo** (✉ *Rua Agripino Lopes de Morais 1100* ☏ *012/3662–1722*). **Police** (☏ *190*).

Visitor & Tour Info **Campos do Jordão Tourist Office** (✉ *At entrance to town, Campos do Jordão* ☏ *012/3664–3525* ⊕ *www.camposdojordao.com.br*).

EXPLORING CAMPOS DO JORDÃO

The brand-new **Amantikir Garden**, created in August 2007, consists of 17 gardens that are inspired by famous international counterparts from around the world. On the grounds you can find a cafeteria and a learning center where there are courses on gardening. Plans are in the works for expanding the area and building a bird-watching center. Reservations are mandatory, as the place receives a limited number of guests per day. An English-speaking guide is available if booked in advanced. ✉ *Estrada Paulo Costa Lenz César, Km 2.8* ☏ *012/3662–2757* ⊕ *www. amantikir.com.br* ▭ *R$15, free on Tues.* ⊙ *Mon.–Sun. 8–5.*

Horto Florestal is a natural playground for *macacos-prego* (nail monkeys), squirrels, and parrots, as well as for people. The park has a trout-filled river, waterfalls, and trails—all set among trees from around the world and one of the last *araucária* (Brazilian pine) forests in the state. ✉ *Av. Pedro Paulo, Km 13* ☏ *012/3663–3762* ▭ *R$3–R$4* ⊙ *Daily 8–5.*

The athletically inclined can walk 3 km (2 mi) and climb the 300-step stone staircase to **Pedra do Baú**, a 6,400-foot trio of rocks inside an ecotourism park north of the city. A trail starts in nearby São Bento do Sapucaí, and it's recommended that you hire a guide. In the park you can also practice horseback riding, canopy walking, trekking, or mountain climbing and spend the night in a dormlike room shared with other visitors. Some of the activities are only available on weekends. ✉ *Km 25, Estrada São Bento do Sapucaí* ☏ *012/3662–1106* ▭ *R$5* ⊙ *Wed.–Sun. 8–6.*

WHERE TO STAY & EAT

$–$$$ ✕ **Baden-Baden.** One of the specialties at this charming German restau-
GERMAN   rant in the heart of town is sauerkraut *garni* (sour cabbage with German sausages). The typical dish serves two and is almost as popular as Baden-Baden's own brewery, which is open to visitors 10–5 on weekdays. ✉ *Rua Djalma Forjaz 93, Loja 10* ☏ *012/3663–3659* ▬ *AE, DC, MC, V.*

$–$$ ✕ **Itália Cantina e Ristorante.** As its name suggests, this place specializes
ITALIAN   in Italian food. The pasta and the meat dishes are delicious, but you can also try trout, lamb, fondue, and even boar dishes. ✉ *Av. Macedo Soares 306* ☏ *012/3663–1140* ▬ *AE, DC, MC, V.*

$–$$$ ▦ **Pousada Villa Capivary.** A stay at this cozy guesthouse puts you in the gastronomic and commercial center of Campos. The friendly staff is helpful and efficient. Most apartments have balconies, and the five suites have whirlpool baths. ✉ *Av. Victor Godinho 131* ☏ *012/3663–1746* 🖷 *012/3663–1736* ⊕ *www.capivari.com.br* ⇗ *10 rooms, 5 suites* ⌂ *In-room: safe. In-hotel: bar* ▬ *AE, DC, MC, V.*

SALVADOR

Though the city of Salvador, founded in 1549, lost its status as capital of Brazil in 1763 when that honor was given to Rio (and later to Brasília), it remains the capital of Bahia. At least 70% of its 2,250,000 population is classified as Afro-Brazilian. African rhythms roll forth everywhere—from buses and construction sites to the rehearsals of percussion groups. The scents of coriander, coconut, and palm oil waft around corners.

Salvadorians may tell you that you can visit a different church every day of the year, which is almost true—the city has about 300. Churches whose interiors are covered with gold leaf were financed by the riches of the Portuguese colonial era, when slaves masked their traditional religious beliefs under a thin Catholic veneer. And partly thanks to modern-day acceptance of those beliefs, Salvador has become the fount of Candomblé, a religion based on personal dialogue with the *orixás,* a family of African deities closely linked to nature and the Catholic saints. The influence of Salvador's African heritage on Brazilian music has also turned this city into one of the musical capitals of Brazil, with many of its exponents like Gilberto Gil, Caetano Veloso, and Daniela Mercury acquiring international exposure.

GETTING HERE & AROUND

Salvador's Aeroporto Deputado Luís Eduardo Magalhães (SSA) is one of the busiest in Brazil. TAM is the only airline with direct flights from the United States. Most international flights require a change of plane in São Paulo. The airport is quite far from downtown—37 km (23 mi) to the northeast. Taxis to central hotels should cost about R$60. To avoid being overcharged, pay your fare in advance at the booth inside the terminal.

Regular buses (R$2) serve most of the city, but they're often crowded and rife with pickpocketing. Fancier executivo buses (R$3.50 to R$4) are a better option.

Comum taxis (white with a blue stripe) can be hailed on the street or at designated stops near major hotels, or summoned by phone. Taxis are metered, and fares begin at R$2.50. Unscrupulous drivers sometimes "forget" to turn on the meter and jack up the fare. In Salvador tipping isn't expected. A company called Cometas runs taxis that are spacious, air-conditioned, and equipped with modern security devices. Although more expensive than regular taxis, these are a good choice for foreign travelers.

Itaparica and the other harbor islands can be reached by taking a ferry or a *lancha* (a small boat carrying up to five passengers), by hiring a motorized schooner, or by joining a harbor schooner excursion—all departing from two docks. Boats depart from the Terminal Turístico Marítimo or Terminal São Joaquim close to the Feira São Joaquim.

Most destinations around Salvador can be easily reached by car. To visit the Discovery Coast, fly to Porto Seguro (723 km/450 mi south of Salvador), and then rent a car to explore other beaches and attractions. For the Cocoa Coast, you can fly directly to Ilhéus, 460 km (286 mi) south of Salvador.

SAFETY & PRECAUTIONS

Salvador is no different from most big cities in Brazil—crime is a concern in most neighborhoods. The Centro Histórico area, especially Cidade Alta during daytime, is one of the safest places in Salvador. There are tourist police stationed on almost every corner. At night stick to the main tourist areas and don't walk down deserted streets. Elsewhere around the city, take a taxi between neighborhoods. Cidade Baixa and the Comércio neighborhood are notorious for petty crime, and pickpocketing is common on buses and ferries and in crowded places.

ESSENTIALS

Airport **Aeroporto Deputado Luís Eduardo Magalhães** (*SSA* ⊠ *Praça Gago Coutinho s/n, São Cristovão* ☎ *071/3204–1214 or 071/3204–1444*).

Banks & Currency Exchange **Banco do Brasil** (⊠ *Largo do Cruzeiro de São Francisco 9, Pelourinho*). **Citibank** (⊠ *Rua Miguel Calmon 555, Comércio*).

Boat Contacts **Terminal Marítimo São Joaquim** (⊠ *Av. Oscar Ponte 1051, São Joaquim*). **Terminal Turístico Marítimo** (⊠ *Av das Naus s/n, Comércio*).

Bus Contacts **Terminal Rodoviário** (⊠ *Av. Antônio Carlos Magalhães 4362, Iguatemi* ☎ *071/3450–3871*).

Emergencies & Medical Assistance **Farmácia Drogadelli** (⊠ *Avenida Adhemar de Barros 59* ☎ *071/3237–3270*). **Hospital Espanhol** (⊠ *Av. 7 de Setembro 4161, Barra* ☎ *071/3264–1500*). **Hospital Português** (⊠ *Av. Princesa Isabel 2, Santa Isabel* ☎ *071/3203–5555*). **Tourist Police** (☎ *071/3116-6817*).

Taxi **Cometas** (☎ *071/3646–6304*). **Rádio-Táxi** (☎ *071/3243–4333*).

Visitor & Tour Info **Bahia Bella Viagens e Turismo-Iguatemi** (⊠ *Centro Empresarial Redenção, Av. Tancredo Neves 1063, Pituba* ☎ *071/3273–8200*). **Bahiatursa** (⊠ *Centro de Convenções da Bahia, Jardim Armação s/n, Armação* ☎ *071/3117–3000*). **Tatur Tourismo** (⊠ *Centro Empresarial Iguatemi, Av. Tancredo Neves 274, Iguatemi* ☎ *071/3450–7216* ⊕ *www.tatur.com.br*).

EXPLORING

Salvador sprawls across a peninsula surrounded by the Baía de Todos os Santos on one side and the Atlantic Ocean on the other. The city has about 50 km (31 mi) of coastline. The original city, referred to as the Centro Histórica (Historical Center), is divided into the Cidade Alta (Upper City), also called Pelourinho, and Cidade Baixa (Lower City).

From the Cidade Histórica you can travel north along the bay to the hilltop Igreja de Nosso Senhor do Bonfim. You can also head south to the point, guarded by the Forte Santo Antônio da Barra, where the bay waters meet those of the Atlantic. This area on Salvador's southern tip is home to the trendy neighborhoods of Barra, Ondina, and Rio Ver-

Salvador

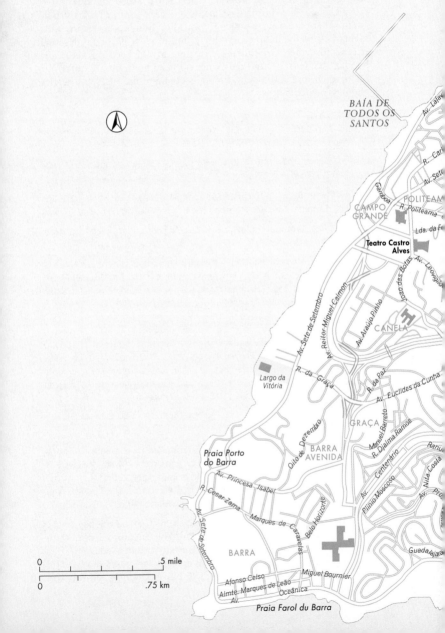

BAÍA DE
TODOS OS
SANTOS

Av. Lafav

R. Car

Av. Sete

Gamboa

POLITEAM

CAMPO
GRANDE

R. Politeama

Lda. da Fe

**Teatro Castro
Alves**

Av. Leovigildo

Caixa de Botas

CANELA

Av. Araújo Pinho

Av. Reitor Miguel Calmon

Av. Sete de Setembro

R. da Graça

R. da Paz

Largo da
Vitória

Av. Euclides da Cunha

GRAÇA

Manuel Barreto

R. Dialma Ramos

Oito de Dezembro

BARRA
AVENIDA

Ranu

Centenário

Av. Nita Costa

Praia Porto
do Barra

Av. Princesa Isabel

Av. Plínio Moscoso

R. Cesar Zama

Belo Horizonte

Marques de Caravelas

Guadalajar

Av. Sete de Setembro

BARRA

Miguel Bournier

Afonso Celso

Almte. Marques de Leão

Av. Oceânica

Praia Farol du Barra

| 0 | | | | .5 mile |
| 0 | | | | .75 km |

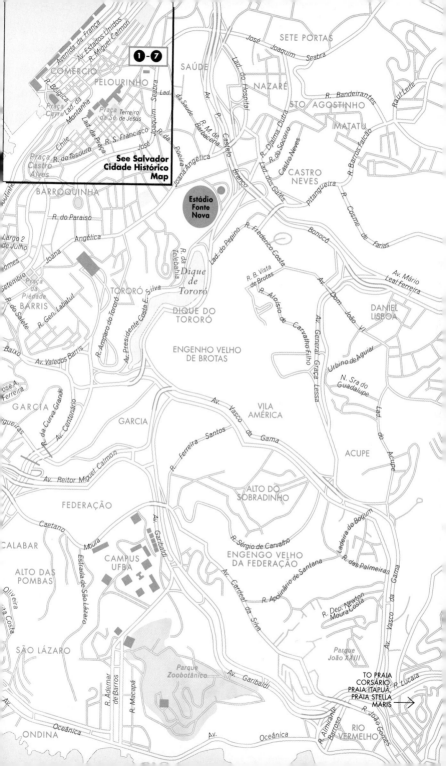

melho, with many museums, theaters, shops, and restaurants. Beaches such as Amaralina, Jardim dos Namorados, and Itapuã, north of Forte Santo Antônio da Barra and along the Atlantic coast, are among the city's cleanest. Many are illuminated at night and have bars and restaurants that stay open late.

CIDADE HISTÓRICO

The heart of the original colonial city, the Cidade Alta section, incorporates the Comércio and Pelourinho neighborhoods and is a riveting blend of European and African cultures. More than 500 of the 2,982 buildings have been restored, earning Salvador the reputation of having the finest examples of baroque architecture in South America. Painted in bright colors, many of the restored buildings are now occupied by restaurants, museums, bars, and shops.

The Cidade Baixa (Lower City) is the section of historic Salvador that fronts the Atlantic Ocean. Its star attraction is the Mercado Modelo, one of Salvador's landmarks, with dozens of stalls that sell everything from Bahian lace dresses and musical instruments to amulets believed to ward off evil or bring good luck. Around the building gathers a mixed crowd of locals and visitors, impromptu entertainers, fortune tellers, and handicrafts vendors.

The area is busy during the day but is practically deserted at night, especially near the base of the Lacerda Elevator. Take a taxi at night.

MAIN ATTRACTIONS

❸ Catedral Basílica. The masonry facade of this 17th-century masterpiece
★ is made of Portuguese sandstone, brought as ballast in shipping boats; the 16th-century tiles in the sacristy came from Macau. Hints of Asia permeate the decoration, such as the facial features and clothing of the figures in the transept altars and the intricate ivory-and-tortoise shell inlay from Goa on the Japiassu family altar, third on the right as you enter. These are attributed to a Jesuit monk from China. The altars and ceiling have a layer of gold—about 10 grams per square meter. ⊠ *Praça 15 de Novembro, Terreiro de Jesus* ☎ *071/3321–4573* ☑ *R$3* ⊙ *Daily 8–11 and 1:30–5:30.*

❺ Igreja de Nossa Senhora do Rosário dos Pretos. Built by and for slaves
★ between 1704 and 1796, the Church of Our Lady of the Rosary has finally won acclaim outside the local Afro-Brazilian community. After extensive renovation, it's worth a look at the side altars to see statues of the church's few black saints. African rhythms pervade the services. ⊠ *Largo do Pelourinho s/n, Pelourinho* ☎ *071/3327–9701* ☑ *Free* ⊙ *Weekdays 8–5, Sat. 9–5, Sun. 10–5.*

❻ Igreja São Domingos de Gusmão da Ordem Terceira. The baroque Church of the Third Order of St. Dominic (1731) houses a collection of carved processional saints and other sacred objects. Such sculptures often had hollow interiors and were used to smuggle gold into Portugal to avoid taxes. Asian details in the church decoration are evidence of long-ago connections with Portugal's colonies of Goa and Macau. Upstairs are two impressive rooms with carved wooden furniture used for church

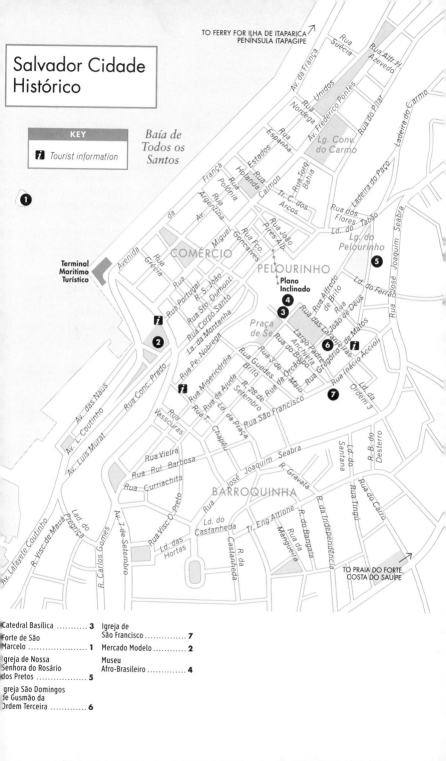

Salvador Cidade Histórico

KEY

i Tourist information

Baía de Todos os Santos

TO FERRY FOR ILHA DE ITAPARICA
PENÍNSULA ITAPAGIPE

Rua Suécia

Rua Alfr. H. Azevedo

Av. da França

Rua Unidos

Rua Nordega

Av. Frederico Pontes

Rua do Pilar

Ladeira do Carmo

Rua Espanha

Lg. Conv. do Carmo

Estados

Rua França

Rua Holanda

Rua Polônia

Argentina

Rua Calmon

Tr. C. dos Arcos

Ladeira do Paço

Rua Torq. Bahia

Rua dos Flores Tabão

Av. da

Av. Miguel Goncalves

Rua Fco.

Rua João Pires Alb.

Ld. do

Lg. do Pelourinho

José Joaquim Seabra

COMÉRCIO

Terminal Marítimo Turístico

Avenida

Rua Grécia

Rua

Rua Portugal

R. S. João

Rua Sto. Dumont

Rua Corpo Santo

La. da Montanha

Rua Pe. Nóbrega

Rua Conc. Prado

PELOURINHO

Plano Inclinado

Rua Alfredo de Brito

Rua das Laranjeiras

Rua São João de Deus

Largo Padre Anchieta

Ld. do Ferrão

Rua Gabriel de Matos

Rua Gregório de Mas

Rua José Joaquim Seabra

Praça de Sé

Rua 3ª de Ordem

Rua Guedes

Rua do Bispo

Rua do Orcado

Rua do Mato

Rua da Ajuda

R. 28 de Setembro

Ld. da Praça

Rua da Misericórdia

Brito

Rua São Francisco

Rua Inácio Accioli

Ld. da Ordem 3

Av. das Naus

Av. L. Coutinho

Av. Luís Murat

Rua Vascúras

Rua

Rua Chabéu

Rua Vieira

Rua Ruí Barbosa

Rua Curriachita

José Joaquim Seabra

R. Gravata

BARROQUINHA

Ld. de Santana

Ld. do R. B. do Desterro

Rua do Carro

Rua Tingi

Av. Lafayete Coutinho

R. Visc. de Mauá

Lad. do Pracinha

Av. Carlos Gomes

Av. 7-de-Setembro

Rua Visc. O. Preto

Ld. das Hortas

Ld. do Castanheda

R. da Castanheda

Tr. Eng. Altione

Rua da Mangueira

R. do Bangata

R. da Independência

TO PRAIA DO FORTE, COSTA DO SAUÍPE

meetings. ⊠ *Praça 15 de Novembro s/n, Terreiro de Jesus* ☎ *071/3242–4185* 🖃 *Free* ☉ *Sun.–Fri. 8–noon and 2–5.*

7 **Igreja de São Francisco.** One of the most impressive churches in Salvador, the Church of St. Francis was built in the 18th century on the site of an earlier church that was burned down during the Dutch invasion in early 1600s. The ceiling was painted in 1774 by José Joaquim da Rocha, who founded Brazil's first art school. The ornate cedar-and-rosewood interior is covered with images of mermaids and other fanciful creatures bathed in gold leaf. Guides say that there's as much as a ton of gold here, but restoration experts maintain there's much less. At the end of Sunday morning mass, the lights are switched off so you can catch the wondrous subtlety of the gold leaf under natural light. The **Convento de São Francisco** (☎ *071/3322–6430*), part of the church complex, has an impressive series of 37 white-and-blue tile panels lining the walls of the cloister, each with a scene from Greco–Roman mythology. The **Ordem Terceira de São Francisco** (☎ *071/321–6968*), on the north side of the complex, has an 18th-century Spanish plateresque sandstone facade—the only one in Brazil—that is carved to resemble Spanish silver altars made by beating the metal into wooden molds. ⊠ *Rua Ordem Terceira, Pelourinho* ☎ *071/322–6430* 🖃 *R$3* ☉ *Mon.–Sun. 8–5.*

Fodor's Choice ★

> ## CANDOMBLÉ
>
> The famous Afro-Brazilian religion called Candomblé was brought over by slaves from Africa. Based on Yoruba, Fon and Bantu beliefs from different regions in Africa, the religion has added some aspects of the Catholic faith over the years. One of the parts of the religion is the belief in 13 principle *orixás*, or deities. In addition, each individual is thought to have his or her own orixá to help guide the way.

4 **Museu Afro-Brasileiro.** Next to the Catedral Basílica, the Afro-Brazilian Museum has a collection of more than 1,200 pieces relating to the city's religious or spiritual history, including pottery, sculpture, tapestry, weavings, paintings, crafts, carvings, and photographs. There's an interesting display on the meanings of Candomblé deities, with huge carved-wood panels portraying each one. The two other museums that share the building are the Memorial de Medicina (Old School of Medicine Memorial) and the Museu Arqueologia e Etnologia (Archaeology and Ethnology Museum); both are closed for extensive renovation. ⊠ *Praça 15 de Novembro s/n, Pelourinho* ☎ *071/3221–2013* 🖃 *R$3* ☉ *Weekdays 9–5.*

CIDADE BAIXA (THE LOWER CITY)

1 **Forte de São Marcelo.** Jorge Amado jokingly called this doughnut-shape fortress near the Terminal Maritimo, the "belly button of the world." Bahia's economy essentially revolved around this spot, with the merchants, the market, and the port clustered practically within arm's reach. The fort, built between 1650 and 1680 in a mix of medieval and colonial styles, housed the Imperial Army for more than 200 years. The troops staved off attacks from buccaneers and other invaders. Inside you can see the armory and soldier's quarters and get a great view of

Fodor's Choice ★

the bay from the lookouts. Hour-long tours in English depart from Terminal Maritimo. ⊠*Av. França s/n, Comércio* ☎*071/3321–5286* 💰*R$ 5* ⏱*Call ahead for hrs.*

❷ Mercado Modelo. From the 17th to the 19th century, slaves were kept in
★ chains in the basement of this building upon arriving from Africa. The market has seen many changes since then. Today it's a convenient place to buy handicrafts. Bargaining is expected here for goods like *cachaça* (sugarcane liquor), cashews, pepper sauce, cigars, leather goods, hammocks, musical instruments, and semiprecious stones. *Repentistas* (impromptu folksingers) and fortune-tellers gather outside. The market is open Monday to Saturday 9–6, Sunday 9–2. ⊠*Praça Visconde de Cayrú 250, Comércio admission* ☎*071/3241–2893.*

CITY BEACHES

In general the farther east and north from the mouth of the bay, the better the beaches. To avoid large crowds, don't go on weekends. Keep an eye on your belongings and take only what you need to the beach—petty thievery is a problem. There are no public bathrooms. You can rent a beach chair and sun umbrella for about R$10.

One of the nicest beaches along Avenida Oceánica is **Praia Corsário,** a long stretch popular with a younger crowd. There are kiosks where you can sit in the shade and enjoy seafood and ice-cold beer. ⊠*Av. Oceánica, south of Parque Metropolitan de Pituaçu, Pituaçu.*

Praia Itapuã. Frequented by the artists who live in the neighborhood, the Itapuã beach has an eclectic atmosphere. There are food kiosks—including Acarajé da Cira, one of the best places to get *acarajé* (a spicy fried-bean snack). The area was once a whale cemetery, and bones are still an occasional find. Inland from Itapuã, a mystical freshwater lagoon, the **Lagoa de Abaeté,** and surrounding sand dunes are now a municipal park. Itapuã's dark waters are a startling contrast to the fine white sand of its shores. ⊠*16 km/10 mi northeast of downtown, Itapuã.*

The northernmost beach in the Salvador municipality along the Avenida Oceánica is **Praia Stella Maris,** popular with surfers and the young crowd. There are myriad food-and-drink kiosks, more than at any other beach—it's the perfect place to sooth your thirst with *água de côco* (coconut water). ⊠*20 km/12 mi north of downtown, after Itapuã, Stella Maris.*

OFF THE BEATEN PATH

★ **Ilha de Itaparica.** The largest of 56 islands in the Baía de Todos os Santos, Itaparica was originally settled because its ample supply of fresh mineral water was believed to have rejuvenating qualities. Its beaches are calm and shallow, thanks to the surrounding reefs, which are avidly sought by windsurfers, divers, and snorkelers. The main port of entry on the north of the island is the town of Bom Despacho, where the ferries from Salvador dock. The best beaches are near the villages of Vera Cruz, Mar Grande, and Conceição, the latter almost entirely owned by Club Med Itaparica.

Instead of buses or taxis, small Volkswagen vans (called *kombis*) provide the most convenient local transportation around the island. You can hail vans and hop from beach to beach along the 40 km (25 mi) of BA 001, the coastal highway that connects Itaparica village on the north part of the island to the mainland via Ponte do Funil (Funnel Bridge) on the southwest side. The drive from Salvador to the island takes about four hours. Bicycle rentals are readily available in the island's towns, so you don't really need a car.

> **FAST FOOD**
>
> Baianas typically make *acarajé*, a delicious street food made of bean dough fried with palm oil and filled with bean paste and shrimp. *Moqueca* is another specialty made with palm oil, coconut milk, and fish or shrimp cooked slowly over a low fire.

Ferries to the island run daily from the **Terminal Marítimo São Joaquim** (⊠ *Av. Oscar Ponte 1051, São Joaquim*). Tickets cost R$3.35 during the week, R$4.35 on the weekend. The ferries run from 5 AM to 11:30 PM and last 40 minutes.

WHERE TO EAT

You can easily find restaurants serving Bahian specialties in most neighborhoods. Pelourinho and Barra, full of bars and sidewalk cafés, are good places to start. There are also many good spots in bohemian Rio Vermelho and a slew of places along Orla, the beachfront drive beginning around Jardim de Alah. The regional cuisine leans toward seafood, but some meat dishes should be tried. And, like anywhere else in Brazil, there are *churrascarias* for beef lovers. One main course often serves two; ask about portions when you order. Beware that regional food is normally spicy and hot.

$$$–$$$$
SEAFOOD
✕ **Bargaço.** Great Bahian seafood dishes are served at this longtime favorite. *Pata de caranguejo* (vinegary crab claws) is hearty and may do more than take the edge off your appetite for the requisite moqueca *de camarão* (with shrimp) or moqueca *de siri mole* (with soft-shell crab); try the cocada for dessert, if you have room. ⊠ *Rua Antonio da Silva Coelho s/n, Jardim Armação* 🕾 *071/3231–3900* ⊕ *www.restaurante bargaco.com.br* ⊟ DC, MC.

$$$
ECLECTIC
✕ **Boi Preto.** Beef is cooked to perfection at one of the best barbecue places in Salvador. Seafood, including lobster, crab, and sushi, and more exotic fare like alligator or wild boar are also on the menu. A piano bar keeps the atmosphere light. ⊠ *Av. Otávio Mangabeira s/n, Jardim Armação* 🕾 *071/3362–8844* ⊕ *www.grupoboipreto.com.br* ⊟ AE, MC, V.

$–$$
BRAZILIAN
✕ **Encontro dos Artistas.** This simple Bahian restaurant has both alfresco and indoor dining. The fish-and-shrimp moqueca, a stew made with coconut milk and *dendê* (a type of palm) oil, is a must here. The charm of this neighborhood establishment lies in its casual ambience, surroundings in a centuries-old part of town, and local clientele, who gather here after work. Service can be slow—order an appetizer or

salad and drinks as soon as you sit down. ⊠ *Rua Francisco Muniz Barreto 13, Pelourinho* ☎ *071/3321–1721* ▤ *AE, DC, MC, V.*

$ ✕ **Escola Pelourinho.** This restaurant, which opened in 1975, is a cooking school where new generations of Bahian chefs hone their skills under supervision of experienced teachers. More than 40 typical Bahian and Brazilian dishes are served buffet style in this old colonial house. It's regarded as one of the best restaurants in town. The bargain prices are an extra incentive. ⊠ *Praça José de Alencar 13/19, Pelourinho* ☎ *071/3324–4550* ⊕ *www.ba.senac.br* ▤ *AE, DC, MC, V* ⊘ *No dinner Sun.*

BRAZILIAN

$$–$$$$ ✕ **Trapiche Adelaide.** It's almost impossible to have a bad meal in this city, but this restaurant along the harbor and near the Mercado Modelo still stands out for its unique blend of Italian, French, and Bahian cuisines. Try the seafood risotto or quail in *farofa* (cassava flour). Having drinks before dinner on the deck overlooking the Todos os Santos Bay is a pleasant way to wind down after a day of sightseeing. ⊠ *Praça dos Tupinambás, Av. Contorno 02, Comércio* ☎ *071/3326–0443* ⊕ *www.trapicheadelaide.com.br* ▤ *DC, MC, V* ⊘ *No dinner Sun.*

BRAZILIAN
Fodor'sChoice
★

$$$–$$$$ ✕ **Yemanjá.** A bubbly underwater theme—replete with aquariums full of colorful fish and sea-goddess murals—sets the tone for the fabulous seafood here. Small portions of acarajé can be ordered as appetizers. The service is somewhat slow, but most patrons don't seem to mind, concentrating instead on plowing through enormous portions of moqueca, or *ensopado,* seafood cooked in a light sauce. Reservations are essential on weekends. ⊠ *Av. Otávio Mangabeira 4655, Jardim Armação* ☎ *071/3461–9010* ⊕ *www.restauranteyemanja.com.br* ▤ *AE, DC, MC, V.*

SEAFOOD
★

WHERE TO STAY

There are only a few hotels in the Cidade Histórico. Heading south into the Vitória neighborhood along Avenida 7 de Setembro there are many inexpensive establishments convenient to beaches and sights. In the fashionable Barra neighborhood, many hotels are within walking distance of cafés, bars, restaurants, and clubs. The resorts in the beach areas of Ondina and Rio Vermelho are a 20-minute taxi ride from downtown. High seasons are from December to March and the month of July. For Carnival, reservations must be made months in advance, and prices are substantially higher.

¢ ▦ **Âmbar Pousada.** The highlight of this small and simple pousada is the service—the staff is attentive to your needs. Location is a draw, too, as here you are just a couple of streets away from the eclectic Barra neighborhood. If you're braving Salvador at Carnival time, the parade passes noisily two blocks away on Avenida Oceânica. The rooms are kept impeccably clean. There's a nice terrace and courtyard. **Pros:** Intimate setting, pleasant rooms. **Cons:** Can be loud during Carnival. ⊠ *Rua Afonso Celso 485, Barra* ☎ *071/3264–6956* ⊕ *www.ambarpousada. com.br* 🛏 *5 rooms* △ *In-room: no TV. In-hotel: public Internet* ▤ *MC, V* ⨀ *BP.*

$ ⊞ **Blue Tree Towers Salvador.** Although it doesn't have the best sea views, the local link of the Blue Tree chain has easy access to the historic center and the beaches. Rooms with king-size beds and other facilities are very comfortable. From here it's a short distance to the many restaurants and bars of the Barra district. **Pros:** Close to everything, nice amenities. **Cons:** Lacking views. ⊠*Rua Monte Conselho 505, Rio Vermelho* ☎*071/2103–2233* ⊕*www.bluetree.com.br* ⇆*200 rooms* ⬧*In-room: safe, refrigerator, dial-up. In-hotel: restaurant, room service, pool, gym, laundry service, public Internet, public Wi-Fi, parking (fee)* ⊟*AE, DC, MC, V* |⊙|*BP.*

$$$ ⊞ **Catussaba Resort Hotel.** In a garden of flowers and palm trees, this
★ hotel has large rooms, some of which have beautiful wicker furniture, with balconies and ocean views. The resort complex opens directly onto Itapuã beach, one of the cleanest and most famous in Salvador. The hotel is 40 km (25 mi) from downtown, near the airport. If you tire of saltwater and sand, head for the large pool area. **Pros:** Spacious rooms, pleasant decor, plenty of amenities. **Cons:** A bit impersonal. ⊠*Alameda da Praia, Itapuã* ☎*0800–998010* ⊕*www.catussaba.com.br* ⇆*186 rooms, 4 suites* ⬧*In-hotel: restaurant, room service, bar, tennis courts, pool, gym, public Internet, parking (no fee)* ⊟*AE, MC, V.*

$ ⊞ **Hotel Catharina Paraguaçu.** Rooms and suites in this 19th-century
Fodor'sChoice mansion are small but comfortable. If you're looking for space, ask for
★ one of the six split-level suites. Extra attention is devoted to the decor, with pottery and embroidery from local artisans. The pousada is family-run and in a neighborhood of many restaurants and bars. It has one room for guests with disabilities, including wheelchair access, unusual for a small hotel. **Pros:** Family-friendlly environment, near dining and nightlife. **Cons:** Not many amenties. ⊠*Rua João Gomes 128, Rio Vermelho* ☎*071/3334–0089* ⊕*www.hotelcatharinaparaguacu.com. br* ⇆*31 rooms* ⬧*In-room: refrigerator. In-hotel: public Internet, no elevator* ⊟*AE, MC, V* |⊙|*BP.*

$$$–$$$$ ⊞ **Pousada das Flores.** The Brazilian–French owners have made this
★ inn, within walking distance of the historical district, one of the city's best options. Rooms are large and have high ceilings and hardwood floors. For peace and quiet as well as an ocean view, opt for a room on an upper floor. If you feel like splurging, request the penthouse, which has a fantastic view of the harbor. Breakfast is served on the patio. **Pros:** Beautiful building, great decor, perfect location. **Cons:** Pricey during high season. ⊠*Rua Direita de Santo Antônio 442, Santo Antônio* ☎*071/3243–1836* ⊕*www.pflores.com.br* ⇆*6 rooms, 3 suites* ⬧*In-room: Wi-Fi. In-hotel: no elevator* ⊟*MC, V.*

$$ ⊞ **Sofitel Salvador.** This branch of the international chain sits in a lushly
☾ landscaped park near Itapuã Beach and the Abaeté Lagoon, about 5 km
Fodor'sChoice (3 mi) from the airport. It's the only hotel in the city with its own golf
★ course, albeit a 9-hole one. As this gleaming white high-rise aims for the business as well as the purely tourist clientele, rooms are more sober than at other beachfront hotels. The Oxum restaurant has an excellent regional menu. There's free transportation to the Centro Histórico. **Pros:** Amenities for business travelers, lovely grounds. **Cons:** Far from the center, Internet connections cost extra. ⊠*Rua da Passargada s/*

n, Itapuã ☎071/3374–8500 ⊕www.sofitel.com ⇝206 rooms ⌂In-room: safe, Ethernet. In-hotel: 2 restaurants, room service, bars, golf course, tennis courts, pools, gym, concierge, children's programs (ages 4–12), laundry service, public Internet, airport shuttle, parking (no fee) ▤AE, DC, MC, V.

NIGHTLIFE & THE ARTS

Pelourinho is filled with music every night and has more bars and clubs than you can count. Activity also centers along the seashore, mainly at Rio Vermelho and between the Corsário and Piatã beaches, where many hotels have bars or discos.

Salvador is considered by many artists as a laboratory for the creation of new rhythms and dance steps. As such, this city has an electric performing arts scene. See the events calendar published by Bahiatursa or check local newspapers for details on live music performances as well as rehearsal schedules. In Pelourinho, groups often have practices open to the public on Tuesday and Sunday nights.

NIGHTLIFE

After dark, Praça Terreiro de Jesus is a hot spot, especially on Tuesday and Saturday nights, when stages are set up here and at other squares around the city for live performances. This plaza is especially popular with tourists because it has been painted, cleaned up, and gentrified. Although there may be impromptu musical performances any night, you can always count on it on Tuesday.

BARS **Sancho Panza** (⊠*Av. Otávio Mangabeira 122, Pituba* ☎071/3248–3571) is a great place for sangria and typical Spanish fare. Sooner or later you must have a *caipirinha* (lime and sugarcane-liquor cocktail) at **Cantina da Lua** (⊠*Largo Terreirro de Jesus 2, Pelourinho* ☎071/33241–7383).

DANCE SHOWS There are Afro-Brazilian dinner shows at the **Solar do Unhão** (⊠*Av. do Contorno 08, Comércio* ☎071/3321–5551). The unforgettable Afro-Bahian show at the **Teatro Miguel Santana** (⊠*Rua Gregório de Matos 49, Pelourinho* ☎071/3322–1962 ⊕*www.balefolcloricod abahia.com.br*) has the town's best folkloric dance troupes. This is an entertaining way to learn about Afro-Brazilian culture.

THE ARTS

CARNIVAL REHEARSALS ★ Afro-Brazilian percussion groups begin Carnival rehearsals—which are really more like creative jam sessions—around midyear. **Associação Cultural Bloco Carnavalesco Ilê Aiyê** (⊠*Rua do Curuzu 288, Liberdade* ☎071/3256–1013), which started out as a Carnival bloco, has turned itself into much more in its 34-year

> **THE SAMBA MAN**
>
> Dorival Caymmi, one of the greatest Brazilian composers, was born in Salvador in 1914. With his beautiful Bahian sambas, Caymmi brought the sights, smells, and sounds of his native state into the popular imagination. One of his most beautiful compositions is called "Minha Jangada Vai Sair Pro Mar" ("My Boat Will Go Out to Sea").

history. It now has its own school and promotes the study and practice of African heritage, religion, and history. Public practices are held every Saturday night at Forte de Santo Antônio, and should not be missed.

★ **Olodum,** Salvador's best-known percussion group, gained international fame when it participated in Paul Simon's "Rhythm of the Saints" tour and recordings. The group has its own venue, the **Casa do Olodum** (⊠ *Rua Maciel de Baixo 22, Pelourinho* ☎ *071/3321–5010* ⊕ *www.narin.com/ olodum*). Olodum also has a percussion school, **Escola Criativa Olodum** (⊠ *Rua das Laranjeiras 30, Novo Horizonte* ☎ *071/3322–8069*).

MUSIC, **Teatro Casa do Comércio** (⊠ *Av. Tancredo Neves 1109, Pituba* ☎ *071/* THEATER & *3273–8732*) hosts music performances and some theatrical produc- DANCE tions. The **Teatro Associação Cultural Brasil-Estados Unidos** (⊠ *Av. 7 de Setembro 1883, Vitória* ☎ *0800/284–2828 or 071/3337–4395* ⊕ *www. acbeubahia.org.br*) has contemporary and classical music, dance, and theater performances by Brazilian and international artists.

SIDE TRIPS FROM SALVADOR

Although Salvador can keep you entertained for more than a week, there are great places for a one- or two-day break in more relaxing environs. On a two-day tour to Morro de São Paulo, you can enjoy the near-pristine beaches and tropical forest. Or plan a day trip to Praia do Forte or the other northern beaches; they're less crowded and more beautiful than those in and near Salvador.

MORRO DE SÃO PAULO

On Ilha de Tinharé, just south of Itaparica, Morro de São Paulo is the most popular place on the island, most of which is covered with thick Atlantic Forest protected by a state park. Private cars are not allowed here; you can walk to the beaches, take tractor-pulled trolleys, or hire a small boat to "beach-hop" about the island.

GETTING HERE & AROUND
To get here from Salvador, take either a *lancha* (small boat carrying up to five passengers) or larger *catamarã* (catamaran) from Salvador's Terminal Marítimo. Lanchas and catamarãs leave daily from 8 AM to 2 PM, and return from Morro de São Paulo from noon to 4 PM. Fares range from R$50 to R$60 and include food, drinks, and live music.

A handful of small flight operators, including AeroStar and Adey, have service to Morro de São Paulo from Salvador. The 20-minute flight costs about $R180. There's only a landing strip at Morro de São Paulo.

SAFETY & PRECAUTIONS
Do not keep your belongings unattended when you're on the beach.

ESSENTIALS
Airline Contacts Adey (☎ *071/3652–1312*).

Capoeira: The Fight Dance

Dance and martial arts in one, *capoeira* is purely Brazilian. The early days of slavery often saw fights between Africans from rival tribes who were thrust together on one plantation. When an owner caught slaves fighting, both sides were punished. To create a smoke screen, the Africans incorporated music and song into the fights. They brought a traditional *berimbau* string-drum instrument (a bow-shape piece of wood with a metal wire running from one end to the other, where there's a hollow gourd containing seeds) to the battles. Tapped with a stick or a coin, the berimbau's taut wire produces a throbbing, twanging sound whose rhythm is enhanced by the rattling seeds. Its mesmerizing reverberations were accompanied by singing and chanting, and when the master appeared, the fighters punched only the air and kicked so as to miss their opponents.

The fights have been refined into a sport that was once practiced primarily in Bahia and Pernambuco but has now spread throughout Brazil. Today's practitioners, called *capoeristas*, swing and kick—keeping their movements tightly controlled, with only hands and feet touching the ground—to the beat of the berimbau without touching their opponents. The goal is to cause one's opponent to lose concentration or balance. Capoeira is traditionally performed in a *roda* (wheel), which refers both to an event of continuous capoeira and to the circle formed by players and instrumentalists. Strength, control, flexibility, artistry, and grace are the tenets of capoeira. In any exhibition the *jogadores*, or players, as they are called—with their backs bending all the way to the floor and their agile foot movements (to avoid an imaginary knife)—as well as the compelling music, make this a fascinating sport to watch.

Banks & Currency Exchange There are no banks in Morro de São Paulo and only one ATM, so get plenty of cash before you arrive

EXPLORING MORRO DE SÃO PAULO

Popular beaches dot the 40-km (25-mi) Atlantic side of Tinharé. Starting at the village of Morro de São Paulo, beaches begin with Primeira (First) and go on to Segunda, Terceira, and so forth. Waters are calm thanks to the coral reef just off the surf, whose abundant marine life (mostly in the form of small fish) makes scuba diving or snorkeling worthwhile. The number of tourists nearly triples from December to February, when Brazilians on their summer vacation fill the pousadas for festival and Carnival season. The southernmost beaches near Boca da Barra are usually quieter even during peak season. The government has begun to charge a R$6.50 tourism tax per person.

NORTH COAST BEACHES

To reach some of Bahia's more pristine and less crowded beaches, head north of Salvador on the Estrada do Coco (Coconut Road), leaving the baroque churches and colonial dwellings behind in favor of miles of quiet road lined with coconut palms.

GETTING HERE & AROUND

At the fishing village and turtle haven of Praia do Forte, take the Linha Verde (Green Line) up the coast. Buses to this string of beaches are readily available, but the convenience of having your own car is justified here.

EXPLORING NORTH COAST BEACHES

Barra do Jacuípe. A river runs down to the ocean at this long, wide, pristine beach lined with coconut palms. There are beachfront snack bars. The Santa Maria/Catuense bus company operates six buses here daily. ✉ *40 km (25 mi) north of Salvador.*

Guarajuba. With palm trees and calm waters banked by a reef, this is the nicest beach of them all, though it's lined with condos. The bus to Barra do Jacuípe continues on to Guarajuba, which has snack kiosks, fishing boats, surfing, dune buggies, and a playground. ✉ *60 km (38 mi) north of Salvador.*

PRAIA DO FORTE

72 km (45 mi) northeast of Salvador.

Praia do Forte was first settled in 1549 by Garcia D'Avila, a clerk for the Portuguese crown. For reasons lost in the mists of history, Garcia D'Avila had acquired a fortune and became a landowner. With foresight he introduced cattle ranching and coconut-palm cultivation in the area. To protect the coast, a medieval-style castle was built that served as a fort—hence the town's name, which means "Fortress Beach." All that remains from the castle is just the outer walls, but it has a helpful visitor center. Today the area's biggest attraction is the headquarters of a sea-turtle preservation center called Projeto Tamar. Bars, restaurants, pousadas, and shops line the three brick-paved streets. Almost everything in town is on the main street, Alameda do Sol.

GETTING HERE & AROUND

To reach Praia do Forte by car from Salvador, take the Estrada do Coco (BA 099) north and follow the signs. From there on, it's called Linha Verde (Green Line), to Costa do Sauípe and the northern beaches all the way to the Sergipe border. Linha Verde has hourly bus service from Salvador to Praia do Forte. The two-hour trip on the un-air-conditioned bus costs R$8.

ESSENTIALS

Internet **Café Connect** (✉ *Alameda das Estrelas s/n* ☎ *71/3676–0431*).

Taxi **Valdécio Franco** (☎ *71/9616–2712*).

Visitor & Tour Info **Centrotour** (✉ *Av. Do Farol, Térreo Praia do Forte* ☎ *71/3676–1091* ⊕ *www.centrotour.com.br*).**Bahia Adventure** (✉ *Km 76, Rodovia BA 099, Costa do Sauípe, Mata de São João* ☎ *712104–8600* ⊕ *www.bahiaadventure.com*). **Odara Turismo** (✉ *Praia do Forte Eco Resort Hotel, Praça da Música s/n, Praia do Forte, Mata de São João* ☎ *071/676–1080*).

EXPLORING PRAIA DO FORTE

Fodor's Choice Five of the seven surviving sea-turtle species in the world roam and
★ reproduce on Brazil's Atlantic coast, primarily in Bahia. The headquarters of **Projeto Tamar,** established in 1980, has turned what was once a small, struggling fishing village into a tourist destination with a mission—to save Brazil's giant sea turtles and their hatchlings. During the hatching season (September through March), workers patrol the shore at night to locate nests and move eggs or hatchlings at risk of being trampled or run over to safer areas or to the open-air hatchery at the base station. Here you can watch adult turtles in the swimming pools and see the baby turtles that are housed in tanks until they can be released to the sea. Eighteen other Tamar base stations on beaches along 1,000 km (621 mi) of coastline in five northeastern Brazilian states protect about 400,000 hatchlings born each year. The headquarters also has educational videos, lectures, and a gift shop where you can buy turtle-theme gifts. From December to February, you can sign up for the "Tartaruga by Night" project to help release hatchlings from the station hatchery to the sea. ⊠*Alameda do Sol s/n* ☎*071/3676–1020* ⊕*www.tamar.org.br* ⊠*R$12* ⊗*Daily 9–7.*

Swim or snorkel in the crystal-clear (and safe) waters of the **Papa Gente,** a 3-meter-deep (10-foot-deep) natural pool formed by reefs at the ocean's edge. Snacks are sold at little huts on the beach, but if you're really hungry, a restaurant, in the Sobrado Da Vila pousada, is nearby.

WHERE TO STAY & EAT

$$–$$$$ ✕ **Sabor da Vila.** It isn't surprising that seafood fresh from the ocean is
SEAFOOD the specialty at this small modest restaurant on Praia do Forte's main street. After visiting Praia do Forte's attractions, stop here for a fish-and-shrimp moqueca. ⊠*Av. ACM 7* ☎*071/3676–1156* ▤*DC, MC, V.*

$$ 🏠 **Pousada Sobrado Da Vila.** Leave your laptop and organizer at home— this laid-back pousada is a place to kick back and relax. Right on the main drag, this lodging has rooms that are plain but comfortable. The restaurant serves Bahian specialties. **Pros:** Relaxing environment, good restaurant. **Cons:** Few amenities. ⊠*Av. ACM 7* ☎*071/3676–1088* ⊕*www.sobradodavila.com.br* ⤶*23 rooms* ৬*In-room: safe, refrigerator. In-hotel: restaurant, bar, public Internet* ▤*MC, V.*

$$$$ 🏠 **Praia do Forte Eco Resort and Thalasso Spa.** Relax in a hammock and
☽ contemplate the sea from your private veranda at this sprawling beach-
Fodor's Choice front resort. You'll be within walking distance of the village in case you
★ need more action, but there's a full roster of activities available including horseback riding, volleyball, kayaking, sailing, and snorkeling. All rooms face the ocean, and a large part of the grounds still has the original Atlantic Forest vegetation that once covered the region. **Pros:** Close to everything, plenty of amenities, relaxing spa therapies. **Cons:** Restaurant open only to resort guests. ⊠*Av. do Farol s/n, Praia do Forte, Mata de São João* ☎*071/3676–4000 or 0800/71–8888* ⊕*www.ecoresort.com.br* ⤶*293 rooms* ৬*In-room: safe, refrigerator. In-hotel: 2 restaurants, bars, tennis courts, pools, gym, beachfront, water sports, children's programs (ages 4–12), public Internet* ▤*AE, DC, MC, V* ⊗*MAP.*

CACHOEIRA

109 km (67 mi) northwest of Salvador.

This riverside colonial town dates from the 16th and 17th centuries, when sugarcane was the economy's mainstay. It has been designated a national monument and is the site of some of Brazil's most authentic Afro-Brazilian rituals. After Salvador it has the largest collection of baroque architecture in Bahia. A major restoration of public monuments and private buildings was finished in 2003, and included revitalized streets and plazas in town. On an excursion to Cachoeira you can walk through the colorful country market and see architecture preserved from an age when Cachoeira shipped tons of tobacco and sugar downriver to Salvador.

GETTING HERE & AROUND

To drive from Salvador, take BR 324 north for about 55 km (34 mi), then head west on BR 420 through the town of Santo Amaro. The trip takes 1½ hours. Santana has daily service from Salvador to Cachoeira.

ESSENTIALS

Banks & Currency Exchange **Banco Bradesco** (⊠ *Aristides Milton 10, Centro*).

Bus Contacts **Santana** (☎ *071/3438–4303*).

EXPLORING CACHOEIRA

The **Capela da D'Ajuda,** built in the 16th century, is one of the most remarkable examples of early baroque architecture in this part of Brazil. ⊠ *Largo D'Ajuda s/n* ☎ *No phone* 🎫 *R$3* ⊘ *Inquire at Museu da Boa Morte to gain entrance to chapel.*

Museu da Boa Morte displays photos and ceremonial dresses worn by members of the Sisterhood of Our Lady of Good Death during their rituals and festivals. You may also meet some of the elderly but always energetic women whose ancestors protested slavery. The ladies at the museum will let you in to see the chapel and the church. ⊠ *Largo D'Ajuda s/n* ☎ *075/3425–1343* 🎫 *By donation* ⊘ *Weekdays 10–1 and 3–5.*

WHERE TO STAY & EAT

¢ 🏨 **Pousada do Convento.** You can stay overnight in one of the large rooms or have a good lunch at this one-time Carmelite monastery that dates from the 17th century. The meeting room adjacent to the hotel main room was formerly a church. **Pros:** Recently remodeled rooms, beautiful colonial furniture. **Cons:** Simple accommodations, few amenities. ⊠ *Praça da Aclamação s/n* ☎ *075/3425–1716* 🛏 *26 rooms* ♿ *In-room: refrigerator. In-hotel: restaurant, pool* ⊟ *MC, V.*

> ### OUR LADY OF GOOD DEATH
>
> Devotion to Nossa Senhora da Boa Morte (Our Lady of Good Death) began in the slave quarters, where discussions on abolition of slavery took place. The slaves implored Our Lady of Good Death to end slavery and promised to hold an annual celebration in her honor should their prayers be answered. Brazil was the last country in the Western Hemisphere to abolish slavery, in 1888.

LENÇÓIS

427 km (265 mi) west of Salvador; 1,133 km (704 mi) northeast of Brasília.

In 1822 a precious-stone frenzy began with the discovery of diamonds in riverbeds around the town of Mucugê. Hundreds of people hoping to make their fortune flooded into the region. This golden age lasted until late in the 1800s, when gems ran out. What remained were towns such as Lençóis, Igatu, and Mucugê, where cobblestone streets are lined with 19th-century colonial houses. Because of the historic and architectural importance of the region, buildings are being restored to give travelers a taste of what life was like in those heady days.

The largest community in the Chapada Diamantina area, as well as the gateway to Chapada Diamantina National Park, Lençóis arose from the hundreds of makeshift tents of white cotton fabric built by *garimpeiros* (gold- and precious stone–seekers). (*Lençóis* means "bedsheet.") The settlement quickly became an important trade hub for precious stones. Many fortunes were made, but the golden age ended in 1889, when and the city was forgotten.

The small town enjoyed a renaissance after it was designated a national monument in 1973. Several *sobrados* (houses) have been restored to their original grandeur. The *mercado municipal* (municipal market), where most of the diamonds were sold, has been completely renovated.

GETTING HERE & AROUND

When driving, the route to Chapada Diamantina from Salvador is fairly straighforward: take BR 342 west to Feira de Santana, then BR 242 to Lençóis. Both roads are in good condition, but expect irregular pavement in some spots. Real Expresso buses make the eight-hour trip from Salvador to Lençóis for about R$35, with departures at 11:30 PM daily and at 7 AM Tuesday, Thursday, and Saturday. Return is at 11:30 PM daily, with additional departures at 7:30 AM Monday, Wednesday, and Friday.

SAFETY & PRECAUTIONS

During festivals, when excessive drinking might occur, it's best to be on the safe side. Stay in groups and stick to the downtown area.

ESSENTIALS

Banks & Currency Exchange **Banco do Brasil** (⊠ *Praça Horacio de Mattos 56, Centro*).

Bus Contacts **Real Expresso** (☎ *075/3334–1112 in Lençóis, 071/450–9310 in Salvador* ⊕ *www.realexpresso.com.br*).

Emergencies & Medical Assistance **Farmacia Maciel** (⊠ *Av. 7 de Setembro s/n, Centro* ☎ *075/3334–1224*). **Municipal de Lençóis** (⊠ *Rua Vai Quem Quer s/n, Centro* ☎ *075/3334–1587*).

Taxi **Lençois Táxi** (☎ *075/3334–1115*).

Visitor & Tour Info Secretaria de Turismo (⊠ *Mercado Cultural, Centro* ☎ *075/3334–1117).* LenTur Turismo Ecológico (⊠ *Av. 7 de Setembro 10, Centro* ☎ *075/3334–1224* ⊕ *www.lentur.com.br).*

EXPLORING LENÇÓIS

One of the region's most popular hiking trails runs along a section of Rio Lençóis called **Rio Serrano.** It's surrounded by exuberant forest, now protected as municipal park. The reddish-color water is due to organic matter from the forest floor. You can bathe and relax in several natural pools—they look a bit like hot tubs—formed on the rock-strewn river-bed. There are also three waterfalls along the way to a scenic overlook of the town and surrounding hills. The trailhead is about 1 km (½ mi) north of Lençóis, after the gate to Portal de Lençóis hotel. ⊠ *End of Rua Altina Alves.*

A steep 6-km (4 mi) cobblestone road connects the BA 142 highway with the community of **Igatú.** During the 19th century several thousand lived in this boomtown. Today the ruins of hundreds of abandoned homes can be explored. ⊠ *113 km (70 mi) south of Lençóis.*

Torrinha. The cave's name, which means "Little Tower," refers to a rock formation outside the entrance. Here you can find a diverse collection of cave formations; besides the usual stalactites and stalagmites, arago-nite flowers, clusters of helectites, and chandeliers abound. There are three different guided tours ranging from 1 to 2½ hours that explore different sections of the cave. ⊠ *From Lençóis, take BR 242 west 25 km (16 mi), then take BA 432, the road to Irecê for about 13 km (8 mi)* ☎ *075/3229–4117* ⊠ *R$20 per group, plus R$10 per person* ⊙ *Daily 9–6.*

WHERE TO STAY & EAT

$ ✕ **Neco's.** One of the oldest eateries in town, it's the place to taste some
BRAZILIAN   of the *garimpeiro* staples like *godó de banana,* a simple but tasty dish combining sun-dried meat and sliced green bananas. ⊠ *Praça Clarim Pacheco 15* ☎ *075/3334–1179* ⊟ *No credit cards.*

$–$$ ⊡ **Hotel Canto das Águas.** One of the first hotels to open after the creation of the national park, Canto das Águas is inspired by the colonial architecture of the nearby historic district. Stone archways open to the garden that surrounds the main building. Nearby is the Rio Lençóis, whose soothing sound inspired the hotel's name, which means "Water Chant." Sleek rooms with balconies are equipped with modern amenities like flat-screen TVs and wireless Internet. **Pros:** Superb location, near the main plaza. **Cons:** Noisy during festivals. ⊠ *Av. Sr. dos Passos 1* ☎ *075/3334–1154* ⊕ *www.lencois.com.br* ⇆ *44 rooms, 8 suites* ⌂ *In-room: refrigerator, Wi-Fi. In-hotel: restaurant, bar, pool* ⊟ *AE, D, MC, V* ⦿ *BP.*

$ ⊡ **Pousada Casa da Geléia.** If you're seeking a home away from home, look no further. The English-speaking owners of this pousada will entertain you with tales of the history of the Chapada. The spacious white-walled rooms are clean and simple. The hearty breakfast will reveal the origin of the inn's name, Jelly House: dozens of homemade jams and jellys that include regional fruits such as umbú, seriguela, and cajú. The owner Zé Carlos is a bird-watching enthusiast, and has escorted tourists and biologists in tours of the Chapada. ⊠*Rua General Viveiros 187* ☎*075/3334–1151* ☞*6 rooms* ⚿*In-room: refrigerator. In-hotel: no elevator* ▤*AE, DC, MC, V* ⭘❙*BP.*

PARQUE NACIONAL CHAPADA DIAMANTINA

60 km (37 mi) west of Lençóis.

Established in 1985, the 1,520-square-km (593-square-mi) national park is one of the most scenic places in Brazil. Here you can find crystal-clear creeks and rivers with abundant rapids and waterfalls and more than 70 grottos and caverns. There are also the tall peaks of the Sincorá Range, the highest point being Barbados Peak (2,080 meters, or 7,000 feet). The flora and fauna of the area, which include many varieties of cactus, orchids, and bromeliads and more than 200 bird species, have been the subject of two extensive studies by the Royal Botanical Gardens at Kew in England. The best time to visit the park is in the dry season from March to October, but expect high temperatures during the day (rarely above 36 C [100 F]). From May to July, temperatures might drop to near 10°C (45°F). The park does not have a visitor center, but there's a small ranger headquarters in the town of Palmeiras.

GETTING HERE & AROUND

The town of Lençóis by far the best gateway to the park.

SAFETY & PRECAUTIONS

Traversing the roads and especially the trails within the park definitely requires experienced guides, as trails are not well marked.

ESSENTIALS

Visitor & Tour Info **Associação dos Condutores de Visitantes** (☎*075/3334–1425*), based in Lençóis, has certified guides to take you to the national park. Itineraries can be arranged to suit your interests and level of fitness.

EXPLORING PARQUE NACIONAL CHAPADA DIAMANTINA

One of the most popular hikes in the national park leads to the country's tallest waterfall, 1,312-foot **Cachoeira da Fumaça** (Smoke Waterfall). Most of the falling water evaporates before reaching the ground, hence the odd name. A 4-km (2-mi) path from the village of Caeté-Açú takes you to the canyon's rim. The most scenic route is a longer trail that leaves Lençóis and reaches the gorge below the falls. The path goes past the impressive Capivara Falls. ⊠*25 km (14 mi) west of Lençóis.*

Vale do Paty, one of the country's most scenic treks, takes you through towering sierras, through caves, and past waterfalls.The 70-km (43-mi) trail starts in Bomba, climbs to Candombá hills, follows a plateau at Gerais de Vieira, then goes alongside the steep Rio Paty toward Andaraí. ⊠*20 km (12 mi) west of Lençóis.*

PORTO SEGURO

730 km (453 mi) south of Salvador.

Not too long ago, Porto Seguro (Safe Harbor) was a serene fishing village. Now it's one of the prime tourist destinations in the country, with international flights from several Europeans cities. Hotels, inns, and restaurants have risen to please nearly every need or taste.

Porto Seguro has an intense atmosphere comparable only to Salvador in Bahia. Picture a city whose main drag is called "Passarela do Alcool" (Booze Walkway). Carnival is a major event here, drawing hundreds of thousands of tourists. The beaches north of the city, such as Mutá, are recommended for those looking for calmer grounds.

GETTING HERE & AROUND

From Salvador, Águia Branca offers daily overnight bus service to Porto Seguro (11 hours, R$120). There are daily flights from Salvador, Rio de Janeiro, and Saõ Paulo on Tam and GOL.

ESSENTIALS

Airport **Aeroporto Porto Seguro** (⊠ *Estr. Aeroporto* ☎ *73/3288–1880).*

Banks & Currency Exchange **Banco do Brasil** (⊠ *Av. Dos Navegantes 22, Centro* ☎ *No phone).*

Bus Contacts **Águia Branca** (☎ *071/3460–4400 or 0800/725–1211).* **Rodoviária** (⊠ *Rua José Borges Souza 35* ☎ *No phone).*

Emergencies & Medical Assistance **Drogaria Plantão** (⊠ *Av 22 Abril, 18 lj 3, Centro* ☎ *73/3268–3370).* **Pronto Socorro** (⊠ *Rua Cova Moca 551, Centro* ☎ *No phone).*

Taxi **Porto Táxi** (☎ *73/3288-1010).*

Visitor & Tour Info **Glória Agência de Viagens e Turismo** (⊠ *Av 22 Abril 400 lj. 10, Centro* ☎ *73/3288-0758).*

EXPLORING PORTO SEGURO

Fodor$Choice ★ One of the most biodiverse places on the planet, **Estação Vera Cruz** is a 6,000-hectare nature preserve. This is the largest private Atlantic Forest protected area in Brazil, owned by one of the world's largest paper pulp mills. The visitor center introduces you to the ecology of the area. From here knowledgeable guides lead you on a 2-km (1.2-mi) trail through the forest. Highlights are the *pau-brasil* (brazilwood) and *jatobá* (South American locust) trees, and birds—especially the colorful toucans and parrots. Call ahead to announce your visit. ⊠ *BR 367, at Km 37.5* ☎ *073/9985–1808* 🖼 *Free* ☉ *By appointment.*

WHERE TO STAY & EAT

$ ITALIAN ✕ **Recanto do Sossego.** This restaurant right on Mutá beach, is popular—on weekends you'll have to wait in line. But it's worth the wait. Fare is Italian—start with appetizers such fish carpaccio and move on to gnocchi with pesto sauce. ⊠ *Praia do Mutá, Av. Beira Mar* ☎ *073/ 3677–1266* ▤ *AE, D, MC, V.*

CLOSE UP

Eating Bahian

When African slaves arrived in Bahia, they added coconut milk, palm oil, and hot spices into Portuguese and Indian dishes, transforming them into something quite new. Additional basic raw materials are lemon, coriander, tomato, onions, dried shrimp, salt, and hot chili peppers. Seafood is the thing in Bahia, and most regional seafood dishes are well seasoned, if not fiery hot. Bahia's most famous dish is *moqueca*, a seafood stew made with fish and/or shellfish, dendê oil, coconut milk, onions, and tomatoes, cooked quickly in a clay pot over a high flame. *Bobó* is equally tasty, but creamier version of moqueca, due to the addition of cassava flour. Other classics include *vatapá*, a thick puree-like stew made with fish, shrimp, cashews, peanuts, and a variety of seasonings; *caruru*, okra mashed with ginger, dried shrimp, and palm oil; *ximxim de galinha*, chicken marinated in lemon or lime juice, garlic, and salt and pepper and then cooked with dendê and peanut oil, coconut milk, tomatoes, and seasonings; and *efo*, a bitter chicorylike vegetable cooked with dried shrimp.

$$ \star $$ **Villagio Arcobaleno.** Porto Seguro's five-star choice is right on hip Taperapuã Beach. Apartments are comfortable and decorated in tune with the tropical surroundings. The hotel maintains a large awning and wooden deck on the beach. **Pros:** Nicely furnished rooms, free Internet. **Cons:** A bit removed from the center. ✉ *Av. Beira Mar, at Km 6.5* ☎ *073/3679–1284* ⊕ *www.hotelarcobaleno.com.br* ⇖ *160 rooms, 5 suites* ♿ *In-room: safe, refrigerator, Ethernet. In-hotel: restaurant, room service, bar, tennis courts, pools, gym, concierge, laundry service, public Internet, airport shuttle* ⊟ *AE, DC, MC, V* ⊞ *CP.*

TRANCOSO

Life here circles around the downtown plaza called "Quadrado" (the Square), where pedestrians have the right of way—no cars allowed. This is where everybody goes for shopping, dining, and people-watching. In recent years Trancoso has become a boomtown of sorts, and a haven for high-society Brazilians from São Paulo, especially.

GETTING HERE & AROUND

Take a ferry to Arraial D'Ajuda. From here take a bus or van to Trancoso. If you're driving, take BA 101 from Arraial d'Ajuda to Trancoso.

.ESSENTIALS

Emergencies & Medical Assistance Ambulance (☎ *192*). **Police** (☎ *190*).

Visitor & Tour Info Trancoso Receptivo (✉ *Rua Carlos Alberto Parracho, s/n, Centro* ☎ *73/3668–1333*).

WHERE TO STAY & EAT

$$–$$$$
SEAFOOD
✕ **Capim Santo.** Capim Santo, right on the central square, is *the* place in Trancoso for seafood. Popular dishes are the fish fillet in shrimp sauce and the lobster. Servings are small. ✉*Rua do Beco 55,* ☎*073/3668–1122* ▤*AE, MC, V* ✆*Closed Sun.*

$$–$$$$
BRAZILIAN
★
✕ **O Cacau.** Unique versions of Bahian dishes are served at this restaurant catering to international visitors. A must is the *arrumadinho*, with sun-dried meat, beans, cassava flour, and spicey *pico de gallo* sauce. ✉*Praça São João 96* ☎*073/3668–1266* ▤*MC, V* ✆*Closed Mon.*

$$$$
★
🖾 **Club Med Trancoso.** Built on the beachfront hills south of Trancoso's village, this Club Med property went to great lengths to merge the sprawling resort with the landscape, with minimal environmental impact. Services are first-rate, as this is one of the higher ranking hotels in this worldwide chain. The spa is very good. The hotel is 6 km (4 mi) south of Trancoso. **Pros:** Beautiful hotel, great service. **Cons:** Not an intimate space. ✉*Km 18, Estrada do Arraial* ☎*073/3575–8400* ⊕*www.clubmed.com.br* ➟*250 rooms, 50 suites* ᐸIn-room: refrigerator. In-hotel: 2 restaurants, room service, bars, tennis courts, pools, gym, spa, beachfront, concierge, laundry service, public Internet, airport shuttle* ▤*MC, V* ⦿*FAP.*

$$$–$$$$
Fodor'sChoice
★
🖾 **Pousada Etnia.** This small pousada is designed for the most demanding guest. The Italian owners also keep an art and antiques shop nearby. Most of the furniture in the pousada's public areas comes from the shop. Each bungalow has a theme decor, like the Moroccan bungalow. Among the draws here are the several massage options and artsy activities taught by art therapists that assist you with painting and pottery that are designed to help you reach the highest level of relaxation. **Pros:** Intimate feel, romantic spot, lovely furnishings. **Cons:** Not for families. ✉*Av. Principal s/n* ☎*073/3668–1137* ⊕*www.etniabrasil.com.br* ➟*8 bungalows* ᐸIn-room: safe, refrigerator, Ethernet. In-hotel: restaurant, room service, pool, gym, public Internet, airport shuttle, no kids under 14, no-smoking rooms* ▤*AE, DC, MC, V* ⦿*FAP.*

THE AMAZON

A trip along the Amazon itself is a singular experience. From its source in southern Peru it runs 6,300 km (3,900 mi) to its Atlantic outflow and averages more than 3 km (2 mi) in width, but reaching up to 48 km (30 mi) across in the rainy season. Of its hundreds of tributaries, 17 are more than 1,600 km (1,000 mi) long. The Amazon is so large it could hold the Congo, Nile, Orinoco, Mississippi, and Yangtze rivers with room to spare. In places it is so wide you can't see the opposite shore, earning it the appellation Rio Mar (River Sea). Although there has been increasing urbanization in the Amazon region, between one-third and one-half of the Amazon's residents live in rural settlements, many of which are along the riverbanks, where transportation, water, fish, and good soil for planting are readily available.

EXPLORING THE AMAZON

Visiting outlying areas in the Amazon usually results in unforgettable adventures, but tropical environments can be hostile, so prepare well and go with a companion if possible. It's a good idea to hire a guide or go with a tour company specializing in backcountry adventures. To join a tour or to choose a destination, contact one of the tour companies we suggest, or consult with a state-run tour agency. Research important health and safety precautions before your trip. A small cut, for example, can turn into a bad infection, and a painful encounter with a stingray's barb can result in a ruined vacation. The more remote your destination, the more seriously you should heed the travel advice and health precautions in this book.

WHEN TO GO

The dry season (low water) between Belém and Manaus runs roughly from mid-June into December, and it's often brutally hot. Shortly before the new year, rains come more often and the climate cools a bit. The average annual temperature is 80°F (27°C) with high humidity. The early morning and the evening are always cooler and are the best times for walking around. The rainy season (high water) runs from December to June. "High water" means flooded forests and better boat access to lakes and wetlands for wildlife spotting. It also means flooded river beaches. Fishing is prime during low water, when fish move from the forest back into rivers and lakes, making them more accessible. Depending on where you are in the Amazon, during the rainy season it may rain every day, or three out of every four days, whereas during the dry season it may rain only one out of four days or less.

AMAZON BY BOAT

Sleep in a hammock on the middle deck of a thatch-roof riverboat or in the air-conditioned suite of an upscale tour operator's private ship. Keep in mind that wildlife-viewing is not good on boats far from shore. Near shore, however, the birding can be excellent. Binoculars and a bird guide can help, and shorebirds, raptors, and parrots can be abundant. Common in many parts of the river system are *boto* (pink dolphins) and *tucuxi* (gray dolphins).

ADVENTURE CRUISES

Adventure cruises combine the luxury of cruising with exploration. Their goal is to get you close to wildlife and local inhabitants without sacrificing comforts and amenities. Near daily excursions include wildlife-viewing in smaller boats with naturalists, village visits with naturalists, and city tours. **G.A.P** (*Great Adventure People* ✉ *19 Charlotte St., Toronto, ON, Canada* ☎ *800/708–7761 or 416/260–0999* ⊕ *www. gapadventures.com*) makes these trips, which run from 9 to 16 days.

TOURIST BOATS

Private groups can hire tourist boats that are more comfortable than standard riverboats. They generally travel close to the riverbank and have open upper decks from which you can observe the river and forest. The better tour operators have an English-speaking regional expert

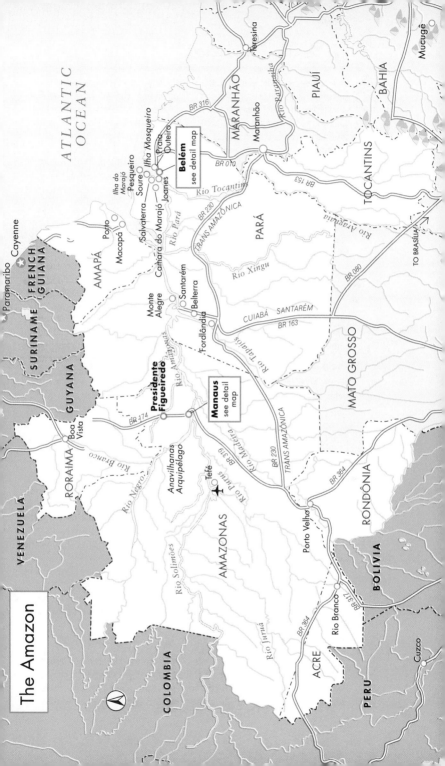

CLOSE UP

Health in the Amazon

Several months before you go to the Amazon, visit a tropical medicine specialist to find out what vaccinations you need. Describe your planned adventure, and get tips on how to prepare.

BITES & STINGS

Tropical forests are home to millions of biting and stinging insects and other creatures. Most are harmless and many, such as snakes, are rarely seen. Mosquitoes can carry malaria and dengue, so it's important to protect yourself (see the Health Tips below). To avoid snake bites, wear boots and pants in the forest and watch closely where you step. Escaping the Amazon without a few bites is nearly impossible—some anti-itch ointment will help you sleep at night.

FOOD & WATER

In rural areas, avoid drinking tap water and using ice made from it. In the cities most restaurants buy ice made from purified water. Beware of where you eat. Many street stands are not very clean. Over-the-counter remedies can ease discomfort. For loose bowels, Floratil can be purchased without a doctor's prescription. Estomazil and Sorrisal (which may contain asprin) are remedies for upset stomach.

INFECTIONS & DISEASES

Dehydration and infections from insect bites and cuts are common. Get plenty of (bottled or purified) water and treat infections quickly. Rabies, Chagas' disease, malaria, yellow fever, meningitis, hepatitis, and dengue fever are present in the Amazon. Research tropical diseases in the Amazon so you know the symptoms and how to treat them should you fall ill. You shouldn't have any problems if you take precautions.

on board—usually an ecologist or botanist. You can either sleep out on the deck in a hammock or in a cabin, which usually has air-conditioning or a fan. Meals are generally provided.

SPEEDBOATS

You can take a speedboat to just about anywhere the rivers flow. Faster than most options, speedboats can be ideal for traveling between smaller towns, a morning of wildlife-viewing, or visiting a place that doesn't have regular transportation, such as a secluded beach or waterfall. You design the itinerary, including departure and return times. Prices and availability vary with distance and locale. Contact tour agencies, talk with locals, or head down to the docks to find a boat willing to take you where you want to go. Work out the price, destination, and travel time before leaving. You may have to pay for the gas up front, but don't pay the rest until you arrive. For trips longer than an hour, bring water, snacks, and sunscreen.

MACAMAZON BOATS

Longer boat routes on the lower Amazon are covered by **MACAMA-ZON** (☎*091/3222–5604 or 091/3228–0774*). Regular departures run between Belém, Santarém, Macapá, Manaus, and several other destinations. The boats are not luxurious but are a step above regional boats. You can get a suite for two from Belém to Manaus with air-conditioning and bath for about R$800. *Camarote* (cabin) class gets you a tiny room for two with air-conditioning and a shared bath. *Rede* (hammock) class is the cheapest and most intimate way to travel, since you'll be hanging tight with the locals on the main decks. Hammocks are hung in two layers very close together, promoting neighborly chats. Arrive early for the best spots, away from the bar, engine, and bathrooms. Keep your valuables with you at all times and sleep with them. Conceal new sneakers in a plastic bag. In addition to a hammock (easy and cheap to buy in Belém or Manaus), bring two 4-foot lengths of -inch rope to tie it up. Also bring a sheet, since nights get chilly.

REGIONAL BOATS

To travel to towns and villages or to meander slowly between cities, go by *barco regional* (regional boat). A trip from Belém to Manaus takes about five days; Belém to Santarém is two days. The double- or triple-deck boats carry freight and passengers. They make frequent stops at small towns, allowing for interaction and observation. You might be able to get a cabin with two bunks (around R$400 for a two-day trip), but expect it to be claustrophobic. Most passengers sleep in hammocks with little or no space between them. Bring your own hammock, sheet, and two 4-foot sections of rope. Travel lightly and inconspicuously.

Booths sell tickets at the docks, and even if you don't speak Portuguese, there are often signs alongside the booths that list prices, destinations, and departure times. Sanitary conditions in bathrooms vary from boat to boat. Bring your own toilet paper, sunscreen, and insect repellent. Food is sometimes served, but the quality ranges from so-so to deplorable. Consider bringing your own water and a *marmita* (carry-out meal) if you'll be on the boat overnight. Many boats have a small store at the stern where you can buy drinks, snacks, and grilled *mixto quente* (ham-and-cheese) sandwiches. Fresh fruit and snacks are available at stops along the way. Be sure to peel or wash fruit thoroughly with bottled water before eating it.

BELÉM

The capital of Pará State, Belém is a river port of around 1.3 million people on the south bank of the Rio Guamá, 120 km (74 mi) from the Atlantic, and 2,933 km (1,760 mi) north of Rio de Janeiro. The Portuguese settled here in 1616, using it as a gateway to the interior and an outpost to protect the area from invasion by sea. Because of its ocean access, Belém became a major trade center. Like the upriver city of Manaus, it rode the ups and downs of the Amazon booms and busts. The first taste of prosperity was during the rubber era. Architects from Europe were brought in to build churches, civic palaces, theaters, and mansions, often using fine, imported materials. When Malaysia's rubber supplanted that of Brazil in the 1920s, wood and, later, minerals provided the impetus for growth.

Belém has expanded rapidly since the 1980s, pushed by the Tucuruvi hydroelectric dam (Brazil's second largest), the development of the

Carajás mining region, and the construction of the ALBRAS/Alunorte bauxite and aluminum production facilities. Wood exports have risen, making Pará the largest wood-producing state in Brazil. As the forests are cut, pastures and cattle replace them, resulting in an increase in beef production.

Belém is more than just a jumping-off point for the Amazon. It has several good museums and restaurants and lots of extraordinary architecture. Restored historic sites along the waterfront provide areas to walk, eat, and explore. Several distinctive buildings—some with Portuguese *azulejos* (tiles) and ornate iron gates—survive along the downtown streets and around the Praça Frei Caetano Brandão, in the Cidade Velha (Old City). East of here, in the Nazaré neighborhood, colorful colonial structures mingle with new ones housing trendy shops.

GETTING HERE & AROUND
There are several daily flights to Belém from Rio and São Paulo. TAM offers heavily discounted flights every weekend, and GOL has frequent promotions. All airlines arrive at the Aeroporto Internacional Val-de-Cans, 11 km (7 mi) northwest of the city. The easiest route from the airport is south on Avenida Julio Cesár and then west on Avenida Almirante Barroso. The 20-minute taxi ride from the airport to downtown Belém costs around R$30.

Most long-distance ships arrive and depart from the Terminal Hidroviário (Av. Marechal Hermes). MACAMAZON and Bom Jesus (based in Macapá) have ships and standard riverboats to Macapá, Santarém, Manaus, and other places.

Belém's local bus service is safe (though you should keep an eye on your belongings) and comprehensive, but a little confusing. Ask a resident for guidance. The bus costs R$1.50.

Although Belém has the most traffic of any Amazon city, in-town driving is relatively easy. Parking is only tricky in a few areas, such as Avenida Presidente Vargas and the Escadinha.

SAFETY & PRECAUTIONS
In Belém watch out for pickpockets everywhere, but especially at Vero-Peso, on Avenida President Vargas, and in Comércio. Avoid walking alone at night or on poorly lighted streets, and don't wear jewelry, especially gold.

ESSENTIALS
Airlines (Local) **Kovacs** (☎ *091/3233–1509*). **Soure** (☎ *091/3233–4986*). **TAF** (☎ *0300/313–2000* ⊕ *www.voetaf.com.br*).

Airport **Aeroporto Internacional Val-de-Cans** (⊠ *Av. Julio Cesár s/n* ☎ *091/3210–6000 or 091/3257–3780* ⊕ *www.aeroportosdobrasil.com.br*).

Banks & Currency Exchange **Banco Amazônia** (⊠ *Av. Presidente Vargas 800, Comércio*). **Banco do Brasil** (⊠ *Aeroporto Internacional Val-de-Cans, Av. Júlio César s/n*). **Casa Francesa Câmbio e Turismo** (⊠ *Trv. Padre Prudêncio 40, Batista Campos* ☎ *No phone*).

Boat Contacts Bom Jesus (☎*091/3272–1423 or 3223–2342*). **MACAMAZON** (☎*091/3222–5604 or 091/3228–0774*).

Bus Contacts Rodoviário São Brás (✉*Av. Almirante Barroso s/n, São Brás* ☎*091/3266–2625*).

Emergencies & Medical Assistance Ambulance (☎*192*). **Fire** (☎*193*). **Hospital:** Hospital e Maternidade Dom Luiz I (✉*Av. Generalíssimo Deodoro 868, Umarizal* ☎*091/3241–4144*). **Pharmacy:** Big Ben (✉*Av. Gentil Bittencourt 1548, Nazaré* ☎*091/3241–3000*). **Police** (☎*190*).

Internet Speednet (✉*Rua Gama Abreu 152, Campina* ☎*091/3222–7506 or 091/ 8147–3937*).

Taxi Coopertáxi (☎*091/3257–1041 or 091/3257–1720*). **Taxi Nazaré** (☎*091/ 3242–7867*).

Visitor & Tour Info Amazon Star Tours (✉*Rua Henrique Gurjão 236, Campina* ☎*091/3212–6244*). **BELEMTUR** (✉*Av. Governador José Malcher 592, Nazaré* ☎*091/3242–0900 or 091/3242–0033*). **Lusotur** (✉*Av. Brás de Aguiar 471, Nazaré* ☎*091/3241–1011* ⊕*www.lusotur.com.br* ☞*City tours and ecotours*). **PARATUR** (✉*Praça Maestro Waldemar Henrique s/n, Reduto* ☎*091/3212–0575* ⊕*www.paratur.pa.gov.br*).

CIDADE VELHA

Cidade Velha (Old City) is the oldest residential part of Belém. Here you'll find colonial houses made of clay walls and tiled roofs, the tallest being only three stories high. However, there are more and more 15-floor apartment buildings invading from the north. Much of Cidade Velha is middle-income with a variety of hardware, auto-parts, and fishing-supply stores. On its northwestern edge, the Forte Presépio lies along the bank of the Rio Guamá.

MAIN ATTRACTIONS

❹ ★ **Casa das Onze Janelas.** At the end of the 18th century, sugar baron Domingos da Costa Barcelar built the neoclassical House of Eleven Windows as his private mansion. Today Barcelar's mansion is a gallery for contemporary arts, including photography and visiting expositions. The view from the balcony is impressive. Take a walk through the courtyard and imagine scenes of the past. This is where the aristocracy took tea and watched over the docks as slaves unloaded ships from Europe and filled them with sugar and rum. ✉*Praç Frei Caetana Brandão, Cidade Velha* ☎*91/4009–8821* 💲*R$2, free Tues.* ☉*Tues.– Fri. 10–6, weekends 10–8*.

❶ **Estação das Docas.** Next to Ver-o-Peso market on the river, three former warehouses have been artfully converted into a commercial–tourist area. All have one wall of floor-to-ceiling glass that provides a full river view when dining or shopping. The first is a convention center with a cinema and art exhibits. The second has shops and kiosks selling crafts and snacks, and the third has a microbrewery and six upscale restaurants. The buildings are air-conditioned and connected by glass-covered walkways and contain photos and artifacts from the port's heyday. ✉*Av. Boulevard Castilho França s/n, Campina* ☎*091/3212–*

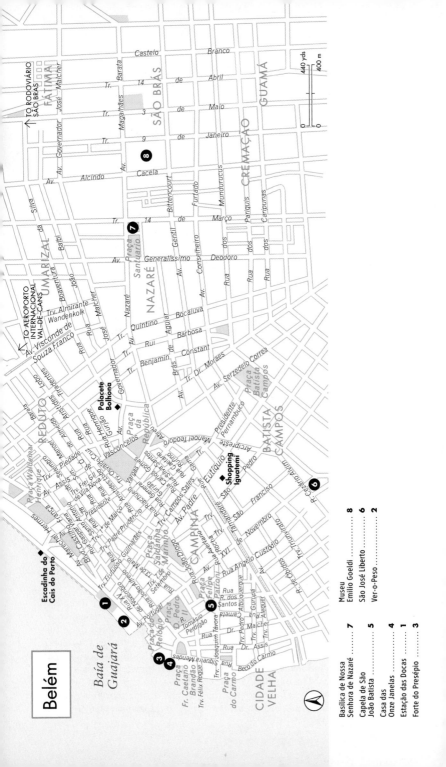

Belém

Baía de Guajará

Escadinha do Cais do Porto

CIDADE VELHA

REDUTO

Praça Waldemar Henrique

Praça da República

Palacete Bolonha

UMARIZAL

TO AEROPORTO INTERNACIONAL VAL-DE-CANS
Av. Visconde de Souza Franco

TO RODOVIÁRIO SÃO BRÁS

FÁTIMA

SÃO BRÁS

NAZARÉ

Praça Santuário

Praça Batista Campos

BATISTA CAMPOS

GUAMÁ

CREMAÇÃO

CAMPINA

Shopping Iguatemi

Praça da Trindade

440 yds
400 m

Basílica de Nossa
Senhora de Nazaré **7**

Capela de São
João Batista **5**

Casa das
Onze Janelas **4**

Estação das Docas **1**

Forte do Presépio **3**

Museu
Emílio Goeldi **8**

São José Liberto **6**

Ver-o-Peso **2**

5525 ✉ *Free* ☺ *Noon–midnight or later.*

❸ Forte do Presépio *(Fort of the Crèche).*
☾ Founded January 12, 1616, this
★ fort is considered Belém's birthplace. From here the Portuguese
launched conquests of the Amazon and watched over the bay. The
fort's role in the region's defense is
evidenced by massive English- and
Portuguese-made cannons pointing out over the water. They are
poised atop fort walls that are 3
yards thick in places. Renovations
completed in 2002 unearthed more
than two dozen cannons, extensive
military middens from the moat,
and native Tupi artifacts. A small
museum of prefort indigenous cultures is at the entrance. Just outside
the fort, cobblestone walkways hug the breezy waterfront. ✉ *Praça
Frei Caetano Brandão, Cidade Velha* ☎ *91/4009–8828* ✉ *R$4, Tues.
free* ☺ *Tues.–Fri. 10–6, weekends 10–8.*

SNAKES IN BELÉM

One of the most popular Amazon
myths is about the *cobra grande*
a huge snake, which lives underneath towns and once in a while
comes out at night to feast on the
inhabitants. Recently, deforestation
has caused the myth to become
reality. Last year alone 21 snakes
were captured in Belém, among
them a 10-foot anaconda. As the
rain forest is destroyed by fires
and logging, these Amazonian
natives search for living space and
food in the city.

---

❷ Ver-o-Peso. Its name literally meaning "see the weight" (a throwback to
the time when the Portuguese weighed everything entering or leaving
the region), this market is a hypnotic confusion of colors and voices.
Vendors hawk tropical fruits, regional wares, and an assortment of
tourist kitsch. Most interesting are the *mandingueiras,* women who
claim they can solve any problem with "miracle" jungle roots and
charms for the body and soul. They sell jars filled with animal eyes,
tails, and even heads, as well as herbs, each with its own legendary
power. The sex organs of the pink river dolphin are a supposedly unri-
valed cure for romantic problems. In the fish market you get an up-
close look at pirarucu, the Amazon's most colorful fish and the world's
second-largest freshwater species. Look for bizarre armored catfish
species, such as the *tamuatá* and the huge *piraíba.* Across the street is
a small arched entrance to the municipal meat market. Duck in and
glance at the French-style pink-and-green-painted ironwork, imported
from Britain. Be sure to visit Ver-o-Peso before noon, when most vendors leave. It opens around 6 AM. Leave your jewelry at home and
beware of pickpockets. ✉ *Av. Castilhos França s/n, Comércio.*

IF YOU HAVE TIME

❺ Capela de São João Batista *(St. John the Baptist Church).* Prodigious
architect Antônio Landi finished this small octagonal church in 1777.
It was completely restored in the late 1996 and is considered the city's
purest example of baroque architecture and the country's first octagonal church. ✉ *Largo de São Joã on Rua João Diogo s/n, Cidade Velha*
☎ *91/3223–2362* ✉ *Free* ☺ *Mon.–Sat. 6:30 AM–9 AM.*

6 São José Liberto In 250 years Belém's old prison, which began as a monastery, became a brewery, then an armory, a nunnery, and eventually the final stop for many criminals. Today's museums and garden seem an attempt to redeem long years of tortuous conditions and bloody rebellions. Behind the enormously thick walls are a gem museum, a prison museum, and several shops. ☒ *Praça Amazonas, Jurunas* ☎ *91/3344–5300* ☒ *R$4* ☉ *Tues.–Sat. 10–10, Sun. 3–10.*

NAZARÉ

Just east of the Cidade Velha, Nazaré's mango tree–lined streets create the sensation of walking through tunnels. Among the historic buildings there's a tremendous variety of pastel colors and European styles. Many of the newer buildings house elegant shops.

7 Basílica de Nossa Senhora de Nazaré. It's hard to miss this opulent Roman-style basilica. Not only does it stand out visually, but there's an enormous *samauma* tree (kapok variety) filled with screeching white-winged parakeets in the plaza out front. The basilica was built in 1908 as an addition to a 1774 chapel, on the site where a *caboclo* (rural, riverside dweller) named Placido is said to have seen a vision of the Virgin in the early 1700s. The basilica's ornate interior is constructed entirely of European marble and contains elaborate mosaics, detailed stained-glass windows, and intricate bronze doors. ☒ *Praça Justo Chermont, Nazaré* ☎ *091/4009–8400, 091/4009–8407 museum* ☒ *Free* ☉ *Daily 6–7.*

Fodor's Choice
★

8 Museu Emílio Goeldi. Founded by a naturalist and a group of intellectuals in 1866, this complex contains one of the Amazon's most important research facilities. Its museum has an extensive collection of Indian artifacts, including the distinctive and beautiful pottery of the Marajó Indians, known as *marajoara*. A small forest has reflecting pools with giant *vitória régia* water lilies. But the true highlight is the collection of Amazon wildlife, including manatees, anacondas, macaws, sloths, and monkeys. ☒ *Av. Magalhães Barata 376, Nazaré* ☎ *091/3249–0477* ☒ *Park R$3, R$2 aquarium, R$2 museum, Tues. free* ☉ *Tues.–Sun. 9–noon and 2–5.*

WHERE TO EAT

$–$$
ITALIAN
★
✕ Dom Giuseppe. From gnocchi to ravioli, flawless preparation of the basics distinguishes this Italian eatery from others. Everyone in town knows this, so reservations are a good idea—particularly on weekends. Don't leave without ordering a scrumptious *dolce Paula* (ice cream-and-brownie dessert). ☒ *Av. Conselheiro Furtado 1420, Batista Campos* ☎ *091/4008–0001* ⊕ *www.domgiuseppe.com.br* ☐ *AE, DC, MC, V* ☉ *No lunch Mon.–Sat.*

$–$$$
JAPANESE
✕ Hatoba Restauranté. This is the best sushi in Belém, which is no small potatoes, since the city has a large Japanese community (second only to that of São Paulo), and many Japanese restaurants. A bonus: Hotoba is in the Estação das Docas, so you can dine along the waterfront. ☒ *Estação das Docas, Campina* ☎ *091/3212–3143 or 091/3088–2900* ☐ *AE, DC, MC, V.*

$-$$ ✕**Lá em Casa.** From inauspicious beginnings has emerged one of Belém's
BRAZILIAN   most popular restaurants. Regional cuisine, prepared to exacting speci-
Fodor'sChoice   fications, has earned Lá em Casa its good reputation. Consider trying
★   Belém's premier dish, *pato no tucupi* (duck in a yellow manioc–herb
sauce served with the mildly intoxicating *jambu* leaf). Crabs on the
half-shell covered with *farofa* (finely ground manioc fried in margarine)
is another good choice, as is *açaí* sorbet for dessert. Sitting on the patio
fringed by tropical vines and bromeliads, you feel like you're dining in
the middle of the forest. ✉*Trv. Dom Pedro Primeiro 546, Umarizal*
☎*091/3242–4222* ⊕*www.laemcasa.com* ▤*AE, DC, MC, V.*

$-$$ ✕**Palafita.** Excellent regional dishes with open-air dining over the river
BRAZILIAN   are why locals enjoy Palafita. Pirarucú fish balls and duck pastries are
among the specialties. Palafita has music on weekend evenings and it's
a one-minute walk from the Forte do Presépio. ✉*Praça da Sé, Rua
Siquiera Mendes 264, Cidade Velha* ☎*091/3212–6302* ▤ *MC, V.*

WHERE TO STAY

$$$ 🏨**Hilton International Belém.** Centrally located on the Praça da República,
★   this Hilton is very similar to the others— comfortable rooms, good
facilities and lots of amenities. Executive rooms have the nicest views
as well as access to a lounge with a VCR, a meeting area, and compli-
mentary food and drink. **Pros:** Great location and excellent facilities.
Cons: Rooms have few decorations, and simple color schemes. ✉*Av.
Presidente Vargas 882, Campina* ☎*091/4006–7000 in U.S.* ⊕*www.
belem.hilton.com* ⇝*361 rooms* ◊*In-room: Internet. In-hotel: restau-
rant, bars, pools, gym* ▤*AE, DC, MC, V.*

¢ 🏨**Hotel Grão Pará.** The oldest hotel in town is also the best deal. Hotel
Grão Pará has few amenities, but has the best price for a modern, clean
room with the basics, sparsely furnished, but with marble sinks in the
bathrooms. The hotel is across the street from the Praça da Republica
and the Teatro da Paz. **Pros:** Inexpensive hotel in the best location.
Cons: No-frill rooms, simply furnished. ✉*Av. Presidente Vargas 718,
Campina* ☎*091/3221–2121* ⊕*www.hotelgraopara.com.br* ⇝*150
rooms* ◊*In-room: refrigerator* ▤*DC, MC, V* ❢*EP.*

$ 🏨**Hotel Regente.** This hotel has excellent service and a prime location
for a reasonable price. Stained-glass windows and soft leather couches
welcome you in an attractive lobby as well as free Internet. Rooms on
the 12th floor are nicer and more modern than those on other floors,
yet they cost the same. **Pros:** Lovely views and a great location. **Cons:**
Internet in the rooms costs R$10. ✉*Av. Governador José Malcher 485,
Nazaré* ☎*091/3181–5000* 🖷*091/3181–5005* ⊕*www.hotelregente.
com.br* ⇝*219 rooms,* ◊*In-room: refrigerator, Internet. In-hotel: res-
taurant, pool* ▤*AE, DC, MC, V.*

$ 🏨**Itaoca Hotel.** It comes as no surprise that this small, reasonably priced
hotel has the highest occupancy rate in town. It's in the center of town,
on the city's main street and right next to the Estação das Docas and
Ver-o-Peso. Its rooms are extremely comfortable, modern, and most
have a fantastic view of the dock area and river. **Pros:** Inexpensive
hotel with great views, and well-equipped rooms. **Cons:** The furnish-

ings in the rooms are outdated, for broadband Internet you have to use the lobby. ⊠ *Av. Presidente Vargas 132, Campina* ☎ *091/4009–2400 or 091/4009–2402* ⊕ *www.hotelitaoca.com.br* ⇌ *32 rooms, 4 suites* ⌂ *In-room: refrigerator, dial-up, safe. In-hotel: restaurant, bar* ▤ *AE, DC, MC, V.*

MANAUS

Manaus, the capital of Amazonas State, is a hilly city of around 1.8 million people that lies 766 km (475 mi) west of Santarém and 1,602 km (993 mi) west of Belém on the banks of the Río Negro 10 km (6 mi) upstream from its confluence with the Amazon. Manaus is the Amazon's most popular tourist destination, largely because of the 19 jungle lodges in the surrounding area. The city's principal attractions are its lavish, brightly colored houses and civic buildings—vestiges of an opulent time when the wealthy sent their laundry to be done in Europe and sent for Old World artisans and engineers to build their New World monuments.

Founded in 1669, Manaus took its name, which means "mother of the Gods," from the Manaó tribe. The city has long flirted with prosperity. Of all the Amazon cities and towns, Manaus is most identified with the rubber boom. In the late 19th and early 20th centuries it supplied 90% of the world's rubber. The 25-year rubber era was brought to a close thanks to Englishman Henry A. Wickham, who took 70,000 rubber-tree seeds out of Brazil in 1876. (Transporting seeds across borders has since been outlawed.) The seeds were planted in Kew Gardens in England. The few that germinated were transplanted in Malaysia, where they flourished. Within 30 years Malaysian rubber ended the Brazilian monopoly.

GETTING HERE & AROUND

Brigadeiro Eduardo Gomes Airport is 17 km (10 mi) north of downtown. Most flights connect in São Paulo. The trip to Manaus Centro from the airport takes 25 minutes and costs about R$49 by taxi. A trip on one of the city buses, which depart regularly during the day and early evening, costs R$2.

If you're looking for a boat from Manaus to another town, a lodge, or a beach, go to the Hidroviária Regional Terminal. At the ticket or tourist information booths you can get information about prices and departure times and days to all the locations. You can also walk down to Porto Flutuante via the bridge behind the terminal to take a look at the regional boats. Their destinations and departure times are listed on plaques.

CARIMBÓ

The carimbó is an indigenous dance and music form, originating in Belém and the island of Marajó that later gave way to the rhythms of the lambada. This music is steeped in the sounds of the Amazon and its folklore, but has also been influenced by African culture. It's accompanied by wooden tambourines. During the dance the woman passes her skirt over the man.

3

The city bus system is extensive, easy to use, and inexpensive (R$2). Most of the useful buses run along Avenida Floriano Peixoto, including Bus 120, which goes to Ponta Negra and stops near the Hotel Tropical. The Fontur bus, which costs about R$14, travels between Centro and the Hotel Tropical several times a day. Manaus has its share of traffic and parking problems, but the driving is calmer than in Belém.

ESSENTIALS

Airlines (Local) **Rico** (☎092/4009–8333 ⊕ www.voerico.com.br).

Airport **Aeroporto Brigadeiro Eduardo Gomes** (✉Av. Santos Dumont s/n ☎092/3652–1210).

Banks & Currency Exchange **Amazonia Câmbio e Turismo Exchange** (✉Av. 7 de Setembro 1199, Centro). **Banco Amazônia** (✉Aeroporto Brigadeiro Eduardo Gomes, Av. Santos Dumont s/n).

Boat Contacts **MACAMAZON** (☎091/3222–5604 or 091/3228–0774).

Bus Contacts **Terminal Rodoviário Huascar Angelim** (✉Rua Recife 2784, Santo Antonio ☎092/3642–5805).

Emergencies & Medical Assistance **Ambulance** (☎192). **Fire** (☎193). **Hospital: Hospital e Pronto Socorro** (✉Av. Cosme Ferreira 3775, São Jose ☎092/3647–1750). **Pharmacies: Drogaria Avenida** (✉Av. Senador Alvaro Maia 748, Centro ☎092/3633–6761). **Police** (☎190).

Taxi **Recife Rádio Táxi** (☎092/3656–6121). **Tucuxi** (☎092/2123–9090).

Visitor & Tour Info **Amazonastur** (✉Rua Saldanha Marinho 321, Centro ☎092/2123–3800 ⊕www.amazonastur.am.gov.br). **Centro de Atendimento ao Turista (CAT)** (✉Av. Eduardo Ribeiro 666, Centro ☎092/3622–0767 ☉Weekdays 8–6). **Fontur** (✉Hotel Tropical, Av. Coronel Teixeira 1320, Ponta Negra ☎092/3658–3052 or 092/3658–3438 ⊕www.fontur.com.br ☉Mon.–Sat. 7–7, Sun. 7–3). **Selvatur** (✉Av. Djalma Batista 276, Carrefour, Flores ☎092/3642–3192 or 92/3642–8777 ⊕www.selvatur.com.br).

EXPLORING CENTRO

Manaus's downtown area has a lot going on. The floating docks are here, with tourist shops nearby. Open markets sell fish, meats, and all sorts of produce, while general stores ply machetes, hoes, hardtack, cassava flour, and boat motor parts to those pursuing a livelihood outside the city. Centro is also the most important historic section of the city. The Teatro Amazonas, the Customs House (Alfândega), and the Adolfo Lisboa Market are here, along with old churches, government buildings, and mansions. The result is a mix of neoclassical, Renaissance, colonial, and modern architecture.

MAIN ATTRACTIONS

❺
☾ **Museu do Índio.** The Indian Museum is maintained by Salesian Sisters, an order of nuns with eight missions in the upper Amazon. It displays handicrafts, weapons, ceramics, ritual masks, and clothing from the region's tribes. ✉Rua Duque de Caxias 296, Centro ☎092/3635–1922 ☷R$5 ☉Weekdays 8:30–11:30 and 2–4:30, Sat. 8:30–11:30.

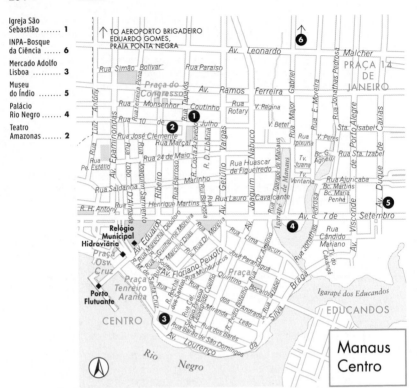

Manaus
Centro

④ Palácio Rio Negro. The extravagant Rio Negro Palace was built at the
★ end of the 19th century as the home of a German rubber baron. Later
it was used as the official governor's residence. Today it houses some
of the city's finest art exhibits and a cultural center. The Museu da Ima-
gem e do Som, on the same property, has three daily screenings of art
films and documentaries Tuesday through Friday and four screenings
daily on weekends. Don't miss the cultural exhibits out back, which
include a caboclo home, an indigenous home, and a cassava-process-
ing house. ⊠*Av. 7 de Setembro 1546, Centro* ☏*No phone* ☎*Free*
☉ *Weekdays 9–6.*

② Teatro Amazonas. Operas and other events are presented regularly. Mon-
Fodor'sChoice day-evening performances are free and usually feature local artists of
★ various musical genres. The Amazonas Philharmonic Orchestra plays
Thursday night and can be seen and heard practicing in the theater
weekdays 9–2. A variety of foreign entertainers, from José Carreras to
the Spice Girls, have performed here. Half-hour tours are conducted
daily 9–4. ⊠*Praça São Sebastião s/n, Centro* ☏*092/3232–1768*
☎*R$10* ☉ *Mon.–Sat. 9–5.*

IF YOU HAVE TIME

① **Igreja São Sebastião.** This neoclassical church (circa 1888), with its charcoal-gray color and medieval characteristics, seems foreboding. Its interior, however, is luminous and uplifting, with white Italian marble, stained-glass windows, and beautiful ceiling paintings. As you stroll through the church plaza and the one in front of the Teatro Amazonas, note the black-and-white Portuguese granite patterns at your feet. They are said to represent Manaus's meeting of the waters. ⊠ *Praça São Sebastião, Centro* ☎ *092/3232–4572* 💳 *Free* ☉ *Usually Mon.–Sat. 9–5, but hrs vary.*

③ **Mercado Adolfo Lisboa.** Vendors sell Amazon food products and handi-
★ crafts at this market. Built in 1882, it's a wrought-iron replica of the original Parisian Les Halles (now destroyed); the ironwork is said to have been designed by Gustave Eiffel himself. ⊠ *Rua dos Barés 6, Centro* ☎ *No phone* ☉ *Daily 6–6.*

ELSEWHERE IN MANAUS

Most of the area surrounding downtown Manaus is not very attractive. The few places of interest include the Natural History Museum and INPA's Bosque da Ciência in Aleixo. The Bosque and nearby Parque Municipal do Mindu in Parque 10 are both forested and good for walks. A taxi will cost around R$30 one-way from downtown to these sites.

MAIN ATTRACTIONS

⑥ **INPA–Bosque da Ciência.** Used as a research station for the INPA (Insti-
☼ tuto Nacional de Pesquisa da Amazônia), this slice of tropical for-
★ est is home to a great diversity of flora and fauna. Some highlights include manatee tanks, caiman ponds, a museum, a botanical garden with an orchidarium, and nature trails. It's a great place for a walk in the shade. ⊠ *Rua Otávio Cabral s/n, Petropolis* ☎ *092/3643–3377* 💳 *R$2* ☉ *Tues.–Sun. 9–4.*

☼ **Meeting of the Waters.** This natural phenomenon is one of the area's big-
Fodor'sChoice gest tourist attractions. At the CEASA port you can rent a boat, or go
★ with a tour company. It takes about an hour to go from CEASA to the Meeting of the Waters, spend some time there, and return. A taxi to CEASA from downtown is about R$30.

IF YOU HAVE TIME

Praia da Ponta Negra. Known as the Copacabana of the Amazon, this beach is next to the Hotel Tropical and has restaurants, bars, sports, and nightlife facilities (including an amphitheater).

WHERE TO EAT

$–$$$$ ✕ **Canto da Peixada.** When Pope John Paul II came to Manaus in 1981,
SEAFOOD   this restaurant was chosen to host him. The dining areas aren't elegant,
★   but the fish dishes are outstanding, and there are 43 types of salad. One platter feeds two. ⊠ *Rua Emilio Moreira 1677, Praça 14* ☎ *092/3234–1066* 💳 *No credit cards* ☉ *Closed Sun.*

¢–$$$$ ✕ **Chez Charufe.** On the banks of the Río Negro, Chez Charufe is in a
BRAZILIAN   lovely location for breezy, open-air dining. Fish dishes as well as beef and chicken are all very good, and it's a 10-minute walk from the Hotel

Tropical. The most expensive dish on the menu is a paella for two, but there are plenty of tasty options for much less. ✉ *Estrada da Ponta Negra, Ponta Negra* ☎ *092/3658–5101* ✐ *charufenasser@hotmail. com* ☰ *AE, DC, MC, V* ☽ *No lunch.*

$$
BRAZILIAN
Fodor$Choice
★

✕ **Churrascaria Búfalo.** Twelve waiters, each with a different cut of chicken, beef, or goat, scurry around this large, sparkling clean restaurant. As if the delectable meats weren't enough, tables are also stocked with side dishes, including manioc root, pickled vegetables, and caramelized bananas. ✉ *Rua Joaquim Nabuco 628-A, Centro* ☎ *092/3633-3773* ⊕ *www.churrascariabufalo.com.br* ☰ *AE, DC, MC, V.*

$$$
ECLECTIC
★

✕ **El Touro Loco.** Excellent regional dishes, unusual and tasty appetizers, pizza, pasta, sushi, salads—El Touro Loco has it all. It also has a fascinating rustic-European decor, and great service in an open-air setting. There's one price for all the food; alcohol and service are separate. ✉ *Av. Do Turismo 215, Tarumã* ☎ *92/3631–2557* ☰ *AE, V.*

WHERE TO STAY

Manaus has several decent in-town hotels, but the jungle lodges outside town are where you should base yourself if you're interested in Amazon adventures. Most jungle lodges have naturalist guides, swimming, caiman "hunts" (the animals are blinded with flashlights, captured, photographed, and released), piranha fishing, and canoe trips. Many jungle lodges (and all of those that we list) are near the Río Negro, where mosquitoes are less of a problem because they can't breed in its acidic black water. Unless otherwise noted, prices at jungle lodges are for two-day, one-night packages, which generally include transport to and from the lodge, meals (not drinks), and a variety of activities that depend on the length of your stay. Air-conditioning, hot water, telephones, and televisions are rare amenities.

IN-TOWN HOTELS

$

🏨 **Central Hotel Manaus.** A good option if you're on a budget, this hotel has simple, clean rooms with standard amenities. It's near the market and the port, and is popular with businessmen on a tight budget. **Pros:** Inexpensive and pleasant. **Cons:** Rooms are plainly decorated. ✉ *Rua Dr. Moreira 202, Centro* ☎ *092/3622–2600* ⊕ *www.hotelcentralmanaus. com.br* ⤴ *50 rooms* ⚷ *In-room: Internet, refrigerator. In-hotel: restaurant* ☰ *AE, DC, MC, V* ⦿ *EP.*

$

🏨 **Hotel Manaós.** Across from Teatro Amazonas and just up the street from the busy part of downtown, Hotel Manaós is in a great spot. Rooms are small but are clean and have nice woodwork. The staff are warm and friendly. **Pros:** One of best locations in town. **Cons:** Rooms are small. ✉ *Av. Eduardo Ribeiro 881, Centro* ☎ *092/3633–5744* ⊕ *www.hotelmanaos.com.br* ⤴ *39 rooms* ⚷ *In-room: Internet, refrigerator. In-hotel: restaurant, bar* ☰ *AE, DC, MC, V* ⦿ *EP.*

$$$$
Fodor$Choice
★

🏨 **Hotel Tropical.** Nothing in the Amazon can match the majesty of this resort hotel. It's 20 km (12 mi) northwest of downtown and overlooks the Río Negro, with a short path to the beach. In addition to a zoo, sports facilities, and two gorgeous pools, the Tropical has its own dock. The location is remote, far from Centro, but a 20-minute cab ride from the airport. The restaurant is a reliable choice for dinners of regional

CLOSE UP

Chico Mendes: Rubber Tapper & Environmental Pioneer

Born in 1944 in the northwestern state of Acre, Chico Mendes was the son of a *seringueiro* (rubber-tree tapper) who had moved across the country in the early 20th century to follow the rubber boom. Chico followed in his father's footsteps as a seringuero in Xapuri, close to the Bolivian border. In the 1960s rubber prices dropped dramatically, and tappers began to sell forests to cattle ranchers who cut them for pastures. In the '70s, to protect forests and the tappers' way of life, Mendes joined a group of nonviolent activists who managed to prevent many ranch workers and loggers from clearing the rubber trees. On the local council of Xapuri, he promoted the creation of forest reserves for rubber and Brazil-nut production. He founded the Xapuri Rural Workers Union and the National Council of Rubber Tappers to educate tappers on forest issues.

In 1987 Mendes was invited to Washington, D.C., to help convince the Inter-American Development Bank to rescind its financial support of a planned 1,200-km (750-mi) road to be constructed through the forest. That same year, Mendes was awarded the Global 500 environmental achievement award from the United Nations, making him an international celebrity.

In 1988 Mendes stopped rancher Darly Alves da Silva from extending his ranch into a reserve. On December 22, 1988, da Silva and son Darcy murdered Mendes outside his home. Upon his death, Chico Mendes made the front page of the *New York Times* and numerous other publications worldwide. Subsequently, Brazil created the Chico Mendes Extractive Reserve near Xapuri, along with 20 other reserves covering more than 8 million acres.

and international fare. **Pros:** Beautifully appointed rooms, luxurious furniture, all the amenities of a high-class resort. **Cons:** Far from all points of interest, expensive commute (R$49) by taxi. ⊠*Av. Coronel Teixeira 1320, Ponta Negra* ☎*092/2123–5000* ⊕*www.tropicalhotel. com.br* ⟿*594 rooms, 8 suites* ♿*In-room: safe, Wi-Fi, refrigerator. In-hotel: 2 restaurants, 2 bars, tennis courts, pools, gym, beachfront* ⊟*AE, DC, MC, V* ⧄*EP.*

JUNGLE LODGES

Though most tour companies will pick you up at the airport and drop you off following your adventure, airport pickup should not be assumed in all situations. It's often included in tour packages, but ask while making arrangements. Local naturalist guides are often available at lodges. Though knowledgeable, they're neither biologists nor teachers. Do not expect accurate information and identification of species or interpretation of ecological relationships. The guides and companies in the Adventure & Learning Vacations chapter are those we recommend.

$$$ 🏠 **Acajatuba Jungle Lodge.** Civilization seems hundreds of miles away at this thatch-hut lakeside lodge. Twenty individual screened round thach-huts are elevated 1 meter (3 feet) aboveground and connected to

the rest of the lodge by walkways. Lighting is provided by 12-volt batteries and kerosene lamps (generators would keep wildlife away), and there's no hot water, but what it lacks in luxury, it more than makes up for by putting you in the middle of the tropical forest. They have many other arrangements including three- and four-night stays. **Pros:** Staying in beautiful large bungalows. **Cons:** Putting up with humidity and cold water. ⊠*60 km (35 mi)/4 hrs west of Manaus, Lago Acajatuba; boats to lodge leave from CEASA port near meeting of waters* ⌑*Conj. Vila Municipal Rua 7 #87, 69057-750 Manaus* ☎*092/3642–0358* ⊕*www. acajatuba.com.br* ⟳*30 rooms* ⌂*In-room: no a/c, no phone, no TV. In-hotel: bar, restaurant, no elevator* ⊟*V* ⦿*FAP.*

$$$$ ⊡ **Ariaú Amazon Towers.** The most famous of the Amazon jungle lodges, Ariaú is made up of four-story wooden towers on stilts and linked by catwalks. The effect is more dramatic when the river floods the ground below from December to June. The feeling of being integrated with nature is a bit lost here due to Ariaú's size, and contact with wildlife is rare, apart from brightly colored macaws and cute semiwild monkeys that visit and make mischief. One suite is the Tarzan House, 100 feet up in the treetops. The packet includes pick-up and drop-off. **Pros:** Excellent food, nicely furnished rooms. **Cons:** Large complex, small rooms. ⊠*60 km (40 mi)/2 hrs northwest of Manaus, Rio Ariaú* ⌑*Rua Leonardo Malcher 699, 69010–170 Manaus* ☎*092/2121–5000* ⊕*www. ariautowers.com.br* ⟳*300 rooms, 8 suites* ⌂*In-room: refrigerator, no phone (some), no TV. In-hotel: 2 restaurants, bars, pools, public Internet* ⊟*AE, DC, MC, V* ⦿*FAP.*

$$$$ ⊡ **Jungle Othon Palace.** It's quite a sight to cruise down the Río Negro and see the neoclassical columns of this luxurious "flotel," built on a steel barge, looming on the horizon. Explore the region by day, and at night return to your air-conditioned cabin for a hot shower or to take a stroll on the observation deck. Packages include airport or hotel pick-up and drop-off in Manaus. **Pros:** Right on the river, all of the usual amenities. **Cons:** Furnishings not as nice as the other lodges. ⊠*35 km (20 mi)/1 hr west of Manaus, Río Negro* ⌑*Joaquim Nabuco, 1133, 69020–031 Manaus* ☎*92/3622–2104 or 92/3212–5409* ⊕*www.jungle palace.com.br* ⟳*34 rooms* ⌂*In-room: refrigerator. In-hotel: restaurant, bar, pool, gym, no elevator* ⊟*DC, MC, V* ⦿*FAP.*

OFF THE BEATEN PATH

Fodor's Choice ★

Mamirauá Sustainable Development Reserve. The largest wildlife reserve in Brazil, Mamirauá is about 1,050 km (650 mi) west of Manaus on the Rio Solimões. The reserve is known for its abundant wildlife, including the endemic, and endangered, red-faced uakari monkey. Guided tours (from Uakari Lodge) take you through the *várzea* (flooded forest) in canoes during the rainy season (January–April) and on foot the rest of the year. Plan to get muddy if you're hiking. Frequent animal sightings include three species of monkeys, colorful birds, and pink river dolphins. Dry season is the best time to see caimans and fish. Since Mamirauá encompasses several communities, cooperation and assistance of local inhabitants in the areas of research, ecotourism, maintenance, and fiscalization help make it successful as a sustainable development reserve.

To get to the reserve, you'll need to fly to Tefé (a one-hour flight from Manaus) and take Mamirauá's boat from there. It's a bit of an effort but well worth it. ⊕*www.mamiraua.org.br.*

$$ ⓣ **Uakari Floating Lodge.** Nearly all visitors to Mamirauá stay at the nearby Uakari Floating Lodge, which has free transportation to and from the reserve. The lodge takes great pride in its efforts to exist in harmony with the local population and the environment—for instance, local guides are hired and most of the lodge uses solar power. Activities include river tours, fishing trips, and guided visits to a local village. Cabin-type rooms have few amenities but are clean and have large windows. Each has a small porch with a hammock. The minimum stay is three nights. Transport to and from the airport is included. **Pros:** Rustic rooms with lots of light. **Cons:** Few amenities. ⊠*30 min by boat from Tefé* ☎*97/3343–4160 or 97/8116–1349* ⊕*www.mamiraua.org. br* ⚲*10 rooms* ᗴ*In-room: no a/c, no phone, no TV. In-hotel: restaurant, bar, airport shuttle, no kids under 12, no elevator* ▤*MC, V* ⓞ*FAP* ☞*R$360 per person double occupancy, 4 days and 3 nights ($240 for 2 per night).*

SPORTS & THE OUTDOORS

JUNGLE & RIVER EXCURSIONS

The most common excursion is a half- or full-day tourist-boat trip that travels 15 km (9 mi) east of Manaus to the point where the coffee-color water of the Río Negro flows beside and gradually joins the coffee-with-cream-color water of the Rio Solimões. According to Brazilians, this is where the Amazon River begins. The waters flow alongside one another for 6 km (4 mi) before merging. Many of these Meeting-of-the-Waters treks include motorboat side trips along narrow streams or through bayous. Some also stop at the Parque Ecológico do Janauary, where you can see birds and a lake filled with the world's largest water lily, the *vitória régia.*

Nighttime boat trips into the forest explore flooded woodlands and narrow waterways. Some stop for trail hikes. Some companies take you by canoe on a caiman "hunt," where caimans are caught and released. Trips to the Rio Negro's upper reaches, where wildlife is a little wilder, are also offered. Such trips usually stop at river settlements to visit with local families. They may include jungle treks, fishing (they supply the gear and boat), and a trip to Anavilhanas, the world's largest freshwater archipelago. It contains some 400 islands with amazing Amazon flora, birds, and monkeys. To arrange any of these excursions, contact an area tour operator.

PRESIDENTE FIGUEIREDO

107 km (64 mi) north of Manaus.

One of the Amazon's best-kept secrets is a two-hour drive north of Manaus. The town of Presidente Figueiredo (founded 1981) has dozens of waterfalls—up to 32 meters (140 feet) in height—and caves with prehistoric paintings and pottery fragments. The area was stumbled on during the construction of BR 174, the only highway that takes you out of the state (to Roraima and on to Venezuela), and was ultimately discovered by explorers looking for minerals, who had based themselves in Presidente Figueiredo. The area is excellent for swimming in blackwater streams and hiking through upland forest. The town has several hotels and restaurants, and there's a hydropower plant and reservoir and an archaeology museum in the area. The Centro de Proteção de Quelonias e Mamiferos Aquaticos (Center for the Protection of Turtles and Aquatic Mammals) is in Balbina, 82 km (51 mi) north of town. Get cash in Manaus because there are only two banks here, and they do not always accept international cards.

GETTING HERE & AROUND
To get to Presidente Figueiredo from Manaus, take the bus labeled ARUANÃ, which runs twice a day (105 km, 1 hour and 30 minutes) from the Terminal Rodoviário Huascar Angelim and costs around R$12.50.

Chile

WORD OF MOUTH

"The people of Chile are really wonderful. Everyone we met on the trip was so nice. It was one of the best trips we have had in many years of travel."

—detraveler

"I LIVE NOW IN A COUNTRY as soft as the autumnal flesh of grapes," begins "Country," a poem by Pablo Neruda. With his odes to the place of his birth, the Nobel Prize winner sang Chile into being and taught us to inhale the bouquet of its salty breezes and its soaring Andean peaks before we hold them to our lips and drink them down.

In the 18 years since its return to democracy, this isolated nation at the end of the world has made great strides on a number of fronts. Corruption is lower here than anywhere in Latin America, leading to the most competitive economy in the region. On the political front, Chileans have democratically elected four presidents since 1990, including Chile's first female president, Michelle Bachelet. From 2003 to 2006, the number of people living below the poverty line was reduced by 5% (from 18.7% to 13.7%), although income inequality is still a significant concern.

Chile's beaches draw sun-worshippers from all over South America, and its towering volcanoes and roaring rivers draw adventure travelers from around the world. Fishing aficionados head south to the Lake District, while armchair archaeologists are attracted to the 5,000-year-old mummies of the Atacama.

Chile is as luminous and pungent, as rustic and romantic, as any of Neruda's poems describing it. It encompasses a bone-dry desert that blooms in a riot of color once or twice a decade, sprawling glaciers that bellow like thunder, and snow-covered volcanoes that perpetually smolder—all in one sliver of land squeezed between the Andes and the Pacific Ocean. In some places the 320-km (200-mi) territorial limit is wider than the country itself, making Chile as much water as earth.

ORIENTATION & PLANNING

GETTING ORIENTED

Santiago. Although it doesn't get the same press as Rio or Buenos Aires, this metropolis of 5 million people is as cosmopolitan as its flashier South American neighbors. Ancient and modern stand side by side in the heart of the city, and the Andes are ever-present to the east.

Viña del Mar & Valparaíso. Anchoring the coast west of Santiago, port city Valparaíso has stunning views from the promenades atop its more than 40 hills. Next door, Viña del Mar, home to Chile's beautiful people, has nonstop nightlife and the country's most popular stretch of shoreline.

El Norte Chico. A land of dusty brown hills, the "little north" stretches for some 700 km (~435 mi) north of Santiago. In the lush Elqui Valley, just about everyone you meet is involved in growing the grapes used to make *pisco*, Chile's national drink. Astronomers flock to the region for the crisp, clear night skies

TOP REASONS TO GO

Contemplating Nature. Norway has fjords. Bavaria has forests. Nepal has mountains. Arizona has deserts. Chile offers all these and more. El Norte Grande's Atacama Desert is the Earth's most arid spot: no measurable precipitation has ever been recorded there. The region's Cerros Pintados form the world's largest group of geoglyphs. Perpetually smoldering Volcán Villarrica in the Lake District is one of the planet's most active volcanoes. And no photo can ever do justice to the ash-gray, glacier-molded spires of Patagonia's Torres del Paine.

Hitting the Slopes. The runs at Vail and Grenoble are closed for the season? Never fear. Since Chile's seasons are the opposite of those of North America, you can ski or snowboard from June to September. Many top resorts, such as La Parva, Valle Nevado, and Portillo, are an easy drive from the capital. Locals often head out in the morning and are back in the city in time for dinner. With the top elevations at most ski areas extending to 3,300 meters (10,825 feet), you can expect long runs and deep, dry snow.

Basking on Beaches. Thousands of Santiaguinos flock to the beaches around Viña del Mar and Valparaíso every summer. To serve the hungry masses are dozens and dozens of seafood shacks, all serving freshly caught fish. The Humboldt Current, which flows northward along the coast of Chile, carries cold water to the Central Coast. If you plan to surf or skin-dive, you need a wet suit; if you plan to swim, you need thick skin. Pristine sands swath the shoreline near Arica and Iquique. During the summer months of January and February they're packed with vacationing South Americans. Outside of these months, you just might have the beach to yourself.

Getting the Goods. Shop for fine woolen items, expertly carved figurines, lapis lazuli jewelry, hand-tooled leather items, Andean textiles, and other handicrafts. Santiago, Valparaíso, and Viña del Mar have everything from large department stores and outlet malls to trendy shops and boutiques. There and elsewhere you can also browse in mercados (markets) and ferias artesenales (artisan fairs). Though bargaining is acceptable, it's less common than in other parts of South America.

Feasting. From the ocean come conger eel, sea bass, king crab, and locos (abalone the size of fat clams). European immigrants brought with them a love for robust country cooking; look for such simple fare as cazuela, a stew of meat, potatoes, and corn on the cob; porotos granados, a thick bean, corn, and squash stew; and humitas, ground corn seasoned and steamed in its own husk. At markets, vendors woo you with pastel de choclo—a corn pie that usually contains ground beef, chicken, and seasonings—as well as empanadas, pastries stuffed with meat or cheese. Chileans are also masters of the parrillada, a method of grilling over hot coals. Not just steak gets grilled: restaurants prepare chicken, fish, seafood, burgers, sausage potatoes, corn, and vegetables parrillada-style, too.

4

El Norte Grande. Stark doesn't begin to describe Chile's great north, a region bordering Peru to the north and Bolivia to the east. This is the driest place on Earth, site of the Atacama Desert, where no measurable precipitation has ever been recorded.

Lake District. The austral summer doesn't get more glorious than in this compact 400-km (250-mi) stretch of land between Temuco and Puerto Montt. It has fast become Chile's vacation central, drawing people to resorts such as Pucón, Villarrica, and Puerto Varas. More than 50 snow-covered peaks, many of them still smoldering volcanoes, offer splendid hiking.

Patagonia. Look up "end of the world" in the dictionary and you might see a picture of Chile's southernmost region. Impenetrable forests and impassable mountains meant that Chilean Patagonia went largely unexplored until the beginning of the 20th century. It's still sparsely inhabited.

CHILE PLANNER

WHEN TO GO

Tourism peaks during the hot summer months of January and February, except in Santiago, which tends to empty as most Santiaguinos take their summer holiday. Though prices are at their highest, it's worth braving the summer heat if you're interested in lying on the beach or enjoying the many concerts, folklore festivals, and outdoor theater performances offered during this period.

CLIMATE

Chile's seasons are the reverse of the Northern Hemisphere's—that is, June through August are Chile's winter months. If you were to move Chile out of its place on the globe and transfer it to corresponding latitudes in the Northern Hemisphere, you would have a nation stretching from Cancún to Hudson Bay. In other words, expect vast north–south climatic differences.

The following are the average daily maximum and minimum temperatures for Santiago

Jan.	85F	29C	May	65F	18C	Sept.	66F	19C
	53	12		41	5		42	6
Feb.	84F	29C	June	58F	14C	Oct.	72F	22C
	52	11		37	3		45	7
Mar.	80F	27C	July	59F	15C	Nov.	78F	26C
	49	9		37	3		48	9
Apr.	74F	23C	Aug.	62F	17C	Dec.	83F	28C
	54	7		39	4		51	11

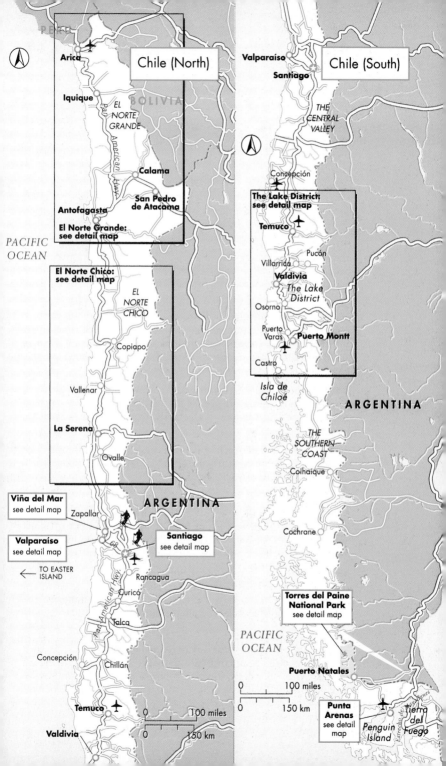

The following are average daily maximum and minimum temperatures for Punta Arenas.

Jan.	58F	14C	May	45F	7C	Sept.	46F	8C
	45	7		35	2		35	2
Feb.	58F	14C	June	41F	5C	Oct.	51F	11C
	44	7		33	1		38	3
Mar.	54F	12C	July	40F	4C	Nov.	54F	12C
	41	5		31	0		40	4
Apr.	50F	10C	Aug.	42F	6C	Dec.	57F	14C
	39	4		33	1		43	6

HOLIDAYS

Shops and services are open on most Chilean holidays except September 18, Christmas Day, and New Year's Day. On these days, shops close and public transportation runs at the bare minimum.

September 18 is Chile's Independence Day, and celebrations last for almost a week. Attending a *fonda* or *ramada* (smaller version of a fonda) is a must. These are parties in which communities gather to eat empanadas, drink *chicha* (a potent drink made from fermented corn), and dance *la cueca,* the national dance. Rodeos are also common this time of year.

Watching the fireworks from Valparaíso or Viña del Mar on New Year's Eve is a remarkable experience. You'll want to wear clothing that can get wet, since Chileans spray each other with champagne.

GETTING HERE & AROUND

Arriving from abroad, American citizens must pay a "reciprocity" fee of $130. Cash and credit cards are accepted. A departure tax of $18 is included in the cost of your ticket.

BY AIR

Miami (9 hour flight), New York (11½ hours), and Atlanta (9 hours) are the primary departure points for flights to Chile from the United States, though flights also leave from Dallas and other cities. Other international flights often connect through Buenos Aires and Lima.

Most international flights head to Santiago's Comodoro Arturo Merino Benítez International Airport (SCL)   (☎2/690–1900 ⊕*www.aero puertosantiago.cl*), also known as Pudahuel, about 30 minutes west of the city. Domestic flights leave from the same terminal.

BY BOAT

Boats and ferries are the best way to reach many places in Chile, such as Chiloé and the Southern Coast. They are also a great alternative to flying when your destination is a southern port like Puerto Natales or Punta Arenas. Navimag (⊕*www.navimag.com)* and Transmarchilay (⊕*www.transmarchilay.cl)* are the two main companies operating routes in the south.

BY BUS

Long-distance buses are safe and affordable. Luxury bus travel between cities costs about one-third that of plane travel and is more comfortable, with wide reclining seats, movies, drinks, and snacks. The most expensive service offered by most bus companies is called *cama* or *semi-cama*, which indicate that the seats fold down into a bed. Service billed as *ejectivo* is nearly as luxurious.

BY CAR

Certain areas of Chile are most enjoyable when explored on your own in a car, such as the beaches of the Central Coast, the wineries of the Central Valley, the ski areas east of Santiago, and the Lake District in the south. Plan your daily driving distance conservatively, as distances are always longer than they appear on maps.

ESSENTIALS

ELECTRICITY

Unlike the United States and Canada—which have a 110- to 120-volt standard—the current in Chile is 220 volts, 50 cycles alternating current (AC). The wall sockets accept plugs with two round prongs.

ENTRY REQUIREMENTS

Citizens of the United States, Canada, Australia, New Zealand, and the United Kingdom need only a passport to enter Chile for up to three months. Upon arrival in Chile, you will be given a flimsy piece of paper that is your three-month tourist visa. This has to be handed in when you leave. You can extend your visa an additional 90 days for a small fee, but do this before it expires to avoid paying a *multa* (fine).

HEALTH & SAFETY

From a health standpoint, Chile is one of the safer countries in which to travel. Altitude sickness—which causes shortness of breath, nausea, and splitting headaches—may be a problem when you visit the Andes.

Food preparation is strictly regulated by the government, so outbreaks of food-borne diseases are rare. But it's still a good idea to use commonsense: don't risk restaurants where the hygiene is suspect and steer clear of raw fruits and vegetables unless you know they've been thoroughly washed and disinfected.

Almost all drinking water receives proper treatment and is unlikely to produce health problems. If you have any doubts, stick to bottled water.

Violent crime is a rarity; far more common are pickpocketing or thefts from purses, backpacks, or rental cars. Women should be careful about walking alone at night in both large cities and small towns. Catcalls are common, but harmless.

Volcano climbing is a popular pastime in Chile, with Volcán Villarrica, near Pucón, and Volcán Osorno the most popular. But some of these mountains are also among South America's most active volcanoes.

CONAF (⊕*www.conaf.cl*), the agency in charge of national parks, cuts off access to any volcano at the slightest hint of abnormal activity.

Emergency Numbers **Ambulance** (☎*131*). **Fire** (☎*132*). **Police** (☎*133*).

LANGUAGE

Chile's official language is Spanish, so it's best to learn at least a few words and carry a good phrase book. Chileans use an astonishing amount of slang—known as "Chilenismos," or "Chileanisms"—on a regular basis. Some common examples are "cachai" and "al tiro." "¿Cachai?" is an interrogative that roughly means "get it?" and supposedly comes from the English expression "to catch." "Al tiro" means "right away," but depending on the Chilean and the circumstances, may indicate a time frame of anywhere from 30 seconds to several hours. Receptionists at most upscale hotels speak English.

MONEY MATTERS

CREDIT CARDS   Credit cards are accepted in most resorts and in many shops and restaurants in major cities, though you should always carry some local currency for minor expenses like taxis and tipping. Once you stray from the beaten path, you can often pay only with cash. Automatic teller machines are widely available in most cities. Most are connected internationally, so that it is often possible to withdraw directly from your account back home.

CURRENCY   The peso ($) is the unit of currency in Chile. Chilean bills are issued in 1,000, 2,000, 5,000, 10,000, and 20,000 pesos, and coins come in units of 1, 5, 10, 50, 100, and 500 pesos. Always check exchange rates in your local newspaper for the most current information; at this writing, the exchange rate was approximately 475 pesos to the U.S. dollar.

TIPPING   In restaurants and for tour guides, a 10% tip is usual unless service has been deficient. Taxi drivers don't expect to be tipped but do leave your small change. Visitors need to be wary of parking attendants. During the day, they should only charge what's on their portable meters when you collect the car but, at night, they will ask for money—usually 1,000 pesos—in advance. This is a racket but, for your car's safety, it's better to comply.

RESTAURANTS & HOTELS

Chile serves an incredible variety of foods. Salmon is caught off the Southern Coast and raised in farms in the Lake District. Other popular catches include sea bass (*corvina*) and conger eel (*congrio*). Shellfish such as mussels and scallops are widely available, and *locos* (abalone) and *jaiba* (crab) are frequently prepared as *chupes* (stews) or *pasteles* (pies). Raw shellfish is best avoided, but cooked with cheese or white wine, lemon, and fresh coriander, it's an excellent introduction to Chilean cuisine. Simply seasoned grilled fish is another Chilean favorite, usually served with steamed potatoes or an *ensalada a la chilena* (sliced tomatoes and onions).

But fish isn't all that's available. *Pastel de choclo* is a typical dish that you'll find just about everywhere in Chile. Served in a heavy clay bowl, it's a mixture of minced beef, chicken, olives, hard-boiled egg, and raisins, topped with a layer of creamy mashed corn.

A *parrillada* is a platter of every cut of meat imaginable—often one order will serve many. Beefsteak *a la pobre* comes with a fried egg or two on top, plus onions and french fries.

Lunch, which usually begins at 1 or 2, is the most important meal of the day. It can take two hours or more. Some Chileans forgo dinner, making do with an *once,* a light evening meal similar in style to a high tea. Once is served from 5 to 8; dinner is eaten later than in North America, usually starting anywhere from 8 to 10.

ACCOMMO-
DATIONS
Chile's urban areas and resort areas have hotels that come with all of the amenities that are taken for granted in North America and Europe, such as room service, a restaurant, or a swimming pool. Elsewhere you may not have television or a phone in your room, although you will find them somewhere in the hotel. Rooms that have a private bath may have only a shower, and in some cases, there will be a shared bath in the hall. In all but the most upscale hotels, you may be asked to leave your key at the reception desk whenever you leave.

Many older hotels in Chile have rooms with wrought-iron balconies or spacious terraces; ask if there's a room *con balcón* or *con terraza* when checking in.

Hotels in Chile do not charge taxes to foreign tourists. Knowing this in advance can save you some cash. When checking the price, make sure to ask for the *precio extranjero, sin impuestos* (foreign rate, without taxes).

Private homes that rent rooms, *residenciales,* are a unique way to get to know Chile, especially if you're on a budget. Sometimes residenciales are small, very basic accommodations and not necessarily private homes. *Hospedajes* are similar. Many rent rooms for less than $10. Some will be shabby, but others can be substantially better than hotel rooms. Contact the local tourist office for details on residenciales and hospedajes.

WHAT IT COSTS IN CHILEAN PESOS (IN THOUSANDS)				
¢	**$**	**$$**	**$$$**	**$$$$**
RESTAURANTS under 3 pesos	3 pesos–5 pesos	5 pesos–8 pesos	8 pesos–11 pesos	over 11 pesos
HOTELS under 15 pesos	15 pesos–45 pesos	45 pesos–75 pesos	75 pesos–105 pesos	over 105 pesos

Restaurant prices are based on the median main course price at dinner. Hotel prices are for two people in a standard double room in high season, excluding tax.

SANTIAGO

Founded in 1541, Santiago today is home to more than 6 million people—nearly a third of the country's total population. It continues to spread outward to the so-called *barrios altos* (upper neighborhoods) east of the center. It's also growing upward, as new office towers transform the skyline. Yet in many ways, Santiago still feels like a small town, where residents are always likely to bump into an acquaintance along the city center's crowded streets and bustling plazas.

Santiaguinos abandon their city every summer during the school holidays that run from the end of December to early March. If you're not averse to the heat, this can be a good time for walking around the city; otherwise spring and fall are better choices, as the weather is more comfortable. Santiago is at its prettiest in spring when gentle breezes sweep in to clean the city's air of its winter smog and the trees that line the streets burst into blossom and fragrance.

In fall, too, the vineyards around the city celebrate the *vendimia*—the grape harvest—with colorful festivals that are an opportunity to try traditional Chilean cuisine as well as some of the country's renowned wines. Santiago nestles in the Maipo Valley, the country's oldest wine-growing district. Some of Chile's largest and most traditional wineries—Concha y Toro and Santa Rita—are within an hour's drive of the city and so too is the lovely Casablanca Valley.

GETTING HERE & AROUND

Santiago's Comodoro Arturo Merino Benítez International Airport, often referred to simply as Pudahuel, is about a 30-minute drive west of the city. Taxis should cost around 16,000 pesos for a trip downtown. Hire one at the desks near customs, rather than using one of the services touted outside. Tickets for bus services cost around 1,500 pesos each at the same desks.

Santiago's excellent subway system, the Metro, is the best way to get around the main part of the city but isn't very extensive. It is comfortable, inexpensive, and safe. The system operates weekdays 6 AM–11 PM, Saturday 6:30 AM–10:30 PM, and Sunday 8 AM–10:30 PM.

You don't need a car if within the city limits, but a car is the best way to see the surrounding countryside.

SAFETY & PRECAUTIONS

Despite what Chileans will tell you, Santiago is no more dangerous than most other large cities and considerably less so than many other Latin American capitals. As a rule of thumb, watch out for your property but, unless you venture into some of the city's outlying neighborhoods, your physical safety is very unlikely to be at risk. Beware of pickpockets particularly in the Centro and on buses.

When it comes to air quality, Santiago ranks as one of the most polluted cities in the world. The pollution is worse in winter, when wind and rainfall levels are at their lowest.

GREAT ITINERARY

DAYS 1 & 2: SANTIAGO

A trip up one of the city's hills—like Cerro San Cristóbal in Parque Metropolitano or Cerro Santa Lucía—lets you survey the capital and its grid of streets. Any tour of a city begins with its historic center; the cathedral and commercial office towers on the Plaza de Armas reflect Santiago's old and new architecture, while the nearby Bohemian quarter of Bellavista, with its bustling markets and colorful shops, was built for walking. Santiago's zippy, efficient metro can also whisk you to most places in the city.

DAYS 3 & 4: VALPARAÍSO & VIÑA DEL MAR

A 90-minute drive west from Santiago takes you to the Central Coast. If you fancy yourself one of the glitterati, you'll go for Viña del Mar and its chic cafés and restaurants and miles of beach. But Valparaíso offers you the charm and allure of a port city, rolling hills, and cobblestone streets with better views of the sea. Nothing says you can't do both; only 10 km (6 mi) separate the two, and a new metro system connects them.

DAYS 5 & 6: SAN PEDRO DE ATACAMA

You certainly *could* drive the nearly 1,500 km (900 mi) to Chile's vast El Norte Grande, but a flight from Santiago to Calama then a quick overland drive to San Pedro de Atacama will take you no more than 3½ hours. That a town with such a polished tourism infrastructure could lie at the heart of one the world's loneliest regions comes as a great surprise. This is one of the most-visited towns in Chile, and for good reason: it sits right in the middle of the Atacama Desert. Explore alpine lakes, ancient fortresses,

DAYS 7, 8, 9, 10: THE LAKE DISTRICT

Head south 675 km (405 mi) from Santiago on a fast toll highway to Temuco, the gateway to Chile's Lake District. About an hour farther south, and just 15 minutes apart on the shores of Lago Villarrica, lie the twin resort towns of flashy, glitzy Pucón and quiet, pleasant Villarrica. Drive south through the region from the graceful old city of Valdivia to Puerto Montt, stopping at the various resort towns. From Puerto Montt, you can take a five-day round-trip cruise through the maze of fjords down the coast to the unforgettable cobalt-blue glacier in Parque Nacional Laguna San Rafael.

DAYS 11, 12, 13, 14: PARQUE NACIONAL TORRES DEL PAINE

From Puerto Montt, take a spectacular morning flight over the Andes to the Patagonian city of Punta Arenas. On the next day drive north to Puerto Natales, gateway to the Parque Nacional Torres del Paine. You'll need at least two days to wander through the wonders of the park. On your final day, head back to Punta Arenas, stopping en route at one of the penguin sanctuaries, and catch an afternoon flight to Santiago, in time to connect with a night flight home to North America or Europe.

ESSENTIALS

Airline Contacts Aerolineas del Sur/Air Comet (☎600/625–0000 in Chile ⊕ www.aircometchile.cl). **American Airlines** (☎800/433–7300 in North America, 2/679–0000 in Chile). **Delta Airlines** (☎800/221–1212 for U.S. reservations, 800/241–4141 for international reservations, 2/690–1555 in Chile ⊕ www.delta.com). **LAN** (☎800/735–5526 in North America, 2/565–2000 in Chile). **United Airlines** (☎800/864–8331 for U.S. reservations, 800/538–2929 for international reservations ⊕ www.united.com).

Airport Comodoro Arturo Merino Benítez International Airport (☎2/690–1900 ⊕ www.aeropuertosantiago.cl).

Bus Companies Manzur Expediciones (✉ Sótero del Río 475, Santiago Centro ☎2/777–4284). **Pullman Bus** (✉ Terminal Alameda, Estación Central ☎2/779–2106). **Skitotal** (✉ Av. Apoquindo 4900, Las Condes ☎2/246–6881). **Tur-Bus** (✉ Terminal Alameda, Estación Central ☎2/270–7500).

Bus Depots Terminal Alameda (✉ La Alameda 3750, Estación Central ☎2/270–7500). **Terminal Los Héroes** (✉ Tucapel Jiménez 21, Estación Central ☎2/420–0099). **Terminal San Borja** (✉ San Borja 184, Estación Central ☎2/776–0645). **Terminal Santiago** (✉ La Alameda 3848, La Alameda ☎2/376–1755).

Currency Exchange American Express (✉ Av. Isidora Goyenechea 3621, Las Condes ☎2/350–6700). **Santander Santiago** (✉ Bandera 140, Santiago Centro ☎600/320–3000 ✉ Av. Providencia 2667, Providencia ☎600/320–3000 ✉ Av. Apoquindo 3575, Las Condes ☎600/320–3000).

Internet Cafés Cyber & Market (✉ Almirante Pastene 62, Providencia ☎2/236–8743). **Isinet** (✉ Calle Londrés 30, La Alameda ☎2/632–9155). **Uribe-Larry** (✉ Merced 618, Parque Forestal ☎2/663–1990).

Medical Assistance Clínica Alemana (✉ Av. Vitacura 5951, Las Condes ☎2/210–1334).**Clínica Las Condes** (✉ Lo Fontecilla 441, Las Condes ☎2/210–4000). **Clínica Santa María** (✉ Av. Santa María 0500, Providencia ☎2/461–2000).**Farmacias Ahumada** (✉ Ahumada 301, at Huérfanos, Santiago Centro ☎2/631–3003).

Postal Services Correo Central (✉ Catedral at Paseo Ahumada, Santiago Centro ☎2/956–5153 ⊕ www.correos.cl).**DHL** (✉ San Francisco 301, Santiago Centro ☎2/280–2000 ✉ Bandera 204, Santiago Centro ☎2/697–1081 ✉ Av. 11 de Septiembre 2070, Providencia ☎2/234–1516).**Federal Express** (✉ Fray Camilo Henríquez 190, Santiago Centro ☎800/363–030 ✉ Av. Providencia 1951, Providencia ☎800/363–030).

Rental Cars Alamo (✉ Airport ☎2/690–1370 ✉ Av. Francisco Bilbao 2846, Providencia ☎2/225–4117). **Avis** (✉2/690–1382 ✉ Airport ☎2/795–3990 ✉ Hotel Radisson, Av. Vitacura 2610, Las Condes ☎2/596–8760). **Bengolea** (✉ Av. Francisco Bilbao 1047, Providencia ☎2/204–9021). **Budget** (✉ Airport ☎2/690–1386 ✉ Av. Francisco Bilbao 1439, Providencia ☎2/362–3205). **Chilean** (✉ Bellavista 0183, Bellavista ☎2/737–9650). **Hertz** (✉ Airport ☎2/601–0477 ✉ Av. Andrés Bello 1469, Providencia ☎2/496–1000). **Rosselot** (✉ Airport ☎2/690–1317 ✉ Av. Francisco Bilbao 2045, Providencia ☎2/381–2200).

Subway Metro de Santiago (☎600/422–3330 ⊕ www.metrosantiago.cl).

Taxi **Alborada** (☎2/246–4900). **Alto Oriente** (☎2/226–2116). **Andes Pacífico** (☎2/225–3064 or 2/204-0104). **Apoquindo** (☎2/211–6073).

Visitor Info **Sernatur Providencia** (⊠ *Av. Providencia 1550, Providencia* ☎2/731–8310 ⊕ *www.sernatur.cl*).

EXPLORING SANTIAGO

It's easy to get your bearings because the Andes Mountains are always there to tell you where the east is. And, to make it even easier, the main districts you'll want to visit—the Centro, Providencia, and Las Condes—form the city's west–east axis, moving gradually up towards the mountains as they become more prosperous. This is the axis served by Line 1 of the subway.

Much of the city, especially communities such as Bellavista, is best explored on foot. The subway is the quickest, cleanest, and most economical way to shuttle between neighborhoods. To travel to more distant neighborhoods, or in the evening after the subway closes, hail a taxi.

SANTIAGO CENTRO

With La Moneda Presidential Palace and its ministries and law courts, Santiago Centro is the place from which Chile is governed and where you'll find most of the historic monuments and museums. But don't think you'll be lost in a sprawling area—it takes only about 15 minutes to walk from one edge of the neighborhood to the other.

Numbered bullets in the margins correspond to numbered bullets on the Santiago Centro & La Alameda map.

❶ **Plaza de Armas.** This square has been the symbolic heart of Chile—and
★ its political, social, religious, and commercial center—since Pedro de Valdivia established the city on this spot in 1541. The Palacio de los Gobernadores, the Palacio de la Real Audiencia, and the Municipalidad de Santiago front the square's northern edge. The Catedral graces the western side of the square. On any given day, the plaza teems with life—vendors selling religious icons, artists painting the activity around them, street performers juggling fire, and tourists clutching guidebooks. ⊠ *Compañía at Estado, Santiago Centro* Ⓜ *Plaza de Armas.*

❷ **Catedral.** Conquistador Pedro de Valdivia declared in 1541 that a house of worship would be constructed at this site bordering the Plaza de Armas. Check out the baroque interior with its line of arches topped by stained-glass windows parading down the long nave and the sparkling silver altar of a side chapel in the south nave. ⊠ *Plaza de Armas, Santiago Centro* ☎2/696–2777 ⊙ *Daily 10–8* Ⓜ *Plaza de Armas.*

❸ **Museo Chileno de Arte Precolombino.** If you plan to visit only one museum
Fodor'sChoice in Santiago, it should be the Museum of Pre-Columbian Art, a block
★ from the Plaza de Armas. The large collection of artifacts of the region's indigenous peoples is displayed in the beautifully restored Royal Customs House. The permanent collection, on the upper floor, showcases textiles and ceramics from Mexico to Patagonia. Unlike many of the city's museums, the displays here are well labeled in Spanish and English.

✉*Bandera 361, at Av. Compañía, Santiago Centro* ☎*2/688–7348* ⊕*www.museoprecolombino.cl* ✆*Tues.–Sat. 3,000 pesos, Sun. free* ☉*Tues.–Sun. 10–6, public holidays 10–2* Ⓜ*Plaza de Armas.*

LA ALAMEDA

Avenida Libertador Bernardo O'Higgins, more frequently called La Alameda, is the city's principal thoroughfare. Along with the Avenida Norte Sur and the Río Mapocho, it forms the wedge that defines the city's historic district.

❽ **Biblioteca Nacional.** Near the foot of Cerro Santa Lucía is the block-long classical facade of the National Library. Although it didn't move to its present premises until 1925, this library, founded in 1813, is one of

the oldest and most complete in South America. The second-floor Sala José Toribio Medina (closed Saturday), which holds the most important collection of early Latin American print work, is worth a look. Three levels of books, reached by curved-wood balconies, are lighted by massive chandeliers. ✉*La Alameda 651, La Alameda* ☎*2/360–5200* ⊕*www.dibam.cl* ✆*Free* ☉*Apr.–mid-Dec., weekdays 9–7, Sat. 9–2; mid-Dec.–Mar., Sun.–Fri. 9–5:30* Ⓜ*Santa Lucía.*

❾ **Cerro Santa Lucía.** The mazelike park of Santa Lucía is a hangout for park-bench smoochers and photo-snapping tourists. Walking uphill along the labyrinth of interconnected paths and plazas takes about 30 minutes, or you can take an elevator two blocks north of the main entrance (no fee). The crow's nest affords an excellent 360-degree view of the city. Be careful near dusk as the park, although patrolled, also attracts the occasional mugger. ✉*Santa Lucía at La Alameda, La Alameda* ☎*2/664–4206* ☉*Nov.–Mar., daily 9–8; Apr.–Oct., daily 9–7* Ⓜ*Santa Lucía.*

❼ **Iglesia San Francisco.** Santiago's oldest structure, greatest symbol, and principal landmark, the Church of St. Francis is the last trace of 16th-century colonial architecture in the city. Construction began in 1586, and although the church survived successive earthquakes, early tremors took their toll and portions had to be rebuilt several times. Inside are rough stone-and-brick walls and an ornate coffered wood ceiling. ✉*La Alameda 834, La Alameda* ☎*2/638–3238* ☉*Daily 8–8* Ⓜ*Santa Lucía, Universidad de Chile.*

❻ **Palacio de la Moneda.** Originally the royal mint, this sober neoclassical edifice designed by Joaquín Toesca in the 1780s and completed in 1805 became the presidential palace in 1846 and served that purpose for more than a century. It was bombarded by the military in the 1973 coup, when Salvador Allende defended his presidency against General Augusto Pinochet before committing suicide there. The two central courtyards are open to the public, and tours of the interior can be arranged by e-mail with at least two days' notice. ⊠ *Plaza de la Constitución, Moneda between Teatinos and Morandé, La Alameda* ☎ *2/690–4000* ✉ *visitas@presidencia.cl* ⊙ *Daily 10:30–6* Ⓜ *La Moneda.*

❺ **Plaza de la Constitución.** Palacio de la Moneda and other government
★ buildings line Constitution Square, the country's most formal plaza. The changing of the guard occurs every other day at 10 am within the triangle of 12 Chilean flags. ⊠ *Moneda at Morandé, La Alameda* Ⓜ *La Moneda.*

PARQUE FORESTAL

A leafy park along the banks of the Río Mapocho gives this tranquil district its name. This is where you'll find the city's main art museums as well as, at its western tip, the bustle of the Mercado Central fish market and, on the other side of the river, the Vega and Vega Chica markets.

❹ **Mercado Central.** At the Central Market you'll find a matchless selection of creatures from the sea. Depending on the season, you might see the delicate beaks of *picorocos,* the world's only edible barnacles; *erizos,* the prickly shelled sea urchins; or heaps of giant mussels. If the fish don't capture your interest, the architecture may: the lofty wrought-iron ceiling of the structure, reminiscent of a Victorian train station, was prefabricated in England and erected in Santiago between 1868 and 1872. Diners are regaled by musicians in the middle of the market, where two restaurants compete for customers. You can also find a cheap, filling meal at a stand along the market's southern edge. ⊠ *Ismael Valdés Vergara 900, Parque Forestal* ☎ *2/696–8327* ⊙ *Sun.– Thurs. 6–5, Fri. 6 AM–8 PM, Sat. 6–6* Ⓜ *Puente Cal y Canto.*

⑫ **Vega Chica and Vega Central.** From fruit to furniture, meat to machinery, these lively markets stock just about anything you can name. Alongside the ordinary items you can find delicacies like *piñones,* giant pine nuts found on monkey puzzle trees. If you're undaunted by crowds, try a typical Chilean meal in a closet-size eatery or *picada.* Chow down with the locals on *pastel de choclo,* a pie filled with ground beef, chicken, olives, and boiled eggs and topped with mashed corn. Be careful with your belongings. ⊠ *Antonia López de Bello between Av. Salas and Nueva Rengifo, Recoleta* Ⓜ *Patronato.*

❿ **Museo de Artes Visuales.** This dazzling museum of contemporary art
★ displays one of the finest collections of contemporary Chilean art. The building is a masterpiece: six gallery levels float into each other with the aid of Plexiglas-sided stairways. ⊠ *José Victorino Lastarria 307, at Plaza Mulato Gil de Castro, Parque Forestal* ☎ *2/638–3502* ⊕ *www.mavi.cl* ✉ *Tues.–Sat. 1,000 pesos (includes Museo Arqueológico de Santiago), Sun. free* ⊙ *Tues.–Sun. 10:30–6:30* Ⓜ *Universidad Católica.*

BELLAVISTA & PARQUE METROPOLITANO

On the north side of the Río Mapocho, nestled in the shadow of the San Cristóbal Hill, Bellavista is Santiago's "left bank," a Bohemian district of cafés, small restaurants, crafts shops, aspiring art galleries, and one of the homes of Nobel poet Pablo Neruda.

⓬   **Cerro San Cristóbal.** St. Christopher's Hill, within Parque Metropoli-
☺   tano, is one of Santiago's most popular tourist attractions. From the western entrance at Plaza Caupolicán you can walk—it's a steep one-hour climb—or take the funicular. Either route leads you to the summit, which is crowned by a gleaming white statue of the Virgen de la Inmaculada Concepción. If you come from the eastern entrance, you can ascend in the cable car or *teleférico* that leaves seven blocks north of the Pedro de Valdivia Metro stop. There is limited parking for 2,000 pesos at the Pío Nono entrance and free parking at the Pedro de Valdivia entrance. ⌂ *Cerro San Cristóbal, Bellavista* ☏ *2/730–1300* ⊕ *www.parquemet.cl* ⌦ *Round-trip funicular 1,400 pesos; round-trip cable car 1,600 pesos* ⊙ *Park: daily 8:30 AM–9 PM. Funicular: Mon. 1–8:30, Tues.–Fri. 10– 8:30, weekends 10–9. Cable car: Mon. 12:30–8, Tues.–Fri. 10:30–8, weekends 10:30–8:30* Ⓜ *Baquedano, Pedro de Valdivia.*

VITACURA

★   **Museo de la Moda.** This Fashion Museum, opened in 2007 by a son of Jorge Yarur Banna, one of Chile's most successful textile barons, hosts small exhibitions using a collection of clothes—mostly women's dresses—that dates back to the 1600s. Housed in the Yarur family's former home, which was designed by Chilean architects in the style of Frank Lloyd Wright in the early 1960s and decorated by a brother of Roberto Matta, one of Chile's most famous painters, the museum offers a fascinating insight into the lifestyle of the Chilean oligarchy in the run-up to the upheaval of Salvador Allende's socialist government and the ensuing military coup. The museum café serves excellent light meals and snacks at reasonable prices and, on weekends, has a special brunch menu. ⌂ *Av. Vitacura 4562, Vitacura* ☏ *2/218-7271* ⊕ *www. mmyt.cl* ⌦ *3,000 pesos* ⊙ *Tues.–Sun. 10–7* Ⓜ *No metro.*

WHERE TO EAT

Dining is one of Santiago's great pleasures. Everything from fine restaurants to informal *picadas,* restaurants that specialize in typical Chilean food, is spread across the city. Menus run the gamut of international cuisines, but don't miss the local bounty—seafood delivered directly from the Pacific Ocean. One of the local favorites is *caldillo de congrio,* the hearty fish stew celebrated by poet Pablo Neruda in his *Oda al Caldillo de Congrio* which is, in fact, the recipe. A *pisco sour*—a cocktail of grape brandy and lemon juice—makes a good start to a meal.

For hearty Chilean fare pull up a stool at one of the counters at Vega Central and enjoy a traditional pastel de choclo. Craving seafood? Head to the Mercado Central, where you can choose from the fresh fish brought in that morning. Or try a trendy new restaurant in neighborhoods like Bellavista.

Remember that Santiaguinos dine a little later than the rest of us. Most restaurants don't open for lunch until 1. Dinner begins at 7:30 or 8, although most places don't get crowded until after 9. Many restaurants are closed on Sunday night.

BELLAVISTA

$$$
SEAFOOD
Fodor'sChoice
★

✕**Azul Profundo.** When it opened, this was the only restaurant on this street near Parque Metropolitano. Today it's one of dozens of restaurants in trendy Bellavista, but its two-level dining room—with racks of wine stretching to the ceiling—ensure that it stands out in the crowd. Choose your fish from the extensive menu—swordfish, sea bass, shark, flounder, salmon, trout, and haddock are among the choices—and enjoy it *a la plancha* (grilled) or *a la lata* (served on a sizzling plate with tomatoes and onions). ⊠*Constitución 111, Bellavista* ☎*2/738–0288* ⌂*Reservations essential* ⊟*AE, DC, MC, V* Ⓜ*Baquedano.*

$$$
CHILEAN
Fodor'sChoice
★

✕**Como Agua Para Chocolate.** Inspired by Laura Esquivel's romantic 1989 novel *Like Water for Chocolate*, this Bellavista standout focuses on the aphrodisiacal qualities of food. One long table is actually an iron bed, with place settings arranged on a crisp white sheet. The food compares to the decor like the film version compares to the book: it's good, but not nearly as imaginative. *Ave de la pasión,* for instance, means Bird of Passion. It may be just chicken with mushrooms, but it's served on a copper plate. ⊠*Constitución 88, Bellavista* ☎*2/777–8740* ⊟*AE, DC, MC, V* Ⓜ*Baquedano.*

$
CHILEAN

✕**Galindo.** Join artists and the young crowd of Bellavista for traditional Chilean food in an old adobe house. This restaurant goes back 60 years when it started life as a canteen for local workmen and, although it gets crowded, it's a great place to try *pastel de choclo* or a hearty *cazuela,* a typical meat and vegetable soup that is a meal in itself. It also has the advantage of being open on Sunday. ⊠*Dardignac 098, Bellavista* ☎*2/777–0116* ⊟*AE, DC, MC, V* Ⓜ*Baquedano.*

CENTRO

$$
CHILEAN
Fodor'sChoice
★

✕**Blue Jar.** This restaurant, only a block from the Palacio de la Moneda, is an oasis of quiet on a small pedestrian street, and its food—simple but creative dishes using the freshest Chilean ingredients—appeals to locals and visitors alike, whether it's a sandwich, a salad and a bowl of soup, a full lunch, or a hearty breakfast. The menu changes monthly but not its hallmark hamburgers made from three different cuts of beef—one for flavor, one for texture, the other for color—with a little bacon fat added, and its wine list has some of Chile's most interesting labels at very reasonable prices. Reservations are advisable for lunch, particularly for an outside table. It closes at 8:30, so arrive early for evening drinks, sandwiches, and snacks. ⊠*Almirante L. Gotuzzo 102, at Moneda, Santiago Centro* ☎*2/696–1890* ⊟*AE, DC, MC, V* ⊘*Closed weekends* Ⓜ*Moneda.*

$$
CHILEAN
★

✕**Confitería Torres.** José Domingo Torres, a chef greatly in demand amongst the Chilean aristocracy of his day, set up shop in this storefront on the Alameda in 1879. It remains one of the city's most traditional dining rooms, with red-leather banquettes, mint-green tile floors, and huge chandeliers with tulip-shaped globes. The food, such

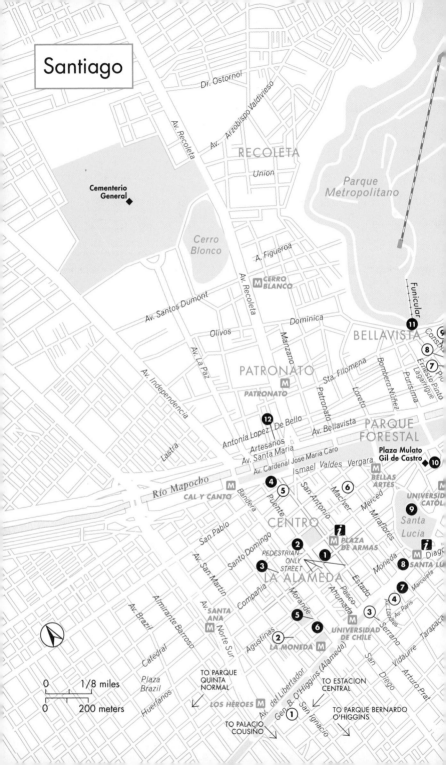

Santiago

Cementerio General ◆

RECOLETA

Dr. Ostornol

Av. Arzobispo Valdivieso

Av. Recoleta

Union

Cerro Blonco

Parque Metropolitano

A. Figueroa

CERRO BLANCO

Funicular

Av. Santos Dumont

Av. Recoleta

Dominica

BELLAVISTA ⑪

⑨

Olivos

Av. La Paz

Manzano

Sta. Filomena

Bombero Núñez

⑧

⑦

PATRONATO

Patronato M

PATRONATO

Loreto

Purísima

Ernesto Pinto Lagarrigue

Av. Independencia

Antonia Lopez De Bello

Av. Bellavista

PARQUE FORESTAL

Lastra

Artesanos ⑫

Av. Santa Maria

Plaza Mulato Gil de Castro ◆ ⑩

Av. Cardenal Jose Maria Caro

Ismael Valdes Vergara

BELLAS ARTES M

UNIVERSID CATOL

Río Mapocho

④

⑤

San Antonio

Maclver

Merced

Miraflores

⑨

Santa Lucia

CAL Y CANTO M

Puente

⑥

Bandera

San Pablo

CENTRO

🛈

Santo Domingo

②

PLAZA DE ARMAS M

🛈

San Martin

③

PEDESTRIAN-ONLY STREET

①

Estado

Moneda

⑧ SANTA LU M Diag

LA ALAMEDA

Compañia

Morande

Paseo Ahumada

③

Av. Londres

Av. Paris

④

⑦ Marcoleta

SANTA ANA

⑤

Av. San Martin

Norte Sur

⑥

UNIVERSIDAD DE CHILE M

Serrano

San Diego

Vidaurre

Arturo Prat

Catedral

Almirante Barroso

Av. Brazil

Agustinas

②

LA MONEDA M

Tarapacá

Plaza Brazil

Huerfanos

TO PARQUE QUINTA NORMAL

LOS HÉROES M

TO PALACIO COUSIÑO

Av. del Libertador Gen. B. O'Higgins (Alameda)

①

San Ignacio

TO ESTACIÓN CENTRAL

TO PARQUE BERNARDO O'HIGGINS

0   1/8 miles
0   200 meters

4

Map labels

TO GRAND HYATT SANTIAGO,
NERUDA EXPRESS, RITZ-CARLTON,
SANTIAGO MARRIOTT HOTEL

TO LAS CONDES

Pedro de Valdivia

Av. Providencia

11 de Septiembre

Av. La Concepción

PEDRO
DE VALDIVIA

Av. Andrés Bello

Av. Antonio Bellet

Av. El Cerro

PROVIDENCIA

Av. Manuel Montt

MANUEL MONTT

Av. Santa María

SALVADOR

Av. Bellavista

de Bello

Av. Pardiñamar

Winkroat

Plaza Baquedano

BAQUEDANO

Av. Bustamante

Av. Vicuña Mackenna

BUSTAMANTE

Paraguay Rancagua

SANTA
ISABEL

Lira

Santa Victoria

Santa Isabel

IRARRÁZABEL

n. Isidoro

Santa Rosa

Francisco

KEY

- 🅼 *Metro stops*
- 🛈 *Tourist information*
- ⊏⊐ *Cable Car Line*
- ❶ *Exploring Sights*
- ① *Hotels & Restaurants*

as *lomo al ajo arriego* (sirloin sautéed with peppers and garlic), now comes from recipes by the mother of owner Claudio Soto Barría. A branch serves snacks and light meals in the Centro Cultural Palacio La Moneda. ⊠ *Alameda 1570, Santiago Centro* ☏ *2/688–0751* ⊟ *AE, DC, MC, V* ⊘ *Closed Sun.* Ⓜ *Universidad de Chile.*

$ ✕ **Donde Augusto.** What was once a simple seafood stand has taken
SEAFOOD   over almost all the interior of Mercado Central. If you don't mind the
Fodor$Choice   unhurried service and the odd tear in the tablecloth, you may have the
★   time of your life dining on everything from sea urchins to baby eel. Go for simple dishes like the *corvina a la plancha* (grilled sea bass), which is mouthwateringly good. Get here early, as it closes at 5 PM Sunday–Thursday and 6 on Saturday; it's open until 8 on Friday. ⊠ *Mercado Central, Santiago Centro* ☏ *2/672–2829* ⊟ *AE, DC, MC, V* ⊘ *No dinner* Ⓜ *Puente Cal y Canto.*

PROVIDENCIA

$$ ✕ **Aquí Está Coco.** The best seafood in Santiago is served here; ask your
SEAFOOD   waiter—or friendly owner "Coco" Pacheco—which fish is the day's
Fodor$Choice   catch. This is a good place to try Chile's famous *machas* (clams), served
★   with tomatoes and Parmesan cheese, or *corvina* (sea bass) grilled with plenty of butter. Don't miss the cellar, where you can sample wines from the extensive collection of Chilean vintages. ⊠ *La Concepción 236, Providencia* ☏ *2/235–8649* ⚱ *Reservations essential* ⊟ *AE, DC, MC, V* ⊘ *Closed Sun.* Ⓜ *Pedro de Valdivia.*

$$$$ ✕ **Astrid y Gaston.** The kitchen is the real star here—every seat in the
CHILEAN   pumpkin-color dining room has a great view of the chefs at work.
Fodor$Choice   You couldn't do better than start with the agnolotti, little pockets of
★   squid-ink pasta stuffed with king crab and cherry tomatoes. After that, try one of the one-of-a-kind entrées, such as the lamb shank drenched in *pisco* (a brandy distilled from small grapes) and served with three kinds of yucca, or the parrot fish with tamarind and ginger. Make sure to peruse the wine list, one of the best in town. Save room for one of Astrid's desserts, such as the creamy confection called *suspiro limeña,* "sigh of a lady from Lima": a meringue-topped dish of dulce de leche. ⊠ *Antonio Bellet 201, Providencia* ☏ *2/650–9125* ⚱ *Reservations essential* ⊟ *AE, DC, MC, V* Ⓜ *Pedro de Valdivia.*

$$ ✕ **Liguria.** This extremely popular picada is always packed, so you
CHILEAN   might have to wait to be seated in the chandelier-lighted dining room or at one of the tables that spill out onto the sidewalk. A large selection of Chilean wine accompanies such favorites as *cazuela* (a stew of beef or chicken and potatoes) and sandwiches of *mechada* (tender and thinly sliced beef). There are three branches in the neighborhood, but each has its own personality. ⊠ *Av. Providencia 1373, Providencia* ☏ *2/235–7914* ⊟ *AE, DC, MC, V* ⊘ *Closed Sun.* Ⓜ *Manuel Montt* ⊠ *Pedro de Valdivia 047, Providencia* ☏ *2/334–4346* ⊟ *AE, DC, MC, V* ⊘ *Closed Sun.* Ⓜ *Pedro de Valdivia* ⊠ *Luis Thayer Ojeda 019, Providencia* ☏ *2/231–1393* ⊟ *AE, DC, MC, V* ⊘ *Closed Sun.* Ⓜ *Tobalaba.*

WHERE TO STAY

Santiago has more than a dozen five-star hotels, many of them in the burgeoning Las Condes and Vitacura neighborhoods. You won't find better service than at newer hotels such as the lavish Ritz-Carlton. But don't write off the old standbys such as Hotel Plaza San Francisco. Inexpensive small hotels are harder to find but they do exist, especially around the Calle Londres in the city center and in the Providencia district.

Note that the 19% sales tax is removed from your bill if you pay in U.S. dollars or with an overseas credit card.

CENTRO

$ **Andes Hostel.** Backpackers and budget-conscious families can ask to block off one of the four- or six-bed dormitories at this excellent hostel, opened in mid-2006. The basement has a well-equipped kitchen and pleasant dining room with three large tables and a television. Older kids love the pool table in the ground-floor lobby–common room. The location—opposite a subway station in the heart of the Parque Forestal, surrounded by museums, cool cafés, and restaurants—is hard to beat. **Pros:** This old house has been beautifully converted, spotlessly clean, great rooftop terrace. **Cons:** Some of the private rooms are very small. ⌂ *Monjitas 506, Santiago Centro* ☎ *2/632–9990* ⊕ *www.andes hostel.com* ↝ *6 rooms, 3 with bath; 9 dormitories* ⌂ *In-hotel: bar, public Wi-Fi, public Internet, no-smoking rooms* ▤ *AE, DC, MC, V* ⧖*CP* Ⓜ *Bellas Artes.*

$$$ **Hotel Fundador.** On the edge of the quaint Barrio París-Londres, the Hotel Fundador has recently been renovated and rooms, although small, are bright and airily attractive. Stroll on the iron bridge across Calle Londres that links the hotel's two halves. Amenities include a small indoor pool. This hotel also has business on its mind, so there are plenty of meeting rooms with high-tech equipment. **Pros:** Tucked away from downtown traffic noise, on the doorstep of a subway station. **Cons:** Not an area for a stroll at night, few restaurants or bars in the immediate vicinity. ⌂ *Paseo Serrano 34, Santiago Centro* ☎ *2/387–1200* 🖷 *2/387–1300* ⊕ *www.hotelfundador.cl* ↝ *119 rooms, 28 suites* ⌂ *In-room: safe, dial-up, refrigerator. In-hotel: restaurant, room service, bar, public Wi-Fi, pool, gym, laundry service, parking (no fee), no-smoking rooms* ▤ *AE, DC, MC, V* ⧖*BP* Ⓜ *Universidad de Chile.*

$$$ **Hotel Plaza San Francisco.** Across from Iglesia San Francisco, at this business hotel you can take a dip in the sparkling indoor pool, work out in the fitness club, or stroll through the art gallery. Recent redecoration has given the hotel a lighter, more modern touch. Its spacious rooms have large beds, and double-paned windows keep out the downtown noise. **Pros:** Helpful English-speaking staff, the Bristol offers interesting cuisine. **Cons:** Other good restaurants and bars are a Metro or taxi-ride away. ⌂ *La Alameda 816, Santiago Centro* ☎ *2/639–3832, 800/223–5652 toll-free in U.S.* 🖷 *2/639–7826* ⊕ *www.plazasanfrancisco. cl* ↝ *136 rooms, 9 suites* ⌂ *In-room: safe, refrigerator, Ethernet. In-hotel: restaurant, room service, bar, pool, gym, public Wi-Fi, laundry*

Fodor's Choice

4

service, no-smoking rooms, parking (no fee) ☐*AE, DC, MC, V* ⦿|*BP*
Ⓜ *Universidad de Chile.*

$$$$ 🏨**Grand Hyatt Santiago.** The soaring spire of the Grand Hyatt resembles
Fodor'sChoice a rocket (and you shoot up a glass elevator through a 24-story atrium).
★   The rooms wrap around the cylindrical lobby, providing a panoramic
view of the Andes. As you might guess from the pair of golden lions
flanking the entrance, the theme is vaguely Asian, which is why two
of the three award-winning restaurants are Thai and Japanese. (Senso,
which is Tuscan, is also well worth a visit.) Duke's, the spitting image
of an English pub, fills to standing capacity each day after work hours.
Pros: The garden is lovely, Atrium Lounge serves famed afternoon teas.
Cons: Out of the way. ⊠*Av. Kennedy 4601, Las Condes* ☎*2/950–*
1234 🖷*2/950–3155* ⊕*www.santiago.hyatt.com* ⇱*287 rooms, 23*
suites ⌂*In-room: safe, refrigerator, Ethernet. In-hotel: 3 restaurants,*
room service, bar, public Wi-Fi, tennis courts, pool, gym, concierge,
laundry service, parking (no fee), no-smoking rooms ☐*AE, DC, MC,*
V ⦿|*BP* Ⓜ*No metro.*

$$ 🏨**Neruda Express.** This "express" branch of the larger Hotel Neruda
(on Avenida Pedro de Valdivia) has recently been redecorated and the
·   rooms are tastefully modern, spacious, and luminous. Ask for one of
the two suites on the second floor or one of the "superior" rooms on the
ninth to 11th floors; they cost the same as a standard room. Although
all windows have double glass, rooms on Avenida Apoquindo still get
traffic noise; those at the back are quieter. **Pros:** On the edge of fashion-
able Las Condes. **Cons:** Fawlty Towers service has its charm but can
also be very irritating. ⊠*Vecinal 40, at Av. Apoquindo, Las Condes*
☎*2/233–2747* 🖷*2/232–1662* ⊕*www.hotelneruda.cl* ⇱*50 rooms, 2*
suites ⌂*In-room: safe, refrigerator, Wi-Fi. In-hotel: public Internet,*
laundry service, parking (no fee), no-smoking rooms ☐*AE, DC, MC,*
V ⦿|*CP* Ⓜ*El Golf, Tobalaba.*

$$$$ 🏨**Ritz-Carlton.** The rather bland brick exterior of this 15-story hotel
belies the luxurious appointments within. Mahogany-paneled walls,
cream marble floors, and enormous windows characterize the splendid
two-story lobby, which faces a small leafy plaza just off busy Avenida
Apoquindo. Elegant furnishings upholstered in brocade, and silk flo-
ral fabrics dominate the large guest rooms. Under a magnificent glass
dome on the top floor you can swim or work out while pondering the
panorama, smog permitting, of the Andes and the Santiago skyline.
Pros: Prime location close to the main El Golf business and restau-
rant area. **Cons:** Almost the same comfort is available in other hotels
at much lower prices. ⊠*El Alcalde 15, Las Condes* ☎*2/470–8500*
🖷*2/470–8501* ⊕*www.ritzcarlton.com* ⇱*187 rooms, 18 suites* ⌂*In-*
room: safe, refrigerator, Ethernet. In-hotel: 2 restaurants, bar, room
service, public Wi-Fi, pool, gym, concierge, laundry service, parking
(no fee), no-smoking rooms ☐*AE, DC, MC, V* ⦿|*BP* Ⓜ*El Golf.*

$$$$ 🏨**Santiago Marriott Hotel.** The first 25 floors of this gleaming copper
tower house the Marriott. An impressive two-story, cream marble
lobby has full-grown palm trees in and around comfortable seating
areas. Visitors who opt for an executive room can breakfast in a private

lounge while scanning the newspaper and marveling at the snowcapped Andes. There are wine tastings in the Latin Grill restaurant and theme evenings, with live music, in the Café Med. **Pros:** Excellent, friendly service in a spacious setting. **Cons:** In a suburban neighborhood, removed from the action. ✉*Av. Kennedy 5741, Las Condes* ☎*2/426–2000, 800/468–4000 toll-free in U.S. and Canada* ⊟*2/426–2001* ⊕*www. santiagomarriott.com* 🖙*280 rooms, 60 suites* ⚒*In-room: safe, refrigerator, Ethernet. In-hotel: 2 restaurants, bar, room service, public Wi-Fi, pool, gym, concierge, laundry service, parking (no fee), no-smoking rooms* ⊟*AE, DC, MC, V* ⦿|*BP* Ⓜ*No metro.*

PROVIDENCIA

$ 🆃**Chilhotel.** This small hotel is one of the few good midrange hotels in Santiago. For about what you'd pay for a dinner for two, you get a room that's clean and comfortable. Those overlooking the palm-shaded courtyard in back are especially lovely. It's in a funky old house, so no two rooms are alike. See a few before you decide. And talk about location—you're on a quiet side street, yet dozens of restaurants and bars are steps away. **Pros:** Excellent service closely supervised by owners; just a 10-minute Metro ride away from downtown sightseeing. **Cons:** Small rooms. ✉*Cirujano Guzmán 103, Providencia* ☎*2/264–0643* ⊟*2/264–1323* ⊕*www.chilhotel.cl* 🖙*17 rooms* ⚒*In-room: safe, refrigerator. In-hotel: restaurant, laundry service, public Wi-Fi, no elevator* ⊟*AE, DC, MC, V* ⦿|*BP* Ⓜ*Manuel Montt.*

$$ 🆃**Hotel Orly.** Finding a treasure like this in the middle of Providencia Fodor'sChoice is nothing short of a miracle. The shiny wood floors, country-manor ★ furnishings, and glass-domed breakfast room make this hotel as sweet as it is economical. Rooms come in all shapes and sizes, so ask to see a few before you decide. Cafetto, the downstairs café, serves some of the finest coffee drinks in town. **Pros:** Attractively decorated, excellent maintenance. **Cons:** Difficult to book on short notice. ✉*Av. Pedro de Valdivia 027, Providencia* ☎*2/231–8947* ⊟*2/334–4403* ⊕*www.orly hotel.com* 🖙*25 rooms, 3 suites* ⚒*In-room: safe, refrigerator. In-hotel: restaurant, room service, laundry service, parking (no fee), public Wi-Fi, no-smoking rooms* ⊟*AE, DC, MC, V* ⦿|*BP* Ⓜ*Pedro de Valdivia.*

NIGHTLIFE

Bars and clubs are scattered all over Santiago, but a handful of streets have a concentration of such establishments. Try pub-crawling along Avenida Pío Nono and neighboring streets in Bellavista. The crowd here is young, as the drinking age is 18. To the east in Providencia, the area around the Manuel Montt Metro station attracts a slightly older and better-heeled crowd.

BARS & CLUBS

El Toro (✉*Loreto 33, Bellavista* ☎*2/737–5937*) is packed every night of the week including Sunday. The tables are spaced close enough that you can eavesdrop on the conversations of the models and other celebrities who frequent the place. For jazz, go to **Perseguidor** (✉*Antonia Lopéz de Bello 0126, Bellavista* ☎*2/777–6763*). At the base of Cerro

Santa Lucía, **Catedral** (⊠*José Miguel de la Barra 407, Parque Forestal* ☎*2/638–4734*) is a smart new bar, popular with the thirties crowd. It serves food but the same building also houses Opera, its upmarket restaurant partner. A secret meeting place during the Pinochet regime, **El Rincón de las Canallas** (⊠*San Diego 379, Santiago Centro* ☎*2/699– 1309*) still requires a password to get in (*Chile libre,* meaning "free Chile"). The walls are painted with political statements such as *Somos todos inocentes* ("We are all innocent"). **Bar Yellow** (⊠*General Flores 47, Providencia* ☎*2/946–5063*) is a newer and more alternative place that has great food as well as drinks. Try the chips, and, if it's on the menu, the Thai soup with shrimp. And the staff really do speak English. Closed Sunday.

SHOPPING

AREAS

Vitacura is, without a doubt, the destination for upscale shopping. Avenida Alonso de Córdova is Santiago's equivalent of 5th Avenue in New York or Rodeo Drive in Los Angeles. "Drive" is the important word here, as nobody strolls from place to place.

Providencia, another of the city's most popular shopping districts, has rows of smaller, less luxurious boutiques. Avenida Providencia slices through the neighborhood, branching off for several blocks into the parallel Avenida 11 de Septiembre. The shops continue east to Avenida El Bosque Norte, after which Avenida Providencia changes its name to Avenida Apoquindo and the neighborhood becomes Las Condes.

SPECIALTY SHOPS

HANDICRAFTS

Fodor's Choice
★ **Artesanías de Chile** (⊠*Av. Bellavista 0357, Bellavista* ☎*2/777–8643* ⊕*www.artesaniasdechile.cl*), a foundation created by the wife of President Ricardo Lagos, is one of the best places to buy local crafts. The work is top quality and you know that the artisans are getting a fair price. The foundation also has shops in the Pueblito Los Dominicos and in the Centro Cultural Palacio La Moneda. The staff at **Pura** (⊠*Av. Isidora Goyenechea 3226, Las Condes* ☎*2/333–3144*) has picked out expertly woven blankets and throws, colorful pottery, and fine leather goods. For everything from masks to mosaics, head to **Manos de Alma** (⊠*General Salvo 114, Providencia* ☎*2/235–3518*).

WINE

El Mundo del Vino (⊠*Av. Isidora Goyenechea 2931, Las Condes* ☎*2/584–1172*) is a world-class store with an international selection, in-store tastings, wine classes, and books for oenophiles. It also has shops in the Alto Las Condes and Parque Arauco shopping malls and in Patio Bellavista. **La Vinoteca** (⊠*Av. Isidora Goyenechea 2966, Las Condes* ☎*2/334–1987*) proudly proclaims that it was Santiago's first fine wineshop. It also has a shop at the airport for last-minute purchases.

VALPARAÍSO & VIÑA DEL MAR

Most people head to the Central Coast for a single reason: the beaches. Yes, some may be drawn by the rough grandeur of the windswept coastline, with its rocky islets inhabited by sea lions and penguins, but those in search of nature generally head south to Chiloé and Patagonia.

The biggest surprise is the charm of Valparaíso, Chile's second-largest city—known locally as Valpo. Valparaíso shares a bay with Viña del Mar but the similarities end there. Valparaíso is a bustling port town with a jumble of colorful cottages nestled in the folds of its many hills. Viña del Mar has lush parks surrounding neoclassical mansions and a long beach lined with luxury high-rises.

4

VALPARAÍSO

10 km (6 mi) south of Viña del Mar via Avenida España, 120 km (75 mi) west of Santiago via Ruta 68.

Valparaíso's dramatic topography—45 *cerros,* or hills, overlooking the ocean—requires the use of winding pathways and wooden *ascensores* (funiculars) to get up many of the grades. The slopes are covered by candy-color houses—there are almost no apartments in the city—most of which have exteriors of corrugated metal peeled from shipping containers decades ago.

Most shops, banks, restaurants, bars, and other businesses cluster along the handful of streets called *El Plan* (the flat area) that are closest to the shoreline. *Porteños* (which means "the residents of the port") live in the surrounding hills in an undulating array of colorful abodes. At the top of any of the dozens of stairways, the *paseos* (promenades) have spectacular views; many are named after prominent Yugoslavian, Basque, and German immigrants. Neighborhoods are named for the hills they cover.

GETTING HERE & AROUND

By car from Santiago, take Ruta 68 west through the coastal mountains and the Casablanca valley, as far as you can go, until the road descends into Valparaíso's Avenida Argentina, on the city's eastern edge. Tur-Bus, Pullman and Condor buses leave several times an hour for Valparaíso and Viña del Mar from Santiago. Walking past all the sights, exploring the museums, and enjoying a meal and drinks makes for a long, full day.

ESSENTIALS

Bus Contacts **Pullman Bus** (☎ *32/221–6663).* **Sol del Pacífico** (☎ *32/221–3776).* **Tur-Bus** (☎ *32/221–2028).* **Valparaíso Bus Depot** (✉ *Av. Pedro Montt 2800* ☎ *32/223–7209).*

Currency Exchange **Banco de Chile** (✉ *Cochrane 785* ☎ *32/356–500).*

Internet **World Next Door** (✉ *Blanco 692* ☎ *32/222–7148).*

Mail & Shipping **DHL** (✉ *Plaza Sotomayor 95* ☎ *32/221–3654).* **Valparaíso Post Office** (✉ *Southeast corner of Plaza Sotomayor).*

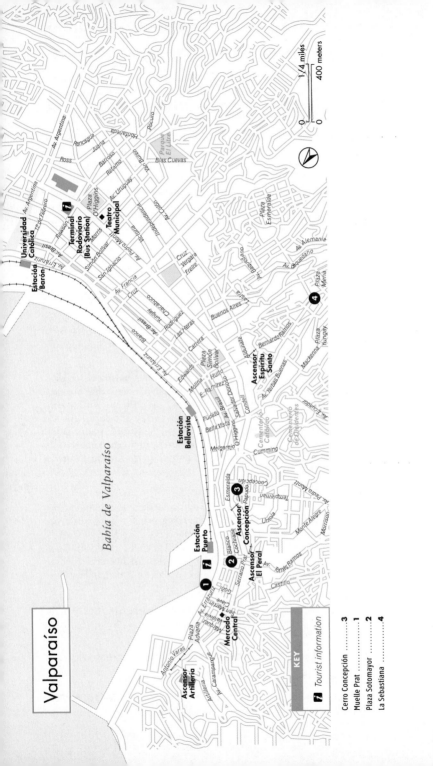

Valparaíso

Bahía de Valparaíso

KEY

i Tourist information

Cerro Concepción **3**
Muelle Prat **1**
Plaza Sotomayor **2**
La Sebastiana **4**

0   1/4 miles
0   400 meters

Medical Assistance **Farmacias Ahumada** (✉ *Pedro Montt No 1881-1895* ☎ *32/221–5524)*.**Hospital Carlos Van Buren** (✉ *San Ignacio 725* ☎ *32/220–4000)*.

Rental Cars **Rosselot** (✉ *Victoria 2675* ☎ *32/352–365)*.

Visitor & Tour Info **Tourism Office** (✉ Condell 1490 ☎ 32/293–9262). Valparaíso Muelle Prat office (✉ *Muelle Prat*

EXPLORING VALPARAÍSO

❸ **Cerro Concepción.** Ride the Ascensor Concepción to this hilltop neighborhood covered with houses and cobblestone streets. The greatest attraction is the view, which is best appreciated from Paseo Gervasoni, a wide promenade to the right when you exit the ascensor, and Paseo Atkinson, one block to the east. Over the balustrades that line those paseos lie amazing vistas of the city and bay. Nearly as fascinating are the narrow streets above them, some of which are quite steep. Continue uphill to Cerro Alegre, which has a bohemian flair. ✉ *Ascensor Concepción, Prat.*

NEED A BREAK?

While exploring Cerro Bellavista, be sure to stop for a coffee at **Gato Tuerto** (✉ *Hector Calvo Jofré 20* ☎ *32/220–867)*, the One-Eye Cat. This meticulously restored 1910 Victorian house, painted eye-popping shades of yellow and blue, affords lovely views. It's also a popular nightspot.

❶ **Muelle Prat.** Though its name translates as Prat Dock, the muelle is actually a wharf with steps leading to the water. Sailors from the ships in the harbor arrive in *lanchas* (small boats), or board them for the trip back to their vessels. It's a great place to watch the activity at the nearby port, and the ships anchored in the harbor. To get a closer look, you can board one of the lanchas—it costs 1,000 pesos for the trip out to a ship and back, or 20,000 pesos for a 60-minute tour of the bay. Here you'll find the tourist information office and a row of souvenir shops. One of the city's best seafood restaurants, Bote Salvavidas, is a few steps away. ✉ *Av. Errázuriz at Plaza Sotomayor.*

❹ **La Sebastiana.** People come to La Sebastiana to marvel at the same ocean ★ that inspired so much of Pablo Neruda's poetry. The house is named for Sebastián Collado, a Spanish architect who began it as a home for himself but died before it was finished. The incomplete building stood abandoned for 10 years before Neruda finished it, revising the design (Neruda had no need for the third-floor aviary or the helicopter landing pad) and adding curvaceous walls, narrow stairways, a tower, and a polymorphous character.

A maze of twisting stairwells leads to an upper room where a video shows Neruda enunciating the five syllables of the city's name over and again as he rides the city's ascensores. His upper berth contains his desk, books, and some original manuscripts. What makes the visit to La Sebastiana memorable, however, is Neruda's nearly obsessive delight in physical objects. The house is a shrine to his many cherished things, such as the beautiful orange-pink bird he brought back embalmed from Venezuela. His lighter spirit is here also, in the carousel horse and the pink-and-yellow barroom stuffed with kitsch. ⊠*Ferrari 692* ☏*32/225–6606* ⊕*www.neruda.cl* ☑*2,500 pesos* ☉*Oct.–Feb., Tues.–Sun. 10:30–7; Mar.–Sept., Tues.–Sun. 10:10–6.*

❷ **Plaza Sotomayor.** Valparaíso's most impressive square, Plaza Sotomayor, serves as a gateway to the bustling port. **Comandancia en Jefe de la Armada,** headquarters of the Chilean navy, is a grand, gray building that rises to a turreted pinnacle over a mansard roof. At the north end of the plaza stands the **Monumento de los Héroes de Iquique,** which honors Arturo Prat and other heroes of the War of the Pacific. In the middle of the square (beware of traffic—cars and buses come suddenly from all directions) is the **Museo del Sitio.** Artifacts from the city's mid-19th-century port, including parts of a dock that once stood on this spot, are displayed in the open under glass. ⊠*Av. Errázuriz at Cochrane.*

WHERE TO EAT

$$–$$$
SEAFOOD
Fodor's Choice
★

✕ **Café Turri.** Near the top of Ascensor Concepción, this 19th-century mansion commands one of the best views of Valparaíso. It also has some of the finest seafood. House specialties such as sea bass or shrimp in almond sauce are alone worth the effort of driving to the coast from Santiago. If you're a seafood lover, splurge on the *jardín de mariscos especial,* which is a huge platter of the catch of the day. Outside there's a terrace and inside are two floors of dining rooms. The old-fashioned service, overseen by the affable owner, is excellent. ⊠*Templeman 147, at Paseo Gervasoni* ☏*32/2252–091, 32/236–5307* ▭*AE, DC, MC, V.*

¢
CHILEAN

✕ **Casino Social J. Cruz M.** This eccentric restaurant is a Valparaíso institution, thanks to its legendary status for inventing the *chorillana* (minced beef with onions, cheese, and an egg atop french fries), which is now served by most local restaurants. There is no menu—choose either a plate of chorillana for two or three, or *carne mechada* (stewed beef), with a side of french fries, rice, or tomato salad. Glass cases choked with dusty trinkets surround tables covered with plastic cloths in the cramped dining room. You may have to share a table. The restaurant is at the end of a bleak corridor off Calle Condell. ⊠*Condell 1466* ☏*32/211–225* ▭*No credit cards.*

¢–$
SEAFOOD

✕ **Donde Carlitos.** A stone's throw from the port are dozens of eateries specializing in whatever was caught that morning. You won't find any fresher fish than at this tiny storefront restaurant near Mercado Central. Through a window on the street you can watch the chefs prying open oysters and rolling razor clams into empanadas. The simple dining room has a half dozen tables under chandeliers shaped like—you guessed it—ships' wheels. ⊠*Blanco 166* ▭*No credit cards* ☉*No dinner.*

$$
ITALIAN
Fodor's Choice
★

✕ **Pasta y Vino.** Everything isn't black and white at this extremely popular restaurant on Cerro Concepción. The innovative food, served in the monochromatic dining room, comes in eye-popping colors. Even the fanciful breads, which seem to swirl out of the basket, are lovely shades of brown. Start with clams on the half shell flavored with ginger and lime, then move on to strawberry gnocchi in a champagne sauce or ravioli filled with duck in a rich port wine reduction. The wine list, focusing on local vintages, is impressive. The hip young staff in floor-length black aprons couldn't be more accommodating. ⊠*Templeman 352* ☎*32/249–6187* ⌖*Reservations essential* ▤*AE, DC, MC, V.*

WHERE TO STAY

$ ▦**Brighton B&B.** This bright-yellow Victorian house enjoys an enviable
Fodor'sChoice   location at the edge of tranquil Cerro Concepción. The house is fur-
★   nished with brass beds and other antiques chosen by owner Nelson Morgado, who taught architecture for two decades at the University of Barcelona. The terrace of its restaurant and three of its six rooms have vertiginous views of the bay. One room has a private balcony that is perfect for a romantic breakfast. Room size varies considerably—only the so-called suite (just a larger room) is spacious—but all are charming. ⊠*Paseo Atkinson 151* ☎*32/222–3513* 📠*32/259–8802* ⊕*www. brighton.cl* ⇨*9 rooms* ⌂*In-room: no a/c, no phone. In-hotel: restaurant, bar, laundry service, no elevator* ▤*AE, DC, MC, V* ⓝ*CP.*

$$–$$$ ▦**Casa Thomas Somerscales.** Perched high atop Cerro Alegre, this palm-
Fodor'sChoice   shaded mansion has an unobstructed view of the sea. As befits an ele-
★   gant home from the 19th century, its rambling hallways and wooden staircases lead to rooms of various shapes and sizes. Ask for Number 8, which has lovely French doors and a private terrace where you can enjoy your breakfast. All rooms at this boutique hotel are impeccably furnished with antique armoires and bureaus and beds piled high with imported linens. Dozens of trendy shops and restaurants are steps away. **Pros:** A chance to imagine life in Valparaíso's Victorian apogee. **Cons:** It's a steep climb back to your room at night. ⊠*San Enrique 446, Cerro Alegre* ☎*32/233–1379* ⊕*www.hotelsomerscales.cl* ⇨*8 rooms* ⌂*In-room: safe, DVD, Internet, Wi-Fi. In-hotel: no elevator* ▤*AE, DC, MC, V* ⓝ*CP.*

$ ▦**Hostal La Colombina.** The location is excellent: on a quiet street just up the hill from the Ascensor Concepción, near Paseo 21 de Mayo in the heart of Cerro Concepción. Dozens of shops and restaurants are on the nearby streets. Rooms in this old house may be sparsely furnished, but they are ample, with high ceilings and wooden floors. Most have big windows, though none of them have much of a view. **Pros:** Good location. **Cons:** A bit austere. ⊠*Concepción 280* ☎*32/223–4980* ⊕*www. lacolombina.cl* ⇨*8 rooms without bath* ⌂*In-room: no a/c, no phone, no TV. In-hotel: bar* ▤*AE, DC, MC, V* ⓝ*CP.*

$–$$$ ▦**Ultramar.** No, you're not seeing spots. Those huge polka dots in the bathroom are part of the whimsical design at Ultramar, the city's first real boutique hotel. The candy-color stripes and bold geometric patterns are like nothing this country has ever seen. They come as a complete surprise, as the hotel is housed in a staid-looking brick building dating from 1907. **Pros:** The café on the first floor hosts occasional art exhibits while terrace boasts eye-popping views of the bay. **Cons:** Just about the only caveat is the location, which is a bit far from the action. ⊠*Tomás Peréz 173, Cerro Cárcel* ☎*32/2210–000* ⊕*www. hotelultramar.cl* ⇨*16 rooms* ⌂ *Cafe, cable TV, in-room safes. No elevator.* ▤*AE, DC, MC, V.*

NIGHTLIFE & THE ARTS

BARS   The huge antique mirrors of **Bar La Playa** (⊠ *Serrano 567* ☎ *32/221–8011*), just west of Plaza Sotomayor, give it a historic feel. It becomes packed with party animals after midnight on weekends in January and February. **Valparaíso Eterno** (⊠ *Almirante Señoret 150* ☎ *32/222–8374*), one block from Plaza Sotomayor, is filled with paintings of Valparaíso and floor-to-ceiling graffiti lovingly supplied by patrons. It opens only on weekends.

LIVE MUSIC   Tango dancing is so popular in Valparaíso that you might think you were in Buenos Aires. On Cerro Concepción, **Brighton** (⊠ *Paseo Atkinson s/n* ☎ *32/222–3513*) has live bolero music on Friday and tango on Saturday, starting at 11 PM. Its black-and-white tile terrace overlooks the city. Dance to live tango music weekends at **Cinzano** (⊠ *Anibal Pinto 1182* ☎ *32/221–3043*), an old-fashioned watering hole facing Plaza Anibal Pinto. Cerro Bellavista's **Gato Tuerto** (⊠ *Hector Calvo Jofré 205* ☎ *32/222–0867*) hosts live Latin music on weekends in a lovely Victorian mansion with a city view.

OUTDOOR ACTIVITIES

BEACHES   If it's beaches you're after, head to Viña del Mar or one of the other resort towns along the coast. Valparaíso has only one notable beach, **Playa Las Torpederas,** a sheltered crescent of sand east of the port. Though less attractive than the beaches up the coast, it does have very calm water. A short bus ride south of the city is **Laguna Verde,** a completely undiscovered stretch of shore that is absolutely gorgeous. There are no eateries, so make sure to pack a picnic.

BOATING   Informal boat operators at **Muelle Prat** take groups on a 60-minute circuit of the bay for 2,000 pesos per person. If you have several people, consider hiring your own boat for 20,000 pesos.

VIÑA DEL MAR

130 km (85 mi) northwest of Santiago.

Viña del Mar has high-rise apartment buildings that tower above its excellent shoreline. Here are wide boulevards lined with palms, lush parks, and mansions. Viña, as it's popularly known, has the country's oldest casino, excellent hotels, and an extensive selection of restaurants. To some, all this means that Viña del Mar is modern and exciting; to others, it means the city is lacking in character. But there's no denying that Viña del Mar has a little of everything—trendy boutiques, beautiful homes, interesting museums, a casino, varied nightlife, and, of course, one of the best beaches in the country.

GETTING HERE & AROUND

From Santiago, take Ruta 68 west through the coastal mountains, turning off to Viña del Mar as the vineyards of the Casablanca valley give way to eucalyptus forests. The spectacular twisting access road (Agua Santa), through hills dotted with Chilean palm trees, drops you on Avenida Alvarez, just a couple of blocks from downtown.

CASABLANCA WINE TASTING

Don't miss the chance to stop at this convenient mid-point for the drive between Santiago and the coast. As you come out of the Zapata tunnel (at kilometer 60 on Ruta 68), vineyards carpet the floor of the Casablanca Valley for as far as the eye can see. Just 30 years ago most winemakers consider this area inhospitable for wine grapes, yet today it is at the forefront of the country's wine industry. Experts have come to recognize the valley's proximity to the sea as its main asset, because cooler temperatures give the grapes more time to develop flavor as they ripen.

Almost all wineries are open to visitors. Choices for activities might include a tour, a tasting, lunch at an on-premises restaurant, or even an overnight stay (all for a price, of course). Although most offer tours on a daily basis, call ahead to ensure someone is available to show you around.

If you want to visit more than one winery, the **Casablanca Valley Wine Producers Association** (⊕ www.casablancavalley.cl ☎ 32/274–3755 or 32/274–3933) runs one-day and two-day visits.

Casas del Bosque, nestled in among rolling vine-covered hills just outside the town of Casablanca, offers a vineyard tour in an old wagon, a tour of the winemaking facilities and a tasting. During March and April, the main harvest months, you can learn even more about the production process with the chance to pick your grapes and take them for selection and pressing. Like many wineries in the valley, Casas del Bosque has its own restaurant, Tanino. ⊠ Hijuela No 2, Casablanca

☎ 2/480–6900 or 32/377–9431 ⊕ www.casasdelbosque.cl.

Viña Matetic, which straddles the border between the Casablanca valley and the adjacent San Anontio valley, may take prize for the region's most stunning bodega. Set into a ridge overlooking vines on both sides, it resembles a futuristic bunker worthy of a James Bond villain, with sloping passageways revealing glimpses into the barrels stored below. A couple of kilometers away, the winery's octagonal restaurant looks out over beautifully manicured gardens, in the middle of which is a recently restored guest house with three elegantly-decorated rooms available to rent. ⊠ Fundo Rosario, Lagunillas Casablanca ☎ 2/583–8660 ⊕ www.mateticvineyards.com.

Chile's vineyard and orchard lands, which are well-protected from many diseases and pests by the Andes mountains, the Pacific Ocean, and the Atacama desert, generally require the use of much fewer pesticides than those in other countries. **Emiliana Orgánico** is a celebration of this fact. Visitors can learn about some innovative organic practices, the most interesting of which is the use of ladybugs and llamas for pest control and fertilization, respectively. Tours can be arranged to include lunch or dinner. ⊠ Ruta 68, km 70, Casablanca ☎ 9/225—5679 ⊕ www.emiliana.cl.

4

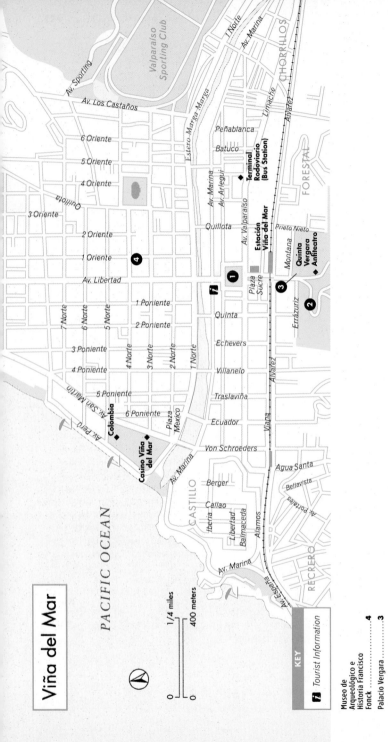

Viña del Mar

PACIFIC OCEAN

Valparaíso Sporting Club

Av. Sporting

Av. Los Castaños

6 Oriente

5 Oriente

4 Oriente

3 Oriente

2 Oriente

1 Oriente

Av. Libertad

1 Poniente

2 Poniente

3 Poniente

4 Poniente

5 Poniente

6 Poniente

7 Norte

6 Norte

5 Norte

4 Norte

3 Norte

2 Norte

1 Norte

Quillota

Plaza México

Av. San Martín

Av. Perú

♦ Colombia

♦ Casino Viña del Mar

Av. Marina

CASTILLO

Berger

Callao

Iberia

Libertad

Balmaceda

Álamos

Av. Marina

Estero-Marga Marga

Peñablanca

Batuco

Av. Marina

Av. Arlegui

♦ Terminal Rodoviario (Bus Station)

Quillota

Av. Valparaíso

Estación Viña del Mar

Plaza Sucre

Quinta

Echevers

Villanelo

Traslaviña

Ecuador

Von Schroeders

Viana

Álvarez

Agua Santa

Bellavista

RECRERO

Av. España

Av. Portales

Limache

Álvarez

CHORRILLOS

T Norte

Av. Marina

FORESTAL

Prieto Nieto

Montana

Quinta Vergara Anfiteatro ♦

Errázuriz

❶

🛈

❹

❸

❷

1/4 miles

400 meters

0

0

ESSENTIALS

Currency Exchange **Banco de Chile** (⊠ *Av. Valparaíso 667* ☎ *32/648–760*).

Internet **OKA Comunicaciones** (⊠ *Av. Valparaíso 242* ☎ *32/713–712*). **286 Rue Valparaíso** (⊠ *Av. Valparaíso 286* ☎ *32/710–140*).

Medical Assistance **Farmacias Ahumada** (⊠ *Av. Valparaíso No. 505* ☎ *32/269–1343*). **Hospital Dr Gustavo Fricke** (⊠ *Av. Alvarez 1532* ☎ *32/265–2200*).

Visitor & Tour Infor **Viña del Mar main office** (⊠ *Av. Libertad at Av. Marina* ☎ *32/269–330*).

Viña del Mar branch office (⊠ *Av. Valparaíso at Villanelo* ☎ *32/683–355*).

EXPLORING VIÑA DEL MAR

4

❹ Museo de Arqueológico e Historia Francisco Fonck. A 500-year-old stone *moai* (a carved stone head) brought from Easter Island guards the entrance to this archaeological museum. The most interesting exhibits are the finds from Easter Island, which indigenous people call Rapa Nui, such as wood tablets displaying ancient hieroglyphics. The museum, named for groundbreaking archaeologist Francisco Fonck—a native of Viña del Mar—also has an extensive library of documents relating to the island. ⊠ *4 Norte 784* ☎ *32/268–6753* ⌦ *1,500 pesos* ⏱ *Tues.–Fri. 10–6, weekends 10–2.*

❸ Palacio Vergara. The neo-Gothic Palacio Vergara, erected after the 1906
★ earthquake as the residence of the wealthy Vergara family, houses the **Museo de Bellas Artes.** Inside is a collection of classical paintings dating from the 15th to the 19th century, including works by Rubens and Tintoretto. A highlight is the intricate parquet floor—you'll be given booties to wear over your shoes so as not to scuff it up. ⊠ *Av. Errázuriz 593* ☎ *32/273–8438 or 32/226–9425* ⌦ *600 pesos* ⏱ *Tues.–Sun. 10–1:30 and 3–5:30.*

❶ Plaza José Francisco Vergara. Viña del Mar's central square, Plaza Vergara is lined with majestic palms. Presiding over the east end of the plaza is the patriarch of coastal accommodations, the venerable Hotel O'Higgins, which has seen better days. Opposite the hotel is the neoclassical Teatro Municipal de Viña del Mar, where you can watch a ballet, theater, or music performance. To the west on Avenida Valparaíso is the city's main shopping strip, a one-lane, seven-block stretch with extra-wide sidewalks and numerous stores and sidewalk cafés. You can hire a horse-drawn carriage to take you from the square past some of the city's stately mansions.

NEED A BREAK?

In search of a great place to watch the sunset? Head to Enjoy Del Mar (⊠ *Av. Perú 100* ☎ *32/500–703*), an ultramodern restaurant right on the beach. Locals eschew the food and come instead for coffee and a view of the sky turning various shades of pink, purple, and green.

❷ Quinta Vergara. Lose yourself on the paths that wind amid soaring eucalyptus trees on the grounds that contain one of Chile's best botanical gardens. An amphitheater here holds an international music festival,

Festival Internacional de la Canción de Viña del Mar, in February.
⊠*Av. Errázuriz 563* ☎*32/477–310* ⊒*Free* ☉*Daily 7–6.*

WHERE TO EAT

$-$$$
STEAK

✕**Armandita.** Meat eaters need not despair in this city of seafood satura-
tion. A rustic restaurant half a block west of Avenida San Martín serves
almost nothing but grilled meat, including various organs. The menu
includes popular dishes such as *lomo a lo pobre* (flank steak served on a
bed of french fries and topped with a fried egg). The *parrillada especial,*
a mixed grill of steak, chicken, ribs, pork, and sausage, serves two or
three people. ⊠*6 Norte 119* ☎*32/268–1607* ⊟*AE, DC, MC, V.*

$$
SEAFOOD
Fodor's Choice
★

✕**Delicias del Mar.** Former television chef Raúl Madinagoitía, who once
had his own program, presides over the kitchen here. The menu lists
such seafood delicacies as Peruvian-style seviche, stuffed sea bass, and
machas *curadas* (steamed clams with dill and melted cheese). Oenophiles are impressed by the extensive, almost exclusively Chilean wine
list. Save room for one of the excellent desserts, maybe crème brûlée,
chocolate mousse, or cheesecake with a raspberry sauce. ⊠*Av. San
Martín 459* ☎*32/290–1837* ⊟*AE, DC, MC, V.*

$-$$$
ITALIAN

✕**San Marcos.** More than five decades after Edoardo Melotti emigrated
here from northern Italy, the restaurant maintains a reputation for first-
class food and service. A modern dining room with abundant foliage
and large windows overlooks busy Avenida San Martín. The menu
includes the traditional gnocchi and cannelloni, as well as *lasagna di
granchio* (crab lasagna) and *pato arrosto* (roast duck). Complement
your meal with a bottle from the extensive wine list. ⊠*Av. San Martín
597* ☎*32/297–5304* ⊟*AE, DC, MC, V.*

WHERE TO STAY

$$$$
Fodor's Choice
★

▦**Hotel Del Mar.** A rounded facade, echoing the shape of the adjacent
Casino Viña del Mar, means that almost every room at this ocean-
front hotel has unmatched views. The exterior is true to the casino's
neoclassical design, but spacious guest rooms are pure 21st century,
with sleek furnishings, original modern art, and sliding glass doors
that open onto balconies. Marble floors, fountains, abundant gardens,
and impeccable service make Hotel Del Mar one of Chile's most luxu-
rious. An eighth-floor spa and infinity pool share the view. A stay here
includes free access to the upscale casino, which evokes Monaco rather
than Las Vegas. **Pros:** The Savinya restaurant was recently named as
Chile's best outside Santiago. **Cons:** The constant chiming of gaming
machines may grate but there are ways to escape. ⊠*Av. San Martín
199* ☎*32/250–0800* ☎*32/250–0801* ⊕*www.enjoy.cl* ⟿*50 rooms,
10 suites* ⌂*In-room: safe. In-hotel: 3 restaurants, bar, pool, spa, con-
cierge, laundry service* ⊟*AE, DC, MC, V* ⦿*BP.*

$$-$$$
★

▦**Hotel Oceanic.** Built on the rocky coast between Viña and Reñaca,
this boutique hotel has luxurious rooms with gorgeous ocean views.
Rooms are cheerful, decorated in bright shades of pink and orange.
The pool area, perched on the rocks below, is occasionally drenched
by big swells. Although there's no beach access, the sands of Salinas
are a short walk away. The restaurant is one of the area's best, serv-
ing French-inspired dishes such as shrimp crepes, *filete café de Paris*

(tenderloin with herb butter), and congrio *oceanic* (conger eel in an artichoke mushroom sauce). **Pros:** Watch the waves on the rock from your hotel terrace. **Cons:** Though the setting is great, it's a long way out of Viña. ✉*Av. Borgoño 12925, north of town* ☎*32/283–0006* 📠*32/283–0390* ⊕*www.hoteloceanic.cl* 🛏*30 rooms, 1 suite* &*In-room: no a/c, safe, dial-up. In-hotel: restaurant, room service, bar, pool, no elevator* ▤*AE, DC, MC, V* ⊚*BP.*

★ 🏨**Sheraton Miramar.** This sophisticated city hotel certainly earns it name, as you can do almost everything here while gazing at the sea. The striking white architecture has quickly made it a landmark in the city, attracting many of the big name stars who perform at the summer music festival. Another highlight is the downstairs Baltus spa, where guests can alternate between a heated pool and one of two outdoor pools, one of which is carved into the rocks and filled by the tide. Fishes and the occasional crab may drift by as you enjoy the view. **Pros:** Difficult to bear comfort with spectacular views. **Cons:** The area around the hotel is blighted by one of Viña's main access roads. ✉*Av. Marina 15* ☎*32/238–8600* 📠*32/283–0390* ⊕*www.sheraton.cl* 🛏*142 rooms, 4 suites* &*In-room: cable TV, safe, Ethernet. In-hotel: 2 restaurants, Wi-Fi, room service, bar, 3 pools* ▤*AE, DC, MC, V* ⊚*BP.*

NIGHTLIFE & THE ARTS

BARS Though it's surrounded by the dance clubs and loud bars of Paseo Cousiño, **Kappi Kua** (✉*Paseo Cousiño 11-A* ☎*32/977–331*) is a good place for a quiet drink. **Margarita** (✉*Av. San Martín 348* ☎*32/972–110*) is a popular watering hole late at night. The namesake cocktail is a killer. **Rituskuan** (✉*Av. Valparaíso at Von Schroeders* ☎*9/305–0340*) is colorful and has excellent beer and electronic music.

CASINO With a neoclassical style that wouldn't be out of place in a classic James Bond movie, **Casino Viña del Mar** (✉*Av. San Martín 199* ☎*32/250–0600*) has a restaurant, bar, and cabaret, as well as roulette, blackjack, and 1,500 slot machines. It's open nightly until the wee hours of the morning most of the year. There's a 3,000-peso cover charge. People dress up to play here, especially in the evening.

SPORTS & THE OUTDOORS

BEACHES Just north of the rock wall along Avenida Peru is a stretch of sand that draws throngs of people December–March. Viña del Mar really has just one **main beach,** bisected near its southern end by an old pier, though its parts have been given separate names: Playa El Sol and Playa Blanca. South of town, on the far side of Cerro Castillo, the small **Playa Caleta Abarca** receives fewer sun worshippers than the main beach. A short drive north of town is the tiny **Las Salinas,** a crescent of sand that has the calmest water in the area.

ISLA NEGRA

6 km (4 mi) south of El Quisco.

"I needed a place to work," Chilean poet and Nobel laureate Pablo Neruda wrote in his memoirs. "I found a stone house facing the ocean, a place nobody knew about, Isla Negra." Neruda, who bought the house in 1939, found much inspiration here. "Isla Negra's wild coastal strip, with its turbulent ocean, was the place to give myself passionately to the writing of my new song," he wrote.

Fodor's Choice

★ A must-see for Pablo Neruda's ardent admirers, **Casa-Museo Isla Negra** is a shrine to his life, work, and many passions. The house, perched on a bluff overlooking the ocean, displays the treasures—from masks and maps to seashells—he collected over the course of his remarkable life. Although he spent much time living and traveling abroad, Neruda made Isla Negra his primary residence later in life. He wrote his memoirs from the upstairs bedroom; the last pages were dictated to his wife here before he departed for the Santiago hospital where he died of cancer. Neruda and his wife are buried in the prow-shaped tomb area behind the house.

Just before Neruda's death in 1973, a military coup put Augusto Pinochet in command of Chile. He closed off Neruda's home and denied all access. Neruda devotees chiseled their tributes into the wooden gates surrounding the property. In 1989 the Neruda Foundation, started by his widow, restored the house and opened it as a museum. Here his collections are displayed as they were while he lived. The living room contains—among numerous other oddities—a number of bowsprits from ships hanging from the ceiling and walls. Neruda called them his "girlfriends."

You can enter the museum only with a guide, but there are excellent English-language tours every half hour. The tour will help you understand Neruda's many obsessions, from the positioning of guests at the dinner table to the east–west alignment of his bed. Objects had a spiritual and symbolic life for the poet, which the tours make evident. ✉ *Camino Vecinal s/n* ☎ *35/461–284* ⊕ *www.neruda.cl* 💰 *3,000 pesos* ⊗ *Tues.–Sun. 10–2, 3–6.*

WHERE TO STAY & EAT

$–$$
SEAFOOD
✕ **El Rincón del Poeta.** Inside the entrance to the Neruda museum, this small restaurant has a wonderful ocean view, with seating both indoors and on a protected terrace. The name translates as Poet's Corner, a theme continued in the small but original menu. Corvina *Neruda* is a sea bass fillet in a mushroom, artichoke, and shrimp cream sauce, and congrio *Garcia Lorca* is conger eel topped with tomato, sausage, and melted cheese. The house specialty is *pastel de centolla* (king crab pie). ✉ *Casa-Museo Isla Negra, Camino Vecinal s/n* ☎ *35/461–774* 🚫 *No credit cards* ⊗ *Closed Mon.*

$–$$
🏨 **La Candela.** Wander along the same rocky shore that Neruda once explored while staying at La Candela. The owner, Chilean folk singer Rosario "Charo" Cofré, was a good friend of the Nerudas—note the photos in the lobby. If there's a crowd, she'll often sing a few songs. Many of the large guest rooms have fireplaces, and about half overlook the sea through the pines. The restaurant serves a vast selection of clams, sea bass, shrimp, and other seafood in numerous sauces. Country-style rooms have pale-wood furnishings and beds piled high with

comforters. **Pros:** Seaside coziness a short walk from Neruda's house. **Cons:** Not somewhere to stay in touch with the rest of the world. ⊠ *De la Hostería 67* ☎ *35/461–254* ⎙ *35/462–531* ⊕ *www.candela.cl* ⇦ *20 rooms* ⟟ *In-room: no a/c, no phone, no TV, Wi-Fi. In-hotel: restaurant, bar, laundry service, no elevator* ⊟ *AE, DC, MC, V* ⎅ *CP.*

EL NORTE CHICO

El Norte Chico's The coastline has some of the best beaches in the country. Offshore there are rocky islands that shelter colonies of penguins and sea lions. Shimmering mountain lakes are home to huge flocks of flamingos. Even the parched earth flourishes twice a decade in a phenomenon called *el desierto florido,* or the flowering desert.

Hidden by the dusty brown hills of El Norte Chico is a sliver of land as lush and green as the Elqui Valley. The people who live along the Río Elqui harvest everything from olives to avocados. The most famous crop is the grapes distilled to make Chile's national drink: pisco. A village named after this lovely elixir, Pisco Elqui, sits high up in the valley.

With unusually clear skies, the Elqui Valley has brought scientists from around the world to peer through the telescopes of the area's many observatories.

LA SERENA

480 km (300 mi) north of Santiago via Ruta 5 (Pan-American Hwy.).

La Serena, Chile's second-oldest city, with several venerable churches and pleasant beaches, got off to a shaky start. Founded by Spanish conquistador Pedro de Valdivia in 1544, La Serena was destroyed by the Diaguitas only four years later. But the Spaniards weren't about to give in, so they rebuilt the city on its original site. Near the mouth of the Río Elqui, La Serena slowly grew until it was visited by British pirate Bartholomew Sharp, who sacked and burned it in a three-day rampage in 1680. Once again the city was rebuilt, and by the time of the silver boom in the late 19th century, it was thriving.

GETTING HERE & AROUND
La Serena is almost exactly 300 mi north of Santiago via the Pan-American Highway. A bus trip will take about six hours from the capital. Daily flights from Santiago take about an hour to reach La Serena's La Florida airport, which is 20 to 30 minutes from downtown via car or taxi.

ESSENTIALS
Air Travel **Aeropuerto La Florida (LSC)** (☎ *51/200–900*). **LAN** (⊠ *Balmaceda 400* ☎ *51/221–551* ⊕ *www.lan.com*).

Bus Contacts **La Serena bus station** (⊠ *Av. El Santo and Amunátegui* ☎ *51/224–573*). **Tur-Bus** (☎ *600/660–6600* ⊕ *www.turbus.cl*).

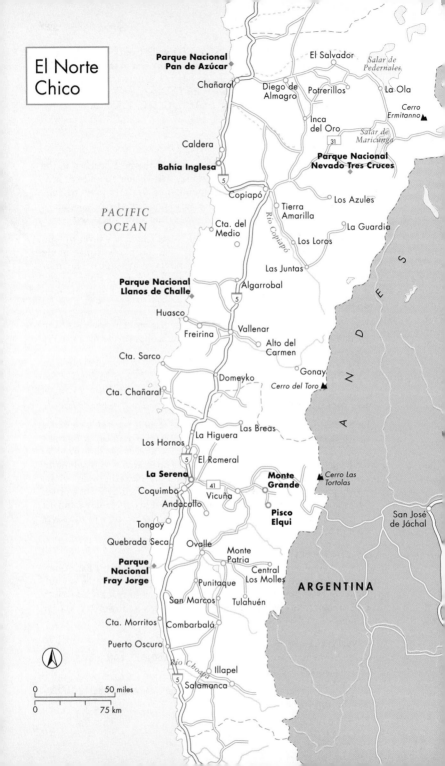

Currency Exchange **Carocol Cambios Herrera Espinosa Ltd.** (⊠*Balmaceda 460, of. 1* ☎*51/229–660*).

Medical Assistance **Hospital Juan de Dios** (⊠*Balmaceda 916* ☎*51/200–560*).

Post Office & Shipping **Correos de Chile** (⊠*Arturo Prat s/n, corner of Matta*). **DHL** (⊠*Arturo Prat 540*).

Rental Cars **Avis** (⊠*Av. Francisco de Aguirre 68* ☎*51/227–171* ⊕*www.avis. com*). **Budget** (⊠*Av. Francisco de Francisco Aguirre 15* ☎*51/218–272* ⊕*www. budget.cl*). **Hertz** (⊠*Av. Francisco de Aguirre 225* ☎*51/226–171* ⊠*La Florida Airport* ☎*51/200–922* ⊕*www.hertz.cl*).

Taxis **Pacifico** (⊠*Los Carreras 572* ☎*51/218–000, 09/614–7298 cell*). **Radio Taxi El Libertador** (⊠*Los Baquedano 2405* ☎*51/252–777 or 51/252–727*).

Visitor & Tour Info **Diaguitas Tour** (⊠*Av. del Mar 3000* ☎*51/214–129*). **Elqui Valley Tour** (⊠*Los Carreras 515* ☎*51/214–846* ⊕*www.elquivalleytour.cl*). **Sernatur, Chilean Tourism Agency** (⊠*Matta 461* ☎*51/225–199*).

EXPLORING LA SERENA

One of the most striking features amid the pleasant streets and hidden plazas of La Serena is the number of churches: there are more than 30, and many of them date as far back as the late 16th century. Most have survived fires, earthquakes, and pirate attacks.

The largest church is the imposing **Iglesia Catedral,** which faces the beautiful Plaza de Armas. French architect Jean de Herbage built this behemoth in 1844, but it wasn't until the turn of the 20th century that the bell tower was added.

Housing many fascinating artifacts—including an impressive collection of Diaguita pottery—the **Museo Arqueológico de La Serena** is a must-see for anyone interested in the history of the region. The Archaeology Museum contains one of the world's best collections of pre-colonial ceramics. Also here is a *moai* (a carved stone head) from Easter Island. The entrance fee allows you entry to the Museo Histórico Gabriel González Videla as well. ⊠*Cordovez at Cienfuegos* ☎*51/224–492* ⊕*www.dibam.cl* ⊠*600 pesos* ⊙*Tues.–Fri. 9:30–5:50, Sat. 10–1 and 4–7, Sun. and holidays 10–1*.

Playa Peñuelas, La Serena's attractive sandy beach, stretches all the way south to the neighboring town of Coquimbo. It's overrun with tourists during high season in summer. **La Herradura,** 2 km (1 mi) south of Coquimbo, has a small but excellent beach. **Playa Totoralillo,** 14 km (9 mi) south of Coquimbo, has beautiful green waters and a white-sand beach.

WHERE TO EAT

$$
STEAK
★
✕**Donde el Guatón.** This European-style steak house, also known as La Casona del Guatón, serves up everything from shish kebab to steak with eggs. With several intimate dining areas off the main salon, this is a great place to enjoy a romantic, candlelit meal. The service, although

friendly, can be overly solicitous. Reservations are recommended. ⊠*Brasil 750* ☎*51/211–519* ☱*AE, DC, MC, V.*

$$ ✕**Restaurant Velamar Beach.** Enjoy a seaside *parrillada* (barbecue) of
SEAFOOD just about any cut of beef imaginable at this longtime favorite. The restaurant literally sits on the sand, so it's a great place to watch the sunset from inside or on the patio. ⊠*Av. del Mar 2300* ☎*51/215–461* ☱*MC, V.*

WHERE TO STAY

$$ 🏨**Hotel Francisco de Aguirre.** Just a block away from the Plaza de Armas, La Serena's most venerable hotel is a rambling, three-story colonial-style building made of wood. Cool off in the pool tucked away in a lush courtyard, or sweat away your worries in the sauna. **Pros:** Newly renovated with top-of-the-line furnishings, central location. **Cons:** A bit impersonal. ⊠*Cordovez 210* ☎*51/222–991* 🖷*51/228–506* ⊕*www.dahoteles.com* ⇋*102 rooms* ⚇*In-room: no a/c, refrigerator. In-hotel: restaurant, room service, bar, pool, laundry service, public Wi-Fi, parking (no fee)* ☱*AE, DC, MC, V* ⦿*BP.*

$$ 🏨**La Serena Club Resort.** A large beachfront hotel in mauve-tinted adobe, this is a good bet for die-hard beachcombers. Yellow-and-blue comforters brighten up the smallish rooms, and upper-story suites have views of the ocean. There is a large pool with a fountain for kids. **Pros:** Near the beach and with a nice pool, too. **Cons:** Rooms are rather small. ⊠*Av. del Mar 1000* ☎*51/221–262* 🖷*51/217–130* ⊕*www.laserenaclubresort.cl* ⇋*49 rooms, 42 suites* ⚇*In-room: no a/c, safe, refrigerator, Wi-Fi. In-hotel: restaurant, bar, tennis court, pool, laundry service, parking (no fee)* ☱*AE, DC, MC, V* ⦿*BP.*

PISCO ELQUI

10 km (6 mi) south of Monte Grande, 43 km (27 mi) east of Vicuña via Ruta D-485.

Once known as La Unión, this pisco-producing village, perched on a sun-drenched hillside, received its current moniker in 1939. Gabriel González Videla, at that time the president of Chile, renamed the village in a shrewd maneuver to ensure that Peru would not gain exclusive rights over the term "pisco." The Peruvian town of Pisco also produces the heady brandy.

GETTING HERE & AROUND

Take Ruta 41 to the turn for Paihuana (Ruta D-485). Follow this serpentine, narrow road about 12 km (7½ mi) into Pisco Elqui. Buses and colectivos run with frequency between La Serena, Vicuña, and Pisco Elqui. A bus or colectivo between Vicuña and Pisco Elqui costs about 1,500 pesos.

ESSENTIALS

Bus Contacts **Solar de Elqui** (☎*51/215–946*). **Valle de Elqui colectivo** (☎*51/411–695 or 51/224–517*). **Via Elqui** (☎*51/312–422*).

STARRY NIGHTS

There are six astronomical observatories in El Norte Chico, and although Vicuña's Mamalluca is the most accessible, you can also visit the others if you make arrangements ahead of time. The Cerro Tololo Observatory (☎ 51/205–200 ⊕ www.ctio.noao.edu), with six telescopes, is in Colina El Pino, 2,200 meters (7,200 feet) above sea level, and can be visited on Saturday by calling ahead. Ten kilometers (6 mi) from Cerro Tololo is the Gemini South Observatory (☎ 51/205–600 ⊕ www.gemini.edu), operated by a consortium of seven nations, which has one of the largest telescopes in the world, an 8.1-meter Cassegrain.

The SOAR Observatory (☎ 51/205–200 ⊕ www.soartelescope.org) features a 4.3-meter telescope; like Cerro Tololo, you can see it by calling ahead.Las Campanas Observatory (☎ 51/207–300 ⊕ www.lco.cl), located at the Observatory of the Carnegie Institute of Washington, 100 km (62 mi) north of La Serena, has twin 6.5-meter Magellan telescopes and can be visited on Saturday by calling in advance. Finally, La Silla Observatory (☎ 56/2463–3280 or 56/2464–4100 ⊕ www.ls.eso.org) in Vitacura, 2½ hours north of La Serena, is administered by the European Southern Observatory, a group of 13 European nations, and can be visited Saturday afternoons from 1:30 to 5 (except July and August) by prior arrangement. La Silla includes the Very Large Telescope (VLT) at Cerro Paranal, which amazingly combines the focal power of four 8.2-meter telescopes into one.

EXPLORING PISCO ELQUI

This idyllic village of fewer than 600 residents has two pisco plants.

★ The **Disteleria Mistral** (☎ 51/451–358 ⊕ www.piscomistral.cl), on the main road, is Chile's oldest distillery. It produces the famous Tres Erres brand, perhaps Chile's finest. In the older section of the plant, maintained strictly for show, you can see the antiquated copper cauldrons and wooden barrels. The distillery arranges daily tours for 4,000 pesos, from 11 AM until 6 PM, followed by tastings where you can sample a pisco sour.

About 4 km (2½ mi) past Pisco Elqui you come upon the **Los Nichos** distillery (☎ 51/411–085), which hosts free daily tours and tastings.

Tiny **Monte Grande,** 6 mi north of Pisco Elqui, recalls a time of simpler pleasures. This picturesque village in the midst of rolling hills is home to both pisco and poetry. On the neighboring hillsides and in the valley below, farmers cultivate the grapes used to make pisco.

Gabriela Mistral, born in nearby Vicuña, grew up in Monte Grande. Her family lived in the schoolhouse where her elder sister taught. The **Casa Escuela** has been turned into a museum and displays some relics from the poet's life. Her tomb is on a nearby hillside. ⊠ Central plaza ☎ 51/451–015 ⬜ 600 pesos ⊙ Tues.–Sun. 10–1 and 3–6.

Chile's National Drink

Distilled from muscat grapes grown in the sunbaked river valleys of El Norte Chico, pisco is indisputably Chile's national drink. This fruity, aromatic brandy is enjoyed here in large quantities—most commonly in a delightful elixir known as a pisco sour, which consists of pisco, lemon juice, and sugar. A few drops of bitters on top is optional. Some bars step it up a notch by adding whipped egg white to give the drink a frothy head. Another concoction made with the brandy is piscola—the choice of many late-night revelers—which is simply pisco mixed with soda. Tea with a shot of pisco is the Chilean answer to the common cold, and it may just do the trick to relieve a headache and stuffy nose. Whichever way you choose to take your pisco, you can expect a pleasant, smooth drink.

WHERE TO STAY

$$ 🏠**Refugio Misterios de Elqui.** These six grass-roof cabanas surround a pleasant pool, where you can relax with a pisco sour and enjoy the delightful sunshine. The views of the mountains from the open-air restaurant are outstanding. **Pros:** Lovely, rustic, and clean. First class all the way. **Cons:** Footpaths a bit steep. ⊠*Arturo Prat s/n* ☎🖩*51/451–126* ⊕*www.misteriosdeelqui.cl* 📞*6 cabanas* △*In-room: no a/c, no phone, no TV. In-hotel: restaurant, bar, pool* ▤*DC, MC, V* ⍾*BP.*

¢–$ 🏠**El Tesoro de Elqui.** Beautiful gardens with flowers of every imagin-
★   able shape and size surround this hotel's nicely decorated cabanas. At the lovely pool you can laze around in the world-famous Elqui Valley sunshine and take in the panoramic view of the Andes. The restaurant, which serves as a meeting place for travelers, has an international menu. The tasty spaghetti Bolognese makes a welcome change from Chilean country cuisine. Ask for one of the rooms with a skylight. **Pros:** Rooms with views of the stars, quiet. **Cons:** Hard to navigate paths at night to reach rooms. ⊠*Arturo Prat s/n* ☎*51/451–069* ⊕*www. tesoro-elqui.cl* 📞*5 rooms* △*In-room: no a/c, no phone, no TV. In-hotel: restaurant, pool* ▤*AE, MC, V* ⍾*BP.*

BAHÍA INGLESA

68 km (42 mi) northwest of Copiapó.

Some of the most beautiful beaches in El Norte Chico can be found at Bahía Inglesa, which was originally known as Puerto del Inglés because of the number of English buccaneers using the port as a hideaway. It's not just the beautiful white sand that sets these beaches apart, however: it's also the turquoise waters, the fresh air, and the fabulous weather. Combine all this with the fact that the town has yet to attract large-scale development and you can see why so many people flock here in summer..

GETTING HERE & AROUND

Follow the Pan-American Highway about one hour north until the small towns of Caldera and Bahía Inglesa come into view: you may smell the salty Pacific before you see the buildings.

WHERE TO STAY & EAT

$
CONTEMPORARY
★

✕ **El Pateao.** With ocean views and the region's best food, this bohemian bistro is a must for anyone staying in the area. The innovative contemporary menu lists such culinary non sequiturs as curry dishes and *tallarines con mariscos* (a pan-Asian noodle concoction served with shellfish and topped with cilantro). On the sand-covered porch you can sit in a comfy chair and watch the sunset. ⊠ *Av. El Morro 756* ☏ *No phone* ▤ *No credit cards.*

$$
Fodor'sChoice
★

🖻 **Hotel Rocas de Bahía.** This sprawling modern hotel, straight from *The Great Gatsby,* has rooms with huge windows facing the sea. You'll also find large beds and Southwestern-style furniture in the rooms. Take a dip in the glistening waters of the bay, or head up to the rooftop pool. **Pros:** Can't beat the views. **Cons:** On same road as main disco in town, which is open until dawn on weekends. ⊠ *Av. El Morro 888* ☏ *52/316–005* 🖷 *52/316–032* ⊕ *www.rocasdebahia.cl* 🛏 *36 rooms* ⌂ *In-room: no a/c, safe. In-hotel: restaurant, room service, pool, bicycles, public Wi-Fi, laundry service* ▤ *AE, DC, MC, V* ⏆ *BP.*

SPORTS & THE OUTDOORS

BEACHES

There are several easily accessible beaches around Bahía Inglesa. **Playa La Piscina** is the town's main beach. The rocky outcroppings and sugary sand are reminiscent of the Mediterranean. **Playa Las Machas,** the town's southernmost beach, is especially relaxing because few tourists have discovered it.

WATER
SPORTS

There are all types of water sports in the area. **Morro Ballena Expediciones** (⊠ *El Morro s/n, on south end of beach* ☏ *No phone*) arranges fishing, kayaking, and scuba-diving trips. The Chilean surfing craze has caught on a bit here, and **Atacama Surf** (☏ *9/484–6769* ⊕ *www.atacamasurf. com*), run by an enterprising Basque transplant, offers bodyboard, kitesurfing, and longboard lessons.

PARQUE NACIONAL PAN DE AZÚCAR

⟳ *100 km (62 mi) north of Caldera.*
★

Some of Chile's most spectacular coastal scenery is in Parque Nacional Pan de Azúcar, a national park that stretches for 40 km (25 mi) along the coast north of the town of Chañaral. Steep cliffs fall into the crashing sea, their ominous presence broken occasionally by whitesand beaches.

Within the park you'll find an incredible variety of flora and fauna. Pelicans can be spotted off the coast, as can sea lions and sea otters, cormorants, and plovers (similar to sandpipers). In the pueblo of Caleta Pan de Azúcar, a tiny fishing village, you can get information from the CONAF-run kiosk (CONAF is the national forestry service, Corporación Nacional Forestal).

Offshore from Caleta Pan de Azúcar is a tiny island that a large colony of Humboldt penguins calls home. You can hire local fisherfolk to bring you here. Negotiate the price, which should be around 7,000 pesos. ✉ *An unpaved road north of cemetery in Chañaral leads to Caleta Pan de Azúcar* ☎ *No phone* ⊕ *www.conaf.cl* 💲 *1,000 pesos* ☉ *Park daily, ranger kiosk daily 8:30–12:30 and 2–6.*

GETTING HERE & AROUND
You can take Route C-120 from Chañaral for 29 km (18 mi) directly into the park, or Route C-110 from Pan-American Highway Km marker 1,410.

WHERE TO STAY
$ 📺 **Hostería Chañaral.** Leaps and bounds above the other places in Chañaral, where you will mostly likely stay the night when visiting the park, the Hostería Chañaral has well-maintained rooms and clean baths with plenty of hot water. A restaurant on the premises serves good seafood. **Pros:** Clean, plenty of hot water. **Cons:** Smallish rooms ✉ *Muller 268* ☎ *52/480–050* 📠 *52/480–554* 🛏 *34 rooms* ⚒ *In-room: no a/c. In-hotel: restaurant, bar, laundry service* ▭ *AE, MC, V* ❮◉❯ *CP.*

EL NORTE GRANDE

A land of rock and earth, terrifying in its austerity and vastness, El Norte Grande is one of the world's most desolate regions. Spanning some 1,930 km (1,200 mi), Chile's Great North stretches from the Río Copiapó to the borders of Peru and Bolivia. Here you will find the Atacama Desert, the driest place on Earth—so dry that in many parts no rain has ever been recorded.

Yet people have inhabited this desolate land since time immemorial, and indeed the heart of El Norte Grande lies not in its geography but in its people. The indigenous Chinchorro people eked out a meager living from the sea more than 8,000 years ago, leaving behind the magnificent Chinchorro mummies, the oldest in the world. High in the Andes, the Atacameño tribes traded livestock with the Tijuanacota and the Inca. Many of these people still cling to their way of life, though much of their culture was lost during the colonial period.

ANTOFAGASTA

565 km (350 mi) north of Copiapó.

Antofagasta is the most important—and the richest—city in El Norte Grande. It was part of Bolivia until 1879, when it was annexed by Chile in the War of the Pacific. The port town became an economic powerhouse during the nitrate boom. With the rapid decline of nitrate production, copper mining stepped in to keep the city's coffers filled.

Many travelers end up spending a night in Antofagasta on their way to the more interesting destinations like San Pedro de Atacama, Iquique, and Arica, but a few sights here are worth a look.

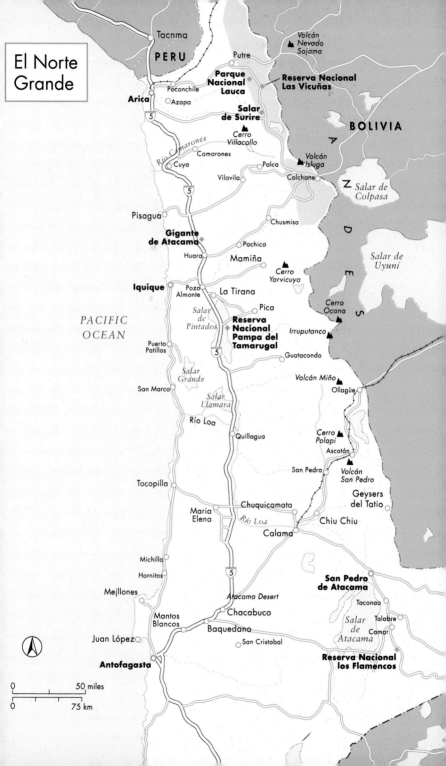

GETTING HERE & AROUND

Antofagasta's airport, 30 minutes from downtown, is a regular stop on Sky Airline's northern run, about a two-hour flight from Santiago. From Caldera in the south, it's a six- to seven-hour ride up the Pan-American Highway by bus or car, but you'll see some of the ocean. The bus terminal on LaTorre is just a short walk from downtown.

ESSENTIALS

Air Travel Aerolineas del Sur/AirComet (☎ 55/452–050 ⊕ www.aircometchile. cl). Cerro Moreno Airport (Antofagasta) (CNF) (☎ 55/269–077). LAN (☎ 55/265–151 ⊕ www.lan.com). Sky Airline (☎ 55/459–090 ⊕ www.skyairline.com).

Bus Contacts Pullman (⊠ LaTorre 2805 ☎ 600/320–3200 ⊕ www.pullman.cl). Tur-Bus (⊠ LaTorre 2751 ☎ 600/660–6600 ⊕ www.turbus.cl).

Currency Exchange Casa de Cambios (⊠ 1818 Sotomayor ☎ 55/312–063).

Medical Assistance Hospital Leonardo Guzman (⊠ Av. Argentina 1962 ☎ 55/204–571 ⊕ www.hospantof.cl).

Post Office & Shipping Correos de Chile (⊠ Washington 2623). DHL (⊠ Arturo Prat 260 ☎ 55/260–209).

Rental Cars Avis (⊠ Av. Baquedano 364 ☎ 55/563–140 ⊕ www.avis.com). Budget (⊠ Av. Pedro Aguirre Cerda 13358 ☎ 55/214–445 ⊕ www.budget.cl). Hertz (⊠ Pedro Aguirre Cerda 15030, Parque Industrial La Portada, Antofagasta ☎ 55/428–042 ⊕ www.hertz.cl).

Visitor & Tour Info Desertica Expediciones (⊠ La Torre 2732 ☎ 55/386–877). Sernatur, Chilean Tourism (⊠ Maipu 240 ☎ 55/264–016).

EXPLORING ANTOFAGASTA

High above Plaza Colón is the **Torre Reloj,** the clock tower whose face is a replica of London's Big Ben. It was erected by British residents in 1910.

The historic customs house, the town's oldest building, dates from 1866. Housed inside is the **Museo Regional de Antofagasta,** which displays clothing and other bric-a-brac from the nitrate era. ⊠ Bolívar 188 ☎ 55/227–016 ⊕ www.dibam.cl/sdm_m_antofagasta/ 🖼 600 pesos ⊙ Tues.–Fri. 9–5, weekends 11–2.

WHERE TO EAT

¢

CHILEAN

✕ **Don Pollo.** This rotisserie restaurant prepares some of the best roasted chicken in Chile—a good thing, because it's the only item on the menu. The thatched-roof terrace is a great place to kick back after a long day of sightseeing. ⊠ Ossa 2594 ☎ No phone ⊟ No credit cards.

$$

SPANISH

★

✕ **Restaurant Arriero.** Serving up traditional dishes from Spain's Basque country, Arriero is the place to go for delicious barbecued meats. A healthy selection of national wines supplements the menu. The restaurant is in a pleasant Pyrenees-style inn decorated with traditional cured hams hanging from the walls. The owners play jazz on the piano almost every evening. ⊠ Condell 2644 ☎ 55/264–371 ⊟ AE, DC, MC, V.

WHERE TO STAY

$$ ⊞**Hotel Antofagasta.** Part of the deluxe Panamericana Hoteles chain,
★ this high-rise on the ocean comes with all the first-class luxuries, from an elegant bar with a grand piano to a lovely kidney-shape pool. The rooms, which have ample bathrooms and plenty of closet space, are comfortably furnished, and some have ocean views. Suites are considerably more expensive ($$$$). A semiprivate beach is just steps from the hotel's back door. **Pros:** Nice beachfront location, top-rate rooms and service. **Cons:** Expensive, a bit sterile. ⊠*Av. Balmaceda 2575* ☎*55/228–811* 📠*55/268–415* ⊕*www.hotelantofagasta.cl* ⇆*145 rooms, 18 suites* ⌂*In-room: safe, refrigerator, Wi-Fi. In-hotel: restaurant, room service, bar, pool, gym, laundry service* ▭*AE, DC, MC, V* ❙○❙*BP.*

$ ⊞**Marsal Hotel.** This modern and clean hotel faces busy Calle Arturo Prat, so be sure to ask for one of the pleasant rooms in the back. All the rooms have nice touches like desks. The service here is quite friendly—the staff goes out of its way to recommend restaurants and arrange excursions. **Pros:** A quick walk from downtown's pedestrian mall, economical. **Cons:** A bit outdated in terms of style and furnishings. ⊠*Arturo Prat 867* ☎*55/268–063* 📠*55/221–733* ⊕*www.marsalhotel.cl* ⇆*18 rooms* ⌂*In-room: no a/c. In-hotel: laundry service, minibar* ▭*AE, DC, MC, V* ❙○❙*CP.*

SAN PEDRO DE ATACAMA

★ *100 km (62 mi) southeast of Calama.*

The most popular tourist destination in El Norte Grande, San Pedro de Atacama sits in the heart of the Atacama Desert and in the midst of some of the most breathtaking scenery in the country. A string of towering volcanoes, some of which are still active, stands watch to the east. To the west is La Cordillera de Sal, a mountain range composed almost entirely of salt. Here you'll find such marvels as the Valle de la Luna (Valley of the Moon) and the Valle de la Muerte (Valley of Death), part of the Reserva Nacional los Flamencos. The number of attractions in the Atacama area does not end there: alpine lakes, steaming geysers, colonial villages, and ancient fortresses all lie within easy reach.

With its narrow streets lined with whitewashed and mud-color adobe houses, San Pedro centers around a small Plaza de Armas teeming with artisans, tour operators, and others who make their living catering to tourists.

GETTING HERE & AROUND

There is direct van shuttle service to San Pedro from the Calama airport, which should be arranged in advance. It's a one-hour-plus drive or bus ride (1,500 pesos) from Calama on Ruta 23. Tur-Bus and a few other companies serve San Pedro. There are myriad tour agencies in San Pedro de Atacama.

SAFETY & PRECAUTIONS

Keep in mind that San Pedro lies at 2,400 meters (7,900 feet). If you're not acclimated to the high altitude, you'll feel tired much sooner than you might expect. Also remember to slather on the sunscreen and drink plenty of water.

ESSENTIALS

There is an emergency clinic in San Pedro on the main plaza, but the nearest proper hospital is in Calama. There are no banks, but on the main plaza there is a Banco de Chile ATM machine across from the regional museum.

Visitor & Tour Info Cosmo Andino Expediciones (⊠ *Caracoles s/n* ☎ *55/851–069*). **Sernatur, Chilean Tourism** (⊠ *Toconao at Gustavo LePaige* ☎ *55/851–420*).

EXPLORING SAN PEDRO DE ATACAMA

The 1744 **Iglesia San Pedro,** to the west of the square, is one of the altiplano's largest churches. It was miraculously constructed without the use of a single nail—the builders used cactus sinews to tie the roof beams and door hinges. ⊠ *Gustavo Le Paige s/n* ☎ *No phone* ⊙ *Daily 9–2 and 3–8.*

Fodor'sChoice The **Museo Arqueológico Gustavo Le Paige** exhibits an awe-inspiring col-
★ lection of artifacts from the region, including fine examples of textiles and ceramics. The museum traces the history of the area from pre-Columbian times through the Spanish colonization. The most impressive exhibit is the well-preserved, fetal-positioned Atacameño mummy with her swatch of twisted black hair. Most of the items on display were gathered by the founder, Jesuit missionary Gustavo Le Paige. ⊠ *Padre Le Paige 380, at Paseo Artesenal* ☎ *55/851–002* ⊕ *www.ucn. cl* ☎ *2,000 pesos* ⊙ *Weekdays 9–noon and 2–6, weekends 10–noon and 2–6.*

NEED A BREAK?
The altiplano sun burns bright and hot in San Pedro, so stop in at Babalu Heladeria (⊠ *Caracoles 160* ☎ *No phone*) to sample one of 52 flavors of ice cream. Stop at Café Cuna (⊠ *Tocopilla 359* ☎ *55/851–999*) for sweet, fresh juices and excellent specials for lunch or dinner. The dining area is in a huge courtyard with chañar trees.

Just 3 km (2 mi) north of San Pedro lies the ancient fortress of **Pukara de Quitor.** This group of stone structures at the entrance to the Valle de Catarpe was built in the 12th century to protect the Atacameños from invading Incas. It wasn't the Incas but the Spanish who were the real threat, however. Spanish conquistador Pedro de Valdivia took the fortress by force in 1540. The crumbling buildings were carefully reconstructed in 1981 by the University of Antofagasta. ⊠ *On road to Valle Catarpe* ☎ *No phone* ☎ *1,200 pesos* ⊙ *Daily 8–8.*

WHERE TO EAT

$$ ✕ **Café Adobe.** With a lattice-covered dining area surrounding a blazing
LATIN fire and a terrace that is open to the stars, Café Adobe is San Pedro's
AMERICAN finest eatery. The regional and international cuisine is excellent, and the
★ animated (at times downright frenetic) waitstaff makes for a unique

dining experience. At night, a white-capped chef grills meat in the center courtyard. Try the perfectly seasoned steaks, the cheesy quesadillas, or any of the pasta dishes. There's an Internet café in the rear. ⊠ *Caracoles 211* ☎ *55/851–132* ▤ *AE, DC, MC, V.*

$ ✕ **Casa Piedra.** This rustic stone structure (*piedra* means "stone") affords
LATIN views of the cloudless desert skies from its central courtyard. As at most
AMERICAN San Pedro eateries, a blazing fire keeps you company. The *congrio* (eel) and salmon are among the best choices on the menu, which includes international and local dishes. Specialty sauces spice up any dinner. ⊠ *Caracoles 225* ☎ *55/851–271* ▤ *AE, DC, MC, V.*

WHERE TO STAY

$$$ 🏨 **Hotel Altiplánico.** This boutique hotel just outside the center of San Pedro has the look and feel of an altiplano pueblo. A river-stone walkway leads you from room to room, each with its own private terrace. Muted whites predominate in the guest chambers, which also have thatched roofs, thick warm comforters, and cool stone-tiled bathrooms featuring nice hot showers. **Pros:** Refreshing pool, friendly service, nice showers. **Cons:** Tricky walk from downtown in the dark—bring a flashlight. ⊠ *Domingo Atienza 282* ☎ *55/851–212* 🖷 *55/851–238* ⊕ *www.altiplanico.cl* ⇆ *29 rooms, 3 apartments* ⌂ *In-room: no a/c, no phone, no TV. In-hotel: restaurant, pool, laundry service, public Wi-Fi, public Internet* ▤ *AE, DC, MC, V* ⊺◎⎮*BP.*

$$$$ 🏨 **Hotel Explora.** Is it a modern monstrosity or an expressionist show-
★ piece? Hotel Explora, built by the same company that constructed the much-lauded Hotel Explora in Parque Nacional Torres del Paine, attracted much criticism for not fitting in with the local architecture. On the other hand, it has also won architectural prizes for its skewed lines and sleek courtyard. The hotel, which has three-, four-, and seven-day all-inclusive stays—with tours, meals, and drinks included—delivers the best service and amenities of any lodging in northern Chile. The wood-and-tile floors and wall-to-wall windows make the views from each room more enjoyable. **Pros:** Top-notch, all-inclusive service. **Cons:** Expensive. ⊠ *Domingo Atienza s/n* ☎ *55/851–110* 🖷 *55/851–115* ⊕ *www.explora.com* ⇆ *52 rooms* ⌂ *In-room: no a/c, safe, Wi-Fi, no TV. In-hotel: restaurant, bar, pools, bicycles, laundry service, public Wi-Fi, airport shuttle, parking (no fee), no-smoking rooms* ▤ *AE, DC, MC, V* ⊺◎⎮*AI.*

$$$ 🏨 **Lodge Andino Terrantai.** An architectural beauty with river-stone walls,
Fodor'sChoice Lodge Andino Terrantai has high-ceilinged rooms highlighted by beau-
★ tiful tile floors and big beds piled with down comforters. Hand-carved furnishings add a rustic feel. Throw open the huge windows to let in the morning breeze. The candlelit restaurant, perfect for a romantic dinner, serves international fare. There's also a tiny, natural-rock plunge pool. The hotel is just a block away from the Plaza de Armas. **Pros:** Beautiful hotel, and great location for walking to the plaza. **Cons:** No room TV. ⊠ *Tocopilla 411* ☎ *55/851–145* 🖷 *55/851–037* ⊕ *www.terrantai.cl* ⇆ *21 rooms* ⌂ *In-room: no TV. In-hotel: restaurant, room service, pool, laundry service, public Wi-Fi* ▤ *AE, DC, MC, V* ⊺◎⎮*BP.*

SPORTS & THE OUTDOORS

BIKING   An afternoon ride to the Valle de la Luna is unforgettable, as is a quick trip to the ruins of Tulor. You can also head to the Salar de Atacama. Bike rentals can be arranged at most hotels and tour agencies. A bike can be rented for a half day for 3,000 pesos and for an entire day for 5,000 pesos.

HIKING   There are hikes in all directions from San Pedro. Good hikes include trips through the Valle de la Muerte, as well as to the ruins of Pukara de Quitor. **Cosmo Andino Expediciones** (⊠ *Caracoles s/n* ☎ *55/851–069*) runs excellent treks with well-informed guides.

HORSEBACK   San Pedro has the feeling of a Wild West town, so why not hitch up your
RIDING   horse and head out on an adventure? Although the sun is quite intense during the middle of the day, sunset is a perfect time to visit Pukara de Quitor or Tulor. An overnight journey to the Salar de Atacama or the Valle de La Luna is a great way to see the region at a relaxed pace. **Herradura** (⊠ *Tocopilla s/n* ☎ *55/851–087* ✍ *laherraduraatacama@ hotmail.com*) provides horses and guides.

SAND   It's like snowboarding, only hotter. Many agencies offer a three-hour
BOARDING   sandboarding excursion into the Valle de la Muerte from 8 AM to 11 AM—the intelligent way to beat the desert heat. These tours run about 12,000 pesos (US$24) and include an instructor. If you're brave and have your own transportation, you can rent just the board for 4,000 pesos (US$8). There is also a combination sandboarding-and-sunset tour for 15,000 pesos which closes the day with a desert sunset over the Valle de la Luna. Contact **Altiplano Aventura** (⊠ *Toconao 441-E* ☎ *55/851–039*) or **Expediciones Corvatch** (⊠ *Tocopilla 406* ☎ *55/851– 087*) for information.

STARGAZING   Chile is known for the visibility of its nighttime skies, due to the exceptionally dry climate. **SPACE** (⊠ *166 Caracoles* ☎ *55/851–935* ⊕ *www. spaceobs.com*) is a small observatory just outside of town with five telescopes and nightly tours operated by a French immigrant to the area.

RESERVA NACIONAL LOS FLAMENCOS

10 km (6 mi) south and east of San Pedro.

Many of the most astounding sights in El Norte Grande lie within the boundaries of the protected Reserva Nacional los Flamencos. This sprawling national reserve to the south and east of San Pedro encompasses a wide variety of geographical features, including alpine lakes, salt flats, and volcanoes.

GETTING HERE & AROUND

Any of the San Pedro tour companies will take you to the Reserva, but if you're in your own vehicle, take the road toward Toconao for 33 km (20½ mi) to the park entrance.

EXPLORING LOS FLAMENCOS

You can get information about the Reserva Nacional los Flamencos at the station run by CONAF, the Chilean forestry service. *⊠CONAF station near Laguna Chaxa ☎No phone ⊕www.conaf.cl ☎2,000 pesos ⊙Daily 8:30–1 and 2:30–6:30.*

★ About 10 km (6 mi) south of San Pedro you arrive at the edge of the **Salar de Atacama,** Chile's largest salt flat. The rugged crust measuring 3,000 square km (1,158 square mi) formed when salty water flowing down from the Andes evaporated in the stifling heat of the desert. Unlike other salt flats, which are smooth surfaces of crystalline salt, the Salar de Atacama is a jumble of jagged rocks. **Laguna Chaxa,** in the middle of Salar de Atacama, is a very salty lagoon that is home to three of the New World's four species of flamingos. The elegant pink-and-white birds are mirrored by the lake's glassy surface. Near Laguna Chaxa, beautiful plates of salt float on the calm surface of **Laguna Salada.**

★ One of the most impressive sights in Reserva Nacional los Flamencos is the 4,350-meter-high (14,270-foot-high) **Laguna Miscanti,** an awe-inspiring blue lake that merits a few hours of relaxed contemplation.

Laguna Miñeques, a smaller lake adjacent to Laguna Miscanti, is spectacular. Here you will find vicuña and huge flocks of flamingos attracted by the warm waters.

★ Very few places in the world can compare to the **Valle de la Luna** (*⊠14 km [9 mi] west of San Pedro*). This surreal landscape of barren ridges, soaring cliffs, and pale valleys could be from a canvas by Salvador Dalí. Originally a small corner of a vast inland sea, the valley rose up with the Andes. The water slowly drained away, leaving deposits of salt and gypsum that were folded by the shifting of the Earth's crust and then worn away by wind and rain. It's best to visit Valle de la Luna in the late afternoon for the incredible sunsets from atop the immense sand dune.

Not far from the Valle de la Luna, just on the other side of Ruta 98 which leads to Calama, are the reddish rocks of the **Valle de la Muerte.** Jesuit missionary Gustavo Le Paige, who in the 1950s was the first archaeologist to explore this desolate area, discovered many human skeletons. These bones are from the indigenous Atacameño people, who lived here before the arrival of the Spanish. He hypothesized that the sick and the elderly may have come to this place to die.

IQUIQUE

390 km (242 mi) northwest of Calama.

Iquique is the capital of Chile's northernmost region, but it wasn't always so important. For hundreds of years it was a tiny fishing community. It was not until the great nitrate boom of the 19th century that Iquique became a major port. Many of the old mansions are badly in need of repair, giving the city a worn-down look.

At the base of a coastal mountain range, Iquique is blessed with year-round good weather. This may explain why it's popular with vacationing Chilean families, who come for the long stretches of white beaches as well as the *zona franca,* or duty-free zone.

GETTING HERE & AROUND

Iquique's Diego Aracena airport (IQQ) is about 45 minutes from downtown proper (35 km [22 mi]; 12,000 pesos in taxi fare) and is served by the three major airlines: Sky, Air Comet, and LAN. Iquique is about seven hours via bus or car from Calama (400 km [249 mi]); once you've turned off the Pan-American Highway it's a narrow, serpentine road down to the town, so don't try passing any of the big trucks or other vehicles that may be slowing you down.

ESSENTIALS

Air Travel **Aerolineas del Sur/AirComet** (☎600/625–0000 ⊕ www.aircomet chile.cl). **Diego Aracena Airport (IQQ)** (☎57/407–000). **LAN** (☎57/427–600 ⊕ www.lan.com). **Sky Airline** (☎57/415–031 ⊕ www.skyairline.com).

Currency Exchange **Agreement Exchange** (⊠ Galeria Lynch 3 y 4).

Medical Assistance **Hospital Dr. E. Torres Galdames** (⊠ Héroes de la Concepción #502 ☎57/395–555 ⊕ www.hospitaliquique.cl).

Post Office & Shipping **Correos de Chile** (⊠ Bolívar 485). **DHL** (⊠ Aníbal Pinto 695, Iquique ☎57/472–820).

Rental Cars **Avis** (⊠ Manuel Rodriguez 730 ☎57/574–330 ⊕ www.avis.com). **Budget** (⊠ Bulnes 542 ☎57/416–322 ⊕ www.budget.cl). **Hertz** (⊠ Aníbal Pinto 1303 ☎57/510–432).

Taxis **Taxi Aeropuerto** (⊠ Baquedano corner of Wilson ☎57/419–004 or 57/415–916).

Visitor & Tour Info **Avitours** (⊠ Baquedano 997 ☎57/429–368 ⊕ www.avitours. cl). **Geotour** (⊠ Baquedano 982 ☎57/428–984 ⊕ www.geotour.cl). **Sernatur, Chilean Tourism** (⊠ Aníbal Pinto 436 ☎57/419–241 ⊕ www.sernatur.cl). **Unita Turismo** (⊠ Baquedano corner of Plaza Prat ☎57/342–300).

EXPLORING IQUIQUE

Life in the city revolves around the **Plaza Prat,** where children ride bicycles along the sidewalks and adults chat on nearly every park bench. The 1877 **Torre Reloj,** with its gleaming white clock tower and Moorish arches, stands in the center of the plaza.

Unlike most cities, Iquique does not have a cathedral on the main plaza. Here instead you'll find the sumptuous **Teatro Municipal,** built in 1890 as an opera house. The lovely statues on the Corinthian-columned facade represent the four seasons. If you're lucky you can catch one of the infrequent plays or musical performances here. ⊠ *Plaza Prat* ☎57/411–292 🎫 *Tickets 1,500–5,000 pesos* ⊗ *Daily 8–7.*

★ For a tantalizing view into the opulence of the nitrate era, visit the Georgian-style **Palacio Astoreca.** This palace, built in 1903, includes such highlights as the likeness of Dionysus, the Greek god of revelry; a giant billiard table; and a beautiful skylight over the central hall. An art- and natural-history museum on the upper level houses modern works by Chilean artists and such artifacts as pottery and textiles. ⊠ *Av. Bernardo O'Higgins 350* ☎*57/425–600* ⊕*www.iqq.cl/palacioastoreca* ☞*Free* ☉ *Tues.–Fri. 10–1 and 4–7, weekends 11–2.*

WHERE TO EAT

$$
SPANISH
Fodor's Choice
★

✕**Casino Español.** This venerable gentleman's club on Plaza Prat has been transformed into a palatial Spanish restaurant, with beautiful Moorish architecture that calls to mind the Alhambra in Granada. The service is good, though rather fussy, and the food is extravagant in the traditional Andalucian style. The paella *Valenciana* is quite good, as is the variety of sauces that accompany the freshly caught fish. Don't miss the *salsa Carolina*, a rich combination of garlic and fresh herbs. Try a side of *pure catalan* (mashed potatoes with bacon, onion, and grilled peppers). ⊠*Plaza Prat 584* ☎*57/423–284* ☝*Reservations essential* ▭*AE, DC, MC, V.*

$$
CONTEMPORARY
★

✕**Taberna Barracuda.** An immensely popular bar and grill, Taberna Barracuda serves everything from tapas to rib-eye steak. The wine list is good, making this an ideal place to sample some of Chile's labels. A general sense of joviality and merriment here harkens back to the decadent days of the nitrate boom. Antiques ranging from brass instruments to time-stained photos decorate the labyrinthine, salitrera-era house. ⊠*Gorostiaga 601* ☎*57/427–969* ☝*Reservations essential* ▭*AE, DC, MC, V* ☉*Closed Sun. mid-June–early Sept.*

WHERE TO STAY

$–$$

⊞**Hotel Arturo Prat.** The only thing this luxury hotel in the heart of Iquique's historic district lacks is access to the ocean. To make up for this, it has a very pleasant rooftop pool area decorated with white umbrellas and navy-blue sails. The rooms are all comfortable and modern, though some look out onto the parking lot. Ask for one of the newer rooms, which are several notches above the rooms in the older section of the hotel. The Arturo faces the central square, and the restaurant, which serves good but somewhat uninspired fare, sits right on Plaza Prat. **Pros:** Central location, friendly staff. **Cons:** A bit cavernous, some rooms nicer than others. ⊠*Anibal Pinto 695* ☎*57/520–000* ☎*57/520–050* ⊕*www.hotelarturoprat.cl* ⇆*81 rooms, 9 suites* ⚬*In-room: no a/c (some), safe (some). In-hotel: restaurant, room service, bar, pool, laundry service* ▭*AE, DC, MC, V* ⦿*BP.*

$
★

⊞**Hotel Atenas.** Housed in a venerable nitrate-era mansion on the beach, Hotel Atenas is truly a taste of the city's history. Antiques and wood furnishings fill most of the rooms. There are more modern rooms in the back, but these are not nearly as charming. The honeymoon suite has a giant tub where you can imagine the nitrate barons bathing in champagne. There's also a pleasant pool in the garden. **Pros:** Near beaches, quaint. **Cons:** Borders on old-fashioned. ⊠*Los Rieles 738* ☎*57/431–100* ☎*57/421–534* ⇆*40 rooms, 3 suites* ⚬*In-room: no a/c, safe. In-hotel: restaurant, room service, pool, laundry service, public Wi-Fi, public Internet* ▭*AE, DC, MC, V* ⦿*CP.*

BEACHES

Just south of the city center on Avenida Balmaceda is **Playa Cavancha,** a long stretch of white, sandy beach that's great for families and often crowded. You can stroll along the boardwalk and touch the llamas and alpacas at the petting zoo. There's also a walk-through aquarium housing a group of *yacares,* small crocodiles that inhabit the rivers of Bolivia, Argentina, and Uruguay. For bars and eateries you'll have to head back to town or the peninsula. If you crave solitude, follow the coast south of Playa Cavancha for about 3 km (2 mi) on Avenida Balmaceda to reach **Playa Brava,** a pretty beach that's often deserted. The currents here are quite strong, so swimming is not recommended. **Playa Blanca,** 13 km (8 mi) south of the city center on Avenida Balmaceda, is a sandy spot that you can often have all to yourself.

EN ROUTE
One of the last nitrate plants in the region, **Humberstone** closed in 1960 after operating for nearly 200 years. Now it's a ghost town where ancient machines creak and groan in the wind. You can wander through the central square and along the streets of the company town, where almost all of the original buildings survive. The theater, with its rows of empty seats, is particularly eerie. ⊠ *45 km (28 mi) east of Iquique on the Pan-American Hwy.* ☎ *57/324–642* ⊠ *1,000 pesos* ☉ *Daily 9–5.*

RESERVA NACIONAL PAMPA DEL TAMARUGAL

96 km (60 mi) southeast of Iquique.

The tamarugo tree is an anomaly in the almost lifeless desert. These bushlike plants survive where most would wither because they are especially adapted to the saline soil of the Atacama. Over time they developed extensive root systems that search for water deep beneath the almost impregnable surface. Reserva Nacional Pampa del Tamarugal has dense groves of tamarugos, which were almost wiped out during the nitrate era when they were felled for firewood. At the entrance to this reserve is a CONAF station. ⊠ *24 km (15 mi) south of Pozo Almonte on Pan-American Hwy.* ☎ *57/751–055* ⊠ *Free.*

Fodor's Choice
★
The amazing **Cerros Pintados** *(Painted Hills),* within the Reserva Nacional Pampa del Tamarugal, are well worth a detour. Here you'll find the largest group of geoglyphs in the world. These figures, which scientists believe ancient peoples used to help them navigate the desert, date from AD 500 to 1400. They are also enormous—some of the figures are decipherable only from the air. Drawings of men wearing ponchos were probably intended to point out the route to the coast to the llama caravans coming from the Andes. More than 400 figures of birds, animals, and geometric patterns adorn this 4-km (2½-mi) stretch of desert. There is a CONAF kiosk on a dirt road 2 km (1 mi) west of the Pan-American Highway. ⊠ *45 km (28 mi) south of Pozo Almonte* ☎ *57/751–055* ⊠ *1,000 pesos* ☉ *Daily 9:30–6.*

GIGANTE DE ATACAMA

84 km (52 mi) northeast of Iquique.

The world's largest geoglyph, the Gigante de Atacama, measures an incredible 86 meters (282 feet). The Atacama Giant, thought to represent a chief of an indigenous people or perhaps created in honor of Pachamama (Mother Earth), looks a bit like a space alien. It is adorned with a walking staff, a cat mask, and a feathered headdress that resembles rays of light bursting from his head. The exact age of the figure is not known, but it certainly hails from before the arrival of the Spanish, perhaps around AD 900. The geoglyph, which is on a hill, is best viewed just before dusk, when the long shadows make the outline clearer. To get here from Iquique, head north on Ruta 5, take Ruta A-483 toward Chusmiza (east), then turn west at Huara and travel for 14 km (8 mi). ⊠*Cerro Unita, 14 km (8 mi) west of turnoff to Chusmiza* ☎*No phone* ☎*Free.*

4

ARICA

301 km (187 mi) north of Iquique.

Arica boasts that it is "the land of the eternal spring," but its temperate climate and beaches are not the only reason to visit this small city. Relax for an hour or two on the Plaza 21 de Mayo. Walk to the pier and watch the pelicans and sea lions trail the fishing boats as the afternoon's catch comes in, or walk to the top of the Morro and imagine battles of days gone by.

Arica is gaining notice for its great surfing conditions, and in 2007 hosted the Rip Curl Pro Search as part of an international competition sponsored by beer giant Foster's. A shop on the main pedestrian mall, **Huntington Surf Shop** (⊠*21 de Mayo 493*) caters to those brought into town by the waves. Arica also has a surfing school, **Escuela de Surf** (☎*58/310–524 or 9/282–5175*).

GETTING HERE & AROUND

Arica is a true international crossroads: planes arrive daily from Santiago (Sky, LAN, Air Comet), buses pull in from La Paz, and colectivos laden with four passengers head in both directions for Tacna and the Peruvian border. The airport is about 15 minutes north of town (a taxi fare is about 5,000 pesos). The bus terminal is a quick five-minute taxi ride to downtown. Arica is about four or five hours north of Iquique by auto or bus (300 km [187 mi]).

ESSENTIALS

Air Travel **Arica Chacalluta Airport (ARI)** (☎*58/211–116*). **LAN** (☎*58/251–641* ⊕*www.lan.com*). **Sky Airline** (☎*58/251–816* ⊕*www.skyairline.com*).

Currency Exchange **Banco Santander** (⊠*21 de Mayo 359* ☎*600/320–3000*).

Hospital **Centro Clinico Militar Arica** (⊠*S. Velasquez 1700* ☎*58/232–478*).

Post Office & Shipping **Correos de Chile** (✉ *Arturo Prat 305*). **DHL** (✉ *Colón 351* ☎ *58/256–753*).

Rental Cars **Budget** (✉ *Colón 996* ☎ *58/258–911* ⊕ *www.budget.cl*). **Avis** (✉ *Gillermo Sanchez 660* ☎ *58/584–821* ⊕ *www.avis.com*). **Hertz** (✉ *Baquedano 999* ☎ *58/231–487* ⊕ *www.hertz.cl*).

Taxis **Taxi Tarapaca** (☎ *58/221–000 or 58/424–000*).

Visitor & Tour Info **Geotour** (✉ *Bolognesi 421* ☎ *58/253–927* ⊕ *www.geo tour.cl*).**Raices Andinas** (✉ *Paseo Thompson, Feria 3 Esquinas* ☎ *58/233–305* ⊕ *www.raicesandinas.com*). **Sernatur, Chilean Tourism** (✉ *San Marcos 101* ☎ *58/252–054*).

EXPLORING ARICA

On Plaza Colón is the **Iglesia de San Marcos,** constructed entirely from iron. Alexandre Gustave Eiffel, designer of that famed eponymous Parisian tower, had the individual pieces cast in France before erecting them in Arica in 1876.

Hanging over the town, the fortress of **El Morro de Arica** is impossible to ignore. This former Peruvian stronghold was the site of one of the key battles in the War of the Pacific. The fortress now houses the **Museo de las Armas,** which commemorates that battle. As you listen to the proud drumroll of military marches you can wander among the uniforms and weapons of past wars. ✉ *Reached by footpath from Calle Colón* ☎ *58/254–091* 🎫 *600 pesos* ⊙ *Daily 8–8.*

Fodor$Choice ★
A newcomer to the museum scene is Arica's **Museo del Mar,** a well-maintained and colorful collection of more than 1,000 seashells and oceanic oddities from around the world. The owner has traveled the globe for more than 30 years to bolster his collection, which includes specimens from Africa, Asia, and you guessed it—Arica. ✉ *Sangra 315* ⊕ *www. museodelmardearica.cl* 🎫 *1,000 pesos* ⊙ *Mon.–Sat. 10–2 and 4–8.*

Fodor$Choice ★
A must for any visitor to El Norte Grande is the **Museo Arqueológico de San Miguel de Azapa.** In an 18th-century olive-oil refinery, this museum houses an impressive collection of artifacts from the cultures of the Chinchorros (a coastal people) and Tijuanacotas (a group that lived in the antiplano). Of particular interest are the Chinchorro mummies, the oldest in the world, dating to 6000 BC. The incredibly well–preserved mummies are arranged in the fetal position, which was traditional in this area. To look into their wrinkled, expressive faces is to get a glimpse at a history that spans more than 8,000 years. The tour ends at an olive press that functioned until 1956, a reminder of the still-thriving industry in the surrounding valley. The museum is a short drive from Arica. You can also make the 20-minute journey by colectivo from Patricio Lynch for about 600 pesos. ✉ *12 km (7 mi) south of town on route to Putre* ☎ *58/205–551* ⊕ *www.uta.cl/masma* 🎫 *1,000 pesos* ⊙ *Jan. and Feb., daily 10–6; Mar.–Dec., daily 9–8.*

WHERE TO EAT

$ ✗**Club de Deportes Náuticos.** This old yacht club with views of the port
SEAFOOD serves succulent seafood dishes in a relaxed terrace setting. One of the
friendliest restaurants in town, this former men's club is a great place
to meet the old salts of the area. Bring your fish stories. ⊠*Thompson
1* ☎*58/254–738* ⊟*MC, V.*

$$ ✗**Maracuyá.** Wicker furniture enhances the cool South Pacific atmo-
SEAFOOD sphere of this pleasant, open-air restaurant that literally sits above the
water on stilts. The international menu focuses on fish. The seafood,
lauded by locals, is always fresh; ask the waiter what the fishing boats
brought in that day. House specialties include octopus grilled in lemon
and olive oil, salmon in an orange sauce, and sea bass in the pine-
apple-flavored *salsa amazonia.* ⊠*Av. Comandante San Martin 0321*
☎*58/227–600* ⊟*AE, DC, MC, V.*

$ ✗**El Rey de Mariscos.** Locals call this the best seafood restaurant in
SEAFOOD town, for good reason. The *corvina con salsa margarita* (sea bass in
a seafood-based sauce) is a winner, as is the *paila marina,* a hearty
soup stocked with all manner of fish. The dreary fluorescent lights and
faux-wood paneling give this restaurant on the second story of a con-
crete-block building an undeserved down-at-the-heels air. ⊠*Colon 565*
☎*58/229–232* ⊟*AE, DC, MC, V.*

WHERE TO STAY

$$–$$$ 🏨**Hotel Arica.** The finest hotel in Arica, this first-class establishment
★ sits on the ocean between Playa El Laucho and Playa Las Liseras. The
rooms, which are elegant if a bit dated, have views of the ocean and
great showers with plenty of hot water. The courteous and attentive
staff can help set up sightseeing tours or book a table at a local eatery.
The hotel's tony restaurant ($), which takes advantage of the ocean
views, serves fresh seafood cooked to order, including crab, octopus,
and tuna. Don't pass up the conger eel chowder. **Pros:** Beautiful setting,
nice restaurant. **Cons:** Somewhat dated, far from downtown. ⊠*Av.
Comandante San Martin 599* ☎*58/254–540* 🖷*58/231–133* ⊕*www.
panamericanahoteles.cl* ⬎*108 rooms, 13 suites, 20 cabanas* ⌂*In-
room: safe. In-hotel: restaurant, room service, tennis court, pool, gym,
children's programs (ages 2–10, summer only), laundry service, refrig-
erator* ⊟*AE, DC, MC, V* ⍣*BP.*

$–$$ 🏨**Hotel El Paso.** This modern lodging in the center of Arica surrounds
a landscaped courtyard and a pool with a swim-up bar. Though not on
the ocean, it's a short walk from any of the city's beaches. The superior
rooms, with newer furnishings and larger televisions, are a far better
value than the standard ones. **Pros:** Modern, close to beach. **Cons:**
Somewhat sterile. ⊠*Av. General Velasquez* ☎*58/230–808* 🖷*58/231–
965* ⊕*www.hotelelpaso.cl* ⬎*71 rooms, 10 suites* ⌂*In-room: no a/c,
safe. In-hotel: restaurant, bar, tennis court, pool, laundry service, parking (no fee), public Internet, refrigerator* ⊟*AE, DC, MC, V* ⍣*BP.*

$ 🏨**Hotel Saint Gregory.** Although it's quite a hike from Arica's city center,
this pleasant oceanfront hotel is great for weary travelers who simply
want to relax on the beach. Some of the rooms and common areas have
dated decor, but the hotel is still a good value. Many rooms have their
own hot tubs. **Pros:** Romantic setting. **Cons:** Far from anything. ⊠*Av.*

Comandante San Martin 1020 🏬58/233–320 ⊕*www.hotelsaint gregory.cl* ⬅*28 rooms, 8 suites* ♿*In-room: kitchen (some). In-hotel: restaurant, bar, pool, airport shuttle, parking (no fee), public Internet* ▭*AE, DC, MC, V* ⦿|*CP.*

NIGHTLIFE

You can join the locals for a beer at one of the cafés lining the pedestrian mall of 21 de Mayo. These low-key establishments, many with outdoor seating, are a great place to spend an afternoon watching the passing crowds. An oddity in Arica is the attire of the servers in various tranquil cafés and tea salons (usually called "café con piernas" or "cafés with legs"): women serve coffee and tea dressed in lingerie.

BEACHES

Part of the reason people flock to Arica is the beaches. The surf can be quite rough in some spots, so look for—and heed—signs that say NO APTA PARA BAÑARSE ("no swimming"). South of El Morro, **Playa El Laucho** is the closest to the city, and thus the most crowded. It's also a bit rocky at the bottom. South of Playa El Laucho you'll find **Playa Brava**, with a pontoon that keeps the kids occupied. At the somewhat secluded white-sand **Playa Chinchorro**, 2 km (1 mi) north of the city, you can rent Jet Skis in high season.

PARQUE NACIONAL LAUCA

★ *47 km (29 mi) southeast of Putre.*

On a plateau more than 4,000 meters (13,120 feet) above sea level, the magnificent Parque Nacional Lauca shelters flora and fauna found in few other places in the world. Cacti, grasses, and a brilliant emerald-green moss called *llareta* dot the landscape. Playful vizcacha—rabbitlike rodents with long tails—laze in the sun, and llamas, graceful vicuñas, and alpacas make their home here as well. About 10 km (6 mi) into the park is a CONAF station with informative brochures. ⊠*Off Ruta 11* 🕾*58/250–570 in Arica* ⊕*www.conaf.cl* ▱*Free.*

Within the park, off Ruta 11, is the altiplano village of **Parinacota,** one of the most beautiful in all of Chile. In the center of the village sits the whitewashed **Iglesia Parinacota**, dating from 1789. Inside are murals depicting sinners and saints and a mysterious "walking table," which parishioners have chained to the wall for fear that it will steal away in the night. An interesting Aymara cultural commentary can be found in the Stations of the Cross, which depict Christ's tormenters not as Roman soldiers, but as Spanish conquistadors. Opposite the church you'll find crafts stalls run by Aymara women in the colorful shawls and bowler hats worn by many altiplano women. Only 18 people live in the village, but many more make a pilgrimage here for annual festivals such as the Fiesta de las Cruces, held on May 3, and the Fiesta de la Virgen de la Canderlaria, a three-day romp that begins on February 2.

About 8 km (5 mi) east of Parinacota are the beautiful **Lagunas Cotacotani,** which means "land of many lakes" in the Quechua language. This string of ponds—surrounded by a desolate moonscape formed by volcanic eruptions—attracts many species of bird, including Andean geese.

Lago Chungará sits on the Bolivian border at an amazing altitude of 4,600 meters (15,100 feet) above sea level. Volcán Parinacota, at 6,330 meters (20,889 feet), casts its shadow onto the lake's glassy surface. Hundreds of flamingos make their home here. There is a CONAF-run office at Lago Chungará on the highway just before the lake. ⊠ *From Ruta 11, turn north on Ruta A-123* ☎*No phone* ⊕*www.conaf.cl* ✉*Free* ☉*CONAF office daily 8–8.*

THE LAKE DISTRICT

4

The Lake District's altitude descends sharply from the towering peaks of the Andes on the Argentine border, to forests and plains, and finally to sea level, all in the space of about 200 km (120 mi). Throughout the region, big volcanoes burst into view alongside the many large lakes and winding rivers. Architecture and gastronomy here are unlike anywhere else in Chile, much of it heavily influenced by the large-scale German colonization of the 1850s and '60s. The Pan-American Highway (Ruta 5) runs straight down the middle, making travel to most places in the region relatively easy.

The Lake District is the historic homeland of Chile's indigenous Mapuche people, who revolted against the early Spanish colonists in 1598, driving them out of the region. After a treaty ended the last Mapuche war in 1881, Santiago recruited waves of German, Austrian, and Swiss immigrants to settle the so-called "empty territory" and offset indigenous domination. The Lake District took on the Bavarian-Tyrolean sheen still evident today.

TEMUCO

675 km (405 mi) south of Santiago on the Pan-American Hwy., Ruta 5.

This northern gateway to the Lake District acquired a bit of pop-culture cachet as the setting for a segment in 2004's *The Motorcycle Diaries,* a film depicting Che Guevara's prerevolutionary travels through South America in the early 1950s. But with its office towers and shopping malls, today's Temuco would hardly be recognizable to Guevara. It's also an odd juxtaposition of modern architecture and indigenous markets, of traditionally clad Mapuche women darting across the street and business executives talking on cell phones, but, oddly enough, it all works.

GETTING HERE & AROUND

At least a dozen bus lines serve Temuco; it's an obligatory stop on the long haul between Santiago and Puerto Montt. The city also hosts Manquehue airport, 6 km (4 mi) southwest of town, which has daily connections to Santiago and other Chilean cities.

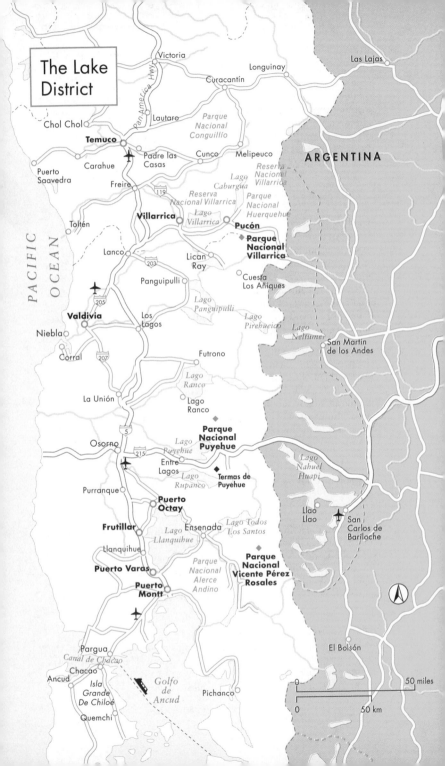

ESSENTIALS

Bus Contacts Buses JAC (⊠ *Corner of Balmaceda and Aldunate* ☎ *45/465–500*). **Cruz del Sur** (⊠ *Terminal de Buses, Av. Vicente Pérez Rosales 1609* ☎ *45/730–310*). **Temuco** (⊠ *Av. Rudecindo Ortega* ☎ *45/257–904*). **Tur-Bus** (⊠ *Lagos 538* ☎ *45/278–161*).

Currency Exchange Germaniatour (⊠ *Manuel Montt 942, Local 5* ☎ *45/958–080*).

Internet Net & Cofee (⊠ *Portales 873* ☎ *45/940–001*).

Medical Assistance Farmacias Ahumada (⊠ *Av. Alemania 505* ☎ *45/246–992*). **Hospital de Temuco** (⊠ *Manuel Montt 115* ☎ *45/212–525*).

Post Office Correos de Chile (⊠ *Av. Diego Portales 801*).

Rental Cars Avis (⊠ *Vicuña Mackenna 448* ☎ *45/237–575*). **Budget** (⊠ *Vicuña Mackenna 399* ☎ *45/232–715*). **Hertz** (⊠ *Las Heras 999* ☎ *45/318–585*).

Visitor & Tour Info Sernatur (⊠ *Claro Solar and Bulnes* ☎ *45/312–857*). **Temuco Tourist Office** (⊠ *Mercado Municipal* ☎ *45/203–345*).

EXPLORING TEMUCO

★ Author Pablo Neruda was Chile's most famous train buff. (Neruda spent his childhood in Temuco and his father was a rail worker.) Accordingly, the city has transformed its old rail yard into the **Museo Nacional Ferroviario Pablo Neruda,** a well-laid-out museum documenting Chile's rail history and dedicated to the author's memory. Thirteen locomotives (one diesel and 12 steam) and nine train carriages are housed in the round engine building. Scattered among the exhibits are snippets from Neruda's writings: "Trains were dreaming in the station, defenseless, sleeping, without locomotives," reads one wistful reflection. Exhibits are labeled in Spanish, but an English-speaking guide is on hand if you need translation. The museum lies a bit off the beaten path, but if trains fascinate you, as they did Neruda, it's worth the short taxi ride from downtown. Twice-monthly tourist rail excursions to Valdivia, using the museum's restored 1940 steam locomotive, are worth an afternoon of your time. ⊠ *Av. Barros Arana 565* ☎ *45/973–940* 💲 *1,000 pesos* ☉ *Tues.–Sun. 9–6.*

The imposing **Monumento Natural Cerro Ñielol** is the hillside site where the 1881 treaty between the Mapuche and the Chilean army was signed, allowing for the city of Temuco to be established. Trails bloom with bright red *copihues* (a bell-like flower with lush green foliage), Chile's national flower, in autumn (March–May). The monument, not far from downtown, is part of Chile's national park system. ⊠ *Av. Arturo Prat, 5 blocks north of Plaza Teodoro Schmidt* 💲 *1,000 pesos* ☉ *Jan.–Mar., daily 8 AM–11 PM; Apr.–Nov., daily 8:30–12:30 and 2:30–6.*

The small **Museo de Chol Chol** in Temuco exhibits a collection of animal-shape ceramics and textiles with bold rhomboid and zigzag designs—both are distinctively Mapuche specialties—as well as old black-and-white photographs. A *fogón,* the traditional cooking pit, graces the center of the museum. ⊠ *Balmaceda s/n* ☎ *45/613–350* 💲 *300 pesos* ☉ *Tues.–Sun. 9–6.*

WHERE TO EAT

$$ ✕ **El Fogón.** Decorated with primary colors—yellow walls, red table-
STEAK cloths, and blue dishes—this place certainly stands out in pastel-hue
Temuco. The Chilean-style *parrillada*, or grilled beef, is the specialty
of the house. Barbecue here has subtler spices than its better-known
Argentine counterpart. The friendly owners will gladly take the time
to explain the menu to the uninitiated. Even though it's close to down-
town, you should splurge on a cab if you're coming to this dark street
at night. ✉*Aldunate 288* ☎*45/737–061* ▭*No credit cards.*

$ ✕ **Mercado Municipal.** In the central market around the produce stalls are
CHILEAN small stands offering such typical Chilean meals as cazuela and pastel
de choclo. Many have actually taken on the trappings of sit-down res-
taurants, and a few even have air-conditioning. The complex closes at
8 in summer and 6 the rest of the year, so late-night dining is not an
option. ✉*Manuel Rodríguez 960* ☎*No phone* ▭*No credit cards.*

$$$ ✕ **La Pampa.** Wealthy local professionals frequent this upscale modern
STEAK steak house for its huge, delicious cuts of beef and the best *papas fritas*
(french fries) in Temuco. Although most Chilean restaurants douse any
kind of meat with a creamy sauce, this is one of the few exceptions:
the entrées are served without anything but the simplest of seasonings.
✉*Caupolicán 0155* ☎*45/329–999* 🍴*Reservations essential* ▭*AE,
DC, MC, V* ☺*No dinner Sun.*

WHERE TO STAY

$ 🏨 **Hotel Continental.** If you appreciate faded elegance and don't mind an
★ uneven floorboard or two, some peeling paint, and few conveniences,
the 1890 Continental is for you. Checkered in black-and-white tiles,
the lobby has leather furniture, antique bronze lamps, and handsome
alerce and *raulí* (native wood) trims. Rooms, painted in ash-blue and
cream tones, have hardwood floors and lofty ceilings. The hotel has
hosted Nobel laureates Pablo Neruda and Gabriela Mistral, and for-
mer president Salvador Allende. The restaurant ($$) serves delicious
French cuisine. Good choices include the steak au poivre and the sal-
ade niçoise. **Pros:** A hotel with character, good location, great food.
Cons: Rooms feel cold and damp, old furniture. ✉*Antonio Varas 708*
☎*45/238–973* 🖶*45/233–830* ⊕*www.turismochile.cl/continental/*
💤*40 rooms, 20 with bath* ♿*In-room: no a/c, no TV (some). In-hotel:
restaurant, bar, no elevator, parking* ▭*AE, DC, MC, V* ℻*CP.*

$$ 🏨 **Hotel Frontera.** This lovely old hotel is really two in one, with *nuevo*
(new) and *clásico* (classic) wings facing each other across Avenida
Bulnes. Tastefully decorated rooms have double-pane windows to keep
out the street noise. Opt for the less expensive rooms in the newer
wing—they're nicer anyway. La Taberna, the downstairs restaurant
on the clásico side ($$), has excellent steak and seafood dining. An
orchestra plays and people dance on weekends. **Pros:** Centrally located,
good restaurant, nice rooms: **Cons:** No Wi-Fi in rooms. ✉*Av. Bulnes
733–726* ☎*45/200–400* 🖶*45/200–401* ⊕*www.hotelfrontera.cl* 💤*90
rooms, 10 suites* ♿*In-room: no a/c, Ethernet (some), refrigerator, safe
(some). In-hotel: restaurant, room service, bar, laundry service, refriger-
ator, executive floor, public Wi-Fi, parking* ▭*AE, DC, MC, V* ℻*BP.*

SPORTS & THE OUTDOORS

CONAF (⊠*Bilbao 931* ☎*45/298–100*) administers Chile's national parks and provides maps and other information about them. In summer it also organizes hikes in Parque Nacional Conguillío. The agency is strict about permits to ascend the nearby volcanoes, so expect to show evidence of your climbing ability and experience.

VILLARRICA

87 km (52 mi) southeast of Temuco via the Pan-American Hwy. and a paved road southeast from Freire.

Today this pleasant town of about 40,000 people, situated on the lake of the same name, is in one of the loveliest, least-spoiled areas of the southern Andes, and has stunning views of the Villarrica and Llaima volcanoes. To Villarrica's eternal chagrin, it lives in the shadow of Pucón, a flashier neighbor several miles down the road. Villarrica has some wonderful hotels that won't give you a case of high-season sticker shock. Well-maintained roads and convenient public transportation make the town a good base for exploring the area.

GETTING HERE & AROUND

Located southeast of Temuco, Villarrica can be reached by a paved, two-lane road, from the town of Freire, or farther to the south, from Loncoche. Several bus lines serve the town. For about 2,000 pesos, buses leave every hour from the Temuco bus terminal and arrive in Villarrica about one hour later.

ESSENTIALS

Bus Contacts **Buses JAC** (⊠*Bilbao 610* ☎*45/467–777*).

Currency Exchange **Christopher Exchange** (⊠*Pedro Valdivia 1033*). **Turcamb** (⊠*Camilo Henriquez 576*).

Internet **Central de Llamadas** (⊠*Camilo Henriquez 567* ☎*45/413–640*).

Medical Assistance **Hospital** (⊠*San Martin 460* ☎*45/411–169*).

Rental Cars **Hertz** (⊠*Picarte 640* ☎*45/218–316*). **Renta Car Castillo** (⊠*Anfion Munoz 415* ☎*45/411–618*).

Visitor & Tour Info **Villarrica Tourist Office** (⊠*Pedro de Valdivia 1070* ☎*45/206–618*).

EXPLORING VILLARRICA

Feria Mapuche is a fine market featuring some of the best local artisans that make Mapuche handicrafts. You'll find all kinds of items, from sweaters and ponchos to wooden figurines. ⊠*Corner of Pedro de Valdivia with Julio Zebers.* ☉*Jan. and Feb., daily 9–noon.*

The municipal museum, **Museo Histórico y Arqueológico de Villarrica**, displays an impressive collection of Mapuche ceramics, masks, leather, and jewelry. A replica of a ruca graces the front yard. It's made of thatch so tightly entwined that it's impermeable to rain. ⊠*Pedro de*

Valdivia 1050 ☎*45/415–706* 💲*200 pesos* ◐*Jan. and Feb., Mon.–Sat. 9–1 and 6–10; Mar.–Dec., Mon.–Sat. 9–1 and 3–7:30.*

WHERE TO EAT

$$
CAFE

✕**Café 2001.** For a filling sandwich, a homemade küchen, and an espresso or cappuccino brewed from freshly ground beans, this is the place to stop in Villarrica. Pull up around a table in front or slip into one of the quieter booths by the fireplace in the back. The *lomito completo* sandwich—with a slice of pork, avocado, sauerkraut, tomato, and mayonnaise—is one of the best in the south. ✉*Camillo Henríquez 379* ☎*45/411–470* ▭*AE, DC, MC, V.*

$$
ECLECTIC

✕**La Cava de Roble.** This is a great, elegant grill with exotic and traditional types of meat and an extensive wine list. One standout dish: deer in cranberry sauce, with quinoa, toasted almonds, cabbage, and spinach. ✉*Valentin Letelier 658* ☎*45/416–446* ▭*AE, DC, MC, V.*

$
ECLECTIC

✕**The Travellers.** Martin Golian and Juan Pereira met by happenstance, and decided to open a place serving food from their homelands—and a few other countries. The result is a place that serves one or two dishes from Germany, Thailand, China, Italy, Mexico, and many countries in between. While you chow down on an enchilada, your companions might be having spaghetti with meatballs or sweet-and-sour pork. Dining on the front lawn under umbrella-covered tables is the best option on a summer evening. ✉*Valentín Letelier 753* ☎*45/413–617* ▭*AE, DC, MC, V.*

WHERE TO STAY

$$
Fodor'sChoice
★

🏨**Hostería de la Colina.** The friendly American owners of this hostería, Glen and Beverly Aldrich, provide attentive service as well as special little touches like homemade ice cream. Rooms in the half-century-old main house are a mix of large and small, with carpets and/or hardwood floors, all tastefully decorated with wood furnishings. Two bright, airy hillside cottages are carpeted and wood paneled and have private patios. There's a hot tub heated by a wood-burning stove, and a serene *vivero* (greenhouse) and garden that attracts birds. The terrace has stupendous views of Lago Villarrica. **Pros:** Homemade ice cream, friendly service, ambience. **Cons:** No TV. ✉*Las Colinas 115, Casilla 382* ☎🏨*45/411–503* ⊕*www.hosteriadelacolina.com* 💤*10 rooms, 2 cabins* ⚷*In-room: no a/c, no phone, no TV. In-hotel: bar, restaurant, room service, water sports, bicycles, laundry service, public Wi-Fi, parking* ▭*AE, DC, MC, V* ⑩*BP.*

$$

🏨**Hotel El Ciervo.** Villarrica's oldest hotel is an unimposing house on a quiet street, but inside are elegant details such as wrought-iron fixtures and wood-burning fireplaces. Spacious rooms, some with their own fireplaces, have huge beds and sparkling bathrooms. Just outside is a lovely pool and a secluded patio. Rates include an enormous German breakfast with loads of fruit, muesli, and fresh milk. El Ciervo also has all-inclusive seven-day tour packages. **Pros:** Spacious rooms. **Cons:** A bit plain. ✉*General Körner 241* ☎*45/411–215* 🖷*45/413–884* ⊕*www.hotelelciervo.cl* 💤*13 rooms* ⚷*In-room: no a/c, Wi-Fi. In-hotel: restaurant, bar, room service, pool, laundry service, public*

Internet, public Wi-Fi, no elevator, parking, no-smoking rooms ☰*AE, DC, MC, V* ⃝|*BP.*

$$ ⌂ **El Parque.** You can take in the commanding views of Lago Villarrica from just about anywhere at this 70-year-old, rustic and quaint retreat—the comfy lobby, the sitting area, the restaurant, or the warmly colored guest rooms. Eleven modern cabins amble down the hill to a private beach and dock. Each cabin, which accommodates two to eight people, comes with a kitchen, fireplace, and terrace. You are on your own here, but lots of personalized attention is yours for the asking. **Pros:** Views of lake, comfortable. **Cons:** Outside of main towns of Pucón and Villarrica. ⊠*Camino Villarrica–Pucón, Km 2.5* ☏*45/411–120* 🖷*45/411–090* ⊕*www.hotelelparque.cl* ⇋*8 rooms, 10 cabins* ⌂*In-room: no a/c, Wi-Fi. In-hotel: restaurant, bar, room service, tennis court, pool, beachfront, laundry service, no elevator, public Wi-Fi, parking, no-smoking rooms* ☰*AE, DC, MC, V* ⃝|*BP.*

PUCÓN

25 km (15 mi) east of Villarrica.

The resort town of Pucón, on the southern shore of Lago Villarrica, attracts all manner of Chileans young and old. There are loads of outdoor activities in the area and this is the place to have fun all 24 hours of the day in southern Chile. Be warned, however, outside of summer, December to March, most stores, restaurants, and pubs here close down.

With Volcán Villarrica looming south of town, a color-coded alert system on the Municipalidad (city hall) on Avenida Bernardo O'Higgins signals volcanic activity. The volcano sits 15 km (9 mi) away, and you'll be scarcely aware of any activity. Indeed, ascending the volcano is the area's most popular excursion.

GETTING HERE & AROUND

Pucón has only a small air strip 2 km (1 mi) outside of town for private planes, but the national airlines such as LAN and Sky fly regularly to Temuco. From Temuco, Buses JAC has frequent service to Pucón. Roads that connect Pucón to Ruta 5, the Pan-American Highway, are paved from both Loncoche and Freire. In Pucón, there are several taxis that can move you about but the town itself is small and in most cases you will just need your two feet.

ESSENTIALS

Bus Contacts **JAC** (⊠*Corner of Palguin and Uruguay* ☏*45/443–693*). **Tur-Bus** (⊠*Palguin 383* ☏*45/481–870*).

Currency Exchange **Banco BCI** (⊠*Fresia 174*). **Banco Santander** (⊠*Av. Bernardo O'Higgins 308*).

Internet **Unid@d G** (⊠*Av. Bernardo O'Higgins 415* ☏*45/444–918*).

Medical Assistance **Hospital San Francisco** (⊠*Uruguay 325* ☏*45/441–177*).

Post Office **Correos de Chile** (⊠*Fresia 183*).

Rental Cars Christopher Car (⊠ *Bernardo O'Higgins 335* ☎ *45/449–013*). **Hertz** (⊠ *Miguel Ansorena 123* ☎ *45/441–664*). **Pucon Rent A Car** (⊠ *Av. Colo Colo 340* ☎ *45/443–052*).

Visitor & Tour Info **Pucón Tourist Office** (⊠ *Av. Bernardo O'Higgins 483* ☎ *45/293–002*).

EXPLORING PUCÓN

Termas Geometricas. Chile is volcano country, and around Pucón are numerous natural hot springs. This is one of the best. Seventeen natural hot-spring pools, many of them secluded, dot the dense native forest. Each thermal bath has its own private bathrooms, lockers, and deck. ⊠ *3 km (2 mi) south of Villarrica National Park* ☎ *9/7477–1708* ⊕ *www.termasgeometricas.cl* 🎫 *14,000 pesos* ⊙ *Jan. and Feb, daily 10–10; Mar.–Dec., daily 11–8.*

Parque Cuevas Volcanicas. After a short hike uphill, you'll find this cave half-way up Volcán Villarrica, right next to a very basic visitor center. The place first opened up in 1968 as a cave for spelunkers to explore, but eventually tourism proved more lucrative. A short tour takes you deep into the electrically illuminated cave via wooden walkways that bring you close to the crystallized basalt formations. Your tour guide may make occasional hokey references to witches and pumas hiding in the rocks, but it's definitely worth a visit—especially on a bad weather day. ⊠ *Volcán Villarrica National Park* ⊕ *www.cuevasvolcanicas.cl* 🎫 *12,000 pesos* ⊙ *Daily 10–7.*

WHERE TO EAT

$
CAFÉ
✗ **Cassis.** Formerly called the Patagonia Express, this is a wonderful café and restaurant. Fruit-filled pastries are baked fresh all day long and the coffee is good. The restaurant has a varied menu of sandwiches, pizza, and more with an extensive wine list. In summer, this is an especially great ice-cream stop—head for one of the tables outside on the sidewalk. This place also stays quite lively on summer nights until about 3 AM. ⊠ *Pedro de Valdivia 333* ☎ *45/444–715* ☐ *AE, DC, MC, V.*

¢
CHILEAN
✗ **Empanadas y Hamburguesas Lleu-Lleu.** This is the place in Pucón to eat Chile's famous empanadas, a sort of hot pastry filled with diverse ingredients. Try the vegetarian empanada. They also have good sandwiches. They are open every day from 10 AM to 7 AM, which makes it a popular destination for the late-night bar crowd. They can also deliver to your hotel. ⊠ *520 General Urrutia* ☐ *No credit cards.*

$$$
SEAFOOD
✗ **La Grilla.** The best seafood in Pucón is served here, so don't be frightened off by the nondescript dining room: basic wooden tables and the ubiquitous nautical theme. You'll receive a free welcoming pisco sour when you arrive. ⊠ *Fresia at Urrutia* ☎ *45/442–294* ☐ *AE, DC, MC, V.*

$$$
LATIN
AMERICAN
✗ **La Maga.** Argentina claims to prepare the perfect parrillada, or grilled beef, but here's evidence that Uruguayans just might do it best. Watch the beef cuts or salmon turn slowly over the wood fire at the entrance. Wood, rather than charcoal, is the key, says the owner, Emiliano Villanil, a transplant from Punta del Este. The product is a wonderfully smoked, natural taste, accented with a hint of spice in the mild *chimi-*

churri (a tangy steak sauce). ⊠*Fresia 125* ☎*45/444–277* ▭*AE, DC, MC, V* ⊘*Closed Mon. Apr.–Dec.*

WHERE TO STAY

$$ 🏠**La Casona de Púcon.** In a beautiful, recently restored 1930s southern Chile-style mansion made entirely of native woods, this bed-and-breakfast opened in late 2007 and is set to become one of Pucón's best lodging options. The rooms are immaculate, tastefully decorated, and the common areas make you feel at home. Located on the town plaza, just a block from the beach, it's also a prestigious address. **Pros:** Homey feeling, tasteful decoration, on the plaza. **Cons:** No restaurant. ⊠*Lincoyan 48* ☎*45/443–179* ⊕*www.lacasonadepucon.cl* ➟*11 rooms, 1 suite* 🛏*In-room: no a/c, safe, Ethernet, Wi-Fi. In-hotel: no elevator, laundry service, public Wi-Fi, airport shuttle, parking, no-smoking rooms* ▭*AE, DC, MC, V* ⦿*BP.*

$ 🏠**¡école!** It's part hostel and part beach house—and takes its name
Fodor'sChoice from a Chilean expression meaning "Right on!" Cozy two-, three-, and
★ four-person rooms can be shared or private. The vegetarian restaurant ($), a rarity in the Lake District, merits a trip in itself. You can choose among truly international options, such as lasagna, burritos, and moussaka, and eat in the sunny courtyard or small dining room. The environmentally conscious staff can organize hiking and horseback-riding trips and expeditions to volcanoes and hot springs, as well as arrange for Spanish lessons and massages. **Pros:** Great food in restaurant, easy to meet other travelers, eco-conscious. **Cons:** Some rooms are noisy, toilets don't always work. ⊠*General Urrutia 592* ☎*45/441–675* ⊕*www.ecole.cl* ➟*21 rooms, 9 with bath* 🛏*In-room: no a/c, no phone, no TV, Wi-Fi. In-hotel: restaurant, bar, public Wi-Fi, no-smoking rooms, no elevator* ▭*AE, DC, MC, V.*

$$ 🏠**Hotel Malalhue.** Dark wood and volcanic rock were used in building
Fodor'sChoice this hotel at the edge of Pucón on the road to Calburga. It's about a 15-
★ minute walk from the hubbub of downtown, but Malalhue's many fans see that as a selling point. The cozy sitting room just off the lobby with fireplace and couches is so inviting you may want to linger there for hours. But the guest rooms, with their plush comforters and pillows, beckon, too. The top-floor "superior" rooms under the gables are more spacious and contain vaulted ceilings; they're a few thousand pesos more than the "standard" rooms, which are perfectly acceptable in their own right and in the same style as the "superiors," though smaller. **Pros:** Rooms are comfortable, sitting room. **Cons:** 15-minute walk to town. ⊠*Camino Internacional 1615* ☎*45/443–130* ▤*45/443–132* ⊕*www.malalhue.cl* ➟*24 rooms* 🛏*In-room: no a/c, safe. In-hotel: bar, restaurant, room service, laundry service, public Internet, public Wi-Fi, no-smoking rooms, parking, no elevator* ▭*AE, DC, MC, V* ⦿*BP.*

$$$ 🏠**Termas de San Luis.** The famous San Luis hot springs are the main attraction of this hideaway east of Pucón. Here you can rent a rustic cabin that sleeps up to six people. Rates include the option of all or some meals—cabins are not kitchen equipped—and free use of the baths. If you're not staying, 5,500 pesos gets you a day of soaking in the thermal springs and mud baths. **Pros:** Access to hot springs. **Cons:** Distance from Pucón. ⊠*Carretera Internacional, Km 27, Catripulli*

☎🖕45/412–880 ⊕*www.termasdesanluis.cl* ➡6 *cabins* ⚙*In-room: no a/c. In-hotel: 2 restaurants, bar, pools, children's programs, no elevator* ▭*No credit cards* ⦿*BP, FAP, MAP.*

SPORTS & THE OUTDOORS

Friendly, French-owned **Aguaventura** (✉*Palguín 336* ☎*45/444–246* ⊕*www.aguaventura.com*) outfits for rafting, as well as canoeing, kayaking, snowshoeing, and snowboarding. They specialize in trekking up the volcano for a ski descent, although you should be an expert skier if you want to join them. Alex Goly, an accomplished guide to all of Chile, works with Aguaventura and can take you on informative natural history and geography climbs in the area.

Anden Sport (✉*Av. Bernardo O'Higgins 535* ☎*45/441–574*) is a good bet for bikes, snowboards, snowshoes, and skis.

Huepil Malal (✉*Km 27, Carretera a Huife* ☎*09/643–2673 or 09/643–3204* ⊕*www.huepil-malal.cl*) arranges horseback riding in the nearby Cañi mountains, with everything from half-day to six-day excursions.

Politur (✉*Av. Bernardo O'Higgins 635* ☎*445/441–373* ⊕*www.politur.com*) can take you rafting on the Río Trancura, trekking in nearby Parque Nacional Huerquehue, on ascents of the Volcán Villarrica, and skydiving.

★ **Sol Y Nieve** (✉*Av. Bernardo O'Higgins and Lincoyan* ☎🖕*45/463–860*) runs rafting trips and hiking and skiing expeditions. It takes groups up Villarrica Volcano.

PARQUE NACIONAL VILLARRICA

Fodor'sChoice   *15 km (9 mi) south of Pucón.*
★

One of Chile's most popular national parks, Parque Nacional Villarrica has skiing, hiking, and many other outdoor activities. The main draw, however, is the volcano that gives the 610-square-km (235-square-mi) national park its name. You don't need to have any climbing experience to reach Volcán Villarrica's 3,116-meter (9,350-foot) summit, but a guide is a good idea. The volcano sits in the park's Sector Rucapillán, a Mapuche word meaning "house of the devil." That name is apt, as the perpetually smoldering volcano is one of South America's most active. CONAF closes off access to the trails at the slightest hint of volcanic activity they deem to be out of the ordinary. It's a steep uphill walk to the snow line, but doable any time of year. All equipment will be supplied by any of the Pucón outfitters that organize daylong excursions for about 30,000 pesos per person. Your reward for the six-hour climb is the rare sight of an active crater, which continues to release clouds of sulfur gases and explosions of lava. You're also treated to superb views of the nearby volcanoes, the less-visited Quetrupillán and Lanín. ✉*15 km (9 mi) south of Pucón* ☎*45/298–221 in Temuco* 🎫*1,100 pesos* ⊗*Daily 8–6.*

SKIING

The popular **Ski Pucón** (✉ *Parque Nacional Villarrica* ☎ *45/441–901* ⊕ *www.skipucon.cl*), in the lap of Volcán Villarrica, is one of the best-equipped ski areas in southern Chile, with 20 runs for varying levels of experience, nine rope tows, three double-chair tows, and equipment rental. The facility offers snowboarding, too. The ski season usually begins early July and can sometimes run through mid-October. High-season rates run 18,000 pesos per day; 15,000 pesos per half day. There are also a restaurant, coffee shop, boutique shop for various skiing accessories, and skiing and snowboard classes. Information about the facility can also be obtained from the Gran Hotel Pucón.

VALDIVIA

120 km (72 mi) southwest of Villarrica.

If you have time for just one of the Lake District's four hub cities, make it Valdivia. The city gracefully combines Chilean wood-shingle construction with the architectural style of the well-to-do German settlers who colonized the area in the late 1800s. But the historic appearance is a bit of an illusion, as the 1960 earthquake destroyed all but a few old riverfront structures. The city painstakingly rebuilt its downtown area, seamlessly mixing old and new buildings. Today you can enjoy evening strolls through its quaint streets and along its two rivers, the Valdivia and the Calle Calle.

Various tour boats leave from the docks at Muelle Schuster along the Río Valdivia for a one-hour tour around nearby Isla Teja. If you have more time, a five-hour excursion takes you to Niebla near the coast for a visit to the colonial-era forts. A four-hour tour north transports you to Puncapa, the site of a 16th-century Jesuit church and a nature sanctuary at San Luis de Alba de Cruces. Each tour company offers all three excursions daily during the December–March high season, and you can always sign on to one at the last minute. Most will not operate tours for fewer than 15 passengers, however, which makes things a bit iffy during the rest of the year.

GETTING HERE & AROUND

Like most other major cities in the Lakes District, Valdivia is served by Ruta 5, the Pan-American Highway. The city also has an airport with frequent flights by national airlines such as LAN, and the nation's bus lines regularly stop here as well.

ESSENTIALS

Bus Contacts **Buses JAC** (✉ *Anfión Muñoz 360* ☎ *63/333–343*). **Cruz del Sur** (✉ *Anfión Muñoz 360* ☎ *63/213–840*). **Valdivia Bus Depot** (✉ *Anfión Muñoz 360* ☎ *63/212–212*).

Currency Exchange **Arauco** (✉ *Galería Arauco, Local 24*). **Banco Santander** (✉ *Pérez Rosales 505*). **Corp Banca** (✉ *Picarte 370*).

Internet **Café Phonet** (✉ *Libertad 127* ☎ *63/341–054*). **Centro Internet Libertad** (✉ *Libertad 7*).

Medical Assistance **Farmacias Ahumada** (✉ *Av. Ramón Picarte 310* ☎ *63/257–889*). **Hospital Regional Valdivia** (✉ *Simpson 850* ☎ *63/297–000*).

Post Office **Correos de Chile** (✉ *Av. Bernardo O'Higgins 575*).

Rental Cars **Assef y Mendez** (✉ *General Lagos 1335* ☎ *63/213–205*). **Autovald** (✉ *Vicente Pérez Rosales 660* ☎ *63/212–786*). **Avis** (✉ *Beauchef 619* ☎ *63/278–455*). **Budget** (✉ *Picarte 1348* ☎ *63/340–060*).

Visitor & Tour Info **Sernatur** (✉ *Av. Arturo Prat 555* ☎ *63/213–596*).**Valdivia Tourist Office** (✉ *Terminal de Buses, Anfión Muñoz 360* ☎ *63/212–212*).

EXPLORING VALDIVIA

Fondly known around town as the "MAC," the **Museo de Arte Contemporáneo** is one of Chile's foremost modern-art museums. This Isla Teja complex was built on the site of the old Anwandter brewery destroyed in the 1960 earthquake. The minimalist interior, formerly the brewery's warehouses, contrasts sharply with ongoing construction of a modern glass wall fronting the Río Valdivia, a project slated for completion by 2010, Chile's bicentennial. The museum has no permanent collection; it's a rotating series of temporary exhibits by contemporary Chilean artists. ✉ *Los Laureles, Isla Teja* ☎ *63/221–968* ⊕ *www.macvaldivia. uach.cl* 🎫 *1,200 pesos* 🕐 *Daily 10–2 and 4–8.*

Just south of the Centro Cultural El Austral lies the **Torreón Los Canelos**, one of two fortress towers constructed in 1774 to defend Valdivia from constant indigenous attacks. Both towers—the other sits on Avenida Picarte between the bus terminal and the bridge entering the city over the Río Calle Calle—were built in the style of those that guarded the coasts of Andalusia, in southern Spain. A wall and moat connected the two Valdivia towers in the colonial era, effectively turning the city into an island. ✉ *General Lagos at Yerbas Buenas.*

Valdivia means beer to many Chileans, and **Cervecería Kunstmann** brews the country's beloved lager. The Anwandter family immigrated from Germany a century-and-a-half ago, bringing along their beer-making know-how. The *cervecería* (brewery), on the road to Niebla, hosts interesting guided tours by prior arrangement. There's also a small museum and a souvenir shop where you can buy the requisite caps, mugs, and T-shirts; plus a pricey restaurant serving German fare. ✉ *Ruta 350 No. 950* ☎ *63/222–570* 🎫 *Free* 🕐 *Restaurant and museum, daily noon–midnight.*

WHERE TO EAT

¢ ✕ **Café Haussmann.** The excellent *crudos* (steak tartare), German-
SEAFOOD style sandwiches, and delicious küchen here are testament to the fact that Valdivia was once a mecca for German immigrants. The place is small—a mere four tables and a bar—but it's that rarest of breeds in Chile: a completely nonsmoking restaurant. ✉ *Av. Bernardo O'Higgins 394* ☎ *63/213–878* ▭ *AE, DC, MC, V* 🕐 *Closed Sun.*

$$ ✕ **La Calesa.** Head to this centrally located, well-known restaurant for
PERUVIAN a good introduction to Peruvian cuisine. Try the *ají* (chicken stew with cheese, milk, and peppers), but be careful not to burn your mouth. Peruvian dishes, particularly the stews, are spicier than their Chil-

ean counterparts. ⊠ *Yungay 735* ☎ *63/225–467* ⊟ *AE, DC, MC, V* ☻ *Closed Sun. No lunch Sat.*

$$ \times$ **Camino de Luna.** The Way of the Moon floats on a barge on the Río
SEAFOOD Valdivia, just north of the Pedro de Valdivia bridge. As the city is only a few miles from the ocean, it's no surprise that seafood is a specialty here. The *congrío calle calle* (conger eel in a cheese-and-tomato sauce) is particularly good. Tables by the windows offer views of Isla Teja. ⊠ *Av. Arturo Prat Costanera s/n* ☎ *63/213–788* ⊟ *AE, DC, MC, V.*

WHERE TO STAY

$ ⊞ **Aires Buenos Hostal.** Well situated near Valdivia's downtown, this ren-
ovated, old and strikingly handsome house is a great find. The price is cheap, but the place is clean, friendly, and warm. It's mostly a back-packers' haven, but there are some private rooms that will make the older crowd feel at home. **Pros:** Price, location. **Cons:** Not many amenities, noise in ground-floor rooms. ⊠ *Garcia Reyes 550* ☎ *63/206–304* ⊕ *www.airesbuenos.cl* ⇨ *10 rooms, 5 with bath* ♨ *In-room: no a/c, no phone, no TV, Wi-Fi. In-hotel: public Internet, public Wi-Fi, parking, no-smoking rooms* ⊟ *AE, DC, MC V* ¶⊙¶ *BP.*

$ ⊞ **Hotel El Castillo.** A grand 1920s German-style house sits at Niebla's main intersection on the riverfront and has been converted into this lovely bed-and-breakfast with lots of knickknacks, antiques, and cuckoo clocks in the common areas. Rooms have more modern amenities, but retain the old wood finishing, and overlook either the river or the pool and back gardens. A new wing has been added, but it blends so seamlessly with the original house that you can't tell where one ends and the other begins. **Pros:** Nice ambience, rooms good. **Cons:** No restaurant. ⊠ *Antonio Ducce* ☎ *63/282–061* ☐ *63/219–133* ✎ *hotelelcastillo@hotmail.com* ⇨ *11 rooms, 2 cabins* ♨ *In-room: no a/c. In-hotel: pools, no elevator, parking, no-smoking rooms* ⊟ *AE, DC, MC, V* ¶⊙¶ *BP.*

$$–$$$ ⊞ **Hotel Naguilán.** You can relax at this charming hotel's poolside gar-
★ den while watching the boats pass by on the Río Valdivia. Rooms in the property's newer building are bigger, with balconies and more modern furnishings; the older rooms, in a building that dates from 1890, are smaller and a bit dated, with lime-green carpeting, but they have more character, and are cheaper. Service-wise, you're in good hands here: as soon as you check in, a waiter will appear to offer you a welcome pisco sour. **Pros:** Good service, river location. **Cons:** No Wi-Fi in rooms. ⊠ *General Lagos 1927* ☎ *63/212–851* ☐ *63/219–130* ⊕ *www.hotel naguilan.com* ⇨ *33 rooms, 3 suites* ♨ *In-room: no a/c, refrigerator (some), dial-up. In-hotel: restaurant, bar, room service, pool, laundry service, no elevator, public Wi-Fi, parking, no-smoking rooms* ⊟ *AE, DC, MC, V* ¶⊙¶ *BP.*

$$$ ⊞ **Hotel Puerta del Sur.** Expect lavish pampering with top-notch service at this highly regarded lodging. Spacious rooms, all with views of the river, are decorated in soft lavender tones. Play a few games of tennis, then hit the pool or relax in the hot tub. You're near the edge of town here, so this is a good place to stay if you have your own car. **Pros:** Good service, lots of activity options. **Cons:** At edge of town. ⊠ *Los Lingues 950, Isla Teja* ☎ *63/224–500* ☐ *63/211–046* ⊕ *www.*

hotelpuertadelsur.com ⇌*45 rooms, 3 suites* ♨*In-room: safe, refrigerator, DVD, Wi-Fi. In-hotel: restaurant, bars, room service, tennis court, pool, gym, spa, bicycles, laundry service, concierge, executive floor, public Internet, public Wi-Fi, parking* ▤*AE, DC, MC, V* ⦿*BP.*

SPORTS & THE OUTDOORS

Valdivia-based tour operator **Pueblito Expediciones** (⊠*San Carlos 188* ☎*63/245–055* ⊕*www.pueblitoexpediciones.cl*) organizes marvelous rafting, kayaking, and nature appreciation trips on nearby rivers. An astonishing variety of wetland birds inhabits this part of the country. **Hualamo** (☎*09/642–3143* ⊕*www.hualamo.com*) lets you get a close look if you join its bird-watching and natural-history tours based out of a lodge 20 km (12 mi) upriver from Valdivia.

PARQUE NACIONAL PUYEHUE

81 km (49 mi) east of Osorno, via Ruta 215.

Chile's most popular national park, Parque Nacional Puyehue draws crowds who come to bask in its famed hot springs. Most never venture beyond them, and that's a shame. A dozen miles east of the Aguas Calientes sector lies a network of short trails leading to evergreen forests with dramatic waterfalls.

Truly adventurous types attempt the five-hour hike to the summit of 2,240-meter (7,350-foot) Volcán Puyehue. As with most climbs in this region, CONAF rangers insist on ample documentation of experience before allowing you to set out. Access to the 1,070-square-km (413-square-mi) park is easy: head due east from Osorno on the highway leading to Argentina. ⊠*Ruta 215* ☎*64/197–4572* 💲*800 pesos* ⊗*Dec.–Feb., daily 8 AM–9 PM; Apr.–Oct., daily 8–8.*

WHERE TO STAY

$$$–$$$$
★
🏨 **Termas Puyehue Wellness and Spa Resort.** Probably Chile's most famous hot-springs resort, this grandiose stone-and-wood lodge sits on the edge of Parque Nacional Puyehue. Make no mistake: the place is enormous, with a slate of activities to match, offering everything from darts to skiing. Yet, despite its huge popularity, and the fact that something is always going on, it can be a surprisingly nice place to relax. Most people come for a soak in the thermal pools. The rooms and common areas here mix starkly modern and 19th-century Germanic features: chrome, hardwoods, and even some modern art happily share the same space. The hotel recently changed to an "all-inclusive" concept in which meals, drinks, excursions, and use of the pools and thermal baths are included in the price of the room. If you're not staying as a guest, an all-day pass for the use of the springs and pools, with meals included, is 30,000 pesos weekdays, 35,000 pesos on weekends and holidays. ⊠*Ruta 215, Km 76, Puyehue* ☎*64/232–881, 2/293–6000 in Santiago* ⊕*www.puyehue.cl* ⇌*137 rooms* ♨*In-room: no a/c, safe, refrigerator, Wi-Fi. In-hotel: 3 restaurants, room service, bar, tennis courts, pools, gym, spa, bicycles, water sports, children's programs, laundry service,*

concierge, public Internet, public Wi-Fi, airport shuttle, parking ⊟*AE, DC, MC, V* ⦶|*BP.*

PUERTO OCTAY

50 km (30 mi) southeast of Osorno, via Ruta 5, the Pan-American Hwy.

The story goes that a German merchant named Ochs set up shop in this tidy community on the northern tip of Lago Llanquihue. A phrase uttered by customers looking for a particular item, "¿Ochs, hay . . .?" ("Ochs, do you have . . .?"), gradually became "Octay." With spectacular views of the Osorno and Calbuco volcanoes, the town was the birthplace of Lake District tourism: a wealthy Santiago businessman constructed a mansion outside town in 1912, using it as a vacation home to host his friends. (That structure is now the area's famed Hotel Centinela.) Puerto Octay doesn't have the frenetic energy of neighboring Frutillar and Puerto Varas, but its many fans enjoy its less-frenzied, more-authentic nature.

GETTING HERE & AROUND

Puerto Octay is easily accessible on paved roads from Ruta 5, the Pan-American Highway. It's less than an hour north of Puerto Montt.

WHERE TO STAY & EAT

$$
GERMAN
✕**Restaurant Baviera.** Because it's on the Plaza de Armas, this is a popular lunch stop for tour groups. Baviera serves solid German fare—schnitzel, sauerkraut, sausage, and küchen are among the favorites. Beer steins and other Bavarian paraphernalia line the walls. ⊠*German Wulf 582* ☎*64/391–460* ⊟*No credit cards.*

$$$
★
Hotel Centinela. Simple and elegant, the venerable 1912 Hotel Centinela remains one of Chile's best-known accommodations. This imposing wood-shingled lodge with a dramatic turret sits amid 20 forested acres at the tip of Península Centinela jutting into Lago Llanquihue. Britain's Edward VII, then Prince of Wales, was the most famous guest (but there's some mystery as to whether his future wife, American divorcée Wallis Simpson, accompanied him). Imposing beds and armoires fill the huge rooms in the main building. The cabins, whose rates include three meals a day delivered to the door, are more modern than the rooms in the lodge. ⊠*Península de Centinela, 5 km (3 mi) south of Puerto Octay* ☎☎*64/391–326* ⊕*www.hotelcentinela. cl* ➭*11 rooms, 1 suite, 18 cabins* ⧄*In-room: no a/c, no TV (some). In-hotel: restaurant, bar, beachfront, no elevator* ⊟*AE, DC, MC, V* ⦶|*BP, FAP.*

$
★
Zapato Amarillo. Backpackers make up the majority of the clientele here, but this is no scruffy youth hostel. This modern alerce-shingled house with wood-paneled rooms affords a drop-dead gorgeous view of Volcán Osorno outside town. Armin Dubendorfer and Nadi Muñoz, the eager-to-please Chilean-Swiss couple that owns it, will arrange guided horseback-riding, hiking, and cycling tours, as well as cheese-fondue evening gatherings. Rates include an excellent buffet breakfast that uses local fruits and dairy products. You also have access to the

kitchen. ⊠*2 km (1 mi) north of Puerto Octay on road to Osorno* 📞🖶*64/210–787* ⊕*www.zapatoamarillo.cl* 🛏*7 rooms, 2 with bath* 🛎*In-room: no a/c, no phone, no TV. In-hotel: bicycles, laundry facilities, public Internet, no elevator* ⊟*No credit cards* ¶*BP.*

FRUTILLAR

30 km (18 mi) southwest of Puerto Octay.

Halfway down the western edge of Lago Llanquihue lies the small town of Frutillar, a destination for European immigrants in the late 19th century and, today, arguably the most picturesque Lake District community. The town—actually two adjacent hamlets, Frutillar Alto and Frutillar Bajo—is known for its perfectly preserved German architecture. Don't be disappointed if your first sight of the town is the nondescript neighborhood (the Alto) on the top of the hill; head down to the charming streets of Frutillar Bajo that face the lake, with their picture-perfect view of Volcán Osorno.

GETTING HERE & AROUND

About 45 minutes north of Puerto Montt, on Ruta 5, Pan-American Highway. Several bus lines make stops here on Santiago–Puerto Montt routes.

ESSENTIALS

Currency Exchange Banco Santander (⊠*Av. Philippi 555* 🖶*65/421–228*).

Medical Assistance Farmacia Frutillar (⊠*Av. Carlos Richter 170*). **Hospital Frutillar** (⊠*Las Piedras* 🖶*65/421–386*).

Visitor & Tour Info Informacion Turistica (⊠*Costanera Philippi in front of boat dock* 🖶*65/421–080*). **Secretaria Muncipal de Turismo** (⊠*Av. Philippi 753* 🖶*65/421–685*).

EXPLORING FRUTILLAR

Each year, in late January and early February, the town hosts **Semanas Musicales de Frutillar,** an excellent series of mostly classical concerts (and a little jazz) in the lakeside Centro de Conciertos y Eventos, a semi-outdoor venue inaugurated for the 2006 festival. Ticket prices are a reasonable 3,000–10,000 pesos. ⊠*Av. Phillipi 1000* 🖶*65/421–290* ⊕*www.semanasmusicales.cl.*

★ You step into the past when you step into one of southern Chile's best museums, the **Museo Colonial Alemán.** Besides displays of the 19th-century agricultural and household implements, this open-air museum has full-scale reconstructions of buildings—a smithy and barn, among others—used by the original German settlers. Exhibits at this complex administered by Chile's Universidad Austral are labeled in Spanish and, *natürlich,* German, but there are a few signs in English. A short walk from the lake up Avenida Arturo Prat, the museum also has beautifully landscaped grounds and great views of Volcán Osorno. ⊠*Av. Vicente Pérez Rosales at Av. Arturo Prat* 🖶*65/421–142* 🎟*1,800 pesos* 🕙*Dec.–Feb., daily 10–7; Mar.–Nov., daily 10–2 and 3–5.*

WHERE TO EAT

$$ ✕ **Club Alemán.** One of the German clubs that dot the Lake District, this
GERMAN restaurant in the center of town has a selection of four or five rotating
prix-fixe menus that cost 3,500 pesos. There will always be a meat and
seafood option—often steak and salmon—with soup, salad, and dessert. Don't forget the küchen. ✉*Philippi 747* ☎*65/421–249* ▭*AE,
DC, MC, V.*

$$ ✕ **Guten Apetit.** Right on the waterfront, with tables both outdoors
GERMAN and inside, this is a warm and friendly place with good food. It's the
standard southern Chilean menu, from clam stews and Barros Lucos
(a classic Chilean sandwich of beef and melted cheese) to large beef
and chicken dishes. But they also have a few German imports such
as Chuletas Kasler, a German pork chop. In summer, a pianist busts
out a variety of tunes from 12:30 to 4 PM every day. ✉*Balmaceda 98*
☎*65/421–145* ▭*AE, DC, MC.*

WHERE TO STAY

$$ ▦ **Hotel Ayacara.** A beautiful, yellow and green house on the lakefront,
this bed-and-breakfast is one of Frutillar's best. The service is friendly,
the rooms are a delight. **Pros:** Fun and friendly. **Cons:** Not much privacy. ✉*Av. Philippi corner of Pedro Aguirre* ☎*65/421–550, 2/430–
7000 in Santiago* ⊕*www.hotelayacara.cl* ▭*8 rooms* ♿*In-room: no
a/c, Wi-Fi. In-hotel: restaurant, room service, bar, beachfront, no elevator, laundry service, public Wi-Fi, parking, no-smoking rooms* ▭*AE,
DC, MC, V* ¶*BP.*

$-$$ ▦ **Hotel Villa San Francisco.** The location of this highly recommended
★ hotel could not be better, situated on a small hill overlooking the lake.
At the tranquil end of the Costanera, or lakeside road, it has a spectacular view of the town and volcanoes while just a minute's walk from
all the sights and sounds of Frutillar. All the rooms have that lake view,
along with their own private terrace. The hotel also has a pleasant pool
and a cozy bar and restaurant. This is a place to relax. Francisco Fayula
de la Corte, its Spanish owner, took over the hotel in 1999 and has
transformed it into Frutillar's top lodging choice. **Pros:** Lakeside view,
good value for price, tranquil but close to town. **Cons:** Some rooms are
small. ✉*Avda. Phillipi 1503* ☎*65/421–531* ⊕*www.villasanfrancisco.
cl* ▭*15 rooms* ♿*In-room: no a/c, Wi-Fi. In-hotel: restaurant, room
service, bar, pool, gym, beachfront, no elevator, laundry service, public
Wi-Fi, parking* ▭*AE, DC, MC, V* ¶*BP.*

$$ ▦ **Salzburg Hotel & Spa.** Rooms at this Tyrolean-style lodge command
excellent views of the lake. Cozy cabins and slightly larger bungalows,
all made of native woods, are fully equipped with kitchens and private
terraces. The staff will gladly organize fishing trips. The restaurant
($$) serves some of the best smoked salmon in the area. **Pros:** Great
view, lots of privacy. **Cons:** Need a car to get around. ✉*Costanera
Norte* ☎*65/421–589* ▤*65/421–599* ⊕*www.salzburg.cl* ▭*31 rooms,
9 cabins, 5 bungalows* ♿*In-room: no a/c, no TV. In-hotel: restaurant,
bar, pool, spa, laundry service, parking, no elevator* ▭*AE, DC, MC,
V* ¶*BP.*

PUERTO VARAS

27 km (16 mi) south of Frutillar via Ruta 5, Pan-American Hwy.

A small but fast-growing resort town on the edge of Lago Llanquihue, Puerto Varas is renowned for its view of the Osorno and Calbuco volcanoes. Stunning rose arbors and Germanic-style architecture grace the many centuries-old houses and churches that dot this tranquil town. Every year new hotels here crop up as tourism continues to rise significantly. Tons of cafés, trendy restaurants, an excellent casino, and a budding bar scene all point towards Puerto Varas's ascendancy as a serious challenge to Pucón, the region's top vacation spot.

GETTING HERE & AROUND

Puerto Varas is only about a 20-minute drive from the center of nearby Puerto Montt, making it a virtual suburb of that large city. Taxis and buses can take you to countryside locations such as Ensenada as well as Puerto Montt for a minimal cost. You can cross to Argentina via bus or boat.

ESSENTIALS

Bus Contacts **Buses JAC** (⊠ *Walker Martinez 227* 🕾 *65/236–000*).**Cruz del Sur** (⊠ *Walker Martinez 239-B* 🕾 *65/231–925*). **Tur-Bus** (⊠ *Salvador 1093* 🕾 *65/233–787*).

Currency Exchange **Banco Santander** (⊠ *Del Salvador 399* 🕾 *65/237–255*). **Travelsur** (⊠ *San Pedro 451* 🕾 *65/236–000*).

Medical Assistance **Clinica Alemana** (⊠ *Otto Bader 810* 🕾 *65/239–100*). **Farmacia Cruz Verde** (⊠ *San Francisco 400* 🕾 *65/234–293*).**Farmacia Salco** (⊠ *Del Salvador 400* 🕾 *65/234–544*).

Post Office **Correos de Chile** (⊠ *San José 242*).

Rental Cars **Hunter Rent-a-Car** (⊠ *San José 130* 🕾 *65/237–950 or 65/522–454*).

Visitor & Tour Info **Casa del Turista** (⊠ *Piedra Plen, in front of Plaza de Armas* 🕾 *65/237–956*). **Oficina de Turismo** (⊠ *San Francisco 441* 🕾 *65/233–477*).

WHERE TO EAT

$

SEAFOOD

✕**Donde El Gordito.** You'll find great seafood here. Some of the fish is personally caught by the avid fisherman owner, El Gordito, who is usually on hand with his wife to wait tables and ring up checks. This little eatery, housed inside a downtown fishmarket, also has entertaining decor, some of it chosen by its owner and some of it given to him by the many tourists that luckily find their way to his food. ⊠*San Bernardo 560* ☎*65/233–425* ⊟*AE, DC, MC, V.*

$$ ✕ **La Olla.** This lakeside restaurant does not look like much, but it serves
SEAFOOD the best fish and seafood dishes in Chile, according to its legion of
★ fans. The specialties of the house are seafood empanadas and other, more simply elegant preparations. The place is almost always full during peak hours, so reserve a table ahead of time. ⊠*Av. Vicente Pérez Rosales 1071* ☎*65/234–605* ⚓*Reservations essential* ⊟*AE, DC, MC, V.*

WHERE TO STAY

$$ ⊡ **Los Alerces Hotel & Cabanas.** Across the street from the town's most popular beach for swimming and tanning, this is a clean, comfortable option. Wood-paneled walls and paintings of flowers predominate. The cabins on-site are a perfect place for a family stay. The hotel pool is inviting, too. **Pros:** Close to beach, large cabins. **Cons:** It's a hike to walk to town. ⊠*Av. Vicente Pérez Rosales 1281* ☎*65/235–985* ⊕*www.hotellosalerces.cl* ⇄*44 rooms, 10 cabins* ⚘*In-room: no a/c, refrigerator, Wi-Fi. In-hotel: restaurant, room service, bar, pool, no elevator, laundry service, executive floor, public Internet, public Wi-Fi, parking, no-smoking rooms* ⊟*AE, DC, MC, V* ⍾*BP.*

$$$ ⊡ **Melia Patagonia.** One of the few legitimate five-star hotels to be found
★ in southern Chile, this relaxing, comfortable hotel is close to downtown. For the hotel's opening in 2007, the Chilean owners entirely renovated and modernized what was once Puerto Varas's most prestigious hotel and casino. Rooms are immaculate, the service personalized and attentive, and the views from the hotel terrace superb. A regular happy hour and live music make Bar Kutral a popular town hangout. **Pros:** Excellent service, attention to detail, spacious rooms, bar. **Cons:** Gym and pool are small, not all rooms have lake views. ⊠*Klenner 349* ☎*65/201–000* ⊕*www.solmelia.com* ⇄*91 rooms, 2 suites* ⚘*In-room: safe, refrigerator, Ethernet, Wi-Fi. In-hotel: 2 restaurants, room service, bar, pool, gym, spa, laundry service, executive floor, public Internet, public Wi-Fi, parking* ⊟*AE, DC, MC, V* ⍾*BP.*

SPORTS & THE OUTDOORS

Fly-fishing is king in the region, with many rivers and the huge Lake Llanquihue making attractive targets. But the region has much more to offer: mountain biking, canyoning, hiking in Vicente Pérez Rosales Park, or just enjoying the lake by kayak. You can also hike up the nearby volcanoes, which makes for an exciting and scenic excursion.

Al Sur Expediciones (⊠*Del Salvador 100* ☎*65/232–300* ⊕*www.alsur expeditions.com*) is known for rafting and kayaking trips on the Class III Río Petrohué. It also runs horseback-riding and fly-fishing trips, and handles hotel reservations and guided tours for Pumalin Park. **Aqua Motion** (⊠*San Pedro 422* ☎*65/232–747* ⊕*www.aqua-motion.com*) is a longtime provider of rafting and kayaking excursions on the nearby Río Petrohué, as well as trekking, horseback riding, helicopter rides, bird-watching, and fly-fishing tours. **Margouya Tours** (⊠*Santa Rosa 318* ☎*65/237–640*) specializes in half- and full-day canyoning and rappelling trips near Volcán Calbuco, in addition to kayaking and hiking excursions. **Miralejos** (⊠*San Pedro 311* ☎*65/234–892* ⊕*www.miralejos.com*) offers trekking, kayaking, mountaineering, horseback-riding trips throughout the region.

For fly-fishing in Puerto Varas, try **Tres Piedras** (⊠*Ruta 225, Km 22, Los Riscos* ☎*65/330–157* ⊕*www.trespiedras.cl*).

PARQUE NACIONAL VICENTE PÉREZ ROSALES

3 km (2 mi) east of Ensenada.

GETTING HERE & AROUND

Take a one-hour drive along Ruta 224, Camino a Ensenada, from Puerto Varas. Several agencies in Puerto Varas offer guided trips and transport to the park.

EXPLORING VICENTE PÉREZ ROSALES

Chile's oldest national park, Parque Nacional Vicente Pérez Rosales was established in 1926. South of Parque Nacional Puyehue, the 2,538-square-km (980-square-mi) preserve includes the Osorno and lesser-known Puntiagudo volcanoes, as well as the deep-blue Lago Todos los Santos. The visitor center opposite the Hotel Petrohué provides access to some fairly easy hikes. The Rincón del Osorno trail hugs the lake; the Saltos de Petrohué trail runs parallel to the river of the same name. Rudimentary campsites are available for 10,000 pesos per person. ☎*65/290–711* ⊉*1,000 pesos* ⊗*Dec.–Feb., daily 9–8; Mar.–Nov., daily 9–6.*

The mountain forms the foundation for Chile's newest ski area, **Ski & Outdoors Volcán Osorno** (⊠*San Francisco 333, Puerto Varas* ☎*65/233–445 or 09/262–3323* ⊕*www.volcanosorno.com*), which offers ski and snowboard rentals and lessons.

One of the Lake District's signature excursions is a binational one. The **Cruce de Lagos** takes in a combination of bus and boat transport from Puerto Varas to San Carlos de Bariloche, Argentina, via the park's Lago Todos los Santos and Argentina's Lago Nahuel Huapi. **Andina del Sud** (⊠*Del Salvador 72, Puerto Varas* ☎*65/232–811* ⊕*www.crucedelagos.cl*) offers the trip starting from Puerto Varas or Puerto Montt.

WHERE TO STAY

$$$$ ▦**Hotel Petrohué.** The common areas in this stately, rustic orange chalet have vaulted ceilings and huge fireplaces. Guest rooms are a mix of dark woods and stone and have brightly colored drapes and spreads. Cabins echo the design of the main building and have their own fireplaces. The hotel's tour office can set you up with cruises on nearby lakes, take you to scale Volcán Osorno if you're an experienced climber, or send you on guided hikes in the park. ⊠*Ruta 225, Km 64, Petrohué s/n* ☎☎*65/212–025* ⊕*www.petrohue.com* ⇆*20 rooms, 4 cabins* △*In-room: no a/c, no phone, safe, no TV. In-hotel: restaurant, bar, pool, bicycles, water sports, beachfront, no elevator, laundry service, parking, no-smoking rooms* ▭*AE, DC, MC, V* ⎮⊚⎮*AI, BP, MAP.*

SPORTS & THE OUTDOORS

Make like Tarzan (or Jane) and swing through the treetops in the shadow of Volcán Osorno with **Canopy Chile** (☎ *65/330–922 or 09/638–2644 ⊕www.canopychile.cl*). A helmet, a very secure harness, 2 km (1 mi) of zip line strung out over 12 platforms, and experienced guides give you a bird's-eye view of the forest below.

PUERTO MONTT

20 km (12 mi) south of Puerto Varas via Ruta 5, Pan-American Hwy.

For most of its history, windy Puerto Montt was the end of the line for just about everyone traveling in the Lake District. Now the Carretera Austral carries on southward, but for all intents and purposes Puerto Montt remains the region's last significant outpost, a provincial city that is the hub of local fishing, textile, and tourist activity. Today the city center is quickly sprouting malls, condos, and office towers—it's the fastest-growing city in Chile—but away from downtown, Puerto Montt consists mainly of low clapboard houses perched above its bay, the Seno de Reloncaví. If it's a sunny day, head east to Playa Pelluco or one of the city's other beaches. If you're more interested in exploring the countryside, drive along the shore for a good view of the surrounding hills.

GETTING HERE & AROUND

Puerto Montt is a main transit hub in the region. Buses from Santiago and all points in southern Chile ramble through here at some point, while many cruise ships dock at the port. Puerto Montt's El Tepual Airport has daily air traffic from all the major airlines that serve Chile. The Pan-American Highway also stops here, while the mostly unpaved Carretera Austral, which winds it ways through Chilean Patagonia, begins south of the city. To cross over into Argentina by boat, buses leave from here and from Puerto Varas. Chiloé Island is less than two hours' drive from Puerto Montt. Take the last part of Ruta 5, or the Pan-American Highway to Pargua, where two ferries cross the Chacao Channel every hour.

ESSENTIALS

Bus Contacts **Cruz del Sur** (⊠ *Av. Diego Portales* ☎ *65/254–731*). **Puerto Montt Bus Depot** (⊠ *Av. Diego Portales* ☎ *65/349–010*). **Tas-Choapa** (⊠ *Av. Diego Portales* ☎ *65/259–320*). **Tur-Bus** (⊠ *Av. Diego Portales* ☎ *65/259–320*).

Currency Exchange **Eureka Turismo** (⊠ *Guillermo Gallardo 65* ☎ *65/250–412*). **Inter Money Exchange** (⊠ *Talca 84* ☎ *65/253–745*).

Internet **Cybercafé Navegante** (⊠ *Illapel 10, Local 304A, Mall Paseo Costanera* ☎ *65/435–858*). **Mundosur** (⊠ *San Martin 232* ☎ *65/295–415*).

Medical Assistance **Farmacias Ahumada** (⊠ *Antonio Varas 651, Puerto Montt* ☎ *65/344–419*).**Hospital Base Puerto Montt** (⊠ *Seminario s/n* ☎ *65/261–100*).

Post Office **Correos de Chile** (⊠ *Av. Rancagua 126*).

Rental Cars Avis (⊠ *Benavente 570* ☎ *65/253–307* ⊠ *Urmeneta1037* ☎ *65/255–065*). **Budget** (⊠ *Antonio Varas 162* ☎ *65/286–277* ⊠ *Aeropuerto El Tepual* ☎ *65/294–100*). **Hertz** (⊠ *Calle de Servicio 1431, Parque Industrial Tyrol* ☎ *65/313–445* ⊠ *Aeropuerto El Tepual* ☎ *65/268–944*).

Visitor & Tour Info Puerto Montt Tourist Office (⊠ *Plaza de Armas* ☎ *65/261– 823*). **Sernatur** (⊠ *Av. de la Décima Región 480* ☎ *65/254–850*).

EXPLORING PUERTO MONTT

About 3 km (2 mi) west of downtown along the coastal road lies the **Caleta Angelmó,** Puerto Montt's fishing cove. This busy port serves small fishing boats, large ferries, and cruisers carrying travelers and cargo southward through the straits and fjords that form much of Chile's shoreline. On weekdays small launches from Isla Tenglo and other outlying islands arrive early in the morning and leave late in the afternoon. The fish market here has one of the most varied selections of seafood in all of Chile.

Beaches at Maullín. About 70 km (43 mi) southwest of Puerto Montt, at this small town near Pargua—the ferry crossing to Chiloé—the Maullín River merges with the Pacific Ocean. It's a spectacular setting. Be sure to visit Pangal Beach, an extensive beach with large sand dunes that is teeming with birds. If you choose to stay overnight, there are cabins and a campground. ⊠ *Ruta 5 south from Puerto Montt, about a 1-hr drive.*

Barely a stone's throw from Cochamó, the mountainous 398-square-km (154-square-mi) **Parque Nacional Alerce Andino,** with more than 40 small lakes, was established to protect some 20,000 endangered alerce trees. Comparable to California's hardy sequoia, alerce grow to average heights of 40 meters (130 feet), and can reach 4 meters (13 feet) in diameter. Immensely popular as a building material for houses in southern Chile, they are quickly disappearing from the landscape. Many of these are 3,000–4,000 years old. ⊠ *Carretera Austral, 35 km (21 mi) east of Puerto Montt* ☎ *65/212–036* ⊡ *1,700 pesos* ⊙ *Daily 9–6.*

WHERE TO EAT

$

CAFÉ

✕ **Café Central.** This old-style café in the heart of Puerto Montt retains the spirit of the 1920s and 1930s. It's a good place for a filling afternoon tea, with its menu of sandwiches, ice cream, and pastries. The raspberry küchen is a particular favorite here. ⊠ *Rancagua 117* ☎ *65/482–888* ⊟ *AE, DC, MC, V.*

$$

SEAFOOD

✕ **Feria Artesanal Angelmó.** Several kitchens here prepare *mariscal* (shellfish soup) and *caldillo* (seafood chowder), as well as *almejas* (clams), *machas* (razor clams), and *ostiones* (scallops) with Parmesan cheese. Separate tables and counters are at each kitchen in this enclosed market, which is 3 km (2 mi) west of Puerto Montt along the coast road. Don't expect anything as formal as set hours, but most open around 11 AM for lunch and serve for about three hours, and then from about 6 to 9 PM for dinner every day in the January–March high season. The rest of the year, most close some days of the week. ⊠ *Caleta Angelmó* ☎ *No phone* ⊟ *No credit cards.*

$$ ✕**Pazos.** One of the best things to do in Puerto Montt is to eat curanto,
SEAFOOD a southern Chilean potpourri of shellfish served together with vari-
Fodor'sChoice ous meats and potatoes. Pazos, located in a large house across the
★ street from the beach in Peulluco, is where you'll want to start. They
also have an array of other seafood delicacies, and meat and chicken
alternatives if you're not up for fish. ⊠*Juan Soler Manfredini, Pel-
luco, across street from beach* ☎*65/252–552* ♠*Reservations essential*
⊟*AE, DC, MC, V.*

WHERE TO STAY

$$–$$$ 🏨**Don Luis Gran Hotel.** This modern lodging down the street from the
cathedral, a favorite among upscale business travelers, has panoramic
vistas of the Seno de Reloncaví. (Rooms on the seventh and eighth
floors have the best views.) The carpeted rooms have undergone a wel-
come renovation and have either queen-size beds or two full-size beds.
A big American-style breakfast, served in a cozy salon, is included in
the rate. **Pros:** Good for business travelers. **Cons:** Not all rooms have
good views. ⊠*Urmeneta at Quillota* ☎*65/259–001* 🖷*65/259–005*
⊕*www.hoteldonluis.cl* 🛏*60 rooms, 1 suite* ♿*In-room: no a/c, safe,
refrigerator (some), Wi-Fi. In-hotel: restaurant, bar, room service, gym,
laundry service, public Internet, public Wi-Fi, parking, no-smoking
rooms* ⊟*AE, DC, MC, V.*

$$ 🏨**Gran Hotel Vicente Costanera.** The grandest of Puerto Montt's hotels
underwent a much-needed face-lift not long ago and, more than ever, it
retains its Gstaad-by-the-sea glory. Its Bavarian-style facade resembles
that of countless other Lake District lodgings, but the lobby's huge
picture window overlooking the Seno de Reloncaví lets you know this
place is something special. The modern guest rooms are comfy, with
carpets and contemporary wood furniture—but do yourself a favor and
spring for a standard room, rather than an economy one. The difference in price is tiny, but the difference in quality of the rooms is substantial. **Pros:** Clean and modern. **Cons:** Low on personality. ⊠*Diego
Portales 450* ☎*65/432–900* 🖷*65/437–699* ⊕*www.granhotelvicente
costanera.cl* 🛏*82 rooms, 4 suites* ♿*In-room: no a/c, safe, refrigerator.
In-hotel: restaurant, bar, room service, concierge, laundry service, airport shuttle, public Internet, public Wi-Fi, parking, no-smoking rooms*
⊟*AE, DC, MC, V* ⏐○⏐*BP.*

$$ 🏨**Holiday Inn Express.** Stunning views of Puerto Montt Bay and the city
★ itself make this place an excellent choice. Combine the view, which
almost all the rooms have (some rooms even have their own private
terrace), with modern facilities, and this is easily one of the best hotels
in the city. As an added bonus, the hotel sits above a large mall that
includes a movie theater with six movie screens. **Pros:** Amazing views.
Cons: Can be noisy. ⊠*Av. Costanera, above Mall Paseo Costanera*
☎*65/566–000* ⊕*www.holidayinnexpress.cl* 🛏*105 rooms* ♿*In-room:
safe, Ethernet, Wi-Fi. In-hotel: restaurant, bar, gym, public Internet,
public Wi-Fi, parking, no-smoking rooms* ⊟*AE, DC, MC, V.*

Chiloé

Steeped in magic, shrouded in mist, the 41-island archipelago of Chiloé is that proverbial world apart, isolated not so much by distance from the mainland—it's barely more than 2 km (1 mi) at its nearest point—but by the quirks of history. Some 130,000 people populate 35 of these rainy islands, with most of them living on the 8,394-square-km (3,241-square-mi) Isla Grande de Chiloé. Almost all are descendants of a seamless blending of colonial and indigenous cultures, a tradition that entwines farming and fishing, devout Catholicism and spirits of good and evil, woolen sweaters and wooden churches.

Getting Around: Some 40 buses per day and frequent ferries make the half-hour crossing between Chiloé and Pargua, near Puerto Montt in the Lake District. If you're like most people, you'll explore Chiloé by car. Because of the island's relatively small size, driving is a pleasure. When best to visit Chiloé? Summer. The islands averages only 60 days of sunshine a year, mostly during the summer months of December to March.

Unless you're one of those rare visitors who approaches the archipelago from the south, **Ancud** is the first encounter you'll have with Chiloé. Founded in 1769 as a fortress city on the northern end of Isla Grande, Ancud was repeatedly attacked during Chile's war for independence. It remained the last stronghold of the Spaniards in the Americas, and the seat of their government-in-exile after fleeing from Santiago, a distinction it retained until Chiloé was finally annexed by Chile in 1826. Sailing and sea kayaking are popular in Ancud. There are several fishing and trekking possibilities as well. Along the coast-line you can see dolphins, penguins, and often whales.

The center of all that is magical and mystical about Chiloé, **Quicaví** sits forlornly on the eastern coast of Isla Grande. More superstitious locals will strongly advise you against going anywhere near the coast to the south of town, where miles of caves extend to the village of Tenaún; they believe that evil witches inhabit them. And many a Quicaví denizen claims to have glimpsed Chiloé's notorious ghost ship, the Caleuche, roaming the waters on foggy nights, searching for its doomed passengers. A brief glimpse of the ship is all anyone dares admit, as legend holds that a longer gaze could spell death.

The small fishing village of **Tenaún**, 12 km (7 mi) south of Quicaví on Isla Grande, is notable for its 1861 neoclassical Iglesia de Tenaún on the Plaza de Armas, which replaced the original 1734 structure built by the Jesuits. The style differs markedly from that of other Chilote churches, as the two towers flanking the usual hexagonal central bell tower are painted a striking deep blue.

Most days travelers in **Dalcahue**, which is 40 km (24 mi) west of Tenaún, stop only long enough to board the ferry that deposits them 15 minutes later on Isla Quinchao. But everyone lingers in Dalcahue if it's a Sunday morning, when they can visit the weekly artisan market. This market, the Feria Artesanal, is held on Avenida Pedro Montt near the waterfront municipal building, and draws crowds who come to shop for Chilote woolens, baskets, and woven mythical figures. Things get under way at about 8 AM and begin to wind down about noon.

Bargaining is expected, though the prices are already quite reasonable.

For many visitors, the elongated **Isla Quinchao**, just southeast of Dalcahue and the easiest to reach of the islands off the east coast of Isla Grande, defines Chiloé. Populated by hardworking farmers and fisherfolk, Isla Quinchao provides a glimpse into the region's past. Head to Achao, Quinchao's largest community, to see the alerce-shingle houses, the busy fishing pier, and the town's centerpiece: the 1706 On Achao's Plaza de Armas, the town's centerpiece is its 1706 Iglesia de Santa María de Loreto, the oldest remaining house of worship on the archipelago. Its typically unadorned exterior contrasts with the deep-blue ceiling embellished with gold stars inside. Rich baroque carvings grace the altar.

Founded in 1567, **Castro** is Chile's third-oldest city and with a population of 20,000, Castro is Chiloé's second-largest city. Next to its wooden churches, palafitos are the best-known architectural symbol of Chiloé. These shingled houses are all along the island's coast. Avenida Pedro Montt, which becomes a coastal highway as it leads out of town, is the best place to see palafitos in Castro. Many of these ramshackle structures have been turned into restaurants and artisan markets.

Visit the much-photographed 1906 Iglesia de San Francisco, whose orange-and-lavender exterior has been described as both "pretty" and "pretty garish." It's infinitely more reserved on the inside. The Museo Regional de Castro, just off the Plaza de Armas, gives the best Spanish-language introduction to the region's history and culture. Packed into a fairly small space are artifacts from the Huilliche era (primarily rudimentary farming and fishing implements) through the 19th century (looms, spinning wheels, and plows). One exhibit displays the history of the archipelago's wooden churches; another shows black-and-white photographs of the damage caused by the 1960 earthquake that rocked southern Chile.

The colorful wooden houses of **Chonchi**, 23 km (14 mi) south of Castro, are on a hillside so steep that it's known in Spanish as the Ciudad de los Tres Pisos (City of Three Stories). Arranged around a scenic harbor, Chonchi wins raves as Chiloé's most picturesque town.

The 430-square-km (166-square-mi) **Parque Nacional Chiloé**, 35 km (21 mi) west of Chonchi hugs Isla Grande's sparsely populated Pacific coast. The park's two sectors differ dramatically in landscape and access. Heavily forested with evergreens, Sector Anay, to the south, is most easily entered from the coastal village of Cucao. A road heads west to the park from the Pan-American Highway at Notuco, just south of Chonchi. Sector Anay is popular among backpackers, who hike the short El Tepual trail, which begins at the Chanquín Visitor Center 1 km (½ mi) north of the park entrance. Cucao beach at the park's southern end extends 1½ km (1 mi). Dunes extend all along this unusually wide beach. This is one of the best beaches in Chile.

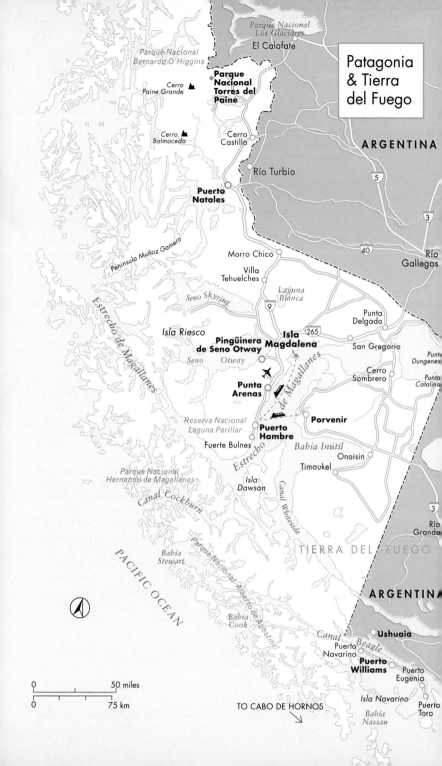

SHOPPING

An excellent selection of handicrafts is sold at the best prices in the country at the **Feria Artesanal Angelmó,** on the coastal road near Caleta Angelmó. Baskets, ponchos, figures woven from different kinds of grasses and straw, and warm sweaters of raw, hand-spun, and hand-dyed wool are all offered. Haggling is expected. It's open daily 9–dusk.

CHILEAN PATAGONIA

The spirit of the region resides in the southernmost province of Magallanes, the waterway of Seno Última Esperanza ("Last Hope Sound"), and the infamous misnomer Tierra del Fuego ("Land of Fire"). It's one of the least inhabited areas in South America, physically cut off from the rest of the continent by two vast ice caps and the Strait of Magellan. The only links with the north are via air or water— or through Argentina. It's amidst this seclusion that you will find the daunting rocky spires of Torres del Paine, horseback sheep-wrangling gauchos, islands inhabited solely by elephant seals and penguin colonies, and the austere landscapes that captivated everyone from Charles Darwin to Butch Cassidy and the Sundance Kid.

PUERTO NATALES

242 km (150 mi) northwest of Punta Arenas.

The land around Puerto Natales held very little interest for Spanish explorers in search of riches. A not-so-warm welcome from the indigenous peoples encouraged them to continue up the coast, leaving only a name for the channel running through it: Seno Última Esperanza (Last Hope Sound).

The town of Puerto Natales wasn't founded until 1911. A community of fading fishing and meat-packing enterprises, with some 20,000 friendly residents, it has recently seen a large increase in tourism and is repositioning itself as a vacation town; it's now rapidly emerging as the staging center for visits to Parque Nacional Torres del Paine, Parque Nacional Bernardo O'Higgins, and other attractions, including the Perito Moreno Glacier across the border in Argentina. A lot of tourism is also generated by the scenic **Navimag cruise** that makes four-day journeys between here and Puerto Montt, to the north.

Hotels and restaurants are simpler than in Punta Arenas, and shops older and more basic. Serious hikers often come to this area and spend four or five days—or more—hiking and camping in **Torres del Paine,** either before or after stopping in Puerto Natales. Others choose to spend a couple of nights in one of the park's luxury hotels, and take in the sights during day hikes from that base.

GETTING HERE & AROUND

Most people fly into the region, landing at Punto Arena's airport. From there Puerto Natales is about a 3 hour drive or bus ride north. Puerto

Natales centers on the Plaza de Armas, a lovely, well-landscaped sanctuary. On a clear day, an early-morning walk along Avenida Pedro Montt, which follows the shoreline of the Seno Última Esperanza (or Canal Señoret, as it's called on some maps), can be a soul-cleansing experience. The rising sun gradually casts a glow on the mountain peaks to the west.

ESSENTIALS

Bus Contacts Buses Fernández (⊠ Eleuterio Ramirez 399 ☎ 61/411–111 ⊕ www.busesfernandez.com).

Internet Cafés El Rincón del Tata (⊠ Arturo Prat 23 ☎ 61/413–845).

Rental Cars Avis (⊠ Av. Bulnes 632 ☎ 61/410–775).

Visitor & Tour Info Sernatur Puerto Natales (⊠ Av. Pedro Montt 19 ☎ 61/412–125).

EXPLORING PUERTO NATALES

A few blocks east of the Seno Última Esperanza is the not-quite-central **Plaza de Armas.** An incongruous railway engine sits prominently in the middle of the square. ⊠ Arturo Prat at Eberhard.

A highlight in the small but interesting **Museo Historico Municipal** is a room filled with antique prints of Aonikenk and Kaweshkar indigenous peoples. Another room is devoted to the exploits of Hermann Eberhard, a German explorer considered the region's first settler. Check out his celebrated collapsible boat. In an adjacent room you will find some vestiges of the old Bories sheep plant, which processed more than 300,000 sheep a year. ⊠ Av. Bulnes 285 ☎ 61/411–263 ≦ 1,000 pesos ⊙ Weekdays 8:30–12:30 and 2:30–8, weekends 2:30–6.

In 1896, Hermann Eberhard stumbled upon a gaping cave that extended 200 meters (650 feet) into the earth. Venturing inside, he discovered the bones and dried pieces of hide of an animal he could not identify. It was later determined that what Eberhard had discovered were the extraordinarily well-preserved remains of a prehistoric herbivorous mammal, *mylodon darwini,* about twice the height of a man, which they called a *milodón.* The discovery of a stone wall in the cave, and of neatly cut grass stalks in the animal's feces led researchers to conclude that 10,000 years ago a group of Tehuelche Indians captured this beast. The cave and a somewhat kitschy life-size fiberglass rendering of the creature are at the **Monumento Natural Cueva de Milodón.** ⊠ 5 km (3 mi) off Ruta 9 signpost, 28 km (17 mi) northwest of Puerto Natales ☎ No phone ≦ 3,000 pesos ⊙ Summer, daily 8 AM–9 PM; winter, daily 9–6.

BORDER CROSSING

There are three crossings to and from Argentina near Puerto Natales. Dorotea Pass is 27 km (17 mi) along Route CH-250 from Puerto Natales. There are 14 km (9 mi) to Río Turbio in Argentina. It's open 24 hours from November to March, 8–midnight April–October. Casas Viejas Pass is located 14 km (9 mi) from Puerto Natales. It's about 19 km (12 mi) to Río Turbio (open all year 8 AM–10 PM). From December to March, Cancha Carrera provides access from Puerto Natales through the Cerro Castillo area to El Calafate.

WHERE TO EAT

$$ ✗**Asador Patagónico.** This bright spot in the Puerto Natales dining scene
CHILEAN is zealous about meat. So zealous, in fact, that there's no seafood on the
★ menu. Incredible care is taken with the excellent *lomo* and other grilled
steaks, as well as the steak carpaccio starter. Though the wine list is
serious, the atmosphere is less so—the place used to be a pharmacy,
and much of the furniture is still labeled with the remedies (*catgut
crin* anyone?) they once contained. There's good music, dim lighting,
an open fire, and a friendly buzz. ⊠*Prat 158* ☎*61/412–197* ☐*AE,
DC, MC, V.*

¢–$ ✗**Café Melissa.** The best espresso in town is found at this café, which
CAFÉ also serves pastries and cakes baked on the premises. In the heart of
downtown, this is a popular meeting place for residents and visitors,
and there's Internet access. It's open until 9 PM. ⊠*Blanco Encalada 258*
☎*61/411–944* ☐*No credit cards.*

¢–$$ ✗**Pez Glaciar.** Eco-friendly vibes waft from this bright newly renovated
SEAFOOD seafood spot. Marine fossils collected from the adjacent fjord, piles of
*National Geographic*s, subtle cuisine, and an English-speaking staff
make this restaurant a hit. The fresh lemon-marinated ceviche is amazing, as are the dinner-plate-size sandwiches served on homemade wheat
bread. The corner location within the Indigo Hotel, overlooking the
water and a backdrop of snowy peaks, makes for a pleasant visit, even
if you come just for a cup of coffee. ⊠*Ladrilleros 105* ☎*61/413–609*
⊕*www.indigopatagonia.com* ☐*AE, DC, MC, V* ☉*Closed in winter;
months vary.*

WHERE TO STAY

$$$ ▦**Altiplanico Sur.** This is the Patagonian representative of the Altip-
lanico line of thoughtfully designed eco-hotels. Nature takes center
stage at Altiplanico Sur. The hotel blends seamlessly with its surround-
ings due to an interesting construction technique which involves the
use of natural materials in its exterior. The roofs are covered with grass
and flowers so it looks like the hotel is cascading down the hillside.
If you are looking for TVs, Wi-Fi, and other modern day accoutre-
ments, there are more appropriate choices. Clean, comfortable, and
well-designed rooms are in a minimalist style, with great views of the
Última Esperanza Sound. The dining area is bright and open. Staff do
their best to help, but sometimes language proves a barrier. **Pros:** You
couldn't be closer to nature. **Cons:** No mod-cons, staff speaks little
English. ⊠*Ruta 9 Norte, Km 1.5, Huerto 282* ☎*61/411–919* ⊕*www.
altiplanico.cl* ⇆*22 rooms* ⌂*In-room: no TV, safe. In-hotel: restaurant*
☐*AE, MC, V.*

$ ▦**Hotel Alberto de Agostini.** The Agostini is one of the modern hotels
that have cropped up in Puerto Natales in the past few years. Small
rooms—some with hot tubs—are unremarkable in decor, but a com-
fortably furnished lounge on the second floor looks out over the Seno
Última Esperanza. **Pros:** Perfectly functional. **Cons:** Rooms small, not
distinctive. ⊠*Av. Bernardo O'Higgins 632* ☎*61/410–060* ☐*61/410–
070* ⊕*www.hotelalbertodeagostini.cl* ⇆*25 rooms* ⌂*In-hotel: restau-
rant, room service, bar, laundry service, public Internet* ☐*AE, DC,
MC, V.*

$$$–$$$$ 🏨 **Hotel CostAustralis.** Designed by a local architect, this venerable three-story hotel is one of the most distinctive buildings in Puerto Natales; its peaked, turreted roof dominates the waterfront. Rooms have wood-paneled entryways, thermo-acoustic windows, and Venetian and Czech furnishings. Some have a majestic view of the Seno Última Esperanza and the snowcapped mountain peaks beyond, and others look out over the city. **Pros:** Great views from bay-facing rooms, good restaurant. **Cons:** Rooms are somewhat bland. ⊠ *Av. Pedro Montt 262, at Av. Bulnes* 🕾 *61/412–000* 🖷 *61/411–881* ⊕ *www.hoteles-australis.com* ⇘ *72 rooms, 2 suites* ⅋ *In-room: safe. In-hotel: restaurant, room service, bar, laundry service, public Internet* ▭ *AE, DC, MC, V* ⏐⊙⏐*BP.*

$$$$ 🏨 **Indigo Patagonia Hotel & Spa.** Rooms in this completely renovated
★ hotel have amazing views down the Canal Señoret, stretching as far as the Mt. Balmaceda glacier and the Paine Grande. Very minimalist modern natural-wood design abounds. Blankets are made of hand-woven wool. With three open-air Jacuzzis and a dry sauna, the rooftop spa is a treat for the senses. Down below common spaces are filled with plush couches and there's a lounge bar where you can enjoy brownies and cappuccinos—or a late-night pisco sour. English is spoken well, as exhibited in the Friday-night shows about Torres del Paine park. Ask for one of the corner rooms, which have windows along two walls. **Pros:** Steeped in ultramodern luxury. **Cons:** Standard rooms do not have bathtubs (though the showers are excellent). ⊠ *Ladrilleros 105* 🕾 *61/413–609* 🖷 *61/410–169* ⊕ *www.conceptoindigo.com* ⇘ *23 rooms, 6 suites* ⅋ *In-room: no TV. In-hotel: restaurant, bar, laundry service, spa, public Wi-Fi* ▭ *AE, DC, MC, V* ⊙ *Closed in winter; months vary.*

$$$$ 🏨 **Remota.** For most of its guests the Remota experience begins a long
Fodor'sChoice way off from the hotel, when they are scooped up from the Punta
★ Arenas airport. On arrival you meet what seems like the entire staff, check into your ultramodern room, have a drink from a top-shelf open bar, and run off to the open-air Jacuzzis and impossibly serene infinity pool—before you unpack. The hotel is the paragon of style, deliberately designed (by the same architect as Explora) in a way that blocks out everything but the exquisite vistas. The staff feels like family, and all meals and excursions are included in the price. Every day a guide proposes a wide range of activities, demanding various levels of exertion, so you are sure to find something to suit your speed. Equipment is supplied and includes everything from Zodiacs to mountain-climbing gear to bikes. Horseback riding with local gauchos is a hard activity to pass up. **Pros:** After a few days the staff feels like family. **Cons:** All-inclusiveness discourages sampling local restaurants. ⊠ *Ruta 9 Norte, Km 1.5, Huerto 279* 🕾 *61/414–040* ⊕ *www.remota.cl* ⇘ *72 rooms* ⅋ *In-room: no phone, no TV, safe. In-hotel: spa, pool, bicycles, restaurant, bar* ▭ *AE, MC, V* ⏐⊙⏐*AI.*

PARQUE NACIONAL TORRES DEL PAINE

Fodor's Choice
★

80 km northwest of Puerto Natales.

Some 12 million years ago, lava flows pushed up through the thick sedimentary crust that covered the southwestern coast of South America, cooling to form a granite mass. Glaciers then swept through the region, grinding away all but the twisted ash-gray spires—the "towers" of Paine (pronounced "pie-nay"), the old Tehuelche word for "blue"— that rise over the landscape of one of the world's most beautiful natural phenomena, now the Parque Nacional Torres del Paine (established in 1959). Snow formations dazzle at every turn of road, and the sunset views are spectacular. The 2,420-square-km (934-square-mi) park's most astonishing attractions are its lakes of turquoise, aquamarine, and emerald green waters; and the Cuernos del Paine ("Paine Horns"), the geological showpiece of the immense granite massif.

Another draw is the park's unusual wildlife. Creatures like the guanaco (a woollier version of the llama) and the *ñandú* (a rhea, like a small ostrich) abound. They are used to visitors, and don't seem to be bothered by the proximity of automobile traffic and the snapping of cameras. Predators like the gray fox make less-frequent appearances. You may also spot the dramatic aerobatics of falcons and the graceful soaring of endangered condors. The beautiful puma, celebrated in a National Geographic video filmed here, is especially elusive, but sightings have grown more common. Pumas follow the guanaco herds and eat an estimated 40% of their young, so don't dress as one.

The vast majority of visitors come during the summer months of January and February, which means the trails can get congested. Early spring, when wildflowers add flashes of color to the meadows, is an ideal time to visit because the crowds have not yet arrived. In summer, the winds are incredibly fierce. During the wintertime of June to September, the days are sunnier yet colder (averaging around freezing) and shorter, but the winds all but disappear. The park is open all year, and trails are almost always accessible. Storms can hit without warning, so be prepared for sudden rain or snow. The sight of the Paine peaks in clear weather is stunning.

VISITOR INFORMATION

CONAF, the national forestry service, has an office at the northern end of Lago del Toro with a scale model of the park, and numerous exhibits (some in English) about the flora and fauna. ✉*CONAF station in southern section of park past Hotel Explora* ☏*61/247–845* ⊕*www. conaf.cl* ✉*Summer 15,000 pesos, winter 5,000 pesos* ☉*Ranger station: Nov.–Feb., daily 8–8; Mar.–Oct., daily 8–12:30 and 2–6:30* ✉*Punta Arenas Branch, Av. Bulnes 0309* ☏*61/238–581* ✉*Puerto Natales Branch, Av. Bernardo O'Higgins 584* ☏*61/411–438.*

EXPLORING TORRES DEL PAINE

There are three entrances to the park: Laguna Amarga (all bus arrivals), Lago Sarmiento, and Laguna Azul. You are required to sign in when you arrive. *Guardaparques* (park rangers) staff six stations around the

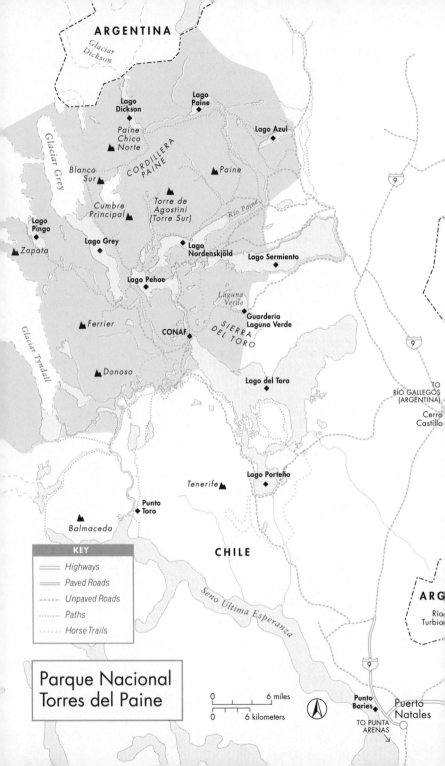

Parque Nacional
Torres del Paine

reserve, and can provide a map and up-to-the-day information about the state of various trails. A regular minivan service connects Laguna Amarga with the Hosteria Las Torres, 7 km (4½ mi) to the west, for 1,000 pesos. Alternatively, you can walk approximately two hours before reaching the starting point of the hiking circuits.

Although considerable walking is necessary to take full advantage of Parque Nacional Torres del Paine, you need not be a hard-core trekker. Many people choose to hike the **"W" route,** which takes four days, but others prefer to stay in one of the comfortable lodges and hit the trails in the morning or afternoon. **Glaciar Grey,** with its fragmented icebergs, makes a rewarding and easy hike; equally rewarding is the spectacular boat or kayak ride across the lake, past icebergs, and up to the glacier, which leaves from Hostería Lago Grey. Another great excursion is the 900-meter (3,000-foot) ascent to the sensational views from **Mirador Las Torres,** four hours one way from Hostería Las Torres. Even if you're not staying at the Hostería, you can arrange a morning drop-off there, and a late-afternoon pickup, so that you can see the Mirador while still keeping your base in Puerto Natales or elsewhere in the park; alternatively, you can drive to the Hostería and park there for the day.

Driving is an easier way to enjoy the park: a new road cuts the distance to Puerto Natales from a meandering 140 km (87 mi) to a more direct 80 km (50 mi). Inside the national park, more than 100 km (62 mi) of roads leading to the most popular sites are safe and well maintained, though unpaved.

You can also hire horses from the Hosteria Las Torres and trek to the Torres, the Cuernos, or along the shore of Lago Nordenskjold (which offers the finest views in the park, as the lake's waters reflect the chiseled massif). The hotel offers tours demanding various levels of expertise (prices start at 25,000 pesos). Alternatively, many Puerto Natales–based operators offer multi-day horseback tours. Water transport is also available, with numerous tour operators offering sailboat, kayak, and inflatable Zodiac speedboat options along the Río Serrano (prices start around 50,000 pesos for the Zodiac trips) towards the Paine massif and the southern ice field. Additionally, the Hostería Lago Grey operates the *Grey II,* a large catamaran making a three-hour return trip twice daily to Glaciar Grey, at 10 AM and 3 PM; as well as dinghy runs down the Pingo and Grey rivers.

WHERE TO STAY & EAT

$$$ **Hosteria Tyndall.** A boat ferries you from the end of the road the few minutes along the Serrano River to this wooden lodge. The simple rooms in the main building are small but cute, with attractive wood paneling. The hallways are poorly lit and the lodge itself can be noisy— a problem solved by renting a log cottage (at $220 a great value for groups of four). There's also a much more basic refugio with dorm-style rooms that are very cheap. Owner Christian Bore is a wildlife enthusiast and bird-watcher; ask him for a tour of the grassy plain looking out toward the central cluster of snowy peaks. Or go fishing—the kitchen

staff will cook your catch for free. The prix-fixe lunch costs $14, dinner $25. **Pros:** Cheaper lodging and dining options than other places in the park. **Cons:** Hallways are poorly lit and the lodge itself can get noisy. ✉ *Ladrilleros 256, Lago Tyndall* 🏠🏠 *61/614–682* ⊕ *www.hosteria tyndall.com* 🛏 *24 rooms, 6 cottages* ⚐ *In-room: no phone, no TV. In-hotel: restaurant, bar, laundry service* ▤ *AE, DC, MC, V* ⦿ *CP.*

$$$$
Fodor'sChoice
★

🏨 **Hotel Explora.** On the southeast corner of Lago Pehoé, this lodge is one of the most luxurious—and the most expensive—in Chile. Although there may be some debate about the aesthetics of the hotel's low-slung minimalist exterior, the interior is impeccable: it's Scandinavian in style, with local woods used for ceilings, floors, and furniture. No expense has been spared—even the bed linens were imported from Spain. A dozen full-time guides tailor all-inclusive park outings to guests' interests. A four-night minimum stay is required, for which you'll pay a minimum of US$4,952 for two people, including airport transfers, three meals a day, drinks, and excursions. Rooms with better views go up to almost double that. Yet, as a testament to the value, the place consistently sells out even during the winter. Nonguests may also enjoy a pricey prix-fixe dinner ($60) at the restaurant. **Pros:** The grande dame of Patagonian hospitality and perhaps the best hotel in all South America. **Cons:** A bank breaker. ✉ *Lago Pehoé* ☎ *2/206–6060 in Santiago* 🖷 *2/228–4655 in Santiago* ⊕ *www.explora.com* 🛏 *44 rooms, 6 suites* ⚐ *In-room: no TV. In-hotel: restaurant, bar, pool, gym, laundry service, airport shuttle, public Internet* ▤ *AE, DC, MC, V* ⦿ *AI.*

$$$$
★

🏨 **Las Torres Patagonia.** Owned by one of the earliest families to settle in what became the park, Las Torres has a long history. Originally an estancia, then a popular hosteria, the facility recently upgraded to a three-night-minimum, all-food-and-excursion-inclusive resort, in the style of Remota and Explora. Stretched across several vast fields, the location is perfect if you want to day-hike to Mirador Torres, one of the park's highlights. Don't forget to check out the informative mini-museum with the stuffed ñandú. **Pros:** Friendly and efficient, with a homey atmosphere. **Cons:** Not cheap. ✉ *Lago Amarga* 🏠🏠 *61/360–364* ⊕ *www.lastorres.com* 🛏 *57 rooms* ⚐ *In room: no TV. In-hotel: restaurant, bar, spa* ▤ *AE, MC, V.*

PUNTA ARENAS

Founded a little more than 150 years ago, Punta Arenas ("Sandy Point") was Chile's first permanent settlement in Patagonia. Great developments in cattle-keeping, mining, and wood production led to an economic and social boom at the end of the 19th century; today, though the port is no longer an important stop on trade routes, it exudes an aura of faded grandeur. Plaza Muñoz Gamero, the central square (also known as the Plaza de Armas), is surrounded by evidence of its early prosperity: buildings whose then-opulent brick exteriors recall a time when this was one of Chile's wealthiest cities.

The sights of Punta Arenas can basically be done in a day or two. The city is mainly a jumping off point for cruises, or for traveling up to

Torres del Paine, which is most pleasantly done by staying in closeby Puerto Natales, a town that's gaining ground over Punta Arenas as a vacation destination..

GETTING HERE & AROUND

Most travelers will arrive at Aeropuerto Presidente Carlos Ibanez de Campo, a modern terminal approximately 12 mi from town. Public bus service from the airport into the central square of Punta Arenas is 2,000 pesos. Private transfers by small companies running minivans out of the airport (with no other pickup points or call-in service) run 3,000 pesos per person, while a taxi for two or more is your best deal at 5,000 pesos.

Set on a windy bank of the Magellan Strait, eastward-facing Punta Arenas has four main thoroughfares which were originally planned wide enough to accommodate flocks of sheep. Bustling with pedestrians, Avenida Bories is the main drag for shopping. Overall, the city is quite compact, and navigating its central grid of streets is fairly straightforward.

ESSENTIALS

Bus Contacts **Buses Fernández** (⊠*Armando Sanhueza 745, Punta Arenas* ☎*61/221–429* ⊕*www.busesfernandez.com*). **Tecni-Austral** (⊠*Lautaro Navarro 975* ☎*61/222–078 or 61/223–205*).

Internet Cafés **Austro Internet** (⊠*Croacica 690* ☎*61/222–297*). **El Calafate** (⊠*Av. Magallanes 922* ☎*61/241–281*).

Medical Assistance **Clinica Magallanes Medical Center** (⊠*Av. Bulnes 1448* ☎*61/211–527*). **Hospital Cirujano Guzman** (⊠*Av. Bulnes at Capitan Guillermos* ☎*61/207--500*). **Hospital Mutual de Seguridad** (⊠*Av. España 1890* ☎*61/212–369*).

Postal Services **DHL** (⊠*Pedro Montt 840, Local 4* ☎*61/228-462* ⊕*www.dhl.com*). **Post Office** (⊠*Bories 911*).

Rental Cars **Avis** (⊠*Roca 1044* ☎*61/241–182* ⊠*Aeropuerto Presidente Ibañez*). **Budget** (⊠*Av. Bernardo O'Higgins 964* ☎*61/241–696* ⊠*Aeropuerto Presidente Ibañez*). **Hertz** (⊠*Av. Bernardo O'Higgins 987* ☎*61/248–742* ⊠*Aeropuerto Presidente Ibañez* ☎*61/210–096*). **International Rent A Car** (⊠*Aeropuerto Presidente Ibañez* ☎*61/212–401*).

Visitor & Tour Info **Punta Arenas City Tourism** (⊠*Plaza Muñoz Gamero* ☎*61/200–610* ⊕*www.puntaarenas.cl*). **Sernatur Punta Arenas** (⊠*Av. Magallanes 960* ☎*61/225-385* ⊕*www.sernatur.cl*).

EXPLORING PUNTA ARENAS

❹ **Cementerio Municipal.** The fascinating history of this region is chiseled ★ into stone at the Municipal Cemetery. Bizarrely ornate mausoleums honoring the original families are crowded together along paths lined by sculpted cypress trees. In a strange effort to recognize Punta Arenas's indigenous past, there's a shrine in the northern part of the cemetery where the last member of the Selk'nam tribe was buried. Local legend

Punta Arenas

Angamos

Burnes

Maipú

Jorge Montt

Quillota

Sarmiento

Armando Sanhueza

Chiloé

Borries

Magallanes

Croacia

Mejicana

Navarro

O'Higgins

Carrera Pinto

Av. Colón

Av. España

José Menéndez

Post Office ▬

❷

❸

Pedro Montt

Waldo Seguel

Cathedral ▬

❶ 🛈

Fagnano

Roca

Armando Sanhueza

Chiloé

José Noguiera

21 de Mayo

Navarro

Errázuriz

Balmaceda

Av. Independencia

Port
◆

Estrecho de Magallanes

KEY

🛈 *Tourist Information*

says that rubbing the statue's left knee brings good luck. ⌧ *Av. Bulnes 949* ☎*No phone* 🎫*Free* ⊙ *Daily dawn–dusk.*

Fodor'sChoice **Isla Magdalena.** Punta Arenas is the launching point for a boat trip to see
★ the more than 120,000 Magellanic penguins at the **Monumento Natural Los Pingüinos** on this island. Visitors walk a single trail, marked off by rope, and penguins are everywhere—wandering across your path, sitting in burrows, skipping along just off the shore, strutting around in packs. The trip to the island, in the middle of the Estrecho de Magallanes, takes about two hours. To get here, you must take a tour boat. If you haven't booked in advance, you can stop at any of the local travel agencies and try to get on a trip at the last minute, which is often possible. You can go only from December to February; the penguin population peaks in January and February. However you get here, bring warm clothing, even in summer; the island can be chilly, and it's definitely windy, which helps with the odor. If you like penguins, you'll have a blast. If you don't like penguins, what are you doing in Patagonia?

❸ **Museo Regional de Magallanes.** Housed in what was once the mansion
★ of the powerful Braun-Menéndez family, the Regional Museum of Magallanes is an intriguing glimpse into the daily life of a wealthy provincial family at the beginning of the 20th century. Lavish Carrara marble hearths, English bath fixtures, and cordovan leather walls are among the original bling. The museum has an excellent group of displays depicting Punta Arenas's past, from European contact to its decline with the opening of the Panama Canal. The museum is half a block north of the main square. ⌧ *Av. Magallanes 949* ☎*61/244–216* 🎫*1,000 pesos* ⊙ *Oct.–Mar., Mon.–Sat. 10:30–5, Sun. 10:30–2; Apr.–Sept., daily 10:30–2.*

❷ **Palacio Sara Braun.** This resplendent 1895 mansion, a national landmark
★ and architectural showpiece of southern Patagonia, was designed by French architect Numa Meyer at the behest of Sara Braun (the wealthy widow of wool baron José Nogueira). Materials and craftsmen were imported from Europe during the home's four years of construction. The city's central plaza and surrounding buildings soon followed, ushering in the region's golden era. The Club de la Unión, a social organization that now owns the building, opens its doors to nonmembers for tours of some of the rooms and salons, which have magnificent parquet floors, marble fireplaces, and hand-painted ceilings. After touring the rooms, head to the cellar tavern for a drink or snack. ⌧ *Plaza Muñoz Gamero 716* ☎*61/241–489* 🎫*1,000 pesos* ⊙ *Tues.–Fri. 10:30–1 and 5–8:30, Sat. 10:30–1 and 8–10, Sun. 11–2.*

NEED A
BREAK?
Tea and coffee house, chocolate shop, and bakery, Chocolatta (⌧ *Bories 852* ☎*61/268–606*) **is a perfect refueling stop during a day of wandering Punta Arenas. The interior is cozy, the staff friendly, and you can hang out, perhaps over a creamy hot chocolate, for as long as you like.**

❶ **Plaza Muñoz Gamero.** A canopy of pine trees shades this square, which is surrounded by splendid baroque-style mansions from the 19th cen-

Tierra del Fuego by Sea

The four-day Navimag trips from Puerto Montt to Puerto Natales, which pass the Amalia Glacier, are immensely popular with backpackers and other visitors. The ship isn't luxurious, but it has a restaurant, pub, and lectures on local culture. Depending on which sort of cabin you choose, cabins are priced US$720–US$845 (380,000 pesos–446,000 pesos) per person for double occupancy in high season, and US$340–US$410 (180,000 pesos–216,500 pesos) per person in low season. Prices include all meals. The boat calls at Puerto Edén, where you can get off and visit the town for a few hours. Navimag tickets can be bought online or at local travel agencies.

If you prefer to travel through the region's natural wonders in comfort, Comapa's affiliate Cruceros Australis runs two ships, the elegant 55-cabin *Mare Australis*, built in 2002, and the even newer 63-cabin *Vía Australis*, constructed in 2005. Both ships have the classic, wood-and-polished-brass design of old-world luxury liners, and both sail round-trip between Punta Arenas and Ushuaia (there are 4-day and 3-day options). On the way, the ships stop at a number of sights, including the Garibaldi Glacier, a breathtaking mass of blue ice. You also ride smaller motorboats ashore to visit Isla Magdalena's colony of 120,000 penguins, and Ainsworth Bay's family of elephant seals. The cruises include lectures in English, German, and Spanish on the region's geography and history, flora and fauna; all multi-course meals and cocktails (including some formidable pisco sours) are included.

Comapa also runs a ferry three times a week between Punta Arenas and Porvenir, and the *Barcaza Melinka*, which makes thrice-weekly trips to Isla Magdalena (during penguin season).

Turismo 21 de Mayo operates two ships, the *Cutter 21 de Mayo* and the *Alberto de Agostini*, to the Balmaceda and Serrano glaciers in Parque Nacional Bernardo O'Higgins. Passengers on these luxurious boats are treated to lectures about the region as the boat moves up the Seno Última Esperanza.

Lago Grey Tours offers boat trips to Glaciar Grey inside the Parque Nacional Torres del Paine.

In El Calafate, Upsala Explorer combines a day at an estancia and a boat trip to Upsala Glacier.

Comapa (⊠ *Av. Magallanes 990, Punta Arenas* ☎ *61/200–200* ⊕ *www. comapa.cl* ⊠ *Av. Bulnes 533 Puerto Natales* ☎ *61/414–300*).

Cruceros Australis (⊠ *Av. El Bosque Norte 0440, Piso 11, Santiago* ☎ *2/442–3110* 🖷 *2/203–5173* ⊕ *www.australis.com*).

Lago Grey Tours (⊠ *Lago Grey* ☎🖷 *61/225–986* ⊕ *www.lagogrey. com*).

Navimag (⊠ *Av. El Bosque Norte 0440, Santiago* ☎ *2/442–3120* 🖷 *2/203–5025* ⊕ *www.navimag.com*).

Turismo 21 de Mayo (⊠ *Ladrilleros 171, Puerto Natales* ☎ *61/411–176* ⊕ *www.turismo21demayo.cl*).

tury. A bronze sculpture commemorating the voyage of Hernando de Magallanes dominates the center of the plaza. Local lore has it that a kiss on the shiny toe of Calafate, one of the Fuegian statues at the base of the monument, will one day bring you back to Punta Arenas. ⊠*José Nogueira at 21 de Mayo.*

WHERE TO EAT

$–$$ ✕**La Leyenda del Remezón.** This cheerful little restaurant stands out
CHILEAN because of its deliciously seasoned grilled fish and meats. The dining room is unpretentious and homey, with a welcoming fireplace, and the day's menu is scrawled onto a chalkboard; if you're lucky, it might include a delicious pisco-marinated goose. Although it's near the port, away from the main part of town, the terrific food and potent pisco sours (brandy mixed with lemon, egg whites, and sugar) make it a walk rewarded. ⊠*21 de Mayo 1469* ☎*61/241–029* ▤*AE.*

¢–$$$ ✕ **Parrilla Los Ganaderos.** You'll feel like you're on the range in this
CHILEAN enormous restaurant resembling a rural *estancia* (ranch). The wait-
★ ers, dressed in gaucho costumes, serve up spectacular *cordero al ruedo* (spit-roasted lamb) cooked in the *salón de parilla* (grill room); a serving comes with three different cuts of meat. Complement your meal with a choice from the long list of Chilean wines. Black-and-white photographs of past and contemporary ranch life are displayed along the walls. The restaurant is several blocks north of the center of town, but it's worth the small detour. ⊠*Av. Bulnes 0977, at Manantiales* ☎*61/214–597* ⊕*www.parrillalosganaderos.cl* ▤*AE, MC, V* ☉*Closed Sun.*

¢–$$$ ✕ **Puerto Viejo.** The paragon of stylish modern design, Puerto Viejo is
CHILEAN down by the old port, appropriately enough. All-glass and untreated-
Fodor'sChoice wood partitions cordon off the smoking section. Seafood is the spe-
★ cialty, but good lamb and steak are also available. Owned by a local farmers' association, its sister restaurant is Los Ganaderos. Reserva-tions are recommended. ⊠*Av. Bernardo O'Higgins 1166* ☎*61/225–103* ⊕*www.puertoviejo.cl* ▤*AE, MC, V* ☉*Closed Sun.*

$–$$ ✕ **Taberna Club de la Unión.** A jovial, publike atmosphere prevails in this
CAFÉ wonderful, labyrinthine cellar redoubt down the side stairway of Sara
Fodor'sChoice Braun's old mansion on the main plaza. A series of nearly hidden rooms
★ in cozy stone and brick have black-and-white photos of historical Punta Arenas adorning the walls. You're likely to hear ragtime and jazz on the stereo while you enjoy beers served cold in frosted mugs, tapas-style meat and cheese appetizers, sandwiches, tacos, pizza, fajitas, and car-paccio (the menu has more bar snacks than dinner entrées). The bar is affiliated with the Club de la Unión headquartered upstairs, and many members relax down here. Unfortunately, due to a lack of proper ven-tilation, this smoker-tolerant venue reeks of cigarette smoke. ⊠*Plaza Muñoz Gamero 716* ☎*61/241–317* ▤*AE, DC, MC, V* ☉*Closed Sun. No lunch.*

WHERE TO STAY

$ **Hostal de la Avenida.** The rooms of this pea-green guesthouse all over-look a garden lovingly tended by the owner, a local of Yugoslav origin. Flowers spill out from a wheelbarrow and a bathtub, birdhouses hang from trees, and a statue of Mary rests in a shrine with a grotto. The rooms offer modest comforts for those on a budget. The ones across the garden, away from the street, are the newest. Beside them is a funky bar that Chilean poet Pablo Neruda would have approved of; it seems hunkered down for blustery winters. **Pros:** Quaint, simple, nice contrast to the big hotels. **Cons:** No Internet. ⊠*Av. Colón 534* ☎*61/247–532* ⟲*10 rooms, 6 with bath* ⚒*In-room: minibar, safe. In-hotel: bar, laundry service, public Wi-Fi* ▤*AE, DC, MC, V* ⵔ*CP.*

$ **Hostal Oro Fueguino.** On a sloping cobblestone street near the obser-
★ vation deck at Cerro la Cruz, this charming little hostelry—tall, narrow, and rambling—welcomes you with lots of color. The first thing you notice is the facade, painted bright orange and blue. Inside are homey wall hangings and lamp shades made of eye-catching fabrics from as far off as India. The dining and living rooms are cheerful, and there's a wealth of tourist information. The warmth is enhanced by the personal zeal of the proprietor, Dinka Ocampo. **Pros:** Much of its charm comes from its quirkiness. **Cons:** Somewhat isolated. ⊠*Fagnano 365* ☎*61/249–401* ⊕*www.orofueguino.cl* ⟲*12 rooms* ⚒*In-room: no a/c. In-hotel: laundry service, public Internet* ▤*AE, DC, MC, V* ⵔ*BP.*

$$$ **Hotel José Nogueira.** Originally the home of Sara Braun, this opulent
★ 19th-century mansion also contains a museum. The location—steps off the main plaza—couldn't be better. Carefully restored over many years, the building retains the original crystal chandeliers, marble floors, and polished bronze details that were imported from France. Rooms are stunning—especially on the third floor—with high ceilings, thick carpets, and period furniture. Suites have hot tubs and in-room faxes. **Pros:** Central location, authentic. **Cons:** None really. ⊠*Bories 959* ☎*61/711–000* ☎*61/711–011* ⊕*www.hotelnogueira.com* ⟲*17 rooms, 5 suites* ⚒*In-room: safe, dial-up. In-hotel: restaurant, bar, laundry service, public Wi-Fi* ▤*AE, DC, MC, V.*

$$ **Hotel Los Navegantes.** This unpretentious older hotel, just a block from the Plaza de Armas, has spacious burgundy-and-green rooms and a nautical theme (an enormous maritime map graces the lobby wall). There's a charming dark-wood bar and a garden-view restaurant that serves delicious roast lamb. **Pros:** Superb mattress and bedding quality. **Cons:** Don't get burned by the radiators; few electrical outlets. ⊠*José Menéndez 647* ☎*61/617–700* ☎*61/617–717* ⊕*www.hotel-losnavegantes. com* ⟲*50 rooms, 2 suites* ⚒*In-room: safe. In-hotel: restaurant, bar, airport shuttle, public Wi-Fi* ▤*AE, DC, MC, V.*

PINGÜINERA DE SENO OTWAY

65 km (40 mi) northwest of Punta Arenas.

Magellanic penguins, which live up to 20 years in the wild, return repeatedly to their birthplace to mate with the same partner. For about 2,000 penguin couples—no singles make the trip—home is this desolate and windswept land off the Otway Sound. In late September the penguins begin to arrive from the southern coast of Brazil and the Falkland Islands. They mate and lay their eggs in early October, and brood their eggs in November. Offspring are hatched mid-November through early December. If you're lucky, you'll see downy gray chicks stick their heads out of the burrows when their parents return to feed them. Otherwise you might see scores of the adult penguins waddling to the ocean from their nesting burrows. They swim for food every eight hours and dive up to 30 meters (100 feet) deep. The penguins depart from the sound in late March.

The road to the sanctuary begins 30 km (18 mi) north of Punta Arenas, where the main road, Ruta 9, diverges near a checkpoint booth. A gravel road then traverses another fierce and winding 30 km (18 mi), but the rough trip (mud will be a problem if there's been recent rain) should reward you with the sight of hundreds of sheep, cows, and birds, including, if you're lucky, rheas and flamingos. The sanctuary is a 1-km (½-mi) walk from the parking lot. It gets chilly, so bring a windbreaker.

The best time to appreciate the penguins is in the morning before 10 AM, or the evening after 5 PM, when they are not out fishing. If you don't have a car, Comapa, like many other tour companies based in Punta Arenas, offers tours to the Pingüinera *(⇨ By Boat in Patagonia & Tierra del Fuego Essentials)*. The tours generally leave from Punta Arenas, return about 3½ hours later, and range in price from 7,000 to 10,000 pesos. ⊠*Off Ruta 9* 📧*2,000 pesos* ⊙*Oct.–Mar., daily 8–7.*

Colombia

WORD OF MOUTH

"Colombia has a lot of energy. Cartegena looks like Spain, like Sevilla with narrow streets, old balconies, and lots of flowers."

—santamonica

Updated
by Richard
McColl

COLOMBIA IS BLESSED IN MANY WAYS. On the continent's northern tip, it's the only South American country that fringes both the Atlantic and Pacific. It's rich in emeralds, coffee, and oil. And because it straddles the equator, it's one of the most lush countries in terms of tropical flora and wildlife—there are more species of birds in Colombia than anywhere else in the world. You can jump on a plane and in less than an hour find yourself in a different dramatic setting—be it the cobblestone streets of a weathered colonial port, the stalls of a crowded market where Guambiano merchants still speak the tongues of their ancestors, or at the base of snow-covered peaks rising sharply from a steamy coastal plain.

Bogotá, Colombia's sprawling capital of more than 7 million people, stands at the end of a vast plateau in the eastern Andes. The poverty and drug violence make the headlines, but rarely covered by the media are the elegant shopping streets, grand high-rises, lovely colonial neighborhoods, and chic nightclubs where stylish young *Bogotanos* (as inhabitants of Bogotá are called) party into the night.

Cartagena, widely revered as the most striking colonial city in South America, is an excellent destination if you want to be on the Caribbean coast. If you equate vacationing with lounging in the sun, the beaches of San Andrés and Providencia islands are Colombia's most compelling. Undeterred by the 640-km (400-mi) trip from the mainland, Colombians escape to the resort islands for weekends of swimming, sunbathing, shopping, and sipping rum at thatch-roof waterfront bars.

Most of the country's 42 million people live in Colombia's western half, where the Andes split into three *cordilleras,* or ridges: Oriental, Central, and Occidental. As you ascend the mighty mountains, subtropical valleys give way to rigid, fern-carpeted peaks where the ever-present mists are brightened only by votive candles placed by truck drivers at roadside shrines. West of Bogotá, quiet villages hug the hillsides en route to Medellín, former base of the eponymous drug cartel of Pablo Escobar. Despite its notorious reputation, Medellín is a pleasant, relatively safe, modern city surrounded by velvety green hills and miles of lush farmland.

ORIENTATION & PLANNING

GETTING ORIENTED

One brief look at the map of South America tells you all that you need to know about Colombia. The country has everything from the Andes, Pacific jungles, colonial treasures, and cosmopolitan cities. Sun-kissed Caribbean beaches will appeal to those looking to kick back, and we challenge any visitor to resist the lure of those in Tayrona National Park. Deliciously verdant rolling hills surround Salento and yield Colombia's coffee crop, and continue deep into the Aburra valley, where the dynamically reborn Medellín surges from the ashes of an infamous history. The culturally rich and diverse capital city

of Bogotá has fine theaters and galleries, and is the main hub for all travel within Colombia, be it to the southwestern salsa capital of Cali, the Amazon at Laeticia, or colonial splendor on show in Cartagena, Mompox, and Popayan.

Bogotá. *Bogotanos* or *Rolos,* as citizens of the capital are called, will often tell you that their city way up on the altiplano is "the Athens of South America"—not for any Greek architecture but for the numbers of well-educated and polite citizens and the cultural riches such as the Museo de Oro and the Donación Botero.

Boyacá. With towns, valleys, and forests that whisper histories of epic battles for independence and yield much of Colombia's emerald wealth, Boyacá has such charming attractions as the colonially splendid Villa de Leyva and the breathtaking Parque Nacional Nevado del Cocuy.

Medellín. Medellín is the blueprint of a Colombian success story. When home to the godfather of international cocaine smuggling, Pablo Escobar, the city was a place to avoid. Now it has made an about turn and draws thousands to its tree-lined hillsides for the annual Feria de las Flores and to sample its unstoppable nightlife.

Southwest Colombia. Stroll about the colorful streets of Salento in Quindo, the coffee producing heartland. In Cali, Colombia's salsa capital blends flavors from the Pacific and the interior, and the result is a balmy city of contrasts; poverty and civil disorder are problems, but the visitor will enjoy long and late clement nights breaking in those dancing shoes. Farther south are Popayan with its restored colonial buildings and the UNESCO World Heritage site of pre-Columbian cultures in San Agustin.

Caribbean Coast. No visit to Colombia would be complete without time spent wandering through the ornate and opulent streets of Cartagena's walled Ciudad Vieja. Farther along the coast the colonial gives way to the hedonistic, as the resort town of Santa Marta acts as the gateway to Tayrona National Park.

San Andrés and Providencia. With more in common with Jamaica and the Cayman Islands, San Andrés and Providencia are two anomalous Caribbean islands in Colombia's abundant crown of riches. San Andrés is the resort island offering package vacations to all and sundry, while Providencia is the protected, less-visited and topographically striking younger sister.

COLOMBIA PLANNER

WHEN TO GO

December through February is the best and driest time to visit Colombia. Colombians also travel during these sometimes hot and humid months, so hotel rooms are harder to come by. While visiting during a festival adds an exciting cultural edge to your trip, you'll experience inflated prices and often overwhelming crowds.

TOP REASONS TO GO

Archaeological Treasures: Archaeological sites and priceless artifacts testify to the cultural richness that thrived in Colombia before European domination. Duck into Bogotá's Museo de Oro to see the world's largest collection of pre-Columbian gold and a comprehensive collection of pre-Columbian artifacts from indigenous cultures. Also in Bogotá is the Museum of Archaeology, which houses splendid pre-Columbian ceramics. And in San Agustin, Huila, visit the marvelous anthropomorphic sculptures.

Beaches: The country's favorite beaches are along the northern coast and on the Caribbean islands of San Andrés and Providencia. These resort islands have gorgeous white-sand beaches that stretch along the coast for miles, and the water is crystal-clear. While Cartagena has popular, if disappointing beaches, Tayrona and Santa Marta, farther along the Caribbean coast, offer exquisite white sand.

Colonial Wonders: Cartagena is Colombia's most visited attraction, but to truly delve into the country's past take a side trip to either Mompox or Popayan—maybe coinciding with their famous Easter week celebrations—to spy other fragments of the wealth the Spanish crown left behind.

CLIMATE

Colombia is often perceived as being a steamy tropical country, but its climate varies greatly with altitude. Along the Caribbean Coast temperatures are an average of 82°F (28°C); in Bogotá, the average is a chilly 54°F (12°C). The valley cities of Medellín and Cali have pleasant weather, with temperatures in between.

There are no real seasons in Colombia, but rainfall and brisk weather are common October to November and April to June. The dry season usually runs December to March in mountainous areas, mid-December to April and July to September in low-lying coastal regions.

The following are the average monthly maximum and minimum temperatures for Bogotá.

Jan.	67F	19C	May	66F	19C	Sept.	66F	19C
	48	9		51	10		49	9
Feb.	68F	20C	June	65F	18C	Oct.	66F	19C
	49	9		51	10		50	10
Mar.	67F	19C	July	64F	18C	Nov.	66F	19C
	50	10		50	10		50	10
Apr.	67F	19C	Aug.	65F	18C	Dec.	66F	19C
	51	10		50	10		49	9

FESTIVALS

Carnaval season (February–March) is particularly festive in Barranquilla. In March or April, Semana Santa (Palm Sunday through

Easter Sunday) processions fill the town of Popayan and Mompox. During the two weeks before Easter, Bogotá hosts the bi-annual Ibero-American Theatre Festival, with international theater and dance troupes performing.

The Flower Festival is held in Medellín in early August. The Folklore Festival takes place in Ibagué, usually during the last week in June. In early November Cartagena's Reinado Nacional de la Belleza has beauty contests and a full week of merrymaking celebrating the city's independence. Between Christmas and New Year's, Bogotá holds a Festival of Lights, and on New Year's Eve there's a fireworks celebration in the Presidential Plaza.

GETTING HERE & AROUND

Colombia charges a departure tax of $20, or $30 for stays over 30 days. The tax is payable in U.S. dollars or the equivalent in pesos.

BY AIR

International airports in Barranquilla, Bogotá, Cali, Cartagena, Medellín, and San Andrés regularly serve destinations in the United States and Europe. Regular flights connect all major Colombian cities. Since the country is fairly large—almost twice the size of Texas—it's usually more practical to fly to far-flung destinations, especially between the Caribbean coast and Medellín and Bogotá.

Airlines in Colombia **Aerorepública** (⊠ *Calle 10 No. 27–51, Oficina 303* ☎ *571/320 9090).* **Aires** (⊠ *Aeropuerto El Dorado* ☎ *571/294–0300).* **Avianca** (⊠ *Avenida 26 No. 92–30* ☎ *571/541–7701).* **Satena** (⊠ *Carrera 10A No. 26–21* ☎ *571/605–2222).*

BY BUS

Bus travel in Colombia is improving; intercity routes are covered by quality buses running at all hours. Remember to keep all your valuable belongings with you on the bus, preferably beneath your feet rather than in the overhead compartment, and be vigilant at bus stations. Buses often stop at police checkpoints, so have your ID close to hand or suffer the unpleasant consequences. In order to ensure the most comfortable journey, ask to see a photo of the type of bus you may end up taking and request seats on any *preferencial* service, which includes food breaks, air-conditioning, reclining seats, and often the delights of a poor B movie.

BY CAR

Driving in Colombia is a bad idea. If you absolutely have to drive, avoid nighttime journeys because of the risk of ambush by guerrillas or thugs impersonating them. It is best to arrive at all destinations before dark. Steer clear of north–south routes to the Caribbean coast and nighttime travel around Popayán and Cali. Keep your car doors locked and windows rolled up at all times.

Also, beware the crumbling, narrow, and winding roads that during rainy season can turn to mud or wash out completely. Always bring a good map, as signs are irregularly posted. Tolls (up to 7,000 pesos) are common. Consider hiring a car and driver or using a taxi for excursions.

BY TAXI

Taxis are readily available in Colombia's larger cities. Calling a taxi is safer than hailing one on the street, because thieves masquerade as taxi drivers, especially at night in heavily touristed areas.

ESSENTIALS

ELECTRICITY

The electrical current in Colombia is 120 volts AC, like that in North America. Sockets take two-prong plugs.

ENTRY REQUIREMENTS

Citizens from the United States, Australia, Canada, the United Kingdom, and New Zealand need only a valid passport to enter Colombia for up to 30 days; tourist visas aren't required. Upon arrival in Colombia, U.S. citizens should register with the embassy.

HEALTH & SAFETY

For the most part you can drink the water in all major cities. In smaller, more remote towns think twice. Colombia's pharmacies are well stocked, although you should bring some basic supplies to combat diarrhea. Some people experience dizziness and headaches upon arrival in Bogotá because of the thin mountain air. Until you acclimatize, avoid alcohol and caffeine, get plenty of sleep, and drink a lot of water and juice. Immunizations against the following diseases are recommended at least three months in advance of your trip: hepatitis A and B, tetanus-diphtheria, measles, typhoid, and yellow fever. The decision whether or not to take malaria pills should be made with your doctor.

Violence perpetrated by the drug cartels, the various armed groups involved in the civil conflict, and gangs of delinquents is a fact of life in Colombia, but with common sense you can avoid most problems. Decades-old civil conflict and the drug trade have made travel outside most major cities more risky than before. Travel to Cali and Popayán is improving, and Medellín, despite its sketchy past, is becoming a boom city.

Avoid black-market money changers or any dubious transaction offering a better rate of exchange—counterfeit bills are a very real problem. Have nothing to do with drug dealers, because many of them freelance as police informers. Possession of cocaine or marijuana can lead to a long sentence in an unpleasant Colombian jail. Don't accept gifts of food, drink, cigarettes, or chewing gum from strangers; there have been reports of travelers being drugged and relieved of their valuables.

Emergency Contacts **United States Embassy** (✉ *Calle 24 Bis No. 48–50, Bogotá* ☎ *571/315–1566*).

LANGUAGE

Spanish is the official language, although you may overhear some of the roughly 90 indigenous languages that are also spoken. English is widely understood on the islands of San Andrés and Providencia, and is commonly spoken in hotels and restaurants.

MONEY MATTERS

Colombia's monetary unit is the peso, which is circulated in the following denominations: 1,000, 2,000, 5,000, 10,000, 20,000 and 50,000. Peso coins come in denominations of 50, 100, 200, and 500. At this writing the official exchange rate was about 1,950 pesos to the U.S. dollar.

U.S. currency and traveler's checks can be exchanged for a small fee in larger hotels, travel agencies, and money exchange offices. You'll get a better rate at banks, although this is not always convenient because of their limited hours (weekdays 9–3). Credit cards give the best exchange rate, so you should use them for cash advances when possible. Either way, keep your exchange receipts to protect yourself against fraud.

You can use credit cards in larger hotels and in the shops and restaurants of major cities, though you should always carry some pesos with you. Automatic teller machines are widely available in most cities. Most are connected internationally, so that it is often possible to withdraw directly from your account back home.

RESTAURANTS & HOTELS

CUISINE From the hearty stews served in the highlands to the seafood soups ladled out along the Caribbean coast, you'll find distinctive regional cuisine everywhere. Beef is popular everywhere, as is chicken. Bogotá's most traditional dish is *ajiaco,* a thick chicken and potato soup garnished with capers, sour cream, and avocado. On the Caribbean coast you're more likely to dip your spoon into a *cazuela de mariscos,* a seafood soup with cassava. On the islands of San Andrés and Providencia the local favorite is *rondón,* a soup made of fish and snails slowly simmered in coconut milk with yucca, plantains, breadfruit, and dumplings.

Restaurants in many cities often close for a few hours between lunch and dinner (roughly 3 to 6). Appropriate attire in restaurants is comparable to U.S. or European standards—dressy for the more formal places, casual everywhere else. In many restaurants, bars, and cafés a 10% service charge is automatically added to the bill; if not, a 10% tip is expected.

ACCOMMO- Prices and standards at high-end hotels in Bogotá are usually compa-
DATIONS rable to those in North America. Outside of the capital, even in such tourist towns as Cartagena and San Andrés, rates for hotel rooms are surprisingly low. Consider staying at small, locally owned hotels where you're more likely to experience Colombian hospitality.

Hotels add a 16% tax to your bill throughout the country. A charge of 2,000 pesos is added for hotel insurance.

WHAT IT COSTS IN PESOS					
	¢	$	$$	$$$	$$$$
RESTAURANTS	under 10,000 pesos	10,000 pesos–15,000 pesos	15,000 pesos–25,000 pesos	25,000 pesos–40,000 pesos	over 40,000 pesos
HOTELS	under 100,000 pesos	100,000 pesos–200,000 pesos	200,000 pesos–280,000 pesos	280,000 pesos–360,000 pesos	over 360,000 pesos

Restaurant prices are per person for a main course at dinner. Lodging prices are for two people in a standard double room in high season, excluding tax.

BOGOTÁ

Bogotá offers abundant contrasts: modern shopping malls and open-air markets, high-rise apartments and makeshift shanties, futuristic glass towers and colonial churches. Simultaneous displays of ostentatious wealth and shocking poverty have been a feature of life here for centuries. In the neighborhood of La Candelaria a rich assemblage of colonial mansions grandly conceived by the Spanish were built by native peoples and financed by plundered gold.

Bogotá, a city of more than 7 million people, has grown twentyfold in the past 50 years. It suffers the growing pains typical of any major metropolis on the continent (insufficient public transportation, chronic air pollution, petty crime) and a few of its own (a scurrilous drug trade and occasional acts of political violence). However, recent mayors have made some progress in cleaning up parks, resurfacing roads, and implementing a new transportation system. In fact, a recent survey indicates that while a majority of Bogotanos feel that the political situation is worsening in Colombia, conditions are improving in Bogotá.

GETTING HERE & AROUND

Aeropuerto El Dorado, a 20-minute taxi ride northwest of downtown, has flights to national and international destinations.

The massive Terminal de Transportes, where long-distance buses arrive and depart, looks more like an airport than a bus station. It's where you'll find all major bus companies (and plenty of thieves, so watch your bags). Buses depart for other major cities about every hour. Since buses are the most common means of transportation for Colombians, they are often more comfortable than those in the United States.

Taxis are required by law to have a meter—make sure your driver turns it on. The minimum charge is 3,000 pesos, plus 50 pesos per 80 meters (260 feet). Fares increase by about a third after dark. It is always safer to call a taxi, especially in the northern parts of Bogotá, where thieves masquerading as taxi drivers have robbed passengers. The taxi companies will tell you the number of the taxi, and when you are picked up the taxi driver will ask you for the last two digits of the phone number from which you called.

A BIT OF HISTORY

Spanish conquistadors built their South American cities in magnificent locations, and Bogotá, which stands on a high plain in the eastern Andes, is no exception. During his disastrous search for the legendary El Dorado, Gonzalo Jiménez de Quesada, the Spanish explorer on whom Miguel de Cervantes reputedly modeled Don Quixote, was struck by the area's natural splendor and its potential for colonization. Though it's a mere 1,288 km (800 mi) from the equator, Bogotá's 8,700-foot altitude lends it a refreshing climate. Jiménez de Quesada discovered one of South America's most advanced pre-Colum-bian peoples, the Muisca. But they were no match for the Spaniards. On August 6, 1538, Jiménez de Quesada christened his new conquest Santa Fé de Bogotá, on the site where the Muisca village of Bacatá once stood.

Bogotá rapidly became an impor-tant administrative center, and in 1740 was made the capital of the viceroyalty of New Granada, an area comprising what is now Colombia, Venezuela, Ecuador, and Panama. With its new status, grand civic and religious buildings began to spring up, often with the hand-carved ceil-ings and sculpted doorways that were the hallmark of New Granada architecture. But by 1900 Bogotá was still a relatively small city of 100,000. It was not until the 1940s that rapid industrialization and the consequent peasant migration to urban centers spurred Bogotá's expo-nential growth.

Renting a car of your own is not advised. It's simply too dangerous.

SAFETY & PRECAUTIONS

Despite the city's reputation, most crimes against tourists are of the purse-snatching and pickpocketing variety, which can be avoided with a little common sense. Avoid displays of wealth, such as expensive jew-elry or watches. Never accept any food or cigarettes from a stranger, and be wary of any unknown person approaching you on the street, especially if they are well dressed and overly friendly. Don't be duped by people claiming to be plainclothes police officers who demand to "register" your money—they are almost certainly thieves. In case of such confrontations, you may want to hand over a 10,000 peso bill to quickly extricate yourself from the situation.

ESSENTIALS

Bus Contacts **Terminal de Transportes** (✉ *Diagonal 23 No. 69–60* ☎ *571/423–3630*). **Autoboy** (☎ *571/900 331–0140*). **Expreso Bolivariano** (☎ *571/416–6464*). **Flota La Macarena** (☎ *571/421–5556*). **Flota Magdalena** (☎ *571/428–7688*). **Los Libertadores** (☎ *571/428–2424*).

Currency Exchange **Banco de la República** (✉ *Carrera 7 No. 14–78*).

Internet Cafés **Café Internet Pura Careta** (✉ *Carrera 5 No. 12–57*). **Cyber Café** (✉ *Carrera 5 No. 12–49*).

Medical Assistance **Clinica del Country** (✉ *Cra 16 No. 82–57* ☎ *571/530–0470*). **Fundacion Santa Fe de Bogota** (✉ *Calle 116 No. 9–02* ☎ *571/629–0766*).

Post Office **Avianca** (✉ *Calle 10 No. 56–06* ✉ *Carrera 50 No. 57–45*).

Taxis **Taxis Express** (✉ *Calle 2 Sur No. 27a–04* ☎ *571/411–1111*). **Taxis Libre** (✉ *Av. Americas No. 51–39* ☎ *571/311–1111*).

Visitor & Tour Info **Punto de Información** (✉ *Carrea 8 and Calle 10* ☎ *571/283–7115* ⊕ *www.turismocolombia.com*). **Vice Ministerio de Turismo** (✉ *Calle 28 No. 13A–15, 18th fl.* ☎ *571/606–7676* ⊕ *www.turismocolombia.com* 🖶 *571/284–8618*).

EXPLORING BOGOTÁ

As you tour the city, take a taxi whenever possible—don't be carefree about strolling around, even during the day, or about lingering in places at night—it's simply not safe to do so. Keep in mind that *carreras* (roads) run north–south and *calles* (streets) run east–west. You'll probably spend much of your time in the charming neighborhood of La Candelaria. To the north of La Candelaria is the downtown area, which is slightly forlorn-looking but holds a handful of bars and restaurants, mostly in La Macarena. Farther uptown and marked by towering office buildings is the Centro Internacional, the city's financial center. To the north is the leafy Zona Rosa, a popular shopping district anchored by an upscale shopping mall called Centro Andino. Farther north along the Carrera 7, at Calle 116, is Hacienda Santa Barbara, another high-end shopping mall built as an extension of an old mansion. A few blocks north of Hacienda Santa Barbara is the plaza of Usaquén, an Andean village that became a neighborhood as Bogotá grew but still maintains its small-town manner.

LA CANDELARIA

At the foot of Guadalupe Peak is Bogotá's oldest neighborhood, La Candelaria, a historic compound of narrow streets lined with astounding colonial structures. It's packed with lovely mansions and exquisite churches. Most of the city's finest museums are found here.

MAIN ATTRACTIONS

⓯ Cerro de Monserrate. Although dense smog often obscures the skyline, the view of chaotic Bogotá from Monserrate Hill is still breathtaking. The panorama extends from the Río Bogotá to La Candelaria, whose red Spanish tiles make it easy to spot, especially in the early morning. The church on top of Monserrate houses an image of the Fallen Christ that is a lure for pilgrims. The *teleférico* (cable car) or the tram leaves every half hour from Monserrate Station near Quinta de Bolívar for the 15-minute journey to the peak. Avoid the hour-long trek up a winding footpath except on Sunday, when it's crowded with pilgrims. Robberies have become all too common. ✉ *Quinta de Bolívar, La Candelaria* ☎ *571/284–5700* 💲 *12,600 pesos during the day and 16,000 pesos in the evening for cable car or tram* ☉ *Mon.–Sat. 10–midnight, Sun. 10–4.*

❽ Donación Botero. In 2000, world-famous artist Fernando Botero made FodorśChoice headlines when he donated dozens of works from his private collection ★ to Colombia. Botero's artwork interprets his subjects from a distinctly

COLOMBIAN HISTORY

Before the arrival of the Spanish, Colombia was sparsely inhabited by indigenous peoples. High in the Andes, the Muisca were master goldsmiths, who may have sparked the myth of El Dorado with their tradition of anointing a new chief by rolling him in gold dust. The legend of El Dorado was an irresistible attraction for a host of European adventurers in search of gilded cities.

The Spanish settled in the region as early as 1510, but it wasn't until conquistador Rodrigo de Bastidas founded the port town of Santa Marta in 1525 that a permanent settlement was established in what is now known as Colombia. He banned the exploitation of the indigenous peoples, but those who followed him had other plans. Explorers like Gonzalo Jiménez de Quesada plundered and pillaged their way inland. After quickly dispatching the local Muisca tribes, he established a Spanish settlement in what is now Bogotá.

Despite their near decimation at the hands of brutal Europeans, Colombia's native peoples have left a lasting mark on the country. The extraordinary carved stones in the southwestern settlement of San Agustín speak of empires once rich in gold, emeralds, and the technological skills necessary to erect statues honoring long-forgotten gods. In the Andes and on the coastal plains you'll find modern descendants of these lost tribes living a life unchanged since Christopher Columbus presumptuously claimed Colombia in the name of King Ferdinand of Spain.

Colombians express with some pride that they live in the oldest democracy in Latin America. Colombia has enjoyed a constitutionally elected government for nearly all of its history. This has not, however, brought stability to the country, and guerrilla activity has echoed in the countryside since the 1940s.

The rise of drug trafficking in the last 25 years has exacerbated the ongoing civil conflict that now involves the government, left-wing guerrillas, and right-wing paramilitary groups. Although the large-scale car bombings and other acts of terrorism that plagued Bogotá and Medellín a decade ago seem like a thing of the past, occasional political assassinations are grim reminders of the violence that is all too common in many parts of the country.

Plans to create jobs and expand Colombian tourism are in the works, and while neither can remedy the country's safety issues, they may help to alleviate some conditions that contribute to crime. Since 2002 President Alvaro Uribe has waged a "mano dura" military campaign aimed at wiping out the guerrillas, and while this may not be wholly possible, the citizens of Colombia are seeing results in improved security and increasing foreign investment. Unfortunately, many people remain as hostages in the jungles, and too often the conflict has spilled over into neighboring Venezuela and Ecuador.

Latin-American standpoint—Colombians affectionately refer to him as "the man who paints fat people." Many of his subjects are well known in Colombia, especially in his native Medellín. The collection includes 123 of his own paintings, sculptures, and drawings. Equally impressive are his donation of 85 original works of renowned European and North American artists. This part of the collection, practically a review of art history since the late 19th century, includes original pieces by Corot, Monet, Matisse, Picasso, Dalí, Chagall, Bacon, and de Kooning. ⊠ *Calle 11 No. 4–41, La Candelaria* ☎ *571/343–1212* ⊕ *www. banrep.gov.co* ⊠ *Free* ⊘ *Mon. and Wed.–Sat. 9–7, Sun. 10–5.*

⑤ **Museo Arqueológico.** The magnificent mansion that houses the Museum of Archaeology once belonged to the Marquís de San Jorge, a colonial viceroy infamous for his cruelty. Today it displays a large collection of pre-Columbian ceramics. ⊠ *Carrera 6 No. 7–43, La Candelaria* ☎ *571/243–0465* ⊠ *3,000 pesos* ⊘ *Tues.–Fri. 8:30–5, Sat. 9.30–5, Sun. 10–4.*

⑥ **Museo de Arte Colonial.** Renovations in 1999 helped preserve this 17th-century Andalusian-style mansion, home of the Museum of Colonial Art. In its substantial collection are paintings by Vasquez and Figueroa, 17th- and 18th-century furniture, and precious metalwork. ⊠ *Carrera 6 No. 9–77, La Candelaria* ☎ *571/341–6017* ⊠ *Children 1,000, students 1,500, adults 2,000 pesos* ⊘ *Tues.–Fri. 9–5, weekends 10–4.*

④ **Museo de Artes y Tradiciones Populares.** A former Augustinian cloister dating from 1583, the Museum of Folk Art and Traditions is one of Bogotá's oldest surviving buildings. Displays include contemporary crafts made by Indian artisans from across the country. A gift shop and a restaurant specializing in traditional Andean cooking are on the premises. ⊠ *Carrera 8 No. 7–21, La Candelaria* ☎ *571/342–1803* ⊠ *2,000 pesos* ⊘ *Mon.–Sat. 8–4. Closed Sun.*

⑬ **Museo de Oro.** Bogotá's phenomenal Gold Museum contains a comprehensive collection of pre-Columbian artifacts. The museum's more than 34,000 pieces (in weight alone worth $200 million) were gathered—often by force—from indigenous cultures, including the Muisca, Nariño, Calima, and Sinú. Don't dismiss them as merely primitive; these works represent virtually all the techniques of modern goldsmithing. Most of the gold is in the guarded top-floor gallery, along with the largest uncut emerald in the world. English audio tours are available. ⊠ *Carrera 6 at Calle 16 (Parque Santander), La Candelaria* ☎ *571/343–2222* ⊕ *www.banrep.gov.co* ⊠ *Tues.–Sat. 3,000 pesos; Sun free* ⊘ *Tues.–Sun. 10–4.*

Fodor's Choice ★

③ **Palacio de Nariño.** The Presidential Palace had to be rebuilt in 1949 following its destruction during "El Bogotazo," an uprising sparked by the assassination of Liberal leader Jorge Eliécer Gaitán. Although it's not open to the public, the guard outside is changed ceremoniously each day at 5 PM. ⊠ *Carrera 7 between Calles 7 and 8, La Candelaria.*

① **Plaza de Bolívar.** Surrounded by stately structures, this square marks the spot where Bogotá was declared the seat of New Granada's colonial government. Today it's popular with photographers snapping pictures, unemployed men intermittently snoozing and chatting, street theater groups performing for a few hundred pesos, and children who never seem to grow bored with chasing pigeons. The Capitolio Nacional, Alcaldía Municipal, and Palacio de Justicia are not open to the public.

On the plaza's east side, the **Catedral Primada de Colombia** was only completed three centuries after construction began in 1565 owing to a series of misfortunes—including the disastrous earthquake of 1785. Its French baroque facade is made from locally mined sandstone. The expansive windows give the immense interior a light, airy feel, even on one of Bogotá's many gray rainy-season days. The ornate altar with gold leaf over heavily carved wood sharply contrasts with the lack of ornamentation elsewhere. In one of the side chapels lies conquistador Gonzalo Jiménez de Quesada's tomb. The church is open Monday through Saturday. Next door, in the **Capilla del Sagrario,** is an exquisite *baldacchino,* a smaller version of the ornate canopy structure in St. Peter's in Rome. The Sanctuary Chapel, open daily, also has a splendid collection of paintings, including works by the Taller de Figueroa and Gregorio Vasquez. ⊠ *Between Carreras 7 and 8 at Calle 10, La Candelaria.*

IF YOU HAVE TIME

❿ Biblioteca Luis Angel Arango. The modern Luis Angel Arango Library sponsors changing international art exhibits. It's also known for its occasional chamber music concerts, which are listed in the local newspapers. ⊠ *Calle 11 No. 4–14, La Candelaria* ☎ *091/343–1212* ⊕ *www.lablaa.org* 🎫 *Free* ☉ *Library Mon.–Sat. 8–8, Sun. 10–4.*

❼ Casa de la Moneda. The former national mint displays coins whose gold content was secretly reduced by the king of Spain, slugs made by revolutionaries from empty cartridges, and currency minted for use exclusively in Colombia's former leper colonies. This museum is part of the complex that houses the Donación Botero and the Colección Permanente de Artes Plásticas. ⊠ *Calle 11 No. 4–93, La Candelaria* ☎ *571/343–1212* ⊕ *www.banrep.org* 🎫 *Free* ☉ *Mon. and Wed.–Fri. 9–7, Sun. 10–5.*

❾ Colección Permanente de Artes Plásticas. This large collection, in the same complex as the Donación Botero, is an overview of Colombian art from the colonial period to the present, including works by such noted artists as Alejandro Obregón, Luis Caballero, and Débora Arango. ⊠ *Calle 11 No. 4–41, La Candelaria* ☎ *571/343–1212* ⊕ *www.banrep.gov.co* 🎫 *Free* ☉ *Mon. and Wed.–Fri. 10–8, Sat. 10–7, Sun. 10–4.*

❷ Iglesia Museo Santa Clara. The simple, unadorned facade of the 17th-century Church of St. Clara gives no hint of the dazzling frescoes—the work of nuns once cloistered here—that bathe the interior walls. The small museum has paintings and sculpture by various 17th-century artists. ⊠ *Carrera 8 No. 8–91, La Candelaria* ☎ *571/337–6762* 🎫 *2,000 pesos* ☉ *Tues.–Fri. 9–5, weekends 10–4.*

Fodor'sChoice
★

⓫ Iglesia de San Francisco. The 16th-century Church of St. Francis is famous for its fabulous Mudéjar interior, carved with geometric designs borrowed from Islamic tradition. Its huge gilded altar is shaped like an amphitheater and has shell-top niches. ⊠ *Av. Jiménez at Carrera 7, La Candelaria* ⊙ *Daily 8–6.*

⓬ Iglesia de la Tercera Orden. The intricate carvings on the mahogany altar at the Church of the Third Order are the most beautiful in Bogotá. A local myth claims that the completion of the altar so exhausted sculptor Pablo Caballero that he died a madman. ⊠ *Carrera 7 at Calle 16, La Candelaria* ⊙ *Daily 8–6.*

⓮ Quinta de Bolívar. Simón Bolívar, the revolutionary hero who drove the Spanish from the northern half of the continent, passed the last years of his life in this rustic house with his mistress, Manuela Saenz. Built in 1800, it was donated to Bolívar in 1820 for his services to the fledgling republic. The house has a distinct Spanish flavor and a lovely garden. Gabriel García Márquez's 1989 novel, *The General in His Labyrinth,* portrays Bolívar's final years. ⊠ *Calle 20 No. 2–91 Este, Barrio Las Nieves* ☎ *571/284-6819* 🎫 *3,000 pesos* ⊙ *Tues.– Fri. 9–5, weekends 10–4.*

CENTRO INTERNACIONAL

The city's financial center, Centro Internacional, lies to the north of La Candelaria. This district, built largely in the 1970s, is fringed by Parque de la Independencia and Parque Bavaria, welcome areas of green in a concrete jungle. Among the modern office buildings you'll find a few interesting museums and the city's Spanish-style bullring.

TOP ATTRACTIONS

⓳ Museo de Arte Moderno. The huge windows in the beautifully designed Museum of Modern Art create a marvelous sense of spaciousness. Peruse the changing exhibits of works by national and international artists. The bookstore stocks (rather pricey) English-language titles on Colombian and international painters. ⊠ *Calle 24 No. 6–00, Centro Internacional* ☎ *571/286-0466* 🎫 *4,000 pesos* ⊙ *Tues.–Sun. 10–7.*

⓱ Museo Nacional. The striking building that houses the National Museum was a prison until 1946; some parts, particularly the narrow top-floor galleries, maintain a sinister air. Designed by English architect Thomas Reed, the museum is arranged to give you a history of Colombia. Everything from ancient artifacts to contemporary art is on display, including works by Fernando Botero and Alejandro Obregón. The first-floor gallery is devoted to changing national and international exhibitions. There's also a café and bookstore. ⊠ *Carrera 7 No. 28–66, between Calles 28 and 29, Centro Internacional* ☎ *571/334-8366* 🎫 *3,000 pesos* ⊙ *Mon.–Sat. 10–6, Sun. 10–5.*

IF YOU HAVE TIME

⓲ Iglesia San Diego. This simple two-aisle church built by Franciscan monks in the early 17th century once stood on a quiet hacienda on the outskirts of colonial Bogotá. Trees and pastures have been replaced by the towering offices of Bogotá's "Little Manhattan." Both the church

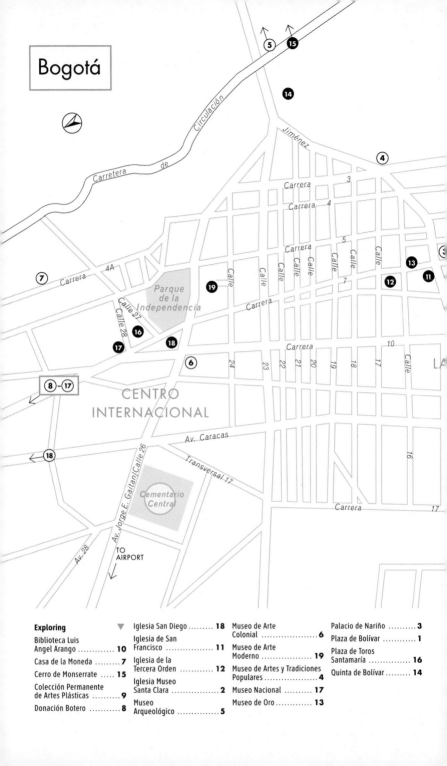

Bogotá

Parque
de la
Independencia

Cementerio
Central

CENTRO
INTERNACIONAL

Carretera de Circulación

Jiménez

Carrera
Carrera
Carrera
Carrera

Calle

Av. Caracas

Transversal 17

Av. Jorge E. Gaitán/Calle 26

Av. 28

TO
AIRPORT

LA

Map Labels

Carrera 2
Carrera 3
Carrera 4
Carrera 5
Carrera 6
Carrera 7
Carrera 8

Calle 9
Calle 8
Calle 7

Pasaje Rivas

Av. 10

CANDELARIA

Calle 13
Calle 12
Calle 11
Calle 10
Calle 9
Calle 8

Av. Caracas

Av. 84

Calle 3

Carrera 18

and its beautiful statue of the Virgin of the Fields, with her crown of intricate gold and silver filigree work, are homages to the city's bucolic past. ⊠ *Carrera 7 No. 26–37, Centro Internacional* ☎ *571/341–2476* ⊠ *Free* ⊗ *Sun.–Fri. 7–7:30, Sat. 7–7:30 and 1–9.*

⑯ Plaza de Toros Santamaría. Bogotá's bullring was designed by Rogelio Salmona in a traditional Andalusian style. For a free peek, the best time to visit is in the morning, when you may see young *toreros* (bullfighters) polishing their skills. Bullfighting season is January through February, but small displays are held throughout the year. ⊠ *Carrera 7 at Calle 26, Centro Internacional* ⊗ *Practice Mon.–Sat. morning. Bullfights Jan. and Feb., Sun. at 3* PM.

WHERE TO EAT

Bogotá's phone book lists more than 1,000 restaurants, and the best offer first-class service and outstanding Colombian cuisine. The most traditional recipes aim to fill the belly and ward off the cold. Soups, such as ajiaco and *puchero* (with chicken, pork, beef, potato, yucca, cabbage, corn, and plantain and accompanied by rice and avocado) are common on local menus. Bogotanos like to start the day off with *santafereño*, a steaming cup of chocolate accompanied by a slab of cheese—you melt the cheese in the chocolate. Lunch is generally served between noon and 2. Restaurants open for dinner around 7, and the more upscale ones stay open until after midnight.

$–$$
ECLECTIC
✗ **Cafetería Romana.** Reminiscent of a 1960s-era diner, this unpretentious eatery in La Candelaria serves an appropriate selection of sandwiches. Breakfast here is typically Colombian—hot chocolate with cheese and bread. ⊠ *Av. Jiménez No. 6–65* ☎ *571/334–8135* ⊟ *AE, DC, MC, V.*

$–$$
ECLECTIC
✗ **Café y Crêpes.** The alpine style of this place celebrates hiking and climbing in the great outdoors, but the mood inside is surprisingly intimate. You can sit on pillows in front of a fire and sip mulled wine. Both sweet and savory crepes are served. ⊠ *Carrera 16 No. 82–17* ☎ *571/236–2688* ⊠ *Diagonal 108 No. 9A–11* ☎ *571/214–5312* ⊟ *AE, DC, MC, V* ⊗ *No lunch Sun.*

$$$–$$$$
LATIN
AMERICAN
✗ **Carbón de Palo.** Bogotá's premier grilled-meat restaurant is a favorite north-end meeting place of senior politicians and plutocrats. The menu is dominated by grilled steak, chicken, and pork, but excellent salads are served with great aplomb. Choose a seat in the delightful indoor patio full of hanging plants. On weekends musicians serenade you with traditional Colombian music. ⊠ *Av. 19 No. 106–12* ☎ *571/214–0450* ⊟ *AE, DC, MC, V* ⊗ *Closed Sun.*

$$$–$$$$
FRENCH
Fodor'sChoice
★
✗ **Casa Medina.** Chef Francisco Rodriguez prepares French dishes, such as medallions of trout smothered in fennel and onion. The stately restaurant, built in 1945 as a private mansion, has been declared a national monument. The dining rooms are strewn with antiques imported by aristocratic Bogotano families. ⊠ *Carrera 7 No. 69A–22* ☎ *571/312–0299* ⊕ *www.hoteles-charleston.com* ⊟ *AE, DC, MC, V.*

$$$–$$$$ ✕**Casa San Isidro.** Specializing in masterfully prepared seafood and
SEAFOOD white-glove service, Casa San Isidro would be worth the trip for the
★ location alone. Perched 2,000 feet over Bogotá on top of the Cerro de
Monserrate, you'll dine fireside as a pianist provides the sound track.
Sample the San Isidro lobster with squid and shrimp, and then wash
it down with your choice of wine from a dozen different countries.
But be sure to leave by midnight, Cinderella, before the last cable car
returns to the streets below. ⊠*Cerro de Monserrate* ☎*571/281–9270
or 571/281–9309* ▭*DC, MC, V* ⊘*Closed Sun.*

$–$$ ✕**Casa Vieja.** Offering typical Colombian dishes, Casa Vieja is known
LATIN for the quality of its ajiaco. Dinner in this belle epoque–style restau-
AMERICAN rant is accompanied by antiques and artwork from Colombia's colonial
past. Three locations serve the Candelaria, the Centro Internacional,
and the northern part of town. ⊠*Av. Jiménez No. 3–63* ☎*571/334–
8908* ⊠*Carrera 10 No. 26–60* ☎*571/336–0588* ⊠*Carrera 11 No.
89–08* ☎*571/257–3903* ▭*AE, MC, V* ⊘*Closed Sun. .*

¢–$$ ✕**Crêpes and Waffles.** This is a unique chain of restaurants serving—sur-
ECLECTIC prise!—crepes and waffles, as well as a delicious selection of ice-cream
desserts. Posters of Colombian artist Fernando Botero's works cover
the walls. ⊠*La Candelaria Av. Jiménez No. 4–55* ☎*571/283–5377*
⊠*Carrera 9 No. 73–33* ☎*571/211–2530* ⊠*Carrera 11 No. 85–79*
☎*571/610–5298* ▭*AE, DC, MC, V.*

$$$–$$$$ ✕**La Fragata.** With its slowly revolving dining room, this is one of the
SEAFOOD capital's more unusual restaurants. Somehow the dimly lit, dark-oak
interior successfully conveys the sensibility of a 19th-century frigate.
The lobster, crab, red snapper, and locally caught rainbow trout are
satisfying but slightly overshadowed by the presentation. ⊠*Calle 100
No. 8A–95, 12th fl.* ☎*571/218–4456* ▭*AE, D, DC, MC, V.*

$$$–$$$$ ✕**Pajares Salinas.** At one of Bogotá's most highly rated restaurants *cal-*
ECLECTIC *los a la madrileña* (tripe stew in slightly spicy sauce) and other Spanish
dishes are among the top choices. The classically elegant dining room is
decorated with works of art from around the world. ⊠*Carrera 10 No.
96–08* ☎*571/616–1524* ▭*AE, DC, MC, V* ⊘*Closed Sun.*

$–$$ ✕**El Patio.** None of the cutlery matches, the plates are a hodgepodge of
ITALIAN styles, and the small dining room is crammed with tables, but all this
simply adds to the restaurant's eccentric charm. It's in a great location
a couple of blocks from the Plaza de Toros Santamaría in the bohemian
neighborhood of La Macarena. Try one of the masterful salads or the
delicious veal parmigiana. ⊠*Carrera 4A No. 27–80* ☎*571/282–6121*
▭*AE, DC, MC, V* ⊘*Closed Sun.*

$–$$ ✕**Sol de Napoles.** Family recipes and fresh bread make this reasonably
ITALIAN priced eatery a longtime favorite among Bogotanos. Try pasta topped
with one of the sauces—the meaty bolognesa and the spicy arrabiata
are favorites, but even the "plain" is enormously satisfying. ⊠*Calle 69
No. 11–58* ☎*571/249–2186* ▭*AE, DC, MC, V* ⊘*Closed Mon.*

5

WHERE TO STAY

Many of Bogotá's better hotels are in the wealthy northern districts— the most alluring parts of the city, and also the safest (with security guards on nearly every corner). If you want to soak up the color of the colonial buildings, or are on a tight budget, book a room in La Candelaria. No matter where you stay, avoid wandering the streets at night.

$$$ **Bogotá Royal.** In addition to modern rooms with good views, this hotel has everything corporate travelers need. The hotel is in Bogotá's World Trade Center in the north end of town, a short taxi ride from many office buildings but far from museums and other attractions. **Pros:** The hotel offers babysitters and has great views. **Cons:** This area on a weekend is vacant and uninhabited. ⊠ *Carrera 8 No. 99–55* ☎ *571/657–8787* 🖷 *571/218–3261* ⊕ *www.hotelsroyal.com* 📱 *143 rooms* ⚐ *In-room: dial-up. In-hotel: 2 restaurants, bars, gym* 🚪 *AE, DC, MC, V.*

$$$$ **Casa Dann Carlton Bogotá.** In a residential neighborhood in northern Bogotá, this hotel has modern rooms and plenty of recreational facilities, including a heated pool. Ask about the golf package, and you'll get to play a round at the Club Pueblo Viejo in the suburb of Chia. Golfers swear they can drive the ball farther at this altitude. **Pros:** Business travelers will enjoy the amenities and uniform decor. **Cons:** Guests are advised when leaving the establishment in the evening to take a taxi everywhere. ⊠ *Calle 94 No. 19–71* ☎ *571/633–8777* 🖷 *571/633–8833* 📱 *242 rooms* ⚐ *In-hotel: restaurant, room service, bar, gym, concierge* 🚪 *AE, DC, MC, V.*

¢   **Hotel Ambala.** Rooms in this small inn are cramped, but they're clean and comfortable. They also have plenty of creature comforts for a lodging in this price range: firm beds and baths with lots of hot water as well as Wi-Fi. **Pros:** Airport and bus terminal pick-up included in the price. **Cons:** Rooms on the street are brighter, but can be noisy, no elevator, very often full. ⊠ *Carrera 5 No. 13–46* ☎ *571/341–2376 or 571/342–2376* 🖷 *571/337–6593* 📱 *24 rooms* 🚪 *MC, V.*

$$$–$$$$ **Hotel de la Opera.** This pair of colonial buildings adjacent to the
★   Teatro Colón in La Candelaria found new life as an elegant hotel. The sleek tile and polished hardwood floors throughout are remarkable, as is the chic furniture imported from Italy. The generously proportioned rooms have high ceilings and huge windows, and some have balconies that open out onto a quiet side street. The Mediterranean cuisine at the hotel's restaurant, La Scala, is wonderful. The Automatico bar is a great place to relax with a brandy. **Pros:** The views are astonishing, and the service impeccable **Cons:** Avoid Calle 10's unofficial guides and beggars. ⊠ *Calle 10 No. 5–72* ☎ *571/336–2066* 🖷 *571/337–4617*

⊕*www.hotelopera.com.co* ⟷*29 rooms* ⟲*In-hotel: 2 restaurants, room service, bar, laundry service* ▤*AE, DC, MC, V.*

$$$ 🖬 **Hotel Real de la T.** This intimate boutique hotel in the heart of the leafy
★ Zona Rosa has understated but luxurious rooms. Business travelers
will appreciate the three phone lines in each room. The adjoining Los
Samanes restaurant is popular for its exquisitely presented Colombian
cuisine. **Pros:** You will not find a better conveniently located hotel.
Cons: Lobby may be dark and foreboding, rooms overlooking Carrera
13 may suffer from the street noise of drunken partygoers on week-
ends. ⊠*Carrera 13 No. 83–19* ☏*571/218–1188 or 571/610–2699*
🖷*571/218–9242* ⊕*www.hotellosurapanes.com.co* ⟷*32 rooms, 16
suites* ⟲*In-room: safe, dial-up. In-hotel: restaurant, room service, bar,
public Wi-Fi, parking (no fee), Internet* ▤*AE, DC, MC, V.*

NIGHTLIFE

Bogotá can easily overwhelm the visitor with its engaging arts and
entertainment opportunities. Just check the local listings in the *GO
Guia del Ocio* (⊕*www.goguiadelocio.com.co*) for an idea of what is
going on. On any given day you might find yourself listening to Celtic
music in a dark left-bank café in the Candelaria or watching a tango
recital in the north; Bogotá delivers on every front.

Bogotá's reputation for street crime hasn't put a damper on its ebullient
nightlife. The two main partying areas are the Zona Rosa, between
Calles 81 and 84 and Carreras 11 and 15, and the nearby Parque 93.
There are also a handful of popular salsa bars in La Candelaria. The
Zona Rosa and Parque 93 are safer than downtown, but travel there
by taxi.

BARS & DANCE CLUBS

Salto del Angel (⊠*Carrera 13 No. 93a–45* ☏*571/236–3139*) plays
rumba at the chic Parque 93 on Thursday, Friday, and Saturday. Dance
on the outdoor patio or in the spacious indoor atrium. **Salomé Pagana**
(⊠*Carrera 14A No. 82–16* ☏*571/221–1895*) has live music in an
intimate environment. Dance to boleros on Tuesday, folk music on
Wednesday, and Cuban salsa on Thursday.

Kukaramákara (⊠*Carrera 15 No. 93–75* ☏*571/642–3166* ⊗*Thurs.,
Fri., and Sat.*) jams in the punters ready to enjoy live Colombian music,
rum, and rumba. Arrive early around 10 PM to ensure a table.

THEATERS

Bogotá has a lively theater scene, though you'll miss a lot if you don't
understand Spanish. Bogotá's biannual **Ibero-American Theater Festival**
fills the two weeks before Easter with performing arts. Theater troupes
arrive from all over the world to perform in Bogotá's numerous theaters
and public parks. Recent festivals have included everything from Aus-
tralian acrobats to African dance troupes. **Teatro La Candelaria** (⊠*Calle
12 No. 2–59* ☏*571/281–4814*) has produced experimental theater for
nearly 40 years. **Teatro Nacional** (⊠*Carrera 20 No. 37–54* ☏*571/323–*

5

0273 or 571/323–0274) presents musicals and popular comedies. Tickets can be purchased in advance at the box office.

OUTDOOR ACTIVITIES

Every Sunday Bogotanos of all shapes and sizes hit the traffic-less streets from early in the morning until 2 PM when the *ciclovia* is in place, giving over main arteries in the ordinarily gridlocked capital to bikers, runners, walkers, and bladers. For those who choose slightly more physical exertions, there are hikes in the surrounding area to be enjoyed. Otherwise, hit the Parque Nacional for some clay-surface tennis or join in the ubiquitous and impromptu soccer game.

BULLFIGHTING

The bullfighting season is January and February, with occasional special events held during the rest of year. All are held at the Plaza de Toros Santamaría near the Parque de la Independencia. Spanish toreros delight the crowds, but Colombia's homegrown bullfighters are also quite exceptional: Bogotá native Cesar Rincón was once the most popular torero in Spain (he has since retired to raise bulls on his own ranch). Tickets can be purchased at the bullring weekdays from 9 AM to 5 PM. You can also get tickets on Sunday before the festivities begin at 3 PM, but you may not be able to secure seats for the more popular fights. Prices range from 10,000 pesos to 400,000 pesos depending on where you are seated, since *sol* (sun) is cheaper than *sombra* (shade).

HIKING

Although there are very real security issues in Colombia, hiking clubs have thrived in Bogotá over the last decade. Do not attempt to hike anywhere on your own—go only on a guided hike. In the region of Boyacá, in which Bogotá is located, there are many safe hikes following *caminos reales,* stone-paved paths often dating from colonial times. **Sal Si Puedes** (⊠*Carrera 7 No. 17–01* ☏*571/283–3765*) is the venerable dean of Bogotá's hiking clubs. Established in 1979, it offers day hikes every weekend, with longer two- and three-day excursions at least once a month. Hikes are rated according to difficulty, and guides are certified by the government.

Caminar Colombia (⊠*Carrera 3 No. 21–46 Apto 802B* ☏*571/241–0065).* Convening every Sunday and often on Saturday, Caminar Colombia promotes and leads hikes of various levels of difficulty through the countryside and highlands about Bogotá. Included in the deal are transport and a guide.

SOCCER

Fútbol games are held on most Sundays at 3:45 PM and Wednesday at 8 PM at **El Campín** (⊠*Carrera 30, between Calles 53 and 63*). There's no need to book ahead except when there's a match between the two most popular local teams—Santa Fé and Millionarios. Tickets are from 5,000 pesos to 30,000 pesos, and can be purchased at the stadium.

SHOPPING

Bogotá's shops and markets stock all types of leather and wool goods designed for life on the high plains. Handwoven *ruanas* (ponchos) are popular; the natural oils in the wool make them almost impervious to rain. Colombian artisans also have a way with straw: *toquilla,* a tough native fiber, is used to make hats, shoes, handbags, and even umbrellas.

MARKETS

In the warren of stalls at the daily **Pasaje Rivas indoor market** (⊠ *Carrera 10 at Calle 10*) look for bargain-price ponchos, blankets, leather goods, and crafts. The **flea market** (⊠ *Calle 24, ½ block east of Carrera 7*) in the Centro Internacional takes over a parking lot alongside the Museo de Arte Moderno on Sunday. It is a good place to hunt for antiques, handicrafts, and just plain junk. An upscale Sunday **flea market** (⊠ *Carrera 7 No. 119B–33*) in Usaquén has a good selection of high-quality local crafts.

SHOPPING CENTERS

Stylish boutiques dominate the chic **Centro Andino** (⊠ *Carrera 11 No. 82–71* ☎ *571/621–3111*), an anchor of the Zona Rosa. There's a U.S.-style food court and a movie theater on the fourth floor. Farther north is the upscale **Hacienda Santa Barbara** (⊠ *Carrera 7 No. 115–60* ☎ *571/612–0388*), constructed as an extension of a colonial-era plantation home. The massive **Unicentro Shopping Center** (⊠ *Av. 15 No. 123–30* ☎ *571/6190730*) in Bogotá's affluent north is one of South America's largest air-conditioned malls, and has a huge selection of stores.

SPECIALTY SHOPS

ANTIQUES

Antiques shops are found mainly in the northern districts of Chapinero, Chicó, and Usaquén. One of the best is **Anticuarios Gilberto F. Hernández** (⊠ *Calle 79B No. 7–48* ☎ *571/249–0041 or 571/248–7572*). **Salón De Antigüedades Lucia Soto De Co** (⊠ *Calle 79B No. 7–40* ☎ *571/248–3436*) stocks both Colombian antiques and colonial art. A good bet for quality antiques in the Candelaria is **Almacen de Antiguedades Leonardo F** (⊠ *Carrera 4 No. 12–34* ☎ *571/334–8312*).

EMERALDS

Seventy percent of the world's emerald supply is mined in Colombia. Value depends on weight, color, clarity, brilliance, and cut, octagonal cuts being the most valuable. Emerald dealers gather to make deals among themselves on the southwest corner of Carrera 7 and Avenida Jiménez during business hours Monday through Saturday. It's interesting to watch the haggling, but don't even think about joining in.

There are countless jewelry shops in the Centro Internacional along Carrera 6 between Calles 10 and 13. **H. Stern** (⊠ *El Dorado International Airport* ☎ *571/283–2819*) sells all kinds of precious gems. In both the Centro Internacional and the Centro Comercial Andino is **Galeria Cano** (⊠ *Edificio Bavaria, Carrera 13 No. 27–98* ☎ *571/242–9114* ⊠ *Edificio Banco Mercantil, Carrera 12 No. 84–07* ☎ *571/635–0529*). It sells emeralds as well as gold jewelry using striking pre-Columbian designs taken from the Museo de Oro.

HANDICRAFTS

In the cloister of Las Aquas, a neighborhood just off La Candelaria, **Artesanías de Colombia** (⊠*Carrera 2 No. 18–58* ☎*571/286–1766*) stocks everything from straw umbrellas to handwoven ponchos. The shop at the **Museo de Artes y Tradiciones Populares** (⊠*Carrera 8 No. 7–21* ☎*571/342–1803*) carries handmade items. **Artesanías El Zaque** (⊠*Centro Internacional, Carrera 10 No. 26–71* ☎*571/342–7883* ⊠*Hotel Tequendama, Interior Centro 28* ☎*571/342–7883*) offers especially good buys on hammocks. **El Balay** (⊠*Carrera 15 No. 75–75* ☎*571/347–1462*) stocks the city's widest selection of souvenirs from around Colombia.

BOYACÁ

Sleepy colonial towns, many originally settled by the pre-Columbian Muiscas, punctuate the rolling green hills and mountains of Boyacá, a region a few hours north of Bogotá. Charming communities such as Villa de Leyva and Paipa have central squares dominated by colonial churches. In this region you'll also find the cloud forest of Santuario de Fauna y Flora Laguna de Iguaque and the parched landscape of the Desierto de la Candelaria.

The area has been spared the unrest that has plagued other parts of Colombia in the last decades, but always exercise caution while visiting.

GETTING HERE & AROUND

The blue buses of Los Libertadores and the transport of Expreso Gaviota from Bogotá's Terminal de Transporte run to Villa de Leyva. Direct buses leave early in the morning; later in the day travelers must take a bus to Tunja and hire a taxi to Villa de Leyva or Paipa.

Car travel in this region is dangerous, not only because of crime but because of the aggressive drivers on the well-traveled route to Tunja. If you do choose to drive, take the route through Tunja for both Villa de Leyva and Paipa. This road is being upgraded to a four-lane highway; expect construction north of the village of Briceño, 20 km (13 mi) from Bogotá.

You can easily hire guides in Villa de Leyva to explore the surrounding area, including the Santuario de Fauna y Flora Laguna de Iguaque. Guías y Travesías and Mónica Luis both have offices near the main plaza in Villa de Leyva.

SAFETY & PRECAUTIONS

Boyacá has been spared the unrest found in other parts of Colombia. To be on the safe side, travel between towns only during the day. Villa de Leyva has very little crime, but beware of pickpockets, particularly around the bus terminal.

VILLA DE LEYVA

40 km (25 mi) west of Tunja.

Walking the cobbled streets of Villa de Leyva, especially in the early morning, takes you back three centuries. The clip-clop of burros laden with the produce from nearby farms, the ringing of bells for early morning mass, and the sun reflecting off the whitewashed buildings along the Plaza Mayor evoke the times when the Spanish ruled over newly conquered lands.

Villa de Leyva carefully preserves its colonial atmosphere—even new buildings must meet rigorous standards. The town's location is as dramatic as its architecture, lodged between lush green fields and forests to the north and an arid desert to the south. You can easily walk between these two wildly divergent climatic zones.

ESSENTIALS

Bus Contacts Expreso Gaviota (☏ *571/428–2424*). **Los Libertadores** (☏ *571/742–2828*).

Internet Cafés Quinternet (✉ *Centro Comercial Casa Quintero, 300 meters from Plaza.* ☏ *No phone*).

Tour Operators Guías y Travesías (✉ *Calle 11 No 8A–30* ☏ *578/732–0742*). **Mónica Luis** (✉ *Carrera 10 No. 12–13* ☏ *578/732–0895*).

Visitor Info Tourist office (✉ *Plaza Mayor, Villa de Leyva* ☏ *578/732–0232*).

EXPLORING VILLA DE LEYVA

Plaza Mayor, one of the largest squares in Colombia, is the place to begin exploring Villa de Leyva. The parish church is on the east side, and the colonnaded galleries running along the northern and southern edges house restaurants and handicraft shops. A helpful tourist office, open daily 9–5, is located at the northeast corner.

A block north of Plaza Mayor is the small grassy park of the **Convento de las Carmelitas,** a cloistered convent with an impressive 17th-century church.

Across from the Convento de las Carmelitas is the **Museo de Arte Religioso de Las Carmelitas,** displaying a large selection of religious art from the first centuries of Spanish rule. ✉ *Carrera 10 at Calle 14* ☏ *578/732–0214* 🎟 *2,000 pesos* ☉ *Weekends only 10–1 and 2–6.*

The **Desierto de la Candelaria,** 7 km (4 mi) east of Villa de Leyva, is covered with marine fossils left behind when the ancient sea that once covered the area receded. The most impressive is El Fósil, a 30-foot skeleton of a kronosaurus. This ancient ancestor of the dolphin swam the seas in the Mesozoic Era, long before the Andes pushed their way out of the ocean. In the middle of the Desierto de la Candelaria is **El Infiernillo** (literally "little hell"), a field of phallic statues dedicated to long-lost fertility rites. The best way to find these sights is by horseback; you can find horses and guides in a field three blocks north of the northwest corner of the Plaza Mayor. Several companies offer tours in air-conditioned vans.

The town of **Ráquira,** 25 km (16 mi) southwest of Villa de Leyva, is famous for its ceramics, sold in shops along the main square. In contrast with the whitewashed buildings of Villa de Leyva, Ráquira is bursting with color.

The **Santuario de Fauna y Flora Laguna de Iguaque,** a national wildlife sanctuary, lies 15 km (9 mi) north of Villa de Leyva. The centerpiece is the lake itself, which the Muiscas believed was the source of all life.

> **MONEY MATTERS**
>
> It is a good idea to exchange money in Bogotá before venturing into Boyacá, especially on weekends. One of the few places to exchange foreign currency is at Banco de la República in Tunja. It is open weekdays 8–11:30 and 2–4. There are ATMs that accept all cards in the Plaza.

Hiking the 8 km (5 mi) trail, which winds its way uphill through cloud forest, isn't easy. Wear practical boots, and be prepared for cold and rainy weather, as the temperature can fall to near freezing. It's worth it when you reach the *páramo,* a climatic zone with a unique plant system. Here you'll find unusual flora such as the ubiquitous *frailejón* (literally, "big friar"), a gray felt-leaf plant from the espletia family. At the trailhead are cabins and a cafeteria. Entry to the Santuario costs 20,000 pesos.

WHERE TO STAY

$ 🏨 **Hospedería Duruelo.** A resort hotel located five blocks uphill from the Plaza Mayor, the hacienda-style Hospedería Duruelo offers a gracious atmosphere and amenities ranging from tennis courts to a Turkish bath. The restaurant serves standard international fare along with typical Colombian entrées. **Pros:** For active visitors the hotel will obligingly organize all travel plans and tours; phone in advance to hear about midweek low price promotions. **Cons:** Did we mention the hill? While only five blocks from the town center, some people will feel the distance from the Duruelo to sites of interest. ⊠ *Carrera 3 No. 12–88* ☎ *578/732–0222 or 578/732–0263* 🛏 *85 rooms* ⚿ *In-hotel: 3 restaurants, bar, tennis court, pool, no elevator* ▭ *AE, DC, MC, V.*

$ 🏨 **El Mesón de los Virreyes.** This well-established lodging is on the Plaza Mayor. Some rooms have a balcony overlooking the flower-bedecked patio. **Pros:** This charming hotel is everything that anyone searching for a weekend retreat might want, privacy and romantic balconies. **Cons:** Rooms overlooking the Plaza during festivals and long weekends may suffer from boisterous revelers. ⊠ *Carrera 9 No. 14–51* ☎ *578/732–0252* 🛏 *31 rooms* ⚿ *In-hotel: restaurant, room service, bar, laundry service, no elevator* ▭ *DC, MC, V.*

SHOPPING

Regional crafts are sold in many small shops surrounding Plaza Mayor and along the adjoining streets. Here you'll find bargains on the wool ponchos worn by locals. Pottery from the nearby town of Ráquira is also a good buy. Saturday morning brings *campesinos* (country people) to town for the weekly **open-air market.** They sell farm-fresh produce in a square two blocks east of Plaza Mayor.

MEDELLÍN

Nestled in the narrow Aburrá Valley, this northwestern city of 2 million people is the capital of Antioquia. The industrious *paisas,* as natives of the province are called, built the successful coffee and textile industries that have enabled Medellín to prosper; today it's the second-largest city in Colombia. Modern and affluent, Medellín has the country's only elevated train system. The city also has several interesting museums, three respected universities, and wide, tree-lined boulevards. But Medellín also has thousands of impoverished citizens whose shanties appear on the city's edges.

Although local and international intervention has lessened the drug trade, the city remains violent and unpredictable. Exercise caution when touring Medellín day or night, and always stick to central areas.

GETTING HERE & AROUND

Medellín has two airports, the Aeropuerto Jose Maria Córdoba in Rionegro is on top of a plateau 38 km (24 mi) southeast of the city. Aerorepública, Avianca, and Satena fly here from Bogotá and other Colombian cities. Downtown there is the older airport, Aeropuerto Olaya Herrera, where smaller propeller aircraft run by Aires and Satena land.

Medellín has two bus stations—the Terminal de Transporte del Norte, where you'll find buses to Bogotá and the Caribbean coast, and the Terminal de Transporte del Sur, which has buses bound for Cali.

Cars are not the safest means of transportation in Medellín, unless you're taking a taxi.

A paved, two-lane highway connects Bogotá and Medellín, and the 560-km (347-mi) journey takes about nine hours.

Medellín has an excellent train system. Because most of the track is elevated, it's a good way to see the city. There are two lines, one running north–south, the other east–west. A one-way fare is 1,050 pesos, and a round-trip ticket costs 2,050 pesos.

SAFETY & PRECAUTIONS

With the death of notorious drug trafficker Pablo Escobar in 1993, car bombings and other random acts of violence seem to be a thing of the past. Politically motivated assassinations and bombings still occur. Exercise the usual caution you would in big cities, especially at night, and take taxis to get around.

ESSENTIALS

Bus Contacts **Terminal de Transporte del Norte** (✉ *Carrera 64C No. 78–344* ☎ *574/267–7075*). **Terminal de Transporte del Sur** (✉ *Carrera 65 No. 8B–91* ☎ *574/361–1499*). **Flota Magdalena** (☎ *574/230–7578*). **Rápido Ochoa** (☎ *574/441–7017*).

Currency Exchange **Banco de la República** (✉ *Calle 50 No. 50–21*).

Internet Cafés **Angimo Café Internet** (✉ *Carerra 42 No. 48–90* ☎ *574/239–6123*). **Las Cabinas** (✉ *Calle 53 No. 47–44* ☎ *574/576–1720*).

5

Medical Assistance **Clínica El Rosario** (⊠ *Carrera 20 No. 2 Sur 185*
☏ *574/326–9216*).

Post Office **Adpostal** (⊠ *Carrera 64C
No. 72-20* ☏ *574/437-3659*).

Taxis **Empresa de Taxis Super** (⊠ *Calle
60 No. 51–65* ☏ *574/513-9700*).

Visitor & Tour Info **Oficina de Turismo**
(⊠ *Calle 42B No. 52-106* ☏ *574/385-
8672*).

TIP

When visiting sights, remember
that calles run east–west and
carreras run north–south. Also be
careful not to walk around after
sunset, as the city can be quite
dangerous.

EXPLORING MEDELLÍN

Medellín is the country's main industrial hub, but don't expect a city
full of smoking chimneys: the factories are well outside of town. Deep-
green mountains that rise sharply around the city provide a bold backdrop to the glass-and-concrete towers of its elegant financial district.
Well-developed tourist facilities in the city proper testify to the region's
relative economic strength.

TOP ATTRACTIONS

❸ **Ermita de la Veracruz.** Distinguishing the interior of the Veracruz Hermitage are its white walls and columns with gilded capitals. Just off
a picturesque plaza, it's a quiet escape from Medellín's noisy streets.
⊠ *Calle 51 No. 52–58* ☏ *574/511–1642* 🎟 *Free* ☉ *Daily 7–6.*

❶ **Jardín Botánico Joaquín Antonio Uribe.** The botanical gardens have more
than 500 plant species, including heliconias, zamias, and azaleas, and
a huge greenhouse teeming with orchids. ⊠ *Carrera 52 No. 73–298*
☏ *574/ 444–5500* 🎟 *4,000 pesos* ☉ *Daily 9–5.*

❷ **Museo de Antioquia.** The Antioquia Museum contains a large collection
of paintings and sculptures by native son Fernando Botero and other
well-known Colombian artists. Botero, known for depicting people and
objects with a distinctive "thickness," donated part of his personal collection to the museum (the bulk of his gift went to Bogotá). ⊠ *Carrera
52 No. 52–53* ☏ *574/251–3636* 🎟 *8,000 pesos* ☉ *Mon.–Sat. 9:30–5,
Sun. and holidays 10–4.*

❹ **Parque Berrío.** This small cement plaza is overwhelmed by the city's
elevated train, the only one of its kind in Colombia. Nearby is the
colonial church of **Nuestra Señora de la Candelaria.** To the south, the
Banco de la República building stands next to a huge female torso
sculpted by native son Fernando Botero. On the bank's other side, a
bronze fountain and marble monument honor Atanasio Girardot, an
18th-century champion of Colombian independence. ⊠ *Carrera 50,
between Calles 50 and 51.*

IF YOU HAVE TIME

❺ **Catedral Basílica Metropolitana.** The Metropolitan Cathedral's ornate cof-
fee-color facade soars above the Parque de Bolívar. Designed by the

Medellín

French architect Charles Carré and built in 1875, it's South America's largest cathedral, and the third-largest brick building in the world. ✉ *Carrera 48 No. 56–64* ☎ *574/513–2269* 💲 *Free* ☉ *Mon.–Sat. 7–noon and 4:30–7, Sun. 7–1 and 4:30–7.*

⑦ Museo El Castillo. The 1930s Gothic-inspired Castle Museum, with beautiful French-style gardens of sweeping lawns and exuberant flower beds, was once the home of a powerful Medellín family. On display are their furniture and international art collection. ✉ *Calle 9 Sur No. 32–269* ☎ *574/266–0900* 💲 *6,000 pesos* ☉ *Weekdays 9–noon and 2–5:30, Sat. 9–11:30* AM.

⑥ Parque de Bolívar. Despite its location in the middle of crowded Medellín, this shady park has a generous amount of open space. In the evening it's popular with young people who congregate on the steps of the nearby cathedral. ✉ *Carrera 49 and Calle 54.*

⑧ Parque de las Esculturas. This small sculpture park near the peak of Cerro Nutibara is a maze of paths dotted with modern and traditional sculptures by Latin American artists. ✉ *Cerro Nutibara.*

⑨ Pueblito Paisa. As you enter this reproduction of an old-time Antioquian village, you'll see a traditional town square with a small church, town hall, barbershop, school, and village store. For your present-day needs, it also has a small restaurant and several souvenir shops. ✉ *Cerro Nutibara.*

OFF THE BEATEN PATH

Santa Fé de Antioquia. Eighty kilometers (50 miles) northwest of Medellín is the province's former capital, Santa Fé de Antioquia. Founded in 1541, the town is now a colonial showpiece, with cobbled streets and whitewashed houses. It's well known for its *orfebrería* (gold work). Visit the workshops on Carrera 10 between the cathedral and the river.

WHERE TO EAT

Traditional Antioquian cooking means hearty peasant fare—plenty of meat, beans, rice, and potatoes. But Medellín is full of high-quality restaurants where you'll find many cuisines. On the first Saturday of every month the **Parque de las Delicias** (✉ *Carrera 73 and Av. 39D*) is packed with food stalls selling everything from *obleas* (thin jam-filled waffles) to *lechona* (roast stuffed pork).

$

LATIN
AMERICAN

✕ **Aguas Claras.** Experience many Colombian dishes in one meal—the hearty *plato típico* is a sampling of 10 different items. The lighter *plato del cura* (priest's plate) is a complete meal of soup, beef, rice, and bread for about $5. The nicest tables are on the balcony, which overlooks a popular pedestrian mall. ✉ *Carrera 49 No. 52–141, 2nd fl.* ☎ *574/231–6642* 🍽 *AE, DC, MC, V.*

$$$–$$$$

ECLECTIC

✕ **Las Cuatro Estaciones.** Medellín's most popular restaurant combines delicious food and first-rate service with an interior that borders on tacky. Choose one of four thematic dining rooms—decorated in gaudy Colombian, European, Asian, and Spanish styles. The house specialty is paella. ⊠*Calle 16B No. 43–79, El Poblado* ☎*574/266–7120* ⊟*AE, DC, MC, V.*

$–$$
LATIN
AMERICAN
Fodor'sChoice
★

✕**El Hato Viejo.** Generous portions draw locals to this second-story restaurant. Waiters in Panama hats serve you on a balcony overflowing with plants or in the large dining room with terra-cotta floors. Try the *sopa de guineo* (plantain soup) before sinking your teeth into *lomito* (tenderloin) or *langostinos* (lobsters). Finish your feast with *brevas con queso* (figs with white cheese). ⊠*Carrera 49 No. 52–170* ☎*574/251–2196 or 574/231–1108* ⊟*AE, DC, MC, V.*

WHERE TO STAY

¢
⌂**La Bella Villa.** Just a few blocks from Parque de Bolívar, this hotel has five floors of modern rooms surrounding a covered courtyard. **Pros:** The accommodating ambience is in striking contrast to the mayhem outside. **Cons:** The hotel could do with some updating. ⊠*Calle 53 No. 50–28* ☎*574/511–0144* ☎*574/512–9477* ⇥*50 rooms* ⌂*In-hotel: restaurant* ⊟*No credit cards.*

$
⌂**Hotel Nutibara.** This stylish hotel from the 1940s recalls a glamorous era. Rooms in the newer building across the street have less personality but cost half as much as those in the main building. From the hotel's downtown location it's a short taxi ride to restaurants and bars. **Pros:** You are close to many museums and galleries. **Cons:** This area gets a little seedy after dark. ⊠*Calle 52A No. 40–56* ☎*574/511–5111* ☎*574/231–3713* ⇥*90 rooms* ⌂*In-hotel: 2 restaurants, bar, pool* ⊟*AE, DC, MC, V.*

$$
⌂**InterContinental Medellín.** This sprawling modern hotel in the hills outside Medellín has spectacular views of the city. The service is friendly, and rooms are well-appointed. The Poblado neighborhood is about 20 minutes by taxi from the city center and 40 minutes from the airport. **Pros:** Jogging trails, tennis courts, and a nearby golf course. **Cons:** Where am I again? Colombia or Fort Worth? ⊠*Calle 16 No. 28–51* ☎*574/319–4450, 800/327–0200 in U.S.* ☎*574/315–4404* ⊕*www.intercontinental.com* ⇥*294 rooms, 45 suites* ⌂*In-hotel: 2 restaurants, bar, tennis court, pool, gym, concierge* ⊟*AE, DC, MC, V.*

SHOPPING

Medellín's **Centro Commercial San Diego** (⊠*Calle 34 No. 43–66* ☎*574/232–0624*) has crafts, jewelry, and clothing shops. You'll find souvenir shops at **Pueblito Paisa** atop Cerro Nutibara. Check the outdoor stalls along **Pasaje Junín,** just south of Parque de Bolívar. For Antioquian crafts, visit the **open-air crafts market** held on the first Saturday of every month at the Parque de Bolívar.

SOUTHWEST COLOMBIA

SALENTO

24 km (15 mi) northeast of Armenia via the Armenia to Pereira Hwy.

For too long Salento's quaint and colorful streets have been the preserve of only the well-informed and adventurous. But visit this charming town in the coffee-producing heartland of Quindío to truly appreciate rural Colombia. Enjoy locally caught trout, take a hike among the mighty wax palms—the national tree of Colombia—of the Valle de Cocora, towering above you, and settle down with a *tinto* harvested from locally grown and roasted coffee beans.

GETTING HERE & AROUND

The fastest and easiest way to reach Salento is to fly to the nearby city of Armenia (24 km/15 mi) or to Pereira (60 km/37 mi). From both regular buses run at almost all hours of the day.

ESSENTIALS

There are precious few modern conveniences in Salento. You are advised to stock up on cash before arriving, since the only bank in town has no ATM and will not change foreign currency or traveler's checks.

WHAT TO SEE

The Butterfly Farm. Housed in the Jardín Botanico del Quindío is an enormous butterfly house. It's home to about 1,500 butterflies, representing 500 different species. Roam the expansive botanical gardens and pay attention to all the diverse species of orchid that grow in Colombia. Don't miss the seven-story lookout point. ⊠ *Km 3, Via al Valle, Calarca* ☎ *576/742–7254* 🖾 *8,000 pesos* ☉ *Daily.*

Valle de Cocora and Los Nevados National Park. Regal wax palms measuring as much as 60 meters (200 feet) in height punctuate the skyline and vistas as the canyon narrows, squeezing the waters of the Río Quindío. There are many hikes, both low-altitude and high-altitude (to the Nevado del Tolima peak), as well as horseback riding opportunities. ⊠ *Valle de Cocora* ☉ *Daily.*

WHERE TO STAY & EAT

$$–$$$ ✕ **Bosques de Cocora.** If visiting Salento, you are strongly recommended
LATIN to go to the Cocora Valley, where beautifully restored fincas now serve
AMERICAN as country-style restaurants and guesthouses. The Bosques de Cocora is the pick of the bunch, offering sumptuous dishes of the local delicacy, trout, and set against a cloud-forest backdrop. ⊠ *Km 10, Valle de Cocora* ☎ *576/759–3212* 🖃 *No credit cards.*

¢ 🏠 **Hostal La Posada del Cafe.** In this delightfully converted colonial house you can relax in the garden's verdant confines or in one of the six simply yet elegantly decorated rooms. The Hostal La Posada del Café is an ideal place to enjoy the wonders of the coffee region. **Pros:** Did we mention tranquillity? **Cons:** If you are looking for upscale accommodation, you are out of luck. ⊠ *Carrera 6 No. 3–08* ☎ *576/759–3012* 🛏 *6 rooms (capacity 22)* 🖨 *576/759–3292* 🖃 *No credit cards.*

SPORTS & THE OUTDOORS

Quindío—though a small Colombian department—is known for its Andean foothills and tumbling rivers. With these come a plethora of adventure activities, including hiking, climbing, horseback riding, kayaking, and rafting.

El Andariego Viajes is a professional outfit offering group expeditions or tailor-made trips to Quindío including rafting, hiking, and other activities. (☎576/637–6135 ⊕*www.elandariego.com.co*).

CALI

Tucked in the fertile Valle de Cauca, Cali is a lively provincial capital and an important agricultural center, responsible for a hefty portion of the country's sugar, coffee, and corn exports. The city's elevation of 3,000 feet contributes to the year-round springlike temperatures. Many people visit during the Christmas–New Year's *feria*, when the city unapologetically devotes itself to merrymaking. *Caleños* are known for their love of Cuban salsa—Celia Cruz and other famous salsa performers play shows in Cali during the feria.

Like Medellín, however, Cali is still a difficult city to enjoy wholeheartedly; the prevalence of street crime requires you to be cautious at all times. The mountains near Cali contain some of the country's most important archaeological sites. Sadly, the enigmatic statues of San Agustín and the painted tombs of Tierradentro are currently off-limits as tourist destinations due to the civil conflict. The violence makes it unadvisable to travel to or from Cali by bus or car.

GETTING HERE & AROUND

Cali's Aeropuerto Alfonso Bonilla Aragón is located about 20 km (12 mi) northeast of the city. Domestic carriers Aerorepública, Aires, Avianca, and Satena have regular flights here from Bogotá, Cartagena, and Medellín. Some international flights arrive here as well. It's a 10-hour trip to Cali from Bogotá or Medellín. Buses leave for these cities about once an hour. All travel by road is risky, so avoid it if at all possible. Civil conflict has been ongoing to the south and west of Cali since 1999, so never take buses to Popayán or Buenaventura.

Driving is dangerous around Cali for the same reasons. The highway between Bogotá and Cali is somewhat safer, but avoid it if at all possible. The 680-km (422-mi) journey to Bogotá takes around 10 hours. Drive during the day and arrive before dark.

SAFETY & PRECAUTIONS

As in other cities in Colombia, you should be on your guard in Cali. Political violence to the south and west of the city has been prevalent since 1999; do not travel by bus or car in those directions.

ESSENTIALS

Bus Contacts **Terminal de Transportes** (✉ *Calle 30N No. 2AN–29* ☎ *572/668–3655*).

Currency Exchange **Banco de la República** (⊠ *Calle 11 No. 4–14*).

Internet Cafés **Cosmonet** (⊠ *Av. 6 Norte No. 17N–65* ☎ *572/668–6522*). **Internet Agil** (⊠ *Av. Roosevelt No. 30–05* ☎ *572/558–3188*).

Medical Assistance **Clínica Fundación Valle de Lili** (⊠ *Carrera 98 No. 18–49* ☎ *572/331–7474 or 331–9090*).

Post Office **Avianca** (⊠ *Calle 12 No. 2AN–37* ⊠ *Calle 9 No. 4–55*).

Rental Cars **Localiza** (⊠ *Aeropuerto Alfonso B. Aragon* ☎ *572/892–0262*).

Taxis **Corpotaxis** (⊠ *Calle 24 No. 4–44* ☎ *572/882–5050*). **Radio Taxi Aeropuerto** (⊠ *Calle 34 No. 3–84* ☎ *572/444–4444*).

Visitor Info **Centro Cultural de Cali** (⊠ *Carrera 5 y Calle 6* ☎ *572/885–8855*).

EXPLORING CALI

Within the rapidly expanding city (it has grown fourfold in the past 40 years) you'll find a small colonial quarter, some interesting museums, and many leafy parks. The city's tree-lined avenues and lazy open-air cafés invite you to linger. In the center is the Paseo de Bolívar, a large park on the north bank of the muddy Río Cali. To the south are the main sights, including most of the interesting old churches.

TOP ATTRACTIONS

❶ **Cerro de los Cristales.** The Hill of the Crystals affords a spectacular view of the city. The monumental statue of Christ at the top is visible for miles. A taxi from downtown should cost about 20,000 pesos round-trip. Be sure to ask the driver to wait for you.

❷ **Iglesia de la Merced.** The Church of Grace, Cali's oldest house of worship, was completed in 1680. It stands on the site where the city's founders celebrated their first religious service in 1536. ⊠ *Carrera 3 No. 6–62* ☎ *572/889–2309*.

❸ **Museo Arqueológico La Merced.** Next door to Iglesia de la Merced, this archaeological museum displays regional pre-Columbian pottery and a scale model of the city. ⊠ *Carrera 4 No. 6–59* ☎ *572/885–5309* ☜ *4,000 pesos* ☾ *Tues.–Sat. 9–1 and 2–6*.

IF YOU HAVE TIME

❺ **Catedral Metropolitana.** Although ground was broken in 1772, construction on the Metropolitan Cathedral was halted during the war for independence. The grand structure wasn't completed until 1841. The pale interior of this massive temple is complemented by its marble columns and brilliantly gilded altar. ⊠ *Calle 11 No. 5–53* ☎ *572/881–1378* ☜ *Free* ☾ *Weekdays 6–noon and 3–8, weekends 7 AM–8 PM*.

❽ **Iglesia de la Ermita.** A neo-Gothic church built between 1930 and 1948, the white-and-blue Hermitage Church has become such an enduring symbol of Cali that it is one of the most common images on postcards. ⊠ *Av. Colombia at Calle 13* ☎ *572/881–8553* ☜ *Free* ☾ *Weekdays 6:30–noon and 2:30–7, Sat. 6:30–noon and 4–5:30, Sun. 8–noon and 5–7*.

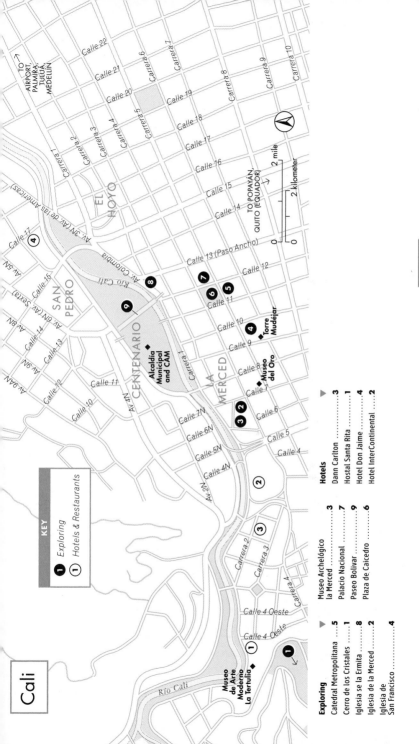

Cali

KEY

● **1** Exploring

① **1** Hotels & Restaurants

Exploring ▶

Catedral Metropolitana **5**
Cerro de los Cristales **1**
Iglesia se la Ermita **8**
Iglesia de la Merced **2**
Iglesia de
San Francisco **4**

Museo Archelógico
la Merced **3**
Palacio Nacional **7**
Paseo Bolívar **9**
Plaza de Caicedro **6**

Hotels ▶

Dann Carlton **3**
Hostal Santa Rita **1**
Hotel Don Jaime **4**
Hotel InterContinental **2**

❹ Iglesia de San Francisco. This large brick church and the adjacent Franciscan monastery date from the early 19th century. The church's brick Torre Mudéjar (Moorish Tower) is considered one of the finest examples of Spanish-Moorish architecture in South America. ✉ *Carrera 6 between Calles 9 and 10* ☎ *572/884–2457* ✉ *Free* ⊙ *Mon.–Sat. 6:30– 11:30 and 4–6:30, Sun. 6:30–11:30 and 4:30–7.*

❼ Palacio Nacional. Intricately carved doors under equally ornate arches adorn the National Palace, on the east side of Plaza de Caicedo. This neoclassical government building houses a small museum that commemorates 300 years of growing and processing sugarcane, for which Cali and the surrounding Valle de Cauca are famous. ✉ *Carrera 4 at Calle 12* ✉ *Free* ⊙ *Weekdays.*

❾ Paseo de Bolívar. Tropical trees shade this large park on the Río Cali's north bank. The modern buildings to the west house municipal offices and are collectively known as the CAM, a term also used by locals to identify the park. ✉ *Av. 6 and Río Cali.*

❻ Plaza de Caicedo. In the middle of this shady square is a statue of Joaquín Caicedo y Cuero, the 18th-century patriot who liberated Cali from the Spanish. ✉ *Carrera 4 between Calles 11 and 12.*

WHERE TO EAT

$-$$
LATIN
AMERICAN
✕ **Obelisco Plaza.** Although you can dine inside, try to snag one of the tables across the street on the bank of the Río Cali. Waiters literally risk their lives crossing the busy Avenida Colombia to deliver your meal. The specialties include bite-size empanadas and *chuzos* (shish kebabs). Because this is a popular late-night hangout, tables fill up early. ✉ *Av. Colombia No. 4* ☎ *572/893–3019* ▭ *DC, MC, V* ⊙ *No lunch.*

$$-$$$
LATIN
AMERICAN
✕ **El Rancho de Jonás.** Specializing in Colombian-style barbecue, El Rancho de Jonás serves up generous portions of grilled beef. This family-run restaurant maintains a dressed-down, informal style. On Sunday you can dance to tropical tunes from the '60s and '70s. ✉ *Autopista Sur with Carrera 43* ☎ *572/513–4444* ▭ *AE, DC, MC, V.*

WHERE TO STAY

$$$
🏨 **Dann Carlton.** Overlooking an attractive residential neighborhood near the Río Cali, the towers of this luxury hotel are filled with comfortable rooms with great views. On balmy days you can cool off in the fourth-floor swimming pool. Restaurante Carlton, with its quirky art deco style, is renowned for its outstanding international fare. **Pros:** You may be forgiven for thinking you are in a far more familiar and chic hotel. **Cons:** Almost everywhere in Cali is saddled with traffic and pollution—the Dann Carlton is no different. ✉ *Av. Colombia 1–60* ☎ *572/893–3000 or 572/893–2000* 🖷 *572/893–4000* ⊕ *www.hotel danncarltoncali.com.co* ⤷ *198 rooms* ♿ *In-hotel: 2 restaurants, bar, pool, gym* ▭ *AE, DC, MC, V.*

$
🏨 **Don Jaime.** This intimate 29-room lodging provides more personalized attention than its larger rivals. The popular café overlooks busy Avenida 6, and the hotel restaurant is among the best in Cali. **Pros:** Breakfast is included, and there is a rapid laundry service. **Cons:** Be wary of rooms that overlook the noisy avenida. ✉ *Av. 6 No. 15N–25* ☎ *572/667–2828*

or 572/667–8287 ✉*572/668–7098* ⭢*29 rooms, 25 with bath* ⚲*In-hotel: restaurant, room service, bar* ▭*AE, DC, MC, V.*

$ ⚏ **Hostal Santa Rita.** This family-run 12-room gem is a true find, and it is most certainly not a hostel in the conventional sense, as it appeals to couples, young professionals, and seasoned travelers. In this neo-colonial building rooms are clean and bright, and the staff make you feel at home. **Pros:** Lodging here you might forget you are in the center of Cali's urban sprawl. **Cons:** Can be hard to find. ✉*Av. 3 Oeste No. 7–131* ☎*572/892–0021* ✉*572/892–6143* ⭢*12 rooms, all with bath* ⚲*In-hotel: no elevator* ▭*AE, DC, MC, V.*

$$ ⚏ **Hotel InterContinental.** Overlooking the Río Cali, this modern luxury hotel is popular among business travelers. The staff is extremely help-ful; concierge Gustavo Ortiz will fill you in on Cali's hottest restau-rants and nightclubs. La Terraza, one of the hotel's four restaurants, specializes in international fare. **Pros:** Right in the middle of things. **Cons:** Have you ever stayed in a hotel perched damlike on a traffic island? ✉*Av. Colombia No. 2–72* ☎*572/882–3225* ✉*572/882–2567* ⊕*www.interconti.com* ⭢*301 rooms* ⚲*In-hotel: 4 restaurants, room service, bar, tennis court, pool* ▭*AE, DC, MC, V.*

SHOPPING

The region's crafts include hand-carved hardwood bowls and serving utensils, finely embroidered blouses and dresses, handwoven ponchos, and *chumbes,* multicolor woolen strips used for belts. One popular craft shop is **Artesanías Pancandé** (✉*Av. 6 No. 17–A53* ☎*572/668–6700*). Look for handmade items at **Artesanías La Caleñita** (✉*Calle 8A 23–C24* ☎*572/556–1172*).

POPAYÁN

130 km (81 mi) south of Cali.

Founded in 1537 by Sebastián de Belalcázar, Popayán quickly became an important administrative center of the viceroyalty of New Granada because of its position on the Cartagena–Quito gold route. Although the town was largely destroyed by an earthquake on Good Friday in 1983, its colonial buildings have all been painstakingly rebuilt. Hotel rooms must be booked months ahead of time for Semana Santa, the week between Palm Sunday and Easter, when the streets are filled with colorful religious processions.

GETTING HERE & AROUND

It is best to fly to Popayán and avoid travel overland. The tiny Aero-puerto Guillermo Leo'n Valencia, located behind the bus terminal, receives two daily Avianca flights from Bogotá.

Popayán is an easy city to navigate, as it's organized in a traditional grid pattern. At the center is Parque Caldas, and in the surrounding streets you'll find most of the points of interest.

SAFETY & PRECAUTIONS

Although you should steer clear of the rough neighborhoods south of Calle 10, you can walk during the day without problems in the old part of town, where most of the sights are located. As always, be aware of your surroundings and keep an eye on your possessions.

Although Popayán itself has been spared, the civil conflict around the city peaks and troughs. Before traveling by bus or car to Cali or to other popular tourist attractions in the area, including Silvia, Tierradentro, San Agustín, and the Parque Nacional Puracé, check with the local authorities.

ESSENTIALS

Airlines **Avianca** (⊠ *Calle 5 No. 5–81* ☎ *572/244–505 or 572/240–575*).

Airports **Aeropuerto Popayán** (⊠ *Via Panamericana* ☎ *572/823–1379*).

Bus Contacts **Terminal de Transporte** (⊠ *Transversal 9 No. 4N–125* ☎ *572/823–1817*).

Currency Exchange **Banco de la República** (⊠ *Carrera 6 No. 2–78*).

Visitor & Tour Info **Aviatur** (⊠ *Calle 4 No. 8–69* ☎ *572/820–8674*).The **Corporacion de Turismo del Cauca** (⊠ *Carrera 5 No. 4–68* ☎ *572/824–2251 or 572/824–0468*).

EXPLORING POPAYÁN

Casa Mosquera. One of Popayán's founding families once owned this now-restored colonial house and the religious art on display inside. Across the street is the Casa Caldas, the local tourist office, where you can pick up a city map. ⊠ *Calle 3 No. 5–14* ☎ *No phone* ☉ *Weekdays 8–noon and 2–6, weekends 9–1.*

★ **Iglesia de San Francisco.** Popayán's most important colonial church is in remarkable condition, thanks to extensive renovation following the 1983 earthquake. The church's bright interior has gilded wooden altars, and its tower holds a 3-ton bell. ⊠ *Calle 4 at Carrera 9* ☎ *572/824–0160* ☑ *Free* ☉ *Daily 7–7.*

Iglesia de San José. This 18th-century church, painted a bright yellow, is one of Popayán's most distinctive structures. Unfortunately, it's open only for masses. ⊠ *Calle 5 at Carrera 8.*

Iglesia de Santo Domingo. After an earthquake destroyed the original chapel, the Dominicans built this church in 1741. It's notable for the stonework around its doorway, which depicts exotic flowers and animals, and for the silver Virgin Mary behind its altar, brought from Spain in 1588. A former monastery next door now houses the regional university. ⊠ *Calle 4 No. 4–15* ☎ *572/824–0533* ☉ *Daily 8–7.*

Museo de Arte Religioso. Housed in a lovely colonial mansion, the Museum of Religious Art has a collection made up predominately of paintings, but it also has some valuable gold and silver artifacts. ⊠ *Calle 4 No. 4–56* ☎ *572/824–2759* ☑ *3,000 pesos* ☉ *Daily 9–2:30 and 3–6.*

Plaza Central. Shaded by tall palms, this square is often called Plaza Caldas, after Francisco José de Caldas, the independence fighter whose statue is here. The city's cathedral, completed in 1906, is to the south; to the east is the 18th-century clock tower. ⊠ *Calles 4 and Carrera 6.*

Puente del Humilladero. The long brick bridge spanning the Río Molino was built at the end of the 18th century, as was the smaller span nearby. ⊠ *Carrera 6 at Calle 2.*

WHERE TO EAT

$–$$
ITALIAN
✕ **Restaurante Italiano.** You won't forget the food served at this small two-level restaurant catercorner to the Iglesia de San Francisco. There's a good selection of pizzas, pastas, salads, and excellent *cremas* (cream soups). ⊠ *Calle 4 No. 8–83* ☎ *572/824–0607* ▭ *No credit cards.*

WHERE TO STAY

$
★
▦ **Casa Familiar el Descanso.** This small pensión down the hill from the tourist office is a bargain. Rooms are simple but clean, and share baths off the central hallway. Breakfast is served in a bright sitting area. Owner Haydee de Varela is a wealth of information about the city. **Pros:** Delightfully simple and homey. **Cons:** If you are looking for something more high-tech, this not the place to be. ⊠ *Carrera 5 No. 2–41* ☎ *572/824–0019* ⇄ *6 rooms with shared bath* ▭ *No credit cards.*

$
▦ **Hotel Camino Real.** Built in 1591 as a women's college, this renovated colonial building off the Plaza Central has tile floors and old, though well-maintained, wooden furniture. Rooms, most of which overlook a patio, have big baths. The first-floor restaurant serves Colombian and European food. **Pros:** You truly feel as if you are staying in the beating colonial heart of Popayán. **Cons:** A room overlooking the Plaza Central will cost you more, otherwise you'll have to make do with an internal view. ⊠ *Calle 5 No. 5–59* ☎ *572/824–1254* 🖷 *572/824–0816* ⇄ *28 rooms* ⚴ *In-hotel: restaurant, no elevator* ▭ *AE, DC, MC, V.*

$$
★
▦ **Hotel Monasterio.** This beautifully restored 18th-century Franciscan monastery wraps around a lovely courtyard with a babbling fountain. Here you'll find well-tended gardens and a view of the tower of the adjacent Iglesia de San Francisco. The generously proportioned rooms are filled with colonial-style furnishings. **Pros:** Oozing style and tranquillity you won't want to leave. **Cons:** Some might find the rooms a mite moody. ⊠ *Calle 4 No. 10–14* ☎ *572/824–2191 or 572/824–4065* 🖷 *572/824–4065* ⇄ *47 rooms* ⚴ *In-hotel: restaurant, bar, sauna, pool, no elevator* ▭ *AE, DC, MC, V.*

SAN AGUSTÍN

36 km (22.5 mi) west of Pitalito via major paved road.

Declared a UNESCO World Heritage in 1995, but off-limits until recently due to the conflict, San Agustín preserves the relics of an advanced pre-Colombian culture that thrived in the area for more than seven centuries. This Agustinian culture is now protected and cherished and on show in verdant parks in the environs of San Agustín, where visitors can stroll back through the centuries marveling at anthropomorphic sculptures symbolizing fertility, maternity, and the alter ego. Outside of Semana Santa visitors will not have trouble finding rooms in decent accommodations in converted colonial homes.

GETTING HERE & AROUND

Flights come into Pitalito's Contador airport some 45 minutes' drive from San Agustín and also into Neiva's Benito Salas airport a further four-hour drive. By bus there are direct services from Bogotá, Popayán, and Cali.

Getting around San Agustín can all be arranged through tour companies, who will contract 4x4 jeeps to shuttle you between the parks and sites of interest.

SAFETY & PRECAUTIONS

For years this part of Huila was the center of guerrilla activity. This is no longer the case, and travel in the immediate San Agustín area is considered safe.

ESSENTIALS

Bus Contacts **Coomotor** (☎571/428–7649). **Cotranshuila** (☎571/429–7760).

Medical Assistance **Clínica Mia Auxiliadora** (✉Calle 6 No. 5–36, Pitalito ☎578/836–0840).

Visitor & Tour Info **Secretaria de Turismo** (☎578/837–3063).

EXPLORING SAN AGUSTÍN

Parque Alto de las Piedras. In the Parque Alto de las Piedras, in addition to more staggeringly well preserved and ornate anthropomorphic and zoomorphic statues and in particular the "double me" alter-ego sculpture, there are some interesting pre-Colombian tombs on display. Visitors can easily while away a few hours here. ✉Parque Alto de las Piedras ⚄3,000 pesos ☉Daily 8–5.

Parque Archeologico San Agustín. In the confines of a well guarded and elysian park can be found the treasures of a disappeared Agustinian culture. Objects such as altars and anthropomorphic statues collected from farmhouses, rescued from private collections, and moved from neighboring communities for their protection are placed respectfully about in this wonderful park. In order to fully appreciate what's on show, you'll need a guide and at least four hours. ✉Parque Archeologico San Agustín ☎578/837–9844 ⚄6,000 pesos ☉Daily 8–4:30.

Parque Archeologico de Tierradentro. Slightly harder to get to over a gravel road is a park recognized for its strikingly decorated hypogea dating from the 6th to the 10th centuries. To visit these famed underground chambers, head to the Alto del Aguacate, Alto del San Andrés, Alto de Segovia, Alto del Duende, and El Tablón. ✉Inza, San Andres de Pisimbalá ⚄6,000 pesos ☉Daily 8–4.

WHERE TO STAY & EAT

¢ **Hacienda Anacaona.** Combining country rustic with colonial chic, the Anacaona is probably the best accommodation from which to explore the ruins and parks of San Agustín. Every room has been thoughtfully decorated and serves as a perfect antidote to aching feet after hours of marveling at treasures from times past. **Pros:** You are in a rural idyll here at the Anacaona **Cons:** The hotel is 2 km from town ⊠*Km 2 via El Estrecho, vereda La Cuchilla* ☎*578/837–9390* ⊕*www.anacaona-colombia.com* ⚒*In Hotel: restaurant, no elevator*

¢–$ **Pizza Manía.** In a town not overwhelmed with quality eateries, Pizza Manía stands out from the ubiquitous roast chicken restaurants as a place where you can easily settle down and enjoy some pretty decent fare. The restaurant seats 15 people and does a brisk trade. ⊠*Carrera 13 No. 3–43* ☎*57/311–248–8983* ▭*No credit cards.*

PIZZA

SPORTS & THE OUTDOORS

It will come as no surprise that there are dozens of outfitters in San Agustín keen to offer their services. Options include touring the parks and surrounding areas on horseback and less tranquil but far more adrenalin-filled white-water rafting on the Grade 1–4 Río Magdalena.

Nueva Lengua International (☎*571/753–2451* ⊕*www.travelsanagustin. com*). Promoting sustainable tourism and with long established links in San Agustín, the Nueva Lengua International offers tours to accommodate your budget.

THE CARIBBEAN COAST

Colombia's sultry Caribbean Coast is linked to Bogotá only by the national flag, the milky Río Magdalena, and a couple of snaking highways. The *costeño* people, driven by salsa and the accordion-heavy *vallenato* music, have an exuberant spirit not seen in the capital.

Toward the western end of the 1,600-km (992-mi) shoreline is Cartagena, Colombia's greatest colonial city. With its barrel-tile roofs and wooden balconies, Cartagena's Ciudad Amurallada resembles many cities in Spain, but the feeling is definitely tropical. The Islas del Rosario, just off the coast, provide plenty of exploring options for snorkelers and divers.

Northeast of Cartagena is Barranquilla, a quiet city that bursts to life during Carnival in February, when it has pre-Lenten festivities. (If you go, fly—do not take a bus or car.)

CARTAGENA

When it was founded in 1533 by Spanish conquistador Pedro de Heredia, Cartagena was the only port on the South American mainland. Gold and silver looted from indigenous peoples passed through here en route to Spain, making Cartagena an obvious target for pirates. The most destructive of these was Sir Francis Drake, who in 1586 torched 200 buildings, including the cathedral, and made off for England with more than 100,000 gold ducats. Cartagena's magnificent city walls and countless fortresses were erected to protect its riches, as well as to safeguard the most important African slave market in the New World. The Ciudad Amurallada attracts many to Cartagena, but it actually comprises a small section of this city of half a million. Most of Cartagena's hotels and res-

> ### DID YOU KNOW?
>
> Despite the strength-sapping heat and carnival-like sensibility, the Caribbean coast has nurtured some of Colombia's best-known writers and artists, including novelist Gabriel García Márquez and painter Alejandro Obregón.

taurants are in the Bocagrande district, an elongated peninsula where high-rise hotels overlook a long, gray-sand beach.

GETTING HERE & AROUND

Cartagena's Aeropuerto Rafael Nuñez lies 3 km (2 mi) east of downtown. There are daily flights from Bogotá and Medellín on domestic carriers Aerorepública, Avianca, and Satena. There are direct international flights from Panama with Copa, from Canada with Air Transat, and from Italy with Lauda Air.

Traveling by car or bus to the Caribbean coast is not impossible yet it is a long haul (20 hours) and should be done during daylight hours only.

SAFETY & PRECAUTIONS

Colombia's Caribbean coast, especially the towns most popular among tourists, is relatively safe. In Cartagena beware of pickpockets in the tourist areas.

ESSENTIALS

Currency Exchange **Banco de la República** (⊠ *Calle 33 No. 3–123*).

Internet Cafés **Café Internet** (⊠ *Plaza Santo Domingo*).

Post Office **Cartagena** (⊠ *Plaza de los Coches, off Av. Venezuela*).

Medical Services **Hospital Bocagrande** (☎ *575/665–5270*).

Visitor Info **Información Turística** (⊠ *Plaza de la Aduana* ☎ *575/655–0640*).

EXPLORING CARTAGENA

❻ Barrio San Diego. The seldom-visited streets of this enchanting north-end district are lined with squat colonial mansions painted white, ocher, and deep blue. Geraniums cascade over balconies, and open doorways reveal lush hidden courtyards. At the northern corner of the city walls you'll find **Las Bóvedas** (The Vaults), a row of storerooms built in the 18th century to hold gunpowder and other military essentials. Today they are occupied by the city's best crafts shops. After you've loaded up on hats, hammocks, and leather goods, take a stroll along the city walls and watch as the setting sun reddens the Caribbean. ⊠ *North of Plaza Fernández de Madrid.*

❶ Casa de Marqués Valdehoyos. Although scantily furnished, this elegant house exudes a powerful aroma of well-to-do colonial life. The sturdy

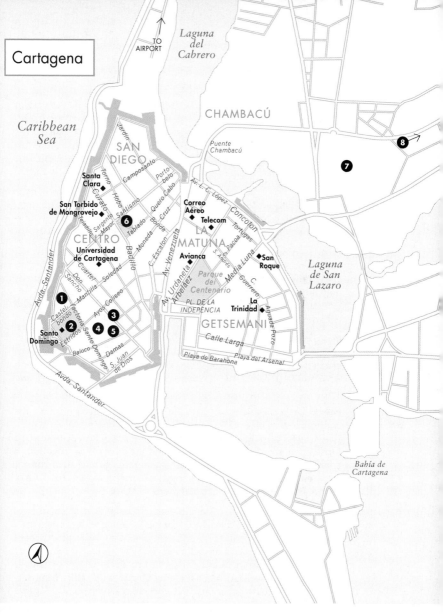

Cartagena

Caribbean Sea

Laguna del Cabrero

TO AIRPORT

CHAMBACÚ

Puente Chambacú

SAN DIEGO

Santa Clara

San Torbido de Mongrovejo

Jardín
Torno
Curato
Holbo
Camposanto
Porto-belo
Quero Cabo
Bonda
Cruz
Av. L. C. López

Correo Aéreo

Telecom

Concolon

CENTRO

Universidad de Cartagena

Sargenta
Mayor
Santísimo
Tablado
Moneda
Escalon
Baditio
C. Escalon
Av. Venezuela

LA MATUNA

Tortugas
Cacoa

Avianca

S. Andres

San Roque

Laguna de San Lazaro

Parque del Centenario

Media Luna
C. Guerrero

1

Castel-bondo
Tractora Santo Domingo
Don Sancho
Mantilla
Cuartel
Soledad
Ayos
Coliseo

Av. Urdaneta Arbelaez

PL. DE LA INDEPENCIA

La Trinidad

2   **3**

4   **5**

Santo Domingo

Estridos
Baloco
Damas
Domingo
S. Juan de Dios

GETSEMANI

Ayuada Pozo

Calle Larga

Playa del Arsenal

Playa de Barahona

Avda. Santander

Avda. Santander

Bahía de Cartagena

7

8

mansion and its shady courtyard, low arches, and elaborate wooden balconies are the products of the marqués's slave-trade fortune. The tourist office inside provides useful maps. ⊠*Calle Factoría No. 36–57* ☎*095/664–0904* ⊠*Free* ☉*Daily 8–noon and 2–6.*

❼ Castillo de San Felipe de Barajas. Designed by Antonio de Arévalo in 1639, the Fort of St. Philip's steep-angled brick and concrete battlements were arranged so that if part of the castle were conquered the rest could still be defended. A maze of tunnels, minimally lit today to allow for spooky exploration, still connects vital points of the fort. ⊠*Av. Pedro de Heredia at Carrera 17* ☎*575/666–4790* ⊠*13,000 pesos* ☉*Daily 8–6.*

❸ Catedral. Plaza de Bolívar is a shady place from which to admire Cartagena's 16th-century cathedral, with its colorful bell tower and 20th-century dome. Inside is a massive gilded altar. ⊠*Plaza de Bolívar.*

❽ Cerro de la Popa. For spectacular views of Cartagena, ascend this hill around sunset. Because of its strategic location, the 17th-century monastery here intermittently served as a fortress during the colonial era. It now houses a museum and a chapel dedicated to the Virgin de la Candelaria, Cartagena's patron saint. ⊠*3 km (2 mi) southeast of Ciudad Amurallada* ☎*575/666–2331* ⊠*6,000 pesos* ☉*Daily 8:30–5.*

Fodor'sChoice
★

❺ Museo del Oro y Arqueología. The Gold and Archaeological Museum displays an assortment of artifacts culled from the Sinús, an indigenous group that lived in the region 2,000 years ago. ⊠*Carrera 4 No. 33–26* ☎*575/660–0778* ⊠*Free* ☉*Tues.–Fri. 10–1 and 3–7, Sat. 10–1 and 2–5.*

❹ Palacio de la Inquisición. A baroque limestone doorway marks the entrance to the Palace of the Inquisition, the headquarters of the repressive arbiters of political and spiritual orthodoxy who once exercised jurisdiction over Colombia, Ecuador, and Venezuela. The ground floor contains implements of torture—racks and thumbscrews, to name but two—and architectural models of bygone Cartagena. ⊠*Carrera 4 No. 33–26* ☎*575/664–7381* ⊠*3,000 pesos* ☉*Daily 9–5.*

Fodor'sChoice
★

❷ Plaza Santo Domingo. The eponymous church looming over the plaza is the oldest in the city. Built in 1539, it has a simple whitewashed interior, bare limestone pillars, a raised choir, and an adjacent cloistered seminary. Local lore says the bell tower's twisted profile is the work of the Devil, who, dispirited at having failed to destroy it, threw himself into the plaza's well. At night the area fills up with tables from surrounding bars and restaurants. ⊠*Calle Santo Domingo and Carrera Santo Domingo.*

WHERE TO EAT

Seafood is the regional specialty, as are *arroz con coco* (rice cooked in coconut milk) and *sancocho de sábalo* (fish prepared in coconut milk with strips of plantains, bananas, and yucca). Tropical *jugos* (juices) are an excellent companion to *carimañolas* (stuffed yucca), *arepas de huevo* (egg-filled pancakes), and *butifarras* (small meatballs).

$$ **✕Café San Pedro.** Although it serves Colombian fare, this restaurant's
CAFÉ eclectic menu also includes dishes from Thailand, Italy, and Japan. You
can also drop by to have a drink and to watch the activity on the plaza
from one of the outdoor tables. ⊠*Plaza San Pedro* ☎*575/664–5121
or 575/664–1433* ▭*DC, MC, V* ⊘*Closed Sun.*

$$$–$$$$ **✕Club de Pesca.** Time slips gently by at this 18th-century fortress in the
LATIN nearby town of Manga. It's easy to linger on the waterfront terrace in
AMERICAN the shade of a giant fig tree, especially when you're savoring one of the
delicate specialties, such as snapper with lemon, soy, tahini, and mint.
⊠*Fuerte de San Sebastián del Pastelillo, Manga* ☎*575/660–4594*
▭*AE, DC, MC, V.*

$$$ **✕Paco's.** Heavy beams, rough terra-cotta walls, wooden benches, and
LATIN tunes from an aging Cuban band are the hallmarks of this downtown
AMERICAN eatery. Drop by for a drink and some tapas, or try the more substan-
tial *langostinos a la sifú* (lobsters fried in batter). You can sit in the
dining room or outside on the Plaza Santo Domingo. ⊠*Plaza Santo
Domingo* ▭*V.*

$$$–$$$$ **✕La Vitrola.** This friendly restaurant on a quiet Ciudad Amurallada
LATIN corner is the result of a New Yorker's love affair with the Caribbean.
AMERICAN You can begin with *ceviche catalina* (fish and octopus marinated in lime
★ juice); then try a *zarzuela de mariscos* (seafood casserole) or perhaps
corvina con salsa de cebollin y jenibre (sea bass with scallion-ginger
sauce). Ceiling fans, historic photos, and live Cuban music complete
the mood. ⊠*Calle Baloco, near Carrera Santo Domingo* ☎*575/664–
8243* ▭*AE, DC, MC, V.*

WHERE TO STAY

$$$$ **⚏Charleston Hotel.** Housed in the historic Convento de Santa Teresa,
★ this 16th-century showplace in the Ciudad Amurallada combines colo-
nial and republican architectural styles. Rooms and suites, sumptu-
ously appointed with rich fabrics and antique furnishings, look out
onto the ocean or the Old City. The best views are from the rooftop
pool and restaurant. **Pros:** The swimming pool is a delight. **Cons:** Be
prepared for the street vendors camped outside. ⊠*Plaza Santa Teresa*
☎*575/664–9494* 🖷*575/664–9447* ⊕*www.hoteles-charleston.com*
⇖*70 rooms, 21 suites* ⚐*In-hotel: 2 restaurants, bar, pool, laundry
service, Internet* ▭*AE, DC, MC, V.*

$$$$ **⚏Hilton.** Every spacious room at this modern hotel on the tip of the
Bocagrande peninsula has a balcony facing the sea. They also have
great views of the terrace and its leafy gardens and three pools. A path
from the hotel leads to a private beach lined with palms, magnolias,
and thatched oyster bars. **Pros:** The narrow streets of the Ciudad Vieja
are left behind. **Cons:** It's a taxi ride back to the delights of the Ciu-
dad Vieja. ⊠*Av. Almirante Brión, Carrera 1 No. 4–00, El Laguito*
☎*575/665–0666, 800/445–8667 in U.S.* 🖷*575/665–2211* ⊕*www.
hilton.com* ⇖*288 rooms, 15 suites* ⚐*In-hotel: 2 restaurants, 2 bars,
tennis court, 3 pools, gym, children's programs (all ages)* ▭*AE, DC,
MC, V.*

$$$$ **⚏Hotel Caribe.** The oldest lodging on Bocagrande, this elegant hotel
resembles a huge sand castle. Bedrooms in the refurbished older build-
ing have more charm than those in the modern wings, though they

5

can be noisy on weekends. Behind the hotel, giant ficus trees shade a large pool. A narrow lane separates the hotel from the beach. **Pros:** In this standard hotel you are close to the beach. **Cons:** Have you seen the beach here? Do not come here if you are looking to escape the package tourism crowd. ⊠ *Carrera 1A No. 2–87, Bocagrande* ☎ *575/665–0155* 🖷 *575/665–4970* ⊕ *www.hotelcaribe.com* 🖙 *346 rooms, 17 suites* 🖧 *In-hotel: 2 restaurants, bar, tennis court, pool, gym* 🖃 *AE, DC, MC, V.*

$$$$

Fodor'sChoice

★

🔲 **Santa Clara.** Beyond the arched porticos and lush courtyard of this elegant hotel in Ciudad Amurallada is a newer wing that holds the pool and the comfortably furnished guest rooms. The former dining room for the convent holds El Refectorio, which serves the city's best French cuisine. **Pros:** You really won't want to leave, every room has a breathtaking view. **Cons:** You will have to leave eventually. ⊠ *Plaza San Diego* ☎ *575/664–6070, 800/221–4542 in U.S.* 🖷 *575/664–8040* ⊕ *www.hotelsantaclara.com* 🖙 *144 rooms, 18 suites* 🖧 *In-room: safe. In-hotel: 3 restaurants, bar, pool, gym, concierge, spa* 🖃 *AE, DC, MC, V.*

$

★

🔲 **Las Tres Banderas.** In the historic San Diego neighborhood, this attractive little 19th-century hotel is an inexpensive option. The rooms, all of which border a narrow courtyard, combine colonial style with modern amenities. **Pros:** So quiet is the street that you may not even notice the hotel is here. **Cons:** Some of the rooms near the back are a little dark ⊠ *Calle Cochera del Hobo No. 38–66* ☎ *575/660–0160* ⊕ *www.hotel3banderas.com* 🖙 *22 rooms* 🖃 *MC.*

NIGHTLIFE

A great way to see the Ciudad Amurallada is to take a romantic ride in a horse-drawn *coche* (carriage), which you can hire in front of the Hotel Caribe or the Charleston Hotel. If you just want to watch the locals, the most popular destination in the Ciudad Amurallada is Plaza Santo Domingo, where several restaurants and cafés have outdoor seating.

A rowdier option is the popular *rumba en chiva*, a bar-hopping bus with a live band on the roof. You'll notice that many Colombians party on the beaches of Bocagrande. Vendors rent plastic chairs and sell cold beer, and roving trios play *vallenato*, the typical regional music.

BARS & DANCE CLUBS

In the Ciudad Vieja, close to the Charleston Hotel is **Ba Bar** (⊠ *Calle San Juan de Dios No. 3–37* ☎ *575/664–7078*), a two-story colonial building that packs in the beautiful and the wealthy. If all the dancing makes you hungry, step outside and feast in one of the elegant neighboring restaurants.

Mr. Babilla (⊠ *Av. del Arsenal No. 893* ☎ *575/664–7005*) is a busy bar with good food and a live salsa band on weekends.

OUTDOOR ACTIVITIES

BEACHES

For white sand and palm trees, your best bet is **Playa Blanca,** about 15 minutes away by boat. Many people opt for a visit to the **Islas del Rosario,** a verdant archipelago surrounded by aquamarine waters and coral reefs. Tour boats leave from the Muelle de los Pegasos, the pier flanked by statues of two flying horses that is just outside the city walls. Plenty of men with boats will also offer to take you on the one-hour journey. Most larger hotels offer a trip to Playa Blanca and Islas de Rosario as part of a package.

FISHING

The **Club de Pesca** (✉ *Calle 24 at Carrera 17* ☎ *575/660–4594*) in Manga can arrange fishing charters.

SCUBA DIVING

The **Caribe Vivo** (☎ *575/664–1417*) at the Hotel Caribe organizes snorkeling trips to the Islas del Rosario and scuba diving at underwater wrecks.

SHOPPING

Las Bóvedas, a series of arched storerooms in the Ciudad Amurallada's northern corner now houses about two-dozen shops with the best selection of local and national crafts. If you're looking for emeralds, visit the jewelry shops on or near Calle Pantaleón, beside the cathedral.

SANTA MARTA

237 km (147 mi) northeast of Cartagena.

Santa Marta lies at the foot of the snowcapped Sierra Nevada, the world's highest coastal range. The mountains are largely protected within Parque Nacional Tayrona. Hidden on their slopes are the pre-Columbian ruins of La Ciudad Perdida.

Although Santa Marta was founded in 1525, modern industry and architecture largely obscure its colonial heritage. Today the city's 200,000 inhabitants rely heavily on the deep-water port, where banana boats are anchored in thick clusters. Most of the cargo is legitimate, but Santa Marta also handles more contraband than any other Colombian port. In the 1970s that meant mostly marijuana; today cocaine reigns supreme. Santa Marta is mostly nonchalant and friendly, but inquisitiveness in this feral, fascinating city is unwise; some of its residents carry weapons as a matter of course.

GETTING HERE & AROUND

Budget travelers come through to Santa Marta overland along a hippie trail that winds its way either from the palaces of Cartagena or from the beaches of Venezuela with interruptions in the paradisiacal Tayrona. If time is short, then Aerorepublica and Avianca have several flights a day from Bogotá, Medellín, and Cali.

SAFETY & PRECAUTIONS

Tourists are advised to stick to the shorefront of Santa Marta and the beaches of nearby Taganga and Rodadero, where security is fine. But remember at all times that the city is an important trans-shipment point for the cocaine trade. At night watch out for pickpockets and bag snatchers and take taxis.

ESSENTIALS

Currency Exchange **Microfinanciera** (⊠ *Calle 13 No. 3–13, Local 210/202* ☎ *575/431–5372*).

Medical Services **Hospital Central Julio Méndez Barreche** (⊠ *Carrera 14 No. 23–42* ☎ *575/438–2147*).

Visitor Info **Fondo de Información Turística de Santa Marta** (⊠ *Calle 10 No. 3–10, El Rodadero* ☎ *575/422–7548*).

EXPLORING SANTA MARTA

The **Museo Arqueológico Tayrona,** in a handsome former customs house on the main square, has a small collection of Tayrona gold and pottery and a model of La Ciudad Perdida. It's worth a look *before* you head to the old city. ⊠ *Calle 14 at Carrera 2* ☎ *575/421–0953* 🎫 *Free* ⊙ *Mon., Wed. 8–noon and 2–6.*

On the seafront, flag down a taxi and head to the **Quinta de San Pedro Alejandrino,** 20 minutes away. This honey-color hacienda is where Simón Bolívar died in 1830. (Ironically, he was a guest of a Spanish royalist.) On the grounds are a huge gleaming monument to the Liberator and a helpful pictorial history of his life. ⊠ *Mamatoco* ☎ *575/433–2994* 🎫 *6,000 pesos* ⊙ *Daily 9–5.*

WHERE TO STAY & EAT

$ 🏨 **Hotel Panamerican.** Despite its austere concrete-block appearance, this friendly hotel has huge, bright rooms with modern amenities. Sea-facing rooms with a balcony are best; you can have air-conditioning for a small charge, but it's scarcely needed with the refreshing sea breezes. **Pros:** Looking out from the hotel you won't have to view the architectural crime that is the Panamerican. **Cons:** The beach out front can get incredibly crowded. ⊠ *Carrera 1 No. 18–23* ☎ *575/421–1238* 🖨 *575/421–4721* 🛏 *46 rooms* 🛎 *In-hotel: restaurant, no elevator* 🟰 *AE, DC, MC, V.*

$ 🏨 **Hotel Turismar (formerly Hotel Tayrona).** For those on a budget, this two-story colonial-style building across from the black-sand beach is your best bet—in fact, it's as good as many that cost twice as much. Comfy rooms have private baths with lots of hot water. Rooms with air-conditioning cost slightly more. There's also a good outdoor restaurant. **Pros:** Cheap and cheerful. **Cons:** Some of the older rooms could do with a makeover. ⊠ *Carrera 1 No. 11–21* ☎ *575/421–2408* 🛏 *24 rooms* 🛎 *In-hotel: restaurant, no elevator* 🟰 *No credit cards.*

$ 🏨 **La Sierra.** Situated in El Rodadero, a resort area 5 km (3 mi) from Santa Marta, this 10-story hotel has large rooms with balconies, many facing the ocean. The restaurant serves an international menu, with seating indoors or on a street-side patio. **Pros:** For an uncomplicated beach holiday, this hotel does the business. **Cons:** Views away from the beach are hardly inspiring. ⊠ *Carrera 1 No. 8–47, El Rodadero* ☎ *575/422–7197* 🖷 *575/422–8198* 🛏 *73 rooms* ♿ *In-hotel: restaurant, bar* ☰ *AE, DC, MC, V.*

OUTDOOR ACTIVITIES

The beaches at Santa Marta are dirty, but just south of town is **El Rodadero,** which has a white-sand beach.

SHOPPING

A block from the Hotel Panamerican, the **Almacenes Típicos El Tiburón** (⊠ *Carrera 2A No. 18–09, Santa Marta*) sells all sorts of Colombian crafts. There is also a store in El Rodadero's Edificio Liberador on Calle 8.

PARQUE NACIONAL TAYRONA

5

38 km (24 mi) east of Santa Marta.

One of Colombia's most popular reserves, Parque Nacional Tayrona has forest-clad slopes, ancient ruins, palm-fringed beaches, and coral reefs, all accessible from the Santa Marta–Riohacha Highway. At **Arrecifes,** a 45-minute walk west of the parking lot along a slippery jungle trail, you can take nourishment at the rustic bars and restaurants with the hippies who inhabit the beautiful beaches nearby. **Pueblito,** an ancient Tayrona village that's being excavated, is a two-hour uphill hike from Arrecifes.

The park's eastern sector around **Cañaveral** is far greener. Get your bearings from the spectacular *mirador* (lookout), and then descend to inspect the giant sculptured monoliths on the beach, which lend something of a *Planet of the Apes* look to the scenery. ⊠ *East of Santa Marta* 🖳 *Foreigners 21,000 pesos* 🕑 *Daily 8–5:30.*

OUTDOOR ACTIVITIES

Spectacular and deserted strips of white sand lie on Parque Tayrona's outskirts. Swimming here is extremely dangerous because of riptides and sharks. Drownings are very common. In order to bathe in the azure waters, head to La Piscina, a tranquil cove some 15 minutes' walk from Arrecifes.

LA CIUDAD PERDIDA

142 km (88 mi) southeast of Santa Marta.

When *guaqueros* (treasure hunters) stumbled upon La Ciudad Perdida (The Lost City) in 1975, they discovered one of the Americas' largest pre-Columbian citadels. Dating from sometime between AD 500 and 700, it's anchored on the rugged northern Sierra Nevada slopes at 3,937 feet, and can only be reached by means of a six-day guided trek or a three-hour helicopter ride.

GETTING HERE & AROUND

Although traveling around the Caribbean coast either by bus or car is getting safer, it's worthwhile going with an organized tour group. In Cartagena, Tesoro Tours arranges everything from city tours to boat trips to the Islas del Rosario. Caliente Tours offers a day trip to the town of Santa Marta (northeast of Cartagena, at the foot of the Sierra Nevada coastal range) and the beaches at El Rodadero. In Bocagrande, Raphael Pérez has a unique trip to the Volcán Totumo, where you can enjoy a mud bath (35,000 pesos).

City tours of Santa Marta can be arranged through Aviatur. The company also offers a boat tour to Acuario Playa Blanca, an aquarium off the coast of Santa Marta. Turcol offers trips to Parque Nacional Tayrona, a reserve with forest-clad slopes, ancient ruins, and palm-fringed beaches as well as the hike to the Ciudad Perdida.

ESSENTIALS

Tour Operators **Aviatur** (⊠ Calle 29 No. 27–05 ☏ 575/423–3159 or 575/421–3848). **Caliente Tours** (⊠ Calle 10 No. 1–61, Edificio Portofino Local 7 ☏ 575/665–5346, 575/665–5347, or 575/660–1516) offers excursions to Las Islas de Rosario and a private island called Isla de Sol. **Raphael Pérez** (⊠ Edificio Hipocampo Local 1, Bocagrande ☏ 575/655–0866) offers a volcano tour, tours to Barranquilla and Santa Marta, a Cartagena City Tour, and a panoramic tour. **Tesoro Tours** (⊠ Carrera 3 No. 6–153, Bocagrande ☏ 575/665–4713). **Turcol** (⊠ Carrera 1C No. 20–15, Santa Marta ☏ 575/421–2256) offers a 5-night/6-day guided hiking trip to the Lost City in the Sierra Nevada.

SANTA CRUZ DE MOMPOX

179 km (111 mi) southeast of Cartagena via Magangue.

Once the crossroads and highway for people and contraband along the mighty Magdalena River and now a colonial relic languishing in the backwaters of the Colombian Caribbean, Mompox (Mompós) is firmly part of the Garciamarquian heartland, with whitewashed streets and ornate churches that echo with tales of South America's liberator Simó Bolívar and the paces of the devout during the city's austere Semana Santa celebrations. Step back in time in a charming destination self-contained on an island, where whole families slumber in rocking chairs in the evening breeze.

GETTING HERE & AROUND

The fastest and easiest ways to reach Mompox are flying into either Cartagena, Barranquilla, or Sincelejo and taking an interurban taxi from there. Daily buses run from Cartagena and Barranquilla.

ESSENTIALS

Change any dollars, euros, or sterling in Cartagena or Barranquilla before coming to Mompox, or suffer the consequences. There are two ATMs on the corner of the Parque Bolívar that accept all cards, but are known to run out of money on Fridays and Saturdays.

Medical Assistance **Hospital San Juan de Dios** (✉ *Calle Real del Medio No. 19–63* ☎ *575/685–6382*).

Visitor Info **Alcaldía de Mompox** (✉ *Palacio San Carlos* ☎ *575/685–5738*).

EXPLORING SANTA CRUZ DE MOMPOX

Casa de Los Portales de la Marquesa. Originally this building made up two mansions but has since been divided up. Two residences still belong to the original families that housed Bolívar on his route through Mompox to Caracas to liberate northern South America. Wander along to the Piedra de Bolívar, which details the dates and days spent in Mompox by the Liberator. ✉ *Albarrada de los Portales* 🎟 *Free.*

El Cementerio Municipal. Finalized in 1789, the ancient cemetery displays elaborate tombstones and mausoleums of the bold and imperious as well as the lowly of Mompox. Look out for the bust of Candelario Obeso, the forefather of black poetry in the Americas, as well as the tombs of early German and Lebanese immigrants looking to make their fortunes. On Wednesday of Easter week Momposinos make the pilgrimage out to the cemetery to place candles on the tombs of family and friends, making for a moving and illuminated spectacle. ✉ *Carrera 4 with Calle 18* 🎟 *Free.*

Iglesia Santa Bárbara Perhaps the architectural icon of Mompox itself, this imposing yellow-painted baroque structure towers over the Magdalena River and dates back to the 16th century. Molds of palms, flowers, and lions adorn its tower. ✉ *Carrera 1 and Calle 14* 🎟 *Free* ⊗ *Daily.*

WHERE TO STAY & EAT

$ ✕ **Dely Bross.** Run by a gentleman from Medellín, this no-frills establishment offers little in the way of *haute cuisine,* but does deliver on the promise of a good feed. Staples of chicken, beef, fried river fish, and the ubiquitous *bandeja paisa* are favorites here. ✉ *In front of Colegio Pinillos* ▭ *No credit cards.*

LATIN AMERICAN

$ ▦ **La Casa Amarilla** New to Mompox is a small and friendly hotel set up by an Englishman enamoured with the town's colonial wonders. More of a guesthouse and hostel than a hotel, La Casa Amarilla is on the bank of the Magdalena and offers dormitory accommodation as well as private rooms around a tended internal garden. ✉ *Carrera 1 No. 13–59* ☎ *575/685–6326* ⊕ *www.lacasaamarillamompos.blogspot. com* ⇆ *4 rooms* ▭ *No credit cards.*

$ ▦ **Hostal Dona Manuela.** The best and most expensive place in town is a sprawling 17th century mansion. All rooms have air-conditioning and cable television, and guests can enjoy the pool. **Pros:** Right in the thick of things, during Semana Santa you will get a first-class view of all the processions. **Cons:** You do not feel the breeze from the river here. ✉ *Calle Real del Medio No. 17–41* ☎ *575/685–5142* ⇆ *23 rooms* ⚭ *In-hotel: pool* ▭ *AE, MC, V.*

SHOPPING

Mompox is recognized for its high-quality carpenters and fine silver-work. Jewelers offer ornate silver earrings and necklaces at negotiable prices. **Taller y Joyería Orvilla Hermanos** (⊠ *Calle Real del Medio No. 17A–76* ☎ *575/684–0130* ⏰ *Weekdays 10–5*). A long-established craftsman in Mompox, Juan Carlos Ortiz Villanueva produces some of the highest quality items in both silver and gold.

Jimmy's (⊠ *Calle Real del Medio No. 15–86* ☎ *575/685–5383* ⏰ *Weekdays 9–4*). On the Calle Real del Medio, Jimmy's displays some of the more delicate jewelry offered in silver in Mompox.

SAN ANDRÉS & PROVIDENCIA

The resort islands of San Andrés and Providencia lie 645 km (400 mi) northwest of the Caribbean coast—closer to Nicaragua than to Colombia. Christopher Columbus was the first European to set foot on the islands during his fourth voyage to the New World. They were later settled by English pilgrims (who landed in their vessel, the *Seaflower,* at about the same time their counterparts came ashore at Plymouth Rock), and then by Jamaican cotton growers. Today the islands' roughly 60,000 residents speak an English patois and Spanish. Frequent air service and San Andrés's duty-free status mean that both islands receive a steady stream of visitors, mostly well-to-do Colombians who dive and snorkel when they aren't sunbathing and shopping.

There is no passenger boat service from the Colombian mainland or between the islands, and no rental cars are available on either island.

SAN ANDRÉS

645 km (400 mi) off Colombia's Caribbean Coast.

As it's only 13 km (8 mi) long, cigar-shape San Andrés is easy to explore by bicycle or motor scooter. Rent one from any of the shops along Avenida Colombia in El Centro. Along the coastal road is **Cueva Morgan,** a small beachfront settlement where the pirate Henry Morgan reputedly stashed his loot after pillaging coastal Cuba and Panama in the 1670s. Beach bums should head for **Johnny Cay,** a tiny islet just off the coast. Boats leave all day from San Andrés's beaches.

The island's duty-free status is responsible for the bland boutiques in the concrete jungle of **El Centro,** San Andrés's commercial center.

GETTING HERE & AROUND

As San Andrés is the package-holiday capital of Colombia, daily flights come in from many mainland cities, including Bogotá, Medellín, Cali, and Barranquilla. Flights book up rapidly on prime Colombian holidays, long weekends, Semana Santa, and in December, but more reasonable tariffs can be secured outside of these dates.

There is a public bus service that circles the island, but the buses are rather old and beat up.

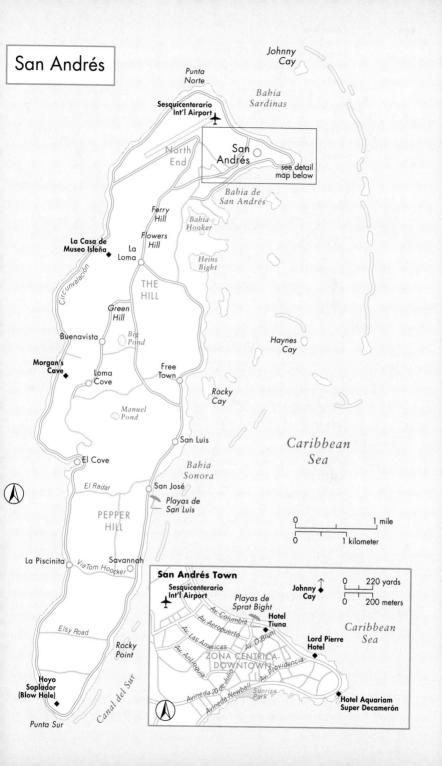

SAFETY & PRECAUTIONS

There is very little to worry about in terms of danger on San Andrés—as the locals say: "There is no maritime guerrilla." The most trouble one may encounter in San Andrés is falling victim to an opportunistic bag-snatcher.

ESSENTIALS

Airports **Aeropuerto Sesquicentenario Gustavo Rojas Pinilla** (🖀 *578/512–6867*).

Currency Exchange **Banco de la República** (✉ *Av. Colón, between Costa Rica and Av. Providencia*). **Cambios y Capitales** (✉ *Av. Providencia No. 1–35 L-106* 🖀 *578/512–3565*).

Post Office **San Andrés** (✉ *Av. Duarte Blum, between Av. 20 de Julio and Av. Colombia*).

Medical Services **Hospital Timothy Britton** (✉ *Av. Colombia Sarie Bay* 🖀 *578/512–7444*).

Visitor & Tour Info **Bluefish Tours** (✉ *Av. Costa Rica C.C. San Andrés L-106* 🖀 *578/512–0751*). **Oficina de Turismo** (✉ *Aeropuerto Sesquicentenario* 🖀 *578/516–110*).

EXPLORING SAN ANDRÉS

La Casa de Museo Islena. Housed in a traditional island dwelling, San Andrés' premier museum goes some way toward detailing the checkered history of San André and Providencia. Tales of pirates, slaves, and missionaries abound, creating the blend of cultures and races found here today. ✉ *Av. Circunvalar, Km 5* 🖀 *578/512–5493*.

Johnny Cay. As if lifted from a soft-drink commercial, Johnny Cay is a small palm-fringed island some 20 minutes by boat from San Andrés. It's best to escape to this deserted Caribbean island on a weekday—on weekends the hordes descend upon the island's white sandy beaches and lather themselves in coconut oil. ✉ *Johnny Cay* ☉ *Daily*.

Morgan's Cave. Leading to the ocean, Morgan's Cave is yet another spot where the famed privateer was supposed to have buried some treasure—a possibility that present-day islanders have seized upon in order to tap into the vibrant tourism market. Two other museums, the Coconut Museum and the Pirate Museum, are nearby. 🖼 *Usually included in an island tour*.

WHERE TO STAY

$ 🖼 **Hotel Aquarium Super Decamerón.** Large rooms with terra-cotta floors occupy 15 towers overlooking the sea. You can enjoy live music shows at night in the Altamar bar. **Pros:** Close to downtown, views from the rooms are spectacular. **Cons:** You may want to leave the hotel to escape the incessant music played at high volume by the pool. ✉ *Av. Colombia 1–19, Punta Hansa* 🖀 *575/665–4400, 578/512–1317 reservations office in Cartagena* 🖷 *578/512–6938* 🛏 *258 rooms* ⚬ *In-hotel: 3 restaurants, bars, pool* 🖃 *AE, DC, MC, V.*

$ 🖼 **Lord Pierre Hotel.** This beachfront hotel has a wide, private pier for sunbathing. Rooms have big beds and bamboo furniture. **Pros:** Close to downtown. **Cons:** All-inclusive resort at times can feel stifling. ☒ *Av. Colombia No. 1B–106* ☎*578/512-7541* 🖷*098/512-5666* 🛏*58 rooms, 2 suites* ♿*In-hotel: 2 restaurants, bar, pool, beachfront* ⊟*AE, DC, MC, V.*

$ 🍴**Tiuna.** Right on the beach, this hotel has clean, comfortable rooms with great views of the ocean. Rates include two meals, making this hotel a good option for the budget traveler. **Pros:** Rooms facing the ocean are something special. **Cons:** Some rooms can be dingy, view is less than inspiring if you face away from the ocean. ☒*Av. Colombia No. 4–31* ☎*578/512-3235* 🖷*578/512-3478* ⊕*www.tiuna.com* 🛏*160 rooms* ♿*In-hotel: restaurant, bar, pool, beachfront* ⊟*AE, DC, MC, V.*

OUTDOOR ACTIVITIES

Whether you are a diving enthusiast drawn by the azure waters or a beach bum just keen to hit a Caribbean island for a few days, there is certainly going to be something for you. Drag yourself away from the perfume boutiques and rent a moped to tour the island, dropping by some of the sights, or rent a Windsurfer, go snorkeling at La Piscinita, or escape to Johnny Cay.

Blue Fish Tours (☒*Av. Costa Rica C.C. San Andrés L-106* ☎*578/512-0751*) offers diving trips, day tours to Johnny Cay, and island tours. It is one of the oldest tour companies on San Andrés.

Diving is one of the island's biggest attractions. You can join a diving trip or rent snorkeling gear from **Aquamarina** (☒*Av. Colombia* ☎*578/512-6649*).

PROVIDENCIA

90 km (56 mi) northwest of San Andrés.

Tiny Providencia, a mere 7 km (5 mi) long, has rugged hills formed from volcanic rock. There's much less development than on San Andrés, which makes it a quiet, easygoing Caribbean retreat. On the west coast is Aguadulce, the island's largest town, where you can rent bicycles and motor scooters or join a boat tour of the surrounding islets. Smaller Santa Isabel, on the island's northern tip, is the governmental center and therefore attracts fewer visitors.

GETTING HERE & AROUND

The only feasible way to reach Providencia is by flying the 15 minutes from San Andrés on one of Satena's two daily flights. Once you are here, you can rent mopeds or choose to hail passing collectivo trucks that swing round the island more or less every 20 minutes.

SAFETY & PRECAUTIONS

There is no crime in Providencia—at worst there may be the odd bag-snatching but then, where would the criminal go?

ESSENTIALS

Post Office **Providencia** (☒*Sucursal Santa Isabel* ☎*578/514-8871*).

Visitor Info **Body Contact** (⊠ *Fresh Water Bay* ☎ *578/514–8283*).

WHERE TO STAY

¢–$ 🏨 **Cabanas Agua Dulce.** These wooden cabins on Aguadulce's beach have clean and simple rooms with ocean views. Adjoining the complex is a no-frills but dependable restaurant and a bar. **Pros:** You are within walking distance of the beach and the limited stores in Aguadulce. **Cons:** If you want technology and Internet access, Providencia is not the place. ⊠ *Aguadulce* ☎ *578/514–8160* 🛏 *35 rooms* ⚓ *In-hotel: restaurant, no elevator* 🖃 *No credit cards.*

TAKE A HIKE

Choose a clear day to hike up the 1,000-foot summit of **El Pico,** which has superb views of the island's necklace of coral cays; it's a 90-minute trek each way from Casa Baja, the village at the bottom.

Ecuador

WORD OF MOUTH

"An amazing trip! I absolutely thought the country and people were so nice and friendly and the Galapagos . . . well what more can I say? An absolutely magical place. We all had such an amazing time on our boat, the *Samba*, and our guide was absolutely wonderful and knowledgeable."

—quimbymoy

"Make sure that the boat you choose [for Galapagos cruising] has a III-level guide. I did not know this until our travel agent pointed out how important it was for us to choose a cruise with the right itinerary and a III-level bilingual guide . . . guess not all boats have the right combination."

—BernieBarb

Updated by
Jeffrey Van
Fleet

IF YOU THINK ECUADOR IS JUST A JUMPING-OFF POINT for the Galápagos Islands, you're missing a great deal. From its Inca treasures and vibrant cities to the variety of its terrain—coastal, rain forest, and mountains—and its many species of birds and wildlife, this Nevada-size nation has much to get excited about.

The equator runs right through Ecuador, which means the night sky brings out the stars in both hemispheres. The mainland has three distinct regions: the Pacific coast, the Andes, which run north to south through the center of the country, and the Amazon basin, in the east.

You'll likely begin or end your journey in the highlands with a visit to Quito, a pleasant mixture of modern and colonial, with stylish galleries and trendy cafés in the New City standing beside the historic Old City's striking colonial architecture. To the west towers the Volcán Pichincha (active since 1998 after 339 years of being dormant), and beyond that swell the Pacific lowlands.

The Pan-American Highway south of Quito is called the "Avenue of the Volcanoes," because it winds past the country's tallest volcanoes on its way to the lovely city of Cuenca. Besides its well-preserved colonial architecture, cobblestone streets, and tradition of artisanal crafts, Cuenca also benefits from its location—south of the country's most important Inca treasure, Ingapirca. West of Cuenca sits Guayaquil, Ecuador's major commercial center, with a progressive city government whose urban-renewal projects have turned the once dilapidated, dangerous city into the country's trendiest locale, alive with museums, restaurants, shops, and promendades that attract street musicians and live concerts.

On the opposite side of the country, Ecuador's piece of the Amazon, El Oriente, spans one-third of the country's landmass but has only about 4% of its population. There are endless waterways to explore, wildlife to discover, and little-known indigenous cultures to encounter deep within this section of the country.

Ecuador's traditional must-see attraction remains, of course, the Galápagos, separated from the mainland by 960 km (600 mi) of ocean. Giant turtles, spiny marine iguanas, lava lizards, sea lions, and countless other species inhabit this barren, volcanic archipelago. Tour the islands by boat and swim with sea lions and snorkel in waters rich with marine life, and you may understand why locals accept their isolation—an increasing standard of modernization these days does help—in exchange for life in what's known as Darwin's "living laboratory of evolution."

After a decade of a revolving door of seven presidents, Ecuador seems to have found political stability under the government of leftist president Rafael Correa. Constitutional reform, petroleum drilling in the Amazon, and chilly relations with neighboring Colombia and the United States remain contentious issues here. (U.S. visitors need not be concerned. Government-to-government dealings may be problematic, but you'll be welcomed warmly.)

Tourism in Ecuador took off in the 1980s, when travelers began look-ing for an alternative to neighboring Peru during its troubled years. They haven't stopped coming here, but Ecuador never seems overrun, and still feels somewhat isolated from the rest of the world. Across the country's majestic, varied landscapes you'll find indigenous peoples who have lived off the earth for generations with comparatively little contact with the West. If you venture into the rural parts of Ecuador, in particular, you'll be pleasantly surprised at how generous a reception you'll receive. And urban dwellers, usually the most jaded segment of any country's population, will welcome you with open arms. Ecuador, after all, is that kind of place.

ORIENTATION & PLANNING

GETTING ORIENTED

Picture mainland Ecuador as a triangle on its side with three vertical stripes. The highland Andes—anchored by the capital, Quito—form the triangle's spine. To the east looms El Oriente, the country's con-tribution to the Amazon basin. To the west of the mountains lies the lowland coast. Far west, out in the Pacific Ocean, scatter the Galápagos Islands, the pearls of the nation's tourism, so popular among visitors that many barely realize Ecuador *has* a mainland. Don't make that oversight if you can help it.

Quito. Ecuador's fun, lively capital sits in the north central part of the country and is one of the continent's great repositories of colonial architecture. The city mixes new in with the old and offers a terrific selection of hotels, restaurants, shopping, and entertainment.

The Northern Highlands. The region north of Quito, typified by the charming town of Otavalo, forms the Ecuador of postcards. The typi-cal visitor takes in this region's artisan markets, lakes, and indigenous culture as a day trip from the capital, but it's just as easy to base your-self out here instead.

The Central Highlands. The highlands south of Quito are Ecuador at its most majestic, a grand promenade through a high-altitude valley passing between rows of volcanoes, many still active. They form the perfect backdrop for the region's burgeoning outdoor-adventure tour-ism market.

Cuenca & the Southern Highlands. Think of the lovely, well-preserved colonial city of Cuenca as a smaller, more manageable version of Quito. It forms the hub for Ecuador's southern highlands, a region containing the country's best-known indigenous ruins.

El Oriente. Ecuador's share of the Amazon watershed forms one-third of the country's territory. Plan on shelling out a few extra bucks to get here, and expect rustic accommodation, although you'll be surprised at the level of comfort you can find out here in the wilderness.

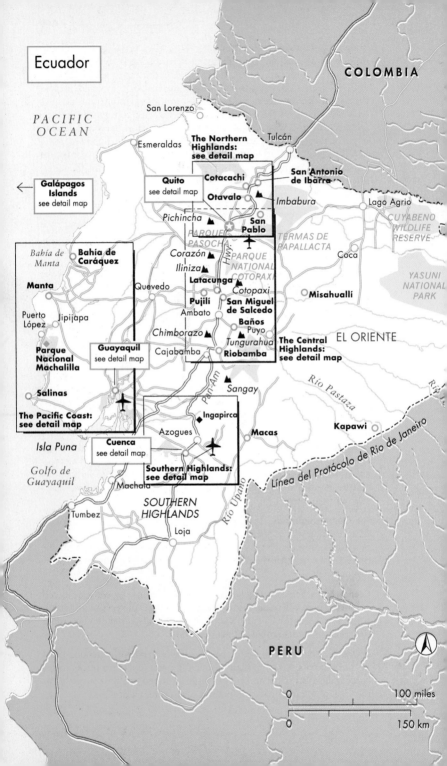

TOP REASONS TO GO

Commune with turtles. Charles Darwin formulated his theory of evolution here in the Galápagos Islands, and a trip here causes you to ponder the mysteries of nature, too. It's expensive to get here, but the islands are one of the world's top wildlife-viewing experiences.

Something old, something new. Quito and Cuenca contain prime examples of preserved colonial quarters that vibrate with modern activity day and night. Both are refreshing examples of urban renewal making use of a proud past.

Journey to the center of the earth. The equator slices across northern Ecuador just north of Quito, making it a tourist-friendly cinch to straddle northern and southern hemispheres at once. Jump from summer to winter or autumn to spring in a single bound.

Shop till you drop. Otavalo, Ecuador's famous market town, hums with shoppers seeking bargains in carvings and woolens, a daily spectacle set against the Northern Highlands' stunning mountain-lake scenery.

Scale a volcano. All manner of tour operators will take you on a hike to the lower slopes of the nearly perfectly coned Cotopaxi volcano, one of Ecuador's iconic symbols, and have you back down in time to catch your breath to brag about it over dinner.

Guayaquil & the Pacific Coast. The Andes seem a world behind when you descend on Ecuador's sultry coast. Guayaquil, the country's largest city and economic powerhouse, will be your gateway to a region known to Ecuadorans for its beaches—Rio it is not, but partake if you have time—and national parks.

The Galápagos Islands. For the typical visitor, Ecuador *is* the Galápagos (and vice-versa), some 70 islands 960 km (600 mi) off the coast. You'll likely take in just a handful during your visit, but that's opportunity enough to observe the amazing selection of wildlife found nowhere else.

ECUADOR PLANNER

WHEN TO GO

Other than in the Galápagos, Ecuador's tourism industry does not observe high and low seasons per se. Hotel rooms become scarce and prices jump noticeably during Christmas and Easter weeks, or when a local community observes an annual celebration. Otherwise, rates remain constant throughout the year.

CLIMATE

Ecuador's climate is remarkably varied, influenced by ocean currents, trade winds, and seasonal changes. The rainy season lasts from December to May and occasionally causes landslides and power outages. Weather in Quito is fairly constant, with warm sunny days giving way to very cool evenings. Guayaquil is muggy during the rainy season, but the rest of the year it is much cooler and drier than you might expect for an area so close to the equator. In the Galápagos Islands the weather is generally hot and humid January to April, with frequent afternoon showers. Cooler temperatures prevail the rest of the year, causing *garua,* the fine mist that envelops the islands. The seas are roughest in September and October, but cruise ships ply the waters year-round.

The following are the average daily maximum and minimum temperatures for Quito.

Jan.	69F	20C	May	69F	20C	Sept.	72F	22C
	46	8		47	8		45	7
Feb.	69F	20C	June	70F	21C	Oct.	70F	21C
	47	8		46	8		46	8
Mar.	69F	20C	July	71F	22C	Nov.	70F	21C
	47	8		44	7		46	8
Apr.	69F	20C	Aug.	71F	22C	Dec.	70F	21C
	47	8		44	7		46	8

HOLIDAYS
Ecuador observes many legal holidays. Expect little to be open and many people to be traveling to visit family and friends.

New Year's Day; Holy Thursday through Easter (Mar. or Apr.); Labor Day (May 1); Battle of Pichincha (May 24); Simón Bolívar's birthday (July 24); Independence Day (Aug. 10); Guayaquil Independence Day (Oct. 9; Guayaquil only); Columbus Day (Oct. 12); All Souls' Day (Nov. 2); Independence of Cuenca (Nov. 3; Cuenca only); Founding of Quito (Dec. 6; Quito only); Feast of the Immaculate Conception (Dec. 8); Christmas.

FESTIVALS & SEASONAL EVENTS
Ecuador's soul lies in its small-town celebrations, usually religious in origin. The countrywide pre-Lenten Carnaval is most exuberant in Cotopaxi Province—local dances and fairs are held in Saquisilí, Pujilí, Latacunga, and Salcedo. Corpus Christi is observed in many mountain towns with fireworks displays. The Fiesta de San Juan enlivens highland towns, especially around Otavalo, on June 24. Otavalo also comes to life during La Fiesta de Yamor, a harvest festival held the first two weeks in September. In Latacunga, September 24 is the Fiesta de la Mamá Negra, which honors Our Lady of Mercy with lively processions featuring costumed dancers. More historic than religious, the Fiestas de Quito, during the first week of December, bring art exhibitions and outdoor concerts. Guayaquil holds similar festivities in early October, Cuenca in early November.

GETTING HERE & AROUND
The Pan-American Highway runs north–south through the heart of the Ecuadoran highlands in the middle of the country, passing near most of the country's important towns and cities—but bypassing Guayaquil by 100 km (60 mi)—and through some of its most spectacular scenery.

To the east is jungle—the Amazon, with little road penetration—and to the west is the Pacific coast. Most attractions are easy to reach by land, although inexpensive flights connecting Quito, Cuenca, and Guayaquil make air travel a convenient option. Flying is essential for visiting the Galápagos Islands and most of El Oriente.

BY AIR

Ecuador's rugged terrain makes domestic air travel a time-saving option worth considering. (Quito–Guayaquil is a quick 35 minutes.) One-way flights between mainland destinations run about $50. Flights to the Galápagos cost upward of $400 round-trip from the mainland. Tame (pronounced *tah*-may), Ícaro, and AeroGal share the domestic market; all can do E-ticketing via their Web sites.

Quito's Aeropuerto Mariscal Sucre and Guayaquil's Aeropuerto José Joaquín de Olmedo both serve as international gateways to Ecuador. Flights that originate in Houston fly to Quito in six hours; those from Miami fly to either Quito or Guayaquil in 4½ hours. See the Essentials sections of individual cities for specific flight information.

AIRLINES IN ECUADOR **AeroGal** (☎ 800/237–642 toll-free in Ecuador, 888/723–7642 in North America ⊕ www.aerogal.com.ec).**Ícaro** (☎ 800/883–567 toll-free in Ecuador ⊕ www.icaro. aero).**Tame** (☎ 800/555–999 toll-free in Ecuador, 800/666–9687 in North America ⊕ www.tame.com.ec).

BY BUS

Major bus companies in Ecuador offer direct service operating between Quito, Cuenca, and Guayaquil. Buses run frequently throughout the country and are extremely cheap: the two-hour ride from Quito to Otavalo costs $2; the 10-hour ride from Guayaquil to Quito is about $8. Theft on buses is a problem—the Quito–Baños route is notorious in this regard—so keep a close eye on your valuables. The luggage compartment below the bus, the overhead rack above you, and even the space under your seat aren't necessarily secure from pilfering. ⚠ **Savvy travelers buy a second ticket and place their luggage in the seat next to them.** Though they cost a bit more, private bus companies such as Panamericana and Reytur are an option you should consider. Their coaches are equipped with niceties such as air-conditioning and restrooms.

BUS INFORMATION **Panamericana** (✉ Av. Colón at Reina Victoria, Quito ☎ 02/257–0900). **Reytur** (✉ Rodrigo de Triana 26–63, Quito ☎ 02/254–6674).

BY CAR

Traffic is congested in cities, and in Quito parking spaces are nearly impossible to find (Guayaquil has numerous parking garages). Outside the major urban areas you'll find that only the major highways are paved. All roads can be treacherous in bad weather. In most parts of the country a four-wheel-drive vehicle is a necessity. On the narrow mountain roads bus drivers are notorious for making dangerous maneuvers, such as passing on curves. If you decide to drive, bring or rent a cell phone for emergencies.

CAR RENTAL   Ecuador recognizes the validity of your home country driver's license for short-term tourist stays. Given the ease here of flying and of renting a taxi by the hour for shorter trips—to say nothing of urban traffic congestion and parking—consider carefully whether you really need to rent a car in Ecuador. (We researched this entire chapter without renting a car.) A vehicle rental can be quite expensive, with rates running higher than $300 for a compact car, and close to $375 for a four-wheel-drive vehicle. Inquire about deductibles for damage and theft, which can be quite high, before agreeing on a price. Examine the car carefully, and make sure it has a jack and spare tire. Outside Quito, Guayaquil, and Cuenca, rental offices are virtually nonexistent.

EMERGENCY ASSISTANCE   No emergency roadside service exists, although passing motorists will frequently stop to help with disabled vehicles. Ask your rental agency for emergency numbers and a list of garages in the area you're traveling in.

GASOLINE   Ecuador's status as a petroleum-producing nation has buffered it from higher gasoline prices seen elsewhere on the continent. Gas is sold by the *galón*: regular leaded, called *extra,* costs about $1.40; unleaded, called *súper,* is roughly $2 per gallon.

PARKING   Park your car at your hotel rather than leaving it on the street, where it is susceptible to theft. Larger hotels are more likely to have fenced parking lots, although surprisingly few lodgings in Quito offer parking at all.

BY TAXI

Taxis are a safe, convenient, and economical way to travel in Ecuador, even when you want to travel long distances. It's easy to negotiate a rate with a driver beforehand for a half- or full-day trip to your destination. A three-hour taxi ride, for example, should only cost about $50, but if you're going only one way, the driver will expect you to pay his return fare, too.

ESSENTIALS

ELECTRICITY

In Ecuador the electric current is 110 volts; North American–style two-pronged plugs are used. Areas outside major cities are subject to frequent power surges.

ENTRY REQUIREMENTS

Only a passport valid for at least six months beyond your departure date from Ecuador is required for U.S., Canadian, U.K., Australian, and New Zealand citizens for stays totaling up to 90 days in a calendar year. Neither Australia nor New Zealand has representation in Ecuador. The Canadian embassy handles consular emergencies for citizens of those countries, but passport matters must be referred to respective embassies in Santiago, Chile.

HEALTH & SAFETY

Food-borne illnesses likely won't be serious problems in Ecuador if you take some precautions and let common sense prevail. Avoid tap water to reduce the risk of contracting intestinal parasites. Drink only bottled water, which is available *con gas* and *sin gas* (with and without carbonation, respectively). Ask for drinks *sin hielo* (without ice). Avoid uncooked or unpeeled vegetables and fruits that may have been washed in tap water. Brush your teeth with bottled water in remote areas or budget hotels. At other hotels, ask if the water is purified; it often is. Eat at street stands at your own risk.

Discuss malaria medications with your doctor if you're traveling to the rain forest or other isolated areas. In the Galápagos the most serious threat you'll face is sunburn—do not underestimate the intensity of the equatorial sun. If you're prone to seasickness and you're planning a cruise around the archipelago, make sure to bring medications. At high altitudes the sun is strong, and altitude sickness can strike. Discuss the advisability of travel to the highlands with your doctor if you have a heart condition or high blood pressure or are pregnant.

Petty crime, such as pickpocketing, is a problem in Ecuador. Use the same precautions you would anywhere—avoid flashy jewelry and watches, hold purses and camera bags close to your body, and avoid handling money in public. Use extra caution in all crowded spaces, such as markets, plazas, and bus terminals. In Quito, be especially wary in the streets and plazas of the Old City, and out for the evening in the La Mariscal district. Take taxis after dark, even if you are going only a few blocks.

6

Emergency Contacts **Canada** (✉ *Av. Amazonas 4153, at Paul Rivet, Quito* ☎ *02/245–5499* ⊕ *ecuador.gc.ca*). **United Kingdom** (✉ *Av. Naciones Unidas, at República de El Salvador, 14th fl., La Carolina, Quito* ☎ *02/256297–0800* ⊕ *www. britishembassy.gov.uk/ecuador* ✉ *Consulate: Av. General Córdova 623, at Padre Solano, Guayaquil* ☎ *04/256–0400*). **United States** (✉ *Av. 12 de Octubre and Av. Patria, La Mariscal, Quito* ☎ *02/256–2890* ⊕ *ecuador.usembassy.gov* ✉ *Consulate: Av. Avenida 9 de Octubre and García Moreno, Guayaquil* ☎ *04/232–3570* ⊕ *guayaquil.usconsulate.gov*).

LANGUAGE

English is the lingua franca of tourism, and you will find many people in travel-related fields who speak excellent English. Those in smaller establishments will likely know only Spanish. The unfamiliar-sounding language you hear in the highlands is the indigenous Quichua, a softer, more grammatically complex relative of Peru's Quechua. Speakers say it more closely resembles the original language spoken by Inca nobility.

MONEY MATTERS

CURRENCY & EXCHANGE

The U.S. dollar is Ecuador's official currency, making currency exchange a non-issue for American visitors. But the country also mints its own coins, equivalent to half-dollars, quarters, dimes, nickels, and pennies, which circulate freely with their U.S. counterparts. The $1 coin bearing the portrait of Native American guide Sacagawea, which never caught on in the United States, is used widely here. Most small businesses have trouble making change for anything over $5. ⚠ **Do not bring $50 or $100**

bills to Ecuador. So many counterfeits circulate that no one will accept them as payment for any bill of any amount, including the $100 Galápagos entrance fee. If you find yourself with these denominations, you have no choice but to exchange them for twenties or smaller at a bank, which *is* capable of determining that your bills are real.

Most large establishments in the cities take credit cards, with Visa and MasterCard the most widely accepted. Some businesses add a surcharge of 3%–10% on credit-card purchases, or may offer a discount if you pay in cash. You can use your card to obtain cash from ATMs, but a surprising number of machines take only Cirrus-affiliated cards. Although it sounds counter-intuitive, get cash from an ATM when the bank is open. Security personnel are present, and if you encounter a problem with your card, you can tend to it immediately. Few businesses take traveler's checks as payment. You can cash American Express traveler's checks for dollars at some banks and casas de cambio.

PRICING Many goods and services—from taxi fares to textiles—are inexpensive by Western standards. Although international chain hotels are pricey, you can stay in perfectly nice places for less than $75.

Sample Prices:. Some sample prices are: cup of coffee, 50¢; bottle of beer, $1.50; soft drink, 50¢; bottle of wine, $10; sandwich, $2; 2-km (1-mi) taxi ride, $1; city bus ride, 20¢; movie, $5; cocktail, $5; theater or concert ticket, $10–$20; museum admission, $2.

TAXES Most hotels add a 12% tax and 10% service surcharge to your bill. Some include this amount when they quote prices, but others do not. Be sure to inquire when you book your room. Restaurants levy the same charges on top of the prices listed on the menu.

TIPPING A tip of 5%–10% is appropriate for waiters in upscale restaurants. (The 10% surcharge often added to a bill is supposedly for service, although whether waiters actually receive it is questionable.) Porters and bellhops should receive the equivalent of 50¢ per bag. Guides expect about $10 per day for each person in a tour group, while drivers expect about $2. Taxi drivers don't expect tips.

PHONES

To call Ecuador from another country, dial the country code of 593, then the area code, then the local number. Include the "0" at the beginning of the area code only when calling long distance within the country. Ecuador completed a nationwide transition to a uniform system of seven-digit local telephone numbers in 2003, but signs, business cards, and stationery (and people) outside Quito occasionally still give the former six-digit numbers. Old habits die hard. Ecuadorans say and write their phone numbers in a "four then three" grouping, for example 2222–001, rather than 222–2001.

Directory assistance, available only in Spanish, is available by dialing 104.

Most public phones accept phone cards, which you can purchase in many shops and newsstands. Some stores charge about 25¢ for a brief call on their private line; look for a sign in a window reading TELÉFONO or LLAMADAS. Many Internet cafés have phones for public use.

An easier alternative is placing a call from an office of Andinatel, the country's national telephone company. Its Pacifictel division serves the coast, the Southern Highlands, and the Galápagos. You'll find offices in most cities and towns. Porta, Alegro, and Movistar, Ecuador's three mobile-phone companies, also operate local offices for placing calls in many communities. Most telephone offices are open daily 8 AM–9 PM.

> ### BIRD LOVER'S PARADISE
>
> Ecuador may be hard to resist if you're an animal and bird lover. More than 1,600 bird species, including crested quetzals, toucans, tanagers, macaws, parrots, cocks-of-the-rock, and 35% of the world's variety of hummingbird species have been counted in the country's cloud forests, dry forests, and rain forests (come in October for the best birding). Rare and endangered tapirs, spectacled bears, llamas, and pigmy silk anteaters live in the Andes.

TELEPHONE OFFICES **Andinatel** (✉ *Av. Colón and Av. Amazonas, La Mariscal, Quito* ✉ *Calderón at Sucre, Otavalo).***Pacifictel** (✉ *Benigno Malo at Presidente Córdova, Cuenca* ✉ *Ballén at Chile, Guayaquil* ✉ *Av. Padre Julio at Española, Puerto Ayora, Galápagos).*

Ecuador's three cellular companies—Alegro, Movistar and Porta—have outlets in every major city and town in the country. All sell chips that can be used in an unlocked GSM mobile phone. Some outlets will sell new phones to you that can be used with their pre-paid calling cards. U.S. companies T-Mobile and AT&T have some coverage in Ecuador. Check with your hometown provider. The abundance of public telephones—they're usually coupled with Internet cafés—makes getting along without a cell phone a possibility, however.

RESTAURANTS & HOTELS

CUISINE You'll eat hearty in Ecuador. Seafood is a mainstay on the coast, though even Quito menus routinely feature fresh fish and seafood. Lobster is a staple on the Pacific coast, and along the north coast seafood is prepared *encocados* (in coconut milk). If you're a very adventurous carnivore, you may want to try succulent suckling pig and guinea pig (called *cuyes*), often roasted—teeth, paws, and all—over a charcoal fire. *Seco de chivo* is a fully garnished lamb stew. *Humitas* are sweet-corn tamales eaten by tradition-minded Ecuadorans only in the late afternoon, generally with black coffee. Other Andean favorites include *llapingachos* (mashed cheese and potato pancakes) and *locro de queso* (a milk-based soup that contains corn, potatoes, and a garnish of fresh avocado). An Ecuadoran specialty, seviche is fish or seafood marinated in lime juice and seasoned with onion, tomato, chili peppers, and cilantro and often served with *cangil* (popcorn), as are most soups. *Churrasco* is a steak fillet with a fried egg, usually accompanied by rice and salad. Typical coastal cuisine includes the staple *arroz con menestra,* huge portions of white rice served with either black beans or lentils, and *patacones,* green bananas fried in oil, smashed, and refried. Many dishes are served with *ají,* a hot sauce, on the side. In the chill of the Andes, you might be offered a *canelazo,* which is cane-sugar liquor heated and mixed with cinnamon and sometimes with fruit juice.

Lunch is the main meal of the day, especially in smaller communities, and most restaurants offer a midday special (*plato del día* or *plato ejecutivo*), typically consisting of meat or fish accompanied by rice, fried potatoes, and a small salad. Prices are reasonable, but watch out, because wines and most liquors are imported and can double the tab.

ACCOMMO-
DATIONS

Accommodations range from modern luxury hotels to centuries-old haciendas that have been converted to *hosterías* (country inns). Although the highland hotels (such as those in Cuenca) offer exposure to local history and culture, those in El Oriente and the Galápagos Islands provide close contact with nature. You'll find rates refreshing, with something to fit any budget; no one has been priced out of the market here. Breakfast is not usually included in the rate, except in *posadas,* or small inns, where either an American or a Continental breakfast is often included.

WHAT IT COSTS (IN U.S. DOLLARS)					
	¢	$	$$	$$$	$$$$
RESTAURANTS	under $10	$10–$12	$12–$15	$15–$18	over $18
HOTELS	under $50	$50–$70	$70–$120	$120–$150	over $150

Restaurant prices are based on the median main course price at dinner. Hotel prices are for two people in a standard double room in high season.

VISITOR INFORMATION

Ecuador's Ministry of Tourism operates a network of iTur information offices in Quito, Guayaquil, Cuenca, Ibarra, and Riobamba—we find Quito's and Guayaquil's branches to be of limited use—and has an informative Web site but is ill-equipped to handle specific pretrip inquiries. Once you're on the ground, city-run tourist offices are a better bet for information (Quito's and Guayaquil's are extraordinary).

Gray Line and Metropolitan Touring are two of the country's biggest and best tour operators.

TOURIST
OFFICE

iTur (☎ *800/004–887 toll-free in Ecuador* ⊕ *www.vivecuador.com*).

TOUR
OPERATORS

Gray Line (☎ *800/472–964 toll-free in Ecuador* ⊕ *www.graylineecuador.com*).
Metropolitan Touring (✉ *Av. República de El Salvador 970, Quito* ☎ *02/246–4780, 800/527–2500 in North America* ⊕ *www.metropolitan-touring.com*).

QUITO

420 km (252 mi) and 35 minutes by air northeast of Guayaquil.

Built on the ashes of the northern Inca capital following the 1533 Spanish conquest, Ecuador's capital city brims with colonial riches. Although set in the north-central part of the country, it makes a convenient launching point for travel to anywhere in Ecuador, including the Galápagos Islands and the Amazon.

Scenic Quito is ensconced in a long, narrow valley at the foot of the restless Volcán Pichincha. The elongated city measures 30 km (19 mi) from north to south, but only 4 km (2 mi) from east to west. This sprawling metropolis of 1.2 million people lies only 24 km (15 mi) south of the equator, but because of its altitude it enjoys a mild climate all year. Quiteños are fond of saying that their city gives you four seasons in one day—a statement supported by the springlike mornings, summery afternoons, autumnal evenings, and wintery nights.

Quito's Old City is a maze of colonial mansions, stately churches, candlelighted monasteries, and crowded cobblestone streets. Wandering the Old City's narrow lanes lined with blue-and-white houses is the highlight of any stay here. Nonetheless, after a morning in the crowded city center, an afternoon in the spacious New City—with its cafés, galleries, and shops—is a welcome change of pace.

GETTING HERE & AROUND

BY AIR   American Airlines and LanEcuador have twice-daily flights between Miami and Quito. Continental flies nonstop from Houston. Delta connects Atlanta with Quito once daily. U.K. visitors can connect in Miami or Atlanta, or in Amsterdam with KLM, or in Madrid with Iberia or with discount airline Air Comet. From Australia or New Zealand, connect in Los Angeles to itineraries on American, Continental, or Delta.

Tame, Ícaro, and AeroGal are Ecuador's domestic carriers; all offer flights several times daily to Guayaquil and Cuenca. Tame also flies between Quito and San Cristóbal and Baltra in the Galápagos Islands and to the mainland towns of Coca, Esmeraldas, Lago Agrio, Loja, Macas, Machala, Manta, Portoviejo, and Tulcán. AeroGal also flies between Quito and Manta, and Baltra and San Cristóbal, as well as Bogotá and Medellín, Colombia. Within South America, LanEcuador connects Quito with Lima and Santiago; TACA Peru connects it with Lima; Avianca with Bogotá; and Santa Bárbara Airlines with Caracas.

Quito's small, aging Aeropuerto Internacional Mariscal Sucre (UIO) is 8 km (5 mi) north of the city center. Stop at the Cooperativa de Taxis Aeropuerto booth beyond the customs barrier to arrange taxi transport. Prices are a fixed $6 for a ride to the New City. The new Aeropuerto Internacional de Quito is under construction near Puembo, about an hour east of the capital, at this writing. The $75 million facility is scheduled to open in 2010.

BY BUS   Buses for most mainland destinations leave from Quito's sprawling Terminal Terrestre Cumandá, south of the Old City. Quito's buses are inexpensive (15¢) and run frequently during the day. Heavy crowds during the morning and afternoon rushes, however, make them less appealing options. Clearly marked EJECUTIVO buses cost 20¢ and guarantee you a seat, making them a more comfortable option. Much faster is the Trole (pronounced *tro*-lay), an electric trolley-bus system running through the center of town along Avenida 10 de Agosto in the

New City and Calle Guayaquil in the Old City. A similar nonelectric system, the Ecovía, generally plies Avenida 6 de Diciembre between the New and Old cities. Fares for both are 25¢.

At this writing, a 30-km (18-mi) light-rail line called the TRAQ (Tren Rápido de Quito) is on the drawing board to replace the saturated Trole system. The 80-kph (48 mph) train will provide the fastest, easiest connection between Old and New Cities and beyond in each direction. Completion is scheduled for 2010.

BY CAR The Pan-American Highway runs right through Quito, which makes driving to most places in the country fairly easy. Short trips are possible to some of the nearby tourist areas but should be carefully planned because road conditions are not always good once you leave the main highway. Do not drive into the Amazon or anywhere near the Colombian border. A better idea is to rent a car and driver. Three of the major international rental agencies—Avis, Budget, and Hertz—have offices in downtown Quito and at Aeropuerto Mariscal Sucre. You can also rent a car from Localiza, an Ecuadoran company, at the airport.

BY TAXI Taxis are inexpensive and an ideal way to get around. A ride between the New and Old cities runs about $2. Most drivers use their meters, which begin tallying the fare at 35¢. Agree on a price beforehand if the driver says the meter isn't working. The fare to most destinations in the city should be $5 or less. Expect a $2 surcharge after dark. Tele Taxi and City-Taxi are reliable companies that will send a driver to pick you up. They will also arrange city tours for $10 per hour.

SAFETY & PRECAUTIONS

Take all the precautions you would traveling in a large city in a developing country and your visit here can be hassle-free. Security in the Old City has improved dramatically with a beefed-up police presence, but streets are dark at night and you should take a taxi after sundown. Nighttime muggings have occurred in the New City's La Mariscal district. Exercise caution and take taxis, even if going just a couple of blocks. A growing number of casual eateries offer wireless Internet service to their customers, but we caution against whipping out a laptop computer in such a public, high-trafficked venue.

ESSENTIALS

Airline Contacts AeroGal (☎02/225–7202). **American** (☎02/226–0900). **Avianca** (☎02/255–6715). **Continental** (☎02/255–7170). **Iberia** (☎02/255–8033). **Ícaro** (☎02/245–0928). **KLM** (☎02/255–7170). **LanEcuador** (☎02/299–2300). **Santa Bárbara Airlines** (☎02/225–4194). **TACA Peru** (☎800/008–222 toll-free in Ecuador). **Tame** (☎02/231–1921).

Airport Contacts Aeropuerto Mariscal Sucre (☎02/294–4900).

Bus Terminal Terminal Terrestre Cu-mandá (✉ *Av. Maldonado 3077, Centro* ☎ *02/257–0529*).

Car-Rental Agencies Avis (☎ *02/255–5890*). **Budget** (☎ *02/330–0979*). **Hertz** (☎ *02/225–4257*). **Localiza** (☎ *800/562–254* ⊕ *www.localiza.com.ec*).

FINDING A COMPUTER

Internet cafés are everywhere in the New City, especially in the La Mariscal neighborhood. You'll find a few in the Old City too.

Currency Exchange Banco Pichincha (✉ *Av. Amazonas 1354, at Av. Colón La Mariscal* ☎ *02/255–5449*). **Vaz Corp** (✉ *Av. Amazonas N21–169, at Roca, La Mariscal* ☎ *02/252–9169*).

Emergency Numbers General emergencies (☎ *911*). **Ambulance** (☎ *131*). **Fire** (☎ *102*). **Police** (☎ *101*).

Medical Assistance Hospital Metropolitano (✉ *Av. Mariana de Jesús at Av. Occidental,* ☎ *02/226–9030* ⊕ *www.hospitalmetropolitano.org*).

Taxi Companies City-Taxi (☎ *02/263–3333*). **Cooperativa de Taxis Aeopuerto** (☎ *02/330–2200*). **Tele Taxi** (☎ *02/241–1119*).

Visitor Info iTur (✉ *Av. Eloy Alfaro 1214, at Carlos Tobar* ☎ *02/222–4971*). **Quito Turismo** (✉ *Venezuela at Espejo* ☎ *02/257–0786* ✉ *Sucre at Benalcázar* ☎ *No phone* ✉ *Calle de la Ronda* ☎ *No phone* ✉ *Reina Victoria at Cordero* ☎ *02/255–1566* ✉ *Av. Patria at 6 de Diciembre* ☎ *02/228-2646* ✉ *Aeropuerto Mariscal Sucre* ☎ *02/330-0163* ⊕ *www.quito.com.ec*). **South American Explorers** (✉ *Jorge Washington 311, at Leonidas Plaza* ☎ *02/222-5228* ⊕ *www.saexplorers.org*).

EXPLORING QUITO

A word on terminology: Quiteños don't use the Old City/New City designations coined by the English-speaking tourism industry. The colonial heart of the city is the Centro or Centro Histórico. To the north lies an amorphous sprawl of modern neighborhoods, most notably comfortable Bellavista and La Floresta, and the bustling La Mariscal, whose large concentration of tourists has led locals to dub it "*Gringolandia.*"

Another word on maps: Quito's north-south elongation makes it a difficult fit for maps, most of which rotate the orientation 90-degrees clockwise. (We do this, too.) Notice that north usually lies to the right of the page on city maps.

Quito has two parallel systems of address numbering: The official scheme employs small green-and-white signs affixed to every building using directions denoted *N, S, E,* and *Oe* (for *oeste,* or west) and followed by a number to denote distance from the city center. Locations in the outer reaches of the city always express their addresses this way; in the center city, people stubbornly stick with the old sequential numbering system.

To help you navigate all this, the phenomenal Quito Turismo, a joint venture between the city government and its police, operates several tourist offices or stands in the city, and offers guided walking tours of the Old City. The Ministry of Tourism's iTur office sits in an out-of-the-way location and has little but a few maps and brochures. A private membership organization of note is South American Explorers, with an amazing selection of information about Ecuador (as well as branch clubhouses in Lima and Cusco, Peru, and Buenos Aires, Argentina).

THE OLD CITY

The oldest part of Quito was founded in 1534 by Spanish explorer Sebastián de Benalcázar on the site of the ancient town of Shyris. The original colonial town was delineated by its four most important monasteries: San Francisco, La Merced, San Agustín, and Santo Domingo. Today informal markets and street vendors still crowd the cobbled routes that run between those ancient monuments, while the interiors of the churches and monasteries are quiet, timeless refuges.

TIMING & PRECAUTIONS

Remember that most museums close on Monday. Most churches keep limited opening hours; you'll have a better chance of seeing the interiors during the morning or late afternoon. Security has improved dramatically in the Old City, but unless you're lodging here, make sure to take a taxi back to your New City hotel. Crime is still a factor on dark center-city streets.

MAIN ATTRACTIONS

❽ Catedral. The city's cathedral is a repository of art from the Quiteña school, which combined themes of Spanish and indigenous cultures: Jesus preaching in the Andes or the Wise Men mounted on llamas in the Nativity scene. The exceptional sculpting abilities of Manuel Chili Caspicara can be appreciated in the 18th-century tableau *The Holy Shroud,* which hangs behind the choir, and in the intricate designs of the rococo Chapel of St. Anne, in the right aisle. The building also houses the volcanic rock-hewn tomb of Quito's liberator, Antonio José de Sucre. A guided tour in Spanish or English is included in your admission price. Enter around the corner on Venezuela. ⊠ *Plaza de la Independencia, visitors entrance at Venezuela N3–117 at Espejo Centro* ☎ *02/257–0371* ☜ *$1.50* ⊙ *Mon.–Sat 9:30–4, Sun. 10–2.*

❻ Iglesia de la Compañía. The "company" referred to here is the Society of Jesus, the powerful Jesuit order that profoundly influenced religious life in colonial South America. In many cities, Quito included, the local Jesuit church outshone the local cathedral. La Compañía is the most impressive of the capital's 86 churches, with 10 side altars and a high altar plated with gold. An ambitious 25-year restoration project was completed in 2006, and if you see nothing else in Quito, don't miss this. The high central nave and the delicacy of its Arab-inspired plasterwork give the church a sumptuous, almost sinfully rich appearance. Indeed, almost half a ton of gold was poured into the ceilings, walls, pulpits, and altars during its 160 years of construction (1605–1765). At the center of the main altar is a statue of the Quiteña saint Mariana de Jesús; her remains are entombed at the foot of the altar. Guided tours in Spanish or English are included in your admission price. ⊠ *García Moreno at Sucre, Centro* ☎ *02/258–4175* ⊕ *www.ficj.org.ec* ☜ *$2,*

FodorsChoice
★

free 1st Sun. of month ⊙ *Weekdays 9:30–5:30, Sat. 9:30–4:30, Sun. 1:30–4:30.*

❺ Iglesia de San Francisco. Established by Franciscan monks in 1536 and
★ said to be the first church built in the Americas, the Church of San Francisco was named for the patron saint of the city. The twin towers, destroyed by an eruption of Volcán Pichincha in 1582, were rebuilt at half their original size in 1893, contributing to the facade's uninspiring appearance. Inside, however, you will find the first New World example of an interior entirely covered with gilded and painted wood. Stationed at the main altar is Bernardo de Legarda's famed 18th-century sculpture *Virgin of the Apocalypse of the Immaculate Conception.* The monastery, at the north end of the complex, now houses a museum of colonial religious art. You can arrange for an English-speaking guide with 24 hours' notice. ⊠*Plaza San Francisco, Centro* ☎*02/228–1124* 🖃*$2* ⊙ *Weekdays 9–1 and 2–6, Sat. 9–6, Sun. 9–noon.*

❾ Plaza de la Independencia. Locals always refer to the city's main square, shaded by palms and pines, as the Plaza Grande. The white, neoclassical **Palacio de Gobierno** (Government Palace), built in the 19th century, occupies the west side of the plaza and is not open to the public. The portico gracing the plaza's northern end, once the archbishop's palace, now holds a variety of stores and businesses, including several souvenir and sweets shops. The main branch of Quito Turismo, the city's topnotch tourist office, flanks the east side of the plaza.

IF YOU HAVE TIME

❷ Calle de la Ronda. Quito's newest urban-renewal venture is a work in nascent progress at this writing. The city has taken one of its most historic streets, swept away the prostitutes and drug dealers, beefed up security, and given grants to owners to refurbish their properties. Galleries, shops, and cafés have begun to open, with more on the way. Flowers deck out the wrought-iron balconies and flags flutter over the winding, two-block cobblestone street. ⊠*Morales, 4 blocks south of Plaza de la Independencia.*

❸ Casa de Sucre. The restored Sucre House, once the residence of Field Marshal Antonio José de Sucre, displays 19th-century furniture and clothing as well as photographs, historical documents, and letters. The house makes an interesting visit if you're a military-history buff, but could probably otherwise be skipped. ⊠ *Venezuela 573, at Sucre, Centro* ☎*02/251–2860* 🖃*$1* ⊙ *Weekdays 9–4:30, Fri. 8:30–1, weekends 10–5.*

⓫ Iglesia de la Merced. The Church of Mercy's beautiful, light-filled interior contains a brilliant statue of the Virgin of Mercy above the main altar. It was sculpted to honor Mary, who supposedly intervened to save Quito from a series of 18th-century earthquakes and volcanic eruptions. The church's 153-foot tower houses the city's largest bell. The adjoining convent, shown by appointment only, features a rich collection of colonial paintings and sculptures. ⊠*Chile at Cuenca, Centro* ☎*02/228–0743* 🖃*Free* ⊙ *Weekdays 8–noon and 2–4.*

6

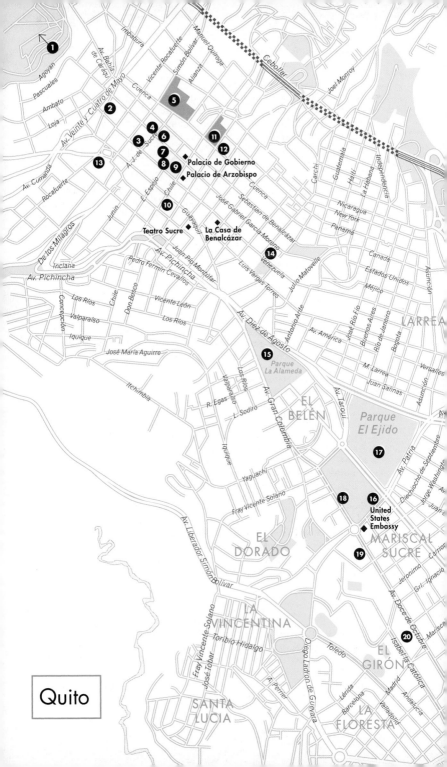

Quito

6

Av. Mariscal Antonio Jos de Sucre

Enrique Rither

Lizarazu

Domigo Espinar

Fernández de Recalde

Pablo Palacio

Jeronimo de Beyton

istorgio Salgado

Bolivia

Universitaria

Moncayo

Munive

Ponce de León

Núñez de Bonilla

Av. La Gasca

Humberto Albornoz

Barros de San Milán

Alejandro de Valdéz

G. de Carvajal

J. Valentín

Fray Gaspar
de Carvajal

Conde Ruiz de Castilla

P. Guerrero

Av. América

SANTA CLARA
DE SAN MILLÁN

Antonio de

Versalles

Av. Diez de Agosto

Aurelio Mosquera

Gral. Vicente Aguirre

Ulloa

Selva Alegre

Bartolome de las Casas

- Robles

Sente R. Roca

Grl. Ulpiano Paez

Toribio

Cristóbal de Acuña

Montes

- Amazonas

tera

Nueve de Octubre

SIMON
BOLÍVAR

Santa María

Av. Grl. E. Alfaro

Inglaterra

Alemania

Italia

Vancrair

Polonia

Hungría

ntimilla

Reina

Av. Río

Amazonas

Foch

Victoria

García

Juan L. Mera

La Rabida

LA
PRADERA

Seis de Diciembre

Luis Cordero

Av. Cristóbal Colón

Reina Victoria

LA
COLÓN

Av. Francisco de Orellana

La Pradera

San Salvador

Diego de Almagro

M. Aguilera

Av. De La República

Alpallana

ardo - Tamayo

21

❼ Iglesia Parroquial del Sagrario. The Church of the Shrine is noted for its beautiful facade in carefully sculpted stone, large gilded altar, and colorful interior, which includes an 18th-century mural of eight arch-angels covering the cupola. The site is undergoing a massive renovation at this writing, but do stop in even if the scaffolding is still up during your visit. ✉ *García Moreno and Espejo, Centro* ▦ *Free* ☽ *Mon.–Sat. 8–11 and 1–6.*

❿ Iglesia de San Agustín. In 1809 Ecuador's declaration of independence was signed in the Church of St. Augustine, and many of the soldiers who fought the Spanish crown are buried here. The gilded crucifix on the main altar offers an impressive example of a style of art called the Quiteña school. The altar displays paintings by Miguel de Santiago about the life of St. Augustine, while more depictions of the saint crowd the side aisles. ✉ *Chile at Guayaquil, Centro* ☎ *02/295–5525* ▦ *$1* ☽ *Weekdays 9–1:30 and 2:30–5, Sat. 9–1.*

⓭ Iglesia de Santo Domingo. The interior of the colonial Church of Santo Domingo may not be as impressive as the Old City's other temples, but it does feature an eye-catching clock and some interesting statues, including the Virgen del Rosario. The adjacent Dominican monastery also holds a small museum of religious art. South of the Plaza Santo Domingo, narrow cobblestone streets lead down to Calle Ronda, one of Quito's first streets. ✉ *Flores at Rocafuerte, Centro* ▦ *Free* ☽ *Weekdays 3–5.*

⓬ Museo de Arte Colonial. The Museum of Colonial Art, housed in a restored 17th-century colonial mansion, includes colonial furniture and 16th- to 18th-century sculpture and paintings by Miguel de Santiago and various other members of the School of Quito. The amusing *Vices and Virtues of the European Countries* is a series of 12 allegorical 18th-century paintings by colonial masters Samaniego and Rodríguez. ✉ *Cuenca 415, at Mejía, Centro* ☎ *02/228–2297* ▦ *$1.50* ☽ *Tues.–Fri. 10–6, Sat. 10–2.*

❹ Museo Casa de María Augusta Urrutia. In the colonial section of Quito is the Museum of Maria Augusta Urrutia, which a grieving widow kept exactly as it had been when her husband was alive. Don't miss the collection of fine French porcelain, beautiful silver dinnerware, and Ecuadoran art from colonial times to the present. Especially interesting are the works of Ecuadoran painter Victor Mideros. ✉ *García Moreno N2–60, at Av. Mariscal Antonio José de Sucre, Centro* ☎ *02/258–0107* ▦ *$2* ☽ *Tues.–Sun. 10–6.*

❶ El Panecillo. The opening of the New City's Teleferiqo has eclipsed this rounded hill (the bread roll) and its stunning views as Quito's most popular lookout point, but the presentation here is more serene and less carnival-like. At the top stands the monumental cast-aluminum statue of the city's protectress, the Virgin of Quito—a copy of Bernardo de Legarda's famous 18th-century sculpture *Virgin of the Apocalypse of the Immaculate Conception,* on display in the Iglesia de San Francisco. Muggers target tourists climbing the long flight of stairs, so hire a taxi to take you to the top—it's safe once you get up there—and wait for

ECUADOR'S NATIONAL HERO

Antonio José de Sucre (1795–1830) accomplished much during his short life. He enlisted in the independence struggle against Spain at age 16, and in a few short years would prove himself to be one of the 19th century's most brilliant military minds. Sucre caught the eye of South American liberator Simón Bolívar and quickly rose through the ranks, becoming one of the leader's generals and confidants by age 24.

After independence, Sucre served as president of Bolivia and Peru, as well as of Colombia's congress. The general, who shone on the battlefield, intensely disliked the rough-and-tumble of post-liberation politics, and resigned his post in Colombia to return to his beloved Quito. Underlings, jealous of Sucre's influence with Bolívar, assassinated Sucre on his journey home. He was interred in Quito's cathedral. The capital's Mariscal Sucre ("Marshal Sucre") airport is named for him. Before 2000, Ecuador's pre-dollarization currency was called the *sucre*. And the name of the Mariscal district, Quito's consummate tourist hangout, also refers to the marshal.

you as you enjoy the view and then to carry you safely back down (about $8 round-trip).

NEED A BREAK? Outdoor cafés are a scarce commodity in the Old City. But Tianguez, a small restaurant/artisan shop makes a pleasant place to while away an afternoon with a gourmet coffee drink—made with fair-trade product—while you write a few cards to the folks back home and watch the passing parade on Plaza San Francisco. A tiny indoor dining area with wooden tables serves effectively on those days when it's too chilly for the green tables and umbrellas on the outdoor patio. Tianguez takes its name from the Quichua word for market (the plaza was a vast outdoor market during Inca times). Tianguez is open daily during the day and Wednesday–Sunday evenings until 11:30 PM, one of the few places to spend an evening in the Old City. ⊠ *Plaza San Francisco, Centro* ☎ *02/223–0609.*

THE NEW CITY

TIMING & PRECAUTIONS

Unlike the compact Old City, the New City encompasses huge distances. You'll likely need to take a taxi between sights. Pick a couple of sights that interest you and focus on them rather than trying to see them all.

MAIN ATTRACTIONS

㉑ **Fundación Guayasamín and Capilla del Hombre.** Ecuador's most famous contemporary artist, Oswaldo Guayasamín (1919–99), held court at a workshop and beautiful museum in the residential neighborhood of Bellavista, befriending everyone from the Rockefellers to Fidel Castro during his long career. On display in three buildings here are pre-Columbian ceramics, colonial sculptures, and paintings from his private collection, as well as a permanent exhibit of his own paint-

ings. Original works by Guayasamín, as well as prints, posters, and
T-shirts, are sold in the gift shop.
Five blocks up the hill is the starkly
modern vision the artist never lived
to see completed: a secular chapel
of art dedicated to the history of
mankind, housing a collection of
his cubist works on the theme of
social injustice in Latin American
history. Take a guided tour in Eng-

lish or Spanish. It's included in your ticket price, and will prove invalu-
able for understanding what you're seeing. An expansion of the Capilla
is underway at this writing, with plans to house the entire collection at
that site upon its completion in late 2009. ⊠ *Fundación: José Bosme-
diano 543; Capilla: Mariano Calvache 245B, at Lorenzo Chávez Bellavista* ☎ *02/244–8492* ⊕ *www.guayasamin.com* 🖾 *$3; $5 for both
sites* ⊙ *Fundación: weekdays 9–1:30 and 3–6:30; Capilla: Tues.–Sun.
10–5.*

🔟 **Museo del Banco Central.** The Central Bank Museum, Quito's most
★ modern museum, features an astonishing collection of pre-Columbian archaeology and Inca artifacts. Brightly lighted cases containing
sculptures from different regions of Ecuador stand next to large-scale
dioramas detailing the minutiae of pre-Columbian life. The first floor
includes an unparalleled collection of gold artifacts; journey upstairs
to an excellent exhibit of colonial paintings and sculptures. Up one
flight more you'll find an impressive collection of modern Ecuadoran
paintings. ⊠ *Northern entrance of Casa de la Cultura, Av. Patria at 6
de Diciembre, La Mariscal* ☎ *02/222–3259* ⊕ *www.museos-ecuador.
com* 🖾 *$2* ⊙ *Tues.–Fri. 9–5, weekends 10–4.*

IF YOU HAVE TIME

🔟 **Basílica del Voto Nacional.** Construction of this neo-Gothic church has
been going on for more than a century, but it still isn't completed. Here
the traditional gargoyles found on such structures are representations
of Ecuadoran jungle animals. The structure bridges the Old and New
cities, literally, figuratively, and stylistically, but falls into neither. Its
115-meter (380-foot) towers are one of Quito's best-known lookout
points. ⊠ *Carchi 122, El Belén* ☎ *02/228–9428* 🖾 *$2* ⊙ *Daily 9–5.*

🔟 **Museo Amazónico.** The Amazon Museum houses an impressive collection of artifacts and utilitarian items from different Amazonian cultures, including cooking pots, bowls, jewelry, hunting implements,
stuffed animals, and shrunken heads. The bookstore, on the first floor,
has a superb collection of (mostly Spanish-language) volumes on Latin
American culture and indigenous peoples. ⊠ *Av. 12 de Octubre 1430,
at Wilson, La Mariscal* ☎ *02/250–6247* 🖾 *$1* ⊙ *Daily 10–4.*

🔟 **Museo de Arte Moderno.** Exhibits at the Museum of Modern Art include
two stories of contemporary Ecuadoran works, such as paintings by
Eduardo Kingman and Oswaldo Guayasamín. There's an excellent col-

lection of pre-Columbian and colonial musical instruments. ⊠*Southern entrance of La Casa de la Cultura, New City* ☎*02/222–3392* ✉*$1* ☉*Tues.–Fri. 10–6, Sat. 10–2.*

⑲ Museo de Jijón Caamaño. On the third floor of the Universidad Católica, the Jijón Caamaño Museum contains a large collection of colonial art, with paintings and sculptures from some of the masters of the school of Quito. There is also a small collection of Ecuadoran and Peruvian archaeological finds. Well-informed docents lead free English-language tours. ⊠*Av. 12 de Octubre at Roca, New City* ☎*02/252–9250* ✉*$1* ☉*Weekdays 9–4.*

⑮ Parque La Alameda. The elongated triangle of La Alameda Park lies between the Old and New cities, near the **Asamblea Legislativa,** a large, modern building that houses the nation's congress. At the center of the park stands **El Observatorio,** the oldest astronomical observatory in South America, rendered useless by the bright city lights. A monument to Simón Bolívar dominates the southern apex of the triangle.

⑰ Parque El Ejido. One of the larger parks in Quito, El Ejido is popular for its extensive playgrounds and courts for *ecuavoli* (three-person volleyball). Theater groups regularly hold impromptu performances here, and there are often open-air art exhibitions on Saturday. You can also usually find a handicraft market in progress on weekends. But as pleasant as it is by day, Parque El Ejido should be avoided once the sun goes down.

☉ Telefériqo. Quito's flashiest attraction whisks you from the foothills of Volcán Pichincha to its height (4,050 meters, or 13,300 feet) courtesy of a fleet of six-passenger gondola cars. Ascending the 1,100 meters (3,620 feet) to the top is accomplished in just 10 minutes. (Lines are long but move quickly, and paying a $3 premium over the regular ticket lets you jump the queue.) At the base you'll find a complex containing a shopping center and an amusement park called Vulqano Park. At the top lie several restaurants and shops, as well as a first-aid station with oxygen in case you develop problems with the high altitude. The volcano's summit lies another 215 meters (700 feet) higher, but don't leave the complex; a few robberies have been reported on the trail to the top. The cable-car trip is worth it, but you need to retain a healthy respect for the altitude. ⚠ **Don't even consider doing this unless you've already become acclimatized to the altitude by having been in the highlands for a few days continuously.** And bring a jacket: it gets cold up here. ⊠*Av. Occidental and La Gasca, Cruz Loma* ☎*02/222–2996, 800/835–333 toll-free in Ecuador* ⊕*www.teleferiqo.com* ✉*$4; fast pass $7* ☉*Telefériqo: Mon. 11–8, Tues.–Thurs. 10–8, Fri. 10–10. Weekends 10 AM–10 PM; Vulqano Park: Mon.–Thurs. 11–9, Fri. 11–11, Sat. 10 AM–11 PM, Sun. 10–9.*

OFF THE BEATEN PATH

Guápulo. Nestled in a secluded valley below the Guayasamín museums, the village of Guápulo is a preserved pocket of colonial architecture only 2 km (1 mi) from Quito's New City. The settlement, with narrow cobblestone lanes lined with two-story white houses trimmed in blue, grew up around its impressive 17th-century church, the **Santu-**

6

ario de Guápulo. The Guápulo Sanctuary contains pieces by some of Quito's most exceptional sculptors and painters; the paintings in the central nave are the work of Miguel de Santiago, and the side altar and pulpit—completed in 1716 and considered masterpieces of colonial art—were carved by Juan Bautista Menacho. ☞ *Free* ☉ *Mon.–Sat. 9–6.* Early September brings Guápulo's annual festival, which features food, drink, and marching bands. To reach Guápulo, walk downhill via the steep staircase directly behind the Hotel Quito, east of the city at Avenida Gonzáles Suárez 2500. To return, make the uphill trek, or take a taxi for about $2.

WHERE TO EAT

Quito's better restaurants are found in the New City. Even at the most glittering establishments, formal attire is never a requirement, but you'll feel out of place in shorts, T-shirts, and jeans, except at places such as The Magic Bean, that consummate foreigners' hangout. Many restaurants close for a break between 3 and 7, and on Sunday some remain shuttered or close early. Some useful phrases are: *a la brasa* (grilled), *al vapor* (steamed), *apanada* (batter-fried/breaded), *brosterizada* (deep fried), *encocado* (cooked in coconut oil), *hornado* (roasted), *reventado* (skillet fried), and *seco* (stewed meat).

NEW CITY

¢
ECLECTIC
✕**Adam's Rib.** The owner hails from New York, but brings a bit of Texas to Quito with hefty servings of smoked baby-back ribs and barbecued chicken. The ample Sunday brunches are an institution among the city's expat community. ✉ *Calama 329, at Reina Victoria, La Mariscal* ☎ *02/256–3196* ▭ *AE, DC, MC, V* ☉ *Closed Sat.*

$$
LATIN
AMERICAN
✕**La Choza.** The mood, music, and menu are strictly Ecuadoran in this restaurant, which opened its doors in 1966. It's across the street from Quito's World Trade Center and draws a large business clientele. There's a garden dining area if you prefer outdoors to indoors. Pastry stuffed with lobster, ricotta, and spinach—baked and topped with fresh mussels, clams, and prawns and covered with a tomato-cream sauce—is one of the mouthwatering specialties here. ✉ *Av. 12 de Octubre N24–551, La Floresta* ☎ *02/223–0839* ▭ *AE, D, DC, MC, V* ☉ *No dinner weekends.*

¢
ECLECTIC
✕**The Magic Bean.** High-quality food and a relaxed vibe draw travelers, expatriates, and locals to "the Bean" to socialize over crisp salads and do business over cappuccinos. Blackberry pancakes and bagels are served for breakfast, while the lunch and dinner menu emphasizes soups, sandwiches, pastas, and shish kebab. The atmosphere is casual and the service friendly; if you're solo, you'll feel very comfortable here. Check out the back wall with a selection of giant *Far Side* cartoons. The Magic Bean also has live music some nights. ✉ *Mariscal Foch 681, at Juan León Mera, La Mariscal* ☎ *02/256–6181* ▭ *AE, DC, MC, V.*

¢
ITALIAN
✕**Pizzeria Le Arcate.** This trendy pizzeria attracts well-heeled patrons who come to choose from 59 types of individual thin-crust pizzas. The emerald-color dining room, with inlaid wood floors, Romanesque columns, and an arched foyer buzzes with conversations in a dozen languages. Crowds reach their peak around 10 PM. The menu also offers a

variety of pasta, fish, and meat dishes. ⊠*Baquedano 358, at Juan León Mera, La Mariscal* ☎*02/223–7659* ▤*DC, MC, V* ☉*Closed Mon. No lunch Sun.*

$ ⤫**La Querencia.** Best known for its superb Ecuadoran dishes—try the
LATIN *seco de chivo* (lamb stewed with fruit) or the langostinos flambéed in
AMERICAN cognac—this restaurant has excellent views of Quito from its rustic
Fodor'sChoice fireside dining room. You can also eat in the serene outdoor garden.
★ Some nights the friendly waiters can be heard singing along to soft Ecuadoran music as they roam the restaurant. ⊠*Av. Eloy Alfaro 2530, at Catalina Aldaz, La Pradera* ☎*02/244–6654* ▤*AE, DC, MC, V* ☉*No dinner Sun.*

¢ ⤫**Las Redes.** Fishing nets hanging from the wall clue you in that the
LATIN specialty here is seafood—cooked Ecuadoran style, naturally. Small and
AMERICAN informal, the restaurant opened in 1969 when Avenida Amazonas was the most popular shopping street in Quito. If you haven't tried corvina yet (a Pacific sea bass), have it here, drowned in shrimp sauce. ⊠*Av. Amazonas 845, at Veintimilla, La Mariscal* ☎*02/252–5691* ▤*AE, DC, MC, V* ☉*Closed Sun.*

$$–$$$ ⤫**Il Risotto.** Fresh roses adorn candlelighted tables, and prints of north-
ITALIAN ern Italy and opera programs from Milan's La Scala decorate the walls,
★ providing a romantic mood at this excellent Italian restaurant. Begin your meal with *insalata del pescatore* (shellfish salad), followed by lobster on a bed of pasta *pomodoro* or a chicken roll with spinach and ricotta cheese. For dessert, order crepes suzette with Grand Marnier or the tiramisu with decadent chocolate and cognac. You can listen to live music Thursday and Friday evenings. ⊠*Eloy Alfaro N34–447, at Portugal, La Pradera* ☎*02/224–6850* ▤*DC, MC, V* ☉*Closed Sat.*

¢–$ ⤫**La Ronda.** During the day businesspeople gather here, in what looks
LATIN like a Bavarian lodge, for traditional meals. Among the best dishes
AMERICAN are *cazuela de mariscos* (a seafood casserole soup) and *pernil* (roast pork) with *llapingachos* (mashed cheese and potato pancakes), peanut sauce, and avocado. During the week dinners are accompanied by guitar music, and folk dancing follows dinner on Sunday. ⊠*Bello Horizonte 400, at Diego de Almagro, La Mariscal* ☎*02/254–0459 or 02/254–5176* ▤*AE, DC, MC, V.*

$–$$ ⤫**La Terraza del Tártaro.** In the heart of the New City, this longtime
ECLECTIC favorite is known for its reliable service and delicious, if simply prepared, meats. The penthouse restaurant atop the Edificio Amazonas—look way up to see the sign, or you'll miss the place as you go by—is cheered by a blazing fire at night; you'll enjoy views of the brilliantly lighted city below. ⊠*Veintimilla 1106, at Av. Amazonas, La Mariscal* ☎*02/252–7987* ▤*AE, DC, MC, V* ☉*Closed Sun.*

$$ ⤫**La Viña.** Everyone raves about this upscale restaurant, which draws
LATIN its share of businesspeople and government officials. If you order a
AMERICAN complete meal from soup to nuts, plus wine, it will cost you around $50, but if you curb your appetite, you could get by for around $15 to $20 total. It is rumored that you could choose from the menu blindfolded and still consistently receive a masterpiece of taste and presentation. ⊠*Isabel la Católica at Cordero, La Mariscal* ☎*02/256–6033* ▤*AE, MC, V* ☉*Closed Sun. No lunch Sat.*

6

WHERE TO STAY

Accommodations range from modern high-rises, which have a range of services from health clubs to babysitting, to family-run inns, where you'll get more personal attention. Almost all the luxury hotels are in the New City, but the best deals are in the pleasant Mariscal neighborhood. Less expensive hotels often lack air-conditioning and heating, although Quito's moderate climate means this usually isn't a worry.

OLD CITY

$$$–$$$$ ⊞**Hotel Patio Andaluz.** It's a less costly alternative to the Hotel Plaza Grande down the street, but a stay here also lets you lodge in the Old City. Rooms in this four-centuries-old mansion are organized around two interior courtyards. All have wood floors, large desks, and flat-screen TVs. Each suite is split-level, with a bedroom and sitting room. We haven't quite got over the unusual layout in some of these, whose bedroom is on the lower entry level and bath on the upper level. **Pros:** Friendly service, central location. **Cons:** Odd room layout, some noise from interior courtyard. ⊠ *García Moreno N6–52 at Olmedo, Centro* ☎ *02/228–0830* ⊕ *www.hotelpatioandaluz.com* ➟ *31 suites* ⚑ *In-room: safe, kitchen (some). In-hotel: restaurant, room service, bar, public Internet* ⊟ *AE, DC, MC, V* ⎅⊙⎅*AI, CP, EP, FAP, MAP.*

$$$$ ⊞**Hotel Plaza Grande.** Arguably Ecuador's most fabulous hotel (with,
Fodor'sChoice   admittedly, prices to match) puts you right on the prime real estate
★   of its namesake plaza. The business dates only from 2007, but the structure was the mansion of early 16th century nobleman Juan Díaz de Hidalgo. "Plush" doesn't begin to describe the art and tapestries that decorate each carpeted room. You have modern amenities such as a flat-screen TV, too. The best rooms face the plaza. Though windows are soundproofed, you need only fling open the French doors and emerge on your private balcony to survey all that goes on below. You have your choice of three restaurants—Ecuadoran, Mediterranean, or French—here, too. **Pros:** Central location, top-notch service. **Cons:** Expensive. ⊠ *García Moreno N5–16, at Chile, Centro* ☎ *02/251–0777* ⊕ *www.plazagrandequito.com* ➟ *15 rooms* ⚑ *In-room: safe, Wi-Fi. In-hotel: 3 restaurants, room service, bar, public Internet* ⊟ *AE, DC, MC, V* ⎅⊙⎅*BP.*

NEW CITY

$ ⊞**Apart-Hotel Antinéa.** Once you check into this charming inn you may never want to check out. Two homes on a shady side street offer a variety of simple but elegant rooms, half of which are spacious apartments with well-stocked kitchenettes. Some open onto flower-filled courtyards, others have private balconies. For a special treat, ask for the room with a fireplace. **Pros:** Cozy atmosphere, friendly staff. **Cons:** Some nighttime crime in neighborhood. ⊠ *Juan Rodríguez E8–20, at Diego de Almagro, La Mariscal* ☎ *02/250–6838* ⊕ *www.hotelantinea. com* ➟ *7 rooms, 8 suites* ⚑ *In-room: no a/c, kitchen, refrigerator, Ethernet. In-hotel: restaurant, room service, gym, no elevator, laundry service, public Internet, parking (fee)* ⊟ *AE, DC, MC, V.*

$$ ⊞**Café Cultura.** This place's name sounds like that of a restaurant—and,
★   indeed, the Sunday brunches are a Quito institution—but it is better

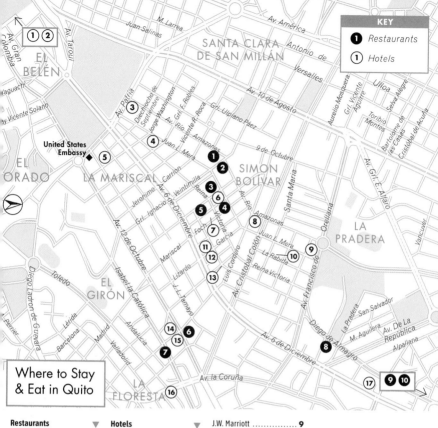

Where to Stay & Eat in Quito

known as one of Ecuador's premier boutique lodgings. The brilliant bougainvillea over the front gate lets you know that this colonial-style hotel—formerly the Center for Arts and Culture of the French Embassy—is something special. The wood-beamed lobby glows when there's a fire in the stone-trim hearth. A mezzanine above leads to the inn's comfortable guest rooms (some warmed by fireplaces). A popular café off the lobby serves breakfast and lunch. All rooms here are no-smoking. **Pros:** Homey atmosphere. **Cons:** Dark rooms. ⊠*Robles at Reina Victoria, La Mariscal* ☎*02/256–4956* ⊕*www.cafecultura.com* ↩*18 rooms, 8 suites* ⸑*In-room: no a/c, no TV. In-hotel: restaurant, no elevator, laundry service, airport shuttle, public Internet, no-smoking rooms* ⊟*AE, DC, MC, V.*

¢ ⌗**La Cartuja.** The present owner, Edurne Ayestarán, came to Ecuador from Spain on holiday and decided to turn this lovely colonial building—once the embassy of Great Britain—into a small hotel. Along with her partner, Inígo Sagarna, she also has a jungle lodge (the Jaguar Lodge) on the Napo River. The hotel's front desk is open 24 hours; the library is stocked with books and magazines. Spanish and international meals are served in the restaurant. You receive a slight discount if you pay in cash. **Pros:** Good budget value. **Cons:** Noisy, some nighttime crime in neighborhood. ⊠*Leonidas Plaza 170, at 18 de Septiembre, La Mariscal* ☎*02/252–3721* ⊕*www.hotelacartuja.com* ↩*12 rooms* ⸑*In-room: no a/c, Wi-Fi. In-hotel: restaurant, room service, bar, no elevator, airport shuttle, public Internet, parking (no fee)* ⊟*AE, DC, MC, V* ⦿*BP.*

$$$$ ⌗**Hilton Colón Quito.** If you love to shop, you'll also love this sleek hotel across from Parque El Ejido. If the shops on the first floor don't strike your fancy, just outside is one of the best shopping strips in Quito. The marble lobby is a bit sterile, and the rooms are functional but nondescript; those on the lower floors can be noisy. **Pros:** Business amenities, good service, near park. **Cons:** Overpriced restaurants. ⊠*Av. Amazonas 110, at Av. Patria, La Mariscal* ☎*02/256–0666, 800/445–8667 in North America* ⊕*www.hilton.com* ↩*333 rooms, 12 suites* ⸑*In-room: refrigerator, safe, Wi-Fi. In-hotel: 4 restaurants, room service, bar, pool, gym, no-smoking rooms* ⊟*AE, DC, MC, V.*

$ ⌗**Hostal La Rábida.** This beautifully restored colonial house is decorated with old mahogany furniture and antiques. All rooms have large private baths. Italian and international cuisine is on the dinner menu; after dinner you can relax and sip a glass of wine in front of the fireplace. Museums, shops, and restaurants are all within walking distance. You'll get a small discount if you pay in cash. **Pros:** Good value, friendly staff. **Cons:** Dark street at night. ⊠*La Rábida 227, at Santa María, La Mariscal* ☎*02/222–1720* ⊕*www.hostalrabida.com* ↩*11 rooms* ⸑*In-room: no a/c, safe. In-hotel: restaurant, room service, bar, no elevator, laundry service, public Wi-Fi, airport shuttle, parking (no fee)* ⊟*AE, DC, MC, V.*

$ ⌗**Hostal La Villa.** This small bed-and-breakfast, which occupies a half-timber Bavarian-style house, has a comfortable, casual style, and it's a convenient base for exploring the city. Internet and fax services are free. The place offers frequent Web-only special rates. **Pros:** Friendly staff, good service. **Cons:** Far from sights. ⊠*Toledo 1455, at Av. Coruña, La Floresta* ☎*02/222–2755* ⊕*www.hostallavilla.com* ⇗*14 rooms, 1 suite* ♿*In-room: no a/c. In-hotel: 2 restaurants, bar, laundry service, public Internet, public Wi-Fi, parking (no fee)* ▭*AE, DC, MC, V* ⫙*BP.*

$$ ▦ **Hotel Río Amazonas.** You might feel as if you're in the Amazon when you enjoy a cocktail at the Terraza Tropical bar, where wicker tables and chairs are set amid lush greenery. The rest of this gleaming glass high-rise, within walking distance of most of the city's museums, is more austere. The restaurant serves up tasty local dishes with a friendly flourish. **Pros:** Good views, nice restaurant. **Cons:** Spartan rooms, some street noise. ⊠*Av. Luis Cordero 1342, at Av. Amazonas, La Mariscal* ☎*02/255–6666, 888/790–5264 in North America* ⊕*www.hotelrio amazonas.com* ⇗*74 rooms, 1 suite* ♿*In-room: refrigerator, safe, Wi-Fi. In-hotel: 2 restaurants, bar, laundry service, airport shuttle, parking* ▭*AE, DC, MC, V.*

$ ▦ **Hotel Sebastián.** This small four-star hotel is in the center of the restaurant and bank district. The large rooms are cheerfully decorated, and the restaurant, Café Mistral, is open daily from 6 AM to 10:30 PM, serving international dishes and specials from Cuenca. The Café and Bar de Antaño is open from 3 to 11 daily for coffee, snacks, and cocktails. **Pros:** Friendly staff, good value. **Cons:** Street noise, some nighttime crime in neighborhood. ⊠*Diego de Almagro 822, at Cordero, La Mariscal* ☎*02/222–2400* ⊕*www.hotelsebastian.com* ⇗*49 rooms, 7 suites* ♿*In-hotel: Wi-Fi. In-hotel: restaurant, bar, laundry service, public Internet, parking (no fee)* ▭*AE, DC, MC, V.*

$$$$ ▦ **J.W. Marriott.** This futuristic pyramid has floor-to-ceiling windows offering expansive views of Volcán Pichincha or the city from every room. A large, glass-enclosed lobby adds elegance. Within walking distance are a business district and several shopping malls. The business crowd comes here for the executive floors and the largest meeting space in Quito, but it's also a good choice if you're just a tourist. **Pros:** Many business amenities, good meeting facilities. **Cons:** Some street noise. ⊠*Av. Francisco de Orellana 1172, at Av. Amazonas, La Pradera* ☎*02/297–2000, 800/228–9290 in North America* ⊕*www. marriott.com* ⇗*241 rooms, 16 suites* ♿*In-room: refrigerator, safe, Ethernet. In-hotel: 3 restaurants, room service, bar, pool, gym, spa, concierge, laundry service, airport shuttle, no-smoking rooms, public Wi-Fi* ▭*AE, DC, MC, V.*

$$ ▦ **Mansión del Ángel.** One of Quito's most luxurious accommodations,
Fodor'sChoice   this hotel is in a lavish mansion dating from the 1930s. A chandelier-
★   lighted stairway leads you upstairs to beautifully decorated rooms with antique four-poster beds. A full American breakfast is included, served in the elegant parlor or on the tile terrace. Museums, restaurants, and shops are steps away. **Pros:** Friendly staff, historic atmosphere. **Cons:** Some nighttime crime in neighborhood, some street noise. ⊠*Wilson E5-29, at Juan León Mera, La Mariscal* ☎*02/255–7721, 800/327–3573 in North America* ⊕*www.mansiondelangel.com.ec* ⇗*10 rooms* ♿*In-room: no a/c. In-hotel: public Internet, laundry service* ▭*MC, V* ⫙*BP.*

$$ **Nü House.** Look up. You can't miss the modern wood exterior, a style never seen in Quito. The furnishings are every bit as modern inside, too. The owner calls it "minimalist," but we call it "comfortable," with added touches such as flat-screen TVs and whirlpool tubs and huge windows in each room. Elevators stop between floors, necessitating your walking up or down four steps to get to your floor. **Pros:** Friendly staff, good restaurant, many amenities. **Cons:** Some nighttime crime in neighborhood. ⊠ *Mariscal Foch E6–12, at Reina Victoria, La Mariscal* ☎ *255–7845* ⊕ *www.nuhousehotels.com* ⇄ *52 rooms, 5 suites* ⌂ *In-room: refrigerator, safe, Ethernet, Wi-Fi (some). In-hotel: restaurant, room service, laundry service, public Internet* ⊟ *AE, DC, MC, V* ⎟⊚⎟ *AI, CP, EP, FAP, MAP.*

¢   **La Posada del Maple.** The friendly mood here (certainly not the small, plain rooms) lures everyone from seasoned travelers to Peace Corps volunteers. It's a friendly, inexpensive B&B, and the price includes a hearty American-style breakfast and all-day coffee, tea, and hot chocolate. **Pros:** Good budget value. **Cons:** Small rooms, some nighttime crime in neighborhood. ⊠ *Juan Rodríguez E8–49, at Av. 6 de Diciembre, La Mariscal* ☎ *02/254–4507* ⊕ *www.posadadelmaple.com* ⇄ *22 rooms, 12 with bath* ⌂ *In-room: no a/c, no phone, no TV. In-hotel: restaurant, no elevator, laundry service, public Internet* ⊟ *MC, V* ⎟⊚⎟ *BP.*

$$ **Radisson Royal Quito Hotel.** Part of Quito's World Trade Center, this
★   hotel is ideally located in the center of the city's financial district. The generously proportioned rooms exude understated elegance. Dine at the popular sushi bar, lively café, or grill. Live bands perform nightly in the Trader's Bar. **Pros:** Good value. **Cons:** Far from sights. ⊠ *Av. 12 de Octubre at Luis Cordero 444, La Floresta* ☎ *02/223–3333, 888/201–1718 in North America* ⊕ *www.radisson.com/quitoec* ⇄ *98 rooms, 14 suites* ⌂ *In-room: refrigerator, safe, Ethernet, Wi-Fi. In-hotel: 3 restaurants, bar, gym, laundry service, airport shuttle, no-smoking rooms, public Internet, public Wi-Fi, parking (no fee), airport shuttle* ⊟ *AE, DC, MC, V.*

$$$ **Sheraton Quito.** This 13-story hotel is right across from a large shopping center and two blocks away from the exposition center. Although it attracts mostly business travelers, it offers enough to do if you just want to relax. The City Pub, in the lobby, has live music. **Pros:** Many business amenities. **Cons:** Far from sights. ⊠ *Av. Naciones Unidas y Av. Republica de El Salvador, La Carolina* ☎ *02/297–0002, 888/625–5144 in North America* ⊕ *www.starwoodhotels.com* ⇄ *130 rooms, 40 suites* ⌂ *In-room: no a/c (some), refrigerator, Ethernet. In-hotel: 3 restaurants, bar, pool, gym, spa, laundry service, airport shuttle, parking (no fee), no-smoking rooms* ⊟ *AE, DC, MC, V.*

$$$$ **Swissôtel Quito.** The hotel has a spacious atrium lobby. Outside there's a pool and lovely gardens. Rooms have dark-wood furnishings. The hotel's four restaurants—French, Italian, international, and Japanese—have excellent reputations. The hotel is within walking distance of several good restaurants. **Pros:** Friendly service, many business amenities. **Cons:** Far from sights. ⊠ *Av. 12 de Octubre 1820, at Cordero, La Floresta* ☎ *02/256–7600, 800/223–6800 in North America* ⊕ *www.swissotel. com* ⇄ *185 rooms, 55 suites, 10 apartments* ⌂ *In-room: DVDs, refrig-*

erator, safe, Ethernet, Wi-Fi. In-hotel: 5 restaurants, room service, bar, tennis court, pool, gym, spa, concierge, laundry service, airport shuttle, public Internet, no-smoking rooms ⊟AE, MC, V ⊚BP.

QUITO ENVIRONS

$ ⚏**San Jorge Eco-Lodge.** A onetime 18th- century Jesuit monastery turned farm in the Andes foothills has now been converted into one of those so-close-but-oh-so-far lodgings. The folks here never tire of reminding you that you're closer to the airport than you would be if you stayed in the New City, but reservations are essential, given the rough road to get here. Cozy rooms are equipped with stone floors, throw rugs, and fireplaces. The whole site sits in the midst of an Audubon-certified reserve, with plenty of bird-watching opportunities. **Pros:** Secluded location, outdoor activities. **Cons:** Far from sights, rough road to get here. ⊠*Km 4, Quito-Minda Rd.* ☎*02/249–3123, 877/565–2596 in North America* ⊕*www.eco-lodgesanjorge.com* ⇆*24 rooms* ⚒*In-hotel: restaurant, pool, no-smoking rooms* ⊟*AE, DC, MC, V.*

AFTER DARK

The air is thin and the nights get cold, but Quito pulses after the sun goes down with plenty of *discotecas* and *salsatecas.* At the *peñas* (clubs where Andean musicians perform), you can listen to traditional Ecuadoran music. Bars usually open in the late afternoon, while dance clubs don't get going until 10 PM. By law, everything shuts down by 2 AM. Cover charges can be as much as $10.

Quito's arts scene has grown significantly in the last few years, too. The free monthly English-language magazine *This Is Ecuador,* the free monthly English-language newspaper *Ecuador Reporter,* and the free Spanish-language monthly magazine *Quito Cultura,* each available in many hotels and restaurants, are good for a look at what's going on around town (and around the country).

Evening crowds throng the streets of La Mariscal, where you'll find the greatest selection of nightlife, but the high tourist quotient attracts a number of thieves, too. Watch your things, your drinks, and yourself, and take a taxi, even if you're only going a few blocks. Bars and restaurants are happy to call one to take you back to your hotel.

BARS

The lively **Bangalo Salon de Te** (⊠*Mariscal Foch 451, between Diego de Almagro and 6 de Diciembre* ☎*02/250–1332*) features a blazing fireplace and nonstop Brazilian music. At **Finn McCool's** (⊠*Pinto 251, at Reina Victoria*), approximates an Irish pub, Quito style, with Guinness on tap. At **Ghoz** (⊠*La Niña 425, at Reina Victoria*), you can munch on Swiss food, play a game of pool, and listen to high-decibel rock and salsa. **Papillón** (⊠*Yanez Pinzón at Av. Colón* ☎*02/252–9411*) blasts pop and techno, which draws a young crowd.

El Pobre Diablo (⊠*Santa María 338, at Juan León Mera* ☎*02/222–4982*) is a gathering place for artists and intellectuals. You'll find a young crowd at **Tijuana** (⊠*Reina Victoria and Santa María* ☎*02/223–8324*).

Varadero (⊠ *Reina Victoria at La Pinta*) has live music on Wednesday, Friday, and Saturday. It fills up with locals early on weekends.

CONCERTS

Ecuador's National Symphony Orchestra—as well as many smaller ensembles—frequently performs at the **Casa de la Música** (⊠ *Valderrama at Av. Mariana de Jesús* ☎02/226–7093). The **Teatro Nacional Sucre** (⊠ *Manabí N8–131, between Guayaquil and Flores* ☎02/257–2823 ⊕*www.teatrosucre.com*) has an active schedule of concerts and dance and opera performances. Tickets run $5–$50.

DANCE

Jacchigua, the national folk ballet, performs Wednesday at 7:30 PM in the **Casa de la Cultura** (⊠ *Av. América at Av. Mariana de Jesús* ☎02/295–2025). Tickets cost $25.

DANCE CLUBS

Enjoy Latin rhythms at **Cali Salsateca** (⊠ *Diego de Almagro 1268, at Av. Orellana*), a popular weekend spot that admits only couples. Locals head to **Salsateca Seseribó** (⊠ *Veintimilla 325, at Av. 12 de Octubre* ☎02/256–3578) to dance to *cumbia,* salsa, and merengue, weekends only; stop by for the free salsa lesson each Saturday at 8:30 PM.

FILM

Cinemas in Quito usually screen Hollywood films a few weeks after their U.S. release in English with Spanish subtitles. **Casa de la Cultura** (⊠ *Av. Patria at Av. 12 de Octubre* ☎02/256–5808) is a good bet for an occasional art film in Spanish.

LECTURES

Fodor's Choice ★ For a fun, intellectual twist on a night out, **South American Explorers** (⊠ *Jorge Washington 311* ☎02/222–5228) holds informal lectures in English each Thursday at 6 PM. Topics range from ways to cope with altitude to planning a trip to the Galápagos. Admission is a nominal $2 for nonmembers, with plenty of popcorn included. They're a great way to meet fellow travelers. The club also holds a lively quiz night (with prizes) the first and third Wednesday of each month at the **Reina Victoria Pub** (⊠ *Reina Victoria at Roca*). Proceedings get under way at 8:30.

PEÑAS

If you're looking for a peña in the Old City, one of the best is **La Taberna Quito Colonial** (⊠ *Marabí at Vargas* ☎02/228–3102). One of the New City's most established peñas is the **Nuncanchi Peña** (⊠ *Av. Universitaria 496, at Armero* ☎02/254–0967). **Peña Pacha Camac** (⊠ *Jorge Washington 530, at Juan León Mera* ☎02/223–4855) is a small place in the Mariscal neighborhood.

SHOPPING

Quito's best shopping area is the New City's Mariscal district. Bounded by Avenidas Amazonas, 6 de Diciembre, Patria, and Colón, the neighborhood is a tightly packed collection of shops and boutiques. Items are reasonably priced, though they don't rival the outlying markets for bargains and color. The quality, however, is often superior. Many stores throughout Quito are closed Saturday afternoon and Sunday, but most shopping malls are open all week.

HANDICRAFTS

The most extensive collection of handicraft shops is in Quito's modern shopping mall, **El Jardín** (⊠ *Av. Amazonas and Av. La República* ☎ *02/246–6570*). **Casa Indo Andina** (⊠ *Roca 606, at Juan León Mera*) sells top-of-the-line items, including original and reproduction pre-Columbian ceramics and colonial religious art, as well as bronze-plated frames and silver jewelry. **El Centro Artesanal** (⊠ *Juan León Mera 804* ☎ *02/254–8235*) specializes in hand-knit sweaters and other items.

Fodor'sChoice ★ **Galería Latina** (⊠ *Juan León Mera 833* ☎ *02/222–1098*) offers an enormous selection of sterling-silver jewelry, ceramic figures, alpaca clothing, and antiques. In addition to regional crafts, **La Bodega** (⊠ *Juan León Mera 614* ☎ *02/222–5844*) has an extensive collection of sweaters in wool and cotton. **Folklore Olga Fisch** (⊠ *Av. Colón 260* ☎ *02/254–1315*) is one of Quito's more expensive, and curious, shopping experiences. The shop is in the colonial home of the late Olga Fisch (1901–90), who worked with craftspeople to turn folk art into modern works of art. The store specializes in handwoven rugs, tapestries, clothing, and pottery inspired by indigenous motifs. While you're here, visit the splendid museum upstairs and have lunch or afternoon tea in the small, informal restaurant in the garden or dinner in the intimate indoor restaurant.

Homero Ortega & Hijos (⊠ *Isabel La Católica N24100, at Madrid* ☎ *02/252–6715* ⊕ *www.homeroortgega.com*), Cuenca's famous Panama hat maker, has a store here in Quito.

MARKETS

You can lose yourself among the stalls at the **Mercado de Santa Clara,** in the New City at the corner of Calle Versalles and Calle Marchena. At this traditional market you'll find fruits and vegetables piled in geometrical patterns, bundles of dried and fresh herbs, barrels of grains, and huge bunches of freshly cut flowers. You can listen to a musician play soulful tunes on the accordion or light a candle to the Virgin Mary at the shrine tucked between the vendors' stalls.

OFF THE BEATEN PATH

Arashá Rain Forest Resort & Spa. Two hours northwest of Quito sits this all-inclusive hotel (packages start at $398) with colorfully painted two-bedroom thatch-roof cottages scattered over the hillsides. On the cusp of a cloud forest, Arashá is 598 meters (1,962 feet) above sea level, with an average temperature of 76°F, and it takes on an ethereal appearance in the early morning as clouds cut the visibility to zero. More than 300 species of birds have been counted along the trails, rivers, and waterfalls. The spa has aromatherapy and moisturizer, facial, and stress-relief treatments. There's also a chocolate factory on-site, so you

Market Day in the Andes

Sunday is market day in villages near Cuenca. Buses leave regularly from Cuenca's Terminal Terrestre, and getting there is half the fun. Drivers pick up anyone who waves them down. Young men lugging pots and pans jump on, leaving their wares piled in the aisle. Women carrying their babies wrapped in shawls drag burlap sacks filled with dried corn to their seats. Farmers taking livestock to the market hold roosters under their arms or strap piglets to the roof. (Larger pigs are more of a problem, and it's not unheard of to see the owner of a squealing sow trying to stuff it into the luggage compartment). By the time you arrive at your destination, the bus itself will seem like a market on wheels.

The largest village is Gualaceo, 38 km (24 mi) east of Cuenca. Well-dressed Cañari women in colorful polleras and jaunty straw or felt hats gather in the main square. Locals buy and sell clothing and kitchen items, but the majority of booths feature piles of fresh produce, sacks overflowing with grains, and barrels filled with spices.

The quietest of the Andean villages, the mining town of Chordeleg, is along a winding road about 5 km (3 mi) south of Gualaceo. The highlight of the market is handmade jewelry. Some complain that the quality of the gold and silver filigree has diminished, but good bargains can still be had. A ring with a startling amount of detail costs less than $5. Handicrafts, embroidered clothing, pottery, and mounds of jewelry are sold in shops surrounding the tree-shaded square. About 24 km (15 mi) beyond Chordeleg is Sigsig, best known for its Panama hats.

–Wayne Hoffman

can see how chocolate is made from cocoa beans (kids love this). Rates include all meals, some drinks (not imported liquor), entertainment (including karaoke and movies), and tours. ⊠*Pedro Vicente Maldonado* ☎*02/276–5348, 02/244–9881 in Quito, 877/828–7733 in North America* ⊕*www.arasharesort.com* ⟿*27 bungalows* ⌅*2 restaurants, pool, spa* ⊟*AE, DC, MC, V.*

THE NORTHERN HIGHLANDS

When the Spanish conquered the territory north of Quito, they introduced sheep to the region. Over time the mountain-dwellers became expert wool weavers and dyers; even today some craftspeople painstakingly collect and prepare their own natural dyes despite the increasing popularity of modern synthetic colors. Many small weaving villages dot the green-and-gold highland valleys, and every weekend artisans make the trek to the colorful market in Otavalo, the largest and most prosperous of these crafts towns. Otavalo's Plaza de Ponchos and adjacent streets bustle each Saturday, with merchants selling weavings, rugs, sweaters, jewelry, and handicrafts. Smaller villages—such as Cotacachi (famous for its leather) and San Antonio de Ibarra (known for its woodwork)—host their own markets, though none on such a grand scale as Otavalo's.

OTAVALO

95 km (58 mi) north of Quito.

Residents of Ecuador's most famous market town proudly retain many of their old customs, including their manner of dress. The women wear embroidered white blouses, blue wraparound skirts, black or blue head cloths, and row upon row of beaded gold necklaces. Though many younger men now sport Western attire, in the nearby villages some still wear the traditional calf-length white pants, white shirt, and dark blue poncho, with a beige felt hat over long braided hair.

GETTING HERE & AROUND

The majority of visitors take in Otavalo as an escorted day tour from Quito. For around $75, taxis can be hired in Quito for a daylong trip to Otavalo and the surrounding countryside. If you want to do it yourself, Otavalo is a good, smooth drive via the Pan-American Highway north of Quito. From Quito's Terminal Terrestre, buses depart every 30 minutes for Otavalo (2 hours) and Ibarra (2½ hours). The round-trip fare should be less than $5. Transportes Otavalo deposits passengers in Otavalo's center.

SAFETY & PRECAUTIONS

Otavalo is reasonably tranquil, but pickpockets navigate the crowded markets. Watch your things.

ESSENTIALS

Bus Information **Transportes Otavalo** (☎ *02/257–0271*).

Currency Exchange **Banco Pichincha** (✉ *Sucre 1413, at Quito* ☎ *06/292–1000*).

EXPLORING OTAVALO

Plaza de Ponchos. Otavalo's premier sight, and one of which you'll be a part, is its Saturday market. This gathering of stalls was once called the Silent Market because there was no loud bargaining or shouting to entice you to buy. Though it's still quiet compared to other markets, times have changed. Today you negotiate your way through a noisy and overwhelming conglomeration of stands crowded with tourists. Once inside the hurly-burly, you deal with the dignified and astute Otavaleños, who speak slowly and softly as they negotiate. For sale are hand-knit sweaters made from sheep or alpaca wool, colorful ponchos, patterned scarves, and Panama hats. You'll also find strings of gold-washed glass beads, worn in multiple strands by Otavalo women, lots of silver, and jewelry embedded with Andean jade. You can usually get discounts of 20% to 30% by bargaining. (Don't bargain *too* hard though. Prices are already reasonable, and that extra couple of dollars will mean a lot more to the vendor than to you.) A produce market is held simultaneously at the Plaza 24 de Mayo; there's also an animal market at the Plaza San Juan. People from the surrounding countryside—many dressed in traditional clothing—come here to bargain for cows, pigs, and other livestock. The animal market begins at 5:30 AM, and most sellers are packing up by 11 AM. The Plaza de Ponchos market

VISITING THE EQUATOR

Ecuador means "equator" in Spanish, and with the line passing just north of Quito, the country offers the world's easiest access for paying your respects to 0° latitude. Three sites compete for your attention, the best known of which has been found not to lie on the equator at all. Two things may surprise you: the pine trees and stiff breezes are likely not how you envisioned equatorial climes; and you weigh a couple of pounds less here, gravity's force being slightly lower.

Ecuador's famous **Mitad del Mundo** (Middle of the World) monument does not sit exactly on the equator. It marks the spot that in 1736 the French Geodesic Mission determined was the latitudinal center of the earth. But GPS satellite technology has demonstrated that the true equator runs about 300 meters (980 feet) north. Visitors today enjoy having their photographs taken as they straddle the painted line here, but, alas, they are really standing entirely in the southern hemisphere. Nonetheless, the site makes an interesting visit. The monument itself is a 30-meter-tall (98-foot-tall) stone obelisk topped by a 2½-ton metal globe. Inside is an Ethnographic Museum with exhibits of the people, clothing, and dwellings of Ecuador's diverse ethnic groups; bilingual guided tours are included in your admission price. The nearby planetarium's show is in Spanish only, and is put on only if at least 15 people are in attendance. The rest of the site is constructed to resemble a colonial village, with most buildings housing souvenir shops. ⊠ 1 km (½ mi) from San Antonio de Pichincha 🖀 02/222–0360 ⊕ www.mitaddelmundo.com 🎫 Site, $2; ethnographic museum,

$3; planetarium, $1.50 ⊙ Mon.–Thurs. 9–6, Fri.–Sun. 9–7.

Just beyond Mitad del Mundo lies **Intiñan,** the site that the Geodesic Expedition meant to find but didn't. The highlight here is a small museum with some basic science exhibits illustrating the effects of physics at 0° latitude. In particular, everyone oohs over the demonstrations of an egg balancing on the tip of a nail without falling, and of the north and south drains with clockwise or counterclockwise swirling water. Your admission ticket includes a guided tour in English or Spanish. ⊠ 200 meters north of Mitad del Mundo traffic circle, hwy. to Calacalí 🖀 02/239–5122 ⊕ www.intinan.org 🎫 $2 ⊙ Daily 9:30–5:30.

If Intiñan approximates high-school science experiments, **Quitsato,** where the equator crosses the Pan-American Highway on the way to Otavalo, offers the subject's most academic treatment of the three sites, with ongoing research into the astronomy, history, and archaeology of equatorial observation. Quitsato's highlight is the enormous, 54-meter (177-foot) walk-on sundial, which, of course, casts no shadow at noon. The Solar Culture Museum here has an informative bilingual talk about peoples' use of the sun in measurements during the pre-Columbian epoch. The site is a standard stop on many of the day tours out of Quito to Otavalo. ⊠ Cayambe, Km 55, Pan-American Hwy. 🖀 02/236–3042 ⊕ www.quitsato.org 🎫 Donation requested ⊙ Daily 9:30–5:30.

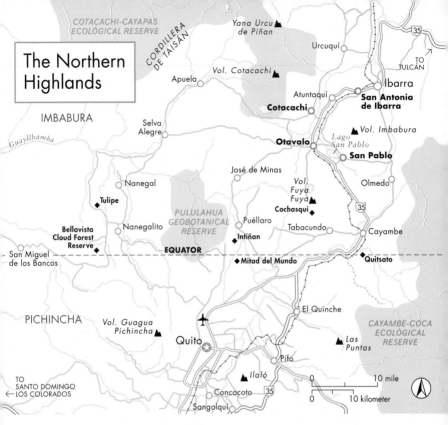

The Northern Highlands

doesn't really begin until 7 or 8 and lasts until about 2 or 3. Although Saturday is the busiest market day, Wednesday runs a close second, and these days something goes on every day of the week.

WHERE TO EAT

¢ ✕ **Mi Otavalito.** One block from the Plaza de Ponchos, this small restaurant has a simple menu that includes fresh trout and pepper steak. Seating is available on a covered patio or in the narrow dining room. The daily lunch specials are a great deal. ⊠*Sucre at Morales* ☎*06/292–2105* ▭*No credit cards*.
LATIN AMERICAN

¢ ✕ **Sisa.** This two-story cultural complex consists of an intimate restaurant on the second floor that serves excellent Ecuadoran cuisine, a ground-floor coffee bar, and a bookstore. The restaurant presents live folk music Friday evening and all day on weekends. ⊠*Abdón Calderón 409* ☎*06/292–0154* ▭*AE, DC, MC, V*.
LATIN AMERICAN

WHERE TO STAY

¢–$$ 🏨 **Ali Shungu.** The Quichua name of this colorful hotel means "good heart," and indeed the American owners go out of their way to make you feel at home. The spacious bedrooms with terra-cotta floors and local weavings surround a flower-filled courtyard, beyond which is Volcán Imbabura in the distance. Two expansive suites are ideal for families. The bright restaurant has wholesome dishes, including vegetarian lasagna and deep-dish chicken pie served with organically grown vegetables. There's live folk music on Friday night. For a real get-away-from-it-all alternative, these folks operate a lodge 5 km (3 mi) southwest of town. Four sparkling, fully equipped houses ($$$) have terra-cotta floors, cactus-braid rugs and wood-burning

> **TIP**
>
> Hotel reservations are essential on Friday night, when many tourists arrive so they can be up early for the Saturday market, the week's biggest affair.

stoves to ward off the night chill. (There's even Wi-Fi access, but come on: leave the laptop at home and enjoy the surroundings.) Both properties are entirely no-smoking. **Pros:** Terrific restaurant in town, good value. **Cons:** Rough road to reach lodge. ⊠*Quito at Miguel Egas* 🕾*06/292–0750* ⊕*www.alishungu.com* 🛏*16 rooms, 2 suites* ♿*In-room: no a/c, Wi-Fi, no phone, no TV. In-hotel: restaurant, bicycles, no elevator, laundry service, no-smoking rooms* ▤*No credit cards.*

$$ ▦**Bellavista Cloud Forest Reserve.** Two hours out of Quito puts you smack-dab up in the heights of Ecuador's best-known cloud forest, replete with trails, waterfalls, orchids, and an amazing 275 bird species to add to your life list. You can do the place as a day trip—a *long* day trip from the capital—but staying here at the reserve's rustic but comfy dome-shape hotel makes a much more relaxing alternative. Rooms, one of which is wheelchair-accessible, have wood floors, basic furnishings and private balconies. (The birds will be your morning alarm clock.) A couple of other small cottages on site offer more seclusion, but all offer you access to surprisingly yummy food considering the isolated location. Various mix-and-match packages let you include tours and transportation. **Pros:** Secluded, ample birding. **Cons:** Rustic rooms. ⊠*Tandayapa, Km 52, Quito-Nanegalito Rd.* 🕾*02/223–2313 in Quito* ⊕*www.bellavistacloudforest.com* 🛏*17 rooms, 16 with bath, 3 cabins* ♿*In-room: no a/c, no phone, no TV. In-hotel: restaurant, no elevator* ▤*AE, DC, MC, V* ⍟*EP, FAP.*

$$ ▦**Hostería Hacienda Pinsaquí.** French and Spanish antiques fill this colo-
Fodor's Choice   nial ranch house, built in 1790, surrounded by palm trees. The huge
★   light-filled suites, which can accommodate up to five people, have canopy beds, fireplaces, and spacious sitting areas. Some rooms have views of Imbabura Volcano. Horseback-riding trips are the hacienda's specialty. **Pros:** Secluded, friendly service, lovely gardens. **Cons:** Chilly at night. ⊠*Pan-American Hwy., 5 km (3 mi) north of Otavalo* 🕾*06/294–6116* ⊕*www.haciendapinsaqui.com* 🛏*20 suites* ♿*In-room: no a/c. In-hotel: restaurant, room service, no elevator, bicycles, laundry service, public Internet, airport shuttle* ▤*MC, V* ⍟*BP.*

AFTER DARK

During the week things are very quiet in Otavalo (some would say downright dull), but the town has a reasonable selection of peñas (small local clubs) that open on weekends. You can't go wrong with either location of **Amauta** (⊠*Jaramillo and Salinas* ⊠*Jaramillo and Morales* 🕾*06/292–0967*). Both open around 8 PM.

SHOPPING

"Shopping" equals "market" in Otavalo. While alpaca goods abound, look (and feel) closely at what you're buying. Alpaca's legendary tenderness approaches that of cashmere, say its many fans. But *too* silky? It's likely a synthetic blend. Too scratchy means that it's probably sheep's wool.

SPORTS & THE OUTDOORS

Few visitors take in more of this area than Otavalo's market, but if you have the time, a couple of tour operators can take you on visits and hikes to surrounding villages. Though not as well known as Baños in the Central Highlands, the nearby Chota (Class II) and Mira (Class III–IV) rivers are gaining attention in rafting circles.

Zulay Viajes (⊠ *Sucre 1014, Otavalo* ☎ *06/292–1217*), owned and operated by indigenous people, offers a variety of trekking and horseback excursions to the area surrounding Otavalo. **IntiExpress** (⊠ *Sucre and Morales, Otavalo* ☎ *06/292–0737*) has a good selection of day trips to highland lakes and villages. **Ecomontes Tour** (⊠ *Sucre and Morales, Otavalo* ☎ *06/292–6244* ⊕ *www.ecomontestour.com*) takes you rafting, as well as on horseback and cycling excursions in the countryside around Otavalo.

SAN PABLO

8 km (5 mi) southeast of Otavalo.

Easily accessible from Otavalo, the highland town of San Pablo is a collection of adobe buildings along the shore of deep-blue Lago San Pablo. The lake sits at the base of the massive 15,190-foot Volcán Imbabura. Lodges on or near the lake are much nicer than those in town.

GETTING HERE & AROUND

Buses run between Otavalo and San Pablo about every 15 minutes, or you can take a taxi for around $3.

SAFETY & PRECAUTIONS

The time-honored backpackers' walk from Otavalo to the lake has been plagued by robberies in recent years. Take a bus or taxi to get here.

ESSENTIALS

Otavalo lies close enough that you can take care of any essentials there.

WHERE TO STAY

$$$–$$$$ 🛏**Hacienda Cusín.** This restored colonial hacienda on the edge of San Pablo is one of the country's most delightful inns. Rooms are filled with period furnishings, and many are warmed by fireplaces. The main buildings, which date from the 17th century, hold the restaurant, bar, and sitting rooms, where you can enjoy the views of the colorful gardens. **Pros:** Secluded, cozy, friendly service. **Cons:** Chilly at night. ⊠ *San Pablo* ☎ *06/291–8013, 800/670–6984 in North America*

⊕ *www.haciendacusin.com* ⇌ *17 rooms, 25 suites* ♿ *In-room: no a/c. In-hotel: restaurant, bar, bicycles, no elevator, public Internet* ▤ *AE, DC, MC, V* ⦿ *BP.*

$–$$ ⬚ **Puerto Lago Country Inn.** Volcanic peaks form a dramatic backdrop for this lakeside country inn just a few miles southeast of Otavalo. The view from the restaurant, built out over the lake, is enough to warrant a stay here. Don't miss the panfried trout, served head and all. Bungalow-style rooms are spacious, with brick walls, wood-beam ceilings, and cozy fireplaces. You can rent a rowboat or kayak, or take an excursion on a festive pontoon boat with live music. Breakfast and dinner are included in the rate. **Pros:** Secluded, good value. **Cons:** Chilly at night. ⊠ *Pan-American Hwy. Km 5½* ☎ *06/292–0920* ⊕ *www. puertolago.com* ⇌ *27 rooms* ♿ *In-room: no a/c, refrigerator. In-hotel: restaurant, bar, water sports, no elevator, public Internet, public Wi-Fi* ▤ *AE, MC, V.*

SPORTS & THE OUTDOORS

The tranquil setting invites hiking, but a few robberies have occurred on remote trails around the lake.

HORSEBACK RIDING

IntiExpress (⊠ *Otavalo* ☎ *06/292–0737)* arranges horseback-riding excursions to San Pablo and other local villages and natural mineral springs.

COTACACHI

15 km (9 mi) north of Otavalo.

Although most people just pass through here on the way to the lake of the same name, the quiet little town of Cotacachi is well worth a visit. The small central plaza is charming, with young children racing around while their grandparents settle back for a little gossip with friends. A few blocks away, Calle 10 de Agosto is lined with shops selling the quality leather goods for which the town is famous. The prices are amazingly low.

GETTING HERE & AROUND

Taxis charge $7 for a one-way trip from Otavalo. Buses to Cotacachi leave every 15–30 minutes throughout the day.

ESSENTIALS

Currency Exchange **Banco de Pichincha** (⊠ *Imbabura at Rocafuerte* ☎ *06/291– 5456)*.

EXPLORING COTACACHI

Laguna de Cuicocha. West of town, a milewide, oblong lake cradles itself in the lower flanks of Volcán Cotacachi. A well-marked hiking trail heads up the crater's rim into an ecological reserve that affords fantastic views of the distant Imbabura and Cayambe volcanoes. Within the lake are islands that can be visited on inexpensive boat tours. ⊠ *18 km (11 mi) west of Cotocachi.*

WHERE TO STAY & EAT

¢ 🖼 **Hostería Mesón de las Flores.** This inexpensive lodging beside the town church provides an authentic Ecuadoran experience. Most rooms are on the second floor surrounding a courtyard restaurant and have small balconies and soft beds. A spacious suite on the third floor is a great deal for a couple. **Pros:** Convenient and authentic. **Cons:** Some noise from the restaurant. ⊠ *García Moreno at Sucre* ☎ *06/291–6009* ⏎ *16 rooms, 1 suite* ⏷ *In-room: no a/c, no phone, no TV. In-hotel: restaurant, bar, no elevator* ⊟ *AE, DC, MC, V* ⏺| *BP.*

$$$ 🖼 **La Mirage Hotel & Spa.** You'll pass trickling fountains and shady courtyards as you wind through flower-filled gardens on the way to your casita on this 200-year-old property. Suites are chock-full of decorative touches, from handcrafted furnishings to crystal chandeliers, antique canopy beds, gilded mirrors, ornate trim, and lavish baths. International cuisine is served in the wood-beamed dining room, part of which looks out onto the lawn, where peacocks roam. Much of the produce is organic and grown in the hotel's own garden. While you're at dinner, staff members slip in to build a fire and place hot water bottles at the foot of your bed, an example of the sort of pampering you can expect throughout a stay here. Aside from the standard massages, the spa has volcanic mud treatments, aromatherapy, massage instruction for couples, and unique shaman treatments. **Pros:** Good restaurant, attentive service. **Cons:** Chilly at night. ⊠ *Av. 10 de Agosto* ☎ *06/291–5237, 800/327–3573 in North America* ⊕ *www.mirage.com.ec* ⏎ *23 suites* ⏷ *In-room: no a/c, Ethernet. In-hotel: restaurant, bar, tennis court, pool, spa, no elevator, no-smoking rooms* ⊟ *DC, MC, V* ⏺| *MAP.*

SAN ANTONIO DE IBARRA

10 km (6 mi) north of Cotacachi.

Renowned for its wood carvings, San Antonio de Ibarra is where you'll find skillful artisans who show off their wares in the shops surrounding the central plaza. Check out the chess sets, which use llamas in place of the horses usually used to signify the knights. Prices range from a few dollars to a few hundred. Luis Potosí on the town's main square is the best known purveyor of fine wood carvings.

GETTING HERE & AROUND

San Antonio de Ibarra is an easy half-day trip if you are based in Cotacahi or Otavalo. From Quito's Terminal Terrestre, buses depart every 30 minutes for San Antonio de Ibarra (2½ hours). The round-trip fare should be less than $5. Flota Imbabura has direct service to Ibarra. From Otavalo, buses depart every 15 minutes throuout the day. Once here, head to the Ibarra branch of iTur, which is open weekdays 8:30–1 and 2–5.

ESSENTIALS

Bus Contact **Flota Imbabura** (☎ *02/223–6940*).

Currency Exchange **Banco Pichincha** (⊠ *Bolívar at Obispo Mosquera* ☎ *06/295–5810*).

Visitor & Tour Info *iTur* (⊠ *García Moreno 376, at Roca Fuerte* ☎ *06/295–8547*).

THE CENTRAL HIGHLANDS

South of Quito the Andes rise sharply on either side of the Pan-American Highway, creating a narrow corridor of fertile valleys that, along with Quito, are home to nearly half of Ecuador's population. Along this 175-km (109-mi) stretch between Quito and Riobamba are most of Ecuador's tallest volcanoes, including one of the tallest active volcanoes in the world, Cotopaxi. Alexander von Humboldt, the German scientist who explored the area in 1802, was so impressed by the landscape that he coined a sobriquet still used today: the Avenue of the Volcanoes.

TERMAS DE PAPALLACTA

65 km (40 mi) east of Quito.

A stunning drive over the eastern range of the Andes brings you to the village of Papallacta. A mile beyond you'll find the Termas de Papallacta, a natural hot springs with eight thermal baths and two cold crystalline pools. It's a beautiful setting, and on a clear day you can see the snowcapped peak of Volcán Antisana. ⊘ *Daily 6* AM–10 PM ☜$5.

GETTING HERE & AROUND
Buses headed to the lowland town of Tena travel every hour past the Termas de Papallacta. You may have to pay the full fare to Tena, which is under $3.

ESSENTIALS
Take care of any essentials before you leave Quito.

WHERE TO STAY

$$ 🖾 **Termas Papallacta Spa & Resort.** This ranch, set 9,000 feet above sea level, is surrounded by natural hot springs. The springs line the Cinnamon Trail, the route taken by Francisco de Orellana in 1542 when he crossed the Andes in search of spices and wound up discovering the Amazon. All rooms have private baths and breathtaking mountain views. Individual cabins scattered around the grounds offer a little more privacy. Walk or ride horses through the rain forest, and bring binoculars to observe the varied species of birds. **Pros:** Relaxing hot springs. **Cons:** Crowded on weekends. ⊠ *Km 67, Carretera Quito–Baeza* ☎ *06/232–0620, 02/256–8989 in Quito, 888/790–5264 in North America* ⊕ *www.termaspapallacta.com* ☜ *32 rooms, 13 cabins* ⌂ *In-room: no a/c. In-hotel: restaurant, pool, spa, no elevator* ☰ *AE, MC, V.*

PARQUE PASOCHOA

38 km (24 mi) southeast of Quito.

Parque Pasochoa, a protected area administered by the Quito-based Fundación Natura, covers 988 acres of high Andean forest. More than 100 species of birds and a variety of butterflies have been identified in the area. Walking trails include short loops and all-day hikes, with the trek to the 13,800-foot summit of Volcán Pasochoa the most strenuous. Camping is permitted in designated areas with water spigots and latrines. ☎ *02/244–7341 or 02/224–6072* 🖃 *$1.50* �he *Daily.*

> **TIP**
>
> Tour operators in Quito offer one-day tours for $40–$85, depending on the group size. If you want to go on your own, buses from Quito stop a couple of miles from the park entrance.

PARQUE NACIONAL COTOPAXI

67 km (42 mi) southeast of Quito.

Folks here will tell you that Cotopaxi, at 5,897 meters (19,347 feet) above sea level, is the highest active volcano in the world. Technically, it's not, but the massive, snowcapped mountain is still one of Ecuador's iconic sights. Although mountaineers risk their lives to reach Cotopaxi's icy summit, you need risk little more than a possible case of lightheadedness to wander around its lower slopes, which are protected within Parque Nacional Cotopaxi.

The drive here is unforgettable. As you make your way past the stands of red pine and into the higher altitudes, you are likely to spot llamas, white-tailed deer, and wild horses, as well as Andean condors and sparrow hawks. Fewer animals roam the semiarid plains called the *páramo,* extending from 10,496 to 15,744 feet. There are no trees here, only small plants that have adapted to the harsh environment. Above the páramo lies the permafrost zone, where giant glaciers extend across the volcano's summit. Cotopaxi is most impressive at dawn, when sunlight sprinkles rays across the surface of the glaciers and casts shadows on the surrounding mountains. 🖃 *$10* ☉ *Daily 7–3.*

GETTING HERE & AROUND

Every Quito tour operator offers day trips to the park for around $40, the way most visitors come here. Getting here on your own is far less convenient: take any of the buses to Ambato that leave from Quito's Terminal Terrestre every 30 minutes. They will drop you off in Lasso, about 10 km (6 mi) from the park entrance. The 30-km (18-mi) ride takes just under an hour and costs $2.

SAFETY & PRECAUTIONS

Two words: altitude effects. Even the easiest Cotopaxi day tours from Quito take you to elevations of 10,000 feet or higher. Have a couple of days at the capital's lofty-enough heights under your belt to acclimatize before attempting a volcano visit.

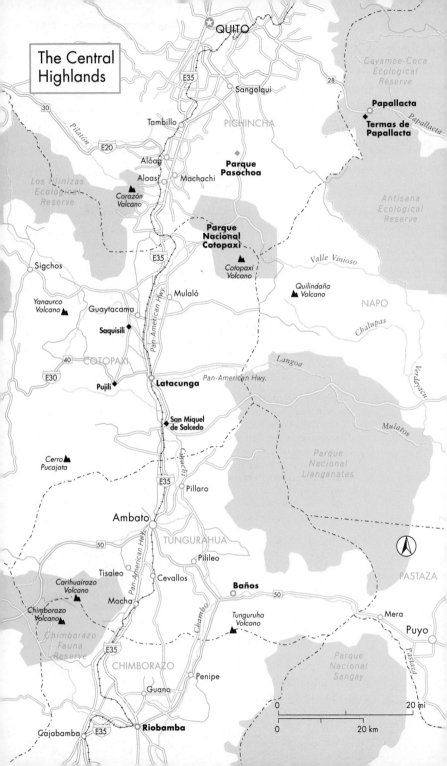

ESSENTIALS

Take care of essentials back in Quito or in Latacunga, the nearest city to Cotopaxi.

WHERE TO STAY

¢ 🖭 **Hostería La Estación.** Owned by the same family for four generations, this log house B&B has a panoramic view of the mountains. Fresh flowers brighten the rooms, which are decorated with antiques. All rooms have private baths. The gracious owners will prepare meals and arrange day hikes for you to Volcán Cotopaxi. The hostería is a half hour from the entrance to Parque Nacional Cotopaxi, near the small village of Machachi. **Pros:** Friendly owners, good budget value, secluded. **Cons:** Rustic rooms. ⊠ *Machachi* 🕾*02/230–9246* ↩*10 rooms* ⌂*In-room: no a/c, no phone. In-hotel: 2 restaurants, no elevator* ⊟*DC.*

¢ 🖭 **Rumipamba de las Rosas.** In an Andean valley 100 km (61 mi) south of Quito, right at the stone gate to the colorful town of Salcedo, is this unexpectedly elegant hostel. Comfortable rooms filled with antiques, a shady pool, and three restaurants—one with seating in a garden—are the perfect antidote for the stresses of modern life. While you're here, explore Salcedo's market. **Pros:** Secluded, cozy. **Cons:** Chilly at night. ⊠*Salcedo* 🕾*03/272–6128, 02/228–0830 in Quito* ⊕*www.rumipamba. com* ↩*31 rooms* ⌂*In-room: no a/c. In-hotel: 3 restaurants, bar, tennis court, pool, no elevator, public Internet, public Wi-Fi* ⊟*AE, DC, MC, V.*

¢–$$ 🖭 **Tierra del Volcán.** Ecotourism is the focus at this rustic lodge in the foothills of Rumiñahui Volcano that acquaints you with the *chagra* (Andean cowboy) lifestyle. Most rooms are tiny nooks with straw ceilings and burlap walls and are only big enough to hold two cotlike single beds. Suites have fireplaces and double beds. The hacienda has horses and conducts riding, biking, hiking, trekking, and climbing trips that last from a few hours to seven days. Cotopaxi National Park is 3 miles away. **Pros:** Secluded. **Cons:** Rustic rooms. ⊠*Machachi* ✛*45 mi southeast of Quito* 🕾*02/223–1806* ⊕*www.volcanoland.com* ↩*12 rooms, 2 suites, without bath* ⌂*In-room: no a/c. In-hotel: restaurant, bicycles* ⊟*AE, MC, V* 🍽*BP.*

LATACUNGA

96 km (58 mi) south of Quito.

The capital of Cotopaxi Province, Latacunga has been rebuilt three times in the wake of massive eruptions of Volcán Cotopaxi, whose perfect, snow-covered cone dominates the city skyline. Juniper trees trimmed in an assortment of geometric shapes grace its main plaza, **Parque Vicente León.** But Latacunga's real attractions? A couple of country lodgings well outside of town, as well as an orbit of colorful market villages.

GETTING HERE & AROUND

Latacunga lies just off the Pan-American Highway south of Quito. From Quito's Terminal Terrestre, buses leave frequently for Latacunga (2 hours). The cost is about $5. Frequent local buses connect Latacunga with Pujilí, Saquisilí, and San Miguel de Salcedo, all accessed by rough roads. Taxis charge $10–$15 for a one-way trip to each.

ESSENTIALS

Currency Exchange **Banco Pichincha** (⊠ *Quito 7195* ☎ *03/281–0304*).

WHERE TO STAY

The region has several hosterías with comfortable rooms. These former haciendas are found outside the towns and villages, so count on country solitude.

¢ ⊞ **The Black Sheep Inn.** It's not easy to get here, but you'll find this ★ place—an ecohostel—is one of the nicest in Ecuador. Prices include vegetarian dinners, farm-fresh breakfasts, tea and coffee all day, purified drinking water, hiking maps, and hot showers. Most rooms have a woodstove fireplace. Dinner is family style. Also available are lunches, home-baked desserts, Chilean wines, cold beer, a full bar, and European-style cheeses. Perched on a hillside outside the village of Chugchilan in Cotopaxi Province, this hostel is five hours southwest of Quito. You can get here by bus, jeep, or taxi. The American owners, Andres Hammerman and Michelle Kirby, will help you make arrangements. **Pros:** Environmentally conscious staff. **Cons:** Rough road to get here, chilly at night. ⊠ *Box 05-01-240, Chugchilan, Cotopaxi* ☎ *03/281–4587* ⊕ *www.blacksheepinn.com* ↪ *9 rooms, 1 bunkhouse* ⅗ *In-room: no a/c. In-hotel: restaurant, bicycles, no elevator* ☰ *No credit cards* ¶⊙¶ *MAP*.

$$$$ ⊞ **Hacienda San Agustín de Callo.** This place has been inhabited for more ★ than five centuries—it began as an Inca fortress and was transformed into an Augustinian monastery after the Spanish conquest. It now belongs to an Ecuadoran family. Two original Inca structures are used as a chapel and a dining room. The hotel is a few miles from Parque Nacional Cotopaxi, where you have access to horseback riding, trout fishing, mountain biking, and trekking. **Pros:** Good restaurant, historic atmosphere. **Cons:** Chilly at night. ⊠ *San Agustín, 5 km (3 mi) from Parque Nacional Cotopaxi* ☎ *03/271–9160, 02/290–6157 in Quito* ⊕ *www.incahacienda.com* ↪ *4 rooms, 2 suites* ⅗ *In-room: no a/c. In-hotel: restaurant, bicycles* ☰ *MC, V* ¶⊙¶ *MAP*.

SHOPPING

Latacunga has its own weekly market, but the highlight of any stay here is really a visit to one of the surrounding market villages.

At the Saturday market held on Latacunga's **Plaza San Sebastián** most of the goods for sale are geared to the locals—fruits, vegetables, and medicinal herbs. Pick up one of the *shigras*, the colorful, handwoven hemp bags used by indigenous people.

In the tiny mountain village of **Pujilí**, 10 km (6 mi) west of Latacunga, colorful markets are held on Sunday and, with much less ado, on Wednesday. Few tourists find their way here, so instead of gringos in T-shirts you'll see locals in bright turquoise or carmine ponchos and miniature fedoras buying and selling produce, pottery, and costume jewelry.

In **Saquisilí**, 13 km (8 mi) northwest of Latacunga, indigenous people in regional dress fill all eight of the village's dusty plazas during the Thursday market, where you can pick through piles of traditional wares—including painted wooden masks of animals and devils.

The market town of **San Miguel de Salcedo,** 14 km (9 mi) south of Latacunga, has pleasant streets and plazas that make it appealing on any day. However, it's most interesting to plan your visit around the Sunday market or the smaller one held on Thursday.

BAÑOS

84 km (53 mi) southeast of Latacunga.

At the base of Volcán Tungurahua and surrounded by heavily forested mountains, tumbling waterfalls, and natural hot springs, Baños is one of Ecuador's top tourist spots. Quiteños have been soaking in the thermal springs for decades. The town's real appeal—as tour operators will attest—are the abundant hiking trails, white-water rafting trips, and horseback excursions in the surrounding highlands, making it the country's outdoor-adventure center.

GETTING HERE & AROUND
Baños lies east of Ambato on the road to Puyo. From Quito's Terminal Terrestre, frequent buses leave for Baños (3½ hours). The fare is $5. The high concentration of tourists means the route is notorious for theft. Watch your things like a hawk (or an Andean condor). Taxi drivers charge around $100 for a trip from Quito. Remember that you must pay the driver's return fare, too.

SAFETY & PRECAUTIONS
For years, the U.S. State Department has issued advisories against overnighting in Baños due to the proximity of the Tungurahua volcano. The mountain—the name is Quichua for "throat of fire"—has been in constant activity since 1999, with major eruptions in 2006 and 2008. Baños itself has not been affected, in spite of impressions painted by the international media. City authorities do have well-rehearsed evacuation plans in place just in case.

ESSENTIALS
Currency Exchange Banco Pichincha (⊠*Ambato at Thomas Alfantes* ☎*03/ 274–0961).*

EXPLORING BAÑOS
In the heart of town, the twin spires of **La Iglesia de la Virgen del Agua Santa** *(Church of the Virgin of the Holy Water)* rise above the tree-lined plaza. The church, whose black-and-white facade is slightly startling, was built to honor Baños's miracle-working patron saint. The huge paintings inside are testimonials from her many exultant beneficiaries.

A few blocks from the church is the small but interesting **Museo Huillancuna** (⊠*Pasaje Velasco Ibarra and Av. Montalvo* ☎*03/274–0973),* a museum that has exhibits about pre-Columbian ceramics, Andean musical instruments, and local history.

Baños is Spanish for "baths," and there are several thermal springs in town. The town's official name is Baños de Agua Santa (Baths of the Holy Water), but no miracles have ever been attributed to the springs. The best of the bunch is a series of pools called **El Salado** *(the Salty One)*. Its six rough-hewn pools, next to a fastmoving stream, overflow with mineral water of various temperatures. The pools are refilled each morning at dawn. ✉ *2 km (1 mi) outside Baños on Vía al Salado* 🖭 *$2* ⊘ *Daily dawn–dusk.*

WHERE TO EAT

¢ ✕**El Higuerón.** Hidden behind bougainvillea and flowering vines, this
CAFE small restaurant serves tasty salads, sandwiches, and pastas. Dine at wooden tables beside sunny windows or head outside to one of the inviting tables on the patio. The owner, William Navarette, is among the region's most knowledgeable mountaineers. ✉ *12 de Noviembre 270* ☎ *03/274-0910* ▭ *MC, V* ⊘ *Closed Wed.*

WHERE TO STAY

$$ 🏠**Hostería Monte Selva.** This quartet of three-room bungalows is nestled on a lush hillside at the edge of town. Each room has several beds and a small bath. Many have views of the town. At the foot of the hill are a swimming pool, a sauna, and a lovely little restaurant. **Pros:** Good location. **Cons:** Rustic rooms. ✉ *Halflants, near Montalvo* ☎ *274-0244* ⊕ *www.monteselvaecuador.com* ⬢ *25 rooms, 3 suites* ⌂ *In-room: no a/c, safe. In-hotel: 2 restaurants, bar, pool, spa, no elevator, laundry service* ▭ *DC, MC, V* ⦿ *BP.*

$$$$ 🏠**Luna Runtún.** Perched high over Baños on the slopes of Volcán Tungurahua, Swiss-run Luna Runtún combines colonial-style architecture with the attention to detail you would expect from a European resort. On your pillow will be fresh flowers carefully selected from the gardens outside. Hike along a route used by rum smugglers in the 1920s, ride horses through the nearby countryside, or join a trip to the hot springs. **Pros:** Secluded, attentive service. **Cons:** Chilly at night. ✉ *6 km (4 mi) from Baños* ☎ *03/274-0882* ⊕ *www.lunaruntun.com* ⬢ *30 rooms, 2 suites* ⌂ *In-room: no a/c, safe. In-hotel: 2 restaurants, bar, spa, no elevator, public Internet* ▭ *AE, DC, MC, V* ⦿ *MAP.*

¢ 🏠**Le Petit Auberge and Restaurant.** After establishing a reputation as one of this town's best restaurants, this place expanded to include inexpensive rooms. All have hardwood floors, white stucco walls, and balconies. Many are warmed by wood-burning fireplaces. The restaurant serves French cuisine, with a menu that includes crepes, ratatouille, and delicious fondues. **Pros:** Good restaurant, great views. **Cons:** Chilly at night. ✉ *Av. 16 de Diciembre at Montalvo* ☎ *03/274-0936* ⬢ *12 rooms* ⌂ *In-room: no a/c, no phone. In-hotel: restaurant, bar* ▭ *AE, DC, MC, V* ⊘ *Restaurant closed Mon.*

¢–$ 🏠**Sangay Spa Hotel.** This family-oriented hotel across the street from the municipal baths has large cabañas behind the pool and spacious rooms with balconies overlooking the nearby Waterfall of the Virgin. From the second-floor restaurant you'll also get nice views. **Pros:**

Helpful staff, good value. **Cons:** Rustic rooms, crowded on weekends. ⊠*Plazoleta Ayora 101* ☎*03/274–0490* ⊕*www.sangayspahotel.com* ↩*63 rooms* ⌂*In-room: no a/c. In-hotel: restaurant, room service, bar, tennis court, pool, laundry service, public Internet* ⊟*AE, DC, MC, V* ⧖*BP.*

SHOPPING

In Baños you'll find plenty of shopping. Most items come from other parts of Ecuador, but there are a few interesting local crafts that can be purchased from the actual craftspeople. Look for hand-carved toucans, turtles, and other tropical creatures. **Recuerdos** (⊠*Maldonado, near Montalvo*) sells balsa-wood carvings of parrots and other birds made in a workshop behind the store. **El Cade** (⊠*Maldonado 681*) sells items carved from the seed of the tagua palm, a hard substance also known as vegetal ivory.

SPORTS & THE OUTDOORS

White-water rafting trips on the Class III Patate, apt for beginners, and the more challenging Class IV Pastaza rivers are the reason many people head to Baños. Cycling fans won't be able to resist the five-hour, 65-km (40-mi) downhill ride from Baños to Puyo. At the bottom you can board a bus, bike and all, for the return trip to Baños. And at least a dozen tour operators offer excellent horseback riding as day trips or overnight excursions.

BICYCLING

Wonderful Ecuador (⊠*Maldonado and Oriente* ☎*03/274–0637*) organizes bicycle tours through the highlands and canoeing expeditions through the jungle.Mountain bikes can be rented at affordable rates at **Bill Mountain** (⊠*Ambato at Maldonado* ☎*03/274–0221*), which also offers cycling tours that wind through subtropical forest and past thundering waterfalls.

HORSEBACK RIDING

Caballos con José (⊠*Maldonado, near Martínez* ☎*03/274–0929*) is a reliable company that offers tours lasting from two hours to several nights. **Huillacuna Tours** (⊠*Santa Clara 206* ☎*03/274–0187*) schedules half- and full-day tours to Runtún. **Río Loco** (⊠*Maldonado and Martínez* ☎*03/274–0929*) offers a variety of excursions outside Baños.

RAFTING

Remote Odysseys Worldwide (⊠*Foch 721, at Juan León Mera, Quito* ☎*02/270–3535* ⊕*www.rowinc.com*) organizes Class III and Class IV white-water trips on the Rió Upano, including side trips to Shuar villages in the Amazon and camping out in Morona-Santiago Province.

RIOBAMBA

105 km (63 mi) south of Latacunga.

Three of Ecuador's most formidable peaks—Chimborazo, Altar, and Tungurahua—are visible from Riobamba, a pleasant town with wide, tree-lined streets and some well-preserved colonial architecture.

Most travelers head to Riobamba because it's the starting point for the famous Devil's Nose train trip. Mudslides have destroyed large sections of the Trans-Andean Railroad, which once ran all the way from Quito to Durán. Plans are underway to rehabilitate the tracks and expand regional rail service once again.

There are good buys at the tourist-oriented Saturday market held in the **Parque de la Concepción** (⊠ *Orozco at Colón*). Look for embroidered belts, hand-knit sweaters, and locally produced jewelry.

> ## MOVE OVER, EVEREST
>
> Locals are fond of identifying Chimborazo as the true world's highest peak, as the planet bulges more at the equator, putting the mountain's summit at a greater distance from the center of the earth than any other point. If you can't visit this part of the country, you can still see Chimborazo, whose name aptly means "throne of ice." portrayed in the coat of arms on Ecuador's flag.

GETTING HERE & AROUND

Riobamba is nestled along the Pan-American Highway 188 km (117 mi) south of Quito. From Quito's Terminal Terrestre, buses leave frequently for Riobamba (4 hours). The fare is about $5. Once in town, you can head to the Riobamba branch of iTur, which is open Monday–Saturday 8:30–5.

ESSENTIALS

Currency Exchange **Banco Pichincha** (⊠ *Primera Constituyente at García Moreno* ☎ *03/296–7416*).

Visitor Info **iTur** (⊠ *Av. Daniel León Borja at Pje. Municipal* ☎ *03/294–1213*).

EXPLORING RIOBAMBA

Across the street from Parque de la Concepción, the **Museo de Arte Religioso** (⊠ *Argentina* ☎ *03/295–2212*) is housed in the beautifully restored Iglesia de la Concepción. The Religious Art Museum has an impressive collection of artifacts from the colonial period.

The hill in the center of the **Parque 21 de Abril** (⊠ *Argentina*) affords an excellent view of the city. On clear days you'll have eye-popping views of several snowcapped volcanoes. The mural here depicts the city's history.

WHERE TO STAY

$ 🏨 **Hacienda Abraspungo.** Reminiscent of a mountain lodge, this place is among the most practical accommodations in the Central Highlands. Each of the clean, comfortable rooms is named after a different mountain peak; several rooms overlook the surrounding hills. Horses, stabled on-site, are available for day treks. The owner, mountaineer Marco Cruz, knows the best hikes in the region. **Pros:** Good budget value, seclusion. **Cons:** Chilly at night. ⊠ *3½ km (2 mi) from Riobamba* ☎ *03/294–0820* ⊕ *www.abraspungo.com.ec* 🛏 *26 rooms, 5 suites* ⚒ *In-room: no a/c, no phone. In-hotel: restaurant, bar, laundry service* ⊟ *AE, DC, MC, V.*

¢ **Hostal Montecarlo.** This century-old house, with its fern-filled central courtyard, is conveniently located in the middle of town. Its elegant yet homey restaurant, around the corner from the hotel, is first-rate. **Pros:** Good budget value, friendly staff. **Cons:** Dark rooms. ⊠*Av. 10 de Agosto 2541* ☎*03/295–3204* ↪*20 rooms* ⊕*www.hotelmonte carlo-riobamba.com* ♿*In-room: no a/c. In-hotel: 2 restaurants, bar, no elevator, public Internet* ⊟*MC, V* ⦿*CP.*

¢ **Hostería El Troje.** This place just outside Riobamba welcomes you back to your spacious room with a crackling fire in the hearth. When there are enough guests, the hotel puts on a show with folk music and dancing before dinner. The owner is one of the most famous mountain climbers in Ecuador. **Pros:** Friendly staff, cozy, good value. **Cons:** Chilly at night. ⊠*4½ km (3 mi) southeast of Riobamba* ☎*03/296–0826* ⊕*www.eltroje.com* ↪*48 rooms* ♿*In-hotel: restaurant, room service, bar, pool, laundry service, public Internet* ⊟*AE, DC, MC, V.*

SPORTS & THE OUTDOORS

Storms and mudslides have put onetime train travel to and from Quito out of business, although plans are afoot to rehabilitate track in this region. Fortunately, the section still intact includes the exhilarating "Devil's Nose," operated by Metropolitan Touring as a combination bus and train trip starting at Riobamba.

Metropolitan Touring (⊠*Av. República de El Salvador 970, Quito* ☎*02/246–4780, 800/527–2500 in North America* ⊕*www.metropoli tan-touring.com*) operates a combination bus and train trip, usually running Tuesday, Thursday, and Saturday,

CUENCA & THE SOUTHERN HIGHLANDS

The less-visited Southern Highlands deserve a more prominent spot on travel itineraries. Cuenca, Ecuador's third largest city, with a collection of colonial architecture that comes close to rivaling Quito's, serves as the gateway to this region. Indigenous ruins in the vicinity are a reminder that Cuenca was the second largest city in the Inca empire, surpassed only by Cusco, in Peru.

CUENCA

442 km (265 mi) and 45 minutes by air south of Quito, 250 km (150 mi) and 35 minutes by air southeast of Guayaquil.

If you've just arrived from Quito or Guayaquil, you might not believe that Cuenca is Ecuador's third-largest city. It hustles and bustles, but with a certain provincial charm. This prosperous and beautiful highland city has retained much of its colonial splendor, and, like Quito's, its city center has been declared a UNESCO World Heritage Site. No building, for example, is allowed to be higher than the highest church steeple, and along its cobblestone streets you'll find colonial mansions with wrought-iron balconies overflowing with potted plants. Here you'll still find old men gossiping in the shady squares and women dry-ing laundry on the grass along the river banks, and on market days—Thursday and Sunday—hundreds of people from surrounding villages crowd into Cuenca's open-air plazas to buy and sell crafts and household items. But despite all that, Cuenca is one of the most advanced cities in Ecuador—it's one of the few cities in Latin America with a controlled water and sewer system.

Cuenca produces fine ceramics and textiles, but is best known for its handsome Panama hats. The *cholas Cuencanas*—female descendants of mixed Spanish and Cañari couples—are striking in their colorful *polleras* (gathered wool skirts in violet, emerald, rose, or marigold), satiny white blouses, and fine straw hats.

GETTING HERE & AROUND

Cuenca's Aeropuerto Mariscal Lamar (CUE), undergoing extensive renovation at this writing, is 2 km (1 mi) from the city center, past the bus terminal. A taxi from the airport to downtown costs around $2. Tame and Ícaro connect Cuenca with Quito and Guayaquil; AeroGal, with Quito.

Cuenca is 442 km (265 mi) south of Quito via the Pan-American Highway, a drive that takes eight hours. Plan on four hours from Guayaquil. The former drive takes you along the Avenue of the Volcanoes, while the latter climbs through subtropical lowlands before beginning a dizzying mountain ascent—8,300 feet in slightly more than 240 km (150 mi). Road conditions between Guayaquil and Cuenca are much better than from Quito. Flying is the better option.

From Cuenca's Terminal Terrestre, 1½ km (½ mi) northeast of the town center, there are daily departures for Quito (9 hours) and Guayaquil (5 hours), both less than $7. Taxis are easy to find on the streets of downtown Cuenca. A trip almost anywhere in town should cost less than $2. A helpful branch of iTur, the national tourist office, sits on the south side of the main square. It's open weekdays 8–8 and Saturday 9–3.

ESSENTIALS

Airport Contact **Aeropuerto Mariscal Lamar** (⊠ *Av. España* ☎ *07/286–2203*).

Bus Contacts **Terminal Terrestre** (⊠ *Av. España* ☎ *07/282–7061*).

Currency Exchange **Banco Pichincha** (⊠ *Gran Colombia at Benigno Malo*).

Medical Assistance **Name Hospital Monte Sinai** (⊠ *Cordero at Av. Solano* ☎ *07/288–5595* ⊕ *www.hospitalmontesinai.org*).

Post Office **Correos de Ecuador** (⊠ *Presidente Correro and Av. Gran Colombia*).

Rental Cars **Hertz** (☎ *07/286–9420*). **Localiza** (☎ *07/280–3198*).

Visitor & Tour Info **iTur** (⊠ *Sucre, between Hermano Miguel and Cordero* ☎ *07/282–1035*).

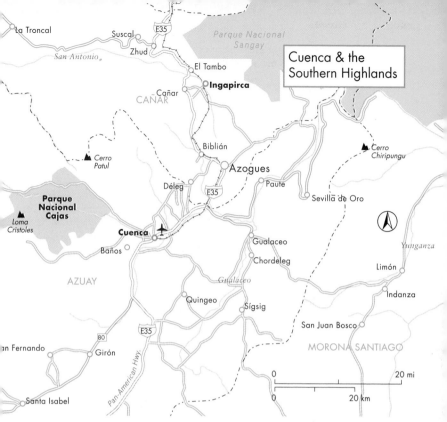

EXPLORING CUENCA

MAIN ATTRACTIONS

2 ★ Catedral de la Inmaculada. Started in 1886 and finished more than 80 years later, the immense cathedral can hold more than 9,000 worshippers. The interior arches tower more than 100 feet high, and light that enters through the stained-glass windows casts a golden glow over the thick brick walls and Italian marble floors. The impressive pillars are Ecuadoran marble, and the choir chairs are hand-carved from native wood. ⊠ *Parque Abdón Calderón* ☎ 07/284–2097 ☉ *Daily 6:30–4:30.*

4 Museo Catedral Vieja. Also called El Sagrario, this lovely church was begun in 1557, the year the city was founded, and served as the headquarters of its archdiocese until a new cathedral on the opposite side of the park was completed in the 1960s. The whitewashed outside gleams after a complete restoration; the inside serves as a museum of religious art. ⊠ *Sucre at Luis Cordero* ☎ 04/283–4636 ☜ *$2* ☉ *Weekdays 9–1 and 2–6, weekends 10–1.*

5 Museo del Monasterio de la Concepción. Cuenca's wealthy Ordóñez family
FodorśChoice donated its spacious home to the Catholic Church in 1599, whereupon
★ it became the cloistered convent of the Order of the Immaculate Concep-

tion, or the Conceptas. Four centuries later, part of this well-preserved edifice houses the Museum of the Monastery of the Conception, which contains an impressive collection of religious art from the 16th to the 19th centuries. This is a must-see stop for an understanding of colonial art, all of which focused on religion, and none of which was ever signed by the artist. (Most pieces here are labeled ANÓNIMO.) The well-informed guides—take a tour conducted in Spanish, English, or French—explain that service to God was deemed more important than any artistic recognition. (That didn't stop some artists from incorporating their own faces in their works.) Most of the collection was contributed by families whose daughters entered the convent. Half the building is still inaccessible, the cloistered nuns emerging only after closing to clean the museum. No one except the museum director has face-to-face contact with them. ⊠*Hermano Miguel 6–33, between Juan Jaramillo and Presidente Córdova* ☎*07/283-0625* ⊕*wwwmuseodelasconceptasorg. ec* ☜*$2.50* ☉ *Weekdays 9–6:30, Sat. 10–1.*

❶ Parque Abdón Calderón. Surrounded by beautiful colonial buildings, Cuenca's central square is one of the loveliest in South America. Manicured trees tower over men discussing politics, grandmothers walking arm in arm, and children running to and fro. The park is dominated by the pale rose Catedral de la Inmaculada towering over its western edge.

IF YOU HAVE TIME

❸ Carmen de la Asunción. The ornate carvings surrounding the doorway of this diminutive chapel are a good example of Spanish baroque design. The interior is typically ostentatious—especially noteworthy is the gilded pulpit encrusted with tiny mirrors. Alas, the church keeps very irregular hours and may not be open when you pass by. ⊠*Mariscal Sucre at Padre Aguirre.*

❼ Iglesia de San Francisco. Built in the 1920s, the Church of St. Francis is famous for its soaring steeple and intricately carved, gold-drenched main altar, which contrasts nicely with its unassuming interior. The church keeps very limited hours. ⊠*Av. Gran Colombia at Padre Aguirre* ☉*Mon.–Wed. 7:30–8:15, Thurs.–Sat. 6:30–7:15, Sun. 7:30–9:30 and 4–5.*

❽ Museo de Arte Moderno. The Museum of Modern Art, housed in a restored convent, features interesting rotating exhibitions of works by Ecuadoran and other Latin American artists. ⊠*Sucre 1578, at Coronel Talbot* ☎*07/283-1027* ☜*Free* ☉ *Weekdays 8:30–1 and 3–6:30, weekends 9–1.*

❻ Plaza de San Francisco. The noisy plaza is filled with vendors hawking a variety of bric-a-brac. Under the northern colonnade, merchants sell more enticing wares—colorful skirts, hand-knit sweaters, and intricate hangings.

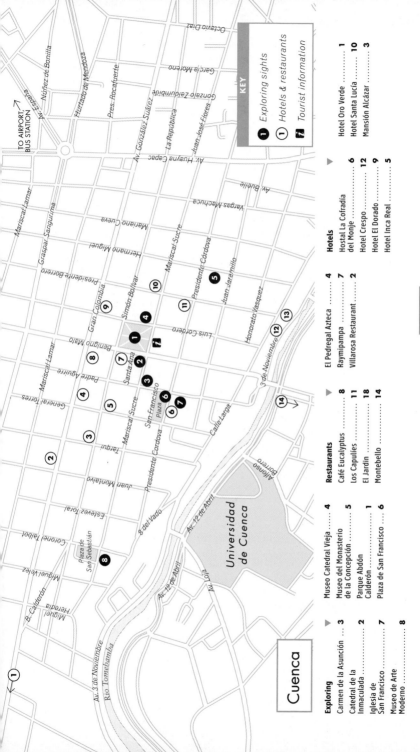

Cuenca

KEY

- ① *Exploring sights*
- ① *Hotels & restaurants*
- 🛈 *Tourist information*

Exploring ▶

Carmen de la Asunción	**3**
Catedral de la Inmaculada	**2**
Iglesia de San Francisco	**7**
Museo de Arte Moderno	**8**
Museo Catedral Vieja	**4**
Museo del Monasterio de la Concepción	**5**
Parque Abdón Calderón	**1**
Plaza de San Francisco	**6**

Restaurants ▶

Café Eucalyptus	**8**
Los Capulíes	**11**
El Jardín	**18**
Montebello	**14**
El Pedregal Azteca	**4**
Raymipampa	**7**
Villarosa Restaurant	**2**

Hotels ▶

Hostal La Cofradía del Monje	**6**
Hotel Crespo	**12**
Hotel El Dorado	**9**
Hotel Inca Real	**5**
Hotel Oro Verde	**1**
Hotel Santa Lucía	**10**
Mansión Alcázar	**3**

6

WHERE TO EAT

ECLECTIC

FodorsChoice

★

✕**Café Eucalyptus.** Quite possibly Ecuador's liveliest restaurant is this downtown, two-floor, all-tapas place. Mix and match to assemble your meal from an astounding selection of appetizers. (Sushi and sashimi are on the menu too.) Eucalyptus also claims to have the country's largest selection of wines and liquors, and we've never seen any evidence to the contrary. Cuenca's U.S. expat community, a 40-, 50-, 60-something crowd, moves the tables together and holds court here Friday evenings. Stop by and say hello. ⊠*Gran Colombia 941, at Benjamín Malo* ☎*07/284–9157* ▤*AE, DC, MC, V* ⊘*No lunch Oct.–Apr.*

> ## TO MARKET, TO MARKET
>
> The flower market, held outside on the Plazoleta El Carmen, is in full bloom every day from sunrise to sunset.

¢

LATIN

AMERICAN

★

✕**Los Capulíes.** This restaurant in a 200-year-old mansion has greenery and fountains. Start with a delicately sweetened empanada, followed by the *plato típico cuencano,* a sampler dish of llapingachos, grilled pork, sweet sausages, and *mote pillo* (boiled corn mixed with onions and eggs). End your meal with a warm glass of *canelazo* (a concoction combining sugarcane, cinnamon, and bitter orange with the rumlike *zhumir*). The music of Andean flutes echoes in the air on weekends, and a bar in an attached building is a favorite hangout. ⊠*Borrero 727* ☎*07/284–5887* ▤*AE, DC, MC, V* ⊘*Closed Sun.*

¢–$

LATIN

AMERICAN

✕**El Jardín.** Hand-painted menus list a variety of steak and seafood dishes. Start with the tangy conch seviche served in a crystal goblet, and then move on to the succulent grilled lobster. Consider a fine Chilean wine with your meal. The relaxed, friendly service here ensures many repeat visitors. ⊠*Larga at Borrero* ☎*07/283–1120* ▤*AE, DC, MC, V* ⊘*Closed Sun. and Mon.*

¢

MEXICAN

✕**El Pedregal Azteca.** If you're tired of the local cuisine, you couldn't do better than stopping in this Mexican eatery. Try the chiles rellenos (deep-fried chili peppers stuffed with cheese) or the specialty of the house, carne asada *a la tampiqueña* (beef grilled with salt and lemon). On weekends there's live music and two-for-one margaritas. ⊠*Av. Gran Colombia 1029, at Padre Aguirre* ☎*07/282–3652* ▤*DC, MC, V* ⊘*Closed Sun.*

¢

LATIN

AMERICAN

✕**Raymipampa.** An unbeatable location adjacent to the Catedral de la Inmaculada doesn't hurt, but it's the reasonably priced food and amiable mood that makes this busy, bilevel restaurant a hit. The extensive menu includes crepes and seviche, and such Ecuadoran favorites as *locro de queso* (a milk-based potato soup garnished with avocado and cheese). ⊠*Benigno Malo 859, at Sucre* ☎*07/283–4159* ▤*MC, V.*

¢

ECLECTIC

FodorsChoice

★

✕**Villarosa Restaurant.** One of the city's best restaurants and a favorite with locals is in a colonial house near the central plaza. Soft music floats through several tastefully decorated salons to the upper balcony, where an open fireplace chases out the evening chill. Try the grilled trout with almonds, then finish with the fruit-and-chocolate fondue. The same family owns the Hotel Santa Lucía. ⊠*Av. Gran Colombia 1222* ☎*07/283–7944* ▤*AE, DC, MC, V* ⊘*Closed weekends.*

WHERE TO STAY

¢ **Hostal La Cofradía del Monje.** Here's a charming little bargain-priced hotel that sits on the Plaza San Francisco. Its seven upstairs rooms overlook a lively little café that serves *típico* Ecuadoran food. Each room contains hardwood floors and stone walls, and most have a little colonial wrought-iron balcony opening to the outside. Most of these overlook the bustling market on the plaza, but the commotion calms down at 6 PM each day. **Pros:** Friendly staff, good budget value. **Cons:** Some noise from retaurant. ⊠*Presidente Córdova 1033, at Padre Aguirre* ☎*07/283–1251* ⊕*www.cofradiadelmonje.com* ⊅*7 rooms* ⚐*In-room: no a/c. In-hotel: restaurant, bar, no elevator* ⊟*MC, V* ⏃*BP.*

$$ **Hotel Crespo.** This hotel overlooking the Río Tomebamba gives you the feeling of staying in a rambling country house. You climb a twisting wooden stairway to the upper rooms, which have lovely views of the river. Scattered about are numerous sitting areas that add to the familiar, homey atmosphere. The restaurant serves excellent French cuisine. **Pros:** Good views, friendly staff. **Cons:** Dark rooms. ⊠*Larga 7–93, at Cordero* ☎*07/284–2571* ⊕*www.hotelcrespo.com* ⊅*39 rooms, 3 suites* ⚐*In-room: no a/c, refrigerator. In-hotel: restaurant, room service, bar, no elevator, laundry service, airport shuttle, public Internet* ⊟*AE, DC, MC, V.*

$$–$$$ **Hotel El Dorado.** Convenient to most of the city's sights, this thoroughly modern eight-story hotel sits just two blocks from Parque Calderón. Rooms at the back of the hotel are quieter than those on the street side. Enjoy a meal at the Inti Sumag restaurant or the Chordeleg Café, or relax with a cocktail at the Samana piano bar. Buffet breakfast and airport transfers are included in the rate. One room is set for wheelchair access. **Pros:** Many business amenities, friendly staff. **Cons:** Some street noise in front rooms. ⊠*Av. Gran Colombia 787, at Luis Cordero* ☎*07/283–1390, 888/790–5264 in North America* ⊕*www.eldoradohotel.com.ec* ⊅*41 rooms, 1 suite* ⚐*In-room: refrigerator, Ethernet, Wi-Fi. In-hotel: restaurant, bar, gym, spa, airport shuttle, public Internet, no-smoking rooms* ⊟*AE, DC, MC, V* ⏃*BP.*

¢ **Hotel Inca Real.** Huddled around three covered courtyards, this sunny hotel is small, but has neat and cheerfully furnished rooms, original art, and unique lighting fixtures. **Pros:** Friendly staff, good budget value. **Cons:** Small rooms. ⊠*General Torres 840, between Sucre and Bolívar* ☎*07/282–3636* ✐*incareal@cue.satnet.net* ⊅*25 rooms* ⚐*In-hotel: 2 restaurants, bar* ⊟*AE, DC, MC, V.*

$$–$$$ **Hotel Oro Verde.** This low-rise hotel has a relaxed, casual environment and feels like a resort in the city. This is the place for animal lovers: three resident alpacas munch on the grassy banks, and peacocks stroll through bushes heavy with pink and yellow roses. It's 2 km (1 mi) from the center of town, so take a taxi unless you're up for a 45-minute walk. The restaurant is famous for its fish—try the trout marinated in brandy. **Pros:** Spacious rooms, many amenities. **Cons:** Far from city center. ⊠*Av. Ordóñez Lazo* ☎*07/283–1200, 800/676–8373 in North America* ⊕*www.oroverdehotels.com* ⊅*74 rooms, 3 suites* ⚐*In-room: refrigerator, safe, Wi-Fi. In-hotel: 2 restaurants, room ser-*

Fodor's Choice ★

6

vice, bar, pool, gym, laundry service, public Internet, airport shuttle
⊟*AE, DC, MC, V.*

$$ ⊞ **Hotel Santa Lucía.** In a beautifully restored building, Santa Lucía has attractive rooms, though its style is more modern than the building itself. Built by the first governor of the Azuay (Cuenca) Province in 1859, it has been in the Vintimilla family for three generations, and is in the center of the historic district. The family decided not to remove a large tree that was growing right in the middle of the courtyard. An American breakfast is included. The restaurant (¢–$$) has excellent service and food: choices include sea bass in marinara sauce with assorted seafood; chicken in a lemon-herb sauce; and a number of risottos and gnocchis. **Pros:** Friendly staff, historic atmosphere. **Cons:** Some noise from courtyard restaurant. ⊠*Antonio Borrero 844, at Sucre* ☎*07/282–8000* ⊕*www.santaluciahotel.com* ⇆*20 rooms* ♿*In-room: safe. In-hotel: restaurant* ⊟*AE, MC, V.*

$$–$$$ ⊞ **Mansión Alcázar.** Fluffy down comforters top beds—some of them
Fodor'sChoice   canopied—in rooms with filmy curtains covering windows that look
★   onto an indoor courtyard with a trickling fountain. A hot water bottle slipped under your covers warms your bed at night. Crystal chandeliers, antique furniture, and art give you the feeling of what life was like more than 100 years ago in this carefully preserved 1891 mansion two blocks from the central plaza. Most rooms have only showers instead of full baths. A couple of rooms have windows looking onto a lovely garden. **Pros:** Sumptuous furnishings, historic atmosphere. **Cons:** Dark interior rooms. ⊠*Bolívar 12–55, at Tarqui* ☎*07/282–3918, 800/327–3573 in North America* ⊕*www.mansionalcazar.com* ⇆*10 rooms, 4 suites* ♿*In-room: Wi-Fi. In-hotel: restaurant, bar, no elevator* ⊟*AE, DC, MC, V* ⦿*BP, MAP.*

AFTER DARK

Cuenca doesn't have a vivid nightlife. Locals usually stay home during the week, venturing forth mostly on weekends. A good source for information on arts events is the daily newspaper *El Mercurio.* Listings are in Spanish, but are easy to decipher. **La Cantina** (⊠*Presidente Borrero at Córdova* ☎*07/283–2339*) is an attractive little bar next to Los Capulíes. Musicians play on weekends. German-owned **Wunderbar** (⊠*Hermano Miguel at Larga* ☎*07/283–1274*) is an intimate bar popular with locals. It's in an old building along the Escalinata, the wide stairway leading down to the river. For dancing, check out **El Conquistador** (⊠*Av. Gran Colombia 665* ☎*07/283–1788*).

THE ARTS

Plays are sometimes performed at **La Casa de la Cultura** (⊠*Luis Cordero 718* ☎*07/282–8175*).

SHOPPING

Panama hats did not originate here, but Cuenca has become the community most associated with their manufacture. Cuenca's artisans produce fine ceramics, textiles, and silver and gold jewelry, too. On a tour of **Homero Ortega & Hijos,** arguably Ecuador's best-known purveyor of Panama hats, you'll see how palm-leaf fibers are transformed into elegant headware. You'll also have the opportunity to buy one for as little as $20 up to $250. ⊠*Av. Gil Ramírez Davalos 3–86* ☎*07/280–9000* ⊕*www.homeroortgega.com* ☉ *Weekdays 9–5, Sat. 9–noon.*

If you're in the market for leather, **Concuero** (⊠*Mariscal Lamar 1137*) sells good-quality shoes, wallets, and handbags. **Fundación Jorge Moscoso** (⊠*Presidente Córdova 614*) has a limited but precious collection of antiques. **Kinara** (⊠*Mariscal Sucre 770*) stocks stylish gold and silver jewelry and shawls made of traditional ikat textiles, in which the threads are knotted and dyed prior to weaving.

Original designs in ceramics, murals, and jewelry are for sale—browsers are welcome—at **Eduardo Vega's Workshop and Gallery.** Vega is Ecuador's most famous ceramicist and designer. The gallery not only sells Vega's beautiful designs, but you'll get a really good cup of coffee here. On El Turi hill, known as the Mirador de Turi, it's also the best spot for a spectacular view of Cuenca. The Galería de Arte 670 has a good selection of Vega designs. ⊠*Hermano Miguel 670* ☉ *Weekdays 9–5, Sat. 9:30–1:30.*

SPORTS & THE OUTDOORS

A contingent of Cuenca-based tour operators offer organized excursions to points of interest in the region, namely Ingapirca and Parque Nacional Cajas. **Gray Line** (☎*800/472–964 toll-free in Ecuador* ⊕*www.graylineecuador.com*) maintains a branch in Cuenca for all manner of city tours and area excursions. The highly regarded **Metropolitan Touring** (⊠*Mariscal Sucre 662* ☎*07/283–1185*) is a branch of the well-known tour operator in Quito, and can arrange area excursions.

INGAPIRCA

Fodor$Choice

★ *70 km (42 mi) north of Cuenca.*

Long before the Inca invaded the region, in the latter half of the 15th century, the fierce and industrious Cañari people ruled Guapdondélig (Plain as Wide and Beautiful as the Sky), the name they gave the fertile highlands surrounding Cuenca. They built some stunning monuments, including the ancient city of Ingapirca.

An important religious and political center for the Cañari, Ingapirca is perhaps better remembered for what the Inca built here after Tupac-Yupanqui conquered the Cañari. The king left behind quite a legacy, including the name, which means "Wall of the Inca." The smaller stone structures, built completely without mortar, are thought to be Cañari temples to the moon, but the massive elliptical structure at the center is an acknowledged temple to the sun built by the Inca. La Cara del Inca, a natural rock formation said to resemble the face of an Inca chief, is a 10-minute hike.

There is a small museum at the entrance, built under the auspices of the Banco Central, which houses artifacts found at the ruins. The cozy restaurant on the hill overlooking the site serves excellent soups and local dishes in front of a fireplace. Getting to the ruins is half the fun. Buses costing less than $2 depart from Cuenca's Terminal Terrestre at

CLOSE UP

Panama Hats Don't Come from Panama

Blame it on Teddy Roosevelt, but Ecuador's signature souvenir bears another country's name. Among Ecuador's most important products is the Panama hat, whose name sticks in the collective craw of proud Ecuadorans. These finely made straw hats—also known as *toquillas,* from the type of straw used to weave them—were named for the country to which they were first exported en masse. President Roosevelt wore one when he toured the Panama Canal, as had many of the workers who constructed the canal, so the hats became forever associated with that Central American country.

The first hats were made by hand in the coastal towns of Jipijapa and Montecristi, and served a dual purpose: their brims protected against the tropical sun, and their tight weave created a container that could be used to carry water. The exceptionally fine *superfino* can take up to eight months to make. Their weave is so tight that they can be rolled up and then expanded with nary a crease evident. Queen Elizabeth and Jack Nicholson are but two of the hat's many celebrity fans.

Today the hats are most associated with the city of Cuenca, but plenty of places around the country sell them. These days quality Panama hats proudly bear the label GENUINE PANAMA HAT MADE IN ECUADOR.

9 and 1. On the return trip your bus is likely to be filled with villagers transporting chickens and other livestock to market. The other option is to take a guided tour. Note that you might want to use a restroom before arriving, as those at the site leave much to be desired. ⊠*5 km (3 mi) east of Cañaris* ☎*07/221–5115* ☞*$6* ⊙*Daily 6–6.*

GETTING HERE & AROUND

You can visit Ingapirca on your own. Buses leave Cuenca's Terminal Terrestre twice daily for the nearby town of Cañaris. The one-way fare is $2 for the two-hour journey. An organized tour that includes the services of a guide is a far easier (and far more informative) option.

ESSENTIALS

There are no real facilities out here. Take care of any important tasks back in Cuenca.

WHERE TO STAY & EAT

¢ **Posada de Ingapirca.** To spend more time at Ingapirca, consider a stay at this posada. Rooms are simple and heated only by space heaters and fireplaces. If you want to see the countryside, you can rent horses for $10 a day; for another $10 you can hire a guide, who will lead you along an old Inca trail. Tables congregate around a cozy fireplace in an excellent restaurant that dishes up fine Ecuadoran cuisine. **Pros:** Close to ruins, good value. **Cons:** Rustic rooms. ⊠*3 mi east of Cañaris, 42 mi north of Cuenca* ☎*07/283–1120 in Cuenca* ✉*santaana@etapaon-line.com.ec* ⇆*19 rooms* ♿*In-hotel: restaurant, bar, no elevator* ☰*AE, DC, MC, V* ⊠*BP.*

PARQUE NACIONAL CAJAS

32 km (20 mi) west of Cuenca.

A short drive from the sunny city of Cuenca are the cold, cloudy moors of the publicly owned, privately administered Parque Nacional Cajas, where the average elevation is 10,500 feet. The rugged terrain is the legacy left by glaciers as they retreated some 5 million years ago. Today the nearly 70,000 acres of this national park are home to Andean condors, hawks, and the elusive gray-breasted mountain toucan, as well as wolves, gazelles, and white-tailed deer. The area's 230 trout-filled lakes are accessible by boat, and fishing trips can be arranged through local tour operators and hotels.

Cajas is best explored with an experienced guide, because visitors can easily become disoriented in the stark landscape. A guide will point out the unique páramo vegetation and select the best place to set up camp each evening. Be prepared for strong sun, cold wind, and the possibility of rain. Sunglasses and sunscreen are necessities. There is a ranger station near the entrance where you can sometimes sleep for a small fee, although if the accommodations are full you'll have to make other plans. ⊕*www.cajaspark.com* 🖃*$10.*

EL ORIENTE

Ecuador's slice of the Amazon basin accounts for roughly one-third of the country's landmass but just 4% of its population. One of the world's biodiversity hot spots, El Oriente is home to hundreds of colorful bird species, including macaws, toucans, and prehistoric-looking hoatzins. Jaguars, pumas, and peccaries are elusive, but you're sure to see howler monkeys, spider monkeys, or tamarins. Pink river dolphins are also easy to spot. An abundance of insects thrive under the jungle canopy, including workaholic leaf-cutting ants, society spiders, and enormous blue morpho butterflies. Myriad plant species coexist, and in some cases even cooperate, with the jungle animals. The giant kapok tree, El Oriente's tallest species, soars nearly 200 feet above the jungle floor. Creeping vines cascade from strangler figs, which in turn envelop other species.

In this exuberant world, eight indigenous peoples continue, to varying degrees, to live their traditional lifestyles. One group still lives a nomadic life and repels any attempts at rapprochement by outsiders. Others allow tourist groups to visit and share their tremendous knowledge of plants and animals.

GETTING HERE & AROUND

BY AIR Tame flies from Quito to Coca's Aeropuerto Francisco de Orellana (OCC) and Lago Agrio's Aeropuerto Nueva Loja (LGQ) daily except Sunday, and to Macas's Aeropuerto Edmundo Carvajal (XMS) Monday, Wednesday, and Friday. Ícaro connects Quito with Coca daily and Lago Agrio three times weekly. Each flight is a 40-minute trip. Several small charter companies specialize in jungle towns and other remote destinations; these are considerably more expensive.

BY BUS The trip from Quito to Lago Agrio takes eight hours by bus. Since Lago Agrio is near the Colombian border, it's best to consult a tour operator about safety in this area. The trip from Quito to Coca takes nine hours. A journey from Cuenca to Macas takes 10–12 hours, but the road is frequently impassable, a condition that comes and goes with the weather. Since El Oriente

PLANNING TIP

Trips to El Oriente—especially in areas close to the Colombia border—should be arranged *only* with a tour operator that is familiar with the area and that keeps up with changing conditions. Independent travel to remote jungle areas is dangerous and not recommended.

has no truly dry season, don't count on being able to negotiate this route overland.

BY CAR Car travel to this region should be undertaken only with much caution and advance preparation. Be forewarned, however, that in some areas of El Oriente you will find yourself driving alongside ugly oil pipelines; roads are periodically blocked by environmentalists protesting petroleum exploration. The trip between Quito and Coca takes eight hours. Misahuallí can be reached in 5–5½ hours by car. Since Macas is so remote, and the road sometimes becomes impassable, you shouldn't attempt to drive. No roads pass near Kapawi, making air travel your only option.

ESSENTIALS

Don't count on much out here in the way of facilities. Your travel should take you directly to your lodge and back without passing through any towns. Your lodge stay is likely paid for in advance anyway, although you should bring cash for tips and beverages, which are frequently not included in your package price.

MACAS

246 km (154 mi) northeast of Cuenca.

The pleasant town of Macas is the gateway to the southern Oriente, which is more heavily settled and has less primary rain forest than the northern sector. Nonetheless, there is still spectacular rain forest to be found. To fly here to explore that rain forest, you'll need to make arrangements with a tour guide.

KAPAWI

184 km (115 mi) east of Macas.

One of the most remote corners of Ecuador, this eastern jungle region near the Peruvian border is the territory of the Achuar people. Kapawi is actually the name of an Achuar village.

WHERE TO STAY

$$$$ **Kapawi Ecolodge & Reserve.** This group of typical Achuar huts—no
★   nails were used in construction—is equipped with modern amenities
like electric lights and private baths. All-inclusive packages last four
to eight days, but you must stay a minimum of four days and three
nights, for a cost of $600. An extra day and night will cost you an
extra $120. This is an excellent experience if you want to see wild-
life and have some contact with the Achuar people. According to an
agreement, the ecolodge will be transferred to the Achuar in 2011.
For birders, Kapawi has a booklet mapping out trails and bird species nesting in the area. In 10 days it isn't unusual to see almost 400.
All meals are included. Remember that round-trip airfare from Quito
will cost you about $225. **Pros:** Secluded, great nature-watching activ-
ity. **Cons:** Difficult to get here. ✉ *Kapawi* ☎ *02/600–9333 in Quito,
800/613–6026 toll-free in North America* ⊕ *www.kapawi.com* ➲ *20
rooms* ⌂ *In-room: no a/c, no phone, no TV. In-hotel: restaurant, bar,
no elevator* ▤ *AE, DC, MC, V* ⚹ *AI.*

$$$$ **Sacha Lodge.** A parrot clay lick and a butterfly farm in the nearby
Parque Nacional Yasuní (Yasuní National Park; close to the Colombian
border) and a 43-meter (135-foot) observation tower built around a giant
kapok tree at the lodge are added attractions at this rustic but comfortable thatch-roof lodge deep in the Amazon. Activities include birding—
more than 60 species have been spotted here—and canoe trips on the
Napo River. **Pros:** Secluded, great nature-watching activities. **Cons:** Difficult to get here. ✉ *Parque Nacional Yasuní* ☎ *09/973–3182, 02/256–
6090 in Quito, 800/706–2215 in North America* ⊕ *www.sachalodge.
com.ec* ➲ *26 cabins* ⌂ *In-room: no a/c, no phone, no TV. In-hotel:
restaurant, bar, laundry service* ▤ *AE, MC, V* ⚹ *AI.*

GUAYAQUIL & THE PACIFIC COAST

Few foreign visitors see Ecuador's Pacific coast beyond the view from
the plane window as they head out to the Galápagos Islands. If you
have the time, this is the center of the country's development—all economic roads lead to Guayaquil, Ecuador's largest city—and vacation
culture—the tourism industry here touts the south coast as the Ruta del
Sol ("route of the sun"), a string of beach resorts, still modest at this
stage, but growing in number all the time.

GUAYAQUIL

420 km (252 mi) and 35 minutes by air southwest of Quito.

Guayaquil is Ecuador's city with the Midas touch. Politics and culture
may center in perpetual rival Quito, but the country's pocketbook lies
here. The city is also one of the world's premier examples of positive
urban renewal. Less than a decade ago, you dared not walk downtown streets night (daytime strolls were no guarantee of safety either).
But an exceptionally ambitious city government, determined to clean
up crime and halt a long downward slide, has transformed the aging

port in a few years into Ecuador's most vibrant city. Change is everywhere you look here, and some two million proud Guayaquileños have become the ultimate civic boosters. "Have you seen the Malecón?" they ask you, pointing to the riverfront promenade lined with museums, restaurants, shops, and ongoing entertainment. They also tout the new museums, the new airport, and the Metrovía, the new urban transportation network. Guayaquil remains a modern, financially minded city and will never attract the same number of visitors as the capital, but it deserves to be a place of pilgrimage for urban fans everywhere for a reassuring look at what a city can do right.

WILDLIFE WATCHING

Few places on the planet offer the kind of close contact with nature that the Galápagos Islands do, but other spots in Ecuador have animal-watching and birding that is no less spectacular. The isolated national parks of El Oriente protect important expanses of the tropical rain forest inhabited by anacondas, anteaters, howler monkeys, river dolphins, and 1,600 species of birds. In the highland forests are avian species ranging from delicate hummingbirds to mighty condors, while the plains that surround those forests offer close encounters with llamas, alpacas, and other Andean ungulates.

GETTING HERE & AROUND

Guayaquil's Aeropuerto Internacional José Joaquín de Olmedo (GYE), new in 2007, is 7 km (4 mi) north of the city center; taxis to downtown cost about $5. From Guayaquil, Tame flies to Quito, Cuenca, Manta, Loja, and Machala, as well as to the Galápagos islands of Baltra and San Cristóbal. AeroGal flies from Guayaquil to Quito, Baltra, and San Cristóbal. Ícaro connects Guayaquil with Quito and Cuenca and Manta with Quito. Internationally, American flies from Miami; Continental, from Houston; Delta from Atlanta; LanEcuador, from Miami, Lima, and Santiago; KLM, from Amsterdam; Iberia and Air Comet, from Madrid; TACA Peru, from Lima; Avianca, from Bogotá; Santa Bárbara Airlines, from Caracas.

Guayaquil is 10 hours by bus from Quito and around 5 hours from Cuenca. The city's main bus station, Terminal Terrestre, is near the airport. Buses ply the coast to various towns all the way to Bahía de Caráquez. The shortest route to Bahía de Caráquez is from Guayaquil, skipping Salinas, going directly northwest up the coast.

Taxis throughout Guayaquil are inexpensive. The average trip should cost $3. Most do not use meters, so be prepared to haggle. Guayaquil's Metrovía, an urban electric trolley-bus system modeled on Quito's Trole, travels north and south, near the Guayas River, with stops at fixed stations. It diverges into two branches that pass through downtown, then rejoin on the other side of the city center.

Guayaquil's branch of iTur is open weekdays 8:30–5, and has a few maps and brochures, but little else. A better bet is the friendly Oficina de Información Turística at the entrance to the Nahím Isaís Museum, open Tuesday–Saturday 10–5.

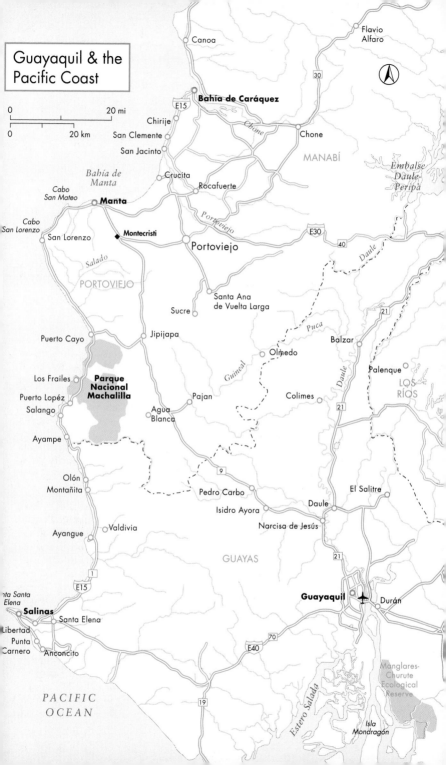

SAFETY & PRECAUTIONS

Downtown streets are reasonably safe, and the riverfront Malecón is exceptionally secure, but pockets of crime do exist. Take taxis at night, and ask the folks at your hotel front desk where you should and should not venture.

ESSENTIALS

Airport Contacts Aeropuerto José Joaquín de Olmedo (⊠ *Av. de las Américas, Guayaquil* ☎ *04/216–9000*).

Currency Exchange Banco de Guayaquil (⊠ *Plaza Icaza 105, at Pichincha*).

Medical Assistance Clínica Kennedy (⊠ *Av. Del Periodista* ☎ *04/228–6963*).

Post Office Correos del Ecuador (⊠ *Avs. Pedro Carbo and Ballén*).

Rental Cars Avis (☎ *04/228–7906*). **Budget** (☎ *04/278–8510*). **Hertz** (☎ *04/216–9035*). **Localiza** (☎ *800/562–254* ⊕ *www.localiza.com.ec*).

Visitor & Tour Info iTur (⊠ *Plaza Icaza 203, at Pichincha, 6th fl.* ☎ *04/256–8764*). **Oficina de Información Turística** (⊠ *Avs. Clemente Ballén and Pichincha* ☎ *04/232–4182* ⊕ *www.visitaguayaquil.com*).

EXPLORING GUAYAQUIL

MAIN ATTRACTIONS

❼ ★ Malecón 2000. Guayaquil's riverfront promenade anchors the city's rebirth. After years of neglect, the 26-block street has been transformed into one of the city's most pleasant attractions. As you stroll along the Río Guayas, you can relax on benches in shady parks or poke into numerous shops, restaurants, the contemporary art museum (MAAC), an IMAX theater, and a planetarium. Across the street from El Malecón is the Palacio Municipal, considered one of the country's best examples of neoclassical architecture. Beside the adjacent Palacio de la Gobernación is Parque Sucre, a sliver of greenery dedicated to war hero Mariscal Antonio José de Sucre. ⊠ *Av. Simón Bolívar between Febres Cordero and Loca* ☎ *04/252–4530* ⊕ *www.malecon2000.com* ⊙ *7 AM–midnight; shops 10–9.*

⓫ Fodor'sChoice ★ Museo Antropológico y Arte Contemporáneo *(MAAC).* If Ecuador doesn't spring to mind when someone mentions art, a visit to Guayaquil's newest museum might change that. Ecuadoran artists began to break the connection with religious-themed art in the late 19th century, and the country's artists have never looked back. Take an English-language guided tour—essential to understanding how the exhibits are laid out. Anthropology, the first A in the museum's name, gets equal treatment as Ecuador's Central Bank's extensive collection of artifacts from the past 10,000 years is displayed on the building's second level. ⊠ *Malecón 2000, at Loja* ☎ *04/230–9400* ⊕ *www.museomaac.com* ⊡ *$3; Sun. $1.50* ⊙ *Tues.–Sat. 10–5:30, Sun. 11–4.*

❻ Fodor'sChoice ★ Museo Nahím Isaías. The Nahím Isaías Museum is one of the country's truly fabulous institutions. Each year about 500 pieces of the astounding permanent collection of religious art from the colonial period is parceled out and displayed. What you see on view this year differs from last year and next year. An informative guided tour—choose between

English or Spanish—that provides the best background on what you see is included in your admission. The museum's flashy Web site (Spanish only) gives you a preview. ⊠*Avs. Clemente Ballén and Pichincha* ☎*04/232–4182* ⊕*www.museonahimisaias.com* 🎫*$1.50; free Sun.* ☉*Tues.–Sat. 10–6, Sun. 11–3.*

IF YOU HAVE TIME

❹ **Catedral Metropolitana.** The twin-spired cathedral, which looms over the western edge of Parque Seminario, is actually one of the city's newer houses of worship. Construction began on the semi-Gothic structure in 1937 and was completed in 1950. Vendors selling hand-carved rosaries and other items crowd the sidewalks outside. ⊠*Parque Seminario.*

⓬ **Cerro Santa Ana and Las Peñas.** Until 2002 this neighborhood at the foot of Cerro Santa Ana (Santa Ana Hill) was a seedy barrio of ramshackle houses where drugs dominated after dark. But from 2001 to 2002 the city poured $8 million into the neighborhood, transforming it in record time into one of the most charming parts of the city. Brightly painted houses, shops, and cafés climb Santa Ana Hill. Old-fashioned streetlamps light the way to the summit—there are 444 steps, thoughtfully (or unthoughtfully) numbered—where you can get an unparalleled view of the city. Perhaps the most amazing aspect of Las Peñas's transformation is that it was done without relocating the neighborhood's residents. Many of them benefited from business grants doled out by the city and now work as shopkeepers or manage cafés. The response from the community has been overwhelmingly positive, and other cities around the globe are following Guayaquil's model.

⓮ **Cementerio General.** Also called Ciudad Blanca, the General Cemetery is
★ one of the city's most impressive sights. More than 200 mausoleums, all in elaborately carved white marble, line the neat paths. Because of a recurring problem with pickpockets, you may want to visit on a guided tour. ⊠*Av. Coronel west of Las Peñas* 🎫*Free.*

⓭ **Iglesia de Santo Domingo.** Guayaquil's oldest church was founded by the Franciscans in 1548. Near Las Peñas, the simple colonial structure was rebuilt after it was destroyed by pirate attacks. Locals also refer to it as the Iglesia de San Vicente.

❿ **Museo Banco del Pacífico.** Just a block from the waterfront, the Pacific Bank Museum has rotating exhibits of archaeological discoveries, as well as a permanent collection of 19th-century South American art. ⊠*Plaza Ycaza 113, at Pichincha* ☎*04/256–6010* 🎫*Free* ☉*Weekdays 8:30–5, weekends 11–1.*

❶ **Museo Casa de la Cultura.** The Museum of Culture features prehistoric stone and ceramic artifacts discovered on La Plata Island off the coast from Guayaquil. There's also an impressive collection of gold items dating to before the arrival of the Spanish. ⊠*Av. 9 de Octubre 1200, at Plaza Moncayo* ☎*04/230–0500* 🎫*$1* ☉*Tues.–Fri. 10–6, Sat. 9–3.*

❺ **Museo Municipal de Guayaquil.** While the Municipal Museum of Guayaquil has many interesting archaeological exhibits, the biggest draw is a collection of *tsantsas*, or shrunken heads. Artifacts from indigenous

Guayaquil

peoples here include beadwork, feather work, tools, and weapons. In the lobby is an unusual 8½-meter (28-foot) totem with 32 vertical figures. ⚠ **Your passport is required for admission, only so an attendant can compile data about who visits and from where.** ⊠ *Av. Sucre, between Av. Chile and Av. Pedro Carbo* ☎ *04/252–4100* ⊕ *www.guayaquil.gov.ec* 💲*Free* ☉ *Tues.–Sat. 9–5.*

❷ ★ **Parque Histórico de Guayaquil.** There are three sections to this park, which opened in 2002: the Architecture Zone, with colonial buildings dating to 1886 (they were restored and moved here); the Traditional Zone, where actors dressed in period costumes re-create life as it was lived in the early 20th century; and the Endangered Wildlife Zone, with rare birds and animals. There are wooden walkways throughout and a small restaurant. This is a very pleasant way to spend a few hours; it's right on the edge of the rain forest. ⊠ *Av. Esmeraldas, Vía a Samborondón* ☎ *04/283–3807* ⊕ *www.parquehistoricoguayaquil.com* 💲*$3; Sun. $4.50* ☉ *Tues.–Sun. 9–4:30.*

❸ **Parque Seminario.** This lovely square, the heart of the city since it was inaugurated in 1895, is known by many names. Because it has the almost obligatory statue of a triumphant Simón Bolívar, many locals call it Parque Bolívar. A more common moniker is Parque de las Iguanas, as dozens of the scaly green creatures can be found lazing about on park benches and across the limbs of trees. The gardens, which still have a marvelous wrought-iron bandstand, are filled with 43 species of indigenous plants. ⊠ *Between Av. Clemente Ballén and Av. Diez de Agosto.*

❾ **La Rotonda.** Imposing marble columns form the backdrop for statues of the men who liberated most of the continent, Simón Bolívar and José de San Martín. The monument commemorates their first (and only) meeting, in Guayaquil in 1822. ⊠ *Malecón at Av. 9 de Octubre* 💲*Free.*

❽ **Torre del Reloj Público.** The Moorish style clock tower, constructed in 1770, is one of the city's most enduring landmarks. Inside is a small exposition of photographs of Guayaquil dating from the early 20th century. ⊠ *El Malecón.*

WHERE TO EAT

$–$$
PERUVIAN
✕ **El Caracol Azul.** This downtown restaurant, specializing in Peruvian-style seafood, is popular with business executives. The interior of the nondescript building is surprisingly attractive, enlivened by a skylight and paintings by local artists. Start off with seviche or *chicharrón de calamar* (deep-fried squid); then move on to langostino *picante* (in a spicy cream sauce). ⊠ *Av. 9 de Octubre at Los Ríos* ☎ *04/228–0461* 🍽*AE, DC, MC, V* ☉ *Closed Sun.*

¢–$
SPANISH
✕ **Casa Baska.** The owner peers out through a tiny window before opening the door to welcome you into this intimate Spanish restaurant, which also goes by the name La Tasca Vasca. The food, cooked up with a Basque flair, couldn't be better. Start with the broiled calamari, large enough to be worn as bracelets, then move on to the flavorful paella. You couldn't do better than end with the expertly prepared crème

caramel. ⊠ *Av. Clemente Ballén 422, at Chimborazo* ☎ *04/253–4599* ⊟ *AE, DC, MC, V* ☉ *Closed Sun. No lunch.*

¢ ✕ **Lo Nuestro Café Restaurant.** Historic photos of Guayaquil crowd the
LATIN   walls of this restaurant in the Urdesa neighborhood. Guayaquil is
AMERICAN   known for its ceviche, and Lo Nuestro's is good, meant to be drenched
in the fresh lime juice that accompanies it. ⊠ *Victor Emilio Estrado
903, at Higueras* ☎ *04/238–6398* ⊟ *AE, DC, MC, V.*

¢ ✕ **La Parrillada del Ñato.** Several long grills make this barbecue restau-
SOUTHERN   rant appear as if it were designed to feed an army. It's a good thing,
too, because legions of hungry carnivores fill the restaurant seven days
a week to feast on racks of ribs, succulent steaks, and an array of other
tasty meat dishes. ⊠ *Av. V. E. Estrada 1219, at Costañera* ☎ *04/238–
7098* ⊟ *AE, DC, MC, V.*

$–$$ ✕ **Trattoria da Enrico.** Tiny shuttered windows set into thick whitewashed
walls reflect this restaurant's Mediterranean influence. The simple exterior doesn't prepare you for the aquarium in the dining room, which is
set into the ceiling. Try the prosciutto and melon appetizer, then move
on to the chicken with a sour cream, vodka, and mushroom sauce.
Musicians playing mandolins wander among the tables. ⊠ *Bálsamos
504, at Ebanos* ☎ *04/238–7079* ⊟ *DC, MC, V.*

WHERE TO STAY

$$–$$$ 🏨 **Grand Hotel Guayaquil.** This landmark hotel near Parque Seminario
and most other downtown attractions shares a city block with the Catedral Metropolitana. Small but comfortable rooms with large windows
let in lots of sun. The health club lets you play squash on two courts,
relax in a sauna, or enjoy the terrace with a great view of the cathedral.
Pros: Central location, decent value. **Cons:** Some worn rooms, thin
walls. ⊠ *Boyaca at Av. 10 de Agosto* ☎ *04/232–9690, 800/334–3782
in North America* ⊕ *www.grandhotelguayaquil.com* 🛏 *182 rooms,
10 suites* 🛆 *In-room: refrigerator, safe, Wi-Fi. In-hotel: 2 restaurants,
room service, bar, pool, gym, laundry service, public Internet* ⊟ *AE,
DC, MC, V.*

$$–$$$ 🏨 **Hampton Inn Guayaquil Downtown.** This small inn behind the beautiful
Fodor'sChoice   San Francisco Church is just a few blocks from the Malecón and close to
★   all the museums. Rooms are well appointed, and all have coffeemakers
and two phone lines. It's rare that a U.S. chain hotel in another country
distinguishes itself as something other than, well, a U.S. chain property.
These folks provide all the amenities you expect from a Hampton Inn,
along with a coziness and friendliness that seems very Ecuadoran. **Pros:**
Top-notch service, good value, central location. **Cons:** U.S. chain status
might unduly turn off those who are looking for truly Ecuadoran-feel-
ing lodging. ⊠ *9 de Octubre 432, at Baquerizo Moreno* ☎ *04/256–
6700, 800/426–7866 in North America* ⊕ *www.hamptoninn1.hilton.
com* 🛏 *95 rooms* 🛆 *In-room: dial-up. In-hotel: restaurant, room service, pool, gym, laundry service, public Internet, public Wi-Fi, airport
shuttle, no-smoking rooms* ⊟ *AE, DC, MC, V* ⏹ *BP.*

$$$$ 🏨 **Hilton Colón Guayaquil.** This majestic hotel outside the city center
Fodor'sChoice   (next to the Expoplaza convention center) has a 10-story atrium lobby.
★   It delivers everything you'd expect from a top-notch business hotel.
The beautiful pool area is surrounded by palm trees. The Large Poli-

centro Shopping Mall is nearby. **Pros:** Business amenities, close to airport. **Cons:** Far from downtown. ⊠*Av. Francisco de Orellana 111* ☎*04/268–9000, 800/445–8667 in North America* ⊕*www.hilton.com* ⟿*273 rooms, 19 suites* ♿*In-room: refrigerator, safe, dial-up, Wi-Fi. In-hotel: 5 restaurants, room service, bar, pool, gym, public Internet, airport shuttle, no-smoking rooms* ▭*AE, DC, MC, V.*

¢　▦**Hotel del Rey.** Visiting soccer players love this pleasant hotel several blocks from Parque Guayaquil. The well-maintained rooms are a bit small, but this is one of the few moderately priced hotels in town that has exercise facilities. **Pros:** Good budget value. **Cons:** Small rooms. ⊠*Aguirre at Andrés Marín* ☎*04/245–3037* ⊕*www.hoteldelrey-ecu. com* ⟿*47 rooms* ♿*In-hotel: restaurant, bar, gym* ▭*DC, MC, V* ⏐⊙⏐*BP.*

$$$–$$$$　▦**Hotel Oro Verde.** The chain's flagship hotel continues to be one of the top choices for business travelers. In addition to comfortable rooms and plenty of amenities, the hotel has a pool, health club, and even a casino. The lobby bar, with live music every night, draws locals. If you're hungry, head to the informal Spice Grill to sample the tasty Szechuan chicken salad. **Pros:** Business amenities, friendly staff, yummy coffee shop. **Cons:** Far from Malecón. ⊠*Av. 9 de Octubre at García Moreno* ☎*04/232–7999, 800/223–6800 in North America* ⊕*www. oroverdeguayaquil.com* ⟿*192 rooms, 45 suites* ♿*In-room: refrigerator, safe, Ethernet. In-hotel: 3 restaurants, room service, bar, pool, gym, public Internet, airport shuttle* ▭*AE, DC, MC, V.*

$$$　▦**Hotel Ramada.** This popular hotel—it's not affiliated with the U.S. chain—is across from El Malecón and the riverfront and within walking distance of Las Peñas. When the heat of tropical Guayaquil gets to be too much, you can sip a cocktail by the pool. Evenings find many guests slipping off to the casino. **Pros:** Close to Malecón, good river views. **Cons:** Wear and tear in some rooms. ⊠*Malecón 606, at Orellana* ☎*04/256–5555* ⊕*www.hotelramada.com* ⟿*76 rooms* ♿*In-room: refrigerator, safe. In-hotel: 3 restaurants, room service, bar, pool, concierge, laundry service, airport shuttle* ▭*AE, DC, MC, V.*

¢　▦**Rizzo Hotel.** A good budget option, this downtown hotel has comfortable rooms with balconies overlooking Parque Seminario. The staff is eager to help you in any way, from suggesting a restaurant to giving tips on nightlife. **Pros:** Good budget value, friendly staff, central location. **Cons:** Small rooms. ⊠*Av. Clemente Ballén 319, at Chile* ☎*04/232–5210* ⊕*www.rizzohotel.com* ⟿*60 rooms* ♿*In-room: refrigerator. In-hotel: 2 restaurants, gym* ▭*AE, DC, MC, V* ⏐⊙⏐*CP.*

$$　▦**UniPark Hotel.** Part of the Oro Verde chain, this comfortable hotel is within walking distance of most of the city's attractions. Across the street from the Parque Seminario, it gives you direct access to an 80-store shopping center. Several excellent restaurants are also on the premises, including a wonderful sushi bar called Unibar. Buffet breakfast is included. The best view is from a parkside room. **Pros:** Good value. **Cons:** Few business amenities. ⊠*Av. Clemente Ballén 406* ☎*04/232–7100, 800/448–8355 in North America* ⊕*www.uniparkhotel. com* ⟿*132 rooms, 7 suites* ♿*In-room: refrigerator, safe, Ethernet, Wi-*

6

A Great Drive

If you're looking for a really splendid car trip—on a good highway—consider driving from Guayaquil up the Pacific coast 280 km (174 mi) to the eco-city of Bahía de Caráquez. There's lots to do along the way—you can lounge on the gorgeous beaches of Machalilla National Park, go deep-sea fishing in Salinas, explore the town of Manta where cruise ships dock, and visit the indigenous village of Montecristi, where the original Panama hats are still made. Once you reach Bahía de Caráquez, you can surf, watch for whales (July–September), and help excavate an archaeological site at the Chirije beach resort. If you prefer not to drive, there is good bus service between towns along the coast (you can also fly to Manta from Quito; from there it's a 45-minute drive to Bahía de Caráquez).

Fi (some). In-hotel: 3 restaurants, room service, bar, gym, concierge, laundry service, airport shuttle, public Internet ⊟AE, DC, MC, V.

AFTER DARK

If you have but one night in Guayaquil—typically visitors have exactly that, waiting for their flights to the Galápagos the next morning—follow up your dinner with a stroll along the Malécon, whose 26 blocks are well populated with activity and security each evening until midnight.

SALINAS

141 km (88 mi) west of Guayaquil.

Guayaquileños flock to the popular if sometimes overcrowded beaches here on holidays and during the hot and humid rainy season. Deep-sea fishing is another draw. The continental shelf drops sharply to the ocean floor just 19 km (12 mi) offshore, providing a fertile feeding ground for Pacific sailfish, swordfish, and amberjack, as well as striped, blue, and black marlin. The biggest catches are made November through May, but fishing continues year-round. An excellent highway connects Salinas and Guayaquil.

GETTING HERE & AROUND

A well-marked four- then two-lane road connects Guayaquil with Salinas. Plan on a drive of about two hours. Buses leave every half-hour throughout the day from Guayaquil's Terminal Terrestre for Salinas. The journey takes about 2½ hours.

ESSENTIALS

Currency Exchange **Banco del Pacífico** (⊠ *General Henríquez at Calle 19* ☎ *04/ 277–4145).*

WHERE TO STAY & EAT

$$ **Puerto Lucía Yacht Club.** If you need a place to anchor your 150-foot yacht, head to this beautiful resort on the Península Santa Elena. (You don't really need a yacht to stay here.) This is a great vacation destination for the entire family; it has everything from deep-sea fishing to rain-forest expeditions. The small suites have balconies overlooking the bay, where you can watch the sun disappear into the ocean. For larger groups, two- and three-bedroom apartments are available. Although the property functions much like a timeshare-condo operation, non-Ecuadoran guests may stay here with advance reservations. **Pros:** Many activities. **Cons:** Crowded on weekends. ⊠ *Av. C. J. Arosemena, Km 2.5* ☎ *04/278–3180, 04/220–6154 in Guayaquil* ⊕ *www.puertolucia.com. ec* ⮌ *24 suites* ⟡ *In-room: refrigerator, safe. In-hotel: restaurant, room service, bar, tennis courts, pools, beachfront, laundry service, public Internet* ⊟ *AE, DC, MC, V.*

> **GO FISH**
>
> The blue waters on this sector of the coast teem with sailfish, albacore, wahoo, dolphin, and marlin, which attract world-class sportfishermen. The prime marlin season on the southern coast is October through April. **Magellan Offshore Fishing Tours** (⊠ *Salinas* ☎ *04/247–83189, 877/426–3347 in North America* ⊕ *www.magellanoffshore.com*) arranges fishing tours on a private yacht called the *Hatteras Paper Moon.* **PescaTours** (⊠ *Salinas* ☎ *04/277–2391, 04/244–3365 in Guayaquil* ⊕ *www.pescatours. ec*) organizes daylong charters for two to six people.

PARQUE NACIONAL MACHALILLA

Fodor'sChoice
★

In Puerto López, 167 km (104 mi) northwest of Guayaquil.

The 136,850-acre Parque Nacional Machalilla is in the extreme southwestern corner of the state of Manabí, and was created in 1979 in an effort to halt the destruction of the country's remaining tropical dry forests. Unlike the lush greenery associated with rain forests, dry-forest vegetation includes kapok trees, prickly pear cactus, and strangler figs. The entrance fee is good for five days and includes access to Isla de la Plata, a 3,000-acre seabird sanctuary where red-footed, blue-footed, and masked boobies make their homes. The waters surrounding the island teem with flying fish, dolphins, and humpback whales that come from Antarctica to bear their young during the June–October season. There are restrooms and changing facilities at the park. ⊠ *The visitor center is on main street in Puerto López* ☎ *05/260–4170* 🎟 *$20.*

GETTING HERE & AROUND

Your gateway to the park is the nearby town of Puerto López, about three hours from Manta and four hours from Guayaquil. Buses ply the route from each, or you can drive. The road floods periodically during the rainy season, making a visit here between June and October a better (and more popular) bet.

ESSENTIALS

Currency Exchange **Banco Pichincha** (⊠ *Av. Machalilla at Calle General Córdova Puerto López* ☎ *05/230–0140*).

WHERE TO STAY & EAT

¢ ✕ **Carmita's Restaurant.** Doña Carmita and her sister have a way with seafood. The signature dish at this simple beachfront eatery, among the best restaurants along the southern coast, is the zesty *pescado al vapor con vegetales* (lemony fish soup with vegetables). A wide variety of drinks, including German and Chilean wines, is available. ⊠ *Malecón s/n, Puerto López* ☎ *05/260–4148 or 05/260–4149* ☰ *V.*

¢ 🏨 **Alandaluz Hostería.** The two- and three-story thatch-roof cabanas face several miles of sand beaches. About 15 minutes south of Puerto López, it is a favorite among tourists, who come to get closer to nature. Many travelers come for a night and end up spending a week, lounging in hammocks and chatting at the open-air bar. The restaurant emphasizes vegetarian fare. **Pros:** Many nature activities, environmentally conscious staff. **Cons:** Cons here. ⊠ *Puerto Rico, Parque Nacional Machalilla* ☎ *04/278–0690, 02/244–0790 in Quito* ⊕ *www.alandaluzhosteria.com* 🛏 *12 rooms, 4 suites, 25 cabins* ⚴ *In-room: no phone, no TV. In-hotel: restaurant, bar, beachfront* ☰ *No credit cards.*

$ 🏨 **Hostería Atamari.** Papayas, palms, and flaming bougainvillea grow among the thatch-roof cottages of this hotel, which is perched on a rocky promontory overlooking the Ayampe Valley and the Pacific Ocean, 28 km (17 mi) south of Puerto López. Trails by the hotel lead to a private beach where hundreds of birds and butterflies hover. Whale-watching season is June–October; from the cliff-top terrace you'll have the best seats in the house. The outdoor restaurant serves fantastic international cuisine, with an emphasis on seafood. **Pros:** Great views. **Cons:** Can be difficult to reach in rainy season. ⊠ *Península de Santa Elena, Ayampe* ☎ *04/278–0430, 02/222–7896 in Quito* ⊕ *atamari.ec.tripod.com* 🛏 *8 cottages, 4 suites* ⚴ *In-hotel: restaurant, pool, no elevator* ☰ *AE, DC, MC, V.*

$ 🏨 **Mantaraya Lodge.** The adobe-style buildings that make up this lodge may remind you a bit of Old Mexico. Nestled among the kapok trees of Parque Nacional Machalilla, the resort has its own guides to take you out on wilderness excursions. You can also join fishing, diving, and whale-watching trips aboard the *Mantarayas II* and *Mantarayas III*. Reservations are made through Advantage Travel in Quito. **Pros:** Many nature tours. **Cons:** No a/c, can be difficult to reach in rainy season. ⊠ *Puerto López* ☎ *02/244–8985 in Quito* ⊕ *www.mantarayalodge.com* 🛏 *15 rooms* ⚴ *In-hotel: 2 restaurants, bar, pool, bicycles* ☰ *AE, DC, MC, V* ❍ *FAP.*

SPORTS & THE OUTDOORS

Guides can be hired at the Parque Nacional Machalilla visitor center in Puerto López for less than $10 a day. When not watching nature here, fishing and horseback riding might be the name of your game.

Machalilla Tours (⊠*Malecón Julio Izurieta, Puerto López* ☎*05/230–0206*) organizes park visits on foot or bicycle, and whale-watching tours.

Advantage Travel (⊠*El Telégrafo E10–63, at Juan de Alcántara, Quito* ☎*02/246–2871*) arranges fishing charters, and can arrange for guides in the national park. Horseback trips to beautiful Los Frailes Cove can be arranged through **Pacarina** (⊠*Puerto López* ☎*05/260–4173*) for less than $5 for a half-day trip.

> ### MANTA & THE MILITARY
>
> Manta owes some of its current prosperity to the presence of a U.S. Air Force base, which shares a runway with the local airport. The United States negotiated a 10-year lease in 1999, and has used the facility as a base from which to conduct aerial surveillance of drug trafficking in neighboring Colombia. The government of Ecuadoran president Rafael Correa, whose relations with the United States have been contentious at times, is not expected to renew the lease and to expel the U.S. military in 2009.

6

MANTA

196 km (118 mi) northwest of Guayaquil.

A onetime sleepy fishing village with an unsuccessful history of warding off pirates, Manta today booms with all the hustle and bustle of a medium-sized city. Ecuador's second-largest seaport's newest incarnation is that of a port of call, with ships of Celebrity, Holland America, Norwegian, Princess, Regent Seven Seas, and Royal Caribbean stopping here on select South America itineraries during the December–April season. Organized shore excursions take you shopping in nearby Montecristi, or via a flight to Quito, then overland to the markets in Otavalo.

GETTING HERE & AROUND

Tame flies between Quito and Manta's Aeropuerto General Eloy Alfaro (MEC).

ESSENTIALS

Airline Contact **Aeropuerto General Eloy Alfaro** (⊠*Av. de las Américas, Manta* ☎*05/229–0005*).

Currency Exchange **Banco de Guayaquil** (⊠*Malecón at Espejo* ☎*05/261–1830*).

EXPLORING MANTA

Malecón. Open-air restaurants and shops front the city's pleasant oceanside promenade, which leads north and south from the cruise-ship docks. ⊠*Av. Chávez.*

Museo Centro Cultural de Manta. Yet another museum operated by Ecuador's Central Bank exhibits artifacts from the Pacific coast's pre-Inca indigenous Manta culture. ⊠ *Malecón at Calle 7* 🕾 *05/262–2956* ⊕ *www.museos-ecuador.com* 🖾 *$1, free Sun.* ⊘ *Tues.–Sat. 10–5, Sun. 11–3.*

SHOPPING

The nearby town of Montecristi, 16 km (10 mi) south of Manta, is regarded as the birthplace of the Panama hat. Even though Ecuador's signature souvenir is primarily identified with Cuenca these days, several hatmakers still hold court here. Many cruise excursions transport you via a refurbished old-fashioned, open-sided Ecuadoran *chiva* bus, compete with musical entertainment.

Bertha Pachay (⊠ *Rocafuerte, Montecristi* 🕾 *09/317–9692*) is one of the town's foremost purveyors of quality Panama hats.

SPORTS & THE OUTDOORS

North of town strings Playa Murciélago, the area's most upscale beach, whose breezy conditions make it popular with windsurfers. Playa Tarquí—a bit rougher, not as clean, but more colorful—lies just south of the docks, on the way to Manta's airport.

BAHÍA DE CARÁQUEZ

14 km (23 mi) from Manta.

This beachfront port town—everyone calls it Bahía for short—built by the Spaniards in 1624, has a delightful small-town resort vibe, with waterfront restaurants that serve delicious meals of organically grown shrimp and fresh crab. The Spaniards were not the first, however, to find this peninsula. Members of the Caras people arrived aboard balsa-wood sailing rafts around 1500 BC, and it's believed that Bahía de Caráquez originally existed as a trading center for shells and crafted ornaments, which were exchanged for gold, copper, and other goods from places as far away as Mexico and Chile.

GETTING HERE & AROUND

Bahía's human-powered, three-wheel taxis make a fun way to get around, but if you're more than two people, or are laden with luggage, be kind to the driver and take a motorized cab instead.

ESSENTIALS

Currency Exchange **Banco de Guayaquil** (⊠ *Río Frío at Bolívar* 🕾 *05/269–2205*).

EXPLORING BAHÍA DE CARÁQUEZ

Casa de la Cultura. A large replica of a raft is in Bahía's Central Bank Museum, which displays archaeological artifacts and costumes. Rafts were built without nails and could hold 50–100 people. ⊠ *Malecón* 🕾 *05/269–0817* ⊕ *www.museos-ecuador.com* 🖾 *$1, free Sun.* ⊘ *Tues.–Sat. 9–4:30, Sun. 11–2:30.*

Isla Corazón. The name of this place just a short boat ride from town translates as "Heart Island." First you'll stop at an off-island welcome center to see a presentation, then you get back on the boat to continue to the island itself. Isla Corazon, which has 174 acres of mangroves, serves as a nesting place for frigate birds—males inflate what looks like a large red balloon to attract females during mating season. You can either walk along boardwalks to explore the forest or canoe around the island. ⌂ *10 km (6 mi) southeast of Bahía de Caráquez* ☎ *No phone* ⌸ *Free* ⏰ *Daily 7–5.*

> **EARTH FRIENDLY**
>
> This town of 25,000 takes pride in being a self-declared "eco-city." Few cars ply the streets, as most transportation is by three-wheel cycle. An environmental learning center serves as an after-school center for children from under-privileged homes, at which kids learn the importance of recycling and environmental issues. Bahía's citizens envision their city as a model of sustainability.

WHERE TO STAY

$ ⌂ **La Piedra.** This small oceanfront hotel gives you access to the beach. You can also tour the town in the hotel's horse-drawn carriage. **Pros:** Good value, great views, nice beach. **Cons:** Spartan rooms. ⌂ *Av. Virgilio Ratti N802* ☎ *05/269–0780* ⌸ *www.cialcotel.com* ⌂ *42 rooms* ⌂ *In-hotel: 2 restaurants, bar, pool, beachfront, no elevator, laundry service* ⌷ *AE, DC, MC, V* ⌷ *BP.*

THE GALÁPAGOS ISLANDS

960 km (600 mi) and 2½ hours by air west of Quito, 960 km (600 mi) and 90 minutes by air northwest of Guayaquil.

Fodor'sChoice ★ A zoologist's dream, the Galápagos Islands afford a once-in-a-lifetime chance to witness animals found nowhere else on the planet. From the moment you step onto these dazzling shores, you're confronted by giant tortoises basking in the sun, lava lizards darting between rocks, and frigates swooping overhead. No one who has walked among these unique creatures will ever forget the experience.

Tourism began in a limited fashion after the Ecuadoran government declared the islands a national park in 1959. Some five decades later, the Galápagos copes with more than 100,000 visitors each year. The delicate balance that exists here is difficult to overstate. Ecologists are concerned that the steadily increasing number of tourists will prove destructive to the irreplaceable environment, as will introduced animals—goats, cats, pigs, dogs, and rats—which interrupt the islands' natural food chain. While more than 250,000 giant tortoises once roamed the islands, there are fewer than 15,000 today due to human hunting and newly introduced predators. El Niño currents also affect marine life, especially in unusually warm years, by raising water temperatures, killing thousands of fish and destroying the food source for marine birds. The Charles Darwin Research Station, based on Santa

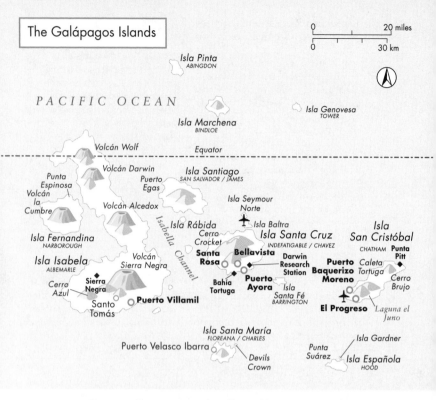

The Galápagos Islands

0   20 miles
0   30 km

PACIFIC OCEAN

Isla Pinta
ABINGDON

Isla Genovesa
TOWER

Isla Marchena
BINDLOE

Volcán Wolf   Equator

Volcán Darwin   Isla Santiago
Puerto   SAN SALVADOR / JAMES
Egas

Punta
Espinosa
Volcán
la
Cumbre   Volcán Alcedox   Isla Seymour
                                        Norte

Isla Rábida   Isla Baltra
Cerro
Crocket   Isla Santa Cruz   Isla
                   INDEFATIGABLE / CHAVEZ San Cristóbal

Isla Fernandina   Santa   Bellavista   CHATHAM Punta
NARBOROUGH   Rosa   Darwin   Pitt
                   Volcán   Research   Puerto Caleta
Isla Isabela   Sierra Negra   Station   Baquerizo Tortuga
ALBEMARLE   Moreno   Cerro
         Sierra   Puerto   Isla   Brujo
Cerro   Negra   Bahía   Ayora   Santa Fé
Azul   Tortuga   BARRINGTON
         Santo ○ Puerto Villamil   El Progreso Laguna el
         Tomás   Juno

Isabella Channel

                   Isla Santa María
                   FLOREANA / CHARLES   Isla Gardner
Puerto Velasco Ibarra   Punta
                            Devils   Suárez   Isla Española
                            Crown   HOOD

Cruz, works to mitigate the effects of human-made and natural disasters and is dedicated to conserving the fragile ecosystem.

GETTING HERE & AROUND

Tame flies once daily from Quito and Guayaquil to Baltra (GPS), a tiny island just north of Santa Cruz, and to San Cristóbal (SCY). AeroGal flies daily to Baltra and San Cristóbal. The flight from Guayaquil takes 90 minutes. Add another hour if you board in Quito. Airfares run $330–$400 round-trip. If you have reservations with a tour or cruise operator, you'll be met at the airport. If you're a do-it-yourself type, a bus-ferry-bus transport combo gets you from Baltra to Puerto Ayora, the largest town on Santa Cruz. San Cristóbal's airport lies near the edge of the town of Puerto Baquerizo Moreno.

As of 2008, all visitors must carry a transit control card (*tarjeta de control de tránsito*) issued by the Instituto Nacional Galápagos (INGALA) (⊕*www.ingala.gov.ec*) to enter the islands. Your tour operator should take care of this step for you if you go with an organized group. Ask. (Not all do.) If not, or if you travel independently, go to INGALA's Web site and register with your name, passport number, and flight details. Print the confirmation page and present it and $10 at INGALA's airport counter in Quito or Guayaquil before you check in for your flight.

You'll be issued the card, which you'll need to show at check-in, and when you enter and depart the Galápagos.

All foreign visitors who enter the Galápagos must pay $100 in cash upon entry, money earmarked for training park rangers and funding conservation efforts. You must pay in U.S. cash—no traveler's checks, no credit cards—and the bills should be in good condition without markings or tears. (Because of Ecuador's glut of counterfeit $50 and $100 bills, bills larger than twenties are not accepted.)

BY BOAT Cruises *to* the Galápagos are mostly nonexistent. Once you're here, you can choose from a wide range of boats for tours around the islands. You book these in Quito or Guayaquil or from abroad. Cheap economy vessels (typically converted fishing trawlers) are often poorly maintained and have guides with only a passing knowledge of English. Stick with tourist-class or luxury vessels, which generally offer three-, four-, and seven-night tours. The price tag per person for a double cabin on a three-night luxury-ship cruise can run $850–$1,500 in low season and $950–$1,800 in high season. Off-peak rates usually apply from May 1 to June 14 and from September 1 to October 14. When you book, be sure to ask if the $100 park tax is included.

Boat tours mean dining and sleeping on board, with much of the sailing done at night to maximize time spent on the islands. Most of these vessels employ multilingual naturalists who are knowledgeable in marine sciences. At least once a day you'll have an opportunity to swim or snorkel. If you want to dive, you should make arrangements beforehand, as it's not offered on all boats.

Storefront travel agencies in Quito and Guayaquil advertise LAST-MINUTE GALAPAGOS TOURS, although there's never any guarantee you'll be able to find space if you wait that long. Quality varies widely with this option, too. Buyer beware. To really save money, you can wait until you arrive on the islands and try to bargain for a cheaper boat fare. Operators of all vessel classes come to the airport selling last-minute tickets. The risk of doing this, however, is that you might not find an available boat, especially during peak seasons.

SAFETY & PRECAUTIONS
The equatorial sun bakes the islands, and there is little shade. Wear a brimmed hat and apply sunscreen liberally.

TIME
It is one hour earlier on the islands than it is on mainland Ecuador.

ESSENTIALS
Airlines The Galápagos-based **EMETEBE** (☎ *05/252–5711 in Baltra, 05/252–0615 in San Cristóbal, 05/252–9155 in Isabela* ⊕ *www.emetebe.com*) operates daily passenger air service between Baltra, San Cristóbal, and Isabela islands in five-passenger Aztec Piper or nine-passenger Twin Islander planes.

Tour Companies Canodros (☎ *04/228–5711 in Guayaquil, 800/327–9854 in North America* ⊕ *www.canodros.com*) operates the all-exterior-suite 293-foot M/V *Galápagos Explorer II*, with 50 cabins, each with twin beds that can be converted to a king-size bed, and a swimming pool and piano bar. You definitely won't feel as if you're roughing it. **Ecoventura** (☎ *04/220–7177 in Guayaquil, 800/633–7972 in North America* ⊕ *www.ecoventura.com*) operates two 16- to 20-passenger yachts, the M/Y *Eric* and M/Y *Sky Dancer*, which it uses on weeklong cruises through the islands. **Enchanted Expeditions** (☎ *02/256–9960 in Quito, 800/327–3573 in North America* ⊕ *www.enchantedexpeditions.com*)—frequently referred to by its former name, Angermeyer's—operates the M/Y *Cachalote I* and the M/Y *Beluga*, both 96-foot schooners that hold 16 passengers for cruises through the islands. **Galápagos Galasam Tours** (☎ *04/230–6093 in Guayaquil* ⊕ *www.galasam-tours. com*) operates eight yachts holding 10–16 passengers. Its catamaran *Millenium*, is an 82-foot cruiser that carries diving gear on board. **Kleintours** (☎ *02/226–7000 in Quito, 888/505–5346 in North America* ⊕ *www.kleintours.com*) operates the 300-foot M/V *Galápagos Legend*, which holds 110 passengers and has cabins all with ocean views. Kleintours also operates two yachts, the 26-passenger M/Y *Coral* and the 20-passenger M/Y *Coral II*. Cruises on the yachts last three, five, or eight days.

The high-end **Metropolitan Touring's** (☎ *02/246–4780 in Quito, 800/527–2500 in North America* ⊕ *www.metropolitan-touring.com*) flagship is the 273-foot M/V *Santa Cruz*, which carries 90 passengers. It was built specifically for the Galápagos. The *Isabela II* is Metropolitan's 40-passenger luxury yacht. Its new 32-passenger *La Pinta*, a 207-foot yacht, cruises through the islands. **Quasar Naútica** (☎ *02/244–6996 in Quito, 800/247–2925 in North America* ⊕ *www.quasarnauticausa.com*) has well-maintained yachts, including the three-masted, ketch-rigged schooner *Alta*. Its most luxurious and fastest yacht is the *Parranda*. **TOPPSA** (☎ *02/224–1345, 866/809–3145 in North America* ⊕ *www.toppsa.com*) is a last-minute booking agency. Its fares are reasonable.

SPORTS & THE OUTDOORS

Not only is there aboveground wildlife to see in the Galápagos, the islands are one of the world's foremost diving and snorkeling destinations, with the opportunity to view hammerhead and Galápagos sharks, eagle rays, and sea lions. December through July means warmer waters.

Galakiwi (☎ *02/252–1562* ⊕ *www.southernexposuretours.co.nz*) is a New Zealand–Ecuadoran company that offers courses and excursions. **Wreck Bay Diving Center** (☎ *02/252–0473*) is based on San Cristóbal and offers courses and excursions.

SANTA CRUZ

Santa Cruz, the most developed and touristed of the islands, sits in the middle of the archipelago. Overlooking Academy Bay on the island's southern shore is the town of **Puerto Ayora,** with hotels, restaurants, shops, and even a few clubs.

GETTING HERE & AROUND

Your airline provides bus transportation from the airport on Baltra to the five-minute ferry crossing that will take you to the island of Santa Cruz itself. On the Santa Cruz side, a public bus or a fleet of white truck-taxis wait to transport you for the 30-minute ride to Puerto Ayora.

CLOSE UP

When & How to Visit the Galápagos Islands

The best months to visit the Galápagos are generally May, June, November and December. Among the 13 principal islands, Santa Cruz and San Cristóbal are the most developed, each with a population of roughly 6,000 year-round residents. Of the two, Santa Cruz has more allure for visitors, with its dozen or so hotels, restaurants, and boutiques. The archipelago's four populated islands can be visited on a limited basis without guides, but the uninhabited islands can be seen only with a guide licensed through the Galápagos National Park Service. It's typical to book your own airfare and prearrange a one- to two-week package that includes guided visits to islands like Española and Isabela. A cruise of 10 days or longer is needed to reach the more remote northern islands or to climb either of Isabela's two accessible volcanic craters.

For the landlubbers among you, a one-island visit is entirely doable, but, of course, limits your exposure to the rest of the archipelago. You can negotiate day jaunts with local boat owners to other islands upon arrival, but these tend to be much smaller (read: more wobbly in the open sea) than the bigger vessels used by cruise operators.

6

ESSENTIALS

Currency Exchange **Banco del Pacífico** (⊠ *Av. Charles DarwinPuerto Ayora* ☎ *05/252–6282*).

Visitor Infor **Santa Cruz Tourist Office** (⊠ *Av. Charles Darwin, Puerto Ayora* ☎ *05/252–6174*).

EXPLORING SANTA CRUZ

Follow the main road east from Puerto Ayora to the expansive grounds of the **Charles Darwin Research Station** and its visitor center, which has an informative exhibit explaining the basics of Galápagos geology, ecology, and weather patterns. Self-guided trails lead to the station's giant tortoise pens, where you can see the only tortoises you're likely to encounter during your visit. Your admission is included in the $100 entry fee you paid upon landing in the islands. ⊠ *Av. Charles Darwin* ☎ *05/252–6146* ⊕ *www.darwinfoundation.org* ⊙ *Daily 7–6* ⊠ *Free.*

Bahía Tortuga (Turtle Bay), 3 km (2 mi) southwest of Puerto Ayora, has a long, white-sand beach where marine iguanas sometimes strut along the water's edge. There are no facilities along the water, but if you walk from town (take the road to Bellavista and turn left past the bank), you'll pass a soda-and-beer stand at the top of a lava-rock staircase. Marine turtles drag their bulky shells up onto the beach to lay their eggs between November and February, with baby turtles hatching in June and July.

Near the small village of **Bellavista** you can explore amazing underground lava tubes. The mile-long tunnels, tall enough to walk through, were created when flowing lava cooled more quickly on the surface than below, forming a crust that enclosed an underground labyrinth. To reach the tunnels from Puerto Ayora, head north on the road to Bellavista; turn east at the cross street and walk about a mile until you find a farm with a sign that announces LOS TÚNELES. A small fee is collected by the owner, who also provides flashlights.

The road to **Santa Rosa**, 13 km (8 mi) beyond Bellavista, is lined with giant elephant grass, avocado and papaya trees, and boughs of yellow trumpet vines, all of which are in marked contrast to the dry, cactus-spotted lowlands. About 2 km (1 mi) beyond Santa Rosa, look for a pair of giant sinkholes called **Los Gemelos** (the Twins), one on either side of the road.

The unattended **National Park Tortoise Reserve** is one of the few places in the archipelago where you can view giant Galápagos turtles in the wild. An unmarked track leads to the reserve from Santa Rosa. Along the way, keep alert for Galápagos hawks, Darwin finches, and short-eared owls. In Santa Rosa a small restaurant across from the church some-times rents horses that you are allowed to ride inside the reserve.

WHERE TO EAT

¢   ✕**La Dolce Italia.** The owners here come from Palermo, but are 11-year
ITALIAN   veterans of life on the islands. They've brought Sicilain and southern Italian cuisine, and the pastas are a nice change of pace from Puerto Ayora's ubiquitous seafood, but do try the seafood fettucine with mush-rooms and cognac sauce. ⊠*Av. Charles Darwin, across from port* ☎*09/455–4668* ▤*MC, V.*

$$ ✕**Four Lanterns.** Expect to see diners sitting around long tables on the
ITALIAN   lantern-lighted outdoor patio enjoying lasagna, gnocchi, or cannel-loni. The proprietor takes pride in her signature dish, fettuccine *mare e monte* (with mushrooms and shrimp). An accepted piece of local wisdom is that all visitors eventually end up at the Four Lanterns. ⊠*Av. Charles Darwin, Puerto Ayora* ☎*No phone* ▤*No credit cards* ☉*No lunch.*

¢   ✕**La Garrapata.** This popular restaurant is run by the offspring of one
SEAFOOD   of the pioneer families of Galápagos. Its outdoor tables attract both tourists and locals. The menu, which is heavy on seafood, also includes a few chicken and pasta dishes. Next door is the popular discotheque La Panga, where salsa music plays until the lights go out or the last patron leaves. ⊠*Av. Charles Darwin, Puerto Ayora* ☎*05/252–6264* ▤*MC, V* ☉*Closed Sun.*

$ ✕**La Tolda Azul.** The first restaurant you'll encounter as you step off the
SEAFOOD   boat in Port Ayora, this place has a small outdoor patio. The menu offers a wonderful selection of lobster dishes served in large portions; the grilled steaks are also good. ⊠*Muelle Municipal, Puerto Ayora* ☎*05/252–6565* ▤*MC.*

WHERE TO STAY

$$$$ ⌑**Finch Bay EcoHotel.** A stay at this totally redone four-star hotel (from 1960) can be combined with day cruises on the yacht *Delphin*—which the hotel owns—or day tours that include snorkeling, diving, sea kayak-ing, hiking, mountain biking, and horseback riding along Santa Cruz's hillside paths. The highlands show a different side of the Galápagos. On kayaking trips behind the hotel you get a close-up look at sharks, sea tur-

tles, rays, and a variety of birds. If you've never paddled a kayak, you can practice off the hotel's beach. Rates include a buffet breakfast. All rooms are no-smoking. **Pros:** Many activities, tours. **Cons:** Far from town. ⊠*Santa Cruz Island at Punta Estrada* ☎*02/246–4780 in Quito, 800/527–2500 toll-free in North America* ⊕*www.finchbay hotel.com* ⊠*21 rooms* ⚹*In-hotel: restaurant, bar, pool, beachfront, bicycles, no elevator, laundry service, airport shuttle, no-smoking rooms, public Internet* ⊟*AE, D, MC, V* ⫶⊙⫶*BP.*

> **DINING**
>
> Most hotels and restaurants are working to upgrade their facilities, but many are still on the rustic side. Some hotels have only cold running water, and rooms often lack electrical outlets. If these things are important to you, be sure to ask before booking.

$$ $$ 🏨**Hotel Red Booby.** No matter that this place sits a few blocks inland; Puerto Ayora is tiny enough that a walk to the ocean is not long. The friendly staff and sparkling rooms with wood furnishings (and a few with their own balconies) make this a good bet. Take a dip in the roof-top pool at the end of a day of sightseeing, and dine at the poolside barbecue, or the more formal restaurant downstairs. **Pros:** Friendly staff, attentive service. **Cons:** Several blocks from ocean. ⊠*Islas Plazas at Av. Charles Binford* ☎*05/252–6485* ⊕*www.hotelredbooby.com. ec* ⊠*26 rooms* ⚹*In-room: no phone. In-hotel: restaurant, bar, pool, no elevator, laundry service, public Internet, public Wi-Fi, no-smoking rooms* ⊟*DC, MC, V* ⫶⊙⫶*BP.*

$$ $$ 🏨**Hotel Silberstein.** This comfortable place is often referred to by its former name, the Hotel Angermeyer, and you'll find a pool with a waterfall and large, pleasant rooms. Dive tours are a specialty here; the hotel has five-day packages for $695, including breakfast and dinner in the hotel and box lunches when out on dives. They also have rooms for travelers with disabilities. **Pros:** Central location. **Cons:** Some noise from traffic on road. ⊠*Av. Charles Darwin y Piqueros, Puerto Ayora* ☎*05/252–6277, 02/226–9626 in Quito* ⊕*www.hotelsilberstein.com* ⊠*24 rooms* ⚹*In-hotel: restaurant, bar, pool, laundry service, public Internet* ⊟*AE, DC, MC, V* ⫶⊙⫶*BP.*

$$ $$$$ 🏨**Royal Palm Hotel.** This small resort on Santa Cruz is the only five-star luxury hotel on the islands. Suites, villas, and rooms blend into the gar-den surroundings within a 500-acre property; all have the proper ame-nities of a mainland high-rise hotel. Features include an observatory with computerized telescopes for stargazing and a Galápagos museum that focuses on the ecology and native species. Tours offered include horseback riding, diving, snorkeling, hiking, birding, sea kayaking, and windsurfing. You also are welcome at the Royal Palm Hotel's Airport VIP room in Baltra. An entire dinner here, without drinks, will run you about $25. **Pros:** Tours, many activities **Cons:** Far from town. ⊠*20 mins northwest of Puerto Ayora* ☎*05/252–7409* ⊕*www.royalpalm galapagos.com* ⊠*10 villas, 4 rooms, 3 suites* ⚹*In-room: refrigerator, DVDs, CDs. In-hotel: restaurant, bar, tennis court, pool, gym, spa, public Internet* ⊟*AE, D, MC, V.*

SHOPPING

Rows of shops line Avenida Charles Darwin in Puerto Ayora, most with a variety of T-shirts, and many with souvenirs from mainland Ecuador, and only a couple of real standouts from the crowd. The profits from your purchase at the small stores inside the grounds of the Charles Darwin Research Station go toward its conservation work.

Galería Aymar (⊠ *Av. Charles Darwin at Los Piqueros* ☎ *05/252–6835* ⊕ *www.galeria-aymara.com*) exhibits the art (painting, sculpture, and jewelry) of 19 Latin American artists, three of whom have taken up residence here on Santa Cruze.

Iguana Factory (⊠ *Av. Charles Darwin at Av. Baltra* ⊕ *www.iguana factory.com*) sells its own distinctive EVOLUTION REVOLUTION T-shirts with Charles Darwin in a variety of poses.

SAN CRISTÓBAL

The capital of Galápagos Province and the largest town on San Cristóbal, **Puerto Baquerizo Moreno** is much less tourist oriented than Puerto Ayora. Two kilometers (1 mi) east of the port is **Frigate Bird Hill,** where both great and magnificent frigates—two species of black seabirds famed for their courtship displays—make their nests. On a clear day it offers sweeping views of the bay.

GETTING HERE & AROUND

White truck-taxis wait in front of the airport to take you for the two-minute trip into Puerto Baquerizo Moreno.

ESSENTIALS

Currency Exchange Banco del Pacífico (⊠ *Av. Charles Darwin at José Villamil* ☎ *05/252–0365*).

EXPLORING SAN CRISTÓBAL

San Cristóbal Interpretation Center. A visitor center just outside Puerto Baquerizo Moreno explains the natural processes that have made the Galápagos such a unique place, delineates efforts to protect and preserve the islands, and serves as an education center for park personnel and naturalist guides. The three exhibits inside are Human History, covering events related to the discovery and colonization of the islands; Natural History, with illustrations of natural events and information on how different species arrived at the islands; and Conservation, an introduction to the struggles of the ecosystems and preservation efforts under way. After viewing the exhibits, take a walk along winding paths leading from the Interpretation Center to Playa Punta Carola (about 35 minutes), a favorite of surfers, or on to Mann Beach for a swim and to Frigate Bird Hill, a nesting place for frigate birds. Along the way are plants, lava lizards, and other animals endemic to this area. ⊠ *2 km (1 mi) southwest of Puerto Baquerizo Moreno* ☒ *Free* ⊙ *Daily 10–8.*

El Progreso, one of San Cristóbal's first colonies, is a small village about 8 km (5 mi) east of Puerto Baquerizo Moreno at the end of one of the island's few roads (buses connect the two towns twice daily). From El

Progreso you can rent a four-wheel-drive vehicle and explore the shores of **Laguna el Junco,** one of the archipelago's few permanent freshwater lakes, 10 km (6 mi) east.

Punta Pitt, at the northeastern tip of the island, is the only place in the Galápagos where you can view three species of boobies—masked, blue-footed, and red-footed—nesting together. Also found here are frigate birds, storm petrels, and swallow-tailed gulls. The site is accessible by motor launch from Puerto Moreno.

WHERE TO STAY & EAT

$ ▥**Miconia Cabañas.** Rooms snake back along a garden strewn with morning glories at this new hotel on Puerto Baquerizo's main street and the nicest lodging on the island. The outside is stone and stucco. Inside are pastel-color rooms, some with refrigerators. The upstairs restaurant specializes in seafood. ⊠*Puerto Baquerizo Moreno* ☎*05/252–0608* ⊕*www.miconia.com* ↗*8 rooms, 4 suites* ♿*In-room: refrigerator (some). In-hotel: restaurant, bar, pool, gym, no elevator, public Internet* ▤*DC, MC, V* ⍟*BP.*

ISABELA

6

Although Isabela is the largest island in the archipelago, it has very little tourism infrastructure. The handful of hotels are very basic, with only intermittent hot water. Sleepy **Puerto Villamil,** founded in 1897 as a center for extracting lime, is the focus of Isabela's tourist trade—nearby are several lagoons where flamingos and migratory birds can be viewed up close, as well as beaches with large populations of herons, egrets, and other birds. Isabela's other community is **Santo Tomás,** 18 km (11 mi) northwest.

The island's signature excursion, is a guided 9-km (5½-mi) trek ascending the 1,370-meter (4,488-foot) **Volcán Sierra Negra.** The volcano erupted in October 2005, but, thankfully, the event threatened none of the island's population—human or animal. Seismologists have kept close watch on any untoward activity, but excursions are open again after a brief suspension. The volcano's crater—roughly 10 km (6 mi) in diameter—is the second-largest in the world. A more ambitious trek, requiring adequate planning and equipment, is 1,100-meter (3,600-foot) **Volcán Alcedox.** The site can be reached only by boat, after which a 10-km (6-mi) trail climbs over rough terrain. You cannot traipse around the island without a guide, and you'll need one here. Your rewards are stunning views and a chance to see the archipelago's largest population of Galápagos tortoises.

Paraguay

WORD OF MOUTH

"Paraguay has a completely different vibe than any other country in Latin America. It is truly unique, and so overlooked. The indigenous Guarani culture is so prevalent (95% of the population speaks the language, the majority much more often than Spanish; only 70% speak Spanish at all, and that drops to about 50% outside of Asunción)."

—realnewlight

Updated by
Jeffrey Van
Fleet

FROM THE SUBLE CHARMS OF ASUNCIÓN, the laid-back capital, to the country's wild countryside and small colonial towns, Paraguay is a country full of surprises and little hideaways. Even the most seasoned travelers, however, scratch their heads when the subject is Paraguay. If the country enters their consciousness at all, it comes as an answer to the trivia question, "Which South American nations have no sea-coast?" (Bolivia is the other.) But Paraguay is more than the answer to a stumper on a quiz show—this Rip Van Winkle of South American nations has finally awakened from almost two centuries of slumber.

Decades of authoritarian rule left Paraguay behind while nearby Argentina and Brazil made rapid economic strides. The country has struggled since 1989—its first year of democracy—to make up for lost time. Although intent on catching up with its neighbors, Paraguay has not completely rubbed the sleep out of its eyes. You'll marvel at the easy pace of life and the old-fashioned courtesies of the people. In Asunción, crowds are seldom a problem when you take in its architectural showplaces. In the wild countryside you'll stumble across villages where you're the only visitor.

A trip to the tranquil southern region of the *ruinas jesuíticas* (Jesuit ruins) transports you to a time when missionaries worked the fields alongside their indigenous Guaraní converts. Some of the world's best fishing can be had in rivers teeming with giant catfish. Anglers can test their skills as clouds of snowy egrets take flight and monkeys swing through trees along the banks. Vultures soar over the sun-scorched plains of the Chaco, an arid scrubland that covers half of Paraguay and is one of the most sparsely populated spots on earth, with less than one inhabitant for each of its 250,000 square km (97,500 square mi).

Intrigued about joining the small number of people who have visited this developing destination? Realize that tourism infrastructure is not what it is in Brazil and Argentina, although things are improving all the time. On top of that, the highway system is underdeveloped, and good accommodations are rare outside Asunción. But there's an upside to visiting one of the least-known countries on the continent: Paraguayans seem genuinely interested in finally becoming part of the international community. They'll start by lavishing attention on you, hoping you'll tell a few friends about their country once you get home.

ORIENTATION & PLANNING

GETTING ORIENTED

Picture Paraguay as a scrunched, lopsided figure-eight. The Río Paraguay splits its two halves, with Asunción, the capital, sitting near the center. The subtropical southeast, the smaller half of the country, distinguished by thick forests and meandering rivers, holds 98% of the country's population. It's also the tourist's Paraguay, giving you access to Asunción and the Jesuit ruins. The other half of the "eight"

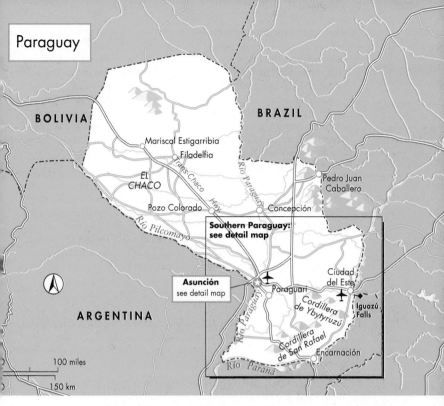

is the desolate Chaco region, little explored and sparsely populated, but important to the country's agriculture.

Asunción. South America's sleepiest capital honestly does hustle and bustle, but at its own relaxed pace. This is the center of all that is Paraguay, where you can take in the country's monuments and history.

Southern Paraguay. A string of 18th century Jesuit missions dates from an era when missionaries and indigenous peoples worked side by side. All can be visited in a hurried one- or more relaxed two-day trip from the capital.

PARAGUAY PLANNER

WHEN TO GO

Paraguay's relative lack of tourists means there aren't well-delineated high and low seasons. There are fewer good hotels in the country than elsewhere on the continent, so reservations are recommended year-round, especially in Asunción.

CLIMATE

Traveling in Paraguay can be uncomfortable from December to March, when the sun beats down on the landlocked country. The heat is intense,

TOP REASONS TO GO

Load Up on Lace. Few words in the language begin with the tilded ñ. A tablecloth or placemat worked in ñandutí fashion is sure to elicit admiration from the folks back home, as well as comments on its unusual name. Artisans craft the delicate spiderweb lacework out of silk or cotton to create Paraguay's signature souvenir.

Reel One In. Believe it or not, southwestern Paraguay is one of the world's foremost freshwater-fishing destinations, with a small handful of resorts catering to the anglers among you. Giant, fighting dorado and catfishlike surubí will test your talents.

Play Explorer. If you seek a less-trodden South American destination than Brazil's beaches or Peru's Machu Picchu, plant your flag in Paraguay. Hospitality is your reward for staking out a claim in this little-known country.

Go On a Mission. Southern Paraguay was the site of a string of colonial-era Jesuit missions where priests and the indigenous Guaraní lived and worked in perfect harmony side by side. The structures remain mostly well preserved, and are, fortuitously, laid out in a circuit, which makes for easy touring.

so don't plan activities for the early afternoon (there's a daily siesta, anyway). The wettest months are December to April, the driest June to August. Torrential cloudbursts can quickly turn unpaved roads into torrents of muddy red water.

The following are the average daily maximum and minimum temperatures for Asunción.

Jan.	93F	34C	May	77F	25C	Sept.	80F	27C
	72	22		55	14		60	16
Feb.	93F	34C	June	72F	22C	Oct.	84F	29C
	72	22		55	13		62	17
Mar.	91F	33C	July	75F	24C	Nov.	88F	31C
	70	21		57	14		66	19
Apr.	82F	28C	Aug.	77F	25C	Dec.	91F	33C
	64	18		57	14		70	21

HOLIDAYS

Pay attention to legal holidays when everything, except your hotel, shuts down entirely, and public transportation is packed with Paraguayans traveling to visit friends and family.

New Year's Day; Heroes Day (March 1); Holy Week (March or April); Labor Day (May 1); Independence Day (May 14–15); Armistice of Chaco War (June 12); Founding of Asunción (August 15); Victory at Boquerón (September 29); Feast of the Immaculate Conception (December 8); Christmas (December 25).

GETTING HERE & AROUND

BY AIR

Few international airlines fly directly to Asunción's Aeropuerto Internacional Silvio Pettirossi. The only way to get to Paraguay is through another South American gateway. Paraguay's TAM Airlines connects in São Paulo with flights from the United States and Europe by its same-named Brazilian partner. It also flies from Buenos Aires, Montevideo, Santiago, and Santa Cruz. Bolivia's AeroSur flies from Santa Cruz and Buenos Aires, and Brazil's Gol from São Paulo.

BY BUS

Intercity buses are inexpensive, fast, and reliable. Long-distance buses—some with air-conditioning, reclining seats, and movies—race between the major centers. Bone-shaking local buses, known as *colectivos*, rattle between villages and along city streets. The 370-km (230-mi) journey from Asunción to Encarnación takes about five hours by bus and costs G50,000; the 330-km (205-mi) trip from Asunción to Ciudad del Este also takes five hours and costs G50,000.

BY CAR

Driving isn't easy in Paraguay—only 25% of the country's roads are paved, and motorists tend to ignore traffic laws. Main highways between hub cities are in decent shape, but side roads quickly degenerate into potholes, or may be closed altogether during the rainy season because of flooding. Beware of animals that wander onto the roads, especially at night. On weekends and around holidays, access roads into and out of Asunción can be jammed with traffic. On the plus side, there are fewer vehicles on the road here than in neighboring Argentina or Brazil.

Although drivers around you won't appear to be doing it, **obey speed limits religiously in Paraguay.** We hear reports of transit police delighting in singling out rental cars for speeding violations and requesting fines on the spot.

Your driver's license is valid here for short-term stays. Seat belts are mandatory. The speed limit is 80 kph (50 mph) on highways and 40 kph (25 mph) in urban areas.

GAS STATIONS   Distances between gas stations can be long, so you should top off your tank regularly. Stations are normally open until midnight. Gasoline costs about G6,000 per liter.

ESSENTIALS

ELECTRICITY

Paraguay operates on a 220 volt, 50-cycle system, with a single-phase AC current.

ENTRY REQUIREMENTS

Citizens of the United Kingdom may enter Paraguay for 90 days with a valid passport that has at least six months' remaining validity. U.S., Canadian, Australian, and New Zealand citizens must obtain a visa before arrival. Embassies in Washington and Ottawa require your application to include your passport with at least six months' remaining validity, two passport-size photos, and the visa form (downloadable in PDF format from their Web sites). Paraguayan embassies in South American capitals might also ask for copies of your bank statements and confirmed flight itineraries.

DID YOU KNOW?

Paraguay is the only country in the world whose flag differs front and back.

Fees, payable in U.S. dollars only, are $45 for a single-entry visa and $65 for multiple entries. There is no Paraguayan representation in Australia or New Zealand. Most travelers from those countries obtain their visas in another South American capital.

Contacts **Embassy of Paraguay** (⊠ *151 Slater St., Suite 501, Ottawa, Ontario* ☏ *613/567–1283* 🖷 *613/567–1679* ⊕ *www.embassyofparaguay.ca*). **Embassy of Paraguay** (⊠ *2400 Massachusetts Ave. NW, Washington, DC* 🖷 *202/483–6960* 🖷 *202/234–4508* ⊕ *www.embaparusa.gov.py*).

HEALTH & SAFETY

Two worrisome public-health problems have gripped Paraguay. Yellow fever, usually found only in remote, swampy regions of South America, has appeared in urban areas, including the suburbs of Asunción. The jury is still out on whether or not the disease actually *is* transmitted in urban locales; for now, the U.S. Centers for Disease Control recommend that all travelers over one year of age be vaccinated no matter what the destination in Paraguay.

No vaccine exists for the mosquito-borne dengue fever, also a problem here. Symptoms are characterized by muscle aches and fever, and dengue's rarer, but more virulent hemorrhagic form can be fatal. Tourists, who are more likely to stay in air-conditioned hotels with well-maintained grounds, are less at risk than the local population. Wearing long sleeves and trousers in the morning and late afternoon, and applying mosquito repellent help limit your exposure.

Although tap water is reputedly safe to drink in Asunción, most visitors stick with bottled water (*agua purificada*) no matter where they travel in Paraguay. Order it *con gas* and *sin gas* (with and without carbonation).

Crime is rising in Paraguay, although you probably won't see much evidence of it during your trip if you take the standard travel precautions. Paraguay's eastern tri-border region with Brazil and Argentina, including the town of Ciudad del Este, has become increasingly dangerous, with a rise in extremist-group violence. It's not a problem if you simply pass through the border at Ciudad del Este to see the world-famous Iguazú Falls, but see the falls from Brazil or Argentina instead. Don't stay in Ciudad del Este overnight.

The United States Embassy is open Monday–Thursday 1–5 and Friday 7:30–11:30. Canada maintains an honorary consulate in Asunción with hours Monday–Thursday 8–4 and Friday 8–noon. An honorary consulate also serves U.K. citizens with weekday hours 8–1 and 3–5:30.

Emergency Contacts Canada (✉ *Prof. Ramírez 3, Asunción* ☎ *021/227-207*). **United Kingdom** (✉ *Eulogio Estigarribia 4846 and Monseñor Bogarín, Asunción* ☎ *021/663-536*). **United States** (✉ *Av. Mariscal López 1776, Asunción* ☎ *021/213-715* ⊕ *Paraguay.usembassy.gov*).

HOURS OF OPERATION

Remember that everything shuts down between noon and 3:30, except for department stores and the odd café. You'll be surprised at how deserted the streets are during those hours, even in Asunción.

LANGUAGE

Paraguay is South America's only officially bilingual country. About half the population speaks the indigenous Guaraní as its first language. If you know some Spanish, don't hesitate to use it. In Asunción the staff at more expensive hotels and restaurants are likely to speak some English. The typical person on the street likely knows none. Outside Asunción it's unusual to find anyone who speaks anything but Spanish or Guaraní.

MONEY MATTERS

CURRENCY & EXCHANGE

Paraguay's currency is the guaraní, designated with a *G* in front of the amount. It comes in bills of 5,000, 10,000, 50,000, and 100,000 guaraníes, with coins of 100, 500, and 1,000 guaraníes. (The G50 coin and G1,000 bill are being withdrawn from circulation.) At this writing the exchange rate was 4,100 guaraníes to the U.S. dollar. Such exchange rates mean prices contain a lot of zeros. Banks and *casas de cambio* here change euros, Argentine pesos, and Brazilian reais in addition to U.S. dollars. It's practically impossible to change guaraníes outside Paraguay, so make sure you spend them or exchange them at the airport before leaving.

You'll find ATMs in the major cities, but rarely in smaller towns. Some machines on Infonet, the country's largest system, accept both Plus and Cirrus cards. Others, annoyingly, accept only one or the other. To be on the safe side, bring cards affiliated with both systems, and contact your bank about changing your password to four digits if you don't already use one—that's what will work here. The ATM at ABN Amro Bank in Asunción *does* take both, as does the machine just beyond the customs exit at Aeropuerto Internacional Silvio Pettirossi.

Most banks are open weekdays 8:45–3. Casas de cambio are open weekdays 8:30–1 and 2:30–6, Saturday 8:30–1. Public offices operate weekdays 7–1, and businesses are open around 7:30 or 8 until midday and then reopen from 3 to 6.

PRICING

Paraguay is an inexpensive country in which to travel, although even the wildly fluctuating currency has gained in value against the dollar in recent years. Going to the theater can cost from G40,000 to G80,000 for special shows or featured artists. Movies are a bargain at G15,000.

Nightlife ranges greatly in price; some of the best clubs charge upward of G8,000 for a cocktail.

Sample Prices: Cup of coffee, G2,000; bottle of beer, G4,000; soft drink, G3,000; bottle of wine, G35,000 (at a liquor store); sandwich, G15,000; crosstown taxi ride, G15,000; city bus ride, G1,000; museum entrance, G2,000–G5,000, though the majority of museums in the country are free.

TAXES The departure tax is $25 to international destinations, payable in U.S. dollars or in guaraníes (about G103,000), and $4 (G16,500) to domestic destinations. (TAM Airlines includes the tax in its ticket prices.) A 10% nonrefundable value-added tax, known as the IVA, is charged on all goods and services. It's included in the prices at bars and restaurants, but it's added to hotel bills. Watch for double-billing: IVA shouldn't be added to food-related bills charged to your room.

TIPPING An appropriate tip in upscale restaurants is about 10% of the bill, more if the service is exceptionally good. In average places, round up the bill to the nearest G1,000. Round up taxi fares to the nearest G500.

PHONES
Paraguay's country code is 595. To call Paraguay, dial the country code, then the area code, omitting the first 0.

Local numbers in urban areas have six digits; a few in Asunción and Ciudad del Este have seven digits. Rural numbers may carry as few as three or four digits. When calling between communities, precede the local number with the three- or four-digit area code. Cellular numbers have area codes beginning with "09." (The country is undergoing a *very* slow process of making the number of digits in phone numbers and area codes uniform.) For local operator assistance, dial 010. For directory assistance, dial 112.

The privatized national telephone company, the Compañía Paraguaya de Comunicaciones (COPACO), has offices in most cities and towns where you can place local and international calls. To place an international call, dial 002 followed by country code, area code and local number. Calls to the United States cost about G4,000 per minute; G5,000 to Canada; and G6,000 to Europe, Australia, and New Zealand. Lines can become congested at peak hours. If you're calling from a hotel, be sure to hang up if there's no answer for about 20 seconds; otherwise, you'll be charged for a three-minute call.

Paraguay has few phone booths, but numerous private telephone offices let you make calls. Look for TELÉFONOS PÚBLICOS or CABINAS TELEFÓNICAS signs.

An unlocked GSM cell phone is your best option for mobile communication in Paraguay. You can purchase phone cards from Claro, Tigo, and Personal, the country's three cellular providers.

Access Codes **AT&T** (☎ *008–11–800*). **British Telecom** (☎ *008–44–800*). **Canada Direct** (☎ *008–14–800*). **MCI** (☎ *008–12–800*). **Sprint** (☎ *008–13–800*).

RESTAURANTS & HOTELS

CUISINE A staple of Paraguayan dining is *parrillada*—large portions of barbecued meats. Beef, including blood sausage and organ meats, is the mainstay, but pork and chicken are also common. *Puchero* is a meat, sausage, vegetable, and chickpea stew that's eaten in the cooler months. *Bori-bori* is a hearty soup with bits of meat, vegetables, and balls molded from cheese and corn. Paraguay's rivers abound with unusual fish, such as the *surubí*, a giant catfish. It's tastiest when served in a dish called *milanesa de surubí* (battered and deep-fried fillets). Another tasty option is the *dorado*, a ferocious predator resembling the salmon. Try it lightly grilled. A soup made from the fish's head and other leftovers is surprisingly delicious.

Usual accompaniments include salads (Paraguay's tomatoes are incredibly flavorful) and *palmitos* (hearts of palm), considered a delicacy. Other side dishes include *sopa paraguaya,* a kind of corn bread made with cheese, eggs, and onions, or *chipá-guazú,* a similar dish in which roughly ground corn is substituted for cornmeal. You also may be served boiled *manioc,* a white, fibrous root with a bland flavor. *Chipá,* a type of bread made from corn flour, ground manioc, and sometimes cheese, is baked in a clay oven called a *tatakua.* It is sold everywhere and is best eaten piping hot. Typical desserts include *dulce de leche,* a pudding made from slow-cooking milk and sugar; papaya preserved in syrup; and such fresh fruits as pineapple, banana, mango, and melon.

Cafés and bars usually sell snacks, mostly fried or grilled foods that can be prepared quickly. The most popular is *milanesa,* thin slices of batter-fried beef, chicken breast, pork, or fish. Other favorites are *empanadas,* envelopes of pastry filled with beef, pork, chicken, corn, or cheese; *croquetas,* sausage-shape minced meat or poultry that is rolled in bread crumbs and deep fried; and *mixtos,* ham-and-cheese sandwiches. Many cafés have a daily lunch special—*plato del día*— that's a good bargain. Paraguayan portions tend to be generous, so don't hesitate to share a dish.

Few Paraguayans are seen without their *guampa,* a drinking vessel made of a cow's horn, metal, or wood, from which they sip a cold infusion of *yerba maté* tea. Maté is drunk hot throughout South America, but the cold version, often mixed with medicinal herbs, is more common here. Pilsners, particularly the Baviera brand, are quite good. If you order beer in a restaurant, an enormous bottle is likely to be brought to your table in an ice bucket. Beer on tap is known as *chopp* (pronounced "shop").

Since restaurants sometimes close between meals, it's important to plan when to eat. Lunch can begin at 11:30, but 12:30 is more typical. Some restaurants stop serving lunch as early as 2. Dinner is often available at 7 PM, with restaurants staying open until 11. More sophisticated dining spots open at 8 PM and serve until shortly after midnight. On Sunday, lunch hours are extended, but late dinner might not be served. Café hours are generally 7 AM–10 PM.

ACCOMMO-
DATION
The largest selection of lodgings is in Asunción, although sheer numbers of hotels remain small. Those that are here offer good value for the rates they charge. Evenings get surprisingly chilly here between June and August, but most upscale hotels have much-appreciated heating during the winter. Any place mid-range or above also offers air-conditioning, a must during the summer. Outside Asunción, hotels are few and far between.

WHAT IT COSTS (IN GUARANÍES)				
¢	$	$$	$$$	$$$$
RESTAURANTS under G$24,000	G$24,000– G$40,000	G$40,000– G$61,000	G$61,000– G$81,000	over G$81,000
HOTELS under G$161,000	G$161,000– G$242,000	G$242,000– G$403,000	G$403,000– G$726,000	over G$726,000

Restaurant prices are based on the median main course price at dinner. Hotel prices are for two people in a standard double room in high season.

VISITOR &
TOUR INFO
The friendly staff at Secretaria Nacional de Turismo (Senatur) in Asunción can dish out advice, pamphlets, and maps at the main office near the Plaza de los Héroes daily 7–7. A branch in the Asunción airport arrivals hall beyond the customs exit is open daily for arriving flights. Little printed information on Paraguay is available in English. What you have in your hands is a rare example.

ASUNCIÓN

1,135 km (704 mi) or two hours by air west of São Paulo, Brazil.

Asunción was founded on August 15, 1537—the Feast of the Assumption, or *Asunción* in Spanish. Take a step back and you'll see traces of the city that was once the colonial capital of southern South America. On the drive from the airport, taxis whisk by the magnificent mansions lining Avenida Mariscal López—a furtive glimpse through a doorway reveals a peaceful patio reminiscent of those in southern Spain. Remnants of Asunción's prosperous past can also be detected in the delicately decorated facades and balconies of belle epoque buildings that have survived the vagaries of fashion, although in some instances they've yielded to commercialism by leasing the ground floor to fast-food joints with blaring neon signs. Alongside the money changers and peddlers of fake Rolex watches who patrol the streets and plazas, indigenous women sell bundles of herbs and roots—centuries-old remedies for every ailment. Contrasting with the hustle and bustle of the nearby commercial center, the pristine columned government buildings overlook the Bay of Asunción as cool breezes rustle through flame trees in the riverside park.

GETTING HERE & AROUND

BY AIR
Asunción's Aeropuerto Internacional Silvio Pettirossi (ASU) is 15 km (9 mi) northeast of downtown. The airport seems to jostle to life with each arrival and departure, and then drifts back to sleep until the the

next flight. Few international airlines serve the airport, and it receives no long-haul flights, making connecting in another South American city necessary to arrive in Asunción.

Taxis are the most practical means of getting to town, and they charge a fixed rate of G93,000. The airport information desk can tell you the exact rate. It can also arrange for an *ómnibus special* whenever there are six or more passengers. This costs G35,000 per person, and will take you to any address in downtown Asunción.

BY BUS All intercity services leave from Terminal de Ómnibus Asunción, located east of downtown. The three major bus companies, La Encarnaceña, Pluma, and Rápido Yguazú, also have information booths on Plaza Uruguaya.

Asunción's spiffy public buses run every 10 minutes during the day. The fare is G2,000. As in all big cities, watch your belongings carefully.

BY CAR Unless you plan to travel out of town, avoid renting a car—driving in Asunción can be a nerve-racking experience. Aggressive bus drivers, confusing routes, and never-ending road construction make even Paraguayans (who rarely follow traffic rules) nervous. Few downtown intersections have stoplights. Negotiate them carefully.

ESSENTIALS

Bus Contacts **La Encarnaceña** (☎ *021/551–745*). **Pluma** (☎ *021/490–128*). **Rápido Yguazú** (☎ *021/557–201*).**Terminal de Ómnibus** (✉ *República Argentina at Fernando de la Mora* ☎ *021/551–740*).

Currency Exchange **ABN Amro Bank** (✉ *Estrella at Alberi* ☎ *021/419–0000*). **American Express** (✉ *Yegros 690* ☎ *021/490–111*). **Cambios Chaco** (✉ *Palma 364* ☎ *021/445–315*). **La Moneda** (✉ *25 de Mayo 127* ☎ *021/494–724*). **Multibanco** (✉ *Aeropuerto Internacional Silvio Pettirossi* ☎ *021/647–199*). **InTerbanco** (✉ *Oliva 349* ☎ *021/494–992*).

Internet **Cyber Shop** (✉ *Estrella 474* ☎ *021/446–290*).

Medical Assistance **Hospital Privado Francés** (✉ *Brasilia at Insaurralde* ☎ *021/295–250*). **Hospital Privado Bautista** (✉ *Av. República Argentina at Andrés Campos Cervera* ☎ *021/600–171*).

Post Office **Dirección General de Correos** (✉ *Alberdi and Benjamín Constant* ☎ *021/498–112*).

Rental Cars **Hertz** (✉ *Aeropuerto Internacional Silvio Pettirossi* ☎ *021/645–100* ✉ *Km 4.5 Av. Eusebio Ayala* ☎ *021/605–708*). **National** (✉ *Yegros 501* ☎ *021/492–157*).

Taxis **Radio Taxi Asunción** (*RTA* ☎ *021/311–080*).

Visitor & Tour Info **Senatur** (✉ *Palma 468 at 14 de Mayo* ☎ *021/441–530* ✉ *Aeropuerto Internacional Silvio Pettirossi* ☎ *021/645–600* ⊕ *www. senatur.gov.py*).

Asunción

Río Paraguay

Puerto Asunción ◆
Aduana

Paraguayo Independiente

Benjamín Constant

Presidente Franco

Av. República
Palacio
Legislativo ◆

Correo ◆

Teatro ◆
Municipal

Palma

Estrella

Ayolas

Juan. E. O'Leary

15 de Agosto

14 de Mayo

Alberdi

Chile

Oliva

Colón

Montevideo

Gen. Díaz

Haedo

Humaitá

KEY

❶ *Exploring sights*

① *Hotels & restaurants*

🛈 *Tourist information*

Piribebuy

Manduvirá

Exploring ▼

Casa de la
Independencia **3**

Casa de los Diputados **4**

Catedral de Nuestra Señora
de la Asunción **8**

Gran Hotel
del Paraguay **13**

Jardín Botánico
y Zoológico **11**

Manzana de la Rivera **6**

Museo de
Bellas Artes **9**

Museo del Barro **12**

Museo del Cabildo **7**

Palacio del Gobierno **5**

Panteón Nacional
de los Héroes **2**

Plaza de los Héroes **1**

Plaza Uruguaya **10**

Restaurants ▼

Il Capo **16**

Churrasquéria
Acuarela **22**

Mburicaó **20**

La Paraguayita **21**

La Pérgola Jardín **15**

0 — 300 yards
0 — 300 meters

Universidad Católica

Av. España

Mariscal López

Eligio Ayala

Asunción

Mcal. Estigarribia

Nuestra Señora de la

Independencia Nacional

25 de Mayo

Yegros

Iturbe

Cerro Corá

Caballero

México

Paraguarí

Antequera

Tacuary

Azara

Luis A. Herrera

Fulgencio R. Moreno

Manuel Domínguez

Parapití

Estados Unidos

EXPLORING ASUNCIÓN

The city is built on a rise overlooking a large bay formed by the Río Paraguay. The *centro* (downtown) runs south–southeast from the bay for about 10 blocks to Teniente Fariña, and it stretches 17 blocks from Colón in the west to Estados Unidos in the east. Most hotels, restaurants, shops, and offices can be found in this rectangle, easily explored in a day. Except for the irregular shoreline along the river, Asunción's streets follow a standard grid. Downtown streets are narrow and generally have one-way traffic. Two major squares—Plaza de los Héroes and Plaza Uruguaya—provide cool resting places in the shade of jacaranda trees. You'll appreciate these during the unbearably hot October–March months. Addresses are frequently expressed in terms of intersections. If the location is close to an intersection, the address may be expressed as "Alberdi *casi* Estrella" (Alberdi "almost at" Estrella).

MAIN ATTRACTIONS

❸ Casa de la Independencia. This 1774 house with whitewashed walls, brick floors, and a lovely patio was once the secret meeting place of revolutionaries plotting to break away from Spain. They entered and left in the dead of night through the *callejón* (alleyway) in back. Relics from the May 1811 revolution, which secured Paraguay's independence, are displayed in this well-maintained museum, as are religious artifacts and furnishings depicting a typical colonial-era home. ⊠*14 de Mayo at Presidente Franco* ☎*021/493–918* ⊕*www.casadelaindependencia. org.py* ⊠*Free* ☉ *Weekdays 7–6:30, Sat. 8–noon.*

❷ Panteón Nacional de los Héroes. Nothing symbolizes Paraguayan history
★ more than the National Pantheon of Heroes, a memorial to the fallen soldiers of the country's hopeless battles and disastrous wars. Construction began in 1864 under the regime of Francisco Solano López, who envisioned a chapel modeled after Les Invalides in Paris. López was soon to lead Paraguay into the catastrophic War of the Triple Alliance. The building was completed in 1936 after the Pyrrhic victory of the Chaco War against Bolivia. López is interred here, as are the remains of two of Paraguay's unknown soldiers. The wars still loom large in Paraguay's consciousness, but commemorative plaques placed on the walls by the old enemies—Argentina, Bolivia, Brazil, and Uruguay— illustrate that all is forgiven if not forgotten. Two sentinels guard the eerily quiet memorial, a place of pilgrimage for every Paraguayan who visits Asunción. ⊠*Mariscal Estigarribia at Plaza de los Héroes* ☎*No phone* ⊠*Free* ☉*Mon.–Sat 6* AM*–6:30* PM*, Sun. 6–noon.*

❶ Plaza de los Héroes. This plaza, whose centerpiece is the Panteón Nacional de los Héroes, is the heart of Asunción. Since the subtleties of Paraguayan life are laid bare in its busy plazas, this is a good place to rest in the shade and watch the locals. Guaraní vendors sell feather headdresses and bows and arrows, artisans display their pottery, and traveling salespeople hawk anything from patent cures to miracle knife sharpeners. You can also climb onto a high chair for a shoe shine or have your picture taken with an old box camera. On public holidays the square is often the scene of live music and folk-dance performances. The plaza's northeast quadrant contains a monument to the victims of torture and execution under the Stroessner dictatorship. ⊠ *Nuestra Señora de la Asunción at 25 de Mayo.*

IF YOU HAVE TIME

❹ **Casa de los Diputados.** Once a convent, then a much-needed blood bank during the Chaco War, then a military museum, then a cultural center, this Spanish colonial building now contains offices for members of Congress. The newly constructed, glass congress building, the Palacio Legislativo, seems to swallow the historic building ⊠ *14 de Mayo at El Paraguayo Independiente* ☏ *021/415–500* 💲 *Free* ⊙ *Weekdays 7–1.*

FRUGAL FUN

Enjoy the pomp of a 15-minute changing-of-the-guard ceremony at the Panteón Nacional de los Heároes Saturdays at 10 AM.

❽ **Catedral de Nuestra Señora de la Asunción.** Inside the newly renovated seat of the Archdiocese of Asunción, portions of which date from 1687, are an enormous gilded altar and many 18th- and 19th-century religious statues and paintings. ⊠ *Plaza Independencia* ☏ *021/449–512* 💲 *Free* ⊙ *Daily 9–11:30 and 6–8.*

❸ **Gran Hotel del Paraguay.** This well-preserved mansion has an illustrious past as the former home of Madame Elisa Lynch, the Irish mistress of Paraguayan dictator Francisco Solano López. Now the oldest hotel in Asunción, and not quite where the action is, it's nonetheless surrounded by verandas and carefully tended tropical gardens. Duck inside to see the collection of 19th-century furniture and paintings and enjoy a cool cocktail at the bar. ⊠ *Calle de la Residenta 902, at Padre Puchen* ☏ *021/200–051.*

⓫ **Jardín Botánico y Zoológico.** The government has improved maintenance at this once-neglected park (a trend that's catching on in other parts of the country as well). Besides plenty of plants and a small zoo, you'll find a fine example of a country house, once the home of President Francisco Solano López. It's now a museum with exhibits on Paraguayan wildlife, ethnology, and history. ⊠ *Gral Artigas and Primer Presidente* ☏ *021/291–255* 💲 *G5,000* ⊙ *Daily 7–5.*

❻ **Manzana de la Rivera.** In a model for urban planners everywhere, the city of Asunción combined this *manzana* (block) of nine historic houses near the river into a pleasing cultural center. The oldest of these, the 1764 Casa Viola, the name by which many Asunceños refer to the complex, serves as a small city museum called the **Museo Memoria de la Ciudad.** The Casa Emaša, once a customs office, now houses **La Galería,** the center's art gallery. The 1914 art nouveau **Casa Clari,** the newest house, is the complex's café. ⊠ *Ayolas 129* ☏ *021/442–448* ⊕ *museo.mca. gov.py* 💲 *Free* ⊙ *Weekdays 7 AM–9 PM, weekends 10–9.*

❾ **Museo de Bellas Artes.** The region's artistic legacy is displayed at the Museum of Fine Arts, which has a collection of paintings and sculpture by Paraguayan and other South American artists. Some of the country's most important documents are found in the museum's archive, but the records are geared toward scholarly research rather than tourist perusal. ✉ *Mariscal Estigarribia at Iturbe* ☎ *021/447–716* 🖂 *Free* ⏲ *Tues.–Fri. 7–6:30, Sat. 8–noon.*

🄲 **Museo del Barro.** Though billed as a modern art museum, the so-called "Museum of Clay" includes colonial and indigenous art, but is actually better known for its collection of pre-colonial Guaraní ceramics. ✉ *Grabadores del Cabichu'í at Cañana* ☎ *021/607–996* ⊕ *www. museodelbarro.com* 🖂 *G8,000* ⏲ *Wed.–Sun. 3:30–8.*

🄷 **Museo del Cabildo.** During the Francia dictatorship, Paraguayans were not permitted to view the exterior of this building, but today you can even tour the interior. Paraguay's constitution was proclaimed on the first floor of the Legislative Palace in 1870. The second floor was added in 1857, destroying the original symmetry of the single-story Jesuit design. Following a long tenure as the Palacio Legislativo (Legislative Palace), the building presently serves as a museum of Paraguayan history. (Paraguay's congress now meets in the gleaming glass building, donated and constructed by the government of Taiwan, across the plaza.) ✉ *Plaza Independencia* ☎ *021/443–094* ⊕ *www.cabildoccr. gov.py* 🖂 *Free* ⏲ *Tues.–Fri. 9–7, weekends 10–5.*

🄵 **Palacio del Gobierno.** The elegant horseshoe-shape Government Palace, with verandas and wide staircases, overlooks the bay, and is Asunción's iconic sight. It's only open to the public on most holidays, but gives tours on Thursday and Friday if you arrange it one day in advance. Of course, you can take in the outside view with its soft white illumination every night from dusk to dawn. ✉ *El Paraguayo Independiente and Ayolas* ☎ *021/419–8220* 🖂 *Free.*

🄳 **Plaza Uruguaya.** So named to honor Uruguay for returning territory it seized in the bloody Chaco War initiated by Paraguay, the plaza is a pleasant respite from the city's heat. On one side is a covered market with a good selection of Latin American literature, and on the other is the 1861 colonnaded **railway station,** shuttered since the discontinuation of rail service. The station now serves as a museum of rail memorabilia, the highlight of which is a well-preserved old steam locomotive, the *Sapucaí,* no longer in use. ☎ *021/447–848 station* ⏲ *Tues.–Fri. 9–5, weekends 9–1* 🖂 *G10,000.*

WHERE TO EAT

$ ✕**Il Capo.** Just opposite La Pérgola Jardín, this small eatery has white-
ITALIAN   washed walls and wooden beams. The homemade pastas, like lasagna *con camarones* (with shrimp) and *melanzana alla parmegiana* (eggplant with tomato and Parmesan), are excellent, and the Italian wine list is reasonably priced. ✉ *Perú 291* ☎ *021/213–022* 🖂 *Austria 1689 and Viena* ☎ *021/608–704* ▭ *AE, DC, MC, V.*

$ ✕**Churrasquería Acuarela.** A 10-minute taxi ride from the centro, this
BRAZILIAN   enormous, 1,300-seat *rodízio*-style restaurant might just be the best
★   value in town. Waiters traverse the dining room with skewers of grilled sausage, chicken, pork, and beef, slicing off as much as you want. You can mosey over to the buffet laden with salads, vegetables, and desserts. For something different, ask for *cupim,* a cut of meat taken from the

hump of the Brahma cattle bred in Paraguay and Brazil. ⊠*Mariscal López 4049 at San Martín* ☎*021/601–750* ⊟*AE, DC, MC, V.*

$$ ✕**Mburicaó.** Chef Rodolfo Angenscheidt honed his skills at the Parisian culinary landmark Maxim's before opening this contemporary restaurant, which has become a favorite of Asunción business executives. Specialties include innovative takes on South American and continental favorites, including fresh Patagonian truffle risotto and surubí with mozzarella and tomato in puff pastry. The airy dining room overlooks a lush patio. ⊠*Prof. A. González Riobóo 737, at Chaco Boreal* ☎*021/611–501* ⊟*AE, DC, MC, V.*

ECLECTIC

$ ✕**La Paraguayita.** Its shaded terrace makes this the best of the numerous parrillas that line Avenida Brasilia. Huge portions of perfectly barbecued beef and pork are accompanied by wonderfully seasoned *sopa paraguaya* and *chipá-guazú.* The chorizo sausages make a good starter, especially when dunked in tangy *criollo,* a spicy onion, tomato, and garlic sauce. ⊠*Brasilia at Siria* ☎*021/204–497* ⊟*AE, DC, MC, V.*

LATIN
AMERICAN
Fodor'sChoice
★

$ ✕**La Pérgola Jardín.** Floor-to-ceiling mirrors, modern black-lacquer furniture, and live saxophone and piano music make this restaurant one of Asunción's most sophisticated dining spots. The service is efficient and friendly, and the ever-changing menu is contemporary. Warning: the piping-hot *pan de queso,* small cheese-flavored rolls, are irresistible. ⊠*Perú 240* ☎*021/214–014* ⊟*AE, DC, MC, V.*

CONTINENTAL

$$ ✕**La Preferida.** Rub shoulders with politicians and diplomats where the two chic dining areas (one of which is no-smoking at peak hours) are set with crisp linen tablecloths and elegant silver and glassware. The house specialty is surubí, served smoked or in a mild curry sauce. Try the excellent *lomo de cerdo à la pimienta* (peppered pork tenderloin)—ask for it if you don't see it on the menu. The Austrian owners have fine-tuned the service, so expect friendliness and efficiency. ⊠*25 de Mayo 1005, at Estados Unidos* ☎*021/210–641* ⊟*AE, DC, MC, V.*

PARAGUAYAN

$ ✕**Talleyrand.** Specialties at this local chain include duck à l'orange, sirloin steak, and surubí. The soft green color scheme and the hunting prints lend the dining rooms a refined colonial style. Talleyrand also has a location at Shopping del Sol. ⊠*Mariscal Estigarribia 932* ☎*021/441–163* ⊠*Av. Aviadores del Chaco at Prof. D. E. González* ☎*021/611–697* ⬧*Reservations essential* ⊟*AE, DC, MC, V* ☉*Mariscal Estigarribia branch closed Sun.*

ECLECTIC

$ ✕**Tío Lucas.** Glossy cream-and-black wallpaper and chic Thonet bentwood chairs give this corner eatery a crisp, modern look. The specialty here is pizza with an astounding variety of toppings to choose from. ⊠*25 de Mayo at Yegros* ☎*021/447–114* ⊟*No credit cards* ☉*Closed Sun.*

ITALIAN

WHERE TO STAY

$$$ ⊞**Asunción Internacional Hotel.** An abundance of greenery greets you as you enter this modern, 15-story hotel. The sleek black-and-white lobby has an executive bar where you can enjoy a cocktail. Many of the rather small rooms, which are redecorated every couple of years, have views of the bay. Each contains a data port where you can plug in your laptop; if you didn't bring it along, the hotel's business center offers four terminals. **Pros:** central location. **Cons:** small rooms. ⊠*Ayolas 520,*

at Oliva ☎*021/494–114* 🖷*021/494–383* ⊕*www.hotelinternacional. com.py* 🛏*74 rooms, 26 suites* ⚒*In-room: refrigerator, safe, Wi-Fi. In-hotel: 2 restaurants, room service, bar, pool, gym, public Internet, airport shuttle, parking (no fee)* ▤*AE, DC, MC, V* ⦿*BP.*

$ ⊡**Asunción Palace Hotel.** Built in the mid-19th century as a private residence for the López family, and transformed into a hospital during the War of the Triple Alliance, this beaux arts–style hotel is now a national landmark. It's certainly charming, though a few of the rooms are noisy. Others are quite nice and peaceful; ask to see one before taking it. All are simply furnished, but this is a good budget option. **Pros:** good budget value, friendly staff. **Cons:** small rooms, some noise. ✉*Colón 415* ☎*021/492–152* 🖷*021/492–153* ✑*aphotel@yahoo.com* 🛏*25 rooms, 2 suites* ⚒*In-room: refrigerator, no TV (some). In-hotel: restaurant, bar* ▤*DC, MC, V* ⦿*BP.*

$–$$ ⊡**Excelsior Inn.** This hotel owned by the owners of the nearby Hotel Excelsior lacks the frills of its pricier sibling. Rooms, many with hardwood floors, are pleasantly furnished with dark greens and golds. Each has an in-room data port—a rarity at this price range. **Pros:** good budget value, friendly staff. **Cons:** some worn rooms. ✉*Alberdi and Manduvirá* ☎🖷*021/496–743* ⊕*www.excelsior.com.py* 🛏*23 rooms, 1 suite* ⚒*In-room: refrigerator, dial-up. In-hotel: laundry service, airport shuttle* ▤*AE, DC, MC, V* ⦿*BP.*

$$$ ⊡**Granados Park Hotel.** Replicating the sensibility of a grand old Latin American hotel, this place gives you colonial style with modern amenities. The attentive staff greets you in an opulent lobby filled with lush greenery. The modern rooms are much more subdued, decorated with carved wooden armoires and handicrafts. **Pros:** central location, services for business travelers. **Cons:** some reports of slow Wi-Fi connections. ✉*Estrella and 15 de Agosto* ☎*021/497–921* 🖷*021/445–324* ⊕*www.granadospark.com.py* 🛏*57 rooms, 12 suites* ⚒*In-room: refrigerator, safe, Wi-Fi. In-hotel: restaurant, room service, bar, pool, gym, concierge, laundry service, public Internet, airport shuttle* ▤*AE, DC, MC, V* ⦿*BP.*

$$$$ ⊡**Hotel Casino Yacht y Golf Club Paraguayo.** This remodeled riverside resort 13 km (8 mi) southeast of Asunción has regained its reputation as one of South America's finest hotels. Some of the rooms, which are decorated with leather furniture, open onto verdant patios where hummingbirds nest in the foliage. You'll find plenty of recreational options here. **Pros:** many activities. **Cons:** far from city, crowded on weekends, some worn rooms. ✉*Av. del Yacht 11, Lambaré* ☎*021/906–121 or 021/906–117* 🖷*021/906–120* ⊕*www.hotelyacht.com.py* 🛏*116 rooms, 12 suites* ⚒*In-room: refrigerator, safe, Wi-Fi. In-hotel: 4 restaurants, room service, bar, golf course, tennis courts, pool, gym, spa, beachfront, laundry service, public Internet* ▤*AE, DC, MC, V* ⦿*BP.*

$$ ⊡**Hotel Cecilia.** Priding itself on personalized attention, this hotel has won a devoted clientele. Rooms are large, though slightly austere. The sixth-floor terrace has a pool with a terrific bay view. Adjacent to the hotel you'll find an excellent deli and pastry shop. **Pros:** close to entertainment, friendly service. **Cons:** spartan rooms, several blocks from sights. ✉*Estados Unidos 341* ☎*021/210–365* 🖷*021/497–111*

⊕*www.hotelcecilia.com.py* ⇌*50 rooms* ☐*In-room: refrigerator. In-hotel: restaurant, room service, bar, pool, gym, laundry service, airport shuttle, parking* ☐*AE, DC, MC, V* ☐*CP.*

$$ ☐**Hotel Chaco.** Friendly, attentive service is the hallmark of this comfortable, if rather unremarkably decorated, lodging. The carpeted rooms are large, but the beds are small. A tasty breakfast is included in the rate. **Pros:** central location, friendly staff. **Cons:** some dark rooms, some small beds. ☒*Caballero 285* ☎*021/492–066* ☐*021/444–223* ⊕*www.hotelchaco.com.py* ⇌*68 rooms, 2 suites* ☐*In-room: Wi-Fi, refrigerator. In-hotel: restaurant, bar, pool, gym, laundry service, airport shuttle, parking (no fee)* ☐*AE, DC, MC, V* ☐*CP.*

$$–$$$ ☐**Hotel Excelsior.** Regency-style fabrics, carved-wood furniture, and Oriental rugs make this one of the city's most elegant hotels, and an ongoing refurbishing is making the place gleam again. You'll sink into the carpeting in the huge, plush, brightly furnished rooms accented with wood carvings and Paraguayan art. The three-story Excelsior Mall is across the street. **Pros:** close to shopping, friendly staff. **Cons:** a few worn rooms, several blocks from sights. ☒*Chile 980* ☎*021/495– 632* ☐*021/496–748* ⊕*www.excelsior.com.py* ⇌*116 rooms, 12 suites* ☐*In-room: safe, Wi-Fi, refrigerator. In-hotel: 2 restaurants, room service, bars, tennis court, pool, gym, laundry service, airport shuttle, parking (no fee), no-smoking rooms* ☐*AE, DC, MC, V* ☐*BP.*

$$$ ☐**Hotel Guaraní Esplendor.** Asunción's landmark Hotel Guaraní opened its doors on the south side of the Plaza de los Héroes in 1961, and for many years was *the* place to stay in the capital. Following a period of disrepair and abandonment, it reopened, refurbished and retooled, in 2008. The outside still says "1960s," but the clean modern lines inside echo this millennium and not the last. The remodeling is a work in progress at this writing: three of the floors are done, with the remaining 16 on the way. **Pros:** central location. **Cons:** ongoing construction noise during day ☒*Oliva at Independencia Nacional* ☎*021/452–099* ⊕*www.guaraniesplendor.com* ⇌*247 rooms* ☐*In-room: refrigerator, safe, Wi-Fi. In-hotel: restaurant, room service, bar, gym, laundry service, concierge, parking (no fee)* ☐*AE, DC, MC, V* ☐*BP.*

$$–$$$ ☐**Hotel Las Margaritas.** Cordial service and opulent, gleaming accommodations are the hallmarks of this lodging. The lobby blooms with plants and works by indigenous artisans and paintings by Michael Burt, one of Paraguay's leading contemporary artists. Rooms come in one of three color schemes (green, light blue, or orange) and all harbor Burt paintings and Guaraní artwork. **Pros:** tastefully decorated rooms, central location. **Cons:** some reports of lackluster service. ☒*Estrella and 15 de Agosto* ☎*021/448–765* ☐*021/448–785* ⊕*www.lasmargaritas. com.py* ⇌*60 rooms, 17 suites* ☐*In-room: refrigerator, safe, dial-up. In-hotel: 2 restaurants, room service, bar, pool, gym, laundry service, public Internet, airport shuttle, parking (no fee)* ☐*AE, DC, MC, V* ☐*BP.*

Fodor'sChoice
★

$ ☐**Hotel Preciado.** Peace Corps volunteers in Asunción on business or pleasure dub this place, just east of downtown, their favorite, and their presence here gives the hotel a youthful exuberance. Modern, high-ceiling rooms are simply furnished with two beds, a desk, and a chair.

★

The low prices make this a solid budget bet. **Pros:** good budget value, friendly vibe. **Cons:** occasional noise, several blocks from downtown, icy a/c. ✉*Azara 840* ☎*021/447–661* 🖷*021/453–937* 🖉*hotelpreciado@yahoo.es* 🛏*22 rooms* ♿*In-room: refrigerator. In-hotel: restaurant, pool, laundry service* 🚫*AE, MC, V* 🍽*BP.*

$$ 🏨 **Hotel Presidente.** Two blocks from the Plaza de los Héroes, this comfortable lodging has conveniences usually reserved for more expensive establishments. All rooms have contemporary furnishings. Business travelers have access to fax machines and computers. **Pros:** central location, good value. **Cons:** small bathrooms, occasionally noisy air conditioning. ✉*Azara 128* ☎🖷*021/494–931* 🖉*hotelpresidente@uninet.com.py* 🛏*44 rooms, 4 suites* ♿*In-room: refrigerator. In-hotel: restaurant, bar, public Internet* 🚫*AE, DC, MC, V* 🍽*BP.*

$$ 🏨 **Mandu'Ará Hotel & Suites.** The suites in this hotel are popular with business travelers. Each includes a sitting room, a dining area, and a kitchenette. The furnishings differ markedly from room to room: "classic" rooms tend toward lots of carved wood, while "contemporary" rooms have more modern furnishings. Both types are equally plush. **Pros:** option to fix own meals. **Cons:** several blocks from downtown. ✉*México 554* ☎🖷*021/490–223* 🌐*www.manduara.com.py* 🛏*82 suites* ♿*In-room: refrigerator, Wi-Fi. In-hotel: restaurant, room service, bar, pool, gym, laundry service, public Internet, airport shuttle* 🚫*AE, DC, MC, V* 🍽*BP.*

$$$ 🏨 **Sabe Center Hotel.** The sleek, orange-brick high-rise facing Plaza Uru-
★   guaya goes out of its way to impress: in the lobby, a giant chandelier shimmers above Oriental rugs, enormous urns, and a grand staircase. Rooms are less regal, but bright and comfortable. A breakfast buffet is included. **Pros:** central location, quiet, huge breakfasts. **Cons:** opulence borders on excess. ✉*25 de Mayo at México* ☎*021/450–093* 🖷*021/450–101* 🌐*www.sabecenterhotel.com.py* 🛏*91 rooms* ♿*In-room: refrigerator, safe. In-hotel: restaurant, room service, bar, gym, laundry service, public Internet, airport shuttle* 🚫*AE, DC, MC, V* 🍽*BP.*

AFTER DARK

Almost all the information about nightlife in Asunción is in Spanish, but the listings you find in publications are easily deciphered. Asunción's free biweekly arts and nightlife newsletter, *Tiempo Libre*, has cinema and theater listings. It's widely available in hotels and restaurants. Look also for the bilingual, monthly *Asunción Quick Guide*, available in hotels, for listings of what's going on.

Asunción doesn't have the nightlife of other Latin American capitals, such as Buenos Aires or Rio de Janeiro, especially during the week. The scene picks up Thursday through Saturday when locals dress up to go out on the town. In many nightspots you'll get turned away at the door if you're wearing jeans and T-shirts. Many upscale places cluster around Avenida Brasilia, Avenida España, and Avenida Mariscal López, about 2 km (1 mi) northeast of the centro. Most charge a small cover.

THE ARTS

Catch dance performances at **Noches del Paraguay** (⊠*Juan Domingo Perón and Cacique Lambaré* ☎*021/332–807*). There's a show every night of the week, but Friday and Saturday are the most popular nights, so make reservations. Weeknight tickets are G20,000; weekends, G40,000.

Originally constructed in 1893, the **Teatro Municipal** (⊠*Presidente Franco and Chile* ☎*021/445–109*) reopened in 2008 following an extensive remodeling, and once again offers a full program of art and cultural entertainment.

Asunción's city cultural center, the **Manzana de la Rivera** (⊠*Ayolas 129* ☎*021/442–448*), presents lectures, concerts, and movies many evenings.

BARS

A visit to the friendly, semi-open-air **Britannia Pub** (⊠*Cerro Corá 851* ☎*021/443–990*) dispels the myth that Asunción has no expat population; they're all here. The always popular **Café Bohemia** (⊠*Senador Long and España*) attracts young and old alike, usually younger on alternative-music nights. As befits the name, **Café Literario** (⊠*Mariscal Estigarribia 456* ☎*021/491–640*) draws aficionados of coffee, wine, books, quiet music, and animated conversation. **Faces** (⊠*Av. Mariscal López* ☎*021/672–768*) is a good place to talk and have a drink. Just west of downtown, the nautical-theme **Choppería del Puerto** (⊠*Palma 1028 at Colón* ☎*021/445–590*) also has a pleasant sidewalk café. It is open 24 hours. **Mouse Cantina** (⊠*Brasilia 803 at Patria* ☎*021/228–794*) gets a little loud at times.

CASINOS

Try your luck at slot machines, roulette, baccarat, and blackjack at the glitzy **Casino de Asunción** (⊠*España 151, at Sacramento* ☎*021/603–160*), open daily 2 PM–6 AM. The **Hotel Casino Yacht y Golf Club Paraguayo** (⊠*Av. del Yacht 11, Lambaré* ☎*021/906–043*), which is about 13 km (8 mi) outside of town, offers all the standard casino games. The casino itself is open daily 9 PM–6 AM.

DANCE CLUBS

The most popular disco in Asunción is **Casapueblo** (⊠*Mariscal López and Mayor Rivarola* ☎*021/611–081*), where you can dance all night to Latin rhythms. Asunción's elite boogie the weekend nights away at **Coyote** (⊠*Sucre 1655, at San Martín* ☎*021/662–816*).

SHOPPING

The best shopping in Asunción falls into two very distinct categories: handicrafts and electronics. Prices for both are among the lowest in South America. Argentinians flock here for bargains on the latter, but prices are actually comparable to those of large discount stores in the United States.

MARKETS & SHOPPING DISTRICTS

Mercado 4, on Avenida Pettirossi, is a crowded market that overflows into neighboring streets. Its stalls are laden with produce, hammocks, and cage after cage of clucking chickens. The tables are set up before dawn, so get an early start to avoid the stifling heat and suffocating crowds. It is open all day, every day, except Sunday afternoons.

You can find lots of handicrafts west of **Plaza de los Héroes** between Palma and Estrella. For quality goods, stick to the specialty stores. Hundreds of small shops here sell imported watches, electronics, cameras, and athletic shoes. Watch out for street vendors selling knock-offs such as "Rolec" watches.

NEED A BREAK?

Across from the Panteón Nacional de los Héroes is the doyenne of Asunción diners, the Lido Bar (Palma at Chile, 021/444–607). The counter loops around the room, painted tan with highlights of brown. Just pull up a stool and an army of pillbox hat-clad waitresses will dish up luscious ice cream and coffee. The icy air-conditioning feels so good that you'll hate to return to the sweltering heat outdoors. Order another slice of pie instead.

CRAFTS SHOPS

FodorśChoice ★ Paraguay's famous ñandutí, the delicate lacework, can be found everywhere in Asunción. One of the best shops for ñandutí is **Ao P'oí Raity** (⊠*F. R. Moreno 155* ☎*021/494–475*). For the best leather goods try **Casa Vera** (⊠*Mariscal Estigarribia 470* ☎*021/445–868*). **Folklore** (⊠*Mariscal Estigarribia at Iturbe* ☎*021/494–360*) sells carved wood items.

SHOPPING MALLS

For department-store items, try the three-story **Excelsior Mall** (⊠*Chile 901* ☎*021/443–015*). **Shopping del Sol** (⊠*Av. Aviadores del Chaco and Prof. D. E. González* ☎*021/611–780*) has specialty shops, a cinema, and a children's play area. **Mariscal López Shopping** (⊠*Quesada 5050* ☎*021/611–272*) has stores selling clothing, books, and records, and computer terminals with free Internet access.

SIDE TRIP FROM ASUNCIÓN

SAN BERNARDINO

The popular holiday resort of San Bernardino, on the shores of Lago Ypacaraí, makes an excellent day trip from the capital. From December to March it's packed with weekenders enjoying the dark blue waters ringed by clean, white sand. Water sports are a popular pastime—windsurfing equipment can be rented at the beaches.

Light, but Long-lasting

Paraguay's signature craft souvenir is the delicate *ñandutí,* a type of spiderweb lacework. Patterns represent plants, animals, or scenes from local legends. Although ñandutí are traditionally made with white silk or cotton, colors are now being added to the designs. Both this and *ao p'oí,* a type of embroidery, are incorporated into such items as tablecloths and place mats. Wood carvings, intricately decorated gourds, and figurines— including Nativity figures—are reasonably priced mementos. Rustic leather items, such as suitcases, knapsacks, and briefcases, are long-lasting and only a fraction of the cost of Argentine goods. Plain white or colorful woven hammocks are another good buy. You'll be able to find all these crafts in stores in Asunción. Craftspeople in the town of Areguá, near Asunción on Lake Ypacaraí, make clay pots and other ceramics. In Luque, near the international airport, you can find Paraguayan harps, guitars, and fine silver filigree jewelry. The town of Itá, 37 km (23 mi) south of Asunción on Ruta 1, is famous for its ceramics, and is the place to come for distinctive black clay pottery.

Looping back toward Asunción, the road passes through **Caacupé**, a mostly Catholic town where the Día de la Nuestra Señora de Los Milagros (Day of Our Lady of the Miracles) is celebrated on December 8. Hundreds of thousands make a pilgrimage to the basilica here.

WHERE TO STAY

$$ ⌃ **Hotel del Lago.** On the shores of Lago Ypacaraí, this low-key century-old Spanish-style hotel underwent a complete refurbishing in 2007, going from country-rustic to country-chic, with amenities such as Wi-Fi and a pool rarely seen in rural Paraguayan lodgings. The restaurant's forte is roast beef or pork, cooked in a wood-fire oven and served with *sopa paraguaya.* **Pros:** historic location, secluded atmosphere. **Cons:** crowded on weekends. ⊠ *Teniente Weiler and Mariscal López* ☎ *0512/232–201* ⊕ *www.hoteldellago.org* ⇌ *23 rooms* ☯ *In-room: refrigerator, safe, DVDs, Wi-Fi. In-hotel: restaurant, room service, pool, laundry service* ☰ *AE, DC, MC, V* ⏏ *BP.*

¢ ⌃ **Hotel Pueblo.** The tranquillity of the forest surrounding this hotel is a
★ welcoming change from the noise and crowds of Asunción. Rooms are simple but comfortable, and all have views of Lago Ypacaraí. Try the restaurant for lunch, where you can order locally prepared surubí and bori-bori. **Pros:** good budget value. **Cons:** spartan rooms. ⊠ *Calle 5 at Paseo del Pebló* ☎ *0512/232–391* ✑ *pueblo@telesur.com.py* ⇌ *12 rooms, 6 suites* ☯ *In-room: no phone, refrigerator. In-hotel: restaurant, pool, no elevator, laundry service* ☰ *AE, DC, MC, V* ⏏ *BP.*

SOUTHERN PARAGUAY

Most of the population of Paraguay outside of Asunción is in this region—particularly in Itá, Villa Florida, Encarnación, and Ciudad del Este. For a scenic trip through Southern Paraguay's history, though,

NO LONGER MARCHING OFF A CLIFF

Paraguay's flamboyant history is one of a small country led by larger-than-life strongmen whose personal goals usually conflicted with the needs of the people. (The old movie stereotype of the mustachioed Latin American leader, decked out in military uniform complete with epaulets, medals, and sunglasses, defined Paraguay until the early 1990s.) The first president, José Gáspar Rodríguez de Francia, whose stern gaze graces the 10,000-guaraní bill, set the tone by calling himself "El Supremo." He preached a policy of complete self-sufficiency, forbidding trade and immigration, and set the stage for Paraguay's history of isolation. He also forbade citizens from looking at his home (now the Palacio Legislativo) or even at him as his carriage passed through the streets. Then came the López family, father and son, the younger of whom, Francisco Solano, led Paraguay into the disastrous War of the Triple Alliance (1865–70) against Argentina, Brazil, and Uruguay; he lost half the country's territory and 80% of the male population. A succession of presidents culminated in the 35-year authoritarian regime of General Alfredo Stroessner, who was toppled in a 1989 coup and died in exile in Brazil in 2006.

The transition to democracy has been lurching at times. The government continues to battle corruption and smuggling, and the financial roller coaster in next-door Argentina and Brazil, Paraguay's primary sources of trade and tourism, has taken its toll here as well. Since freedom of the press was restored, daily accounts of grievances against current officials fill the country's now-lively media. Yet, we vote to label Paraguay as a glass half full rather than half empty. The 2008 election of former bishop Fernando Lugo to the presidency ended six decades of one-party monopoly and raised new hopes that the government will better address the plight of its poor. And that Paraguay functions as well as it does, given its odd history, is a testament to the will of its people, who are determined to take that newfound democracy and make their country work.

be sure to stop at the seven 17th-century Jesuit missions along the 405-km (253-mi) drive from Asunción to Jesús. They date from as far back as 1609, when the newly formed Compañía de Jesús (Society of Jesus, better known as the Jesuits) was granted permission by the Spanish crown to move the nomadic Guaraní people, threatened by slave traders from Brazil, into self-sufficient agricultural communities. Each community, called a *reducción* (literally meaning "reduction"), had a population of about 3,000 Guaraní under the charge of two or three priests who taught them agricultural and other practical skills such as stonemasonry and metalwork, as well as the rudiments of Christianity. Each reducción was centered on a large plaza with a chapel, the priests' living quarters, and usually a school. The main buildings, most often constructed of red sandstone blocks, had terra-cotta-tile roofs, wide verandas, and covered walkways. The experiment, however, was so successful that the Spanish monarchs banned the Jesuits from their

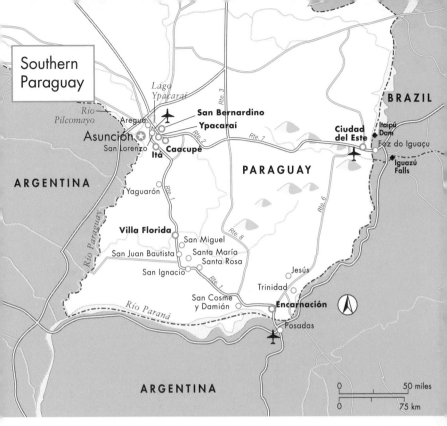

New World empire in 1767. The 100,000 Guaraní soon returned to their old way of life and the missions fell into disrepair.

ITÁ

37 km (23 mi) south of Asunción on Ruta 1.

Famous throughout Paraguay for its ceramics, Itá is the place to come for its distinctive black clay pottery. You'll pass a government-run handicraft exhibition before you reach town. On February 3 the town celebrates the Feast of St. Blas, the patron saint of Paraguay, with singing, dancing, a parade, and horse racing.

GETTING HERE & AROUND

Some Asunción-based tour operators include shopping day-trips to Itá among their offerings. The buses of La Encarneceña serve Villa Florida on its route between Asunción and Encarnación.

ESSENTIALS

Bus Information **La Encarnaceña** (☎ *071/203–440*).

VILLA FLORIDA

141 km (87 mi) south of Itá on Ruta 1.

Fodor'sChoice
★
Farms give way to rolling grasslands as you approach Villa Florida, the grazing grounds of white Nelore cattle. Cowboys in wide-brim hats tend the herds on horses saddled in sheepskin, while goats stealthily graze in hibiscus- and bougainvillea-filled gardens outside tiny, rustic cottages along the Río Tebicuary. The river, which once marked the western border of the Jesuit mission area, now has several popular beaches; anglers know it well as a prime spot for catching dorado and surubí. The town is not particularly pretty, but there is a good selection of hotels and restaurants, and sunsets over the water are magnificent.

THE ONE THAT GOT AWAY

Paraguay's fishing is considered to be among the best in the world. Anglers come chiefly to catch dorado (spectacular fighters that leap high into the air when hooked) and surubí (giant catfish that take off like an express train when you reel them in). Dorado are generally between 9 and 27 pounds, although some weigh up to 40 pounds. Surubí weighing as much as 44 pounds are not uncommon, but the real trophies are more than 90 pounds. The top spots for anglers are in the southwest—Ayolas, on the Río Paraná, and Villa Florida, on the Río Tebicuary.

GETTING HERE & AROUND

Your own vehicle is ideal for getting here, since the lodgings and activities we include are not right in town. The buses of La Encarneceña serve Villa Florida on its route between Asunción and Encarnación.

ESSENTIALS

Bus Information **La Encarnaceña** (☎ *021/551–745*).

WHERE TO STAY

$$ 🏠 **Estancia Santa Clara.** This ranch, 24 km (14 mi) north of Villa Florida, is downright plush compared to most of the other agriculture tourism lodgings in Paraguay. You can roll up your sleeves and rope steers, milk cows, pick vegetables, or bake bread if you really want a hands-on experience. You can also ride horses, hike bird-filled trails, or curl up in a hammock with a good book. Rooms in the rambling orange stucco house have vaulted wooden ceilings. Rates include all meals. **Pros:** quiet, secluded location, chance to "live" on the farm, good value. **Cons:** little to do if not interested in activities offered. ✉ *Ruta 1, Km 141, Caapucú* ☎ *0981/405–020 cell phone* 🏠📞 *021/605–729 in Asunción* ⊕ *www.estanciasantaclara.com.py* 🛏 *8 rooms* ♨ *In-room: no phone, no TV. In-hotel: restaurant, pool* ⊟ *No credit cards* ¶⊙*FAP.*

¢ 🏠 **Hotel Centu Cué.** Comfortable bungalows scattered along the banks
Fodor'sChoice
★
of the Río Tebicuary make up this isolated lodge frequented mainly by anglers in search of the one that won't get away. Lounging on the 2-km (1-mi) private beach and taking a dip in the river are also a popular activities. At the nautical-theme restaurant, mounted heads of enormous fish and photos of proud fishermen with their catches may mock

your day's accomplishments. What else would you eat here but dorado or surubí, grilled or in a casserole, caught just a few yards from the table? **Pros:** terrific restaurant, secluded location. **Cons:** little to do if not interested in fishing. ⊠ *7 km (4 mi) off Ruta 1 at Km 163, Desvío* ☎*083/240–219* ➪*30 rooms, 5 cabins* ⚄*In-room: no phone. In-hotel: restaurant, beachfront* ⊟*No credit cards* ⦿|*FAP.*

¢ ⊡ **Hotel Nacional de Turismo.** Colonial-style rooms open onto a shady courtyard at this friendly hotel. Camping areas near the river have been set aside for fishing enthusiasts. The restaurant serves grilled meats and poultry; a must is the milanesa, made with freshly caught surubí. The chef is eager to please, and will be happy to prepare whatever you desire. Rates include a big breakfast. **Pros:** good budget value. **Cons:** spartan rooms. ⊠*Ruta 1, Km 162* ☎*083/240–207* ➪*25 rooms* ⚄*In-hotel: restaurant, pool, laundry service* ⊟*No credit cards* ⦿|*BP.*

ENCARNACIÓN

150 km (90 mi) southeast of Villa Florida on Ruta 1.

Encarnación was the site of the long-gone Itapúa mission, but you'd never know it today. Linked by bridge to the Argentine town of Posadas, Encarnación is a somewhat dreary border town that serves as a convenient stopping point for many a weary traveler. The town has seen an influx of Eastern European immigrants. Its most incongruous sight is the small, ornate Ukrainian Orthodox church on Plaza Artigas.

GETTING HERE & AROUND

BY AIR Most visitors fly into Paraguay's Aeropuerto Internacional Silvio Pettirossi, but just across the border from Encarnación in Posadas, Argentina, is the domestic Aeropuerto Libertador General San Martín (PSS), with daily flights from Buenos Aires' Aeroparque Jorge Newbery.

BY BUS Buses between Asunción and Encarnación leave frequently. The five-hour trip costs about G50,000. You can get off the bus along Ruta 1 to visit any of the Jesuit missions. When you are ready to leave you can flag down another, which will pick you up unless it is full. Rapido Iguazú has buses running between Asunción and Encarnación. La Encarnaceña runs the same route, as well between Encarnación and the ruins at Trinidad and Jesús.

BY CAR Ruta 1, which runs from Asunción to Encarnación, is fairly well maintained, although there are occasional potholes. From Encarnación, the poorly maintained Ruta 6 stretches northeast for 280 km (175 mi) to Ciudad del Este, near the Brazil and Argentine borders. This route takes you to Iguazú Falls.

ESSENTIALS

Airport **Aeropuerto Libertador General San Martín** (⊠*Posadas, Argentina* ☎*54/752/451–903*).

Banks **ABN Amro Bank** (⊠*Mariscal Estgarribia and Caballero, Encarnación* ☎*071/201–872*). **Guaraní Cambios** (⊠*Mariscal Estigarribia 307, Encarnación*

⌨*071/204–301).* **Interbanco** (✉ *Tomás Romero Pereira at Carlos Antonio López, Encarnación* ⌨ *071/203–428).*

Bus Information **La Encarnaceña** (⌨ *071/203–440).* **Rapido Iguazú** (⌨ *021/551–601).*

Visitor & Tour Info **Secretaria Nacional de Turismo** (✉ *Tomás Romero Pereira 126, Encarnación* ⌨ *071/203–508).*

EXPLORING ENCARNACIÓN

The **Museo de Arte Sacro**, a small museum in the center of town, is devoted to religious art. ✉ *Artigas and 14 de Mayo* ⌨ *071/201–845* 🎟 *Free* ⏱ *Weekdays 3–7.*

WHERE TO STAY

CRUISING IN PARAGUAY?

Paraguay may be landlocked, but it is entirely possible to take a cruise here. **Crucero Paraguay** ✉ *Perú 689, Asunción* ⌨ *021/223–217* ⊕ *www.crucero paraguay.info* offers three-day/two-night cruises up the Río Paraguay to the remote Chaco region, and six-day/five night trips to the heavily forested Pantanal region in the northeast part of the country. The 27-cabin *Paraguay* makes each trip at least monthly, and more frequently in the December—February summer season.

$$ 🏨 **Encarnación Resort.** Amid spacious gardens, this hotel is a quiet 3 km (2 mi) from town and makes a pleasant place stay if you're doing the mission route and don't want to trek back to Asunción. The restaurant's menu has Paraguayan specialties, including milanesa, *sopa paraguaya,* and cassava. **Pros:** good value, good base for tour of missions. **Cons:** some worn rooms. ✉ *Ruta 1, Km 361, Villa Quiteria* ⌨ *071/207–248* ⊕ *www.encarnacionresort hotel.com.py@itacom.com.py* ⤳ *102 bedrooms, 4 suites* ♿ *In-room: refrigerator. In-hotel: restaurant, room service, bar, tennis court, gym, pool, laundry service, no-smoking rooms* ☰ *AE, DC, MC, V* ⦿*BP.*

¢ 🏨 **Hotel Cristal.** This nine-story hotel has modern rooms decorated with original artwork. The restaurant, which fills up at lunch with local businesspeople, serves contemporary fare and local fish dishes. **Pros:** good restaurant, good budget value. **Cons:** some worn rooms, some street noise. ✉ *Mariscal Estigarribia 1157* ⌨ *071/202–371* 🖷 *071/202–372* ⤳ *86 rooms* ♿ *In-room: no phone, refrigerator. In-hotel: restaurant, pool* ☰ *AE, MC, V* ⦿*BP.*

$$ 🏨 **Tirol del Paraguay.** Built on a hillside 25 km (16 mi) from Encarnación, this hotel has spectacular views of the rolling countryside, and makes a convenient base for visiting the Jesuit ruins at Trinidad and Jesús. Rustic rooms with reddish brick walls are furnished with sturdy wood furniture. Accommodations are in single-story bungalows that surround four swimming pools fed by natural springs, which are said to have therapeutic properties. (Some people come here to take the waters.) Rates include all meals. **Pros:** secluded location, ideal base for visiting missions at Trinidad and Jesús. **Cons:** need a car to stay here. ✉ *Ruta 6, 8 km (5 mi) from Trinidad, Capitán Miranda* ⌨ *071/202–388* 🖷 *071/205–555* ⊕ *www.hoteltirol.com.py* ⤳ *60 rooms* ♿ *In-room: refrigerator. In-hotel: restaurant, bar, tennis court, pools, laundry service* ☰ *AE, DC, MC, V* ⦿*FAP.*

CIUDAD DEL ESTE

280 km (175 mi) northeast of Encarnación, 333 km (200 mi) east of Asunción.

Quintessential border town Ciudad del Este mixes a bit of sleaze with a lot of shopping (and, reputedly, an equal amount of smuggling). Expect little in the way of history here—the city dates only from 1957. The draw for tax-weary Argentines and Brazilians is block after block of stores offering goods less expensive than in their own countries. For North Americans and Europeans, prices are no lower than those of a large discount store, however, and the warning "Buyer beware" comes to mind when evaluating merchandise quality here. Ciudad del Este makes a convenient gateway from the west to the Iguazú Falls, straddling the Argentine-Brazilian border. Rising crime in the city itself means we recommend not basing yourself here, but enjoying the falls from Brazil, 26 km (16 mi), or Argentina, 23 km (14 mi), away. A couple of attractions here on the Paraguayan side can be enjoyed hassle-free, most conveniently as day trips from the other two countries.

As a border city, Ciudad del Este sees its share of crime. The tri-border region with Brazil and Argentina has also become a haven for extremist groups in recent years. You'll be fine with day visits to the attractions we list, but we recommend not staying the night here.

GETTING HERE & AROUND

TAM Airlines flies at least once daily from Asunción to Ciudad del Este's Aeropuerto Alejo García (AGT). Frequent buses ply the Asunción–Ciudad del Este route; the five-hour trip costs about G50,000.

ESSENTIALS

Airports **Aeropuerto Alejo García** (⊠ *Ciudad del Este* ☎ *061/518–352*).

Bus Information **Rapido Iguazú** (☎ *061/510–396*).

Currency Exchange **MaxiCambios** (⊠ *Av. Adrán Jara at Curupayty* ☎ *061/509–511*).

EXPLORING CIUDAD DEL ESTE

Centro Hidroeléctrico de Itaipú. South America's great engineering marvel is the world's largest hydroelectric facility, and spans the Paraná river between Paraguay and Brazil. Construction on the dam, as tall as a 65-story building, was completed in 1984. The installation supplies 19% of Brazil's power needs and an astounding 91% of Paraguay's. Admission is free from the Paraguayan side. (The visitor center on Brazil's side charges for visits.) Take in an informative 90-minute tour and/or a spectacular sound-and-light show on weekend nights. ⊠ *Hernandarías, 18 km. (11mi.) north of Ciudad del Este* ☎ *061/599–8040* ⊕ *www.itaipu.gov.py* 🎟 *Free* ☉ *Tours: weekdays 8, 9:30, 2, 3, Sat. 9, 9:30, 10:30, 2, 3, Sun. 8, 9:30, 10:30; Sound-and-light show: Fri. and Sat. 9* PM *Oct.–Feb. (arrive by 7:30), 8* PM *Mar.–Sept. (arrive by 6:30).*

VISITING THE JESUIT MISSIONS

Paraguay's most compelling architectural attractions are the ruins of some 30 Jesuit missions in the southeast part of the country. Although Spanish missionaries came to what is now Paraguay in 1588, little remains of their earliest dwellings. What you'll find are fascinating traces of 17th-century *reducciónes* (literally, "reductions"). Here the Jesuits organized the indigenous Guaranís—a nomadic people—into farming communities, and worked with them side-by-side, providing vocational training and religious and secular education.

You can do a mission tour in your own car—if you don't mind negotiating some unpaved roads. The benefit of having your own car is that you can take it easy and spend a few days exploring. If you prefer not to drive, you can opt for a hurried day with an Asunción tour operator. The sites you'll see run the spectrum—from the well-preserved San Cosmé y Damián, where many of the structures still serve the community, to the never finished, but intriguing, abandoned structures at Jesús.

Franciscan missionaries attempted to fill the void left after the Jesuits were expelled from the Spanish empire in 1767. They centered their efforts in **Yaguarón** but met with less success in maintaining the reducción communities established by their predecessors.

The town's restored 18th-century Iglesia de San Buenaventura was the centerpiece of Paraguay's post-Jesuit Franciscan missions. Inside, you'll find brightly colored wooden statues carved by Guaraní artists. ✉ *11 km (7 mi) south of Itá on Ruta*

1 ☎ *0533/32–229* ✉ *Free* ⊙ *Tues.–Sat. 8–11:30 and 2–5, Sun. 8–11:30.*

You'll pass through San Miguel, where locals tempt you with hand-woven woolen blankets, rugs, and ponchos, and San Juan Bautista, with quaint colonial houses lining cobblestone streets, before reaching **Santa María.** Nearly 7,000 Guaraní lived here in the early 18th century, and some of the original houses have been restored.

The Museo Jesuítico has some 70 Guaraní carvings and statues; the latter represent the life of Jesus. (The museum keeps no fixed hours; if the door is locked, you may have to ask around for the priest to let you in.) ✉ *Santa María, 37 km (22 mi) south of San Miguel on Ruta 1* ☎ *0781/283–222* ✉ *G5,000.*

The Jesuits established Paraguay's first mission in **San Ignacio** in 1610, and today the Museo Jesuítico displays the country's best collection of Guaraní wood carvings and other period artifacts, including gilded pulpits, door panels, and statues. A depiction of St. Paul pointing to new lands in need of salvation is most striking; at his feet are carved faces with Guaraní features. The building itself, with its thick adobe walls, is believed to be the oldest surviving structure in Paraguay, dating from the establishment of the mission in 1609. ✉ *Ruta 1, look for sign, 18 km (11 mi) south of Santa María* ☎ *082/232–223* ✉ *G5,000* ⊙ *Weekdays 2–5:30, Weekends 8–11.*

The ringing of bells from the red sandstone bell tower, built in 1698, can still be heard in the town of

Santa Rosa, one of the era's largest reducciónes.

In the small museum you can see frescoes from the old altar of the local chapel. You'll also find a group of centuries-old carvings representing the Annunciation. ⊠ *Ruta 1, look for sign, 19 km (12 mi) east of San Ignacio* 🕾 *0858/285–221* 💲 *G2,000* ⊙ *Weekdays 7–11:30.*

Just as Ruta 1 reaches Coronel Bogado, a 25-km (15-mi) paved highway leads to the village of **San Cosmé y Damián,** near the banks of the Río Paraná.

Follow the signs along a dirt track to the red sandstone mission buildings, currently in use as a Jesuit school. They once held an astronomical observatory. Many original houses are still in use. ⊠ *San Cosmé y Damián, 95 km (59 mi) southeast of Santa Rosa* 🕾 *No phone* 💲 *G2,000* ⊙ *Dec.–Mar., daily 7–7; Apr.–Nov., daily 7–5:30.*

Fodor's Choice ★ The region's most impressive ruins, superior even to those of Argentina and Brazil, are at **Trinidad.** The red sandstone reducción, built between 1712 and 1764, stands on a hilltop, enabling its full size to be appreciated. After the expulsion of the Jesuits, much of it was destroyed by an unscrupulous local official who ripped out stones to build his own residence, causing the structure to collapse. Many of the church walls and arches remain intact, however, even though open to the elements. Note the elaborately carved doors and wall friezes depicting angels playing the clavichord, harp, and other musical instruments. The only building with a roof is the sacristy,

with intricate relief work above the main entrance. Also surviving are the school and cloister foundations and a sandstone tower. Restoration is ongoing. ⊠ *Trinidad, 28 km (17 mi) northeast of Encarnación* 🕾 *No phone* 💲 *G2,000* ⊙ *Dec.–Mar., daily 7–7; Apr.–Nov. daily 7–5:30.*

The Jesuits began construction of the hilltop church of **Jesús del Tavarangue** a mere eight years before their expulsion from the New World. Though never finished, this is the most distinctive of the region's mission churches. Moorish-style arches make up the building's three entrances and lead to what were to be three naves and three altars. Vegetation and earth have covered much of the nearby reducción community. Painstaking excavations are under way. ⊠ *Ruta 6, 10 km (6 mi) north of Trinidad* 🕾 *No phone* 💲 *G2,000* ⊙ *Dec.–Mar., daily 7–7; Apr.–Nov. daily 7–5:30.*

7

Museo de la Tierra Guaraní. This small but well-designed "Museum of the Guaraní Land" documents 10,000 years of human settlement in the region. Exhibits focus on the interweaving of culture, environment, and technology, taking you from the era of rudimentary tools to the opening of the nearby Itaipú Dam. This is one of the few museums in Paraguay to offer ample signage in English, as well as Spanish and Portuguese. ✉ *11 km (7 mi) south of Ciudad del Este* ☎ *061/599–8782* 🎫 *Free* 🕐 *Mon. 2:30–5, Tues.–Sat. 8–noon and 2:30–5, Sun. 8–11:30.*

Peru

WORD OF MOUTH

"That first look was awesome. My daughter and I literally stopped in our tracks and just stared—and then looked at each other in total amazement. We both had these big expectations and were afraid we'd be disappointed, but we weren't. [Machu Picchu] lived up to every expectation imaginable! The scale was immense; the details elaborate; the stonework an almost unbelievable engineering feat. It was beautiful, and there was an air of mystery just as I'd hoped! We were mesmerized."

—althom1122

THE PERU TRAVEL EXPERIENCE IS A UNIQUE JOURNEY of history, culture, food, and fantastic natural backdrops. The "Lost City of the Incas" is the big reason why people come to Peru. The Machu Picchu ruins were built around the 1450s, only to be abandoned a hundred years later. For centuries it stayed hidden. But in 1911, it was rediscovered by an American historian.

There's much more to see beyond Machu Picchu. Puzzle over the mysterious Nazca Lines from the sky. Enjoy city life in the Spanish influenced Lima, Trujillo, and Arequipa, and their colonial-era homes, churches, monasteries, and museums. The islands of Lake Titicaca reveal a slice of raw ancient Andean culture. It's as if time has frozen while Quechua and Aymara families live and work off the land, eating and dressing as they did in the 16th century.

For natural wonders, Colca Canyon and Cotahuasi Canyon are the two deepest canyons in the world, and Cordillera Blanca mountain range in the north has 50 mountains higher than 18,000 feet.

Peru is a nation on the threshold of change. Emerging from decades of corrupt governments, the Andean country is now seen as an economic power in Latin America, despite half of its population living under poverty. Travel infrastructure has also been improving. Thanks to more domestic flights, Peru is much easier to move about these days. Almost every worthwhile destination is within a two-hour flight from Lima. Train travel is limited, but easy to use. Traveling by car is trickier—roads are better than before, but signs aren't well-posted. Buses go everywhere, and come in all classes and sizes. In cities, cabs are available and cheap. But check for an official license.

ORIENTATION & PLANNING

GETTING ORIENTED

Lima. In Peru's cultural and political center experience some of the best dining in the Americas, vibrant nightlife, and great museums and churches. See the *Catedral* and the catacombs at the Iglesia de San Francisco, and stroll about Miraflores for shops and eats.

The South. Head south for wines and piscos around Ica, duneboarding in Huacachina, the mysterious Nazca Lines, and the marine life of Paracas National Perserve. Colca and Cotahuasi canyons are the world's two deepest canyons. Peru's "second city" Arequipa may also be its most attractive. Lake Titicaca is the world's highest navigable lake and home to the floating Uros Islands.

Cusco & the Sacred Valley. Cusco (11,500 feet above sea level) is a necessary stop on your journey to Machu Picchu. The former Inca capital has fine restaurants, hotels, churches, and museums. Take day trips to the Pisac market, and to Inca ruins at Sacsayhuamán and Ollyantaytambo.

TOP REASONS TO GO

Machu Picchu & the Inca Trail: This "Lost City of the Incas" is the big reason why people come to Peru. The Machu Picchu ruins were built around the 1450s, only to be abandoned 100 years later. Spanish conquistadors never found it and for centuries it stayed hidden. But in 1911, it was rediscovered by an American historian. If you're adventurous, and in good shape, the four-day Inca Trail is the classic route to Machu Picchu.

Lake Titicaca: At 3,812 meters, Puno's Lake Titicaca is the highest navigable lake in the world. More than 25 rivers empty into it, and according to Inca legend, it was the birth place of the Sun God who founded the Inca dynasty. On Isla Taquile, like other islands here, Quechua-speaking people reserve the traditions of their ancestors.

Nazca Lines: It's thought that between 900 BC and AD 600, the Nazca and Paracas cultures constructed the Nazca Lines: geometric figures drawn into the Pampa Colorado (Red Plain) in Nazca, a city south of Lima. Three hundred geoglyphs and 800 straight lines make up these mysterious figures. No one knows why these massive drawings—which include representations of a lizard, monkey, condor, and spider—were created. The only way to get a good view is to take a flightseeing tour.

Sun, surf & seafood: During the summer months (December–March), beach lovers around Peru head west to enjoy a day of surfing the Pacific Ocean waves, sunbathing on immaculate beaches, and devouring the country's freshest seafood.

Machu Picchu & the Inca Trail. The great Machu Picchu, crowded or not crowded, misty rains or clear skies, never ceases to enthrall, and the Inca Trail is still the great hiking pilgrimage. Stay in Aguas Caliente for the best access.

The North Coast & the Northern Highlands. Go up the coast for some of South America's best beach life and inland to the Cordillera Blanca for some of the world's highest mountains. Many of Peru's greatest archaeological discoveries were made in the north. Don't miss Chan Chan on Trujillo's outskirts.

PERU PLANNER

WHEN TO GO

Seasons flip in the southern hemisphere, but this close to the equator, "summer" and "winter" mean little. Think instead of "dry" and "rainy" seasons. Also the climates of the Costa (coast), the Sierra (mountains) and the Selva (jungle) are different.

Peru's tourist season runs from May through September, the dry season in the Sierra and Selva. The best time to visit is May through July, when the cool, misty weather is on the Costa, and the highlands are dressed in bright green under blue skies. When it's dry in the Sierra and the Selva, it's wet on the Costa, and vice versa. (But the coast doesn't get much rain *any* time of year.)

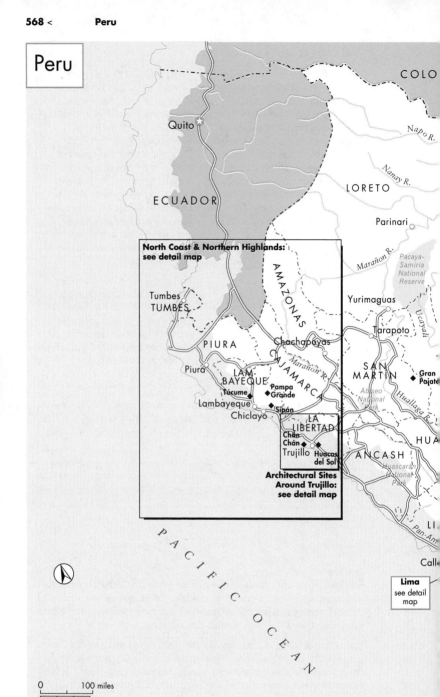

Peru

COLO

Quito

Napo R.

ECUADOR

Nanay R.

LORETO

Parinari

North Coast & Northern Highlands:
see detail map

Marañon R.

Pacaya-
Samiria
National
Reserve

Tumbes
TUMBES

AMAZONAS

Yurimaguas

Ucayali

Tarapoto

PIURA

Chachapoyas

Piura

CAJAMARCA

Marañon R.

SAN
MARTIN

Gran
Pajaté

LAM-
BAYEQUE

Pampa
♦ Grande

Abiseo
National
Park

Huallaga R.

Túcume ♦

Lambayeque

♦ Sipán

LA
LIBERTAD

HUA

Chiclayo

Chan
Chan ♦

♦ Huacas
del Sol

ANCASH

Trujillo

Huascarán
National
Park

Architectural Sites
Around Trujillo:
see detail map

LI

Pan-Am.

P A C I F I C

Call

Lima
see detail
map

O C E A N

0	100 miles
0	150 km

It never rains in the coastal desert, but a dank, heavy fog called the *garúa* coats Lima from June through December. Outside Lima, coastal weather is clearer and warm.

FESTIVALS

Fireworks and processions honor the **Virgen de la Candelaria** (February 2) in Puno and the Highlands, with the faithful following images of the Virgin Mary through the streets. Dancers depict the struggle between good and evil. (The demons always lose.)

Semana Santa (March or April) brings elaborate Holy Week processions countrywide. Ayacucho portrays the week's agony and triumph with ornate porter-borne floats emerging from palls of incense to the accompaniment of clanging bells.

Cusco's spectacular **Inti Raymi** (June 24) marks the winter solstice and reenacts age-old Inca pageantry that beseeches the sun to return. The fortress ruins of Sacsayhuaman form the stage for that proverbial cast of thousands.

Predawn firecrackers rouse you out of bed. Not to worry: the revolution has not started. It's the kick-off to Peru's two-day **Independence Day** (July 28–29) parades. Independence was won in 1821.

Lima and the Central Highlands revere the **Señor de los Milagros** (October 18–28), a colonial-era image of a dark-skinned Christ that survived a 1655 earthquake that destroyed much of the capital. The devout, clad in purple robes and white sashes, carry heavy statues of Christ through the streets.

GETTING HERE & AROUND

BY AIR

Almost all international flights into Peru touch down at Aeropuerto Internacional Jorge Chávez (☎ 01/517–3100 ⊕ *www.lap.com.pe/ingles*), on the northwestern fringe of Lima. If you're flying from other Latin American cities, Lan has flights from most major airports in the region.

Within Peru, flying is the best way to travel between most cities and towns. Lan departs several times each day for Arequipa, Cusco, Juliaca, Puerto Maldonado, and Trujillo. Aero Cóndor has daily flights to Arequipa Cusco, and Iquitos. and Star Perú flies to Arequipa, Cusco, Juliaca, Iquitos, and Trujillo.

Airline Contacts Aero Cóndor (☎ 01/614–6014 ⊕ www.aerocondor.com.pe). **Aerolineas Argentinas** (☎ 800/333–0276 in North America, 01/513–6575 in Lima ⊕ www.aerolineas.com.ar). **Aeroméxico** (☎ 800/237–6639 in North America, 01/421–3500 in Lima ⊕ www.aerolineas.com.ar). **Air Canada** (☎ 888/247–2262 in North America, 01/241–1457 in Lima ⊕ www.aircanada.com). **American Airlines** (☎ 800/433–7300, 01/211–7000 in Lima ⊕ www.aa.com). **Avianca** (☎ 800/284–2622 in North America, 01/444–0747 in Lima ⊕ www.avianca. com). **Continental Airlines** (☎ 800/523–3273 for U.S. and Mexico reservations, 800/231–0856 for international reservations, 01/712–9230 in Lima ⊕ www.continental.com). **Copa** (☎ 800/359–2672 in North America, 01/610–0808 in Lima ⊕ www.copaair.com). **Delta Airlines** (☎ 800/221–1212 for U.S. reservations,

800/241–4141 for international reservations, 01/211–9211 in Lima ⊕ www.delta. com). **Lan** *(☎ 866/435–9526 in North America, 01/213–8200 in Lima ⊕ www.lan. com).* **Star Perú.** *☎ 01/705–9000 ⊕ www.starperu.com.*

BY BUS

The bus system in Peru is extensive, and fares are quite reasonable. Remember, however, that distances can be daunting. It's best to use buses for shorter trips, such as between Lima and Ica or between Cusco and Puno. That way you can begin and end your trip during daylight hours. If you stick with one of the recommended companies, like Cruz del Sur (☎ *01/225–6163 ⊕ www.cruzdelsur.com.pe*) or Ormeño (☎ *01/472–1710 ⊕ www.grupo-ormeno.com.pe*), you can usually expect a comfortable journey.

BY CAR

Driving is a heart-stopping experience, as most Peruvians see traffic laws as suggestions rather than rules. That said, there are a few places in Peru where having a car is a benefit, such as between Lima and points south on the Pan-American Highway. If you rent a car, keep these tips in mind: outside cities, drive only during daylight hours, fill your gas tank whenever possible, and make sure your spare tire is in good repair.

Consider hiring a car and driver through your hotel, or making a deal with a taxi driver, for some extended sightseeing.

BY TRAIN

PeruRail (☎ *084/238–722 ⊕ www.perurail.com*) runs trains along three different routes: between Cusco and Machu Picchu, between Ollantaytambo and Machu Picchu, and between Cusco and Lake Titicaca. Tickets can be purchased at train stations, through travel agencies, or sometimes on the Internet.

ESSENTIALS

ELECTRICITY

The electrical current in Peru is 220 volts, 50 cycles alternating current (AC). A converter is needed for appliances requiring 110 voltage. U.S.-style flat prongs fit most outlets.

ENTRY REQUIREMENTS

Visitors from the United States, Canada, the United Kingdom, Australia, and New Zealand require only a valid passport and return ticket to be issued a 90-day visa at their point of entry into Peru.

Make two photocopies of the data page of your passport, one for someone at home and another for you, carried separately from your passport. While sightseeing in Peru, it's best to carry the copy of your passport and leave the original hidden in your hotel room or in your hotel's safe. Never, ever, leave one city in Peru to go to another city without carrying your passport with you.

HEALTH & SAFETY

Peru is safer than it has been in years, but standard travel precautions apply. Remember: you represent enormous wealth to the typical person here; the budget for your trip might exceed what many Peruvians earn in a year. Conceal your valuables, watch your things, avoid deserted locales, walk purposefully, take taxis at night, and be vigilant around scenes of commotion that may be engineered to distract you.

In terms of health and sanitation, few visitors experience anything worse than a bout of traveler's diarrhea. If you stick to upscale eateries in well-trodden destinations, you may minimize even those problems. Be wary of raw foods (peel your fruit!), and avoid drinking tap water entirely (and ice cubes). Check with your local public health department about any pre-travel immunizations or precautions (hepatitis, typhoid, malaria) recommended for Peru, and give yourself several weeks, since some procedures may require multiple injections.

HIGH ALTITUDE   Peru's lofty heights present you with both majesty and menace. Treat that altitude with respect. Its consequences, locally known as *soroche,* affect visitors. For most, it's little more than a shortness of breath, which can be minimized by resting the first couple of days and a good intake of nonalcoholic liquids. It occasionally requires immediate descent to lower altitudes. Peruvians swear by tea brewed from coca leaves, a completely legal way (legal here, at least) to prevent symptoms. We recommend a pre-trip check with your doctor to see if any underlying conditions (hypertension, heart problems, pregnancy) might preclude travel here.

LANGUAGE
Spanish is Peru's national language, but many indigenous languages also enjoy official status. Many Peruvians claim Quechua, the language of the Inca, as their first language, but most also speak Spanish. Other native languages include the Tiahuanaco language of Aymará, which is spoken around Lake Titicaca, and several languages in the rain forest. But English is now routinely taught in schools, and many older people have taken classes in English.

A word on spelling: since the Inca had no writing system, Quechua developed as an oral language. During the past 30 years, a new sensitivity to the country's indigenous roots have led Peruvians to try to recover consistent, linguistically correct transcriptions of Quechua words. As you travel you may come across different spellings and pronunciations of the same name. An example is the city known as Cusco, Cuzco, and sometimes even Qosqo.

MONEY MATTERS
Peru's national currency is the nuevo sol (S/). Bills are issued in denominations of 5, 10, 20, 50, and 100 soles. Coins are 1, 5, 10, 20, and 50 céntimos, and 1, 2, and 5 soles. At this writing, the exchange rate was almost exactly S/3 to the U.S. dollar.

ATMs (*cajeros automáticos*) are widely available, especially in Lima, and you can get cash with a Cirrus- or Plus-linked debit card or with a major credit card.

A 19% *impuesto general a las ventas* (general sales tax) is levied on everything except goods bought at open-air markets and street vendors. It's usually included in the advertised price and should be included with food and drink.

RESTAURANTS & HOTELS

Food in Peru is hearty and wholesome. Thick soups made of vegetables and meat are excellent. Try *chupes,* soups made of shrimp and fish with potatoes, corn, peas, onions, garlic, tomato sauce, eggs, cream cheese, milk, and whatever else happens to be in the kitchen. Corvina, a sea bass caught in the Pacific Ocean, is superb, as is a fish with a very large mouth, called *paiche,* that is found in jungle lakes and caught with spears. *Anticuchos* (marinated beef hearts grilled over charcoal) are a staple. Peru's large-kernel corn is very good, and it's claimed there are more than 100 varieties of potatoes, served in about as many ways. And there is always *ceviche,* raw fish marinated in lemon juice and white wine then mixed with onions and red peppers and served with sweet potatoes, onions, and sometimes corn.

Top-notch restaurants serve lunch and dinner, but most Peruvians think of lunch as the day's main meal, and many restaurants open only at midday. Served between 1 and 3, lunch was once followed by a siesta, though the custom has largely died out. Dinner can be anything from a light snack to another full meal. Peruvians tend to dine late, between 7 and 11 PM. Most smaller restaurants offer a lunchtime *menú,* a prix-fixe meal ($2–$5) that consists of an appetizer, a main dish, dessert, and a beverage.

At hotels, it's always good to take a look at your room before accepting it; especially if you're staying in a budget hotel. If it isn't what you expected, there might be several other rooms from which to choose. Expense is no guarantee of charm or cleanliness, and accommodations can vary dramatically within a single hotel. Many older hotels in some of the small towns in Peru have rooms with charming balconies or spacious terraces; ask if there's a room *con balcón* or *con terraza* when checking in.

Bed-and-breakfasts are a popular option all over Peru, but especially in tourist areas like Cusco, Arequipa, and Puno. Many are in charming older buildings, including colonial-era homes built around flower-filled courtyards. Breakfast ranges from a roll with butter and jam to a massive buffet.

WHAT IT COSTS IN NUEVO SOLES					
	¢	$	$$	$$$	$$$$
RESTAURANTS	under S/20	S/20–S/35	S/35–S/50	S/50–S/65	over S/65
HOTELS	under S/125	S/125–S/250	S/250–S/375	S/375–S/500	over S/500

Restaurant prices are per person for a main course. Hotel prices are for a standard double room, excluding tax.

LIMA

When people discuss great cities in South America, one that is often overlooked is Lima. But Peru's capital has an oceanfront setting, colonial-era splendor, sophisticated dining, and nonstop nightlife.

In 1535 Francisco Pizarro found the perfect place for the capital of Spain's colonial empire. On a natural port, the so-called Ciudad de los Reyes (City of Kings) allowed Spain to ship home all the gold the conquistador plundered from the Inca. Lima served as the capital of Spain's South American empire for 300 years.

It's true that the city—clogged with traffic and choked with fumes—doesn't make a good first impression. But wander around the regal edifices surrounding the Plaza de Armas, among the gnarled olive trees of San Isidro, or along the winding lanes in the coastal community of Barranco and you might find yourself charmed.

GETTING HERE & AROUND

If you're flying to Peru, you'll almost certainly touch down at Aeropuerto Internacional Jorge Chávez, on the northwestern fringe of Lima.

Taxis are the best way to get around Lima. Use only taxis painted with a company's logo and that have the driver's license prominently displayed. It's best to negotiate the fare before you get in. A journey between two adjacent neighborhoods should cost between S/4 and S/7; longer trips should be about S/10 to S/15. If you call a taxi, the price will be roughly double. Well-regarded companies include Taxi Amigo (☎01/349–0177) and Taxi Móvil (☎01/422–6890).

SAFETY & PRECAUTIONS

Drink only bottled water and order drinks *sin hielo* (without ice). Avoid lettuce and other raw vegetables.

El Centro is safe during the day, but as the locals head home in the late afternoon, so should you. The neighborhood is dicey at night. Residential neighborhoods like Miraflores, San Isidro, and Barranco have far less street crime, but you should be on your guard away from the main streets. Always be alert for pickpockets in crowded markets and on public transportation.

For robberies, contact the Tourist Police. The department is divided into the northern zone (☎01/424–2053), which includes El Centro, and the southern zone (☎01/460–4525), which includes Barranco, Miraflores, and San Isidro. English-speaking officers will help you negotiate the system. For emergencies, call the police (☎105) and fire (☎116) emergency numbers.

ESSENTIALS

Currency Exchange **Banco de Credito** (✉ *Av. José Larco and Schell, Miraflores* ✉ *Av. José Pardo between Recavarren and Libertad, Miraflores*). **Banco Santander** (✉ *Carabaya and Ucayali, El Centro*). **Interbank** (✉ *Av. José Larco and Schell, Miraflores* ✉ *Jr. de la Unión and HuancavelicaEl Centro*).

SPENDING YOUR TIME

DAY 1: LIMA

On your first morning, tour the Plaza de Armas. In the afternoon, see Iglesia de San Francisco and the Museo de Arte de Lima and shop at the outdoor Feria Artesanal. Have dinner in Miraflores.

DAYS 2 & 3: ICA

Head south on the Pan-American highway to Ica, Peru's wine-growing area. Arrange for an afternoon tour of one of the wineries and Ica's Museo Histórico Regional. The next day jump in a 4WD and drive through the desert and then test your skills at sand boarding down the dunes surrounding the *Huacachina* oasis.

DAY 4: NAZCA

In the morning take a five person plane to survey the lines and drawings of Nazca from the air before leaving by bus or car for Paracas. On an afternoon boat trip to the Balestas Islands you'll see sea lions, birds, and tiny Humboldt penguins, passing by the large candelabra etched on a cliff.

DAYS 5 & 6: PUNO

From Lima take an early-morning flight to Juliaca, a commercial center with an airport that serves Puno and the Lake Titicaca region. Puno's 3,830-meter (12,500-feet) altitude can take your breath away. The next day take a boat tour of the lake, stopping at the Uros Islands and Isla Taquile.

DAYS 7 & 8: CUSCO

From Puno take the train to Inca capital of Cusco, a 330 meter (1,083-foot) drop in altitude. Spend the day visiting Qorikancha, the MAP museum, and other architectural gems. The following day tour the Sacred Valley, stopping for the stone fort of Sacsayhuaman, the handicraft market and fantastic ruins at Pisac, and finally at Ollantaytambo for the Inca fortress ruins.

DAYS 9 & 10: MACHU PICCHU

Catch the early train in Cusco to Aguas Calientes. Take the bus up the mountain to Machu Picchu, the majestic ancient citadel. For bragging rights climb Huaynu Picchu, the backdrop mountain for incredible views of the ruins below. A night in Aguas Calientes gives you time at Machu Picchu without the crowds.

DAYS 11–14: HUARAZ

From Lima, drive or take an early-morning bus to Huaraz and spend the day acclimatizing while exploring the city and the nearby Wari ruins of Wilcahuaían. For the next couple days take less strenuous day trips to pristine mountain lakes and the ruins of Chavín de Huantar.

DAYS 15 & 16:

From Huaraz go to Trujillo. Explore the Plaza de Armas at your leisure. The Libertador Hotel on the Plaza is a good spot for lunch or dinner. The next day visit the beach resort of Huanchaco for lunch and spend the afternoon lounging on the beach. Local fishermen set out in their *caballitos de totora,* or reed boats. In the afternoon travel to the adobe-brick city of Chán Chán.

8

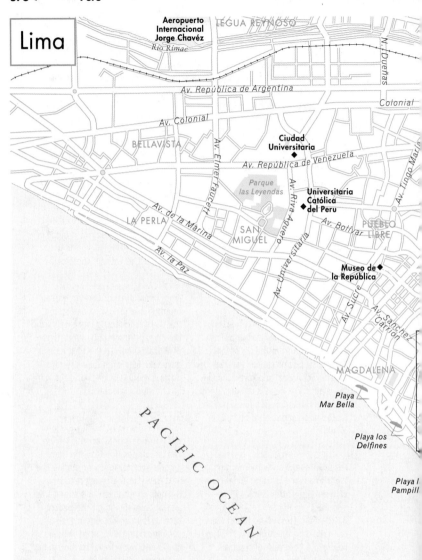

Lima

Aeropuerto Internacional Jorge Chavéz

LEGUA REYNOSO

Río Rímac

N. Dueñas

Av. República de Argentina

Colonial

Av. Colonial

BELLAVISTA

Ciudad Universitaria

Av. República de Venezuela

Av. Elmer Faucett

Av. Riva Agüero

Parque las Leyendas

Universitaria Católica del Peru

Av. Tingo María

LA PERLA

Av. de la Marina

SAN MIGUEL

Av. Botívar

PUEBLO LIBRE

Av. la Paz

Av. Universitaria

Museo de la República

Av. Sucre

Av. Sanchez Carrión

MAGDALENA

Playa Mar Bella

Playa los Delfines

PACIFIC OCEAN

Playa l Pampill

0   1 mile

0   1 km

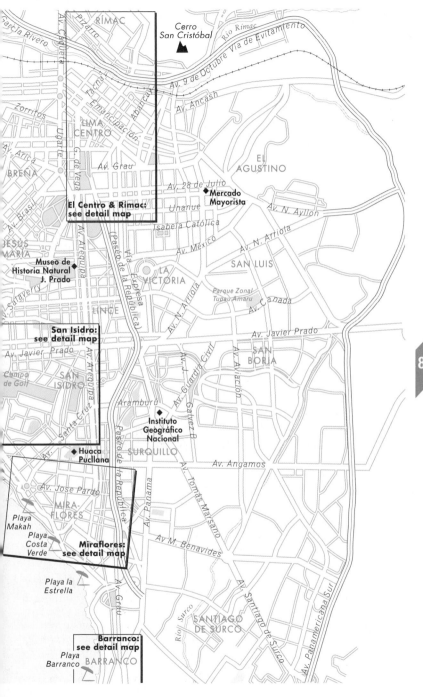

Hospitals Clinica Anglo-Americana (✉ *Av. Alfredo Salazar, San Isidro* ☎ *01/221–3656*). **Clinica El Golf** (✉ *Av. Aurelio Miro Quesada, San Isidro* ☎ *01/264–3300*).

Internet Cafés Dragon Fans (✉ *Calle Tarata 230, Miraflores* ☎ *01/446–6814*). **Jedi** (✉ *Av. Diagonal 218, Miraflores* ☎ *01/447–9290*).

Pharmacies Farmacia Deza (✉ *Av. Conquistadores 144, San Isidro* ☎ *01/441–5860*). **InkaFarma** (✉ *Av. Benavides 425, Miraflores* ☎ *01/314–2020*).

Mail Miraflores (✉ *Av. Petit Thouars 5201* ☎ *01/445–0697*). **San Isidro** (✉ *Av. Libertadores 325* ☎ *01/422–0981*).**DHL** (✉ *Calle Los Castaños 225, San Isidro* ☎ *01/517–2500*). **FedEx** (✉ *Pasaje Mártir José Olaya 260, Miraflores* ☎ *01/242–2280*). **UPS** (✉ *Av. del Ejercito 2107, San Isidro* ☎ *01/264–0105*).

Rental Car Avis (✉ *Av. Larco 1080, Miraflores* ☎ *01/446–4533*). **Budget** (✉ *Moreyra 569, San Isidro* ☎ *01/442–8703*). **Hertz** (✉ *Av. Cantuarias 160, Miraflores* ☎ *01/447–2129*). **National** (✉ *Av. España 453, El Centro* ☎ *01/433–3750*).

Visitor Info iPerú (✉ *Jorge Basadre 610, San Isidro* ☎ *01/421–1627* ✉ *Malecón de la Reserva and Av. José Larco, Miraflores* ☎ *01/445–9400* ⊕ *www.peru.info*). **Oficina de Información Touristica** (✉ *Paseo de los Escribanos 145, El Centro* ☎ *01/315–1505*).

EXPLORING LIMA

EL CENTRO

In the colonial era, Lima was the seat of power for the viceroyalty of Peru. It held sway over a swath of land that extended from Panama to Chile. With power came money, as is evident by the grand scale on which everything was built. At least half a dozen churches would be called cathedrals in any other city. And the Plaza de Armas, the sprawling main square, is spectacular.

But history has not always been kind to El Centro. Many buildings are victims of neglect. But after years of decline, things are changing for the better.

An unhurried visit to the historic district's main attractions takes a full day, with at least an hour devoted to the Museo de Arte Nacional and the Museo de la Inquisición. Don't bypass the guided tour of the underground catacombs of the Iglesia de San Francisco.

Chances are you're staying in Miraflores or San Isidro, which are a quick taxi ride from El Centro. Since taxis take the expressway, you're downtown in 10 minutes. Once you're there, the only way to get around is by foot. No problem, as the historic area is rather compact.

MAIN ATTRACTIONS

5 Casa Torre Tagle. Considered one of the most magnificent structures in South America, this mansion sums up the graceful style of the early 18th century. Flanked by a pair of elegant balconies, the stone entrance is as expertly carved as that of any of the city's churches. It currently serves as a governmental building and is not open to the public, but you can often get a peek inside. You might see the tiled ceilings, carved columns, and a 16th-century carriage. Across the street is **Casa Goy-**

eneche, which was built some 40 later in 1771, and was clearly influenced by the rococo movement. ✉ *Jr. Ucayali 363.*

❷ **Catedral.** The first church on the site was completed in 1625. The layout for this immense structure was dictated by Francisco Pizarro, and his basic vision has survived complete rebuilding after earthquakes in 1746 and 1940. Inside are impressive baroque appointments, especially the intricately carved choir stalls. Because of changing tastes, the main altar was replaced around 1800 with one in a neoclassical style. At about the same time the towers that flank the entrance were added. Visit the chapel where Pizarro is entombed. ✉ *East side of Plaza de Armas* ☎ *01/427–9647* 💲 *S/10* ⏰ *Mon.–Sat. 10–4:30.*

❹ **Iglesia de la Merced.** Nothing about this colonial-era church could be
★ called restrained. Take the unusual baroque facade. Instead of stately columns, the powers-that-be decided they should be wrapped with carefully carved grapevines. Inside are a series of retables that gradually change from baroque to neoclassical styles. The intricately carved choir stalls, dating from the 18th century, have images of cherubic singers. The first house of worship to be built in Lima, Our Lady of Mercy was commissioned by Hernando Pizarro, brother of the city's founder. ✉ *Jr. de la Unión at Jr. Miro Quesada* ☎ *01/427–8199* 💲 *Free* ⏰ *Tues.–Sun. 8–1 and 4–8.*

❸ **Iglesia de San Francisco.** Bones—including thousands and thousands of
☺ human skulls—are piled in eerie geometric patterns in the crypt of this
*Fodor's*Choice church. ■**TIP**➜ **This was the city's first cemetery, and the underground**
★ **tunnels contain the earthly remains of some 75,000 people, which you visit on a tour (available in English).** The Church of Saint Francis is the most visited in Lima, mostly because of these catacombs. But it's also the best example of what is known as "Lima Baroque" style of architecture. The handsome carved portal would later influence those on other churches, including the Iglesia de la Merced. The central nave is known for its beautiful ceilings painted in a style called *mudejar* (a blend of Moorish and Spanish designs). ✉ *Jr. Ancash 471* ☎ *01/427–1381* 💲 *S/5* ⏰ *Daily 9:30–5:45.*

❻ **Iglesia de San Pedro.** The Jesuits built three churches in rapid succession on this corner, the current one dating from 1638. It remains one of the finest examples of early-colonial religious architecture in Peru. The facade is remarkably restrained, but the interior shows all the extravagance of the era, including a series of baroque retables thought to be the best in the city. ■**TIP**➜ **Don't miss the side aisle, where gilded arches lead to chapels decorated with beautiful hand-painted tiles.** Many have works by Italians like Bernardo Bitti, who arrived on these shores in 1575. His style influenced an entire generation of painters. In the sac-

8

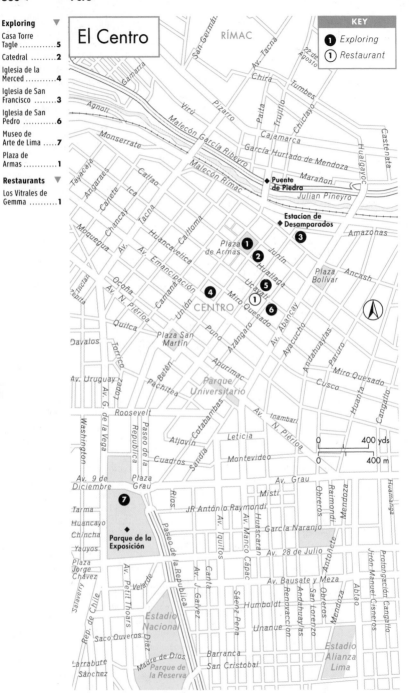

risty is *The Coronation of the Virgin,* one of his most famous works.
✉*Jr. Ucayali at Jr. Azángaro* ☎*01/428–3010* 🎟*Free* 🕑*Mon.–Sat. 7–12:30 and 5–8.*

❼ Museo de Arte de Lima. The facade is covered with graffiti, probably because it adjoins a busy bus stop. But the rest of the Museum of Art is lovingly cared for. Built in 1872 as the Palacio de la Expedición, this mammoth neoclassical structure was designed by Gustav Eiffel (who later built the famous tower). It contains a bit of everything, from pre-Columbian artifacts to colonial-era furniture to modern art. One of the highlights is the collection of 2,000-year-old weavings from Paracas. ✉*Paseo Colón 125* ☎*01/423–6332* 🌐*museoarte.perucultural.org.pe* 🎟*S/12* 🕑*Thurs.–Tues. 10–5.*

❶ Plaza de Armas. This massive square has been the center of the city since
★ 1535. Over the years it has served many functions, from an open-air theater for melodramas to an impromptu ring for bullfights. Huge fires once burned in the center for people sentenced to death by the Spanish Inquisition. Much has changed over the years, but one thing remaining is the bronze fountain unveiled in 1651. ■TIP➔ **It was here that José de San Martín declared the country's independence from Spain in 1821.** ✉*Jr. Junín and Jr. Carabaya.*

SAN ISIDRO

Like nearby Miraflores, San Isidro is big on shopping—plenty of boutiques sell designer goods, bars serve up the latest cocktails, and restaurants dish out cuisine from around the world. At its main attraction, Huaca Huallamarca, you can clamor around the ruins of this ancient temple.

The best way to travel between San Isidro's widely dispersed attractions is by taxi. Walking through the neighborhood takes no more than a few hours. This is probably Lima's safest neighborhood.

❶ Huaca Huallamarca. The sight of this mud-brick pyramid catches many people off guard. The structure, painstakingly restored on the front side, seems out of place among the neighborhood's towering hotels and apartment buildings. The upper platform affords some nice views of the San Isidro. There's a small museum with displays of objects found at the site, including several mummies. This temple, thought to be a place of worship, predates the Incas. ✉*Av. Nicolás de Rivera and Av. El Rosario* ☎*01/224–4124* 🎟*S/5.50* 🕑*Tues.–Sun 9–5.*

MIRAFLORES

With flower-filled parks and wide swaths of green overlooking the ocean, no wonder travelers flock to this seaside suburb. There are plenty of boutiques, galleries, and museums, as well as bars, cafés, and restaurants.

At its center is Parque Miraflores, sitting like a slice of pie between Avenida José Larco and Avenida Diagonal. On the eastern side is the Parroquia Virgen Milagrosa, the neighborhood's largest church. The colonial-style building next door is the Municipalidad de Miraflores, where most governmental business takes place.

8

All the stores along Avenida José Larco stay open for early-evening window shoppers. About a half hour of walking will lead you to the ocean, where you'll want to spend another hour or so strolling along the cliff. Miraflores is about 20 minutes from El Centro by taxi.

MAIN ATTRACTIONS

1 **Pucllana.** Rising out of a nondescript residential neighborhood is this
★ mud-brick pyramid. You'll be amazed at the scale—this pre-Inca *huaca,* or temple, covers several city blocks. The site, which dates back to at least the 4th century, has ongoing excavations, and new discoveries are often being announced. ■ TIP→ **Archaeologists working on the site are usually happy to share their discoveries about the people who lived in this area hundreds of years before the Inca**. A tiny museum highlights some recent finds. Knowledgeable guides are available in Spanish and English. This site is off the beaten path, but plenty of restaurants are nearby, including the on-site Huaca Pucllana. ⊠ *General Borgoño, 2 blocks north of Av. Angamos Oeste* ☎ *01/445–8695* ⊕ *pucllana.peru cultural.org.pe* ⊴ *S/7* ⊙ *Wed.–Mon. 9–4:30.*

2 **Parque Miraflores.** What locals call Parque Miraflores is actually two parks. The smaller section is Parque Central, which has frequent open-air concerts. Shoeshine boys will ask whether you need a *lustre* when you stop to listen to the music. The honking noise you hear is the ice-cream vendors that patrol the park on bright yellow bicycles. A tourist-information kiosk sits on the south side. Across a pedestrian street full of local artists showing off their latest works is Parque Kennedy, where the babble from a lively crafts market fills the evening air. On the eastern side is the pretty Parroquia Virgen Milagrosa (Miraculous Virgin Church). A few sidewalk cafés are behind the church. ⊠ *Between Av. José Larco and Av. Diagonal.*

BARRANCO

Barranco is a magnet for young people who come to carouse in its bars and cafés. Sleepy during the day, the neighborhood comes to life around sunset when artists start hawking their wares and its central square and bars begin filling up with people ready to party.

MAIN ATTRACTIONS

2 **Museo-Galería Arte Popular de Ayacucho.** An unassuming facade makes it easy to miss, but inside you'll find one of the country's best collections of folk art. One especially interesting exhibit concerns the cajones San Marcos, the boxlike portable altars that priests once carried from village to village. Peasants began to make their own, placing scenes of local life inside. These dioramas, ranging in size from less than an inch to more than a foot wide, are still made today. ⊠ *Av. Pedro de Osma 116* ☎ *01/247–0599* ⊴ *Free* ⊙ *Tues.–Sat. 9–6.*

3 **Museo Pedro de Osma.** Even if there was no art inside this museum,
Fodor's Choice it would still be worth the trip to see the century-old mansion that
★ houses it. The mansard-roofed structure—with inlaid wood floors, delicately painted ceilings, and breathtaking stained-glass windows in every room—was the home of a wealthy collector of religious art. The

best of his collection is permanently on display. The finest of the paintings, the 18th-century *Virgen de Pomato,* represents the Earth, with her mountain-shape cloak covered with garlands of corn. A more modern wing contains some fine pieces of silver, including a lamb-shape incense holder with shining ruby eyes. Make sure to explore the manicured grounds. ⊠ *Av. Pedro de Osma 423* ☎ *01/467–0141* ⊡ *S/10* ⊙ *Tues.–Sun. 10–6.*

❶ Puente de los Suspiros. The roman-
★ tically named Bridge of Sighs is a lovely wooden walkway shaded with flowering trees. You won't have to wait long to see couples walking hand in hand. The bridge crosses over the Bajada de Baños, a cobblestone walkway that leads to Playa Barranquito. On the far side is La Ermita, a lovely little chapel painted a dazzling shade of red. ⊠ *East of Parque Municipal.*

> ### LOVE PARK
>
> **Parque del Amor.** You might think you're in Barcelona when you stroll through this lovely park. Like Antonio Gaudí's Parque Güell, the park that provided the inspiration for this one, the benches are decorated with broken pieces of tile. Here, however, they spell out silly romantic sayings like *Amor es como luz* ("Love is like light"). The centerpiece is a controversial statue of two lovers locked in a lewd embrace. ⊠ *Av. Diagonal.*

PUEBLO LIBRE

Instead of hurrying past, residents of Pueblo Libre often pause to chat with friends. There's a sense of calm here not found elsewhere in the capital. Plaza Bolívar, the park at the heart of Pueblo Libre, is surrounded by colonial-era buildings, many of which have shops and restaurants.

MAIN ATTRACTIONS

Museo Nacional de Antropología, Arqueología, e Historia del Perú. The country's most extensive collection of pre-Columbian artifacts can be found at this sprawling museum. Beginning with 8,000-year-old stone tools, Peru's history is peeked at through the sleek granite obelisks of the Chavín culture, the intricate weavings of Paraca peoples, and the colorful ceramics of the Moche, Chimú, and Inca civilizations. A fascinating pair of mummies from the Nazca region are thought to be more than 2,500 years old; they are so well preserved that you can still see the grim expressions on their faces. Not all the exhibits are labeled in English, but you can hire a guide for S/15. ⊠ *Plaza Bolívar* ☎ *01/463–5070* ⊕ *mnaah.perucultural.org.pe* ⊡ *S/11* ⊙ *Tues.–Sat. 9–5, Sun. 9–4.*

Fodor's Choice **Museo Arqueológico Rafael Larco Herrera.** Fuchsia bougainvillea tumbles
★ over the white walls surrounding the home of the world's largest private collection of pre-Columbian art. The oldest pieces are crude vessels dating back several thousand years. Most intriguing are the thousands of ceramic "portrait heads" crafted more than a millennium ago. Some owners commissioned more than one, allowing you to see how they changed over the course of their lives. The *sala erótica* reveals that these ancient artists were surprisingly uninhibited. Everyday objects are

adorned with images that are frankly sexual and frequently humorous. This gallery is across the garden from the rest of the museum, so you can distance the kids from it. Guides are a good idea, and are just S/25 per group. ⊠ *Av. Bolívar 1515* ☎ *01/461–1835* ⊕ *www.museolarco. org* 🖾 *S/25* ⊙ *Daily 9–6.*

OFF THE BEATEN PATH

Pachacàmac. Dating back to the first century, this city of plazas, palaces, and pyramids, many of them painstakingly restored, was for centuries a stronghold of the Huari (Wari) people. Here they worshipped Pachacámac, creator of the world. It was a pilgrimage site, and people from all over the region came to worship here. In the 15th century the city was captured by the Inca, who added structures such as the *Acclla-huasi,* the Palace of the Chosen Women. When the Spanish heard of the city, they dispatched troops to plunder its riches. In 1533, two years before the founding of Lima, they marched triumphantly into the city, only to find a few remaining objects in gold. Today you can visit the temples, including several that were built before the time of the Incas. The Incas built several more structures, including the impressive Templo del Inti, or Temple of the Sun. Here you'll find a grand staircase leading up to the colonnaded walkways surrounding the temple. The site has a small but excellent museum. Although it's a quick drive from the city, the easiest way to see Pachacámac is by a half-day guided tour offered by Lima Tours and several other agencies in Lima. ⊠ *31 km (19 mi) south of Lima on Carretera Panamericana Sur* ☎ *01/430–0168* ⊕ *www.pachacamac.perucultural.org.pe* 🖾 *S/5.50* ⊙ *Daily 9–5.*

WHERE TO EAT

BARRANCO

$–$$
PERUVIAN

✕**Manos Morenas.** A century-old house behind an iron gate contains one of the most atmospheric restaurants in Barranco. Past the brilliant blue facade is a warmly lighted dining room bustling with women in colorful headwraps serving tasty Peruvian fare. The ají de gallina, a spicy stewed hen, is the best you'll find anywhere. If you're brave, sample the *anticuchos,* skewers of beef hearts. At night Manos bursts to life with music and dancing. ⊠ *Av. Pedro de Osma 409,* ☎ *01/467–0421* ⌂ *Reservations essential* ⊟ *AE, MC, V.*

¢–$
PERUVIAN
★

✕**Las Mesitas.** Filled with a dozen or so marble-topped tables, this charming old-fashioned café is a block north of Parque Municipal. Share a few *humitas,* steamed tamales that you season with pickled onions or bright yellow hot sauce. The best are those stuffed with chicken, onions, and green corn. If the floor's pinwheel design doesn't put you off balance, then the spinning dessert display certainly will. Try the *mazamorra morada,* a sweet pudding of cornmeal and candied fruit. ⊠ *Grau 341,* ☎ *01/477–1346* ⊟ *MC, V.*

$–$$
SEAFOOD
★

✕**Vida.** Facing a cobblestone street, this butter-yellow building has an unbeatable location. Wide windows in the dining room let you watch young lovers stroll across the Puente de los Suspiros. With the ocean practically at the door, it's no surprise the focus is seafood. Try the sea bass wrapped in prosciutto and sautéed in pisco, or the swordfish

Barranco

KEY

❶ *Exploring*

① *Restaurants & Hotels*

grilled in squid ink. ⊠*Bajada de Baños 340,* ☎*01/252–8034* ⌲*Reservations essential* ⊟*AE, DC, MC, V* ☉*Closed Mon. No dinner Sun.*

EL CENTRO

$
PERUVIAN
★

✕**Los Vitrales de Gemma.** Tucked into the courtyard of a beautiful colonial-era building, this is one of the prettiest restaurants in the historic district. The food, creative takes on old recipes, is just as appealing. Start with a spinach salad tossed with bacon, walnuts, and slices of apples, then move on to *pescado en salsa langotinos* (fish in lobster sauce) or *espagueti fruotos del mar* (pasta with seafood). ⊠*Jr. Ucayali 332* ☎*01/426–7796* ⊟*AE, DC, MC, V* ☉*Closed Sun.*

MIRAFLORES

$$–$$$
CONTINENTAL
Fodor'sChoice
★

✕**Astrid y Gaston.** You can't help but watch the kitchen door—each dish the waiters carry out is a work of art. Take the *pato asado con mil especies* (roast duck with 1,000 spices): the honey-brown breast is accompanied by a steamed pear and a pepper bubbling over with basil risotto. Other dishes, like the pasta with squid and artichokes, are just as astonishing. Take advantage of the wine list—it's one of the best in town. In a colonial-style building on a quiet street, the restaurant is lovely, with pumpkin-color walls and original artwork. ⊠*Cantuarias 175, Lima 18* ☎*01/444–1496* ⊟*AE, MC, V* ☉*Closed Sun.*

8

Miraflores

KEY

❶ *Exploring*

① *Restaurants & Hotels*

$$–$$$$ ✕**Huaca Pucllana.** You feel like a part of history at this beautiful restau-
PERUVIAN rant, which faces the ruins of a 1,500-year-old pyramid. Excavations
Fodor'sChoice are ongoing, so you can watch archaeologists at work as you enjoy
★ the breezes on the covered terrace. Rough-hewn columns hold up the
dining room's soaring ceiling. This is *novo andino* cuisine, which puts
a new spin on old recipes. Yellow peppers stuffed with shrimp are a
great way to start, and the *cabrito al horno* (roasted kid) is a work of
art. ⊠ *Av. General Borgoña* ☎ *01/445–4042* ⊜ *Reservations essential*
⊟ *AE, DC, MC, V.*

$–$$ ✕**El Señorío de Sulco.** It's no surprise that the food is so good when you
PERUVIAN learn that owner Isabel Alvarez authored several cookbooks. Start with
chupe de camerones, a hearty soup combining shrimp and potatoes,
then move on to *arroz con pato,* duck stewed in dark beer and seasoned with coriander. For dessert there's the meringue-topped *suspiro
de limeña,* which literally means "sigh of a lady of Lima." Arrive early
to watch the sun set over the ocean. ⊠ *Malecón Cisneros 1470, Lima
18* ☎ *01/441–0389* ⊜ *Reservations essential* ⊟ *AE, DC, MC, V* ☾ *No
dinner Sun.*

$–$$ ✕**Las Tejas.** As it's a few steps down from the street, it would be easy to
PERUVIAN pass by this family-run restaurant. That would be a shame, as it serves
up some of the neighborhood's tastiest traditional cuisine. The staff will
explain each dish, what part of the country it comes from, and how it's

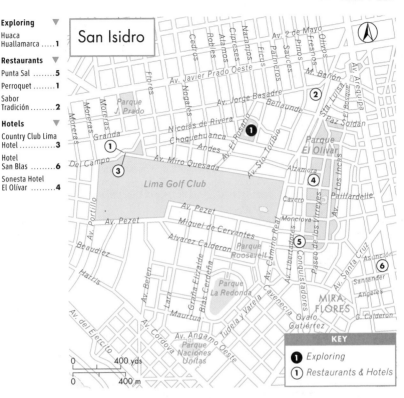

Exploring ▼

Huaca
Huallamarca **1**

Restaurants ▼

Punta Sal **5**

Perroquet **1**

Sabor
Tradición **2**

Hotels ▼

Country Club Lima
Hotel **3**

Hotel
San Blas **6**

Sonesta Hotel
El Olívar **4**

San Isidro

Lima Golf Club

KEY

❶ *Exploring*

① *Restaurants & Hotels*

0   400 yds

0   400 m

made. ■**TIP**➔ This is the best place to sample lomo saltado, slices of pork sautéed with tomatoes and onions and served over fried potatoes. You know the food is fresh, as it's prepared in the open-air kitchen inches away from the tables scattered around the covered terrace. ⊠*Diez Canseco 340, Lima 18* ☎*01/444–4360* ⊟*AE, DC, MC, V.*

$$–$$$ ✕**La Tranquera.** A butcher's front window couldn't display more cuts of
STEAK   meat than the glass case along the wall of this local landmark. Check out the different cuts, then inform your waiter which one you want and how it should be cooked. It will arrive at your table atop a charcoal brazier, sizzling from the grill. ■**TIP**➔ **Even the smallest steaks, labeled junior, are the size of a dinner plate. If you have a lighter appetite, the costillas a la barbacoa are basted with a tangy barbecue sauce that doesn't overwhelm the flavor of the ribs.** ⊠*Av. José Pardo 285, Lima 18* ☎*01/447–5111* ⊟*AE, DC, MC, V.*

SAN ISIDRO

$$–$$$ ✕**Perroquet.** There's not a more elegant dining room than Perroquet,
PERUVIAN   tucked away in the Country Club Lima Hotel. You feel pampered in the main room, with its upholstered chairs and tables almost overloaded with polished crystal and china. If it's a cool evening, you might prefer the terrace and its glittering chandeliers. There are traditional dishes, but they have a modern flair. Try the lamb's shin simmered for three

hours in red wine and cilantro seeds, or the salmon in a passion-fruit glaze served over a bed of looks. After dinner, retire to the English Bar for an aperitif. ⊠ *Country Club Hotel, Los Eucaliptos 50* ☎ *511/611–9000* ⚐ *Reservations essential* ⊟ *AE, D, DC, MC, V.*

$–$$

SEAFOOD

★

✕**Punta Sal.** Walls covered with stones worn smooth by the ocean add an elegant touch to San Isidro's best seafood restaurant. But the real excitement is on the platters streaming out of the kitchen. Order the *tiradito criollo,* and the slices of fish arrive covered in a vivid sauce made from yellow peppers. This place has won every award in the book, undoubtedly because the chefs constantly look to other countries for inspiration. This is one of the few *cebicherías* serving carpaccio. You can ask that your sole or sea bass be cooked one of 10 different ways. ⊠ *Av. Conquistadores 948, San Isidro,* ☎ *01/441–7431* ⊠ *Malecón Cisneros at Av. Tripoli, Miraflores* ☎ *01/242–4524* ⊟ *AE, DC, MC, V* ⊗ *No dinner.*

¢–$

SEAFOOD

✕**Sabor Tradición.** Locals can't get enough of this restaurant—maybe because the fish dishes are so good, or maybe because the prices, including the lunch specials, are so reasonable. Deciding on an entrée can be difficult. If you're in the mood for shrimp, you'll find it prepared at least half a dozen ways, including *picante de camarones* (shrimp in a spicy sauce). It's a good thing that the chef lets you sample. ⊠ *Av. Santa Luisa 156, Lima 27* ☎ *01/441–8287* ⊟ *AE, DC, MC, V* ⊗ *Closed weekends. No dinner.*

WHERE TO STAY

The best lodgings are on quiet streets in the mostly residential neighborhoods of Miraflores and San Isidro. These areas are safe, so you don't have to worry about taking a stroll during the day, and they're quick cab rides to El Centro.

BARRANCO

¢

🏨**Hospedaje Domeyer.** Barranco is the artist hangout, so it's no surprise that the hotel's common areas are furnished in what might called "thrift store chic." Bronze sculptures are scattered about and paper lanterns hang from above. It all somehow works with the old house's vividly colorful tile floors. Rooms have high ceilings and tall windows with shutters you can throw open to catch the ocean breezes. **Pros:** Near dozens of restaurants, quiet street. **Cons:** Hippy aesthetic means common areas are often a jumble, bathroom walls don't extend to the ceiling. ⊠ *Jr. Domeyer 296, Lima 04* ☎ *01/247–1413* 🛏 *13 rooms* ⚐ *In-room: VCR. In-hotel: bar, laundry service* ⊟ *AE, DC, MC, V.*

MIRAFLORES

$

Fodor'sChoice

★

🏨**La Castellana.** A favorite for years, this exuberantly neoclassical structure resembles a small castle. The foyer, where wrought-iron lanterns cast a soft glow, is a taste of what is to come. Beyond are lovely touches like stained-glass windows and a towering turret. All the wood-shuttered rooms are lovely, but especially nice are No. 10, which overlooks the sunny courtyard, and No. 15, which has a private balcony facing the front. The friendly staff goes above and beyond the call of duty, even helping with things like airplane reservations. This inn remains immensely popular, so make reservations far in advance. **Pros:** Gorgeous colonial-style building, near dozens of restaurants, great value. **Cons:** Neighborhood can be noisy on weekends, newer section not quite as charming. ⊠*Grimaldo del Solar 222, Lima 18* ☎*01/444–3530* ⊕*www.hotel-lacastellana.com* ⇦*29 rooms* ⌂*In-room: safe. In-hotel: restaurant, bar* ☐*AE, DC, MC, V.*

$–$$
Fodor'sChoice
★

▦**Hotel Antigua Miraflores.** In a salmon-color mansion dating back more than a century, this elegantly appointed hotel is perhaps the city's loveliest lodging. Black-and-white marble floors and perfectly polished railings greet you as you stroll through the antiques-filled lobby. Up the wooden staircase are guest rooms with hand-carved furniture. Those in front have more character, whereas the more modern rooms in the newer section curve around a graceful fountain. Known for its impeccable service, the hotel sees repeat business year after year. **Pros:** Gorgeous architecture, pleasant staff, residential neighborhood. **Cons:** Long walk to Miraflores sights, newer rooms have less charm. ⊠*Grau 350, Lima 18* ☎*01/241–6116* ⊕*www.peru-hotels-inns.com* ⇦*15 rooms* ⌂*In-room: Wi-Fi. In-hotel: restaurant, bar, gym, public Internet* ☐*AE, DC, MC, V.*

$–$$
▦**Leon de Oro.** A statue of a lion stands guard at this boutique hotel in the heart of Miraflores. Don't expect the usual bright colors and colonial-style furniture. Instead you'll find muted shades and crisp lines in the generously sized rooms. The butter-soft linens on the queen-size beds and polished marble in the baths will leave you feeling pampered. For real luxury, spend a bit more on a suite and settle into your own hot tub. **Pros:** On a quiet street, professional staff, nice buffet breakfast. **Cons:** Feels more European than Peruvian, long walk to most dining options. ⊠*Av. La Paz 930, Lima 18* ☎*01/242–6200* ⊕*www.leondeoroperu.com* ⇦*44 rooms, 2 suites* ⌂*In-room: safe. In-hotel: restaurant, room service, bar, laundry service* ☐*AE, DC, MC, V* ��*BP.*

$$$$
Fodor'sChoice
★

▦**Miraflores Park Plaza.** Surprisingly few of the city's hotels are near the ocean, which is why this hotel is in such demand. ■**TIP➡ If you think the views from your room are breathtaking, just head up to the rooftop pool overlooking the entire coastline.** Rooms have sitting areas that make them as big as suites, and computer connections and fax machines. Better suited for couples are the suites, which have hot tubs strategically placed beside the beds. **Pros:** Unobstructed ocean views, lots of atmosphere, near many restaurants. **Cons:** Not walking distance to Miraflores sights. ⊠*Malecón de la Reserva 1035, Lima 18* ☎*01/242–3000* ⊕*www.mira-park.com* ⇦*64 rooms, 17 suites* ⌂*In-room: safe, refrigerator, VCR, Wi-Fi. In-hotel: 2 restaurants, room service, bars, pool, gym, spa, laundry service, public Internet, public Wi-Fi, airport shuttle* ☐*AE, MC, V.*

SAN ISIDRO

$$$$
Fodor'sChoice
★

▦**Country Club Lima Hotel.** Priceless paintings from the Museo Pedro de Osma hang in each room in this luxurious lodging. The hacienda-style hotel, dating from 1927, is itself a work of art. Just step into the lobby, where hand-painted tiles reflect the yellows and greens of the stained-glass ceiling. The air of refinement continues in the rooms, all

8

of which are draped with fine fabrics. Many have private balconies that overlook the oval-shaped pool or the well-tended gardens. Locals frequently come by for high tea in the stained-glass atrium bar or traditional fare in the elegant Perroquet restaurant. **Pros:** Architectural gem, doting service, one of the city's best restaurants. **Cons:** A bit removed from the action, newer sections lack the old-fashioned charm. ⊠*Los Eucaliptos 590, Lima 27* ☎*01/211–9000* ⊕*www.hotelcountry.com* ⤵*75 rooms* ⌂*In-room: safe, refrigerator, Ethernet. In-hotel: restaurant, room service, pool, gym, laundry service, public Internet, public Wi-Fi, airport shuttle* ⊟*AE, DC, MC, V.*

$ 🏨**Hotel San Blas.** The best deal in San Isidro—maybe in the entire city—
★ is this little gem. Its price tag is below that of many budget hotels, while its amenities are equal to those of quite a few resorts. The rooms are as big as suites and have niceties like modem connections and soundproof windows. Jacuzzis turn the baths into spas. A well-equipped meeting room on the ground floor that accommodates 30 people opens out into a sunny patio. The café in the lobby is on call if you order up a midnight snack, even if it's three in the morning. **Pros:** Spacious rooms, pretty terrace, generous breakfast buffet. **Cons:** On a busy street, long walk to restaurants. ⊠*Av. Arequipa 3940, Lima 18* ☎*01/222–2601* ⊕*www.hotelsanblas.com.pe* ⤵*30 rooms* ⌂*In-room: safe, refrigerator, Wi-Fi. In-hotel: room service, bar, laundry service, public Internet, public Wi-Fi, airport shuttle* ⊟*AE, DC, MC, V* ⍨*BP.*

$$$$ 🏨**Sonesta Hotel El Olívar.** Stretching along an old olive grove, this lumi-
★ nous hotel has one of the most relaxed settings in San Isidro. This is especially true if you avail yourself of the sundeck and pool on the top floor. Rooms are amply proportioned, especially those with private balconies overflowing with greenery. The clientele is mostly business travelers, so the rooms have computer connections and space to spread out. Italian cuisine is served at El Olivar, where you're treated to a view of the park. Ichi Ban serves up a vast selection of sushi and sashimi. **Pros:** Lovely location overlooking a park, top-notch dining, near shops and boutiques. **Cons:** Chain-hotel feel, far from sights. ⊠*Pancho Fierro 194, Lima 27* ☎*01/221–2121* ⊕*www.sonesta.com* ⤵*134 rooms, 11 suites* ⌂*In-room: safe, refrigerator, Ethernet. In-hotel: 2 restaurants, room service, bar, pool, gym, laundry service, public Internet, public Wi-Fi, airport shuttle* ⊟*AE, DC, MC, V.*

NIGHTLIFE

BARS

When you're in Barranco, a pleasant place to start off the evening is **La Posada del Mirador** (⊠*Ermita 104, Barranco* ☎*01/477–9577*). The bar has a second-story balcony that looks out to sea, making this a great place to watch the sunset. Facing Barranco's main square is **Juanito's** (⊠*Grau 274, Barranco* ☎*No phone*), one of the neighborhood's most venerable establishments. Built by Italian immigrants in 1905, the former pharmacy retains its glass-front cabinets. Today, however, the bottles inside are filled with wine and spirits. If you prefer a good

Pena Party

The most popular weekend destinations are *peñas*, bars that offer *música criolla*, a breathless combination of Peruvian, African, and other influences. The music is accompanied by flashily costumed dancers whipping themselves into a frenzy. Depending on the venue, these shows can be exhilarating or just plain exhausting. Ask locals to recommend one not geared to tourists. Most peñas start the show at 10:30 or 11 and continue until the wee hours of the morning.

The most upmarket of the peñas is found in Barranco at **Manos Morenas** (⊠ *Av. Pedro de Osma 409, Barranco* ☎ *01/467–0421*). Extravagantly costumed performers hardly seem to touch the ground as they re-create dances from around the region. The musicians, switching instruments half a dozen times during a song, are without equal. The place feels like a theme park, partly due to the long tables of picture-taking tourists. Vying for the tourist market is **La Candelaria** (⊠ *Av. Bolognesi 292, Barranco* ☎ *01/247–1314*), which is recognizable from the fiery torches flanking the front door. In the main room, the dancers have plenty of room to show off their steps. The facade may be dull, but the attitude is anything but at **De Rompe y Raja** (⊠ *Jr. Manuel Segura 127, Barranco* ☎ *01/247–3271*). Slightly off the beaten path, this peña attracts mostly locals to its shows with *música negra*, a black variant of *música criolla*.

Junius (⊠ *Av. Independencia 125, Miraflores* ☎ *01/617–1000*) has dinner shows featuring traditional dances. It's geared mostly to tourists. An older crowd heads to **Sachún** (⊠ *Av. del Ejército 657, Miraflores* ☎ *01/441–4465*). The draw, it seems, are the sentimental favorites played by the band.

pilsner, try **Freiheit** (⊠ *Lima 471, Miraflores* ☎ *01/247–4630*). The second-story establishment is a favorite among college students.

SHOPPING

CLOTHING

★ Lots of stores stock clothing made of alpaca, but one of the few to offer articles made from vicuña is **Alpaca 111** (⊠ *Av. Larco 671, Miraflores* ☎ *01/447–1623* ⊠ *Larcomar Malecón de la Reserva and Av. José Larco, Miraflores* ☎ *01/241–3484*). This diminutive creature, distant cousin of the llama, produces the world's finest wool. It's fashioned into scarves, sweaters, and even knee-length coats. There are branches of the store in Hotel Los Delfines, Miraflores Park Hotel, and Sonesta Posada del Inca El Olívar.

★ **Anonima** (⊠ *Av. Libertadores 256, San Isidro* ☎ *01/222–2382*) is known for its handmade glass bowls, vases, and other objects in wonderfully wacky color combinations. For one-of-a-kind pieces, **Coral Roja** (⊠ *Recavarren 269, Miraflores* ☎ *01/447–2552*) sells work made on the premises. The little red building is the place to go for original designs.

8

TOURS

Lima has many top tour operators with experienced English-speaking guides for local and country-wide sightseeing. The most professional is Lima Tours, which offers tours of the city and surrounding area as well as the rest of Peru. The company is one of the few that conducts tours for gay groups. Lima Vision has some excellent city tours, including several that include lunch at a traditional restaurant or a dinner show. Other well-regarded companies include Condor Travel, Setours, and Solmartour.

Operators Condor Travel (⊠ *Av. Amando Blondet 249, San Isidro* ☎ *01/442–0935* ⊕ *www.condortravel.com.pe*). **Lima Tours** (⊠ *Belén 1040, El Centro* ☎ *01/619– 6900* ⊕ *www.limatours.com.pe*). **Lima Vision** (⊠ *Jr. Chiclayo 444, Miraflores* ☎ *01/447–7710* ⊕ *www.limavision.com*). **Setours** (⊠ *Av. Comandante Espinar 229, Miraflores* ☎ *01/446–9229* ⊕ *www.setours.com*). **Solmartour** (⊠ *Av. Grau 300, Miraflores* ☎ *01/444–1313* ⊕ *www.solmar.com.pe*).

THE SOUTH

By Katy
Morrison
& Michelle
Hopey

With wines and piscos to taste in Ica, dunes to board down in Huacachina, mysterious Lines to puzzle over in Nazca, and tranquil fishing villages to relax in in Pucusana and Cerro Azul, this part of Peru will seduce and charm you.

When the earthquake struck the coast of Pisco on August 15, 2007, it was a double calamity for the region. The quake leveled much of Pisco and left the fishing industry in tatters due to boat damage also severely affected the region's tourism.

Arequipa, Peru's second largest city, is a Spanish-colonial maze, with volcanic white sillar buildings, well-groomed plazas, and wonderful food, museums, and designer alpaca products. Arequipa is close to Colca Canyon, where many head to see the famed gorge for its stunning beauty, depth, and Andean condors.

Second in tourism to Machu Picchu, Lake Titicaca is home to the Floating Islands. The Los Uros islands are nearly 40 man-made islands—constructed from the lake's tortora reeds—and are literally floating. The natives are the Quechua and Aymara peoples, who still speak their respective languages.

Puno, an agricultural city on the shores of Titicaca is the jumping-off point for exploring the lake, and is Peru's folkloric capital. A dusty-brown city most of the time, Puno is a colorful whirlwind during festivals. Each November and February, Puno puts on two spectacular shows for local holidays.

CLOSE UP

Surfing

South of Lima you'll find a string of sandy beaches, most of them backed by massive sand dunes. The water is cold and rough, the waves are big, and lifeguards are nonexistent.

Sound appealing? Then pick up your board and head south to see why Peru is becoming one of South America's hottest surfing destinations.

For a sure bet, head to **Punta Hermosa,** a town near Km 44 on the Pan-American Highway (about an hour's drive south of Lima), which with its numerous reefs and coves has the highest concentration of quality surf spots and breaks all year round.

Fancy yourself a pro? The largest waves in South America, some 7 meters (20 feet) high, roll into nearby **Pico Alto,** with nearly 20 good breaks around the Pico Alto Surf Camp. Paddle out from Punta Hermosa via Playa Norte to reach the reef, although be warned—these waves are for the very experienced and crazy only!

Excellent surfing is also much closer to shore at the town of **Cerro Azul,** at Km 132 of the Panamericana. Long tubular waves break right in front of the town, so be prepared for an audience. A pleasant fishing village, Cerro Azul is a popular weekend and holiday destination and the beach gets crowded during peak times. Go mid-week if you want the place to yourself.

Peru doesn't have a huge surfing tradition, but to see where a small slice of local history was made, head to **Punta Rocas,** 42 km south of Lima, where in 1965 Peruvian surfer Felipe Pomar converted himself into something of a national hero when he won the World Surfing Championships. The reef-break here provides a classic wave for beginners and advanced surfers alike.

Surfing in Peru is best from March to December, with May probably being ideal. Although the climate is dry year-round, in winter the Pacific Ocean can get very chilly (although it's never particularly warm and wetsuits are advisable year-round), and coastal fog can leave you with little to look at.

–Katy Morrison

TAMBO COLORADO

Fodor's Choice ★ *48 km (30 mi) southeast of Pisco.*

Tambo Colorado is one of Peru's most underrated archaeological sites. This centuries-old burial site, extremely well-preserved in this bone-dry setting, was discovered beneath the sand dunes by Peruvian archaeologist Julio Tello in 1925. Dating back to the 15th-century, Tambo Colorado or Pucahuasi in Quechua (*Huasi* means "resting place," and *puca* means "red," after the color of the stone it was built from), is thought to have been an important Inca administrative center for passing traffic on the road to Cusco. It was also where Inca runners waited to relay messages. With runners waiting at similar stations every 7 or so kilometers, messages could be passed from one end of the country to the other in just 24 hours.

8

The site comprises several sections laid out around a large central plaza. Notice that the plaza's distinctive trapezoid shape is reflected throughout the site—look for trapezoid windows and other openings—and thought to have been an earthquake-proofing measure, necessary in this extremely volatile region. The site has withstood the test of time, but that hasn't stopped generations of visitors from etching personalized graffiti into its walls. A small museum is on-site, which has some of Julio Tello's original finds, including funeral *fards* (burial cocoons), dating from 1300 BC to AD 200 and wrapped in bright cotton and wool textiles embroidered with detailed patterns. Some skulls showed evidence of trepanation, a sophisticated medical procedure involving the insertion of metal plates to replace sections of bone broken in battles where rocks were used as weapons. Samples from Tello's original dig are also on display at the Museo Julio Tello near Paracas. ⊠ *Paracas Bay* 🕾 *No phone* 🕾 *S/7.50* ⊙ *Daily 9–5.*

ISLAS BALLESTAS

15 km (10 mi) south of Pisco.

Spectacular rocks pummeled by waves and wind into *ballestas* (arched bows) along the cliffs mark the Islas Ballestas, a haven of jagged outcrops and rugged beaches that shelter thousands of marine birds and sea lions. You're not allowed to walk on shore, but you wouldn't want to—the land is calf-deep in *guano* (bird droppings). Anyway, a boat provides the best views of the abundant wildlife: sea lions laze on the rocks surrounded by penguins, pelicans, seals, boobies, cormorants, and even condors, which make celebrity appearances for the appreciative crowds in February and March. On route to the islands is Punta Pejerrey, the northernmost point of the isthmus and the best spot for viewing the enormous, cactus-shape **Candelabro** carved in the cliffs. It's variously said to represent a symbol of the power of the northern Chavín culture, a Masonic symbol placed on the hillside by General Jose San Martín, leader of the liberation movement, or a pre-Inca religious figure.

GETTING AROUND

To visit Islas Ballestas, you must be on a registered tour, which usually means an hour or two cruising around the islands among sea lions and birds. Motorboat tours usually leave from the El Chaco jetty at 8 and 10 AM. It takes about an hour to reach the park from the jetty; you're close when you can see the Candelabra etched in the coastal hills. A two-hour tour costs around S/50. Some tours continue on to visit the Paracas Peninsula during the afternoon for around S/25 extra.

Several companies in Pisco sell Paracas–Ballestas packages. One of the most reputable is **Paracas Overland** (🕾 *056/533–855* ⊕ *www.paracasoverland.com.pe*).

Ballestas Expeditions (🕾 *056/532–373*), whose owner Lucho Astorayme has been going out to the islands since he first accompanied his fisherman dad more than 30 years ago, is another reputable tour operator.

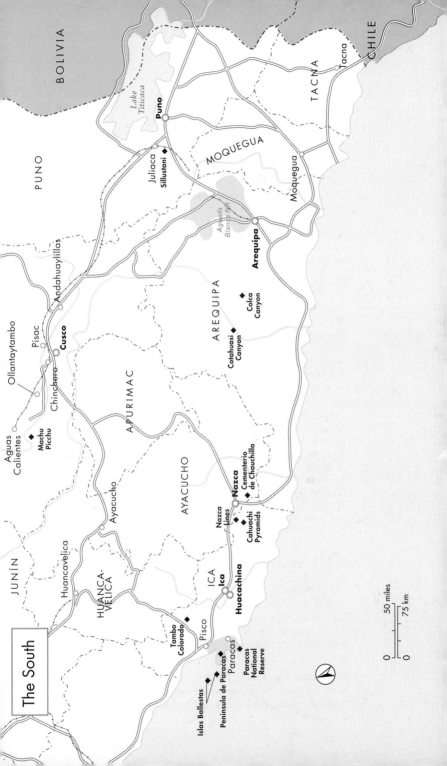

The South

BOLIVIA

CHILE

Tacna

TACNA

MOQUEGUA

Moquegua

Lake
Titicaca

Puno

PUNO

Juliaca
Sillustani

Arequipa

Agua da Blanca

AREQUIPA

Colca
Canyon

Cotahuasi
Canyon

Andahuaylillas

Pisac

Cusco

Ollantaytambo

Chinchero

APURIMAC

Aguas
Calientes

Machu
Picchu

AYACUCHO

Ayacucho

Nazca

Cementerio
de Chauchilla

Nazca
Lines

Cahuachi
Pyramids

Huancavelica

HUANCA-
VELICA

JUNÍN

ICA

Ica

Huacachina

Tambo
Colorado

Pisco

Paracas

Islas Ballestas

Península de Paracas

Paracas
National
Reserve

0   50 miles

0   75 km

PARACAS NATIONAL RESERVE

15 km (10 mi) south of Pisco.

This stunning coastal reserve, on a peninsula south of Pisco, teems with wildlife. Pelicans, condors, and red-and-white flamingos congregate and breed here; the latter are said to have inspired the red-and-white independence flag General San Martín designed when he liberated Peru. On shore you can't miss the sound (or the smell) of the hundreds of sea lions, while in the water you might spot penguins, sea turtles, dolphins, manta rays, and even hammerhead sharks.

Named for the blustering *paracas* (sandstorms) that buffet the west coast each winter, the Reserva Nacional de Paracas is Peru's first park for marine conservation. Organized tours take you along the thin dirt tracks which crisscross the peninsula, passing by sheltered lagoons, rugged cliffs full of caves, and small fishing villages. This is prime walking territory, where you can stroll from the bay to the **Julio Tello Museum,** and on to the fishing village of **Lagunilla** 5 km (3 mi) farther across the neck of the peninsula. Adjacent to the museum are colonies of flamingos, best seen June through July (and absent January through March, when they fly to Sierra). Hike another 6 km (4 mi) to reach **Mirador de Lobos** (Sea-Lion Lookout) at Punta El Arquillo. Carved into the highest point in the cliffs above Paracas Bay, 14 km (9 mi) from the museum, is the **Candelabra.** Note that you must hire a guide to explore the land trails.

PISCO COUNTRY

Spend any amount of time in the south of Peru, and it won't be long before someone offers you a pisco, Peru's national liquor and a southern specialty. At up to 40% proof it can be too much for some palates, so if you're unused to drinking spirits straight up remember that the secret to pisco drinking is to first swirl the pisco around the glass, and then, before taking a mouthful, inhale the vapors. Exhale as you swallow for a much smoother and more pleasurable drop! Salud!

GETTING AROUND

Minibus tours of the entire park can be arranged through local hotels and travel agencies for about S/25 for five hours. From Paracas, you can catch a slow motorboat to the reserve and islands.

BEACHES

Most beaches at Paracas are rugged and scenic, top-notch for walking but dangerous for swimming due to rip tides and undertow. Beware in the shallows, too—there are often stingrays and giant jellyfish. Calmer stretches include La Catedral, La Mina, and Mendieta, as well as Atenas, a prime windsurfing section. Dirt roads lead farther to Playa Mendieta and Playa Carhaus. Small, open restaurant shacks line the more popular beaches.

WHERE TO STAY & EAT

$ ✕ **El Chorito.** Spacious, light-filled, and with minimalist white decor and
SEAFOOD   polished wood, this eatery would not look out of place in a much larger
★   and more cosmopolitan city. The emphasis is on seafood, dished up in

delicious creations such as conchitas à la parmesana (baked mussels with Parmesan cheese). The dish to try is the *cebiche asesino,* or "killer ceviche," which packs a spicy punch. ⊠*Av. Paracas s/n, in front of Plazuela Abelarolo Quiñorez* ☎*056/545–045* ⊟*AE, MC, V.*

¢   **Refugio del Pirata.** Friendly and terrifically located for those heading out to early-morning boat tours, this ramshackle guesthouse is popular with backpackers and tour groups alike. The slightly worn-looking rooms may be nothing to write home about, but the breakfast terrace with views over the port is the best spot in town from which to catch up on postcard writing or enjoy a pisco sour. Try to get a room with sea views; those that face the internal corridor are small and dark. **Pros:** Terrific terrace with port views, easy to organize tours via the affiliated travel agency on the ground floor. **Cons:** No restaurant, rooms lack style. ⊠*Av. Paracas, Lote 6* ☎*056/545–054* ⋗*14 rooms* ⌂*In-room: no phone. In-hotel: bar, no elevator, laundry service, public Internet, parking (no fee)* ⊟*No credit cards.*

ICA

56 km (35 mi) southeast of Paracas.

A bustling commercial city with chaotic traffic and horn-happy drivers, Ica challenges you to find its attractive side. Step outside the city center, however, and you'll see why this town was the Nazca capital between AD 300 and 800, and why the Nasca people couldn't have picked a better place to center their desert civilization. Set in a patch of verdant fields and abutted by snow-covered mountains, Ica is serene, relaxing, and cheerful, with helpful residents—likely due as much to the nearly never-ending sunshine as to the vast selection of high-quality wines and piscos produced by dozens of local bodegas. This is a town of laughter and festivals, most notably the Fiesta de Vendimia, the wine-harvest celebration that takes place each year in early March. Ica is also famous for its pecans and its high-stepping horses called *caballos de paso.*

The city's colonial look comes from its European heritage. Ica was founded by the Spanish in 1536, making it one of the oldest towns in southern Peru. The city suffered badly in the August 2007 earthquake, however, and sadly many of the colonial-era buildings, including most of the famous churches, were destroyed.

GETTING AROUND

Surrounded as it is by vineyards, tourism in Ica is all about wineries. Most are close to the city and are easily accessed by road. If you don't have your own car (or you don't want to be designated driver on a winery trip), pick the wineries you'd like to see and ask a taxi driver to make you a price. Or hop on one of the prearranged tours offered by most hotels. The going rate for a four-hour taxi ride taking in three wineries close to the city is around S/50; if you go on a formal tour you'll pay up to S/40 per person.

ESSENTIALS

Bus Contacts Ormeños (⊠*Lambayeque 180* ☎*056/215–600).*

Currency Exchange **Banco de Crédito** (⌧ *Av. Grau 105* ☎ *056/235–959*).

Internet Café **Cetelica** (⌧ *Huánico* ☎ *056/221–534*).

Mail **Post Office** (⌧ *Lima y Moquegua* ☎ *056/221–958*). **DHL** (⌧ *Av. San Martín 398* ☎ *056/234–549*).

Visitor Info **Inrena** (⌧ *Petirrojos 355* ☎ *01/441–0425*). **Tourist Office** (⌧ *Cajamarca 179*).

WINERIES

If you can't imagine anything better than sampling different varieties of wine and pisco at nine in the morning, then these winery tours are most definitely for you. Most wineries in the Ica region make their living from tourism and devote a good portion of the winery tour in the tastings room. Tours are free although the guides do appreciate tips.

Peruvians like their wines sweet and their pisco strong. If you're unused to drinking spirits straight up, follow this tried and true Peruvian technique for a smoother drop—after swirling the pisco around the glass, inhale the vapors. Before exhaling, take the pisco into your mouth and taste the flavor for four seconds. As you swallow, exhale!

After suffering earthquake damage in 2007, this 16th-century farm hacienda has taken the opportunity to overhaul its now very modern operation. Internationally renowned, **Bodega Hacienda Tacama** produces some of Peru's best labels, particularly the Blanco de Blancos. Stroll through the rolling vineyards—still watered by the Achirana irrigation canal built by the Inca—before sampling the end result. The estate is about 11 km (7 mi) from town. ⌧ *Camina a la Tinguiña s/n* ☎ *056/228–395* ☜ *Free* ☼ *Weekdays 9–2*.

Look for **Bodega El Carmen,** a small winery on the right side of the road, when you're driving south into Ica; it makes a good stop for sampling fine pisco. Look for the ancient grape press, which was made from an enormous tree trunk. ⌧ *3 km (2 mi) north of Ica, Guadalupe* ☎ *056/233–495* ☜ *Free* ☼ *Mon.–Sat. 10–4*.

A sunny brick archway welcomes you to the large, pleasant **Bodega Vista Alegre,** which has been producing fine wines, pisco, and sangria since it was founded by the Picasso brothers in 1857. The largest winery in the valley, this former monastry is a popular tour bus stop so come early to avoid the groups. Tours in English or Spanish take you through the vast pisco and wine-making facilities at this industrial winery, before depositing you in the tasting room. Take a taxi or city buses 8 or 13 to get there. *Don't walk from downtown Ica,* as robberies have been reported along this route. ⌧ *Camina a la Tinguiña, Km 205* ☎ *056/238–735* ☜ *Free* ☼ *Weekdays 9–2*.

One of the more fun alcohol-making operations to visit is **Bodega Lazo,** owned by Elar Bolivar, who claims to be a direct descendent of the Libertador Simón Bolívar himself (some locals shrug their shoulders at this boast). Nonetheless, Elar's small artisanal operation includes a creepy collection of shrunken heads (Dutch tourists, he says, who didn't pay their drink tab), ancient cash registers, fencing equipment, and copies of some of the paintings in Ica's regional museum. The question is, who really has the originals—Elar or the museum? As part of your visit, you can taste the bodega's recently made pisco, straight from the barrel. Some organized tours include this bodega as part of a tour. It's not a safe walk from town, so take a cab if you come on your own. ✉*Camino de Reyes s/n, San Juan Bautista* ☎*056/403–430* 💲*Free.*

A favorite stop on the tour circuit, the family-run **Bodega El Catador** produces wines and some of the region's finest pisco. If you're here in March, watch out for the annual Fiesta de Uva where the year's festival queen tours the vineyard and gets her feet wet in the opening of the grape-pressing season. If you miss the festival, check out the photos in the small museum near the restaurant. The excellent Taberna restaurant and bar is open for lunch after a hard morning's wine tasting. If you don't want to drive, take a taxi or wait at the second block of Moquegua for Bus 6 (S/1), which passes by about every half hour. ✉*Pan-American Hwy. S, Km 294, Fondo Tres Equinas 102* ☎*056/403–295* 💲*Free* ⊙*Daily 8–6.*

SIGHTS

Soaring ceilings, ornate stained-glass windows and the fact that it's the only one of Ica's colonial era churches left standing after the 2007 earthquake makes **Iglesia San Francisco** the city's grandest religious building. Yet even this colossal monument didn't escape the quake unscathed. If you look on the floor toward the front of the church you can see the gouges left in the marble blocks by falling pieces of the church altar. It's said that the statues of the saints stood serenely throughout the quake and didn't move an inch. ✉*At Avs. Municipalidad y San Martín* ☎*No phone* 💲*Free* ⊙*Mon.–Sat. 6:30–9:30 and 4:30–7:30.*

Fodor's Choice
★ It may be a little out of the way, but don't let that stop you from visiting the fantastic **Museo Histórico Regional** with its vast and well-preserved collection on regional history—particularly from the Inca, Nazca, and Paracas cultures. Note the quipas, mysterious knotted, colored threads thought to have been used to count commodities and quantities of food. Fans of the macabre will love the mummy display, where you can see everything from human mummies to a mummified bird. The squeamish can head out back to view a scale model of the Nazca Lines from an observation tower. You can also buy maps (S/0.50) and paintings of Nazca motifs (S/4). The museum is about 1½ km (1 mi) from town. It's not advisable to walk, so take the opportunity to jump into one of the distinctive three-wheeled *mototaxis* that will make the trip for around S/2. ✉*Ayabaca s/n* ☎*056/234–383* 💲*S/11, plus S/4 camera fee* ⊙*Weekdays 8–7, Sat. 9–6, Sun. 9–1, or by appointment.*

WHERE TO EAT

¢–$
PERUVIAN
✕**El Otro Peñoncito.** Three generations have had a hand in this family business, one of the oldest and most respected restaurants in Ica. Dishing up traditional Peruvian cuisine and the self-proclaimed best pisco sours around, this classic spot is a welcome change from the usual fried chicken and rice joints on every other corner. Local specialties include the *pollo a la Iqueña* (chicken in a rich pecan, pisco, and spinach sauce)

8

and the traditional *papa a la huancaina* (potatoes with cheese sauce). ⊠*Bolívar 255* ☏*056/233–921* ⊟*No credit cards.*

$$
PERUVIAN
✗ **La Taberna.** After a hard morning's wine tasting, stop in this cheerful open-air restaurant in Bodega El Catador to top up your carbohydrates and soak up the pisco. Like an outdoor rural dining room, this pleasant spot dishes up local specialties such as *carapulcra con sopa seca* a stew of dried potatoes and dried meat, washed down with one of El Catador's excellent wines. If you want to keep up the pace, Catador's bar with its extensive range of piscos is within arm's reach. ⊠*José Carrasco González, Km 296* ☏*056/403–295* ⊟*AE, MC, V.*

WHERE TO STAY

$$–$$$
★
☷**Hotel Las Dunas.** For a taste of the good life, Peruvian style, head to this top-end resort on the road between Ica and Huacachina. A cluster of whitewashed buildings at the foot of the dunes, this colonial-style holiday resort is a favorite getaway for Peruvian families. Llamas roam freely in the grounds. The ponds and canals that run between the buildings are full of fish. Spacious rooms have balconies overlooking lush lawns, and suites have sunny courtyards and whirlpools. You can dine poolside or in a breezy gazebo at the restaurant and enjoy such dishes as flounder with seafood sauce and spicy *lomo saltado* an enormous pile of stir-fried beef, tomatoes, chips and rice. Rent sand boards, play golf on the dunes, ride horseback, or fly over the Nazca Lines (S/350) from the hotel's airstrip. Book weekdays to save 20%. **Pros:** Beautiful grounds, activities for children, top restaurant. **Cons:** Out of town, resort aesthetic, rooms look a little frumpy for the price. ⊠*La Angostura 400* ☏*056/256–224* ✑*dunas@invertur.com.pe* ⇝*130 rooms, 3 suites* ♿*In-room: no a/c (some), safe, refrigerator, Wi-Fi (some). In-hotel: restaurant, bars, golf course, tennis court, pools, gym, bicycles, no elevator, laundry service, public Internet, parking (no fee), no-smoking rooms* ⊟*AE, DC, MC, V.*

$–$$
☷**Ocucaje Sun & Wine Resort.** The focus is on all the best of southern Peru: sunshine and good wines. Popular with well-heeled Limeños, it feels like a comfortable Spanish country home, but rooms have all the amenities. Well outside Ica, this remote bodega and resort is all about relaxation and restoring your spirits—which you can do by lying beside the attractive pool, getting a spa massage, or exploring the nearby historic sights. A continental breakfast is available for S/15 and during the evening the restaurant dishes up the usual criollo and Peruvian fare, just with slightly more style. Wash it all down with an excellent wine from the award-winning bodega. **Pros:** Beautiful grounds, excellent wines from the award-winning bodega, tourist services. **Cons:** Remote location, inaccessible via public transport. ⊠*Pan-American Hwy. S, Km 334, Av. Principal s/n* ☏*056/836–101* ⊕*www.hotelocucaje.com* ⇝*55 rooms* ♿*In-room: refrigerator. In-hotel: restaurant, room service, bar, tennis court, pool, gym, spa, bicycles, no elevator, laundry service, parking (no fee)* ⊟*AE, DC, MC, V.*

HUACACHINA

5 km (3 mi) southwest of Ica.

Drive 10 minutes through the pale, mountainous sand dunes southwest of Ica and you'll suddenly see a gathering of attractive, pastel-color buildings surrounding a patch of green. It's not an oasis on the horizon, but rather the lakeside resort of Laguna de Huacachina, a palm-fringed lagoon of jade-color waters whose sulfurous properties are reputed to have healing powers. The view is breathtaking: a collection of attractive, colonial-style hotels in front of a golden beach and with a backdrop of snow-covered peaks against the distant sky. In the 1920s Peru's elite traveled here for the ultimate holiday, and today the spacious resorts still beckon. The lake is also a pilgrimage site for those with health and skin problems, and for sand boarders who want to tackle the 100-meter (325-foot) dunes and budget travelers who pitch tents in the sand or sleep under the stars.

WHERE TO STAY & EAT

¢ ✕**Arturo's Restaurant Taberna.** In a town severely lacking dining options, PERUVIAN this new restaurant holds some promise. With plastic furniture and a concrete floor, it's not winning any style prizes, but the hearty Peruvian cooking hits the spot with most meals going for around S/7 to S/10 it's by far the best deal on food in town. Owner Arturo has grand plans to turn it into a more upmarket eatery, so expect changes. There's a good selection of wines from the local bodegas, and prices are almost as cheap as buying direct from the winery. ⊠*Av. Perotti, Lote 3* 🕾*No phone* ▤*No credit cards.*

¢ 🏨**El Hauchachinero.** Hands-down Huacachina's best budget lodging, Fodor'sChoice this is a beautiful bargain in the oasis of Peru. Clean, safe, and with its ★ own little bar featuring a mural of Ica's now-disappeared camel herd, this place is very popular, so call ahead or risk missing out. Thoughtful design touches are everywhere, from the Peruvian art and artesanía adorning the walls to the gorgeous bamboo fittings and wooden balconies and walkways. If you want to relax, the pool area with its hammocks for lounging in is super inviting. If you're feeling more adventurous, head out on a dune buggy and sand-boarding tour. The collection of raucous parrots will ensure that you're up in time for breakfast. **Pros:** Fantastic pool area with hammocks for lounging, dune-buggy service and sandboard rental, attractively furnished rooms and common areas. **Cons:** Often full, noisy parrots. ⊠*Av. Perotti, Balnearia de Huacachina* 🕾*056/271–435* ⊕*www.elhuacachinero.com* 🛏*21 private rooms, 3 shared rooms* ♿*In-room: no phone, no TV. In-hotel: bar, pool, no elevator, laundry facilities, parking (no fee)* ▤*No credit cards* ☉*CP.*

$$–$$$ 🏨**Hotel Mossone.** Imagine life as it was in Huacachina's heyday in the Fodor'sChoice oasis's original hotel. With a picture-postcard location fronting onto ★ the lagoon and gorgeous Spanish colonial–style architecture, this graceful spot is as popular now as it was in the 1920s. An internal courtyard lined with tall ficus trees is the focal point of this century-old mansion. Watch out for Jennifer, the (male) tortoise who likes to stroll here during the day. Rooms look out onto gardens overflowing with flowers

8

SAND BOARDING

Ever fancied having a go at snow-boarding but chickened out at the thought of all those painful next-day bruises? Welcome to the new adventure sport of sand boarding, a softer and warmer way to hit the slopes. Surrounded by dunes, Huacachina is the sand-boarding capital of the world: every year European sports fans arrive here in droves to practice for the international sand-surfing competitions on Cerro Blanco, the massive dune 14 km (8 mi) north of Nazca.

With no rope tows or chairlifts to get you up the dunes, the easiest way to have a go at sand boarding is to go on a dune buggy tour, offered by just about every hotel in town. In these converted vehicles you'll be driven (quickly) to the top of the dunes, upon which you can board, slide, or slither down to be picked up again at the bottom. Drivers push their vehicles hard, so be prepared for some heart-stopping moments. Carola del Sur guesthouse has the biggest fleet of dune buggies and runs two tours daily at 10 AM and 4 PM. The tours last around two hours and cost S/40.

and the elegant bar and restaurant have splendid lake views. The hotel provides free bicycles and sand boards for guests, but if you're staying elsewhere you can still stop in for excellent *comida criolla* (cuisine rich in peppers, onions and other spices), especially *papas a la huancaina.* a potato dish served with a creamy mustard sauce. **Pros:** Fantastic location in front of the lagoon, great pool, the elegant lounge bar is the best spot in town from which to watch the sun set over the dunes. **Cons:** Rooms look a little tired, hotel is often full with tour groups. ⊠*Balneario de Huacachina s/n* ☎*056/213–630, 01/261–9605 in Lima* 🖨*034/236–137* 🛏*41 rooms* ⌂*In-room: safe, refrigerator. In-hotel: restaurant, bar, pool, billiards room, bicycles, laundry service, public Internet, parking (no fee)* ▤*AE, DC, MC, V.*

NAZCA

Fodor's Choice   *120 km (75 mi) southeast of Ica.*
★

What do a giant hummingbird, a monkey, and an astronaut have in common? Well, apart from the fact that they're all etched into the floor of the desert near Nazca, no one really seems to know. Welcome to one of the world's greatest mysteries—the enigmatic Nazca Lines. A mirage of green in the desert, lined with cotton fields and orchards and bordered by crisp mountain peaks, Nazca was a quiet colonial town unnoticed by the rest of the world until 1901, when Peruvian archaeologist Max Uhle excavated sites around Nazca and discovered the remains of a unique pre-Colombian culture. Set 598 meters (1,961 feet) above sea level, the town has a dry climate—scorching by day, nippy by night—that was instrumental in preserving centuries-old relics from Inca and pre-Columbian tribes. The area has more than 100 cemeteries, where the humidity-free climate has helped preserve priceless jewelry, textiles, pottery, and mummies. Overlooking the parched scene is the 2,078-meter (6,815-foot) Cerro Blanco, the highest sand dune in the world

Even with the knowledge of the Nazca culture obtained from the archeological discoveries, it was not until 1929 that the **Nazca Lines** were discovered, when American scientist Paul Kosok looked out of his plane window as he flew over them (✉ *Pampas de San José, 20 km (12 mi) north of Nazca town*). Almost invisible from ground level, the Lines were made by removing the surface stones and piling them beside the lighter soil underneath. More than 300 geometrical and biomorphic figures, some measuring up to 300 meters (1,000 feet) across, are etched into the desert floor, including a hummingbird, a monkey, a spider, a pelican, a condor, a whale, and an "astronaut," so named because of his goldfish-bowl-shape head. Theories abound as to their purpose, and some have devoted their lives to the study of the Lines. Probably the most famous person to investigate the origin of the Nazca Lines was Kosok's translator, German scientist Dr. Maria Reiche, who studied the Lines from 1940 until her death in 1998.

GETTING AROUND

Be prepared: Nazca is all about tours and it may seem like everyone in town is trying to sell you one at once. The minute you poke your nose outside the bus door you'll be swamped with offers for flights over the lines, hotels, and trips to the Chauchilla cemetery. Be wise about any offers made to you by touts at the bus station—if it's cheap, there's probably a good reason why. That said, a tour with a reputable agency is a great way to catch all of Nazca's major sites. Recommended agencies include Alegria Tours and Nasca Trails.

All buses arrive and depart from the óvalo (roundabout). To see the lines from ground level, taxis will make the 30-minute run out to the mirador for around S/40. Flights over the lines are best in early morning before the sun gets too high and winds make flying uncomfortable. Standard flights last around 30 minutes and cost between $40US and $60US, depending on the season. You'll also have to pay an airport tax of S/10 (watch out for cheeky operators who will try and tell you that the tax is $10US, it's not!). You can buy flight tickets from travel agencies and many hotels in town, or directly from the airline offices near the airport. Buying tickets in advance will save you time. Tickets are available on the spot at the airport but as planes won't take off until all seats are filled you may spend most of your morning hanging around the dusty Panamerica Sur watching while others take off and land.

FLIGHTS FOR THE LINES Nazca Lines tours on Aero Cóndor, which depart from the small Aeropuerto Nazca, cost S/191 for a 40-minute flight plus lunch, a tour of Nazca's archaeological museum, and a trip to the *mirador*. Note that these flights are often overbooked year-round. Less expensive flights on Aero Ica and upstarts Aero Montecarlo, Aero Palpa, Aeroparacas, Alas Peruanas, TAE, Travel Air, and Taxi Aereo have similar services. As these latter lines are small operations with varying office hours, check at the airport for schedules. Most sightseeing flights depart from Nazca, although Aero Paracas also originates in Lima and Pisco. Arrive early to check-in for your flight, as many are full and there's a chance you'll get bumped if you're late.

Carriers **Aero Condor** (✉ *Camino Real 355, San Isidro, Lima* ☎ *01/442-5215* ✉ *Panamericana Sur, Km 446, Nazca* ☎ *056/522-402* ⊕ *www.aerocondor. com.pe*). **Aero Ica** (✉ *Hotel Maison Suisse, Nazca* ✉ *Tudela and Varela 150, Lima* ☎ *01/440-1030*). **Aero Palcazu** (✉ *Calle León Bauman 101, San Borja Sur, Lima* ☎ *061/990-0247*). **Aero Paracas** (✉ *Teodoro Cardenas 470, Lince, Lima* ☎ *01/265-8073 or 01/265-8173* ✉ *Lima 169, Nazca* ☎ *056/521-027* ✉ *Panamericana Sur, Km 447* ☎ *056/522-688*). **Sabsa** (✉ *Panamericana Sur, Km 447, Nazca* ☎ *056/523-863*).

ESSENTIALS

Bus **Cruz del Sur** (✉ *Av. Los Incas* ☎ *034/522-484* ⊕ *www.cruzdelsur.com.pe*). **Wari Tours** (✉ *Pan-American Hwy.* ☎ *056/534-967*).

Currency Exchange **Banco de Crédito** (✉ *Lima y Grau*).

Internet Cafés **Speed Service** (✉ *Bolognesi 299* ☎ *056/522-176*).

Mail **Post Office** (✉ *Jr. F. de Castillo 379* ☎ *056/522-947*).

Medical Services **Hospital de Apoyo** (✉ *Calle Callao s/n* ☎ *056/522-486*). **Es Salud** (✉ *Juan Matta 613* ☎ *056/522-446*).

Police **Comisaría Sectorial** (✉ *Av. Los Incas* ☎ *056/522-2084*).

EXPLORING NAZCA

To see where a lifelong obsession with the Nazca lines can lead you, head to the **Casa-Museo Maria Reiche,** former home of the German anthropologist who devoted her life to studying the mystery of the lines. There's little explanatory material among the pottery, textiles, mummies, and skeletons from the Paracas, Nazca, Wari, Chincha, and Inca cultures, so don't expect any of the area's mysteries to be solved here, but the museum does a great job of showing the environment in which Maria lived and worked, and her vast collection of tools, notes, and sketches is impressive. A scale model of the lines is behind the house. Take a bus from the Ormeño terminal to the Km 416 marker to reach the museum, which is 1 km (½ mi) from town. ✉ *Pan-American Hwy., Km 416, San Pablo* ☎ *034/255734* 💰 *S/3.50* ⏱ *Daily 9–4.*

For an overview of the Nazca culture and the various archaeological sites in the region, the Italian-run **Museo Antonini,** is the best museum in town. The displays, made up of materials excavated from the surrounding archaeological digs, are heavy on scientific information and light on entertainment, although the display of Nazcan trophy skulls will appeal to the morbid among us and textiles fans will appreciate the display of painted fabrics from the ancient adobe city of Cahuachi. All the signage is in Spanish, so ask for the translation book at the front desk (there's only one copy, however). Don't miss the still-working Nascan aqueduct in the back garden. ✉ *Av. de la Cultura 600* ☎ *056/265–421* 💰 *S/15, S/20 with a camera* ⏱ *Daily 9* AM–7 PM.

AROUND NAZCA

Within a walled, 4,050-square-yard courtyard west of the Nazca Lines are the **Cahuachi Pyramids,** an ancient ceremonial and pilgrimage site. Six adobe pyramids, the highest of which is about 21 meters (70 feet), stand above a network of rooms and connecting corridors. Grain and water silos are also inside, and several large cemeteries lie outside the walls. Used by the early Nazca culture, the site is estimated to have existed for about two centuries before being abandoned about AD 200. Cahuachi takes its name from *qahuachi* (meddlesome). El Estaquería, with its mummification pillars, is nearby. Tours from Nazca visit both sites for around S/60 and take four hours. ⊠ *34 km (21 mi) west of Nazca* ☎ *No phone* ⊠ *Free* ⊙ *Daily 8–5.*

WHERE TO EAT

¢ ✕ **Restaurant Don Carlos.** For a truly local experience, follow the crowds PERUVIAN to this tiny restaurant, which dishes up tasty Peruvian meals in huge portions. The restaurant won't dazzle you with its design, but what it lacks in style it more than makes up for with home-style Peruvian cuisine just like your grandmother used to make it (or your grandmother's Peruvian cousin). The set-lunch—a soup, a main course, and a drink—is a steal at only S/4.50 and you may need to fight to get a table. The menu changes daily but specialties include *aji de gallina,* chicken in creamy hollandaise sauce served with boiled rice and a sliced egg. There's no street sign; look for "Restaurant" painted over the door. ⊠ *Calle Fermín del Castillo 375* ☎ *056/524–087* ⊟ *No credit cards.*

¢–$$ ✕ **Via La Encantada.** This stylish eatery on restaurant row adds some PERUVIAN class to the Nazca dining scene. With food that is as modern as the **Fodor's**Choice decor, this is the best spot in town to try Peruvian-fusion cuisine. The ★ *pollo a lo Oporto,* chicken in a port wine sauce, is a stand-out, as is the cocktail list, including tri-color Macchu Pichu pisco. Head upstairs for a spot on the balcony overlooking the street, and while there, sneak a peek through the back window and you can see the parrilla chef working over the restaurant's giant barbecue. ⊠ *Calle Bolognesi 282* ☎ *056/524–216 or 056/964–3426* ⊟ *V.*

WHERE TO STAY

$ ▦ **Casa Andina.** A relative newcomer, this hotel, part of a national chain, **Fodor's**Choice offers the best value for the money of any of Nazca's top-end lodgings. ★ Catering to business travelers and tourists, the smartly furnished rooms come fully equipped with safes and Wi-Fi Internet access, and a small business center has computer access and endless coffee and tea. Those interested strictly in pleasure can instead spend their time relaxing by the hotel's small pool. **Pros:** Wi-Fi Internet access in rooms, welcoming service. **Cons:** Small pool. ⊠ *Bolognesi 367* ☎ *056/523–563* ⊕ *www.casa-andina.com* ⇆ *60 rooms* ♿ *In-room: safe, Wi-Fi. In-hotel: restaurant, bar, pool, no elevator, laundry service, public Internet, public Wi-Fi, parking (no fee), no-smoking rooms* ⊟ *AE, DC, MC, V* ⦿ *CP.*

$$ ▦ **Hotel Nazca Lines.** Mixing colonial elegance with all the mod-cons, **Fodor's**Choice this top-end hotel is a Nazca landmark. Formerly the home of Maria ★ Reiche, this historic hacienda has long drawn international tourists and adventurers seeking to solve the mysteries of the lines. Stylish colonial rooms with private terraces and piped-in music deliver a touch of the

8

good life, and the enormous central courtyard with its inviting pool make it hard to drag yourself away to explore the lines. With nightly planetarium shows and lectures about the lines, you can attempt to solve the mystery without leaving poolside. Delicious meals served on a tiled walkway beside the courtyard are worth the expense, and non-guests can have lunch and use the pool for S/16. The hotel is extremely charming—the staff, perhaps overwhelmed by the tour groups that march nightly through the doors, not so much. **Pros:** Magnificent pool, nightly lectures, colonial charm. **Cons:** Busy staff, tour groups, expensive. ✉ *Jr. Bolognesi* ☎ *056/522–293, 01/261–9605 in Lima* 🖷 *056/522–112* 🛏 *78 rooms* ᗙ *In-room:safe, refrigerator. In-hotel: restaurant, bar, pool, no elevator, laundry service, public Internet, public Wi-Fi, parking (no fee), no-smoking rooms* 🟰 *AE, DC, MC, V.*

COTAHUASI CANYON

★ *50 km (31 mi) north of Colca Canyon.*

Colca Canyon may be the region's most famous natural attraction, but at 3,354 meters (11,001 feet), Cotahuasi is the world's deepest gorge, beating Colca Canyon by 163 meters (534 feet). It's nearly twice as deep as the Grand Canyon. The canyon has been carved by the Río Cotahuasi, which changes into Río Ocuña before connecting to the Pacific. Its deepest point is at Ninochaco, below the quaint administrative capital of Quechualla, and accessible only by kayak; kayak explorations first documented the area in the mid-1990s and measured its depth. Since then, paddling Cotahuasi river's Class V rapids is to kayakers what scaling Mount Everest is to mountaineers.

The ride from Arequipa to the Cotahuasi Canyon ranks with the great scenic roads of the world. As you pass Corire and Toro Muerto, the road rides the western side of snow-capped Nevado Coropuno (21,079 feet), Peru's third-highest volcano, for spectacular views as you descend into the valley of Cotahuasi. Logistically speaking, it's a bumpy 11- to 13-hour bus ride or 10 hours by four-wheel drive from Arequipa. The pavement ends in Chuquibamba. Some of the road from Chuquibamba to Cotahuasi, the longest stretch of the ride, is in the process of being graded. There's no fee to enter the canyon.

GETTING HERE

Cotahuasi Canyon is a travel destination in the making, but outside of expert extreme sports enthusiasts, few people venture here. Unless you're taking a bus, driving anything but a 4x4 is asking for trouble. The jagged, rocky dirt roads are full of cliffs and narrow corners. Dry for most of the year, the roads get muddy from December to April (rainy season), a time

ADVANCE PREP

Cotahuasi is not traveler-savvy yet so it's not possible to show up in a town, buy a map, hire a guide, and get on your way. You'll want to buy a map of the canyon at the Instituto Geográfico Militar in Lima or at the South American Explorers in Lima or Cusco.

when you're also likely to encounter random streams flowing across the road.

Hire a guide, regardless of season and not just for safety. Since this region is so remote, you're likely to see a lot more with a guide. All buses travel through the night; three bus companies go from Arequipa to Cotahuasi daily, each leaves around 5 PM, arriving in Cotahuasi village in time for sunrise: Transportes Cromotex (☎054/421–555), Transportes Reyna (☎054/430–612), and Alex Bus (☎054/424–605).

COTAHUASI VILLAGE & VICINITY

Cotahuasi is the largest town in the region and the first you'll stumble upon. In the hills at 2,680 meters (8,620 feet), whitewashed colonial-style homes line slim, straight lanes before a backdrop of Cerro Hiunao. Most visitors kick-off their stay in this Quechua-speaking community of 3,500 residents, where there are a few hostels, restaurants, a small tienda (grocery store), a bell tower, and Plaza de Armas. It's also where most hiking trails begin or end. Many families rent burros (mules) to tourists to help carry their load, especially kayakers who walk eight hours down to the gorge with their boats.

Below the village of Cotahuasi is the valley of Piro, the gateway to the canyon, which is close to Cataratas de Sipia, a 150-meter (462-foot), 10-meter-wide waterfall. Sipia Falls is the most visited attraction in the entire canyon. Three hours farther south along a thin track against the canyon wall—which climbs to 400 meters (1,312 feet) above the river— you'll reach Chaupo, a settlement surrounded by groves of fruit trees.

OUTDOOR ACTIVITIES

Many operators in Arequipa and Cusco offer multiday excursions. Most tours are at least four days, five nights and some last up to 17 nights. A few local hikers provide custom tours for visitors as well.

HIKING Cotahuasi Canyon is an awesome place to explore by foot. The backdrop of snow-capped Volcano Coropuna and Solimana is fantastic, the high desert plains offer a rest from the steep upward rocky canyon terrain, and the untouched villages provide a cultural aspect. Temperatures remain about 65°F–70°F during the day, dipping below 45° on any given night. Ancient Inca paths wind throughout the canyon and its terraces. Beware, many of these ancient trails are narrow, rocky, and hang over the side of the canyon. Newer trails parallel some of the ancient ones, and are generally safer.

8

VALLEY OF THE VOLCANOES

This spectacular, 65-km (40-mi) crevasse north of Colca Canyon includes a line of 80 extinct craters and cinder cones. Looming over the scene is active Volcán Coropuna, the third highest peak in Peru. Andagua, at the head of the valley, has the best tourist facilities in the area. The valley is about five hours by a rocky, half-paved, half-dirt road from Colca Canyon. There are several multi-day hikes from Colca Canyon that must be arranged in Arequipa. If you're going to Cotahuasi or Colca Canyon, you're bound to pass through this high-altitude valley.

Sipia Falls is a solid three- to four-hour trek from Cotahuasi Village and it's a hard-on-your knees hike down that includes two bridge crossings, but the first taste of being in the canyon is a surreal experience. It's also possible to reach the falls by hailing a colectivo or in your own 4x4 from the Cotahuasi road to the Sipia Bridge where the road ends. From here it's a 45-minute hike to the falls.

> ### SCARY BRIDGES
>
> A hallmark of Cotahausi Canyon is its bridges, which are all hanging (and swinging) across the Río Cotahuasi. They're cool to look at, nerve-racking to consider, but there's only one way over.

WHITE-WATER RAFTING   Kayakers and white-water rafters can challenge the rapids anywhere from the upper Cotahuasi, near the village, almost to the Pacific. The river is divided into four sections: the Headwaters, beginning upstream from Cotahuasi village, Aimaña gorge, Flatwater Canyon, and the Lower Canyon.

White-water season is June through November when the rapids are Class III to V. But the best time to go is mid-May to mid-June. The water is snowmelt so wetsuits are necessary.

COLCA CANYON

30 km (19 mi) north of Toro Muerto.

Carved into the foothills of the snow-covered Andes and sliced by the silvery Río Colca, Colca Canyon drops 3,182 meters (10,607 feet) down. The more adventurous can embark on a multiday hike into the canyon—typically a two-, three-, or five-day excursion. Bird lovers (and anyone with an eye for amazement) can visit the Cruz del Condor. Culture seekers can spend a night with a native family. Light hikers and archaeology aficionados can observe points along the rim, or those seeking pure relaxation can hit one of the all-inclusive lodges with horseback riding and thermal baths.

Cruz del Condor is a haunt for the giant birds, particularly at dawn, when they soar on the winds rising from the deep valley. At 1,200 meters (4,000 feet), the "condor cross" precipice between the villages Pinchollo and Cabanaconder is the best place to spot them. From June to August, you're likely to spot close to 20 or more condors during a morning visit. By October and November many of the female birds are nesting, so your chances of eyeing flocks are slim, but you'll likely spot a few birds.

GETTING AROUND

By hiring a private guide, renting a four-wheel-drive vehicle, joining a tour from Arequipa, or going by bus you can explore the area. Arequipa is the jumping-off point for nearly everyone headed to Colca Canyon. Chivay is the first town you'll come to. The ride takes about five hours from Arequipa.

Taxis are a good way to go from town to town if long hikes or mountain biking isn't your thing. Taxis line up around the Plaza de Armas in Chivay. Most rides will cost S/15–S/20.

CHIVAY

The largest town in the Colca Canyon region is Chivay, a small, battered-looking village with a population of 3,000. Most tourist facilities are here, which are not many, but include restaurants, hotels, a medical clinic, and a tourist information center. As you approach Chivay, you'll pass through a stone archway signifying the town entrance, where AUTOCOLCA, the government authority over Colca Canyon, stops cars to ask if they are headed to see the condors. If you're headed to Cruz del Condor or any of the churches in the 14 villages you must purchase a S/35 entry ticket, which will be asked for again at the entrance of the Mirador. Nearly all agency tours do not include this entry fee in their all price.

Chivay marks the eastern end of the canyon's rim, the other end is Cabonconde, a developing village where most multiday hikes into the canyon begin and end. As you come into Chivay the road splits off into two: one, less traveled because of its rocky rutted surface, goes along the canyon's northern edge to the villages of Coporaque, Ichupampa, and Lari; the other follows the southern rim and although it's a bumpy dirt road, it's better for travel and leads to Cruz del Condor, and the small towns of Yanque, Maca, and Cabanaconde.

OUTDOOR ACTIVITIES

HIKING **Along the Canyon:** Along the south side of the canyon it's possible to do an easy hike from the observation points between Cruz del Condor and Pinchollo. Paths are along the canyon rim most of the way; however, in some places, you have to walk along the road. The closer to Cruz del Condor you are the better the paths and lookouts get.

Into the canyon: Trails into the canyon are many as well as rough and unmarked, so venture down is with a guide. Several adventure tour operators provide governmental certified hiking guides; local guides are also easily found. Packages range from two- to eight-day treks. The Cabanaconde area is the entry point for most of these.

WHITE-WATER RAFTING   The Río Colca is a finicky river. Highly skilled paddlers long to run this Class IV–V river. Depending upon the season, the water level and the seismic activity of the local volcanoes, the rapids change frequently. In some areas it's more than a Class V and in other areas it's slow enough that it could be considered a Class II–III.

WHERE TO STAY & EAT

Chivay is tiny, but has plenty of small budget hotels and a few restaurants. You'll come into town on 22 de Agosto, which leads to the Plaza de Armas, where you'll find **Lobo's Pizzeria**, **McElroy's Pub** (a gringo magnet owned by a true Irishman), and **El Balcón de Don Zacarias,** which serves very good traditional food.

$ ⬚**Pozo del Cielo.** Across the river
★ on top of a hill on the outskirts of
Chivay sits one of the most quaint
lodges in the valley. A series of cha-
lets are made of adobe, wood, and
stone. Simple rooms have beds piled
with warm blankets and include a
modern bathroom. The dark-wood
window shades and low wooden
doorways seem out of a fairy tale.

> **BRING CASH!**
>
> There are no ATMs in the Colca
> Canyon or valley area, nor is it
> possible for credit cards to be
> processed. Soles and U.S. dol-
> lars (no bills larger than $10) are
> accepted.

All rooms lead to the main lodge by narrow, outdoor cobbled stone
pathways. In the lodge the restaurant is composed of endless windows
and an adobe fireplace. The views over Chivay, the valley, and volcanoes are stunning. Good novo-Andino food is served and there's always
hot tea. **Pros:** Hot-water bottles at bedtime for extra warmth, on the
outskirts of Chivay, good views. **Cons:** Must walk outside to get to
breakfast, no bureaus or closets. ⊠*In Chivay: Calle Huáscar B-3 Sacsayhuaman. In Arequipa: Pasaje Apurímac 113* ☎*054/531–041 Chivay, 054/205–838 Arequipa* ☎☎*054/202–606* ⊕*www.pozodelcielo.
com.pe* ⟳*20 rooms* ⌂*In-room: no a/c, no phone, safe (some), no TV
(some). In-hotel: restaurant, room service, bar, no elevator, laundry
service, parking (no fee), no-smoking rooms* ▭*AE, MC, V* ⑩|*BP.*

$$$$ ⬚**Las Casitas del Colca.** It doesn't get better than this, at least not in
Fodor's Choice Colca. The region's newest hotel is also the most luxurious, and by far
★ the most expensive. It's an all-inclusive resort with cooking and painting classes, fly-fishing, horseback riding, hiking tours, and a full-service
spa. Thatch-roof bungalows with terraces have spectacular views over
the silvery Río Colca. All outdoor terraces also have small private hot
springs tubs, an open-fire pit, and couches. Rooms are bright with
comfortable furnishings, including wrought-iron beds piled with heaps
of elegant bedding and leather armchairs. The smooth stone floors are
heated and the deep bathtubs have glass ceilings so at night you can
also soak in the amazing stars above. An on-site novo-Andino restaurant serves creative fare made using vegetables from the garden. All
meals are offered à la carte. **Pros:** All-inclusive, heated floors, private
hot springs. **Cons:** Pricey. ⊠*Parque Curiña Yanque* ☎*051/610–8300*
☎☎*051/242–3365* ⊕*www.lascasitasdelcolca.com* ⟳*19 rooms, 1 suite*
⌂*In-room: no a/c, safe, refrigerator, no TV, Wi-Fi. In-hotel: restaurant,
room service, bar, pools, spa, bicycles, no elevator, laundry service, concierge, executive floor, public Internet, public Wi-Fi, parking (no fee),
no-smoking rooms* ▭*AE, MC, V* ⑩|*AI.*

$ ⬚**La Casa de Mama Yacchi.** Perhaps the best food around, and the best
pillows, too. Owned by the same folks of Casa de Mi Abuela in Arequipa, this rustic thatched-roof hotel is a great economical choice. Its
main lodge is cozy and the restaurant specializes in local fare, such as
the alpaca barbeque, and there's a good bar. The rooms are simple bungalows with standard beds and excellent bedding. On the north rim,
in Coporaque, it's very peaceful. Horseback riding and hikes can be
arranged daily. **Pros:** Delicious food, good water pressure, and pillows.
Cons: Gets cold, far from Cruz del Condor. ⊠*Calle Jerusalén 606,*

Coporaque ☎*054/241–206* 🖷*054/242–761* ⊕*www.lacasademamay acchi.com* 💬*50 rooms* ♿*In-room: no a/c, no phone, safe. In-hotel: restaurant, bar, no elevator, laundry service, parking (no fee), no-smoking rooms* ⊟*No credit cards* Ⓞ*BP.*

AREQUIPA

150 km (93 mi) south of Colca Canyon, 200 km (124 mi) south of Cotahuasi Canyon.

Cradled by three steep, gargantuan, snow-covered volcanoes, the charming white-stoned Arequipa shines under the striking sun at 2,350 meters (7,709 feet). This settlement of 1 million residents grew from a collection of Spanish-colonial churches and homes constructed from white *sillar* (petrified volcanic ash) gathered from the surrounding terrain. The result is unique—short gleaming white buildings contrast with the charcoal-color mountain backdrop of El Misti, a perfectly shaped cone volcano.

Arequipeños call their home *Cuidad Blanca,* "White City," and the "Independent Republic of Arequipa"—they have made several attempts to secede from Peru and even designed the city's own passport and flag. On August 15, parades, fireworks, bullfights, and dancing celebrate the city's founding.

Arequipa enjoys fresh, crisp air, and warm days averaging 23°C (73°F) and comfortable nights at 14°C (57°F). To make up for the lack of rain, the Río Chili waters the surrounding foothills, which were once farmed by the Inca and now stretch into rows of alfalfa and onions.

GETTING AROUND

Walking is the best option around the city center. Most sights, shops, and restaurants are near the Plaza de Armas. Most sites are open morning and afternoon, but close for a couple of hours midday. Churches usually open 7 to 9 AM and 6 to 8 PM, before and after services. Taxis are everywhere and cost about S/3 to get around the center or to Vallecito.

In Arequipa the airport is large and it's easy to hail a taxi to your hotel. Many hotels also offer pick-up and drop-off. The cost is about S/15.

PRECAUTIONS   Wear comfortable walking shoes, and bring a hat, sunscreen, a Spanish dictionary, some small change, and a good map of town. Be street-smart in the Arequipa market area—access your cash discreetly and keep your valuables close. At 2,300 meters (7,500 feet) Arequipa is quite high. If you're coming directly from Lima or from the coast, carve out a day or two for acclimatization.

ESSENTIALS

Currency Exchange **Banco Continental BBVA** (✉*San Francisco 108*).**Banco de Crédito BCP** (✉*San Juan de Dios 123* ☎*054/283–741*). **Caja Municipal Arequipa** (✉*La Merced 106*).

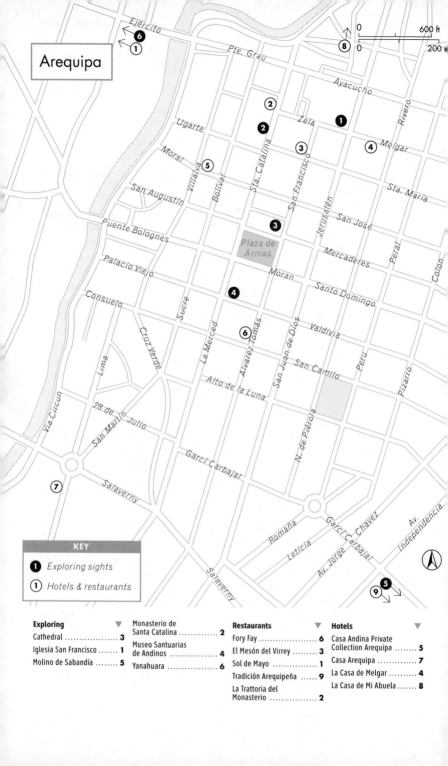

Arequipa

KEY

- ① Exploring sights
- ① Hotels & restaurants

Internet Cafés **C@tedral Internet** (⊠*Pasaje Catedral 101* ☏054/282–074). **Cybermarket** (⊠*Santa Catalina 115* ☏054/284–306).

Mail **Serpost Arequipa** (⊠*Calle Moral 118* ☏054/215–247 ⊕*www.serpost.com. pe* ☽*Mon.–Sat. 8–8, Sun. 9–2*). **DHL** (⊠*Santa Catalina 115* ☏054/234–288).

Medical Assistance **Clínica Arequipa SA** (⊠*Puente Grau y Av. Bolognesi* ☏054/253–416 or 054/253–424). **Hospital Goyeneche** (⊠*Av. Goyeneche s/n, Cerado* ☏054/231–313). **Honorio Delgado Espinoza Regional Hospital** (⊠*Av. A. Carrión s/n* ☏054/231–818, 054/219–702, or 054/233–812).

Police **Police** (⊠*Av. Emmel 106, Yanahuara* ☏054/254–020). **Policía de Turismo** (⊠*Jerusalén 315* ☏054/201–258).

Rental Car **Akal Rent A Car** (⊠*Av. Bolognesi 903 Cayma* ⊕*www.akalrentacar. com*). **Avis Arequipa** (⊠*Ugarte 216* ⊕*www.avisperu.com*). **Exodo** (⊠*Manuél Belgrado F-1, Urb. Alvarez Thomas* ☏054/423–756). **Hertz** (⊠*Palacio Viejo 214,* ☏054/282–519 ⊕*www.hertz.com* ⊠*Rodriguez Ballón Airport* ☏054/443–576).

Taxi **Taxi Turismo Arequipa** (☏054/458–888 or 054/459–090 ⊕*www.taxiturismo. com.pe*). **454545** (☏054/454–545).

Visitor Info **Iperu Oficina de Información Turística** (⊠*Portal de la Municipalidad 110, Plaza de Armas,* ✎*iperuarequipa@promperu.gob.pe* ⊠*Santa Catalina 210, Casona Santa Catalina* ☏054/221–227 ⊠*Rodríguez Ballón Airport, 1st fl., Main Hall* ☏054/444–564). **Touring and Automobile Club of Peru** (⊠*Goyeneche 313* ☏054/603–131 or 054/603–333 ✎*arequipa@touringperu.com.pe*).

EXPLORING AREQUIPA

❸ ★ Catedral. You can't miss the imposing twin bell towers of this 1612 cathedral, whose facade guards the entire eastern flank of the Plaza de Armas. As the sun sets the imperial reflection gives the Cathedral an amber hue. The inside has high-vaulted ceilings above a beautiful Belgian organ. The ornate wooden pulpit, carved by French artist Rigot in 1879, was transported here in the early 1900s. In the back, look for the Virgin of the Sighs statue in her white wedding dress, and the figure of Beata Ana de Los Angeles, a nun from Santa Catalina monastery who was beatified by Pope John Paul II when he stayed in Arequipa in 1990. A fire in 1844 destroyed much of the cathedral, as did an 1868 earthquake, so parts have a neoclassical look. In 2001 another earthquake damaged one of the bell towers, which was repaired to match its sister tower. ⊠*Plaza de Armas, between Santa Catalina and San Francisco* ☏*054/23–2635* 🎫*S/7* ☽*Daily 7:30–11:30 and 4:30–7:30.*

❶ Iglesia de San Francisco. This 16th-century church has survived numerous natural disasters, including several earthquakes that cracked its cupola. Inside, near the polished silver altar, is the little chapel of the Sorrowful Virgin, where the all-important Virgin Mary statue is stored. On December 8, during Arequipa's Feast of the Immaculate Conception, the Virgin is paraded around the city all night atop an ornate carriage and surrounded by images of saints and angels. A throng of pilgrims carry flowers and candles. Visit the adjoining convent S/5 to see Arequipa's largest painting and a museum of 17th-century religious furniture and paintings. ⊠*Zela 103* ☏*054/223–048* 🎫*Free*

⊙ *Church: Mon.–Sat. 7 AM–9 AM and 5–8, Sun. 7–noon and 5–8. Convent: Mon.–Sat. 9–12:30 and 3:30–6. Closed Sun.*

❺ Molino de Sabandía. There's a colorful story behind the area's first stone
★ *molina* (mill), 7 km (4 mi) southeast of Arequipa. Built in 1621 in the gorgeous Paucarpata countryside, the mill fell into ruin over the next century. Famous architect Luis Felipe Calle was restoring the Arequipa mansion that now houses the Central Reserve Bank in 1966 when he was asked to work on the mill project. By 1973 the restoration of the volcanic-stone structure was complete—and Calle liked the new version so much that he bought it, got it working again, and opened it for visitors to tour. Bring your swimsuit and walking shoes in good weather; there's a pool and trails around the lovely countryside. Adjoining the site is Yumina, which has numerous Inca agricultural terraces. If you're not driving, flag a taxi for S/16 or take a colectivo from Socabaya in Arequipa to about 2 km (1 mi) past Paucarpata. ⊠ *8 km (5 mi) south of Arequipa, Sabandia* ☎ *No phone* ⊠ *S/7* ⊙ *Daily 9–6.*

❷ Monasterio de Santa Catalina. A city unto itself, this 5-acre complex of
☉ mud-brick, Iberian-style buildings surrounded by vibrant fortress like
Fodor's Choice walls and separated by neat, open plazas and colorful gardens, is a work-
★ ing convent and one of Peru's most famed cultural treasures. Founded in 1579 and closed to the public for the first 400 years, Santa Catalina was an exclusive retreat for the daughters of Arequipa's wealthiest colonial patrons. Visitors can catch a peek at life in this historic monastery. Narrow streets run past the Courtyard of Silence, where teenage nuns lived during their first year, and the Cloister of Oranges, where nuns decorated their rooms with lace sheets, silk curtains, and antique furnishings. Though about 400 nuns once lived here, fewer than 30 do today. Admission includes a one-hour guided tour (tip S/10–S/20) in English. Afterward, head to the cafeteria for the nuns' famous *torta de naranja* (orange cake), pastries, and tea. There are night tours on Tuesday and Thursday, but check the times before you go, as they sometimes change. ⊠ *Santa Catalina 301* ☎ *054/229–798* ⊠ *S/30* ⊙ *Daily 9–5; last entry at 4; night tours Tues. and Thurs. 7–9.*

❹ Museo Santuarios Andinos. Referred to as the Juanita Museum, this fasci-
Fodor's Choice nating little museum at the Universidad Católica Santa Maria holds the
★ frozen bodies of four young girls who were apparently sacrificed more than 500 years ago by the Inca to appease the gods. The "Juanita" mummy, said to be frozen around the age of 13 was the first mummy found in 1995 near the summit of Mt. Ampato by local climber Miguel Zarate and anthropologist Johan Reinhard. When neighboring Volcán Sabancaya erupted, the ice that held Juanita in her sacrificial tomb melted and she rolled partway down the mountain and into a crater. English-speaking guides will show you around the museum, and you can watch a video detailing the expedition. ⊠ *La Merced 110* ☎🖂 *054/215–013* ⊠ *S/11* ⊙ *Mon.–Sat. 9–6, Sun. 9–3.*

❻ Yanahuara. The eclectic little suburb of Yanahuara, northwest of the
★ city, is perfect for lunch or a late afternoon stroll. The neighborhood is above Arequipa and has amazing views over the city at the lookout

constructed of sillar stone arches. On a clear day views of volcanos El Misti, Chachani, and Picchu can be had. Stop in at the 1783, mestizo-style Iglesia Yanahuara. The interior has wrought-iron chandeliers and gilt sanctuaries surrounding the nave. Ask to see the glass coffin that holds a statue of Christ used in parades on holy days. To reach Yanahuara, head across the Avenida Grau bridge, then continue on Avenida Ejército to Avenida Lima, and from here, it's five blocks to the Plaza. It's a 15-minute walk or an 8-minute cab ride from the city center.

WHERE TO EAT

Comida Arequipa (Arequipan cuisine) is a special version of *comida criolla*. Perhaps the most famous dish is *rocoto relleno,* a large, spicy red pepper stuffed with meat, onions, and raisins. Picanterías are where locals head for good, basic Peruvian meals and cold Arequipeña beer served with *cancha* (fried, salted corn).

¢–$ ✕**Fory Fay Cevicheria.** Ask any Arequipeño to name their favorite fish
SEAFOOD   joint and Fory Fay tops the list. For more than 22 years they've served
Fodor'sChoice   some of the freshest ceviche (raw fish marinated in lime juice) around.
★   Its owner, the personable Alex Aller, grew up in the coastal port of Mollendo and travels there daily to check on the catch. Fishing bric-a-brac and photos of New York, where Aller once lived, line the walls. ⊠*Alvarez Thomas 221* ☏*054/242–400* ▭*AE, MC, V.*

$–$$$ ✕**El Mesón del Virrey.** This spacious upscale restaurant is donned in
PERUVIAN   antiqued Spanish-colonial motif. The meat-heavy menu is infused with
★   Italian and coastal influences. Quinoa con Camarones (quinoa with shrimp) is one of the best dishes in Arequipa. Much like a risotto, the quinoa is cooked in a creamy tomato sauce with vegetables and a large fresh jumbo-size shrimp that looks more like a lobster. Lamb, beef, alpaca, and ostrich can also be enjoyed. The pisco sour is one of the best around. Hear live music nightly from 8 to 10. ⊠*San Francisco 305* ☏*054/202–080* ▭*AE, D, MC, V.*

$–$$$ ✕**Sol de Mayo.** This charming garden restaurant in the colonial Yana-
PERUVIAN   huara neighborhood is worth the expense to taste true Arequipan cook-
★   ing. Specialties include *ocopa arequipeña* (boiled potato slices in spicy sauce and melted cheese), and *rocoto relleno* (spicy peppers stuffed with cheese, meat and raisins). Only open for lunch. ⊠*Jerusalén 207, Yanahuara* ☏*054/254–148* ▭*AE, D, MC, V.*

$ ✕**Tradición Arequipeña.** It may be a S/8 taxi ride to this restaurant in
PERUVIAN   the Paucarpata district, but locals come in droves for the fantastic
Fodor'sChoice   Arequipan food. The decor is Peruvian country, but the flavors lean
★   toward Creole. Get ready for *cuy chactado* (deep-fried guina pig) and *ocopa arequipeña* (potato-based dish with garlic, olives, onion, and fresh cheese). If you crave seafood, try the *Chupe de Camarones* (a creamy shrimp chowder). Open from noon to 7, it's primarily a lunch-only venue Sunday through Thursday, but on Friday and Saturday it doesn't close until 10 (sometimes later) when live music can be heard, including an orchestra on Saturday nights. Reservations recommended. ⊠*Dolores 111, Paucarpata* ☏*054/426–467* ▭*AE, D, MC, V.*

8

$ ✕ **La Trattoria del Monasterio.** Designed by Gaston Acurio, of Lima's elite
ITALIAN   Astrid y Gaston restaurant, the Italian food is some of the best in Peru.
Fodor'sChoice   Its location in the Monasterio de Santa Catalina (the entrance is out-
★   side the compound) is enough to make this place special. Homemade
pastas, raviolis, gnocchi, risottos, paired with seafood, meats and creative, savory sauces are offered. There's an extensive wine list. ⊠ *Santa
Catalina 309* ☎ *054/204–062* ▤ *AE, V.*

WHERE TO STAY

$$$$ ⊡ **Casa Andina Private Collection Arequipa.** Over-priced, but as upscale
★   as it gets, this is the place to go for top-of-line amenities. Housed in
the city's former coin mint and national historical monument, this
mid-size hotel opened in February 2008. Draped in Andean weaves
and adorned with newfangled furniture, the rooms are large, yet cozy
with plush modern bedding and elegant fixtures. Many rooms have
romantic views of the city. Two colonial courtyards beg for a night
walk. The gourmet restaurant serves creative novo-cuisine in its hip
dining area and there's even a coin museum in honor of the building's
history. **Pros:** New, comfortable bedding, large bathrooms, top-of-the-
line. **Cons:** Expensive. ⊠ *Ugarte 403* ☎ *054/226–907* ▤ *054/226–908*
⊕ *www.casa-andina.com* ⟲ *41 rooms, 1 presidential suite, 6 regular
suites* △ *In-room: no a/c, safe, refrigerator (some), DVD (some), Wi-
Fi. In-hotel: restaurant, bar, laundry service, concierge, executive floor,
public Internet, public Wi-Fi, airport shuttle, parking (fee), no-smok-
ing rooms* ⊙| *BP.*

$–$$ ⊡ **Casa Arequipa.** With seven individually designed rooms, all donned
Fodor'sChoice   in luxuriously high-quality motif and bedding, every last detail has
★   been thought of—and applied. It's so personalized it's like you're visiting your best friends. This neocolonial boutique hotel books up fast
and has won several awards. Filled with antique furnishings typical of
the region, the hand-carved beds are piled high with alpaca blankets
and 400 count sheets to counter the cool Andean air, and there are
room heaters as well. The extra charm comes from those who run it,
the hospitable staff (they'll retrieve your luggage from the airport if
it's delayed, iron your clothes, and throw you a party for your birthday). A lavish breakfast buffet includes an assortment of coffee, tea,
breads, fruits, and eggs, served in the dining room. In an upscale, residential neighborhood, it's a 10- to 15-minute walk from the center of
town. **Pros:** Impeccable service, new and comfortable bedding, quiet
neighborhood, large rooms, will arrange trips to Colca Canyon. **Cons:**
Not near any stores, need a taxi at night. ⊠ *Av. Lima 409, Vallecito*
☎ *054/284–219, 202/518–9672 from U.S.* ⊕ *www.arequipacasa.com*
⟲ *7 rooms* △ *In-room: no a/c, safe, DVD (some), Wi-Fi. In-hotel: restaurant, room service, bar, no elevator, laundry service, concierge, public Internet, public Wi-Fi, airport shuttle, parking (no fee), no-smoking
rooms* ▤ *AE, DC, MC, V* ⊙| *BP.*

¢   ⊡ **La Casa de Melgar.** In a beautiful tiled courtyard surrounded by
★   fragrant blossoms and dotted with trees is this 18th-century home,
believed to have been the one-time temporary residence of Mariano

Melgar, Peru's most romantic 19th-century poet. This brightly blue and adobe-color Spanish-colonial has double rooms that have towering, vaulted brick ceilings, as well as private baths with hot water. The single suite has an original cookstove from its early days. A small on-site café, Flor de Café serves breakfast. **Pros:** High on the charm-scale, garden is great for relaxing, quiet, close to shops and restaurants. **Cons:** Rooms can get cold in rainy season, some have thin walls, front desk staff can be curt. ✉ *Melgar 108* 📠*054/222–459* ⊕*www.lacasade melgar.com* 🖙*30 rooms, 1 suite* ♿*In-room: no a/c, safe. In-hotel: café, no elevator, laundry service, parking (no fee)* ⍣*CP* ▭*V.*

$ 　🛏**La Casa de Mi Abuela.** An old stone wall circles this famous budget-
☾　traveler haunt. Extensive gardens, with 2,000 square meters of green
★　space grace this compound-like resort, but the English-speaking owners show their sense of humor in its centerpiece: a rusted Fiat van. The basic, wood-paneled standard rooms with well-worn furniture and tiny bathrooms do the job, but for only $10 more, the new junior garden suites—with contemporary furnishings and amenities—are much nicer. Regardless of the room, the elaborate breakfast buffet in the garden terrace is hard to top. At night you can clean up, read a book in a hammock, listen to the live piano music at the bar or take a dip in the pool. It's a five- to seven-minute walk to the Plaza de Armas. **Pros:** Best breakfast buffet in town, free airport pick-up, large grounds, security gate. **Cons:** Standard room bathrooms are old and small, lots of tour groups. ✉ *Calle Jerusalén 606* 📞*054/241–206* 📠*054/242–761* ⊕*www.lacasademiabuela.com* 🖙*57 rooms* ♿*In-room: no a/c, safe (some), kitchenette (some), refrigerator (some), Wi-Fi. In-hotel: restaurant, bar, pool, no elevator, laundry service, concierge, public Internet, public Wi-Fi, airport shuttle, parking (fee)* ▭*AE, DC, MC, V* ⍣*BP.*

SHOPPING

Arequipa has the widest selection of Peruvian crafts in the south. Alpaca and llama wool is woven into brightly patterned sweaters, ponchos, hats, scarves, and gloves, as well as wall hangings, blankets, and carpets. Look for *chullos* (woolen knitted caps with ear flaps and ties), transported from the Lake Titicaca region. Ceramic *toros* (bulls) are a local favorite to hold flowers or money, and you can even see them sitting in the rafters of homes to bring good luck.

PUNO

975 km (609 mi) southeast of Lima.

Puno doesn't win any beauty pageants—brown unfinished cement homes, old paved roads, and a dusty desert has been the landscape for years. It's a sharp contrast to Puno's immediate neighbor, Lake Titicaca. Some people arrive in town, and scram to find a trip on the lake. Don't let the dreary look of Puno stop you from exploring its shores; it's considered Peru's folklore capital.

Puno retains traits of the Aymará, Quechua, and Spanish cultures that settled on the northwestern shores of the lake. Their influence is in the art, music, dance, and dress of today's inhabitants, who call themselves

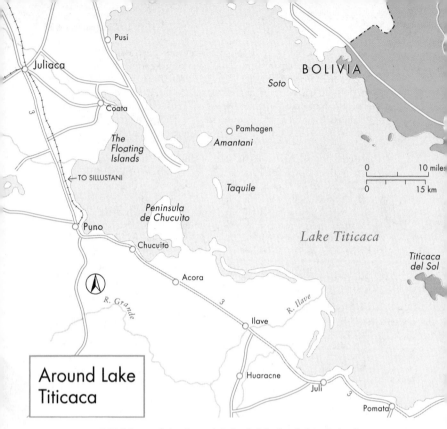

Around Lake Titicaca

"Children of the Sacred Lake." Much of the city's character comes from the continuation of ancient traditions—-at least once a month a parade or a festival celebrates some recent or historic event.

GETTING AROUND
Restaurants, shops, Internet services, banks, and drug stores line the four-block pedestrian-only street Jirón Lima, between Pino Park (sometimes called Parque San Juan after the San Juan Bautista Church nearby) and the Plaza de Armas.

Puno has tricycle taxis, which resemble Asian tuk-tuks, and are driven by bicycle peddlers with a supped-up carriage and costs only S/1 to go nearly anywhere in the city. However, if you're heading to a mirador high up on the hill, and you don't want the peddler to keel over, take an auto taxi, which costs S/3.

SAFETY
Walking around the port after dark is not smart. When the sun goes down, the port gets desolate and unsuspecting tourists become targets for crime. So if you're at the handicraft market or are getting back from an outing on the lake, and suddenly it's dusk, catch a cab.

Festival Time!

While anytime of year is suitable for traveling to Puno and Lake Titicaca, visiting during a festival of dance, song, and parades is ideal. The streets are flooded with people; the folklore experience is passionate and very fun. Preserving the choreography of more than 140 typical dances, Puno's most memorable celebration is the *Festival of the Virgin de la Candelaria* (candle), held on February 2 and during carnival. A cast of several hundred elaborately costumed Andean singers, dancers, and bands from neighbor-ing communities parades through the streets carrying the rosy-white complexioned statue of the Virgin. During the rest of the year, the statue rests on the altar of the San Juan Bautista Church. Puno week, as it's informally known occurs the first week of November and is equally fun. When Puno isn't having a celebration, it reverts to its true character, that of a small, poor Andean agriculture town. On the lake, Isla Taquile celebrates a vivid festival the last week of July.

ESSENTIALS

Bus Contacts Cruz del Sur (✉ *Terminal Terrestre C-10* 🕾 *051/368–524* ⊕ *www. cruzdelsur.com.pe*). **CIVA** (✉ *Terminal Terrestre C-35* 🕾 *051/365–882*). **Imexso** (✉ *Terminal terrestre C-14* 🕾 *051/369–514*). **Inka Express** (✉ *Jr. Melgar N 226,* 🕾 *051/365–654*). **Panamericano** (✉ *Terminal Terrestre C-12* 🕾 *051/354–001*).

Currency Exchange Banco de Crédito BCP (✉ *Jr. Lima 510* 🕾 *051/352–119*). **Banco Continental BBVA** (✉ *400 Jr. Lima*). **Scotiabank** (✉ *Plaza de Armas, corner of Duestra and Jr. Lima*).

Internet Cafés La Casa del Corregidor (✉ *Deustua 576* 🕾 *051/351–921* ⏰ *Tues.–Sat. 10–10*). **Choz@Net** (✉ *Jr. Lima 339, 2nd fl.* 🕾 *051/367–195*). **Top Net** (✉ *208 Duestra*).

Mail Serpost Puno (✉ *Av. Moquegua 269* 🕾 *051/351–141* ⏰ *Mon.–Sat. 8–8*).

Medical Assistance Carlos Monge Medrano Hospital (✉ *Kil. 2 of Huancane Hwy., sector San Ramon, Juliaca* ⏰ *Daily 24 hrs* 🕾 *051/321–901, 051/321–750, 051/321–131, 051/321–370*). **Manuel Nuñez Butron National Hospital** (✉ *Av. El Sol 1022* ⏰ *Daily 24 hrs* 🕾 *051/351–021 or 051/369–286, 051/369–696*).

Police Police (✉ *Jr. Deustua 530* 🕾 *051/366–271 or 051/353–988*). **Policía de Tourismo** (✉ *Jr. Deustua 538* 🕾 *051/354–764, 051/354–774, or 051/353–3988*).

Taxi Radio Taxi Milenium (🕾 *051/353–134*). **Servitaxi Turistico** (🕾 *051/369–000*). **Tonocar Titikaka** (🕾 *051/368–000*).

Train PeruRail (✉ *Estacion Puno, La Torre 224* 🕾 *084/238–722* ⊕ *www.perurail.com* ⏰ *Weekdays 7–5, weekends 7–noon*).

Visitor Info Iperu Oficina Información Turística (✉ *Corner of Jr. Deustua and Jr. Lima, Plaza de Armas,* 🕾 *051/365–088* ✎ *iperupuno@promperu.gob.pe*).

EXPLORING PUNO

Fodor'sChoice **La Casa del Corregidor.** Reconstructed more than five times, this 17th-
★ century colonial structure, once a chaplaincy, is now a brightly colored
cultural center. It was originally home to Silvestre de Valdés, a Catholic
priest who served as a *corregidor* (a Spanish official who acts as governor, judge, and tax collector) and oversaw construction of the nearby
Catedral. The house had a long history of changing owners until its
present owner, Sra. Ana Maria Piño Jordán, bought it at public auc-
tion. Now a vibrant cultural locale, with an arts cooperative, it houses
a fair-trade café and a few upscale handicraft stores. The exhibition
hall displays works by local artists, and hosts music events. ⊠*Deustua
576* ☎*051/351–921 or 051/365-603* ⊕*www.casadelcorregidor.com.
pe* ☽*Mon.–Sat. 9–10, Sun. 2–8.*

★ **Museo Carlos Dreyer.** An exhibit of 501 gold pieces, called the "Great
Treasure of Sillustani" has classified the intimate museum as one of
the most important regional archaeological museums in southern Peru.
The museum is named for famed Puno painter and antiques collector, Carlos Dreyer Spohr. You can view the oil canvasses by Dreyer
and explore exhibits of pre-Hispanic and colonial art, weavings, silver,
copper works, delicate Aymará pottery, pre-Inca stone sculptures, and
historical Spanish documents on the founding of Puno. ⊠*Conde de
Lemos 289* ☎*S/15* ☽*Mon.–Sat. 9:30–7:30, Sun, 2–7:30.*

★ **Museo de la Coca & Costumbres.** A hidden gem, this museum pays tribute
to the infamous coca leaf and Peruvian folklore. The quaint museum,
tucked away on a second-floor building is sliced into rooms, one that
houses the folklore exhibit and the other displays everything you'd
ever want to know about the coca leaf. Presented in English and Spanish, displays are well-constructed with educational videos and photographs. The mission is not to promote coca, but merely to share
the plants' history and culture. You can enlist the help of a bilingual
guide if you wish or mosey on your own. The folklore exhibit displays
elaborately constructed costumes worn during festivals and shares the
history behind the dances. ⊠*Jr. Deza 301* ☎*051/977–0360* ⊕*www.
museodelacoca.com* ☎*S/5* ☽*Daily 9–1 and 3–8.*

WHERE TO EAT

¢–$$ ✕**Coco K'intu.** It's probably the best restaurant to hit town since Apu
PERUVIAN Salkantay opened its doors 13 years ago. Not surprising, both are
Fodor'sChoice owned by members of the Martinez family. It's novo-Andino cuisine at
★ its finest, taking traditional food and making creative, sophisticated,
down-right delicious entrées. The food bursts with flavor, especially the
sopa Incasica, a thick, creamy quinoa soup with peppers and onions,
and a kick of spice. Slow-cooked alpaca entrées include the *alpaca con
salsa de maracuya,* a tender alpaca steak cooked in a passionfruit sauce.
The creative concoctions go on and on. Open for breakfast, lunch, and
dinner. ⊠*Jr. Lima 401* ☎*051/365–566* ▭*V.*

¢–$ ✕**Apu Salkantay.** Dark rustic wooden fixtures and an adobe wood stove,
PERUVIAN along with a cozy ambience and modern novo-Andino cuisine, keep
this candle-lighted restaurant a favorite with tourists and locals. While
we think the best-tasting pizza is made here, there's a whole delectable

menu to choose from. For lunch or dinner try the *Trucha ahumadas* (smoked trout), or the blackberry beef, an alpaca steak, fresh soup, or one of the flavorful vegetarian dishes, all prepared with natural ingredients. Service can be a little slow, but perhaps they're perfecting their product, so order-up a hot mulled wine and relax by the fire. ⊠*Lima 425* ☎*051/363–955* ▭*V.*

¢–$ ✕**Don Piero.** Colorful paintings of Quecha people partaking in various
PERUVIAN rituals hang above you as you enjoy such typical dishes as barbecued chicken, fresh fish (pejerrey and *trucha*—trout) fried in oil and garnished with potatoes and toasted chili peppers. Local musicians entertain on most nights. It's open for breakfast, lunch, and dinner. ⊠*Lima 364* ☎*051/365–943* ▭*No credit cards.*

WHERE TO STAY

Puno can be cold so bring warm clothes. Not even the fanciest hotels have internal heating systems, but most have portable electric heaters.

$ 🏨**Hotel La Hacienda.** Panoramic views of Lake Titicaca and its sur-
★ roundings can be viewed from the endless window-filled restaurant atop of this Spanish-colonial hotel, two blocks from Plaza de Armas. All rooms are spacious, bright, and clean. The bedding, especially the pillows, is plush. Most rooms have big bay windows for a view of the city or lake. A grand spiral staircase extends through all six floors. **Pros:** Free Internet, large bathrooms, complimentary pisco sour upon arrival. **Cons:** Can be noisy along Avenida Deustra. ⊠*Deustua 297* ☎*051/365–134* ⊕*www.lahaciendapuno.com* ⇌*58 rooms* ⚐*In-room: no a/c, safe, Wi-Fi. In-hotel: restaurant, room service, bar, laundry service, concierge, public Internet, public Wi-Fi, airport shuttle, no-smoking rooms* ▭*DC, MC, V* ⏹*BP.*

¢–$ 🏨**Intiqa Hotel.** Looking as if it were lifted out of Soho, all the rooms
★ are spacious, sleek, and modern, and have lots of natural light, flat-screen TVs with Direct TV, plush brown bedding, and polished hardwood floors. Indigenous art hangs on the walls. Stained-glass windows, which permeate light from the hotel's large atrium, line the hallways. A service-oriented staff is helpful and can help plan local trips. **Pros:** Big bathrooms, spacious rooms, new. **Cons:** Breakfast café doesn't have enough seating. ⊠*Tarapacá 272* ☎*051/366–900* ⊕*www.intiqahotel.com* ⇌*17 rooms* ⚐*In-room: no a/c, safe, Wi-Fi. In-hotel: restaurant, laundry service, public Wi-Fi, airport shuttle, parking (no fee), no-smoking rooms* ▭*AE, MC, V* ⏹*CP.*

$$$$ 🏨**Titilaka.** Peru's Inkaterra, an elite ecotourism hotel group, now has a
★ property in Lake Titicaca. While the facade won't woo you, the sleek and luxurious inside matches the classic euro-contemporary motif Inkaterra is known for. All rooms have nice furnishings, high-quality linens, plasma TVs, and heated floors. The new resort is all-inclusive and offers an off-the-beaten-path location, overlooking the lake next to the Chucuito Peninsula, on Peninsula Titilaka, about a 30-minute boat ride from Puno. Titilaka offers excursions to the islands, gourmet cuisine, massage services, and a heated outdoor pool. **Pros:** All inclusive, heated floors. **Cons:** Secluded, far from Puno. ⊠*Huenccalla, Centro Poblado Menor de Titilaca, District of Plateria, Peninsula Titilaka*

8

☎*800/422–5042 from USA, 511/610–0400 in Peru* ⊕*www.inkaterra. com* ⇱*18 suites* ⌂*In-room: refrigerator, Wi-Fi. In-hotel: restaurant, room service, bar, pool, spa, beachfront, water sports, no elevator, laundry service, concierge, executive floor, public Wi-Fi, airport shuttle, parking (no fee), no-smoking rooms* ⊟*AE, MC, V* ⏿*AI.*

LAKE TITICACA

Forms Puno's eastern shoreline.

Stunning, unpredictable, and enormous, Lake Titicaca is a world of unique flora, fauna, cultures, and geology. Lago Titicaca, which means lake of the grey (titi) puma (caca) in Quechua, borders Peru and Bolivia, with Peru's largest portion to the northwest. While Peru boasts the largest port in Puno, Bolivia's side has Isla del Sol and Isla de la Luna, two beautiful islands with great views and Inca ruins.

The Bahía de Puno, separated from the lake proper by the two jutting peninsulas of Capaschica and Chucuito, is home to the descendents of the Uro people, who are now mixed with the Aymará and Quechua. The lakeshores are lush with totora reeds—valuable as building material, cattle fodder, and, in times of famine, food for humans.

GETTING AROUND

A boat is necessary for traveling the lake. Most people go to the islands with a tour, but colectivo boats in Puno Bay will transport you for S/10–S/25. Most boats are super slow, super old, and they won't leave port unless at least 10 people are smushed aboard. A four-hour trip will take only an hour in one of the newer speedboats that the higher-end tour companies now use.

EXPLORING THE FLOATING ISLANDS

Islas los Uros, known as the Floating Islands, are man-made islands woven together with mud and tótora reeds that grow in the lake shallows. Replenished often with layers because the underbelly reeds rot, these tiny islands resemble floating bails of hay. Trips to the Los Uros typically take three hours and can be arranged from the port in the Puno Bay or with a guide through one of the many agencies in town. While some travelers marvel at these 40-plus islands, some call them floating souvenir stands. Yes, locals sell trinkets, but visiting the floating islands is a glimpse into one of the region's oldest cultures, the Uros. Now mixed with Aymara culture it's a form of human habitation that evolved over centuries. The closest group of "floating museums" is 10 km (6 mi) from Puno.

The islanders make their living by fishing, trapping birds, and selling visitors well-made miniature reed boats, weavings, and collages depicting island life. You can hire an islander to take you for a ride in a reed boat.

TAQUILE ISLAND

35 km (22 mi) west of Puno in the high altitude sunshine, Taquile's brown dusty landscape contrasts with green terraces, bright flowers,

and the surrounding blue waters. Snow-capped Bolivian mountains loom in the distance.

Taquile folk are known for weaving some of Peru's loveliest textiles, and men create textiles as much as the women. Islanders still wear traditional dress and have successfully maintained the cooperative lifestyle of their ancestors. The annual Taquile festival the third week of July is a great time to visit.

Taquile is on a steep hill with curvy long trails, which lead to the main square. There are two ways to reach the top of Taquile where there are Inca and Tiahuanaco ruins—you can climb up the 528 stone steps, or take a longer path.

AMANTANI ISLAND

The island of Amantani is 45 km (28 mi) from Puno and almost two hours away by boat from taquile. Amantani has pre-Columbian ruins, and a larger, mainly agrarian society, whose traditional way of life has been less exposed to the outside world until recently. Not as pretty as Taquile, Amantani is dusty and brown.

Most of the younger generations speak Spanish and even a smidgen of English, but the older generation speaks only Quechua. Amantani has a population of 3,500 Quechua. Sacred rituals are held in its two pre-Inca temples, dedicated to the earth's fertility.

TOURS OF LAKE TITICACA

Excursions to the floating islands of the Uros as well as to any of the islands on Lake Titicaca can be arranged through tour agencies in Puno. Most tours depart between 7:30 and 9 AM, as the lake can become choppy in the afternoon. You also can take the local boat at the Puno dock for about the same price as a tour, although boats don't usually depart without at least 10 passengers.

Operators All Ways Travel (✉ *Jr. Tacna 285* ☎ *051/355–552* ⊕ *www.allwaystrav elperu.com*). **Condor Travel** (✉ *Tarapacá* ☎ *051/364–763* ⊕ *www.condortravel. com.pe*). **Edgar Adventures** (✉ *Jr. Lima 328* ☎ *051/353–444* ⊕ *www.edgaradven tures.com*). **Kingdom Travel** (✉ *Jr. Lima 369* ☎ *051/364–318* ✎ *kingdomperu@ hotmail.com*). **Kontiki Tours** (✉ *Jr. Melgar 188* ☎ *051/353–473* ⊕ *www.kontiki peru.com*). **Solmartour** (✉ *Jr. Libertad 229–231* ☎ *051/352–901* ⊕ *www.solmar. com.pe*). **Titikayak Kayak Tours** (✉ *Jr. Bolognesi 334* ☎ *051/367–747* ⊕ *www. titikayak.com*). **Turpuno** (✉ *Jr. Lima 208 Ofic. 5 Segundo Piso,* ☎ *051/352–001* ⊕ *www.turpuno.com*).

CROSSING TO BOLIVIA

You'll hear lots of talk about crossing Lake Titicaca from Peru to Bolivia via hydrofoil or catamaran. At this time you can not go completely across without stopping at the border and walking from Peru into Bolivia or vice versa. You can still use hydrofoils and catamarans in your journey to Bolivia's side of the lake from Copacabana on the Bolivian side, then on to the Sun and Moon islands for an overnight or two on Sun Island.

Bolivia now requires U.S. citizens to obtain a visa to travel in the country. For a price tag of $100, the visa is good for up to 90 days in a calendar year. The application can be done by mail or in person at any Bolivian Consulate, not by the Internet. Additionally a yellow fever vaccination certificate is also necessary to show upon entry.

If you're taking a bus from Puno, three hours into the ride the bus will stop just after Yunguyo for border-crossing procedures. Most higher-end bus services hand you immigration forms on the bus. As you leave Peru you'll get off to get an exit stamp from the Peruvian immigration, and then walk through to the small Bolivian immigration building, where you get an entrance stamp and will have to show your visa. From there you catch up with your bus, which will be waiting for you. Keep all immigration documents, your passport and visa safe; you may need these when leaving Bolivia.

Tour Companies Crillón Tours (⊠ *Av. Camacho 1223, La Paz* ☎ *591/02/233–7533* ⊕ *www.titicaca.com* ✍ *Titicaca@entelnet.bo*). **Crillón Tours** (⊠ *1450 S. Bayshore Dr., Suite 815, Miami, FL* ☎ *305/358–5853* ✍ *darius@titicaca.com*). **Transturin** (⊠ *Av. Arce 2678, La Paz, Bolivia* ☎ *591–2/242–2222* ⊕ *www.transturin.com*).

CUSCO & THE SACRED VALLEY

By Katy
Morrison
& Jeffrey Van
Fleet

Cusco has stood for nine centuries in this fertile Andean valley, 3,500 meters (11,500 feet) above sea level. Once the capital of the Inca empire, Cusco fell to Spanish conquistadors in 1533, when the empire was weakened from civil war. Peruvian independence was declared in 1821, and now Cusco is home to the indigenous mestizo culture of today.

The Río Urubamba passes, at its closest, about 30 km (18 mi) north of Cusco and flows through a valley about 300 meters (980 feet) lower in elevation than Cusco. The northwestern part of this river basin, romantically labeled the Sacred Valley of the Inca, contains some of the region's most appealing towns and fascinating pre-Columbian ruins. A growing number of visitors are heading here directly upon arrival in Cusco to acclimatize. The valley's altitude is slightly lower and its temperatures slightly higher, and make for a physically easier introduction to this part of Peru.

CUSCO

If you arrive in Cusco with the intention of hopping on the train to Machu Picchu the next morning, you'll probably only have time to take a stroll though the Plaza de Armas and visit Qorikancha (Temple of the Sun) and the Catedral. However, we recommend spending at least two days in Cusco before venturing off to Machu Picchu, giving yourself time to acclimate to the altitude and get to know this city of terra-cotta roofs and cobblestone streets.

Cusco takes its newest role as tourist favorite in stride, and absorbs thousands of travelers with an ample supply of lodgings, restaurants,

ACCLIMATIZING THE COCA WAY

Take it easy! Cusco is a breathless 3,300 meters (10,825 feet) above sea level—a fact you'll very soon appreciate as you huff and puff your way up its steep cobbled streets. With 30% less oxygen in the atmosphere, the best way to avoid altitude sickness is to take it easy on your first few days. There's no point in dashing off on that Inca hike if you're not acclimatized—altitude sickness is uncomfortable at best and can be very dangerous.

Locals swear by *mate de coca,* an herbal tea brewed from coca leaves that helps with altitude acclimatization. Indigenous peoples have chewed the leaves of the coca plant for centuries to cope with Andean elevations. But the brewing of the leaves in an herbal tea is considered a more refined and completely legal way to ingest the substance, in Andean nations at least. Most restaurants and many hotels have a pot steeping constantly.

and services. That a polished infrastructure exists in such a remote, high-elevation locale is a pleasant surprise.

GETTING AROUND

Cusco's Aeropuerto Internacional Teniente Alejandro Velasco Astete (CUZ) is about 15 minutes from the center of town. An army of taxis waits at the exit from baggage claim, and charge S/5 to take you to the city center.

Cusco's center city is most enjoyably explored on foot. Many of the streets open to vehicular traffic are so narrow that it's simply faster to walk. Cusco streets have a habit of changing names every few blocks, or even every block. Many streets bear a common Spanish name that everyone uses, but have newly designated street signs with an old Quechua name in order to highlight the city's Inca heritage: the Plaza de Armas is Haukaypata, the Plaza Regocijo is Kusipata, Triunfo is Sunturwasi, Loreto is Intikijlli, Arequipa is Q'aphchijk'ijllu, and intermittent blocks of Avenida El Sol are labeled Mut'uchaka. And so on.

HEALTH & SAFETY

ALTITUDE SICKNESS Known as *soroche,* you'll likely encounter altitude sickness at Cusco's 3,500-meter (11,500-foot) elevation. Drink lots of fluids but eliminate or minimize alcohol and caffeine consumption. Most large hotels have an oxygen supply for their guests' use. The prescription drug acetazolamide can help. Check with your physician about this, and about traveling here if you have a heart condition or high blood pressure, or are pregnant.

Warning: Sorojchi pills are a Bolivian-made altitude-sickness remedy whose advertising pictures a tourist vomiting at Machu Picchu. Its safety has not been documented, and we don't recommend trying it.

SAFETY Security has improved dramatically in Cusco. A huge police presence is on the streets, especially around tourist centers such as the Plaza de Armas. Nonetheless, petty crime, such as pickpocketing, is not uncom-

Buying a Boleto Turistico

Offering access to 16 of Cusco's best-known tourist attractions, the *boleto turístico* is the all-in-one answer to your tourism needs. Or is it? The scheme, in which you pay S/70 (S/35 for ISIC student card holders), certainly has its critics. Most agree that the ticket represents good value only if you visit nearly all the sites included. Under the scheme, however, no site can charge its own entry fee—so if you want to visit one, you pay for them all! Certain big name attractions (such as the Cathedral) have withdrawn from the boleto turisico in order to levy their own fees. Regardless, if you want to see sites like Sacsayhuamán and Pisac, you have to buy the ticket, which can be purchased at either location of the **Oficina Ejecutiva del Comité Boleto Turístico** (*OFEC* ⊠ *Av. El Sol 103* ☎ *084/227–037* ⊠ *Garcilaso and Heladeros* ☎ *084/226–919* ⊕ *www.boletoturisticodelCusco.com*), open Monday through Saturday 8 to 5 and Sunday 8 to 2.

For S/40 you can buy a *boleto parcial* (partial ticket) good for admission for one day only at Sacsayhuamán, Qenko, Puka Pukara, and Tambomachay, the four Inca ruins nearest Cusco. Another partial ticket, also S/40, is valid for two days at farther-flung ruins of Pisac, Chinchero, and Ollantaytambo in the Sacred Valley and Tipón and Pikillacta in the South-eastern Urubamba Valley.

If you're interested in only Cusco's cathedral and Qorikancha, as are many short-term visitors, then the boleto turístico is of no use. The cathedral, the Church of La Compañía, the church of San Blas, and the religious art museum are now united under their own *boleto intergral* (integral ticket), which you can purchase at the cathedral for S/15 (S/7.50 with an international student ID). The ticket is valid for 10 days, and the price includes a headset audioguide at each location. If you're not interested in visiting all four, it's possible to pay individual admission prices, but the four-in-one price is a bargain, and the sights are close together.

The Qorikancha, arguably Cusco's most fabulous tourist sight, levies its own admission price; it's not a member of the boleto turístico partnership. The equally wonderful Museo Inka and Museo de Arte Precolombino also charge admission independently.

mon: use extra vigilance in crowded markets or when getting on and off buses and trains. Robbers have also targeted late-night, early-morning revelers stumbling back to their hotels.

WATER   Tap water is not safe to drink here. Stick with the bottled variety, *con gas* (carbonated) or *sin gas* (plain).

ESSENTIALS

Airport Aeropuerto Internacional Teniente Alejandro Velasco Astete (⊠ *Av. Velasco Astete s/n* ☎ *084/222–611*).

Bus Contacts Cruz del Sur (⊠ *Pachacutec 510* ☎ *084/221–909*). **Ormeño** (⊠ *San Juan de Dios 657* ☎ *084/227–501*).

Currency Exchange Banco de Crédito (⊠ *Av. El Sol 189* ☎ *084/263–560*). **Banco Wiese Sudameris** (⊠ *Maruri 315* ☎ *084/264–297*).

Internet Cafés **Intinet** (✉ *Choquechaca 115* ☎ *084/258-390*). **Mundo** (✉ *Santa Teresa 172* ☎ *084/260-285*). **Telser** (✉ *Calle del Medio 117* ☎ *084/242-424*).

Mail **SERPOST** (✉ *Av. El Sol 800* ☎ *084/224-212*). **DHL** (✉ *Av. El Sol 627* ☎ *084/244-167*). **Scharff International/FedEx** (✉ *Pardo 978* ☎ *084/223-140*).

Medical Assistance **Clínica Pardo** (✉ *Av. de la Cultura 710, Plaza Tupac Amaru* ☎ *084/240-387* ⊕ *www.clinicapardo.com*). **Hospital Regional** (✉ *Av. de la Cultura s/n* ☎ *084/223-691*).

Police **Policia Nacional** (☎ *084/249-659*). **Tourist Police** (✉ *Monumento a Pachacutec, Av. Saphi s/n* ☎ *084/249-654*).

Rental Car **Avis** (✉ *Garcilaso 210* ☎ *084/241-824*). **Herz** (✉ *Av. El Sol 808* ☎ *084/248-800*). **Explores Transportes** (✉ *Plateros 356* ☎ *084/261-640*). **OSDI Rent-a-Car** (✉ *Urb. Mateo Pumacahua B-10* ☎ *084/251-616*).

Taxi **Alo Cusco** (☎ *084/222-222*). **Llama Taxi** (☎ *084/222-000*). **Taxi Turismo Cusco** (☎ *084/245-000*).

Train **Peru Rail** (✉ *San Pedro station, Cascapara near Santa Clara* ☎ *084/233-551* ⊕ *www.perurail.com* ✉ *Wanchaq station, Pachacutec near Tullumayo* ☎ *084/238-722* ⊕ *www.perurail.com*).

Visitor Info **Dirección Regional de Industria y Turismo** (Dircetur) (✉ *Mantas 117* ☎ *084/222-032* ⊙ *Weekdays 8–7, Sat. 8–2*). **iPerú** (✉ *Av. El Sol 103* ☎ *084/252-974* ⊙ *Daily 8:30–7:30*)

EXPLORING CUSCO

AROUND THE PLAZA DE ARMAS

❹ **Catedral.** Dominating the Plaza de Armas, the monumental Cathedral is one of Cusco's grandest buildings. Built in 1550 on the site of the palace of the Inca Wirachocha and using stones looted from the nearby Inca fortress of Sacsayhuaman, the Cathedral is a perfect example of the imposition of the Catholic faith on the indigenous population. The grander the building, went the theory, the more impressive the faith. With soaring ceilings, baroque carvings, enormous oil paintings, and glittering gold-and-silver altars, the Cathedral certainly seemed to achieve its aim.

Today Cusco's Cathedral is one of the town's star attractions, noted mainly for its amazing collection of colonial art that mixes Christian and non-Christian imagery. Entering the Cathedral from the Sagrada Familia chapel, head to your right to the first nave where you'll find the famous oil painting depicting the earthquake that rocked the town in 1650. Among the depictions of burning houses and people fleeing, you'll see a procession in the Plaza. Legend has it that during the earthquake, the citizens took out from the Cathedral a statue of Jesus on the cross and paraded it around the Plaza—halting the quake in its tracks. This statue, now known as the Señor de los Temblores, or Lord of the Earthquakes, is Cusco's patron, and you'll find him depicted in many Cusqueñan paintings—you'll recognize him by his frilly white skirt.

FodorsChoice ★

8

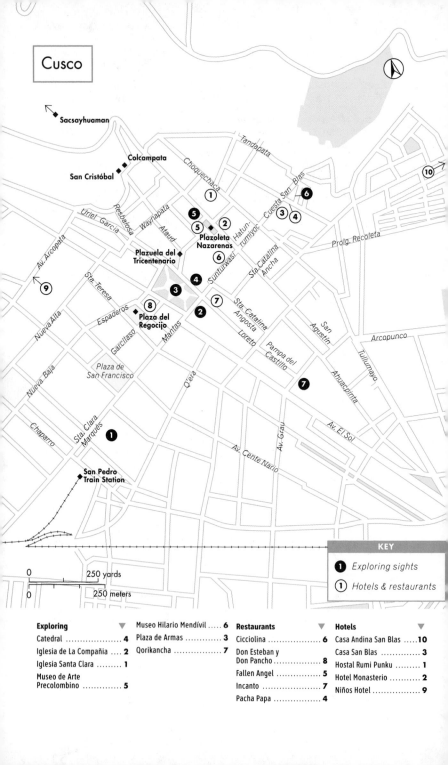

Cusco

Sacsayhuaman

Colcampata

San Cristóbal

Tandapata

Choquechaca

Cuesta San Blas

6

1

Resbalosa

Waynapata

Ataud

5

5

2

3 4

Uriel Garcia

Plazoleta
Nazarenas

Hatun-
rumiyoc

Prolg. Recoleta

Av. Arcopata

Plazuela del
Tricentenario

6

Sunturwasi

Sta. Catalina
Ancha

9

Sta. Teresa

4

3

7

Nueva Alta

Espaderos

8

Plaza del
Regocijo

2

Sta. Catalina
Angosta

San
Agustin

Arcopunco

Garcilaso

Mantas

Loreto

Pampa del
Castillo

Tullumayo

Nueva Baja

Plaza de
San Francisco

Q'era

Ahuacpinta

7

Chaparro

Sta. Clara

Marqués

1

Av. El Sol

Av. Grau

San Pedro
Train Station

Av. Cente Nario

KEY

1 *Exploring sights*

1 *Hotels & restaurants*

0   250 yards

0   250 meters

The cathedral's centerpieces are its massive, solid-silver altar, and the enormous 1659 María Angola bell, the largest in South America, which hangs in one of the towers and can be heard from miles away. Behind the main altar is the original wooden *altar primitivo* dedicated to St. Paul. The 64-seat cedar

HEY TOURIST!

The ubiquitous TOURIST INFORMATION signs are storefront travel agencies anxious to sell you tours rather than provide unbiased, official sources of information.

choir has rows of carved saints, popes, and bishops, all in stunning detail down to their delicately articulated hands. ⊠*Haukaypata (Plaza de Armas)* ☎*084/254–285* ⊠*S/16 or Boleto Integral* ☉*Daily 10–6.*

❷ Iglesia de La Compañía. With its ornately carved facade, this Jesuit church on the Plaza gives the Cathedral a run for its money in the beauty stakes. The Compañía, constructed by the Jesuits in the 17th century, was intended to be the most splendid church in Cusco, which didn't sit too well with the archbishop. The beauty contest between the churches grew so heated that the pope was forced to intervene. He ruled in favor of the Cathedral, but by that time the Iglesia was nearly finished, complete with baroque facade to rival the Cathedral's grandeur. The interior is not nearly so splendid, however, although it's worth seeing the paintings on either side of the entrance depicting the intercultural marriage between a Spanish conquistador and an Inca princess. ⊠*Haukaypata (Plaza de Armas)* ☎*No phone* ⊠*S/10 or Boleto Integral* ☉*Mon.–Sat. 9–11:45 and 1–5:30, Sun. 9–10:45 and 1–5:30; Masses: Mon.–Sat. 7* AM, *noon, 6, and 6:30* PM, *Sun. 7:30, 11:30* AM, *and 6 and 7* PM.

❸ Plaza de Armas. With park benches, green lawns, and splendid views of the Cathedral, Cusco's gorgeous colonial Plaza de Armas invites you to stay awhile. What you see today is a direct descendant of imperial Cusco's central square, which the Inca called the Haukaypata (the only name indicated on today's street signs) and it extended as far as the Plaza del Regocijo. According to belief, this was the exact center of the Inca empire, Tawantinsuyo, the Four Corners of the Earth. Today, continuing the tradition, it's the tourism epicenter. From the Plaza you'll see the Cathedral and Iglesia de la Compañía on two sides, and the graceful archways of the colonial *portales,* or covered arcades, lining the other sidesOn Sunday mornings a military parade marches on the cathedral side of the plaza, drawing hundreds of spectators and a few protesters.

NORTH OF THE PLAZA DE ARMAS

❺ Museo de Arte Precolombino. For a different perspective on pre-Colombian Fodor'sChoice ceramics head to this spectacular new museum, known as MAP, where ★ art and pre-Colombian culture merge seamlessly. Twelve rooms in the 1580 Casa Cabrera, which was used as the convent of Santa Clara until the 17th century, showcase an astounding collection of pre-Colombian art from the 13th to 16th centuries, mostly in the form of carvings, ceramics, and jewelry. The art and artifacts were made by the Huari and Nasca, as well as the Inca, cultures. The stylish displays have excellent

Tours of Cusco

The typical tour of the Cusco region combines the city with the Sacred Valley and Machu Picchu in three whirlwind days, including the full boleto turístico. We recommend devoting five days to get the most out of your visit—including one day to get acclimated to the high altitude.

Many excellent tour operators and travel agents are in Cusco, and some have offices in Lima. Several companies specialize in adventure tours, others in rafting excursions, still others in llama-assisted treks.

Several outfitters offer rafting trips on the Río Urubamba, close enough to Cusco to be done as a day excursion from the city. The river is navigable year-round, with rains turning it into a Class V from November–May, but a more manageable Class III the rest of the year. All also do multiday trips to the Río Apurimac, outside the Sacred Valley south of Cusco, during its May–December rafting season.

SELECTING A TRAVEL AGENCY

"Holaaaa—trip to Machu Picchu?" With so many touts in Cusco's streets hawking tours to Peru's most famous sight, it's tempting to just buy one in order to make them stop asking. Anyone who offers an Inca Trail trek departing tomorrow should be taken with more than a grain of salt—Inca Trail walks need to be booked months in advance. Don't make arrangements or give money to someone claiming to be a travel agent if they approach you on the street or at the airport in Cusco or Lima. Instead choose an agency that has a physical address. Better yet, select one that is listed in this book or on www.peru.info. Below are several reputable travel agencies.

Action Valley operates an adventure park near Poroy with double-cord bungee jumping, catapult swing, paragliding, and environmentally friendly paintball. Guides speak German and Hebrew in addition to English and Spanish. ✉ *Santa Teresa 325, Cusco* ☎ *084/240–835* ⊕ *www. actionvalley.com.*

Amazing Peru organizes group and individual guided tours, including two types of trips to Cusco and Machu Picchu. Transportation services and accommodations are top-notch, and the guides are flexible and extremely helpful. ☎ *01/243–7704 in Lima, 800/704–2915 in North America* ⊕ *www.amazingperu.com.*

Andina Travel specializes in trekking, especially alternatives to the Inca Trail, as well as offering all the standard Sacred Valley and Machu Picchu tours. ✉ *Plazoleta Santa Catalina 219, Cusco* ☎ *084/251–892* ⊕ *www. andinatravel.com.*

Tame rafting trips on the Urubamba River are operated year-round by **Apumayo Expediciones** ✉ *Garcilaso 265, Cusco* ☎🖶 *084/246–018* ⊕ *www.apumayo.com.*

Enigma specializes in small, customized adventure trips throughout the region. Enjoy trekking, rafting, mountain climbing, mountain biking, or horseback riding led by professional guides. ✉ *Jr. Clorinda Mato de Turner 100, Cusco* ☎ *084/222–155* ⊕ *www. enigmaperu.com.*

Explorandes is large and long-running company that organizes customized guided trips and expeditions through the Andes in Peru and Ecuador, including rafting and trekking trips around Cusco. ✉ *Av. Garcilazo 316, Cusco* ☎ *084/238–380, 01/445–*

0532 in Lima ⊕ www.explorandes.com.

Globos de los Andes floats you above the Sacred Valley on hot-air balloon tours. ✉ Av. de la Cultura 220, Cusco ☎ 084/232-352 ⊕ www.globosperu.com.

Inkaterra is a top-end agency specializing in nature-orientated trips to Machu Picchu, but can customize tours that include Cusco and the Sacred Valley with however much guide accompaniment as you need. ✉ Andalucía 174, Miraflores, Lima ☎ 01/610-0400 in Lima, 084/245-314 in Cusco, 800/442-5042 toll-free in North America ⊕ www.inkaterra.com.

Instinct leads Cusco city tours, Inca Trail hikes, walking and rafting trips along the Tambopata River, and more. ✉ Av. de la Cultura 1318, Cusco ✉ Calle 25 No. 129, San Isidro, Lima ☎ 084/233-451 ⊕ www.instinct-travel.com.

Marle's Travel Adventure offers trekking excursions and rents or sells camping equipment, in addition to doing all the standard Sacred Valley tours. ✉ Plateros 328, Cusco ☎ 084/233-680 ✍ marlestraveladventure@yahoo.com.

Mayuc is known for its rafting excursions but also offers good city and Sacred Valley tours. ✉ Portal de Confiturías 211, Haukaypata, Plaza de Armas, Cusco ☎ 084/242-824 ⊕ www.mayuc.com.

Overseas Adventure Travel offers fully escorted 11-day tours of Cusco and the surrounding region with groups no larger than 16 people. A popular OAT add-on is a trip to Ecuador's Galápagos Islands.

☎ 800/493-6824 in North America ⊕ www.oattravel.com.

River Explorers takes you on one- to six-day rafting and kayaking excursions on the Urubamba and Apurimac rivers, and offers the standard trekking tours. ✉ Plateros 328, Cusco ☎ 084/233-680 ⊕ www.riverexplorers.com.

Urubamba-based **Sacred Valley Mountain Bike Tours** rents mountain bikes for $25 per day and $15 per half-day, and leads cycling excursions throughout the valley. ✉ Jr. Convención s/n, Urubamba ☎ 084/201-331 ⊕ www.machawasi.com.

Cusco-based **SAS Travel** has made a name for itself in trekking circles, but can also customize tours and accommodations in the region. ✉ Garcilaso 270 ✉ Portal de Panes 167, Haukaypata, Plaza de Armas, Cusco ☎ 084/249-194 or 084/255-205 ⊕ www.sastravelperu.com.

Swissraft-Peru runs multiday trips on class II, II, IV, and V rapids. ✉ Heladeros 129, Cusco ☎ 084/264-124 ⊕ www.swissraft-peru.com.

For a tame adventurer, **Wilderness Travel** has a Peru Llama Trek that follows an off-Inca trail route to Machu Picchu where llamas carry your gear and you have the trail to yourself until near the end. ✉ 1102 9th St., Berkeley, CA ☎ 510/558-2488, 800/368-2794 in U.S. ⊕ www.wildernesstravel.com.

Mainly for experienced adventurers, **X-treme Tourbulencia** leads mountain climbing and biking, trekking, and multisport trips. ✉ Plateros 358, Cusco ☎ 084/224-362 ⊕ www.x-tremetourbulencia.com.

8

labels in Spanish and English that place the artifacts in their artistic and historical context. On the walls is commentary from European artists on South American art. Swiss artist Paul Klee wrote: "I wish I was newly born, and totally ignorant of Europe, innocent of facts and fashions, to be almost primitive." Most Cusco museums close at dark but MAP remains open every evening. ✉*Plazoleta Nazarenas 231* ☎*084/233–210* 💵*S/20* ⊙ *Daily 9 AM–10 PM.*

⑥ **Museo Hilario Mendívil.** As San Blas's most famous son, the former home of 20th-century Peruvian religious artist Hilario Mendívil (1929–77),

FodorsChoice
★

makes a good stop if you have an interest in Cusqeñan art and iconography. Legend has it that Mendívil saw llamas parading in the Corpus Christi procession as a child and later infused this image into his religious art, depicting all his figures with long, llamalike necks. In the small gallery are the maguey-wood and rice-plaster sculptures of the Virgin with the elongated necks that were the artist's trademark. There's also a shop selling Mendívil style work. ✉*Plazoleta San Blas 634* ☎*084/232–231* 💵*Free* ⊙ *Mon.–Sat. 9–1 and 2–6.*

San Blas. For spectacular views over Cusco's terra-cotta rooftops head to San Blas, the traditional old Bohemian quarter of artists and artisans and one of the city's most picturesque districts. Recently restored, its whitewashed adobe homes with bright-blue doors shine anew. The area is fast becoming the trendiest part of Cusco, with many of the city's choicest restaurants and bars opening their doors here. The Cuesta de San Blas (San Blas Hill), one of the main entrances into the area, is sprinkled with galleries that sell paintings in the Cusqueña-school style of the 16th through 18th centuries. Many of the stone streets are built as stairs or slopes (not for cars) and have religious motifs carved into them.

SOUTH OF THE PLAZA DE ARMAS

① **Iglesia Santa Clara.** Austere from the outside, this incredible 1588 church takes the prize for most eccentric interior decoration. Thousands of mirrors cover the interior, competing with the gold-laminated altar for glittery prominence. Legend has it that the mirrors were placed inside in order to tempt locals into church. Built in old Inca style, using stone looted from Inca ruins, this is a great example of the lengths that the Spanish went to in order to attract indigenous converts to the Catholic faith. ✉*Santa Clara* ☎*No phone* 💵*Free* ⊙ *Daily 7–11:30 and 6–7:30.*

➐ Qorikancha. Built during the reign of the Inca Pachacutec to honor the
Fodor'sChoice Sun, Tawantinsuyos' most important divinity, Qorikancha translates as
★ "Court of Gold." All that remains today is the masterful stonework.
4,000 priests and attendants are thought to have lived within its confines. Walls and altars were plated with gold, and in the center of the
complex sat a giant gold disc, positioned to reflect the sun and bathe
the temple in light. Much of the wealth was removed to pay ransom
for the captive Inca ruler Atahualpa during the Spanish conquest, blood
money paid in vain since Atahualpa was later murdered.

An ingenious restoration to recover both buildings after the 1953
earthquake lets you see how the church was built on and around the
walls and chambers of the temple. In the Inca parts of the structure left
exposed, estimated to be about 40% of the original temple, you can
admire the mortarless masonry, earthquake-proof trapezoidal doorways, curved retaining wall, and exquisite carvings that exemplify the
artistic and engineering skills of the Inca. Bilingual guides lead tours
every day except Sunday; the service is included in your admission
price. ⊠*Pampa del Castillo at Plazoleta Santo Domingo* 🕾*No phone*
🕾*Ruins and church, S/10; museum, Boleto Turístico* ⊗*Ruins and
church, Mon.–Sat. 8:30–5:30, Sun. 2–5; museum, Mon.–Sat. 9–5:30,
Sun. 9–1.*

WHERE TO EAT

¢–$$ ✕**Fallen Angel.** Suppress your gasps as you walk in: images of heaven,
CONTINENTAL hell, earth, limbo, and purgatory, and everything in between greet you.
Fodor'sChoice This was one of Francisco Pizarro's houses, and it's doubtful that he
★ envisioned anything so avant-garde. You'll dine off bathtubs that dou-
ble as fish tanks, watched over all the while by baroque angels (not the
waiters!). The steak-driven menu, just like the decoration, is absolutely
fabulous darling. ⊠*Plazoleta Nazarenas 221* 🕾*084/258–184* 🖃*AE,
DC, MC, V* ⊗*No lunch Sun.*

$–$$ ✕**Cicciolina.** Everyone seems to know everyone and greet each other
MEDITERRANEAN with a peck on the cheek at this second-floor eatery, part lively tapas
Fodor'sChoice bar, part sit-down, candle-light restaurant. The bar wraps around the
★ kitchen area where a small army of cooks prepare your food. You'll
strain to see as they set out each new platter of tapas—perhaps some
bruschetta or prawns and sweet potato in wasabi sauce—and be
tempted to say, "I want one of those." The restaurant half of Cicciolina is much more subdued, with a complete selection of homemade
pastas with Mediterranean sauces on the menu. You can order off the
restaurant menu in the tapas bar, but not the other way around. ⊠*Sunturwasi 393, Triunfo* 🕾*084/239–510* 🖃*AE, DC, MC, V.*

$–$$ ✕**Incanto.** Stylish contemporary design in an Andean setting has made
MEDITERRANEAN this large upmarket restaurant near the Plaza a hit with those looking
for a classy night out. Dishing up Mediterranean-Andean fusion cuisine
as well as more traditional dishes such as delicious thin-crust pizza, this
has got to be the only place in the world where you'll find ravioli of *aji
de gallina,* a traditional creamy chicken sauce usually served with rice,
on the menu. Wander down the back to the open kitchen, and don't

forget to have a look at the original Inca wall on the way. ⊠*Catalina Angosta 135* ☎*084/254-753* ⊕*www.Cuscorestaurants.com* ▤*AE, DC, MC, V.*

$
PERUVIAN
✕**Don Esteban y Don Pancho.** Contemporary Andean cuisine is the flavor of this addition to Cusco's dining scene. Starched white tablecloths and impeccable service lend a polished air, although design touches such as a cobbled floor and natural fibers are reminders that you're in the Andes. The menu is as well-crafted as the service, with traditional Peruvian Criolle dishes. The carapulcra, dried potato with pork ribs, and the traditional bean dish tacu tacu are stand outs. Even if you don't eat, drop in for cocktails—the Chicha Tu May, which puts a twist on the pisco sour by adding a dash of ruby-red chicha, is a happiness inducer. ⊠*Portal Espinar 144, Plaza Regocigo* ☎*084/244–664* ⊕*www.donesteban ydonpancho.com* ▤*AE, DC, MC, V.*

$–$$$
PERUVIAN
Fodor'sChoice
★
✕**Pacha Papa.** If you've been putting off trying the famous Andean dishes of guinea pig or alpaca, then wait no longer. This fabulous restaurant is hands-down the best place in town for Peruvian food. Based on a typical open-air quinta, wooden tables are scattered around a large patio, warmed on those chilly Andean nights by the huge bread oven, which takes pride of place at the front, and an underground oven where one of the star dishes, pachamanca, is cooked then disinterred before your eyes. The menu takes influences from all over Peru and the waiters are happy to explain what makes each dish special. Try the delicious anticuchas de alpaca, skewers of tender alpaca meat with local spices, and don't miss the sensational adobo de chancho, a tangy pork stew with meat that melts in your mouth. The star dishes of cuy al horno, baked guinea-pig, or the underground-oven baked *pachamanca* stew where different types of meats are slow roasted together with potatoes and aromatic herbs (pacha is Quechua for ground, manca means pot) have to be ordered 24 hours in advance, so plan ahead. ⊠*Plazoleta San Blas 120* ☎*084/241–318* ▤*AE, DC, MC, V.*

WHERE TO STAY
Lodgings in Cusco keep shockingly early checkout times. (Flights to Cusco arrive early in the morning.) Expect to have to vacate your room by 8 or 9 AM, though this is less strictly enforced in the off-season. Most lodgings will hold your luggage if you're not leaving town until later in the day.

$$$
★
⌂**Casa Andina San Blas.** Taking its lead from the Spaniards, Casa Andina is slowly colonizing Cusco all over again with five branches now in various locales throughout the city. Part of a national chain, all of the Casa Andina hotels exude professionalism and are great value for money. Fortunately for them, this is where the resemblance ends, as each hotel differs in style. The San Blas branch, in a colonial house perched up on the hillside offers great views over the city's terra-cotta rooftops. The modern and comfortable rooms are tastefully furnished with Andean touches. **Pros:** Good value for top-end lodgings, excellent location with spectacular views over Cusco, professional atmosphere and pleasant service. **Cons:** Can be a hard walk uphill to get here, some

rooms have subpar views over the neighboring houses. ✉*Chihuampata 278* ☎*084/263–694* ⊕*www.casa-andina.com* ⇦*38 rooms* ⚹*In-room: safe. In-hotel: restaurant, bar, laundry service, no elevator, public Internet, public Wi-Fi, airport shuttle, no-smoking rooms* ▤*AE, DC, MC, V.*

$$ ★ **Casa San Blas.** This small hotel with a large staff—there's a 2-to-1 staff-to-guest ratio—prides itself on exceptional service. Regular rooms are quite comfortable, with colonial-style furniture and hardwood floors, but with more mod-

> ### CORN A HUNDRED WAYS
>
> Corn is the other staple of the Peruvian diet—wander the streets of Cusco long enough and you'll soon see it being popped, steamed, and roasted into a healthy carbo-snack. *Chicha,* a corn beer drunk at room temperature and sold from rural homes that display a red flag (and in many restaurants) is a surprisingly tasty take on the old corn cob.

ern amenities than this restored 250-year-old house would imply. The top-floor suites and one apartment are similar in style, but larger, with wood-beamed ceilings and great views over the city. The spacious apartment is a great option for those considering a longer stay, and has a fully equipped kitchen. All rooms are decorated with handmade textiles (each with a design reflecting the room's name), which can be purchased if you want a keepsake. The hotel sits a block off the Cuesta San Blas, the "staircase" street leading up from the Plaza de Armas, and could not be more central for sightseeing. **Pros:** Exceptionally warm welcome from the staff, the massage service is a great way to soothe away those sightseeing aches, fantastic location. **Cons:** Regular rooms are relatively pricey, it's a steep uphill walk to get here, the adjoining restaurant is extremely small (but cozy!). ✉*Tocuyeros 566, San Blas* ☎*084/237–900, 888/569–1769 toll-free in North America* ⊟*084/251–563* ⊕*www.casasanblas.com* ⇦*12 rooms, 4 suites, 1 apartment* ⚹*In-room: safe, Wi-Fi. In-hotel: restaurant, bar, no elevator, laundry service, public Internet, public Wi-Fi, airport shuttle, no smoking rooms* ▤*AE, DC, MC, V* ⎟○⎟*BP.*

$ **Hostal Rumi Punku.** A massive stone door—that's what Rumi Punku means in Quechua—opens onto a rambling complex of balconies, patios, gardens, courtyards, terraces, fireplace, and bits of Inca wall scattered here and there. It all links a series of pleasantly furnished rooms with hardwood floors and comfy beds covered with plush blankets. The top-level sauna and gym has stupendous views of the city. **Pros:** Great views from the upstairs sauna, good hot water 24 hours a day, charming rambling layout. **Cons:** Lots of stairs, no restaurant, located a huff and puff up the hill. ✉*Choquechaca 339* ☎*084/221–102* ⊟*084/242–741* ⊕*www.rumipunku.com* ⇦*20 rooms* ⚹*In-room: Wi-Fi. In-hotel: bar sauna, no elevator, laundry service, public Internet, public Wi-Fi* ▤*AE, DC, MC, V* ⎟○⎟*CP.*

$$$$ Fodor'sChoice ★ **Hotel Monasterio.** Indisputably Cusco's top hotel is this beautifully restored 1592 monastery of San Antonio Abad, a national historic monument. Planners managed to retain the austere beauty of the complex—the lodging even counts the original chapel with its ornate gold

8

altar and collection of Cusqueño art—yet updated the compact rooms with stylish colonial furnishings and all the mod-cons such as remote operated window blinds and TVs that pop out of cabinet tops. The public spaces such as the elegant lounge bar and serene cloisters will take your breath away. For those having trouble getting it back, the hotel even offers an in-room oxygen enrichment service. For S/100 per night you can elect to have your room pressurized with a flow of enriched oxygen, much like in an airplane cabin, duplicating conditions of those 1,000 meters (3,300 feet) lower than Cusco. **Pros:** Stylish rooms with all the conveniences, stunning public spaces, attentive service. **Cons:** Rooms are small for the price-tag, *everything* (including Internet access) is charged, the piped choral music can get annoying. ⊠*Palacio 136, Plazoleta Nazarenas* ☎*084/240–696, 01/242–3427 in Lima* ⊕*www.monasterio.orient-express.com* ⇔*120 rooms, 6 suites* ⚲*In-room: safe, refrigerator. In-hotel: 2 restaurants, bar, spa, concierge, laundry service, public Internet, public Wi-Fi* ⊟*AE, DC, MC, V* ⊺⃝*BP.*

¢ ⊡ **Niños Hotel.** If you prefer lodging with a social conscience—and even
★ if you don't—this is a great budget find; proceeds from your stay at the "Children's Hotel" provide medical and dental care, food, and recreation for 250 disadvantaged Cusqueño children who attend day care on the premises and cheerfully greet you as you pass through the courtyard. Rooms tend toward the spartan side, with painted hardwood floors but firm, comfy mattresses and an endless supply of hot water. A few other rooms as well as four apartments with shared bath, for longer stays, are down the street on Calle Fiero. The catch? The place is immensely popular. Make reservations weeks in advance. **Pros:** Wonderfully welcoming staff, charming colonial building, you can sleep soundly with the knowledge that your money is going to a good cause! **Cons:** Slightly out of the way, some rooms are small. ⊠*Meloq 442* ☎☎*084/231–424* ⊕*www.ninoshotel.com* ⇔*20 rooms, 13 with bath* ⚲*In-room: no phone, no TV. In-hotel: no elevator, laundry service, no-smoking rooms* ⊟*No credit cards.*

SHOPPING

Maqui Arte (⊠*Sunturwasi [Triunfo] 118* ☎*084/246–493*) has high-quality alpaca products, including sweaters, jackets, and even colorful alpaca shoes.

Alpaca gets the camelid's share of attention for use in making fine garments, but **La Casa de la Llama** (⊠*Palacio 121* ☎*084/240–813*) sells a fine selection of expensive clothing made from the softer hairs sheared from its namesake animal's chest and neck. It's difficult to tell the difference in texture between llama and adult alpaca, at least in this shop.

Several artisan markets and cooperatives populate the city. The **Center for Traditional Textiles of Cusco** (⊠*Av. El Sol 603* ☎*084/228–117*) is a nonprofit organization dedicated to the survival of traditional textile weaving. Weavers from local villages work in the shop, and the on-site museum has informative exhibits about weaving techniques and the customs behind traditional costume. Sweaters, ponchos, scarves, and wall hangings are sold at fair-trade prices.

SIDE TRIPS FROM CUSCO

These sights are easy to visit by car during a day trip from Cusco; you'll find only very rugged lodging if you choose to stay.

SACSAYHUAMÁN

2 km (1 mi) north of Cusco.

Fodor's Choice
★
Towering high above Cusco, the ruins of Sacsayhuamán are a constant reminder of the city's Inca roots.

Construction of the site began in the 1440s, during the reign of the Inca Pachacutec. It's thought that 20,000 workers were needed for Sacsayhuamán's construction, cutting the astonishingly massive limestone, diorite, and andesite blocks—the largest is 361 tons—rolling them to the site, and assembling them in traditional Inca style to achieve a perfect fit without mortar. The probable translation of Sacsayhuamán, "city of stone," seems apt. The Inca Manco Capac II, installed as puppet ruler after the conquest, retook the fortress and led a mutiny against Juan Pizarro and the Spanish in 1536. Fighting raged for 10 months in a valiant but unsuccessful bid by the Inca to reclaim their empire.

Today only one-fifth of the original complex is left; nonetheless, the site is impressive. Sacsayhuamán's three original towers, used for provisions, no longer stand, though the foundations of two are still visible. The so-called Inca's Throne, the Suchuna, remains, presumed used by the emperor for reviewing troops. Today those parade grounds, the Explanada, are the ending point for the June 24 Inti Raymi festival of the sun, commemorating the winter solstice and Cusco's most famous celebration.

If you don't have a car, take a taxi, or if you want to test yourself, the ruins are a steep 25-minute walk up from the Plaza de Armas. A large map at both entrances shows the layout of Sacsayhuamán, but once you enter, signage and explanations are minimal. Self-appointed guides populate the entrances and can give you a two-hour tour for S/30. Most are competent and knowledgeable, but depending on their perspective you'll get a strictly historic, strictly mystical, strictly architectural, or all-of-the-above type tour. (But all work the standard joke into their spiel that the name of the site is pronounced "sexy woman.") ⊠*Km 2, Hwy. to Pisac* ☎*No phone* ⊠*Boleto Turístico* ⊗*Daily 7–6.*

TIPÓN

26 km (15½ mi) southeast of Cusco.

Everyone has heard that the Incas were good engineers, but for a real look at just how good they were at land and water management, head to Tipón. Twenty kilometers or so south of Cusco, Tipón is a series of terraces, hidden from the valley below, crisscrossed by stone aqueducts and carved irrigation channels that edge up a narrow pass in the mountains. A spring fed the site and continually replenished a 900-cubic-meter reservoir that supplied water to crops growing on the terraces. So superb was the technology that several of the terraces are still in use today, and still supplied by the same watering system developed

8

centuries ago. The ruins of a stone temple of undetermined function guard the system, and higher up the mountain are terraces yet to be completely excavated. Unfortunately, the rough dirt track that leads to the complex is in wretched condition. If you visit, either walk up (about two hours each way) or go in a four-wheel-drive vehicle (about 45 minutes to the site and 30 minutes back). ⊠ *4 km (2½ mi) north of Km 23, Hwy. to Urcos* ☎ *No phone* 🎫 *Boleto Turístico* ⊗ *Daily 7–6.*

PIKILLACTA
6 km (3½ mi) east of Tipón, 7 km (4 mi) south of Oropesa.

For a reminder that civilizations existed in this region before the Incas, head to Pikillacta, a vast city of 700 buildings from the pre-Inca Wari culture, which flourished between AD 600 and 1000. Over a 2 km site you'll see what remains of what was once a vast walled city with enclosing walls reaching up to 7 meters (23 feet) in height and many two-story buildings, which were entered via ladders to doorways on the second floor. Little is known about the Wari culture, although the empire once stretched from near Cajamarca to the border of the Tiahuanaco empire based around Lake Titicaca. It's clear, however, that they had a genius for farming in a harsh environment and like the Incas built sophisticated urban centers such as Pikillacta (which means the "place of the flea"). At the thatch-roofed excavation sites, uncovered walls show the city's stones were once covered with plaster and whitewashed. Across the road lies a beautiful lagoon, Lago de Lucre. ⊠ *Km 32, Hwy. to Urcos* ☎ *No phone* 🎫 *Boleto Turístico* ⊗ *Daily 7–6.*

A pleasant climate, fertile soil, and proximity to Cusco made the Urubamba River valley a favorite with Inca nobles, many of whom are believed to have had private country homes here. Inca remains, ruins, and agricultural terraces lie throughout the length of this so-called Sacred Valley of the Inca. Cusco is hardly the proverbial urban jungle, but in comparison the Sacred Valley is positively captivating with its lower elevation, fresher air, warmer temperatures, and rural charm. You may find yourself joining the growing ranks of visitors who base themselves out here and make Cusco their day trip, rather than the other way around.

GETTING AROUND
Highways are good—the main east-west road crossing the valley is potholed between Pisac and Urubamba, but in better shape beyond Urubamba to Ollantaytambo—and traffic is relatively light in the Sacred Valley, but any trip entails a series of twisting, turning roads as you head out of the mountains near Cusco and descend into the valley. ■ TIP → The road to Machu Picchu ends in Ollantaytambo; beyond that point, it's rail only.

PISAC
9 km (5 mi) north of Taray.

The colorful colonial town of Pisac, replete with Quechua-language masses in a simple stone church, a well-known market, and fortress ruins, comes into view as you wind your way down the highway from Cusco. Pisac, home to about 4,000 people, anchors the eastern end of the Sacred Valley. The level of congestion (and fun) increases dramatically each Tuesday, Thursday, and especially Sunday with one of Peru's most celebrated markets, but more spectacular are the ruins above.

EXPLORING PISAC

Pisac Market. Each Tuesday, Thursday, and Sunday, fruits, vegetables, and grains share the stage with ceramics, jewelry, and woolens on the central plaza and spill over into the side streets. Sellers set up shop

BOLETO TURÍSTICO

Three Sacred Valley sites (the ruins at Pisac, Chinchero, and Ollantaytambo) fall under Cusco's Boleto Turístico scheme (*See Buying a Boleto Turístico at the start of this chapter.*) The ticket's 10-day validity lets you take in these three attractions as well, and is the only way to gain admission. An abbreviated S/40 ticket, valid for two days, gains you admission to the three sites in the valley.

about 8 am on market days and start packing up at about 3 PM. The market is not so different from many others you'll see around Peru, only larger. Go on Sunday if your schedule permits; you'll have a chance to take in the 11 am Quechua Mass at the Iglesia San Pedro Apóstolo and watch the elaborate costumed procession led by the mayor, who carries his varayoc, a ceremonial staff, out of the church afterward. Sunday afternoon sees bands and beer tents—this is small-town Peru at its best. ☉ *Sun., Tues., and Thurs. 8–3 or 4.*

Pisac Ruins. From the market area, drive or take a taxi S/10–S/15 one-way up the winding road to the Inca ruins of Pisac. Archaeologists originally thought the ruins were a fortress to defend against fierce Antis (jungle peoples), though there's little evidence that battles were fought here. Now it seems that Pisac was a bit of everything: citadel, religious site, observatory, and residence, and may have served as a refuge in times of siege. The complex also has a temple to the sun and an astronomical observatory, from which priests calculated the growing season each year. Narrow trails wind tortuously between and through solid rock. You may find yourself practically alone on the series of paths in the mountains that lead you among the ruins, through caves, and past the largest known Inca cemetery (the Inca buried their dead in tombs high on the cliffs). Just as spectacular as the site are the views from it. 🎫*Boleto Turístico* ☉*Daily 7–6.*

WHERE TO STAY & EAT

¢ ✕**Samana Wasi.** The Quechua name of this basic restaurant on the central square translates as "house of rest," and the owner claims that this
PERUVIAN is Peruvian cuisine, fresh and made-to-order. It doesn't get any fresher than the trout caught in the nearby Urubamba River. These folks also dish up a spicy *cazuela de gallina* (chicken stew). If it's a nice day, grab one of the tables on the shady interior courtyard. ⊠*Plaza Constitución 509* ☎*084/203–018* ▭*No credit cards.*

$$ ▦**Hotel Royal Inka Pisac.** Just outside of town is the newest branch of Peru's Royal Inka hotel chain, and the closest lodging to the Pisac ruins.

Bright carpeted rooms congregate around acres of wooded and flowered grounds, and have print spreads and drapes and white walls. All third-level rooms have a fireplace. With all the activities and facilities here, a rarity in the Sacred Valley, you really never have to leave the grounds. **Pros:** Lots of activities. **Cons:** Outside of town. ⊠*Km 1½, Carretera a Pisac Ruinas* ☎*084/203–064, 800/664–1819 in North America* ☎*084/203–065* ⊕*www.royalinkahotel.com* ☞*80 rooms* ♤*In-room: no a/c, safe. In-hotel: 2 restaurants, room service, bar, tennis court, pool, bicycles, no elevator, no-smoking rooms* ⊺⊘*BP.*

OLLANTAYTAMBO
19 km (11 mi) west of Urubamba.

Ollantaytambo makes a superb base for exploring the Sacred Valley and has convenient rail connections to Machu Picchu. It's also the kick-off point for the Inca Trail. You'll start here at nearby Km 82 if you wish to hike to the Lost City. Walk up for to discover the **fortress of Ollantaytambo,** one of the most fantastic ruins in the Sacred Valley.

EXPLORING OLLANTAYTAMBO
Fortress of Ollantaytambo. Walk above the town to a formidable stone structure where massive terraces climb to the peak. It was the valley's main defense against the Antis from the neighboring rain forests. Construction began during the reign of Pachacutec but was never completed. The rose-color granite used was not mined in this part of the valley. The elaborate walled complex contained a temple to the sun, used for astronomical observation, as well as the Baños de la Ñusta (ceremonial princess baths), leading archaeologists to believe that Ollantaytambo existed for more than defensive purposes. The fortress was the site of the greatest Inca victory over the Spanish during the wars of conquest. The Manco Inca fled here in 1537 with a contingent of troops after the disastrous loss at Sacsayhuamán and routed Spanish forces under Hernando Pizarro. The victory was short-lived: Pizarro regrouped and took the fortress. ⊠ *Plaza Mañay Raquy A Boleto Turístico* ☉ *Daily 7–6.*

Ollantaytambo Heritage Trail. This self-guided trail allows you to tour the original layout of the town, following a series of blue plaques that outline important sites. Attribute the town's distinctive appearance to Inca organization. They based their communities on the unit of the cancha, a walled city block, each with one entrance leading to an interior courtyard, surrounded by a collection of houses. The system is most obvious in the center of town around the main plaza. You'll find the most welcoming of these self-contained communities at Calle del Medio.

WHERE TO STAY & EAT
$ ▥ **Albergue Ollantaytambo.** Everyone in town knows the Albergue, right at the train station, owned by exuberant longtime American resident and artist Wendy Weeks. Dark-wood rooms here are spacious but rustic, with historic black-and-white photos from the region. The lodging has homey touches like a wood-fired sauna, huge breakfasts, and a cozy sitting room. Reserve in advance: the place is popular with groups about to embark on, or just returning from, the nearby Inca Trail. **Pros:**

Convenience to rail station, relaxing sauna. **Cons:** It's no secret. ⊠*Estación de Ferrocarril* ☎☎*084/204–014* ⊕*www.elalbergue.com* ⇄*12 rooms* ⟳*In-room: no a/c, no TV. In-hotel: restaurant, room service, bar, bicycles, no elevator, laundry facilities* ⊟*V* ⍓*BP.*

$$ 🔲 **Hotel Pakaritampu.** Ollantaytambo's best lodging has a Quechua name

Fodor's Choice that translates as "house of dawn." Fireplaces, and reading rooms with

★ Cusqueño art, invite you to settle in with a good book and a hot cup of coffee on a chilly evening. Rooms, with modern furnishings, plush blue comforters, and green-tile bathrooms, extend through two buildings. The on-grounds orchard supplies the fruit that ends up on your breakfast plate, and in the Peruvian cuisine served in the restaurant. **Pros:** Tranquil setting, good restaurant. **Cons:** Not for the party types. ⊠*Av. Ferrocarril s/n* ☎*084/204–020, 01/242–6278 in Lima* ☎*084/204–105* ⊕*www.pakaritampu.com* ⇄*32 rooms, 1 suite* ⟳*In-room: no a/c, no TV. In-hotel: restaurant, bar, no elevator, laundry service, public Internet* ⊟*AE, V* ⍓*BP.*

MACHU PICCHU & THE INCA TRAIL

The exquisite architecture of the massive Inca stone structures, the formidable backdrop of steep sugarloaf hills, and the Urubamba river winding far below have made Machu Picchu the iconic symbol of Peru. It's a mystical city, the most famous archaeological site in South America, and one of the world's must-see destinations.

The world did not become aware of Machu Picchu's existence until 1911 when Yale university historian Hiram Bingham (1875–1956) announced that he had "discovered" the site. "Rediscovery" is a more accurate term; area residents knew of Machu Picchu's existence all along. This "lost city of the Inca" was missed by the ravaging conquistadors and survived untouched until the beginning of the 20th century.

Ever since Bingham came across Machu Picchu, its history has been debated. It was likely a small city of some 200 homes and 1,000 residents, with agricultural terraces to supply the population's needs and a strategic position that overlooked—but could not be seen from—the valley floor.

WHEN TO GO

All the high-season/low-season trade-offs are here. Winter (June through August) means drier weather and easier traveling, but it's prime vacation time for those in the northern hemisphere. Don't forget that three major observances—Inti Raymi (June 24), Peru's Independence Day (July 28), and Santa Rosa de Lima (August 30)—fall during this time, and translate into exceptionally heavy crowds of Peruvian travelers. For near-ideal weather and manageable crowds, consider a spring or fall trip.

In January and February the weather could wreak havoc with your travel plans. But it's also the time when you can enjoy Machu Picchu without the crowds.

8

GETTING AROUND

Travel to Machu Picchu is so efficient that it's almost too easy. The most common method is to hop on the PeruRail from Cusco to Aguas Calientes or you can do as the Incas did and walk the path, which is a four-day jaunt and highlight for those who do it. ■TIP→You cannot drive here.

EXPLORING MACHU PICCHU

If you arrive without an admission ticket, you must purchase one in Aguas Calientes at the Instituto Nacional de Cultura (⊠ *Avenida Pachacutec s/n,* ☉ *open daily 5 am–10 pm*) just off the Plaza de Armas. There is no ticket booth at the ruins' entrance.P *084/211–067, 084/211–256 in Aguas Calientes S/120, S/60 with international student identity card. Daily 6* AM*–5:30* PM.

A snack bar is a few feet from where the buses deposit you at the gate to the ruins, and the Machu Picchu sanctuary lodge, the only hotel up here, has a s/100 lunch buffet open to the public. Bathrooms cost s/1, and toilet paper is provided. There are no bathrooms inside the ruins.

It gets warm, and the ruins have little shade. Sunscreen, a hat, and water are musts. Officially, no food or drinks are permitted, but you can get away with a bottle of water. Large packs must be left at the entrance.

CATCHING THE BUS

If you're a day-tripper, follow the crowd out of the rail station about two blocks to the Consettur Machu Picchu shuttle buses, which ferry you up a series of switchbacks to the ruins, a journey of 20 minutes. Buy your s/40 round-trip ticket at a booth next to the line of buses before boarding.

Buses leave Aguas Calientes for the ruins beginning at 6:30 AM and continue more or less hourly, with a big push in mid-morning as the trains arrive. The last bus up leaves about 1 PM. Buses start coming back down about 11:30 AM, with a last departure at 5:40. If you're heading back to Cusco, take the bus back down at least an hour before your train departs.

SIGHTS

Everyone must go through the main entrance to have their ticket stamped. From there you work your way up through the agricultural areas and to the urban sectors. There are almost no signs inside to explain what you're seeing; booklets and maps are for sale at the entrance.

The English-language names to the structures within the city were assigned by Bingham. Call it inertia, but those labels have stuck, even though the late yale historian's nomenclature was mostly offbase.

The Guardhouse is the first structure you encounter after coming through the main entrance. The Inca carved terraces into the hillsides to grow produce and minimize erosion. Corn was the likely crop cultivated.

CLOSE UP

Train to Machu Picchu

At least two PeruRail trains depart from Cusco's San Pedro station daily for Aguas Calientes, near Machu Picchu. The Vistadome leaves at 6 AM and arrives in Aguas Calientes at 9:40. It returns from Aguas Calientes at 3:30 PM, arriving in Cusco at 7:25. A second Vistadome service departs at 6:15 AM. The round-trip fare is S/429. Snacks and beverages are included in the price, and the cars have sky domes for great views. The return trip includes a fashion show and folklore dancing.

The Backpacker train leaves Cusco at 7 AM, arriving in Aguas Calientes at 10:40. It leaves Aguas Calientes at 5 PM, getting back to Cusco at 9:25. The round-trip fare is S/290. Conditions are comparable to second-class trains in Western Europe and are quite comfortable.

Trains stop at Poroy, Ollantaytambo, Km 88 (the start of the Inca Trail), and Km 104 (the launch point of an abbreviated two-day Inca Trail). Arrival is in Aguas Calientes, where you catch the buses up to the ruins.

Purchase tickets in advance from the PeruRail sales office at Cusco's Wanchaq Station, weekdays from 7 to 5, and weekends and Peruvian holidays from 7–noon—note that PeruRail does not accept credit cards—or from a travel agency. (Most tour packages include rail tickets as well as bus transport to and from Aguas Calientes and Machu Picchu and admission to the ruins, and lodging if you plan to stay overnight.)

PeruRail's luxury Hiram Bingham train departs from Poroy station, about 15 minutes outside Cusco, eliminating the tedious switchbacks necessary for the other trains to get out of and into the city. Departure time is a more leisurely 9 AM daily except Sunday, arriving at Aguas Calientes at 12:30 PM. Return service leaves Aguas Calientes at 6:30 PM, returning to Poroy at 10. The S/1,775 round-trip price tag includes brunch on the trip to Machu Picchu, bus transport from Aguas Calientes up to the ruins and back, admission to the ruins, guide services while there, and an afternoon buffet tea at the Machu Picchu Sanctuary Lodge. The trip back entails cocktails, live entertainment, and a four-course dinner.

If you're staying in the Sacred Valley, PeruRail operates a daily Vistadome train departing from Ollantaytambo at 7 AM, with arrival in Machu Picchu at 8:20. Other trains leave Ollantaytambo at 10:30 AM and 2:55 PM, arriving at Aguas Calientes about 75 minutes later. Return trains leave Aguas Calientes at 8:35 AM and 1:20 and 4:45 PM. Round-trip fare is S/362. A daily Backpacker train departs Ollantaytambo at 9:05 AM, arriving at Aguas Calientes at 11. Return from Aguas Calientes is at 4:20 PM, with arrival in Ollantaytambo at 6. Round-trip fare is S/260.

PeruRail's service is generally punctual. Schedules and rates are always subject to change, and there may be fewer trains per day to choose from during the December to March low season.

INFORMATION

Asociación de Agencias de Turismo de Cusco (⊠ *Nueva Baja 424, Cusco* ☎ *084/222–580*). **PeruRail** (⊠ *San Pedro station, Cascapara near Santa Clara, Cusco* ☎ *084/233–551* ⊕ *www.perurail.com* ✉ *Wanchaq station, Pachacutec near Tullumayo, Cusco* ☎ *084/238–722* ⊕ *www.perurail.com*).

8

The House of the Terrace Caretaker and Funeral Rock are a 20-minute walk up to the left of the entrance, and provide the quintessential Machu Picchu vista. Nothing beats the view in person, especially with a misty sunrise. Bodies of nobles likely lay in state here, where they would have been eviscerated, dried, and prepared for mummification.

The Temple of the Sun is a marvel of perfect Inca stone assembly. On June 22 (winter solstice in the southern hemisphere), sunlight shines through a small, trapezoid-shape window and onto the middle of a large, flat granite stone presumed to be an Inca calendar. Looking out the window, astronomers saw the constellation Pleiades, revered as a symbol of crop fertility. Bingham dubbed the small cave below the royal tomb, though no human remains were found here.

Fountains. A series of 16 small fountains are linked to the Inca worship of water.

Palace of the Princess, a likely misnomer, is a two-story building that adjoins the temple.

The Principal Temple is so dubbed because its masonry is among Machu Picchu's best. The three-walled structure is a masterpiece of mortarless stone construction.

Sacristy. At this secondary temple next to the primary temple, priests may have prepared themselves for ceremonies.

Temple of the Three Windows. A stone staircase leads to the three-walled structure. The entire east wall is hewn from a single rock with trapezoidal windows cut into it.

Intihuatana. A hillock leads to the "hitching post of the sun." Every important Inca center had one of these vertical stone columns (called gnomons), but their function is unknown. The Spanish destroyed most of them, seeing the posts as objects of pagan worship. Machu Picchu's is one of the few to survive—partially at least. Its top was accidentally knocked off in 2001 during the filming of a Cusqueña beer commercial.

The Sacred Rock takes the shape in miniature of the mountain range visible behind it.

Temple of the Condor is so named because the positioning of the stones resembles a giant condor, the symbol of heaven in the Inca cosmos. The structure's many small chambers led Bingham to dub it a "prison," a concept that did not likely exist in Inca society.

HIKES FROM MACHU PICCHU

If you come by train, you can take a 45-minute walk on a gentle arc leading uphill to the southeast of the main complex. **Intipunku,** the sun gate, is a small ruin in a nearby pass. This small ancient checkpoint is where you'll find that classic view that Inca Trail hikers emerge upon. The walk along the way yields some interesting and slightly different angles as well. Some minor ancient outbuildings along the path occasionally host grazing llamas. A two- or three-hour hike beyond the

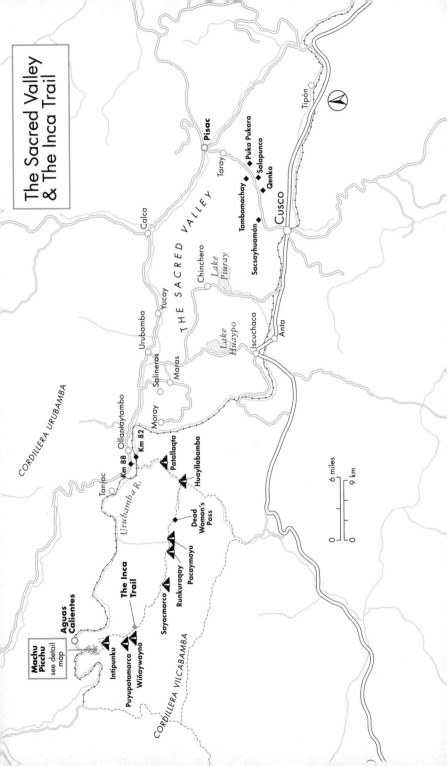

The Sacred Valley
& The Inca Trail

CORDILLERA URUBAMBA

Urubamba R.

Taniac

Km 88

Ollantaytambo

Km 82

Moray

Patallaqta

Huayllabamba

Dead Woman's Pass

Pacaymayu

Runkuraqay

Sayacmarca

The Inca Trail

Intipunku

Puyupatamarca

Wiñaywayna

Machu Picchu
see detail map

Aguas Calientes

CORDILLERA VILCABAMBA

Salineras

Maras

Urubamba

Yucay

Chinchero

Lake Piuray

Lake Huaypo

Iscuchaca

Anta

Calca

THE SACRED VALLEY

Pisac

Taray

Tambomachay

Puka Pukara

Salapunco

Qenko

Sacsayhuamán

CUSCO

Tipón

6 miles

9 km

0

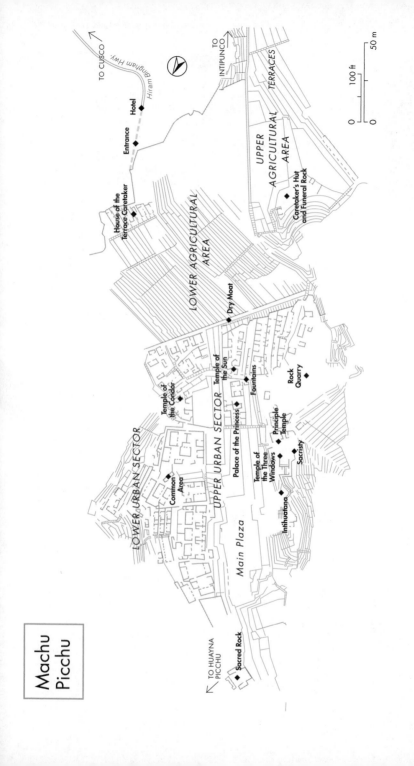

Machu Picchu

TO CUSCO

Hiram Bingham Hwy.

Hotel

Entrance

House of the Terrace Caretaker

TO INTIPUNCO

UPPER AGRICULTURAL TERRACES

LOWER AGRICULTURAL AREA

UPPER AGRICULTURAL AREA

Caretaker's Hut and Funeral Rock

Dry Moat

Temple of the Condor

Temple of the Sun

Rock Quarry

Fountains

Palace of the Princess

Principle Temple

LOWER URBAN SECTOR

UPPER URBAN SECTOR

Common Area

Temple of the Three Windows

Sacristy

Intihuatana

Main Plaza

TO HUAYNA PICCHU

Sacred Rock

0   100 ft
0   50 m

Intipunku along the Inca Trail brings you to the ruins of **Huiñay Huayna**, a terrace complex that climbs a steep mountain slope and includes a set of ritual baths.

Built rock by rock up a hair-raising stone escarpment, the **Inca Bridge** is yet another example of Inca engineering ingenuity. From the cemetery at Machu Picchu, it's a 30-minute walk along a narrow path.

The **Huayna Picchu** trail, which follows an ancient Inca path, leads up the sugarloaf hill in front of Machu Picchu for an exhilarating trek. Climbers must register at the entrance to the path behind la Roca Sagrada (Sacred Rock). Limited to 400 visitors daily, no one is permitted entry after 1 PM—the limit is reached long before 1 PM in the high season—and all must be out by 4 PM. The walk up and back takes at least two hours and is only for the sure-footed. Bring insect repellent; the gnats can be ferocious. An alternate route back down takes you to the temple of the moon. The map at the entrance to the Huayna Picchu trail designates it as the Great Cave.

INCA TRAIL

The Inca Trail (camino Inca in Spanish), a 50-km (31-mi) sector of the stone path that once extended from Cusco to Machu Picchu, is one of the world's signature outdoor excursions. Nothing matches the sensation of walking over the ridge that leads to the lost city of the Inca just as the sun casts its first yellow glow over the ancient stone buildings.

There are limits on the number of trail users, but you'll still see a lot of fellow trekkers along the way. The four-day trek takes you past ruins and through stunning scenery, starting in the thin air of the highlands and ending in cloud forests. The orchids, hummingbirds, Andean condors, and spectacular mountains aren't bad either.

You must go with a guide. You must use a licensed tour operator, one accredited by the Unidad de Gestión Santuario Histórico de Machu Picchu, the organization that oversees the trail and limits the number of hikers to 400 per day, including guides and porters. There are some 30 such licensed operators in Cusco.

WHEN TO GO

May through September is the best time to make the four-day trek; rain is more likely in April and October and a certainty the rest of the year. The trail fills up during the dry high season. Make reservations months in advance if you want to hike then—weeks in advance the rest of the year. The trek is doable during the rainy season, but can become slippery and muddy by December. The trail closes for maintenance each February.

GETTING READY

Tour operators in Cusco will tell you the Inca Trail is of "moderate" difficulty, but it can be rough going, especially the first couple of days. You must be in decent shape, even if your agency supplies porters to carry your pack—current regulations limit your load to 20 kg (44 lb). The trail is often narrow and hair-raising.

As the mountains sometimes rise to over 13,775 feet, be wary of altitude sickness. (give yourself two or three days in Cusco or the sacred valley to acclimatize.)

Your gear should include sturdy hiking boots, a sleeping bag (some outfitters rent them); clothing for cold, rainy weather, a hat, and a towel. Also bring plenty of sunblock and mosquito repellent. Toilet paper is essential.

AGUAS CALIENTES

But for the grace of Hiram Bingham, Aguas Calientes would be just another remote, forgotten crossroads. There are but two major streets—Avenida Pachacutec leads uphill from the Plaza de Armas, and Avenida Imperio de los Incas isn't a street at all, but the railroad tracks; there's no vehicular traffic on the former except the buses that ferry tourists to the ruins. You'll have little sense of Aguas Calientes if you do the standard day trip from Cusco. But the town pulses to a very lively tourist beat with hotels, restaurants, Internet cafés, hot springs, and a surprising amount of activity even after the last afternoon train has returned to Cusco.

ESSENTIALS

Currency Exchange Banco de Crédito (⊠ *Av. Imperio de los Incas s/n* ☎ *084/211–342*).

Internet Cafés Inkanet (⊠ *Av. Imperio de los Incas s/n* ☎ *084/211–077*).

Mail SERPOST (⊠ *Av. Pachacutec 20*).

WHERE TO EAT

$–$$
FRENCH
Fodor'sChoice
★
✕ **Indio Feliz.** An engaging French-Peruvian couple manage the best restaurant in Aguas Calientes, and this pink bistro is possibly the only restaurant in town *not* to have pizza on its menu. Quiche lorraine, ginger chicken, and spicy *trucha macho* (trout in hot pepper and wine sauce) are favorites here, and are usually part of the more reasonably priced (S/40) prix-fixe menu, all to the accompaniment of homemade bread. Top it off with a fine coffee and apple pie or flan for dessert. The restaurant presents each diner with a tiny ceramic pot or bowl as its calling card. ⊠ *Lloque Yupanqui 4* ☎ *084/211–090* ☐ *AE, MC, V* ☉ *No dinner Sun.*

¢–$
ARGENTINE
✕ **Pueblo Viejo.** Lively conversation fills this restaurant just off the Plaza de Armas. Everyone gathers around the grill where cuts of beef, lamb and trout are prepared Argentine parrillada style, with rice, vegetables, and fries. Off to the side is the requisite clay oven where pizzas are baked, yet this is one of the few places that does not trumpet the pizza on its menu. ⊠ *Pachacutec s/n* ☎ *084/211–193* ☐ *AE, DC, MC, V* ☉ *No lunch Sun.*

INCA TRAIL DAY BY DAY

The majority of agencies begin the Inca Trail trek at **km 82** after a two- to three-hour bus ride from Cusco.

Day 1. Compared to what lies ahead, the first day's hike is a reasonably easy 12 km (7½ mi). You'll encounter fantastic ruins almost immediately. An easy ascent takes you to the first of those, **Patallaqta** (also called llactapata). The name means "town on a hillside" in quechua, and the ruins are thought to have been a village in Inca times. Bingham and company camped here on their first excursion to Machu Picchu. As at most Inca sites, you'll see three levels of architecture representing the three spiritual worlds of the inca— the world above (a guard tower), the world we live in (the main complex), and the world below (the river and hidden aqueducts).

At the end of the day, you arrive at **Huayllabamba** (also called as wayllamba), the only inhabited village on the trail and your first overnight

Day 2. It's another 12-km (7½-mi) hike, but with a gain of 1,200 meters (3,940 feet) in elevation. The day is most memorable for the spectacular views and muscular aches after ascending **Dead Woman's Pass** (also known as warmiwañuscca) at 4,200 meters (13,780 feet). The pass is named for the silhouette created by its mountain ridges—they resemble a woman's head, nose, chin, and chest.

A tricky descent takes you to **Pacaymayu,** the second night's campsite, and you can pat yourself on the back for completing the hardest section of the Inca Trail.

Day 3. Downhill! You descend to the subtropical cloud forest where the

amazon basin begins. There's some of the most stunning mountain scenery you'll see during the four days. The ruins of **Runkuraqay** were a circular Inca storage depot for products transported between Machu Picchu and Cusco.

You also pass by **Sayacmarca**, possibly a way station for priests traversing the trail.

Most excursions arrive by mid-afternoon at **Huiñay Huayna** (also known as wiñaywayna), the third-night's stopping point, at what may now seem a low and balmy 2,712 meters (8,900 feet). The first possibility of a hot shower and a cold beer are here.

There is time to see the ruins of **Puyupatamarca** (also known as phuyupatamarca) a beautifully restored site with ceremonial baths, and perhaps the best ruins on the hike. At this point you catch your first glimpse of Machu Picchu peak, but from the back side.

Day 4. This is it. Day 4 means the grand finale, arrival at **Machu Picchu**, the reason for the trail in the first place. You'll be roused from your sleeping bag well before dawn to arrive at the ruins in time to catch the sunrise. You'll be amazed at the number of fellow travelers who forget about their aching muscles and sprint this last stretch.

The trail takes you past the **Intipunku,** the sun gate. Bask in your first sight of the ruins and your accomplishment, but you'll need to circle around and enter Machu Picchu officially through the entrance gate.

8

WHERE TO STAY

$ **Hotel Presidente.** Orange, and open, the Presidente is the best moderately priced hotel in Aguas Calientes. Carpeted rooms have modern furnishings, and about half have big windows and balconies that overlook the Río Vilcanota. These folks also manage three hostales (small hotels)—the Continental, the Machupicchu, and the Plaza—with simpler furnishings nearby. **Pros:** Good value, some good views. Cons: Nothing fancy. ⊠ *Av. Imperio de los Incas s/n, Aguas Calientes* ☎ *084/211–034* 🖶 *084/229–591* ✉ *sierraandina@gmail.com* ⇌ *28 rooms* ⅏ *In-room: no a/c, no TV (some). In-hotel: restaurant, no elevator, laundry service* 🖃 *No credit cards* ❙�◎❙ *BP.*

$$$$

Fodor'sChoice

★

Inkaterra Machu Picchu . A five-minute walk from the center of town takes you to this stunning ecolodge in its own minitropical cloud forest. The stone bungalows, none with the same design, have a rustic elegance, with exposed beams and cathedral ceilings. Activities include a one-day Inca Trail trek, bird-watching excursions, and orchid tours, as well as a twilight nature walk. The restaurant overlooking the surrounding hills is first-rate—try the delicious *crema de choclo* (corn chowder). The place was renamed in 2007, but everyone still refers to it as the Machu Picchu Pueblo Hotel. **Pros:** Natural setting, many activities. **Cons:** Expensive. ⊠ *Av. Imperio de los Incas s/n, Aguas Calientes* ☎ *084/211–032, 01/610–0404 in Lima, 800/442–5042 in North America* 🖶 *084/211–124, 01/422–4701 in Lima* ⊕ *www.inkaterra. com* ⇌ *83 rooms, 2 suites* ⅏ *In-room: no a/c, no TV. In-hotel: 2 restaurants, room service, bar, pool, spa, laundry service, public Internet* 🖃 *AE, DC, MC, V* ❙◎❙ *MAP.*

$$$$ **Machu Picchu Sanctuary Lodge.** This hotel at the entrance to Machu Picchu puts you closest to the ruins, a position for which you pay dearly. But not only will you have the thrill of watching the sun rise over the crumbling stone walls, you'll be the first ones through the ruins' gate in the morning, and have the place to yourself after most of the tourists depart each afternoon. The lodge has been completely renovated by Orient Express, which has taken over the property. The restaurant has an excellent international menu that makes it worth a special trip, and serves a popular S/100 buffet lunch open to the public. **Pros:** Prime location at ruins' entrance. **Cons:** Expensive. ⊠ *Machu Picchu* ☎ *084/211–094, 01/610–8300 in Lima, 800/237–1236 in North America* 🖶 *084/211–246* ⊕ *www.machupicchu.orient-express.com* ⇌ *29 rooms, 2 suites* ⅏ *In-room: no a/c, no phone, safe, refrigerator, VCR. In-hotel: 3 restaurants, room service, bar, no elevator, laundry service, no-smoking rooms* 🖃 *AE, DC, MC, V* ❙◎❙ *FAP.*

¢ **Plaza Hostal.** The small Plaza faces the river on the road heading out of town up to the ruins. Rooms are simply furnished. Opt for one with its own small balcony. An ample breakfast is included in the rates and served at the Hotel Presidente around the corner. **Pros:** Good location and price. **Cons:** Some rooms better than others. ⊠ *Carretera a Machu Picchu* ☎ *084/211–192* 🖶 *084/229–591* ✉ *sierraandina@gmail.com* ⇌ *7 rooms* ⅏ *In-room: no a/c, no phone, no TV. In-hotel: no elevator, laundry service* 🖃 *No credit cards* ❙◎❙ *BP.*

$$$$ **Sumaq Hotel.** At this hotel at the edge of town on the highway head-
Fodor's Choice ing up toward the ruins, the list of nice touches and amenities goes on
★ and on: grand staircases, elegant restaurant with a terrific cross selection of Peruvian cuisine, huge rooms, some with fireplace, all with
wood-beam ceilings, flat-screen TVs, box spring mattresses, porcelain
basin sinks, and sinfully fluffy towels. Sumaq means "beautiful" in
Quechua and the name is apt. Rates include a breakfast buffet and
lunch or dinner. **Pros:** Many amenities, great restaurant. **Cons:** Luxury
costs. ⊠*Carretera a Machu Picchu, Aguas Calientes* ☎*084/211–059,
01/447–0579 in Lima* 🖷*084/211–114, 01/445–7828 in Lima* ⊕*www.
sumaqhotelperu.com* ➲*60 rooms* ☖*In-room: safe, refrigerator, DVD,
Wi-Fi. In-hotel: restaurant, room service, bar, spa, laundry service,
public Internet* ▭*AE, DC, MC, V* ⏷⦿*MAP.*

THE NORTH COAST & THE CORDILLERA BLANCA

Updated by
Aviva Baff

From pyramids to sun-drenched beaches, the north coast offers great
diversity in landscape, weather, and activities. The north coast was,
until recently, largely ignored by foreign tourists, but all the way up
this sun-drenched stretch of coastal desert you'll find plenty of places
to explore and relax, including well-preserved colonial architecture,
numerous ancient ruins, excellent restaurants, reasonable beach resorts,
and a friendly and relaxed people.

Stunning snow-capped peaks, natural hot springs and incredible international food make the Cordillera Blanca and the adventure vacation
town of Huaraz one of the north's most popular areas. With more
than 40 peaks above 6,000 meters (19,500 feet) and the second highest peak in all the Americas, this provides spectacular views and outdoor activities.

8

TRUJILLO

561 km (350 mi) northwest of Lima on Pan-American Hwy.

The well-preserved colonial architecture, pleasant climate, and archeological sites have made Trujillo a popular tourist destination. The Plaza
de Armas and beautifully maintained colonial buildings make central
Trujillo a delightful place to while away an afternoon. Occupied for
centuries before the arrival of the Spaniards, ruins from the Moche and
Chimú people are nearby, as is a decent museum. Combine this with a
selection of excellent hotels, restaurants, and cafés, and you'll see why
Trujillo, officially founded in 1534, competes with Arequipa for the
title of Peru's "Second City." The only serious problem for tourists is
trying to fit in the time to visit all the sights—literally, since many places
close from 1 to 4 for lunch.

GETTING AROUND

Almost everything is within walking distance in the center of the city
and for everything else there are reasonably priced taxis. If you don't

have a car, ask your hotel to arrange for a taxi for the day or to tour a specific place. For the archaeological sights, another option is to join a day tour from a travel agency.

ESSENTIALS

Currency Exchange Scotia Bank (⊠ *Pizarro 314* ☎ *044/256–600* ⊕ *www. scotiabank.com.pe*).

Mail Post Office (⊠ *Av. Independencia 286* ☎ *044/245–941*). **DHL** (⊠ *Av. Pizarro 318* ☎ *044/233–630* ⊕ *www.dhl.com.pe*).

Medical Assistance Belén Hospital (⊠ *Bolívar 350* ☎ *044/245–281*).

Rental Car Trujillo Rent-a-Car (⊠ *Prolongación Bolivia 293* ☎ *044/420–059*).

Visitor Info iPerú (⊠ *Jr. Pizarro 402* ☎ *044/294–561* ⊕ *www.peru.info*).

EXPLORING TRUJILLO

ARCHAEOLOGICAL SITES

Begin your archaeological exploration at the **Museo del Sitio.** The entrance fee includes admission to the museum, plus Chán Chán, Huaca Arco Iris, and Huaca Esmeralda, so hold onto your ticket (you may also go directly to the ruins and purchase the same ticket there, for the same price). From Trujillo, take a taxi or join a tour from an agency. Each location is a significant distance from each other. Guides are available at the entrance of each site for S/10 more (S/20 Chán Chán) and are strongly recommended. At the museum, and all sites listed below, there are clean restrooms and a cluster souvenir stalls and snack shops, but no place to buy a full meal. ⊠ *Carretera Huanchaco, 5 km (3 mi) northwest of Trujillo* ☎ *044/206–304* 💳 *S/11, includes admission to Chán Chán, Huaca Arco Iris, and Huaca Esmeralda* ☉ *Daily 9–4:30.*

Fodor'sChoice
★
Chán Chán. The sprawling adobe-brick capital city, whose ruins lie 5 km (3 mi) west of Trujillo, has been called the largest mud city in the world. It once held boulevards, aqueducts, gardens, palaces, and some 10,000 dwellings. Within the city were nine royal compounds, one of which, the royal palace of Tschudi, has been partially restored and opened to the public. Although the city began with the Moche civilization, 300 years later, the Chimú people took control of the region and expanded the city to its current size. Although less known than the Incas, who conquered them in 1470, the Chimú were the second-largest pre-Columbian society in South America. Their empire stretched along 1,000 km (620 mi) of the Pacific, from Lima to Tumbes.

Huaca Arco Iris. Filled with intriguing and unusual symbolic carvings, and with an urban backdrop, is the restored Huaca Arco Iris or Rainbow Pyramid. Named for the unusual rainbow carving (the area rarely sees rain), it's also known as the Huaca El Dragón, or Pyramid of the Dragon, because of the central role dragons play in the friezes. This structure, built by the early Chimú, also has a repeating figure of a mythical creature that looks like a giant serpent. On the walls, mostly reconstructions, you will see what many archaeologists believe are priests wielding the knives used in human sacrifices. Half-moon shapes the bottom of most of the friezes indicate that the Chimú probably

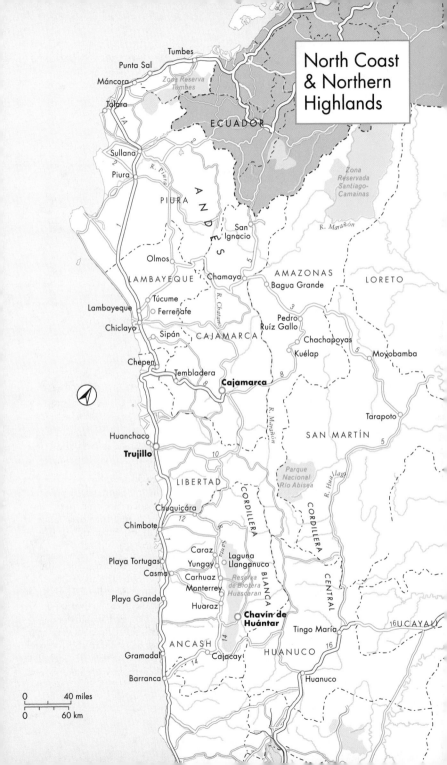

North Coast
& Northern
Highlands

Tumbes
Punta Sal
Máncora
Tótora
1A
ECUADOR
Zona Reserva
Tumbes
Sullana
2
Piura
R. Piura
PIURA
A N D E S
San
Ignacio
Zona
Reservada
Santiago-
Camainas
R. Marañón
Olmos
LAMBAYEQUE
Chamaya
AMAZONAS
Bagua Grande
LORETO
5
Túcume
Ferreñafe
Lambayeque
Chiclayo
Sipán
R. Chatama
Pedro
Ruíz Gallo
3
Chachapoyas
Kuélap
Moyobamba
5
CAJAMARCA
Chepen
Tembladera
8
Cajamarca
8
R. Marañón
Tarapoto
SAN MARTÍN
5
Huanchaco
Trujillo
10
R. Hual lago
LIBERTAD
Parque
Nacional
Río Abisea
Chuquicára
12
Chimbote
1
CORDILLERA
Caraz
Yungay
Santa
Laguna
Llanganuco
Reserva
de Biofera
Huascaran
CORDILLERA
CENTRAL
Playa Tortugas
Casma
Carhuaz
Monterrey
Huaraz
BLANCA
Playa Grande
Chavín de
Huántar
Tingo María
16 UCAYALI
ANCASH
HUANUCO
16
Gramadal
Cajacay
14
Barranca
Huanuco

0 — 40 miles
0 — 60 km

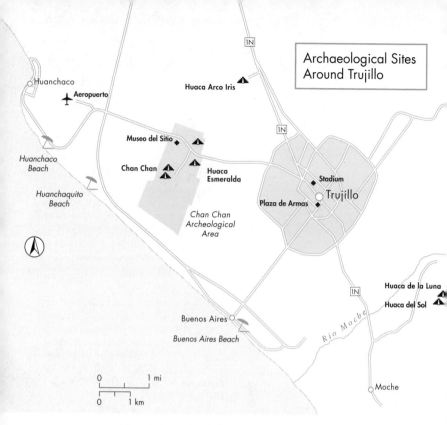

Archaeological Sites Around Trujillo

Huanchaco

Aeropuerto

Huaca Arco Iris

Huanchaco Beach

Museo del Sitio

Chan Chan

Huaca Esmeralda

Huanchaquito Beach

Chan Chan Archeological Area

Stadium

Trujillo

Plaza de Armas

Huaca de la Luna

Huaca del Sol

Buenos Aires

Buenos Aires Beach

Río Moche

Moche

0   1 mi

0   1 km

worshipped the moon at this temple. ⊠ *Pan-American Hwy., 5 km (3 mi) north of Trujillo* ☎ *No phone* ☎ *S/11, includes admission to Chán Chán, Huaca Esmeralda, and Museo del Sitio* ☉ *Daily 9–4:30.*

Fodor'sChoice **Huaca de la Luna & Huaca del Sol.** When you consider that these temples
★ were built more than 3,000 years ago, the mud and adobe pyramids near the Pan-American Highway and Río Moche are quite impressive. The Moche people were the first to spread its influence over much of the north coast and all subsequent civilizations, including the Chimú and Incas, built upon what this group began.

The smaller of the two pyramids—the only one you can actually tour—is the **Huaca de la Luna,** the Pyramid of the Moon. The adobe structure is painted with anthropomorphic and zoomorphic reliefs. The Moche expanded the pyramid several times during their reign, covering up the exterior's original reliefs. Since 1990 archaeologists have slowly uncovered the ancient layers of the pyramid. Walk through to its very heart to glimpse some of its first facades. On most days you're able to watch archaeologists as they uncover multicolor murals. Facilities include a visitor center at the entrance, with a small craft market, cafeteria, restrooms, and parking area (free).

Although the nearby **Huaca del Sol,** or the Pyramid of the Sun, sits along the same entry road, it's not yet ready for the public. Standing more than 40 meters (130 feet) high—slightly shorter than it originally stood—with more than 140 million bricks, this is the largest adobe-brick structure in the New World. ⊠ *10 km (6 mi) southeast of Trujillo* ☎ *044/834–901* ⊕ *www.huacadelaluna.org.pe* ☜ *S/11* ☉ *Daily 9–4.*

EL CENTRO SIGHTS

Casa de la Emancipación. This branch of Banco Continental is unlike any bank you've ever been in. Go through the central courtyard and up to the small art gallery on the right. Enjoy the current exhibition, anything from modern to traditional artwork, and see a scale model of Trujillo when it was a walled city. ■ **TIP➜** Continue to the back, taking in the chandeliers, the large gold mirrors and the small fountain, and imagine the day that, in this house, the city declared its independence from Spain on December 29, 1820. It later became the country's first capitol building and meeting place for its first legislature. ⊠ *Pizarro 610* ☎ *044/246–061* ☜ *Free* ☉ *Mon.–Sat. 9–12:30 and 4–6:30 (frequent special events may affect these hrs).*

☾ **Museo del Juguete.** Puppets, puzzles, toys, games ... what could be more fun than a toy museum? This private museum houses a large collection of toys from all over the world and shows the transformation of toys through the centuries. The toys from pre-Colombian Peru are especially interesting, giving a seldom-seen view into the daily lives of ancient people. You can't play with the toys so it may not be appropriate for very young children. ⊠ *Jiron Independencia 705* ☎ *044/208–181* ☜ *S/3* ☉ *Mon.–Sat. 10–6, Sun. 10–2.*

Plaza de Armas. Brightly colored, well-maintained buildings and green grass with walkways and benches, make this one of the most charming central plazas. Fronted by a 17th-century cathedral and surrounded by the colonial-era mansions that are Trujillo's architectural glory, this is not, despite claims by locals, Peru's largest main plaza, but it's one of the nicest.

WHERE TO EAT

$–$$ ✕ **Las Bóvedas.** This elegant restaurant in the Hotel Libertador offers
PERUVIAN   diners a beautiful space and delicious food. An impressive *bóveda,* or
★   vaulted brick ceiling, line the walls of the dining room and plants fill the niches. The house specialty is the local delicacy, shámbar, garnished with *canchita* (fried bits of corn). It's served only on Monday. ⊠ *Independencia 485* ☎ *044/232–741* ☐ *AE, DC, MC, V.*

¢–$ ✕ **De Marco.** Come to this noisy but cheerful eatery for good Peruvian
★   and Italian dishes, excellent coffee, an enormous selection of desserts, and free filtered water. Try the *seco de cabrito,* a local delicacy made of stewed goat. If you eat the freshly baked bread on the table, there's a small fee (S/0.25 each), but the special herbed butter is no extra charge. ⊠ *Pizarro 725* ☎ *044/234–251* ☐ *AE, DC, MC, V.*

$–$$ ✕ **San Remo.** People come here for the best pizza in town. Select from a large list of pizzas, with every topping imaginable, or choose one of the many other dishes, mostly pasta, but also meat and poultry options.

8

The deer head in the entryway, the stained-glass windows, and the small wooden bar add to an old-school atmosphere. There's an excellent selection of South American and European wines. ⊠*Av. Húsares de Junín 450* ☎*044/293–333* ▤*AE, DC, MC, V* ⊙*No lunch.*

WHERE TO STAY

$ 🏨**Gran Bolívar.** A modern hotel hides behind the historic facade of this centrally located lodging. The spacious rooms overlook a courtyard filled with streaming sunlight. Inside the hotel is a full-service tourist agency, which offers a decent selection of local tours. Ask to see a few rooms beforehand, as some are nicer than others. **Pros:** Colonial architecture, beautiful central courtyard, central location, good staff. **Cons:** Some rooms have lots of light, others have very little. ⊠*Jr. Bolívar 957* ☎▤*044/222–090 or 044/223–521* ⊕*www.perunorte.com/gran bolivar* ➴*21 rooms, 7 suites* ⚹*In-room: no a/c (some). In-hotel: restaurant, room service, bar, gym, spa, laundry service, billiards, airport shuttle, parking (no fee)* ▤*AE, DC, MC, V* ⊙⏐*CP.*

$ 🏨**Gran Hotel El Golf.** If you want to stay outside the city, this modern hotel is the best place to stay. The rooms face a large pool, surrounded by beautifully landscaped gardens and palm trees. It's a good choice for families since it has open areas for kids to play. There's a nearby golf course. **Pros:** Quiet, attractive setting. **Cons:** Can be isolating without a car. ⊠*Los Cocoteros 500, El Golf* ☎*044/282–515* ▤*044/282–231* ⊕*www.granhotelgolftrujillo.com* ➴*112 rooms, 8 suites* ⚹*In-room: safe, Wi-Fi (some). In-hotel: restaurant, public Internet, room service, bar, pools, gym, laundry service, airport shuttle, parking (no fee), no-smoking rooms* ▤*AE, DC, MC, V* ⊙⏐*CP.*

$$–$$$ 🏨**Hotel Libertador.** On the Plaza de Armas, this elegant, upscale hotel is
★   the best choice in Trujillo. With beautiful colonial architecture, room details like pre-Colombian designs, locally tooled leather and wood furniture, and wrought-iron wall lamps, along with all the modern amenities. Look at your room in advance as some are smaller and don't have much natural light. If you fancy people-watching, ask for a room in the front with a small balcony facing the street. **Pros:** Central location and beautiful architecture. **Cons:** Some rooms are better than others. ⊠*Independencia 485* ☎*044/232–741* ⊕*www.libertador. pe* ➴*73 rooms, 5 suites* ⚹*In-room: safe, Wi-Fi. In-hotel: restaurant, room service, bar, pool, gym, sauna, Wi-Fi, laundry service, parking (no fee), no-smoking rooms* ▤*AE, DC, MC, V* ⊙⏐*BP.*

HUANCHACO

12 km (7½ mi) northwest of Trujillo.

Less than half an hour away from the city, Huanchaco is a little beach community where surfers, tourists, affluent *Trujillianos*, families, and couples easily mix. With excellent restaurants, comfortable hotels and never-ending sunshine, this is a nice place to unwind for a couple of days or to live it up at one of the many annual *fiestas.* The Festival del Mar is held every other year during May, the Fiesta de San Pedro held every June 29, and multiple surfing and dance competitions happen throughout the year.

■ TIP→ Head to the beach in the late afternoon to watch fishermen return for the day, gliding along in their caballitos de totora, traditional fishing boats that have been used for more than 1,000 years. These small, unstable boats, made from totora reeds, can be seen in Moche ceramics and other pre-Columbian handiwork. The boat's name, *caballitos*, means "little horse" and comes from how fishermen kneel on them.

Although people come to Huanchaco for the beach, one of Peru's oldest churches, **El Santuario de Huanchaco**, on a hill overlooking the village, is a nice sidetrip. The Sanctuary of Huanchaco was built on a Chimú ruin around 1540. In the second half of the 16th century a small box containing the image of *Nuestra Señora del Socorro* (Our Lady of Mercy) floated in on the tide and was discovered by locals. The image, which is kept in the sanctuary, has been an object of local veneration ever since. ⊠ *At Andrés Rázuri and Unión* ☎ *No phone* ☑ *Free* ☉ *Daily 8–6.*

THE BEACHES

Playa Malecón, north of the pier, is the town's most popular beach and is filled with restaurant afer restaurant. Local craftspeople sell their goods along the waterfront walk. Rocky **Playa Huankarote**, south of the pier, is less popular for swimming, but there's good surfing.

WHERE TO EAT

¢–$ ✕**Big Ben.** Skip the first floor and head upstairs to the terrace for great
SEAFOOD views of the beach. Enjoy Huanchaquero specialties, including *cangrejo reventado* (baked crab stuffed with eggs) and *ceviche de mococho* (algae ceviche). Only open 11–6, this open-air restaurant serves lunch and sunset drinks from a special wine list or cocktail menu. Huanchaquero specialties include *cangrejo reventado* (baked crab stuffed with eggs) and *ceviche de mococho* (algae ceviche). ⊠ *Av. Victor Larco 836* ☎ *044/461–378* ⊕ *www.bigbenhuanchaco.com* ☰ *AE, DC, MC, V* ☉ *No dinner.*

¢–$ ✕**Club Colonial.** An excellent menu, beautifully decorated, and the abso-
SEAFOOD lute best place to watch the sunset, this is one of the finest places to
Fodor'sChoice dine in northern Peru. Club Colonial combines recipes from the Old
★ World with ingredients from the New World, coming up with wonderful combinations of fresh seafood, pasta, greens, meats, and more. There's everything from Basque-style sea bass to crepes covered with tropical fruit. The restaurant is filled with colorful colonial artifacts and has a cozy bar and an outdoor terrace. The a new location is on a newly created street, so asking for directions can be tricky. It's closer to the surfers' section of the beach than the fishermen's area. ⊠ *Av. La Rivera 171* ☎ *044/461–015* ☰ *AE, MC, V.*

WHERE TO STAY

$ 🏨**Las Palmeras.** Across from the tranquil Playa Los Tumbos, a beach on
★ the northern end of the waterfront, Las Palmeras is a welcoming hotel once you get past the gated entrance. Its spotless rooms have terraces; most have great views of the ocean. A narrow garden with a small pool makes your stay very relaxing. Since the hotel is gated in, there's a feel-

ing of privacy. At this writing, the hotel is in the process of building a new restaurant in front of the hotel. **Pros:** Pristine and comfortable rooms, very quiet and relaxing. **Cons:** Difficult to find behind a closed gate, prices vary based on location of the room. ⊠*Av. Victor Larco 1150* 🖼044/461–199 ⊕*www.laspalmerasdehuanchaco.com* ↘*20 rooms, 1 suite* ♨*In-room: no phone, no TV. In-hotel: restaurant, pool, laundry service, room service, no elevator* ▭*V.*

THE CORDILLERA BLANCA

The Cordillera Blanca is one of the world's greatest mountain ranges. The soaring, glaciated peaks strut more than 6,000 meters (19,500 feet) above sea level—only Asia's mountain ranges are higher. Glaciers carve their lonely way into the green of the Río Santa valley, forming streams, giant gorges, and glorious gray-green alpine lagoons. On the western side of the valley is the Cordillera Negra. Less impressive than the Cordillera Blanca, its steep mountains have no permanent glaciers and are verdant and brooding. Driving along the paved stretch of road through the valley offers spectacular views of both mountain ranges

Climbers come during the dry season to test their iron on the more than 40 peaks in the area exceeding 6,000 meters (19,500 feet). The 6,768-meter (21,996-foot) summit of Huascarán is the highest in Peru and is clearly visible from Huaraz on sunny days.

HUARAZ

400 km (248 mi) north of Lima.

Peru's number-one trekking and adventure-sports destination, Huaraz is an easy starting point for those wishing to explore the vast wilderness of the Cordillera Blanca. Unfortunately, the town has been repeatedly leveled by natural disasters. In the later part of the 20th century three large earthquakes destroyed much of Huaraz, claiming more than 20,000 lives.

Despite the setbacks and death toll, Huaraz rallied, and today it's a pleasant town filled with good-natured people. Being the most popular tourist destination in northern Peru, Huaraz also has a great international scene; while the town has few sights, the restaurants and hotels are some of the best in the region. ■TIP➜ Many businesses close between September and May, when the town practically shuts down without its hoards of climbers and trekkers. It can be hard to find an outfitter at this time; call ahead if you plan a rainy-season visit.

GETTING AROUND

Huaraz is a small town and you can walk almost everywhere. Or, if you've just arrived and are feeling a little breathless from the altitude, take a taxi for 3 to 5 soles. To enjoy any of the nearby treks and sights, hire a guide as it's not safe to go alone.

ESSENTIALS

Currency Exchange Banco de Crédito (⌧ *Av. Luzuriaga 691* ☎ *043/421–170* ⊕ *www.viabcp.com*). **Scotia Bank** (⌧ *José de Sucre 760* ☎ *043/721–500* ⊕ *www.scotiabank.com.pe*).

Mail **Post Office** (⌧ *Av. Luzuriaga 702* ☎ *043/421–030*).

Medical Assistance **Hospital Victor Ramos Guardia** (⌧ *Av. Luzuriaga, Cuadra 8* ☎ *043/421–861*).

Rental Car **Monte Rosa** (⌧ *Jr. José de la Mar 691* ☎ *043/421–447*).

Visitor Info **iPerú** (⌧ *Pasaje Atusparia* ☎ *043/428–812* ⊕ *www.peru.info*).

EXPLORING HUARAZ

The small **Museo Arqueológico de Ancash** displays some very unique items, including a mummified baby and teenager, created by covering the dead with salt, *muña* (wild mint), *quinua* (a cornlike plant), and *izura* (pink earth). Upstairs numerous skulls bear the scars (or rather holes) from trepanation, the removal of bone from the skull. Additionally, the museum has Chavín textiles and ceramics, and a delightful little park accessible through the bottom floor. Here you'll find original carved stones, benches, and a little café. ⌧ *Av. Luzuriaga 762* ☎ *043/721–551* ⊕ *www.huaraz.com/museo* ☑ *S/5.60, includes a guide* ⊙ *Mon.–Sat. 8:15–6:30, Sun. and holidays until 5.*

The **Mirador de Retaquenua,** lookout point has an excellent view of Huaraz, the Río Santa, and the surrounding mountains. It's a 45-minute walk up, but the directions are complicated so it's best to hire a guide or just take a taxi. ⌧ *Av. Confraternidad Inter Sur and Av. Confraternidad Inter Este.*

North of the city is a small archaeological site called **Wilcahuaín.** The Wari temple, dating back to AD 1100, resembles the larger temple at Chavín de Huántar. Each story of the crumbling three-tiered temple has seven rooms. There's a small museum and recently built basic bathroom facilities and a limited restaurant. Trained and knowledgeable local students will be your guide for a small tip (suggested minimum tip: S/15). ⌧ *8 km (5 mi) north of Huaraz* ☎ *No phone* ☑ *S/5* ⊙ *Daily 6–6.*

OFF THE BEATEN PATH

Glaciar Pastoruri. A popular day trip from Huaraz is a visit to the Glaciar Pastoruri, where you can hike around the glacier and visit a glowing blue-ice cave. On this trip you'll ascend to well above 4,000 meters (13,000 feet), so make sure you're used to the high altitude. Wear warm clothing, sunscreen, and sunglasses, as the sun is intense. Drink lots of water to avoid altitude sickness. The easiest and safest way to get here is with a tour company from Huaraz. The tour costs about S/20 to S/30 and takes eight hours. Admission to the glacier is S/5. You can also hire diminutive horses to take you up to the glacier from the parking lot for about S/15. It's not the most spectacular glacier in the world, but if you've never seen one up close, it's worth the trip. The glacier is south of Huaraz, off the main highway at the town of Recuay.

WHERE TO EAT

¢–$ ✕**Creperie Patrick.** With a breezy terrace upstairs and a cozy bistro
FRENCH downstairs, this French eatery is an excellent choice. There's couscous
Fodor'sChoice and fondue, as well as hard-to-find local dishes such as grilled alpaca.
★ Don't miss the sumptuous dessert crepes and good wine selection. After
almost 20 years in Peru, chef and owner Patrick has begun to make
homemade delicacies including his own liquors, jams, mustards, gra-
nola, and more. ⊠*Av. Luzuriaga 422* ☎*044/426–037* ▤*No credit
cards* ⊗*No lunch Oct.–Apr.*

¢–$ ✕**El Horno.** With a terrace area for sunny afternoons and a recently
ITALIAN expanded dining room for the evenings, El Horno is a good stop any
★ time. ■TIP➜ **Here you'll find some of the finest pizzas in Huaraz—baked
by a Frenchman, no less.** The doughy crusts are superb and the service
faultless. Excellent salads, sandwiches, pastas, and barbecued meats
are also on the menu. If you are, by some chance, looking for French
books, there is a French-only book exchange here as well. ⊠*Parque
del Periodista 37* ☎*043/424—617* ⊕*www.elhornopizzeria.com* ▤*No
credit cards* ⊗*Closed on Sundays; No lunch during the low season.*

WHERE TO STAY

$ ▦**Hotel Colomba.** The best hotel to come if you—or your kids—are
↻ high-energy and want activities. In addition to a beautiful garden setting around this hacienda-turned-hotel, there's a rock-climbing wall,
soccer field, basketball court, gameroom, gym, and playground. The
staff is well-trained and friendly. **Pros:** Family friendly, lots of activities.
Cons: Some rooms are better than others, but all cost the same (ask for
a room in the back with parquet floors). ⊠*Jr. Francisco de Zela 210,
Independencia* ☎*043/421–501 or 043/422–273* ⊕*www.huarazhotel.
com* ➲*20 rooms* ⌂*In-hotel: room service, laundry service, public
Internet, public Wi-Fi, parking (no fee)* ▤*AE, DC, MC, V* ⍟*BP.*

$ ▦**Hotel San Sebastián.** Perched on the side of a mountain, this hotel has
★ great views of the Cordillera Blanca. Many rooms have small balconies
and shady terraces are scattered about the hotel. Built in the Spanish-colonial style, the hotel exudes rustic charm with plenty of pine
furniture and natural sunlight. The owner is Selio Villón, a mountain
guide with more than 20 years of experience. **Pros:** Reasonable rates
with first-rate accommodation. **Cons:** Hotel keeps expanding, doubling
its capacity in two years, losing some of its "family" charm. ⊠*Jr. Italia 1124* ☎*043/426–960 or 043/426–386* ▤*043/422–306* ⊕*www.
sansebastianhuaraz.com* ➲*30 rooms, 1 junior suite* ⌂*In-hotel: room
service, laundry service, public Internet, Wi-Fi, parking (no fee), no
elevator* ▤*V.*

OUTDOOR ACTIVITIES

CLIMBING & If dreams of bagging a 6,000-meter (19,500-foot) peak or trekking
TREKKING through the wilderness haunt your nights, Huaraz is the place for you.
Huaraz sits at a lofty 3,090 meters (10,042 feet), and the surrounding
mountains are even higher. Allowing time to acclimatize is a life-saving
necessity. ■TIP➜ **The climbing and trekking season runs from May through
September—the driest months.**

Even if you're an experienced hiker, you shouldn't venture into the backcountry without a guide. So many outfitters are in the area that looking for a qualified company can become overwhelming. Visit a few places, and make sure you're getting what you really want. **Casa de Guís** (⊠*Parque Ginebra 28/G* ☎*043/427–545* ⊕*www.casadeguias. pe*) is an association of certified freelance guides who offer excellent advice and personalized trips, including mountaineering and trekking as well as rock- and ice-climbing courses.

WHITE-WATER RAFTING — There's good rafting on the Río Santa with Class 3 and 4 rapids. The freezing cold glacial river water brings heart-pumping rapids. The most-often-run stretch of river runs between Jangas and Caraz. The river can be run year-round, but is at its best during the wettest months of the rainy season, between December and April. Be prepared with the right equipment; the river is cold enough to cause serious hyperthermia. **Monttrek** (⊠*Av. Luzuriaga 646, upstairs* ☎*043/421–124* ⊕*www.monttrek peru.com*) is one of the best rafting outfitters in Huaraz.

CHAVÍN DE HUÁNTAR

★ *110 km (68 mi) southeast of Huaraz.*

Although the ruins appear unimpressive at first—most of the area was covered by a huge landslide in 1945—underground you'll discover a labyrinth of well-ventilated corridors and chambers. They're illumined by electric lights that sometimes flicker or fail altogether—it's wise to bring your own flashlight. Deep inside the corridors you'll come upon the **Lanzón de Chavín.** This 4-meter-high (13-foot-high) dagger-like rock carving represents an anthropomorphic deity (complete with fangs, claws, and serpentine hair); it sits elegantly at the intersection of four corridors. Built by the Chavín, one of the first civilizations in Peru, little is known about this ancient culture, although archaeologists believe they had a complex religious sysem. The main deity is always characterized as a puma or jaguar. Lesser deities, represented by condors, snakes, and other animals, were also revered.

This is a fascinating archaeological site that you can day-trip to from Huaraz. Chavín de Huántar sits on the southern edge of Chavín, a tiny village southeast of Huaraz. On the drive from Huaraz you get good views of two Andean peaks, Pucaraju (5,322 meters/17,296 feet) and Yanamarey (5,237 meters/17,020 feet). Construction on the road may delay your journey—check on conditions before setting out. Tours from Huaraz visit the ruins, a small on-site museum, and the alpine Laguna de Querococha during the eight-hour tour. The tour costs about S/30 per person, not including the entrance fee to the ruins. If you'd prefer to get here on your own, regular buses run between Huaraz and Chavín, you can hire a guide at the entrance to the ruins. ☎*No phone* ✉*S/11* ⊙*Daily 8–4.*

CLOSE UP

Tours of Cusco, the Sacred Valley & Machu Picchu

The typical tour of the Cusco region combines the city with the Sacred Valley and Machu Picchu in three whirlwind days, including the full boleto turístico. We recommend devoting five days to get the most out of your visit—including one day to get acclimated to the high altitude.

Many excellent tour operators and travel agents are in Cusco, and some have offices in Lima. Several companies specialize in adventure tours, others in rafting excursions, still others in llama-assisted treks.

SELECTING A TRAVEL AGENCY

"Holaaaa—trip to Machu Picchu?" With so many touts in Cusco's streets hawking tours to Peru's most famous sight, it's tempting to just buy one in order to make them stop asking. Anyone who offers an Inca Trail trek departing tomorrow should be taken with more than a grain of salt—Inca Trail walks need to be booked months in advance. Don't make arrangements or give money to someone claiming to be a travel agent if they approach you on the street or at the airport in Cusco or Lima. Instead choose an agency that has a physical address. Better yet, select one that is listed in this book or on www.peru.info. Below are several reputable travel agencies.

Action Valley operates an adventure park near Poroy with double-cord bungee jumping, catapult swing, paragliding, and environmentally friendly paintball. Guides speak German and Hebrew in addition to English and Spanish. ✉ *Santa Teresa 325, Cusco* ☎ *084/240–835* ⊕ *www. actionvalley.com.*

Amazing Peru organizes group and individual guided tours, including two types of trips to Cusco and Machu Picchu. Transportation services and accommodations are top-notch, and the guides are flexible and extremely helpful. ☎ *01/243–7704 in Lima, 800/704–2915 in North America* ⊕ *www.amazingperu.com.*

Andina Travel specializes in trekking, especially alternatives to the Inca Trail, as well as offering all the standard Sacred Valley and Machu Picchu tours. ✉ *Plazoleta Santa Catalina 219, Cusco* ☎ *084/251–892* ⊕ *www. andinatravel.com.*

Tame rafting trips on the Urubamba River are operated year-round by **Apumayo Expediciones** ✉ *Garcilaso 265, Cusco* ☎🖷 *084/246–018* ⊕ *www.apumayo.com.*

Enigma specializes in small, customized adventure trips throughout the region. Enjoy trekking, rafting, mountain climbing, mountain biking, or horseback riding led by professional guides. ✉ *Jr. Clorinda Mato de Turner 100, Cusco* ☎ *084/222–155* ⊕ *www. enigmaperu.com.*

Explorandes is a large and long-running company that organizes customized guided trips and expeditions through the Andes in Peru and Ecuador, including rafting and trekking trips around Cusco. ✉ *Av. Garcilazo 316, Cusco* ☎ *084/238–380, 01/445–0532 in Lima* ⊕ *www.explorandes. com.*

Globos de los Andes floats you above the Sacred Valley on hot-air balloon tours. ✉ *Av. de la Cultura 220, Cusco* ☎ *084/232–352* ⊕ *www. globosperu.com.*

Inkaterra is a top-end agency specializing in nature-orientated trips to Machu Picchu, but can customize tours that include Cusco and the Sacred Valley with however much guide accompaniment as you need. ⊠*Andalucía 174, Miraflores, Lima* ☎*01/610–0400 in Lima, 084/245–314 in Cusco, 800/442–5042 toll-free in North America* ⊕*www.inkaterra.com.*

Instinct leads Cusco city tours, Inca Trail hikes, walking and rafting trips along the Tambopata River, and more. ⊠*Av. de la Cultura 1318, Cusco* ⊠*Calle 25 No. 129, San Isidro, Lima* ☎*084/233–451* ⊕*www.instinct-travel.com.*

Marle's Travel Adventure offers trekking excursions and rents or sells camping equipment, in addition to doing all the standard Sacred Valley tours. ⊠*Plateros 328, Cusco* ☎*084/233–680* ✍*marlestraveladventure@yahoo.com.*

Mayuc is known for its rafting excursions but also offers good city and Sacred Valley tours. ⊠*Portal de Confiturías 211, Haukaypata, Plaza de Armas, Cusco* ☎*084/242–824* ⊕*www.mayuc.com.*

Overseas Adventure Travel offers fully escorted 11-day tours of Cusco and the surrounding region with groups no larger than 16 people. A popular OAT add-on is a trip to Ecuador's Galápagos Islands. ☎*800/493–6824 in North America* ⊕*www.oattravel.com.*

River Explorers takes you on one- to six-day rafting and kayaking excursions on the Urubamba and Apurimac rivers, and offers the standard trekking tours. ⊠*Plateros 328, Cusco* ☎*084/233–680* ⊕*www.river explorers.com.*

Urubamba-based **Sacred Valley Mountain Bike Tours** rents mountain bikes for $25 per day and $15 per half-day, and leads cycling excursions throughout the valley. ⊠*Jr. Convención s/n, Urubamba* ☎*084/201–331* ⊕*www.machawasi.com.*

Cusco-based **SAS Travel** has made a name for itself in trekking circles, but can also customize tours and accommodations in the region. ⊠*Garcilaso 270* ⊠*Portal de Panes 167, Haukaypata, Plaza de Armas, Cusco* ☎*084/249–194 or 084/255–205* ⊕*www.sastravelperu.com.*

Swissraft-Peru runs multiday trips on class II, II, IV, and V rapids. ⊠*Heladeros 129, Cusco* ☎*084/264–124* ⊕*www.swissraft-peru.com.*

For a tame adventurer, **Wilderness Travel** has a Peru Llama Trek that follows an off-Inca trail route to Machu Picchu where llamas carry your gear and you have the trail to yourself until near the end. ⊠*1102 9th St., Berkeley, CA* ☎*510/558–2488, 800/368–2794 in U.S.* ⊕*www.wildernesstravel.com.*

Mainly for experienced adventurers, **X-treme Tourbulencia** leads mountain climbing and biking, trekking, and multisport trips. ⊠*Plateros 358, Cusco* ☎*084/224–362* ⊕*www.x-tremetourbulencia.com.*

8

LAGUNAS DE LLANGANUCO

FodorsChoice
★
Make sure your memory card is empty when you go to see these spectacular glaciers, gorges, lakes, and mountains. Driving through a giant gorge formed millions of years ago by a retreating glacier, you arrive at **Lagunas de Llanganuco.** The crystalline waters shine a luminescent turquoise in the sunlight; in the shade they're a forbidding inky black. Waterfalls of glacial melt snake their way down the gorge's flanks, falling lightly into the lake. There are many *quenual* trees (also known as the paper-bark tree) surrounding the lakes. Up above, you'll see treeless alpine meadows and the hanging glaciers of the surrounding mountains. At the lower lake, called Lago Chinancocha, you can hire a rowboat (S/3 per person) to take you to the center of the lake. A few trailside signs teach you about local flora and fauna. The easiest way to get here is with an arranged tour from Huaraz (about S/25 plus S/5 entrance fee). The tours stop here and at many other spots on the Callejón de Huaylas, finishing in Caraz.

Laguna Llanganuco is one of the gateways to the **Parque Nacional Huascarán,** a 340,000-hectare park created in 1975 to protect and preserve flora and fauna in the Cordillera Blanca. ■ TIP➡ This incredible mountain range has a total of 663 glaciers and includes some of the highest peaks in the Peruvian Andes. Huascarán, which soars to 6,768 meters (21,996 feet), is the highest in Peru. The smaller Alpamayo, 5,947 meters (19,327 feet), is said by many to be the most beautiful mountain in the world. Its majestic flanks inspire awe and wonder in those lucky enough to get a glimpse. The monstrous Chopicalqui and Chacraraju rise above 6,000 meters (19,500 feet).

The giant national park attracts campers, hikers, and mountain climbers. Check with guide agencies in Huaraz for maps, trail information, and insider advice before heading out. ✉ *Federico Sal y Rosas 555* ☎ *043/422–086* 💳 *S/5 day pass, S/65 multiday pass* ◷ *Daily 6–6.*

Uruguay

WORD OF MOUTH

"My favorite place in Uruguay depends a lot on the time of the year. In summer it would be Punta del Este, but in winter Montevideo. It all depends on what you prefer and how many days you will spend there."

—Graziella5b

"If you need a 'vacation from the vacation,' Colonia is a wonderful place. Find a small restaurant, and converse with the locals at the bar. It's a lot of fun."

—tompack

Updated by
Jeffrey Van
Fleet

THE SMALLEST COUNTRY COVERED IN THIS BOOK just might be called "the Little Nation that Could." On a continent with a turbulent past, Uruguayans have parlayed their human and natural resources into a history of success. A strong middle class, a high standard of living, relative prosperity, and a long tradition of peace, good government, and democracy have defined Uruguay (although that last feature did disappear for a dozen years in the last century). The country has enacted landmark legislation that made it the first in South America to sever relations between church and state, to grant women the right to vote, to permit same-sex civil unions, and to enact a generous social-welfare system.

Wedged between Brazil and Argentina, two of the continent's tourism powerhouses, Uruguay misses out on the attention it deserves. Most visitors come from its two large neighbors, and they know what the country has to offer. For example, Brazilians, with plenty of world-class beaches to call their own, still flock to Punta del Este, Uruguay's very own tony coastal resort. The draw? There's safety and security that, quite frankly, can be lacking in, say, Rio.

Like next-door Argentina, Uruguay has cosmopolitan flair. That's not surprising, since about half of its population lives in Montevideo, the capital. Uruguay's small number of original inhabitants, the seminomadic Charrúa people, were attacked first by the Portuguese, who settled the town of Colonia in 1680, then by the Spanish, who in 1726 established a fortress at Montevideo. That left the country with almost an entirely homogeneous population of Spanish, Italian, British, and Portuguese descent, the most European of South American countries. The country takes pride in the number of world-famous artists it produces. Galleries here are full of works by masters such as sculptor José Belloni (1880–1965) and painters Joacquín Torres-García (1874–1949), Pedro Figari (1861–1938), and Pedro Blanes Viale (1879–1926). Uruguayans like to claim their country as the birthplace of the internationally renowned tango singer Carlos Gardel (1809–1935), although the Argentines and French also vie for this honor.

As in Argentina, the legendary gaucho is Uruguay's most potent cultural fixture, and it's difficult to pass a day without some reference to these cowboys who once roamed the country singing their melancholy ballads. You can still see remnants of the gaucho lifestyle on active ranches throughout the country.

ORIENTATION & PLANNING

GETTING ORIENTED

Uruguay is one of South America's smallest countries, both in area (it's roughly the size of England) and population. Montevideo anchors the coast, and most of the population and action hugs the water line. Vast ranches and farms fill the hilly, sparsely developed interior. Montevideo's only cosmopolitan rival is Punta del Este, one of a hand-

Uruguay

0 ___ 50 miles
0 ___ 75 km

BRAZIL

Artigas

Sequeira

Rivera

Tranqueras

Concordia · Salto

Tacuarembo

Vichadero

CUCHILLA DE HAEDO

Paysandu

Melo

Lago Artificial
de Rincón del Bonete

Rio Branco

Laguna
Merín

Lago Artificial
de Baygorria

Paso
de los Toros

CUCHILLA GRANDE

Vergara

Fray
Bentos

Durazno

Treinta y Tres

Mercedes

Trinidad

Sarandí
Grande

Cerro
Colorado

Lascano

Dolores

Carmelo

Florida

Aguas
Dulces

ATLANTIC
OCEAN

Colonia del Sacramento
see detail map

San
Ramon

Aigua

Minas

Rocha

Buenos
Aires

Canelones

93

Rio de la Plata

Montevideo
see detail map

Piriápolis

San Carlos

La Barra
de Maldonado

Punta del Este
see detail map

ARGENTINA

Punta
Ballena

Punta
Ballena

Rio Uruguay

ful of Atlantic Ocean resorts popular with well-heeled Brazilians and Argentines.

Montevideo. True to developing-country patterns, all roads, literal and figurative, lead to Montevideo. Uruguay's friendly capital strings for miles along the southern coast with an odd positioning that means, you can walk south, north, or west from the center city to reach the water.

The South Coast. Head west from Montevideo along the coast for pleasures of the soul and the lovely old city of Colonia del Sacramento. East lie the pleasures of the flesh and Punta del Este, one of the world's trendiest beach communities.

URUGUAY PLANNER

WHEN TO GO

Between October and March the temperatures are pleasant—it's warm and the country is in bloom. Unless you're prepared to tangle with the multitude of tourists that overwhelm Punta del Este in January and February, late spring (November–December) and late winter (March) are the most appealing months to lounge on the beach.

CLIMATE

Uruguay's climate has four distinct seasons. Summer (January–March) can be hot and humid, with temperatures as high as 90°F. Fall (April–June) is marked by warm days and evenings cool enough for a light sweater. Winter (July–September) is cold and rainy, with average temperatures generally below 50°F. Although it seldom reaches freezing, the wind off the water can give you quite a chill. Spring (October–December) is

THE "EASTERN REPUBLIC"

The country's official name is the República Oriental del Uruguay, denoting the republic east of the Uruguay River, which forms today's border with Argentina. Though calling someone "Oriental" is decidedly a no-go in English, Uruguayans happily, colloquially refer to themselves as *los Orientales.*

much like the fall, except that the trees will be sprouting, rather than dropping, their leaves.

The following are average daily maximum and minimum temperatures for Montevideo.

Jan.	83F	28C	May	64F	18C	Sept.	63F	17C
	62	17		48	9		46	8
Feb.	82F	28C	June	59F	15C	Oct.	68F	20C
	61	16		43	6		49	10
Mar.	78F	25C	July	58F	14C	Nov.	74F	23C
	59	15		43	6		54	12
Apr.	71F	22C	Aug.	59F	15C	Dec.	79F	21C
	53	12		43	6		59	15

HOLIDAYS

New Year's Day; Three Kings' Day (January 6); Good Friday–Easter (March or April); Disembarkation of the 33 Exiles (April 19); Labor Day (May 1); Battle of Las Piedras (May 18); Artigas's Birthday (June 19); Constitution Day (July 18); Independence Day (August 25); Columbus Day (October 12); All Souls' Day (November 2); Christmas.

FESTIVALS & SEASONAL EVENTS

Almost every town in Uruguay celebrates Carnaval, the weeklong festival that immediately precedes the beginning of Lent. The entire country participates in the *comparsas,* the festive mix of singing, dancing, drinking, eating, and general merrymaking. Carnaval overtakes Montevideo with parades, dancing in the streets, and general all-hours revelry. Semana Criolla, celebrated the week before Easter in the Montevideo suburb of Carrasco, is an excellent way to observe traditional gaucho activities. Montevideo holds an annual cattle fair in August.

TOP REASONS TO GO

Bask in Colonial Splendor. There's little that could be called old in this modern, progressive country—except for the once-walled 1680 Portuguese settlement of Colonia del Sacramento. Flowers spill over balconies, balladeers serenade their sweethearts, and lanterns illuminate the streets of this well-preserved colonial city.

Frolic with the Rich and Famous. One visit to Uruguay's tony Punta del Este, and Brazil's beaches will forever seem a tad too déclassé. From December through February, fun-in-the-sun crowds flock here;

they mostly hail from Argentina, but Punta's resorts and boutiques draw an ever-growing number of visitors from other countries, too.

Ride 'Em, Cowboy. The gaucho embodies the country's spirit, and these rugged cowboys still mount their trusty horses to round up livestock on vast ranges. Sometime in the 19th century the process was transformed into the *criolla*, the Uruguayan-style rodeo. If your time is limited, you don't even need to leave urban Montevideo to see the spectacle: the capital's El Prado district is the site of the best rodeos.

GETTING HERE & AROUND

BY AIR

Most international flights land at Montevideo's Aeropuerto Internacional de Carrasco, about 24 km (15 mi) east of downtown. Nearly all Montevideo-bound flights are routed through Buenos Aires. Uruguay's Pluna Airlines flies to Buenos Aires, São Paulo, and Madrid. Aerolineas Argentinas flies from Buenos Aires. TAM Airlines connects Montevideo with Asunción and São Paulo. Brazil's low-cost airline Gol flies from São Paulo. TACA connects Montevideo with Lima. If you fly a strictly Argentina-Uruguay itinerary, you'll likely depart from Buenos Aires' domestic airport, the Aeroparque Jorge Newbery. Through flights on American use the capital's international airport at Ezeiza.

Service to the Aeropuerto Internacional de Punta del Este is frequent from many South American cities during the resort's December–March high season, but almost nonexistent the rest of the year.

BY BOAT

Ferries cross the Río de la Plata between Argentina and Uruguay several times daily. They travel to Montevideo or Colonia, where you can get a bus to Montevideo and Punta del Este. The best companies are Aliscafos, Buquebus, Ferry Lineas Argentina, and Ferry Tur.

BY BUS

You can go almost anywhere in Uruguay by bus. Some are quite luxurious, with air-conditioning, movies, and snack service. Departures are frequent and fares low. Most companies are based in Montevideo and depart from its state-of-the-art Terminal Tres Cruces, whose Web site lists all bus schedules to and from Montevideo.

BY CAR

From Argentina you can transport your car across the Río de la Plata by ferry. Alternatively, you can cross the Argentina-Uruguay border in three places: Puerto Unzue-Fray Bentos, Colón-Paysandu, or Concordia-Salto. From Brazil you can cross the border either at Chuy, the Río Branco, Rivera, or via the bridge at Quarai-Artigas.

Roads between Montevideo and Punta del Este or Colonia del Sacramento are quite good, as are the handful of major highways. In the countryside, roads are usually surfaced with gravel. If you want to leave the main roads, it's best to speak with locals about current conditions before setting off. Trips will often take longer than expected, so budget extra time. On the up side, country roads often have very little traffic and spectacular scenery.

Car-rental rates are often higher in Uruguay than in the United States because of the value-added tax. For an economy-size car, expect to pay around US$55 per day. Uruguayans tend to drive carefully, but visitors from Argentina have the reputation of driving with wild abandon. Since almost all roads have only two lanes, keep an eye out for passing vehicles.

GAS STATIONS Gas is expensive in Uruguay, and will cost you up to about 26 pesos per liter. Major stations operated by Shell, Esso, Texaco, and Ancap (the national petroleum company) are open daily until 9 PM or later.

ESSENTIALS

ELECTRICITY

Uruguay runs on 220-volt power. The two-pronged plugs, such as those used in Europe, are standard here.

ENTRY REQUIREMENTS

U.S., U.K., Canadian, Australian, and New Zealand citizens may visit Uruguay for stays up to 90 days with only a passport valid for at least six months beyond departure from the country.

HEALTH & SAFETY

It's a good idea to avoid tap water, as pipes in many older buildings are made of lead. Almost everyone drinks locally bottled *agua mineral* (mineral water), which is available *con gas* or *sin gas* (with or without carbonation).

Uruguay would win most "Safest South American Country" competitions, but standard travel precautions apply. Keep an eye on your purse or wallet, avoid unnecessary displays of wealth, and avoid wandering back streets of Montevideo at night.

Emergency Contacts **General Number** (📞 *911, for police, fire, or ambulance emergencies nationwide*). **U.S. Embassy** (✉ *Lauro Müller, No. 1776 Centro, Montevideo* 📞 *02/418–7777* 🌐 *montevideo.usembassy.gov*). **Canadian Embassay**

(⊠ *Plaza Independencia 749, Ciudad Vieja, Montevideo* ☎ *02/902–2030* ⊕ *uruguay. gc.ca*). **U.K. Embassy** (⊠ *Marco Bruto 1072, Buceo, Montevideo* ☎ *02/622–3630* ⊕ *britishembassy.gov.uk/uruguay*).

LANGUAGE

Spanish is the official language of Uruguay, spoken with an accent similar to that of neighboring Argentina. Many Uruguayans, especially those conneted with the tourist industry, speak at least a little English.

MONEY MATTERS

CURRENCY & EXCHANGE Uruguay's currency is the peso uruguayo, designated with a $ sign in front of the number. Given the potential for confusion, we spell out of the word *pesos* when giving local prices, and only use the $ sign to indicate dollar prices. Bills come in 20-, 50-, 100-, 200-, 500-, 1,000-, and 2,000-peso denominations. Coins are available in 50 centésimos, 1, 2, 5, and 10 pesos.

At this writing the exchange rate was just under 20 pesos to the U.S. dollar. All banks and *casas de cambio* (exchange houses), which are plentiful in Montevideo, will change dollars, euros, Argentine pesos, and Brazilian reales. Many change traveler's checks too, but plan on a 3% surcharge.

PRICING Uruguay devalued its peso by half in 2001 and went overnight from one of the world's most expensive countries to a reasonably priced one for visitors. The falling U.S. dollar has made Uruguay slightly more expensive again, but you'll find the quality of meals, hotels, and services quite good for the money.

Sample prices: cup of coffee, 20 pesos; bottle of beer, 30 pesos; soft drink, 20 pesos; bottle of house wine, 180 pesos; sandwich, 30 pesos; 1-km (½-mi) taxi ride, 20 pesos; city bus ride, 13 pesos.

TAXES Throughout the country a value-added tax, called IVA, of 14% is added to hotel and restaurant bills. This tax is usually included in the rate. Almost all other goods and services carry a 23% IVA charge. To most foreign destinations you can expect to pay an airport-departure tax of US$31. (American Airlines includes the tax in its ticket prices.) If you're headed to Argentina, instead, you'll only pay $17.

TIPPING In restaurants a flat 10% tip is considered adequate. For any other services, such as tour guides and valet services, a 20-peso tip is appreciated. Tips are optional for taxi rides.

PHONES

To call Uruguay from abroad, dial the country code of 598, and then the area code, minus the initial zero. To call locally, dial the digits of the numbers without any prefix. In Montevideo, a local number has seven digits; in Punta it has six; in Colonia it has five. To dial domestically to another region, include the regional code and then the number. The Montevideo area code is 02; Punta del Este's code is 042; Colonia's is 052.

Public phones use phone cards in denominations of 60, 100, 200, and 500 pesos, available for purchase at newsstands and other small businesses. You can also place calls at one of the offices of Antel, the national telecommunications company, though at a much higher rate.

An unlocked GSM phone is your best option for cellular communication in Uruguay. Claro and Movistar, the country's two mobile providers, sell phone cards.

RESTAURANTS & HOTELS

CUISINE   Beef is the staple of the Uruguayan diet. It's cheap, abundant, and often grilled in a style borrowed from the gauchos, and known as

---

WHERE'S THE BEEF?

Argentina may leap to mind when discussing South American beef, but some 12 million head of cattle, primarily Hereford and Angus, graze Uruguay's grasslands—this in a nation of roughly 3 million people. ("Grass-fed" and "all-natural" are the buzz terms the $800 million industry here uses to promote its beef.) Uruguay publicized its best-known export in April 2008 with a Guinness-record-setting barbecue in Montevideo: 1,250 cooks prepared 12,000 kg. (13 tons) of beef on 1.5 km (about one mile) of grills.

---

parrillada. A meal in a a Uruguayan steak house, should be on your agenda. Beef is also made into sausages, such as *chorizo* and *salchicha*, or is combined with ham, cheese, bacon, and peppers to make *matambre.* Seafood is also popular here—especially the *lenguado* (flounder), *merluza* (hake), and *calamar* (squid). Try the *raya a la manteca negra* (squid ray in blackened butter). If you are not up to a full meal, try the *chivito,* a steak sandwich with thin strips of beef. Uruguayan wines under the Bouza, Santa Rosa, and Calvinor labels, a step up from table wine, are available in most restaurants. *Clericó* is a mixture of white wine and fruit juice, while *medio y medio* is part sparkling wine, part white wine.

Lunch is served between noon and 3; restaurants begin to fill around 12:30 and are packed by 1:30. Many restaurants do not open for dinner until 8 PM, and are rarely crowded before 10 PM. Most pubs and *confiterías* (cafés) are open all day. Formal dress is rarely required. Smart sportswear is acceptable at even the fanciest establishments.

ACCOMMO-   Hotels here are generally comfortable and good value for your money.
DATION   Most include breakfast in their rates. All but the most basic hotels have air-conditioning—you'll appreciate it during the hot summers. *Hosterías* are country inns that not only offer modest rooms but are open for dinner as well. Menus tend to be limited, though the food served is unfailingly hearty.

Lodging at the beach requires reservations no matter what the time of year. Rooms fill up quickly (and prices increase dramatically) during the December–February high season. Rates go down during the shoulder months of November and March, but you can still count on good weather. Many hotels close for a few weeks between Easter and late May and/or in September.

One of the nicest ways to experience Uruguay's vast unspoiled countryside is to stay at an *estancia*. These ranches usually raise animals for the country's most-prized exports—wool, beef, and leather. Although some exist solely as tourist attractions, most estancias are fully operational. You may meet the *estancieros* (ranchers) and stay in quarters that date from the colonial period. The highlight is accompanying the gauchos while they herd cattle, shear sheep, or sit around a fire roasting up sausages for lunch.

Accommodations at estancias range from comfortable to luxurious, and meals are generally included. Some estancias have swimming pools and tennis courts, and most let you explore the countryside on horseback and swim in local rivers and lakes. All provide a chance to breathe the fresh air of the open range.

WHAT IT COSTS (IN URUGUAYAN PESOS)				
¢	$	$$	$$$	$$$$
RESTAURANTS under 120	120–200	200–300	300–400	over 400
HOTELS under 1,000	1,000–1,500	1,500–2,500	2,500–3,500	over 3,500

Restaurant prices are based on the median main course price at dinner. Hotel prices are for two people in a standard double room in high season.

VISITOR INFORMATION

Contact Ministerio de Turismo (✉ *Rambla 25 de Agosto 1825, Ciudad Vieja, Montevideo* ⊕ *www.uruguaynatural.com*).

MONTEVIDEO

Uruguay's only real metropolis has its share of glitzy shopping avenues and modern office buildings. But few visitors come here specifically in search of urban pleasures. This city of 1½ million doesn't have the whirlwind vibe of Rio de Janeiro or Buenos Aires, but it's a fine old city with sumptuous, if worn, colonial architecture, and a massive coastal promenade that—as it passes fine beaches, restaurants, and numerous parks—recalls the sunny sophistications of the Mediterranean. In fact, if you've been to Buenos Aires, Montevideo may strike you as a smaller, more manageable, less expensive incarnation of Argentina's capital.

Built along the eastern bank of the Río de la Plata (River of Silver), Montevideo takes full advantage of its location. When the weather's good, La Rambla, a 22-km (14-mi) waterfront avenue that links the Old City with the eastern suburbs and changes names about a dozen times, gets packed with fishermen, ice-cream vendors, and joggers. Around sunset, volleyball and soccer games wind down as couples begin to appear for evening strolls. Polls consistently rate Montevideo as having the highest quality of life of any city in Latin America. After one visit here, especially on a lovely summer evening, you just might agree.

9

GETTING HERE & AROUND

BY AIR   Uruguay's principal airport, Aeropuerto Internacional de Carrasco (MVD), is 24 km (15 mi) east of Montevideo. A gleaming new terminal is under construction at this writing and scheduled to open in 2009. It will replace the present crowded and, quite fankly, dreary facility, A taxi to downtown costs about 550 pesos; plan on 620 pesos to reach the Ciudad Vieja. A city bus (marked CIUDADELA) is cheap—about 26 pesos—but the drawback is that it takes an hour to reach downtown.

WHAT'S IN A NAME?
Stories abound about the origin of Montevideo's unusual name. The generally accepted account holds that Magellan, traveling along the coast from Brazil in 1520, counted off six hills from the Brazilian border and thus named the city Monte (mountain) vi (roman numeral six) de (from) eo (*este a oeste,* or east to west).

BY BOAT & FERRY   Buquebus operates hydrofoil service between Buenos Aires and the ports at Montevideo and Colonia. The trip takes less than three hours to Montevideo and less than four hours to Colonia. A round-trip ticket between Buenos Aires and Montevideo costs about 3,000 pesos. A package that includes a round-trip ticket between Buenos Aires and Colonia and a shuttle bus to or from Montevideo costs about 2,000 pesos.

BY BUS   Montevideo's public buses are a great alternative to taxis, which can be difficult to find during peak hours. Buses crisscross the entire city 24 hours a day. You don't need exact change, and the price for any trip within Montevideo is only 13 pesos.

Colonia is serviced by several regional bus lines, including Cot and TURIL. The three-hour ride costs less than 400 pesos.

BY CAR   Because La Rambla, Montevideo's riverside thoroughfare, extends for dozens of miles, driving is a good way to see the city. Roads are well maintained and drivers obey the traffic laws—a rarity in South America. It's easy to rent a car, both downtown and at the airport. In Montevideo you can rent from several major international companies, including Avis, Budget, and Dollar, and from smaller companies such as Inter Car and Multicar.

BY TAXI   All cabs have meters that count *fichas,* or pulses, each 1/10 km (1/20 mi). When you arrive at your destination, the driver will take out an official chart that calculates the fare from the number of pulses elapsed. You can hail taxis on the street with ease, or call one to pick you up at your hotel. A ride to the airport from the Old City costs about 500 pesos.

SAFETY & PRECAUTIONS

Although Montevideo doesn't have the problems with crime that larger cities in South America do, it's best to watch your wallet in crowded markets, and to avoid walking down deserted streets at night. Most of Montevideo's residents stay up quite late, so the streets are usually full of people until 1 AM. The city bus authority discourages boarding empty buses at night. Look for the helpful tourist police decked out in blue berets and yellow vests that say POLICÍA TURÍSTICA. They patrol Avenida 18 de Julio, the Ciudad Vieja, and the Mercado del Puerto. Most are bilingual or can round up a colleague who is. Some are accompanied by canine members of the force decked out in matching yellow jackets.

ESSENTIALS

Air Contacts **Aerolíneas Argentinas** (☎ *02/902–3691* ⊕ *www.aerolineas.com. ar*). **American** (☎ *02/916–3929*). **Pluna-Varig** (☎ *02/902–1414* ⊕ *www.pluna. aero*).

Bank **Cambio Matriz** (✉ *Sarandí 556, Ciudad Vieja* ☎ *02/915–0804*).

Boat Contacts **Buquebus** (☎ *02/408–8120* ⊕ *www.buquebus.com*). **Terminal Tres Cruces** (✉ *Bulevar General Artigas 1825, Centro* ☎ *02/408–8710* ⊕ *www. trescruces.com.uy*).

Bus Contacts **Cot** (☎ *02/409—4949 in Montevideo*). **TURIL** (☎ *02/900—5185 in Montevideo* ⊕ *www.turil.com.uy*).

Car-Rental Contacts **Avis** (☎ *02/903–0303*). **Dollar** (☎ *02/402–6427*).

Internet **Babylon** (✉ *18 de Julio 1236, Centro* ☎ *02/900–9361*).

Medical Assistance **Hospital Británico** (✉ *Av. Italia 2420* ☎ *02/487–1020* ⊕ *www.hospitalbritancio.org.uy*).

Taxis **Taxi Aeropuerto Internacional de Carrasco** (☎ *02/600–0323*).

Visitor Info **Información Turística de la Intendencia at City Hall** (✉ *18 de Julio 1360, Centro* ☎ *1950–1830*). **Ministerio de Turismo** (✉ *Calle Colonia 1021, Centro* ☎ *02/900–1078* ✉ *Terminal Tres Cruces, Bulevar General Artigas 1825, Centro* ☎ *02/409–7399* ✉ *Aeropuerto Internacional de Carrasco* ⊕ *www. uruguaynatural.com*).

EXPLORING MONTEVIDEO

Modern Montevideo expanded outward from the peninsular Ciudad Vieja, the Old City, still noted for its narrow streets and mix of elegant colonial and art deco architecture. El Prado, an exclusive enclave a few miles north of the city center, is peppered with lavish mansions and grand parks. When you remember that these mansions were once summer homes for aristocratic Uruguayans who spent most of the year elsewhere, you'll get some idea of the wealth this small country once enjoyed.

CIUDAD VIEJA

TIMING & PRECAUTIONS

Ciudad Vieja is fairly compact, and you could walk from one end to the other in about 15 minutes. Take care at night, when the area is fairly deserted and feels a little sketchy.

MAIN ATTRACTIONS

② Mercado del Puerto. For Montevideo's quintessential lunch experience, head to the old port market, a restored building of vaulted iron beams and colored glass, and a terrific example of urban renewal at its best. The market shields 14 stalls and eateries where, over large fires, the best *parrillas* (grilled beef) in the city are cooked. It's a mix of casual lunch-counter places and sitdown restaurants. The traditional drink here is a bottle of *medio y medio* (champagne mixed with white wine). Many other eateries congregate outside around the perimeter of the building. ⌧*Rambla 25 de Agosto, between Av. Maciel and Av. Pérez Castellano, across from port, Ciudad Vieja* ☏*No phone* ⊕*www. mercadodelpuerto.com.uy* ⊘*Daily 11–6.*

FodorsChoice
★

① Museo del Carnaval. Move over Rio. Montevideo's annual Carnaval celebration may be more low-key than that of its northern neighbor, but it lasts for a full 40 days. This museum honoring the celebration sits next to the Mercado del Puerto and displays the elaborate costumes and photos of the processions that make up pre-Lenten carnival here. A guided tour is included in your admission price (which happens to be free). ⌧*Rambla 25 de Agosto 1825, Ciudad Vieja* ☏*02/916–5493* ⌧*Free* ⊘*Nov.–Mar., daily 10–6; Apr.–Oct., daily 11–5.*

⑬ Plaza Independencia. Portions of Independence Square were once occupied by the *ciudadela,* a fort built originally by the Spanish but deemed militarily useless and destroyed in 1833. All that remains of the original walls is the Puerta de la Ciudadela, the triumphal gate to the Old City. In the center stands a 30-ton statue of General José Gervasio Artigas, the father of Uruguay and the founder of its 19th-century independence movement. At the base of the monument, two flights of polished granite stairs lead to an underground mausoleum that holds Artigas's remains. The mausoleum is a moving memorial: bold graphics chiseled in the walls of this giant space detail the feats of Artigas's life. Two uniformed guards dressed in period uniforms stand at solemn attention beside the urn in this uncanny, rarely visited vault. There's a changing of the guard Friday at 12:30, and a parade at the mausoleum on Saturday at 11:30 AM.

Looming over the north side of the plaza, the 26-story **Palacio Salvo** was the tallest building in South America when it was erected in 1927 (it's still the second-tallest building in Uruguay). Today this gorgeous Art Deco edifice is simply an office building. A speaker on the Avenida 18 de Julio side of the building plays the strains of *La Cumparsita,* a famous tango, each day at noon and 6 PM.

IF YOU HAVE TIME

❿ El Cabildo. The old City Hall is where the Uruguayan constitution was signed in 1830. This two-story colonial edifice houses an impressive collection of paintings, antiques, costumes, and rotating history exhibits. Fountains and statuary line the interior patios. English-speaking guides are available. ⊠ *Calle Juan Carlos Gómez at Calle Sarandí, Ciudad Vieja* ☎ *02/915–9685* ☞ *Free* ⊗ *Wed.–Fri. 1:30–5:30, Sat. 11–4:30, Sun. 1:30–5:30.*

❸ Casa de Lavalleja. This Spanish neoclassical home was built in 1783 and later became the home of General Juan A. Lavalleja, who distinguished himself in Uruguay's war for independence. This pristine colonial home with lovely wrought-iron balconies displays manuscripts and historical memorabilia. ⊠ *Calle Zabala 1469, Ciudad Vieja* ☎ *02/915–1028* ☞ *Free* ⊗ *Tues.–Fri. 1–5.*

❻ Casa de Rivera. Once the home of General Fructuso Rivera, Uruguay's first president, the Rivera House was acquired by the government in 1942. Exhibits inside this pale yellow colonial house with an octagonal cupola document the development of Uruguay from the colonial period through the 1930s. ⊠ *Calle Rincón 437, Ciudad Vieja* ☎ *02/915–1051* ☞ *Free* ⊗ *Tues.–Fri. 1–5, Sat. 11–4.*

❾ Club Uruguayo. Uruguay's most prestigious private social club, founded in 1878, is headquartered in this eclectic, three-story neoclassical national monument on the south side of Plaza Matriz. The club is open for tours (anytime) to the public, and friendly, English-speaking guides will happily show you up the marble staircases so you can marvel at the elegant salons. The club was formed for high society of European descent. Today its approximately 400 exclusive members gather for meals and to play bridge. ⊠ *Calle Sarandí 584, Ciudad Vieja* ☎ *No phone* ☞ *Free* ⊗ *Daily 7 AM–10 PM.*

❼ Iglesia Matriz. This cathedral, the oldest public building in Montevideo, has a distinctive pair of dome-cap bell towers that stand guard over the plaza below. Besides its rich marble interior, colorful floor tiling, stained glass, and dome, the Matriz Church is most notable as the final resting place of Uruguay's most important political and military figures. ⊠ *Calle Ituzaingó 1373, at Calle Sarandí, Ciudad Vieja* ☎ *02/915–7018* ⊕ *www.arquidiocesis.net* ⊗ *Daily 9–7; mass Sun. 9–1.*

❿ Palacio Estévez. On the south side of Plaza Independencia, Estévez Palace, one of the most beautiful old buildings in the city, was the seat of government until 1985, when the president's offices were moved to a more modern building. This building, unfortunately closed to the public, is used on occasion for ceremonial purposes. ⊠ *Plaza Independencia, Ciudad Vieja.*

❹ Palacio Taranco. Built in 1908 atop the rubble of Uruguay's first theater, the ornate Taranco Palace, in the Ciudad Vieja, is representative of the French-inspired architecture favored in fin-de-siècle Montevideo. Even the marble for the floors was imported from France. Today you can survey that bygone glory in rooms filled with period furniture, statuary, draperies, clocks, and portrait paintings. A cultural center within has

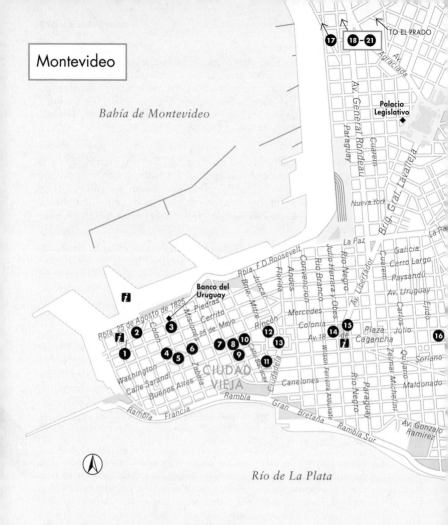

Montevideo

Bahía de Montevideo

TO EL PRADO

Palacio Legislativo

CIUDAD VIEJA

Río de La Plata

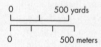

0 — 500 yards

0 — 500 meters

KEY

🛈 *Tourist information*

a calendar of performances and live music. ⊠*Calle 25 de Mayo 376, Ciudad Vieja* ☎*02/915–1101* ⌨*Free* ⊙*Tues.–Sat. 12:15–6, Sun. 2–6; guided tour Tues.–Sun. 4:30.*

❽ Plaza Matriz. The ornate cantilever fountain in the center of this tree-filled square (known to most as Plaza Constitución) was installed in 1871 to commemorate the construction of the city's first water system.

❺ Plaza Zabala. At this charmed spot in the heart of the Ciudad Vieja it's easy to image the splendor of the old Montevideo. Around the fountain and flowers of the park are the turn-of-the-century Taranco mansion and bank headquarters in—a refreshing sight in the Old City—renovated older buildings.

⓫ Teatro Solís. Named in honor of the discoverer of the Río de la Plata, Juan Diaz de Solís, the 1856 Solís Theater is famed for its fine acoustics. Sharing the building is the **Museo Nacional de Historia Natural** (National Museum of Natural History). Both theater and museum reopened in 2008 following extensive renovations. ⊠*Calle Buenos Aires 652, Ciudad Vieja* ☎*1950–3323* ⊕*www.teatrosolis.org.uy.*

CENTRO

Montevideo's main street, the Avenida 18 de Julio, runs through the heart of the city's center. You'll find everything here—shops and museums, cafés and plazas, bustling traditional markets, chrome-and-steel office towers, and places for you to change money. The avenue runs east from Plaza Independencia, away from the Ciudad Vieja, passing through bustling Plaza Fabini and tree-lined Plaza Cagancha.

TIMING It's a 20-minute walk from Plaza Independencia to the Palacio Municipal. If shopping is your main interest, you may want to devote an entire afternoon to browsing and buying along the avenida.

⓮ Museo del Gaucho y la Moneda. The Cowboy and Coin Museum is in a ★ rococo 19th-century mansion near Calle Julio Herrera y Obes, four blocks east of Plaza Independencia. Here you'll find articles from the everyday life of the gauchos, from traditional garb to the detailed silver work on the cups used for *mate* (an indigenous herb from which tea is brewed). Ancient South American and European coins are on the first floor. Tours in English are available with two days' notice. ⊠*Av. 18 de Julio 998, Centro* ☎*02/900–8764* ⌨*Free* ⊙*Weekdays 9–5.*

⓰ Museo de Historia del Arte (MuHAr). In the Palacio Municipal (an ambitious name for this unremarkable brick city hall) you'll find the Museum of Art History, which has the country's best collection of pre-Columbian and colonial artifacts. You'll also find Greek, Roman, and Middle Eastern art, including ceramics and other artifacts. On the street level is the Biblioteca de Historia del Arte (Library of Art History). ⊠*Calle Ejido 1326, Centro* ☎*02/908–9252* ⊕*www.montevideo.gub.uy/cultura* ⌨*Free* ⊙*Museum Tues.–Sun. noon—5:30. Library weekdays 9:30–4:30.*

⓯ Plaza Fabini. In the center of this lovely, manicured square is the Monumento del Entrevero, a large sculpture depicting a whirlwind of gauchos, *criollos* (mixed-blood settlers who are half native, half European), and native Uruguayans in battle. It's one of the last works by sculptor José Belloni (1882–1965). An open-air market with food and other items takes place here every morning. ⊠ *Av. 18 de Julio, Centro.*

EL PRADO

The district known as El Prado lies roughly 6 km (4 mi) north of Plaza Independencia. You could make the long uphill walk along the busy Avenida Agraciada, but it's a lot easier in a taxi. It is pleasant to walk along Avenida Buschental in fall and spring when the trees are in full color. The Jardín Botánico (Botanical Garden) inside the Parque Prado is a worthwhile stop, where you can admire thousands of plant species, many of which were brought to Uruguay in the 19th century by Charles Racine.

⑱ Museo de Bellas Artes. The Museum of Fine Arts, known locally as the Blanes Museum, is housed in an elegant colonial mansion that once belonged to Uruguay's foremost 19th-century painter, Juan Manuel Blanes. He was entirely self-taught, and did not begin painting until he was in his fifties. His realistic portrayals of gauchos and the Uruguayan countryside compose the core of the museum's collection. ⊠ *Av. Millán 4015, El Prado* ☎ *02/336–2248* ⊕ *www.montevideo.gub.uy/museoblanes* ☜ *Free* ☉ *Tues.–Sun. noon–6.*

㉑ Museo del Fútbol. "Other countries have their history," Helenio Herrera, Uruguay's most famous soccer coach once said. "We have our fútbol." Indeed, *fútbol*—that's "soccer" to U.S. readers—is played anywhere there's space, by boys (and a growing number of girls) of all ages. Uruguay both hosted and won the first World Cup competition in 1930 here at the Estadio Centenario. In the bowels of the stadium is this museum dedicated to the country's soccer heritage. It's worth a detour if you're a big fan of the sport. Hours are limited. ⊠ *Av. Ricaldoni s/ n, El Prado* ☎ *02/480–1259* ⊕ *www.museodelfutbol.com.uy* ☜ *Free* ☉ *Fri. noon–7, Sat. 10–5.*

㉒ Museo de la Memoria. The question still pains Uruguayans who remember the era: How did South America's strongest democracy dissolve into 12 years of brutal military dictatorship? This museum documents the history of the 1973–85 period that people here call simply the *dictadura,* during which an astounding 2% of the population experienced arrest for "political crimes" at some time or other. It won't be a stop on most visitors' Montevideo itineraries, but if you're a student of Latin American history and politics, it's worth a look. ⊠ *Av. Las Instrucciones 1057, El Prado* ☎ *02/355–5891* ⊕ *www.montevideo.gub. uy/cultura/museodelamemoria* ☜ *Free* ☉ *Tues.–Sun. 11–5.*

⑲ Parque Prado. The oldest of the city's parks is also one of the most popular. Locals come to see El Rosedal, the rose garden with more than 800 different varieties, and the fine botanical garden. Also in the park you'll find the statue called *La Diligencia,* by sculptor José Belloni. There are free guided tours in Spanish only of the park 10–11 and 4:30–5:30. ⊠ *Av. Agraciada, El Prado* ☎ *02/336–4005* ☉ *Daily 7–7.*

⑰ **Sagrada Familia.** Too tiny to require flying buttresses, the ornately Gothic Holy Family Church is complete in all other respects. A troop of gargoyles peers down at you, and the finely wrought stained-glass windows become radiant when backlit by the sun. ⊠ *Calle Luis Alberto de Herrera 4246, El Prado* ☎ *02/203–6824* ⊙ *Mass weekdays 7 PM; Jan. and Feb., Sat. 7 PM, Sun. 8 PM.*

> **SOCCER**
>
> Try to attend a *clássico,* a match between Montevideo's two great rival professional teams, Nacional and Peñarol, played amid the screams and encouragement of passionate supporters at the capital's Estadio Centenario.

WHERE TO EAT

Menus don't vary much in Montevideo—meat is always the main dish—so the food may not provide a distraction from the blinding light (even the most fashionable restaurant in Montevideo seems to be brightly illuminated).

CIUDAD VIEJO

¢ ✕ **Café Bacacay.** This small and smartly designed restaurant facing
URUGUAYAN Teatro Solís attracts a young, hip crowd. The owner takes special care in preparing the excellent salads, such as the Bacacay (spinach, raisins, carrots, nuts, and hearts of palm topped with croutons) or the Sarandí (lettuce, celery, chicken, apples, carrots). ⊠ *Bacacay 1310, at Calle Buenos Aires, Ciudad Vieja* ☎ *02/916–6074* ⊕ *www.bacacay.com.uy* ⊟ *AE, MC, V* ⊙ *Closed Sun.*

$ ✕ **La Pasiva.** For an ice-cold beer, this popular *chopperia* (beer house)
CAFÉ is a late-night favorite. The specialties are frankfurters (10 pesos), chivitos, and other bar food. In good weather you can socialize at the outdoor tables in Plaza Matriz, which does close at 7 on weeknights. This Montevideo staple has franchises throughout the city, including a prominent location on Plaza Fabini. ⊠ *Calle Sarandí at Calle J.C. Gómez, Ciudad Vieja* ☎ *02/915–7988* ⚞ *No reservations* ⊟ *MC, V* ⊙ *Closed Sun. No dinner Sat.*

CENTRO

$ ✕ **Mesón Viejo Sancho.** What draws the post-theater crowds to this
URUGUAYAN friendly but plain restaurant near Plaza Cagancha are gargantuan portions of smoked pork chops and fried potatoes. ⊠ *Calle San José 1229, Centro* ☎ *02/900–4063* ⊟ *MC, V* ⊙ *Closed Sun.*

$$ ✕ **El Viejo Buzón.** This unassuming restaurant serves excellent parrilla
URUGUAYAN and inexpensive, homemade pastas. The *pollo deshuesado* (boneless breast of chicken stuffed with ham and mozzarella and served with mushroom sauce) is worth the trip. For dessert, try the *charlot* (vanilla ice cream with warm chocolate). Stop by Friday evenings for the tango show. ⊠ *Calle Hocquard 1813, Centro* ☎ *02/203–3971* ⊟ *MC, V* ⊙ *No dinner Sun.–Wed.*

9

ELSEWHERE IN & AROUND MONTEVIDEO

¢ ✕**La Casa Violeta.** Meats are the specialty at this beautiful restaurant
URUGUAYAN facing Puerto del Buceo, one of the prettiest spots in the city. Parrilla is served in the method called *espeto corrido*—grilled meats are
brought to your table on a long skewer so you can slice off whatever
you want. There's also a good selection of salads. There's a big deck
shaded with umbrellas and with attractive views of the port and surrounding homes. ⊠*Rambla Aremeña 3667, corner of 26 de Marzo,
Puerto del Buceo, Pocitos* ☎*02/628–7626* ⊟*AE, MC, V.*

¢ ✕**Doña Flor.** Housed in a century-old home in the suburb of Punta Carre-
FRENCH tas, this quiet, elegant restaurant has a diverse menu heavily indebted to
the French (the pâté is rich as butter and twice as smooth). It's currently
open only for banquets of 10 or more persons. In summer this location
closes so the staff can give its full attention to a sister restaurant in Punta
del Este. ⊠*Bulevar Artigas 1034, Punta Carretas* ☎*02/708–5751*
⌘*Reservations essential* ⊟*AE, DC, MC, V* ☺*Closed Dec.–Apr.*

WHERE TO STAY

Many downtown hotels are grouped around the big three squares,
Plaza Independencia, Plaza Fabini, and Plaza Cagancha. In the weeks
before and after Carnaval in February, rooms become hard to come by.
Otherwise, rooms are plentiful in summer, when beach-bound residents
desert the city.

CENTRO

¢ ▥**Lancaster.** Hidden behind tall poplars in a corner of Plaza Cagancha,
this 11-story hotel in the heart of the city may be past its glory days,
but it makes a fine budget lodging choice if you're not too fussy. Rooms
are sunny and large, with tall French doors that open out onto the
square. **Pros:** Central location, friendly staff, good value. **Con:** Worn
rooms. ⊠*Plaza Cagancha 1334, Centro* ☎*02/902–1054* ⊕*www.lan
caster-hotel.com* ⇆*76 rooms* ◊*In-room: refrigerator, Wi-Fi (some).
In-hotel: restaurant, bar, laundry service, public Internet* ⊟*AE, DC,
MC, V* ◉|*BP.*

$$ ▥**Oxford.** Glass walls, broad windows, and mirrors give the small
lobby an open but intimate feel, much like that of the hotel itself.
Rooms at this English-style hotel are immaculate, the staff friendly and
helpful. Despite its location near Plaza Cagancha, the hotel is remark-
ably quiet. **Pros:** Central location, attentive staff. **Cons:** Some oddly
configured rooms, small bathrooms. ⊠*Calle Paraguay 1286, Centro*
☎*02/902–0046* ⊕*www.hoteloxford.com.uy* ⇆*66 rooms* ◊*In-room:
Ethernet, refrigerator, safe. In-hotel: restaurant, room service, bar, pub-
lic Internet, parking (no fee)* ⊟*AE, DC, MC, V* ◉|*BP.*

$$$–$$$$ ▥**Radisson Montevideo Victoria Plaza.** The luxurious glass-and-brick
structure overlooks Plaza Independencia and blend harmoniously with
the surrounding architecture, including that of the original Victoria Plaza
Hotel. The café on the 24th floor is the best public space for views of
the old and new city, and the on-site casino is the capital's largest. **Pros:**
Great location for sightseeing, attentive staff, many amenities. **Cons:**
Some reports of window frames that rattle with temperature changes.

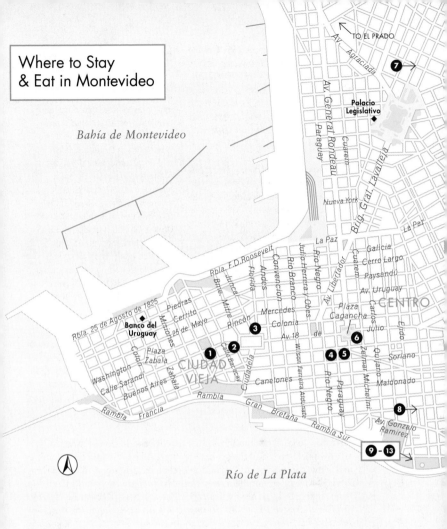

Where to Stay & Eat in Montevideo

Bahía de Montevideo

Río de La Plata

CENTRO

CIUDAD VIEJA

Banco del Uruguay

Palacio Legislativo

TO EL PRADO

0	500 yards
0	500 meters

Plaza Independencia 759, Centro ☎*02/902–0111* ⊕*www.radisson. com/montevideouy* ⇱*190 rooms, 64 suites* ⌂*In-room: Ethernet, refrigerator. In-hotel: 2 restaurants, room service, bar, pool, gym, spa, laundry service, public Internet, airport shuttle* ▤*AE, DC, MC, V* ¶○¶*BP.*

$$$ 🏨**Sheraton Montevideo.** The city's biggest new hotel is removed from the Old City, and, decidedly modern, feels a world away. Attached to the flashy Punta Carretas shopping center, the hotel offers the comforts of a corporate luxury hotel only a five-minute walk from one of the city's many fine beaches. You will need a cab, however, to reach most sights. Note that there's also a Sheraton Four Points location in the city's financial district. **Pros:**

Attentive staff, many amenities, adjoins mall. **Con:** Far from downtown and sights. ✉*Victor Soliño 349, Punta Carretas* ☎*02/710–2121* ⊕*www.starwoodhotels.com/sheraton* ⇱*207 rooms, 10 suites* ⌂*In-room: Ethernet, kitchen (some), refrigerator, safe. In-hotel: restaurant, room service, bar, tennis courts, pool, gym, spa, concierge, laundry service, public Internet, airport shuttle* ▤*AE, DC, MC, V* ¶○¶*BP.*

ELSEWHERE IN MONTEVIDEO

$$–$$$ 🏨**Armon Suites.** This hotel in a quiet neighborhood east of downtown is an all-suites hotel, and the spaces are huge. All have a small kitchenette, making it a good option if you don't feel like eating out all of the time. **Pros:** Good value, ample-size suites, can prepare own food **Con:** Far from sights. ✉*21 de Setiembre 1885, Pocitos* ☎*02/712–4120* ⊕*www. armonsuites.com.uy* ⇱*40 rooms* ⌂*In-room: refrigerator, kitchen, safe, Wi-Fi. In-hotel: Restaurant, room service, bar, pool, spa, service, public Internet, parking (no fee)* ▤*AE, DC, MC, V* ¶○¶*BP.*

$ 🏨**Ermitage.** The Ermitage is in an unprepossessing, sandstone-front
★ building overlooking the lovely Plaza Tomás Gomensoro, and is a good, affordable choice if you want to be near the shore. It's in a calm residential zone a block from Pocitos Beach and is also a 10-minute drive from the Old City. You'll find plenty of other guests sitting over a drink or playing cards in the wood-panel lobby—decorated with a large photomural of Playa Pocitos in 1928. Rooms are furnished with replicas of 1920s-style furniture and light fixtures—to reflect that gentler, more stylish era of city history. **Pros:** Wonderful historic building, good value, friendly staff. **Con:** Far from sights. ✉*Calle Juan Benito Blanco 783, Pocitos* ☎*02/710–4021 or 02/711–7447* ⊕*www.ermitagemontevideo. com* ⇱*100 rooms* ⌂*In-room: refrigerator, safe, Wi-Fi. In-hotel: restaurant, laundry service, parking (no fee)* ▤*AE, DC, MC, V* ¶○¶*BP.*

¢ ⚐ **Hostería del Lago.** On a beautiful lake about 12 km (7 mi) east of
★ downtown, this sprawling Spanish colonial hotel is the kind of place
that encourages relaxation. Bask by the pool, play a few games of tennis, or head out on a horse for an afternoon of exploring the parkland.
The split-level rooms, all the size of suites, have wood-beam ceilings
and carpeted floors. **Pros:** Secluded site, beautiful lake. **Cons:** Requires a
car, not immediately convenient to city. ⊠*Av. Arizona 9637, Carrasco*
☎*02/601–2210* ⊕*www.hosteriadelago.com* ⇆*60 rooms* ♨*In-room:
refrigerator. In-hotel: 2 restaurants, room service, bar, tennis court,
pool, laundry service, airport shuttle* ▭*AE, DC, MC, V.*

AFTER DARK

In Montevideo you'll find quiet, late-night bars, hip-hop clubs, and
folk-music shows. The entertainment and cultural pages of local papers
are the best sources of information; particularly useful is the *Guía del
Ocio*, a magazine inserted into the Friday edition of the daily newspaper *El País*. With few exceptions, bars and clubs come to life around
1 AM and don't close until it's time for breakfast.

DANCE CLUBS
The retro set flocks to **Aquellos Años** (⊠*Calle Beyrouth 1405, Pocitos*),
which has music from the '50s and '60s. You can hear live music and
dance to house hits at **Mariachi** (⊠*Gabriel Pereira 2964, Pocitos* ☎*No
phone*).

Milenio (⊠*25 de Mayo and Ciudadela, Ciudad Vieja*) is popular with
the MTV generation. **New York** (⊠*Calle Mar Artico 1227* ☎*02/600–
0444*) draws an older crowd. In front of Playa Ramirez in Parque
Rodó, **W Lounge** (⊠*Rambla Wilson s/n, Punta Carretas* ☎*02/712–
5287*) gets a large crowd on weekends. It transforms from a bar to a
disco at 1 AM.

PUBS
Amarcor (⊠*Calle Julio Herrera y Obes 1231, Centro* ☎*02/900–1207
or 02/901–9281*) is popular with young artists, actors, and intellectuals. **Riff Gallery Pub** (⊠*Bul. España 2511, Centro* ☎*No phone*) is the
only bar in the city devoted to jazz, with live shows on Thursday and
Saturday. The **Shannon Irish Pub** (⊠*Mitre 1318, Ciudad Vieja*) in the
Old City draws a young crowd. It has good rock music and an unpretentious vibe.

TANGO SHOWS
La Casa de Becho (⊠*New York 1415, Centro* ☎*02/400–2717*), the
house that once belonged to Mattos Rodríguez, the composer of "La
Cumparsita," has weekend shows for a younger crowd. Call first,
because reservations are necessary, and the frequency of the shows
depends on the time of year. **Joven Tango** (⊠*Calle San José 1314, Centro* ☎*02/908–1550*) is the best place in the city to learn tango. Shows
are frequent; call for times.

9

SHOPPING

Let's face it: Montevideans head to Buenos Aires when they want to go on an extra-special shopping excursion. But quality and selection are decent here, and prices are lower than in Argentina. Stores in Centro, along Avenida 18 de Julio, offer the standard selection of urban merchandise. The truly fun shopping experience is to be found in the city's markets.

MARKETS

Weekend *ferias* (open-air markets) are the best place for leisurely browsing among a warren of crafts stalls. Government regulations dictate that all ferias must close in the early afternoon, so make sure to arrive by 10 AM. **Feria Tristán Narvaja,** started over half a century ago by Italian immigrants, is Montevideo's top attraction on Sunday. (It's only open on Sunday, a day when all other markets, and much of the city, are closed. Hours run about 9–4.) Running off 18 de Julio at Calle Tristán Narvaja, a 5- to 10-minute walk from the Old City and in the Centro district, the fair is plentifully stocked with secondhand goods. The Saturday morning market—although a few stands stay open until about 3 PM—at **Plaza Biarritz** in the neighborhood of Pocitos, sells crafts, clothes, and some antiques. **Plaza Cagancha,** between Avenida 18 de Julio and Calle Rondeau in Centro, has a crafts market every day except Sunday.

A fun market in Centro, a few blocks from the Palacio Municipal at the corner of Calle San José and Calle Yaguarón, is the **El Mercado de la Abundancia.** Inside are a tango dance center, four good choices for a lunchtime *parrillada,* and, downstairs, a crafts market from 10 AM–8 PM every day but Sunday.

SHOPPING CENTERS

There are three major shopping centers in Montevideo, offering everything from designer clothing to gourmet foods to art supplies. **Montevideo Shopping** (⊠ *Av. Luis Alberto de Herrera and Calle General Galarza, Punta Carretas*) is near Parque Rodó. **Portones de Carrasco** (⊠ *Avs. Bolívia and Italia, Carrasco*) is a 2-story, 250-store indoor mall with a movie theater. **Punta Carretas Shopping Center** (⊠ *Calles Ellauri and Solano, Punta Carretas*), housed in a former prison, is the city's largest and most upscale mall. It's near the Sheraton Montevideo, a 10-minute cab ride from the Old City.

SPECIALTY STORES

ANTIQUES

Calle Tristán Narvaja north of Avenida 18 de Julio is packed with antiques shops. In the Old City, the streets north of Plaza Constitución are also lined with such stores. **El Rincón** (⊠ *Calle Tristán Narvaja 1747, Centro* ☎ *02/400–2283*) is one of the area's best antiques dealers. **El Galeón** (⊠ *Juan Gómez 1327, Centro* ☎ *02/915–6139*) sells antiques and rare books. The **Louvre** (⊠ *Calle Sarandí 652, Ciudad Vieja* ☎ *No phone*), an antiques store, is the only source for handmade and painted trinket boxes—the perfect *recuerdos* (souvenirs).

GEMSTONES & JEWELRY

Amatistas Del Uruguay (✉ *Calle P. Sarandí 604, Ciudad Vieja* ☎ *02/916–6456*) specializes in amethysts, topazes, and other gems. **Gemas de América** (✉ *Av. 18 de Julio 948, Centro* ☎ *02/902–2572*) carries amethyst and topaz jewelry, agate slices, and elaborate objects made of precious gems. **La Limeña** (✉ *Calle Buenos Aires 542, Centro* ☎ *No phone*) has good prices on unset stones.

HANDICRAFTS

Ema Camuso (✉ *Av. 8 de Octubre 2574, Centro* ☎ *No phone*) offers a sophisticated and sporty line of hand-knit sweaters, all permanently on sale at factory prices. **Manos del Uruguay** (✉ *Av. de la Herrera 1290, Centro* ☎ *02/628–4401* ⊕ *www.manos.com.uy* ✉ *Calle San José 111, Centro* ☎ *02/900–4910* ✉ *Montevideo Shopping, Punta Carretas* ☎ *No phone*) has three locations with a wide selection of woolen wear and locally produced ceramics. **Tiempofunky** (✉ *Bacacay 1307, Ciudad Vieja* ☎ *02/916–8721*) sells clothing, candles, lamps, soaps, and contemporary crafts and design items, on a pleasant street in the Old City.

LEATHER

Although Buenos Aires has more stylish choices, Montevideo is a good source for inexpensive leather. Shops near Plaza Independencia specialize in hand-tailored coats and jackets made out of nutria (fur from a large semiaquatic rodent). **Peletería Holandesa** (✉ *Calle Colonia 894, Centro* ☎ *02/901–5438*) carries leather clothing. **Péndola** (✉ *Calle San José 1087, Centro* ☎ *02/900–1524*) has a particularly good selection of leather apparel. Try **Casa Mario** (✉ *Calle Piedras 641, Centro* ☎ *02/916–2356* ⊕ *www.casamarioleather.com*) for good leather clothes. They offer free transportation, which your hotel can arrange. Custom-made boots are available from **Damino Botas** (✉ *Calle Rivera 2747, Centro* ☎ *02/709–7823*).

SPORTS & THE OUTDOORS

Ample park space and miles of coastline make flat, relatively safe Montevideo one of the world's great cities for runners and joggers. The city holds a dozen or so races each year, mostly 5- or 10-km, but also including the Latin America-famous San Felipe and Santiago marathon in mid-December.

The Web site for the **Confederación Atlética del Uruguay** *(Uruguayan Athletics Confederation)* (⊕ *www.atlecau.org.uy*) lists schedules for races—in Spanish only—each year.

THE SOUTH COAST

A technicality of geography: though Uruguay's entire coast appears to front the ocean, everything west of famed vacation spot Punta del Este—sister resort Piriápolis, lovely pre-independence Colonia del Sacramento, and Montevideo itself—is the Río de la Plata, the world's widest river, which fans out to 219 km (131 mi) at its broadest point. The Plate, to use its name in English, swirls in a mix of fresh- and salt-water with the changing winds and tides. Beyond the *punta,* the point from which Punta del Este gets its name, looms the Atlantic Ocean, and the coast takes on a more rugged, end-of-the-world look.

COLONIA DEL SACRAMENTO

Fodor's Choice *180 km (113 mi) west of Montevideo.*
★

It's hard not to fall in love with Colonia del Sacramento, a UNESCO World Heritage Site, and one of South America's most beautiful cit-ies. Founded in 1680, the city was subject to a long series of wars and pacts between Spain and Portugal, which eventually gave up its claim. Its many small museums are dedicated to the story of its tumultuous history. Like Cartagena, Quito, and Cusco, Colonia offers the best of an old colonial city, with wonderfully preserved architecture, rough cobblestone streets, and an easy grace and tranquillity evident in its people and pace. There are more bicycles than cars here, which adds to the serenity of this roughly six-by-six-block Old City that juts out on a small peninsula into the Río de la Plata. Colonia is often the first (and sometimes only) destination in Uruguay most visitors see; it's easily done as a day trip from Buenos Aires, or makes a convenient gateway to the country if arriving from Argentina.

The best sightseeing activity in Colonia, however, is simply walking through its Barrio Histórico (Old Town). Porteños (as citizens of Bue-nos Aires are known) come to Colonia for romantic getaways or a break from the city. It makes sense to follow their example: you don't get enough time here on a day trip to really relax or see the city at its own pace. A night in one of its many colonial-style B&Bs offsets travel costs and time and makes a visit here far more rewarding.

GETTING HERE & AROUND

There's frequent daily bus service from the Tres Cruces terminal in Montevideo to Colonia del Sacramento. Two companies that serve the entire region are Copsa and Cot. It's a beautiful drive from Montevideo to Colonia del Sacramento, and it will take you about three hours on Ruta 1 west. Renting a car is the simplest way to explore the coast.

Hydrofoils and ferries cross the Río de la Plata between Buenos Aires and Uruguay several times a day. Boats often sell out, particularly on summer weekends, so book tickets at least a few days in advance. Buquebus provides two kinds of service for passengers and cars: Colo-nia Express operates the cheapest and fastest services to Colonia, via a 50-minute catamaran trip; the slower ferry takes around three hours. In Buenos Aires the Buquebus terminal is at the northern end of Puerto Madero, accessible by taxi or by walking seven blocks from Leandro N. Alem subte station along Trinidad Guevara and Avenida Alicia M. de Justo to the intersection with Cecilia Grierson. Colonia's ferry port is undergoing renovation work and is rather chaotic. The shortest way to the Barrio Histórico is to turn left out of the port car park into

Florida—it's a six-block walk. Walking is the perfect way to get around this part of town; equally practical—and lots of fun—are golf carts and sand buggies, which you can rent from Thrifty.

■TIP➔Signs and transportation schedules frequently shorthand the name of the city to simply COLONIA.

ESSENTIALS

Bank Banco República (⊠Av. Gral. Flores 151).

Bus Contacts Cot (☎052/23–121). TURIL (☎052/24–5318).

Ferry Contacts Buquebus (☎11/4316—6500 in Buenos Aires ⊕ www.buquebus. com). Colonia Express (☎11/4313–5100 in Buenos Aires, 52/29676 in Colonia ⊕ www.coloniaexpress.com).

Medical Assistance Hospital de Colonia (⊠18 de Julio and Rivera ☎52/20–762).

Rental Cars Thrifty (☎52/22–939 ⊕ www.thrifty.com.uy).

Taxi Taxis Colonia (☎52/22–920).

Visitor Info Colonia del Sacramento Tourist Board (⊠General Flores and Rivera ⊠Manuel Lobo between Ituzaingó and Paseo San Antonio ☎52/23–700 ⊕ www.colonia.gub.uy).

EXPLORING COLONIA

Begin your tour of the town at the reconstructed Portón de Campo or city gate, where remnants of the old bastion walls lead to the river. A block farther is Calle de los Suspiros, the aptly named Street of Sighs, a cobblestone stretch of one-story colonial homes that can rival any street in Latin America for sheer romantic effect. It runs between a lookout point on the river, called the Bastión de San Miguel, and the Plaza Mayor, a lovely square filled with Spanish moss, palms, and spiky, flowering *palo borracho* trees. The many cafés around the square are ideal places to take it all in. Clusters of bougainvillea flow over the walls here and in the other quiet streets of the Barrio Histórico, many of which are lined with art galleries and antiques shops.

Another great place to watch daily life is the Plaza de Armas Manoel Lobo, where you'll find the Iglesia Matriz, the oldest church in Uruguay. The square itself is crisscrossed with wooden catwalks over the ruins of a house dating to the founding of the town. The tables from the square's small eateries spill from the sidewalk right onto the cobblestones: they're all rather touristy, but give you an excellent view of the drum-toting candombe squads that beat their way around the old town each afternoon.

You can visit all of Colonia's museums with the same ticket, which you buy from the Museo Portugués or the Museo Municipal for 50 pesos. You can use the ticket on two consecutive days.

❸ **Casa Nacarello.** A colonial Portuguese residence has been lovingly re-created inside this 17th-century house on the main plaza. (⊠*Plaza*

Mayor and Henríquez de la Peña ⌨50 pesos, includes all Colonia Museums ☉Daily 11:15–4:45).

❹ **Faro.** Towering over the Plaza Mayor, Colonia's landmark lighthouse dates from 1857. Your reward for climbing it is great views over the Barrio Histórico and the Río de la Plata. ⌧*Plaza Mayor ⌨30 pesos ☉Daily 11–4.*

❶ **Museo del Azulejo.** This small 18th-century building near the river displays a small collection of the beautiful handmade French tiles that adorn fountains all over Colonia. (⌧*Misiones de los Tapies and Paseo San Gabriel ⌨50 pesos, includes all Colonia museums ☉Daily 11:15–4:45).*

❷ **Museo Municipal.** It houses a sundry collection of objects related to the city's history. (⌧*Plaza Mayor and Misiones de los Tapies ⌨50 pesos, includes all Colonia museums ☉Daily 11:15–4:45).*

❺ **Museo Portugués.** Colonia's best museum documents the city's ties to Portugal. It's most notable for its collection of old map reproductions based on Portuguese naval expeditions. A small selection of period furnishings, clothes, and jewelry from Colonia's days as a Portuguese colony complete the offerings. Exhibits are well labeled, but in Spanish only. (⌧*Plaza Mayor between Calle de los Suspiros and De Solís ⌨50 pesos, includes all Colonia museums) ☉Daily 11:15–4:45)*

WHERE TO EAT

In Colonia, prices are displayed in dollars at all hotels and many restaurants.

$$
$$ PIZZA ✕ **La Bodeguita.** Each night, this hip restaurant serves incredibly delicious, crispy pizza, sliced into bite-size rectangles. The backyard tables overlook the river, and the interior is cozy, with rust- and ocher-color walls. ⌧*Calle del Comercio 167 ☎052/25–329 ▭No credit cards ☉No lunch.*

$$$ URUGUAYAN ✕ **La Florida.** The black-and-white photos, lace tablecloths, and quaint knickknacks that clutter this long, low house belie the fact that it was once a brothel. It still has private rooms, but it's dining that politicians and the occasional celeb rent them for these days. You, too, can ask to be seated in one, but consider the airy back dining room, which has views over the river. It's hard to say whether it's the flamboyant French-Argentine owner's tall tales that keep regulars returning or his excellent cooking. Specialties include kingfish, sole, and salmon cooked to order: you can suggest sauces of your own or go with house suggestions like orange-infused cream. ⌧*Florida 215 ☎094/29–3036 ▭AE, MC, V.*

$$ URUGUAYAN ✕ **El Mesón de la Plaza.** Simple dishes—many steak-based—made with good-quality ingredients have made this traditional restaurant a favorite with visitors to Colonia. The comprehensive wine list showcases Uruguayan vineyards hard to sample anywhere outside of the country. Try to get one of the outside tables that sit right on the peaceful Plaza de Armas. ⌧*Vasconcellos 153 ☎052/24807 ▭MC, V.*

$$ URUGUAYAN ✕ **Pulpería de los Faroles.** There's nothing particularly special about the pastas and grilled fish this tavern-style restaurant does, but the 300-

Colonia del Sacremento

0   1/8 mile

0   1/8 km

Campo Municipal

Dayman

Cnel. Arroyo

Casa de la Cultura ◆

Feria Artesanal ◆

Dr. Daniel Fosalba

⑧

Rivadavia

⑦

Lavalleja

Alberto Mendez

Gral. Rivera

🛈

De España

De Santa Rita

Del Virrey Cebayos

Banco Repúblicas

De Comercio

Av. Gral. Flores

Av. Gral. Flores

De Portugal

Iglesia Matriz ◆

Paseo de San Gabriel

① ②

⑤

De la Playa

Plaza de Armas

Manuel Lobo

18 de Julio

③

④

❶

Misiones de los Tapes

❷

Plaza Mayor

Portón del Campo

Turzaingó

Washington Barbot

Intendente Suárez

Manuel Lobo

Hospital ◆

③

De las Flores

❸

Henriquez de la Peña

❺

🛈

⑥

⑩

❹

De San Pedro

de los Suspiros

Florida

Bastión de San Miguel ◆

Centro Cultural AFE ◆

Ferry Terminal 🛳

Río de la Plata

KEY

🛈   *Tourist information*

🛳   *Ferry*

❶   *Exploring sights*

①   *Hotels & Restaurants*

← TO BUENOS AIRES

year-old stone house it's in is gorgeous. Outside tables on the Plaza Mayor are the perfect place for a coffee or drinks and nibbles. ✉*Misiones de los Tapies 101* ☎*052/30–271* 💳*No credit cards.*

$$ URUGUAYAN ★ ✕ **Sacramento.** It's in the heart of the Barrio Histórico, but chef Nicolás Díaz Ibarguren's fresh take on local ingredients is very now. The fish of the day comes in a cashew crust and chili sauce, and the minty, garlicky lamb is served with fried polenta chips. Set on a quiet corner, the renovated old house is light and breezy during the day, and its modern, dark wooden tables are candlelit at night. ✉*Calle del Comercio and De la Playa* ☎*052/29–245* 💳*AE, MC, V* ⏲*Closed Wed.*

WHERE TO STAY

Since Colonia is the comsummate day trip from Montevideo or Buenos Aires, few visitors actually spend the night here. Consider breaking that mold; there's no shortage of sumptuous lodgings to choose from.

IN COLONIA

$ **Posada Don Antonio.** Rooms open onto long galleries that overlook an enormous split-level courtyard at Posada Don Antonio, the latest incarnation of a large, elegant building that has housed one hotel or another for over a century. With their plain white walls and drab green carpets, rooms lack the character promised by the architecture outside, but they're clean and functional and have comfy beds with wrought-iron bedsteads. **Pros:** The sparkling turquoise pool, surrounded by loungers; a location two blocks from the Barrio Histórico; low rates don't preclude proper hotel perks. **Cons:** Staff are sometimes indifferent, at other times rude; plain, characterless rooms; ill-fitting doors let in noise from the courtyard. ✉*Ituzaingó 232,70000* ☎*052/25–344* 🌐*www.posadadonantonio.com* *38 rooms* *In-room: refrigerator. In-hotel: room service, pool, laundry facilities, public Internet, no elevator* 💳*AE, MC, V* *CP.*

$ ★ **Posada de la Flor.** This colonial-style hotel is on a quiet street leading to the river, and is arranged around a sunny courtyard. Quilts and old china decorating the walls of the bright dining room announce a country-cottage vibe. You feel even more at home after attacking the unlimited breakfast spreads or gazing at the river over a glass of wine on the roof terrace—the owner's happy for you to bring your own. The simple, clean rooms have cheery quilts and are named after flowers: it's worth paying a few dollars more for the more spacious ones, like "Nomeolvides," or "Forget-me-not." The posada is a pleasant five-minute walk from Plaza Mayor. **Pros:** Peaceful location near the river and Barrio Histórico, gorgeous breakfast area and roof terrace, great value. **Cons:** Standard rooms a little cramped; damp spots on some ceilings; ground-floor rooms open to the courtyard and can be noisy. ✉*Calle Ituzaingó 268* ☎*052/30–794* 🌐*www.guiacolonia.com.uy/posadadelaflor* *14 rooms* *In-room: safe, no phone, no TV (some). In-hotel: laundry service, no elevator* 💳*No credit cards* *CP.*

$$ **Posada Plaza Mayor.** A faint scent of jasmine fills the air at this lovely old hotel. Rooms open onto a large, plant-filled courtyard with a fountain. The main building dates from 1840 (a part at the back is even older) and the original stone walls are visible in most rooms, which also

have gloriously high ceilings and pretty flowered bedspreads. There are peaceful river views from the first-floor dining room and from the garden tucked behind the building, whose deck chairs rival those in the courtyard. **Pros:** Beautiful green spaces; on quiet Barrio Histórico street; cheerful, accommodating staff. **Cons:** Cramped bathrooms; three cheapest rooms are small and lack the atmosphere of other standard rooms; high price of deluxe rooms isn't justified by the amenities. ✉*Calle del Comercio 111* ☎*52/23–193* ⊕*www.posadaplazamayor. com* ⊲*15 rooms* ♿*In-room: refrigerator, no TV. In-hotel: room service, laundry service, no elevator* ⊟*AE, DC, MC, V.*

$$$ ★ 🖳**Sheraton Colonia.** This riverside hotel and spa is fast becoming a favorite with weekend visitors from Buenos Aires. It's easy to see why. Materials like copper, terra-cotta, and golden-colored stone add warm touches to the airy, light-filled atrium. So does the massive wood-fronted fireplace, which is always lit in winter. Rooms have handmade woolen bed throws that take the edge off the elegant, but rather generic, furniture. You can walk straight out onto the golf course and the sandy river beaches—who cares about the muddy water when you've got two gorgeous pools (one heated) to play in? Plan your visit mid-week, when the rooms and spa packages are heavily discounted. **Pros:** Excellent value, considering the quality of accommodations; peaceful location; river views from many rooms; great spa. **Cons:** It's a 15-minute drive or taxi-ride north of the Barrio Histórico; lots of noisy kids on weekends; staff are slow and sometimes unhelpful. ✉*Cont. Rambla de las Américas s/n, 70000* ☎*054/29–000* ⊕*www.sheraton.com/coloniasite* ⊲*88 rooms, 4 suites* ♿*In-room: refrigerator, safe, dial-up. In-hotel: 2 restaurants, room service, bar, 9-hole golf course, 2 pools, gym, spa, laundry service, no-smoking rooms.* ⊟*AE, DC, MC, V* ⑩*CP.*

COLONIA & ENVIRONS

$$$$ FodorsChoice ★ 🖳**Four Seasons Carmelo.** Serenity pervades this harmoniously decorated resort an hour west of Colonia del Sacramento. Everything is done in a fusion of Asian styles—from yoga classes at the incense-scented and bamboo-screen health club to bungalows (considered "standard rooms") with private Japanese gardens (and marvelous outdoor showers). In the evening, torches illuminate the paths, which meander through sand dunes. **Pros:** All rooms are spacious; fabulous, personalized service; on-site activities compensate for distance from sights and restaurants. **Cons:** Despite copious netting and bug spray, mosquitos can get out of hand; food quality is erratic; noisy Argentine families can infringe on romantic getaways. ✉*Ruta 21, Km 262, Carmelo* ☎*054/29–000* ⊕*www.fourseasons.com/carmelo* ⊲*20 bungalows, 24 duplex suites* ♿*In-room: safe, refrigerator, cable TV, VCR. In-hotel: 2 restaurants, room service, 18-hole golf course, tennis courts, 2 pools (1 indoors), gym, fitness classes, sauna, spa, bicycles, horseback riding, lobby lounge, library, children's programs (ages 5–12), laundry service, airport shuttle, Internet, meeting rooms, no-smoking rooms* ⊟*AE, DC, MC, V.*

9

AFTER DARK

Much of Colonia's nightlife centers on its restaurants, which become default drinking and bar snacking spots after 11 or 12. In summer, outdoor tables on the Plaza Mayor, which is often lit with torches, are particularly atmospheric.

Locals in their twenties and thirties rub shoulders with visitors at **Colonia Rock** (⊠*Misiones de los Tapies 157* ☎*52/28–189*), a popular, laid-back bar on the Plaza Mayor. There's live music and even karaoke on Fridays and Saturdays.

EN ROUTE

Argentina and Chile grab all the attention in discussions of South American wines, but Uruguay counts some 15 wineries of its own. On the way back to Montevideo from Colonia, take a detour and stop by the **Bouza Winery,** one of the few open for daily visits. For a real treat (1,000 pesos), reserve a full sit-down dinner with samplings of wines to accompany each course. ⊠*Km 13.5, Las Violetas* ☎*2/323–3872* ⊕*www.bodegabouza.com* ☎*Tours 200 pesos; with sampling 430 pesos* ☉*Tours daily 11* AM *and 4* PM.

PIRIÁPOLIS

98 km (61 mi) east of Montevideo.

In 1890 Francisco Piria, an Argentine born of Italian parents, purchased the land between the town of Pan de Azúcar and the Río de la Plata. It became his private residence, but Piria saw the tourism potential of the land and began developing his "Piriápolis" to resemble a French coast town. Piriápolis is nowadays a laid-back beachfront enclave that lacks the sophistication—and the exorbitant prices—of nearby Punta del Este, but it's popular with middle-class Uruguayans. Piriápolis has plenty of stores and restaurants, a casino, and the grand Argentino Hotel, the town's crown jewel, built in the old European tradition with spas and thermal pools.

GETTING HERE & AROUND

Many bus lines travel daily between Montevideo's Terminal Tres Cruces and Piriápolis's Terminal de Omnibus. Two companies that serve the entire region are Copsa and Cot.

ESSENTIALS

Bus Contacts Copsa (☎*042/89–205*). **Cot** (☎*042/86–810*). **Terminal de Omnibus** (⊠*Misiones and Niza*).

Visitor & Tour Info Piriápolis Tourist Office (⊠*Rambla de los Argentinos 1348* ☎*043/22–560*).

EXPLORING PIRIÁPOLIS

Castillo de Piria. Since Piriápolis was the town that Piria built, it's no surprise that its patron would construct the best house for himself. His 1897 Italianate residence sits north of town on expansive palm-strewn grounds. A tour offers a glimpse at turn-of-the-century life of Uruguay's upper class. ⊠*4 km (2½ mi) north of Piriápolis* ☎*No phone* 🖃*Free* ⊙*Dec.–Mar., daily 10–6; Apr.–Nov., weekends 10–3.*

Cerro Pan de Azúcar. The 339-meter (1,100 foot) so-called "Sugar-loaf Hill" north of Piriápolis passes for a mountain in flat Uruguay, but the views are stupendous east toward Punta del Este and west toward Montevideo. The climb isn't bad, but plan on two hours each to ascend and descend. At the top sits a 35-meter (115-foot) concrete cross with a narrow spiral staircase inside. The views from the top of the cross are no better than from the base. ⊠*10 km (6 mi) north of Piriápolis* ☎*No phone* 🖃*Free* ⊙*Daily 7–6.*

BEACHES

Pirápolis's sand stretches 25 km (15 mi) from town east toward Punta del Este. Although seven beaches, all public, can be delineated, only two—Rambla and Hermosa—receive regular cadres of high-season visitors and have amenities (food stands, parking, lifeguards) to cater to them. The crowds and number of facilities dwindle markedly during the off-season.

Playa de la Rambla. The calm, in-town beach lines the Rambla de los Argentinos, the coastal road. It reflects Piriápolis: middle-class Uruguayan, popular, and a mix of families and young singles.

Playa Grande. Gritty sand and rough waters mean fewer people frequenting this beach east of town.

Playa Verde. "Verde" means green in Spanish. The swirling mix of fresh- and saltwater here gives things a greenish tint. The waters are rough for swimming.

Playa Hermosa. The so-called Beautiful Beach lies several kilometers east of town, with fine, golden sand and a population of families with children.

Playa de San Francisco. The waves make this beach popular with surfers, but you should think twice about swimming here.

Playa Punta Colorada. Local fishermen bring in their catch of the day along this stretch of coast that sees few tourists.

Playa Punta Negra. Few people venture out to this isolated dark-sand beach. If you do, you'll likely have it to yourself.

WHERE TO STAY

$$–$$$$ ⚏**Argentino Hotel.** This belle epoque–style structure deserves its honor
★ as a national historic monument. Argentine president Baltasar Brum attended the groundbreaking in 1920; when completed a decade later the hotel was one of the continent's grandest. Elegantly furnished rooms have French doors and balustraded balconies overlooking the ocean. If this isn't stress-reducing enough, the hotel is renowned for its Piriavital health spa. The casino is renowned in South America. **Pros:** Wonderful ambience in historic hotel, lower-priced rooms good value. **Cons:** Higher-priced rooms not as good value. ⊠*Rambla de los Argentinos* ☎*043/422–572* ⊕*www.argentinohotel.com* 🛏*300 rooms, 56*

suites ⟨In-room: *refrigerator. In-hotel: 3 restaurants, room service, bar, tennis courts, pools, gym, spa, laundry service* ☰*AE, DC, MC, V* ⟨○⟨*BP, MAP, FAP.*

PUNTA DEL ESTE

35 km (21 mi) east of Piriápolis.

Part Hamptons, part Cote d'Azur, part South Beach (with a dash of Vegas tossed in for good measure), Punta del Este is a flashy destination. "Punta"—five minutes here and you'll shorten the name just as everyone else does—and the handful of surrounding beachfront communities are, famously, jet-set resorts—places where lounging on golden sand and browsing designer boutiques constitute the day's most demanding activities. The resort takes its name from the "east point" marking the division of the Río de la Plata on the west from the Atlantic Ocean to the east. It also lends its name to the broader region encompassing the nearby communities of Punta Ballena and La Barra de Maldonado.

Punta celebrated its centennial in 2007, but little more than a half a century ago it was a fishing village nearly covered by dunes. Its shores were first discovered by sunseekers escaping winter in Europe and, to a lesser extent, North America. South Americans were soon to follow—more than 100,000 Argentines flock to its beaches each January.

GETTING HERE & AROUND

Most visitors headed to the beach fly into Montevideo's Aeropuerto Internacional de Carrasco (MVD). Flights arrive from many South American cities, in high season only, directly to the Aeropuerto Internacional de Punta del Este (PDP), about 24 km (15 mi) east of town.

Many bus lines travel daily between Montevideo's Terminal Tres Cruces and and Punta del Este's Terminal Playa Brava. Two companies that serve the entire region are Copsa and Cot.

To get to Punta del Este from Montevideo, follow Ruta 1 east to the Ruta 93 turnoff. The road is well maintained and marked, and the trip takes about 1½ hours. Rental agencies, such as Avis, Budget, and Dollar, are in downtown Punta del Este.

SAFETY & PRECAUTIONS

The preponderance of Brazilian visitors, all of whom will tell you they feel far more secure here than in Rio, is testament to Punta's reassuring level of security. Nevertheless, in any locale that sees a high concentration of tourists it pays to watch your things. Swimming is not safe at several of the beaches, especially those on the Atlantic side of the point. Never swim alone, and gauge your abilities carefully.

ESSENTIALS

Airport Aeropuerto Internacional de Punta del Este (⊠ *Camino del Placer* ☎ *042/59777*).

Bus Contacts Copsa (☎ *042/89205*). **Cot** (☎ *042/86–810*).**Terminal Playa Brava** (⊠ *Rambla Artigas and Calle Inzaurraga, Punta del Este*).

Hotels ▼
L'Auberge **7**
Casapueblo
Club Hotel **2**
Conrad Resort
& Casino **4**
Las Cumbres
Hotel-
Art & Spa **3**
Hotel
Salzburgo **6**
Palace Hotel **5**
La Posta del
Cangrejo **8**
Serena Hotel.....**1**

Restaurants ▼
Andrés **3**
La Bourgogne ...**4**
Restaurante
Ciclista **1**
Yacht Club
Uruguayo **2**

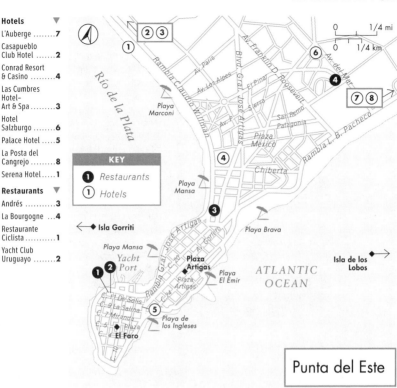

KEY

❶ Restaurants
① Hotels

Punta del Este

Visitor & Tour Info **Maldonado Tourist Office** (✉ *Parada 1, Calles 31 and 18, Punta del Este* ☎ *042/46510*). **Punta del Este Tourist Office** (✉ *Rambla Artigas and Izaurraga* ☎ *042/44–069* ⊕ *www.turismo.gub.uy*).

EXPLORING PUNTA DEL ESTE

MAIN ATTRACTIONS

Avenida Gorlero. Punta is circled by the Rambla Artigas, the main coastal road that leads past residential neighborhoods and pristine stretches of beach. Avenida Gorlero, Punta's main commercial strip, runs north–south through the heart of the peninsula and is fronted with cafés, restaurants, and elegant boutiques, Yves St. Laurent and Gucci among them.

Casapueblo. A hotel and museum at the tip of a rocky point with tremendous views of the Río de la Plata is the main draw in Punta Ballena, east of Punta del Este. Creator Carlos Páez Vilaró calls his work a "habitable sculpture" and it defies architectural categorization. With allusions to Arab minarets and domes, cathedral vaulting, Grecian whitewash, and continuous sculptural flourishes that recall the traceries of a Miró canvas, this curvaceous 13-floor surrealist complex climbs up a hill and looks like nothing else in South America.

Begun in 1968, Casapueblo is a continually evolving work. Says the artist: "While there be a brick near my hands, Casapueblo will not stop growing." The spaces include an excellent series of galleries dedicated to his work. Here you can see photos of the artist with friends like Picasso and peruse copies of his books. One of Páez's books tells the true story of his son Carlos Miguel, who survived a plane crash in the Andes, a story made into the 1993 film *Alive*. ⊠ *Punta Ballena* 🕾 *042/578–485* 🖃 *150 pesos* 🕙 *Daily 10–dusk.*

Isla de los Lobos. This island is home to one of the world's largest colonies of sea lions. You can view them from tour boats that leave regularly from the marina. Its 1907 lighthouse stands at 509 meters (190 feet).

> ## A CAVALCADE OF STARS
>
> Visitors to Punta del Este during its first heyday in the '50s and '60s rubbed shoulders with the likes of Ingmar Bergman and Yul Brynner. Even Brigitte Bardot, that then-icon of similarly themed St-Tropez, appeared here periodically. Today the town regularly rolls out the red carpet for supermodel Naomi Campbell and Latin singer Shakira. Ricky Martin, Madonna, Enrique Iglesias, Antonio Banderas, Pamela Anderson, Ralph Lauren, Bob Dylan, Eric Clapton, and Leonardo DiCaprio have done the Punta circuit, too. You never know who you might see. In season, that is.

IF YOU HAVE TIME

Arboreto Lussich. Inland lies a huge arboretum perfumed with the scent of eucalyptus. Its creation was the labor of love of Croatian-Uruguayan botanist Antonio Lussich (1848–1928). Its 4,000 acres contain 350 species of trees from outside Uruguay as well as 70 domestic species. Guided tours are in Spanish only. 🕾 *No phone* 🖃 *Free* 🕙 *Jan. and Feb., daily 8–8; Mar.–Dec., daily 9–6.*

Isla Gorriti. You can take a boat from the marina to this pine-covered island with a good restaurant. Gorriti was once the site of a prison, making it Uruguay's own little Devil's Island.

BEACHES

This stretch of coast has dozen or so beaches, each with its own high-season personality. All bets are off on activity levels the rest of the year, and remember: what's hot one season may be so "last year" the next. Punta is that kind of place. Locals frequently shorthand things to the *mansa* (calm) side fronting the Río de la Plata—many sections are fine for swimming—and the *brava* (rough) side lining the Atlantic Ocean—its waves draw surfers but should make you think twice about going into the water. By law, all beaches in Uruguay are public. Unless mentioned, all have parking and facilities (during the high season, at least).

RÍO DE LA PLATA SIDE

Playa Chihuahua. Uruguay's only sanctioned nude beach—look for the PLAYA NATURISTA ("naturist beach") sign—sits out near the airport west of Punta Ballena and divides into a straight and a rather cruisy gay section. Be cool about it if you go: no cameras, no binoculars, no gawking.

Playa Solanas. The famous Casapueblo museum and hotel sit above this calm beach at Punta Ballena with shallow water shielded from the wind. That makes it a favorite of families with small children. Great sunset views are a plus here, too.

Playa Chiringo. Things turn a bit rougher here, just east of Punta Ballena, with grittier sand and deeper water. Chiringo catches full sun at midmorning but shadows descend as the afternoon progresses, and the sun sets behind Punta Ballena. As with Chileno and Pinares beaches, wind and waves make swimming riskier here.

Playa Chileno. The wind picks up dramatically here, making this beach a favorite among windsurfers.

Playa Pinares. Deep water and rocky sand make this a beach you'll likely have to yourself. Expect little in the way of facilities.

Playa Mansa. Things turn calm again at Punta's longest beach. Decent sand, shallow water, many food stands, and proximity to the center of town make it the area's most family-oriented stretch of coast. Catch good sunset views here, and take in one of the late-afternoon beach aerobics classes, too.

ATLANTIC SIDE

Playa de los Ingleses. The mood changes as you round the peninsula's tip. This beach still contains the same fine sand found on on Playa Mansa, but the wind and waves pick up dramatically. Venture into the water at your own risk. You're still close to the center of Punta, meaning this beach sees many nonswimming visitors. Restaurants lining this so-called Englishmen's Beach were the spots for afternoon tea in a bygone era.

Playa El Emir. High waves make rocky El Emir, named for a long-ago Middle Eastern emir who vacationed here, popular with surfers but somewhat dangerous for swimmers.

Playa Brava. The golden sand and numerous food stands here draw a young crowd that mostly stays on the beach rather than braving the rough water. Brava is the place to take in the sunrise after a night of partying and before going home to bed. Look for the whimsical *La Mano,* a giant sculpture with the fingers of an enormous hand appearing to claw its way out of the sand. The work gives the beach its colloquial name, Playa de los Dedos (Beach of the Fingers).

La Barra. A mostly locally patronized beach sits at La Barra de Maldonado where the Riáo Maldonado spills into the ocean. If you do go into the water—remember, swimming poses risks here—note that the stirring of the currents creates a vibration in the sand beneath your feet.

Playa Montoya. Just east of La Barra lies this run-of-the-mill beach, whose young crowd rarely goes in the water and always seems to have a volleyball or soccer game going.

Playa Manantiales. Locals have dubbed this trendy stretch of sand "Playa Bikini." The swimwear skews a tad more daring here. At this favorite of celebrity visitors, you never know who you'll spot playing beach volleyball or doing morning aerobics.

José Ignacio. This tiny community sits just enough outside the Punta orbit to make a visit here a day trip. Sitting on a miniature Punta-style peninsula, José Ignacio has its own calmer Playa Mansa and rougher Playa Brava.

WHERE TO EAT

$$ ✕**Andrés.** Operated by a father and son, both of whom answer to
LATIN Andrés, this small restaurant on the Rambla Artigas, the oceanside
AMERICAN promenade, offers fine dining at moderate prices. Most of the tables are outdoors under a canopy, so you can appreciate the excellent service while also enjoying the sea breeze. The fish Andrés (served in a white wine and tomato sauce), spinach or cheese soufflés, and grilled meats are exquisite. ⊠ *Parada 1, Edificio Vaguardia* ☎ *042/481–804* ▤ *V* ☉ *Closed Mon.–Wed. Mar–Nov. No lunch Thurs. and Fri., and no dinner Sun. Mar.–Dec.*

$$ ✕**La Bourgogne.** A shaded terra-cotta terrace gives way to a breezeway
LATIN with arched windows. This opens onto a large split-level dining room
AMERICAN with antique sideboards. The food, served by impeccably clad waiters
★ who go about their business with cordial authority, is prepared with only the finest and freshest of ingredients; the breads are baked on the premises (an adjoining bakery sells them by the loaf), and the herbs and berries are grown in the backyard garden. The desserts are sublime—the sampler is a good way to try them all. ⊠ *Av. del Mar at Calle Pedragosa Sierra* ☎ *042/482–007* ⚖ *Reservations essential* ▤ *AE, MC* ☉ *Closed May–Aug. and Mon.–Wed. Sept.–Apr.*

¢ ✕**Restaurante Ciclista.** This no-frills restaurant serves the best inexpen-
ECLECTIC sive meals in Punta. Choose from a menu of over 100 items, from soups to pastas. The *tortilla de papas* (potato pancake) is extremely hearty. ⊠ *Calle 20 at Calle 27* ☎ *042/440–007* ▤ *AE, DC, MC, V.*

$ ✕**Yacht Club Uruguayo.** Loved by locals, this small eatery has a great
SEAFOOD view of Isla Gorriti. The menu includes a bit of everything, but the specialty is seafood. Perennial favorites are *brotola a la Roquefort* (baked hake with a Roquefort sauce) and *pulpo Provençal*, likely to be the most tender octopus you've ever eaten. ⊠ *Rambla Artigas between Calles 6 and 8* ☎ *042/441–056* ▤ *AE, DC, MC, V.*

WHERE TO STAY

Punta hotels operate on a many-tiered rate system. Prices go through the roof Christmas and Easter weeks. Standard high-season rates apply in January, and go slightly lower in February. March and December see prices a bit lower still, and then November creeps down a bit more, with some real bargains to be found the rest of the year. On the "rest of the year" topic, lodgings may close for a few weeks in the off-season. Always check ahead.

$$$–$$$$ ▣ **L'Auberge.** This hotel is in the heart of Parque del Golf, Punta's chicest neighborhood, and can be spotted for miles around. An 18th-century stone water tower, which now contains guest rooms, rises from a double-wing chalet. Rooms are tastefully adorned with antiques; a few quarters even have working fireplaces. Some of Punta del Este's finest beaches are several blocks away, but the vast lawns and lovely terrace gardens create a world apart from the crowded beach. **Pros:** Secluded neighborhood, friendly staff. **Con:** Not on beach. ✉ *Barrio Parque del Golf* ☎ *042/482–601* ⊕ *www.laubergehotel.com* ⌁ *36 rooms* ⌂ *In-room: refrigerator, safe. In-hotel: restaurant, room service, bar, pool, laundry service, public Internet* ▤ *AE, DC, MC, V.*

$$$$ ▣ **Casapueblo Club Hotel.** It would be hard not to feel like an artist in
★ this whitewashed marvel. Merely riding the old-style iron elevators and walking the sinuous hallways (there are no right angles here) is an experience. Spacious rooms have wooden floors and handsome antique furniture. Each also has a different name—Paloma (Dove), for example, or Luna Negra (Black Moon)—that determines the design of the handmade tiles in your bathroom. The restaurant has a wide terrace with fine coastline views. **Pros:** Secluded location, conversation-starting architecture, interesting adjoining museum. **Cons:** Far from Punta action, difficult to procure space in summer. ✉ *Punta Ballena* ☎ *042/578–611* ⊕ *www.clubhotel.com.ar* ⌁ *72 rooms* ⌂ *In-room: refrigerator. In-hotel: restaurant, room service, bar, pools, gym, spa, laundry service, public Internet* ▤ *AE, DC, MC, V.*

$$$–$$$$ ▣ **Conrad Resort & Casino.** Spectacularly lit fountains and gardens, an
Fodor'sChoice   abundant use of marble, and stunning art by Uruguayan painter Car-
★ los Páez Vilaró make this an extraordinary resort. Even though the off-season is quieter, things hop here year-round. Every room has a terrace with views of the beaches. The most prominent draw is the Las Vegas–style casino—the country's best. Head to the blackjack tables, or try your luck at one of the nearly 500 slot machines. The entertainment here reads like a Who's Who of *farándula*—that's showbiz, Spanish/ Latin American style—but Eric Clapton and Bob Dylan are among the U.S. stars who have performed here, too. **Pros:** Always something going on, friendly staff, phenomenal shows. **Con:** Not a good choice if you crave intimate surroundings. ✉ *Rambla Claudio Williman at Parada 4, Playa Mansa* ☎ *042/491–111* ⊕ *www.conrad.com.uy* ⌁ *296 rooms, 30 suites* ⌂ *In-room: refrigerator, safe. In-hotel: 5 restaurants, room service, bar, pool, laundry service, public Internet, no-smoking floors* ▤ *AE, DC, MC, V.*

$$$–$$$$ ▣ **Las Cumbres Hotel–Art & Spa.** The area's newest lodging is perhaps its most un-Punta-like. You're nowhere near the beach as you climb a 160-meter (520-foot) hill north of Punta Ballena out near the airport. The difference in elevation translates into temperatures a couple of degrees cooler, as well as a great views and a wooded, get-away-from-it-all locale. The rambling ranch building appears to have been transplanted from the U.S. West. Modern art festoons guest rooms and public areas. All rooms have flat-screen TVs; some have fireplaces. **Pros:** Quiet location, attentive staff, cooler temperatures than in town. **Cons:** Far from Punta, need car to stay here. ✉ *Ruta 12, Km 3.5, Laguna del Sauce*

9

☎042/578–689 ⊕www.cumbre.com.uy ⚑19 rooms, 9 suites ⚬In-room: DVDs. In-hotel: restaurant, room service, bar, pool, gym, spa, public Internet, public Wi-Fi ▤AE, DC, MC, V ⊘May ‖⊙‖BP.

$–$$ ⊞**Hotel Salzburgo.** This delightful hotel occupies a white-stucco, three-story chalet with polished slate floors and exposed beams. Its rooms have ceiling fans, modern baths, and fine views framed by flower-filled window boxes. **Pros:** Friendly owner, secluded neighborhood. **Con:** Not near beach. ⊠*Calle Pedragosa Sierra at El Havre* ☎042/488–851 ⊕www.hotelsalzburgo.com ⚑29 rooms ⚬In-room: refrigerator, safe. In-hotel: restaurant, bar, laundry service, public Internet, parking (no fee) ▤AE, DC, MC, V.

¢   ⊞**Palace Hotel.** Housed inside one of Punta's oldest structures—a three-
★   story Spanish colonial masterpiece complete with an airy interior court-yard—this hotel is a stone's throw from the beach (at the end of the Gorlero shopping strip). The restaurant has one of the country's largest wine cellars. **Pros:** One of Punta's most historic buildings, convenient to beach, good budget value. **Con:** Difficult to procure space in summer ⊠*Calle Gorlero at Calle 11, 20100* ☎042/441–919 or 042/441–418 ⚑47 rooms ⚬In-room: refrigerator. In-hotel: restaurant, room ser-vice, bar, public Internet ▤MC, V ‖⊙‖BP.

$$$$ ⊞**La Posta del Cangrejo.** You're about 20 minutes farther east from
★   Punta's center if you stay out here, but La Posta's many fans appreci-ate the relative isolation. From its stylish lobby to its relaxed lounge and restaurant, this hotel takes an informal approach to luxury. The Mediterranean theme—red-tile floors and white-stucco walls—comple-ments the impeccably decorated rooms; each is furnished with hand-stenciled antiques and canopy beds and has views of either the beach or the small garden. The staff is warm and accommodating. The adjoin-ing seafood restaurant is outstanding. Although rates here are on the pricey side—worth it, of course—Cangrejo offers numerous Web-only promotions during the off-season. **Pros:** Friendly staff, terrific restau-rant, good off-season deals. **Con:** Difficult to get space in summer, need a car to stay here. ⊠*Ruta 10, Km 160.5, La Barra de Maldonado, 20001* ☎042/770–021 ⊕www.lapostadelcangrejo.com ⚑29 rooms ⚬In-room: safe. In-hotel: restaurant, bar, pool, laundry service, public Internet ▤AE, DC, MC, V ‖⊙‖BP.

$$$$ ⊞**Serena Hotel.** Few Punta hotels actually sit on the beach. This is the rare exception: a stay here puts you steps from tranquil Playa Mansa and all its amenities. Walls are blindingly white inside and out, and huge picture windows in all rooms provide a view of the ocean. Children under 16 are not permitted. **Pros:** Right on beach, no kids (if that's your thing). **Con:** Notan option for families with young children ⊠*Rambla Williman Parada 24, 20100* ☎042/233–441 ⊕www.serenahotel.com.uy ⚑32 rooms ⚬In-room: refrigerator. In-hotel: restaurant, room ser-vice, bar, pool, spa, public Internet ▤AE, DC, MC, V ‖⊙‖BP.

AFTER DARK

Nightlife and tastes change capriciously from season to season. Expect fast-paced evenings in bars and nightclubs that might open as late as 1 AM and only reach a fever pitch around sunrise. Many places are open only in high season, and have covers as steep as 800 pesos.

DANCE CLUBS

Hop in a cab and head for **Gitane** and **La Plage** (⊠*Rambla Brava, Parada 12* ☎*042/441–240*), two dance places in one that seem to survive season after season on the road toward La Barra. Both places play booming house music. In La Barra, **Space** (⊠*Central La Barra* ☎*No phone*) occupies an enormous warehouse bursting with five different bars. Any taxi driver will know the way.

LIVE ENTERTAINMENT

For many visitors, the **Conrad Resort & Casino** (⊠*Rambla Claudio Williman at Parada 4* ☎*042/491–111*) defines nightlife in Punta with its casino and a year-round slate of Las Vegas–style shows by some of the biggest stars in Latin entertainment. Even if you don't recognize the names, taking in a performance at the area's largest hotel is *de rigueur.*

SPORTS & THE OUTDOORS

Water, water everywhere means that surfing (on the brava side) and swimming (on the mansa side) abound. But you'll also find plenty of land-based activities to keep you occupied. Some things are quite informal: someone's always getting up a game of beach volleyball or soccer, and you're free to join in the aerobics sessions you see on various beaches.

GOLF

Club de Golf (☎*042/82–127*) charges a typical $90 greens fee for 18 holes of golf. You can play a round of golf at **Club de Lago** (☎*042/78423*), which has tennis courts as well.

HORSEBACK RIDING

Mosey over to **Club Hípico Parque Burnett** (☎*042/30765*), an equestrian center on the distant outskirts of Punta, in Pinares, for an afternoon of trail riding. Montevideo-based **Estancias Gauchas** (⊠*Bacacay 1334, Montevideo* ☎*2/916–3011*) offers various trips from Punta del Este to estancias where you can ride horses and take part in the gaucho life. There are French and English-speaking guides.

POLO

From December 15 to February 28 there are several polo tournaments in Punta del Este, the most famous of which are the Medellín Polo Cup and the José Ignacio Tournament, attended by some of the best players from South America and Europe.

SHOPPING

An essential part of visiting Punta is exploring the colorful **Feria Artesanal** at the intersection of El Ramanso and El Corral. It's open weekends 5 PM–midnight all year; between Christmas and Easter it's open daily 6 PM–1 AM. Popular items include gourds for sipping mate (herb tea), and leather and silver crafts.

Venezuela

WORD OF MOUTH

"One [way to visit Venezuela] is to take a guided tour. Another suggestion would be to fly into Caracas, take a guided tour of the city, and then take a ferry to Margarita Island from the port of La Guaira. Because of the increase in crime in Venezuela, a guided tour may be the safest way to go."

—howie67

"If you're planning to spend a week in Venezuela, take a plane to Caracas's International Airport, and then fly to Los Roques for a week. It's the best you can do: Amazing beaches and safe. Just take into consideration that there's not a developed tourist infrastructure, so things may be a bit rustic."

—ramoram

Updated by
Heidi Leigh
Johansen

BEYOND THE DRAMATIC FRONT-PAGE NEWS concerning the policies of President Hugo Chávez lies a lush, welcoming Venezuela—one of tropical jungles, diverse wildlife and birds, and, of course, that gorgeous turquoise Caribbean water. Though most people discuss this country's politics more often than these impressive attributes, most Venezuelans will tell you, when asked, that theirs is the most plentiful and gorgeous of all the South American countries—one with luscious chocolate, rich coffee, flavorful rum, miles and miles of breathtaking Caribbean shores, sizzlingly hot women (just turn on the TV come Miss Universe season), and let's not forget that thick, rich substance the world seems to love so much: oil.

Not so many years ago, the 2,750-km (1,700-mi) Venezuelan coastline was the first glimpse of the country for almost all visitors. Christopher Isherwood, who arrived here on an ocean liner in 1950, wrote that "its mountains rose up sheer and solemn out of the flat sea, thrown into massive relief by tremendous oblique shafts of light from the rising sun. The gorges were deep in crimson shadow, the ridges were outlined in dazzling gold."

For natural beauty, Venezuela is indeed a land of surprising diversity. In the Caribbean you'll find Los Roques, which has the most spectacular snorkeling and diving in the region. Some of the islands that make up the archipelago virtually disappear with the high tide. Closer to the mainland is lovely Isla Margarita, a popular destination for sunseeking Venezuelans, Brazilians, Europeans, and, increasingly, North Americans.

In the country's western reaches, snow glistens year-round in the northernmost fingers of the Andes. The longest and highest cable-car system in the world provides stunning views of the surrounding mountainside. The Río Orinoco, mustering its might from a million sources in Colombia and Brazil, meanders through the broad grasslands that cover about a third of the country. You'll spot brilliantly colored tropical birds that are found only here, including the rare jabiru stork. In the far southeast, flat-top mountains called *tepuis* tower over Parque Nacional Canaima. These same geological formations inspired Sir Arthur Conan Doyle's novel *The Lost World*. The park is also home to the world's highest waterfall, Angel Falls, which plummets over 2,647 feet into a bizarre landscape of inky black lagoons and rare plant life.

For hundreds of years Venezuela was grindingly poor, disregarded because it lacked the mineral riches of neighbors such as Peru and Ecuador. Then in 1914 huge deposits of oil were discovered in what was thought to be a barren region near Lago Maracaibo. Venezuela, one of the founding members of the Organization of Petroleum Exporting Countries (OPEC), would be the world's largest oil exporter for the next 50 years. Sleepy towns transformed into booming metropolises, and the country continued to grow with the energetic impatience of its youthful population (about 70% are under 35 years old).

Two failed coups in 1992 marred Venezuela's reputation as South America's most enduring democratic state. In an ironic twist, the 1998 elections saw the leader of the attempted takeovers, Hugo Chávez, swept into office. He won strong support from the poor for his promise of fairer wealth distribution, but has angered middle and upper classes over his populist policies. In early 2003, a 63-day nationwide strike calling for Chávez's ouster crippled the country and choked its lifeblood of petroleum, ending with an uneasy impasse between the two sides. More recently, Chávez saw a major loss when voters rejected a proposed referendum that, among many other changes, would have granted the president indefinite re-election. Ch[ac]vez has also officially changed the name of the country from Venezuela to La Republica Bolivariana de Venezuela (or the Bolivarian Republic of Venezuela). And in early 2008 the currency of the country was changed from the bolívar to the bolívar fuerte (or the "strong bolivar"), colorful new paper money and coins included. With the new currency three zeroes were dropped: 1,000 bolívares became 1 bolívar fuerte. This was an attempt on the government's part to minimize inflation, but many economists remain dubious that the change will help.

ORIENTATION & PLANNING

GETTING ORIENTED

Beach lovers should waste no time in getting to the translucent waters of the Caribbean coast, specifically those around Isla Margarita and Los Roques. You might be surprised to see that the continent's mighty Andes take up such a prominent portion of Venezuelan territory, but for a taste of what the capital once was like, head to Andean towns such as Mérida, set against the sublime backdrop of mountains. The Orinoco River basin and Canaima National Park, itself the size of Belgium, occupy Venezuela's eastern sector. Deep in the south is the jungly Amazonas, named, of course, for the hemisphere's largest river. Los Llanos, vast, wildlife-filled grasslands, sit in the center of it all.

Caracas. A sprawling, lively, colorful capital, Caracas enjoys a sublime spot just inland from the Caribbean Coast, sheltered by the Ávila and its surrounding mountains. Though there's plenty of this city that should be avoided—weary locals will be the first to tell you so—there are also many neighborhoods, restaurants, museums, and shops waiting to be explored.

The Caribbean Coast. Miles upon miles of Venezuela's diverse coastline—rocky, pebbled, dark, and, of course, beige and sugary soft—are waiting to be explored, but it does take an adventurous spirit and a bit of time to explore this region by car: driving in this country can be hassling, and getting directions from the locals even more difficult. If you go for it, though, it'll surely be a trip of a lifetime.

Isla Margarita. Come to this large, diverse island during Semana Santa (holy week) and you'll see that many people have caught on to its allure. But plan your trip outside the busy seasons and you'll feel like you have this tropical paradise to yourself, with plenty of lovely

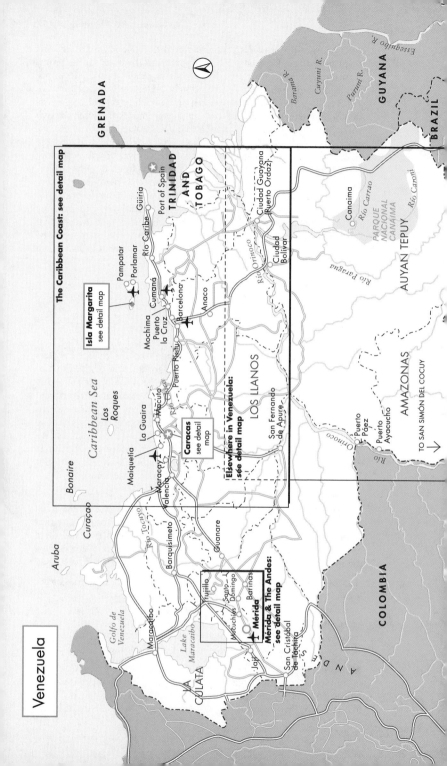

Venezuela

The Caribbean Coast: see detail map

GRENADA

TRINIDAD AND TOBAGO

Port of Spain

Güiria

Río Caribe

Pampatar

Porlamar

Isla Margarita see detail map

Cumaná

Mochima

Puerto la Cruz

Barcelona

Anaco

Ciudad Guayana (Puerto Ordaz)

Ciudad Bolívar

Río Orinoco

Puerto Píritu

Los Roques

Caribbean Sea

Bonaire

Curaçao

Aruba

La Guaira

Maiquetía

Macuto

Caracas see detail map

Maracay

Valencia

Río Tocuyo

Barquisimeto

Guanare

Maracaibo

Golfo de Venezuela

Lake Maracaibo

LA COSTA

Trujillo

Santo Domingo

Barinas

Mucuchíes

Mérida & The Andes: see detail map

Jají

San Cristóbal de Táchira

ANDES

COLOMBIA

LOS LLANOS

San Fernando de Apure

Elsewhere in Venezuela: see detail map

Río Orinoco

Puerto Páez

Puerto Ayacucho

AMAZONAS

TO SAN SIMÓN DEL COCUY →

Canaima

Río Carrao

PARQUE NACIONAL CANAIMA

AUYÁN TEPUY

Río Paragua

Río Caroní

Barama R.

Cuyuni R.

Puruni R.

Esequibo R.

GUYANA

BRAZIL

TOP REASONS TO GO

Fly Like an Angel. You probably know Kerapa Kupai Mapú, the world's highest waterfall, as Angel Falls, named for barnstormer pilot Jimmy Angel, who crash-landed here in 1937. Your approach to this amazing cascade (15 times higher than Niagara Falls), deep within Canaima National Park, can be via boat, plane, or feet.

Scale the Andes. South America's preeminent mountain range simply juts into Venezuela. Pleasant university town Mérida anchors the country's highland region, and makes the perfect antidote to the urban sprawl of Caracas. Take a ride on the world's longest, highest cable-car system, and make a leisurely day trip through artisan towns that dot the mountains.

Bask on a Caribbean Beach. St. Bart's has nothing on Margarita, the continent's one true Caribbean island. Venezuelans call their favorite vacation destination *La Perla del Caribe* (the Pearl of the Caribbean), and the island, with its white-sand beaches, smart hotels, yummy restaurants, and historic sites, really does live up to the hype.

Hone Your Bird-Watching Skills. With more than 1,300 species of birds, Venezuela is one of the world's top destinations for avid ornithologists. In Los Llanos you will be awed by immense flocks of roseate spoonbills, giant egrets, green ibis, scarlet ibis, and jabiru storks. In the Andes, you can watch the magnificent soaring flights of condors. On the Caribbean coast, numerous lagoons shelter flocks of pink flamingos.

beaches, colonial towns, and shops to explore—plus grilled red snapper and cold beers to complete your days.

Mérida & Environs. Perhaps Venezuela's most spectacular landscape, Mérida and the Andean region around it simply beg to be explored. In addition to the lush green landscape strewn with boulders and chilly streams, there are wood crafts to be seen, friendly people to meet, museums to peruse, and delicious food to enjoy.

10

VENEZUELA PLANNER

WHEN TO GO

The most popular time to visit is between December and April. During holidays, prices are higher and it's more difficult to find accommodations. During the rainy season from May to October—when there is still plenty of good weather—crowds are rare and hotel prices drop significantly.

CLIMATE

Caracas and much of Venezuela boast a year-round mild climate, with temperatures ranging between 65°F and 75°F during the day and rarely dropping below 55°F at night. Expect it to be colder in the higher altitudes of the Andes. Some coastal areas are hotter and more humid, but you can usually depend on a cool breeze.

The following are the daily maximum and minimum temperatures for Caracas.

Jan.	79F	26C	May	81F	27C	Sept.	82F	28C
	60	16		66	19		64	18
Feb.	80F	27C	June	80F	27C	Oct.	81F	27C
	62	17		65	18		64	18
Mar.	81F	27C	July	80F	27C	Nov.	82F	28C
	62	17		65	18		62	17
Apr.	80F	27C	Aug.	84F	29C	Dec.	80F	27C
	64	18		65	18		61	16

HOLIDAYS

All the days listed below are major holidays, when banks, schools, and many private businesses are closed. Holy Week is a big vacation time for Venezuelans. Caracas basically shuts down. Also, companies usually give vacation from around December 15 through January 15.

New Year's Day; Holy Thursday and Good Friday; Proclamation of Independence Day (April 19); Labor Day (May 1); Battle of Carabobo (June 24); Independence Day (July 5); Simón Bolívar's birthday (July 24); Columbus Day (October 12); Christmas Eve and Day.

GETTING HERE & AROUND

BY AIR

Major U.S. carriers serving Venezuela include American, Continental, and Delta. Venezuela's Aeropostal flies to Caracas from Miami. Most fly into Aeropuerto Internacional Simón Bolívar, located about 25 km (16 mi) from downtown Caracas in the coastal area of Maiquetía. Charters fly directly to the Caribbean island of Isla Margarita.

A number of regional airlines provide regular service throughout Venezuela. Among them are Aeropostal, Aereotuy, Avior, and Santa Bárbara. Bad weather or periodic disruptions in fuel flow can cause flight cancellations. ■TIP→ **Note that 2007 and 2008 saw several plane crashes in Venezuela. Though safety standards are said to remain stringent in this country, you should do your research before booking any flights, and never take charter flights on old planes.** Allow some flexibility in your itinerary, and do not plan out-country air travel for the very end of your stay in Venezuela.

AIRLINES IN VENEZUELA **Aereotuy** (☎ 0212/212–3110, 0212/212–3111, or 0212/212–3112 ⊕ www.tuy. com/home_eng.html). **Avior** (☎ 0212/955–3811 ⊕ www.avior.com.ve/). **Santa Bárbara** (☎ 212/204–4000 ⊕ www.sbairlines.com/eng/default.html).

BY BUS

Buses connect the Brazilian town of Manaus to the Venezuelan town of Santa Elena de Uairén, a trip that takes six hours and costs Bs.F100. Almost all of Venezuela can be traversed by bus, the least expensive and often most agreeable way to see the country. Your best bet is using the private carriers, usually referred to as *rápidos* (express buses). Private companies typically accept reservations and offer comforts such as assigned seats, air-conditioning, toilets, and on-board attendants.

BY CAR

Although the Venezuelan highway system is still a work in progress, more than 80% of the country's roads are paved. Driving can get you places you wouldn't otherwise get to see. However, Venezuelans often drive as if the traffic rules are merely suggestions. It's important to drive defensively. Avoid using your car at night, when poorly lit roadways and erratic drivers make things especially dangerous.

GAS STATIONS Oil-rich Venezuela has among the world's cheapest gas prices. A liter of unleaded gas (*sin plomo*) costs Bs.F 0.10. The national oil company, Petroleos de Venezuela (PDV), operates 24-hour stations on major highways. Shell, Texaco, and others also have stations.

ESSENTIALS

ELECTRICITY

Venezuela operates on a 110 volt, 60-cycle system, with a single-phase AC current.

ENTRY REQUIREMENTS

Australian, British, Canadian, New Zealand, and United States citizens who fly to Venezuela are issued 90-day tourist cards, free of charge, immediately upon arrival with presentation of a passport that has at least six months' remaining validity. Keep the flimsy second copy of the tourist card you receive when you arrive; you'll need it to leave the country. Procure a visa in advance from a Venezuelan embassy abroad if you plan to arrive overland. Most land immigration posts charge $3 to $5 for a tourist card.

HEALTH & SAFETY

In Caracas and other large cities, food in reputable hotels and restaurants should be safe. A sudden change of diet, however, can result in an upset stomach, which is often misinterpreted as a form of food poisoning. Avoid raw fruits and vegetables, uncooked fish, and tap water. Bottled water is readily available throughout the country, as are good beer and a wide variety of soft drinks. Pharmacies in different neighborhoods take turns staying open all night; you can spot them by the sign *turno*, or consult local newspapers for lists of open *farmacias* (pharmacies).

Crime, both petty and violent, is prevalent in Caracas, but less so in other parts of Venezuela. Use common sense wherever you travel. Always be aware of your surroundings and avoid unnecessary displays of wealth. Political demonstrations are common in Caracas, as well as in Mérida, and there's always the potential for such gatherings to turn violent. It is illegal for foreigners to engage in anything deemed "political activity."

EMERGENCY   **Police, Ambulance & Fire (country-wide general number)** (☎*171*). **United**
CONTACTS   **States Embassy** (✉ *Calle F at Calle Suapure, Colinas de Valle Arriba* ☎ *0212/975–6411 or 0212/975–7831*).

LANGUAGE

Spanish is the official language of Venezuela, but many words in common usage are unique to the country, especially regarding foods. For instance, Venezuelans call a banana a *cambur*; a watermelon a *patilla*; a papaya a *lechosa*; and a passion fruit a *parchita*. ■TIP→ If you really want to sound like a local, sprinkle the word *chevere* (CHEH-veh-reh) into your conversation: that's the best way to say "cool" or "all right."

MONEY MATTERS

CURRENCY & EXCHANGE
The bolívar was the official unit of currency in Venezuela until the end of 2007. In early 2008 the bolívar fuerte (Bs.F) was introduced, which comes in bills of 2, 5, 10, 20, 50, and 100. Coins come in 1, 5, 10, 12.5, 25, and 50 *céntimos* (cents) and 1 bolívar denominations. At press time, the exchange rate was a fixed, government-regulated Bs.F2.15 to the U.S. dollar.

In hopes of stemming the flight of dollars from Venezuela, the government has implemented rigid currency controls. Italcambio, the largest of the *casas de cambio* (exchange houses), is permitted to exchange cash dollars and American Express traveler's checks denominated in dollars for bolívares fuertes, but not vice-versa. (Most banks will not exchange currency, and none will accept traveler's checks.)

You can use your ATM card in some machines to obtain bolívares fuertes, but it is impossible to obtain dollars here. Gauge your cash-spending needs accordingly to avoid being stuck at the end of your trip with local currency that is impossible to change back. ⚠ There will be no shortage of black-market currency dealers approaching you quietly about changing money in public places, but the so-called *mercado negro* is officially illegal and a dangerous risk for robbery. That said, it's hard to ignore the fact that you can get over twice the number of bolívares fuertes per dollar through the black market. Therefore it shouldn't come as a surprise that the black market is thriving here.

PRICING
Venezuela can be a relatively inexpensive country, although the prices are greatly inflated in Caracas and on Isla Margarita. Going to the theater can cost from Bs.F.40 to Bs.F.200 for special shows or featured artists. Movies are comparable to prices in the United States, at Bs.F.20. Nightlife ranges greatly in price; some of the best clubs charge upward of Bs.F.18 for a cocktail.

Sample Prices: Cup of coffee, Bs.F2–Bs.F3; bottle of beer, Bs.F6; soft drink, Bs.F2; bottle of wine, Bs.F20 (at a liquor store); sandwich, Bs.F10–Bs.F20; crosstown taxi ride, Bs.F20; city bus ride, Bs.F1; museum entrance, Bs.F2, though the majority of museums in the country are free.

TAXES
Venezuela has a nonrefundable 9% sales tax, known as the IVA, which is added to the price of all articles except basic foodstuffs and medicine. At hotels, foreigners must pay a 10% tourist tax. You will find it added to your bill. The airport departure tax (usually included in your ticket) for international flights leaving Venezuela is $75 or Bs.F161.

TIPPING Restaurants usually add 10% to the bill for service, but you are expected to tip an additional 10%. Tipping hotel porters, hair stylists, and guides up to 10% is customary. Taxi drivers do not expect a tip unless they carry suitcases.

PHONES

All telephone numbers have seven digits. Area codes begin with a "0" followed by a three-digit number. Use the zero only for long-distance calls from other parts of Venezuela, not for calls from other countries. A "0412" or "0414"or "0416" code designates a mobile phone number. To call a Venezuelan number from another country, dial the international access code, the country code of 58, and then the area code. Be prepared for frequent busy signals.

Public pay phones accept phone cards, starting in denominations of 5 bolívares fuertes at kiosks and newsstands marked TARJETA INTELIGENTE (smart card). To speak with a local directory assistance operator, dial 113.

RESTAURANTS & HOTELS

CUISINE Venezuela's larger cities boast a wide variety of restaurants, from Spanish *tascas* (casual restaurants with bars) to French bistros to Japanese sushi bars. But while you're here, you should sample Venezuela's own unique cuisine. The national dish, *pabellón criollo,* consists of shredded beef served with rice, black beans (*caraotas negras*), fried ripe plantains (*tajadas*), and local white cheeses such as *queso de mano.* Venezuelans love beef, and restaurants that specialize in grilled meats (called *restaurantes de carne*) are popular with locals. Stop at an *arepera* and try an *arepa,* a grilled cornmeal pocket stuffed with anything from fresh cheese to *reina pepiada,* or avocado-and-chicken salad. If you visit during the Christmas season, try the delicious holiday specialty called *hallacas,* which are a combination of chicken, almonds, olives, and pork, in a cornmeal shell wrapped in aromatic banana leaves.

Excellent fish and shellfish dominate in the coastal areas and on Isla Margarita and Los Roques. You can choose from grouper, snapper, mackerel, tuna, swordfish, lobster, crab, shrimp, and clams. In the Andean regions, treat yourself to rainbow trout.

10

Don't leave Venezuela without sampling at least one of these scrumptious, typical desserts: *bien me sabe* (coconut cake), *torta de guanábana* (a tart fruitcake), *merengón de nispero* (meringue cake), and the always popular *cascos de guayaba* (guava shells with white cheese). As a Caribbean nation, Venezuela excels at rum production (*ron* in Spanish). A small bottle of aged Santa Teresa fits nicely in your pack to take home. Venezuela also produces some surprisingly good domestic wines, such as Viña Altagracia or the sparkling Pomar from Lara State, in the northwest region of the country.

Lunch, the main meal of the day, begins around noon and lasts until about 3. A light dinner is eaten between 7 and 10 PM; don't count on being served much past 10:30 PM, except in the Las Mercedes district of Caracas, where some restaurants remain open until midnight. Some restaurants offer a prix-fixe meal at lunchtime known as the *menu ejecutivo.* This includes a *primero* (appetizer of soup or salad); a *segundo,* the main course; and *postre* (dessert). Espresso or *guayoyo,* a weaker drip coffee, is included.

High-end restaurants may have dress codes, so inquire when making reservations. For most other dining establishments, a woman can't go wrong in an informal dress or a man in a collared shirt with optional tie.

ACCOMMO-
DATIONS
Venezuela offers lodging options to suit almost every price range and comfort level—from the resort citadels of Caracas to the colorful, three-room posadas of Los Roques. Take in a view of the Andes from the window of a restored 17th-century monastery or from the cobblestone courtyard of a renovated coffee hacienda nestled in the cloud forest above Mérida. In Los Llanos you can stay on a working cattle ranch or in the guest facilities of a biological field station. Those who seek adventure by day and comfort by night will relish the prime location and amenities offered by the Arekuna camp near Parque Nacional Canaima.

Luxury hotels rarely include meals when quoting rates, but many of the smaller lodgings in the Andes do include breakfast (and sometimes dinner) in their room rates. Remember that prices jump 10%–20% during holiday periods, particularly during Christmas, pre-Lenten Carnival, and Holy Week.

WHAT IT COSTS IN BOLIVARES FUERTES				
	¢	$	$$	$$$	$$$$
RESTAURANTS	Under $13	$13–$21.5	$21.5–$32 5	$32–$43	over $43
HOTELS	Under $86	$86–$129	$129–$215	$215–$387	Over $387

Restaurant prices are based on the median main course price at dinner. Hotel prices are for two people in a standard double room in high season.

VISITOR INFORMATION
One good source of Venezuela travel information is the U.S.-based Venezuelan Tourism Association.

CONTACT **Venezuelan Tourism Association** (🖂 *Box 3010, Sausalito, CA 94966* ☎ *415/331–0100*).

CARACAS

On a wall facing the Plaza el Venezolano, Simón Bolívar is quoted as follows: SI SE OPONE LA NATURALEZA LUCHAREMOS CONTRA ELLA Y LA HAREMOS QUE NOS OBEDEZCA (If nature opposes us, we'll struggle against her and make her obey us). Nowhere in Venezuela is the legacy of Bolívar's defiant proclamation more apparent than in Caracas itself. Whether gazing at the city's sprawling skyline from the 17th-story window of a high-rise hotel or strolling in the shadows of looming concrete edifices, one wistfully dreams of what Caracas might have been like had its sudden growth spurt occurred during any other architectural moment than the 1970s.

What redeems Caracas are the Caraqueños themselves: a diverse, young, and lively population that colors the grimy streets of the capital with music and enthusiasm. The sophisticated tastes of the nearly 5.5 million inhabitants demand the parades of boutiques and fine restaurants that crowd commercial areas. Hip, fast-paced, and altogether cosmopolitan, Caraqueños still manage to retain a warmth and amiability you may not expect to encounter in a city this vast.

A FESTIVE COUNTRY

During February's Carnaval the entire country goes on a Mardi Gras–like binge; in Caracas nearly everyone vacates the city and heads for the beach. Also in February, Mérida celebrates its Feria del Sol (Festival of the Sun) with bullfights, open-air salsa, and merengue performances. In mid-March Paraguachí on Isla Margarita celebrates the Feria de San José. In the week before Easter the country celebrates Semana Santa (Holy Week).

Although Caracas is a rambling metropolis, its places of interest can be explored comfortably in a day or two. Interesting museums and cultural centers, lovely parks, and refined dining establishments are all connected by a quick taxi ride or the city's efficient subway system. The weather, too, facilitates exploring: At 3,000 feet above sea level, Caracas enjoys one of the world's most agreeable climates, with an average daily temperature of 24°C (75°F).

■**TIP**➔ **Be advised, however, that Caracas well deserves its reputation as a dangerous city.** The main tourist areas are generally safe during the day, but always be on your guard. Even residents do not go out alone in most neighborhoods after dark, when muggings and other violent crimes are shockingly frequent. Taxis are the safest means of transportation after dark.

GETTING HERE & AROUND

BY AIR Caracas is served by Aeropuerto Internacional Simón Bolívar (CCS), about 25 km (16 mi) from downtown in the coastal area of Maiquetía. The trip into town from the airport is via a busy four-lane highway and takes between 30 and 45 minutes, depending upon your destination in Caracas. Cab fare to downtown Caracas costs about Bs.F150. The official fare is posted next to the taxi stand outside the international terminal.

Robberies of tourists by drivers of unofficial cabs are all too common. To be on the safe side, take a taxi from the dispatcher outside the international terminal.

BY BUS There are two inconveniently located and exceedingly unsavory public bus terminals serving Caracas. For travel to destinations west of the city, buses leave from Terminal La Bandera. The Terminal del Oriente serves destinations to the eastern part of the country. Far more convenient—and

10

much safer—is the *servicio especial* (special service) offered by Aeroexpresos Ejecutivos. All buses depart from the company's own clean, quiet terminal in the Bello Campo district. Two other reliable private companies are Expresos del Oriente and Expresos Alianza.

Clean, air-conditioned buses called *MetroBus* leave all Metro stops for areas outside the reach of the subway system. The cost is Bs.F0.70. If used within four hours of purchase, a ticket is also valid for a one-way ride on the Metro. Smaller public buses called *carritos* or *por puestos* connect all parts of the city, but they are no quicker in heavy traffic.

BY CAR   Heavy traffic, a lack of parking, and the city's baffling layout combine to render Caracas a driving challenge for residents, let alone visitors. If you can avoid it, do not rent a car to explore the city. However, if you're here for a long visit, and you want to explore, driving to the west or east of Caracas can be an incredibly memorable experience. Note, though, that nonadventurous types need not apply!

BY SUBWAY   ⚠ **Avoid using the Metro as much as possible. It just isn't safe. If you must use it, do so only during the day.** The speedy trains traverse the city between Palo Verde in the east and Propatria in the west, with connecting north–south lines from Capitolio and Plaza Venezuela. One-way tickets, which can be purchased in all stations, are Bs.F0.50, depending on distance traveled. Save your ticket; you'll need it to exit the turnstile out of the station. If you plan to use the Metro frequently, opt for the convenience of a *multi abono* card (Bs.F4.50), valid for 10 rides anywhere on the system. These cards save you the hassle of waiting in long lines for individual tickets. (The stations' automated ticket-vending machines are frequently out of order.) Route maps are posted at ticket booths and inside each car, but not on the platforms. The Metro operates daily 4:30 AM–11 PM. Cars get very crowded during the 6–9 and 5–8 rush hours.

BY TAXI   Licensed taxis have yellow license plates and carry secured signs that say *libre* (free) on the roof, while *pirata* (pirate) varieties have signs that are obviously detachable. When selecting a taxi off the street, settle only on official cars—tales of robbery by pirata drivers are legion—and agree on the rate before you depart. Unless you are traveling only a couple of blocks, Bs.F8 is a standard fare anywhere in the central city area between Capitolio and Altamira. Note that fares increase by as much as 50% at night and on weekends. Once en route, don't be surprised if your driver cuts corners and ignores stop signs and red lights as he maneuvers through downtown traffic. Many larger hotels have their own taxi companies. Ask your hotel or restaurant to call you a taxi if you go out at night.

SAFETY & PRECAUTIONS

Pickpocketers and muggers, often violent, are serious problems for residents and visitors alike. Most downtown areas, including those popular with tourists, are usually safe during the day, though you should be careful absolutely everywhere you go. Note that even residents do not go out alone on foot in most neighborhoods after dark. Use taxis at night, even if you are traveling a short distance.

When visiting the city, never wear expensive clothing or flashy jewelry, and don't handle money in public. It's a good idea to keep your money in a pocket or a hidden money belt rather than a wallet, which is easier to steal. On buses, in the subway, and in crowded areas, hold purses or camera bags close to your body (or, better yet, leave most belongings in the hotel lock box when you are out exploring); thieves use knives to slice the bottom of a bag and catch the contents as they fall out.

Avoid all political demonstrations. They're quite common in Caracas and occasionally result in clashes between demonstrators and police.

ESSENTIALS

Bus Company **Aeroexpresos Ejecutivos** (☎ 0212/266–2321 or 0212/263–3266 ⊕ www.aeroexpresos.com.ve).

Car-Rental Agencies **Avis** (☎ 0212/959–5822, 0212/355–1190 at airport). **Budget** (☎ 0212/603–1300, 0212/355–2799 at airport). **Hertz** (☎ 0212/905–0430, 0212/614–5623 at airport).

Currency Exchange **Italcambio** (⊠ Edificio Belmont, Av. Luis Roche, Altamira, Caracas ☎ 0212/562–9555 ⊕ www.italcambio.com ⊠ Centro Comercial Sambil, Av. Libertador, Chacao, Caracas ☎ 0212/265–5087 ⊠ Aeropuerto Internacional Simón Bolívar, Maiquetía, Caracas ☎ 0212/355–1080).

Medical Assistance **Clínica El Ávila** (⊠ Av. San Juan Bosco at 6a Transversal, Altamira ☎ 0212/276–1111).

Visitor Info **INATUR** (⊠ Edificio Conde, Bellas Artes ☎ 0212/574–2220, 0800/462–8871 in Venezuela ⊕ www.inatur.gob.ve/portal/ ⊠ Aeropuerto Internacional Simón Bolívar ☎ 0212/507–8607).

EXPLORING CARACAS

Set amid rolling hills, Caracas lacks a single downtown area. However, the city can be divided into four principal areas of interest: El Centro and its Plaza Bolívar ringed by historic buildings; Parque Central and the surrounding Bellas Artes district; Las Mercedes with its many boutiques and restaurants; and the walled villas, apartment buildings, and shops of Altamira and La Castellana.

The main subway line runs across much of the city, supplemented by two short southern spurs. It's clean and great for traveling around Caracas. Buses confound first-time visitors because service is sporadic and routes are difficult to ascertain. *Por puestos*—the small vans that will pick you up and drop you off anywhere on their set routes—are fine for short point-to-point hops. Taxis are often hampered during the day by gridlock, but they are a good, safe option for getting around downtown, especially if you use a hired car or taxi recommended by your hotel.

Numbers in the text correspond to numbers in the margin and on the Caracas maps.

10

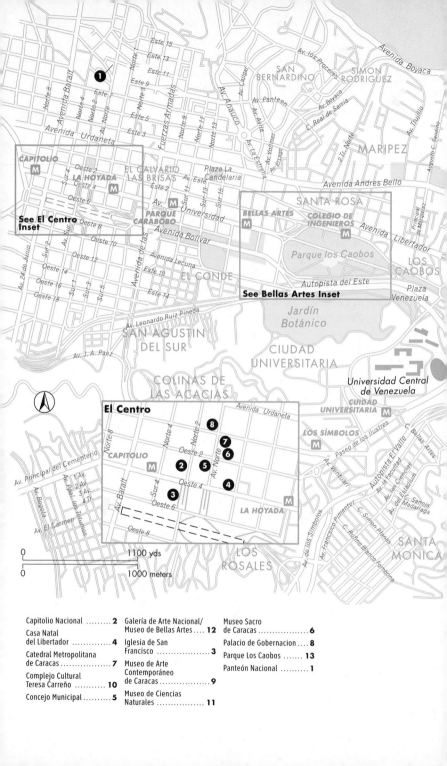

Caracas

Parque Nacional El Ávila

Avenida Boyaca

ALTA FLORIDA

CHAPELLIN

EL PEDREGAL

LAS PALMAS

LA FLORIDA

Caracas Country Club

COUNTRY CLUB

ALTAMIRA

LA CAMPINA

Av. J. B. Arismendi

LA CASTELLANA

Av. El Bosque

C. Maturin

Av. Ppal. del Country Club

Av. El Saman

Av. Blandin

PLAZA VENEZUELA

SABANA GRANDE

CAMPO ALEGRE

3 Av. Tr.

C.V.F. Rivas

ALTAMIRA

SABANA GRANDE

Avenida Libertador

C. 3A

CHACAO

BELLO CAMPO

CHACAITO

(Av. A. Lincoln)

CHACAITO

Av. Francisco de Miranda

CHACAO

LOS CHAGUARAMOS

Av. Tamanaco
Av. Venezuela
Av. Guaicaipuro

EL ROSAL

Distribuidor Altamira

Autopista del Este - Francsico Fajardo

Av. Bello Monte

LAS MERCEDES

Bellas Artes

SANTA ROSA

BELLAS ARTES

Avenida Libertador

COLEGIO DE INGENIEROS

Parque los Caobos

Autopista del Este

EL CENTRO

El Centro is the oldest part of Caracas, a city founded by Spanish conquistador Diego de Losada in 1567. Colonial buildings are clustered around the lush Plaza Bolívar. Numerous benches are almost always occupied by aging Venezuelans vehemently discussing the latest political events or admiring the passing Caraqueña girls. In the center is an imposing statue of Simón Bolívar, the hero of Venezuelan Independence. Unfortunately, El Centro has become a crowded, seedy, and crime-ridden area in the past decade or so. Your best option for visiting the area is to hire a guide, or a car or taxi through your hotel that can take you to various attractions and wait outside while you explore. Be sure to leave valuables at your hotel. If you do decide to go by subway (Capitolio is the best subway stop for this area), be cautious and go during the day.

TIMING & PRECAUTIONS

With the exception of the Panteón Nacional, which is a 15-minute walk from Plaza Bolívar, the sights in El Centro are very concentrated. Remember that museums are closed in the middle of the day and all day Monday. Unfortunately, this area has become quite unsafe for exploring during the day; after dusk it gets even rougher. Your best bet is to ask your hotel if they have guided tours to the plaza, or to hire a car through your hotel that will wait for you as you peek at the sights. Keep in mind that it's very unwise at this point to bring a flashy camera or purse along with you.

MAIN ATTRACTIONS

② **Capitolio Nacional.** Venezuela's Congress is housed in the neoclassical National Capitol, a pair of buildings constructed on the site of the 17th-century convent of the Sisters of the Conception. President Guzmán Blanco, who ordered the disbanding of all convents, razed the original building in 1874. On the site he built the Federal and Legislative palaces. The paintings in the oval Salón Elíptico by Venezuelan artist Martin Tovar y Tovar are quite impressive, especially those on the ceiling. The bronze urn in the room contains the 1811 Declaration of Independence. (In deference to decorum, you must tuck in your shirt when you enter this room.) ⊠*Av. Norte 2 at Av. Oeste 2, El Centro* ⊠*Free* ⊙*Daily 9–12:30 and 3–5* Ⓜ*Capitolio.*

④ **Casa Natal del Libertador.** The birthplace of Simón Bolívar is a pilgrimage site for Venezuelans, who honor him as "El Libertador." The house has very little to offer about the great man himself, but is a lovely example of a spacious and airy old colonial house in the midst of downtown's hustle and bustle. Monumental wall paintings by Tito Salas in the front room that retell the stories of Bolívar's heroic battles are well worth a look. ⊠*Av. Traposos at Av. San Jacinto, El Centro* ☎*0212/541–2563* ⊠*Free* ⊙*Tues.–Fri. 9–noon and 1–4:30, weekends 10–noon and 1–4:30* Ⓜ*Capitolio.*

③ **Iglesia de San Francisco.** Filled with richly gilded altars, this church dating from 1593 was the site of Simón Bolívar's proclamation as "El Libertador" (the Liberator) and of his massive funeral 12 years after

FodorśChoice
★

his 1830 death. It remains the loveliest example of colonial architecture in Caracas. ⊠*Av. Bolsa at Av. San Francisco, El Centro* ☎*0212/484–5707* ☜*Free* ⊙*Daily 7–noon and 3–6* Ⓜ*Capitolio.*

❻ Museo Sacro de Caracas. The Museum of Religious Art of Caracas, a for-
★ mer sacristy and ecclesiastical prison built in 1844 adjoining the cathedral, now houses ornate religious statues and lavish costumes from the
colonial era. Especially noteworthy in the first salon is the ornate silver
canopy made to cover the statue of Our Lady of the Rosary. Downstairs you'll find an intriguing, albeit rather macabre, common grave
where remains of the religious are interred in sealed niches. ⊠*Plaza
Bolívar, El Centro* ☎*0212/861–6562* ☜*Bs.F1* ⊙*Tues.–Sat. 8:30–4,
Mon. 11–4* Ⓜ*Capitolio.*

❶ Panteón Nacional. Five blocks north of Plaza Bolívar, the striking National
★ Pantheon's exquisite marble interior holds the remains of 138 Venezuelan political and historical figures, including Simón Bolívar. The walls
and ceilings are graced with murals depicting some of the most famous
battles for independence. ⊠*Av. Panteón, El Centro* ☎*0212/862–1518*
☜*Free* ⊙*Tues.–Sun. 10–noon and 1–4:30* Ⓜ*Capitolio.*

IF YOU HAVE TIME

❼ Catedral Metropolitana de Caracas. With its original facade unaltered
since it was built at the end of the 17th century, the Metropolitan
Cathedral towers over Plaza Bolívar. The main altar is a magnificent
Baroque creation gilded with more than 300 pounds of gold leaf.
Don't miss the Bolívar family chapel on the right-hand side. ⊠*Plaza
Bolívar, El Centro* ☎*0212/862–1518* ☜*Free* ⊙*Tues.–Sun. 8–1 and
3–6* Ⓜ*Capitolio.*

❺ Concejo Municipal. This graceful colonial building, set around a manicured courtyard, is considered the cradle of Venezuelan statehood.
On July 5, 1811, the National Congress met here and approved the
Declaration of Independence. Today the building houses the **Museo
Criollo,** which exhibits a permanent collection of works by noted Venezuelan painter Emilio Boggio (1857–1920) and scale-model miniatures
by Raúl Santana that depict every imaginable aspect of Venezuela's
early culture. ⊠*Plaza Bolívar, El Centro* ☎*0212/915–1585* ☜*Free*
⊙*Tues.–Fri. 9:30–11 and 2:30–5, weekends 10–4* Ⓜ*Capitolio.*

❽ Palacio de Gobernación. The art deco–style Government Palace, built
in 1935, now houses political offices and a ground-floor gallery with
rotating exhibits of international and Venezuelan art. ⊠*Plaza Bolívar,
El Centro* ☎*0212/564–3080* ☜*Free* ⊙*Tues.–Sat. 10–6* Ⓜ*Capitolio.*

BELLAS ARTES
The cultural center of Caracas, Bellas Artes hosts almost all the major
exhibitions and performances that come to Venezuela. This zone
encompasses the giant twin towers of Parque Central and the museums of Parque Los Caobos.

10

TIMING & PRECAUTIONS

Visiting all of the sights of Bellas Artes will take half a day. Allow an hour and a half to visit the museums on weekdays, a bit more on weekends, when they tend to be crowded. All museums are closed on Monday. As with other areas in Caracas, be cautious here.

MAIN ATTRACTIONS

⑩ Complejo Cultural Teresa Carreño. World-class ballet, opera, and classical concerts are regularly presented at this modern cultural center named for Venezuela's most famous classical pianist. Hanging from the theater roof is the kinetic sculpture *Yellow Pendants,* by Venezuelan artist Jesús Soto. Adjacent to the complex are a bookstore and the Teatro Ateneo de Caracas, home of a popular movie theater screening art films. ✉*Plaza Morelos, Bellas Artes* ☎*0212/574–9122* Ⓜ*Bellas Artes.*

HISTORY

Skyscrapers and freeways might make you forget that Caracas is the repository of Venezuelan history. Colonial-era buildings line the narrow streets of El Centro, the old city center. The capital also contains many monuments to Venezuelan hero Simón Bolívar, often referred to as simply "El Libertador"—after all, this is the man who liberated much of South America, and who lends his name to the country's official name: the Bolivarian Republic of Venezuela.

⑫ Galería de Arte Nacional. Known around town as the "GAN," the interesting National Art Gallery, across the circular Plaza Morelos from the Museum of Natural Science, displays more than 4,000 works of art from Venezuela's proud past. It shares a building with the **Museo de Bellas Artes,** which exhibits a random selection of art from all around the globe. The top floor is a terrace offering views over Parque Los Caobos and much of Caracas. ✉*Plaza de los Museos, Bellas Artes* ☎*0212/578–1818 for gallery, 0212/578–1816, 0212/578–1819 for museum* ✉*Free* ☉*Tues.–Fri. 9–5, Sat.–Mon. 10–5* Ⓜ*Bellas Artes.*

Fodor'sChoice
★

⑨ Museo de Arte Contemporáneo de Caracas Sofía Imber. This excellent contemporary art museum displays paintings by Picasso, Miró, and Bacon. There are also 3-D works by renowned Venezuelan artist Jesús Soto. Housed on the edge of the Parque Central complex, this is one of the best collections of modern art in South America. ✉*Parque Central, Bellas Artes* ☎*0212/573–8289* ✉*Free* ☉*Daily 9–5* Ⓜ*Bellas Artes.*

Fodor'sChoice
★

IF YOU HAVE TIME

⑪ Museo de Ciencias Naturales. The Museum of Natural Science includes archaeological, botanical, and zoological displays (stuffed animals against rather dismal backdrops). The Pre-Columbian displays, however, are particularly interesting, as are the overviews of early American life, such as demonstrations of the farming methods of indigenous peoples. ✉*Plaza de los Museos, Bellas Artes* ☎*0212/577–5103* ✉*Free* ☉*Weekdays 9–5, weekends 10:30–6* Ⓜ*Bellas Artes.*

⑬ Parque Los Caobos. One of the city's oldest parks, Parque Los Caobos has towering mahogany trees planted to celebrate Venezuela's independence. The lovely old fountain, ringed by bronze sculptures, is a taste

The Ávila

Parque Nacional El Ávila. Ask most Caraqueños what defines their city the most, and you'll often hear "El Ávila!" The mountains of Parque Nacional El Ávila rise some 3,300 feet over the northern edge of Caracas, then slope down its other side directly into the Caribbean. The national park is a favorite destination for weekend hikers, as its southern side is criss-crossed with trails. Novices prefer the daylong hike that leads to Pico Ávila, while more experienced hikers take

the two-day trek to Pico Naiguatá. The park is easily accessible from the Altamira neighborhood in eastern Caracas. If you don't feel like hiking, you can ride up in a cable car.

San José de Galipán, a settlement on the coastal side of Mount Ávila, makes a nice destination if you've been hiking all morning. Horses are available there for further exploring. The town's cool climate makes it perfect for growing flowers to sell in Caracas.

of the Caracas of a century ago. ⊠*Av. México, Bellas Artes* Ⓜ*Bellas Artes.*

WHERE TO EAT

$$$$
MEDITERRANEAN
Fodor'sChoice
★

✕**Antigua.** For a romantic evening in Las Mercedes, head to this antique-strewn restaurant that defines itself as a "gastronimic boutique." The Mediterranean-influenced risottos, pizzas, and pastas are consistently good, and the wine list is fabulous. Skip the eggplant carpaccio and cocao-filled raviolis in favor of a simpler menu items. While you nibble, you may spend even more time staring at the incredible collection of colorful antique plates, chandeliers, furniture, and bric-a-brac here, but stay focused, because the dessert is well worth it: try crème brûlée tinted with *ponche crema* (a creamy holiday booze) and *milhojas de dulce de leche* (millefeuille with caramel). ⊠*Calle Madrid, between Mucuchíes and Monterrey, Las Mercedes 1050* ☎*0212/991–9056* ⊟*AE, MC, V.*

¢
LATIN
AMERICAN
Fodor'sChoice
★

✕**El Budare Del Este.** An old-school Caracas arepa joint, Budare serves up freshly made arepas and cachapas with flair and a wee bit of atti-tude. There's a huge variety of stuffing options for your arepas; among the most popular are local cheeses such as *queso de mano* and *queso telita*. Also scrumptious are the meat options, including *carne mechada* (shredded beef) and *reina pepiada* (avocado-and-chicken salad). Be sure to get a *batido de fruta,* or a fruit shake—we recommend *parchita* (passionfruit) or *lechosa* (papaya). This is the best place to end any bar-hopping or theater-going evening: the restaurant is open 24/7, 365 days a year—yes, even on Christmas. ⊠*Av. Rio Janeiro, between Trinidad and Mucuchíes, Las Mercedes 1050* ☎*0212/992–6940* ⊟*MC, V.*

$$$

✕**Gourmet Market.** Serene white spaces define this simple but delicious eatery just outside of the main Las Mercedes thoroughfares, in El Rosal. Just a short walk from the Marriott and THE Hotel, Gourmet Market invites diners to feast alfresco on well-prepared risottos, pastas, brusquetas, and sandwiches (including such favorites as caprese, New

10

CLOSE UP

Coffee in Caracas

Un café con leche, por favor—that is: "One coffee with milk, please." And, if you're a fan of good coffee, you'll love café-hopping in Caracas. The local beans are top quality, the machines are almost all of Italian origin, and the technique is pure and simple. Listed below are a few of our favorite places to grab a cup of joe and some beans to take home—the ultimate souvenir or gift.

Arabica (⊠*Av. Andrés Bello, between Av. Francisco de Mirando and Tranv. de Los Palos Grandes, Altamira/Los Palos Grande* ☎*0212/285–3469*) is hands-down the best coffee in the city—it also may be the priciest. Choose from the delectable desserts, order a coffee, and sit outside to watch the world go by.

Las Nieves (⊠*Calle Pichincha, El Rosal* ☎*0212/952–0372*) is true old-school Caracas—the same baristas seem to have been pulling delicious, *crema*-topped espressos here for years. All of the high-quality pastries and goodies are made here: it's a true family affair. Parking can be a pain outside, but be patient, because it's worth the wait.

St. Honoré (⊠*1era Calle con Av. Andrés Bello, Altamira/Los Palos Grande* ☎*0212/286–9396*) is near the fabulous store **Casa Curuba** and just across the street from rival café **Arabica.** This is less hip than Arabica, but just as well loved and scrumptious. Grab a *cachito de jamón* (a ham-stuffed croissant) and enjoy the friendly hubbub on the outdoor patio. These same owners opened up a bakery called **Tisserie** in New York City, at the northwest corner of Union Square.

Le St. Tropez (⊠*Av. Blandín, C. San Ignacio, Nivel Chaguaramos, Local CH2-22, La Castellana* ☎*0212/731–5629*) sits right across the street from a massive church in the Castellana neighborhood. The sweet owner serves up yummy couscous dishes on Thursdays, but the real draw here are the simple, fresh sandwiches, desserts, and pastries—not to mention the divine coffee.

York–style tuna, and smoked turkey). A well-edited wine list and helpful waiters attract loads of couples and businesspeople here for lunch, but come dinnertime the scene is more romantic, with lighted bamboo and shrubs protecting the patio from street noise. ⊠*Calle Guaicaipuro, Quinta Otawa, El Rosal 1050* ☎*0212/951–3884* ▤*AE, MC, V.*

$$
ITALIAN ✕ **Da Guido.** This well-loved, casual, family-style restaurant, with hams hanging from the ceiling and colorful murals depicting the Italian countryside, is filled with locals who enjoy its classic dishes and affordable prices. Manager Eliseo Peserico and his friendly waiters have been serving up delicious gnocchi, ravioli, and fettuccine for more than 30 years. House specialties include roasted lamb and cornish hen with polenta. The meat dishes are the real attraction here. ⊠*Av. Mariscal Francisco Solano, Local 8, Sabana Grande* ☎*0212/763–0937* ▤*AE, MC, V* Ⓜ*Plaza Venezuela.*

$$$
LATIN
AMERICAN ✕ **Haras Grill.** Located in a popular shopping mall called El Recreo, this meat restaurant makes up for the fact that it's on the mall's second floor with friendly, rustic charm and bright, floor-to-ceiling photo murals

of Venezuelan farmland. The waiters are helpful, and the clientele is mostly shoppers, though some people make the effort to come here just for the consistently good grilled meats, *arepas,* and cold beers. ⊠ *Av. Casanova, Torre Norte, Piso 2, Local Top 2-1, El Recreo Bello Monte* ☎ *0212/761–3945* ⊟ *AE, MC, V.*

$$$$
ECLECTIC

✕ **Lola.** When Sean Penn visited Caracas in 2007, rumor has it he came to sleek, modern Lola for lunch. Perhaps he, too, was perplexed by the wide range of cuisines the menu has to offer: Italian pasta, Moroccan tagine, Chinese dim sum, Venezuelan grilled fish, and fresh Indian naan. This eccentricity (or perhaps indecisiveness) is more than made up for by the incredible bi-level modern space. Try a steak, lamb, or fish dish, and leave room for an inspired dessert, especially the deconstructed *bienmesabe,* a traditional Venezuelan coconut-and-liqueur cake. ⊠ *5ta transv., Av. San Juan, Bosco 1050* ☎ *0212/263–9596* ⌓ *Reservations essential Jacket* ⊟ *AE, MC, V* ⊗ *Closed Sun.*

$$$$
LATIN
AMERICAN
Fodor'sChoice
★

✕ **Maute Grill.** With a huge central indoor courtyard, Maute Grill is a popular spot for families, couples, and business types. On the menu you will find delectable grilled steaks cooked to your exact specifications. Stick to the traditional Venezuelan cuts such as *solomo* (sirloin), *lomito* (tenderloin), or the ever-popular *punta trasera* (top rump). Be sure to order a side of perfectly hand-fashioned *arepitas* (little arepas) and yucca. Delicious! ⊠ *Av. Rio de Janeiro, between Calles New York and Trinidad, Quinta el Portal, Las Mercedes* ☎ *0212/991–0892* ⊟ *AE, MC, V.*

$$$
JAPANESE

✕ **Sakura.** A great neighborhood sushi joint in Altamira, Sakura is run by a friendly Japanese chef who speaks both Spanish and English with his diverse clientele. Begin your meal with the *tempura mixta* (mixed tempura) and go with the chef's tasting menu, which will include various traditional rolls and scrumptious pieces of fresh sushi. Our favorite place to sit is at the bar, with a pot of steaming green tea. ⊠ *1era Av., Edificio 1st Av., Planta Baja, Altamira* ☎ *0212/285–5394* ⊟ *AE, MC, V.*

$$$$
MEDITERRANEAN
★

✕ **Spizzico.** Grab a seat on the open-air second-floor balcony for a more elegant meal or head downstairs to get your fill of wood-oven, thin-crust pizza. An impeccable wine list complements such dishes as *pasta con hongos* (wild-mushroom pasta) and mouth-watering roasted rabbit. Valet parking, friendly service, and a nice long bar keep the customers coming. ⊠ *Av. Principal La Castellana, between Chaguaramos and El Bosque, La Castellana 1050* ☎ *0212/267–8484* ⊟ *AE, MC, V.*

10

$$$
LATIN
AMERICAN

✕ **Tarzilandia.** Lush tropical vegetation filled with parrots, tree frogs, and turtles has been part of the experience at this Caracas landmark since it opened in 1950. It's truly memorable just to arrive here: the mostly open-air restaurant is perched just below the Ávila, and the moment you walk through the front gate you see cages of colorful birds and waiters scurrying about carrying trays laden with cuts of meat. There's definitely a theme-park feeling here, but it's fun just the same, espeically on a sunny, breezy afternoon. On the menu you will find well-prepared (if not life-changing) grilled steaks and seafood. The mango flambé à la mode is a delightful way to end your meal. ⊠ *Av. San Juan de Bosco at Decima Transversal, Altamira* ☎ *0212/261–8419* ⊟ *AE, MC, V.*

WHERE TO STAY

$$$$ 🏨**Embassy Suites.** This 20-floor tower in the financial district caters to the needs of business travelers. The soaring atrium, which lets in the Caracas sunlight, is a great place to relax over breakfast. The suites all have separate living rooms, except for 24 new rooms that have balconies instead. **Pros:** Comfortable for business travelers, central location. **Cons:** On a major street that can be unsafe at night, somewhat bland. ⊠*Av. Francisco de Miranda and Av. El Parque, El Rosal* ☎*0212/276–4200* ⊕*www.embassysuitescaracas.com* ⬇*224 suites, 24 rooms* ⚴*In-room: safe, dial-up. In-hotel: restaurant, bars, pool, gym, concierge, laundry service, no-smoking rooms, parking (no fee)* ⊟*AE, D, MC, V.*

> ### COLONIA TOVAR
>
> Colonia Tovar, 65 km (40 mi) west of Caracas, is an intriguing mountain village colonized by German immigrants in the 1840s. Because it remained isolated until the 1930s, the community retains a German character nearly as authentic as any you'll find in the Black Forest—except for those wild parrots and verdant jungle. Given its cooler climate, you'll quickly forget that this breezy mountain retreat is so close to the Caribbean. The real joy is hiking in the surrounding hills.

$$$$ 🏨**J.W. Marriott Caracas.** The newest and most up-to-date hotel in Cara-
Fodor'sChoice cas is also the most popular, and with good reason: in a city where it
★ can feel like many hotels haven't been renovated or refurbished since the end of the last century, the Marriott, in El Rosal, is shiny and well kept. Rooms are as you'd expect them to be for this hotel chain: business-friendly, clean, and comfortable. Though it doesn't hold a candle to nearby THE Hotel in terms of personality, it certainly is a dependable spot. **Pros:** Great business facilities and know-how, clean rooms, central location. **Cons:** Lacking verve, very large at 17 stories. ⊠*Av. Venezuela, at Calle Mohedano, El Rosal 1060* ☎*0212/957–2222* ⊕*www.marriott.com* ⬇*134 rooms, 135 suites* ⚴*In-room: safe, refrigerator. In-hotel: 3 restaurants, bar, parking (fee), spa, outdoor pool, gym, no-smoking rooms* ⊟*AE, DC, MC, V* ⊺⦿|*CP.*

$$$$ 🏨**THE Hotel.** The first true boutique hotel in Caracas is hard on the
Fodor'sChoice wallet, but easy on the eyes. A Thai- and Buddhism-inspired under-
★ tone is accented by modern touches such as gleaming Mac computers in the lobby, Philippe Starck–designed clear acrylic chairs, and a wine bar that will impress oenophiles. Rooms are exeedingly comfortable, with comfy beds, robes, open showers, glass and marble finishes, and iPod-friendly Bose stations. Be sure to head up to the lovely rooftop on Thursdays for "Chill Nights," which offer 2-for-1 drinks and a cooler-than-thou atmosphere. Be sure to check the Web site before you book for good deals on rooms in low season. ⊠*Calle Mohedano, El Rosal 1060* ☎*0212/951–0268* ⊕*www.thehotel.com.ve* ⬇*32 rooms, 30 suites* ⚴*In-room: safe, refrigerator. In-hotel: restaurant, bar, Internet, gym, spa, pool* ⊟*AE, DC, MC, V* ⊺⦿|*CP.*

$$$ 🏨**Hotel Paseo Las Mercedes.** There's no hiding the fact that this hotel needs a serious renovation, but you also can't ignore its central location in a lovely mall with some of the best shopping and dining right nearby. If you can get past the 1980s-style floral bedspreads and the wear-and-tear, you will enjoy staying here—the staff is friendly, the amenities are solid, and the price is right. **Pros:** Great location, mall downstairs with cinemas and cafes, friendly atmosphere, lovely pool. **Cons:** Close to highway, bad views, needs a facelift. ⊠ *Final Av. Principal Las Mercedes, Las Mercedes* ☎ *0212/993–1244* ⊕ *www.hotelpaseo lasmercedes.com* ↗ *196 rooms* ⚼ *In-hotel: restaurant, bar, public Wi-Fi, parking (free), gym, pool* ⊟ *AE, MC, V* ⱺ *CP.*

$$$$ ⚏ **Tamanaco InterContinental.** A time-tested beacon of old-school Caracas, this venerable pyramid-shape hotel sits on a bluff above the Las Mercedes neighborhood in the southeastern section of the city. It's the oldest of the city's luxury hotels and still well maintained after all these years. Its most stunning facility, a free-form pool, loops around any which way but rectangularly. You can take a dip after working out at the health club or playing a few games on the tennis courts. The bar, El Punto, is a gathering place of choice for the city's elite and influential. Rooms are spacious and comfortable. **Pros:** Old-world charm, consistant service, great location. **Cons:** Needs renovation, perched over a busy street. ⊠ *Av. Principal de Las Mercedes, Las Mercedes* ☎ *0212/909–7111* ⊕ *www.ichotelsgroup.com/* ↗ *486 rooms, 55 suites* ⚼ *In-room: safe, dial-up. In-hotel: 3 restaurants, bars, tennis courts, pool, gym, concierge, laundry service, no-smoking rooms, parking (no fee)* ⊟ *AE, D, MC, V.*

AFTER DARK

Monday must be the only night Caraqueños get any sleep, because Tuesday seems to be the unofficial start of the weekend. By Saturday the whole population appears to be out on the town. As in much of Latin America, the nightlife doesn't really get swinging until close to midnight. The trendy Las Mercedes neighborhood, packed with cafés, restaurants, bars, and dance clubs, is the place to be on Friday and Saturday. Although Caracas is generally pretty casual, clubs often require men to wear jackets. Take a taxi after dark no matter where you go or how short the distance.

10

BARS & DANCE CLUBS

There's no shortage of bars in Caracas, whether hole-in-the-wall establishments with semi-warm beer or gleaming, modern hotel clubs with champagne and cocktails. Salsa and merengue are more popular in Venezuela than in any other South American country, which means that both types of music can be found in almost any club in the city. Many begin the night playing pop, then switch to salsa and merengue when the crowd gets warmed up. The dance floors immediately fill with young couples gyrating hip to hip.

Fodor's Choice ★ San Ignacio, a mall in La Castellana, is hands-down the best place to go for nightlife: there are cafés, clubs, bars, wine joints, and eateries. The best part, though, is that it's all enclosed in a safe mall, with plenty of young revelers to join you in the fun. Our favorite place here is **Souka**, a lounge/dance club/bar that is both friendly and über-cool. The trend-

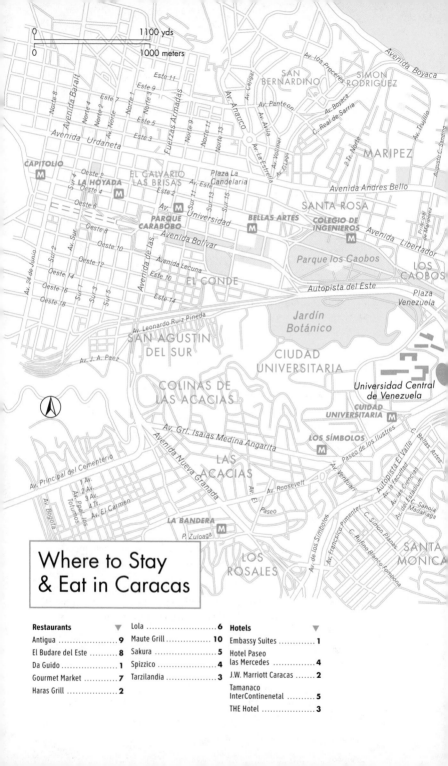

Where to Stay & Eat in Caracas

KEY

1 Restaurants

① Hotels

Parque Nacional El Ávila

ALTA FLORIDA

CHAPELLIN

EL PEDREGAL

LAS PALMAS

LA FLORIDA

Caracas Country Club

COUNTRY CLUB

ALTAMIRA

LA CAMPIÑA

LA CASTELLANA

PLAZA VENEZUELA

SABANA GRANDE

CAMPO ALEGRE

CHACAO

BELLO CAMPO

SABANA GRANDE

ALTAMIRA

CHACAITO

CHACAO

LOS CHAGUARAMOS

EL ROSAL

Distribuidor Altamira

LAS MERCEDES

CHULAVISTA

Av. Boyaca

Avenida Libertador

Autopista del Este - Francisco Fajardo

Autopista Caracas-Baruta

iest and hippest peeps in Caracas make it a point to stop by here on a regular basis. (⊠*Av. Blandín, La Castellana* ☎*0212/263–5249*). In Las Mercedes, **Auyama** (⊠*Calle Londres, Las Mercedes* ☎*0212/991–9489*) is a popular place for a cocktail before heading to the clubs. It also serves reasonably priced food. The most popular salsa club is also is in what has unfortunately become a seedy and unsafe area. However, if you must get your dance on, go for it at **El Maní Es Así** (⊠*Calle El Cristo at Av. Francisco Solano López, Sabana Grande* ☎*0212/763–6671*) with that cautionary note in mind. It's always packed with a crowd covering a wide age range.

CAB IT TO EL HATILLO

On the southern outskirts of Caracas is the hillside village of El Hatillo, a destination well worth the 30-minute taxi ride. Its narrow stone streets are lined with 17th-century buildings housing dozens of charming shops, boutiques, galleries, and popular restaurants. Here you'll find unique handicrafts and indigenous artifacts, original artwork, and rare antiques from all over Venezuela. The restored village is clearly intended for tourists, but it somehow has managed to preserve its colonial style.

SHOPPING

Caraqueños are style-conscious, which accounts for the city's numerous modern shopping centers. Jewelry (especially gold) and leather goods (including shoes, handbags, and luggage) are some of the best purchases in Caracas, but don't expect a steal. Prices are often high in the wake of sobering inflation.

CENTERS

Caracas is home to two of the most gargantuan shopping centers on the continent. **Centro Sambil** (⊠*Av. Libertador, Chacao* ☎*0212/267–9302*), the largest mall in South America, is a five-level behemoth packed with more than 500 shops, restaurants, theaters, and even amusement-park rides. The **Central Comercial Ciudad Tamanaco** (⊠*Calle La Estancia, Las Mercedes* ☎*0212/271–7435*), east of Las Mercedes in the suburb of Chuao, attracts crowds with its upstairs cinemas, fast-food restaurants, and swanky boutiques. **San Ignacio** (⊠*Av. Blandín, La Castellana* ☎*0212/263–5249*) is a mall in La Castellana with fine shopping (such as Merrell, Dockers, Swatch, and Guess, plus much more interesting boutiques) and even better nightlife.

Las Mercedes has its own sprawling shopping complex, **Paseo de Las Mercedes** (⊠*Av. Principal de Las Mercedes, Las Mercedes* ☎*0212/991–7242*). **El Recreo** (⊠*Paseo El Recreo, Bello Monte* ☎*0212/762–7228*) is the newest of the large-scale malls and boasts the best food court in the city.

DISTRICTS

With the growing popularity of shopping malls, traditional shopping districts have suffered a decline. One area that continues to draw crowds, even if it is somewhat seedy and unsavory, is the **Bulevar**

de Sabana Grande. Once a main traffic thoroughfare, this is a bustling promenade where Caraqueños converge to browse in the tiny shops or chat over a *marrón grande* (large coffee) in one of the many cafés that line the streets. The area can be crowded, so beware of pickpockets.

★ Besides its restaurants and clubs, **Las Mercedes** is overflowing with fancy boutiques and fashionable shops. The most exclusive are often tucked into side streets. Avoid its main strip, Avenida Principal de Las Mercedes, which has an overwhelming collection of cheap clothing stores.

MARKETS

One of the most popular markets is the Thursday- and Saturday-morning **Mercadito de Chacao**, where you can stroll through the stands overflowing with fruits and vegetables. It's a block from Avenida Francisco de Miranda in the Chacao district.

> **EL BÉISBOL**
>
> On a continent where soccer is nearly a religion, Venezuela's obsession with *béisbol* (baseball) is a notable exception. The popularity of the sport is due in large part to the thriving professional winter league, where North American players such as Johnny Bench, Pete Rose, and Darryl Strawberry all honed their skills. Atlanta Braves slugger Andres Galarraga, born in Caracas, is a hero in his hometown. The centrally located stadium at the **Universidad Central de Venezuela** (✉ *Ciudad Universitaria* ☎ *0212/572–2211*) is the best venue for baseball or soccer. Tickets can be purchased

SPECIALTY SHOPS

Fodor'sChoice **El Buzcón** (✉ *Centro Comercial Paseo Las Mercedes, Las Mercedes*
★ ☎ *0212/993–8242*) is a fantastic book shop in the basement of the Paseo Las Mercedes Mall. You can find used art books, books about Venezuela, calendars to take home with photographs of local animal life, and even colorful journals. On the same floor of the mall you'll find a great little chocolate shop called **Kakao** (✉ *Centro Comercial Paseo Las Mercedes, Las Mercedes* ☎ *0212/993–5583*)—choose an artistic little box emblazoned with artwork by local artists, and fill it with the elegant chocolates behind the counter. Flavors range from Earl Grey to *parchita* (passionfruit), *ron* (rum), and even *culo de bachaco* (literally "ass of the ant"), a spicy concoction that really is filled with ground-up ants—a traditional delicacy in some parts.

Fodor'sChoice **Casa Curuba** (✉ *Edificio Everi, 5th Av. at 4th Transversal, Altamira*
★ ☎ *0212/283–9368*) is a sumptuous world of wood and design. The great variety of Venezuelan hardwoods provides a surprising palette of color and grain. The objects, from hand-carved iguanas to contemporary rocking chairs, reflect a longtime collaboration between skilled artisans of Lara state and prominent Venezuelan designers.

10

THE CARIBBEAN COAST

Sometimes referred to as *La Ruta del Sol* (the Route of the Sun), the 563-km (350-mi) stretch of highway along the Caribbean Coast from Caracas to Puerto La Cruz and, farther east, to Cumaná, is at once gloriously picturesque and treacherous. Seldom far from the water's edge, most of the Autopista del Oriente (Eastern Highway) follows the myriad loops and twists of the natural shoreline, past unspoiled bays and isolated hamlets. Roadside vendors sell *cocos fríos* (cold coconuts) and *cachapas* (a delicious corn pancake folded around cheese), while gas stations blast salsa and merengue and offer up good coffee, a quick rest, and, of course, dirt-cheap gasoline.

> ### FISHING
>
> Los Roques is one of the top bonefishing destinations in the world, and many visitors come to Venezuela specifically to cast for the quick-running sport fish. You can catch *pavón*, huge peacock bass, in Los Llanos and in the Río Orinoco, where you may also enjoy the added thrill of angling for feisty piranha. Trout fishing is a popular diversion in the Andes, where local tour operators host a variety of expeditions to well-stocked, scenic lakes. A few restaurants will even fry up your catch.

Much of the coastline is protected from development, but small posadas are occasionally nestled among the palm trees along the shore. Sprawling resorts line the broad beaches near both Puerto La Cruz and Cumaná.

PUERTO LA CRUZ

318 km (198 mi) east of Caracas.

The region's main tourist hub, Puerto La Cruz has attractive waterways reminiscent of those found near wealthy communities in Florida, lined with marinas and lovely villas. Visitors flock to the maze of shops and restaurants along Paseo Colón, a busy thoroughfare that runs along the beach. At night the crowds move to the bars and dance clubs in town.

Although Puerto La Cruz's own beaches are dangerously polluted, its main attractions are the alluring islands of nearby Parque Nacional Mochima. At the eastern end you'll find boats to the national park that charge Bs.F25–Bs.F40 for round-trip service. Puerto La Cruz is also a jumping-off point for ferries to Isla Margarita, which depart from the western end of Paseo Colón.

OFF THE BEATEN PATH

Barcelona. Capital of the state of Anzoátegui, Barcelona was founded more than 300 years ago by Spanish settlers. Today it is Puerto La Cruz's gritty next-door neighbor, and, most important, the site of the region's largest airport. Barcelona's colonial-era vibe makes it a pleasant day trip from the resort-town style of its neighbors. Go to the corner of Plaza Boyacá, the city's tree-lined main square, where you can visit and photograph the **Iglesia de San Cristóbal,** a stunning church built in 1748. Perhaps more impressive is the adjacent Palacio del Gobierno (Govern-

The Caribbean Coast

Bonaire (Neth.)

Caribbean Sea

Islas Los Roques
Parque Nacional Archipélago Los Roques

Puerto Cabello

Higuerote

Macuto
La Guaira
Maiquetía
Caracas
Los Teques

TO BARQUISIMETO, MARACAIBO

Valencia
Maracay
La Victoria
San Juan de los Morros
DISTRITO FEDERAL
MIRANDA
CORDILLERA DE LA COSTA
ARAGUA

Tinaquillo
CARABOBO

El Baúl
COJEDES
Río Cojedes

El Sombrero
Calabozo
Embalse de Guárico
GUÁRICO
PARQUE NACIONAL AGUARO-GUARIQUITO

Altagracia de Orituco

Valle de la Pascua

LLANOS

Puerto Píritu
Barcelona
Puerto La Cruz
Pozuelos

Aragua de Barcelona

Anaco
El Tigre
ANZOÁTEGUI

Mochima
Cumaná

Santa Barbara

Cariaco
SUCRE

Río Caribe
Pastelhued Houses

Güiria
Golfo de Paria
Parque Nacional Península de Paria
Trinidad

P.N. Turuépano

Portamar
Isla de Margarita
see detail map

Cave of Guácharo

Maturín
MONAGAS

DELTA AMACURO
Tucupita

Barrancas
Ciudad Guayana
Río Orinoco

Caribbean Sea

50 miles
50 kilometers

ment Palace), built in 1671. Today it houses the **Museo de la Tradición,** which has rotating exhibits of colonial and religious art. ⊠*Plaza Boyacá* ☎*0281/277–3481* ☎*Free* ☉*Daily 9–12:30 and 3–5.*

GETTING HERE & AROUND
Conferry shuttles passengers and cars four times daily between Puerto La Cruz and Punta de Piedras, 25 km (16 mi) west of Porlamar, Margarita. Gran Cacique serves Margarita six times daily from Puerto La Cruz.

Several regional airlines fly regularly between the domestic terminal of Aeropuerto Internacional Simón Bolívar in Caracas and Barcelona, including Avior and Aeropostal. Both lines also fly between Barcelona and Isla Margarita. Barcelona's Aeropuerto José Antonio Uzcatéqui (BLA) is 3 km (2½ mi) south of the city. There are dozens of car rental places at the airport.

ESSENTIALS
Air Contacts (Barcelona) **Aeropostal** (☎*0281/277–1735*). **Avior** (⊠*Aeropuerto José Antonio Uzcatéqui, Barcelona* ☎*0281/287–2080*).

Boat Contacts **Conferry** (⊠*Terminal Los Cocos, Puerto La Cruz* ☎*0281/267–7847* ⊕*www.conferry.com*). **Gran Cacique** (⊠*Terminal Los Cocos, Puerto La Cruz* ☎*0281/263–0935* ⊕*www.grancacique.com.ve*).

Visitor & Tour Info **Coranztur (Barcelona)** (⊠*Av. 5 de Julio at Calle Las Flores, Barcelona* ☎*0281/275–0474*).**Coranztur (Puerto La Cruz)** (⊠*Paseo Colón at Calle Maneiro, Puerto La Cruz* ☎*0281/268–8170*). **Macite Turismo** (⊠*Centro Commercial Paseo Mar, Calle Sucre at Paseo Colón* ☎*0281/265–5703* ⊕*www. maciteturismo.com*).

WHERE TO STAY
$$$ ☷ **Gran Hotel Puerto La Cruz.** This expansive hotel at the end of the Paseo Colón is next to the marina where the boats take off for excursions to the nearby islands. Spacious, if dingy, rooms overlook the lush gardens and pool. **Pros:** Location, spaciousness. **Cons:** Rooms need refurbishing, service is lacking. ⊠*Paseo Colón* ☎*0281/265–3611* ☞*220 rooms* ♿*In-room: safe. In-hotel: restaurant, bar, pool, diving, water sports, golf* ☱*AE, D, MC, V.*

$$$$ ☷ **Punta Palma Hotel.** Built at the end of the bay, this hotel has an enviable view of Puerto La Cruz and the mountains to the west—best of all, though, is its small slice of beachfront, including a private moorage and beach. Most of its colorfully decorated rooms have balconies and overlook the pool, marina, and small private beach. Be sure when you are booking to ask for a room with a view of the water. Also, when you are enjoying the lovely breakfast buffet poolside, take a look over the edge of the patio and you'll see dozens of iguanas sunning themselves—there are so many iguanas that live in this rockery, in fact, that biologists have taken to studying them here. ⊠*Prolongación Av. La Península, Cerro El Morro* ☎*0281/280–0800* ⊕*www.hotelpuntapalma.com.ve* ☞*181 rooms, 3 suites* ♿*In-room: safe, refrigerator. In-hotel: 3 restaurants, bars, public Internet, tennis courts, pools, laundry service* ☱*AE, D, MC, V.*

CLOSE UP

Parque Nacional Los Roques

If you are looking for a spalike vacation, then this is your place. Los Roques has several "posadas" or bed-and-breakfasts ranging from rustic and simple to elegant and exclusive. An archipelago composed of some 350 tiny islands sprinkled in the dazzling Caribbean, Parque Nacional Los Roques is a 30-minute (propeller-aircraft) flight north from Caracas. Only one of those islands, Gran Roque, boasts a bona fide town, tiny as it is. A few others have private weekend retreats or fishermen's shacks, while most are completely uninhabited. Some are so small they disappear at high tide. The sandy beaches of Parque Nacional Los Roques are uncommonly white, even by uncompromising Caribbean standards. Coral reefs here are home to more than 300 species of fish.

A national park since 1976, Parque Nacional Los Roques is subject to strict federal regulations that protect it from overdevelopment. New construction is prohibited on any of the islands. Every structure on Gran Roque—which enjoys fresh water from a desalinization plant and electricity from a generator—existed before the archipelago became a national park. Many have been extensively remodeled and are meticulously maintained as *posadas* (small inns). A handful of bars and eateries make up the rest of the businesses. A mid-19th-century lighthouse, its windmill-like appearance revealing its Dutch heritage, overlooks the town from a small hill nearby.

Los Roques is considered one of the finest locales for hooking bonefish and other types of fish. You can head out in powerboats or in *peñeros* (local fishing boats). Sea kayaking is also popular, and some of the islands have emerged as premier sailboarding destinations. More sedate pastimes include scuba diving and snorkeling. Sunbathing, however, remains the most popular activity. Approximately 60 posadas line the sandy roads of Gran Roque. Most have two to six rooms with private or shared bath and a common dining area. Except during the peak season you should have no difficulty finding lodging on the island. Italian-born innkeeper Elena Battani's heritage is evident throughout the exquisite **Posada Mediterráneo**, from the simple furnishings of the rooms to the white stone staircase leading to the rooftop terrace hung with sun-shaded hammocks. Join her for a chat at the rustic wooden dining table on her flowering vine-laden front patio. **Pros:** Heaven on earth, good food, trip of a lifetime. **Cons:** Getting here, rustic. ✉ *Calle Las Flores 99, Isla Gran Roque* ☎ *0414/329–0621* 🌐 *www.posadamediterraneo.com* *6 rooms* *In-room: no phone, safe, no TV. In-hotel: restaurant, no elevator* *AE, MC, V* *FAP.*

AFTER DARK

You won't have to look far to find bars and dance clubs in Puerto La Cruz, as all are along Paseo Colón or adjacent streets. A popular part of the scene is the vibrant **Harry's Pub** (✉ *Calle Bolívar 53* ☎ *No phone*), a casual watering hole with an interesting mix of young locals and seasoned wayfarers.

SPORTS & THE OUTDOORS

FISHING

Boat owners throughout the region will take you fishing in their small wooden peñeros. Bargain for the best price—the going rate is about $5 per person for a half-day excursion. The friendly staff at **Macite Turismo** (⊠ *Centro Comercial Paseo Mar, Calle Sucre at Paseo Colón* ☏ *0281/265–5703* ⊕ *www.maciteturismo.com*) offers full-day trips to Isla Tortuga for barracuda fishing.

WATER SPORTS

In Puerto La Cruz, **Explosub** (⊠ *Paseo Colón* ☏ *0281/267–3256*) offers snorkeling and scuba-diving trips, as well as excursions to Parque Nacional Mochima. If you are not already an experienced diver, Explosub also offers certification classes. In neighboring El Morro, **Odisea** (⊠ *Av. Américo Vespucio*) rents sailboats, Windsurfers, and pedal boats at the Hotel Doral Beach.

CUMANÁ

75 km (47 mi) east of Puerto La Cruz.

The oldest European settlement on South America's mainland, Cumaná was founded by the Spanish in 1521. Most of its colonial buildings were destroyed by a string of earthquakes that devastated the town. It's a hike to get here, but those who make the effort almost always come away with rave reviews. The scenery and outlying beaches, in particular, are fabulous.

GETTING HERE & AROUND

Several regional airlines fly regularly between Caracas and and Cumaná, including Avior and Santa Bárbara. Avior also flies between Cumaná and Isla Margarita, and Santa Bárbara also connects Cumaná with Mérida. The flight takes about one hour and will cost about $250 (Bs. F537). Aeropuerto Antonio José de Sucre (CUM) in Cumaná is 4 km (2 mi) southeast of the city. You can rent a car from one of the many agencies that have desks at the airport.

Conferry shuttles passengers and cars between Cumaná and Punta de Piedras, 25 km (16 mi) west of Porlamar, Margarita. It also travels between Puerto La Cruz and Margarita. Gran Cacique travels between Margarita and Cumaná six times daily.

ESSENTIALS

Air Contacts **Avior** (☏ *0281/287–1294 or 0212/955–3811*). **Santa Bárbara** (☏ *0293/467–2933 or 0212/204–4000*).

Boat Contacts **Gran Cacique** (⊠ *Terminal Puerto Sucre, Cumaná* ☏ *0293/433-0909 or 0293/433-0744* ⊕ *www.grancacique.com.ve*).

EXPLORING CUMANÁ

After the last major earthquake in 1929, the **Iglesia de Santa Inés** was rebuilt a few blocks south of Plaza Bolívar. Inside are a few items from the colonial period.

ON THE ROAD AGAIN

A car is a nice option for this part of the country, as you can travel at your own pace and stop at beautiful beaches along the coastal route. The often-congested Autopista del Oriente connects Caracas with Barcelona, Puerto La Cruz, Cumaná, and smaller towns beyond. It has plenty of roadside services. If you are taking a bus between Caracas and Puerto La Cruz, hire a car to reach smaller towns, such as Río Chico or Puerto Píritu. Keep in mind that driving in Venezuela can be a bit frazzling and scary, so a trip along the coast, while wonderful, can be stressful, mostly because of confusing traffic signs, dazed or speedy drivers, and menacing (but usually harmless) police checkpoints.

Rent a car in Caracas and head east out of town in the early morning (traffic in the capital is absolutely hideous after 7 AM). Bring along some *cachitos de jamón* (ubiquitous ham-filled croissants) to munch on while you pass through Caracas, then the shanty-filled outskirt of Petare, then the lush, ever-changing landscape along the coast. Keep in mind that you should have a cell phone, some small-denomination cash, and all of the necessary documents needed to travel by rental car. Also be forewarned that traveling by car here is to be undertaken by the brave and adventurous: there are potholes, windy roads, and, *peajes* (pay tolls, which, at this writing, weren't charging but still existed) and, most famously, *alcabalas* (police checkpoints). There are also fruit stands, friendly locals, lovely scenery, and many beaches to be explored. Small, charming towns along the way include Río Chico, El Guapo, Clarines, and Puerto Píritu; larger cities such as Barcelona and Puerto La Cruz are also major stopping points. If you decide to go beyond Puerto La Cruz by land, you'll pass the small town of Santa Fe to reach the turnoff for Mochima, the launching point for boat trips to the tranquil beaches of **Parque Nacional Mochima**, which encompasses hundreds of small islands. Contract a *peñero* to take you to any of the nearby beaches, where you can spend a relaxing morning or afternoon lazing around in the sun. It's about $10 per person, but the rate is negotiable.

One block south of Plaza Bolívar, the **Ateneo de Cumaná** (⊠ *Calle Antonio* ☎ *0293/431–1284*) hosts dance and opera evenings in addition to periodic exhibits of contemporary and colonial art.

Overlooking Cumaná from its hilltop perch, **Castillo de San Antonio de la Eminencia** is one of two forts commissioned in the 1680s to protect what was at the time the world's largest salt deposit. The four-point fort was built entirely of coral and outfitted with 16 guns.

The fort **Castillo de Santiago de Araya,** is on treeless Araya Peninsula. Ferries leave daily from Cumaná's harbor for the 90-minute trip.

It's estimated that **Cueva del Guácharo,** Venezuela's largest cave, has at least 9 km (5½ mi) of subterranean passageways. Groups are led into the dank caverns by guides who tote kerosene lanterns so as not to upset the light-sensitive *guácharos*—a nocturnal species of fruit-eating birds. Visitors are not allowed to bring anything inside, including purses, flashlights, or cameras. To reach the cave from Cumaná, take Highway 9 south toward Caribe for about 65 km (40 mi) and follow signs; there are bathrooms, guided tours, and a a visitor center available at the mouth of the caves. ⊠*Parque Nacional El Guácharo* 🚗*About Bs.F5* ⊗*Daily 8–4.*

WHERE TO STAY

$$$$ 🏨**Premier Cumanagoto.** Attention to detail makes this beachfront hotel among the finest hotels outside of Caracas. Large wrought-iron perches holding colorful macaws border the open-air, Mediterranean-style lobby, which has a terra-cotta floor and plenty of old-world charm. Bars and restaurants take full advantage of the Caribbean breezes with outdoor seating. The generously proportioned rooms have terraces overlooking the beautiful pools and gardens below. ⊠*Final Av. Universidad* 🕾*0293/430–1577* 📠*163 rooms, 11 suites* ⚒*In-room: safe. In-hotel: 3 restaurants, bar, golf course, tennis court, pools, gym, spa* 🖃*AE, D, MC, V.*

LA GUAIRA

20 mi (32 km) northwest of Caracas.

In 1999 heavy rainfall resulted in horrific mud- and landslides that crippled the region between Maiguetía and Naiguata; some reports say that up to 30,000 perished. This swath of land includes the once-charming town of La Guaira. Uprooted trees, broken sidewalks, and buried buildings meant the loss of the colonial charm that once existed here. Though Venezuela is still fairly unprepared for major influxes of tourists, and the political tensions in this country consistently keep mainstream travelers at arm's length, this small town is still on its way to becoming a major cruise port. The town itself doesn't have much to offer in the way of services, so most cruise-ship passengers are loaded immediately onto Caracas-bound buses. The beaches nearby aren't much to look at (being so close to such a major port), so beachgoers will be bused along the coast as well.

ISLA MARGARITA

Venezuelans are enormously fond of the island they call the *Perla del Caribe,* or the "pearl of the Caribbean." Its status as a duty-free port and its proximity to the mainland make it the top vacation spot for Venezuelans. Come here to explore miles of white sandy beaches, glittering hotels and restaurants, vibrant nightlife, and 16th-century forts and national parks, all of which have transformed Isla Margarita into an increasingly popular destination for other travelers as well.

Isla Margarita is split into two sections linked by an 18-km (11-mi) spit of sand. Most of the island's 400,000 residents occupy the more developed eastern half, especially the bustling city of Porlamar and adjoining Pampatar. Others are found in the much smaller city of La Asunción,

MARGARITA'S MAIN BEACHES

Playa El Agua: Easily the most famous and crowded beach on the island, palm-lined Playa El Agua is a remarkable stretch of fine white sand that runs along the coast a short drive north of Pampatar. For much of its 4-km (2-mi) length, restaurants and bars lure sunbathers with blaring salsa music and ice-cold beers. In high season this is the place to show off your bikini, not to relax.

Playa Manzanillo: Hungry for some fresh fish soup? This is a fishermen's bay on the north side of the island, complete with shacks selling cold beer and good seafood overlooking bobbing wooden boats and tangles of rope and net. Though it's not the best spot on the island for swimming, it is good for a dip and a lazy afternoon punctuated with photo ops and yummy snack from the sea.

Playa Pampatar: You'll most certainly pass by this stretch of sand when you go to downtown Pampatar to visit the sights and have a meal at one of the popular restaurants along the main drag. Also home to many fishermen, the beach has a positively lovely view.

Playa Parguito: Laid-back but still quite popular, this is the stretch of beach south of Playa El Agua that surfers love to frequent. It's basically a smaller version of Playa El Agua, offering restaurants, bumpin' music, and a bit of a scene.

Playa Puerto Cruz: Two massive hotels reign over this exquisite, if sometimes choppy, beach: Dunes and Hesperia. There's a short uphill walk to a lighthouse on one end of the beach, and a delicious ½-mi of sand that begs to be walked. You could spend days here.

Playa El Yaque: Close to the airport, this southern-side beach is windsurfer and kite-surfer central—in fact, it's internationally known for its smooth surface and high winds. It's a great place to people-watch and take a stroll but, not surprisingly, the swimming's not great.

the capital of the region that also encompasses the neighboring islands of Coche and Cubagua.

10

PORLAMAR & PAMPATAR

Porlamar, with more than a third of Isla Margarita's population, is the island's center of commerce. Since it was granted free-port status in 1973, its store-lined avenues have been mobbed with tourists in search of tax-free bargains. Many of the goods found here are no cheaper than on the mainland, however. Porlamar is also the most cosmopolitan city on Isla Margarita, boasting many restaurants, bars, clubs, and casinos. This area is home to the Hilton hotel and several large shopping malls, most notably the Centro Comercial Sambil. It's also, unfortunately, a place where plenty of abandoned construction projects stand surrounded by spray-painted walls. This strange mixture of divine coastline, urbanization, and half-baked projects makes for a less-than-ideal spot for many vacationers. Most sunseekers simply say, why come to this island to stay in a city? Others point out that you can have the best of both worlds—coastline, ocean, shopping, nightlife, and restaurants—if you stay in or near Porlamar.

Just 10 km (6 mi) northeast of Porlamar is the sleepy, charming town of Pampatar, once a small fishing village. Fishing craft of all sizes line the bay and sandy beach here, offering up a gorgeous range of fish, from *pargo* (red snapper) to *mero* (grouper). Farther inland a culinary awakening is taking place—in fact, Pampatar has replaced its older sibling to the south as *the* place to wine, dine, and dance.

GETTING HERE & AROUND

Direct flights from Caracas and other Venezuelan cities, ·as well as scheduled or charter flights from a number of North American and European cities, make Isla Margarita an easy destination. Most major domestic carriers have daily service from Caracas, Cumaná, Valencia, and Maracaibo to Isla Margarita's Aeropuerto Internacional del Caribe (PMV), 29 km (18 mi) south of Porlamar. Aereotuy flies between Porlamar and Los Roques.

Conferry shuttles passengers and cars four times daily between Puerto La Cruz on the mainland and Punta de Piedras, 25 km (16 mi) west of Porlamar. Gran Cacique serves Margarita six times daily from both Cumaná and Puerto La Cruz. Crossings take from two to four hours and cost Bs.F50 per passenger and Bs.F100 per car. The bus company Unión Conductores de Margarita makes the 12-hour road/ferry trip from Caracas to Isla Margarita for less than Bs.F26.

Taxis and vans serve as public transportation throughout Isla Margarita, but roads are good and renting a car is a great way to reach the more secluded stretches of sand off the beaten track. At Aeropuerto Internacional del Caribe near Porlamar, Hertz is a good option. In downtown Porlamar, try Beach Car Rental.

ESSENTIALS

Air Contacts **Aeropostal** (☎0212/708–6300 ⊕www.aeropostal.com). **Aereotuy** (☎0212/212–3110 ⊕www.tuy.com).**Conviasa** (☎0212/507–8820 ⊕www.conviasa.aero/).

Boat Contacts **Conferry** (✉Terminal Los Cocos, Puerto La Cruz ☎0281/267–7847 ⊕www.conferry.com). **Gran Cacique** (✉Terminal Puerto Sucre, Cumaná ☎0293/431–2589 ⊕www.grancacique.com).

Bus Contact **Unión Conductores de Margarita** (✉Terminal de Oriente, Caracas ☎0212/541–0035 ✉Puerto La Cruz ☎0281/267–3426).

Car-Rental Contacts **Budget** (✉Aeropuerto Internacional del Caribe ☎0295/269–1490 or 0295/269–1292).**Hertz** (✉Aeropuerto Internacional del Caribe ☎0295/269–1237).

Currency Exchange **Italcambio** (✉Centro Comercial Jumbo, Porlamar ☎0295/265–9392).

Tour Information **Turaser Venezuela** (✉Av. Bolívar, Urb. Playa El AngelPampatar ☎0295/262–0166 ⊕www.turaser.com).

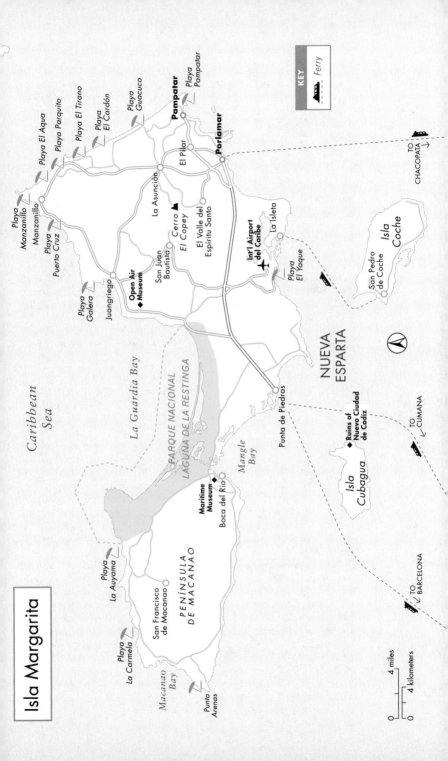

Isla Margarita

Caribbean Sea

Playa La Carmela

Macanao Bay

Punta Arenas

Playa La Auyama

San Francisco de Macanao

PENÍNSULA DE MACANAO

Mangle Bay

Boca del Río

Maritime Museum ◆

PARQUE NACIONAL LAGUNA DE LA RESTINGA

La Guardia Bay

Playa Galera

Juangriego

Playa Puerto Cruz

Playa Manzanillo

Manzanillo

Playa El Agua

Playa Parquito

Playa El Tirano

Playa El Cardón

Playa Guacuco

Pampatar

Playa Pampatar

San Juan Bautista

Open Air Museum ◆

Cerro El Copey ▲

La Asunción

El Valle del Espíritu Santo

El Pilar

Porlamar

Punta de Piedras

Int'l Airport del Caribe ✈

La Isleta

Playa El Yaque

San Pedro de Coche

Isla Coche

TO CHACOPATA →

Isla Cubagua

Ruins of Nueva Ciudad de Cadiz ◆

NUEVA ESPARTA

← TO CUMANA

← TO BARCELONA

KEY

⛴ Ferry

0 | 4 miles
0 | 4 kilometers

Visitor Info Corpotur (⊠ *Aeropuerto Internacional del Caribe, Porlamar* ☎ *No phone*).

EXPLORING PORLAMAR & PAMPATAR

Pampatar was founded nearly 500 years ago. Its strategic importance is clear when you visit the **Castillo de San Carlos de Borromeo** on the waterfront in the center of town. Constructed entirely of coral, the fort was built by the Spanish in 1662 after the original was destroyed by the Dutch. The port town is now known more for its myriad yachts and the fortnightly ferries that set sail for nearby Trinidad.

In the center of town is the **Iglesia Santísimo Cristo,** which features a bell tower with an outside staircase—an architectural oddity found on several churches on Isla Margarita.

☾ A giant Ferris wheel leads you to the island's largest amusement park, **Diverland** (⊠ *Av. Jóvito Villalba, Pampatar* ☎ *0295/262–0813*). There are 16 attractions, including a roller coaster and water slide.

A few blocks east of Porlamar's shady Plaza Bolívar is the **Museo de Arte Contemporáneo Francisco Narváez,** named after the native Margariteño sculptor whose works also can be viewed on the grounds of the Bella Vista Hotel. Here you'll find a permanent collection of Narváez's works, plus a rotating exhibit of national and international artworks. ⊠ *Calle Igualdad at Calle Diaz* ☎ *0295/261–8668* ☜ *Bs.F1* ☾ *Tues.– Fri. 9–5, weekends 10–3.*

WHERE TO EAT

$$$$
MEDITERRANEAN
Fodor'sChoice
★

✕ **Casa Caranta.** In the very heart of Pampatar lies this inviting Mediterranean trattoria. International clientele mix with locals for romantic dinners or drinks at the well-stocked bar (try a mojito or a frozen Casa Caranta cocktail). The specialties of the house include homemade fettucini with a rotating menu of sauces, and fresh fish such as *dorado* (mahimahi) in a variety of preparations—try it drizzled in red curry sauce or simmering in a fragrant broth. This old colonial house also serves as an art gallery: local artwork and charming antiques are tastefully exhibited throughout. Strong, hand-pulled coffee and fresh pies (lime, coconut, chocolate, *yum*) are the way to end your feast. ⊠ *Blvd. Histórico, Pampatar 6316* ☎ *0295/262–8610 or 0414/793– 5248* ⚠ *Reservations essential* ▭ *AE, MC, V* ☾ *Closed Sun. during low season. No lunch.*

$$$
VENEZUELAN

✕ **Casa E' Maya.** For a sublimely fresh and delectable *criollo* (typical Venezuelan) lunch of fish, fried plantains, beets, and *lechosa* (papaya) smoothies, come to low-key Casa E' Maya, where the soft-spoken owner will fry or grill up straight-from-the-ocean *catalana* fish, which is a Margariteña specialty. There are no menus, but if you're up for a place off the beaten path, this is a great place to choose. ⊠ *Casa Luisa Caceres de Arismendi No. 64, diagonally across from El Cículo Militar, Pampatar* ☎ *0295/267–0422* ▭ *No credit cards* ☾ *Closed Sun. No dinner.*

$$$

✕ **Charlie.** Head for Charlie, in Pampatar, to dine on always-on-the-mark pasta. The cozy space is perfect for families or couples; you'll see a mixed clientele happily sipping *vino tinto* (red wine) and often ordering the house specialty: *linguini neri,* fresh pasta cooked up with

To Macanao

Exploring Macanao, the western portion of Margarita, is a great way to spend a day off from the beach. Hire a driver through your hotel or, even better, rent a car: this arid, mysterious area is great fun to explore with your own four wheels.

The mangrove forests of **Parque Nacional Laguna de la Restinga** cover the 20-km (12-mi) thread of sand that makes up the tenuous link between the main part of the island and the Península de Macanao. Here you'll find a variety of colorful birds, such as the scarlet ibis. The park has an unspoiled beach and a sprinkling of fishermen's huts where you can buy the catch of the day. There are also nearly 50 small, traditional wooden boats that can take visitors on small trips through the mangrove forests.

From Parque Nacional Restinga, loop around the peninsula, where you'll pass by Punta Arenas, a touristy little spot that is worth a stop just to see the "playa salvaje," or savage beach:

wind-swept, sun-bleached, and utterly desolate in comparison to the glizty beaches on the other side of the island.

On the southern side of the peninsula, in Boca del Río, 50 km (30 mi) west of Porlamar, stands the **Museo Marino de Margarita,** a museum whose eight exhibit halls serve as a repository for Venezuela's astounding variety of marine life. The museum is home to a small collection of marine life, including sharks, turtles, and fish. The best part of the complex, though, are the exhibits, vintage photographs, and bilingual explanations focusing on the history of sea exploration in northern South America. There are even detailed exhibits of nautical knot tying and painstakingly assembled model boats. Be sure to check out the two-headed baby shark on the frst floor. It's this fun, eclectic mixture of information and the tangible local pride that goes into this museum that make it a must-see. ☎ 0295/291–3231 💳 Bs.F6 ⊙ Daily 9–4:30.

squid in its own ink. ⊠ *Calle Joaquin Maneiro, Pamapatar 6316* ☎ *No phone* 🖃 *AE, MC, V* ⊙ *No lunch.*

$$
FRENCH ✕ **Cocody.** Not far from Playa Bella Vista, this restaurant pairs well-prepared, standard French cuisine with fine wines in romantic elegance. You can also dine under the palms on the open-air terrace overlooking the beach. ⊠ *Av. Raúl Leoni, Porlamar* ☎ *0295/261–8431* 🖃 *AE, MC, V.*

$
VENEZUELAN ✕ **Guayoyo.** A large, multilevel open-air bar/restaurant perched just below the Flamingo Beach Hotel in Pampatar, Guayoyo (Spanish for a local coffee) is a hip place to spend a night on the town. The food isn't quite as memorable as the views over the ocean at sunset—the eatery is built right into the cliffside. Still, they do grill up a yummy *dorado,* or mahimahi. ⊠ *Calle El Cristo, Sector La Caranta, Pampatar, in front of Flamingo Beach hotel, 6316* ☎ *0295/262–4514* 🖃 *AE, DC, MC, V* ⊙ *No lunch.*

$$$$
MEDITERRANEAN ✕ **Paladar.** Put on your strappy heels (or your swankiest tie) for a night out in Pamapatar at this whitewashed Mediterranean restaurant. Good service, white linens, and a small but interesting menu make for a festive dinner. Fresh salads, pastas, and fish dishes such as salmon with

10

papaya compote are all good bets. ⊠*Calle Joaquin Maneiro No. 51, Pampatar 6316* ☏*0295/267–0309* ⚐*Reservations essential, Jacket* ⊟*AE, DC, MC, V* ⊘*No lunch.*

WHERE TO STAY

$$$ 🏨**Flamingo Beach Hotel.** Tarnished old-school glamour defines the public spaces at this hotel perched on the edge of Pampatar's turquoise bay. Though rumors swirl that this hotel will be getting a much-needed facelift soon, for now rooms remain basic. Be sure to ask for a room with a view of the ocean; rooms of the top floor are the best. A glass elevator whisks you up to rooms, some of which overlook the ocean. Breakfast is included, and you can enjoy it overlooking the pretty pool area and the ocean beyond. Just across the street are **Café Guayayo** and the happening night club **Mykonos. Pros:** Plenty of personality, awesome pool area. **Cons:** Tired rooms, a walk from downtown. ⊠*Calle El Cristo, Sector La Caranta, Pampatar* ☏*0295/262–5111* ☏*0295/262–0271* ⊕*www.enlared.net/flamingo* ⇱*169 rooms* ⚲*In-room: safe. In-hotel: restaurant, bar, pool, beachfront, water sports, Wi-Fi* ⊟*AE, MC, V.*

$$$ 🏨**Hilton Margarita.** Close to the sands of Playa Moreno, this vener-
⟳ able, family-friendly hotel offers a great location—five minutes from the center of the city. If you're not planning on renting a car on the island, or you want to be short cab ride from Pampatar's restaurants and nightlife, this is a reasonable option. The upper-floor rooms in the white tower are spacious and have slanted balconies overlooking the sea, but you'll probably spend most of your time lying by the lovely pool, playing a few matches on the lighted tennis courts, or heading out for waterskiing. A good restaurant option here is **La Scala**; the Vegas-style casino is a popular nightspot. **Pros:** Good location if you want to be in Porlamar, consistent service, private beach. **Cons:** Rooms need renovating, lacking personality. ⊠*Calle Los Uveros, Costa Azul* ☏*0295/260–1700* ⊕*www.hilton.com* ⇱*322 rooms, 11 suites* ⚲*In-room: safe, refrigerator. In-hotel: 4 restaurants, bars, room service, tennis courts, pool, gym, water sports, laundry service, airport shuttle, no-smoking rooms* ⊟*AE, D, MC, V.*

$$$$ 🏨**Lagunamar.** This vast complex just north of Pampatar spans a huge swath of coastline. There's plenty to keep sun-worshipers busy, from waterskiing to windsurfing to relaxing by one of the pools. Meals are included in the rate, the dining options ranging from a poolside café to a glittery Italian restaurant. **Pros:** Private beach, everything's taken care of (it's all-inclusive). **Cons:** A bit isolated and predictable. ⊠*Vía Agua de Vaca, Playa Guacuco* ☏*0295/400–4033* ⊕*www.lagunamar.com.ve* ⇱*216 rooms, 190 suites* ⚲*In-room: safe, refrigerator. In-hotel: 5 restaurants, bars, tennis courts, pools, gym, beachfront, water sports, laundry service* ⊟*AE, DC, MC, V.*

WHERE TO STAY ELSEWHERE ON THE ISLAND

$$$$ 🏨**Dunes.** Extremely popular with sun-seeking Europeans as well as
⟳ well-to-do Venezuelans, Dunes feels a bit like camp in its all-inclusive-ness—there's even a cinema alongside one of its many pools. What it lacks in charm and room elegance (rumor has it that much-needed renovations are coming), the hotel makes up for with well-kept grounds,

El Valle del Espíritu Santo & La Asunción

Founded as the capital of the island in 1529, **El Valle del Espíritu Santo,** just north of Porlamar, has a splendid pink-and-white church honoring the Virgen del Valle, patron saint of eastern Venezuela. Pilgrims journey here year-round, but especially on her feast day in early September.

The stained-glass windows of the **Santuario de la Virgen del Valle,** a twin-towered chapel on the main plaza, are worth a visit. A small museum open most afternoons contains the thousands of tokens, jewelry, and holy medals left by supplicants.

From the mountains in the center of the island there are striking views as the road slowly descends to **La Asunción,** the small capital of the region. The sleepy little town, ignored by the bargain-hunting throngs, is the opposite of the bustling Porlamar. A

handful of pretty colonial buildings are found around La Asunción's tree-covered Plaza Bolívar.

Built in 1568, the **Catedral de Nuestra Señora** is one of the oldest churches in Venezuela. Of particular interest is its three-tiered tower—the country's only surviving example of a colonial church tower.

Overlooking the main square, the **Castillo de Santa Rosa,** with its famous dungeon, is one of seven fortifications constructed by the Spanish to guard against pirate attacks.

Parque Nacional Cerro El Copey, along the road between Porlamar and La Asunción, has the highest point on the island. The mountain soars to 3,109 feet. From here you can often spot the smaller islands of Coche and Cubagua.

amenities, and sublime beachfront real estate. Unlike its colossal white neighbor up the beach, Hotel Hesperia Isla Magarita, Dunes blends in well with the countryside, no small feat considering the many buildings and rooms it has on offer. If nightly variety shows by the pool and so-so food with tons of foreigners are all right with you in exchange for beautiful pools, great kids' programs, and a perfect walking beach, then perhaps this is the right place for you. **Pros:** The beach, everything is taken care of. **Cons:** Theme park–like all-inclusiveness. ⊠ *Valle de Pedro González, Calle Campo Elias, Playa Puerto Cruz 6136* ☎ *0295/250–0000* ⊕ *www.dunesmargarita.com* ↩ *282 rooms* ⚘ *In-room: safe* ☰ *AE, DC, MC, V* ⏍ *AI.*

$$$$ 🖼 **Hesperia Playa El Agua.** This sprawling resort enjoys one of the best pieces of real estate around, smack in front of Playa El Agua. A smattering of low-slung, colorful buildings, as well as a few larger towers house elegant rooms. Be sure to ask questions when you book, as there are some more recently renovated spaces. There will be little time to enjoy those rooms, though, with the beach activity, various pools, bars, and tennis courts on offer here. You can even get your hair done and a deep-tissue massage before heading out with your towel—or as a reward on the way back! **Pros:** Location, location, location, great amenities. **Cons:** Somewhat impersonal, with a mini-city feeling. ⊠ *Av. 31 de Julio* ☎ *0295/400–8160* ⊕ *www.hesperia.com* ↩ *430 rooms,*

10

152 bungalows ⚒*In-room: safe, refrigerator. In-hotel: 3 restaurants, 2 bars, tennis courts, 5 pools, gym, spa* ☰*AE, D, MC, V* ❍*AI.*

$$$$ ▦ **Hotel Costa Linda Beach.** A short walk away from bumping (and beau-
★   tiful) Playa El Agua, this family-run hotel offers up both comfort and charm. Colonial flourishes add personality to the terra-cotta and blue spaces. If you want to spring for the best room, ask for No. 208. Rooms on the second floor offer views of the sea from a hammock-equipped balcony; rooms on the first floor simply look out onto the small pool area. Breakfast is included in the rustic, open-air restaurant—a perfect way to start your day. **Pros:** Family-run, small, intimate, within walk-ing distance of Playa El Agua. **Cons:** Tiny pool, a bit pricey. ✉*Calle Miragua, Playa El Agua* ☎*0295/249–1303* ⊕*www.hotelcostalinda. com* ↪*43 rooms* ⚒*In-room: safe. In-hotel: restaurant, bar, pool, gym, no elevator* ☰*AE, MC, V* ❍*CP.*

$$$ ▦ **Hotel Hesperia Isla Margarita.** With a soaring atrium lobby, this gigantic white hotel resides on the north side of the island near Pedro González. It has the island's only 18-hole golf course and an almost deserted stretch of beach right behind it—alas deserted but for this larger-than-necessary bright-white edifice—so there are plenty of out-door activities to indulge in here, especially swimming and walking along the beach. A sumptuous buffet breakfast is included in the rate. **Pros:** The beach, attention to detail. **Cons:** Large eyesore of a building. ✉*Playas Puerto Viejo y Puerto Cruz, Pedro González* ☎*0295/400–7111* ⊕*www.hesperia.com* ↪*295 rooms, 17 suites* ⚒*In-room: safe, refrigerator. In-hotel: 2 restaurants, bars, golf course, tennis courts, pools, gym, spa* ☰*AE, D, MC, V* ❍*AI.*

AFTER DARK

You'll likely find yourself in need of some refreshments after a day at the beach. Conveniently, nearly all restaurants in Porlamar and Pam-patar have stocked, lively bars; if you're looking for more of a scene, check out the options below. Porlamar hot spots come and go with alarming frequency, but one place that seems to have settled in for the time being is **Señor Frog's** (✉*Av. Bolívar, Costa Azul* ☎*0295/262–0270*), the mustard-yellow Mexican restaurant (the one near the Hilton with a fake cow hanging from its roof) that transforms itself into a lively dance club at night.

★ In Pampatar, head out to the edge of the town, right next to the Fla-mingo Beach Hotel, where you can choose from two hot nightclubs. **Beach Bar** (✉*Calle El Cristo, Sector Punta Ballena* ☎*0295/267–2392* ⊕*www.beachbar.com.ve*) is just what its name suggests: a low-key, laid-back club perfect for sipping a few after-beach cocktails. **Myko-nos** (✉*Calle El Cristo, Sector Punta Ballena* ☎*0295/267–1850*) is an elegant Greek-inspired lounge: grab an ice-cold Pinot Grigio and watch the sunset while the DJ spins.

SHOPPING

Although Isla Margarita is a major destination for Venezuelan day-trip-pers taking advantage of the duty-free prices, real bargains are hard to find. Your best bets are liquor and jewelry. Aside from the less expen-sive shops along Bulevar Guevara and Bulevar Gómez, shoppers are attracted to boutiques along **Avenidas Santiago Mariño** and **4 de Mayo.** More and more shoppers are heading to the ubiquitous malls that are taking over the island. One of the most popular is the massive **Jumbo Mall** on 4 de Mayo. The stadium-size **Centro Sambil** has 137 stores and is the offspring of its mammoth parent shopping center in Caracas. For everything from pots and pans to insect repellant to flip-flops, go to the immense **Rattan** in Porlamar.

> **ATTENTION, SHOPPERS!**
>
> Isla Margarita is a duty-free extravaganza where you'll find international clothing and leather goods, liquor, tobacco, and perfume. Lovely cloth hammocks, well known for their fine craftsmanship and immense size, are another favorite purchase here; many beachside vendors set up shop daily, with dozens of colorful hammocks for visitors to peruse.

★ **Rattan** (⊠ *Av. 4 de Mayo, Porlamar* 6136 ☎*0295/263–2411* ⊕*www.rattanmargarita.com*) is great for everyday shopping such as clothing, imported goods, sunscreen, sunglasses, and bug spray—this is Margarita's answer to Target. **Sambil** (⊠*Avs. Bolívar, Jovito Villalba, and Principal de San Lorenzo 6136* ☎*0295/260–2593* ⊕*www.sambilmall.com/margarita*) is the mother of all Venezuelan malls: you can find some great bargains here. **Tierra de Arte** (⊠*Av. Principal No. 15, Pampatar* ☎*0295/772–6496*) is a great little shop in downtown Pampatar specializing in local crafts, including woven bags, handmade miniature wooden boats, hammocks, and carvings.

MÉRIDA & THE ANDES

The changes are swift and unmistakable: from the treacherously winding outlying roads of Caracas and then low-lying, reddish valleys, you suddenly feel the air change as you begin your ascent into the Andes. Along the Trans-Andina Highway you pass stone-strewn fields sprouting wheat and coffee and tile-roof hamlets clinging to hillsides before reaching the *páramo,* the arid region above the timberline. Friendly, red-cheeked *andinos* (Andean people) walk perilously close to the edges of the highways, sometimes wearing traditional woven throws and *sombreros* to protect them from the glaring sun. Roadside stands selling coffee, honey, and bananas compete with larger establishments offering up tables and meals of arepas, cachapas, and chicken. After hitting an altitude of 13,146 feet at Paso Pico El Aguila (Eagle Peak Pass), the highway descends past towns such as Apartaderos, San Rafael de Mucuchíes, and Mucuchíes before reaching the capital city of Mérida. This ride is one of the most exhilaratingly beautiful in all of Venezuela: if you can afford the time, the car rental, and are up to the challenge, then go for it—it's truly an adventure you won't soon forget.

10

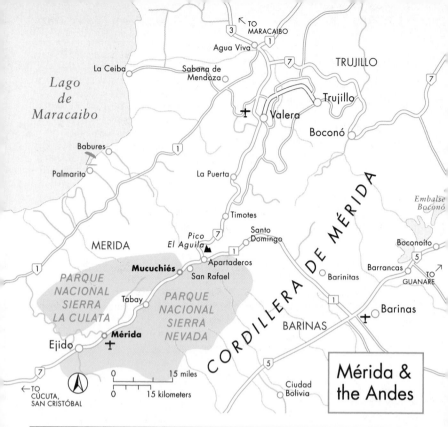

MÉRIDA

622 km (422 mi) southwest of Caracas.

Mérida is cradled in a valley between the two arms of the Andes, yet this is anything but a sleepy mountain village. It is a city whose spirit is decidedly young, hip, sporty, and bohemian. Home of one of Venezuela's largest universities, the Universidad de los Andes, Mérida has all the pleasures of an academic center, including eclectic bookstores, lively coffeehouses, and an arts scene that ranges from refined and traditional to wild and spontaneous. What defines this city even more than its people, though, may be the stunning mountains surrounding it on all sides. You'll find yourself often staring at the sky (either in awe of the jagged mountains or in hope that the ubiquitous afternoon clouds will disperse), and taking deep breaths of the fresh mountain air. This is one place where you'll really need a car—whether it's rented or hired by the day—because some of the best adventures on offer are outside of the city and down bumpy little roads with no signage. In fact, if there's one activity to do here, it's weaving your way from the city toward San Rafael de Mucuchíes and back—you'll likely return loaded down with local honey, wooden crafts, and perhaps a straw hat or three.

GETTING HERE & AROUND

Mérida's Aeropuerto Alberto Carnevali (MRD), five minutes by taxi from the city center, is served by Avior and Santa Bárbara with 12 flights daily from Caracas.

The Trans-Andina Highway is one of the most scenic routes in the country, with wonderful towns along the way where you'll be tempted to stop, even if only to refill you tank and have a quick *café con leche* (coffee and milk). The spectacular 12-hour journey from Caracas begins on Highway 51 west to Valencia. From here, follow the road to Barinas, then Barinitas, where the ascent to the Andes begins. Budget and Davila are reputable agencies at Mérida's Aeropuerto Alberto Carnevali. With either agency, expect to pay close to Bs. F196 per day for the smallest car. There are morning and evening departures from Terminal la Bandera in Caracas to Terminal Antonio Paredes in Mérida. The grueling 10- to 13-hour trip costs less than Bs. F60. Purchase your ticket at least a day in advance at the station. Expreso Mérida is a reputable company that services the route. Buses from Mérida's Terminal Antonio Paredes head to all the smaller mountain towns along the Trans-Andina Highway, including Jají, Apartaderos, and Mucuchíes.

Travel through this Andean region can be arranged according to your own desires and interests through the U.S.-based Lost World Adventures or through its partner in Mérida, Montaña Adventures. Other reputable Mérida-based companies include Natoura Adventure Tours and VenAventours. There is a state tourism office, Cormetur, near the airport in Mérida. Some staff members speak English. The Institute of National Parks, Inparques, also has an office in Mérida that can assist you with camping permits.

SAFETY & PRECAUTIONS

The center of Mérida is relatively safe during the day, but use caution at night; as in any tourist destination, always be aware of your surroundings and avoid unnecessary displays of wealth. Being a university town, the city sees its share of political demonstrations, which you should avoid.

10

ESSENTIALS

Air Contacts **Avior** (⊠ *Centro Comercial Canta Claro, Av. Las Américas* ☎ *0274/244–2563* ⊕ *www.avior.com.ve/*). **Santa Bárbara** (⊠ *Aeropuerto Alberto Carnevali, Mérida* ☎ *0274/262–0381* ⊕ *www.sbairlines.com/eng/default.html*).

Bus Contact **Expreso Mérida** (⊠ *Terminal la Bandera* ☎ *0212/693–5559 or 0414/7371110*).

Car-Rental Contacts **Budget** (☎ *0274/263–1758*). **Davila** (☎ *0274/263–4510*).

Currency Exchange **Italcambio** (⊠ *Aeropuerto Internacional Alberto Carnevalli, Mérida* ☎ *0274/263–2977*).

Visitor & Tour Info **Cormetur** (⊠ *Av. Urdaneta at Calle 45, Mérida* ☎ *0274/263–0814 or 0254/993–7239* ⊕ *www.merida.com.ve*). **Inparques** (⊠ *Calle 19, between Avs. 5 and 6, Mérida* ☎ *0274/252–9876*). **Lost World Adventures** (☎ *404/373–*

5820, 800/999–0558 in U.S. @*www.lostworldadventures.com*). **Montaña Adventures** (✉*Av. Las Américas, Edificio Las Américas, Mérida* ☎*0274/266–1448*). **Natoura Adventure Tours** (✉*Calle 24 Nos. 8–237, Mérida* ☎*0274/252–4075 or 0274/252–4216* @*www.natoura.com*). **VenAventours** (✉*Av. 3, between Calles 17 and 18, Mérida* ☎*0416/473–5460* @*www.venaventours.com/abadiatours*).

EXPLORING MÉRIDA

Founded in 1558, Mérida grew up around the **Plaza Bolívar,** a bustling center that attracts meandering students, locals, and artisans hawking their wares during the day and flocks of young couples along with shadier characters in the evening. The best time to come is mid-morning, before Mérda's famous midday heat makes things too hazy, and, hopefully, in time to catch the views of the mountains.

Facing the main square is the embellished baroque facade of the **Catedral Metropolitana.** Although construction began in 1787, the cathedral wasn't completed until 1958. Its geometric designs make this one of Venezuela's most striking churches. A visit to the plaza for a rest in the shade (with a view of the cathedral, of course) is an absolute must.

Dedicated to the artist responsible for the famous stone chapel in nearby San Rafael de Mucuchíes, the **Casa de Cultura Juan Félix Sánchez** *(Juan Félix Sánchez Cultural House)* hosts exhibitions of paintings and sculptures by regional artists. This lovingly restored colonial house is found on Plaza Bolívar, opposite the cathedral. ✉*Plaza Bolívar* ☎*0274/252–6101* 🎫*Free* ⊙*Weekdays 8:30–noon and 2:30–6:30, weekends 9–5.*

★ The **Museo de Arte Colonial** *(Colonial Art Museum)* houses a rich collection of religious art from the 16th to 19th centuries and also showcases rotating exhibitions with plenty of local flavor. Though the space is small, it's utterly worth the small entry fee to enjoy the sun-splashed space and to soak up some rays in the open-air courtyard. ✉*Av. 4 at Calle 20* ☎*0274/252–7860* 🎫*Bs.F5* ⊙*Tues.–Fri. 8–noon and 2–6, weekends 8:30–12:30.*

The **Museo Arqueológico** *(Archaeological Museum)* has the region's finest collection of figurines, ceramics, and tools from the pre-Hispanic cultures that once dominated this part of the Andes. ✉*Av. 3 Independencia, Edificio Rectorado* ☎*0274/240–2344* 🎫*Bs.F1* ⊙*Tues.–Sun. 8–11:30 and 2–5:30.*

The **Museo de Arte Moderno** *(Modern Art Museum)* contains an excellent permanent collection of works by some of Venezuela's most heralded contemporary painters. It faces Parque Reloj de Beethoven (Beethoven's Clock Park), noted for a well-known clock that ushers in the hour with music from the great composer. ✉*Centro Cultural Tulio Febres Cordero, Av. 2 at Calle 21* ☎*0274/252–9664* 🎫*Free* ⊙*Weekdays 9–noon and 3–6, weekends 10–5.*

NEED A BREAK?

At least once during your sojourn in Mérida, head to Heladería Coromoto (✉*Av. 3 No. 28–75* ☎*0274/252–3525* ⊙*Tues.-Sun. 2–10*) for a scoop of ice cream with the flavor of rose petals, local beer, or even *chicharrón* (fried pork skin). Proprietor Manuel S. da Oliviera holds a proud place in the *Guinness Book of Records* for producing the most flavors (840 and counting). Dare your companions to sample the sausage or smoked trout, and order for yourself a cone topped with ginger, corn, *arroz con leche* (rice pudding), or plain old strawberry. We were tempted by the more mysterious flavors, such as *El Nido de Amor* ("the nest of love") and *No Me Odies* ("Don't hate me").

> **WORD OF MOUTH**
>
> "If you're considering a visit to Venezuela, Mérida is really one of the best places to visit in the entire country: beautiful weather; amazing scenery; delicious food; plenty of outdoor activities; not too expensive; wonderful!"
>
> —orangecats

Fodor'sChoice
★ Five blocks east of Plaza Bolívar is Parque Las Heroínas, where you can catch the **Teleférico de Mérida.** Built in 1957 by French engineers, it is the longest and highest cable-car system in the world. In under an hour, the Teleférico ascends in four breathtaking stages to the 15,634-foot Pico Espejo, a mountain peak 892 feet taller than Switzerland's Matterhorn.

The 13-km (8-mi) journey carries you to four stations—Barinitas, La Montaña, La Aguada, and Loma Redonda—before reaching Pico Espejo, where you'll be treated to a great view of Pico Bolívar, Venezuela's highest peak, at 16,428 feet. The first car departs around 7 AM, the last around noon. ■TIP➡ **Head out early in the day to beat the clouds that often obscure the views by late morning.** Dress appropriately for the snowy heights, as the temperature change can be quite dramatic, and evaluate carefully your ability to make the trip if you have high blood pressure or a heart condition. The Loma Redonda stop houses a medical station for passengers having trouble with the altitude. Along the way, you'll encounter restaurants, coffee shops, bars, souvenir stores, and an Internet café to let the folks back home know what lofty heights you've reached. Reservations are mandatory during the high season, which lasts from Christmas to Easter, and during that time must be procured at least the day prior from the ticket office on Parque Las Heroínas, or via phone or fax. Your reservation will carry a specific departure time, and you're expected to show up an hour in advance to secure your place. The system is much more flexible the rest of the year. ✉ *Parque Las Heroínas* ☎ *0274/252–5080* 🖷 *0274/252–9174* 🌐 *www.telefericodemerida.com* ✇ *Baranitas to Pico Espejo Bs.F60* ☉ *Dec.–Apr., daily 7:30–noon; May–Nov., Wed.–Sun. 8 AM–11 AM (11:30 AM on weekends).*

OFF THE BEATEN PATH
Los Nevados. From Lomas Redonda, the second-highest point on the Teleférico, you can hire donkeys, mules, or horses for a descent to Los Nevados, a secluded mountain village that was once a garrison for Spanish conquistadors. Following an initial sharp ascent through a thick forest called the Bosque de los Coloraditos, you'll begin a four- to five-hour ride down a rocky path followed by pre-colonial indigenous peoples. Weary and winded, you finally come upon the red-tile roofs

10

of Los Nevados. There are unpretentious accommodations in local posadas. For the return trip, take a four-wheel-drive vehicle back to Mérida. This route takes you through tiny hamlets, past generations-old farms, colonial ruins, and some of the most spectacular scenery in the Andes.

WHERE TO EAT

$$$ ✕ **La Abadía Restaurante.** Sit out back
VENEZUELAN   on the terrace on a warm night and
order a fresh salad, soup, or well-prepared *lomito* (meat) at this young, energetic restaurant run by the Abadía Group, which also has tours and another restaurant nearby. Young couples, tourists, and families come here more for the atmosphere than the food, but it's a reliable choice if you want a simple meal in a cozy, festive environment. ⊠*Av. 3, between Calles 17 and 18* ☎*0274/251–0933* ▤*MC, V.*

$$$$ ✕ **Comedor Xinia & Peter.** This adorable inn outside of Méridea serves
VENEZUELAN   delicious, memorable dinners on the weekend. Make reservations well
★   in advance, and come prepared to feast on a five-course prix-fixe meal; *creama de auyama* (cream of pumpkin soup), *lomito de res* (a meat dish), and *tres leche de parchita* (a traditional Venezuelan milk-based cake with a touch of passion fruit) were our favorites. ⊠*La Mucuy Baja, Tabay* ☎*0416/874–7698* ⌂*Reservations essential* ▤*MC, V* ☽*Open for weekend dinners only.*

$$$ ✕ **Miramelindo.** This intimate restaurant is noted for its succulent Basque
SPANISH   cuisine. The exquisitely prepared entrées include *robalo en salsa verdea*
★   (striped bass in green sauce). Also ask about the daily specials. ⊠*Hotel Chama, Calle 29 at Av. 4* ☎*0274/252–9437* ▤*AE, V.*

$$$$ ✕ **Papiros.** Situated on the gorgeous grounds of Estancia San Francisco,
VENEZUELAN   in the hills outside of downtown Mérida, Papiros is an elegant, quiet
★   respite from the hubbub of downtown. Overlooking the well-maintained grounds of the hotel, you can dine on fresh-from-the-stream *trucha* (trout) served with yellow lentil and cilantro sauce. Even better, perhaps, are the restaurant's meats: the preparations of lamb, pork, and beef are all mouthwateringly good. A good wine list and tasty desserts (such as pumpkin soufflé) add to the charm. ⊠*Carretera Vía la Culata, Km 10, Sector Alto Viento, Finca San Francisco* ☎*0414/744–0076 or 0416/970–3725* ⌂*Reservations essential Jacket* ▤*AE, DC, MC, V*

WHERE TO STAY

$$$ ▥ **Estancia San Francisco.** The imposing white wall outside this vast prop-
★   erty and the lovely hillside drive up toward the reception area are your first two clues that this hotel is out of the ordinary. Indeed it is: it sits on a whopping 500,000 square meters of lush, walkable Andean land. At this country inn you can catch trout in a private lagoon and have the chef cook it up for dinner with freshly baked *arepas* (made with whole-wheat flour in the Andes). Little extras like the down pillows and comforters, cushy bathrobes, and cozy fireplaces make this deluxe

mountain retreat worth every bolívar fuerte. All the two-level suites feature spectacular views of the valley; the more luxurious three-bedroom chalets have their own kitchens. **Pros:** Quiet, secluded, gorgeous. **Cons:** Far from town, some chalets have odd layouts. ⊠*Carretera Via La Culata, 10 km (7 mi) northwest of Mérida* ☎*0274/416–2000* 🖷*0274/974–3000* ⊕*www.estancia.com.ve* ⟲*20 suites, 12 chalets* ⌂*In-room: no a/c. In-hotel: restaurant, bar, bicycles, laundry service, no elevator* ▭*AE, MC, V* ⦿|*MAP.*

$$ 🏨**Hotel Belensate.** A top choice among picky Venezuelans and an insti-
★ tution in Mérida, Mediterranean-style Belensate is close enough to downtown Mérida that you can get there in just a few minutes, but far enough away that you can soak up the quiet and peace of the surrounding mountains. Rooms, many of which have two floors, are scattered in various buildings across the hotel's sprawling grounds. The open-air dining takes place in well-tended gardens and next to a gorgeous swimming pool. Quite child- and family-friendly, the hotel also caters to couples willing to share the pool with youngsters. La Era, the restaurant right off the lobby, is a great place to have a cold beer and an antipasti plate. They also serve simple risottos, seafood, salads, and meat dishes. **Pros:** Great location, comfortable, well-kept grounds. **Cons:** Rooms are tired, not all rooms have views. ⊠*Urbanización La Hacienda* ☎*0274/266–2963* ⊕*www.hotelbelensate.com* ⟲*93 rooms, 7 cabins* ⌂*In-room: no a/c (some), safe (some). In-hotel: 2 restaurants, bar, pool, laundry service, Wi-Fi* ▭*AE, DC, MC, V.*

$$ 🏨**Posada Casa Sol.** Hands-down the most elegant little posada in town,
Fodor's Choice this quiet gem a short walk from the Plaza Bolívar is the best place to
★ stay, whether you are coming to Mérida for two nights or two weeks. Behind the plain colonial facade lies an elegance rarely found in this country—yet. Kathrin Kocher, the owner, is definitely on the cutting edge. She has covered the multilevel space with simple tiles, lovely window coverings, sublime and understated colors, and tastefully edited local artwork and crafts. The beds are new and the sheets are of high quality. Views of the surrounding mountains are lovely from the rooms that have balconies. Sit by the open-air pond in the lobby, or grab a cushy, mod chair to read some magazines before you hit the town—or use this as your ultimate refuge during the hottest hours of the day. A small restaurant serves simple meals. **Pros:** Chic, great service, small, intimate. **Cons:** No parking, not all rooms have views/balconies. ⊠*Av. 4, between Calles 15 and 16, 5105* ☎*0274/252–4164* ⊕*www.posada casasol.com* ⟲*14 rooms, 2 suites* ⌂*In-room: safe, Wi-Fi. In-hotel: no elevator* ▭*MC, V* ⦿|*EP.*

$$ 🏨**El Tisure.** From the tiny window of your room in this bland, if centrally located, building you can glimpse the amazing surrounding mountain ranges. In addition to a superb location in the center of town, the yellow-and-adobe-brick Tisure offers clean, simple rooms—just be sure to ask to see yours first, as some have better views, and more light, than others. **Pros:** Centrally located, clean. **Cons:** Charmless, dark rooms. ⊠*Av. 4 Bolívar 17–47* ☎*0274/252–6072* 🖷*0274/262–6061* ⟲*33 rooms* ⌂*In-room: no a/c. In-hotel: 2 restaurants, bar, laundry service* ▭*AE, MC, V.*

10

AFTER DARK

In the towns of the Andes, hotel bars are often the only choice for after-dark excitement. Many host performances by local musicians, particularly on weekends. You should take care to avoid walking around downtown alone at night; crime has escalated in the past five years here, so be aware at all times. **La Abadía Restaurante** (⊠ *Av. 3, between Calles 17 and 18* ☎ *0274/251–0933*) is a festive, young restaurant serving simple, international food that's also a great spot to have a drink or two if you want a quieter, earlier night on the town. Ask for a seat out back on the terrace.

Not too far away, also in downtown Mérida, the Abadía Group has opened a lovely wine-and-tapas bar called **La Abadía del Ángel** (⊠ *Calle 21, between Avs. 5 and 6, 5101* ☎ *0274/252–8013*).

In Mérida the enthusiastic crowds of young people at **Birosca Carioca** (⊠ *Calle 24 at Av. 2, Los Tapiales* ☎ *No phone*) swing into the wee hours with live salsa, reggae, and hip-hop.

SHOPPING

The best souvenirs to be found in Mérida are the traditional carved wooden sculptures (often depicting saints, Simóon Bolívar, or angels) made in small surrounding mountainside villages such as Tabay. If possible, head straight to the source—driving around Tabay looking for streetside vendors and ARTESANÍAS (crafts) signs pointing toward homes is our favorite way to go—but you can also have a look around the nearly 500 stalls of the **Mercado Principal de Mérida** (⊠ *Av. Las Américas at the Viaducto Miranda bridge*), which offer everything from *flores* (flowers) to *frutas* (fruits) to crafts and *recuerdos* (souvenirs). Begin your morning by sampling traditional Andean *pasteles* (pocketlike pastries) filled with pork, chicken, or beef. You can take home a *cuatro* (traditional four-string guitar) or a supposedly hand-loomed blanket from any of the dozens of shops that crowd the top two floors. The quality here has taken a nosedive in recent years (though it's still great fun to explore these stalls), so consider making your big purchases at the stores listed below.

Fodor's Choice
★
Sift through the cheesy mass-produced stuff to find great handicrafts by local artists at **La Calle Mayor** (☎ *0274/262–1862 or 0274/252–0111*), on the third floor of the Mercado Principal. For gift-worthy jams, jellies, pickled goods, dried fruits, and sweets, go past the fruit-and-vegetable section on the first floor to **Labrantía** (☎ *0274/657–6854*). **Galería Tierra y Arte** (☎ *0274/262–1473*), on the third floor of the Mercado Principal, has some great wooden pieces among some ghastly artwork—take your time and you can score a few gems. **Morera** (☎ *0274/657–5520*), if tiny, has some of the best textile work in Mérida. In the back hallway on the second floor of the Mercado Principal, this glass-enclosed shop twinkles with possibility: choose between turquoise, magenta, chocolate-brown, and ivory woven throw pillows; handmade silk scarves; lush throws; and intricate, mixed-fiber table runners. You can't go wrong here. ■ TIP→ If you really fall in love with the shop, take a short cab ride

to their mountainside outpost (⊠*Pedregosa Alta, Via Principal, Km 3.6* ☎*0274/266–1545*) and shop with a view.

SPORTS & THE OUTDOORS

Mérida is one sporty own—why shouldn't it be, nestled as it is among mountains, cold rivers, and rock-strewn pastures? Whether you want to hike, fish, or simply take a drive to a national park, ask your hotel first about outdoor activities on offer—nearly all the innkeepers and hotel owners try their best to include opportunities to take trips. You can also call the resourceful **Abadía Tours** (☎*0274/25–0933*), in downtown Mérida—they can help you arrange trips of all types.

FISHING

Anglers flock to Mérida, where the mountains are liberally sprinkled with small lakes stocked with rainbow and brown trout. In remote reaches, hooking a 15-pound trophy is commonplace. Getting there, however, isn't always easy. Fishing season runs between March 30 and September 30.

HIKING

Mérida is the base for three- to seven-day treks into the Andes. Rocky trails trod during the early 19th century by armies struggling for independence from Spain make for good hiking. **Montaña Adventures** (⊠*Av. Las Américas* ☎*0274/266–1448*) arranges multiday excursions to El Tisure, the secluded village of Los Nevados, and Paso Pico El Aguila. Another company offering trekking in the region is **Páramo Tours** (⊠*Centro Commercial Oasis, Piso 2, Viaducto Campo Elias, Mérida* ☎*0274/244–8855*).

MUCUCHÍES

52 km (30 mi) east of Mérida.

The Trans-Andina Highway brings you to Mucuchíes, founded in 1596 on the site of a precolonial village. (You'll spot the prefix *mucu*—meaning "place of" in the indigenous language—at the beginning of the names of many Andean villages. This one means "Place of Cold.") The starkly beautiful landscape—scrub-filled fields and barren hillsides—includes a handful of pristine lakes and plenty of rocky, cold-water streams. This is truly some of the most fascinating landscape in all of Venezuela—get your cameras ready.

GETTING HERE & AROUND

If you've taken a flight to Mérida, the best way to explore the surrounding areas is by car (rented or hired for the day). If you are driving from Caracas to Mérida, Mucuchíes is one of the first small Andean towns you'll pass through. The roads here are quite twisty, though, so only consider a car rental if you're comfortable driving on this kind of road.

10

THE ROUTE TO MÉRIDA

From Barinas, you'll start ascending into the cooler, crisper Andes. The following are the major towns and villages you'll pass on Carretera Andina en route to Mérida.

■ Barinitas: This is a good gasoline stop on your way up the mountain (though there are gas stations all along this route).

■ Santo Domingo: A large town with lots of trout restaurants.

■ Pico el Aguila: Take a moment to breathe in deep—this is the highest point on this road.

■ Apartaderos: Stop for a moment to enjoy this cute little colonial town with some fun craft shops and small restaurants.

■ San Rafael de Mucuchíes: Though it's tiny, and crisscrossed by a very treacherous road filled with fast-moving vehicles, San Rafael is a real gem, with one of the most famous *capillas*, (chapels) in all of Venezuela—that of Jean Félix Sánchez *(see below)*.

■ Mucuchíes: This charming, if overflowing, Andean town has lots of hotels and posadas to choose from, along with a great *criollo* (traditional Venezuelan) restaurant at Posada Restaurant Los Andes *(see below)*.

■ Musui: Hike up to hot springs or just stop for a hot coffee in this small, welcoming village.

■ Tabay: Turn left off the highway toward Cabañas de Xinia & Peter (see below) and discover a thriving mountainside community of woodworkers and artisans. Lovely magenta flowers and wild mountain scenery make it one of our favorite stops.

EXPLORING MUCUCHÍES

The nearby town of San Rafael de Mucuchíes is the site of the renowned **Capilla de Juan Félix Sánchez,** built by the reclusive, iconoclastic local artist for whom it is named. As he single-handedly built this stone chapel in honor of the Virgin of Coromoto, Juan Félix came to be greatly loved throughout this region.

OFF THE BEATEN PATH

Mucubají. With five beautiful lakes and several waterfalls, this section of Parque Nacional Sierra Nevada is the ideal area in which to get to know the páramo. The well-designed and informative displays at the visitor center introduce you to the flora and fauna of the region. Travel on foot or horseback along the clearly marked scenic trails to Pico Mucuñuque, which soars to 13,800 feet. While you're enjoying the mountain air, remember that there isn't much of it. Keep your pace slow and take time to smell the frailejones. Mucubají is 2 km (1 mi) from Apartaderos on the road to Barinas.

WHERE TO STAY & EAT

$ ★ **Los Balcones de la Musui.** You reach this colonial-era hacienda, which clings to a mountain ridge, via a steep road that takes you literally into the clouds. When it's clear, which is virtually every morning, the view from each of the cozy rooms is breathtaking. Colorful hammocks slung on the lower-level patio command the same view. A two-hour hike takes you to the Aguas Termales de la Musui, a local hot spring where you'll catch sight of Humboldt Glacier. The restaurant ($–$$) serves food worth going out of your way to sample; don't pass up the trout. **Pros:** Near fabulous hot springs, friendly. **Cons:** Isolated—you have to drive virtually everywhere. ⊠*Trans-Andina Hwy., near Mucuchíes* ☏*0414/974–0712* ⊘*balconesmusui@cantv.net* ⌁*12 rooms, 6 cabins* ⌂*In-room: no a/c. In-hotel: restaurant, bar* ⊟*MC, V.*

$$$ ⊞**Cabañas Xinia y Peter.** This tranquil refuge near Tabay is run by a
★   Venezuelan-German couple who work hard to make you feel at home. Every detail is perfect, from the fresh flowers on the tables to the thick comforters piled on the beds. The two tile-roof cabins have handcrafted furnishings and fully equipped kitchens, making them perfect for an extended stay. The staff can arrange for horseback, fishing, and hiking tours. The place is popular, so reservations are necessary at both the hotel and the restaurant. At this writing, the inn was undergoing a major expansion, which was to add a major new restaurant area, as well as 12 new rooms. **Pros:** Gorgeous scenery, attentive service, serene. **Cons:** Not great for children. ⊠*La Mucuy Baja, Tabay* ☏*0416/874– 7698* ⊕*www.xiniaypeter.com* ⌁*2 cabins, 4 rooms* ⌂*In-room: no phone. In-hotel: restaurant, airport shuttle, no elevator* ⊟*No credit cards* ⦿*MAP.*

★   ⊞**Posada San Rafael del Páramo.** True Andean charm and rusticity merge at this family-run posada perched on the Trans-Andean highway. Crafts adorn nearly every available inch; an open-air courtyard lets the sun stream into the inn come morning. Delicious breakfasts are enjoyed on the terrace or small restaurant filled with simple wooden chairs. **Pros:** Family-run simplicity and charm at its very best. **Cons:** On a major thoroughfare, very simple. ⊠*Trans-Andina Hwy., 500 meters before Capilla de Piedra* ☏*0274/872–0938* ⌂*In-room: no phone, no a/c. In-hotel: restaurant, parking* ⊟*No credit cards* ⦿*CP.*

$ ✕**Restaurante/Posada Los Andes.** For authentic Andean cuisine, stop by
LATIN   this rustic, charming lodge on the main street of Mucuchíes. The pro-
AMERICAN   prietor, Renata Pirrone, serves up *trucha a la plancha* (grilled stream
★   trout), hearty lentil stews, simple chicken dishes, and hot coffee, among other comforting foods. The rooms here are simple, with shared bathrooms, and the views out the back are wonderful—go upstairs after your meal for a quick photo op. If you do decide to stay here, room No. 6 has the best view. **Pros:** Small, intimate, the real deal. **Cons:** Rustic, shared bathrooms, on a loud street. ⊠*Calle Independencia 25* ☏*0274/872–0151* ⋈*Reservations not accepted* ⊟*No credit cards* ⦿*Breakfast, lunch, and early dinner served (doors close between 6 and 7 most nights).*

AFTER DARK

The best way to enjoy your evenings in smaller Andean towns is to nestle close to the fire that will inevitably be lit at your inn or posada, have a drink at the bar, and tuck in early. There's no nightlife to speak of here, but we can tell you for sure that waking up early with the sun makes it more than worth going to bed early.

10

SHOPPING

Fodor'sChoice **La Casa del Paramo** (⊠*San Isidro 29, Apartaderos* ☎*0274/888–0132*)
★ is great one-stop shopping for Andean souvenirs: there are three rooms
filled with local wood carvings, paintings, sculptures, and jewelry to
peruse.

ELSEWHERE IN VENEZUELA

Whether you want to visit the "Serengeti of South America" (aka
Los Llanos), the incredibly remote and surreal southeast region of
the country, or the amazingly lush watershed of the Ri[ac]o Orinoco,
taking a week or two to head into the lesser-traveled regions of Venezuela is recommended the trip of a lifetime. But keep in mind that
the farther afield you travel, the more useful—in terms of navigation,
know-how, safety, and gear—a tour operator will be. Decide the area
you want to explore, make a list of the top experiences you'd like to
have, and then choose your tour operator accordingly. There's no
doubt that traveling to remote areas is trying in this country, with
its insufficient tourism infrastructure and frequent social and political unrest, but it's also worth the time and effort if you're craving a
memorable, captivating adventure.

LOS LLANOS

Known as the "Serengeti of South America," Los Llanos is an alluring
destination for anyone interested in wildlife. Covering nearly a third of
Venezuela's total area, the sprawling grasslands of Los Llanos are just
a short flight away from Caracas—through San Fernando de Apure or
Barinas—but they feel a world away from the bustling capital. The air
sings with birdcalls instead of car horns, and the unpaved roads are
more likely to carry iguanas searching for a sunny spot than commuters
looking for a parking space.

Los Llanos (literally "the Plains")
has two distinct seasons, each
offering opportunities to see a wide
variety of animals and birds. From
May to November the plains are
inundated with water and crisscrossed by powerful rivers, forc-
ing land animals to scramble for
higher ground as the rains unleash
their fury. Flooding submerges the
smaller roads, making it a bit more
difficult to get around. This is the
best time, however, to observe the
large river otters, and to see clusters
of capybaras and troops of howler
monkeys gather in small patches of
gallery forest. This is also the time

PASO PICO EL AGUILA

About 10 km (6 mi) past Apartaderos, the Trans-Andina Highway
leads you to the incredible views
from the 14,000-foot Paso Pico
El Aguila (Eagle Peak Pass),
Venezuela's highest roadway.
Paso Pico El Aguila marks the
spot where Simón Bolívar and his
army crossed the Andes in 1813
on their way to fight for independence from the Spanish. Near a
statue commemorating this triumphant crossing sits a café serving
fresh trout and steaming cups of
calentado (a regional drink made
with liquors and herbs).

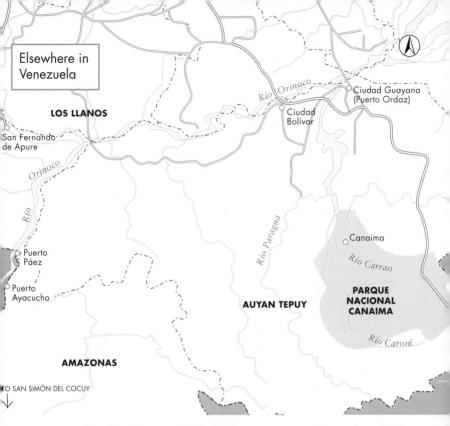

LOS LLANOS

San Fernando
de Apure

Río Orinoco

Ciudad Guayana
(Puerto Ordaz)

Ciudad
Bolívar

Orinoco

Río

Río Paragua

Canaima

Río Carrao

Puerto
Páez

Puerto
Ayacucho

AUYAN TEPUY

**PARQUE
NACIONAL
CANAIMA**

Río Caroní

AMAZONAS

TO SAN SIMÓN DEL COCUY

when Los Llanos cools off; daytime temperatures hover above 90°F, but the evenings are comfortably mild.

With the end of the rainy season in December, the landscape begins a dramatic transformation. Standing water quickly evaporates in the heat of the tropical sun, revealing the bright greens, yellows, and golds of the grasses. By the end of the dry season in April, the mighty rivers have become trickles, and only a few pools remain. Temperatures soar to over 110°F during the day, but it's worth enduring the heat, as the dry season is the best time to view wildlife. Four-wheel-drive vehicles can head in almost any direction across the parched landscape, bringing you to where the animals have gathered around the few remaining pools of water.

Spanish settlers established the first cattle ranches in Los Llanos in 1548, and within 200 years the expansive ranches, known as *hatos,* had spread across the region. Today, amid the more exotic wildlife, thousands of cows still roam the range, driven by cowboys known as *llaneros.* The best way to see Los Llanos is to stay at one of the half-dozen hatos set up to accommodate guests. Sometimes you can eat dinner with the llaneros in the dining hall or head out with them for a cerveza in one of the little towns that dot the region.

The "Serengeti of South America"

The first animals you'll notice are the scary ones. In Los Llanos, the vast grasslands that make up nearly a third of Venezuela, roadside pools teem with crocodiles—both the endangered Orinoco caiman and the more common spectacled caiman, which locals call "babas." Anacondas, some more than 20 feet long, slither across your path. If you're lucky you'll spot a puma—and if you're really lucky, it'll be far away.

But there's much more to see in Los Llanos, often called the "Serengeti of South America." Bird lovers will delight in spotting dozens of species—majestic hawks to diminutive burrowing owls, well-camouflaged herons to brightly colored tanagers. Spoonbills and storks, flycatchers and kingfishers, parrotlets and cormorants abound in this isolated region. Since the landscape is perfectly flat and sparsely wooded, they're all easy to see. The most spectacular of these is the scarlet ibis; when hundreds of them return home to roost at sunset, they cluster so closely together that they seem to turn entire trees bright red.

During the dry season you can catch sight of giant anteaters lumbering across plains punctuated by knee-high termite mounds. The rainy season finds the tree branches filled with sun-worshipping iguanas that occasionally lose their grip and tumble into the waters below. No matter what time of year you visit you'll see hundreds of capybaras (called *chiguires* in Venezuela), cute, furry brown mammals that are equally comfortable on land or in water. Weighing more than 100 pounds when fully grown, they're the world's largest rodents.

A guided excursion is the best—and safest—way to observe wildlife in this remote region. A naturalist at one of the many lodges will take you out in a jeep or a converted pickup truck, driving along dirt roads and across patches of parched earth to get as close to animals as possible. At first you'll need help spotting wildlife, but once you get the hang of it, you'll find you can see an amazing variety of animals at close range, without binoculars. Often you can get out of the jeep and walk right among them.

Boating down the Río Apure, or one of the mighty river's tributaries, is the only way to see what the rest of Los Llanos has to offer. Freshwater dolphins will jump and play around your boat as you drift downstream watching the egrets build their nests in the branches above the water. You might want to stop on a sandbar to do some fishing—for piranhas. Catching these hungry little creatures is a fast-paced sport. Baiting a hook with chunks of raw meat, you toss a line (no rods are necessary) into the deceptively calm water. Schools of piranhas gather immediately, leaping out of the water in a frenzy to grab the bait with their jagged teeth. The trick here is to yank on the line before the bait disappears, which can happen in seconds. With some practice, you'll be able to catch enough of the salad-plate-size fish for dinner. Just brace yourself for the boat ride back to your lodge; the river won't seem so tranquil now that you know the water is infested with these little carnivores.

–Wayne Hoffman

Although sparsely populated, Los Llanos is considered by many to be the cultural heart of Venezuela. It's no coincidence that the traditional music of Venezuela—called *joropo*—was born in Los Llanos. Locals still gather after dark to listen to these lilting folk songs, sung over the sounds of maracas, harps, and four-stringed guitars called cuatros. In outdoor bars with dirt floors, couples dance while joropo bands alternate rousing tunes that celebrate the bravery of the llaneros with ballads that recount the difficult lives these cowboys must endure.

GETTING HERE & AROUND

To reach Los Llanos, take one of the daily flights from Caracas to San Fernando de Apure, Barinas, and Guanare. Cities such as Barinas and San Fernando de Apure in Los Llanos are accessible by bus from Caracas and other major cities. Aereotuy connects Ciudad Bolívar with Puerto Ayacucho once weekly. Another option is having a tour company take care of the details. Orinoco Tours, based in Caracas, specializes in ecotourism. The savvy staff of Lost World Adventures specialize in tailoring an independent travel itinerary around your interests. The founder of this U.S.-based company once lived in Venezuela, so he knows his way around. The company specializes in small-group expeditions throughout Venezuela—including Los Llanos—and other South American countries.

ESSENTIALS

Airlines **Aerotuy** (⊠ *Edificio Gran Sabana, Blvd. de Sabana Grande, Sabana Grande, Caracas* ☎ *0212/212–3106* ⊕ *www.tuy.com*).

Tour Operators **Lost World Adventures** (⊠ *337 Shadowmoor Dr., Decatur, GA* ☎ *404/373–5820 or 800/999–0558* 🖷 *404/377–1902* ⊕ *www.lostworldadventures. com*). **Orinoco Tours** (⊠ *Edificio Galerías Bolívar, Bulevar de Sabana Grande* ☎ *0212/761–8431* 🖷 *0212/761–6801* ⊕ *www.orinocotours.com*).

WHERE TO STAY

$$$$ ⊞**Estación Biológica El Frío.** Besides being a working ranch, this place also functions as a biological research center. So in addition to the wildlife that exists across the region, Hato El Frio also houses animals that are the subject of conservation efforts and biological studies, from tortoises to pumas. Want to see a caiman up close? Accompany one of the biologists in residence when they head out for the daily feeding. These knowledgeable—and English-speaking—scientists take you on twice-daily excursions in trucks or boats, answering any questions about the varied flora and fauna. There's also ample opportunity to mingle with the llaneros, whose quarters are a short distance away. The cowboys and researchers work closely together, frequently coming together for an outdoor barbecue or a night out in the local village.

Facilities are basic but comfortable. Fans and a cool breeze make it comfortable enough for sleeping, even in the summer. There is no hot water, but even the "cold" water in these sun-drenched grasslands is warm enough for bathing. Meals are hearty and always fresh, as the ranch produces its own eggs, meats, and dairy products. You can bet that the fruit that made your juice was still on the tree that morning.

10

Trips to Hato El Frío must be arranged through a travel agent such as Caracas-based Orinoco Tours. The tour company can also arrange for a car to transfer you from the airport in the town of San Fernando de Apure, two hours away. ⊠*145 km (90 mi) west of San Fernando de Apure* ☎*0240/808–3662 or 0416/540–9371* ⊕*www.elfrioeb.com* ☞*10 rooms* ⚅*In-room: no a/c, no phone, no TV. In-hotel: restaurant, airport shuttle, no elevator* ⦿*AI.*

PARQUE NACIONAL CANAIMA

Here, in Venezuela's remote southeast, is a surreal landscape of pink beaches and black lagoons, where giant waterfalls plunge from the summits of prehistoric table-top mountains called *tepuis,* formations that harbor some of the most unusual life on earth. A trip to Venezuela is not complete without a visit to these mist-enshrouded plateaus that inspired Sir Arthur Conan Doyle's *The Lost World.*

Fodor'sChoice
★

This unique region is protected by Parque Nacional Canaima, which covers an area the size of Belgium. Most of the park is extremely remote, so the only way to see it is by boat or plane. Most people head to Canaima to see **Angel Falls,** the world's tallest waterfall. This spectacular torrent of water plummets 2,647 feet—more than twice the height of the Empire State Building, and 15 times higher than Niagara Falls—from atop the giant Auyantepuy mesa. Indigenous people knew the falls as "Kerapa kupai merú,"(the fall to the deepest place). But this natural phenomenon acquired its English-language moniker after its sighting by barnstorming U.S. pilot Jimmy Angel, who crash-landed on Auyantepuy's vast surface in 1937 while in search of gold. Angel, his wife, and two companions spent 11 days descending on foot from the tepui back to civilization and told the world of his "discovery." Angel's ashes were scattered over the falls after his 1956 death. The eastern half of Parque Nacional Canaima is crossed by a road, and this region is referred to as the Gran Sabana. Three- to four-day excursions to the Gran Sabana are made in four-wheel-drive vehicles and will carry you to waterfalls, indigenous villages, and vantage points that provide breathtaking views of the tepuis. These round-trip excursions generally begin in Ciudad Bolívar or Ciudad Guayana, working slowly south toward Santa Elena de Uairén. The especially adventurous can hire a Pemón guide and scale a large tepui called Roraima, an undertaking that requires a minimum of five days. At the top, you find yourself in an unearthly lunarlike landscape.

GETTING HERE & AROUND

Aereotuy flies regularly between Caracas and Canaima and Ciudad Bolívar, and connects Ciudad Bolívar with Puerto Ayacucho once weekly. There is no bus service at all to Canaima. Alternatively, the tour company Lost World Adventures creates small-group tours to suit travelers' specific interests. Eco-oriented Orinoco Tours will take you there too; they're based in Caracas.

ESSENTIALS

Airlines Aerotuy (⊠*Edificio Gran Sabana, Blvd. de Sabana Grande, Sabana Grande, Caracas* ☎*0212/212–3106* ⊕*www.tuy.com*).

Tour Operators Lost World Adventures (⊠*337 Shadowmoor Dr., Decatur, GA* ☎*404/373–5820 or 800/999–0558* 🖷*404/377–1902* ⊕*www.lostworldadventures. com*). **Orinoco Tours** (⊠*Edificio Galerías Bolívar, Bulevar de Sabana Grande* ☎*0212/761–8431* 🖷*0212/761–6801* ⊕*www.orinocotours.com*).

WHERE TO STAY

$$$$
Fodor'sChoice
★

Arekuna. This self-contained luxury camp is on the bank of the Río Caroni, just outside the boundaries of Parque Nacional Canaima. After a full day of land and water excursions, enjoy a glorious sunset from the hilltop dining area before retiring to a stylish cabaña, where attention to detail is evident in the hand-painted sinks and the curious figures carved into the walls. All of the building materials are produced locally and the entire camp is powered by solar energy. Most importantly, the hotel is staffed by extremely personable, multilingual guides who create a fun, informative atmosphere. Packages for this 90-person facility, including round-trip airfare, lodging, meals, and guided excursions, start at $375 per couple, and are arranged through charter airline Aerotuy. ⊠*Parque Nacional Canaima* ☎*0212/761–6247* ⊕*www.tuy. com* ➬*30 rooms* ⚖*In-room: no a/c, no phone, no TV. In-hotel: restaurant, bar, laundry service, no elevator* ⏏*AI*.

AMAZONAS

Venezuela's largest region is Amazonas, an ironic name given that virtually the entire area lies within the watershed of the mighty Río Orinoco and not the Amazon. Amazonas contains two gargantuan national parks that together cover an area of almost 48,000 square km (30,000 square mi), feature varied flora and fauna, and comprise the homeland of many native peoples, most notably the Yanomami. Tourist facilities in this vast area are limited to a small number of lodges that are connected to the outside world through the region's only sizable town, Puerto Ayacucho.

GETTING HERE & AROUND

To reach Amazonas, you can fly daily from Caracas to Puerto Ayacucho, the region's only tourist hub. Aereotuy connects Ciudad Bolívar with Puerto Ayacucho once weekly. Amazonas is not as accessible by bus; you can get to Puerto Ayacucho from Caracas via San Fernando de Apure, but it's at least a 16-hour trip. Tour groups are another option; check out the highly reputable Lost World Tours. Also worth their salt, Alpi Tour is based in Caracas and specializes in adventure tourism to the Amazonas and other regions. Orinoco Tours, based in Caracas, too, will organize an eco-friendly trip for you.

ESSENTIALS

Airlines Aerotuy (⊠*Edificio Gran Sabana, Blvd. de Sabana Grande, Sabana Grande, Caracas* ☎*0212/212–3106* ⊕*www.tuy.com*).

10

Tour Operators **Alpi Viajes** (✉ *Av. Sucre, Centro Parque Boyacá, Piso 1, Oficina 2, Caracas* ☎ *0212/283–1433* ⊕ *www.alpi-group.com*). **Lost World Adventures** (✉ *337 Shadowmoor Dr., Decatur, GA* ☎ *404/373–5820 or 800/999–0558* 🖶 *404/377–1902* ⊕ *www.lostworldadventures.com*). **Orinoco Tours** (✉ *Edificio Galerías Bolívar, Bulevar de Sabana Grande* ☎ *0212/761–8431* 🖶 *0212/761–6801* ⊕ *www.orinocotours.com*).

WHERE TO STAY

$$$$ 🏨 **Yutajé Camp.** This camp in the Manapiare Valley, just east of Puerto Ayacucho, appeals to families who prefer the comfort of real beds, private baths, and sit-down meals. Built and run year-round by José Raggi, the camp has a 5,000-foot airstrip and accommodations for about 30. During the day you trek through the jungle in search of howler monkeys, or float down a river to view spectacular waterfalls. A two-night package from Caracas, including air and meals, runs about $450 per person. ✉ *Reservations: Alpi Viajes, Av. Sucre, Centro Parque Boyacá, Torre Centro, Piso 1, Oficina 2, Caracas* ☎ *0212/283–1433* 🔥 *In-room: no a/c, no phone, no TV. In-hotel: restaurant, no elevator* 🍽 *AI.*

Adventure & Learning Vacations

WORD OF MOUTH

"In one word—yes! Antarctica is worth every penny . . . but this comes from someone who did a small-ship expedition with 2–3 landings daily. There are few places that would give a wildlife and nature enthusiast more pleasure than Antarctica."

—eenusa

"Man, seeing the majestic mountain ranges of Cerro Torre and Fitz Roy was unbelieveable. I didn't know of such remarkable beauty until I saw them. Luckily, we came on days with good weather. The next two days consisted of hiking to Cerro Torre and Fitz Roy. The 6-hour hike to Fitz Roy was definitely more challenging than Cerro Torre's hike...but SO worth it."

—rampup82

Updated by
Nicholas Gill

WITH TERRAIN RANGING FROM TOWERING Andean peaks to vast grasslands, deserts, wetlands, glaciers, and the huge Amazonian rain forest, South America's natural attractions are virtually unsurpassed. This topographical diversity guarantees ideal settings for almost any type of active or ecotourism adventure. Additionally, the continent claims some of the world's most renowned archaeological sites, a number of indigenous cultures, and an impressive array of wildlife, creating the perfect destination for off-the-beaten-path cultural experiences. You can explore the Amazon by riverboat, trek, ski, or climb the Andes, kayak along a fjord-studded coast, or view the Galápagos Islands' astonishing wildlife up close.

As in the past, today's travelers yearn to see the world's great cities, historical sites, and natural wonders. The difference is that today far fewer travelers are content to experience all this from the air-conditioned comfort of a huge bus. Even tour operators known for their trips' five-star comfort have included in most itineraries soft-adventure components, such as hiking, canoeing, biking, or horseback riding, and added "best available" lodgings to satisfy the increased demand for visits to more traditional locales.

Choosing a tour package carefully is always important, but it becomes even more critical when the focus is adventure or sports. You can rough it or opt for comfortable, sometimes even luxurious accommodations. You can select easy hiking or canoeing adventures or trekking, rafting, or climbing expeditions that require high degrees of physical endurance and technical skill. Study multiple itineraries to find the trip that's right for you.

This chapter describes selected trips from some of today's best adventure-tour operators. Wisely chosen special-interest vacations lead to distinctive, memorable experiences—just pack flexibility and curiosity along with the bug spray.

For additional information about a specific destination, contact the country's tourist office (often attached to the embassy) or the **South American Explorers Club** (✉ *126 Indian Creek Rd., Ithaca, NY* ☎ *607/277–0488 or 800/274–0568* ⊕ *www.saexplorers.org*). This nonprofit organization is a good source for current information regarding travel throughout the continent. The Explorers Club also has clubhouses in Buenos Aires, Quito, Lima, and Cusco.

CHOOSING A TRIP

With hundreds of choices for special-interest trips to South America, there are a number of factors to keep in mind when deciding which company and package will be right for you.

How strenuous a trip do you want? Adventure vacations are commonly split into "soft" and "hard" adventures. Hard adventures, such as strenuous treks (often at high altitudes), Class IV or V rafting, or ascents of some of the world's most challenging mountains, generally require excellent physical conditioning and previous experience. Most hiking, biking, canoeing/kayaking, and similar soft adventures can be enjoyed by persons of all ages who are in good health and accustomed to a reasonable amount of exercise. A little honesty goes a long way—recognize your own level of physical fitness and discuss it with the tour operator before signing on.

How far off the beaten path do you want to go? Depending on the tour operator and itinerary selected for a particular trip, you'll often have a choice of relatively easy travel and comfortable accommodations or more strenuous going with overnights spent camping or in basic lodgings. Ask yourself if it's the *reality* or the *image* of roughing it that appeals to you. Stick with the reality.

Is sensitivity to the environment important to you? If so, then determine whether it is equally important to the tour operator. Does the company protect the fragile environments you'll be visiting? Are some of the company's profits designated for conservation efforts or put back into the communities visited? Does it encourage indigenous people to dress up (or dress down) so that your group can get great photos, or does it respect their cultures as they are? Many of the companies included in this chapter are actively involved in environmental organizations and projects with indigenous communities visited on their trips.

What sort of group is best for you? At its best, group travel offers curious, like-minded people with whom to share the day's experiences. Do you enjoy a mix of companions or would you prefer similar demographics—for example, age-specific, singles, same sex? Inquire about the group size; many companies have a maximum of 10 to 16 members, but 30 or more is not unknown. The larger the group, the more time spent (or wasted) at rest stops, meals, and hotel arrivals and departures.

If groups aren't your thing, most companies will customize a trip just for you. In fact, this has become a major part of many tour operators' business. The itinerary can be as loose or as complete as you choose. Such travel offers all the conveniences of a package tour, but the "group" is composed of only you and those you've chosen as travel companions. Responding to a renewed interest in multigenerational travel, many tour operators also offer designated family departures, with itineraries carefully crafted to appeal both to children and adults.

The client consideration factor—strong or absent? Gorgeous photos and well-written tour descriptions go a long way in selling a company's trips. But what's called the client consideration factor is important, too. Does the operator provide useful information about health (suggested or required inoculations, tips for dealing with high altitudes)? A list of frequently asked questions and their answers? Recommended readings? Equipment needed for sports trips? Packing tips when baggage is restricted? Climate info? Visa requirements? A list of client referrals? The option of using your credit card? What is the refund policy if you must cancel? If you're traveling alone, will the company match you up with a like-minded traveler so you can avoid the sometimes exorbitant single supplement?

Tour Operators

Below you'll find contact information for all tour operators mentioned in this chapter. For international tour operators, we list both the tour operator and its North American representative. For example, Exodus is represented in North America by Adventure Center. Although those listed hardly exhaust the number of reputable companies, these tour operators were chosen because they are established firms that offer a good selection of itineraries. Such operators are usually the first to introduce great new destinations, forging ahead before luxury hotels and air-conditioned buses tempt less hardy visitors.

Abercrombie & Kent ✉ 1520 Kensington Rd., Oak Brook, IL ☎ 630/954–2944 or 800/554–7016 ⊕ www.abercrombiekent.com.

Adventure Center ✉ 1311 63rd St., Suite 200, Emeryville, CA ☎ 510/654–1879 or 800/227–8747 ⊕ www.adventurecenter.com.

Adventure Life ✉ 1655 S. 3rd St. W, Suite 1, Missoula, MT ☎ 406/541–2677 or 800/344–6118 ⊕ www.adventure-life.com.

Alpine Ascents International ✉ 121 Mercer St., Seattle, WA ☎ 206/378–1927 ⊕ www.AlpineAscents.com.

Amazon Nature Tours ☐ Box 128, Jamestown, RI 02835 ☎ 401/423–3377 or 800/688–1822 🖶 401/423–9630 ⊕ www.amazon-nature-tours.com.

American Alpine Institute ✉ 1515 12th St., Bellingham, WA ☎ 360/671–1505 ⊕ www.mtnguide.com.

Amizade ☐ Box 110107, Pittsburgh, PA 15232 ☎ 412/441–6655 or 888/973–4443 ⊕ www.amizade.org.

Andes Adventures ✉ 1323 12th St., Suite F, Santa Monica, CA ☎ 310/395–5265 or 800/289–9470 ⊕ www.andesadventures.com.

Angel-Eco Tours ✉ 53 Remsen St., Suite 6, Brooklyn, NY ☎ 212/656–1240 or 888/423–3864 ⊕ www.angel-ecotours.com.

A Taste of Peru ✉ 6363 Christie Ave., Apt. 927, Emeryville, CA ☎ 510/655–0566 ⊕ www.atasteofperu.com.

Augusto Albuquerque ✉ Rua Rio Javarí 36, Vieralves, Manaus ☎ 092/3635–6868 ✉ mgasouza@ig.com.br.

Austin-Lehman Adventures ☐ Box 81025, Billings, MT 59108 ☎ 800/575–1540 ⊕ www.austinlehman.com.

Australian & Amazonian Adventures ✉ 2711 Market Garden, Austin, TX ☎ 512/443–5393 or 800/232–5658 ⊕ www.amazonadventures.com.

Big Five Tours & Expeditions ✉ 1551 S.E. Palm Ct., Stuart, FL ☎ 772/287–7995 or 800/244–3483 ⊕ www.bigfive.com.

BikeHike Adventures ✉ 200-1807 Maritime Mews, Vancouver, British Columbia , Canada ☎ 604/731–2442 or 888/805–0061 ⊕ www.bikehike.com.

Boojum Expeditions ✉ 14543 Kelly Canyon Rd., Bozeman, MT ☎ 406/587–0125 or 800/287–0125 ⊕ www.boojum.com.

Brazil Nuts ✉ 1854 Trade Center Way, Naples, FL ☎ 239/593–9959, 239/593–0267, or 800/553–9959 ⊕ www.brazilnuts.com.

Bushtracks Expeditions ✉ 6335 Mountain View Ranch Rd., Healdsburg,

CA ☎*800/995-8689* ⊕*www.bush tracks.com.*

Butterfield & Robinson ✉*70 Bond St., Suite 300 Toronto, Ontario , Canada* ☎*416/864-1354 or 866/551-9090* ⊕*www.butterfield.com.*

Colorado Mountain School ✉*341 Moraine Ave., Estes Park, CO* ☎*800/836-4008* ⊕*www.total climbing.com.*

Country Walkers ✉*Box 180, Waterbury, VT* ☎*802/244-1387 or 800/464-9255* ⊕*www.country walkers.com.*

Culinary Tour Peru ✉*Tarata 160, Miraflores, Peru* ☎*511/243-6074* ⊕*www.culinarytour.com.pe.*

Dragoman Overland ✉*Camp Green, Debenham, Suffolk , U.K.* ⊕*www. dragoman.com.* This company is represented in North America by Adventure Center (contact information under A, above).

Earth River Expeditions ✉*180 Towpath Rd., Accord, NY* ☎*845/626-2665 or 800/643-2784* ⊕*www. earthriver.com.*

Earthwatch ✉*3 Clocktower Pl., Suite 100, Maynard, MA* ☎*978/461-0081 or 800/776-0188* ⊕*www.earthwatch. org.*

Ecotour Expeditions ✆*Box 128, Jamestown, RI 02835* ☎*401/423-3377 or 800/688-1822* ⊕*www. naturetours.com.*

ElderTreks ✉*597 Markham St., Toronto, Ontario, Canada* ☎*416/588-5000 or 800/741-7956* ⊕*www. eldertreks.com.*

Equitours ✆*Box 807, Dubois, WY 82513* ☎*307/455-3363 or 800/545-0019* ⊕*www.equitours.com.*

Exodus This company is represented in North America by Adventure Center (contact information under A, above). ✉*9 Weir Rd., London , England* ⊕*www.exodustravel.com.*

Experience Plus! ✉*415 Mason Ct., #1, Fort Collins, CO* ☎*970/484-8489 or 800/685-4565* ⊕*www.Experience Plus.com.*

Explore! Worldwide This company is represented in North America by Adventure Center (contact information under A, above). ✉*Hampshire GU14 7 PA, U.K.* ⊕*www.explore.co.uk.*

Explore Bolivia ✉*2510 N. 47th St., Suite 207, Boulder, CO* ☎*303/545-5728 or 877/708-8810* ⊕*www. explorebolivia.com.*

Far Horizons ✆*Box 2546, San Anselmo, CA 94979* ☎*415/482-8400 or 800/552-4575* ⊕*www.farhorizons. com.*

Field Guides ✉*9433 Bee Cave Rd., Bldg. 1, Suite 150, Austin, TX* ☎*512/263-7295 or 800/728-4953* ⊕*www.fieldguides.com.*

Fishing International ✉*5510 Skylane Blvd., Suite 200, Santa Rosa, CA* ☎*707/542-4242 or 800/950-4242* ⊕*www.fishinginternational.com.*

FishQuest ✉*152 N. Main St., Hiawassee, GA* ☎*706/896-1403 or 888/891-3474* ⊕*www.fishquest.com.*

Fly Fishing And ✆*Box 1719, Red Lodge, MT 59068* ☎*406/425-9452* ⊕*www.flyfishingand.com.*

Tour Operators

Focus Tours ✉ Box 22276, Santa Fe, NM ☎ 505/989–7193 ∰ www.focus tours.com.

Frontiers ✆ Box 959, Wexford, PA 15090 ☎ 724/935–1577 or 800/245–1950 ∰ www.frontierstravel.com.

Galápagos Network ✉ 5805 Blue Lagoon Dr., Suite 160, Miami, FL ☎ 305/262–6264 or 800/633–7972 ∰ www.ecoventura.com.

G.A.P. Adventures ✉ 19 Charlotte St., Toronto, Ontario , Canada ☎ 416/260–0999 or 800/708–7761 ∰ www.gapadventures.com.

Gecko's This company is represented in North America by Adventure Center (contact information under A, above). ✉ 380 Lonsdale St., Melbourne , Australia ∰ www.geckosadventures.com.

Geographic Expeditions ✉ 1008 General Kennedy Ave., San Francisco, CA ☎ 415/922–0448 or 800/777–8183 ∰ www.geoex.com.

Global Adventure Guide ✉ 14 Kennaway Rd., Unit 3, Christchurch , New Zealand ☎ 800/732–0861 in North America ∰ www.globaladventure guide.com.

Global Crossroad ✉ 11822 Justice Ave., Suite A-5, Baton Rouge, LA ☎ 972/252–4191 ∰ www.global crossroad.com.

Global Vision ✉ 252 Newbury St., No. 4, Boston, MA ☎ 888/653–6028 ∰ www.gviusa.com.

Green Tracks Amazon Cruises ✉ 10 Town Plaza, PMB 231, Durango, CO ☎ 800/892–1035 or 970/884–6107 ∰ www.amazontours.net.

Heliconia Amazônia Turismo ✉ Rua José Clemente 500, Room 214, Manaus, AM, Brazil ☎ 092/3234–5915 ✆ 092/3633–7094 ∰ www. heliconia-amazon.com.

Hidden Trails ✉ 659A Moberly Rd., Vancouver, British Columbia , Canada ☎ 604/323–1141 or 888/987–2457 ∰ www.hiddentrails.com.

Ibike/International Bicycle Fund ✉ 4887 Columbia Dr. S, Seattle, WA ☎ 206/767–0848 ∰ www.ibike.org.

Inca ✉ 1311 63rd St., Emeryville, CA ☎ 510/420–1550 ∰ www.inca1.com.

International Expeditions ✉ One Environs Park, Helena, AL ☎ 205/428–1700 or 800/633–4734 ∰ www.ietravel.com.

Joseph Van Os Photo Safaris ✆ Box 655, Vashon Island, WA 98070 ☎ 206/463–5383 ∰ www.photo safaris.com.

Journeys International ✉ 107 Aprill Dr., Suite 3, Ann Arbor, MI ☎ 734/665–4407 or 800/255–8735 ∰ www.journeys-intl.com.

Kaiyote Tours ☎ 970/556–6103 ∰ www.kaiyotetours.com.

KE Adventure Travel ✉ 3300 E. 1st Ave., Suite 250 Denver, CO ☎ 303/321–0085 or 800/497–9675 ∰ www.keadventure.com.

Latin American Escapes ✉ 3209 Esplanade, Suite 130, Chico, CA ☎ 530/879–9292 or 800/510–5999 ✆ 530/879–9290 ∰ www.latin americanescapes.com.

Ladatco Tours ✉ 2200 S. Dixie Hwy., Suite 704, Coconut Grove, FL ☎ 800/327–6162 ∰ www.ladatco. com.

Lindblad Expeditions ✉ 96 Morton St., New York, NY ☎ 212/765–7740 *or 800/397–3348* ⊕ *www.expeditions. com.*

Manu Nature Tours ✉ *Av. Pardo 1046, Cusco, Peru* ☎ *51-84/252–271* ⊕ *www.manuperu.com.*

Maxim Tours ✉ *268 Rte. 206, Flanders, NJ* ☎ *973/927–0760 or 800/655–0222* 📠 *973/927–1417* ⊕ *www.maximtours.com.*

Mountain Madness ✉ *3018 S.W. Charlestown St., Seattle, WA* ☎ *206/937–8389 or 800/328–5925* ⊕ *www.mountainmadness.com.*

Mountain Travel Sobek ✉ *1266 66th St., Suite 4, Emeryville, CA* ☎ *510/594–6000 or 888/687–6235* ⊕ *www.mtsobek.com.*

Myths and Mountains ✉ *976 Tee Ct., Incline Village, NV* ☎ *775/832–5454 or 800/670–6984* ⊕ *www.mythsand mountains.com.*

Nature Expeditions International ✉ *7860 Peters Rd., Suite F-103, Plantation, FL* ☎ *954/693–8852 or 800/869–0639* ⊕ *www.naturexp.com.*

Nature Quest ✉ *Box 22000, Tel- luride, CO* ☎ *800/369–3033* ⊕ *www. naturequesttours.com.*

Oceanic Society Expeditions ✉ *Fort Mason Center, Bldg. E, San Francisco, CA* ☎ *415/441–1106 or 800/326– 7491* ⊕ *www.oceanic-society.org.*

Off the Beaten Path ✉ *7 E. Beall, Bozeman, MT* ☎ *800/445–2995* ⊕ *www.offthebeatenpath.com.*

OutWest Global Adventures This company operates gay- and lesbian- oriented tours. ☎ *Box 2050, Red Lodge, MT 59068* ☎ *406/446–1533 or 800/743–0458* ⊕ *www.outwest adventures.com.*

PanAmerican Travel Services ✉ *320 E. 900 S, Salt Lake City, UT* ☎ *800/364–4359* ⊕ *www.panam tours.com.*

Perol Chico ✉ *Peru* ☎ *511/9822– 3297* ⊕ *www.perolchico.com.*

Peru Bike ✉ *Nueva Castilla Calle A, D-8 Surco, Peru* ☎ *511/449–5234* ⊕ *www.perubike.com.*

Peruvian Andes Adventures ✉ *Olaya 532, Huaraz, Peru* ☎ *51- 43/421–864* ⊕ *www.peruvianandes. com.*

PowderQuest Tours ✉ *7108 Pine- tree Rd., Richmond, VA* ☎ *206/203– 6065 or 888/565–7158* ⊕ *www. powderquest.com.*

Quark Expeditions ✉ *1019 Post Rd., Darien, CT* ☎ *203/656–0499 or 800/356–5699* ⊕ *www.quark expeditions.com.*

Remote Odysseys Worldwide (ROW) ☎ *Box 579, Coeur d'Alene, ID 83816* ☎ *208/765–0841 or 800/451– 6034* ⊕ *www.ROWinternational.com.*

Rod & Reel Adventures ✉ *32617 Skyhawk Way, Eugene, OR* ☎ *541/349–0777 or 800/356–6982* ⊕ *www.rodreeladventures.com.*

Santana ✉ *Rua dos Andrades 106, Centro, Manaus* ☎ *092/3234–9814* 📠 *092/3233–7127* ⊕ *www.santana ecologica.com.br.*

Small World Adventures ☎ *Box 1225, Salida, CO 81201* ☎ *800/585– 2925* ⊕ *www.smallworldadventures. com.*

Snoventures ✉ *Cedar Ave., Hudder- sfield U.K.* ☎ *775/586–9133 in North America* ⊕ *www.snoventures.com.*

Tour Operators

South American Journeys
✉ 9921 Cabanas Ave., Tujunga, CA
☎ 818/951–8986 or 800/884–7474
⊕ www.southamericanjourneys.com.

Southwind Adventures ✑ Box
621057, Littleton, CO 80162
☎ 303/972–0701 or 800/377–9463
⊕ www.southwindadventures.com.

Swallows and Amazons ✑ Box
523, Eastham, MA 02642 ☎ 508/255–
4794 ⊕ www.swallowsandamazons
tours.com.

The World Outdoors ✉ 2840
Wilderness Pl., Suite D, Boulder, CO
☎ 303/413–0938 or 800/488–8483
⊕ www.theworldoutdoors.com.

Tours International ✉ 12750 Briar
Forest Dr., Suite 603, Houston, TX
☎ 800/247–7965 ⊕ www.tours
international.com.

Travcoa ✉ 4340 Von Karman
Ave., Suite 400, Newport Beach, CA
☎ 949/476–2800 or 800/992–2003
⊕ www.travcoa.com.

Victor Emanuel Nature Tours
✉ 2525 Wallingwood Dr., Suite 1003,
Austin, TX ☎ 512/328–5221 or
800/328–8368 ⊕ www.ventbird.com.

Wilderness Travel ✉ 1102 9th St.,
Berkeley, CA ☎ 510/558–2488 or
800/368–2794 ⊕ www.wilderness
travel.com.

Wildland Adventures ✉ 3516 N.E.
155th St., Seattle, WA ☎ 206/365–
0686 or 800/345–4453 ⊕ www.
wildland.com.

WildWings ✉ 577–579 Fishponds Rd., Fishponds, Bristol U.K.
☎ 0117/965–333 ⊕ www.WildWings.
co.uk.

WINGS ✉ 1643 N. Alvernon, Suite
109, Tucson, AZ ☎ 520/320–9868 or
888/293–6443 ⊕ www.wingsbirds.
com.

World Expeditions ✉ 580 Market
St., Suite 225, San Francisco, CA
☎ 415/989–2212 or 888/464–8735
⊕ www.worldexpeditions.com.

Yanna Ecofishing ☎ 092/3232–2522
🖷 092/3232–2397 ⊕ www.yanna.
com.br.

Zegrahm & Eco Expeditions ✉ 192
Nickerson St., #200, Seattle, WA
☎ 206/285–4000 or 800/628–8747
⊕ www.zeco.com.

Are there hidden costs? Make sure you know what is and is not included in basic trip costs when comparing companies. International airfare is usually extra. Sometimes domestic flights are additional. Is trip insurance required, and if so, is it included? Are airport transfers included? Visa fees? Departure taxes? Gratuities? Equipment? Meals? Bottled water? All excursions? Although some travelers prefer the option of an excursion or free time, many, especially those visiting a destination for the first time, want to see as much as possible. Paying extra for a number of excursions can significantly increase the total cost of the trip. Many factors affect the price, and the trip that looks cheapest in the brochure could well turn out to be the most expensive. Don't assume that roughing it will save you money, as prices rise when limited access and a lack of essential supplies on-site require costly special arrangements.

CRUISES

ANTARCTICA CRUISES

Founded to promote environmentally responsible travel to Antarctica, the **International Association of Antarctica Tour Operators** (☎ *970/704–1047* ⊕ *www.iaato.org*) is a good source of information, including suggested readings. Most companies operating Antarctica trips are members of this organization and display its logo in their brochures.

Season: November–March.
Location: Most cruises depart from Ushuaia, Argentina.
Cost: From $2,995 (triple-occupancy cabin) for 12 days from Ushuaia.
Tour Operators: Abercrombie & Kent; Adventure Center; Adventure Life; Big Five Tours & Expeditions; ElderTreks; G.A.P. Adventures; Lindblad Expeditions; Mountain Travel Sobek; Quark Expeditions; Travcoa; Wilderness Travel; Zegrahm & Eco Expeditions.
Ever since Lars-Eric Lindblad operated the first cruise to the "White Continent" in 1966, Antarctica has exerted an almost magnetic pull for serious travelers. From Ushuaia, the world's southernmost city, you'll sail for two (sometimes rough) days through the Drake Passage and then on to the spectacular landscapes of Antarctica. Most visits are to the Antarctic Peninsula, the continent's most accessible region. Accompanied by naturalists, you'll travel ashore in motorized rubber craft called Zodiacs to view penguins and nesting seabirds. Some cruises visit research stations, and many call at the Falkland, South Orkney, South Shetland, or South Georgia islands. Adventure Center, Adventure Life, and Big Five Tours & Expeditions offer sea kayaking and, at an extra cost, the chance to camp for a night on the ice.

Expedition vessels have been fitted with ice-strengthened hulls; many were originally built as polar research vessels. On certain Quark Expeditions itineraries you can travel aboard an icebreaker, the *Kapitan*

Khlebnikov, which rides up onto the ice, crushing it with its weight. This vessel carries helicopters for aerial viewing.

When choosing an expedition cruise, it's wise to inquire about the qualifications of the on-board naturalists and historians, the maximum number of passengers carried, the ice readiness of the vessel, onboard medical facilities, whether there is an open bridge policy, and the number of landings attempted per day.

GALÁPAGOS CRUISES

Season: Year-round.
Location: Galápagos Islands.
Cost: From $2,195 for eight days from Guayaquil.
Tour Operators: Abercrombie & Kent; Adventure Life; Austin-Lehman Adventures; Ecotour Expeditions; ElderTreks; Galápagos Network; G.A.P. Adventures; Inca; Lindblad Expeditions; Mountain Travel Sobek; Nature Expeditions International; Oceanic Society Expeditions; Travcoa; Wilderness Travel; Wildland Adventures; WildWings; World Expeditions.

To say there's no place like it is not hyperbole. The Galápagos Islands are isolated in the Pacific some 950 km (600 mi) west of South America. Their abundant wildlife inspired Charles Darwin's theory of evolution by natural selection. Even today, about two-thirds of the birds and most reptiles on this barren archipelago are found nowhere else. Following a flight from Guayaquil or Quito, Ecuador, you'll board a comfortable vessel and spend 5–11 days visiting as many as 12 islands (eight is typical), where the ship's naturalists will lead guided nature walks. You'll find the wildlife (sea lions, land and marine iguanas, huge tortoises, and numerous birds quite unafraid, but strict rules for shore visits are enforced. Visitors must follow established pathways, stay with the guide, and not give food or water to any wildlife. Pathways are rough and often rocky, but the pace is not hurried. Most operators include time for swimming or snorkeling with the sea lions. Vessels vary from 8- to 20-passenger motorized sailing yachts to the 100-passenger M/V *Galápagos Explorer II.* Some itineraries combine the Galápagos with stays in the Amazon or Andes; almost all include time in Quito and/or Guayaquil. Among Galápagos Network's many offerings are 8- and 11-day programs aimed at serious divers. The character of your trip will probably depend less on the number of islands visited than on the quality of the naturalists who are leading you around.

OCEAN CRUISES

Season: October–April.
Locations: Cruise lines are finding South American ports of call increasingly popular among travelers. Bordered by long Atlantic and Pacific coasts, the continent offers an abundance of choices. Many itineraries visit Argentina (Buenos Aires and Ushuaia), Brazil (Belém, Fortaleza, Rio de Janeiro, and Salvador), and Chile (Antofagasta, Arica, Cape Horn, Coquimbo, Puerto Montt, Punta Arenas, and Valparaíso). Other

typical ports of call include Cartagena, Colombia; Guayaquil, Ecuador; Devil's Island, French Guiana; Callao (for Lima) and Paracas (for Nazca Lines), Peru; Punta del Este and Montevideo, Uruguay; and Caracas, Venezuela. Some ships set sail in the Caribbean and stop at one or two islands before heading south. West coast departures might include one or more Mexican ports before reaching South America. Partial navigations of the Amazon River, frequently as far as Manaus, are becoming more frequent, as are stops at the Falkland Islands. Although circumnavigation of the continent is possible (50 or more days), 14- to 21-day cruises are the norm.

Vessels vary in the degree of comfort or luxury they offer, as well as in what is included in the price. Guided shore excursions, gratuities, dinner beverages, and port taxes are often extra. Peruse brochures carefully, and ask questions to ensure your choice of vessel is the right one for you.

Cost: Prices vary according to the ship, cabin category, and itinerary. Figure $1,550 to $4,495 for a 14-day cruise, excluding international airfare.

Cruise Companies: The following operators offer cruises calling at various South American ports.

Celebrity Cruises (☎800/647–2251 ⊕www.celebrity.com). **Crystal Cruises** (☎888/722–0021 ⊕www.crystalcruises.com). **Fred. Olsen Cruise Lines** (☎800/843–0602 ⊕www.fredolsencruises.com). **Holland America Line** (☎877/724–5425 ⊕www.hollandamerica.com). **Norwegian Cruise Line** (☎800/327–7030 ⊕www.ncl.com). **Princess Cruises** (☎800/774–6237 ⊕www.princess.com). **Regent Seven Seas Cruises** (☎877/505–5370 ⊕www.rssc.com). **Seabourn Cruise Line** (☎800/929–9391 ⊕www.seabourn.com). **Silversea Cruises** (☎800/722–9955 ⊕www.silversea.com).

PATAGONIA COASTAL & LAKE CRUISES

Cruising the southern tip of South America presents you some of the earth's most spectacular scenery: fjords, glaciers, lagoons, lakes, narrow channels, waterfalls, forested shorelines, fishing villages, penguins, and other wildlife. Although many tour operators include a one- or two-day boating excursion as part of their Patagonia itineraries, the companies listed below offer from 4 to 12 nights aboard ship.

ARGENTINA & CHILE

Season: October–April.

Locations: Chilean fjords; Puerto Montt and Punta Arenas, Chile; Tierra del Fuego and Ushuaia, Argentina.

Cost: From $1,395 for 12 days from Buenos Aires.

Tour Operators: Abercrombie & Kent; Adventure Life; Big Five Tours & Expeditions; Explore! Worldwide; International Expeditions; Mountain Travel Sobek; Off the Beaten Path; Wilderness Travel; Wildland Adventures.

Boarding the comfortable M/V *Mare Australis* or M/V *Via Australis* in Punta Arenas, Chile, or Ushuaia, Argentina, you'll cruise the Strait of Magellan and the Beagle Channel, visiting glaciers, penguin rookeries, and seal colonies before heading north along the fjords of Chile's western coast. With Adventure Life and Abercrombie & Kent you'll savor the mountain scenery of Torres del Paine National Park before or following the cruise, while Mountain Travel Sobek and International Expeditions visit Tierra del Fuego National Park. Several of the companies also include Cape Horn National Park. Wilderness Travel allows time for hiking at Volcano Osorno and in Alerce Andino National Park; the latter protects the second-largest temperate rain-forest ecosystem in the world. Following a five-day cruise, Off the Beaten Path travelers fly to Puerto Montt for a three-night stay at nearby Lake Llanquihue, with opportunities for hiking in the mountains. Along with the typical sea voyage, Wildland Adventures cruise in a 50-foot yacht along the Chiloé Archipelago, a region rich in folklore about ghost ships, witch-like *brujas,* and magical sea creatures, with stops at the virgin forest of Parque Pumalín (an eco-traveler favorite) and the Carretera Austral.

RIVER CRUISES

The Amazon, home to more than 200 species of mammals and 1,800 species of birds, and providing 30% of the earth's oxygen, is the world's largest and densest rain forest. Stretching 6,300 km (3,900 mi), the Amazon is the world's longest river. From its source in the Peruvian Andes, the river and its tributaries snake through parts of Bolivia, Ecuador, Colombia, and Brazil before emptying into the Atlantic. Whatever your style of travel, there's a boat plying the river to suit your needs. Sleep in a hammock on the deck of a thatch-roof riverboat or in the air-conditioned suite of an upscale vessel. A typical river program includes exploring tributaries in small boats; village visits, perhaps with a blowgun demonstration; piranha fishing; nocturnal wildlife searches; and rain-forest walks with a naturalist or indigenous guide to help you learn about plants, wildlife, and traditional medicines

BRAZIL

Season: Year-round.

Locations: Anavilhanas Archipelago; Lago Janauári Ecological Park; Manaus; Río Branco; Río Negro.

Cost: From $1,050 for seven days from Manaus.

Tour Operators: Amazon Nature Tours; Big Five Tours & Expeditions; Ecotour Expeditions; G.A.P. Adventures; Heliconia Amazônia Turismo; Latin American Escapes; Maxim Tours; Nature Expeditions International; Southwind Adventures; Swallows and Amazons; Travcoa.

River journeys along the Brazilian Amazon typically begin in Manaus and feature 3–10 days on the water, plus time in Manaus and, sometimes, Rio de Janeiro. On Big Five's 14-day trip you'll follow three days in Rio with a four-day cruise aboard the comfortable *Amazon Clipper Premium,* then continue on to Salvador and Iguaçu Falls. Travcoa's guests cruise aboard the Amazon's first luxury ship, the *Iberostar Grand Amazon;* after three days on the river you'll visit Brazil's capital, Brasília, before spending time in the Pantanal and Rio. Amazon Nature Tours, Latin American Escapes, Ecotour Expeditions, Nature Expeditions, and Southwind Adventures use the 18-passenger motorized yacht *Tucano* for their Amazon cruises, which ply the mostly uninhabited Río

Negro. On G.A.P.'s 42-day itinerary, explore the Amazon from Belém to Manaus and visit Bahia and Ceara states; the trip concludes with 10 days in Venezuela. Swallows and Amazons offer a variety of river programs, ranging from a traditional riverboat to a six-cabin air-conditioned houseboat with shared baths to a motorized yacht with private baths. Itineraries run from 4 to 11 days, and all include a visit with traditional *caboclo*, or river people. For Heliconia, Maxim Tours, and most of the tour operators' programs, a cruise highlight is the "Meeting of the Waters," where the dark waters of the Río Negro join the lighter waters of the Amazon.

PERU

Season: Year-round.
Locations: Iquitos to Tabatinga; Pacaya-Samiria National Reserve; Río Marañón; Río Ucayali.
Cost: From $799 for four days from Iquitos.
Tour Operators: Big Five Tours & Expeditions; G.A.P. Adventures; Green Tracks Amazon Cruises; International Expeditions; Oceanic Society Expeditions; Tours International.

Peru vies with Brazil as a destination for Amazon cruises. In fact, one G.A.P. program combines the two countries, beginning its 10-day cruise in Iquitos, Peru, and ending in Manaus, Brazil. This company offers a great variety of Amazon trips. With Big Five Tours & Expeditions, International Expeditions, and Tours International, you'll sail along the Amazon, Río Ucayali, and Río Marañón aboard modern vessels designed in the style of classic 19th-century riverboats. These trips include a visit to Pacaya-Samiria National Reserve, known for its 85 lakes, 250 fish species, 449 species of birds, 132 types of mammals, and 22 varieties of orchids. Oceanic Society Expeditions also feature Pacaya-Samiria on a nine-day trip, paying special attention to the behavior of freshwater dolphins. Green Tracks Amazon Cruises explore the Amazon and its tributaries on the 12-cabin M/V *Arapaima*, built in 2007. Tours International trips spend four or seven days sailing from Iquitos to *tres fronteras* (three borders), the spot where Peru, Brazil, and Colombia meet.

LEARNING VACATIONS

CULTURAL TOURS

Among the many types of travel, some find the most rewarding to be an in-depth focus on one aspect of a country's culture. This could mean exploring the archaeological remains of great civilizations, learning about the lives and customs of indigenous peoples, or trying to master a foreign language or culinary skills.

ARGENTINA

Season: March–October.
Locations: Buenos Aires; Mendoza; northwestern Argentina.
Cost: From $1,430 for nine days from Buenos Aires.

Tour Operators: Adventure Life; ElderTreks; Myths and Mountains.

Argentina's northwest is rich in cultural history as well as scenic beauty. With Adventure Life, spend seven days exploring this area. You'll view fossilized animals, ancient paintings and engravings on rock faces, neolithic remains where historic adobe huts sit atop sand dunes; and the city of Salta. Several hikes are on the itinerary. ElderTreks combines visits to several of these sites with time in Bolivia and Chile; included is a three-day trek in western Argentina. For a literal taste of Argentina, join Myths and Mountains' 10-day Adventurous Cook's Tour. Led by a renowned Argentine gastronomist, you'll take part in culinary workshops in Buenos Aires and wine tastings in Mendoza; there's even a typical barbecue on a working *estancia* (ranch). The program includes some hiking and horseback riding as well.

BOLIVIA

Season: March–November.

Locations: Cochabamba; Inkallajta; Lake Titicaca; Potosí; Sucre; Tiahuanaco; Uyuni Salt Flats.

Cost: From $1,003 for nine days from La Paz.

Tour Operators: Adventure Life; Amizade; Big Five Tours & Expeditions; Explore Bolivia; Explore! Worldwide; G.A.P. Adventures; Gecko's; Ladatco Tours; South American Journeys.

With archaeological sites, a salt desert, the world's highest navigable lake, a mining past, and indigenous Amazonian people, Bolivia, not surprisingly, is the subject of many culturally focused tours. Several of the above companies take you to Sucre, the Uyuni Salt Flats (the world's largest), and Potosí; the last was once the site of a major Spanish mint. On Explore Bolivia's trip, you'll camp on the Salar de Uyuni and by Laguna Colorada (Red Lagoon). Following travel in these same areas, Explore! Worldwide moves on to the jungle for a three-night ecolodge stay in Madidi National Park, followed by time at Lake Titicaca, while G.A.P. includes San Pedro de Atacama, in Chile, plus Cusco and Machu Picchu, in Peru. Adventure Life's itinerary offers an in-depth focus on the Salar de Uyuni, including a visit to a historic hotel built of salt, and Isla de Pescadores, an island surrounded by salt. Amizade organizes service projects such as joining local people in converting a cowshed into a school near Cochabamba or working with orphans, the elderly, or the mentally and physically challenged. Spanish lessons are part of the program.

BRAZIL

Season: Year-round.

Locations: Amazon; Rio de Janeiro; Salvador.

Cost: From $943 for eight days from Salvador.

Tour Operators: Abercrombie & Kent; Amizade; Brazil Nuts; Focus Tours; G.A.P. Adventures; Maxim Tours; Nature Expeditions International; Swallows and Amazons; Wilderness Travel.

If your interest is learning about other cultures, consider Swallows and Amazons' Caboclo program, which focuses on the lifestyle and culture of the Amazonian river people, the caboclos. You'll stay at the company's rain-forest camp in the Anavilhanas Archipelago Biological

Reserve, and get to know the local family that lives on the property. Activities include canoeing, fishing, rain-forest walks, and overnight camping. Nature Expeditions' multifaceted itinerary features a three-day Amazon cruise; two days in Salvador, the spiritual and cultural center of the Bahia region; Rio; Petropolis, where you'll visit the home of a Macumba practitioner to learn about this unique religion with roots in voodoo; Paraty; and Iguaçu Falls. Maxim Tours lets you determine the number of days you'd like in the architectural and historical gems of Ouro Prêto, Olinda, and Salvador. The Afro-Brazilian and Bahian culture of Salvador and its environs are the focus of Brazil Nuts' 8-day tour. Following 10 days in Venezuela, G.A.P. Adventures moves on to the Brazilian Amazon, then works its way down the coast to Rio, exploring such points as São Luis, Fortaleza, Recife, and Salvador along the way. To add a rewarding dimension to your trip, consider an Amizade work project in Santarém, an Amazonian city of 300,000 people, where you'll help construct a center for street children.

CHILE
Season: Year-round.
Locations: Atacama Desert; Easter Island; Santa Cruz.
Cost: From $1,795 for seven days from Santiago.
Tour Operators: Abercrombie & Kent; Big Five Tours & Expeditions; Far Horizons; G.A.P. Adventures; Ladatco Tours; Myths and Mountains; Nature Expeditions International; PanAmerican Travel Services; South American Journeys; Tours International; World Expeditions.
In the Pacific Ocean 3,680 km (2,300 mi) west of the Chilean mainland, remote Easter Island is famed for its *moais,* nearly 1,000 stone statues whose brooding eyes gaze over the windswept landscape. Abercrombie & Kent, Far Horizons, Myths and Mountains, and Nature Expeditions are among the tour operators that will take you there. Far Horizons' departure is timed for the annual Tapati festival. Vying with Easter Island as a cultural experience, the Atacama, generally considered the world's driest desert, is a region of bizarre landscapes, ancient petroglyphs (designs scratched or cut into rock), geoglyphs (designs formed by arranging stones or earth), and mummies. Many of the above companies have Atacama programs. For a cultural experience of another sort, join PanAmerican Travel's 9-day round of Chilean vineyards, where you'll enjoy tours, tastings, and even the occasional vineyard lunch; on World Expedition's 8-day Chile Wine Route by bike, you'll cycle from vineyard to vineyard in the Rosario, Casablanca, and Aconcagua valleys. G.A.P. Adventures takes you from Santiago to Buenos Aires, stopping for tastings at wineries and cooking classes along the way in Mendoza and Córdoba in their 10-day Gourmet Adventure.

ECUADOR
Season: Year-round.
Locations: Amazon; Quito.
Cost: From $630 for eight days from Quito.
Tour Operators: Gecko's; Myths and Mountains.
On Myths and Mountains' Shamans of Ecuador itinerary, travel through jungles and highlands for 10 days, meeting with shamans and

learning about their rituals and healing practices. For their African Pulse itinerary, Myths and Mountains explores African roots and heritage in Ecuador by participating in drum and weaving workshops and performances by *payadores* (performers of a type of improv poetry). Speaking with the local people is sure to add an important dimension to any journey, and Gecko's 7-day conversational Spanish school in Quito helps you do just that. You'll live and eat with an Ecuadoran family and receive 28 hours of one-on-one tutoring.

PERU

Season: Year-round.

Locations: Islas Ballestas; Chachapoyas region; Chán Chán; Kuelap; Sipan.

Cost: From $745 for seven days from Lima.

Tour Operators: Abercrombie & Kent; A Taste of Peru; Bushtracks Exeditions; Culinary Tour Peru; Experience Plus!; Explore! Worldwide; Far Horizons; Gecko's; Global Crossroad; Green Tracks Amazon Cruises; Inca; Myths and Mountains; South American Journeys; Tours International; Wildland Adventures; World Expeditions.

Since virtually all tours to Peru, including most of those described below, take in Cusco (also spelled Cuzco) and Machu Picchu, the emphasis here will be on other noteworthy sites or activities. Chán Chán (capital of the ancient Chimú Empire and one of the largest pre-Columbian cities yet discovered), the fortress of Kuelap, and Sipan (where archaeologists unearthed the most spectacular tomb in the western hemisphere) are highlights of programs offered by most of the above operators. Some itineraries also include flights over the Nazca Lines; visits to the Islas Ballestas (sometimes called the Little Galápagos), the mountaintop ruins of Pachacamac, or the well-preserved pre-Inca mummies of Leymebamba. Catching on rapidly in Peru are culinary tours, and A Taste of Peru's 8-day itinerary is one of the most in-depth. Your journey takes you to local markets, cooking demonstrations by well known Peruvian chefs, and visits to the major sights in Lima and Cusco. On one Myths and Mountains' tour you'll travel with a Peruvian artist and weaver, visiting homes and studios while learning about ancient weaving techniques. Inca's program includes a by-appointment-only view of a textile collection and a visit to the Paracas Necropolis, where 400 mummies and ancient weavings were found. Far Horizons' trip features a private collection of Andean art viewed in the owner's home and dinner with the excavator of San José Moro, a Moche cemetery. With Tours International you'll trek, ride horses, and camp near an archaeological complex, while with South American Journeys you'll travel by floatplane to an Achual indigenous village for meetings with the chief, and enjoy jungle hikes and hunting activities with the Achual. Immerse yourself in Lima's culture while improving your conversational Spanish skills with the one-week home-stay language programs of Gecko's and World Expeditions. Global Crossroad gets up close to rural life in Peru in their month-long immersion program that combines a week of language study, two weeks of volunteer work in a community service project, and a week of tours in the Andes and Amazon.

SCIENTIFIC RESEARCH TRIPS

11

Joining a research expedition team gives you more than great photos. By assisting scientists, you can make significant contributions to a better understanding of the continent's unique ecosystems and cultural heritages. Flexibility and a sense of humor are important assets for these trips, which often require roughing it.

ARGENTINA

Season: Year-round.
Locations: Patagonia **Cost:** $3,500 for 6 weeks from San Carlos de Bariloche, Argentina.
Tour Operator: Globalvision.
On Globalvision's Patagonian Exploration and Wildlife Research Expedition you will explore remote regions of both Chilean and Argentinean Patagonia while taking part in numerous conservation projects. The 6- or 12-week programs take you from San Carlos de Bariloche to collect data on condors on the Patagonian steppe, climb volcanoes, trek across Chile's Northern Ice Cap, and record mammal species with local rangers and scientists.

BRAZIL

Season: Year-round.
Locations: Cananéia Estuary; Emas National Park; Pantanal.
Cost: From $2,946 for 13 days from Campo Grande.
Tour Operator: Earthwatch.
Earthwatch has six projects in Brazil, all focused on wildlife. Working by boat and on land on the Cananéia Estuary, volunteers will help to establish data for guiding local tourism development and protecting the region's biodiversity. Emas National Park harbors many mammal, reptile, and bird species. Scientists here are involved in assessing the distribution and numbers of carnivores in the park, and volunteers will help in this endeavor by capturing and radio-collaring jaguars, foxes, pumas, and wolves. In the Pantanal, the largest freshwater wetland on the planet, assist a multinational team of scientists in collecting data on the area's plants and animals to aid in the development of a sound conservation plan. Special projects focus on bats, giant river otters, and amphibians and reptiles.

ECUADOR

Season: May–August; November–January.
Location: Amazon, Loma Alta Ecological Reserve; Tangara Reserve.
Cost: From $2,546 for 12 days from Quito.
Tour Operator: Earthwatch, Globalvision.
Though covering only 1.6% of South America's land mass, Ecuador is home to more than half the continent's bird species. Many inhabit threatened ecosystems. You'll help survey a remote tropical forest to track seasonal shifts in bird populations and perform such tasks as setting up and checking mist nets. Volunteers will visit the cloud forests of the Santa Lucia Reserve (where bears, jaguars, ocelots, and coatimundis roam free), collect aerial photos, and gather data on trees, plants, and animals. Working to educate the community in Globalvision's small

center along the Río Napo, the focus of their 5- or 10-week programs is helping to conserve the diverse wildlife of the Ecuadorian Amazon. You'll work alongside students and teachers and receive on-site training to carry out a variety of projects involving scientific investigation and education.

PERU

Season: December–February.
Location: Tambopata National Reserve.
Cost: From $2,746 for 12 days from Puerto Maldonado.
Tour Operators: Earthwatch.
Take part in a study of tourism's impact on macaws at Tambopata National Reserve as a scientist seeks to learn if they are being "loved to extinction." Traveling to clay licks by riverboat and on foot, you'll observe the macaws' daily behavior and reactions to tourists. You'll stay at both the Tambopata Research Center and the Refugio Amazonas and have enough free time to wander nearby trails searching for the more than 500 species of birds recorded in the reserve.

THE OUTDOORS

AMAZON JUNGLE CAMPING & LODGES

Because the Amazon and its tributaries provide easy access to remote parts of the jungle, river transport often serves as the starting point for camping and lodge excursions. Many lodges and camps are within or near national parks or reserves. Accommodations range from hammocks to comfortable rooms with private hot-water baths. Nature walks, canoe trips, piranha fishing, and visits to indigenous villages are typically part of rain-forest programs led by naturalists or indigenous guides.

BOLIVIA

Season: Year-round.
Locations: Madidi National Park.
Cost: From $795 for seven days from La Paz.
Tour Operators: Adventure Life; Explore Bolivia.
Considered one of the most pristine tropical rain forests in South America, Madidi National Park, home to howler monkeys, capybaras, anacondas, caimans, and countless species of birds and butterflies, is the site of Chalalán EcoLodge. Reached by a five-hour dugout canoe journey along the Ríos Beni and Tuichi from the frontier town of Rurrenabaque, the lodge is owned and operated by an indigenous Quechua community. Adventure Life bases its seven-day journey here for rain-forest explorations and insights into the traditional crafts, beliefs, and customs of the Quechua.

BRAZIL

Season: Year-round.
Locations: Amazon Ecopark; Jau National Park; Manaus; Río Negro.
Cost: Beginning at about $1,400 for eight days from Manaus.

Tour Operators: Ecotour Expeditions; Focus Tours; Heliconia Amizônia Turismo; International Expeditions; Latin American Escapes; Maxim Tours; Naturequest; PanAmerican Travel; Swallows and Amazons.

Most jungle adventures here begin with a boat trip up the Río Negro, the main tributary of the Amazon. With Swallows and Amazons, there are 19 trips throughout the Brazilian Amazon ranging from 7 to 15 days, including stays Araras Lodge, the company's floating jungle hotel, and canoe trips between Jau National Park and the Rio Branco. From this base, make various excursions as outlined in the introduction to this section. Naturequest has created a rustic jungle lodge and riverboat safari combination. With International Expeditions you'll explore the rain forest and watery byways from your base at remote Uakari Lodge's cluster of floating cabañas. Focus Tours' program features the rain forest, rivers, and wildlife of the Alta Floresta region. Maxim Tours offers short stays at the comfortable Pousada dos Guanavenas or the more rustic Amazon Lodge. PanAmerican Travel's 12-day itinerary also begins with a transfer by boat from Manaus to a rain-forest lodge. In this case, it's the Amazon Ecopark, on the banks of the Rio Tarumã. Here biologists and zoologists have initiated several wildlife preservation projects, including a monkey jungle, a bird sanctuary, and a botanic garden.

COLOMBIA

Season: Year-round.
Locations: Leticia.
Cost: From $495 for four days from Bogotá.
Tour Operators: PanAmerican Travel Services.

Tours to Colombia are becoming far more common than they were just a few years ago. PanAmerican Travel Services offers a 4-day excursion to Colombia's foothold on the Amazon that can be added to any of their Colombia tours. After arriving in Leticia, you'll head to Amacayacu National Park, where you'll visit Indigenous villages and search for pink river dolphins and Victoria Amazonica, the world's largest water plant—which around these parts still goes by the name Victoria Regia.

ECUADOR

Season: Year-round.
Location: Amazon basin.
Cost: From $595 for four days from Quito.
Tour Operators: Abercrombie & Kent; Adventure Life; Big Five Tours & Expeditions; Galápagos Network; G.A.P. Adventures; Inca.

Scientists estimate that the Ecuadoran Amazon has 1,450 species of birds and as many as 20,000 varieties of plants. Operators use several comfortable lodges located throughout the region: Sacha Lodge, a cluster of cabañas nestled deep in the rain forest, plus a 40-meter (130-foot) observation tower and a 287-meter (940-foot) canopy walkway; La Selva Lodge, a group of cabins overlooking the waters of Lago Garzacocha; Napo Wildlife Center, with 10 luxurious cabañas and a 37-meter (120-foot) canopy tower; and Kapawi, a pioneering ecolodge on the Río Pastaza, where the majority of the staff are indigenous Achuar people. Galápagos Network offers 4- and 5-day stays at all four properties, while Abercrombie & Kent utilizes Napo Wildlife Center, Big Five favors Kapawi, Adventure Life and Inca stay at Sacha Lodge, and G.A.P. uses Kapawi and Sacha.

PERU

Season: Year-round.

Location: Amazon basin.

Cost: From $1,050 for five days from Quito.

Tour Operators: Abercrombie & Kent; Adventure Life; Big Five Tours & Expeditions; Bushtracks Expeditions; G.A.P. Adventures; International Expeditions; Journeys International; Myths and Mountains; South American Journeys; Southwind Adventures; Tours International; Wildland Adventures.

At Tambopata Macaw Research Center you'll witness hundreds of macaws and parrots returning each morning to nibble bits of clay from a riverside ledge. Another popular destination is Manu Biosphere Reserve, home to the Amazon's largest-known tapir lick and lakes inhabited by giant river otters and a variety of waterbirds. Most of the above companies visit one or both of these sites. Among other Peruvian jungle lodges are Explorama and ExplorNapo, used by International Expeditions and Tours International; Manu Wildlife Center (Wildland); Ceiba Tops Lodge & Resort (Abercrombie & Kent, International Expeditions, and Tours International); Pacaya-Samiria (Big Five); and the new Heath River Wildlife Center, owned by the Esé Eja indigenous community (G.A.P., South American Journeys, and Wildland Adventures).

VENEZUELA

Season: Year-round.

Locations: Río Orinoco.

Cost: $265 for four days from Puerto Ayacucho.

Tour Operator: Australian & Amazonian Adventures.

Based right on the river at Orinoquia Lodge, you'll visit indigenous villages to learn about medicinal plants, forms of agriculture, and the making of baskets, hammocks, and traps. Enjoy the Tobogan de la Selva, a pool-filled natural water slide, and a boat trip along the Orinoco searching for freshwater dolphins and otters.

BIRD-WATCHING TOURS

When selecting a bird-watching tour, ask questions. What species might be seen? What are the guide's qualifications? Does the operator work to protect natural habitats? What equipment is used? (In addition to binoculars, this should include a high-powered telescope, a tape recorder to record and play back bird calls [as a way of attracting birds], and a spotlight for night viewing.)

ANTARCTICA

Season: January; November and December.

Locations: Antarctic Peninsula; Falkland Islands; South Georgia.

Cost: From $14,595 for 19 days from Ushuaia.

Tour Operator: Victor Emanuel Nature Tours; WildWings.
Arguably the ultimate travel adventure, Antarctica exerts a strong pull
on nature lovers. Now a trip has been designed to focus on the special
interests of serious birders. With Victor Emanuel you'll be traveling
aboard the *Clipper Adventurer* in the hope of seeing wandering, light-
mantled and royal albatrosses; snow petrels and several other petrel
species; as well as large colonies of king and macaroni penguins. Wild-
Wings cruises to Antarctica, as well as South Georgia and the Falkland
Islands, aboard the *Akademik Ioffe* or *Vavilov*. Zodiac boats bring you
ashore for land excursions.

ARGENTINA

Season: November and December.
Locations: Andes; Chaco; Iguazú; Pampas; Patagonia.
Cost: From $2,230 for eight days from Salta.
Tour Operators: Focus Tours; Kaiyote Tours; Victor Emanuel Nature
Tours; WINGS.
Whatever part of Argentina you visit, expect to see a great variety
of bird species, including many endemic to this region. Focus Tours'
21-day program concentrates on the northern region, where feathered
inhabitants such as the plumbeous sierra-finch, Salinas Monjita, and
Steinbach's canastero live. Kaiyote's itinerary takes 19 days and covers more than 2,200 mi, stopping in Posadas, Ibera, El Soberbio, and
Iguazú. Victor Emanuel offers three Argentine programs: two to the
northern areas for such endemic birds as Oustalet's and Cordoba cin-
clodes and the other covering Patagonia and Tierra del Fuego. Possible
sightings on the latter include the rufous-backed negrito, Andean condor, and Humboldt penguin. WINGS's three itineraries visit the high
Andes, the Pampas, and Iguazú Falls.

BOLIVIA

Seasons: October; February–April.
Locations: Amazon; Andes; Chaco; Cochabamba; Santa Cruz.
Cost: From $3,480 for 16 days from Santa Cruz.
Tour Operators: Explore Bolivia; Field Guides; WINGS.
Thanks to its varied geography, Bolivia has some 1,300 bird spe-
cies, representing 40% of those found in all of South America. Up to
213 species have been recorded by one tour group on a single day.
Depending on the WINGS itinerary you select, you could visit the
Central Andes; the Amazon; the area around Santa Cruz; or Refugio
Los Volcanes and the Chaco Desert. Explore Bolivia's 15-day program covers Bolivia from the lowlands to the Andes, climbing from an
altitude of 427 meters to 4,724 meters (1,400 to 15,500 feet). Thus,
the variety of birds observed is huge. With Field Guides' Bolivia's
Avian Riches program, you will spend 16 days exploring the Bolivian Andes with an optional 4-day stint in the Amazon observing the
blue-throated macaw.

BRAZIL

Seasons: Year-round.
Locations: Amazon; Emas National Park; Iguaçu Falls; Itatiaia National
Park; Northeast; Pantanal; Southeast.

Cost: From $1,550 for seven days from Manaus.
Tour Operators: Field Guides; Focus Tours; Swallows and Amazons; Victor Emanuel Nature Tours; WINGS.

Bird habitats in Brazil range from coastal rain forests to cloud forests to open plains, and with dozens of itineraries between them, the above tour operators cover all topographies. The Pantanal, a vast area of seasonally flooded grassland, has the hyacinth macaw, bare-faced curassow, Toco toucan, and yellow-billed cardinal, while the newly described cryptic forest-falcon and bare-headed parrot are but two of many exotic species inhabiting the Amazon and coastal jungles. Brazilian avian life is so rich that Focus Tours has four tours here, Wings runs six, Victor Emanuel Nature Tours has eight, and Field Guides offers ten.

CHILE

Seasons: October and November.
Locations: Atacama Desert; Lake District; Patagonia.
Cost: From $3,999 for 16 days from Santiago.
Tour Operators: Focus Tours; WINGS.

Chile spans a number of distinctive vegetational and altitudinal zones, ensuring a varied and abundant avian population. On a 16-day journey to the northern and central regions, Focus Tours participants visit the ski areas of Farellones and Valle Nevado to spot the rare crag chilia, an earth-creeper-like bird; Los Cipreses Reserve, stronghold of the burrowing parrot; La Campana National Park, which holds five of Chile's eight endemic species; the Andes for the rare and threatened white-tailed shrike-tyrant; plus the arid Atacama and Lauca National Park. WINGS's itinerary covers the country from Tierra del Fuego in the south to the Atacama Desert in the north, also spending time in Patagonia and the Lake District.

COLOMBIA

Season: January.
Locations: Bogotá; Amazon.
Cost: From $3,840 for 22 days from Bogotá.
Tour Operators: Kaiyote Tours.

Colombia has the highest diversity of bird life in the world, and tour operators are taking advantage of the stabilized situation in the country. Kaiyote's 22-day itinerary takes in the Andes surrounding Bogotá, then heads for 11 days in the Brazilian and Colombian Amazon before coming back to the Colombian capital.

ECUADOR

Season: Year-round.
Locations: Amazon; Andes; Galápagos Islands; Southwest Coast.
Cost: From $1,135 for seven days from Quito.
Tour Operators: Field Guides; Victor Emanuel Nature Tours; WINGS.

Some birders have described one of Ecuador's nature reserves as "one of the birdiest places on earth." In each region, from the Amazon to the Andes to the Galápagos, you'll find hundreds of distinct species. More than 500 species have been recorded at the Napo Wildlife Center, which is visited on one of Victor Emanuel's six programs in this country. The company's other trips travel to the Andes and the Galápagos, with one northern Andes itinerary focused on the region's 40 to 60 hummingbird species. WINGS offers five itineraries in Ecuador, ranging from the Amazon to the Yanacocha Reserve, Vilcabamba, the Manglares de Churute Reserve, and Oriente. Field Guides' 10-day program, one of their seven trips, is based at a hacienda in the cloud forest at an altitude of 2,073 meters (6,800 feet). The bird list here features the recently discovered bicolored antvireo and the rare mountain avocetbill.

PERU

Season: Year-round.
Locations: Amazon basin; Andes; Northern Peru.
Cost: From $3,090 for 10 days from Lima.
Tour Operators: Field Guides; Tours International; Victor Emanuel Nature Tours; WINGS.

With habitats ranging from the Amazon to the Andes to the coastal desert, Peru claims in excess of 1,800 bird species. WINGS's three itineraries cover Manu National Park, considered one of the world's premier birding sites; other Amazonian regions; and northern Peru. Field Guides takes in Manu, Abra Malaga, Machu Picchu, and the North Coast on their six itineraries. Tours International's birding trips focus on Tambopata, Colca, and Paracas, while Victor Emanuel offers four itineraries, two concentrating on the Amazon, one on the central region including the Paracas Peninsula and Cordillera Blanca, and the fourth on the north, with visits to Tumbes, Marañón Canyon, and the Andes.

VENEZUELA

Season: Year-round.
Locations: Andes; Gran Sabana; Henri Pittier National Park; Los Llanos.
Cost: From $3,590 for nine days from Caracas.
Tour Operators: Victor Emanuel Nature Tours; WINGS.

With topography ranging from cloud forests to the Andes, the *tepuis* (mountains with sheer sides and flat tops), saline lagoons, grasslands, and a number of national parks, Venezuela offers an abundance of birding opportunities. More than 500 species are found in Henri Pittier National Park alone, and both Victor Emanuel and WINGS take you there. Each company offers three distinct itineraries in Venezuela. Victor Emanuel's eastern Venezuela trip has been nicknamed the "Harpy Eagle Tour," a tribute to the success rate of viewing these magnificent birds.

NATURAL HISTORY

Many operators have created nature-focused programs that provide insight into the importance and fragility of South America's ecological treasures. The itineraries mentioned below take in the deserts, glaciers, rain forests, mountains, and rivers of this continent, as well as the impressive variety of its wildlife.

ARGENTINA & CHILE

Season: October–April.

Locations: Atacama Desert; Buenos Aires; Lake District; Patagonia; Santiago.

Cost: From $790 for four days from Bariloche.

Tour Operators: Abercrombie & Kent; Adventure Life; Big Five Tours & Expeditions; ElderTreks; G.A.P. Adventures; Geographic Expeditions; Inca; Journeys International; Myths and Mountains; Nature Expeditions International; Off the Beaten Path; PanAmerican Travel Services; South American Journeys; Southwind Adventures; Wilderness Travel; Wildland Adventures; World Expeditions, Zegrahm & Eco Expeditions.

The southern tip of Argentina and Chile, commonly referred to as Patagonia, has long been a prime ecotourism destination, and nature lovers will find no lack of tour offerings for this region. You'll view the glaciers of Los Glaciares National Park, where the Moreno Glacier towers 20 stories high; the soaring peaks of Torres del Paine; the fjords of the Chilean coast; and a Magellanic penguin colony. Most itineraries spend some days in the Lake District, possibly traversing the fantastic Cruce del Lagos ferry route between the countries. Many programs include day walks and, often, a one- to three-day cruise. Several operators feature a stay at a historic ranch, Estancia Helsingfors. The Atacama Desert of northern Chile is nature of another sort. Abercrombie & Kent has a "Fire and Ice" itinerary, combining the deep south with this arid zone. Zeghram Expeditions' 15-day program explores the natural highlights of Patagonia with stops in Torres del Paine, the Perito Moreno glacier, and the Península Valdéz.

BOLIVIA

Season: Year-round.

Locations: Madidi National Park; Noel Kempff Mercado National Park; Ríos Iténez and Paucerna; Santa Cruz.

Cost: From $795 for four days from La Paz.

Tour Operator: Adventure Life; Wildland Adventures.

Noel Kempff Mercado National Park's 2.4 million acres contain 525 bird, 91 mammal, and 18 reptile species, plus numerous plants. It is one of the most isolated and concentrated wildlife reserves in all South America, and contains a diverse combination of ecosystems. Wildland Adventures' 9-day itinerary also takes in several impressive waterfalls along various rivers, and offers boat trips up to five hours by motorized canoe. Madidi National Park is home to some of the most pristine rain forest on the planet, filled with sloths, howler monkeys, giant otters, jaguars, and herds of peccaries. Adventure Life explores the park while staying at the posh Chalalan Ecolodge. All of the above companies can take you here to hike the forest trails and visit the river to see dolphins, giant otters, and endangered black caimans.

BRAZIL

Season: Year-round.

Locations: Bonito; Iguaçu Falls; Pantanal.

Cost: From $831 for five days from Campo Grande.

Tour Operators: Australian & Amazonian Adventures; Big Five Tours & Expeditions; Brazil Nuts; Bushtracks Expeditions; Ecotour Expeditions; ElderTreks; Explore! Worldwide; G.A.P. Adventures; Geographic Expeditions; International Expeditions; Latin American Escapes; Maxim Tours; Naturequest; Oceanic Society Expeditions; Southwind Adventures; Travcoa; Wilderness Travel.

Covering 89,000 square mi, the Pantanal is the world's largest freshwater wetland. Most of the above companies operate Pantanal programs; many are based at Refúgio Ecológico Caiman, which offers comfortable lodgings and a staff of naturalists who lead excursions by truck, by boat, on horseback, and on foot. Jabiru storks and other wading birds, anteaters, monkeys, caimans, capybaras, and possibly jaguars are among the wildlife you might see. Oceanic Society's trip, led by two animal specialists, spends six days at a lodge on the Río Pixiam and includes an excursion to an area with the world's highest recorded number of jaguar sightings per day. ElderTreks combines the Pantanal, the Amazon, and Iguaçu on a 15-day trip. Australian & Amazonian Adventures offers two programs in lesser-known regions of the Pantanal. Before traveling to the wetlands, Bushtracks participants observe hyacinth macaws and maned wolves at Hyacinth Cliffs Lodge, then continue on to Greenwing Valley Reserve to see brown capuchin monkeys, sometimes called Einstein monkeys because of their ability to use rock tools as hammers and anvils. With G.A.P. you'll spend days in Rio, Parati, and Iguaçu, as well as the Pantanal.

ECUADOR

Season: Year-round.

Locations: Amazon; Antisana Reserve; Cotopaxi; Galápagos; lakes of Riobamba.

Cost: $1,825 for 13 days from Quito.

Tour Operators: Abercrombie & Kent, Ecotour Expeditions; Gecko's.

It's the smallest Andean country, but Ecuador is impressively scenic and culturally diverse. Abercrombie & Kent's 10-day journey introduces many of its natural wonders. At Antisana Reserve you'll view volcanoes and a variety of flora and fauna, including, perhaps, the Andean condor. Continuing on to Baños, gateway to the Amazon rain forest, there will be the chance for horseback riding, hiking, mountain biking, or simply enjoying the volcanic hot springs and waterfalls. Reaching the central lake region of Riobamba, board a train for rooftop views of the landscape. With Ecotour Expeditions you'll take in a few days in Quito and five more in Oriente Lodge, while Gecko's takes in not just the Galápagos but makes a foray into the Amazon and visits the Cotopaxi Volcano on their 13-day Ecuador and the Galápagos program.

PERU

Season: Year-round.

Locations: Colca Canyon; Manu Biosphere Reserve; Tambopata-Candamo Reserve.

Cost: From $1,345 for 12 days from Cusco.

Tour Operators: Adventure Life; Big Five Tours & Expeditions; Elder-Treks; G.A.P. Adventures; Manu Nature Tours; Southwind Adventures; Tours International; World Expeditions.

The Peruvian portions of the Amazon lay claim to some of the highest biodiversity on the planet. The Manu Biosphere Reserve alone holds numerous world records in birdlife, mammals, reptiles, amphibians, freshwater fish, insects, and plants. Manu Nature Tours and other operators bring you to the highly protected cloud forest and stay at Manu Lodge or one of various tent camps set throughout the park. Elsewhere the 3.7 million acres Tambopata-Candamo Reserve is primarily known for its Macaw Research Center, where a huge nutrient-rich clay lick attracts hundreds of parrots and parakeets and at least six species of macaws. The reserve has some 500 bird species, 11 varieties of monkeys, and various mammals, including ocelots and jaguars. All the above operators have trips to Tambopata, ranging from three to seven days. Adventure Life and World Expeditions also offer itineraries in Arequipa, called the White City because of its many buildings made of light-color volcanic rock, and Colca Canyon, the world's deepest canyon. With Tours International, choose a 3-day stay at Posada Amazonas, built in traditional style using palm fronds, wood, wild cane, and clay. The lodge, deep in the Madre de Dios rain forest, is a joint venture with the Esé eja Native Community and the Tambopata Research Center.

VENEZUELA
Season: Year-round.
Locations: Andes; Angel Falls; Canaima; Los Llanos; Orinoco Delta.
Cost: From $2,600 for 15 days from Caracas.
Tour Operators: Angel-Eco Tours; Explore! Worldwide; PanAmerican Travel Services.

Besides 1,250 species of birds and 250 kinds of mammals, Venezuela also has mountains, tropical forests, mesas, and waterfalls. A highlight of any journey is Canaima National Park and a view of Angel Falls, either from the base or by light aircraft. The avalanche of water drops 807 meters (2,647 feet), twice the height of the Empire State Building. PanAmerican's 14-day journey visits the falls, the Orinoco Delta, and Caracas, following eight days in neighboring Guyana. Some camping is part of the program. Adventure Life divides its 15-day package between Canaima and the falls, the Orinoco Delta, and Los Llanos. Three overnights are in jungle shelters and two in hammock camps. Angel-Eco Tours offers multiple trips varying from two days to two weeks in Venezuela's isolated Amazon regions, including combinations of Canaima, Angel Falls, and the Orinoco River basin.

OVERLAND SAFARIS

The brochure for a company that operates overland trips exclusively states in bold print: NOT YOUR EVERYDAY JOURNEY. Although definitely not for everyone, this type of travel is sure to take you far from the beaten path. It's also a great way to immerse yourself in a number of cultures and landscapes. Expect to travel by truck, bus, train, boat, or

The Outdoors > **791**

custom-built expedition vehicle—no air-conditioned coach tours here. Occasionally, you may find yourself in lodges or inns, but much of the time you'll be sleeping outdoors. Know that you're expected to help pitch tents, cook, and do other chores. The camaraderie that evolves often sparks lifelong friendships. You should be tolerant of others, willing to forego some creature comforts, and be a good sport about taking part in group activities. Companies often rank trip segments from easy to extreme. This type of trip generally attracts an international mix of physically fit adventurers between ages 18 and 50. Although the operators listed below do not have fixed upper age limits for participants, those over 60 will likely be asked to complete a health questionnaire. Note that this practice is not limited to overland journeys; many companies follow this procedure when trips involve strenuous activities or roughing it.

Season: Year-round.
Locations: Throughout South America.
Cost: From $1,320 for 32 days from La Paz, plus $390 for a "kitty," which funds such expenses as camp food, group activities, and park entrance fees.
Tour Operators: Dragoman Overland; Exodus; G.A.P. Adventures; Gecko's.
These companies offer trips that cover most of South America, ranging in length from 4 to 22 weeks. Itineraries are typically composed of segments that you can take separately or combine into a longer trip. Most programs visit between three and nine countries.

PHOTO SAFARIS

An advantage of photo tours is the amount of time spent at each place visited. Whether the subject is a rarely spotted animal, a breathtaking waterfall, or villagers in traditional dress, you get a chance to focus both your camera and your mind on the scene before you. The tours listed below are led by professional photographers who offer instruction and hands-on tips. If you're not serious about improving your photographic skills, these trips might not be the best choice, as you could become impatient with the pace.

ANTARCTICA
Season: October; January and February.
Locations: Antarctic Peninsula; Falkland, South Georgia, and South Orkney Islands.
Cost: From 11,795 for 28 days from Ushuaia.
Tour Operator: Joseph Van Os Photo Safaris.
Photograph seabirds, Adélie and gentoo penguin colonies, albatross nesting areas, and elephant and fur seals, plus the spectacular landscapes of Antarctic. With Joseph Van Os you'll travel for 28 days aboard their research expedition ship *Ushuaia,* which carries its own fleet of Jacques Cousteau-designed Zodiac landing craft. Highlights include Paulet Island, home of Adélie penguin colonies, and cruising the Neumayer and Lemaire channels.

ARGENTINA & CHILE

Season: March and April.
Locations: Central Patagonia; Easter Island; Los Glaciares and Torres del Paine national parks.
Cost: From $5,395 for 15 days from Buenos Aires.
Tour Operators: Joseph Van Os Photo Safaris.
Timed for vibrant fall colors among ice fields, snowcapped mountains, glaciers, and rushing streams, Joseph Van Os has a 15-day departure during the Patagonian fall (during the months of the northern hemisphere's spring). The trip visits the famed sites of Torres del Paine and Los Glaciares national parks and lesser-known regions such as central Patagonia. They also offer an itinerary that splits two weeks in Easter Island and Cusco and Machu Picchu.

BRAZIL

Season: August
Locations: Iguaçu Falls; Pantanal; Atlantic Rain Forest; Caraça Natural Park; Chapada National Park; Caratinga Biological Station
Cost: $3,999 for 21 days
Tour Operator: Focus Tours
Focus Tours custom designs photo tours for groups. It also has a package tour that takes you to six unique Brazilian habitats to shoot wildlife up close. Each destination has a number of endemic species, and all are known as places with exceptional biodiversity. A maximum of six participants ensures that all have window seats in ground transportation. Highlights include the Pantanal, the largest freshwater wetlands on the planet, sparsely populated by humans but abundantly populated by animals. From small boats and other vehicles you can photograph jabiru storks, caimans, capybaras, marsh deer, giant anteaters, and, with luck, the camera-shy jaguar. The price includes meals, accommodations, land transportation, and a naturalist guide.

ECUADOR

Season: Year round.
Locations: Galápagos Islands.
Cost: From $4,150 for 10 days from Guayaquil.
Tour Operators: Lindblad Expeditions.
Confronted with the rugged landscapes and incredible array of unafraid wildlife, few visitors to the Galápagos leave without wishing they knew just a bit more about composing and executing that perfect image. Joining a photo expedition will ensure that you return home without such regrets. Lindblad's special photo departures utilize the 80-passenger ship *Polaris* to call at a number of islands known for such appealing photo subjects as sea lions, blue- and red-footed boobies, iguanas, and frigate birds.

PERU

Season: April and May.
Locations: Cusco; Machu Picchu; Tambopata Reserve.
Cost: From $2,885 for 10 days from Lima.
Tour Operators: Joseph Van Os Photo Safaris; Tours International.

Arguably the most photographed site in South America, Machu Picchu inspires more than the usual vacation photos. With each of these operators a professional photographer helps you determine the best angles and lighting for your images of the world's most famous Incan site. With Joseph Van Os you'll visit Cusco and the Incan citadel before jetting off to Chile's Easter Island. Tours International's photo journey is based at Tambopata Reserve, noted for its abundant wildlife, including some 500 bird species.

SPORTS

A sports-focused trip offers a great way to get a feel for the part of the country you're visiting and to interact with local people. A dozen bicyclists entering a village, for instance, would arouse more interest and be more approachable than a group of 30 stepping off a tour bus. Although many itineraries do not require a high level of skill, it is expected that your interest in the sport focused on in a particular tour be more than casual. On the other hand, some programs are designed for those who are highly experienced. In either case, good physical conditioning, experience with high altitudes (on certain itineraries), and a flexible attitude are important. Weather can be changeable, dictating the choices of hiking and climbing routes. If you're not a particularly strong hiker or cyclist, determine whether support vehicles accompany the group or alternate activities or turnaround points are available on more challenging days.

BICYCLING

ARGENTINA & CHILE

Season: October–March.

Locations: Atacama Desert; Bariloche; Lake District; Mendoza; Patagonia; Salta.

Cost: From $2,545 for eight days from San Carlos de Bariloche.

Tour Operators: Australian & Amazonian Adventures; Butterfield & Robinson; Experience Plus!; Global Adventure Guide.

Global Adventure's 15-day journey, graded moderate with some uphill challenges and occasional single-track riding, twice crosses the lower Andes as you ride along paved and dirt roads through forests and past volcanoes. The itinerary encompasses both the Lake District and Patagonia, with occasional options for rafting, canyoning, or volcano climbing. Nicknamed a "two-wheeled tango," Butterfield & Robinson's 9-day trip travels from Santiago, Chile, to Buenos Aires, Argentina (not totally by bike!), stopping in Chile's Atacama Desert and Argentina's wine country along the way. Starting in Bariloche, Experience Plus! cycles up to 93 km (58 mi) a day around Lake Llanquihue for views of volcanoes; there's also the chance for Class III rafting on Río Petrohué. Choose from four biking journeys with Australian & Amazonian Adventures, one to Chile's Lake District, another biking from Salta to San Miguel de Tucumán, and others traversing the Andes between the countries. Most nights are spent camping.

BOLIVIA

Season: July.

Locations: Altiplano; Lake Titicaca; La Paz; Zongo Valley.

Cost: From $2,800 for 12 days from Arica, Chile.

Tour Operator: Global Adventure Guide.

Bolivia is thought of as the be-all and end-all of South American mountain biking, and with Global Adventure's two itineraries you can discover why. A 12-day journey starts in the city of Arica, Chile, ascends one of the world's highest roads to traverse the Atacama Desert, crosses the border into Bolivia, and concludes in the capital, La Paz. The journey follows 16th-century trade routes, biking up to 68 km (41 mi) a day. The company's second program is a high-altitude training camp where you'll put in lots of road miles under the tutelage of a renowned sports coach. The route goes from sea level to an altitude of more than 4,707 meters (15,443 feet), and each night's location is selected to give incremental gains in altitude. This training camp is designed for experienced cyclists and triathletes under the eye of one of the world's top sports coaches, Dr John Hellemans.

ECUADOR

Season: June and July.

Locations: Avenue of the Volcanoes; Baños; Pulalahua Reserve; Quito.

Cost: From $525 for five days from Quito.

Tour Operators: Australian & Amazonian Adventures; Ibike/International Bicycle Fund.

Both of Ibike's programs begin with acclimatization in Ecuador's capital, Quito. From there one itinerary heads north to Imbabura Province, sightseeing among the region's markets, churches, pre-Columbian sites, and varied ecological zones. The second journey ranges from the Avenue of Volcanoes to the Amazon basin. A focus of both trips is people-to-people experiences. These trips are recommended for physically fit intermediate and expert cyclists. Australian & Amazonian Adventures offers two Ecuadorian programs, varying from four to five days. Bike through such beauty spots as Cotopaxi National Park, the Chota Valley, Pululahua Cloud Forest Reserve, and Quilotoa Crater Lake, stopping at Indian markets, waterfalls, and hot springs en route.

PERU

Season: May–October.

Locations: Amazon; Andes; Cusco; Machu Picchu.

Cost: From $1,799 for nine days from Cusco.

Tour Operators: BikeHike Adventures; KE Adventure Travel; Peru Bike.

All the above operators visit Machu Picchu. BikeHike Adventures uses all-terrain mountain bikes to explore a network of backcountry roads, dirt trails, villages, and ancient ruins in the Sacred Valley. On KE Adventures' 15-day journey, follow a network of Inca trails to cycle high in the Andes, only to make a seemingly endless 4,000-meter (13,000-foot) descent to a camp at the edge of Manu National Park. The biking is sometimes technical, always challenging. Peru Bike has numerous trips throughout the country, ranging from 6-day trips in

Cusco and the Sacred Valley and day trips in the coastal valleys near Lima to longer itineraries in the central jungle and Chachapoyas.

VENEZUELA
Season: Year-round.
Locations: Andes; La Grita Circuit.
Cost: $2,690 for 15 days from Caracas.
Tour Operator: KE Adventure Travel.
KE Adventure Travel focuses on Venezuela's Andes, including La Grita Circuit in the northwest of the country and various roads off the beaten track. You'll cover 50–60 mi daily for 15 days, while staying at camp-sites and hotels. It's a challenging trip, with hairpin descents and vicious climbs, including one to Paso del Aguila at 13,146 feet.

CANOEING, KAYAKING & WHITE-WATER RAFTING

White-water rafting and kayaking can be exhilarating experiences. You don't have to be an expert paddler to enjoy many of these adventures, but you should be a strong swimmer. Rivers are rated from Class I to Class V according to difficulty of navigation. Generally speaking, Class I–III rapids are suitable for beginners, while Class IV and V rapids are strictly for the experienced. Canoeing is a gentler river experience.

BRAZIL
Season: Year-round.
Location: Amazon.
Cost: $1,100 for eight days from Manaus.
Tour Operator: Swallows and Amazons.
Following a day's journey along the Río Negro, overnight in a small rain-forest lodge owned by Swallows and Amazons. The next day, set out on a six-day canoeing and camping adventure, exploring various tributaries and the lakes, channels, and flooded forest of the Anavil-hanas Archipelago. Hike, fish, swim, and visit the local river people, camping at night on beaches or in the jungle.

CHILE
Season: November–March.
Locations: Chiloé Archipelago; Northern Patagonia; Río Futaleufú.
Cost: From $680 for four days from Castro, in Chiloé.
Tour Operators: Adventure Life; Australian & Amazonian Expeditions; Earth River Expeditions; Hidden Trails; PanAmerican Travel Services.
Chile has both scenic fjords for sea kayaking and challenging rivers for white-water rafting. With PanAmerican Travel, sea kayakers can spend nine days exploring the fjords, waterfalls, and hot springs of the country's rugged coast, camping at night. Australian & Amazonian Adventures offers 3- to 6-day kayaking experiences. On the 4-day itinerary you'll discover the islands of the Chiloé Archipelago, a region rich in folklore, while the 6-day program explores the fjords of northern Patagonia. For the experienced rafter, the Class IV and V rapids of Río Futaleufú, often considered the best rapids in the world, offer many challenges. Its sheer-walled canyons boast such well-named rapids as Infierno and Purgatorio. Earth River's 10-day program here includes a

rock climb up 98-meter (320-foot) Torre de los Vientos and a Tyrolean traverse where, wearing a climbing harness attached to a pulley, you pull yourself across a rope strung above the rapids. With tree houses and riverside hot tubs formed from natural potholes, overnight camping becomes an exotic experience. Earth River also offers a kayaking journey over a chain of three lakes, surrounded by snowcapped mountains. Access is by floatplane. Hidden Trails and Adventure Life have Futaleufú rafting trips; the latter's program offers, in addition to shooting the rapids, horseback riding in the mountains, kayaking, and fishing.

ECUADOR
Season: Year-round.
Locations: Amazon basin; Galápagos; Oriente; Río Upano.
Cost: From $1190 for seven days from Quito.
Tour Operators: Australian & Amazonian Adventures; Hidden Trails; Remote Odysseys Worldwide (ROW); Small World Adventures.
Río Upano's Class II–IV rapids have become synonymous with world-class rafting. Experience these "big volume" rapids with Hidden Trails or Australian & Amazonian Adventures. Between the put-in site and the take-out 105 km (65 mi) later, the river will have tripled in volume. Australian & Amazonian also has rafting journeys on several other Class II and III Ecuadoran rivers such as the Toachi and Blanco. From Small World Adventures' lodge in the Oriente, you can kayak or raft more than 100 km (60 mi) of several rivers, including the Ouijos (Class III and IV) and Jondachi (Class IV and V). In just one day you'll run more than 25 rapids. This company operates multiple kayaking journeys as well. Australian & Amazonian Adventures has created kayaking programs along the Río Shiripuno into the land of the Huaorani people. Following 3–5 hours on the water daily, enjoy rainforest hikes, camping, and learning about local life from your Huaorani guide. Although several companies offer yacht-based kayaking on Galápagos itineraries, ROW has created the first true sea-kayaking trip here, camping on secluded beaches. Because of strict Ecuadoran government controls, the adventure was 10 years in the making, but it's now a reality.

PERU
Season: May–November.
Locations: Colca Canyon; Cotahuasi Canyon; Lake Titicaca; Río Apurímac; Río Tambopata.
Cost: From $524 for four days from Cusco.
Tour Operators: Australian & Amazonian Adventures; Earth River Expeditions; Myths and Mountains.
The moderate-to-difficult rapids of the Class III and IV Río Tambopata lead to the Tambopata-Candamo Reserve, while the wilder ride of the Class III–V Río Apurímac cuts through gorges and canyons under towering Andean peaks. Cotahuasi Canyon rafting takes you through Class IV and V white water on the Andes' western slopes. All three adventures can be booked with Australian & Amazonian Adventures. For serious rafters, the Class V Río Colca is one of the deepest and most

inaccessible canyons in the world. In fact, it has been termed the Everest of river canyons. Earth River takes you here and helps you master the challenges. Australian & Amazonian Adventures also travels to the world's highest navigable lake, Lake Titicaca, for 4- and 12-day kayaking trips and camping on its shores.

FISHING

ARGENTINA & CHILE

Season: Year round.
Locations: Chiloé; Lake District; Patagonia.
Cost: From $3,250 for seven days from Balmaceda, Chile.
Tour Operators: Fishing International; FishQuest; Fly Fishing And; PanAmerican Travel Services; Rod & Reel Adventures.

For anglers, Argentina and Chile are the southern hemisphere's Alaska, offering world-class trout fishing in clear streams. An added bonus is the availability of landlocked salmon and golden dorado, known as the river tiger. Bilingual fishing guides accompany groups, and accommodations are in comfortable lodges with private baths. Although November is the usual opening date for freshwater fishing, the season begins two months earlier at Lago Llanquihue because of the large resident fish population. Rod & Reel takes advantage of this, basing participants at a lodge near Osorno volcano. With Fly Fishing And, your 10 days will be divided between El Encuentro and La Patagonia lodges, meaning you can fish several rivers and creeks, while PanAmerican's seven-day program breaks up lodge stays with a night of riverside camping. Fishing International offers an Argentina program fishing the Ibera marshes for dorado and a Chile trip based at an *estancia* (ranch) where you can fish two rivers for brown trout weighing up to 15 pounds; they also organize trips to lodges throughout both countries, including Tierra del Fuego. FishQuest has four itineraries, offering fishing at a variety of rivers for brown and rainbow trout, dorado, giant catfish, and salmon.

BRAZIL

Season: September–May.
Location: Amazon.
Cost: From $2,495 for six days from Bélem.
Tour Operators: Augusto Albuquerque; Fishing International; FishQuest; Frontiers; G.A.P Adventures; Rod & Reel Adventures; Santana; Swallows and Amazons; Yanna Ecofishing.

Although pirapitinga, pirarucú, jancundá, and many other exotic fish inhabit the Amazon, it is the legendary peacock bass that anglers describe as the ultimate adversary. With Swallows & Amazons you can fish the Ríos Negro and Cuieiras plus several lakes, while based on a traditional riverboat with hammocks or mats for beds. Yanna Ecofishing has all the amenities of a typical upscale Amazon fishing company, including a luxury regional boat and small BassTracker fishing boats. Santana has well-run tucunaré sportfishing tours in Manaus that are popular with North Americans. Augusto Albuquerque runs a small operation setting up fishing tours for small groups to out-of-the-way places. Depending on the trip, your base will be a fishing camp, a five-star resort, or a comfortable live-aboard yacht. Fishing International will even take you by small plane to some very remote places. On Rod & Reel's Amazon trip you'll live aboard a comfortable 30-meter (100-foot) yacht while reeling in peacock bass. Frontiers offers several choices of accommodations on the Brazilian Amazon: a fly-fishing-only lodge, floating cabins, a luxury live-aboard riverboat, or a four-person houseboat with air-conditioned rooms and private baths. FishQuest also utilizes the floating cabins, as well as lodge and yacht accommodations. The company takes you to tributaries and lagoons where it's not uncommon to catch two- or three-dozen peacock bass per day. One itinerary focuses on an estuary known for pirarucú, the world's largest freshwater fish, known for its fighting spirit and long runs and leaps.

VENEZUELA

Season: Year-round.
Locations: Casiquiare watershed; La Guaira; Lake Guri; Los Roques; Río Caura.
Cost: From $1,995 for five days from Caracas.
Tour Operators: FishQuest; Frontiers.
Venezuela has an enviable reputation for both saltwater and freshwater fishing. Los Roques, an archipelago that's a short flight from Caracas, offers exciting bonefishing, while Guri Lake and Río Caura are top spots for peacock bass, some exceeding 15 pounds. Other challenges are the payara, described as "a salmon with a bad attitude," giant catfish, and the fierce aymara. Frontiers and FishQuest will take you to Los Roques. The latter company also operates packages to Río Caura, a tributary of the Orinoco; the Casiquiare watershed, where the chance of landing a trophy pavon in the 20-pound range compensates for some sacrifice of creature comforts; and La Guaira, off the northern coast, for the grand slam of fishing: billfish, blue and white marlin, and sailfish, as well as dolphin, wahoo, and tuna.

HIKING, RUNNING & TREKKING

South America's magnificent scenery and varied terrain make it a terrific place for trekkers and hikers. The southern part of Argentina and Chile, known as Patagonia, and Peru's Inca Trail are especially popular. Numerous tour operators offer hiking and trekking trips to these regions, so study several offerings to determine the program that's best suited to your ability and interests. The trips outlined below are organized tours led by qualified guides. Camping is often part of the experience, although on some trips you stay at inns and small hotels. Itineraries range from relatively easy hikes to serious trekking and even running.

ARGENTINA & CHILE

Season: October–April.
Locations: Atacama Desert; Lake District; Patagonia; Salta.
Cost: From $1,619 for 15 days from El Calafate, Argentina.
Tour Operators: Adventure Life; American Alpine Institute; Andes Adventures; Australian & Amazonian Adventures; BikeHike Adventures;

Butterfield & Robinson; Country Walkers; Geographic Expeditions; KE Adventure Travel; Mountain Travel Sobek; Southwind Adventures; The World Outdoors; Wilderness Travel; Wildland Adventures; World Expeditions.

Patagonia may be the most trekked region in South America. All the above companies have programs here, ranging from relatively easy hikes (Butterfield & Robinson, Country Walkers) to serious treks that gain up to 800 meters (2,625 feet) in elevation daily and ice and snow traverses using crampons (American Alpine Institute). Almost every operator runs tours to Torres del Paine in Chile and places just across the border around El Calafate, Argentina, often combining the two; just a few operate in Tierra del Fuego or the Southern Ice Fields (Wildland Adventures and Mountain Travel Sobek among them). Adventure Life's program lets you overnight in igloo-shape tents at EcoCamp in Torres del Paine. In addition to its hiking trip, Andes Adventures offers an 18-day running itinerary with runs of as much as 31 km (19 mi) per day. Other options include an Atacama Desert trek with KE Adventure Travel that includes an ascent of Licancabur Volcano or a Futaleufú Canyon trek with Wilderness Travel.

BOLIVIA

Season: March–October.

Locations: Cordillera Apolobamba; Cordillera Quimsa Cruz; Cordillera Real; Lake Titicaca.

Cost: From $1120 for seven days from La Paz.

Tour Operators: American Alpine Institute; Explore Bolivia; KE Adventure Travel; Mountain Madness; Mountain Travel Sobek; Wildland Adventures.

Bolivia's majestic mountain ranges offer some challenging treks. The extreme altitude makes the going even tougher, so operators allow time for acclimatization in La Paz, the world's highest capital, or at Lake Titicaca, the world's highest navigable lake. All the above companies have trekking itineraries ranging from 4 to 22 days through the 121 km (75 mi) of the Cordillera Real. On some journeys you'll cross up to six passes in excess of 4,500 meters (15,000 feet). In addition to its 22-day Cordillera Real trek, KE Adventures has a 17-day itinerary in the Cordillera Quimsa Cruz that features a four-day traverse beneath the west and north sides of Mt. Illimani, Bolivia's third-highest peak. Mountain Travel Sobek and Mountain Madness have a 14-day trans-Andean trek beginning in La Paz and ending in Santiago. Explore Bolivia offers 4-day treks in the Cordillera Real and Zongo Valley, as well as a 9-day trek in the Apolobamba range. On all ventures llamas or other pack animals will tote your gear, but you can expect to spend nights camping at high elevations.

BRAZIL

Season: Year-round.

Locations: Amazon basin; Bahia; Jau National Park; Rio de Janeiro.

Cost: From $466 for four days from Rio.

Tour Operators: Australian & Amazonian Adventures; G.A.P Adventures; Swallows and Amazons.

For an up-close jungle experience, join Swallows and Amazons for 11 days of trekking and camping in Jau National Park, during which you walk an average of six hours daily through thick vegetation, then relax at night in a jungle camp. This company also operates a 7-day hiking and camping adventure between the Rios Cuieiras and Jaraqui, focusing on jungle biodiversity, animal tracking, and jungle survival skills. Australian & Amazonian Adventures' itinerary centers around scenic Chapada Diamantina, in Bahia state, and the colonial city of Lençóis. You'll hike valleys, ravines, and mountains while exploring caves, waterfalls, natural chutes, and the region's heritage as a source of precious stones. A visit to a diamond prospecting ghost town is a highlight. G.A.P. Adventures runs longer (45 days or more) trekking tours that take you to the Pantanal, Iguaçu, and Rio.

ECUADOR

Season: Year-round.
Locations: Chimborazo, Cotopaxi, and Sangay national parks; Cuenca; Otavalo Valley; Riobamba.
Cost: From $1,309 for seven days from Quito.
Tour Operators: Andes Adventures; Australian & Amazonian Adventures; KE Adventure Travel; Mountain Travel Sobek; World Expeditions.

Two mountain ranges slice through Ecuador, making for some great trekking. Here you'll find the Avenue of Volcanoes, one of the largest concentrations of volcanoes in the world. Treks lead to glacier-clad peaks, national parks, and cloud forests. On Australian & Amazonian Adventures' "Volcanoes and Haciendas" program, each day's hike ends at a colonial hacienda, while World Expeditions combines seven days of trekking with day hikes, thermal springs, camping, and the exciting Devil's Nose train journey, where the best views are from the roof. Mountain Travel Sobek has a strenuous 11-day volcano trek with a maximum altitude of nearly 20,000 feet. On KE Adventure Travel's arduous 12-day trek you'll traverse river valleys, cross several 4,000-meter (13,000-foot) passes, and camp beside mountain lakes. With Andes Adventures, choose between 12 trekking or running routes in the country, ranging from 4 to 14 days over dramatic landscapes including volcanic craters, Amazon lowlands, or the stone steps of an Inca trail.

PERU

Season: April–November.
Locations: Blanca, Huayhusah, and Vilcabamba mountain ranges; Colca Valley; Inca Trail; Mt. Ausangate; Mt. Salcantay.
Cost: From $601 for four days from Cusco.
Tour Operators: Adventure Life; American Alpine Institute; Andes Adventures; Australian & Amazonian Adventures; Country Walkers; Experience Plus!; Gecko's; Geographic Expeditions; KE Adventure Travel; Mountain Madness; Mountain Travel Sobek; Peruvian Andes Adventures; Southwind Adventures; Tours International; Wilderness Travel; Wildland Adventures; World Expeditions.

The Inca Trail, stretching from the Urubamba Valley to Machu Picchu, has become one of South America's most popular destinations for trekkers. The 45-km (28-mi) mountain trail is mostly level, but the altitude makes it challenging. All the above companies offer Inca Trail treks. Several also lead more difficult Andean treks at altitudes in excess of 4,000 meters (13,000 feet), treks to other regions of the country such as the Mantaro Valley, Lares Valley, Cordillera Blanca, Ausangate, and alternative Inca trails. Each of these tour operators offers 3–7 trekking itineraries in Peru. In addition to treks, Andes Adventures has three running programs here, including a 44-km (27.5-mi) marathon and a circuit around Mt. Ausangate. Peruvian Andes Adventures focuses on the Cordillera Blanca and Huayhuash. In recent years a more diverse range of tours has trickled into many operators' repertoires as increased fees and severe overcrowding on the Inca Trail have meant many hikers are looking for alternatives. Mountain Travel Sobek and Country Walkers recently began offering the Machu Picchu Inn to Inn trek that is being raved about in almost every travel publication worldwide. The high-altitude trek stops each night in a comfortable lodge with excellent meals and hot showers and ends at Machu Picchu. Experience Plus! combines hiking in the Sacred Valley with a week-long trip cruising the Galápagos.

VENEZUELA
Season: Year-round.
Locations: Angel Falls; Canaima; Mérida; Mt. Roraima; Pico Bolivar.
Cost: From $759 for five days from Ciudad Bolivar.
Tour Operators: Australian & Amazonian Adventures; Explore! Worldwide; KE Adventure Travel; World Expeditions.
Trekkers often head to 2,810-meter (9,220-foot) Mt. Roraima, rumored to be the setting of Arthur Conan Doyles's *The Lost World.* All the above tour operators organize treks here, including a nontechnical ascent of the summit. With KE Adventure Travel your trip also features camping near Angel Falls, plus two days of relaxation on the islands of Los Roques. Australian & Amazonian Adventures itineraries spend several nights camping in the vicinity of Mt. Roraima or five days trekking to Angel Falls, while on World Expeditions' 11-day trip, enjoy a 5-day trek to and ascent of Venezuela's highest peak, Pico Bolívar. A six-day Roraima trek and a four-day journey by motorized canoe are part of Explore! Worldwide's 15-day adventure.

HORSEBACK RIDING

ARGENTINA
Season: Year-round, lower elevations; November–March, Andes.
Locations: Corrientes; Nahuel Huapi National Park; Lake District; Patagonia; Tunuyan Valley.
Cost: From $649 for six days from Mendoza.
Tour Operators: Boojum Expeditions; Equitours; Hidden Trails.
Few countries have a greater equestrian tradition than Argentina. Equitours introduces you to the country's gaucho culture at a 15,000-acre *estancia* (cattle ranch). You ride through the grasslands and beech forests of Lanin National Park and spend several nights camping. Hidden Trails offers eight itineraries in Argentina that explore the forests,

mountains, and lakes of Patagonia, the vast wilderness around Canyon del Diabolo, and the Serrucha mountain range, also several estancia-based adventures where you'll ride more than 32 km (20 mi) a day and, perhaps, join the gauchos as they round up cattle and horses. With Boojum Expeditions, ride sure-footed Criollo horses high in the mountains and along rugged trails. As the company warns, this is not a place to learn to ride.

BRAZIL

Season: Year-round
Locations: Highlands; Pantanal
Cost: From $1,445 for seven days from Campo Grande
Tour Operators: BikeHike Adventures; Hidden Trails

Observe the flora and fauna as you ride through the vast Pantanal with Hidden Trails on a "Wildlife Safari Ride" that includes picnics, camping, and ranch stays, plus sightseeing and a show in Rio. The company also has an eight-day "Aparados da Serra," where you journey the Serra Geral between Rio Grande do Sul and Santa Catarina. Meet local ranchers and gauchos and, perhaps, participate in a local rodeo. BikeHike Adventures incorporates horseback riding into its multisport excursions (⇨ *below*).

CHILE

Season: October–April; year-round, Atacama.
Locations: Atacama Desert; Patagonia; Easter Island; Río Hurtado Valley.
Cost: From $1,100 for six days from Rapa Nui.
Tour Operators: Equitours; Hidden Trails.

On Equitours's 12-day "Patagonia Glacier Ride" you cross the pampas to Torres del Paine National Park, a region of mountains, lakes, and glaciers. Nights are spent camping or in lodges. Hidden Trails has 15 itineraries: you can opt for a ride in southern Chile into the Andes along historic mule trails created by gold diggers; join an Atacama Desert adventure and ride over the crusted salt of the Salar de Atacama, across expanses of sand, and past ancient ruins and petroglyphs; explore moais, caves, craters, and beaches on Easter Island; or choose from four Patagonia programs. If getting off the beaten path appeals to you, consider the company's Glacier Camping Ride, which ventures into remote areas accessible only on foot or horseback.

ECUADOR

Season: Year-round.
Location: Andes; Avenue of Volcanoes.
Cost: From $795 for seven days from Quito.
Tour Operators: Equitours; Hidden Trails.

Journeying into the heart of the Eucadorean Andes, Hidden Trails' eight itineraries offer exciting rides through cloud forests, desertlike landscapes, high mountains, pastoral valleys, or along the famed Avenue of Volcanoes. In more remote areas overnights are in simple accommodations; otherwise, they are spent in historic haciendas, in some cases dating to the 17th century. One program stays on a working farm where you can join the *chagras* (Andean cowboys) in rounding up horses and cattle. On most trips expect to ride from four to eight hours per day. Equitours offers a hacienda-to-hacienda ride through the Zuleta Valley and Cotopaxi National Park, with elevations reaching 2,500–4,300 meters (8,000–14,000 feet).

PERU

Season: March–November.

Locations: Arequipa; Colca Canyon; Cusco; Leymebamba; Machu Picchu.

Cost: From $720 for three days from Cuzco.

Tour Operators: Australian & Amazonian Adventures; Equitours; Hidden Trails; Perol Chico.

Astride a Peruvian Paso horse, a breed dating to the colonial era that originated in Spanish Andalusia, explore the terraces of the Sacred Valley of the Incas and the ancient city of Machu Picchu on programs offered by Equitours and Hidden Trails. You'll also mingle with descendants of the Inca and learn about their culture. Another Hidden Trails itinerary combines Machu Picchu and the Sacred Valley with a descent into the Amazon and the Manu Bisophere Reserve. Perol Chico focuses on the Sacred Valley, Arequipa, and the Colca Canyon with trips from 4 to 12 days. With Australian & Amazonian Adventures, saddle up in the village of Leymebamba and head for the Lake of the Condors, a mystical place from which 219 well-preserved mummies were recovered in 1998. The trip also visits the fortress of Kuelap, called the Machu Picchu of the North, and the pyramids of Túcume.

URUGUAY

Season: Year-round.

Locations: Laguna Negra; Montevideo; Santa Teresa National Park.

Cost: From $1,950 for 15 days from Montevideo.

Tour Operators: Boojum Expeditions; Hidden Trails.

Uruguay's coastline boasts wide beaches dotted with small communities of artists and fishermen. With Boojum Expeditions, explore the unspoiled coastlines on Criollo and Spanish Barb horses accompanied by gaucho helpers on their 8-day Beach Ride. You'll overnight at cozy inns and take your meals in restaurants. This is a comfortable trip with no camping. Those with more time might combine this ride with Boojum's Patagonia journey for a "Coastline to Condors" adventure. Hidden Trails operates two rides in Uruguay. One itinerary includes eight days of riding across a traditional cattle-breeding area to the coast, with time to discover the diversity of wildlife at the UNESCO-designated Bañados del Este Biosphere Reserve. You'll stay in some of Uruguay's oldest and best-preserved haciendas. A second itinerary, based at two estancias, offers the chance to learn about rural activities and ride through a forest of *ombúes*, strange trees with thick, twisting branches spreading over the ground.

MOUNTAINEERING

Only the most towering peaks of Asia vie with the Andes in the challenges and rewards awaiting mountaineers. This is no casual sport, so ask questions, and be honest about your level of fitness and experience. Safety should be the company's—and your—first priority. Are the guides certified by professional organizations such as the American Mountain Guides Association? Are they certified as wilderness first responders and trained in technical mountain rescue? What is the climber-to-guide ratio? Are extra days built into the schedule to allow for adverse weather? Is there serious adherence to "leave no trace" environmental ethics? Several of the tour operators mentioned below have their own schools in the United States and/or other countries that offer multilevel courses in mountaineering, ice climbing, rock climbing, and avalanche education.

ANTARCTICA

Season: November–January.
Location: Mt. Vinson.
Cost: $29,500 for 22 days from Punta Arenas.
Tour Operator: Alpine Ascents International; Mountain Madness.
If you have a solid mountaineering background and are accustomed to cold-weather camping, this could be the ultimate mountaineering adventure. A short flight from Patriot Hills in Antarctica brings you to the base camp of Antarctica's highest peak. With loaded sleds, move up the mountain, establishing two or three camps before attempting the 4,897-meter (16,067-foot) summit of Mt. Vinson. Although the climb itself is considered technically moderate, strong winds and extreme temperatures, as low as -40°F, make this a serious challenge. Additionally, Alpine Ascents offers the chance to ski from the 89th to the 90th parallel. Aircraft will bring you within 70 mi of the South Pole; then ski the rest of the way. This unique adventure can be made independently or as an extension of the Vinson climb.

ARGENTINA & CHILE

Season: November–February.
Locations: Mt. Aconcagua.
Cost: From $2,980 for 11 days from Calafate, Argentina.
Tour Operators: Alpine Ascents International; American Alpine Institute; Colorado Mountain School; KE Adventure Travel; Mountain Madness; World Expeditions.
At 6,960 meters (22,835 feet), Argentina's Mt. Aconcagua is the highest peak in the world outside of a few in the Himalayas. Though some routes are not technically difficult, Aconcagua is quite demanding physically, and requires the use of ice axes, crampons, and ropes. All the above operators offer climbs of Aconcagua, some via the more difficult Polish glacier route; frequent high winds and ice make this route very challenging, and only for those with extensive mountaineering experience at high altitudes. American Alpine Institute has a second expedition with ascents of the Cerro Marconi Sur and Fitzroy massifs in southern Patagonia. On this program you'll also traverse part of the Patagonian Ice Cap.

11

BOLIVIA

Season: June–September.
Location: Cordillera Real.
Cost: From $2,700 for 11 days from La Paz.
Tour Operators: Alpine Ascents International; American Alpine Institute; Colorado Mountain School; KE Adventure Travel; Mountain Madness; World Expedtions.

Stretching for 160 km (100 mi), Bolivia's Cordillera Real has some of the continent's finest and most varied alpine climbing. Large crevasses and a glacial face at a 40- to 45-degree incline will challenge even those with lots of experience. Twenty-two mountains are 5,800 meters (19,000 feet) or higher, justifying Bolivia's designation as the Tibet of the Americas. The highest peak, Illimani, soars to 6,462 meters (21,201 feet). Most of the above operators offer climbs of Illimani. Other popular ascents include Ancohuma, Huayna Potosí, Illampu, and Pequeno Alpamayo. American Alpine Institute offers four Bolivian climbing itineraries, while Mountain Madness, in addition to climbs, operates a glacier mountaineering course here. World Expeditions' 17-day trip includes strenuous trekking, a few days on Lake Titicaca, and a 3-day attempt to summit Huayna Potosí. The climb is suitable for intermediate mountaineers in excellent physical condition who are familiar with the use of crampons and ice axes.

ECUADOR

Season: November–March.
Locations: Antisana; Cayambe; Chimborazo; Cotocachi; Cotopaxi; Illiniza Sur.
Cost: From $1,975 for 9 days from Quito.
Tour Operators: Alpine Ascents International; American Alpine Institute; Colorado Mountain School; KE Adventure Travel; Mountain Madness.

With challenges for all levels of ability, Ecuador's volcanoes have become a major destination for climbers. All the companies above organize climbs of 6,311-meter (20,701-foot) Chimborazo, 5,878-meter (18,996-foot) Cayambe, or 5,897-meter (19,347-foot) Cotopaxi. Chimborazo is the highest summit in Ecuador, Cayambe claims the tropics' most massive glaciers, and Cotopaxi is the second-highest active volcano on earth. Most itineraries attempt to summit three or four major volcanoes. In addition to the climbs mentioned above, American Alpine Institute and Colorado Mountain School have trips focusing on Artisana and Illiniza Sur. These are considered good expeditions for intermediate climbers. Mountain Madness operates 12-day climbing courses in Ecuador that are designed for beginners who want to learn the fundamentals of snow-, ice-, and glacier climbing.

PERU

Season: June–August.
Locations: Alpamayo; Ancocancha; Chopicalqui; Huascarán; Ishinca; Pisco Oeste; Toclaraju; Urus.
Cost: From $3,190 for 15 days from Lima.

Tour Operators: American Alpine Institute; Alpine Ascents International; Colorado Mountain School; Mountain Madness; Peruvian Andes Adventures.

Considered one of the world's most beautiful mountains, Alpamayo's pyramid-shape peak soars 5,947 meters (19,512 feet). Strong alpine skills are necessary for this climb, as is the ability to handle ice at a 60 degree incline. Huascarán, Peru's highest mountain at 6,768 meters (22,205 feet), has two extinct volcanic summits separated by a deep saddle. Prerequisites for Huascarán include high-altitude climbing experience and the ability to scale 45-degree ice with a full pack. The Peruvian Andes are the highest, most glaciated tropical mountains in the world. Even so, advanced beginners can handle some peaks here. All the above companies operate expeditions in the magnificent Cordillera Blanca. One of American Alpine Institute's four climbing programs in Peru is designed for beginner and intermediate levels.

MULTISPORT

Only a few years ago, multisport offerings were so sparse that the topic didn't merit inclusion in this chapter. Since then, such trips have grown in popularity every year, and now form an important part of the programs of many adventure tour operators. Innovative itineraries combine two or more sports, such as biking, fishing, canoeing, hiking, horseback riding, kayaking, rafting, and trekking.

ARGENTINA & CHILE
Season: November–April.
Locations: Lake District; northern Chile; Patagonia; Río Futaleufú, Chile.
Cost: From $1862 for 10 days from Buenos Aires, Argentina.
Tour Operators: American Alpine Institute; Australian & Amazonian Adventures; BikeHike Adventures; Earth River Expeditions; Hidden Trails; Mountain Madness; Mountain Travel Sobek; Nature Expeditions International; The World Outdoors; Wilderness Travel; World Expeditions.

Whether you choose the Lake District or Patagonia, the setting for your active vacation will be one of great beauty. Mountain Travel Sobek and Hidden Trails combine horseback riding with sea kayaking in Southern Patagonia, while Mountain Madness offers hut-to-hut trekking and glacier walking in the Torres del Paine area along with kayaking on the Río Serrano. With Nature Expeditions you'll have soft-adventure options most days, such as hiking, rafting (Class II and III rapids), and horseback riding. BikeHike has two multisport trips in Argentina and Chile; you can hike, raft, sea-kayak, bike, and ride horses in the Lake District or hike, ride horses, and sandboard in northern Chile. If you want to try serious rafting, consider one of the Río Futaleufú trips, such as those run by Earth River Expeditions and the World Outdoors; these programs also include hiking and horseback riding.

BOLIVIA

Season: June; August.

Locations: Altiplano; Cordillera Real; Lake Titicaca; Salar de Uyuni; Yungas Lowlands.

Cost: From $1,475 for nine days from La Paz.

Tour Operators: Explore Bolivia; Mountain Travel Sobek.

Bolivia's diverse topography means the chance to enjoy many outdoor sports. Explore Bolivia offers two adventures: a 14-day journey focuses on hiking (up to five hours a day) and rafting the Class II–IV rapids of the Río Tuichi, with most nights spent camping, while a second itinerary includes kayaking, hiking, and horseback riding with overnights divided between camps, hotels, and haciendas. Mountain Travel Sobek combines hikes in the Cordillera Real with 4WD tours in the Salar de Uyuni and northern Chile.

BRAZIL

Season: April–October.

Locations: Bonito; Rio de Janeiro; Serra do Cipó.

Cost: From $1,899 for nine days from Belo Horizonte.

Tour Operator: Australian & Amazonian Adventures; BikeHike Adventures; Mountain Travel Sobek; Swallows and Amazon.

Nearly a continent's worth of adventure on its own, Brazil has a multitude of landscapes, making it ideal for taking on a number of sports in one trip. BikeHike's 9-day adventure starts off with a 3-day trek through the Cipó mountain range, including an ascent of 1,676-meter (5,500-foot) Pico do Breu, followed by river kayaking, horseback riding across wide-open plains, and an 18-meter (60-foot) rappel down a waterfall. There's even an aerial zip-line running from forest into water; gear up in a harness and take off! Australian & Amazonian Adventures has come up with a fresh way to take in Rio's most famous sites. View Tijuca, the world's largest urban forest, by peddling through it on a mountain bike; follow a hiking path for about two hours, then make a 24-meter (80-foot) climb to stand atop that Rio landmark, Sugarloaf; kayak to Cotunduba Island for snorkeling and swimming, and climb four pitches (5.8 grade) to reach the top of Corcovado. Horseback riding, rafting, hang gliding, rappelling, and surfing are other options. With Mountain Travel Sobek you'll take a 3-day rafting trip down the Rio Novo, spend a few days hiking in the state of Tocantins, explore the beaches of Rio, and summit Sugarloaf. Swallows and Amazon's multisport trips include mountain biking, canyoning, snorkeling, and trekking in various locations.

ECUADOR

Season: Year-round.

Locations: Amazon basin; Andean Highlands; Galápagos; Ríos Arajuno, Jatunyacu, Quijos, and Toachi.

Cost: From $1,495 for nine days from Quito.

Tour Operators: Australian & Amazonian Adventures; Adventure Life; Austin-Lehman Adventures; BikeHike Adventures; G.A.P. Adventures; Mountain Travel Sobek; Myths and Mountains; Remote Odysseys Worldwide (ROW); The World Outdoors.

Ecuadorian multisport adventure locales range from the Amazon to the Andes to the Galápagos Islands. BikeHike Adventures' itineraries hit all three regions with a hiking, horseback-riding, biking, and sea-kayaking program in the Galápagos and an Andes-to-Amazon trip that takes in the first three sports mentioned plus rafting and an inner-tube float. G.A.P. has combined two days on mountain bikes, a three-day trek with camping, and three days of rafting the Class IV rapids of the Río Quijos. With Adventure Life, take a mountain trek, raft the Río Toachi, and try volcano biking, including at least one exhilarating descent down a steep slope. The World Outdoors's itinerary combines kayaking, biking, hiking, and horseback riding along the Avenue of Volcanoes and in the Galápagos, while Austin-Lehman Adventures, Mountain Travel Sobek, and ROW offer Galápagos sea-kayaking, snorkeling, and swimming, plus hiking up Sierra Negra Volcano and camping near the rim.

PERU

Season: April–December.
Location: Amazon; Andes; Lake Titicaca; northern Peru.
Cost: From $1,799 for seven days from Lima.
Tour Operators: Adventure Life; Austin-Lehman Adventures; Australian & Amazonian Adventures; BikeHike Adventures; Explore! Worldwide; G.A.P. Adventures; KE Adventure Travel; Mountain Travel Sobek; OutWest Global Adventures; The World Outdoors.

What better way to see it all than by horseback, mountain bike, or raft or on foot? Itineraries range from moderately easy to challenging, and run from 6 to 21 days. Although most programs feature Cusco, Machu Picchu, and a trek that includes at least part of the Inca Trail, KE Adventures and Adventure Life add time in the Amazon, and many companies include rafting on the Ríos Urubamba or Kosñipata. Australian & Amazonian Adventures has a variety of multisport itineraries in Peru. One combines hikes, horseback rides, and steep climbs in the country's north with visits to the cliff-side funerary statues at Karajia and the fortress of Kuelap, while another features hiking, biking, sea-kayaking, and sailing on Lake Titicaca. BikeHike's four 8- to 12-day programs all include mountain biking, horseback riding, and hiking; two feature rock climbing. With Austin-Lehman, you'll enjoy hiking, rafting (Class II and III rapids), horseback riding, and mountain biking while overnighting in upscale accommodations, including a museum hotel that was once a 16th-century monastery and was built on the foundation of an Inca palace.

VENEZUELA

Season: Year-round.
Location: Andes; La Culata National Park; Mérida State.
Cost: $2,199 for 12 days from Caracas.
Tour Operator: BikeHike Adventures.

Enjoy Venezuela's snowcapped mountains, cloud forests, and *páramo* tropical highlands as you bike and hike along backcountry roads and hidden trails and raft down rushing rivers. Such travel virtually guarantees interaction with village people, offering insights into their traditions. On BikeHike's 12-day itinerary you'll take part in the sports mentioned plus rock climbs and rappels. Bike up to 70 km (38 mi) per day at altitudes ranging from 762 to 4,023 meters (2,500 to 13,200 feet) and bounce through the Class III and IV rapids of the Río Siniguis.

11

SKIING & SNOWBOARDING

When ski season's over in the northern hemisphere, it's time to pack the gear and head for resorts in Argentina or Chile. Advanced and expert skiers will find seemingly endless terrain, and powder hounds will discover the ultimate ski. However, adventures aplenty await beginner and intermediate skiers as well. Snowboarders, too, will find the southern mountains much to their liking. In addition to marked trails, there's off-piste terrain, often with steep chutes and deep powder bowls, plus backcountry areas to try. Those with strong skills could opt for heliskiing on peaks reaching 4,200 meters (13,600 feet) as condors soar above. Many of the resorts exude a European ambience with a lively nightlife scene. The tour operators mentioned below have created all-inclusive ski packages covering airport–hotel and hotel–ski mountain transfers, accommodations, two meals daily, and lift tickets for a number of mountains and resorts in both Argentina and Chile; many packages combine the two countries. Costs vary with the accommodations selected. Prices quoted are per person double occupancy; costs are even lower if four persons share a room. Be aware that less expensive packages, while providing the services mentioned, generally are not guided tours. Eight-day guided packages start around $1,795.

ARGENTINA

Season: June–October.
Locations: Catedral Bariloche; Cerro Bayo; Chapelco; La Hoya-Esquel; Las Leñas.
Cost: From $2,495 for seven days from Bariloche.
Tour Operators: Ladatco Tours; PowderQuest Tours; Snoventures.
Argentina's Bariloche, an alpine-style resort town nicknamed Little Switzerland, is 13 km (8 mi) from the slopes of Cerro Catedral. This ski area offers more than 1,500 skiable acres with 105 km (65 mi) of trails and is a good choice for skiers of all levels. The resort is in the midst of a several-years expansion project that will double lift capacity and open new terrain. Your lift ticket is valid for skiing at both Catedral and the adjacent resort of Robles. Also accessed by a flight to Bariloche, the ski center of Cerro Bayo, on the northwestern tip of Lake Nahuel Huapi, is generally not crowded, and offers steep powder runs and excellent backcountry hiking. Some packages combine Catedral, Cerro Bayo, and La Hoya; the latter is a government-owned and -operated resort near the town of Esquel, where easy hikes lead to steep bowls and chutes, some with inclines of as much as 60 degrees. With 56 km (35 mi) of downhill trails and a vertical drop of 1,200 meters (4,000 feet), plus more than 100 couloirs (steep gullies) and vast off-piste and backcountry areas, Las Leñas is considered by many to be South America's premier ski destination. Appealing especially to the expert skier, Las Leñas has served as summer training ground for several Olympic ski

teams. Between Bariloche and Las Leñas near the resort town of San Martin de los Andes, Chapelco offers challenges for skiers and riders at all levels. The mountain claims access to great backcountry bowls. Ladatco Tours has a seven-day package to Catedral Bariloche, while PowderQuest and Snoventures have multiple offerings for all ski destinations mentioned with a wide variety of accommodation choices to suit most budgets. Many of their packages combine stays at two or more ski areas.

CHILE

Season: June–October.

Locations: El Colorado; La Parva; Portillo; Pucón; Termas de Chillán; Valle Nevado.

Cost: From $730 for a seven-day nonguided inclusive package from Santiago.

Tour Operators: Ladatco Tours; PowderQuest; Snoventures.

A short drive from Santiago, Valle Nevado has more than 300 acres of groomed runs and an 800-meter (2,600-foot) vertical drop. Famous for powder, it's also home to the Andes Express, a chair lift so super-fast you can get in extra runs each day. From Valle Nevado you can interconnect with the slopes of nearby El Colorado and La Parva, making for a vast amount of skiable terrain. First-rate heli-skiing, heli-boarding, and even hang gliding can be taken out of Valle Nevado; the off-piste is excellent, as well. A snowboard camp is based here coached by North American AASI level-three certified instructors. Participation in the seven-day program, divided into first-time and advanced groups, can be arranged by PowderQuest. Near the base of Mt. Aconcagua, the highest mountain in the western hemisphere, Portillo is ranked on numerous lists as one of the top 10 ski resorts in the world. Several national ski teams have their off-season training here. The heli-skiing is enviable, and Portillo's lively après-ski life comes as an added bonus. Yet another world-class resort, Termas de Chillán, has what one tour operator terms "killer slopes," plus a network of forest tracks for cross-country skiers. Its 28 runs along 35 km (22 mi) of groomed trails include one that at 13 km (6 mi) is South America's longest. Boasting one of Chile's deepest snow packs, the resort offers varied terrain on two volcanoes for skiing or snowboarding, plus a thermal area comprised of nine pools for end-of-the-day relaxation. At the small resort of Pucón, on the edge of Lago Villarrica, ski on the side of Chile's most active volcano. You can hike to the crater to gaze at molten magma, then ski or snowboard back down. Bordering two national parks plus a national reserve, Pucón boasts great snowshoeing. PowderQuest and Snoventures offer inclusive packages to all the resorts mentioned. Ski weeks without guides run in the $730–$800 range. PowderQuest's main focus is guided tours of 8–16 days, with time spent at as many as seven resorts in both Argentina and Chile. Ladatco offers packages to Valle Nevado, Portillo, and Chillán.

PORTUGUESE VOCABULARY

	ENGLISH	PORTUGUESE	PRONUNCIATION
BASICS			
	Yes/no	Sim/Não	**see**ing/nown
	Please	Por favor	pohr fah-**vohr**
	May I?	Posso?	**poh**-sso
	Thank you (very much)	(Muito) obrigado	(**mooy**n-too) o-bree **gah**-doh
	You're welcome	De nada	day **nah**-dah
	Excuse me	Com licença	con lee-**ssehn**-ssah
	Pardon me/what did you say?	Me desculpe/O que disse?	mee des-**kool**-peh/o.k. **dih**-say?
	Could you tell me?	Poderia me dizer?	po-day-**ree**-ah mee dee-**zehrr**?
	I'm sorry	Sinto muito	**seen**-too mooyn-too
	Good morning!	Bom dia!	bohn **dee**-ah
	Good afternoon!	Boa tarde!	**boh**-ah **tahr**-dee
	Good evening!	Boa noite!	**boh**-ah nohee-tee
	Goodbye!	Adeus!/Até logo!	ah-**deh**oos/ah-**teh loh**-go
	Mr./Mrs.	Senhor/Senhora	sen-**yor**/sen-**yohr**-ah
	Miss	Senhorita	sen-yo-**ri**-tah
	Pleased to meet you	Muito prazer	**mooy**n-too prah-**zehr**
	How are you?	Como vai?	**koh**-mo **vah**-ee
	Very well, thank you	Muito bem, obrigado	**mooy**n-too **beh**-in o-bree-**gah**-doh
	And you?	E o(a) Senhor(a)?	eh oh sen-**yor**(**yohr**-ah)
	Hello (on the telephone)	Alô	ah-**low**
NUMBERS			
	1	um/uma	oom/**oom**-ah
	2	dois	**doh**ees
	3	três	trehys
	4	quatro	**kwa**-troh
	5	cinco	**seen**-koh

ENGLISH	PORTUGUESE	PRONUNCIATION
6	seis	sehys
7	sete	**seh**-tee
8	oito	**ohee**-too
9	nove	**noh**-vee
10	dez	**deh**-ees
11	onze	**ohn**-zee
12	doze	**doh**-zee
13	treze	**treh**-zee
14	quatorze	kwa-**tohr**-zee
15	quinze	**keen**-zee
16	dezesseis	deh-zeh-**sehys**
17	dezessete	deh-zeh-**seh**-tee
18	dezoito	deh-**zoh**ee-toh
19	dezenove	deh-zeh-**noh**-vee
20	vinte	**veen**-tee
21	vinte e um	**veen**-tee eh **oom**
30	trinta	**treen**-tah
32	trinta e dois	**treen**-ta eh **doh**ees
40	quarenta	kwa-**rehn**-ta
43	quarenta e três	kwa-**rehn**-ta e **treh**ys
50	cinquenta	seen-**kwehn**-tah
54	cinquenta e quatro	seen-**kwehn**-tah e **kwa**-troh
60	sessenta	seh-**sehn**-tah
65	sessenta e cinco	seh-**sehn**-tah e **seen**-ko
70	setenta	seh-**tehn**-tah
76	setenta e seis	seh-**tehn**-ta e **seh**ys
80	oitenta	ohee-**tehn**-ta
87	oitenta e sete	ohee-**tehn**-ta e **seh**-tee
90	noventa	noh-**vehn**-ta
98	noventa e oito	noh-**vehn**-ta e **oh**ee-too
100	cem	**seh**-ing

ENGLISH	PORTUGUESE	PRONUNCIATION
101	cento e um	**sehn**-too e **oom**
200	duzentos	doo-**zehn**-tohss
500	quinhentos	key-**nyehn**-tohss
700	setecentos	seh-teh-**sehn**-tohss
900	novecentos	noh-veh-**sehn**-tohss
1,000	mil	meel
2,000	dois mil	**doh**ees meel
1,000,000	um milhão	oom mee-lee-**ahon**

DAYS OF THE WEEK

Sunday	Domingo	doh-**meehn**-goh
Monday	Segunda feira	se-**goon**-da **fey**-rah
Tuesday	Terça feira	**tehr**-sah **fey**-rah
Wednesday	Quarta feira	**kwahr**-tah **fey**-rah
Thursday	Quinta feira	**keen**-tah **fey**-rah
Friday	Sexta feira	**sehss**-tah **fey**-rah
Saturday	Sabado	**sah**-bah-doh

MONTHS

January	Janeiro	jah-**ney**-roh
February	Fevereiro	feh-veh-**rey**-roh
March	Março	**mahr**-soh
April	Abril	ah-**breel**
May	Maio	**my**-oh
June	Junho	**gyoo**-nyoh
July	Julho	**gyoo**-lyoh
August	Agosto	ah-**ghost**-toh
September	Setembro	se-**tehm**-broh
October	Outubro	owe-**too**-broh
November	Novembro	noh-**vehm**-broh
December	Dezembro	deh-**zehm**-broh

COLORS

Black	preto	**preh**-toh

ENGLISH	PORTUGUESE	PRONUNCIATION
blue	azul	a-**zool**
Brown	marrom	mah-**hohm**
Green	verde	**vehr**-deh
pink	rosa	**roh**-zah
Purple	roxo	**roh**-choh
Orange	laranja	lah-**rahn**-jah
red	vermelho	vehr-**meh**-lyoh
White	branco	**brahn**-coh
Yellow	amarelo	ah-mah-**reh**-loh

USEFUL PHRASES

Do you speak English?	Fala inglês?	**fah**-lah een-**glehs**?
I don't speak Portuguese.	Não falo portugues.	nown **fah**-loh pohr-too-**ghehs**
I don't understand (you)	Não lhe entendo	nown **lyeh** ehn-**tehn**-doh
I understand	Eu entendo	**eh**-oo ehn-**tehn**-doh
I don't know	Não sei	nown say
I am American/British	Sou americano (americana)/inglês (inglêsa)	sow a-meh-ree-**cah**-noh (a-meh-ree-**cah**-nah)/een-**glehs** (een-**gleh**-sa)
What's your name?	Como se chama?	**koh**-moh seh **shah**-mah
My name is . . .	Meu nome é . . .	mehw **noh**-meh eh
What time is it?	Que horas são?	keh **oh**-rahss **sa**-ohn
It is one/two/three . . . o'clock	É uma/São duas, três . . .hora/horas	eh **oom**-ah/**sa**-ohn **doo**-ahss, treys **oh**-rah/**oh**-rahs
Yes, please/No, thank you	Sim por favor/Não obrigado	seing pohr fah-**vohr**/ nown o-bree-**gah**-doh
How?	Como?	**koh**-moh
When?	Quando?	**kwahn**-doh
This/Next week	Este/próxima semana	**ehss**-tah/**proh**-see-mah se-**mah**-nah
This/Next month	Este/próximo mêz	**ehss**-te/**proh**-see-moh mehz

ENGLISH	PORTUGUESE	PRONUNCIATION
This/Next year	Este/próximo ano	**ehss**-te/**proh**-see-moh **ah**-noh
Yesterday/today/ tomorrow	Ontem/hoje/amanhã	**ohn**-tehn/**oh**-jeh/ ah-mah-**nyan**
This morning/afternoon	Esta manhã/tarde	**ehss**-tah mah-**nyan**/**tahr**-deh
Tonight	Hoje a noite	**oh**-jeh ah **noh**ee-tee
What?	O que?	oh **keh**
What is it?	O que é isso?	oh **keh** eh **ee**-soh
Why?	Por quê?	pohr **keh**
Who?	Quem?	**keh**-in
Where is . . .?	Onde é . . .?	**ohn**-deh eh
the train station?	a estação de trem?	ah es-tah-**sah**-on deh train
the subway station?	a estação de metrô?	ah es-tah-**sah**-on deh meh-**tro**
the bus stop?	a parada do ônibus?	ah pah-**rah**-dah doh **oh**-nee-boos
the post office?	o correio?	oh coh-**hay**-yoh
the bank?	o banco?	oh **bahn**-koh
the hotel?	o hotel . . .?	oh oh-**tell**
the cashier?	o caixa?	oh **kahy**-shah
the museum?	o museo?	oh moo-**zeh**-oh
the hospital?	o hospital?	oh ohss-pee-**tal**
the elevator?	o elevador?	oh eh-leh-vah-**dohr**
the bathroom?	o banheiro?	oh bahn-**yey**-roh
the beach?	a praia de . . .?	ah **prahy**-yah deh
Here/there	Aqui/ali	ah-**kee**/ah-**lee**
Open/closed	Aberto/fechado	ah-**behr**-toh/ feh-**shah**-doh
Left/right	Esquerda/direita	ehs-**kehr**-dah/ dee-**ray**-tah
Straight ahead	En frente	ehyn **frehn**-teh
Is it near/far?	É perto/longe?	eh **pehr**-toh/**lohn**-jeh

ENGLISH	PORTUGUESE	PRONUNCIATION
I'd like to buy . . .	Gostaria de comprar . . .	goh-tah-**ree**-ah deh cohm-**prahr**
a bathing suit	um maiô	oom mahy-**owe**
a dictionary	um dicionário	oom dee-seeoh-**nah**-reeoh
a hat	um chapéu	oom shah-**peh**-oo
a magazine	uma revista	**oo**mah hev-**vees**-tah
a map	um mapa	oom **mah**-pah
a postcard	cartão postal	kahr-**town** pohs-**tahl**
sunglasses	óculos escuros	**ah**-koo-loss ehs-**koo**-rohs
suntan lotion	um óleo de bronzear	oom **oh**-lyoh deh brohn-zeh-**ahr**
a ticket	um bilhete	oom bee-lye**h**-teh
cigarettes	cigarros	see-**gah**-hose
envelopes	envelopes	eyn-veh-**loh**-pehs
matches	fósforos	**fohs**-for-rohss
paper	papel	pah-**pehl**
sandals	sandália	sahn-**dah**-leeah
soap	sabonete	sah-bow-**neh**-teh
How much is it?	Quanto custa?	**kwahn**-too **koos**-tah
It's expensive/cheap	Está caro/barato	ehss-**tah** **kah**-roh/bah-**rah**-toh
A little/a lot	Um pouco/muito	oom **pohw**-koh/**mooy**n-too
More/less	Mais/menos	**mah**-ees/**meh**-nohss
Enough/too much/too little	Suficiente/demais/ muito pouco	soo-fee-see-**ehn**-teh/ deh-**mah**-ees/**mooy**n-toh **pohw**-koh
Telephone	Telefone	teh-leh-**foh**-neh
Telegram	Telegrama	teh-leh-**grah**-mah
I am ill.	Estou doente.	ehss-**tow** doh-**ehn**-teh
Please call a doctor.	Por favor chame um medico.	pohr fah-**vohr** shah-meh oom **meh**-dee-koh
Help!	Socorro!	soh-**koh**-ho

ENGLISH	PORTUGUESE	PRONUNCIATION
Help me!	Me ajude!	mee ah-**jyew**-deh
Fire!	Incêndio!	een-**sehn**-deeoh
Caution!/Look out!/ Be careful!	Cuidado!	kooy-**dah**-doh

ON THE ROAD

Avenue	Avenida	ah-veh-**nee**-dah
Highway	Estrada	ehss-**trah**-dah
Port	Porto	**pohr**-toh
Service station	Posto de gasolina	**pohs**-toh deh gah-zoh-**lee**-nah
Street	Rua	**who**-ah
Toll	Pedagio	peh-**dah**-jyoh
Waterfront promenade	Beiramar/orla	behy-rah-**mahrr/ohr**-lah
Wharf	Cais	**kah**-ees

IN TOWN

Block	Quarteirão	kwahr-tehy-**rah**-oh
Cathedral	Catedral	kah-teh-**drahl**
Church/temple	Igreja	ee-**greh**-jyah
City hall	Prefeitura	preh-fehy-**too**-rah
Door/gate	Porta/portão	**pohr**-tah/pohr-**tah**-on
Entrance/exit	Entrada/saída	ehn-**trah**-dah/ sah-**ee**-dah
Market	Mercado/feira	mehr-**kah**-doh/**fey**-rah
Neighborhood	Bairro	**buy**-ho
Rustic bar/snack bar	Lanchonete	lahn-shoh-**neh**-teh
Shop	Loja	**loh**-jyah
Square	Praça	**prah**-sah

DINING OUT

A bottle of . . .	Uma garrafa de . . .	**oo**mah gah-**hah**-fah deh
A cup of . . .	Uma xícara de . . .	**oo**mah **shee**-kah-rah deh
A glass of . . .	Um copo de . . .	oom **koh**-poh deh

ENGLISH	PORTUGUESE	PRONUNCIATION
Ashtray	Um cinzeiro	oom seen-**zehy**-roh
Bill/check	A conta	ah **kohn**-tah
Bread	Pão	**pah**-on
Breakfast	Café da manhã	kah-**feh** dah mah-**nyan**
Butter	A manteiga	ah mahn-**tehy**-gah
Cheers!	Saúde!	sah-**oo**-deh
Cocktail	Um aperitivo	oom-ah-peh-ree-**tee**-voh
Dinner	O jantar	oh **jyahn**-tahr
dish	Um prato	oom **prah**-toh
Enjoy!	Bom apetite!	bohm ah-peh-**tee**-teh
Fork	Um garfo	oom **gahr**-foh
Fruit	Fruta	**froo**-tah
Is the tip included?	A gorjeta esta incluída?	ah gohr-**jyeh**-tah ehss-**tah** een-clue-**ee**-dah
Juice	Um suco	oom **soo**-koh
Knife	Uma faca	oomah **fah**-kah
Lunch	O almoço	oh ahl-**moh**-ssoh
Menu	Menu/cardapio	me-**noo**/kahr-**dah**-peeoh
Mineral water	Água mineral	**ah**-gooah-mee-neh-**rahl**
Napkin	Guardanapo	gooahr-dah-**nah**-poh
No smoking	Não fumante	nown foo-**mahn**-teh
Pepper	Pimenta	pee-**mehn**-tah
Please give me	Por favor me dê	pohr fah-**vohr** mee deh
Salt	Sal	sahl
Smoking	Fumante	foo-**mahn**-teh
Spoon	Uma colher	**oo**mah koh-ly**ehr**
Sugar	Açucar	ah-**soo**-kahr
Waiter	Garçon	gahr-**sohn**
Wine	Vinho	**vee**-nyoh

SPANISH VOCABULARY

	ENGLISH	SPANISH	PRONUNCIATION
BASICS			
	Yes/no	Sí/No	see/no
	Please	Por favor	pore fah-**vore**
	May I?	¿Me permite?	may pair-**mee**-tay
	Thank you (very much)	(Muchas) gracias	(**moo**-chas) **grah**-see-as
	You're welcome	De nada	day **nah**-dah
	Excuse me	Con permiso	con pair-**mee**-so
	Pardon me	¿Perdón?	pair-**dohn**
	Could you tell me?	¿Podria decirme?	po-dree-ah deh-**seer**-meh
	I'm sorry	Lo siento	loh see-**en**-to
	Good morning!	¡Buenos dias!	**bway**-nohs **dee**-ahs
	Good afternoon!	¡Buenas tardes!	**bway**-nahs **tar**-dess
	Good evening!	Buenas noches!	**bway**-nahs **no**-chess
	Goodbye!	¡Adiós!/¡Hasta luego!	ah-dee-**ohss/ah**-stah **lwe**-go
	Mr./Mrs.	Señor/Señora	sen-**yor**/sen-**yohr**-ah
	Miss	Señorita	sen-yo-**ree**-tah
	Pleased to meet you	Mucho gusto	**moo**-cho **goose**-to
	How are you?	¿Cómo esta usted?	**ko**-mo es-**tah** oo-**sted**
	Very well, thank you	Muy bien, gracias.	**moo**-ee bee-**en**, **grah**-see-ahs
	And you?	¿Y usted?	ee oos-**ted**
	Hello (on the telephone)	Diga	**dee**-gah
NUMBERS			
	1	un, uno	oon, **oo**-no
	2	dos	dos
	3	tres	tress
	4	cuatro	**kwah**-tro
	5	cinco	**sink**-oh
	6	seis	saice

ENGLISH	SPANISH	PRONUNCIATION
7	siete	see-**et**-eh
8	ocho	**o**-cho
9	nueve	new-**eh**-vey
10	diez	dee-**es**
11	once	**ohn**-seh
12	doce	**doh**-seh
13	trece	**treh**-seh
14	catorce	ka-**tohr**-seh
15	quince	**keen**-seh
16	dieciséis	dee-**es**-ee-**saice**
17	diecisiete	dee-**es**-ee-see-**et**-eh
18	dieciocho	dee-**es**-ee-**o**-cho
19	diecinueve	dee-**es**-ee-new-**ev**-ah
20	veinte	**vain**-teh
21	veinte y uno/ veintiuno	**vain**-te-**oo**-noh
30	treinta	**train**-tah
32	treinta y dos	train-tay-**dohs**
40	cuarenta	kwah-**ren**-tah
43	cuarenta y tres	kwah-**ren**-tay-**tress**
50	cincuenta	seen-**kwen**-tah
54	cincuenta y cuatro	seen-**kwen**-tay **kwah**-tro
60	sesenta	sess-**en**-tah
65	sesenta y cinco	sess-**en**-tay **seen**-ko
70	setenta	set-**en**-tah
76	setenta y seis	set-**en**-tay **saice**
80	ochenta	oh-**chen**-tah
87	ochenta y siete	oh-**chen**-tay see-**yet**-eh
90	noventa	no-**ven**-tah
98	noventa y ocho	no-**ven**-tah-**o**-choh
100	cien	see-**en**
101	ciento uno	see-**en**-toh **oo**-noh

ENGLISH	SPANISH	PRONUNCIATION
200	doscientos	doh-see-**en**-tohss
500	quinientos	keen-**yen**-tohss
700	setecientos	set-eh-see-**en**-tohss
900	novecientos	no-veh-see-**en**-tohss
1,000	mil	meel
2,000	dos mil	dohs meel
1,000,000	un millón	oon meel-**yohn**

DAYS OF THE WEEK

Sunday	domingo	doe-**meen**-goh
Monday	lunes	**loo**-ness
Tuesday	martes	**mahr**-tess
Wednesday	miércoles	me-**air**-koh-less
Thursday	jueves	hoo-**ev**-ess
Friday	viernes	vee-**air**-ness
Saturday	sábado	**sah**-bah-doh

MONTHS

January	enero	eh-**neh**-roh
February	febrero	feh-**breh**-roh
March	marzo	**mahr**-soh
April	abril	ah-**breel**
May	mayo	**my**-oh
June	junio	**hoo**-nee-oh
July	julio	**hoo**-lee-yoh
August	agosto	ah-**ghost**-toh
September	septiembre	sep-tee-**em**-breh
October	octubre	oak-**too**-breh
November	noviembre	no-vee-**em**-breh
December	diciembre	dee-see-**em**-breh

COLORS

black	negro	**neh**-groh
blue	azul	ah-**sool**
brown	café	kah-**feh**

ENGLISH	SPANISH	PRONUNCIATION
green	verde	**ver**-deh
pink	rosa	**ro**-sah
purple	morado	mo-**rah**-doh
orange	naranja	na-**rahn**-hah
red	rojo	**roh**-hoh
white	blanco	**blahn**-koh
yellow	amarillo	ah-mah-**ree**-yoh

USEFUL PHRASES

Do you speak English?	¿Habla usted inglés?	**ah**-blah oos-**ted** in-**glehs**
I don't speak Spanish.	No hablo español.	no **ah**-bloh es-pahn-**yol**
I don't understand (you)	No entiendo	no en-tee-**en**-doh
I understand (you)	Entiendo	en-tee-**en**-doh
I don't know	No sé	no seh
I am American/British	Soy americano (americana)/inglés(a)	soy ah-meh-ree-**kah**-no (ah-meh ree-**kah**-nah)/in-**glehs**(ah)
What's your name?	¿Cómo se llama usted?	**koh**-mo seh **yah**-mah oos-**ted**
My name is . . .	Me llamo . . .	may **yah**-moh
What time is it?	¿Qué hora es?	keh **o**-rah es
It is one/two/three . . . o'clock	Es la una . . .Son las dos, tres	es la **oo**-nah/sohn lahs dohs, tress
Yes, please/No, thank you	Si, por favor/No, gracias	**see**, pohr fah-**vor**/no **grah**-see-us
How?	¿Cómo?	**koh**-mo
When?	¿Cuando?	**kwahn**-doh
This/Next week	Esta semana/la semana que entra	es-teh seh-**mah**-nah/ lah seh-**mah**-nah keh **en**-trah
This/Next month	Este mes/el próximo mes	**es**-teh mehs/el **proke**-see-moh mehs
This/Next year	Este año/el año que viene	**es**-teh **ahn**-yo/el **ahn**-yo keh vee-**yen**-ay

ENGLISH	SPANISH	PRONUNCIATION
Yesterday/today/tomorrow	Ayer/hoy/mañana	ah-**yehr**/oy/mahn-**yah**-nah
This morning/afternoon	Esta mañana/tarde	**es**-tah mahn-**yah**-nah/**tar**-deh
Tonight	Esta noche	**es**-tah **no**-cheh
What?	¿Qué?	keh
What is it?	¿Qué es esto?	keh es **es**-toh
Why?	¿Por qué?	pore **keh**
Who?	¿Quién?	kee-**yen**
Where is . . .?	¿Dónde está . . .?	**dohn**-deh es-**tah**
the train station?	la estación del tren?	la es-tah-see-**on** del **train**
the subway station?	la estación del tren subterráneo?	la es-tah-see-**on** del train soob-tair-**ron**-a-o
the bus stop?	la parada del autobus?	la pah-**rah**-dah del oh-toh-**boos**
the post office?	la oficina de correos?	la oh-fee-**see**-nah deh koh-**reh**-os
the bank?	el banco?	el **bahn**-koh
the hotel?	el hotel?	el oh-**tel**
the store	la tienda?	la tee-**en**-dah
the cashier?	la caja?	la **kah**-hah
the museum?	el museo?	el moo-**seh**-oh
the hospital?	el hospital?	el ohss-pee-**tal**
the elevator?	el ascensor?	el ah-**sen**-sohr
the bathroom?	el baño?	el **bahn**-yoh
Here/there	Aquí/allá	ah-**key**/ah-**yah**
Open/closed	Abierto/cerrado	ah-bee-**er**-toh/ser-**ah**-doh
Left/right	Izqierda/derecha	iss-key-**er**-dah/dare-**eh**-chah
Straight ahead	Derecho	dare-**eh**-choh
Is it near/far?	¿Esta cerca/lejos?	es-**tah** **sehr**-kah/**leh**-hoss

ENGLISH	SPANISH	PRONUNCIATION
I'd like . . .	Quisiera . . .	kee-see-**ehr**-ah
a room	un cuarto/una habitacion	oon **kwahr**-toh/**oo**-nah ah-bee-tah-see-**on**
the key	la llave	lah **yah**-veh
a newspaper	un periódico	oon pehr-ee-**oh**-de-koh
a stamp	un sello de correo	oon **seh**-yoh deh koh-**reh**-oh
I'd like to buy . . .	Quisiera comprar . . .	kee-see-**ehr**-ah kohm-**prahr**
cigarettes	cigarillos	ce-ga-**ree**-yohs
matches	cerillos	ser-**ee**-ohs
a dictionary	un diccionario	oon deek-see-oh-**nah**-ree-oh
soap	jabón	hah-**bohn**
sunglasses	gafas de sol	**ga**-fahs deh sohl
suntan lotion	loción bronceadora	loh-see-**ohn** brohn-seh-ah-**do**-rah
a map	un mapa	oon **mah**-pah
a magazine	una revista	**oon**-ah reh-**veess**-tah
paper	papel	pah-**pel**
envelopes	sobres	**so**-brehs
a postcard	una tarjeta postal	**oon**-ah tar-**het**-ah post-**ahl**
How much is it?	¿Cuánto cuesta?	**kwahn**-toh **kwes**-tah
It's expensive/cheap	¿Está caro/barato?	**es**-tah **kah**-roh/bah-**rah**-toh
A little/a lot	Un poquito/mucho	oon poh-**kee**-toh/**moo**-choh
More/less	Más/menos	mahss/**men**-ohss
Enough/too much/too little	Suficiente/desmasiado/ muy poco	soo-fee-see-**en**-teh/deh-mah-see-**ah**-doh/**moo**-ee **poh**-koh
Telephone	Teléfono	tel-**ef**-oh-no
Telegram	Telegrama	teh-leh-**grah**-mah
I am ill.	Estoy enfermo(a)	es-**toy** en-**fehr**-moh(mah)

ENGLISH	SPANISH	PRONUNCIATION
Please call a doctor.	Por favor llame a un medico	pohr fah-**vor ya**-meh ah oon **med**-ee-koh
Help!	¡Auxilio! ¡Ayuda! ¡Socorro!	owk-**see**-lee-oh/ah-**yoo**-dah/soh-**kohr**-roh
Fire!	¡Incendio!	en-**sen**-dee-oo
Caution!/Look out!	¡Cuidado!	kwee-**dah**-doh

ON THE ROAD

Avenue	Avenida	ah-ven-**ee**-dah
Broad, tree-lined boulevard	Bulevar	boo-leh-**var**
Fertile plain	Vega	**veh**-gah
Highway	Carreterra	car-reh-**ter**-ah
Mountain pass	Puerto	poo-**ehr**-toh
Street	Calle	**cah**-yeh
Waterfront promenade	Rambla	**rahm**-blah
Wharf	Embarcadero	em-bar-cah-**deh**-ro

IN TOWN

Cathedral	Catedral	kah-teh-**drahl**
Church	Templo/iglesia	**tem**-plo/ee-**glehs**-see-ah
City hall	Casa do gobierno	**kah**-sah deh go-bee-**ehr**-no
Door/gate	Puerta/portón	poo-**ehr**-tah por-**ton**
Entrance/exit	Entrada/salida	en-**trah**-dah/sah-**lee**-dah
Inn, rustic bar, or restaurant	Taverna	tah-**vehr**-nah
Main square	Plaza principal	plah-thah prin-see-**pahl**
Market	Mercado	mer-**kah**-doh
Neighborhood	Barrio	**bahr**-ree-o
Traffic circle	Glorieta	glor-ee-**eh**-tah
Wine cellar, wine bar, or wine shop	Bodega	boh-**deh**-gah

DINING OUT

A bottle of . . .	Una botella de . . .	**oo**-nah bo-**teh**-yah deh

ENGLISH	SPANISH	PRONUNCIATION
A cup of . . .	Una taza de . . .	**oo**-nah **tah**-thah deh
A glass of . . .	Un vaso de . . .	oon **vah**-so deh
Ashtray	Un cenicero	oon sen-ee-**seh**-roh
Bill/check	La cuenta	lah **kwen**-tah
Bread	El pan	el pahn
Breakfast	El desayuno	el deh-sah-**yoon**-oh
Butter	La mantequilla	lah man-teh-**key**-yah
Cheers!	¡Salud!	sah-**lood**
Cocktail	Un aperitivo	oon ah-pehr-ee-**tee**-voh
Dinner	La cena	lah **seh**-nah
dish	Un plato	oom **plah**-toh
Menu of the day	Menú del día	meh-**noo** del **dee**-ah
Enjoy!	¡Buen provecho!	bwehn pro-**veh**-cho
Fixed-price menu	Menú fijo o turistico	meh-**noo fee**-hoh oh too-**ree**-stee-coh
Fork	El tenedor	el ten-eh-**dor**
Is the tip included?	¿Está incluida la propina?	es-**tah** in-cloo-**ee**-dah lah pro-**pee**-nah
Knife	El cuchillo	el koo-**chee**-yo
Large portions of savory snacks	Raciones	rah-see-**oh**-nehs
Lunch	La comida	lah koh-**mee**-dah
Menu	La carta, el menu	lah **cart**-ah, el meh-**noo**
Napkin	La servilleta	lah sehr-vee-**yet**-ah
Pepper	La pimienta	lah pee-me-**en**-tah
Please give me	Por favor déme	pore fah-**vor deh**-meh
Salt	La sal	lah sahl
Savory snacks	Tapas	**tah**-pahs
Spoon	Una cuchara	oo-nah koo-**chah**-rah
Sugar	El azucar	el ah-**thu**-kar
Waiter!/Waitress!	¡Por favor Señor/Señorita!	pohr fah-**vor** sen-**yor**/sen-yor-**ee**-tah

INDEX

Photo Credits: 8, *javarman/Shutterstock.* 9 *(left), Robert Wróblewski/Shutterstock.* 9 (right), *Simple-Foodie.* 10 (top), *Colman Lerner Gerardo/Shutterstock.* 10 (bottom), *Jamie Carroll/iStockphoto.* 11, *Tom Higgins/Shutterstock.* 12, *Giulio Andreini/Marka/age fotostock.* 13 (left), *Alan Kearney/viestiphoto.com.* 13 (right), *Bill Murray/viestiphoto.com.* 14, *Joe Viesti/viestiphoto.com.*

NOTES

NOTES

ABOUT OUR WRITERS

ADVENTURE & LEARNING VACATIONS

Nicholas Gill, who updated the Adventure Vacations chapter, is a food and travel writer and photographer based in both Lima, Peru, and New York City. He has authored and contributed to numerous guidebooks on Latin America.

ARGENTINA

Expat writers Brian Byrnes, Andy Footner, and Victoria Patience put their considerable experience and talent to work covering their adopted home of Buenos Aires. Victoria also covered the side trips from the city. Eddy Ancinas, who's married to an Argentine and who visits the country frequently, covered Mendoza and the Lakes District. David Miller, Tim Patterson, and Johnathan Yevin are the team of intrepid writers who covered southern and Atlantic Patagonia.

BOLIVIA

Paul Kaye, who updated the Bolivia chapter, was born on the south coast of England but got as far away as possible as soon as he could. He first came to Bolivia in 1998 and took about two weeks to fall in love with the country. Like all relationships, this affair has had its ups and downs, with the Salar de Uyuni, his own marriage, and the mountains of the Cordillera amongst the highs, and anything involving traffic, politics, bureaucracy or portly little policemen amongst the lows.

BRAZIL

Writers and adventurers Lucy Bryson, Doug Gray, Katya Hodge, and Stephen Silva teamed up to complete the Rio de Janeiro section, while Alastair Thompson tackled Side Trips from Rio. Ana Cristina, Daniel Corry, and Simon Tarmo updated São Paulo and Side Trips from São Paulo. Fulbright scholar and PhD candidate Anna Katsnelson singlehandedly explored Salvador, the Bahia coast, and the Amazon. All of the writers are hard-core Brazilophiles.

CHILE

In Chile, Ruth Bradley updated the Santiago chapter while carrying out her duties as a correspondent for *The Economist*. Tom Azzopardi, a journalist who lives in Santiago but dreams of the beach, updated Valparaíso and Viña del Mar. Margaret Snook took on the update for the Central Valley wineries. The longtime Chile resident and freelance journalist Jimmy Langman covered Chiloé, the Lake District, and the South Coast. Jonathan Yevin updated Tierra del Fuego.

COLOMBIA

With over six years' experience in Latin America under his belt, British-born freelance journalist Richard McColl moved to Colombia, citing the country as the last true frontier in South America. When he's not filing stories for various news outlets and magazines in the United Kingdom and the United States, he works as a freelance expedition guide in Bolivia, Brazil, Ecuador and Peru, and takes his downtime on the much-overlooked Colombian Pacific coast or at his colonial house in the Colombian town of Mompos.

ECUADOR, PARAGUAY & URUGUAY

In addition working on the Peru chapter, Central America–based writer and Wisconsin native Jeffrey Van Fleet updated the Ecuador, Paraguay, and Uruguay chapters. Jeffrey never passes up the chance to partake of the more cosmopolitan pleasures to be found in South America. He has contributed to Fodor's guides to Costa Rica, Guatemala, Peru, Chile, Argentina, and Central America.

PERU

Mark Sullivan, former Fodor's editor and extensive South America traveler, updated the Lima section. Katy Morrison, a travel writer from Australia who can't stop exploring South America, wrote about Cusco and southern Peru. Costa

12-08

Rica–based freelancer Jeffrey Van Fleet updated Machu Picchu and the Sacred Valley. Michelle Hopey tramped about and updated Colca and Cotahuasi Canyons, Arequipa, and Lake Titicaca. Former corporate Manhattanite turned teacher Aviva Baff, now living in Lima, updated the North Coast and Northern Highlands, while archaeologist and ski buff Oliver Wigmore wrote about the Cordillera Blanca.

VENEZUELA

One-time Fodor's editor Heidi Johansen thoroughly enjoyed exploring Venezuela's mysterious Andes, basking on the sun-drenched shores of Margarita Island, and unearthing hidden gems in the urban explosion of Caracas. Prior to her time in Venezuela, Heidi spent two months traveling through China and Laos. She's currently working as a writer and editor in Seattle, Washington.

WITHDRAWN